DATE DUE			

Mass Communication Review Yearbook

Editorial Board

Mass Communication Review Yearbook

Volume 4

1983

Ellen Wartella
D. Charles Whitney

Editors

Sven Windahl

Associate Editor

SAGE PUBLICATIONS
Beverly Hills / London / New Delhi

Copyright © 1983 by Sage Publications, Inc.

For information address:

SAGE Publications, Inc.
275 South Beverly Drive
Beverly Hills, California 90212

SAGE Publications India Pvt. Ltd.
C-236 Defence Colony
New Delhi 110 024, India

SAGE Publications Ltd
28 Banner Street
London EC1Y 8QE, England

Printed in the United States of America

International Standard Book Number 0-8039-2016-4

International Standard Series Number 0196-8017

FIRST PRINTING

Contents

About the Editors

ELLEN WARTELLA is research assistant professor in the Institute of Communications Research. Her research on children and television has been published in a variety of communication journals and edited collections. She is coauthor of *How Children Learn to Buy* and editor of *Children Communicating,* Volume 7 of the Sage Annual Reviews of Communication Research. She is on the editorial board of the *Journal of Broadcasting* and is a member of the Broadcast Educators Association, the International Communication Association, the International Association for Mass Communication Research, and the Society for Research in Child Development. She is head of the Communication Theory and Methodology Division of the Association for Education in Journalism, and has been a consultant to the Federal Trade Commission and the Federal Communications Commission.

D. CHARLES WHITNEY is research assistant professor in the Institute of Communications Research and assistant professor of journalism at the University of Illinois at Urbana-Champaign. He is a member of the Association for Education in Journalism, the International Association for Mass Communication Research, the International Communication Association, and the executive board of the Midwest Association for Public Opinion Research. His research has focused on sociological approaches to the study of mass communicators and on mass communication and public opinion. He is coeditor, with James S. Ettema, of *Individuals in Mass Media Organizations: Creativity and Constraint,* Volume 10 of the Sage Annual Reviews of Communication Research.

SVEN WINDAHL is senior lecturer in sociology and information techniques at the University College of Växjoe and the University of Lund. He has published in a number of communication journals and is coauthor, with Denis McQuail, of *Communication Models for the Study of Mass Communication.* Since 1976 he has been a principal investigator on a media panel research program at the University of Lund, and in 1981-1982 was visiting professor in the School of Journalism and Mass Communication at the University of Minnesota.

Preface

In our second year as editors of this series, we continue to be awed by the diversity and quality of scholarship in mass communication research world-wide. The problems associated with mass communication demand urgent concern and serious criticism, and many answers, all of them as yet tentative, are being provided. While the volume cannot do full justice to this panoply of scholarship, we are grateful for the opportunity to assemble it, and in this task we have been aided by a number of individuals.

First among these are the editorial board members listed in the front matter of this volume. The recommendations of these scholars have formed the backbone of this series.

Our associate editor, Sven Windahl, has continued to render invaluable assistance, and we could not regard his advice more highly.

Closer to home, we would especially like to thank Everett Rogers for his timely aid in obtaining the Polish manuscript reprinted in Part VI and to Roberta Astroff, a doctoral student in the Institute of Communications Research at the University of Illinois, for the translation of the Spanish contribution in the same secton.

Others at the University of Illinois have helped us considerably. Among them are our colleague Willard D. Rowland, Jr., whose advice was especially helpful in compiling Part VIII of this yearbook; doctoral students William May and Linda Maguire, who offered editorial assistance; and Marvene Blackmore and Anita Specht, whose secretarial and clerical assistance cannot be overestimated. We are also grateful to the university's College of Communications and Institute of Communications Research and its faculty and staff for assistance.

We wish to thank you all.

—Ellen Wartella
D. Charles Whitney

INTRODUCTION

Ellen Wartella and D. Charles Whitney

We noted a year ago that this series has achieved some stability and that this yearbook, if it is to serve any useful purpose, should above all highlight the diversity that marks research on mass communication. We reaffirm that here. This series endeavors to collect what represents the best in mass communication studies—best, in the world of G. Cleveland Wilhoit, our predecessor as editor, because they "integrate ongoing work, . . . chart new directions, or . . . are typical studies in an important area."

In our search for such chapter and articles, we are aided by an outstanding editorial board of about 40 internationally regarded scholars. Among them, they have recommended several hundred recent articles and manuscripts for inclusion in this volume, and from among their recommendations and those of others, we have selected the thirty-eight readings that appear here. They are from varied sources. The selections include fifty-four different authors from eight nations; they are drawn from seventeen different journals and from eight books, the remaining selections being original manuscripts. As we note below in more detail, they are a diverse lot; the field, if such a field as mass communication research can be said to exist, includes work on a number of problems that represent both the hurdles and the opportunities comprising such a field.

SCOPE OF THE YEARBOOK

This volume comprises eight sections. They include parts on the effects perspective; the comprehension of media content, with special attention to television; feminism and the mass media; the notion of culture in media studies; five studies of mass communicators; four discussions of the role of the state in media performance; and four chapters each on new technology and the "information age" and on American telecommunications policy. Of these, the sections on feminism and on technology and policy deserve special mention, because these are areas in which scholarship is burgeoning in response to pressing social needs. Two other new sections, those on the role of the state and on various conceptualizations of culture and media, and these three, moreover, signal an attempt on our part to broaden the range of what is included in this series and to depict the issues around which scholars of various approaches are formulating current research questions.

Missing from this volume are two sections readers found in all previous numbers in this series: theoretical perspectives and international mass communication. We did not include a theoretical perspectives section for two reasons. First is that in the past year, theoretical development in mass communication appears to us to have been incremental, with various positions continuing to develop without major restructuring. Second, and to us more important, we have tried to include in each section works with theoretical substance within their own topical substrates, viewing development of theory as tied to a topical context. There were, similarly, two reasons for not adding a separate international communications sections. First is the last year's international section, following the MacBride Commission report (UNESCO, 1980), dealt with international communication policy, and this year we chose to focus on policy research in a single nation. Second is that, as a glance at the contents will attest, we feel that by including works from authors in a number of nations in most of the sections of the volume, we have attempted to make the work international in character. Nonetheless, we likewise expect that future volumes in the series will return to a direct concern with comparative, transnational, and international mass communication studies.

PART I:
MEDIA EFFECTS

We have gathered six contributions under this heading, and a glance at the titles indicates that our selections reflect research traditions that have been especially prominent in the recent past: the effects of media on children and youth and on presentations of social reality, and a research literature on political communication.

We have made four selections, including the first three in this part of the Collins chapter in Part II, from the 1982 update of the important and influential 1972 U.S. Surgeon General's report on television and social behavior. When the 1982 report appeared, it was framed incorrectly by most of the U.S. press as another violence report. As is noted in the summary chapter from the recent report, which we have reprinted as part of Chapter 1, violence-effects research constitutes rather a small part of the enterprise for this update, with attention also directed to television's health-promoting possibilities, to cognitive and emotional functioning, to imaginative play and prosocial behavior, to socialization and conceptions of social reality, to the medium's influence on family and interpersonal relations, to the role of television in society, and to education and learning about television. Moreover, as noted in this chapter, citing Murray (1981), the recent past has seen an enormous increase in the amount of research on television: Murray's bibliography on television and youth from 1946 to 1980 shows that two-thirds of the entries were from studies published between 1975 and 1980. The 1982 report also appears to signal a shift, reflected here in the Rice, Huston, and Wright chapter and in Part II in the Collins chapter, away from a social learning theory of television effects to a cognitive psychology that requires clearer attention to the intervention of the formal features of a medium and its presentation and to the characteristics of attention and comprehension of the message in making generalizations about television effects. Our final selection from this report is the chapter by Hawkins and Pingree, a critical review of the literature on television and social reality.

The other three chapters in Part I fall under the general rubric of political communication. In introducing the first of these, it is necessary to note that we have not included in this volume a separate section or discussion on the agenda-setting hypothesis, the subject of the Iyengar, Peters, and Kinder chapter, and with which the Whitney and Becker chapter in Part V is consistent. In part this is because, as Iyengar et al., and many other recent commentators have noted, support for the hypothesis at the aggregate level, employing survey data, has been weak to nonexistent. But their study, and the one in Part V, indicate that with experimental data and at the individual level, the hypothesis is alive and well. The final two selections in this section deal with Noelle-Neumann's now-familiar notion of a "spiral of silence" and relate it to Allport's venerable idea of pluralistic ignorance. Katz's critical discussion of Nelle-Neumann focuses on why, conceptually, the spiral might not be found to obtain under many circumstances; Taylor offers survey evidence for specifying under what conditions it might obtain. The reader, moreover, may note a concurrence between Taylor's discussion of dominance and momentum in campaigns and the discussion by Iyengar et al. of "priming" in agenda-setting.

PART II:
UNDERSTANDING TELEVISION

We have included seven chapters, most of them brief, in this section. The first four, taken from a recent issue of the *Journal of Marketing,* may be read together, for together they raise several substantive issues: First is that televised messages are routinely misunderstood by a significant fraction of those attending to them; second is that "social-categorical" variables, at least in the present research, offer remarkably little in the way of power to predict misunderstanding; third, miscomprehension, in the words of one author, is "measurement-bound"; and finally, comprehension of media content and more especially its miscomprehension have clear policy implications for those who produce such content and for those who regulate it.

These themes are explored in some detail by the other authors in this section. In his brief review of research on news recall, Gunter points a finger at television journalists and their modes of news production. The final two selections were reviews of models for understanding how media content is understood. Woodall, Davis, and Sahin consider episodic memory and semantic network models, and Collins suggests that the active nature of the viewing process has important implications for the processing of content and for behavioral effects of television on children.

In toto, these chapters present us with the vexing problem of how media can influence individuals if those media are not uniformly understood, and they provide some answers.

PART III:
FEMINISM AND THE MEDIA

A section such as this has appeared in no other volume in this series, despite the fact that media depictions of various groups, women among them, have presented important research questions since well before this series began. The four selections here present some of the varieties of approach that are useful in addressing questions of media depictions of women.

MaryAnn Yodelis Smith's review of eight recent books related to women and media elaborates a research schematic and especially argues for a more analytical history of women and media and for further study of institutional-level contexts of media production of images of women.

Robinson documents that the 1970s saw a change in U.S. and Canadian magazine depictions of the role and status of women, but certain "blind spots" in coverage related to practical methods of achievement of equality in work and other opportunities remain in such depictions.

Angela McRobbie's engaging semiotic analysis of the English teen magazine *Jackie* argues that it depicts an ideology of romantic individualism.

Finally, Thelma McCormack's analysis of soap operas suggests that this form has evolved from treating women as mothers to treating them as wives and currently as consumers.

PART IV:
MEDIA AND CULTURE

The entries in this section were chosen explicitly because they employ different notions of culture. Nonetheless, there are commonalities. All the authors are concerned with the role of audience and producers in the production of mass-mediated carriers of cultural content. Where they vary is in the relative emphasis they give to producer and to audience, and to the methodologies they employ.

David Nord suggests that much American writing on popular culture is restricted by reliance on overly simple economic models of culture production; understanding convention and formula in popular culture requires an understanding of the economics of production.

Roughly consistent with this approach is the biographical chapter by Gaye Tuchman, whose examination of Victorian publishers' readers "demonstrate how economic and cultural practices are embedded in one another."

In a quantitative treatment of press mentions of authors, Karl Erik Rosengren furnishes evidence of the sort of cultural indicators research he advocated two years ago in this series.

A very different approach is that of Dick Hebdige, who in his chapter on "Americanization" of British taste-subcultures argues that their members are not necessarily passive consumers in the cultural process; rather, they have an active hand in adapting cultural products to their own needs and meanings.

PART V:
MASS COMMUNICATORS

Five chapters are offered here, and each is a report of research on the individuals, organizations, and institutions producing mass communications. In part this section is organized around lines suggested by the initial chapter in this section, in which John Dimmick and Philip Coit demonstrate the utility, in theory organization and generation, of dividing the field by level of analysis under study; they moreover provide a multilevel data analysis to illustrate their method.

In the next selection, Kepplinger, operating at an individual level, attempts to show that cameramen are aware of, and employ, formal and technical modes of filming political figures that are consistent with their existing images of such candidates, despite articulating craft norms to the contrary.

Whitney and Becker, in their field-experimental study, look to a structural, industry-level explanation—the wire services' assignment of priorities to different forms of news—to explain consistencies in news editors' selections of some news items and their rejection of others. As they point out, wire service editors thus help to shape more local news agendas.

Powell and Friedkin suggest that understanding how public television programmers decide what will be aired requires elaboration of a variety intra- and extraorganizational pressures on such programmers, set within a context of the sources of funding for such programming.

Finally, Dreier's descriptive study is at the nexus between institutional and societal levels, in the Dimmick and Coit taxonomy. By identifying linkages between newspaper corporations and the U.S. power structure, Dreier argues that the nation's elite press helps to maintain and reinforce an ideology of corporate liberalism.

PART VI:
MEDIA PERFORMANCE AND STATE STRUCTURE

In some respects, this section may be viewed as an extension of the preceding one. Here the concern is with how mass media presentations reflect, refract, and are tied to the state apparatuses in which they are prepared.

In the initial chapter, reviewing recent research on their knowledge gap hypothesis, Olien, Donohue, and Tichenor underscore a theme reflected in other chapters in this section, that mass media strongly tend to reflect power relationships in societies, and even in times of serious stress, "the weight of media coverage is structured in large part to reinforce . . . the power structure." Societies in crisis especially furnish excellent research conditions for studying the role of media in the modern state. The remaining three selections in this section are studies of three contemporary states in crisis.

Philip Schlesinger examines coverage, particularly that of the BBC, in a particular crisis, the takeover of the Iranian embassy in London in 1980. The institutional arrangements between the press and the government during the crisis, he argues, raise disturbing questions about the future conduct of each.

The Polish contribution, by Tomasz Goban-Klas, deals with a small part of one of the major crises of our time, the great ferment in that nation. Treated here are the events during 1980, a period that saw the formation of Solidarity, and examined in some detail are failure of the official press and the emergence of alternatives that helped to propel social change.

Finally, de Moragas Spa outlines the development of the media, not entirely a smooth and felicitous one, in a continuing "crisis," the forging of a new form of government in post-Franco Spain. Of special interest is his discussion of the meaning and fragile nature of political legitimacy.

These chapters together raise interesting questions about the role of media in various political climates, and a comparative reading of them is both enlightening and disturbing.

PART VII:
NEW TECHNOLOGY AND THE INFORMATION AGE

This section is all too brief; it would be impossible at this stage to do adequate justice to the task of keeping track of technological development in information generation and dissemination alone, much less to do what we have tried to do here, which is to offer some views on the meaning of new developments. What we provide here, then, are four, among many, considerations of how new media technologies will be organized and used, along with some appraisal of how the institutional arrangements growing up around these technologies may alter the landscape around them. As is usually the case in such discussions, the appraisals range from the optimistic to the dispassionately neutral to the pessimistic and to all three at once.

In the first selection, Fombrun and Astley are interested in how major corporations are coping with technological innovations in communications; their data suggest that corporate strategies of absorption and networking are erasing long-held functional distinctions in the information industries; the long-term consequences of this trend, they say, are not clear.

However, the authors of the next two sections do argue that there are clear, and negative, trends in the development of new media technologies. Herbert Schiller suggests that the major corporations are seeking to rework the notion of information from one of a social good to one of a private and hence salable, exploitable commodity. Philip Elliott's concern in the following chapter is that the emergence of a transnational corporate information economy will lead, among other things, to the disappearance of a liberal "public sphere" in which questions can be debated.

Finally, David Weaver's examination of video text operations suggests that both optimism and pessimism prevail after various experiments with such systems.

PART VIII:
AMERICAN TELECOMMUNICATIONS POLICY

The four chapters in this section represent both academic critics and industry perspectives in telecommunications regulation, and reading them leads to the conclusion that the issues in such regulation are far from resolved.

The terms used in the debate over control of American telecommunications—"competition," "deregulation," and the "marketplace"—are, as these chapters attest, subject to differing interpretations, and these interpretations can be grounded in the bases from which the participants argue.

In his chapter, Dallas Smythe suggests that deregulation of American radio represents well "the struggle to redefine the border between the public and private sectors," and that at present the public sector is very nearly out of sight.

Closely allied with this view is that of Willard Rowland, who suggests that recent telecommunications legislation, and some of its "failures," lead to the conclusion that when the air clears, about all one can say is that the regulatory issues have narrowed, largely to the benefit of the largest corporate telecommunications interests.

By contrast, however, FCC Chairman Mark Fowler and Daniel Brenner, and former FCC Chairman Richard Wiley, argue in their chapters, that marketplace forces and minimal regulation better serve the public interest, where competition can, by regulation, be assured.

CONCLUSION

As have the three previous volumes in this series, this one concludes by noting the diversity of mass communication research. This diversity is expressed in a number of ways: Studies in the present volume span half a dozen loci of concern, from media effects on the individual, to the text, to production by individual communicators, to production by media organizations and institutions, to culture and subculture. Diversity of method is also apparent, and as has been noted in previous volumes, such diversity seems to be waxing more than waning. Included in this volume are reports not only of the usual laboratory experiments and field surveys but also of documentary and historical research and several methodologically distinguishable forms of textual analysis. This diversity extends to theory as well; as we noted last year and as Professor Wilhoit did before us, nothing like theoretical closure appears on the horizon; indeed, the sources of theory, the citations of previous work from inside and outside mass communication, to thinkers both classical and contemporary, seem to become more diverse as the years pass.

Behind this diversity, however, stands the one clear conclusion we can draw about this year's selections: This is a book about pressing social problems. The appearance of an update of the 1972 Surgeon General's report signals that television's impact on youth remains an urgent concern. The pessimism observable in several of the technology and policy chapters reflects the thought of some that media developments are not proceeding in a reasonable, democratic, humane direction. Behind the chapters on media performance and the state are concerns that neither the media nor government is meeting public aspirations. Our section on feminism suggests that here too problems abound.

Clearly, the problem orientation in mass communication studies is not new; it almost defines the field. What we hope this volume does is to give expression to the twin needs of practical recognition of real human communication difficulties and to critical, theoretical, and philosophical approaches to them. The former have been, in the field and in this series, more in the foreground. We are more capable of recognizing problems than of adequately framing them for resolution. It remains our hope, however, that the latter—attention to rigorous critical, theoretical, and philosophical concerns—will demand more attention in the future.

REFERENCES

MURRAY, J. P. (1981) Television and Youth: 25 Years of Research and Controversy. Boys Town, NE: Boys Town Center for the Study of Youth Development.

UNESCO (1980) Many Voices, One World: Report of the UNESCO International Commission for the Study of Communication Problems (S. MacBride, president). Paris: UNESCO.

U.S. Surgeon General's Scientific Advisory Committee on Television and Social Behavior (1972) Television and Social Behavior. Washington, DC: Government Printing Office.

PART I

MEDIA EFFECTS

Previous volumes in this series have begun with a section on theoretical perspectives in mass communication. By not including such a section here, we are not saying that theory is to be dispensed with. On the contrary, we would like to signal that theory is, as always, both implicit and explicit. We begin here with a somewhat traditional concern with the effects of mass communication and have chosen works that exemplify two concerns that have prevailed throughout the systematic study of mass communication: the effects of media and their messages on children and in the realm of public affairs.

The first three entries in this section are drawn from the ten-year update of the 1972 U.S. Surgeon General's report on television and social behavior. While the 1972 report concerned itself largely with the effects of televised violence, the 1982 report has a broader focus and relies less on social learning theory and considerably more on an emerging cognitive psychology, as the first two chapters in this section make clear.

Our third selection from that report serves as a bridge to the remaining selections in the part. Hawkins and Pingree are concerned with the effects of televised messages on perceptions of social reality, and in the fourth selection, Iyengar, Peters, and Kinder approach a similar concern experimentally in terms that those familiar with agenda-setting studies will immediately recognize.

The final two chapters in the section address similar questions, and both draw heavily from Elisabeth Noelle-Neumann's notion of a "spiral of silence" and Floyd Allport's idea of "pluralistic ignorance." Both are saying that whatever we learn of "social reality" from the media may well be conditioned by what we feel, in Noelle-Neumann's phrase, on our "social skins."

The 1982 National Institute of Mental Health report, "Television and Behavior: Ten Years of Scientific Progress and Implications for the Eighties," is an update of the 1972 U.S. Surgeon General's violence study. Included here are the introductory and summary chapters of the summary report of the 1982 update, selections that illustrate the changes research on television and behavior have undergone in the past decade. Of particular note is that the issue of television's role in instigating real-life violence, while still a topic of research, no longer constitutes the majority of research on television and behavior. As is noted in the following chapter, inroads have been made in the past decade in examining the rule of television in the context of American life, how it affects consumer and sex role socialization, its impact on family life, the affective and cognitive demands of watching and making sense of television, as well as the educational implications of television watching.

1

TELEVISION AND BEHAVIOR
Ten Years of Scientific Progress
and Implications for the Eighties

National Institute of Mental Health

The Surgeon General's Scientific Advisory Committee Report—1972

Among the great inventions in the electronic age, television is one of the most beguiling. A sound-and-light show appealing to the prepotent senses of vision and hearing, it draws attention like a magnet. Infants as young as 6 months gaze at it; little children sit in front of it for hours at a time; and millions of elderly, sick, and institutionalized people keep contact with the outside world mainly through television. An integral part of everyday life, it helps to determine how people spend their time, what they learn, what they think and talk about; it influences their opinions and helps shape their behavior. Few other inventions have so completely enveloped an entire population. More Americans have television than have refrigerators or indoor plumbing.

It is no wonder, then, that students of human behavior have been attracted to television as a field of research, as a vast arena for the study of behavior in today's technological world. It is no less wonder that the American public is concerned about the effects of television on their lives and the lives of their children. Some people think it has a malignant influence; others praise it as a boon to society. Wanting to know about the effects of television, the public has turned to the scientific community for answers.

Spurred on by both curiosity and a need to find answers to practical questions, scientists have been busy during the past decade at many kinds of television research. Such research did not arise suddenly. Investigations into the effects of television began in the late 1940s, almost as soon as television began to appear in American homes, continued at a relatively slow pace in the 1950s, and accelerated in the 1960s.

In 1969, the increase in research on television began with a request by Senator John G. Pastore to the Secretary of the Department of Health, Education, and Welfare. As Chairman of the Senate Subcommittee on Communications of the Senate Commerce Committee, Senator Pastore wrote, "I am exceedingly troubled by the lack of any definitive information which would help resolve the question of whether there is a casual connection between televised crime and violence and antisocial behavior by individuals, especially children. . . ." The Senator asked the Secretary to direct the Surgeon General of the U.S. Public Health Service to appoint a committee to "conduct a study to establish scientifically what effects these kinds of programs have on children."

The Department swung rapidly into action. The Surgeon General directed the National Institute of Mental Health to take responsibility for the committee and to provide necessary staff. The Scientific Advisory Committee on Television and Social Behavior

From National Institute of Mental Health, *Television and Behavior: Ten Years of Scientific Progress and Implications for the Eighties,* Vol. 1: Summary Report, Chapter 1, "Ten Years of Scientific Progress: An Overview," and Chapter 10, "Implications for the Eighties "(Rockville, MD: National Institute of Mental Health, 1982), pp. 1-8, 87-91. This work is in the public domain.

was appointed, and one million dollars were provided for new research. Scientists throughout the country submitted proposals; the most promising proposals received approval; and their authors were funded to conduct the research. The studies were completed within 2 years, unusual speed for the behavioral sciences. In December 1971, the committee sent its report to the Surgeon General. The report, entitled *Television and Growing Up: The Impact of Televised Violence,* summarized the state of knowledge at that time. It was accompanied by five technical volumes of reports in which the contributing scientists described their studies in detail.

The report confirmed the "pervasiveness of television in the United States," stating that almost everyone watched some television programs and that many people watched for many hours a day. The report pointed out that little was known about the reasons people view so much television or choose particular programs. The report also confirmed that there was a great deal of violence on television. On entertainment television during 1967 and 1968, there were about eight violent incidents per hour.

The report's major conclusion, often quoted, was: "Thus, there is a convergence of the fairly substantial experimental evidence for a *short-run* causation of aggression among some children by viewing violence on the screen and much less certain evidence from field studies that extensive violence viewing precedes some *long-run* manifestations of aggressive behavior. The convergence of the two types of evidence constitute some preliminary indication of a casual relationship, but a good deal of research remains to be done before one can have confidence in these conclusions."

The committee itself wrote that these tentative and limited conclusions were not entirely satisfactory but that they did represent much more knowledge than was available when the committee began its work.

Ten Years Later

During the 1970s, much of the necessary research was done, and—to anticipate findings that will be described later—it can be said that the evidence for a causal relationship between excessive violence viewing and aggression goes well beyond the preliminary level. Scientists in this decade have also broadened the research. They have been trying to find the many interrelated and intricate factors that operate in television programing and viewing—who watches television and why, what children see and hear on television, what people learn from television and how they learn it. Among other topics, they analyze television's effects on social life and values.

As a result of the Surgeon General's committee effort, a new generation of scientists was spawned. Some of the scientists who undertook research projects in

the late 1960s are still working the field. Many of the younger people brought into the projects as assistants and associates developed a continuing interest and are now contributing their talents and efforts to television research. They include investigators from all the behavioral sciences, notably psychology, psychiatry, and sociology, as well as from public health and communications. They do their work in many settings, including universities and the television industry itself. Much of the research is supported by the government and private foundations, but many of the smaller projects have no major outside funding. During the past decade, at almost all conventions of behavioral scientists, there have been sessions on television research which has become an established specialty.

Although the number of scientists doing television research has increased, it is still small compared to the magnitude of the research problems. Many more investigators from all fields are needed if research is to find answers to the questions concerned citizens ask.

Because scientists from many fields have been at work, the studies have taken different approaches. Some, for example, concentrate on analyses of program content, others observe children before and after they have looked at violent programs, and still others observe children after they have looked at benign and prosocial programs. Many of the projects are done in the laboratory under strict experimental conditions; others are naturalistic field studies and observations. These two approaches complement one another. The laboratory studies tell whether or not something can happen, the possibility of occurrence. The field studies tell how commonly something does happen, the likelihood of occurrence. When both kinds of studies point in the same direction, their conclusions are mutually reinforcing.

The amount of television research increased significantly during the 1970s. This increase is documented in a bibliography published in 1980; the bibliography covers articles, books, and other materials in the field of research on television and youth published, primarily in English, between 1946 and 1980.[1] Up to 1970, there were about 300 titles, and from 1970 through 1980 there were another 2,500, of which more than two-thirds were published in 1975 or later. Put another way, 90 percent of all the publications appeared in the last 10 years. No one knows whether this acceleration will continue at such a rate, but television is so much a part of present-day human existence that the amount of research will undoubtedly increase and delve even more into all facets of the relationships between television and human behavior.

Much of the research on effects of television has been concerned with its impact on children. It is easier to gather data on young people, as most of them are in schools or other settings that make them accessible to the investigators. Also, it is more important to learn about television's influence on the growing child. It is essential to know what the many hours a day spent watching television are doing to them at a time when they are developing and learning about the world and the people around them. Children are an audience qualitatively different from adults, and they may be an audience more vulnerable to television's messages. It may also be significant that there is now a generation of young adults who have grown up with television and whose children are now second-generation television viewers. The effects on them probably are not the same as on previous generations who were adults when they first became acquainted with television.

The Television Audience

The Surgeon General's committee asked who watches television, and its report replied, "almost everyone." That was true in the late 1960s and it is still true in the early 1980s. Some people watch occasionally, for special events or at certain times, but many Americans watch television everyday. Their viewing times range from an hour or two to many hours daily, and some even keep the set on all day long. One survey showed that for large numbers of people television ranks third among all activities (after sleep and work) in the number of hours devoted to it.

One could go on citing figures about the pervasiveness and ubiquity of television. It should be remembered, however, that these figures are estimates. If *TV Guide* states that 85 million people watched *Roots,* it does not mean that the roofs were snatched off all the houses and apartments in the United States and the people in front of television sets counted one by one. The figures are projections from small samples and are subject to all the errors—and the scientific accuracy—found in such projections.

Most of the audience figure estimates come from surveys. Surveys conducted by telephone are much in use now, although mail and door-to-door surveys are still used occasionally. Another technique is exemplified by the famous Nielsen ratings which derive from television use in about 1,200 homes where the set is hooked up to a computer indicating when the set is on and which channel it is turned to. Other procedures merely ask people if they look at television, how often, which programs, and so on. This kind of questioning is sometimes done by interviewers and sometimes through written questionnaires. People have also been asked to keep television logs or diaries of their viewing. In a few instances, ordinarily in conjunction with other studies, direct observations of families or other groups, such as children or institutionalized persons, have been made by visitors to the home or institution.

On the basis of these surveys and observations, quite a bit is known about who looks at television. Because many different methods have been used and compared, this information, as a whole, is probably accurate and reliable.

For research purposes, the audience is often categorized in terms of amount of viewing. Some scientists use simple terms like "heavy" and "light" viewers or "high" and "low" amount of viewing. In some situations, a person who looks at television more than 4 hours a day is called a "heavy" viewer. A "light" viewer might be defined as a person who views about an hour a day or less. Where to draw additional lines in between is sometimes a topic of scientific controversy. There are, of course, the "constant" viewers who watch television almost all their waking hours, and there are some confirmed "nonviewers." The definitions vary, depending on who is doing the research and on the purpose of the research.

Surveys confirm what most people already suspect—television appeals to all ages, though not equally. Babies look at it for rather brief intervals and, as they grow older, tend to look at it more and more. By age 2 or 3, some children spend large amounts of time before the set and apparently have some understanding of what is going on. The amount of viewing continues at a relatively high level, then drops off somewhat when children reach their teens. In young adulthood it increases again, especially for parents with young children. Viewing time tends to drop in the busy years of middle age, but later in life television again becomes a major attraction and may be watched for many hours a day. It is sometimes the principal recreation for elderly people.

Amount of viewing seems to vary with other characteristics of people. Minority groups tend to watch more than others, on the average, and women more than men. Some surveys show that people in lower socioeconomic groups view somewhat more than those in the middle class. People who watch a lot of television tend to be less educated than those who do not watch as much, yet among college students television is a favorite pastime. People in hospitals, prisons, and other institutions often look at television when they get the chance.

It appears that, although almost everyone watches television, those who do not have much else to do watch it most often. Many people, for example the elderly and the unemployed, use television to fill time, to do something instead of nothing. Some researchers have concluded that these are people who do not choose to watch specific programs; they are not really selective in what they look at. They watch by the clock, turning on the set at free times, no matter what is being shown. Television is a ritualized or habitual activity.

In general, the surveys indicate that the television audience has not changed appreciably during the past 10 years. Americans' viewing habits seem to have been established early in the history of television.

Doing Research on Television and Behavior

Like all scientists, behavioral scientists who study television, draw their conclusions from evidence they have gathered and organized to answer specific questions. The kind of evidence they collect depends on the aspect of television and behavior they are studying and on which stage in a rather long process they are concerned with. Some simple distinctions may help clarify the complexity of the overall process, which in turn explains why each researcher tries to simplify the problem by limiting a study to a small portion of the total process.

The heart of the process includes a television set showing a particular program and a person sitting in front of it watching and listening to the program. Supposedly, the researcher then tries to study the effect of the program on this viewer. But the effects of television cannot be understood in such simple terms. Because the program on television is sometimes *selected* by the viewer the researcher must also consider the role of the viewer in any possible causal relationships. Moreover, the typical audience often consists of a number of persons who must somehow agree on the program they will watch. They interact with one another about the program and about other things as well. All these social relationships in the immediate viewing situation have been called the "social context" of viewing and must be taken into account. The researcher may also want to look beyond the television presentation and its audience in the immediate social context to the longer term behavioral outcomes. Television's interrelations with the viewer's psychological processes may also be a focus of inquiry. In any case, the context in which behavior occurs is important.

Television presentations themselves became a prime target of research almost since television began. Virtually any topic on television which is suspected of having behavioral effects is likely to be examined. For example, there have been content analyses of the incidence of violent portrayals, depictions of minorities, prosocial acts, families, sexual references, people in various professions, and so forth. In many of these areas, research has not progressed beyond the analyses of the content. There are good reasons for this limitation; some of the suspected effects are very difficult to measure satisfactorily as, for example, the impact of sexually oriented programs. But in other areas, the research community has moved well along in examining the effects of television's content on the viewer.

Two different approaches have been followed in the study of television's influence on the behavior of the viewing audience. One group of researchers, grounded mostly in laboratory psychology, is conducting *experimental* studies in which an audience is temporarily brought together to view programs selected for research purposes. This approach leads to strong conclusions about the immediate impact on behavior that the researcher subsequently observes. As a rule, social context is eliminated from consideration by holding it constant within the experimental session so that it does not affect the results. A second group of researchers approached the study of television's uses and effects in natural *field* settings. Field studies attempt to take social context factors into account by measuring them and making their interactions with the television experience a part of what is studied. This approach usually takes the form of field surveys, which produce evidence of correlation between various factors but which are not scientifically as satisfactory as the controlled experiment in trying to isolate the specific effect of any single factor.

Two intermediate approaches have occasionally been used by researchers who hope to couple some of the precision of the experimental study with the greater generalizability and breadth of the field study. One is the *field experiment,* such as, systematically exposing audiences to different television programs while they remain in their normal viewing situations at home. The other is the *panel study* in which the same individuals are interviewed, tested, or otherwise observed over time. The panel study examines natural variation over time (rather than at a specific time, as in the field survey) on the assumption that changes occur both in the person's exposure to television presentations and in a pattern of behavior that might be affected by those presentations.

Field experiments and panel studies are relatively rare in research on television and behavior. They tend to arouse controversy among scientists; there are those who prefer the greater certainty of cause-effect evidence provided by the laboratory experiment and those who seek greater generality in field research. Field experiments are practicable on only a narrow range of topics, and often the experimental procedures seem to effect more change in the person's life than just that which the person is shown on television. Panel studies run the risk of "contamination" of the person who is repeatedly interviewed on the same topic. Because the subjects in the research are interviewed or tested repeatedly, they may not represent the larger population that has not been asked the same questions.

Disagreement among researchers is often the product of disagreement about the kind of evidence that is required to draw a conclusion. Such evidence in turn grows out of the aspect of the overall process that they are attempting to study and the specific type of television presentation or behavior that is at stake. Some students of behavioral effects, for example, may find the research detailing various imbalances—overrepresentation or underrepresentation—in the demographic makeup of the total cast of characters on television to be of little import. They say that, because there is no evidence that there are socially deleterious behavioral outcomes associated with these television portrayals, the portrayals and imbalances can be shrugged off. On the other hand, some observers, including those in one of the offended demographic groups—minorities, women, the elderly, the disabled, and so on—may see the imbalances in content as sufficient grounds for action and reform, regardless of the demonstrability of the effects.

One task of developing a theory is to tie together the many areas of content analysis with the rather fewer areas where learning and other effects have been demonstrated experimentally or tested for their generality in field studies. For example, can a laboratory finding that young people imitate aggressive acts they have seen on television be extended either to social behavior in the real world or to the unmeasured impact on behavior of televised presentations of, say, prostitution or bigotry? As the total scope of research has broadened, some researchers have been willing to accept these generalizations.

While the research on television and behavior is by no means complete, it is expanding at an accelerating pace. New applications and versions of research methods are being used, and scientists can now draw conclusions more confidently than they could from the much more limited research of 10 years ago.

Highlights of Ten Years of Research

Television's Health-Promoting Possibilities

In its programs, television contains many messages about health, messages that may be important to promotion of health and prevention of illness. Television seems to be doing a rather poor job of helping its audience to attain better health or better understanding of health practices. This is, of course, not a goal of commercial television; nevertheless, incidental learning from television stories and portrayals may be contributing to lifestyles and habits that are not conducive to good health. Portrayal of mental illness on television is not frequent, but when it does appear, it is related to both violence and victimization; compared with "normal" characters, twice as many mentally ill characters on television are violent or are the victims of others' violence. Even though very few characters on television are ill, many more doctors are evident than are in real life. Much of television's content seems to foster poor nutrition, especially in commercials for sweets and snack foods. Children who watch a lot of television have poorer nutritional habits than children who do not watch as much. Alcohol consumption is common; it is condoned and is presented as a part of the social milieu. When people drive cars, which occurs often on television, they almost never wear seat belts. Correlational studies suggest that people's attitudes are influenced by these portrayals. One study, for example, indicated that television ranked second to physicians and dentists as a source of health information.

There has been almost no research on people in institutions, even though it is known that they often watch television. One study in a psychiatric setting found that staff believed television had a beneficial effect on patients, especially the chronic and elderly. Increased use of television for therapeutic purpose should be considered; for example, films and videotape have been used successfully to help people learn to cope with fears and phobias. An experimental study of emotionally disturbed children reported that, for some of the children, prosocial programs increased their altruistic behavior and decreased their aggressive behavior. More research is needed to explore the therapeutic potential of television.

With the pervasiveness of television viewing, it can be assumed that campaigns to promote better health would be effective. There have been campaigns on community mental health, against drug abuse and smoking, for seat-belt wearing, for dental health, and against cancer, venereal disease, and alcoholism. An example of a successful campaign to reduce risk of cardiovascular disease in California had programs in both English and Spanish and face-to-face instruction, in addition to the television messages, for some of the groups. After 2 years, communities exposed to the campaign, even without the personal instruction, had significantly reduced the likelihood of heart attack and stroke, while in a "control" community where there was no campaign risk levels remained high. Carefully planned and evaluated campaigns built on an understanding of the ways in which messages are conveyed and incorporated into people's lives hold great promise.

Cognitive and Emotional Functioning

Research on cognitive processes has asked such questions as: What are the factors involved in paying attention to television? What is remembered? How much is understood? The research shows that duration of paying attention is directly related to age. Infants watch sporadically; little children gradually pay more attention visually until, at about age 4, they look at television about 55 percent of the time, even when there are many other distractions in the room. Auditory cues are very important in attracting and holding attention. Up to the second and third grades, children cannot report much of what they see and hear on television, but they probably remember more than they can report, and memory improves with growing up. Young children remember specific scenes better than relationships, and they often do not understand plot or narrative. Making inferences and differentiating between central and peripheral content are difficult for young children, but these skills also improve with age. The changes may be partly developmental and partly the result of experience with television.

The "medium as the message" came to be studied again in the 1970s. Much of what children, and others, see on television is not only the content. They learn the meaning of television's forms and codes—its camera techniques, sound effects, and organization of programs. Some of the effects of television can be traced to its forms, such as fast or slow action, loud or soft music, camera angles, and so on. Some researchers suggest that fast action, loud music, and stimulating camera tricks may account for changes in behavior following televised violence.

Although television producers and viewers alike agree that television can arouse the emotions, there has been very little research on television's effects on emotional development and functioning. It is known that some people have strong emotional attachments to television characters and personalities and that children usually prefer characters most like themselves. Research on television and the emotions should be given a top priority.

Violence and Aggression

The report of the Surgeon General's committee states that there was a high level of violence on television in the 1960s. Although in the 1970s there was con-

siderable controversy over definitions and measurement of violence, the amount of violence has not decreased. Violence on television seems to be cyclical, up a little one year, down a little the next, but the percentage of programs containing violence has remained essentially the same over the past decade.

Senator Pastore's question can be asked again: What is the effect of all this violence? After 10 more years of research, the consensus among most of the research community is that violence on television does lead to aggressive behavior by children and teenagers who watch the programs. This conclusion is based on laboratory experiments and on field studies. Not all children become aggressive, of course, but the correlations between violence and aggression are positive. In magnitude, television violence is as strongly correlated with aggressive behavior as any other behavioral variable that has been measured. The research question has moved from asking whether or not there is an effect to seeking explanations for the effect.

According to observational learning theory, when children observe television characters who behave violently, they learn to be violent or aggressive themselves. Observational learning from television has been demonstrated many times under strict laboratory conditions, and there is now research on when and how it occurs in real life. Television is also said to mold children's attitudes which later may be translated into behavior. Children who watch a lot of violence on television may come to accept violence as normal behavior.

Although a causal link between televised violence and aggressive behavior now seems obvious, a recent panel study by researchers at the National Broadcasting Company found no evidence for a long-term enduring relation between viewing violent television programs and aggressive behavior. Others doing television research will no doubt examine this new study to try to learn why it does not agree with many other findings.

Imaginative Play and Prosocial Behavior

Since children spend many hours watching the fantasy world of television it can be asked whether television enriches their imaginative capacities and whether it leads to a distortion of reality. Evidence thus far is that television does not provide material for imaginative play and that watching violent programs and cartoons is tied to aggressive behavior and to less imaginative play. Most young children do not know the difference between reality and fantasy on television, and of course, they do not understand how television works or how the characters appear on the screen. Television, however can be used to enhance children's imaginative play if an adult watches with the child and interprets what is happening.

During the past 10 years research on television's influence on prosocial behavior has burgeoned. As a result evidence is persuasive—children can learn to be altruistic, friendly and self-controlled by looking at television programs depicting such behavior patterns. It appears that they also learn to be less aggressive.

Socialization and Conceptions of Social Reality

Most studies on socialization have been in the form of content analyses concerned with sex, race, occupation, age and consumer roles. There are more men than women on entertainment television, and the men on the average are older. The men are mostly strong and manly, the women usually passive and feminine. Both, according to some analysts are stereotyped but the women are even more stereotyped than the men. Lately there has been more sexual reference, more innuendo, and more seductive actions and dress. Both parents and behavioral scientists consider television to be an important sex educator not only in depictions specifically related to sex but in the relationships between men and women throughout all programs.

For a while, after organized protest removed degrading stereotyped portrayals from the air, there were almost no blacks to be seen on television. About 12 years ago, they emerged again, and now about 10 percent of television characters are black. There are not many Hispanics, Native Americans or Asian Americans.

Television characters usually have higher status jobs than average people in real life. A large proportion of them are professionals or managers, and relatively few are blue-collar workers.

The elderly are underrepresented on television, and, as with the younger adults, there are more old men than old women.

Research shows that consumer roles are learned from television. Children are taught to be avid consumers; they watch the commercials, they ask their parents to buy the products, and they use or consume the products. Not much research has been done with teenagers, but they seem to be more skeptical about advertisements.

In general, researchers seem to concur that television has become a major socializing agent of American children.

In addition to socialization, television influences how people think about the world around them or what is sometimes called their conceptions of "social reality." Studies have been carried out on the amount of fear and mistrust of other people, and on the prevalence of violence, sexism, family values, racial attitudes, illness in the population, criminal justice, and affluence. On the whole, it seems that television leads its viewers to have television-influenced attitudes. The studies on prevalence of violence and mistrust have consistent results: People who are heavy viewers of television are more apt to think the world is violent than are light viewers. They also trust other people less and believe that the world is a "mean and scary" place.

The Family and Interpersonal Relations

There are many television families—about 50 families can be seen weekly—and most of them resemble what people like to think of as the typical American family. The husbands tend to be companions to their wives and friends to their children; many of the wives stay home and take care of the house and children. Recently, however, on entertainment television there have been more divorces, more single-parent families, and more unmarried couples living together. In black families, there are more single parents and more conflict than in white families. The actual effects of these portrayals on family life have been the subject of practically no research.

Television, of course, takes place in the context of social relations, mainly in the family. Parents do not seem to restrict the amount of time their children spend in front of the television set, nor do they usually prevent them from looking at certain programs. They seldom discuss programs with their children except perhaps to make a few favorable comments now and then. Many families look at television together, which brings up the question of who decides what to look at. Usually the most powerful member of the family decides—father first, then mother, then older children. But, surprisingly often, parents defer to the wishes of their young children.

Television in American Society

Television seems to have brought about changes in society and its institutions. Television's effects on laws and norms have been the subject of discussion, but no firm conclusions have been reached. Television, according to some observers, reinforces the status quo and contributes to a homogenization of society and a promotion of middle-class values. Television's ubiquity in bringing events—especially violent and spectacular events—throughout the world to millions of people may mean that television itself is a significant factor in determining the events. Television broadcasts of religious services bring religion to those who cannot get out, but they also may reduce attendance at churches and thus, opportunities for social interactions. Television has certainly changed leisure time activities. For many people, leisure time means just about the same as television time; their off-duty hours are spent mainly in front of the television set. Many of these effects of television, however, are still speculative and need further research to provide more accurate and reliable information.

Education and Learning About Television

Parents, teachers, and others blame television for low grades and low scores on scholastic aptitude tests, but causal relationships are complex, as in television and violence, and they need careful analysis. Among adults, television viewing and education are inversely related: the less schooling, the more television viewing. Although children with low IQs watch television more than others, it is not known if heavy viewing lowers IQ scores or if those with low IQ choose to watch more television. There have been no experimental studies on these questions. Research on television and educational achievement has mixed findings. Some studies found higher achievement with more television viewing, while others found lower, and still others found no relation. There seems to be a difference at different ages. At the lower grades, children who watch a moderate amount of television get higher reading scores than those who watch either a great deal or very little. But at the high school level (a time when heavy viewing tends to be less common), reading scores are inversely related to amount of viewing, with the better readers watching less television.

In terms of educational aspiration, it appears that heavy viewers want high status job but do not intend to spend many years in school. For girls, there is even more potential for conflict between aspirations and plans; the girls who are heavy viewers usually want to get married, have children, and stay at home to take care of them, but at the same time they plan to remain in school and to have exciting careers.

Finally, one of the most significant developments of the decade is the rise of interest in television literacy, critical viewing skills, and intervention procedures. "Television literacy" is a way to counteract the possible deleterious effects of television and also to enhance its many benefits. Several curricula and television teaching guides have been prepared, containing lessons on all facets of television technology and programing—camera techniques, format, narratives, commercials, differences between reality and fantasy, television's effect on one's life, and so on. Use of these educational and intervention procedures has demonstrated that parents, children, and teachers can achieve much greater understanding of television and its effects, but whether this understanding changes their social behavior is not yet known.

Reference

(1) Murray, J. P. Television and youth: 25 years of research & controversy. Boys Town, Neb.: The Boys Town Center for the Study of Youth Development, 1981.

Implications for the Eighties

It is now time to look at the total array of research on television and behavior in the 1970s and to discern the import and implications for the coming decade.

First, an impressive body of scientific knowledge has been accumulated since 1972, when the report of the Surgeon General's Advisory Committee was published. Some 3,000 reports, papers, and books have been published. The number of scientists engaged in research on television began to proliferate as a result of the report of the Surgeon General's committee, and the number has continued to grow. Yet, in relation to the magnitude of the research field and the many questions to which answers are urgently needed, the number of scientists involved in the study of television is still miniscule compared with other research specialists. If the momentum of research productivity achieved in the 1970s is to continue into the 1980s, the number will have to be increased.

When the Surgeon General's committee completed its report, the members believed that their task was not really finished. What had been a seemingly straightforward question of scientific evidence quickly developed extensive ramifications. While the original question on televised violence had been partially answered, the framework in which the question had been posed raised larger issues abou television and behavior. Now, 10 years later, the committee's concern with these larger issues becomes even more urgent and timely.

The research findings of the past decade have reaffirmed the powerful influence of television on the viewers. Almost all the evidence testifies to television's role as a formidable educator whose effects are both pervasive and cumulative. Television can no longer be considered as a casual part of daily life, as an electronic toy. Research findings have long since destroyed the illusion that television is merely innocuous entertainment. While the learning it provides is mainly incidental rather than direct and formal, it is a significant part of the total acculturation process. Furthermore, indications are that future technological developments in programming, distribution, and television usage will probably increase television's potential influence on the viewer.

Extending over all other findings is the fact that television is so large a part of daily life. Within American society, television is now a universal phenomenon. About half the present population never knew a world without it. Television is, in short, an American institution. It has changed or influenced most other institutions, from the family to the functioning of the government.

In the 1980s, television will no doubt continue to be pervasive and ubiquitous in American life. Information about its role and its effects will be needed by all those who will help to shape television's future and to make decisions about it. Beside the general public, these groups include parents; professionals in fields like education and public health; organizations that represent special interests such as those of children, ethnic groups, mental health, and business; local, State, and Federal governmental agencies; the research community; and the television industry itself.

In contrast to previous research, the bulk of the current findings no longer focuses on specific cause-effect or input-output results. Television viewing is so entrenched in American daily life that it can only be regarded as a major socializing influence almost comparable to the family, the schools, the church, and other socializing institutions. Socialization can be thought of as the accumulation of the many specific learning experiences throughout one's life. It is not limited to the developing child, although children have an especially strong need to acquire knowledge and skills as they grow up. But at any age, a person represents the product of cumulative learning, and thinking and behavior are affected by a mixture of recent learning and of learning earlier in life. As people go through life-cycle transitions, the importance of television changes for them. Old people, for example, are more like very young people in their use of television than they are like middle-age adults. Further studies of socialization and general learning from television need be continued with children and expanded to include the entire lifespan.

Health

With television a central feature of daily life, it is somewhat surprising that little attention has been given to its influences on physical and mental health. Television's portrayals of mentally ill persons as often being either violent or victimized is particularly unfortunate, because it may be contributing to the well-known stigma borne by those suffering from mental illness. The widespread consumption of alcoholic beverages on television, together with the fact that such consumption is presented as a pleasant aspect of social life with no deleterious consequences, may also be fostering attitudes and subsequent behavior that reinforce the use of alcohol by viewers. Similarly, the portrayals of snacks and other nonnutritious foods may be affecting eating habits, especially of children. Health portrayals on television thus are distorted frequently and have the possibility of unwittingly encouraging poor health. But the fact that very little smoking appears on television is noteworthy and perhaps an indication that television has been responsive to an important health problem. Other efforts to eliminate depictions detrimental to good health would not inhibit the dramatic impact of the programs and could have positive social consequences.

Another area, perhaps more difficult to implement, would be the possibility of programing for special populations, such as institutionalized individuals in psychiatric settings, in homes for the elderly, and in hospitals. This kind of programing offers an excellent opportunity for constructive change.

In the 1980s, it can be predicted that there will be increased use of television for health campaigns. Such campaigns should be very carefully planned and the more recent theories and practices of evaluation research applied to them. Campaigns can be a valuable resource to improve the Nation's health, but they require at least the talent and financial backing that go into making a good commercial.

There have been no attempts to assess in systematic studies the direct effect of television viewing on health. For example, the passivity of television viewing has not been studied in connection with physical fitness of children and adults. The relationship, if any, of the amount of physical exercise to the amount of viewing time is not known, nor is there any clue concerning whether early and continued heavy viewing establishes enduring patterns of passive, rather than active, participation in daily life. Eating behavior during television viewing could be significant. For example, eating junk foods while watching television is common, and it is possible that some adults link television viewing with drinking wine and beer. The cumulative effects of these conditioned eating and drinking patterns might have serious long-term effects.

Television as a stressor needs to be studied. At times, it can be stress reducing and at other times stress enhancing. The noise levels of television may operate as a chronic stressor for some persons. It is not known whether stress can be induced by the synergistic effect of television arousal and other psychosocial variables that may be operating.

There is a dearth of studies on the psychophysiological implications of television watching. Possible areas for research, to name only a few, include sleep and sleep disturbances, autonomic nervous system functioning, rigorous studies on brain lateralization, biological rhythms, and perhaps even on neurotransmitters, all as related to television. A practical question here is: Are there children suffering chronic fatigue from staying up late to look at television? The decade of the 1980's needs biomedical pioneers to begin this kind of important research.

The suggestion by the Surgeon General's committee that it would be well to explore television's health-promoting possibilities may at last be a major research direction.

Cognitive Processes

Several issues have emerged from the innovative research on cognitive processes in the 1970s, all with implications for continued research into the 1980s.

Children growing up with television must learn cognitive strategies for dealing with the medium. At very early ages, children already demonstrate active and selective viewing strategies, for example, watching animation, turning away from dialog they do not understand, turning back when music or sound effects suggest lively action or "pixillation" (animated activity). Age factors as well as properties of the medium interact to determine how children develop useful viewing strategies.

Television differs from real life by using structural symbols or codes that may be difficult to understand. A character who is remembering things from the past may fade out of view, and actual past scenes then show the character's memories. Children at young ages may not recognize these "flashback" conventions and be confused. Conventions, such as split screens (screen divided into two parts with a different picture on each part), may not be understood, and magical effects, for example, superheroes leaping over buildings, may be taken literally. While children eventually learn television conventions and viewing strategies and incorporate some of them into more general thinking, there are suggestions that some forms of presentation are more effective than others in helping children to learn the television codes and also in enhancing general cognitive effectiveness.

Age differences are highly significant in television viewing. These differences, which themselves reflect differences in conceptual capacities (for example, the inability of preschoolers to engage in conversation), lead to sizable differences in how much sense children can make of stories on television. Structural factors, such as rapid shifts of scene, may lead young children to misunderstand the intended plots, to overemphasize the more obvious features of a story (for example, violence), and to be confused about causality. The fact that young children do not easily relate consequences to earlier actions makes the adult interpretation of the story quite different from that of the child. The contention is often made that children's programs, or adult programs watched by children, really are prosocial programs because the "bad guy" gets punished at the end. What is not recognized in this argument is the critical fact that young children simply do not see the relation between the punishment and the earlier antisocial behavior. This finding can be generalized to include a large number of other age-specific responses to, and attributes of, television viewing. The dilemma—and the challenge—raised by these research findings is that it is difficult to produce programs that simultaneously satisfy the needs and capabilities of a widely diverse audience.

Although there is some evidence that young children's imaginativeness and the stories they use in spontaneous play are enhanced by television materials, the predominant evidence suggests that heavy viewing is associated with lower imagination and less creativity. Under special circumstances with carefully designed programing and with adult mediation, children can increase their spontaneous playfulness, imagination, and enjoyment after television viewing. There is reason to believe, however, that under conditions of unsupervised viewing children may not learn necessary distinctions between "realism" and "fantasy" in stories.

More research is needed to explore ways of presenting material that will maximize not only attention but also comprehension and reflective thought. More research also needs to be done on effective learning. The research should address such questions as: What combinations of structure and content maximize interest, attention, and learning effectiveness of television for different age groups.

Emotional Development and Functioning

Children show a wide range of emotional reactions to television. The evidence suggests that moderately rapid pacing leads to arousal and enjoyment in children. For adolescents and young adults, a good balance of lively pace and some (but not too much) humor may enhance attention and comprehension. There is not yet adequate evidence to support some current beliefs that children have been led by lively television programing to be inattentive to verbal presentations and detailed material presented in the classroom. While children can learn to be more empathic and to express or understand emotions from television presentations with guidance from adults, the data on heavy viewing suggest that they tend to be less empathic or to show negative reactions, such as unhappy or fearful emotions.

The decade of the 1970s did not produce much research on the emotions and television. Increasing attention to this area is highly desirable in the 1980s.

Violence and Aggression

Recent research confirms the earlier findings of a causal relationship between viewing televised violence and later aggressive behavior. A distinction must be made, however, between groups and individuals. All the studies that support the causal relationships demonstrate group differences. None supports the case for particular individuals. As with most statistical analyses of complex phenomena, group trends do not predict individual or isolated events. This distinction does not, of course, minimize the significance of the findings, even though it delimits their applicability. Moreover, no single study unequivocally confirms the conclusion that televised violence leads to aggressive behavior. Similarly, no single study unequivocally refutes that conclusion. The scientific support for the causal relationship derives from the convergence of findings from many studies, the great majority of which demonstrate a positive relationship between televised violence and later aggressive behavior.

During the 1970s, research on violence and aggression yielded interesting new information. Recent studies have extended the age range in which the relationship between televised violence and aggressive behavior can be demonstrated. Earlier research had been primarily with children from 8 to 13 years old. The evidence has now been extended to include preschoolers at one end of the age spectrum and older adolescents at the other. In addition, most of the earlier studies had indicated that boys, but not girls, were influenced by watching televised violence, while recent research in both the United States and other countries shows similar relationships in samples of girls as well as boys.

Despite some argument about how to measure the amount of television violence, the level of violence on commercial television has not markedly decreased since the Surgeon General's committee published its report. What this means for the 1980s is difficult to discern. If one extrapolates from the past 20 years, it can be predicted that violence on television will continue to be about the same. Yet there may be various social forces and groups that will work to bring about a diminution.

Research evidence accumulated during the past decade suggests that the viewer learns more than aggressive behavior from televised violence. The viewer learns to be a victim and to identify with victims. As a result, many heavy viewers may exhibit fear and apprehension, while other heavy viewers may be influenced toward aggressive behavior. Thus, the effects of televised violence may be even more extensive than suggested by earlier studies, and they may be exhibited in more subtle forms of behavior than aggression.

Although violence and aggression are no longer the central focus of television research, there is still a need to study them. More research is needed to distinguish how individual predisposition may interact with and influence the effects of television violence. These studies should include, for example, the relations of age, sex, race, socioeconomic status, and social setting to the effects of violence.

Prosocial Behavior and Socialization

Potentially, as research suggests, children (and to some degree adults) can learn constructive social behavior, for example, helpfulness, cooperation, friendliness, and imaginative play, from television viewing, especially if adults help them grasp the material or reinforce the program content. It is less certain whether these positive benefits are actually being achieved, since analyses of television content and form suggest that such potentially useful material is embedded in a complicated format and is viewed at home by children under circumstances not conducive to effective generalization. Additional research is required to determine the conditions under which prosocial behavior is most likely to be learned.

If almost everybody is learning from television, the question of television's influence needs to be rephrased in terms not only of what specific content is acquired but of what constraints or qualifications television imposes on people's learning capacities. Thus, television content reflecting certain stereotypes may limit or distort how people view women, ethnic groups, or the elderly, for example, and how people interpret the extent to which there are dangers that confront them in daily life.

There is a clear need to study family beliefs and styles as they may be influenced by heavy television viewing. And there has been little research on interpersonal relations as they have an effect on, and as they are influenced by, television.

Educational Achievement and Aspiration

The evidence now supports the opinion that heavy television viewing tends to displace time required to practice reading, writing, and other school-learning skills. These effects are particularly noticeable for children from middle socioeconomic levels who might in the past have spent more time in practicing reading. Television on the whole also seems to interfere with educational aspirations. The cultivation effects leading to increased cognitive skills and educational aspirations in heavy-viewing girls from lower socioeconomic levels are evident, suggesting that amount of viewing may influence social class or IQ groups differently. Unfortunately, studies examining the value of specific types of programing for reading interest and skill development have not been carried out.

The sheer attractivness of television may preempt other activities which were part of daily life, such as sports or hobbies, social activities like playing cards, and, for children, studying and homework activity. Thus the medium's pervasive attraction may also be interfering with certain social and cognitive skill developments formerly acquired through direct exchanges between people or through reading. In this sense, television viewing may be influencing how people learn generally, not only from watching television.

Critical Viewing Skills

Recognition of the pervasiveness of television has led during the past decade to the beginnings of a new effort to teach children and others to understand the medium. Several school curricula have been constructed. Programs for elementary school children that include teacher-taught lessons, sometimes with videotape segments to enhance effectiveness, have been tested increasingly in the schools. Accumulating evidence suggests that such educational programs are welcomed by teachers and pupils and that the programs do produce changes in awareness of television production, special effects, the nature of commercials, the excesses of violence, and so on. Longer term effects of genuine critical viewing at home or of reduced viewing or more selective viewing have yet to be demonstrated. Teaching about television is considered by many television researchers to be one of the most significant practical developments of the 1970s, one that needs to be continued, expanded, and evaluated in the 1980s.

New Technologies

The report of the Surgeon General's committee predicted that new technologies would result in many changes in television programing and viewing. These changes were slow in coming, but it appears that they will be made in the 1980s. Cable television and videodiscs may gradually alter the content of entertainment television. They also may make it feasible to have different programing for various special populations. Interactive television is considered by many people to be a desirable advance because it will require greater effort and thus result in more effective learning.

Ten years ago, the report of the Surgeon General's committee led to significant increases in the research on television and behavior. This research also expanded in many directions from the original focus on the effects of televised violence. Now, 10 years after the appearance of that report, it is clear that research on television is still growing and expanding and that the research in the 1970s has opened new vistas and posed new questions. Compared with the 1970s, the decade of the 1980s should witness an even greater intensity of necessary research effort on television and behavior.

Rice, Huston, and Wright argue that research attention to the forms of television, those formal features of the medium that demarcate it from other mass media presentations, are powerful predictors of children's attention to and comprehension of televised content. Further study, they suggest, will allow generalizations about separating the effects attributable to form from those associated with content and will clarify the interaction between the two. Mabel L. Rice, Aletha C. Huston, and John C. Wright are at the Center for Research on the Influences of Television on Children (CRITC) at the University of Kansas.

2

THE FORMS OF TELEVISION
Effects on Children's Attention, Comprehension, and Social Behavior

Mabel L. Rice, Aletha C. Huston, and John C. Wright

When television swept the United States and other industrialized countries in the 1950s, much of the research was concerned with the effects of this new medium on the lives and minds of the citizenry, especially children. By the 1960s, research about television had turned to studies of the content rather than the medium itself. Yet the content of television is not unique to the medium. Violence, prosocial actions, stereotypes, and the like can be presented in print, still pictures, or oral descriptions. What is unique about television is the *form* in which information is presented. Television is a visual medium in which a stream of constantly changing images can be generated by techniques that are not replicated in real-world experience. Camera cuts, pans across scenes, zooms in and out, slow and fast motion, and special effects of all kinds are used in unique ways—musical accompaniments, sound effects, unusual cries and noises, canned laughter, and faceless narrators. Finally, of course, television is a verbal medium. The verbal and linguistic conventions of television are not unique. They are the language conventions of the real world, but the ways in which language is used to convey content (rather than the content it conveys) is an important *formal* property of the television medium.

In the past few years, the attention of researchers studying television's influence on children has returned to the forms of the medium itself as distinct from the content presented with those forms. The purpose of this review[1] is to present the recent research on television forms and child viewing and to suggest some issues in need of resolution. Because most of the research is in the early stages of exploring new terrain, the unresolved issues outnumber the solid conclusions, and many of the findings must be regarded as tentative.

Both theoretical and practical concerns have led to the study of television form. McLuhan's (1964) early suggestion that television contained representational codes fundamentally different from those of print remained a vague formulation, until Salomon (1979) and Huston-Stein and Wright (1977) began to elaborate the implications of that notion for developmental theory. Salomon focused particularly on the influence of visual media codes on children's mental processing and mental skills. Huston-Stein and Wright attempted to place television forms (both visual and auditory) in the context of a broader theory of developmental change in patterns of attention and information processing.

The practical concerns of producing effective educational programing have been a second impetus for research on television form. Much of this work has been carried out in conjunction with the Children's Television Workshop productions, *Sesame Street* and *The Electric Company*. The goal is to identify the program attributes or production techniques that are maximally effective in gaining and holding children's attention and in communicating information to them in ways they will understand and remember.

A third reason for studying form has been increasing suspicion that many effects attributed to television content may be partially due to the forms in which the content is presented. We have argued, for example, that some of the aggression-arousing effects of violent television may be a result of the high levels of "hype" typically accompanying violence as well as the violent content. Similarly, most of the research on the effects of

[1] Much of this research and the preparation of this review were supported by a grant to CRITC from the Spencer Foundation.

prosocial television on very young children has used *Mister Rogers' Neighborhood,* a program notable for its slow pace, gentle style, and unusual language forms. It is possible that some of the positive effects of that program may be a function of its verbal and nonverbal formal properties.

One may question whether it is possible to distinguish crisply between content and form. Although they can be defined independently, we acknowledge that in practice the forms of television and content messages co-occur in systematic ways. The relationship is probably analogous to that between grammar and meaning in verbal language. Among linguists there is a growing belief that the grammar of verbal language cannot be isolated from semantic meanings (e.g., Fillmore's case grammar 1968). To the degree that form and content are confounded in the real world, all studies of television content are subject to the criticism that their results may be partially a function of the forms in which that content was presented. Theory and research focusing on form independent of content may redress the imbalance so that their interactive effects can be better understood.

Representational Codes of Television

Verbal and nonverbal forms are the representational codes of television. Because children view television at a very early age, it is tempting to assume that these representational codes are simple and of little interest. However, television is a medium that can be processed at differing levels of complexity. There is a difference between superficial consumption of interesting audiovisual events and mental extraction of information from coded messages, a distinction formulated by Salomon (1979). He used the term "literate viewing" to refer to "a process of information extraction by the active negotiation of the coding elements of the message" (p. 189). The notion of "literate viewing" is closely related to the more informal term "media literacy." With age and viewing experience, children's attention to, and comprehension of, television program changes (e.g., Collins 1979; Krull and Husson 1979; Wright et al. 1980). It is presumed that these developmental changes reflect increasing facility with television's conventions and content, i.e., the beginning television viewer is not "media literate" but instead gradually acquires such competence as a function of experience with the medium and the attainment of certain minimal cognitive abilities.

Just because one can become a literate viewer at an early age and without conscious effort does not demonstrate that the task is simple. The representational codes of television range in complexity from literal visual depiction to the most abstract and arbitrary symbols, including verbal language and audiovisual metaphor. The child's task is not an easy one. The change from infants' sensory-motor awareness of alternations in patterns of visual and verbal stimuli (Hollenbeck and Slaby 1979) to the literate viewing skills of elementary school-age children involves a major qualitative advance, accompanied by developmental growth in related perceptual and cognitive skills.

Levels of Representation

The simplest level of representation is literal visual and/or auditory portrayal of real-world information, e.g., a shot of a car moving on the highway. A child's ability to process this level is presumably dependent primarily on perceptual and cognitive skills used in interpreting real-world stimuli. But even at this literal level, object recognition at unusual angles of viewing, lighting, and distance requires perceptual generalization and constancies not yet fully developed in the youngest viewers.

On the second level of representation are media forms and conventions that do not have an exact real-world counterpart. some of these, such as cuts and zooms, are analogs of perceptual experience. For example, a zoom-in is a perceptual analog of moving close to an object. Other media conventions are more distinct from real-world experience. Dissolves, slow motion, musical accompaniments, sound effects, and electronically generated visual special effects are relatively specific to film and television. These features provide a structure for the presentation of content in a manner analogous to syntax in language. A literate viewer must be able to decode the structural meanings of formal features. For example, fades and dissolves often indicate major transitions in time, place, or content; cuts are more often used for minor shifts from one character or viewing angle to another (Huston-Stein et al. 1979). In children's programs, distinctive visual "markers" are used to separate programs from commercials; the literate viewer must understand their function. This understanding is not automatic. For example, 5- and 6-year-olds did not understand the meaning of separators between programs and commercials in one recent study (Palmer and McDowell 1979).

Media codes can also serve as models for mental representation or mental skills. That is, the child can adopt the media forms as modes of representations in her own thinking. Salomon (1979) has demonstrated, for example, that children can learn to analyze a complex stimulus into small parts by observing camera zooms in and out. Apparently, the camera provided a model of the mental process of focusing on specific parts of the stimulus. Media codes can be internalized as forms of mental representation, as suggested by McLuhan (1964), so that people can think in moving pictures with flashbacks, fast and slow motion, changes from color to black and white, and other media conventions (Salomon 1979).

The forms of television can also take on connotative meaning, either because of their repeated association with certain content themes or because of their metaphorical similarity to real-world objects and symbols. For example, rapid action, loud music, and sound effects are often associated with violence in children's programs (Huston et al. 1981). Commercials for masculine sex-typed toys are made with high action, rapid cuts, and loud noise, whereas feminine sex-typed toys are advertised with fades, dissolves, and soft music (Welch et al. 1979). The forms themselves may come to signal violence or sex typing to children, even when the content cues are minimal or nonexistent.

The third level of representation consists of symbolic forms not unique to the medium. Such forms may be nonlinguistic (e.g., a red stoplight) or linguistic. It is also possible for verbal language to encode forms at the other two levels. For example, dialog can encode the literal representation of reality (the first level), as when a speaker describes on-screen objects or events, or dialog can encode the conventional significance of a production feature (the second level), as when a fade is accompanied by the line "Once upon a time, long, long ago. . . ." In this sense of double encoding, it is possible for the first two levels to be nested in the linguistic codes. Such piggybacking of representational means could aid children in understanding the message and also, by association, facilitate their mastery of the codes themselves (cf. Rice and Wartella 1981).

It is apparent that the second and third levels of representational codes found in children's television programs not only have different surface characteristics but also are derived from different sources or experiences. The second level of representation, specific knowledge, is probably acquired largely as a function of experience with the medium. That is not the case with the third level, where symbols are shared by the wider culture. By definition, these codes have currency outside the medium of television and can be learned without viewing television. They also have a different utility in the world, leading to slightly different reasons for investigating them. The media-specific codes are important insofar as they reveal what is involved in a child's processing of televised information. The verbal language of television is of special interest insofar as it contributes to a child's processing of televised messages and other media codes and also, perhaps more importantly, as it serves to facilitate a child's mastery of the general linguistic code (cf. Rice in press).

While the representational functions of the linguistic system have been described by linguists in a long research tradition, the production conventions, or codes, of television have only recently come to the attention of behav-

ioral scientists. The first step in understanding these codes and their functions is to develop descriptive taxonomies for formal features and to describe the ways in which they are used in television productions.

Most descriptions of formal features have been developed for the purpose of studying television's influence on children. This is not to imply that formal features are without relevance for adults or that studies conducted with adult subjects are without implications for understanding children's television viewing experiences. A general discussion of how formal features may influence adult viewers is, however, beyond the scope of this review; only those studies immediately pertinent to child-directed issues and investigations are presented. Readers interested in the effects of television forms on adult audiences may wish to refer to television and film broadcasting and production publications, where issues of form are often discussed in regard to editing techniques. For example, Messaris et al. (1979) argue that editing techniques (the sequence and composition of visual shots) influenced how adult audiences perceived the nature of the interchanges between Carter and Ford during the televised 1976 presidential debates.

Descriptive Analyses of Television Forms

Two groups have attempted descriptions of the occurrence and co-occurrence of formal features in existing television programs. One such analysis of adult programs was based on the information theory construct, "entropy" (Watt and Krull 1974). Entropy or form complexity was defined by the "variability" of sets, characters, and speakers and by the "unpredictability" with which each set, character, or speaker might appear next. Operationally, the entropy measure included the number of different sets, characters, and speakers, and the amount of time during which each of these appeared in the program. These investigators coded a sample of adult programs and demonstrated by factor analysis that the formal features of the programs could be clustered in two major groupings: "dynamism" (roughly the rate of change in scenes and characters) and "unfamiliarity" (roughly the variability or number of different scenes and characters). In a later study, these investigators found that form complexity was correlated with violent content in prime time programs (Watt and Krull 1977). Wartella and Ettema (1974) used the same coding system on a set of commercials designed for children and adults but found that the two factors emerging were visual and auditory features.

Formal features of children's television programs have been analyzed in our work (Huston et al. 1981) to determine what features co-occur, what features characterize animated and live programs, and how formal features differ as a function of target audience or production goals. In two samples of children's programs selected from Saturday morning, prime time, and daytime educational programing (primarily PBS), action (physical activity of characters), variability of scenes (number of different scenes), and tempo (rate of scene and character change) were grouped with visual special effects, rapid cuts, loud music, and sound effects. This package of features was labeled "perceptually salient" because it was characterized by high intensity, rapid change, and rapid motion.

Commercial programs for young children are packed with these perceptually salient forms. Although such formal features are more frequent in animated than in live shows, Saturday morning live programs have higher rates of perceptually salient features than prime time or educational programs. This pattern of heavy reliance on perceptual salience suggests an image of the child in the minds of producers as a being whose attention must be captured and held by constant action, change, noise, and visual onslaught. Although much of what children watch is family adult programing, these children's programs may be particularly important developmentally because they constitute the child's earliest experience with the medium. They may set the standard for what the child expects from television. In addition, they are less likely than adult programs to be mediated or buffered by parents' or adults' viewing with the child. We do not know what effects early experience with heavily saturated television "hype" and violence has on later development, later viewing patterns, or on tastes and preferences in the medium, but these questions are critically important for future research.

Educational programs for young children use some perceptually salient visual features that characterize Saturday morning programs, though at more moderate levels. They combine these features, however, with other forms that have considerable potential for helping children to understand, rehearse, and remember a message. These include child dialog—probably the best form of speech to gain and hold children's attention—as well as songs, long zooms, and moderate levels of physical activity. All of these features provide opportunities for reflection, rehearsal, and review of content. Songs are frequently used to repeat themes and as a device for helping children to rehearse. Long zooms involve slow presentation and/or emphasis of important content. Because young children often understand content that is demonstrated in action, the moderate levels of action may be a particularly important means of conveying information in a form that is interesting and comprehensible to a young child. Educational programs package their content in a set of forms that is quite different from commercial programing for children, and they appear to be

designing programs that have good potential to hold attention *and* to communicate a message effectively.

The findings concerning forms in children's programs can also be seen from the perspective of media literacy and its antecedents (Wright and Huston in press). Recall that Saturday morning cartoons were characterized by high levels of action, variability, and tempo. These clusters consist of perceptually salient events, such as physical activity, music, sound effects, scene changes, and visual special effects. The conspicuous nature of these features may allow the features themselves to become the message. That is, the child may pay more attention to *how* the information is conveyed than to *what* the message is, especially when the plot lines are thin to begin with. Unnoticed in the entertainment value of the features is the tutorial nature of the experience. The child is receiving explicit cues about how messages are communicated on television. In this case, the relationship between form and content is the opposite of the usual assumption. That is, the forms overpower the content (from the young viewer's perspective), whereas the problem is usually regarded as a matter of the content controlling the form (from the producer's perspective).

Linguistic Codes

The coding systems inherent in verbal language constitute another component of the forms of television. In television programs, verbal language is a code within a code. Descriptive studies of the language of children's television can provide information for two purposes: (1) Knowing the nature of television's linguistic conventions or codes and how they interact with other forms of communication in children's programs is a critical part of any attempt to understand how children process televised information; and (2) analysis of television's linguistic codes may show how they are adjusted in different programs to different levels of linguistic competence in the viewer and therefore how they may, under certain conditions, play an important role in furthering language acquisition itself.

In a pilot study of the linguistic structure of children's programing in relation to formal feature use, Rice (1979) analyzed 25 categories of linguistic coding in six programs. The programs represented animated stories with high, low, and no dialog (respectively, *Fat Albert, Bugs Bunny,* and *Road Runner*); a live program representing situation comedy (*Gilligan's Island*); and educational programs differing in age of intended audience and format (*Mister Rogers' Neighborhood* and *The Electric Company*). Three sets of linguistic descriptors were scored: (1) "Communication flow" consisted of measures of length, variability, rate, and repetition of utterances; (2) "language structure" contained measures of grammatical completeness, descriptive qualifiers, and stressed single words; (3) "meaning/content" variables included focusing (i.e., giving selective prominence to a particular linguistic constituent), nonliteral meanings, explicit instructions, novel words, and immediacy of reference.

Distinctive patterns of language usage were evident in the two educational programs. *Mister Rogers' Neighborhood*, the educational program for preschoolers, presented a moderate pattern of verbal communication: a moderate amount of dialog, without the use of nonliteral meanings or novel words, combined with moderate amounts of focusing and some use of stressed single words. *The Electric Company*, an educational program designed for early school-age children, used the most dialog of all the shows sampled and incorporated techniques for drawing attention and interest to dialog (e.g., focusing, stressed single words, novel words, nonliteral meanings) while at the same time adjusting for easier comprehension of grammatical forms (e.g., short comments, partial grammatical units, low variability in length) and content (e.g., reference to immediately present events). While it is widely recognized that the purpose of *The Electric Company* is to enhance children's reading skills, the fact that it does so by means of intensive verbal presentation is generally overlooked. Both *Mister Rogers' Neighborhood* and *The Electric Company* used techniques that are likely to facilitate children's comprehension of language (stressed single words, focusing), but the latter also used a more complex pattern of verbal presentation designed to challenge the more linguistically competent school-age viewer.

Unlike the educational programs, the commercial programs containing dialog showed little evidence that language codes were adjusted to the level of the child viewer. *Bugs Bunny* and *Fat Albert* contained frequent nonliteral meanings and little focusing. *Gilligan's Island* was particularly high in descriptive qualifiers and nonreferential content. Although *Fat Albert* and *The Electric Company* both presented complex linguistic patterns, they differed in the amount of adjustment to facilitate the viewer's ease of processing. *Gilligan's Island* was unique, i.e., it did not share any distinctive language features with the other shows.

Comparison of the linguistic features with the formal production features of the six programs revealed that the shows with low amounts of dialog (*Bugs Bunny* and *Road Runner*) were high in action, pace, cuts, fades, zooms, visual special effects, vocalizations, sound effects, and music. All of these production features are perceptually salient ones that attract and hold visual attention in young viewers. The two verbally complex shows, *The Electric Company* and *Fat Albert,* each contained some distinctive uses of salient formal features: *Fat Albert* had very high pace, frequent cuts, pans, and background music; *The Electric Company* had a high number of vocalizations. *Mister Rogers' Neighborhood* and *Gilligan's Island* demonstrated lower rates of nonlinguistic formal features.

Such findings suggest a continuum of difficulty of representational coding in this range of children's programs. We would expect linguistic coding to be more difficult for young viewers than the perceptually salient visual and auditory nonverbal codes. The packaging of cartoons, such as *Bugs Bunny* and *Road Runner,* seems well suited to young children of limited media or linguistic competence. Similarly, the simple, comprehensible speech in *Mister Rogers' Neighborhood* is well suited to a preschool audience. More complex packaging in shows aimed at an older audience requires considerable linguistic sophistication and comprehension of distinctive uses of formal features. In some cases, the codes are judiciously mixed in packages of information presentation well suited to the communicative competencies of the intended audience. A moderate level of complexity may be important to maintain interest among older relatively sophisticated viewers.

Just as the conventional meanings of production features can be suggested by exaggerated, perceptually salient presentations used to convey redundant content, so there is evidence of adjustments of the linguistic and production codes that are designed to draw attention to and clarify language forms themselves. For example, the frequent focusing operations and stressed single words on *Mister Rogers' Neighborhood* and *The Electric Company* serve to draw attention to the language codes. Furthermore, in these two programs, the meanings of the linguistic forms are often explicitly depicted. Frequently, the content is a visual representation of the verbal meaning, sometimes highlighted by attention-maintaining visual production techniques, such as cuts to a closer focus or different perspective. At least some children's programs appear to combine language adjustments with selective and supportive use of nonlinguistic salient features, at first to supplement and later to challenge the emerging cognitive competencies of the child viewer.

The language of commercials aimed at children warrants explicit attention from researchers insofar as the intent goes beyond the communication of messages to the selling of products. Presumably, the effectiveness of commercials is dependent upon the nature of the linguistic codes presented (i.e., their basic understandability), their referential accuracy, and their use within the social context. Bloome and Ripich (1979) analyzed the social message units of commercials and how the messages related to plot or social context and/or the product. They found that many of the product-tied references were ambiguous in regard to certain features of products, such as the use of flavorings. Also, there was a subtle shift within commercials from using language in a social context to using language to promote products. Language served to establish the social occasion and then to lead the child to a product and its role in enhancing the social occasion.

The Influence of Television Forms on Children's Mental Processes

When children watch television, they can just sit passively and stare at the set if they choose, but a growing body of empirical evidence suggests that this is not the usual level of response. Instead, children are more likely to become involved in the viewing experience, to work at extracting information from coded messages, to respond cognitively, affectively, and socially to program content. They are mentally and socially active viewers (Wright et al. 1978; Singer 1980). At least some (if not most) of their mental responses are influenced by how the information is packaged, i.e., the media-specific and general representational codes employed (Rice and Wartella in press). The ones for which there is empirical evidence are discussed here: children's visual attention while viewing, and their understanding of television forms, program events, and relationships among characters.

Formal Features and Attention

Visual Attention to Television Forms. Studies using different types of programs found that certain production features or program attributes attract and hold children's visual attention while viewing television (Anderson et al. 1979; Anderson and Levin 1976; Anderson et al. 1977; Wartella and Ettema 1974; Wright et al. 1980; Rubinstein et al. 1974). Even though different systems of scoring production features have been used, there is consistency in the findings. First, auditory features, such as lively music, sound effects, children's voices (but not adult dialog), peculiar voices, nonspeech vocalizations, and frequent changes of speaker attract and hold children's attention. Second, conventional visual features, such as cuts, zooms, and pans have less influence, but visual special effects do attract children's attention. Third, in most studies, high levels of physical activity or action elicit and maintain children's attention. Fourth, changes in scene, characters, themes, or auditory events are especially effective in eliciting attention, though they are less important for maintaining it once the child is looking. Features that lose children's attention include long complex speeches, long zooms, song and dance, men's voices, and live animals (Anderson and Levin 1976; Anderson et al. 1979; Susman 1978; Rubinstein et al. 1974; Bernstein 1978).

Auditory Attention

The finding that auditory events, action, and change elicit and hold children's visual attention, while visual features have less influence, serves to remind us that audition and vision interact in a complex manner during information processing. While there is considerable evidence describing visual attention, little information is available describing auditory attention (or the interaction of the two modalities) while viewing television. Any general conceptual model of how children attend to television (including the factors that are proposed as controlling attention) must take into account both visual and auditory attention. The measurement of auditory attention while maintaining a naturalistic viewing situation has been a challenging experimental problem. Looking behavior can be recorded directly in a reliable and unobtrusive manner; listening is a private mental event that is not amenable to direct unobtrusive measurement. A number of techniques for directly measuring auditory attention are being explored in several laboratories.

Pending satisfactory measures, auditory attention can be inferred by testing comprehension of material presented in the auditory modality or material presented when the child is not looking at television. Repeated findings that children receive and understand fairly complex messages from exposure to *Mister Rogers' Neighborhood,* despite low rates of visual attention, have led to speculation that children were often listening even when they were not looking (Tower et al. 1979). Obviously, auditory attention can facilitate comprehension only for material that is presented in an auditory modality, usually speech. Studies in our laboratory, involving microanalysis of short time intervals within a program, indicate close connections among visual presentation of content, visual attending, and recall (Calvert et al. 1981). Similar precision in specifying the mode through which content is presented would be required to infer that auditory attention mediated comprehension.

Auditory attention can also be inferred by observing visual attention to the screen (or lack thereof) and by observing what children talk about while viewing. If they are talking about things unrelated to the television content, they are probably not listening. Even if they are looking at the set, their attention may be only at the level of monitoring instead of active processing. On the other hand, auditory features, such as foreground music and children's speech, recruit visual attention for children who are looking away from the screen—evidence that some form of auditory processing is taking place.

Form and Content Interactions. One of the original reasons for our interest in television form was the hypothesis that formal features in children's television were more important determinants of attention than violent content. The relative contributions of form and violent content are difficult to disentangle because conventions of production lead to correlations of certain forms with violence. Violence in children's programs is usually portrayed with high levels of action and salient auditory and visual features (Huston-Stein et al. 1979). Yet, formal features can be separated conceptually and operationally from violent content. In one study of preschoolers, we selected programs that were high in both action and violence, or high in action and low in violence, or low in both action and violence. (We were unable to find a low action, high violence program.) Children's total attention differed as a function of action, not violence. That is, they were as attentive to high action without violence as they were when it accompanied violence, and less attentive to low action (Huston-Stein et al. 1981).

A more molecular analysis was performed for these three programs and for four other cartoons by dividing each program into 15-second intervals and correlating attention with formal features and violent content. Multiple regressions were performed to determine which features were the best predictors of attention in each program. Violence did not enter any of the seven multiple regressions as a predictor that contributed significant variance independently of formal features, but considerably more data on different programs and different age groups are needed to establish the generality of this null conclusion (Huston-Stein 1977).

Form, Content, and Viewership Ratings. The relation of form and content to children's interest in television programs has also been studied by analyzing feature occurrence rates in nationally broadcast television programs in relation to national audience ratings for different ages, sexes, and regions of the country. For a sample of 34 Saturday morning programs, high action and violent content were predictors of viewership for preschool children. Each made an independent contribution. Among children from age 6 to 11, variability and tempo were the best predictors of viewership (Wright et al. 1980). In a similar analysis of general adult audience ratings in relation to violent content of prime time adventure programs, violence accounted for a minuscule and nonsignificant portion of the variance in viewership (Diener and DeFour 1978).

How Formal Features Influence Attention

Salience and Informativeness. Basic research on young children's attention indicates that perceptual sa-

lience of the stimulus environment is one determinant of attention. The attributes of a stimulus that make it salient include intensity, movement, contrast, change, novelty, unexpectedness, and incongruity (Berlyne 1960). Many of the production features that attract and hold young children's attention fit these criteria defining perceptual salience. We have proposed a developmental model hypothesizing that perceptual salience is a particularly important determinant of attention for very young viewers and/or for viewers with little media experience (Huston-Stein and Wright 1977; 1979).

The theory guiding our work was derived from the more general theoretical work of Wright and Vlietstra (1975) concerning developmental change from "exploration" to "search" in children's modes of information getting. Exploration as a mode of response is governed by the most salient features of the stimulus environment. It involves short duration, discontinuous, and impulsive responding to whatever features of the environment are perceptually dominant from moment to moment. Habituation to the salient features of a particular stimulus environment occurs as one becomes more familiar with it. Application of this model to television experience leads to the hypothesis that, among the youngest and least experienced viewers, the viewing experience consists of the consumption of perceptually salient events as entertainment in their own right. The child's attention is controlled primarily by feature salience. Until the powerful effects of salience have partially habituated, the child is essentially a passive consumer of audiovisual thrills and does not engage in deeper levels of processing (Wright et al. 1981).

Consummatory stimulus-controlled exploration gives way in familiar contexts to perceptual search, a kind of information getting in which the activity is instrumental, rather than consummatory, active rather than passive, and guided by the child's desire to abstract information, rather than by just entertainment, from perceived events. The child's progress from perceptual exploration to perceptual search is believed to be as much or more a function of familiarization through experience and habituation as it is a consequence of cognitive maturation, though, of course, the two are usually confounded. Thus, the older and more experienced viewers are more interested in the content of a program and its meaning and less responsive to salient formal features. When older children do attend to formal features, they may use them as syntactic markers to develop a structural framework in which to organize and integrate their comprehension of content meaning (Wright et al. 1980).

Singer (1980) also proposed that high rates of salient audiovisual events on television absorb children's attention, not only because they are perceptually interesting, but because they are affectively involving. His theory does not, however, contain the proposition that developmental shifts will occur as consequences of cognitive development and familiarity with the medium. Instead, he seems to imply that extensive exposure to salient features in the medium will inhibit other forms of interest (e.g., books and verbal media) and will leave the child focused on the absorbing stimulus features of the moving picture on the screen.

Studies comparing attention patterns of preschool children (age 4–6) with those of children in middle childhood (age 8–10) have supported the hypothesis that younger children are more attentive to salient formal features than are older children (Wartella and Ettema 1974; Wright et al. 1980). In our studies, preschool children attended to high levels of action and audiovisual "tricks," (visual special effects, sound effects, and unfamiliar scenes), but elementary school children were not differentially attentive to these features. Contrary to prediction, however, older children were more attentive than younger ones to programs with rapid pace (i.e., frequent scene and character changes). These studies support the hypothesis that young children's attention is affected by the perceptual salience of television's formal features.

There is less support for the complementary hypothesis that older children's attention is guided more by the informativeness of features, perhaps because informativeness depends on the program context and the child's level of processing. When children try to follow a plot or engage in a logical search for meaning, they probably attend to features that provide cues about time sequences, locations, characters, and events in the program. Studies by Krull and Husson (1979), in fact, suggest that older children may attend to form cues that signal content and form changes during the upcoming 1 or 2 minutes. Preschool children did not show these anticipatory patterns of attention to formal cues. Media literate children may learn temporal associations so they can anticipate what will occur in a program. Older children also attend differentially to informative action and signals associated with scene changes, bit changes, and changes to and from commercials.

Comprehensibility. A somewhat different perspective on the relationship between attention and formal features is proposed by Anderson and his associates, who link attention with the comprehensibility of program content (e.g., Anderson 1979). They suggest that features such as animation or children's voices may serve as signals that the content is designed for children and is therefore likely to be comprehensible. Children may attend to such features, not because of the inherent qualities of the features, but because their media experience leads them to expect meaningful and understandable program content. The fundamental determinant of attention, according to this formulation, is the comprehensibility of the content. Two sets of data are used to support this hypothesis. In one study (Lorch et al. 1979), children's attention to *Sesame Street* was manipulated experimentally by varying the availability of toys and distractions during viewing. Despite the fact that the nondistraction treatment produced very high levels of attention, it did not produce improved comprehension. Within the distracted group, however, the children who attended more comprehended more of the content. This finding was interpreted as demonstrating that comprehensibility guided attention rather than attention determining comprehension. In a subsequent study (Anderson 1979), children attended less to a television program in which the speech was incomprehensible because it was backwards or in a foreign language than to a program with understandable speech. Although the influence of comprehensibility on attention has been tested thus far only by varying language features of programs, the hypothesis suggests that the comprehensibility of nonlinguistic formal features should affect attention through a similar mechanism.

This line of research provides important evidence that very young children are actively processing content when they watch television rather than merely passively consuming audiovideo thrills. It does not, however, establish that feature salience and other noncontent aspects of television programs are unimportant influences on children's attention. In the studies varying comprehensibility, feature salience has been held constant (and fairly high). If salience were low, would comprehensibility alone hold children's attention? Again, the relatively low rates of attention usually found for *Mister Rogers' Neighborhood* suggest not, despite its outstanding comprehensibility. Second, the full range of comprehensibility has not been systematically explored. It is clear that complex, incomprehensible material loses children's attention in comparison to moderately easy, comprehensible material, but one cannot extrapolate that finding to conclude that very easy material would produce more attention than moderately difficult but still comprehensible content. In fact, the model to be proposed here suggests that both extremes of comprehensibility will be less likely to maintain attention than material in the middle range. Moreover, the model explicitly cautions against trying to define moderate comprehensibility as a stimulus feature without taking into account both the cognitive level and the viewing experience of the child.

An Integrative Model of Attention and Development. These seemingly divergent explanations of the determinants of attention can be integrated in the framework of one established model for attention and interest as a function of familiarity and complexity (Hunt 1961).

'That model is illustrated in figure 1. The abscissa is a compound of familiarity and complexity of both form and content. On the left end are highly familiar and oft-repeated bits, like the standard introductions and closings of familiar program series, whose informative content is minimal, and whose formal features have become habituated and no longer elicit attention among habitual viewers. The joint processes of habituation and familiarization (Wright 1977) serve continually to depress attention on the left side of the inverted U-shaped function. By contrast, the forms and content at the high end of the abscissa are unfamiliar, complex, and incomprehensible to the child viewer. They, too, elicit little interest and attention because the child is incapable of understanding their meaning and their relation to other parts of the program. Their decoding requires comprehension of standards the child has not yet acquired and logical integration for which the child is not yet cognitively ready. They also often make reference to outside infor-

mation and contextual knowledge that only adult viewers possess. Thus, attention on the right side of the curve is also low, owing to incomprehensibility. But cognitive development and the child's growing store of background information will, over time, tend to raise attention on the right, just as familiarization and habituation tend to reduce it on the left. The result is a developmental migration of the curve describing a child's attention from left to right as a function of cognitive development and viewing experience. What was interesting for its perceptual salience or simple content becomes boring by its redundancy, and what was incomprehensible or formally complex, and therefore ignored, gradually becomes meaningful and informative in the decoding process and, therefore, of greater interest. If the abscissa is defined in terms of the form and content of a televised stimulus, the location of the curve for a particular child along that gradient is a function of cognitive level (on the right) and viewing history (on the left).

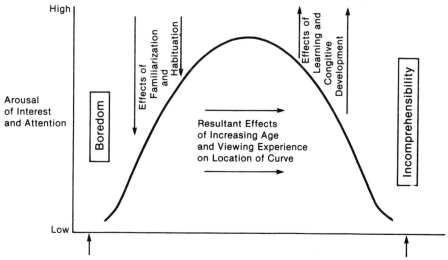

Figure 1. Theoretical model.

How Formal Features Influence Comprehension

As children attend to television, their immediate task is how to interpret the information they receive, what to make of the messages. The medium's representational codes influence this process of comprehension in a number of ways. The media-specific codes themselves require some interpretation, as do the general representational codes, such as language. The coding systems also interact with content in ways that can enhance or interfere with how easily the content can be understood.

Media-Specific Codes and Mental Skills. Recall our opening remarks about how television does not literally present events as we perceive them in the real world. Instead, the representational codes package messages in a manner that requires mental transformations in order to interpret them. The linkage between forms and mental processes can be quite specific and intimate. Salomon (1979) proposed that some production features may be viewed as representing certain mental skills or mental operations. For example, zooming in and out literally portrays the mental operation of relating parts to a whole. Camera cuts that make the image jump from one part of a physical space to another, or from one view of an object to another, correspond to the mental operations of coordinating spaces and taking different perspectives.

Salomon (1979) distinguishes two different ways in which production features can function in relationship to mental processes, at two different levels of interpretative difficulty: One is the function of "supplanting" the skill. That is, the camera essentially performs the operation for the viewer; presumably, the viewer can learn the skill from watching through the eye of the camera. A zoom-in is an example of a camera operation that supplants the skill of analyzing a complex array into subparts or isolating one small part at a time. The second function of media codes is to "call upon" an already existing skill in the viewer. For example, a cut to close-up shot presumes that the viewer can already relate small parts to a larger whole: It does not perform the operation as a zoom does.

Data on both Israeli and American children support the hypothesis that the understanding of and ability to use common media codes increase with age and, in some cases, with media experience. Younger and less experienced viewers benefit more from media formats or formal features that supplant the intellectual skills to which they relate. Older and more experienced viewers understand recurring formats that call upon related mental skills better than do younger and less experienced viewers (Salomon 1979; Palmer 1978). For example, children who were skilled at visual analysis performed better when shown a "cut to close up" format than when shown zooms (Salomon 1974).

Salomon (1979) argues that the relationship between media codes and children's mental processing is not just a one-way process of using mental skills to interpret media codes. Instead, the influence is reciprocal—experience with media codes actually cultivates the existing mental skills to which they relate; the media codes can become part of children's mental schemata, resulting in their ability to think in terms of such codes as zooms and camera cuts. Salomon cautions, however, that the media-specific codes are not the only messages to affect cognition, and not all of television's codes function in this capacity. He suggests that those codes that are unique to television and have a wide potential field of reference are those most likely to contribute to viewers' mental schemata.

The supplanting function of media form was tested in our laboratory in two studies designed to teach conservation of number by showing children animated television sequences demonstrating that the number of objects was independent of their spatial configuration. Pairs of white and black squares separated into designs, danced around one another, and played games; then they returned to their original arrangement with a narrator's reminder that there were still the same number of blacks and whites. Training improved conservation on a televised posttest of number conservation, but did not generalize to a live test, in the first study. In the second, training influenced performance on both televised and live post-tests (Butt and Wright 1979).

Language Codes. There are several aspects of verbal language that have relevance for how children comprehend the messages of television. The first is how children comprehend the verbal dialog itself. This question has yet to be the subject of explicit empirical investigation (beyond a few observations of how children interpret disclaimer phrases in commercials). We can presume however, that children interpret televised verbal information according to the same linguistic processing strategies and constraints that they draw upon in the presence of live speakers. In other words, insofar as the general representational codes of television are like their real-world counterparts, children probably interpret them in much the same way as they do in other social contexts. The second aspect of verbal language with relevance for comprehension is the fact that, unlike the media-specific representational codes, viewers can produce the general codes themselves to communicate their reactions to and understandings of television. Viewers can process the messages of television and then respond in some of the same codes; indeed, they can literally imitate and rehearse the verbal messages, if they choose to do so.

In one study, we explored what children talk about when they watch television as a function of the amount of dialog present in the programs. Preschool and third-grade children watched four shows that differed in the amount of dialog (one show with none, two with moderate amounts, and one with a high frequency of dialog). The children watched in pairs, and they were free to pursue other play activities. Their comments while viewing were transcribed and coded for content categories. The children made the most comments about the television program when viewing the program with no dialog. This trend was more pronounced among the third-graders than the preschoolers. Furthermore, the television-related comments fell in a distinctive pattern: more descriptions of actions and events, more emotional and self-referenced comments (e.g., "I like this part"), more questions about program content, and more statements of knowledge of recurrent program themes for the no-dialog program than for any of the other three. There were very few directly imitative responses (Rice 1980).

The most obvious interpretation of these findings—that children listen when there is dialog and talk when there is no dialog—does not completely account for the results. The total amount of talking was highest in the no-dialog show, but second highest in the high-dialog show. Children talked to one another extensively during a program with frequent dialog, but they more often talked about topics that were irrelevant to the program. In the program without dialog, the absence of dialog, as well as the fact that the program was familiar and repetitive, appeared to stimulate children to talk about the program. Whether or not similar effects would occur for programs that were less repetitive or familiar is not yet clear, but in a program that is interesting, familiar, and simple to understand, it appears that the absence of dialog may elicit comments about aspects of a program that are of interest to children.

Verbal Mediation of Content. Another aspect of verbal language with relevance for television viewing is that it can be used to mediate and direct more general mental processes, such as attention, comprehension, and recall. Verbal labels and explanations have been used in a number of experiments to clarify children's understanding of program content. In one study, preschool children imitated sharing from a television program more when the program included verbal labeling of the characters' behavior than when the behavior was not labeled (Susman 1976). In another investigation, verbal explanations of program themes inserted in a cartoon with a moderately complex plot were relatively ineffective in improving comprehension, but the same explanations provided by an adult viewing with the child aided comprehension considerably. In particular, children who received the adult explanations recalled the temporal order of events in the program and were able to make inferences about implicit content better than controls. They also attended more to the program. Temporal integration and inferential processing of televised information are skills that are difficult for third graders, yet even 4- to 6-year-olds were able to do them better than chance after the adult explanations (Watkins et al. 1980). Other studies have demonstrated similar benefits for kindergarten-age children from verbal labeling of central program themes (Friedrich and Stein 1975).

Television Form and Plot-Relevant Content. Many television programs are narratives; that is, they tell a story consisting of interrelated events. The content of such stories can be distinguished as plot-relevant (central content) or irrelevant to the plot (incidental content). Developmental changes in comprehension of such content have been explored in some detail (Collins 1979). Through second grade, children have limited and fragmented comprehension of story material, fifth graders do better, and eighth graders comprehend most of the story. In particular, younger children tend to recall material that is incidental and irrelevant to the plot, whereas older children appear better able to select central content messages. Younger children also have difficulty in integrating facets of the story that are separated in time (e.g., connecting an action with its motives and consequences), and they have difficulty inferring content that is implicit in the story but is not explicitly shown. All of these findings are based on children's responses to adult prime time dramas (Collins 1979). The specific ages at which changes in comprehension occur may be slightly different for other types of programs, such as those made for children, but the direction of developmental trends is probably the same.

While developmental differences in children's understanding of television content undoubtedly reflect cognitive developmental changes, they may also vary, depending on the form in which content is communicated. In general, children understand information presented visually, so that character actions can be observed, better than they understand information presented in verbal form without accompanying visual cues. In addition, high action and other perceptually salient features maintain children's attention better than dialog and narration, so children may retain the content presented with salient features better than content conveyed primarily through dialog. Obviously, the combination of visual and verbal cues is likely to be most effective (Friedlander et al. 1974).

In one study (Calvert et al. 1979), children's recall of a televised story was measured for four types of content: Central or incidental content was presented with formal features that were either high or low in perceptual salience. High salience features included visual features and moderately high action; low salience features included adult and child dialog. Central content questions often involved inferences; incidental content usually consisted of isolated factual events. Children remembered central, theme-relevant content better when it was presented with highly salient formal features than when it was presented with low salience techniques. Young children (kindergarten age) benefited from attention to such salient features more than older children (third and fourth graders).

Some parallels appear in a study of commercials in which visual cues and words in the form of slogans or labels actually conflicted with the more abstract verbal message. Visual cues and word slogans suggested that the advertised products contained fruit, although the "higher level" abstract verbal message indicated no fruit content. Children from kindergarten through sixth grade accepted the false message conveyed by the visual and associative word cues. Apparently they did not understand the abstract implied message that there was no real fruit in the products (Ross et al. 1981).

Salomon's work (1979) also indicates that children understand content messages better when they understand the formats used to present the content. For instance, children who were good at relating parts to a whole, and who could, therefore, understand a close-up format, learned more content from a film using cuts to close-ups than did children who were less skilled in understanding that format.

These findings suggest that associating content with certain media codes may increase comprehension of the content, if the production feature is familiar and understood by the child and if it focuses attention on central rather than incidental content. If the child does not understand the code represented by the feature or if the feature focuses attention away from the central content, it may interfere with comprehension. These conclusions may apply to the verbal codes of television as well as to media-specific production features.

To conclude this section on how children's comprehension of television is influenced by the representational codes, we can offer some general observations: The child viewer has the job of making sense of the medium at several different levels: the codes themselves, the immediate content, and more abstract interrelationships relevant to story lines. The representational codes are implicated at each of these levels. Children learn to interpret the media-specific codes as a function of age and viewing experience. Furthermore, certain media codes may come to be incorporated in children's general mental schemata. The general representational code of verbal language has a twofold relevance for increasing our understanding of

how children comprehend television: (1) We need to be aware of the particular interpretative demands presented by the verbal dialog as a linguistic code; and (2) children's own verbal comments while viewing can provide further clues about how they comprehend television's messages (cf. Rice and Wartella 1981). The psychological dimensions of television codes can be used to enhance children's comprehension of plot-relevant content: The association of attention-getting features or codes that are readily understood with content central to the story should contribute positively to children's ability to understand the plot.

The Influence of Television Forms on Social Behavior

The initial questions we raised about the effects of formal features on social and task-related behavior implied that form and content might have separable effects on children's behavior. Because certain formal features are correlated with content in existing television fare (e.g., action and noise with violence or slow pace with prosocial behavior), previous findings concerning the effects of violent or prosocial television content could have been partially due to the form rather than the content of those programs (Huston-Stein and Wright 1977).

If form and content have somewhat different effects, some important practical implications for commercial and educational television could result. If salient formal features are primarily responsible for drawing child viewers to cartoons and other commercial programs, but violent content is the main cause of aggressive behavior, then commercial producers might reduce violence in children's programs and substitute nonviolent content presented with salient features. Conversely, prosocial and educational programs might increase their audiences by the use of certain salient formal features without compromising their content.

The theoretical issues examined in our research derived from a comparison of two basic models: observational learning and arousal. Specific and separate effects of form and content can be predicted from observational learning theory. According to that model, viewers should imitate particular types of television content—aggressive content should lead to aggressive behavior and prosocial content to prosocial behavior. Children might also imitate formal features—high action might lead to increased motoric activity; high pace might lead to rapid shifting from one activity to another. Arousal theory leads to contrasting predictions (Zillmann et al. 1974). That model suggests that *either* salient formal features or "exciting" content can lead to a state of generalized arousal; the specific behaviors manifested as a result will depend on the immediate environmental cues and the predispositions of the child. Increases in either aggressive or prosocial behavior could occur if there were appropriate environmental cues. The principal difference between observational learning theory and arousal theory is that the latter leads to a prediction that both form and content of television can stimulate behavior that is quite different from what has been observed in the program, whereas the former predicts that viewers will imitate whatever was presented. Arousal theory has received some support in studies of adults. Both nonaggressive content designed to induce arousal (e.g., erotic content) and formal feature complexity or salience have been demonstrated to induce physiological arousal and aggressive behavior when the stimulus situation provides cues for aggression (Bryant and Zillmann 1979; Watt and Krull 1976; Zillmann et al. 1974).

Two studies in our laboratory provide support for the notion that salient formal features can instigate aggressive behavior in children, even in the absence of violent content. In the first study, animated children's programs containing different levels of action and violence constituted the treatment conditions. There were three programs: high action/high violence, high action/low violence, and low action/low violence. A control group saw no television (Huston-Stein et al. 1981). In the second study, advertisements with different levels of salient formal features—action, pace, visual special effects—were shown in the commercial breaks of a nonaggressive program. There was virtually no aggression in the program or any of the commercials (Greer et al. 1980). Pairs of preschool children were observed in a play situation containing a variety of toys before and after viewing the experimental programs.

In both studies, high levels of salient formal features stimulated aggressive behavior, despite the diverse content and formats of the programs and commercials. When cartoons were shown, children tended to be more aggressive after high action programs than after low action or no television at all. Violent content did not add to the level of aggression found after high action alone. When advertisements were shown, highly salient formal features without violent content led to higher levels of aggression than low salience features. These findings provide support for the notion that arousing form can lead to increased aggression even without the modeling of violent content, just as it aroused more attention with or without violence. An alternative interpretation is that children have learned to associate salient formal features with violent content through experience with the medium, so that they respond to salience as though it contained violence even without explicit content cues. In either case, the results fail to provide producers of children's television with a way of attracting viewers that avoids the adverse effects of violent programing.

The hypothesis that children will imitate formal features—high action or rapid shifts from one thing to another—has received little support. In the two studies described above, there were no differences in motor activity level as a function of program form or content, though the measure may have been restricted by the fact that children were observed in a small room. Negative findings also appeared in an experiment comparing Sesame Street programs with rapid versus slow pace (i.e., short, frequently changing bits versus long, infrequently changing bits). There were no differences in impulsivity or task persistence as a function of program pace (Anderson et al. 1977). However, in a field study of Israeli children who were less experienced with television than are American children, those who watched Sesame Street regularly did show less perseverance on a routine task than a control group of nonviewers (Salomon 1972).

. It appears that no simple causal segregation has yet been, or will be, easily achieved between the effects of television form and content on young children's social behavior. Both form and content can influence arousal. Arousal both enhances attention to the program and enhances the likelihood that its form, its content, and other situational cues present at the time of viewing will be responded to by the child viewer. Separating arousal attributable to formal complexity from arousal attributable to exciting content is another difficult research task that lies ahead.

Concluding Remarks

The empirical study of the forms of television, its representational codes, is in the early stages of investigation. The ultimate goal is to determine how children perceive, interpret, and assimilate the forms of television as an integral part of their viewing experience, how they come to acquire this knowledge, and what impact it has upon their general mental processing. Among the immediate issues is the nature of the relationships among children's viewing history, general cognitive development and the manner in which they respond to television's representational codes.

Another important question is how children may incorporate or generalize television forms to their own mental or social development. To the extent that the forms can be imitated or are similar to possible performance modes, children could, in effect, learn to use the forms themselves. We have already touched on several possibilities: Salomon claims that visual media formats (e.g., cuts, zooms) acquire representational status in children's thought processes; the verbal language of television may, in some circumstances, serve to introduce children to certain linguistic knowledge; action of characters or shifts of activities may elicit similar responses in the social/motoric behaviors of child viewers.

More specifically, though there is fairly strong evidence that certain media-specific codes attract and hold visual attention, we need to know more about auditory attention, how linguistic features influence attention, and the nature of the interaction among forms, content, attention, and developmental change (including both intellectual change and accumulated viewing experience). Still another set of questions revolves around the ways in which formal features of television affect children's comprehension of content. To the extent that such effects occur, are they a function of attention-eliciting and maintaining functions of formal features, or do they reflect the fact that certain formal features are themselves representational codes that children can readily understand? A related issue is raised by critics who suggest that salient, high-paced formats may, in fact, detract from comprehension. It seems overly simple to argue that particular television forms are either "good" or "bad" for comprehension. Instead, the research task is to analyze under what circumstances, in what combinations, and for what types of children particular features enhance or detract from comprehension.

The investigation of television form promises to contribute information that will allow greater specificity in our conceptions of how children process the medium of television. In particular, it will be possible to separate effects attributable to form from those associated with content and to clarify the interaction of the two aspects of television. Closely related to this possibility is another: The study of television codes leads directly to inferences about particular processing abilities of children; the match between televised information and children's mental processes is very close in certain television forms. Furthermore, as we learn more about the representational codes of television, how children come to understand them and use them to comprehend content, we also learn about the general principles of symbol formation, a knowledge with relevance for many aspects of child development. Finally, if, as seems entirely possible, future generations of Americans will do much of their information processing via interactive electronic audiovisual displays and will receive most of their entertainment and much of their education via television, then the development of "media literacy" may become almost as important as that of basic reading skills, whether or not we are ready to acknowledge it.

References

Acker, S. R. & Tieman, R. K. *Non-conservation of size of televised images: A developmental study.* Paper presented at the meeting of the Society for Research in Child Development, San Francisco, 1979.

Anderson, D. R. *Active and passive processes in children's TV viewing.* Paper presented at the meeting of the American Psychological Association, New York, 1979.

Anderson, D. R., Alwitt, L. F., Lorch, E. P., & Levin, S. R. Watching children watch television. In G. Hale & M. Lewis (Eds.), *Attention and the development of cognitive skills.* New York: Plenum, 1979.

Anderson, D. R., & Levin, S. R. Young children's attention to *Sesame Street. Child Development,* 1976, *47,* 806–811.

Anderson, D. R., Levin, S. R., & Lorch, E. P. The effects of TV program pacing on the behavior of preschool children. *AV Communication Review,* 1977, *25,* 154–166.

Berlyne, D. E. *Conflict, arousal, and curiosity.* New York: McGraw Hill, 1960.

Bernstein, L. J. *Design attributes of Sesame Street and the visual attention of preschool children.* Unpublished doctoral dissertation, Columbia University, 1978.

Bloome, D., & Ripich, D. Language in children's television commercials: A sociolinguistic perspective. *Theory into Practice,* 1979, *18,* 220–225.

Bryant, J., & Zillmann, D. Effect of intensification of annoyance through unrelated residual excitation on substantially delayed hostile behavior. *Journal of Experimental Social Psychology,* 1979, *15,* 470–480.

Bryant, J., Heze, R., & Zillmann, D. Humor in children's educational television. *Communication Education,* 1979, *28,* 49–59.

Butt, Y., & Wright, J. C. *Televised training of preschoolers in number conservation.* CRITC Report 24a. Center for Research on the Influences of Television on Children, University of Kansas, Lawrence, Kansas, 1979.

Calvert, S. C., Huston, A. C., Watkins, B. A., & Wright, J. C. *The effects of selective attention to television forms on children's comprehension of content.* Paper presented at the meeting of the Society for Research in Child Development, Boston, 1981.

Calvert, S. C., Watkins, B. A., Wright, J. C., & Huston-Stein, A. *Recall of television content as a function of content type and level of production feature use.* Paper presented at the meeting of the Society for Research in Child Development, San Francisco, 1979.

Collins, W. A. Children's comprehension of television content. In E. Wartella (Ed.), *Children Communicating: Media and Development of Thought, Speech, Understanding.* Sage Annual Reviews of Communication Research, Vol. 7, Beverly Hills: Sage, 1979.

Diener, E., & DeFour, D. Does television violence enhance program popularity? *Journal of Personality and Social Psychology,* 1978, *36,* 333–341.

Fillmore, C. J. The case for case. In E. Bach & R. T. Harms (Eds.), *Universals in linguistic theory.* New York: Holt, Rinehart & Winston, 1968.

Friedlander, B. Z., Wetstone, S., & Scott. Suburban preschool children's comprehension of an age-appropriate information television program. *Child Development,* 1974, *45,* 561–565.

Friedrich, L. K., & Stein, A. H. Prosocial television and young children: The effects of verbal labeling and role playing on learning and behavior. *Child Development,* 1975, *46,* 27–38.

Greer, D., Potts, R., Wright, J. C., & Huston-Stein, A. *The effects of television commercial form and commercial placement on children's attention and social behavior.* Paper presented at the meeting of the Southwestern Society for Research in Human Development, Lawrence, Kansas, 1980.

Hollenbeck, A. R., & Slaby, R. G. Infant visual and vocal responses to television. *Child Development,* 1979, *50,* 41–45.

Hunt, J. McV. *Intelligence and experience.* New York: Wiley, 1961.

Huston, A. C., Wright, J. C., Wartella, E., Rice, M. L., Watkins, B. A., Campbell, T., Potts, R. Communicating more than content: Formal features of children's television programs. *Journal of Communication*, 1981, *31*(3), 32–48.

Huston-Stein, A. *Television and growing up: The medium gets equal time.* Invited address to Divisions 15 and 7 at the meeting of the American Psychological Association, San Francisco, 1977.

Huston-Stein, A., Fox, S., Greer, D., Watkins, B. A., & Whitaker, J. The effects of action and violence in television programs on the social behavior and imaginative play of preschool children. *Journal of Genetic Psychology*, 1981, *138*, 183–191.

Huston-Stein, A., & Wright, J. C. *Modeling the medium: Effects of formal properties of children's television programs.* Paper presented at the meeting of the Society for Research in Child Development, New Orleans, 1977.

Huston-Stein, A., Wright, J. C., Rice, M. L., Potts, R., Watkins, B. A., Zapata, L., Calvert, S., Greer, D., Plehals, R., & Thissen, D. *Formal features of children's television programs: Structure, patterns of use, and correlations with content.* CRITC Report 4b, Center for Research on the Influences of Television on Children, University of Kansas, Lawrence, Kansas, 1979.

Krull, R., & Husson, W. Children's attention: The case of TV viewing. In E. Wartella (Ed.), *Children communicating: Media and development of thought, speech, understanding.* Beverly Hills: Sage, 1979.

Lorch, E. P., Anderson, D. R., & Levin, S. R. The relationship of visual attention to children's comprehension of television. *Child Development*, 1979, *50*, 722–727.

McLuhan, H. M. *Understanding media: The extensions of man.* New York: McGraw-Hill, 1964.

Messaris, P., Eckman, B., & Gumpert, G. Editing structure in the televised versions of the 1976 presidential debates. *Journal of Broadcasting*, 1979, *23*, 359–369.

Palmer, E. L. *A pedagogical analysis of recurrent formats on Sesame Street and The Electric Company.* Paper presented at the International Conference on Children's Educational Television, Amsterdam, 1978.

Palmer, E. L., & McDowell, C. N. Program/commercial separators in children's television programming. *Journal of Communication, 1979, 29*(3), 197–201.

Rice, M. L. Cognitive aspects of communicative development. In R. L. Schiefelbusch & J. Pickar (Eds.), *Communicative competence: Acquisition and intervention.* Baltimore: University Park Press, in press.

Rice, M. L. *Television as a medium of verbal communication.* Paper presented at the meeting of the American Psychological Association, New York, 1979.

Rice, M. L. *What children talk about while they watch TV.* Paper presented at the meeting of the Southwestern Society for Research in Human Development, Lawrence, Kansas, 1980.

Rice, M. L., & Wartella, E. Television as a medium of communication: Implications for how to regard the child viewer. *Journal of Broadcasting*, in press.

Ross, R., Campbell, T., Huston-Stein, A., & Wright, J. C. Nutritional misinformation of children: A developmental and experimental analysis of the effects of televised food commercials. *Journal of Applied Developmental Psychology*, 1981, *1*, 329–345.

Rubinstein, E. A., Liebert, R. M., Neale, J. M., & Poulos, R. W. *Assessing television's influence on children's prosocial behavior.* Occasional paper 74–11. Stony Brook, New York: Brookdale International Institute, 1974.

Salomon, G. *Educational effects of Sesame Street on Israeli children.* Hebrew University of Jerusalem, 1972. (ERIC Document Files #070 317.)

Salomon, G. Internalization of filmic schematic operations in relation to individual differences. *Journal of Educational Psychology*, 1974, *66*, 499–511.

Salomon, G. *Interaction of media, cognition, and learning.* San Francisco: Jossey-Bass, 1979.

Singer, J. L. The power and limitations of television: A cognitive-affective analysis. In P. Tannenbaum (Ed.), *The entertainment functions of television.* Hillsdale, N.J.: Erlbaum, 1980.

Susman, E. J. *Visual imagery and verbal labeling: The relation of stylistic features of television presentation to children's learning and performance of prosocial content.* Unpublished doctoral dissertation, Pennsylvania State University, 1976.

Susman, E. J. Visual and verbal attributes of television and selective attention in preschool children. *Developmental Psychology*, 1978, *14*, 565–566.

Tower, R. B., Singer, D. G., Singer, J. L., & Biggs, H. Differential effects of television programming on preschoolers' cognition, imagination, and social play. *American Journal of Orthopsychiatry*, 1979, *49*, 265–281.

Wartella, E., & Ettema, J. S. A cognitive developmental study of children's attention to television commercials. *Communication Research*, 1974, *1*, 69–88.

Watkins, B. A., Calvert, S., Huston-Stein, A., & Wright, J. C. Children's recall of television material: Effects of presentation mode and adult labeling. *Developmental Psychology*, 1980, *16*, 672–679.

Watt, J. H., & Krull, R. An information theory measure for television programming. *Communication Research*, 1974, *1*, 44–68.

Watt, J. H., & Krull, R. An examination of three models of television viewing and aggression. *Human Communication Research*, 1977, *3*, 99–112.

Welch, R. H., Huston-Stein, A., Wright, J. C., & Plehals, R. Subtle sex-role cues in children's commercials. *Journal of Communications*, 1979, *29*(3), 202–209.

Wright, J. C. *On familiarity and habituation: The situational microgenetics of information getting.* Paper presented at the meeting of the Society for Research in Child Development, New Orleans, 1977.

Wright, J. C., Calvert, S., Huston-Stein, A., & Watkins, B. A. *Children's selective attention to television forms: Effects of salient and informative production features as functions of age and viewing experience.* Paper presented at the meeting of the International Communication Association, Acapulco, Mexico, 1980.

Wright, J. C., & Huston, A. C. The forms of television: Nature and development of television literacy in children. In H. Gardner & H. Kelly (Eds.), *Children and the worlds of television.* A quarterly sourcebook in the series *New Directions in Child Development.* San Francisco: Jossey-Bass, in press.

Wright, J. C., Huston-Stein, A., Potts, R., Rice, M., Calvert, S., Greer, D., Watkins, B. A., Thissen, D., & Zapata, L. *The relation of formal features of children's television programs to viewership by children of different ages: A tale of three cities.* Paper presented at the meeting of the Southwestern Society for Research in Human Development, Lawrence, Kansas, 1980.

Wright, J. C., & Vlietstra, A. G. The development of selective attention: From perceptual exploration to logical search. In H. W. Reese (Ed.), *Advances in child development and behavior.* Vol. 10. New York: Academic Press, 1975.

Wright, J. C., Watkins, B. A., & Huston-Stein, A. *Active vs. passive television viewing: A model of the development of TV information processing in children.* Paper presented at the meeting of the American Psychological Association, Toronto, 1978.

Zillmann, D., Hoyt, J. L., & Day, K. D. Strength and duration of the effect of aggressive, violent, and erotic communications on subsequent aggressive behavior. *Communication Research*, 1974, *1*, 286–306.

Hawkins and Pingree note that the evidence concerning the causal direction of television's impact on social reality is not sufficient for strong conclusions, but that it is fairly consistent and suggests that television can teach about social reality. The relationship between viewing and social reality, they further suggest, may be reciprocal: Viewing causes a social reality to be constructed in a certain way, but this construction may also direct viewing behavior. The chapter further presents theoretical arguments for, and evidence bearing on, five processes that may be involved in cultivation effects. Robert P. Hawkins is associate professor in the School of Journalism and Mass Communication, and Suzanne Pingree is assistant professor in the Department of Agricultural Journalism at the University of Wisconsin.

3

TELEVISION'S INFLUENCE ON SOCIAL REALITY
Robert P. Hawkins and Suzanne Pingree

We have noted and deplored the paucity of research about the manner in which values with respect to many areas of behavior, including violence, are transmitted, and about the role played by television and other mass media in this communication. In the long run, societal values are shaped by a great variety of environmental forces and institutions; television programs may contribute a great deal or only a small amount to the process. (Surgeon General's Scientific Advisory Committee on Television and Social Behavior 1971, p. 115).

The committee's call stimulated a great response in research since 1971. The committee also forecast the future by suggesting the inadequacy of a direct-effects model of television's influence on society. In this review,[1] we will consider one area of effects research—how television's content is used in the construction of social reality. As the committee implied, however, and as becomes clear later, television's influence on constructions of social reality is probably a complex and indirect process in interaction with "a great variety of environmental forces and institutions."

Does Television Affect Social Reality?

The Problem of Demonstrating Television Influence on Social Reality

Demonstrating the influence of television on individuals' conceptions of the world—their social reality—faces

all the usual problems of television effects research (lack of unexposed groups, causal ordering, and control of third variables), with two added complications. First, if the relevant messages of television are patterns present only in the aggregate, experimental tests of television's influence will be far less generalizable than usual, unless they are grandiose field experiments. Second, and even more important, if the patterns in television content reflect norms of society (as seems likely), television's influence will be that of stabilizing and reinforcing the status quo—something difficult to document with statistics designed to measure differences, not the absence of differences.

One of the main conclusions of Klapper's review of mass communication effects (1960) was that the mass media act largely in concert with other influences and as reinforcers of already held beliefs, but he based this conclusion largely on the scarcity and small size of *change* effects rather than on direct evidence of reinforcement. And many a conclusion about mass communication states, roughly, "the most important effect of mass communication is no effect at all," accepting that statement as either a truism or an untestable hypothesis.

A major contribution of the Cultural Indicators group at the Annenberg School of Communications has been to take that hypothesis and attempt to devise ways to test it. One way takes advantage of the distinction between television reflecting the objective world or reflecting a set of values and norms about that world. Although the television world seems realistic, it contains systematic distortions and biases, such as more violence than in real life, underrepresentation of women, minorities, the young and the old, and exaggerated relationships between various forms of success and sex, age, and occupation. Standard survey techniques can determine whether or not there is any association between the

[1] The editors of *Communication Research, Human Communication Research, Journal of Communication, Journalism Quarterly,* and *Public Opinion Quarterly* helped us contact authors of relevant but as-yet unpublished papers; many of these papers are a substantial departure from previous work, and their inclusion makes this paper very different and much better than it would otherwise have been. Steven H. Chaffee provided comments and suggestions.

From Robert P. Hawkins and Suzanne Pingree, "Television's Influence on Social Reality," in National Institute of Mental Health, *Television and Behavior: Ten Years of Scientific Progress and Implications for the Eighties,* Vol. 2: Technical Reviews (Rockville, MD: National Institute of Mental Health, 1982), pp. 224-247. This work is in the public domain.

amount of exposure to these distorted images and the belief that the real world matches the distorted television images.

For example, the U.S. Statistical Abstract for 1974 provided the information that 10 percent of all crimes are violent crimes, whereas content analyses show that 77 percent of all major television characters who commit crimes also commit violence. A survey respondent can be asked "What percent of all crimes are violent crimes like murders, rape, robbery, and aggravated assault?" with a forced choice between two wrong answers, 15 percent and 25 percent. One of the wrong answers is closer to the "real world" of the Statistical Abstract, and the other is closer to the "TV world" statistic; an association with television viewing is demonstrated if heavy viewers are more likely than light viewers to give the "television answer."

Making the inference that television is the cause of this television-bias effect, of course, requires the usual pursuit of potentially spurious third variables, but the television versus real-world bias comparison allows for an additional argument about causal order. Because the television bias answers are so different from the real world, direct experience seems unlikely to be the source of these beliefs for the heavy television viewers. Thus, a reversed causal direction (having these television bias conceptions of the world leads one to prefer television because it matches one's beliefs) is less plausible.

From these results, it is a relatively small step to argue that television provides reinforcement for all those cases where the real and normative worlds concur. Even so, there is another important step in the cultivation of social reality. Demonstrating that people apply the demographic characteristics of the television world to their beliefs about the demographic characteristics of the real world would indicate television's influence, but these demographic beliefs themselves are probably not as important as the further, more generalized beliefs. The influence argument takes a final step as follows: If viewing a biased picture of the world on television has led someone to believe that the real world matches those biases, the overestimates of violence, law enforcement occupations, and so on generalize to beliefs, such as personal fear of violence, acceptance of authority, etc. This is intriguing, but it is a separate hypothesis that is as yet untested.

Recent reports have concentrated on the more interesting, general aspects of social reality. For example, respondents have been asked to agree or disagree with such statements as "Is it dangerous to walk alone in a city at night" and "Would you say that most of the time people try to be helpful or that they are mostly just looking out for themselves?" Once again, an association with viewing is a prerequisite for inferring television

influence, but controlling for third variables and establishing causal order become even more important since these variables seem more open to other influences.

One final methodological point deserves mention. Gerbner and his colleagues make a great deal of the argument that television's influence is one of social control, stability, maintenance of the social order, etc. It is important not to confuse these reinforcement predictions with a null hypothesis; a positive correlation between television viewing and social reality beliefs does not necessarily reflect change by heavy television viewers. It may be that heavy television viewing prevents the drift away from the norms that would otherwise happen and is responsible for a less television-like social reality for light television viewers.

What the Research Says

In table 1, we summarized most of the research. This review will focus on these studies for the most part. This summary covers 24 different samples,[2] 48 separate published and unpublished papers; and 12 independent researchers and research groups.[3]

The 24 samples range in size from 57 to 4,254, and cover many geographical areas. Several are national samples (NORC, CPS, Harris, ORC, Starch); these tend to be adult samples. Other adult samples include one from the southwest, one from California, one from Cincinnati, one from Madison, Wisc., and two from Philadelphia. The adult samples outside the United States include two from Great Britain and one from Canada. Samples of children are from New Jersey, New York, Philadelphia, and Australia.

Television viewing measures also exhibit a range from average number of evenings per week that television is viewed at least 1 hour (Cincinnati) to viewing diaries (Madison, Wisc.; Philadelphia mother-child dyads; Toronto, Canada; and Perth, Western Australia). Some measures ask about frequency of exposure to various program types (Arizona; CPS National Election Study), the rest ask about number of hours viewed on an "average day," or "usually," or "yesterday," or "on a school

---

[2] The samples that Gerbner et al. (1977–79a,b) report for New Jersey and New York schoolchildren are treated here as two separate samples. The New Jersey longitudinal panel (1974–77) is not, however, since all of the children in this panel were in both of the New Jersey samples.

[3] Most of the 45 papers were written by Gerbner and Gross and associates. We have chosen to describe colleagues and graduate students working with Gerbner and Gross as part of their group and not as independent researchers; this is obviously arguable. Besides researchers named in joint authorship with Gerbner or Gross, these researchers include Gonzales, Harr-Mazer, Morgan, and Rothschild.

Table 1

Television Viewing and Constructions of Reality: Brief Overview of Research

Sample	Authors	Television Measure	Controls	Relationship	
Arizona Southwestern City Registered Voters $N=133$ to 215	Volgy and Schwarz, 1980	Exposure to medical programs, entertainment programs, and ethnic programs	None reported	Positive affect toward doctors (medical shows) Sexism (entertainment shows) Concern about racial problems (ethnic shows)	+ + +
California Three Counties Adults $N=762$	Haney and Manzolati, 1980	Number of hours per day	Sex, income, age, occupation, education; zero-order correlations with TV viewing and dependent variables	Attitudes about criminal justice 11/21	+
Cincinnati Area Project 1975: Adults $N=470$ to 475	Fox and Philliber, 1978	Average number of evenings/week watch TV at least 1 hour	Income, occupation, education, and all together; perceptions of veracity; sex, age, and race	Perceptions of affluence	0
CPS National Election Study 1976: Adults $N=2,335$	Gerbner, et al., 1978a; 1978b	Frequency of viewing police-crime shows	Age, sex, education	Fear of walking alone at night Protection: Dog Locks Gun Avoid areas Interpersonal mistrust	+ + + + 0 +
	Neville, 1980	Frequency of viewing police/crime, national news, local news, daytime entertainment	Age, sex, race, income, education, all together	Interpersonal mistrust with— Police/crime Daytime News	 + + 0
Harris Poll for National Council of Aging 1974: Adults $N=4,254$	Gonzalez, 1979	Number of hours "yesterday"	Education, income, sex, age, race	Negative beliefs about older people	+
	Gerbner, et al., 1980a	Number of hours "yesterday"	Education, income, sex, age	Negative beliefs about older people	+

day," etc., (California Adults; NORC General Social Surveys; New Jersey and New York schoolchildren; ORC; Philadelphia schoolchildren; and Starch).

Most of the studies use controls at one point or another, and these controls are typically demographics such as age, sex, and education. The use of controls in cultivation analyses is a significant issue in evaluating the research, as discussed further in the next section.

Until recently, most of this research centered on aspects of social reality related to the violent content of television, including fearfulness (usually of walking alone at night), interpersonal mistrust, and perceived prevalence of violence. Several researchers studied other areas of social reality in the last few years, so that we now have research on the link between television viewing and attitudes about doctors (Volgy and Schwarz 1980), sex-

Table 1

Television Viewing and Constructions of Reality: Brief Overview of Research (Cont.)

Sample	Authors	Television Measure	Controls	Relationship	
Madison, WI Women: Adults 1979 N = 57	Pingree, et al., 1979	Minutes viewing soap operas, evening, from 2-day viewing diary	Age, education, income, occupation, all together	Interpersonal mistrust (soaps) Prevalence of violence Traditional family values (soaps) Family structures (prime time)	+ 0 + +
NORC General Social Survey 1975: Adults N = 1,452	Gerbner, et al., 1977a, 1977b	Number of hours on the average day	Sex, age, education, income, newspaper reading, church attendance, race	Interpersonal mistrust U.S. out of world affairs*	+ +
N = 1,333	Hughes, 1980	Number of hours on the average day	Sex, age, race, education, income, hours worked/week, numbers of memberships, population size, all together	U.S. out of world affairs	+
NORC General Social Survey 1977: Adults N = 1,516	Gerbner et al., 1978a; 1978b	Numbers of hours on the average day	Age, sex, education	Fear walk alone at night Anomie: Lot of average man worse Child into world Public officials not interested	+ + + +
N = 1,312 to 1,377	Hughes, 1980	Number of hours on the average day	Sex, race, education, income, age, hours worked/week, number of memberships, church attendance, population size, all together	Fear walk alone at night Anomie: Lot average man worse Child into world Public officials not interested Approval of violence: Adult hitting Police hitting Own guns Pistol	0 ∩ 0 ∩ 0 − 0 0
NORC General Social Surveys 1975, 1977, 1978 N = 1,838	Gerbner & Signorielli, 1979	Number of hours on average day	Age, sex, race, education, newspaper reading, income	Sexism	+

Table 1 continues on next page.

ism (Volgy and Schwarz 1980; Gerbner and Signorielli 1979; Rothschild 1979; Morgan 1980); family values and structures (Pingree et al. 1981; Morgan and Harr-Mazer 1980; Harr-Mazer 1980); concern about racial problems (Volgy and Schwarz 1980), beliefs about older people (Gonzalez 1979; Gerbner and Signorielli 1979; Gerbner et al. 1980a), perception of population illness (Robertson et al. 1979), attitudes about criminal justice (Haney and Manzolati 1980), and perceptions of affluence (Fox and Philliber 1978).

As a first attempt to answer the question that this section addresses, and treating entries in table 1 as data points, there are two answers. If the unit of analysis is samples the answer is "yes," television use does appear to have a significant influence on constructions of social reality. Of the 24 samples, 17 show significant positive relationships, 5 show no relationship, and 2 are disputed. On the other hand, if we look at the 12 independent researchers or research groups for their interpretations of their own work, 7 of the 12 believe the relationship

Table 1

Television Viewing and Constructions of Reality: Brief Overview of Research (Cont.)

Sample	Authors	Television Measure	Controls	Relationship	
	Hirsch, 1980	Number of hours "on an average day"	Education, sex, age, race; all together	Alienation* and anomie†	+ ∩
				Fear walk alone at night†	∪
				Approve violence†	∩
				Interpersonal mistrust†	+
				Approve suicide†	−
N=382	Hirsch, 1980	Number of hours "on an average day" compares nonviewers vs. light, heavy vs. extremely heavy	Age, sex, education	18 items used to form the six scales used above	
				Nonviewers vs. light viewers:	
				13 items	−
				5 items	+
				Heavy vs. extreme viewers:	
				11 items	−
				1 item	0
				6 items	+
New Jersey School children 1975–76: 6th, 7th, 8th, 9th grades N=466	Gerbner et al., 1977a; 1977b	Number of hours per day, including morning, afternoon, and evening usually spend watching	Sex, age, newspaper reading, father's education, IQ, all together	Prevalence of violence	+
	Gerbner et al., 1978a; 1978b	Number of hours per day, including morning, afternoon and evening usually spend watching	Age, sex, parent's education	All right to hit	+
				Fear walk alone at night	+
	Gerbner et al., 1980a	Number of hours per day, including morning, afternoon, and evening, usually spend watching	IQ, social class, sex, grade	Old age starts early	+

between television viewing and social reality to be spurious, and the answer is "no."

Of course, this isn't fair. The latter analysis gives single pieces of research as much weight as entire programs, and the former says nothing about the complexity of findings or quality of the various research findings. It is to this task that we now turn.

There are two crucial issues in evaluating the area. First, is the relationship between television viewing and constructions of television-biased social reality an artifact of uncontrolled or improperly controlled third variables—in other words, is it spurious? Second, if the relationship persists despite controls, what is its causal order?

Spuriousness. Evidence in support of a relationship can be found in many studies and for many areas of social reality. There is the most evidence for areas of social reality related to violence.

Demographic Measures. For measures closely tied to the demographics of television content, the research consistently shows small and significant correlations. For example, Gerbner et al. (1977a,b) asked New Jersey schoolchildren questions such as those listed in table 2. These questions were conbined into an index, and when the index was correlated with television viewing, the zero-order correlation was .16 ($p < .001$). Partialing on sex, grade, newspaper reading, father's education, socioeconomic status, and IQ changed the correlation very

Table 1

Television Viewing and Constructions of Reality: Brief Overview of Research (Cont.)

Sample	Authors	Television Measure	Controls	Relationship	
New Jersey Schoolchildren 1976–77: 7th and 8th grades N=214 to 339	Gerbner et al., 1979a; 1979b	Number of hours per day, including morning, afternoon, and evening, usually spend watching	Sex, grade, ethnic group, newspaper reading, network newsviewing, father's education	Prevalence of violence Fear walk along at night Interpersonal mistrust	+ + +
New Jersey Schoolchildren 1974–77 Panel 6th-8th/7th-9th /8th-10th grades N=216	Morgan & Harr-Mazer, 1980	Number of hours "on an average day"	SES, IQ, sex, grade, family structure, mother's education, religious background	Family: Early for marriage & childbirth Projected family size	+ +
	Morgan, 1980	Number of hours "on an average day"	IQ, grade, mother works, father's occupation, education	Sexism: girls only	+
	Gross & Morgan, 1980 (last 2 years only)	Number of hours "on an average day"	SES, family context	Interpersonal: Mistrust (depends on family context) Prevalence of violence	+ +
	Gerbner et al., 1980b; 1980c (last 2 years only)	Number of hours "on an average day"	SES, IQ, and 2nd year scores	Interpersonal mistrust Perceived danger	+ +
New York Schoolchildren (Bankstreet) 1976: age 9–11, 12–14 N=133	Gerbner et al., 1977a; 1977b	Number of hours per day, including morning, afternoon, and evening usually spend watching	Sex, age, newspapers, SES, all together Sex, age, SES, newspaper	Prevalence of violence Interpersonal mistrust	+ +
	Gerbner et al., 1978a; 1978b	Number of hours per day, including morning, afternoon, and evening usually spend watching	Age, sex, father's education	All right to hit Fear walk alone at night	+ +
New York Schoolchildren (Private School) 1977: grades 5–8, 9–12 N=123	Gerbner et al., 1979a; 1979b	Number of hours per day including morning, afternoon, and evening usually spend watching	Sex, grade, SES, achievement, experience as victim	Prevalence of violence Fear walk alone at night Activities of police	+ + +
ORC 1974 Adults	Gerbner et al., 1977a; 1977b	Number of hours "yesterday"	Sex, age, education, newspaper reading, all together	Prevalence of violence	+

Table 1 continues on next page.

Table 1

Television Viewing and Constructions of Reality: Brief Overview of Research (Cont.)

Sample	Authors	Television Measure	Controls	Relationship	
ORC national sample, 1979, Adults $N=5,534$	Gerbner et al., 1980b; 1980c	Number of hours on the average weekday	Sex, age, income, newspaper reading, education, race, urban proximity; all together	Perceived danger	+
Philadelphia: Adults $N=593$	Harr-Mazer, 1980	Amount of viewing on an average day	Age, education, sex, religion, income, race, newspaper reading, children under 18	Child's role in society restricted	+
Philadelphia 1977: Mother-Child Dyads 3rd, 5th, 7th grades $N=675$	Robertson, Rossiter & Gleason 1979	Exposure to medical ads: past week and month viewing of randomly selected list of TV shows (not during school or after 11:30 p.m.)	Grade	Perception of population illness	0
Philadelphia Schoolchildren 3rd and 5th grades	Rothschild, 1979	On a school night, (weekend) how many hours of TV	Sex, group cohesiveness, group affiliation, grade, SES, achievement level, all together	Depends on group cohesiveness: Interpersonal mistrust Sexism Occupational aspirations	0 + +
Starch 1973 Adults $N=573$	Gerbner et al., 1977a; 1977b	Hours/day	Sex, age, education, newspaper reading, TV news, all together	Prevalence of violence	+
Outside USA					
British Gallup Poll 1976: Adults 16 and over $N=258$	Wober, 1978	Hours/day	Sex, age, social class	Interpersonal mistrust Prevalence of violence	0 0
Portsmouth (UK) survey 1976: Adults $N=842$	Piepe, Crouch, & Emerson, 1977	?	?	Interpersonal mistrust Prevalence of violence	0 0

little, and, although it was reduced to $r=.12$ with simultaneous partialing on all the above variables, it remained significant. This pattern was replicated by Gerbner et al. (1977a, b) in their New York sample of schoolchildren ($r=.18$), and with adult samples from the 1974 ORC ($r=.08$) and the 1973 Starch surveys ($r=.06$), although the partial correlation is smaller after all controls for the two adult samples than it is for the two child samples.

Gerbner et al., (1979a,b) also dealt with New York and New Jersey schoolchildren and with questions on prevalence of violence. They report results for both samples for television biases in estimates of the number of people involved in violence and for the New Jersey schoolchildren for the number of people who commit serious crimes. Results show an overall significant "cultivation differential" (percent of heavy viewers giving a

Table 1

Television Viewing and Constructions of Reality: Brief Overview of Research (Cont.)

Sample	Authors	Television Measure	Controls	Relationship	
Toronto Adults 1977 $N=364$ to 405	Doob & Macdonald, 1979	TV programs last week coded overall & violent vs. nonviolent	Sex, age, geographical area, high-low crime, radio news, newspaper, all together	Fear of crime factor: only in high crime areas Prevalence of violence	0, + +
Perth (Western Australia) 1977 2nd, 5th, 8th, 11th graders $N=1,085$	Hawkins & Pingree, 1980; 1981 Pingree & Hawkins, 1981	4-day viewing diary, frequency of exposure to content types, number of hours yesterday	Content types, age, sex, perceived reality, media studies, newspaper reading, SES, all together	Interpersonal mistrust Prevalence of violence	+ +

+ Significant positive relationship.   0 No relationship.   − Reversal.   ∩ Curvilinear.
* Controls for sex, education, age only.
† Excludes nonviewers and extreme viewers; our selection, see text.

television bias answer minus the percent of light viewers giving a television bias answer). The cultivation differential varies somewhat in their tables within levels of control variables. This variation does not indicate spuriousness; spuriousness would be indicated if the cultivation differential disappeared at all levels of a control variable. However, unlike the 1977 reports of correlational analyses, the effect of simultaneous controls is not given in the 1979 reports. It could be that each demographic variable accounts for a separate part of the cultivation differential, and, if all were controlled together, the differential would disappear. Still, we suspect that this would not be the case here, based on the close tie between television content and the questions used and on the previous results reported in Gerbner et al. (1977a,b). In support of this, Gross and Morgan's analysis of the last 2 years of the New Jersey Panel shows significant correlations for seventh and eighth graders between viewing and perceived prevalence of violence that hold across levels of family structure with father's education and occupation simultaneously controlled.

The last American study using the demographic prevalence of violence approach is an analysis of the different relationships between television content types and social reality (Pingree et al. 1979). There was no significant relationship between perceived prevalence of violence and either soap opera viewing or prime time viewing, although the prime time viewing correlation was stronger and in the right direction ($r=.21$). The small sample size of this study ($N=57$) makes it difficult to treat its results as anything but suggestive.

Outside America, Pingree and Hawkins (1981) report confirming results for the prevalence of violence variables

($r=.20$), despite controls individually and together for age, sex, perceptions of reality, media studies, newspaper reading, current events knowledge, SES, and Australian-American similarity. This may be overcontrolled, since some of these variables (e.g., perceived reality) are process variables and not necessarily causally prior to television use.

In a study of fear of victimization with Canadian adults, Doob and Macdonald (1979) report results for a 25-item set of questions related to the nature and frequency of crime and violence. For 14 of the 25 questions, they report significant relationships to television viewing that do not substantially drop when the area in which the subject resides is controlled, suggesting that real-world differences in the actual level of crime do not mediate this relationship. Although this would appear to support the cultivation position for prevalence of violence, it is not clear whether it does or not, since Doob and Macdonald did not control for other characteristics.

A possible disconfirmation of cultivation of prevalence of violence comes from Great Britain (Wober 1978). Wober analyzed the results of a national opinion poll that asked two cultivation-related questions, one dealing with prevalence of violence phrased in terms of one's chances of being a victim of violence and the other with interpersonal mistrust. The two items were summed to form a "security scale," which was not related to viewing. Wober argues that this summing is a more powerful procedure than single-item scales. However, Wober's security scale is a mixture of the demographic approach and the interpersonal mistrust approach. As noted above, these two approaches are hypothesized to measure the

Table 2

Data Sources for Questions Included in Index Reflecting
Television Answers Relating to Violence and Law Enforcement
(Gerbner et al., 1977b)*

Question ("TV Answer" in Italics)	Data Source	
	"Real World"	"World of Television"
During any given week, what are your chances of being involved in some kind of violence? *About one in ten?* About 1 in 100?	.32 violent crimes per 100 people (1970 U.S. Census)	64.4% of characters are involved in violence (Table 1)
What percent of all males who have jobs work in law enforcement and crime detection? One percent? *Five percent?*	1% (1970 U.S. Census)	15% of all TV male characters (Cultural Indicators data, 1969–76)
What percent of all crimes are violent crimes like murders, rape, robbery and aggravated assault? Fifteen percent? *Twenty-five percent?*	10% (Statistical Abstract of the U.S., 1974)	77% of all TV major characters who commit crimes (as criminals) also commit violence (Cultural Indicators data, 1969–76)
Does most fatal violence occur between *strangers* or between relatives or acquaintances?	16% of homicides occur between strangers, 64% occur between family members or friends (National Commission on the Causes and Prevention of Violence, 1969)	58% of homicides committed by strangers (Cultural Indicators data, 1967–76)

* Used with permission of the authors.

same construction of social reality, but it is not logically necessary that they do.

But there is a more serious problem with this study related to differences in television content and viewing in Great Britain and the United States. Wober cites a study showing that heavy television viewers (4 or more hours per day) expose themselves to 10.7 violence-containing programs per week. In contrast, an American heavy television viewer (also 4 or more hours per day) would watch almost 24 hour-long programs containing violence per week. Thus, an American heavy viewer sees more than twice as much violence as a British heavy viewer. In fact, the British heavy viewer sees *less* violence than many American *light* viewers. Wober's comparison is between light and extremely light viewers of violence, and his negative results are not surprising.

This issue does force recognition of a hidden assumption: It is not just that exposure to violence leads in a linear fashion to construction of a violent social reality. There must be a certain *threshold* level of a social reality content for television influence to occur.

An example of the need for attention to content prevalence is a study of the effects of medical commercials on children by Robertson et al. (1979). They measured the exposure of third, fifth, and seventh graders to medical

commercials, using a randomly selected list of 35 programs combined with actual incidence of commercials by program. They also measured perception-of-population illness with four questions estimating the incidence of symptoms in the population (e.g., how many times a month do people get headaches?). Results showed no relationship ($r = .00$) between children's perception of population illness and exposure to medical commercials, despite "the considerable depiction of illness on television, both on doctor shows and in medicine commercials." However, there were only two doctor shows on prime time in 1977 when the data were gathered ($M*A*S*H$ and *Quincy, M.D.*), and these programs said little about headaches. Similarly, the children's exposure to medical commercials was light, amounting to less than 15 commercials per week. At most, this would seem to be very light exposure to the relevant content, and greater exposure than this is probably necessary.

This study also suggests the relative weakness of the demographic approach when it is tied neither to careful content analysis nor to real-world statistics. It is not possible to evaluate an answer for real-world or television-world bias when the statistical answer is unknown, and thus these questions lose their causal strength.

We are left with two studies that use the demographic approach, and neither of them is based on content analysis. Both use simultaneously applied controls, however, which help deal with third variable explanations and build the case for causal arguments. Pingree et al. (1979) used questions concerning the demography of the American nuclear family to test the hypothesis that prime time cultivates a rosy picture of the stability of the nuclear family (e.g., low divorce rate, two-parent families). Results showed that, despite controls for age, education, occupation, and income together, a significant relationship between prime time television viewing and "television-biased" stable family persisted ($r = .34$, $p < .01$). These results can only be viewed as suggestive, however, since the sample size is so small.

In a study slightly better supported by content analysis, Fox and Philliber (1978) dealt with perceptions of affluence, arguing that television overrepresents middle- and upper-class characters and thus an affluent lifestyle. If this is true, then heavy viewers should construct a social reality that overestimates the extent of affluence in American society. The affluence measure was an average of answers to seven questions, such as "how many Americans out of 100 have homes that cost more than $40,000?" Their measure of television use was "on the average, how many evenings a week do you watch TV at least one hour?" This weak measure of viewing seriously undermines what would be a strong analysis—using both simultaneous controls and interactions of viewing and other variables.

Their results show a small but significant relationship between television viewing and perceptions of affluence that is reduced by controls applied separately (income, occupation, and especially education) and is eliminated by all three together. Fox and Philliber's study, then, makes clear the need for controls, especially controls on characteristics that have an obvious relationship to the dependent variable (e.g., income, occupation, and education with perceptions of affluence). Further, their analyses show clearly that controlling separately is not sufficient: When controls that each reduce the relationship a little are applied together, they reduce it enough so that it is no longer significant.

Value-System Measures. The measures of social reality that are a step removed from the demography of television we label "value-system" measures. The intent is to measure some aspect of the meaning of the action of television, to tap the underlying value system of television content. As in the research on demographic variables, value-system research has dealt mostly with television violence: fearfulness of walking alone at night, acquisition of protective devices, alienation, greater acceptance of physical violence, and interpersonal mistrust or wariness.

Table 3 shows results from a New Jersey school sample for the question, "Is it dangerous to walk alone in a city at night?" Results show an overall cultivation differential that is significant, but the effect varies within levels of control variables. This does not indicate spuriousness; but controls are apparently not applied together. Similar results are found in the same sample with a slightly different phrasing of the question, in a New York schoolchildren sample for both "a city at night" and "your own neighborhood," and for both samples in a previous year (Gerbner et al. 1978a,b). Questions concerning fear of walking alone at night were also analyzed for two adult samples. Gerbner et al. (1978a,b) report, for the CPS 1976 data and for the NORC 1977 General Social Survey, significant cultivation differentials between light and heavy viewers that vary somewhat within controls (see table 1 for controls).

Other items asked about approval of hitting (e.g., "How often is it all right to hit someone if you are mad at them?") and about activities of the police (e.g., "When police arrive at a scene of violence, how much of the time do they have to use force and violence?") for schoolchildren, and about the use of protective measures (e.g., "bought a dog for purposes of protection") in the CPS National Election Survey. With individual controls, Gerbner et al. find significant cultivation differentials for all but one of the protection measures (1978a,b; 1979a,b):

Two recent reanalyses of the same NORC data provide a strikingly different picture by using multiple controls simultaneously and by including additional dependent variables (Hughes 1980a; Hirsch 1980). By introducing simultaneous controls for a number of potential third variables (see table 1 for controls), Hughes found that the relationship between viewing and fear of walking alone at night was reduced to nonsignificance. Hughes also examined several other variables that Gerbner et al. (1978a,b) report in their NORC (1975 data) analyses. The relationship between viewing and a question about America staying out of world affairs is weakened but remains significant. And for two anomia questions that Gerbner et al. found significant in the 1977 NORC data ("Most public officials are not really interested in the problems of the average man," and "In spite of what some people say, the lot of the average man is getting worse"), the relationships remain significant but appear *curvilinear*: Medium viewers show the most agreement.

Hughes also analyzed four questions from the NORC data sets that had not been reported by Gerbner et al. For two questions about approval of violence similar to those reported by Gerbner et al. (1978a,b), for schoolchildren ("Are there any situations that you can imagine in which you would approve of a man punching an adult male

Table 3

Percent of Adolescents Who Consider Walking Alone in the City at Night Dangerous (Gerbner et al., 1979b)

	Giving Television Answer								
			Television Viewing[1]						
	Total		Light		Heavy		(% Heavy–	Total	
	%	N	%	N	%	N	% Light)	gamma	N
Overall	83	(339)	79	(139)	86	(200)	+ 7	.24*	407
Controlling for									
Sex:									
Male	78	(140)	76	(62)	80	(78)	+ 4	.14	179
Female	87	(199)	83	(77)	90	(122)	+ 7	.32*	228
Grade in School:									
7th	91	(153)	75	(53)	85	(100)	+10	.31*	189
8th	85	(186)	83	(86)	88	(100)	+ 5	.20	218
Ethnic Group:[2]									
Ethnic	84	(84)	82	(37)	86	(47)	+ 4	.12	100
Non-Ethnic	83	(228)	79	(85)	86	(143)	+ 7	.25*	274
Newspaper Reading:									
Everyday	81	(126)	80	(62)	82	(64)	+ 2	.05	155
Sometimes	84	(211)	78	(75)	88	(136)	+10	.36*	250
Network News Watching:									
Almost Daily	87	(81)	83	(29)	90	(52)	+ 7	.28	93
Once in a While	83	(147)	81	(64)	85	(83)	+ 4	.13	177
Hardly Ever	83	(110)	76	(45)	88	(65)	+12	.38*	133
Father's Education:									
No College	83	(147)	77	(51)	96	(96)	+ 9	.28	178
Some College	83	(153)	79	(70)	87	(83)	+ 8	.30	184

[1] "Altogether, about how many hours a day do you usually spend watching TV, including morning, afternoon, and evening?" Light: less than 4 hours; Heavy: 4 hours and more.

[2] Those who perceive themselves as members of a special group of Americans, such as Italian-Americans, Chinese-Americans, Afro-Americans, etc.

* $p \leq .05$ (tau).

Data Source: New Jersey School.
Interview Date: December 1976; May 1977.
Method: Self-Administered Questionnaire.
Question (WLKRSK3B): "Is it dangerous to walk alone in a city at night?"
Used with permission of the authors.

stranger" and a similar question about police striking male citizens), the relationships were the *reverse* of what had been found with the schoolchildren (light viewers were the most likely to approve of violence), and one of the two relationships remained significant even under multiple controls.

Hirsch's reanalysis replicates that of Hughes using different statistical procedures and adding 10 items unreported by Gerbner to the reanalysis of eight that were reported by Gerbner et al. In addition, by combining samples from the 1975, 1977, and 1978 NORC surveys, Hirsch was able to isolate the two "tails" of the viewing distribution: Nonviewers were separated from "light" viewers (for Gerbner et al. 0–2 hours per day; for Hirsch 1–2 hours), and "extreme" viewers (more than 8 hours per day) were separated from "heavy" viewers (for Gerbner et al., 4 or more hours; for Hirsch, 4–7 hours).

Hirsch presents comparisons of nonviewers versus light viewers and heavy versus extreme viewers and finds reversal of the cultivation hypothesis for a substantial majority of the 18 items. That is, when compared to light viewers, nonviewers are fairly consistently more fearful, more approving of violence and suicide, and have higher levels of anomia and alienation. Extreme viewers, on the other hand, are less fearful, alienated, etc. than heavy viewers. Hirsch takes these results as contradicting the cultivation hypothesis.

When the 18 items are collapsed into six scales, the upper part of table 4 illustrates several of Hirsch's points. First, while even the joint predictive power of television viewing, education, sex, and race is very small for these six dependent variables, television's contribution is small and shrinks substantially when other variables are controlled ("unadjusted beta" and "adjusted beta" columns, respectively). Furthermore, the cultivation differential between nonviewers and extreme viewers is (1) usually very small compared to that of other predictors, (2) almost always the reverse of predictions, and (3) there is a linear relationship across the five categories of viewing for only one of the six dependent variables.

This would appear to be a dramatic disconfirmation of cultivation. However, the extremes of the distribution (the 4 percent nonviewers and the 4 percent extreme viewers) are unusual enough that they probably differ from other groups on possibly relevant third variables, so that ascribing their scores to a failure of the television influence hypothesis seems to us unreasonable. Therefore, on the bottom of table 4 we compared only the light, moderate, and heavy viewers and generally find larger cultivation differentials than before between light and heavy viewers, although these are still much smaller than those of the control variables such as education. Still, these differentials are negative (although smaller) as often as positive, and more importantly, three of the six appear to be best explained as curvilinear relationships.

Several factors could account for this difference in results between Hirsch and Hughes and Gerbner et al. First, the questions may be a source of some of the disagreement. Hughes' (1980a) NORC questions asked people to *imagine a situation*, while Gerbner et al. asked children *how often is it all right*. Hughes himself makes a similar argument about differences in questions concerning the protection measures. And the rationale for applying the cultivation hypothesis to the six alienation items and the four suicide items (Hirsch 1980) is so lacking that we tend to discount these results. Gerbner et al. (1980d), in responding to Hughes, report that the approval-of-violence items analyzed by both Hughes and Hirsch were discarded for inadequate reliability, although it is not at all clear just what the alphas they report are based on; we tend to accept this measure as useful, even though it results from a single item. Second, children and adults are not always comparable, and perhaps adults surveyed in the NORC General Social Surveys are not comparable to the adults in the CPS National Election study. Nevertheless, there is surely more to the difference than sample differences: Gerbner et al. (1978a,b), Hughes (1980a), and Hirsch (1980) differ in some of their results with the *same* sample and questions.

This leads to the issue of controls: Gerbner et al. apply controls one at a time; Hughes and Hirsch apply more controls and use them simultaneously. When controls are

Table 4

Summary Statistics on Television Viewing's "Separate and Independent Contribution"
to the Variance Explained on:

Variable	Multiple R^2 for Television Viewing, Education, Sex, and Race	Unadjusted Eta for Television Viewing	Adjusted Beta of Television Viewing	High-Low Differential for Largest Contributor to R^2	High-Low Differential (None vs. Extreme) for Television Viewing
Alienation	0.08	0.11	0.06	−20.64 (Education)	−2.42 +
Anomia	0.13	0.16	0.08	−28.50 (Education)	−2.36 ∩
Fear	0.18	0.06	0.03	39.68 (Sex)	−6.13 ∪
Actual Violence	0.07	0.09	0.05	16.67 (Education)	−3.33 ∩
Mean World	0.12	0.13	0.06	−25.03 (Education) 22.19 (Race)	3.81 +
Suicide	0.07	0.10	0.06	10.91 (Education)	−6.91 −

NOTE: Above from Hirsch, P. The "scary world" of the nonviewer and other anomalies: A re-analysis of Gerbner et al.'s findings of cultivation analysis. *Communication Research*, 7:403–456, 1980, Sage Publications, Inc., with permission of the publisher and the author.

Variable	High-Low Differential (Light vs. Heavy) for Television Viewing	Nature of Relationship for Light, Medium, and Heavy Viewing
Alienation	4.44	+ Positive
Anomia	5.11	∩ Curvilinear
Fear	−1.08	∪ Curvilinear
Actual Violence	−4.02	∩ Curvilinear
Mean World	4.47	+ Positive
Suicide	−2.37	− Negative

applied simultaneously, the cultivation effect of Gerbner et al., which should have a linear or at least monotonic form, either flattens out or becomes curvilinear in all cases but one.

This would appear to be a disconfirmation of the cultivation hypothesis; it raises serious questions about the control procedures used in many studies. Apparently, individual control variables applied separately are not as effective as when applied in concert:[4] Each may be accounting for different pieces of the variance, and we would never be able to see this by controlling sequentially. Alternatively, Hughes' (1980) and Hirsch's (1980) procedures may also be inappropriate—for a different reason. Although controlling for third variables leaves a relationship of television and a social reality variable that is independent of those third variables, it may mislead us by removing relationships that are conditional on third variables. For example, even if a positive correlation between viewing and belief is reduced to zero because of education's relation to one or the other, subgroups on education (or even subgroups on another variable with no zero-order relation to viewing or beliefs) can still differ in the degree of association between viewing and beliefs.

Furthermore, the application of control variables should be theoretically motivated and interpreted, with special care given to consideration of the causal order of the control variable and the two variables of interest. Changing a zero-order correlation by removing a causally prior third variable suggests that the original relationship may have been partially spurious (without ruling out conditional), but changing the relationship by removing the covariance of an intervening third variable should suggest an interpretation of indirect influence through intervening processes. And, while curvilinear relationships between viewing and beliefs after the application of causally prior controls suggest that the relationship between viewing and beliefs cannot be explained by monotonic theories or be assumed to apply universally, these unexpected relationships demand further explanation—not the simple negation of the original simple hypothesis.

Recently, Gerbner et al. (1980b,c) presented some analyses that begin to respond to these critiques and suggestions by both simultaneously employing multiple controls and checking for subgroup differences. For the

anomia items from the 1977 NORC survey reanalyzed by Hughes and Hirsch, partialing simultaneously on eight variables reduces the television-belief relationship to zero for two education subgroups, but not for the third: The correlation between viewing and anomia remains unchanged ($r = .14$) for those respondents with some college education. And there were similar subgroup results for the combination of income level and where one lives for an index labeled "perceptions of danger."

Subgroup differences can also be found in Doob and Macdonald's (1979) study of Toronto adults living in areas that varied in amount of real-world crime. Doob and Macdonald were testing the hypothesis that "people who watch a lot of television may have a greater fear of being victims of violent crime, because, in fact, they live in more violent neighborhoods." Using a recall-diary of television viewing for 1 week and a measure of fear-of-crime, Doob and Macdonald found an overall significant relationship between television use and fear of crime. However, when city-suburb, level of crime, sex, and age are entered in a multiple regression before television viewing, this relationship disappears. What is suggestive of conditional effects is that Doob and Macdonald also report the television-fear correlation separately for the four city-suburb and level of crime areas and find a significant correlation ($r = .24$) only in the high-crime city area (the correlation in the high-crime suburb is similar at .16, while the correlations for the other two groups are much smaller). Unfortunately, however, these subgroup correlations are not partialed for sex and age, nor were interactions of television with area included in the multiple regression, so these differences can only be taken as suggestive.

Moving away from fear-alienation-protection, but still related to television violence, is a value-system area called "interpersonal mistrust" or "wariness." These variables usually have some variation on "Can most people be trusted, or are they just looking out for themselves?"

Gerbner et al. (1977a,b; 1979a,b) found significant differences for light and heavy viewers for school children with variations within control variables such as age, sex, ethnic group, newspaper reading, network news viewing, and father's education. Similarly, they found a television-viewing interpersonal mistrust relationship with adults in the CPS sample and in the 1975 NORC sample with controls such as sex, age, education (CPS sample) in addition to income, newspaper reading, church attendance, and race (NORC sample). Again, the controls are applied separately. However, Neville's (1980) reanalysis of CPS data in a path analysis with age, sex, race, income, and education showed a significant contribution of both prime time and daytime television to interpersonal mistrust. In Australia, Hawkins and Pingree (1980a)

---

[4] We suspect that the efficacy of Hughes' control procedures is the result of controlling variables together rather than the additional control variables Hughes uses. In an analysis we suggested, Hughes dropped one of the strongest predictors of television watching (hours worked per week) and reanalyzed the data: Results were the same as when hours worked per week were included as a control procedure. (Hughes 1980b).

similarly found a significant correlation under simultaneous controls. Thus, the relationship has received support when examined with multiple control variables together.

One other study deserves mention to emphasize the need to relate influence hypotheses explicitly to television content. In most cases, value-system measures are only implied by television content. But Haney and Manzolati (1980) found 21 attitudes about criminal justice as consistent themes in dramatic television programs (e.g., crime is a product of the criminal's personality and not of societal structures and law violations by police to apprehend criminals are acceptable). For 11 of these 21 items, heavy viewers were more likely than light viewers to agree. Adequate controls were not applied, but the study is noteworthy in demonstrating that hypotheses about television influence on value systems can be based more directly on content analyses and not simply on implications derived from content demographics.

Areas of social reality that have been studied in addition to violent television content deal mostly with value systems related to traditional sex roles, family structure, and images of older people.

In analyses of a 1974 Harris Poll, Gonzalez (1979), Gerbner et al. (1980a), and Gerbner and Signorielli (1979) report significant television viewing-value system relationships for negative beliefs about older people. These include beliefs that the proportion of older people is declining, that people do not live as long as they used to, and that older people are less healthy than they used to be. Gerbner et al. (1980a) report significant relationships for negative images: "Older people are not open-minded and adaptable, are not bright and alert, and are not good at getting things done." These relationships were controlled separately with variables such as age, education, income, sex, race, and contact with the elderly. Similarly, Gerbner et al. (1980a) found that, compared with light viewers, heavy viewers among schoolchildren thought that "people become old" at a younger age.

For traditional sex roles, Volgy and Schwarz (1980) report higher levels of sexism among adults heavily exposed to entertainment programs, but since neither measures nor controls are reported, this study is impossible to evaluate. Rothschild (1979) reports conditional results for some subgroups that withstand simultaneous controls, and Gerbner and Signorielli (1979) find a sexism cultivation differential between light and heavy viewers in their analysis of NORC's General Social Survey data from 1975, 1977, and 1978. Their controls, while not applied simultaneously, suggest a "leveling" effect for cultivation of sexism: Within levels of some control variables, television-sexism relationships work in opposite ways. Gerbner and Signorielli (1979) argue that this implies that television cultivates a certain *level* of sexist

orientation, bringing some toward traditional roles from a nontraditional orientation and some the reverse.

Research on family structure value systems is scarcer. Harr-Mazer (1980) found significant relationships between viewing and measures of child victimization and seeing children's societal roles as more restricted. Since this work is still underway, details of measures and analyses are unclear, but relationships were found to be stronger for younger and college-educated respondents. Also, significant results for family structure value systems and viewing were found for some subgroups by Pingree et al. (1979) and Morgan and Harr-Mazer (1980).

Finally, Volgy and Schwarz (1980) also report significant relationships between viewing medical shows and affect toward doctors and between viewing ethnic shows and concern about racial problems. However, we are told nothing about their measures or analysis techniques.

Summary. Is there a relationship between television viewing and social reality? Most studies show evidence for a link, regardless of the kind of social reality studied. These studies cover a diverse range of areas including prevalence of violence, family structures, interpersonal mistrust, fear of victimization, traditional sex roles, family values, images of older people, attitudes about doctors, and concern about racial problems.

There does seem to be a relationship then, but is it real, or is it an artifact of some third variable? The research does not easily answer this question. It may lie partly in the kinds of social reality we are concerned with. Relationships between viewing and demographic measures of social reality closely linked to television content appear to hold despite controls.

This is only partially true for value-system measures. For measures concerned with interpersonal mistrust, the research shows a similar pattern to that with demographic measures. However, this is not the case for fear of victimization and for alienation. Simultaneously applied controls reduce the relationship below significance, produce curvilinear patterns, or reverse the relationship of beliefs and viewing. The few conditional results hint that these odd overall patterns may result from the combination of subgroups for which there is no relationship with subgroups for whom a positive relationship persists. Given the mixed evidence, our conclusions here must be tentative: The zero-order relationships reported between television viewing and these aspects of value systems *may* be spurious, or the relationship may hold up only under certain conditions.

The other value system areas also require more sophisticated analyses, but in any case there are so few studies in each area [5] that little can be said until the work has been replicated.

Causal Order. A relationship between two variables says nothing about the nature of that relationship. One could cause the other, or vice versa, or both could work reciprocally, or a third variable could cause both. Fortunately, we have several kinds of evidence to help explore the causal direction of the TV-social reality relationship—experiments, longitudinal analyses, and indirect evidence.

Experiments. First, it should be pointed out that use of the experimental method of study cultivation goes against a basic assumption of the cultivation approach, namely, that effects occur over time and through repeated exposure to bits and pieces of information and to value systems that favor a particular construction of the world (Gerbner and Gross 1976). However, experiments are the best evidence for causal direction, and, to the extent that any social reality effects can be demonstrated experimentally, the case for the cultivation hypothesis is strengthened. Tan (1979) studied the effects of exposure to television beauty ads on perceptions of the importance of beauty, sex appeal, and youth in various "real-life" roles. He showed high school girls 15 commercials that either emphasized beauty or did not mention or show beauty themes. Tan's results support the argument that television content causes change in social reality; exposure to beauty themes in commercials produced higher ratings of the importance of beauty for two of the five roles.

Bryant et al. (1981) also found evidence that television influences social reality beliefs in a study of anxiety, likelihood and fear of victimization, and likelihood of retribution for violence. Bryant et al. used controlled television diets for a 6-week period and randomly assigned undergraduates to light viewing, heavy viewing of violence ending with justice, and heavy viewing of violence ending with injustice. Their results showed that heavy viewers were more anxious and fearful, regardless of retributive justice, although there was suggestive evidence that cultivation of fear and anxiety is more pronounced when violence is unjustly rewarded. There was also evidence for a reciprocal relationship between viewing and violence: Heavy viewers of violence with retributive justice subsequently exposed themselves to more violent television. This does not imply, however, that anxiety per se causes viewing, since heavy viewers of

injustice exposed themselves to *less* action drama subsequent to their diets. Thus, this experiment supports the hypothesis that the television viewing-social reality link is causal with television as the source and also refines the hypothesis to include a weaker reciprocal link.

Longitudinal Analysis. Morgan (1980) used the New Jersey schoolchildren panel for 3 years to make causal inferences about value-system measures concerning sexism. Using sexism scores in the third year as the dependent variable, Morgan conducted a hierarchical multiple regression. His results show that, for girls, amount of viewing in the first year significantly predicts sexism in the third year that is not attributable to earlier sexism or demographics. For boys, the relationship is reversed: Earlier sexism predicts third-year total television viewing.

And using the same sample, Gerbner et al. (1980b,c) report a path analysis of 2-years' television viewing, interpersonal mistrust, and perceptions of danger (a mixed demographic and value-systems index). Controlling for IQ, SES, and second-year values of the social reality variables, Gerbner et al. found that second-year television viewing still contributes to the adolescents' third-year social reality beliefs, indicating a causal contribution of television viewing. It is worth noting that second-year values of both social reality variables contribute to third-year viewing, so that the reciprocal causal link is supported as well.

Indirect Evidence. Gerbner and Signorielli's (1979) "leveling" argument also has causal implications, although as an argument it carries less force than an experiment or a longitudinal analysis. If television viewing is positively related to sexism for a group relatively low on sexism, but negatively related for a group relatively high on sexism, a counter-explanation based on an untested control variable requires an *interaction* of that control variable with either television viewing or sexism *and* the subgrouping variable. This is not impossible, but it does eliminate the simple ways for the control variable to produce a spurious relationship.

Some suggestive evidence against reverse causation can be found in Hawkins and Pingree (1981). We separated the influence of television into component parts corresponding to viewing specific content types. Quite different relationships to social reality beliefs were found with residuals of viewing content types partialed on total viewing—an estimate of watching more or less of that type than predicted based on sample norms and the individual's total viewing. These changed relationships refute the reverse causation argument that social reality beliefs lead people to television that matches those beliefs for confirmation. *Viewing* crime-adventure programs provided the strongest relationship for prevalence of vio-

[5] Actually, there is a good deal of evidence to support a relationship between acceptance of traditional sex roles and television viewing, but the variables are not quite within the cultivation approach (see Greenberg, this volume).

lence and interpersonal mistrust, but *choosing* to watch relatively more or less crime-adventure than one's total viewing would predict is unrelated to such beliefs. As in previous work by Chaffee (Chaffee 1972; Chaffee and Tims 1976), the link through preference or selection is unsupported, leaving the viewing effects explanation more plausible, at least for this study.

Two surveys by Wober (1979, 1980) provide an example of another indirect test that can be made. Wober compared ratings and "appreciation" scores for viewers in cities with high and low crime rates. Viewing action-adventure programs differed relatively little between cities, but appreciation scores varied considerably. In one survey, viewers in the more violent city seemed to like crime-adventure programs less, suggesting to Wober that "they have had enough of the real thing." In the other survey, however, the appreciation scores were reversed, suggesting that real-world violence leads to seeking vicarious violence on television.

Summary. The evidence concerning the causal direction of television's impact on social reality is not sufficient for strong conclusions. It is fairly consistent, however, and suggests that television *can* teach about social reality and that the relationship between viewing and social reality may be reciprocal: Television viewing causes a social reality to be constructed in a certain way, but this construction of social reality may also direct viewing behavior.

How Cultivation Effects Occur: Conditions and Processes

The cultivation of social reality has generally been treated sociologically, so that the psychological process(es) responsible for the sociological effects are generally summed up as "learning." For example, Gross and Morgan (in press) write, "A basic premise of Cultivation Analysis is that what happens to most people, most of the time, is more important than individual or discrete effects *for policy decisions*" (p. 11, emphasis added). And in describing variation in the cultivation differential across different levels of control variables (e.g., table 3), the Cultural Indicators group consistently acknowledges the differences but emphasizes the fact that the cultivation differentials almost always remain greater than zero (even though often too small for statistical significance).

But, it is equally plausible to look at figures such as those in table 3 and emphasize the differences in the positive cultivation differentials rather than the consistency of direction, asking "How does cultivation work, anyway?" What sorts of processing are involved in social reality construction based on television content? We will present theoretical arguments for and evidence bearing on five processes that may be involved: (1) information-processing abilities and cognitive-structural constraints, (2) critical awareness of and approach to television, (3) direct experience or other sources providing confirmation or disconfirmation of television's messages, (4) social-structural influences, and (5) cultivation identified with specific content and selective viewing instead of habitual viewing of television in general.

Processing Abilities

To the extent that individual construction is required for television to influence social reality, we need to expand on the notion of "learning" to more particular understandings of processes involved. And, if individual differences in processing abilities or cognitive structures are responsible for differences in cultivation, these abilities will provide an indication of some of the processes involved. The variety of conditional hypotheses involving processing abilities is potentially quite large, so we will mention only a few examples here and then discuss the few results available that bear on them.

Inferring patterns from discrete events might make IQ an important factor, with low IQ an inhibitor of cultivation effects. The evidence here is sparse. Gerbner et al. (1979b) do report separate cultivation differentials at high, medium, and low relative levels of achievement for their New York sample of schoolchildren. In estimating the proportion of people involved in violence, the cultivation differential is significant for low and medium achievement, but not for high achievement. However, this is not the appropriate statistic for concluding that there is less cultivation for the high achievement subgroup. What is needed is a test of the *differences* of the cultivation·differential—something analogous to tests of the difference between two correlation coefficients. Such a test is not reported, but it appears that the cultivation differential of the high achievement group is not much less than that of the other two groups. Other dependent variables show a mix of patterns of achievement, but the subsample sizes are too small for meaningful comparisons.

Achievement, even as a surrogate for IQ, subsumes too much and thus is rather distant from processing abilities that would give us an idea of what goes on as television influences social reality. Ideally, one should determine individual performance on various processing abilities and then use these individual differences in conditional analyses for the same sample of individuals.

Comparisons across age groups would provide a surrogate method of comparison whenever one can trace developmental changes in processing abilities that parallel changes in cultivation. For example, one could predict stronger television influences on young children, based on cognitive-developmental theories suggesting that concrete-operational reasoning may be more inflexible and dogmatic than formal-operational reasoning. As an example, Cordua et al. (1979) showed children a videotaped visit to the office of Doctor Nancy and Nurse David and then asked the children to pick the doctor's and nurse's names out of a list of two male and two female names. Even tested immediately, first and fourth graders were overwhelmingly certain that the doctor had been a man and the nurse a woman. Seventh graders, in contrast, got the gender correct at immediate post-test, although they too slipped back in a 1-week retest. Such inflexible thinking could make concrete-operational children more affected by television message systems (cumulatively quite stereotyped), because they might accept and generalize the dominant messages, ignoring the few deviant ones. Adolescents and adults might partially balance the main message by noting the exceptions and admitting the possibility of others.

Also, greater influence for young children could be predicted on the basis of their tendency to acquire more incidental than central plot information. Because crucial message elements for social reality construction—things like the sex, age, and social class of victors and vanquished or the marital status of women (married) and men (single)—resemble information described in developmental literature as "incidental," those viewers with a "strong filter" focusing on central information and discarding incidental information may be less influenced by television viewing. In general, this focusing ability seems to be an age-related acquisition, with children older than 10–12 much more likely to ignore incidental information.

There are other intertwined processing abilities that suggest young children will not use television content to construct their social reality before adolescence. A variety of studies suggest that young children (before ages 8–10) have difficulty comprehending and making use of the order of isolated events in a plot (Leifer et al. 1971), lose track of order and relationships between events separated in a plot (Collins 1973), have difficulty making inferences about the causes and meanings of televised actions (Collins et al. 1978), and have difficulty understanding, let alone applying, dramatic characters' motives and the consequences of their actions (Leifer and Roberts 1972). Young children may simply not understand enough of what they watch to be cultivated by it.

Two samples from the Cultural Indicators group provide comparisons across transitional age ranges (New York schoolchildren and Bank Street children). Cultivation was reported in their youngest group (fourth to sixth grade) as strong as in the seventh to ninth graders at the same school (Gerbner et al. 1978a). There is even some suggestion in the New York schoolchildren sample of greater cultivation for fifth to eighth graders than for ninth to twelfth graders (Gerbner et al. 1979b). However, apparently stable correlations between viewing and interpersonal mistrust at fifth, eighth, and eleventh grade in the Perth sample changed after being partialed on SES: The relationship at fifth and eighth grade was reduced essentially to zero, while the correlation at eleventh grade was unaffected (Hawkins and Pingree 1980a).

Critical Attention to Television

A second set of hypotheses has to do with viewers' attitudes toward television and critical weighing of television messages. The perceived reality of television, for example, has been hypothesized to control involvement with viewing and the relevance of what is viewed, and these are believed to lead to greater effects of viewing (see Hawkins 1977 for a fuller review). Although this interaction prediction (between viewing and perceived reality) has been challenged by direct effect findings (Pingree 1978; Reeves 1978), the fact that the dependent variables have themselves to do with conceptions of reality in general make these hypotheses once again relevant. With social reality variables like prevalence of violence and interpersonal mistrust, perceived reality worked only in interaction with whether Perth students had taken a media studies course, only in reverse of expectations: Stronger cultivation correlations occurred at *lower* levels of perceived reality whenever perceived reality located significant differences cultivation (Hawkins and Pingree 1980a).

What may be important here is not the beliefs about television but what they may indicate about the "activity" with which people watch television. It may be that "inactive" viewing is necessary for social reality effects or that "active" viewing inhibits the influence. In one study (Pingree et al. 1981), social reality effects were compared for soap opera fans (who had paid to attend a soap opera convention and luncheon with several stars) and a random sample of women from the same city. The evidence suggested that the fans watched much more actively and discussed the programs with friends. Amount of soap opera viewing and soap opera-biased social reality were related for the random sample of women but not for the fans, suggesting that active processing and involvement may inhibit cultivation.

We are skeptical of interpreting this in a counterargument framework (Roberts and Maccoby 1973), because that would imply that the media consumer sees a particular point of view in a television message and argues against it during or immediately after message receptions. We suggest instead the term "critical consumer" processes, by which we mean evaluation of information during reception, greater retention of the bits and pieces of information provided by television, awareness of exceptions to patterns, more active search (not simply exposure) for confirming or disconfirming information, a more rational weighing of evidence in constructing social reality, and so on.

Besides the characteristics of active involved television viewing that prevent social reality effects, it is equally appropriate to suggest that uninvolved or passive reception can *enhance* some kinds of effects. Advertising researchers propose that, instead of a progression from attentive learning to evaluation and attitude formation and finally behavior, our understanding of much of television viewing, especially viewing commercials, will be increased if we consider an uninvolved, disinterested viewer assimilating only the simplest facts, names, and jingles, and then only into short-term memory. Examples include the purchase of low-cost interchangeable consumer goods (or voting for minor local candidates) based on short-term memory cues, with little intervention of preformed attitudes (Ray 1973).

The potential contribution of the low-involvement model may stem from the nature of the relevant television messages, as interpreted by Gerbner and his colleagues, even though these messages are quite different from the short-term learning from commercials. Advertisements constructed to take advantage of the low-involvement model make the brand name, jingle, and other simple characteristics as salient as possible, repeating the ad as often as is economically feasible. Putting across the crucial message elements for social reality construction is probably not the primary goal of producers of entertainment television. But for the viewer, because these elements are seldom crucial to plots of individual dramas, attention to them may be very similar.

If so, unfocused attention to plot-incidental items bears a strong resemblance to that of young children who do not focus on central information. The difference may be that, while young children *cannot* focus on central information, perhaps many adults (or most adults some of the time) can but *do not* focus, and thus they are more open to television influence on their social reality when they do not focus.

Experience

Even if television influences the construction of social reality, it does not do so in a vacuum. Viewers have their own experience, other mass media, friends, family, and their beliefs as filters for television's images. These factors may form conditions for television influence in at least three ways.

First, for any given television message, some minimum degree of *confirmation* from real-world experience, other sources, or even preexisting beliefs about social reality may be necessary to validate the television message; below that minimum threshold, the relationship between viewing and beliefs may be attenuated or absent (Gerbner et al. 1980*b,c* propose the same processes under the label "resonance"). Second, messages different from those of television coming from a heavily used or relied-on source could provide sufficient *disconfirmation* that the amount of exposure to television becomes less relevant or even irrelevant. Third, Gerbner et al. (1980*b,c*) suggest that, for some social reality beliefs, television's portrayals both form and match the *mainstream* of beliefs. Many population subgroups share these beliefs for other reasons, and the amount of television viewed adds little; but for divergent population subgroups, the extent of viewing becomes important, with the beliefs of heavy viewers in the divergent group converging on the population mainstream.

The characteristics of an individual's experience that might be relevant could make a long and expandable list. For example, the pressures and experiences of lower SES lifestyles could provide confirmation of television messages about interpersonal mistrust and possibly about the prevalence of violence and fear of crime. Confirmation of television's messages about violence could come from exposure to news media or personal experience or personal knowledge of victimization. And confirmation/disconfirmation mainstreaming based on experience should not be limited to violence. The impact of television sex-role portrayals might be quite different for children whose mothers work outside the home, thus providing them with a counter-example to television's stereotyping of women.

Examples that follow the mainstreaming pattern are easy to find. For example, in the NORC 1975 sample (Gerbner et al. 1977*a,b*), a significant cultivation differential exists for interpersonal mistrust at middle-and upper-income levels, but not for those with low incomes. And when the NORC 1975 and 1978 samples are combined (Gerbner et al. 1980*b,c*), a significant correlation between viewing and interpersonal mistrust persists despite simultaneous controls for those with some college, but not for those without a college education, whose level of mistrust is uniformly high. And for nonwhites, whose interpersonal mistrust is relatively high, the partial correlation with television viewing is negative (instead of positive, as with whites), further suggesting a television role in converging viewpoints on the "mainstream." Likewise, for the three "anomia" items in the NORC 1977 survey, Gerbner et al. (1980*b,c*) report that the correlation with viewing is unaffected only for the some college subgroups, who again score lowest as a whole on anomia. Other results give some indication of mainstreaming patterns for some sex and age differences.

Confirmation (or "resonance") results seem less common, but several examples are available, starting with Doob and Macdonald's (1979) Toronto results on fear of victimization. Television viewing and fear were significantly related only in the high-crime city area; this may suggest that living in such an area provides confirmation that television's messages are relevant and to be believed. Note, however, that the less localized perceptions of violence derivable from newspapers and television news do not make a consistent difference in television influence (Gerbner et al. 1979a,b; Hawkins and Pingree 1980), although this leaves aside the issue of news directly influencing social reality.

Gerbner et al. (1980b,c) report a partial replication of Doob and Macdonald's results, although their subgroupings on income within cities and suburbs cannot provide as clean an indicator as the Toronto police statistics broken down for 210 individual patrol districts. Still, after the application of simultaneous controls, the relationship between viewing and a perception-of-danger index remained positive and significant for low-income city residents but was zero for high-income city residents for whom the questions were somewhat less relevant. However, income located no differences in the positive correlations for suburban residents, making the interpretation of these findings less clear.

No good evidence for the disconfirmation pattern has been found, even though one 1977 survey was designed to test for confirmation and disconfirmation relationships (Hawkins and Pingree 1980).

This is an apt point to emphasize that mainstreaming, confirmation (resonance), and disconfirmation should all be regarded as hypotheses. They have been applied post hoc to describe subgroup differences, and psychological processes have been proposed as explanations, but they have not been applied predictively. As Hirsch (1980; 1981) points out, one could easily argue (as Gerbner et al, originally suggested in earlier publications) that women, blacks, and the poor ought to be *most* affected by portrayals of television violence, since they are the subgroups most at risk in the real world and the most victimized on television. Yet, relationships between violence-related beliefs and television viewing are often weakest in these groups. In addition, given the large number of control variables on which subgroups could be formed, we must also evaluate these isolated subgroups against chance.

These hypotheses are complex and controversial enough (Gerbner et al. 1981; Hirsch 1981b) that strong tests require not just predictions but actually going beyond the basic three variables of the relationship. If interpersonal mistrust is high for low-education groups and

unrelated to viewing, while mistrust rises to similar high levels for high-education groups as viewing increases, a "mainstreaming" interpretation would be greatly strengthened if we could demonstrate that television's messages are in fact at the "mainstream" point on the graph. Similarly, arguments for why viewing does not affect less educated groups would be more convincing if the rest of their symbolic environment were examined with the same care that content analysis gives to television.

The one other difference that might be explained by experience may be the difference between adolescent and adult samples. In general, the relationships are much weaker in the adult samples, although statistical significance is maintained by the much larger sample sizes. We argued before that children younger than about 10 may lack some processing abilities necessary to construct social reality from television. What we may have here instead is an application of what has become almost a communication research truism—that effects of communication are strongest when competing sources of information and preexisting knowledge are lowest. For adolescents, these social reality beliefs are still in the process of formation and thus more amenable to influence. Perceived relevance of the topic might play a role here as well. Morgan and Harr-Mazer (1980) report pronounced increases with age in the correlation of viewing and family expectations for adolescents, with the largest shift coming between eighth and ninth grades for projected age of family formation and between seventh and eighth grades for anticipated family size.

The interesting thing about all of this discussion is the implication of a relatively rational process and perhaps even an awareness of weighing and balancing information from different sources. Such weighing and balancing are generally presumed in information seeking but are foreign to our discussion of television's influence within the low-involvement model. There is room, however, for this apparent contradiction to be resolved, because emphasizing individual constructions of social reality separates television's influence into at least two steps. First, the individual must acquire from television various bits of information about actions and characterization and associations between these bits of information; this may be best explained as incidental learning within the low-involvement model. Second, the individual may use these bits of information to construct more general and integrated conceptions of the world, and it is probably here that the "higher" processes like inference or weighing television against other sources of information occurs.

Social Structure

There are at least two interesting studies in which the nature of the intimate social groups surrounding the individual seem to make a difference in television's influence. Rothschild (1979) categorized third- and fifth-grade children's peer groups as cohesive or non-cohesive, depending on whether all children nominated each other reciprocally or whether there was a non-reciprocal link. Since children could belong to multiple groups, they were categorized in four groups: purely cohesive, mixed (belong to both cohesive and semi-cohesive), purely semi-cohesive, or no group membership. It appears that group cohesiveness inhibits or may even reverse predicted cultivation influences for gender-related qualities, occupational aspirations, and interpersonal mistrust. Rothschild interprets her findings as indicating that the increased social interaction in groups provides a rich set of alternative information which may counteract television's messages.

Gross and Morgan (in press) report cultivation differences in the New Jersey panel survey of adolescents based on four characteristics of the family context. These are protectiveness (the tendency to restrict viewing), utility (parents' perception of the usefulness and reality of television), conflict over television viewing, and independence (students' access to television in terms of who selects what they see). High parental protectiveness, utility, and low conflict over television wipe out correlations with television for interpersonal mistrust, although not for the prevalence of violence. Those who have greater independence of access appear more cultivated for prevalence of violence, but only in the third year. The amount of family intervention capability suggested here is striking and encouraging.

Specific Viewing

Gerbner et al. (1979a) assert that two key assumptions underlie Cultural Indicators research:

One is that commercial television, unlike other media, presents an organically composed total world of interrelated stories (both drama and news) produced to the same set of market specification. Second, television audiences (unlike those for other media) view largely non-selectively and by the clock rather than by the program. Television viewing is a ritual, almost like religion, except that it is attended to more regularly.

It is possible however, to argue separately with each of these assumptions. First, content analyses have not been reported by program type, despite the fact that different content types may present differences in patterns of action and characterization. And, if people vary in their mix of viewing different types of programs, then these content differences would make for differential influence across types of television content (see Hawkins and Pingree, 1981). Table 5 (Hawkins and Pingree 1981) presents the cultivation correlation from the Perth sample for total viewing and each of 10 independent types of

Table 5

Correlations Between Content Types and Belief in Mean World and Violence in Society (Hawkins & Pingree, 1980a)

	Mean World	Violence in Society
Television news............	.04	−.03
Television documentaries ...	.01	.01
Situation comedies.........	.05	.06*
Crime-adventure shows.....	.06*	.16***
Drama....................	−.04	−.01
Music / variety..............	.03	−.02
Game shows..............	.03	.14***
Cartoons..................	.00	.14***
Children's shows...........	.00	.07*
Sports....................	.01	.02

Note: Each correlation coefficient reported for a specific program type is actually a partial correlation coefficient, with the total amount of viewing all other types of content partialed out. *p<.05.   ***p<.001.

television content coded from viewing diaries. Because the *amounts* people view of different types are not independent of each other, each correlation for a content type is partialed on all other viewing, so that these partials may be taken to represent the independent contribution of varying content types.

While the relationships between viewing and social reality beliefs can only be indirect evidence of symbolic message differences between different content types, it is clear from table 5 that differences do exist. Even within the Cultural Indicators group's overall "dramatic programs" category, corresponding to our divisions of situation comedies, crime-adventure, drama, and cartoons, the types are not uniformly related to the social reality measures, and the most parsimonious explanation must be that the symbolic messages presented in these program types are not uniform with respect to social reality beliefs.

Hawkins and Pingree (1981) also examine the intercorrelations of viewing these program types and total viewing and report differences in selective versus habitual viewing of these content types, with crime-adventure, cartoons, and news viewed relatively habitually and comedy viewed much more selectively. Thus, two of the three content types most related to social reality (crime-adventure and cartoons) are predictable from other viewing, suggesting that the omnivorous habits of heavy viewership are responsible for such viewing. However, habitual television watching itself (as an unmeasured third variable) cannot be posited to account for the content-specific relationships, since comedy and news viewing are much more weakly or even negatively related to social reality, thus strengthening the causal arguments made earlier.

Summary

Figure 1 illustrates how these processes and the limited data relevant to them might fit together. The act of viewing television, even cumulatively over long periods of time, is only the beginning of television influence on social reality. And it should be obvious that we think it is crucial for message-systems analysis to move down at least to the level of content types. The next step in television's influence is learning (probably incidentally) various bits and pieces of action, characterization, and so on, and their associations with one another and with demographic characteristics. In determining how well this learning proceeds, such factors as attention to television, memory capacities, focusing strategies, and involvement may be important conditional or intervening variables (and we have drawn the arrow from these conditions to the link between viewing and learning and not to learning itself, to signify this intervention). We suspect that the actual construction of social reality is a separate following step, conditioned by such things as inference skills, social structures such as family and friends, and the competing or complementing information of other experience (we also note here that these conceptions of reality can be *directly* influenced by experience as well). Finally, if social reality has any importance at all, it should serve as a guide to actual behavior. What is needed now is work that takes account of these separate steps and treats each of them as an empirical question.

Summary

The evidence is relatively supportive of television's influence on *some* aspects of social reality, especially in areas related to violence and for the demographic measures on prevalence of violence and the value-system measures on interpersonal mistrust. There are also suggestive evidence for other areas of social reality (sexism, ageism, family structure) and a small amount of experimental and longitudinal evidence for television as the cause of certain social reality constructions. On the other hand, some relationships, especially those between television viewing and value-system measures, are seriously attenuated, made curvilinear, or even made negative by the application of simultaneous controls.

We should point out that relationships that are significant between television viewing and social reality are generally on the weak side of moderate in strength. It would be a considerable overstatement of the area to assign preeminence to television as a shaper of culture. However, asserting the opposite—that television's contribution is trivial—likewise misses some important points.

First, the cultivation hypothesis (and the whole cultural indicators approach) has the joint disadvantages for theory testing of being both global and subtle. Those characteristics of television content hypothesized to be important are meanings present only *implicitly* and only *cumulatively* across the sum total of all television messages. Quite apart from whether such implicit meanings are extracted the same way by all or even most members of a population, testable hypotheses depend on the researcher's own interpretation of the most likely meaning. But researchers, after all, bring a particular vision of their own to television, and this vision could lead to interpretations of messages slightly different from those of most members of the mass audience, thus systematically deflating any observable television effect.

As if these problems were not enough, it should be obvious that present measurements of television viewing and of what people believe about the world, the reality they have constructed, are extremely crude. What has been measured as interpersonal mistrust and prevalence of violence probably has *something* to do with the social

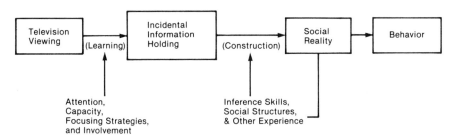

Figure 1. A model of conditions in cultivation.

reality potentially cultivated by television, but they could be much better. Happily, there are indications that measurement in this area is improving, as with Doob and Macdonald's (1979) much greater variety of questions about violence.

It is probable that television's effect on social reality is underestimated by the relatively weak relationships. It should also be clear, however, that the theory that has directed the research needs to be changed. Television's influence on individual constructions of reality can no longer be described as direct but must be viewed as a complex process that takes place within individual contexts. We need to modify the theory to recognize the conditional nature of television's influence: Under some conditions, television does seem to contribute to constructions of reality, but in others it does not. A new focus on the conditions that specify effects would encourage a deeper interest in the viewing situation itself as well as the context of viewing. Are heavy television viewers watching television in the same way as light viewers? Are they more or less attentive, selective?

The theory would similarly be enriched if more attention was paid to explanations for *how individuals use television* to construct social reality. Research findings suggesting conditional effects will be much better explained when we have some idea of the processes involved in the construction of social reality.

Appendix

It has been apparent in reviewing this research that not everyone appreciates the importance of tying content of television to a study of how that content might affect social reality, and it has been obvious that hardly anyone (ourselves included) has been analyzing their data properly. In this appendix, we present some methodological/procedural principles that seem to be essential for meaningful results.

1. Assessing Content

First, some sort of content analysis is necessary so that the existence of a pattern can be established and documented. Some failures to find a television viewing-social reality relationship probably happen because the pattern isn't there (and the researcher assumed it but didn't test for it) or because the researcher's view of the meaning of certain events and relationships presented on television is peculiar, not something that many others would see. It is the carefully documented and relatively objective patterns in content that, when used to construct questions about social reality, give this approach its advantage over

other survey research in ascribing a causal direction to television.

Related to this is the issue of pattern frequency. It's probable that a certain level of a set of events must be present for the pattern to influence an individual's social reality. Since this issue has not previously been raised, we can only guess at what that level is, but it seems worthy of study in its own right.

In addition, there are clear variations in patterns across types of television content: Crime-adventure programs are more violent than situation comedies or daytime serials. The television diet of viewers is not always going to be the same as the mix of what is available. To the extent that this is true, researchers who use more specific viewing measures, such as television-use diaries, will have more meaningful results. Exposure measures need to be capable of specifying at least this level of detail, and it is quite likely that better understanding of viewing situations (attention, selectivity, and so on) will lead to better understanding of whether and how television content influences social reality.

2. Controls

Most researchers who routinely study television effects control for other variables. It is obvious that demographic characteristics such as social class could be accounting for both television viewing and a violent construction of reality. It is not so obvious that applying controls separately is not sufficient to control for spuriousness. There are at least some areas of social reality where simultaneously applied controls reduce a previously significant relationship below significance, when these same controls did not individually affect the significance of the relationship. Thus, it is crucial to control *simultaneously;* controls applied one at a time may each account for a separate, small piece of the variance, leading the researcher to conclude that the relationship is general and holds despite controls.

However, finding that simultaneously applied controls are effective in dramatically altering a relationship or reducing it below conventionally accepted levels of significance is *not sufficient* evidence for calling the relationship spurious, for several reasons.

First, controlling for a third variable or a set of third variables leaves us with an independent (of those other variables) relationship between television viewing and social reality. Assuming that the set of control variables is sufficient (never demonstrable), this independent relationship can be regarded as the whole story when the control variables are causally prior to both viewing and social reality. It is sometimes possible to make this assumption, but more often it is not. Whenever there is a possible reciprocal relationship between a third variable and television viewing or social reality, or whenever the third variable may intervene, the results of an analysis that controls for third variables are likely to be an underestimate of the true relationship. In such a case, the control for third variables still leaves the independent relationship between viewing and social reality but improperly removes any indirect causation through third variables or reciprocal relationships. Instead of using these controls to provide "yes" or "no" answers to simple hypotheses, we would be much better off to do some complex thinking about theoretical relationships both before applying controls (to direct them rationally) and after (to take advantage of the shifting relationships as a guide to more adequate theory).

A second problem with controls arises out of our *routine* use of controls. It is easy to forget that demographic characteristics are reifications of very meaningful processes. They are locators that are simpler to use than the processes themselves, but as demographics they mean nothing. For example, if we find that sex can change a television viewing–social reality relationship, we still need to come up with an *explanation* or a process to account for the effect of sex on this relationship. Sex in itself does not offer us any insight; rather, the explanation lies with some behavior pattern or set of experiences or situations that is located by sex. And this process should interest us. Researchers who remember this are much likelier to be interested in the meaning of a relationship that is changed by a control variable and ultimately to gain a richer understanding of how people use television.

Third, wholesale controlling can obfuscate potential conditional relationships. For example, if a control variable such as socioeconomic status reduces a viewing–social reality relationship to nonsignificance, it, would usually be concluded that socioeconomic status really accounts for both and that there is no true relationship. But it could be that the expected relationship holds in one social class and works exactly the opposite in the other. That such possibilities are often unexamined reflects a use of controls that is not theoretically based; theory building is the poorer for it.[6]

Thus, it is crucial in this area to control for third variables. It is essential to apply these controls simultaneously. But it is also imperative that the use of controls be directed by theoretical systems so that the conditions under which individuals use television to construct social reality can be illuminated.

In sum, we are suggesting as guidelines for research on television's influence on constructions of social reality that researchers (1) need to establish the presence of relevant content and exposure to that content; and (2) need to conduct conditional analyses using simultaneous controls that are directed by theory. Further, we suggest that the original hypothesis that television's peculiar distortions of social reality directly, although subtly, affect heavy viewers' constructions of social reality, needs to be rephrased. We should ask, "How does an individual construct social reality?" and "What sorts of thought processes by the individual and what real-world experiences are necessary for television to contribute to constructions of social reality?"

---

[6] Readers wishing to pursue the logic of third-variable analyses further would do well to consult the chapter in Babbie (1979) on the elaboration model as a carefully explained introduction to the problem.

References

Babbie, E. *The practice of social research* (2nd ed.). Belmont, Calif.: Wadsworth, 1979.

Bryant, J., Carveth, R., & Brown, D. Television viewing and anxiety: An experimental examination. *Journal of Communication*, 1981, *31* (1), 106–119.

Chaffee, S. H. Television and adolescent aggressiveness (Overview). In G. A. Comstock, & E. A. Rubinstein (Eds.), *Television and social behavior, (Vol. 3.) Television and adolescent aggressiveness.* Washington, D.C.: U.S. Government Printing Office, 1972.

Chaffee, S. H., & Tims, A. R. Interpersonal factors in adolescent television use. *Journal of Social Issues*, 1976, 32 (4), 98–115.

Collins, W. A. The effect of temporal separation between motivation, aggression, and consequences: A developmental study. *Developmental Psychology*, 1973, 8, 799–802.

Collins, W. A., Wellman, H., Keniston, A., & Westby, S. Age-related aspects of comprehension of televised social content. *Child Development*, 1978, *49*, 389–399.

Cordua, G., McGraw, K., & Drabman, R. Doctor or nurse: Children's preceptions of sex-typed occupations. *Child Development*, 1979, *50* 590–593.

Doob, A., and Macdonald, G. Television viewing and fear of victimization: Is the relationship causal? *Journal of Personality and Social Psychology*, 1979, *37*, 170–179.

Fox, W., & Philliber, W. Television viewing and the perception of affluence. *Sociological Quarterly*, 1978, *19*, 103–112.

Gerbner, G., & Gross, L. Living with television: The violence profile. *Journal of Communication*, 1976, *26*(1), 173–199.

Gerbner, G., & Gross, L. Editorial response: A reply to Newcomb's "Humanistic critique." *Communication Research*, 1979, *6*, 223–230.

Gerbner, G., Gross, L., Eleey, M., Jackson-Beeck, M., Jeffries-Fox, S., & Signorielli, N. TV violence profile No. 8. *Journal of Communication*, 1977, *27*,(2), 171–180.(a)

Gerbner, G., Gross, L., Eleey, M., Jackson-Beeck, M., Jeffries-Fox, S., & Signorielli, N. Violence Profile No. 8: Trends in network television drama and viewer conceptions of social reality 1967–1976. Annenberg School of Communications, University of Pennsylvania, 1977.(b)

Gerbner, G., Gross, L., Jackson-Beeck, M., Jeffries-Fox, S., & Signorielli, N. Cultural Indicators: Violence Profile No. 9. *Journal of Communication*, 1978, *28*(3) 176–207.(a)

Gerbner, G., Gross, L., Jackson-Beeck, M., Jeffries-Fox, S., & Signorielli, N. Violence profile No. 9: Trends in network television drama
and viewer conceptions of social reality 1967-1977. Annenberg
School of Communications, University of Pennsylvania, 1978. (b)

Gerbner, G., Gross, L., Signorielli, N., Morgan, M., Jackson-Beeck,
M. The demonstration of power: Violence profile No. 10. *Journal of
Communication*, 1979, *29*, (3) 177-196(a).

Gerbner, G., Gross, L., Signorielli, N., Morgan, M., Jackson-Beeck,
M. Violence Profile No. 10: Trends in network television drama and
viewer conceptions of social reality 1967-1978. Annenberg School of
Communications, University of Pennsylvania, 1979.(b)

Gerbner, G., Gross, L., Signorielli, N., & Morgan, M. Aging with
television: Images on television drama and conceptions of social reality. *Journal of Communication*, 1980, *30*, 37-47.(a)

Gerbner, G., Gross, L., Morgan, M., & Signorielli, N. The "mainstreaming" of America: Violence profile No. 11. *Journal of Communication*, 1980, *30*, (3) 10-29.(b)

Gerbner, G., Gross, L., Morgan, M., & Signorielli, N. *Violence profile
No. 11: Trends in network television drama and viewer conceptions
of social reality, 1967-1979.* Annenberg School of Communications,
University of Pennsylvania, 1980.(c)

Gerbner, G., Gross, L., Morgan, M., & Signorielli, N. Some additional
comments on cultivation analysis. *Public Opinion Quarterly*, 1980,
44, 408-410.(d)

Gerbner, G., Gross, L., Morgan, M., & Signorielli, N. A curious
journey into the scary world of Paul Hirsch. *Communication Research*, 1981, *8*, 39-72.(e)

Gerbner, G., & Signorielli, N. *Women and minorities in television
drama 1969-1978.* Annenberg School of Communications, University of Pennsylvania, Philadelphia, 1979.

Gonzales, M. *Television and people's images of old age.* Unpublished
master's thesis. Annenberg School of Communications, University of
Pennsylvania, Philadelphia, 1979.

Gross, L., & Morgan, M. Television and enculturation. In J. Dominick & J. Fletcher (Eds.), *Broadcasting Research Methods.* Boston:
Allyn & Bacon, in press.

Haney, C. & Manzolati, J. Television criminology: Network illusions
of criminal justice realities. In E. Aronson, (Ed.), *Readings about the
social animal.* San Francisco: Freeman, 1980.

Harr-Mazer, H. Television's victimized children. *Unpublished master's thesis.* Annenberg School of Communications, University of
Pennsylvania, Philadelphia, 1980.

Hawkins, R. The dimensional structure of children's perceptions of
television reality. *Communication Research*, 1977, *4*, 299-320.

Hawkins, R., & Pingree, S. Some processes in the cultivation effect.
Communication Research, 1980, *7*, 193-226.

Hawkins, R., & Pingree, S. Uniform content and habitual viewing:
Unnecessary assumptions in social reality effects. *Human Communication Research*, 1981, *7*, 219-301.

Hirsch, P. The "scary world" of the nonviewer and other anomalies: A
reanalysis of Gerbner et al.'s findings of cultivation analysis. *Communication Research*, 1980, *7*, 403-456.

Hirsch, P. On not learning from one's own mistakes: A reanalysis of
Gerbner, et al.'s findings on cultivation analysis. Pt. II. *Communication Research* 1981, *8*, 3-37.(a)

Hirsch, P. Distinguishing good speculation from bad theory: Rejoinder
to Gerbner et al. *Communication Research*, 1981, *8*, 73-96.(b)

Hughes, M. The fruits of cultivation analysis: A re-examination of the
effects of television watching on fear of victimization, alienation, and
the approval of violence. *Public Opinion Quarterly*, 1980, *44*,
287-302.(a)

Hughes, M. Personal Communication, April, 1980.(b)

Klapper, J. *The effects of mass communication*, Glencoe, Ill.: Free
Press, 1960.

Leifer, A. D., Collins, W. A., Gross, B. M., Taylor, P. H., Andrews,
L. & Blackmer, E. R. Developmental aspects of variables relevant to
observational learning. *Child Development*, 1971, *42*, 1509-1516.

Leifer, A. D., & Roberts, D. F. Children's responses to television
violence. In J. Murray, E. A. Rubinstein, & G. A. Comstock (Eds.),
Television and social behavior (Vol. 2). *Television and social learning.* Washington: U.S. Government Printing Office, 1972.

Morgan, M. *Longitudinal patterns of television viewing and adolescent
role socialization.* Unpublished doctoral dissertation. Annenberg
School of Communications, University of Pennsylvania, 1980.

Morgan, M. & Harr-Mazer, H. *Television and adolescent's family life
expectations.* Annenberg School of Communications, University of
Pennsylvania, 1980.

Neville, T. *Television viewing and the expression of interpersonal
mistrust.* Unpublished doctoral dissertation. Princeton University,
Princeton, N.J., 1980.

Piepe, A., Couch, J., & Emerson, M. Violence and television, *New
Society*, 1977, *41*, 536-38.

Pingree, S. The effects of nonsexist television commercials and perceptions of reality on children's attitudes about women. *Psychology of
Women Quarterly*, 1978, *2*, 262-276.

Pingree, S., & Hawkins, R. U.S. programs on Australian television:
The cultivation effect. *Journal of Communication*, 1981, *31*(1),
97-105.

Pingree, S., Starrett, S., & Hawkins, R. *Soap opera viewers and social
reality.* Unpublished manuscript, Women's Studies Program, University of Wisconsin-Madison, 1979.

Ray, M. Marketing communication and the hierarchy of effects. In
P. Clarke (Ed.), *New models for mass communication research*, Beverly Hills: Sage, 1973.

Reeves, B. Perceived TV reality as a predictor of children's social
behavior. *Journalism Quarterly*, 1978, *55*, 682-689, 695.

Robertson, T., Rossiter, J., & Gleason, T. Children's receptivity to
proprietary medicine advertising. *Journal of Consumer Research*,
1979, *6*, 247-255.

Rothschild, N. *Group as a mediating factor in the cultivation process
among young children.* Unpublished master's thesis. Annenberg
School of Communications, University of Pennsylvania, 1979.

Tan, Alexis. TV beauty ads and role expectations of adolescent female
viewers. *Journalism Quarterly*, 1979, *56*, 283-288.

Volgy, T., & Schwarz, J. Television entertainment programming and
sociopolitical attitudes. *Journalism Quarterly*, 1980, *57*, 150-155.

Wober, J. M. Televised violence and paranoid perception. The view
from Great Britain. *Public Opinion Quarterly*, 1978, *42*, 315-321.

Wober, J. M. *Experience of television, and of the world at large: Some
Scottish evidence.* Independent Broadcast Authority Research Summary, London, December 14, 1979.

Wober, J. M. *Use of television in relation to events in the environment:
More evidence on violence.* Independent Broadcast Authority Research Summary, London, January 11, 1980.

Two experiments manipulating problem placement and salience demonstrate substantial individual agenda-setting effects in this chapter. Iyengar, Peters, and Kinder further suggest that such effects may be greatest among the politically naive, who seem to be unable to challenge the pictures and narrations appearing on their television sets. Shanto Iyengar and Mark D. Peters are on the political science faculty at Yale University, and Donald R. Kinder is at the Institute for Social Research, University of Michigan.

4

EXPERIMENTAL DEMONSTRATIONS OF THE "NOT-SO-MINIMAL" CONSEQUENCES OF TELEVISION NEWS PROGRAMS

Shanto Iyengar, Mark D. Peters, and Donald R. Kinder

[The press] is like the beam of a searchlight that moves restlessly about, bringing one episode and then another out of the darkness into vision.

W. Lippmann (1922)

Four decades ago, spurred by the cancer of fascism abroad and the wide reach of radio at home, American social scientists inaugurated the study of what was expected to be the sinister workings of propaganda in a free society. What they found surprised them. Instead of a people easily led astray, they discovered a people that seemed quite immune to political persuasion. The "minimal effects" reported by Hovland and Lazarsfeld did much to dispel naive apprehensions of a gullible public (Lazarsfeld, Berelson, and Gaudet 1944; Hovland, Lumsdaine, and Sheffield 1949). Moreover, later research on persuasion drove home the point repeatedly: propaganda reinforces the public's preferences; seldom does it alter them (e.g., Katz and Feldman 1962; Patterson and McClure 1976; Sears and Chaffee 1978).[1]

Although politically reassuring, the steady

stream of minimal effects eventually proved dispiriting to behavioral scientists. Research eventually turned elsewhere, away from persuasion, to the equally sinister possibility, noted first by Lippmann (1922), that media might determine what the public takes to be important. In contemporary parlance, this is known as agenda setting. Cohen put it this way:

the mass media may not be successful much of the time in telling people what to think, but the media are stunningly successful in telling their audience what to think about (1962, p. 16).

Do journalists in fact exert this kind of influence? Are they "stunningly successful" in instructing us what to think about? So far the evidence is mixed. In a pioneering study that others quickly copied, McCombs and Shaw (1972) found that the political problems voters thought most important were indeed those given greatest attention in their media. This apparently successful demonstration, based on a cross-sectional comparison between the media's priorities and the aggregated priorities of uncommitted voters in one community, set off a torrent of research. The cumulative result has been considerable confusion. Opinion divides over whether media effects have been demonstrated at all; over the relative power of television versus newspapers in setting the public's agenda; and over the causal direction

We are grateful to Robert P. Abelson for his comments on an earlier version of this manuscript and to the National Science Foundation (Political Science Program) and the National Institutes of Health, which supported the research.

[1]Our abbreviated history of this vast literature is necessarily incomplete, conspicuously so at two points. In the first place, "minimal consequences" has critics of its own, Robinson (1976) being the most vocal. Robinson argues that network news and public affairs programming are largely responsible for the sharp increases in Americans' political cynicism over the past fifteen

years. In the second place, we do not mean to suggest that researchers should abandon tests of persuasion. "Minimal consequences" is an apt phrase to describe effects of short-term media presentations, but over the longer haul, media effects produced by repetitive presentations may prove to be substantial.

From Shanto Iyengar, Mark D. Peters, and Donald R. Kinder, "Experimental Demonstrations of the 'Not-So-Minimal' Consequences of Television News Programs,'" *American Political Science Review*, Vol. 76, No. 4 (December 1982), pp. 848-858. Reprinted by permission of the American Political Science Association.

of the relation between the public's judgments and the media's priorities. (For reviews that vary in their enthusiasm, see Becker, McCombs, and McCleod 1975; Erbring, Goldenberg, and Miller 1980.) A telling indication of this confusion is that the most sophisticated cross-sectional study of agenda setting could do no more than uncover modest and mysteriously context-dependent effects (Erbring, Goldenberg, and Miller 1980). In short, "stunningly successful" overstates the evidence considerably.

But the problem may rest with the evidence, not the hypothesis. Along with Erbring and his colleagues, we believe that much of the confusion is the result of the disjuncture between cross-sectional comparisons favored by most agenda setting researchers, on the one hand, and the agenda setting hypothesis, which implies a dynamic process, on the other. If problems appear and disappear—if they follow Downs's (1972) "issue-attention cycle"—then to look for agenda setting effects cross-sectionally invites confusion. If they are to be detected, agenda setting effects must be investigated over time.

Though few in number, dynamic tests of agenda setting do fare better than their cross-sectional counterparts. Funkhouser (1973), for example, found substantial concurrence between the amount and timing of attention paid to various problems in the national press between 1960 and 1970 and the importance accorded problems by the American public. These results were fortified by MacKuen's more sophisticated and more genuinely dynamic analysis (MacKuen and Coombs 1981). MacKuen discovered that over the past two decades fluctuations in public concern for problems like civil rights, Vietnam, crime, and inflation closely reflected changes over time in the attention paid to them by the national media.

For essentially the same reasons that motivate dynamic analysis, we have undertaken a pair of experimental investigations of media agenda setting. Experiments, like dynamic analysis, are well equipped to monitor processes like agenda setting, which take place over time. Experiments also possess important advantages. Most notably, they enable authoritative conclusions about cause (Cook and Campbell 1978). In our experiments in particular, we systematically manipulated the attention that network news programs devoted to various national problems. We did this by unobtrusively inserting into news broadcasts stories provided by the Vanderbilt Television News Archive. Participants in our experiments were led to believe that they were simply watching the evening news. In fact, some participants viewed news programs dotted with stories about energy shortages; other participants saw nothing about energy at all. (Details about the procedure are given below in

the Methods section.) By experimentally manipulating the media's agenda, we can decisively test Lippmann's assertion that the problems that media decide are important become so in the minds of the public.

Our experimental approach also permits us to examine a different though equally consequential version of agenda setting. By attending to some problems and ignoring others, media may also alter the standards by which people evaluate government. We call this "priming." Consider, for example, that early in a presidential primary season, the national press becomes fascinated by a dramatic international crisis, at the expense of covering worsening economic problems at home. One consequence may be that the public will worry more about the foreign crisis and less about economic woes: classical agenda setting. But in addition, the public's evaluation of the president may now be dominated by his apparent success in the handling of the crisis; his management (or mismanagement) of the economy may now count for rather little. Our point here is simply that fluctuations in the importance of evaluational standards may well depend on fluctuations in the attention each receives in the press.

Another advantage of experimentation is the opportunity it offers to examine individual-level processes that might account for agenda setting. Here we explore two. According to the first, more news coverage of a problem leads to the acquisition and retention of more information about the problem, which in turn leads to the judgment of the problem as more important. According to the second, news coverage of a problem provokes the viewer to consider the claims being advanced; depending on the character of these ruminations, agenda setting will be more or less powerful.

In sum, we will: (1) provide authoritative experimental evidence on the degree to which the priorities of the evening newscasts affect the public's agenda; (2) examine whether network news' priorities also affect the importance the public attaches to various standards in its presidential evaluations; and (3) further exploit the virtues of experimentation by exploring individual cognitive processes that might underlie agenda setting.

Method

Overview

Residents of the New Haven, Connecticut area participated in one of two experiments, each of which spanned six consecutive days. The first experiment was designed to assess the feasibility of our approach and took place in November 1980, shortly after the presidential election. Experiment

2, a more elaborate and expanded replication of Experiment 1, took place in late February 1981.

In both experiments, participants came to two converted Yale University offices to take part in a study of television newscasts. On the first day, participants completed a questionnaire that covered a wide range of political topics, including the importance of various national problems. Over the next four days participants viewed what were represented to be videotape recordings of the preceding evening's network newscast. Unknown to the participants, portions of the newscasts had been altered to provide sustained coverage of a certain national problem. On the final day of the experiment (24 hours after the last broadcast), participants completed a second questionnaire that again included the measures of problem importance.

Experiment 1 focused on alleged weaknesses in U.S. defense capability and employed two conditions. One group of participants (N = 13) saw several stories about inadequacies in American defense preparedness (four stories totalling eighteen minutes over four days). Participants in the control group saw newscasts with no defense-related stories (N = 15). In Experiment 2, we expanded the test of agenda setting and examined three problems, requiring three conditions. In one group (N = 15), participants viewed newscasts emphasizing (as in Experiment 1) inadequacies in U.S. defense preparedness (five stories, seventeen minutes). The second group (N = 14) saw newscasts emphasizing pollution of the environment (five stories, fifteen minutes). The third group (N = 15) saw newscasts with steady coverage of inflation (eight stories, twenty-one minutes). Each condition in Experiment 2 was characterized not only by a concentration of stories on the appropriate target problem, but also by deliberate omission of stories dealing with the two other problems under examination.

Participants

Participants in both experiments responded by telephone to classified advertisements promising payment ($20) in return for taking part in research on television. As hoped, this procedure produced a heterogeneous pool of participants, roughly representative of the New Haven population. Participants ranged in age from nineteen to sixty-three, averaging twenty-six in Experiment 1 and thirty-five in Experiment 2. They were drawn primarily from blue collar and clerical occupations. Approximately 30 percent were temporarily out of work or unemployed. Blacks made up 25 percent and women, 54 percent of the participants in Experiment 1 and 10 percent and 61 percent, respectively, in Experiment 2.

Participants were first scheduled for one of several daily sessions. Each of these sessions, with between five and ten individuals, was then randomly assigned to one of the two conditions in Experiment 1, or one of the three conditions in Experiment 2.[2] Random assignment was successful. Participants in the defense condition in Experiment 1 did not differ at all in their demographic characteristics, in their political orientations, or in their political involvement from their counterparts in the control condition, according to day 1 assessments. The sole exception to this pattern—the control group had a significantly larger proportion of black participants (38 vs. 15 percent, $p < .05$)—is innocuous, since race is unrelated to the dependent variables. And in Experiment 2, across many demographic and attitudinal pretreatment comparisons, only two statistically significant differences emerged: participants in the defense condition reported watching television news somewhat more often ($p < .05$), and participants in the pollution condition were somewhat less Democratic ($p < .03$). To correct for this, party identification has been included as a control variable, where appropriate, in the analyses reported below.

Manipulating the Networks' Agenda

On the evening before each day's session, the evening national newscast of either ABC or NBC was recorded. For each of the conditions being prepared, this broadcast was then copied, but with condition-inappropriate stories deleted and condition-appropriate stories inserted. Inserted stories were actual news stories previously broadcast by ABC or NBC that were acquired from the Vanderbilt Television News Archive. In practice, the actual newscast was left substantially intact except for the insertion of a news story from the VTNA pool, with a condition-irrelevant story normally deleted in compensation. All insertions and deletions were made in the middle portion of the newscast and were spread evenly across experimental days. In Experiment 1 the first newscast was left unaltered in order to allay any suspicions on the part of the participants, and for the next three days a single news story describing inadequacies in U.S. military preparedness was inserted

---

[2] Initially, each condition in both experiments was to be represented by three independent groups of viewers so that condition, session, and time of day would be independent. This arrangement prevailed in Experiment 2 but not in Experiment 1, where early attrition forced us to combine the defense sessions, thus confounding condition and time of day. Fortunately, this adjustment does not threaten the integrity of the experimental design, as comparisons reported in text show.

into the broadcasts. Similar procedures were followed in Experiment 2, except that we added material to all four newscasts. The stories comprising the treatments in both experiments are listed and described in the Appendix.[3]

Avoiding Experimental Artifacts

In both experiments we undertook precautions to guard against "demand characteristics" (Orne 1962)—cues in the experimental setting that communicate to participants what is expected of them. In the first place, we initially presented to participants a diverting but wholly plausible account of our purpose: namely, to understand better how the public evaluates news programs. Participants were told that it was necessary for them to watch the news at Yale to ensure that everyone watched the same newscast under uniform conditions. Second, editing was performed with sophisticated video equipment that permitted the cutting, adding, and rearranging of news stories without interrupting the newscast's coherence. Third, though key questionnaire items were repeated from pretest to posttest, they were embedded within a host of questions dealing with political affairs, thus reducing their prominence. The success of these precautions is suggested by postexperimental discussions. Not a single participant expressed any skepticism about either experiment's real purpose.

We also tried to minimize the participants' sense that they were being tested. We never implied that they should pay special attention to the broadcasts. Indeed, we deliberately arranged a setting that was casual and informal and encouraged participants to watch the news just as they did at home. They viewed the broadcasts in small groups, occasionally chatted with their neighbors, and seemed to pay only sporadic attention to each day's broadcast. Although we cannot be certain, our experimental setting appeared to recreate the natural context quite faithfully.

Results

Setting the Public Agenda

We measured problem importance with four questions that appeared in both the pretreatment and posttreatment questionnaires. For each of eight national problems, participants rated the

problem's importance, the need for more government action, their personal concern, and the extent to which they discussed each with friends. Because responses were strongly intercorrelated across the four items, we formed simple additive indices for each problem. In principle, each ranges from four (low importance) to twenty (high importance).[4]

The agenda setting hypothesis demands that viewers adjust their beliefs about the importance of problems in response to the amount of coverage problems receive in the media. In our experiments, the hypothesis was tested by computing adjusted (or residualized) change scores for the importance indices and then making comparisons across conditions. Adjusted change scores measure the extent to which pretest responses underpredict or overpredict (using OLS regression) posttest responses (Kessler 1978). Participants whose posttest scores exceeded that predicted by their pretest scores received positive scores on the adjusted change measure; those whose posttest scores fell short of that predicted received negative scores.

Table 1 presents the adjusted change scores for each of the eight problems inquired about in Experiment 1. In keeping with the agenda-setting hypothesis, for defense preparedness *but for no other problem,* the experimental treatment exerted a statistically significant effect ($p < .05$). Participants whose news programs were dotted with stories alleging the vulnerability of U.S. defense capability grew more concerned about defense over the experiment's six days. The effect is significant substantively as well as statistically. On the first day of the experiment, viewers in the experimental group ranked defense sixth out of eight problems, behind inflation, pollution, unemployment, energy, and civil rights. After exposure to the newscasts, however, defense ranked second, trailing only inflation. (Among viewers in the control group, meanwhile, the relative position of defense remained stable.)

Experiment 2 contributes further support to

---

[3]Had participants viewed the actual newscasts each evening and compared them to the version presented on the subsequent day, they might well have discovered our alterations. This possibility was circumvented by instructing participants not to view the national network newscasts at home during the week of the study.

[4]The wording of these items is given below:

Please indicate how important you consider these problems to be.

Should the federal government do more to develop solutions to these problems, even if it means raising taxes?

How much do you yourself care about these problems? These days how much do you talk about these problems?

Index reliability was assessed with Cronbach's Alpha. In Experiment 1, the obtained values for the defense importance indices were .77 and .79. In Experiment 2, the alpha values ranged from .69 to .89.

Table 1. Adjusted Change Scores for Problem
Importance: Experiment 1

Problem	Condition	
	Defense	Control
Defense*	.90	−.79
Inflation	−.49	.23
Energy	−.40	.22
Drug addiction	−.19	−.48
Corruption	−.67	.05
Pollution	−.58	.60
Unemployment	.28	.54
Civil rights	−.27	−.27

*$p < .05$, one-tailed t-test.

classical agenda setting. As in Experiment 1, participants were randomly assigned to a condition—this time to one of three conditions, corresponding to an emphasis upon defense preparedness, pollution, or inflation. Changes in the importance of defense, pollution, and inflation are shown in Table 2. There the classical agenda setting hypothesis is supported in two of three comparisons. Participants exposed to a steady stream of news about defense or about pollution came to believe that defense or pollution were more consequential problems. In each case, the shifts surpassed statistical significance. No agenda setting effects were found for inflation, however. With the special clarity of hindsight, we attribute this single failure to the very great importance participants assigned to inflation before the experiment. Where twenty represents the maximum score, participants began Experiment 2 with an average importance score for inflation of 18.5!

As in Experiment 1, the impact of the media agenda could also be discerned in changes in the rank ordering of problems. Among participants in the defense condition, defense moved from sixth to fourth, whereas pollution rose from fifth to second among viewers in that treatment group. Within the pooled control groups, in the meantime, the importance ranks of the two problems did not budge.

Taken together, the evidence from the two experiments strongly supports the classical agenda

setting hypothesis. With a single and, we think, forgivable exception, viewers exposed to news devoted to a particular problem become more convinced of its importance. Network news programs seem to possess a powerful capacity to shape the public's agenda.

Priming and Presidential Evaluations

Next we take up the question of whether the media's agenda also alters the standards people use in evaluating their president. This requires measures of ratings of presidential performance in the designated problem areas—national defense in Experiment 1, defense, pollution, and inflation in Experiment 2—as well as measures of overall appraisal of the president. For the first, participants rated Carter's performance from "very good" to "very poor" on each of eight problems including "maintaining a strong military," "protecting the environment from pollution," and "managing the economy." We measured overall evaluation of President Carter in three ways: a single five-point rating of Carter's *"overall performance* as president"; an additive index based on three separate ratings of Carter's *competence;* and an additive index based on three separate ratings of Carter's *integrity.*[5]

In both Experiments 1 and 2, within each condition, we then correlated judgments of President Carter's performance on a particular problem with rating of his overall performance, his competence, and his integrity. (In fact these are partial correlations. Given the powerful effects of partisanship on political evaluations of the kind

[5]On the importance of and distinction between competence and integrity, consult Kinder, Abelson, and Peters 1981. The specific trait terms were smart, weak, knowledgeable (competence), and immoral, power-hungry, dishonest (integrity). The terms were presented as follows: How well do the following terms describe former President Carter: extremely well, quite well, not too well, or not well at all? The average intercorrelation among the competence traits was .43 in Experiment 1 and .62 in Experiment 2. For the integrity traits the correlations were .60 and .30.

Table 2. Adjusted Change Scores for Problem Importance: Experiment 2

Problem	Condition		
	Pollution	Inflation	Defense
Pollution	1.53**	−.71	−.23
Inflation	−.11	.11	−.06
Defense	−.44	−.34	.76*

*$p < .05$.
**$p < .01$.

under examination here, we thought it prudent to partial out the effects of party identification. Party identification was measured in both experiments by the standard seven-point measure, collapsed for the purpose of analysis into three categories.)

At the outset, we expected these partial correlations to conform to two predictions. First, when evaluating the president, participants will weigh evidence partly as a function of the agenda set by their news programs. Participants exposed to stories that question U.S. defense capability will take Carter's performance on defense into greater account in evaluating Carter overall than will participants whose attention is directed elsewhere; that is, the partial correlations should vary according to the broadcasts' preoccupations, in keeping with the priming hypothesis. Second, the priming effect will follow a semantic gradient. Specifically, priming is expected to be most pronounced in judgments of Carter's overall performance as president, somewhat less apparent in judgments of his competence, a personal trait relevant to performance; and to be least discernible in judgments of his integrity, a personal trait irrelevant to performance.

Experiment 1 treated our two predictions unevenly. As Table 3 indicates, the first prediction is corroborated in two of three comparisons. Steady coverage of defense did strengthen the relationship between judgments of Carter's defense performance and evaluations of his overall job performance, and between judgments of Carter's defense performance and integrity, as predicted. However, the relationship reverses on judgments of Carter's competence. And as for our second prediction, Experiment 1 provides only the faintest encouragement.

More encouraging is the evidence provided by Experiment 2. As Table 4 indicates, our first prediction is upheld in eight of nine comparisons, usually handsomely, and as predicted, the effects are most striking for evaluations of Carter's overall performance, intermediate (and somewhat irregular) for judgments of his competence, and fade away altogether for judgments of his integrity.

In sum, Experiments 1 and 2 furnish considerable, if imperfect, evidence for priming. The media's agenda does seem to alter the standards people use in evaluating the president. Although the patterns are not as regular as we would like, priming also appears to follow the anticipated pattern. A president's overall reputation, and, to a lesser extent, his apparent competence, both depend on the presentations of network news programs.

Mediation of Agenda Setting

Having established the consequences of the media's priorities, we turn finally to an investigation of their mediation. One strong possibility is information recall. More news coverage of a problem leads to the acquisition and retention of more information. More information, in turn, leads individuals to conclude that the problem is important.

Participants in both experiments were asked to describe "what the news story was about" and "how the story was presented" for each story they could recall something about. We coded both the number of stories as well as the volume of information participants were able to recall. We then correlated recall with participants' posttest beliefs about the importance of the target problem, controlling for their pretest beliefs.

In Experiment 1 the partial correlation using the number of defense stories recalled was $-.13$ (ns); in the case of volume of defense information recalled it was even tinier ($-.03$). The recall hypothesis also failed in Experiment 2. Here, for reasons of parsimony, we pooled the importance and recall data across the three conditions. The appropriate partial correlation between the number of news stories recalled and posttest importance, controlling for pretest importance was $-.20$ (ns). Recall of information seems a most unlikely mediator of agenda setting.

The failure of the recall hypothesis led us to consider a second possibility, that agenda setting might be mediated by covert evaluations triggered by the news stories. This hunch is consistent with

Table 3. Correlations between Overall Evaluations of Carter and Judgments of Carter's Performance on Defense as a Function of News Coverage: Experiment 1

	Coverage emphasizes defense	Coverage neglects defense
Carter's overall performance	.59	.38
Carter's competence	.03	.58
Carter's integrity	.31	.11

Table entries are first-order Pearson partial correlations, with party identification held constant.

Table 4. Correlations between Overall Evaluations of Carter and Judgments of
Carter's Performance on Specific Problems as a Function of News Coverage: Experiment 2

	Coverage emphasizes defense	Coverage neglects defense
Carter's overall performance	.88	.53
Carter's competence	.79	.58
Carter's integrity	.13	−.17

	Coverage emphasizes pollution	Coverage neglects pollution
Carter's overall performance	.63	.42
Carter's competence	.47	.56
Carter's integrity	.33	.15

	Coverage emphasizes inflation	Coverage neglects inflation
Carter's overall performance	.63	.39
Carter's competence	.71	.38
Carter's integrity	.07	.08

Table entries are first-order Pearson partial correlations, with party identification held constant.

a growing body of experimental research in which people are invited to record their thoughts as a persuasive message is presented. These thoughts are later classified as unfavorable, favorable, or as neutral to the persuasive message. It turns out that attitude change is predicted powerfully by the intensity and direction of such covert evaluations: the greater the number of unfavorable reactions, the lower the level of attitude change and vice versa. (For a detailed review of these experiments see Petty, Ostrom, and Brock 1980.)

This result extends with little effort to agenda setting. Viewers less able or willing to counterargue with a news presentation should be more vulnerable to agenda setting. To test this hypothesis, participants in Experiment 2 were asked to list "any thoughts, reactions, or feelings" about each news story they recalled. These responses were then scored for the number of counterarguments, with an average inter-coder correlation across the three treatment problems of .86. Consistent with the covert evaluation hypothesis, such counterarguing was inversely related to increases in problem importance. The partial correlation between the number of counterarguments (concerning news stories about the treatment problem) and posttest importance, controlling for initial importance was −.49 ($p < .05$) in the defense treatment group; −.35 (ns) in the inflation treatment group; and −.56 ($p < .05$) in the pollution treatment group. Pooled across conditions, the partial correlation was −.40 ($p < .05$).[6]

[6]Typical counterarguments were: in the defense condition a viewer reacted to a story depicting Soviet

And who are the counterarguers? They are the politically involved: those who claimed to follow public affairs closely, who reported a higher level of political activity, and who possessed more political knowledge. Of these three factors, political knowledge appeared to be the most consequential. In a regression analysis, pooling across the experimental groups, counterarguing was strongly predicted only by political knowledge (Beta = .43, $p < .05$).[7]

To summarize, agenda setting is strengthened to the degree audience members fail to counterargue. Agenda setting appears to be mediated, not by the information viewers recall, but by the covert evaluations triggered by the news presentations. Those with little political information to begin with are most vulnerable to agenda setting. The well informed resist agenda setting through

superiority over the U.S. in the realm of chemical warfare by saying, "The story was very one sided and made me feel even more strongly that the military is over-funded." In the pollution condition, a viewer reacted to a story on the evils of toxic waste: "Overdone—reporter admitted to no evidence to link this with lung disease." Counterarguments with respect to inflation news were comparatively rare. Most came in the form of remarks critical of President Reagan's proposed cuts in social programs.

[7]And who are the politically knowledgeable? Presumably they are people who over some interval in their past paid special and abiding attention to media presentations bearing on their perhaps idiosyncratic interests, and hence developed a particular point of view —a point of view that current media presentations have difficulty budging.

effective counterarguing, a maneuver not so available to the less informed.[8]

Conclusion

Fifty years and much inconclusive empirical fussing later, our experiments decisively sustain Lippmann's suspicion that media provide compelling descriptions of a public world that people cannot directly experience. We have shown that by ignoring some problems and attending to others, television news programs profoundly affect which problems viewers take seriously. This is so especially among the politically naive, who seem unable to challenge the pictures and narrations that appear on their television sets. We have also discovered another pathway of media influence: priming. Problems prominently positioned in television broadcasts loom large in evaluations of presidential performance.[9]

How long do these experimental effects persist? We cannot say with certainty. Our results are generally consistent with MacKuen's time-series analysis of agenda setting, which finds news media to exert persisting effects on the judgments the public makes regarding the country's most important problems (MacKuen and Combs 1981). We also know that our experimental effects survive at substantial levels for at least twenty-four hours, since posttests in both experiments were administered a full day after the final broadcast. This is a crucial interval. The dissemination of television news is of course periodic, typically following cycles of twenty-four hours or less. The regularity and frequency of broadcasts mean that classical agenda setting and priming are, for most people, continuous processes. When news presentations develop priorities, even if rather subtle

---

[8] These results work against the claim that the classical agenda setting and priming effects are special products of artificially high levels of attention induced by our experimental setting. In the first place, as we argued earlier, attention did not seem to be artificially high. Second, the information recall results imply the greater the attention, the *less* (marginally) beliefs are changed. Third, the counterarguing results imply, similarly, that the more "alert" viewers are, the *more* able they are to defend themselves against the media's priorities. All this suggests that our experimental setting, if anything, *underestimates* the influence of network news.

[9] In a pair of experiments conducted since the two reported here, we found additional strong support both for classical agenda setting and for priming. The new experiments demonstrated also that priming depends not only on making certain evidence prominent but also on its relevance; priming was augmented when news presentations portrayed the president as responsible for a problem (Iyengar, Kinder, and Peters 1982).

ones as in our experiments, viewers' beliefs are affected—and affected again as new priorities arise.

Political Implications

We do not mean our results to be taken as an indication of political mischief at the networks. In deciding what to cover, editors and journalists are influenced most by organizational routines, internal power struggles, and commercial imperatives (Epstein 1973; Hirsch 1975). This leaves little room for political motives.

Unintentional though they are, the political consequences of the media's priorities seem enormous. Policy makers may never notice, may choose to ignore, or may postpone indefinitely consideration of problems that have little standing among the public. In a parallel way, candidates for political office not taken seriously by news organizations quickly discover that neither are they taken seriously by anybody else. And the ramifications of priming, finally, are most unlikely to be politically evenhanded. Some presidents, at some moments, will be advantaged; others will be undone.

Psychological Foundations

On the psychological side, the classical agenda setting effect may be a particular manifestation of a general inclination in human inference—an inclination to overvalue "salient" evidence. Extensive experimental research indicates that under diverse settings, the judgments people make are swayed inordinately by evidence that is incidentally salient. Conspicuous evidence is generally accorded importance exceeding its inferential value; logically consequential but perceptually innocuous evidence is accorded less (for reviews of this research, see Taylor and Fiske 1978; Nisbett and Ross 1980).

The analogy with agenda setting is very close. As in experimental investigations of salience, television newscasts direct viewers to consider some features of public life and to ignore others. As in research on salience, viewers' recall of information seems to have little to do with shifts in their beliefs (Fiske, Kenny, and Taylor 1982). Although this analogy provides reassurance that classic agenda setting is not psychologically peculiar, it also suggests an account of agenda setting that is unsettling in its particulars. Taylor and Fiske (1978) characterize the process underlying salience effects as "automatic." Perceptually prominent information captures attention; greater attention, in turn, leads automatically to greater influence.

Judgments are not always reached so casually, however; according to their retrospective accounts, our participants occasionally quarreled with the newscasts and occasionally actively agreed with them. Counterarguing was especially common among the politically informed. Expertise seems to provide viewers with an internal means for competing with the networks. Agenda setting may reflect a mix of processes therefore: automatic imprinting among the politically naive; critical deliberation among the politically expert.

Alterations in the standards by which presidents are evaluated, our second major finding, may also reflect an automatic process, but of a different kind. Several recent psychological experiments have shown that the criteria by which complex stimuli are judged can be profoundly altered by their prior (and seemingly incidental) activation. (For an excellent summary, see Higgins and King 1981.) As do these results, our findings support Collins's and Loftus's (1975) "spreading-activation" hypothesis. According to Collins and Loftus, when a concept is activated—by extended media coverage—other linked concepts are made automatically accessible. Hence when participants were asked to evaluate President Carter after a week's worth of stories exposing weaknesses in American defense capability, defense performance as a general category was automatically accessible and therefore relatively powerful in determining ratings of President Carter.

Methodological Pluralism

Over twenty years ago, Carl Hovland urged that the study of communication be based on field *and* experimental research (Hovland 1959; also see Converse 1970). We agree. Of course, experimentation has problems of its own, which our studies do not fully escape. That our participants represent no identifiable population, that our research setting departs in innumerable small ways from the natural communication environment, that the news programs we created might distort what would actually be seen on network newscasts—each raises questions about the external validity of our results. Do our findings generalize to other settings, treatments, and populations—and to the American public's consumption of evening news particularly? We think' they do. We took care to avoid a standard pitfall of experimentation—the so-called college sophomore problem—by encouraging diversity in experimental participants. We undertook extra precautions to recreate the natural communication environment: participants watched the broadcasts in small groups in an informal and relaxed setting. And we were careful not to tamper with standard network practice in constituting our experimental presentations.

Limitations of experimentation—worries about external validity especially—correspond of course

to strengths in survey-based communication research. This complementarity argues for methodological pluralism. We hope our results contribute to a revitalization of Hovland's dialogue between experimental and survey-based inquiries into political communication.

References

Becker, L. B., McCombs, M. C., and McCleod, J. 1975. The development of political cognitions. In *Political communication: issues and strategies for research.* ed. S. H. Chaffee, Beverly Hills: Sage.

Cohen, B. 1963. *The press and foreign policy.* Princeton: Princeton University Press.

Collins, A. M., and Loftus, E. F. 1975. A spreading-activation theory of semantic processing. *Psychological Review* 82:407-28.

Converse, P. E. 1970. Attitudes and non-attitudes: continuation of a dialogue. In *The quantitative analysis of social problems.* ed. E. R. Tufte, Reading, Mass.: Addison-Wesley.

Cook, T. D., and Campbell, D. T. 1978. *Quasi-experimentation.* Chicago: Rand-McNally.

Downs, A. 1972. Up and down with ecology—the "issue attention cycle." *Public Interest* 28:38-50.

Epstein, E. J. 1973. *News from nowhere.* New York: Random House.

Erbring, L., Goldenberg, E. N., and Miller, A. H. 1980. Front-page news and real-world cues: a new look at agenda setting by the media. *American Journal of Political Science* 24:16-49.

Fiske, S. T., Kenny, D. A., and Taylor, S. E. 1982. Structural models for the mediation of salience effects on attribution. *Journal of Experimental Social Psychology* 18:105-27.

Funkhouser, G. R. 1973. The issues of the sixties: an exploratory study of the dynamics of public opinion. *Public Opinion Quarterly* 37:62-75.

Higgins, E. T., and King, G. 1981. Category accessibility and information-processing: consequences of individual and contextual variability. In *Personality, cognition, and social interaction,* ed. N. Cantor and J. Kihlstrom. Hillsdale: Lawrence Erlbaum.

Hirsch, P. M. 1975. Occupational, organizational and institutional models in mass media research. In *Strategies for communication research.* ed. P. Hirsch et al., Beverly Hills: Sage.

Hovland, C. I. 1959. Reconciling conflicting results derived from experimental and survey studies of attitude change. *American Psychologist* 14:8-17.

Hovland, C. I., Lumsdaine, A., and Sheffield, F. 1949. *Experiments on mass communication.* Princeton: Princeton University Press.

Iyengar, S., Kinder, D. R., and Peters, M. D. 1982. The evening news and presidential evaluations. Unpublished manuscript.

Katz, E., and Feldman, J. 1962. The debates in the light of research: a survey of surveys. In *The great debates.* ed. S. Krauss, Bloomongton: Indiana University Press.

Kessler, R. 1978. The use of change scores as criteria in longitudinal research. *Quality and Quantity* 11: 43-66.

Kinder, D. R., Abelson, R. P., and Peters, M. D. 1981. Appraising presidential candidates: personality and affect in the 1980 campaign. Paper delivered at the Annual Meeting of the American Political Science Association, New York City, September.

Lazarsfeld, P., Berelson, B., and Gaudet, H. 1944. *The people's choice.* New York: Columbia University Press.

Lippmann, W. 1922. *Public opinion.* New York: Harcourt, Brace.

MacKuen, M. J., and Coombs, S. L. 1981. *More than news: media power in public affairs.* Beverly Hills: Sage.

McCombs, M. C., and Shaw, D. 1972. The agenda setting function of the mass media. *Public Opinion Quarterly* 36:176-:87.

Nisbett, R. E., and Ross L. 1980. *Human inference: strategies and short-comings of social judgment.* Englewood Cliffs, N.J.: Prentice-Hall.

Orne, M. T. 1962. On the social psychology of the psychology experiment. *American Psychologist* 17: 776-:83.

Patterson, T. E., and McClure, R. D. 1976. *The unseeing eye: the myth of television power in national elections.* New York: G. P. Putnam.

Petty, R. E., Ostrom, T. M., and Brock, T. C. 1981. *Cognitive responses in persuasion.* Hillsdale: Lawrence Erlbaum.

Robinson, M. J. 1976. Public affairs television and the growth of political malaise. *American Political Science Review* 70:409-32.

Sears, D. O., and Chaffee, S. H. 1979. Uses and effects of the 1976 debates: an overview of empirical studies. In *The great debates, 1976: Ford vs. Carter.* ed. S. Krauss, Bloomington: Indiana University Press.

Taylor, S. E., and Fiske, S. T. 1978. Salience, attention and attribution: top of the head phenomena. In *Advances in experimental social psychology, Vol. 11.* ed. L. Berkowitz, New York: Academic Press.

Appendix

Day	Network	Length (min)	Content
Experiment 1			
1	ABC	1.40*	Increases in defense spending to be proposed by the incoming Reagan Administration.
2	ABC	4.40	Special assignment report on the declining role of the U.S. as the "arsenal of democracy." Story notes the declining level of weapons production since the early seventies and points out the consequences on U.S. ability to respond militarily.
3	NBC	4.40	Special segment report on U.S. military options in the event of Soviet aggression in the Persian Gulf region. Story highlights Soviet superiority in conventional forces and tanks and suggests that a U.S. "rapid deployment force," if used, would be overwhelmed.
4	ABC	1.10*	Air crash in Egypt during joint U.S.-Egyptian military exercises.
		4.30	Special assignment report on the low level of education among incoming military recruits. Describes resulting difficulty in the use of advanced equipment and shows remedial education programs in place.
Experiment 2			
Defense			
1	ABC	4.40	Declining role of the U.S. as the "arsenal of democracy" (see above).
2	NBC	4.00	Special report on the readiness of the National Guard. Notes dilapidated equipment being used and lack of training among members.
3	NBC	3.00*	Growing U.S. involvement in El Salvador; draws parallel with Vietnam.
4	ABC	2.00	Deteriorating U.S.-USSR relations over El Salvador.
4	ABC	4.00	Special report on U.S. capability to withstand a chemical attack. Story highlights the disparity in the production of nerve gases between the U.S. and USSR and notes the vulnerability of U.S. forces to chemical weapons.
Pollution			
1	ABC	2.20	Congressional hearings on toxic waste in Memphis.
		2.10	Report on asbestos pollution in the soil and resulting dangers to health for residents of the area.

Appendix (continued)

Day	Network	Length (min)	Content
2	ABC	2.40	Toxic dumping in a Massachusetts community and the high rate of leukemia among the town's children.
3	NBC	2.10*	Underground coal fire in Pennsylvania; carbon monoxide fumes entering residents' homes.
4	ABC	5.10	Special feature on the growing dangers from toxic waste disposal sites across the nation. Sites shown in Michigan, Missouri, Louisiana, and California.

Inflation

Day	Network	Length (min)	Content
1	ABC	2.30*	Reagan's approach to inflation to concentrate on government spending reductions. Results of a public opinion poll concerning cuts in government spending reported.
		2.20*	Taxpayers in Michigan protest the high level of taxes.
2	ABC	2.20*	Reagan's plans to deal with inflation discussed.
		4.10	Special report on supply-side economics as a means of controlling inflation; views of various economists presented.
3	NBC	3.00*	Latest cost of living statistics announced in Washington and reaction from the Administration and Congress.
		1.20*	Reaganomics discussed at a House committee hearing.
4	ABC	3.00	Special report on economic problems in the U.S. and the prospects for improvement under the Reagan Administration.
		2.30*	Democrats attack the proposed cuts in social services and programs.

*Story appeared live in original newscast.

In the first of two commentaries we present here on the relationship between Noelle-Neumann's theory of a "spiral of silence" and Floyd Allport's notions of "pluralistic ignorance," Elihu Katz compares the role of communication in her thesis to the "liberating" role of publicity implicit in the treatment of pluralistic ignorance; raises the question of the conditions under which individuals might be expected to break a spiral of silence and considers a case in the opposite direction, where "everybody knows," and "everybody knows that everybody knows"; and relates Noelle-Neumann's image of powerful media to similar claims by others. Katz is director of the Communications Institute at the Hebrew University, Jerusalem, and professor in the Annenberg School of Communications at the University of Southern California.

5

PUBLICITY AND PLURALISTIC IGNORANCE
Notes on "The Spiral of Silence"

Elihu Katz

It is strange, but true, that public opinion research, mass communications research and public opinion theory have become disconnected. It is difficult even to explain how any one of these can exist without the others, and yet the fact is that each has wandered off on its own. It is to the great credit of *Elisabeth Noelle-Neumann* that she has taken the lead in trying to bring them together again.[1] Beginning with her call for a "return to a theory of powerful mass media", *Noelle-Neumann* has been trying to show how the dynamics of media production and the dynamics of opinion formation interact, and how the process of this interaction can be described empirically by means of creative polling techniques.[2] There may be room for debate over her inferences from the data, but nobody can underestimate the importance of her attempt to put the whole together.

If I may be permitted to summarize this effort impressionistically, drawing on a number of papers all at once,[3] I would state her argument as follows: (1) Individuals have opinions; (2) Fearing isolation, individuals will not express their opinions if they perceive themselves unsupported by others; (3) A 'quasi-statistical sense' is employed by individuals to scan the environment for signs of support; (4) Mass media constitute the major source of reference for information about the distribution of opinion and thus for the climate of support/nonsupport; (5) So do other reference groups (but the relative importance of these is not clear, on which see below – EK); (6) The media tend to speak in one voice, almost monopolistically; (7) The media tend to distort the distribution of opinion in society, biased as they are by the (leftist) views of journalists; (8) Perceiving themselves unsupported, groups of individuals – who may, at times, even constitute a majority – will lose confidence and withdraw from public debate, thus speeding the demise of their position through the self-fulfilling spiral of silence. They may not change their own minds, but they stop recruitment of others and abandon the fight; (9) Society is manipulated and impoverished thereby (for the absence of dialogue and/or the repression of truth – these inferences are not spelled out by *Noelle-Neumann*). Thus the "powerful effect" assigned to mass communication is a subtle one. The media are not perceived as agents of direct influence, but rather as reporters on the distribution of (acceptable) opinion. The media are used by individuals as indicators to determine who may speak and who should remain silent. The extreme case – illustrated in two recent

From Elihu Katz, "Publicity and Pluralistic Ignorance: Notes on 'The Spiral of Silence,'" in Horst Baier, Hans Mathias Kepplinger, and Kurt Reumann, eds., *Public Opinion and Social Change: For Elisabeth Noelle-Neumann* (Wiesbaden: Westdeutscher Verlag, 1981), pp. 28-38. Reprinted by permission.

German elections — is one of "pluralistic ignorance" in which individual supporters of one of the major political parties believed their cause to be doomed because they inferred from the media that "everyone" believed the other side would win, and began to believe so themselves.

Assuming that this exposition of the "spiral of silence" is reasonably accurate, I should now like to comment on a number of aspects of the thesis. My object is not to evaluate findings — indeed, I shall not consider empirical findings at all — but to discuss underlying assumptions, raise questions about certain elements of the theory, attempt to relate it to ongoing work of myself and others, and to explore its implications for our image of modern society and its future. For lack of an integrated theory of my own, I shall do this in the form of notes and comments, in no formal order, for which I ask the reader's indulgence. Specifically, I would like (1) to compare the role of communication in *Noelle-Neumman's* thesis to the "liberating" role of publicity implicit in the traditional treatment of pluralistic ignorance, by which individuals learn what they had not known before, namely, that others think as they do; (2) to raise the question of the conditions under which individuals might be expected to break a spiral of silence; (3) to consider a case at the opposite extreme where "everybody knows" something and "everybody knows that everybody knows", and thus where publicity might be expected to be merely redundant; (4) to relate *Noelle Neumann's* image of powerful media to similar claims by others.

1. Publicity and pluralistic ignorance. Floyd Allport's concept of pluralistic ignorance has been used by social psychologists to explain ostensibly rapid social change.[4] When everybody believes that he is the only one who thinks something, and does not talk about his opinion for fear of violating a moral taboo or an authoritarian ruler, or of just being unpopular, it sometimes happens that a wave of publicity will sweep through the community, informing people that everybody else (or many others) think as they do. In such cases, what appears to be revolutionary change — say, the uprising in Poland in 1956, or the changed status of homosexuals following publication of the *Kinsey* Report — may not be the product of a basic change in attitude but, rather, the result of changed perception of the distribution of opinion. In this view, communication is perceived as liberating. The Emperor's New Clothes, of course, is the classic example. The tailors duped the vain Emperor into believing that only wise men could see his golden-threaded suit. Nobles and officials believed it, too, or at least they acted as if they did, for fear of betraying their incompetence. So did the common people, perhaps out of fear. Only the child — with nothing to lose — declared publicly that the Emperor was naked.

Silence, it appears, is a reaction to taboo, fear and shame — for those who think differently than what they perceive others to be thinking. *Asch* finds that some people actually begin to *see* things as they think the others do.[5] Most people, however, continue to think as they thought, deferring to the majority either out of self-doubt or self-protection. Even a single truth-teller is enough to wipe out the effect on the naive subject of a large majority.[6] The experimental literature has focused only rarely on this enlightening function of interpersonal communication.

Most laboratory research has examined only the pressures toward conformity exerted by groups on their members. By comparison with such studies of small groups, communications theory and research has focused as much on the enlightening, as on the repressive, role of communication. Of course the media propound false consciousness! But in democratic societies, where the media may speak out against authority, or where journalistic norms require balance, something close to truth is often to be seen and heard, or at least inferred.[7] Truth-telling liberates people from their reticence to reveal their true thoughts to others, thus reviving a social network which has become atomized or atrophied by perceptions of the consensus, true or false.

Noelle-Neumann wants us to consider the dark side of mass communication. Even in the democracies, media — like interpersonal communication — can impose acquiescence and silence, in defiance of the free flow of information. People will become disconnected from each other, warns *Noelle-Neumann*, if the media practice misrepresentation and monopolization. People, searching for support, will scan their environments in vain if the distribution of opinions is misrepresented and if the media arbitrarily shut out the plurality of voices. Such monopolization (*Noelle-Neumann* calls it "consonance") offers no basis for selctivity, and one readily finds oneself outside the ostensible consensus. *Noelle-Neumann* feels that the communications literature has underestimated this state of affairs and the powerful media that sustain it. *Lazarsfeld* and *Merton* noted that monopolization of the media does, indeed, produce more powerful effects, but they do not associate media monopolization with Western democracy.[8] *Noelle-Neumann* does, thus ironically joining forces with the critical school, from the other side of the political spectrum. There is "consonance" in media, and it is on the right, say the Frankfurt School and their descendants. *Noelle-Neumann* sees it on the left, and brings data to bear.

Has the concentration of media ownership, and the professionalization of journalism, really led to a narrowing of the range of opinion offered to the public? Is the narrowing, if there is one, biased towards the left, in spite of the economic and political interests of those who control the media?[9] Does television news typically reflect the ideological leanings of its editors and reporters? *Should* the press be expected to mirror — in news and editorials — the gamut of opinion in the population? Should reality, as reported by journalists, be expected to coincide with the reality of, say, the Central Bureau of Statistics or of opinion polls?[10] *Noelle-Neumann* appears to be saying yes to all of these questions and it remains for the rest of us to join in the debate.

2. Breaking the silence. When will individuals apeak out against a consensus? *Asch* found certain of his subjects self-confident and fiercely dedicated to the independence of their own observations; some were independent but withdrawn; some maintained their independence because of their commitment to carrying out the assigned task.[11] Reviewing the experimental literature on conformity, *Kretch* et al. suggest that individuals are more independent when status in the group is less important to them, or when they can expect to be rewarded by an outsider for non-conformity, as when a prize is offered for being right or for being independent.[12] A recent paper by *James Coleman* takes us a step further.[13] Like the laboratory experimenters, *Coleman* assumes that individuals are motivated by self-interest; this may sometimes lead to action which takes no account of the group or action which is contingent on what the others do. Such contingent behavior, however, may be similar or opposite to the others' actions. (Unlike *Coleman*, *Noelle-Neumann* appears to assume that self-interest is regularly expressed in terms of conformity.) *Coleman* asks us to consider the conditions under which a rational individual, calculating his self-interest, will make his behavior or his thought contingent on that of others, or in *Coleman's* words, will invest in others the authority to determine his own behavior. Among his illustrations from collective behavior, *Coleman* tells us of some individuals, trapped with a crowd in a fire, who will run for the exit under any circumstances, while some will run only if others do. People *closer* to the door are more likely to run first, says *Coleman*, since they have most to gain by running: those who make their running contingent on whether others run have less to gain by running.

These same dynamics, suggests *Coleman*, can help explain the phenomenon of milling crowds who seem suddenly to erupt in revolution or in dissidence. Typically, in such situations discontented people gather around some symbolic target. They do not act at first because they (1) know that the police, or some other agency of enforcement will punish them for illegal action, and (2) they are not certain about how others in the crowd think. In such circumstances, members of the crowd continue to circulate, keeping one eye on the police and another on the crowd. If somebody acts, however, others will quickly follow. The actor is, typically, somebody who has little to gain from obedient behavior, and/or who is perceptive enough to know that the others are with him. Once he has acted, the *ratio* of possible loss to possible gain changes. That is, each successive actor is less likely to be caught and punished as the crowd overwhelms the police and the attractions of expressive or revolutionary action increasingly outweigh its dangers. This takes us a step beyond *Noelle-Neumann's* assertion that "at the beginning and toward the end of changes in the climate of opinion, minorities — avant garde and hard core — are more willing to stand up for their opinion than the majority, while during the hot phase, when the new opinion actually begins to prevail, those who think that they are, or soon will be, the majority, are more willing to do so."[14]

But in most of the statements of *Noelle-Neumann* the emphasis is on conformity rather than independence. People seek affiliation and thus celebrate the unity of their shared perceptions; those who feel outside this consensus fall silent. *Noelle-Neumann's* majorities are social beings; the minorities speak only to each other and, gradually, to no one at all. She has very little to say about independents, or about those who have more distant reference groups. Ostensibly, the independents are the heroes of democracy. They not only stand up for their opinions, but in situations of pluralistic ignorance, they ignite the process of rapid social change. But it is evident — consider *Coleman's* example of the rioting crowd — that pluralistic ignorance may sometimes keep passion in check. It is sometimes a functional fiction — not only for the society, but for the individual as well — to assume that one's fellows do not share one's baser feelings and prejudices. A liberating communication — an independent voice spreading knowledge of shared passions — may also shatter a society. It is no wonder that advocates of free speech prefer also to assume that their fellows are reasonable.

3. Publicity as commitment. Communication may be liberating, we have seen, or it may be an agent of repression. It may stimulate further communication, or it may cause silence to spread. In the one case, communication may be seen to correct a false impression; it permits "true consciousness" to prevail. In the opposite case, communication is the agent of pluralistic ignorance, or of false consciousness, causing people to misperceive what their similarly-situated fellows think or believe. In both cases, communication is used to transmit information about what relevant others are thinking or doing. It is obvious that when people want to know what others think, communication of such information will have an effect. But consider the curious case where everybody knows something, and everybody knows that everybody knows, and yet communication of that piece of information will have an effect nevertheless. The history of the State of Israel provides a number of case-studies of this phenomenon.[15] In the 1950s, for example, Jewish immigrants were permitted to leave Poland for Israel. This fact was never publicly acknowledged, either in Poland or in Israel, and strict censorship on this matter was imposed on the Israeli press. Yet, it is almost certain that everybody who mattered — Poland, Israel, the United States, the Soviet Union — all knew, and each knew that the others knew. The very same dynamics are evident in the imposition of censorship on publication of the primary source from which Israel received its oil in the '50s and '60s. In this case, too, it is likely that all relevant actors knew, and knew that the others knew. Certeinly informed public opinion in Israel knew, and it is likely that decision-makers in Iran, the Arab states, as well as the U.S. and Russia all knew, and were aware that the others knew. Then why the taboo on publication? What difference would such information make.

That it would make a difference is evident from the reaction to the adoption by the Knesset of the Law of Jerusalem in the Summer of 1980. The Law declares Jerusalem the capital of Israel, thus reiterating officially a situation which had existed *de facto* and perhaps even *de jure*. Foreign embassies which had been located in Jerusalem since the establishment of the State in 1948 — attesting to the widespread recognition that everybody knew, and that everybody knew that everybody knew — felt constrained to leave the capital. A related example comes from the Eastern bloc: a "new economic order" was established in one of the Eastern European countries and everybody, including government, acted in accord with it. But there was a strict taboo on mention of this in the press, and when the first violation did occur, repercussions were drastic. Entire nations may collectively mis-represent themselves with full knowledge that they are living schizophrenically.

One could multiply examples from both the public and the private spheres. Many cities have acknowledged pockets of violation or deviance. So-called blue-laws which require shops to remain closed on the Sabbath in certain American cities are often violated, with the knowledge and tacit consent of buyers, police and municipalities. Similarly, the existence and location of red-light districts is often well-known. Yet a letter to the editor of a newspaper, or a speech in Parliament — even when they do not add any information at all, since everybody knows and everybody knows that everybody knows — will cause authorities to enforce the norm. In the private sphere, it is not unusual for all parties involved in a case of adultery — even the "deceived" spouse — to know and to know that everybody knows, and yet to wish to keep the matter unpublicized. The knowledgeable spouse may even insist that he doesn't "want to know". A gossip columnist can change all that. Similar dynamics are involved in social change. Persons favoring legalized abortion or homosexual practice, for example, may purposely insist on publicizing what is already known in order to challenge the norm. Their object, paradoxically, is to publish what is already known by all to be the case — not to add information, but to make it "public" or "official".

The classic literature of communication is aware of this norm enforcing role of communication.[16] Exposing deviance and thus rallying society to reinforce a norm is a familiar function of mass communication. But the assumption is that the journalist has exposed something "new". Why should exposing something "old" — something that everybody already knows — make such a difference? It is true that there will always be somebody who doesn't know, and it is equally true that there will always be somebody who didn't know that the other knew — but let us assume, for the moment, that there are no such people. Let us assume that everybody knows and everybody knows that everybody knows and ask how it is that publication matters. The symbolic-interactionist will answer in terms of the idea of negotiated reality.[17] So long as the information is not published — that is, so long as it is not "public" — there is flexibility open to all concerned in the assignment of meaning. "This shop isn't open on Sundays; we are just doing some repair work." But if Poland or Iran or the Blue Laws are mentioned by name, if the red-light district is signposted, it leaves no room for ambiguity.

More specifically, publication of a violation — even one about which all know — calls for a reaction of our public selves. While we can tolerate a certain form of deviance privately and unofficially, we cannot allow ourselves to do so publicly and officially. Publicly, the norm must either be upheld or defied: there is no room for ambiguity. It follows that we can probably tolerate a higher level of dissonance privately than publicly. Our public selves are more consistent. Thus, publication — even in a situation where everybody knows, and everybody knows that every knows — has consequences because it forces people to *take account* of the fact that the others know. Prior to publication, an actor may act *as if* only he knew — because he does not have to acknowledge that the others know as well. (Note that this is the very opposite of the case of pluralistic ignorance where each person believes that he is the only one who knows. In the present case, all know that the others know. But in both cases one acts as if the others think differently.)

When news of the broken norm is published, however, one can no longer act as if the others do not know. In this "public" situation, where the norm-violator has to take account of his audience, he must decide whether to retreat into consonance, or publicly declare that he is *committed* to the violation, that is, to some new norm. In other words, the fact of publication of an act of norm-violation forces the violator to face up to the demands of the norm-upholders or to defy them openly. In choosing defiance, he may well base his decision on his perception of the extent to which those who have tacitly concurred in his deviance will now give him open support. Whereas the stone-thrower in *Coleman's* crowd, or the would-be charismatic leader, must employ his refined quasi-statistical sense to judge whether the crowd agrees with him and will follow him, the norm-violator in the present instance already knows that the others agree privately. His problem is whether they will agree *publicly*, or in other words, whether they will follow him in public. A community cannot tolerate the public flaunting of immorality/illegality, as if to say "I really mean it". Even despots — who sense that the people support them — sometimes do not make public their horrific actions and do not make them into laws for fear that *public* opinion will not tolerate them.[18]

4. Publicity, False Consciousness, Silence, Mass Society. Noelle-Neumann's spiral of silence theory brings us back to theories of the mass society. The essentials of these theories, from which the earliest models of mass communication were derived, consist of atomized individuals, on the one hand, and powerful agencies of remote social control, on the other. The more the media speak in one voice, and the more people are disconnected from each other, from intermediate organizations (church, trade union, political party, voluntary organizations, etc.) and from their past, the more absolute is the rule of the media and their masters. Empirical research on mass communication beginning with the late '30s argued that this model did not seem to apply. Mass media campaigns were less effective than was expected because the voice of the media was not monolithic; people belonged to organizations and to primary groups, and their exposure to media influence was mediated by two important filters: (1) selectivity — which protects prior opinions and attitudes from being overwhelmed, and (2) interpersonal relations which are forums for pre-testing, forming and changing opinions and attitudes. Subsequent models of mass communication are based on transferring to the people some part of the power originally attributed to the media.[19]

The current call for a return to theories of powerful media — of which *Noelle-Neumanns's* is a major representative — must show that the mediating processes of selectivity and interpersonal relations were inapplicable when they were originally enunciated or are inapplicable now. In his critique of *Personal Influence*, *Gitlin* claims they were inapplicable then.[20] Interpersonal communication, he says, is only a conduit through which media influence is relayed and has no real relevance therefore, except to distract public attention from the omnipotent media. Moreover, says *Gitlin*, personal influence was the primary source for only 48 % of *political* decisions (as compared with much higher proportions for decisions in the fields of marketing, fashions and movie-going) and thus its role in politics is misre-presented in *Katz* and *Lazarsfeld*. The mass society has long been with us, says *Gitlin*.

Not so, say *Gerbner* et al.,[21] or, indeed, *Noelle-Neumann*. These authors, and others, are saying that the theories of mass society of 50 years ago are now (again?) becoming truly applicable to the modern, democratic societies of the West. They think that things have changed. They believe, first of all, that television is different from its predecessors. Viewing television is a more "total" experience, appealing, as it does, to eyes and ears, providing information, entertainment, and companion-ship — in short, a symbolic environment in place of the real world outside. *Noelle-Neumann* has data to show that television owners lose interest in their jobs, appa-rently preferring to stay home.[22] *Gerbner* et al. argue that the image of urban vio-lence as augmented by television helps to keep people home, and thus disconnec-ted from the larger society.

As was noted above, the effect of television viewing for *Noelle-Neumann* is an indirect one: by portraying the (false) climate of opinion, TV causes people to per-ceive a reality different from the one which surrounds them. Similarly, *Gerbner* et al. argue that reality as perceived by heavy television viewers is a reflection of what they have seen and heard on television and not in the real world. Thus, a vicious circle is at work in which people fear the world portrayed by television because of its violence (*Gerbner*) or its misrepresentation of the climate of opinion (*Noelle-Neumann*), causing people to feel lonely, retreat into their nuclear cells to watch television, talking neither to neighbor nor spouse, but to be satisfied, apparently, with their many hours of viewing. Cut off as they are from work and other affilia-tions, they are all the more vulnerable to manipulation by the media. Moreover, says *Noelle-Neumann*, the message of the media is monopolistic, due to the journa-lists' professional proclivity to peek over each other's shoulders and to their shared ideological leanings. Thus, selectivity and interpersonal communication are neutra-lized as mediating factors, and the media of mass communication may indeed be described as "powerful".

It is extremely interesting that *Gitlin, Gerbner* and *Noelle-Neumann,* despite their very different theoretical and ideological orientations, share the idea that the media are active agents of false consciousness, constraining people to misperceive their environment and their own place in it. Following in the steps of the Frankfurt School, *Gitlin* argues that the media suppress opposition and reinforce existing au-thority by making things look much better than they are. *Gerbner* et al. agree that the media reinforce the status quo, by depoliticizing people, by teaching them their proper place in the status system, and by inculcating fear of social interaction. For a different set of reasons, already reviewed, *Noelle-Neumann* also notes a with-drawal from social interaction and political activity (along with an overall increase in political interest) but she sees the media as agents for undermining establish-ments rather than as agents for their glorification.

In a general way, these more subtle, more sociological definitions of effect are familiar from the theoretical writings of critics of mass communication and mass society. They are anchored in the belief that the media can "construct reality" and impose their construction on defenseless minds. The innovation in the work of this generation of critics — of whom *Noelle-Neumann* and *Gerbner* are leading representatives — is in their painstaking efforts to spell out the processes — social and psychological — through which these effects are thought to take place and to put empirical tests to some of the steps in the process. Such theorizing also constrains those who disagree to be precise! In the last few years, the work of the *Gerbner* team has engendered such reactions, and a sharp but focussed debate is presently in progress between *Gerbner* and certain critics.[23] *Noelle-Neumann's* data have not yet been subject to such criticism, at least not in English-language journals. The progress of science clearly warrants such debate. In a word, one must ask whether we are entering a new era of mass society? Are modern media reducing the political choices offered to citizens of Western democracies? Are the media serving as substitutes for reference and membership groups? Are individuals less involved and less active in their organizational affiliations? Is there a retreat from interpersonal communication on public affairs? Are people becoming more silent? I will not attempt to answer these questions, since I have not set out to criticize the available data or to marshall new data of my own. I would like to elaborate on only one of the above questions which seems to me a key to the others: Are mass media usurping the place of refernce groups?[24]

Central to *Noelle-Neumann's* thesis is the notion that the media have come to substitute for reference groups. It is strongly implicit in the *Noelle-Neumann* papers that people decide whether or not to be silent on the basis of the distribution of opinion reported (often incorrectly) by the media. But *Noelle-Neumann* herself is ambivalent in her presentation of this point. The spiral of silence theory itself cannot so easily dismiss the direct influence of actual membership and reference groups. Consider two examples: (1) In discussing the data on recall of how one voted, *Noelle-Neumann* points out that recall is distorted not so much by national or even regional election results as by the distribution of votes within demographic and social groupings with which respondents are identified. (2) When groups retreat into silence, or when conflict polarizes opinion, *Noelle-Neumann* tells us that one's membership group becomes more salient as a reference group. In such circumstances, individuals are likely to misperceive the world not because they use the media as reference but because they have their own proximate groups to which they refer. In these two examples, and elsewhere, *Noelle-Neumann* reminds us of the importance of real-life reference groups, contact with whom is not, typically, mediated by mass communications. This is not just a minor point. It is basic to our entire perspective on society whether the media are usurping and monopolizing the role of reference groups. If reference groups are alive and well, individuals will not so quickly fall silent in the face of mass-communicated information about the opinion attributed by journalists to some vaguely defined majority, or by journalists to themselves. And discussion can continue. If reference groups are declining and people becoming more victimized by pluralistic ignorance and fear of isolation, we are in trouble, indeed.

Notes

1 *Tamar Liebes* assisted me in exploring the interrelations among the ideas of *Elisabeth Noelle-Neumann* and those of *James Coleman, Todd Gitlin, George Gerbner* and others noted below. I also wish to thank Professor *Marc Galanter* who is interested in pluralistic ignorance from the point of view of the law, as well as Professor and Mrs. *David Weiss-Halivni*, Professor *Ruth Katz*, Dr. *Yvette Biro* and *Pierre Motyl* who contributed and clarified in various ways. Members of the faculty-student interdepartmental seminar in social psychology at the Hebrew University, under the leadership of Professor *Shalom Schwartz*, helpfully reacted to an earlier version of the paper.

2 Elisabeth Noelle-Neumann, "Return to the Concept of Powerful Mass Media", in H. Eguchi and K. Sata (eds.) *Studies of Broadcasting*, No. 9, NHK, Tokyo, 1973, pp. 67–112.

3 In addition to the 1973 paper, *ibid.*, I draw on the following writings of Elisabeth Noelle-Neumann: "Spiral of Silence: A Theory of Public Opinion", *Journal of Communication*, Vol. 24, 1974, pp. 43–51; "Turbulences in the Climate of Opinion: Methodological Applications of the Spiral of Silence Theory", *Public Opinion Quarterly*, Vol. 41, 1977, pp. 143–158; and "Mass Media and Social Change in Developed Societies", in Elihu Katz and Tamas Szecsko, (eds.), *Mass Media and Social Change*, London: Sage Ltd., 1981.

4 Textbook discussions of the concept of "pluralistic ignorance" can be found in Theodore Newcomb, *Social Psychology*, Dryden, New York 1950, and in David Krech, Richard S. Crutchfield and Egerton L. Ballachey, *Individual in Society*, McGraw-Hill, New York, 1972.

5 Solomon E. Asch, "Effects of Group Pressure Upon the Modification and Distortion of Judgments", in E. Maccoby, T. Newcomb and P. Hartley (eds.) *Readings in Social Psychology*, 3rd edition, Holt, New York 1958. See also the *Crutchfield* technique as described in Kretch et al., *Individual in Society, op. cit.*, pp. 509–512.

6 *Ibid.*

7 In this connection see the recent reviews by *J.G. Blumler* of research paradigms in American and European communication studies and the democratic contexts in which they are pursued, "Mass Communications Research – A Transatlantic Perspective", *Journalism Quarterly*, Vol. 55, 1978. pp. 219–230 and "Mass Communication Research in Europe", *Media, Culture and Society*, Vol. 2, 1980, pp. 367–376, esp. pp. 373–375.

8 Paul F. Lazarsfeld and Robert K. Merton, "Mass Communication, Popular Taste and Organized Social Action", (1948), reprinted in Wilbur Schramm and Donald Roberts (eds.) *Process and Effects of Mass Communication*, University of Illinois Press, Urbana Ill. 1971.

9 A sophisticated discussion of this problem is Alvin Gouldner, *Dialectics of Ideology and Technology*, Macmillan, London 1976.

10 This is an assumption in such recent works as Glasgow University Media Group, *Bad News*, Routledge and Kegan Paul, London 1976, where official statistics of man-days lost in strikes is compared with extent of media coverage of the same strikes.

11 Asch, "Effects of Group Pressure ...", *op. cit.*

12 Kretch et al., *Individual in Society, op. cit.* pp. 512 ff.

13 James S. Coleman, "Authority Systems", *Public Opinion Quarterly*, Vol 44, 1980, pp. 143–163.

14 Noelle-Neumann, "Turbulences ...", *op. cit.*, p. 151.

15 These cases are discussed in Dina Goren, *Secrecy and the Right to Know*, Turtledove Press, Tel Aviv, 1979.

16 See Lazarsfeld and Merton, "Mass Communication, Popular Taste ...", *op. cit*

17 See Anselm Strauss, *Negotations*, Josey-Bass, San Francisco, Calif., 1978.

18 Interpreting the despotism of Pharaoh toward the Hebrews, the 13th Century biblical commentator, *Rabbi Moses ben Nahman (Nahmanides)* anticipated this point. When Pharaoh says to his advisors "let us outwit them" (Exodus 1 : 10) *Nahmanides* observes that the king feared that an open attack upon the Hebrews would cause defections in the army ("in the face of an arbitrary attack on a people who had come to Egypt at the invitation of a former king") and moreover, that *"the people would not give permission to the king* to act so unjustly ... Pharaoh's order to act deviously (was) so that the Israelis would not realize that he was acting against them out of hate." Ironically, when *Moses* made public Pharaoh's scheming, the Israelites turned against *Moses* in anger. By putting Pharaoh's conspiracy into the open (i. e. now that everybody knows), "the Egyptians will increase their hatred

of us and libel us by saying that we are rebelling against the throne. They will no longer have to resort to trickery; they will kill us." Free translation, paraphrasing, underlining and parentheses are mine — E.K.

19 For a discussion of these models, see Elihu Katz, "On Conceptualizing Media Effects", in Thelma McCormack (ed.) *Studies in Communication*, Vol. I, JAI Press, Bridgeport, Conn., 1980.

20 See Todd Gitlin, "Media Sociology: The Dominant Paradigm", *Theory and Society* Vol. 6, 1978, pp. 205–253. This paper is in sharp criticism of Elihu Katz and Paul Lazarsfeld, *Personal Influence*, The Free Press, Glencoe, 1956.

21 See George Gerbner and Larry Gross, "Living with Television: The Violence Profile", *Journal of Communication*, Vol. 26, 1976, pp. 173–199, and a series of subsequent papers by these authors and their associates, in the same journal, in succeeding years.

22 "Mass Media and Social Change . . .", *op. cit.*

23 See Paul M. Hirsch, "The 'Scary World' of the Nonviewer and Other Anomalies: A Reanalysis of Gerbner et al's Findings on Cultivation Analysis, Part I and Part II", *Communication Research*, Vol. 7, 1980, pp. 403–456, and Vol. 8, 1981; Michael Hughes, "The Fruits of Cultivation Analysis: A Reexamination of Some Effects of Television Watching", *Public Opinion Quarterly*, Vol. 44, 1980, pp. 287–302; J. M. Wober, "Televised Violence and Paranoid Perception: The View from Great Britain", *Public Opinion Quarterly*, Vol. 42, 1978, pp. 315–321. A detailed reply appears in George Gerbner, Larry Gross, Michael Morgan and Nancy Signorielli, "A Curious Journey into the Scary World of Paul Hirsch", *Communication Research*, Vol. 8, 1981.

24 The classic discussion of this concept is Robert K. Merton and Alice Kitt, "Contributions to the Theory of Reference Group Behavior", in R. K. Merton and P. F. Lazarsfeld (eds.) *Studies in the Scope and Method of the American Soldier*, Free Press, Glencoe, 1950, pp. 40–105. See also continued discussions of this topic in the several recent editions of R.K. Merton, *Social Theory and Social Structure*, Macmillan-Free Press, New York. Pioneer of this field is Herbert H. Hyman, "The Psychology of Status", *Archives of Psychology*, 1942, No. 269.

This chapter presents a formal analysis of Noelle-Neumann's spiral of silence and Allport's notion of pluralistic ignorance. Taylor develops a set of five hypotheses about the relationships among variables in each model of how individuals perceive public opinion and tests them, noting points of success and failure for each model. A general argument is made linking the spiral of silence and theories of the perception of public opinion to the analysis of the general class of social choice situations where people's expectations influence outcomes. D. Garth Taylor is assistant professor of political science at the University of Chicago.

6

PLURALISTIC IGNORANCE AND THE SPIRAL OF SILENCE
A Formal Analysis

D. Garth Taylor

DO PEOPLE accurately perceive public opinion? The "spiral of silence" and "pluralistic ignorance" are theories that draw on psychological principles of perception, communication, and certainty to answer this question. The theory of the spiral of silence states that one's perception of the distribution of public opinion motivates one's willingness to express political opinions. The act of self-expression, however, changes the global environment of opinion, altering the perceptions of other persons and, ultimately, affecting their willingness to express their own opinions. Because individuals monitor their social environment as one cue to opinion and action, opinions with visible adherents appear to be more widely held than they are in fact. The appearance of strength becomes a self-fulfilling prophecy; those who think they are in the majority are more willing to speak out, those who think they are in the minority have an extra incentive to remain silent. The description of the plight of those who believe they are in the minority gives the name to this theory: the spiral of silence (Noelle-Neumann 1974; 1977; 1979). In recent writings on this theory, Noelle-Neumann emphasizes the importance of this phenomenon for

Reprinted by permission of the publisher from "Pluralistic Ignorance and the Spiral of Silence: A Formal Analysis," by D. Garth Taylor, *Public Opinion Quarterly,* Vol. 46, pp. 311-355. Copyright 1982 by The Trustees of Columbia University.

analyzing the development of public opinion: "The link between [one's] personal convictions and the results of his observations of the social environment . . . is the principal feature in the process of opinion formation" (1974:50).

In this article, as in Noelle-Neumann's writings, it is important to keep a clear distinction between individuals' private opinions, the willingness of each individual to express his opinion, and public opinion. For purposes of this exposition, public opinion can be thought of as the sum of expressed private opinions. According to the theory of the spiral of silence, individuals' opinions are more or less constant (at least in the short run), individual willingness to express one's opinion changes depending on perceptions, and therefore public opinion changes because of the perceptual process.

The other theory to be discussed in this paper is about the accuracy of people's environmental perceptions. If perception of the distribution of opinion in the social environment is a principal part of the process of public opinion formation, then it is of some interest to know whether or not people perceive the environment accurately. Recent studies of this question have produced some empirical generalizations that at first appear to raise problems for any easy interpretation of the spiral of silence. Fields and Schuman (1976) note the tendency for people to believe that others agree with them. This pattern is called the "looking-glass perception." In the same article Fields and Schuman suggest that there is a conservative bias to opinion perceptions. In their article they found that those favoring civil liberties and racial liberalism were actually in the majority on several questions but were rarely believed to be a majority by themselves or by others in the sample. The problem of the accurate perception of the majority position has also been taken up by O'Gorman (1975; 1979; 1980; O'Gorman and Garry 1976). He reintroduces the term "pluralistic ignorance" to describe the situation when a minority position in public opinion is incorrectly perceived to be the majority position and vice versa.[1]

Each of the two theories analyzes some aspect of the role of social perception in public opinion formation. The analysis of the spiral of silence takes the perceptions of public opinion as given and examines the effect of these perceptions on subsequent actions or intended

[1] O'Gorman's definition is a little narrower than that of others who have used the term. Allport (1924) describes the attitudes of submission and conformity that regulate a person's actions and opinions in public or in "crowd" situations. Allport does not, however, use the term "pluralistic ignorance" in the discussion (pp. 304–309). Merton (1968) refers to any uncertainty about the distribution of opinion in a reference group as pluralistic ignorance (pp. 430–431). Empirical studies of pluralistic ignorance have usually ended up testing whether or not the majority correctly perceives the majority position.

actions. The literature on pluralistic ignorance is concerned with the accuracy of such perceptions. The predominant finding from the literature on pluralistic ignorance is that perceptions are not necessarily accurate and that it is hard to find any correlation between others' opinions and one's own opinions. Fields and Schuman, for instance, conclude that there is a distinct "air of unreality to the whole public perception process [that] makes it difficult to argue that people are being directly influenced by the actual opinions of others" (1976:442).

Comparing the usual findings from these two theories, we have, in the spiral of silence, a theory of opinion expression that takes as a causal antecedent the perceptions of others' opinions. However, according to the theory of pluralistic ignorance, we cannot expect that such perceptions will be accurate. Noelle-Neumann notes that her findings "do not negate the fact or importance of patterned misperceptions of other people's opinions. Rather . . . [they] may help clarify some conditions and consequences of such misperceptions" (1977:144).

The goal of this paper is to show how to clarify one's understanding of the conditions and consequences of public (mis)perception of public opinion. We will explore the meaning of the specific variables and the causal linkages relating these two theories at a considerably more formal level than has been done in the previous literature. To this end the next section of this paper is devoted to a more extended formal and theoretical discussion than is normally the case for an empirical research report. Once the theoretical guideposts are in place, the paper turns to an analysis of the theories of pluralistic ignorance and the spiral of silence as they apply to some issues in American environmental politics. Survey data were recently collected by the National Opinion Research Center in Waukegan, Illinois. Public opinion on water pollution, air pollution, and nuclear regulation was studied using the questions and questionnaire formats that have been previously used to study pluralistic ignorance and the spiral of silence for other issues and in other countries. With these data, it is possible to analyze many of the theoretical and empirical interconnections between the two theories of public opinion and to learn a great deal about the motivations of people in the arena of environmental politics. This is the task of the second half of this paper.

Variables and Hypotheses in the Theory of the Spiral of Silence

The spiral of silence begins with the premise that the individual assesses the distribution of opinions in the social environment by evaluating the strength, commitment, urgency, and the chances of success of certain proposals and viewpoints. To paraphrase Noelle-Neumann's work (1974:44 ff.): If the individual discovers he agrees with the prevailing view it boosts his self-confidence and enables self-expression without the danger of social isolation. If he finds his views are losing ground he will become more uncertain and therefore less inclined to express his opinion to others. These different patterns of behavior influence others' quasi-statistical pictures of opinion. The tendency of one to speak up and the other to remain silent starts off a spiraling process which increasingly establishes one opinion as the prevailing one.

The basic premise of the theory is that through social interaction people influence each other's willingness to express opinions. The self-interest that people protect by monitoring the environment and shaping their expression of opinions is their fear of social isolation. The interpersonal nature of the theory of the spiral of silence is linked to classical theories of social influence: "Nor is there one in ten thousand who is stiff and insensible enough to bear up under the constant dislike and condemnation of his own club" (Locke, 1961). Just as the Federalist sought to defend certain democratic institutions, Madison extended the spiral of silence to include those without club memberships:

> The strength of opinion in each individual and its practical influence on his conduct depend much on the number which he supposes to have entertained the same opinion.
> The reason of man . . . is timid and cautious when left alone and acquires firmness and confidence in proportion to the number with which it is associated (Federalist No. 49).

It is helpful to diagram the spiral of silence in a formal model showing the variables that are implicit in the theory, the position of each variable, and the causal connections between the variables. In its simplest form—i.e., without the qualifications and special cases that are in the literature—the spiral of silence postulates a causal ordering among four variables, with one feedback loop. The four variables are: one's opinion on an issue; one's perception of the predominant public opinion; one's assessment of the likely future course of public opinion; and one's willingness to support one's opinion with action, verbal statements, or other signs of commitment.

To help specify the empirical predictions from this theory, let us assume the variables are coded in the following way:

Variable 1: One's Opinion on an Issue
        0 = minority position
        1 = majority position

Variable 2: Perception of the Predominant Position
    0 = what is, in fact, the minority
    1 = what is, in fact, the majority
Variable 3: Assessment of the Future Trend
    0 = more support for what is presently, in fact, the
        minority
    1 = more support for what is, in fact, the majority
Variable 4: Willingness to Express One's Opinion
    0 = no
    1 = yes

The causal order among these variables is shown in Figure 1. One's opinion and one's assessment of the predominant public opinion are assumed to be related. The theory of the spiral of silence is primarily concerned with other factors and takes this relationship as given. Some of the factors in this relationship are discussed below, where we specify the variables involved in the "looking-glass perception" and the theory of pluralistic ignorance. For now we will note the relationship between the first two variables in Figure 1 as a double-headed arrow.

One's opinion and one's assessment of the predominant public opinion are both assumed to influence one's judgment of the future course of opinion. Again, this relationship will be discussed more directly when we examine the literature on pluralistic ignorance.

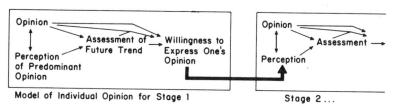

Figure 1. Depiction of Stages and Models for Individual Opinion
in the Sprial of Silence

The fourth variable is willingness to express one's opinion.[2] At one point in her discussion Noelle-Neumann states that "willingness to expose one's views publicly varies according to one's assessment of the frequency distribution and the trend of opinions in the social environment" (Noelle-Neumann 1974:45). In terms of the variables shown in Figure 1, this means that one's willingness to express one's opinion depends on an interaction between one's opinion (majority or

[2] Noelle-Neumann is primarily concerned with changes in actions expressing the degree of one's support. Rarely is it found that the direction of one's opinion (e.g. a vote change) is a result of the pressures exerted by the spiral of silence.

minority) and one's perception of the future trend in public opinion. For those who favor the majority position, willingness to express one's opinion is greater for those who see a trend toward greater public support for that position. For those who favor the minority position, willingness to express oneself is greater for those who see a trend toward the minority position. This implies an interaction between variables 1, 3, and 4. We do not draw in a similar interaction between 1, 2, and 4 because, according to the theory, one's perception of the predominant opinion affects one's assessment of the future trend (and so we draw in this arrow), but does not *directly* affect one's willingness to express support for one's position. This, at least, appears to be the conclusion from Noelle-Neumann's research: "If there is a divergence in the assessment of the present and future strengths of a particular view, it is the expectation of the future position which will determine the extent to which the individual is willing to expose himself" (Noelle-Neumann 1974:45).

The "spiral" of silence comes about because the amount of support that is shown for an opinion affects the public's perception of the strength or predominance of that opinion at some later stage in the development of public opinion. We can portray the spiraling process with a multistage model for opinion evolution. Figure 1 presents a schematic diagram showing the first stage and part of the second. The lefthand side of Figure 1 shows the ordering of variables in the individual-level model predicting willingness to express one's opinion at any point in time. The heavy arrow leading away from the Expression variable is not a path in the model for explaining individual responses or individual changes but the way of representing the cumulative effect of individual changes in probabilities of self-expression on the aggregate mixture of public opinion. This aggregate mixture of public opinion is the stimulus for an individual's perception of public opinion in the second stage of the process of the development of public opinion. (Recall that public opinion is defined, under this model, as the aggregate expressed opinion and not the aggregate of individual beliefs.)

As time passes, individual expressions of opinion have a cumulative effect that may alter the perceived environment of public opinion. It is possible that at some later time, indicated as Stage 2 in the diagram, the perception of public opinion is changed because of the impact of changes in the willingness of individuals to express themselves. The heavy arrow linking that willingness at time 1 to perceptions of the predominant opinion at time 2 represents the crucial aggregate perception in the spiral of silence. The population at time 2 is evaluating a different mixture of public and private messages.

The new perceived mixture of public and private messages operates, in Stage 2, as a new, independent causal force in further stimulating changed perceptions of the future and changed levels of willingness to express one's own views. A complete model for public opinion formation would show several stages. Within each stage there is a short-term individual-level process of perception and opinion expression. Between stages there is an aggregate process of longer-run changes in the distribution of perceived public opinion. As issues evolve over a slightly longer period of time, these changes serve as new, independent sources of further change in the individuals who are themselves members of the public being studied.

The variables and causal connections in Figure 1 show what we can call the usual pattern of predictions for the theory of the spiral of silence. In the literature on the spiral of silence there are many counter examples and reports of special situations where the connections hypothesized in Figure 1 are found not to apply. One purpose of this article, however, is to distill a baseline or reference model for the usual working of the spiral of silence. From the analysis so far, we can make two predictions that ought to be empirically supported if the spiral of silence (as it usually operates) is an appropriate description of the microdynamics of willingness to express one's opinion on a political issue:

Hypothesis A: Those who believe there is a trend in support of their position are more likely than those who do not to express their opinion.

Hypothesis B: Those who perceive majority support for their position are more likley than those who do not to express their opinions. This pattern, however, is statistically explained by controlling for one's assessment of the future trend.

The remaining hypotheses tested in this article do not arise directly from the theory of the spiral of silence. Rather, we note that further specification and testing of the theory of the spiral of silence implies that we pay attention to the variables and propositions that are normally associated with the theory of pluralistic ignorance. Therefore, we now take a closer look at this second theory.

Variables and Hypotheses in the Theory of
Pluralistic Ignorance

The empirical studies of pluralistic ignorance have analyzed, for a range of dependent variables and within a range of settings, the extent to which people believe others agree with them and the consequences this certainty has for the perceived levels of public support for certain opinions. In terms of Figure 1, the empirical literature on pluralistic ignorance is concerned with a more careful spelling out of the relation between one's opinion and one's perception of the predominant present or future trend in public opinion. The key explanatory factor that is introduced is a psychological tendency to be certain of one's opinions and to attribute to others the tendency to agree with oneself—the looking-glass perception.

Empirical studies of pluralistic ignorance have not attempted to measure certainty directly. Rather, the findings typically show the relation between one's own opinion and the perception of the predominant opinion.[3] A schematic table showing this relationship is shown in Figure 2.

In Figure 2, P_1 is an index of the certainty of those who are, in fact, in the majority. P_2 is an index of the certainty of those who are in the minority. With these symbols, one can calculate the proportion who think A is the majority position as a function of the distribution of actual opinion and the level of uncertainty of those holding each position:

$$P_a = P_1 P_A + (1 - P_2) P_B \qquad (1)$$

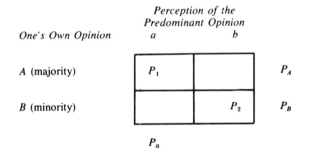

where P_A = Proportion thinking A (assumed to be majority position)
$\quad P_a$ = Proportion who think A is the majority position
$\quad P_1$ = Proportion of those thinking A who think A is majority
$\quad P_2$ = Proportion of those thinking B who think B is majority

Figure 2. A Schematic Representation of the Type of Cross-Tabulation Typically Used to Study Pluralistic Ignorance

[3] The empirical studies of pluralistic ignorance analyze (or theorize about) the relation between one's opinion and one's perception of the majority opinion. Other descriptions of the phenomenon of pluralistic ignorance sometimes take other variables into account or focus more attention on the outcome of the process (e.g. Allport's (1924) observations on the conservatizing effect of large groups). This paper, however, is a review and synthesis of empirical studies of pluralistic ignorance and the spiral of silence. Therefore, the more narrow definition of the term "pluralistic ignorance" is used here.

This equation is a formal way of saying that the proportion who believe A to be the majority position is affected by the certainty of those who believe A, the proportion who believe A, and by the ununcertainty of those who believe B. The exact pattern of certainty is, from a substantive point of view, quite important because a small decrease in certainty has a greater effect on the perception of the dominant public opinion if it is the majority who become uncertain rather than the minority who become unsure.

The aggregate level of misperception of the majority opinion (i.e., the amount of pluralistic ignorance) is usually described by comparing P_A with P_a. As a measure of aggregate misperception, this index may obscure more than it reveals. For one thing, if everyone is completely certain—if the looking-glass perception completely controls one's views—then there is no aggregate misperception. The index would show no pluralistic ignorance even though the minority group was 100 percent wrong in its views. One cause of this outcome is that the index is combining numbers that should be studied separately. The study of pluralistic ignorance should focus on the amount and distribution of certainty and uncertainty. For instance, in the data reported by Fields and Schuman every case of "ignorance" is explained by the lack of certainty of the majority (P_1 was small).

A deeper cause of the problem with the index is that the majority position, the perceived majority, rates of uncertainty, and the level of misperception are all aggregate measures that are being used to study individual-level dynamics of opinion. Because of this there is an indeterminancy in calculating the amount of pluralistic ignorance for any individual person or for any particular issue. Given the framework that has been developed for analyzing the question, the only index of ignorance that makes sense for the whole population is one that recognizes that 100 percent of the population lives in an area where A is the majority opinion. Therefore the index of pluralistic ignorance should be $1.0 - P_a$. But this focuses the research on variation in P_a alone. The only way to focus attention on the original question of the match between actual and perceived opinion distributions is to start with a research design that is comparative: across issues, over time, and/or between groups. Inferences about the causes and consequences of pluralistic ignorance can be made only by analyzing variation over these comparative domains.

Figure 1, showing the variables in the theory of the spiral of silence, does not include the variable "certainty." The theory of the spiral of silence takes that part of the psychological process as given or as exogenous to the primary variables of interest. However, the theory of pluralistic ignorance, and particularly the principle of looking-glass perception, makes the following predictions about the relations between the first three variables in Figure 1:

Hypothesis C: Those who favor the majority position tend to believe that the majority currently favors their position. (Opinion and Perception are positively related).

Hypothesis D: Those who favor the majority position tend to believe that the future trend is toward greater support for their position. (Opinion and Assessment of the Future are positively related.)[4]

An Additional Deduction and Hypothesis

The fifth hypothesis tested in this paper does not arise directly from Noelle-Neumann's writings on the spiral of silence, nor does it arise from the articles that have been published on the theory of pluralistic ignorance. The final hypothesis comes from considering the dynamic properties that are expected to emerge when (or if) public opinion passes through stages as they are shown in Figure 1. We begin the discussion with a formal derivation of this dynamic property.

Let us assume that the principle of the looking-glass perception holds. Additionally, let us say that those in the majority and those in the minority are equally certain that the public predominantly agrees with them (in terms of the parameters in Figure 2, $P_1 = P_2 > .5$). Then, for issues of this character, we deduce by hypotheses C and D that the majority position is seen by the average member of the public as the predominant view in the present and likely to be even more so in the future. This means that the type of person who is most likely to be interviewed in a sample survey of the population is a member of the majority who thinks that public opinion is (and will be even more) on his side. If we assume that hypotheses A and B are also correct, then a person in the majority who thinks he has majority public support (call this a type *M* person) and a person in the minority who thinks he has majority public support (type *m*) will be the kinds of people most likely to express themselves.

Let us add to the postulates we have so far made the assumption that the strength of the propensity to convert the perception of majority support into willingness to express oneself is the same for those in the majority and those in the minority. If these few hypotheses and assumptions are true then, because of the fact that there are more

---

[4] Noelle-Neumann does not explicitly say it, but her more extended discussion of the theory implies there is an interaction: the influence of one's opinion on one's perception of the future course of opinion is stronger for those who believe they are in the majority. This interactive relationship could be represented in Figure 1 with a joint arrow connecting the third variable with the first two variables.

type M people than type m people, any particular member of the public is more likely to hear (or see) expressions of opinion by members of the majority than by members of the minority. (The fact that this is not always true should not deter us from the formal exercise. Deviations from this pattern must be explained by one of the hypotheses or assumptions being wrong. It is an interesting research question to determine for particular instances which assumptions are incorrect—e.g., when are majorities uncertain of support.)

If the formal aspects of this model are assumed to be true at any particular point in time, then further propositions result when we consider the stages of development of public opinion as represented in Figure 1. As public opinion develops, the mixture of expressed public opinion at time 1 becomes the stimulus for people's perceptions of public opinion at time 2. Using the diagram in Figure 1 as a guide, what further dynamic properties of public opinion can we infer from this?

A change in the perceived majority position may cause a change in the strength or direction of one's own opinion (depending on how the principles of certainty and the looking-glass perception actually work). We have admitted this possibility with the double-headed arrow between opinion and perception (but see footnote 2). Regardless of how we decide this issue, a change in the perceived majority position is clearly, by the model, expected to cause a change in one's assessment of the future trend.

Thinking again about the types of people in the population, we see that at stage 2 the modal member of the public is a member of the majority who notices an increase in support for the majority and increases his expectation slightly that the majority position will eventually be the predominant position in public opinion. Since we believe hypothesis B, we expect an increase in the perception of support for one's position will translate into an increased willingness to express support for one's position. (This results from applying dynamic reasoning to the static correlations shown in Figure 1.)

If the model is so far correctly specified, then over any span of time those in the majority are more likely than those in the minority to notice increased support for their position and therefore should be more willing to express their opinions. This reflection on the dynamic properties of Figure 1 leads to the fifth hypothesis:

Hypothesis E: Those who favor the majority position are more willing to express their opinions.

Since this hypothesis is not suggested by any particular proposition in the literature on pluralistic ignorance or the spiral of silence, we need to be clear on where it comes from. We have assumed that hypotheses A to D are correct and that: (1) there is a similar level of certainty between those in the majority and those in the minority position on an issue; and (2) there is a similar tendency for those in either position to convert their perception of support into willingness to express their opinion. Hypothesis E has raised comment from everyone who has read earlier drafts of this article: how does it happen, then, that minority positions are sometimes seen as the majority position in public opinion? How do minority positions ever successfully displace majority positions?

To answer these questions we must first remind ourselves that hypothesis E predicts that it is public opinion—i.e., the aggregate expressed opinion or the aggregate perceived opinion—that gravitates toward majority dominance absent other factors. Majority dominance in perceived public opinion may not actually occur in all circumstances because of countervailing opinion change (due to social movements, governmental leadership, or whatever) or because one of the hypotheses or assumptions in our formal statement of the spiral of silence does not hold true. One purpose of the formal analysis in this paper is to point out where and how to think about the weak links when the baseline predictions are not supported.

One likely candidate for the weak link is the certainty of those in the majority position. The findings of Fields and Schuman establish that for some issues the majority is quite insecure, so much so as to cause a substantive divergence between perceived public opinion and the aggregate of private beliefs. The trend data reported by Noelle-Neumann (1977) could be further analyzed to determine empirically whether this is actually the cause of the breakdown of hypothesis E in the cases she reports.

In the next part of this paper we will test the five hypotheses using a recently completed survey of public opinion on three issues in environmental politics.

Data and Analysis

The original plan for the analysis in this part of the paper was to describe the variables collected and use the diagram for Stage 1 in Figure 1 as the "map" for a multiple-regression/path analysis of the data. By stepping through the model, we would first examine the issues raised in the discussion of pluralistic ignorance, then by focusing on the later parts of the causal chain we would examine the hypotheses generated by combining the theory of pluralistic ignorance with the theory of the spiral of silence. It is not possible to pursue this strategy because several key hypotheses fail to be confirmed. The sign of the relationship between whether one is in the majority or minority position on an issue and perception of majority support in public opinion is not in the same direction for all issues. Furthermore, the effect of one's perception of the predominant opinion on willingness to express one's own opinion is different for those in the majority than for those in the minority. Because of the complex patterns in the data, we will employ less formidable analytic tools than originally planned. We begin with a description of the data and then proceed with a step-by-step analysis of the path diagram. For three issues in regulatory politics—air pollution, water pollution, and nuclear energy—we will examine the following topics:

a. The distribution of actual opinions and the extent of pluralistic ignorance.
b. The correlates of perceived support for one's own opinion.
c. Differences by issue in a and b.
d. The effect of perceived support on willingness to commit oneself to each issue.
e. Differences by issue in d.

DATA

In the fall of 1980 the National Opinion Research Center conducted a 500-case survey of public opinion in the city of Waukegan, Illinois, under contract with the city government. The survey, part of a program for community needs assessment developed by the mayor's office, covered many topics of interest to students of urban development and the quality of life in industrial towns. The issues of water pollution, air pollution, and nuclear regulation are particularly salient in this town, situated about 30 miles north of Chicago and built around a natural harbor on Lake Michigan which is currently polluted with PCBs. The cleanup campaign and lawsuits that have been filed on behalf of the city have been the subject of frequent local and regional attention. Just before the field period for this survey there was a mild scare about radiation leakage and improper administrative procedures at a nuclear power plant in Zion, Illinois, about 20 miles north of Waukegan.

The questions used to measure opinions were exactly the same in wording (except for the description of the environmental problems) as the items reported in Noelle-Neumann's studies of the spiral of silence. (These questions, it will be recalled, include the key concepts in the literature on pluralistic ignorance.) One procedural difference between this study and those cited earlier is that we began the questions in each area with a general test of interest and information:

Have you heard or read about the problem of chemicals polluting the harbor here in Waukegan?

This was followed by the measure of the respondent's opinion:

Here is a card with two people discussing the problem of chemicals polluting the harbor. Person A says there should be stronger steps to prevent industry from putting chemicals in the harbor. Person B disagrees. Person B says chemicals are something we have to live with because Waukegan needs the industry. Which person do you agree with more?

Then follow-up questions measured the respondent's willingness to commit to the issue, his view of the predominant view in public opinion, and his assessment of the future:

Do you feel strongly enough about this that you would donate money if you could afford it to a group that supported your position?[5]

Would you say most of the people in Waukegan are for stronger steps to control chemicals in the harbor, or would you say most accept the chemicals as something that can't be avoided?

How do you think it will be in the future? How will people view the problem a year from now? Do you think more or fewer people will favor stronger steps to control chemicals in the harbor?

The battery of questions for air pollution and nuclear regulation followed the same format. The conversation about air pollution was:

Person A says air pollution is something we have to live with because we need to use cars and keep factories. Person B says there should be stronger steps to control these sources of pollution. Which person do you agree with more?

The tradeoff in nuclear regulation was posed as:

Person A says nuclear power plants should be more closely regulated. Person B disagrees. Person B says we need the electricity so much that we should not try to regulate nuclear power more closely. Which person do you agree with more?

The interviewers did not report any problems administering this section of the questionnaire. Their perception was that people understood the questions, the card made it easy to follow the arguments, and respondents understood the point of the questions: the tradeoff between productivity and regulation.

---

[5] Willingness to donate money is not the same as willingness to express one's opinions in other ways. We assume that people who will donate money are also willing to engage in other kinds of persuasive or communicative behavior. We did not ask about other modes of expression that are often used in this kind of research—e.g. bumper stickers, buttons, etc.—because these questions would signal too much identification with the environmentalist and nuclear protest movements that were quite active at the time of the survey. The fear is that such questions would have biased responses in some way because of people's opinions of these protest movements.

Looking back to Figure 1, we see that the relationship between one's opinion and one's perception of the majority opinion is the first step in the causal chain for the spiral of silence. These are also the variables compared in most empirical studies of pluralistic ignorance. Therefore, the first step in our analysis of the spiral of silence is to examine the extent of pluralistic ignorance for each issue.

The first question we must ask to assess the degree of pluralistic ignorance is: What is the distribution of public opinion on our three topics with respect to regulation? If we validly presented the tradeoff between productivity and regulation, then we must conclude that the residents of Waukegan prefer regulation by a substantial margin for each issue. Table 1 shows that when the total population is considered (including those without opinions or information about the issue), the level of support for regulation is 67 percent for water pollution, 68 percent for nuclear energy, and 61 percent for air pollution. If we consider only those who said they had heard about the problem (80 percent said they were aware for each issue) then the level of support for regulation jumps to between 80 and 90 percent, depending on the particular area.

The second question we must ask to assess the extent of pluralistic ignorance is: What proportion correctly perceives the majority position? The literature on pluralistic ignorance cited earlier in this paper includes the don't know/uninvolved in the base for calculating the proportion correctly perceiving the majority position. Table 1 shows that when this procedure is followed, there is a high level of pluralistic

Table 1. Public Opinion on Water Pollution, Air Pollution, and Nuclear Regulation

	Water Pollution	Air Pollution	Nuclear Regulation
Opinion: Favor stronger regulations			
Total population	67%	61%	68%
Those with opinions (P_A)	89	80	89
Perception: Believe majority favors stronger regulations			
Total population	46	37	47
Those with opinions (P_a)	61	48	62
Future: Expect greater support for regulation in the future			
Total population	54	46	47
Those with opinions	70	61	71
Expression of opinion: Would donate money if they could afford it			
Those favoring greater regulation	72	72	72
Those opposed to greater regulation	45	51	49

ignorance for our issues. Less than 50 percent accurately perceive the majority position in each area of public opinion. If we exclude the uninvolved, the measured level of pluralistic ignorance is much lower—about 60 percent correctly perceive the majority position on water pollution and nuclear regulation and 48 percent correctly perceive the majority position on air pollution. It is interesting to note that the percentage who correctly perceive the majority position is lower for the issue that, in fact, has the weaker majority (air pollution). The close tracking of actual opinion and the perception of the predominant view is found in other studies as well: "If an opinion decreases by only a few percentage points it also decreases in the opinion climate. That is, 'most people hold this view' goes down by distinctly more percentage points" (Noelle-Neumann, 1979:147).

Do these results show that there is pluralistic ignorance about our three issues? Probably, because according to the recommended index $(1.0 - P_a)$, between 39 and 52 percent of those with informed opinions are unaware of the true majority position on each issue. The second index of pluralistic ignorance that was discussed $(P_A - P_a)$ also shows some mismatch between public opinion and the perception of public opinion.

HYPOTHESIS C: PERCEPTION OF MAJORITY SUPPORT

Hypothesis C, based on the theory of pluralistic ignorance, is that people will tend to perceive majority support for their own opinions. Table 2 shows that this prediction is weakly confirmed in our survey data. For each issue, between 50 and 65 percent of those who favor regulation perceive majority support for regulation. For each issue about 60 percent of those who oppose regulation see majority support for opposition.

According to the data presented in the Fields and Schuman article (1976), the level of pluralistic ignorance of public opinion was greatest

Table 2. Interest Group Differences in the Perception of Current Public Opinion

	Water Pollution	Air Pollution	Nuclear Regulation
See majority support for position			
Those favoring greater regulation (P_1)	64%	50%	64%
Those opposed to greater regulation (P_2)	60	58	57
See majority opposition to position			
Those favoring greater regulation	18	29	21
Those opposed to greater regulation	28	36	24
Undecided or don't know about public opinion			
Those favoring greater regulation	18	21	19
Those opposed to greater regulation	12	6	15

for certain issues—race relations and support for civil liberties—where the liberal majority was particularly uncertain or lacked confidence in the prevalence of its views. The authors suggest on the basis of their findings that there is a conservative bias to public perception of public opinion. If we translate the suggestion from the Fields and Schuman article into a hypothesis for the data presented here it would be that the liberals (pro-regulation advocates) are more uncertain of the strength of their opinion than the anti-regulation respondents.

Table 2 shows that this hypothesis is not supported. The percentage seeing majority support is high for advocates of either position—a strong case of looking-glass perception—and the relation between majority/minority status and the perception of majority support is weak and not always in the same direction.

MAJORITY CERTAINTY AND CHANGES IN PUBLIC OPINION

With the data in Tables 1 and 2 we can illustrate an extremely important feature of our dynamic model for the spiral of silence. We recall from formula 1 that P_a, the proportion correctly perceiving the majority position, can be calculated as a function of: the certainty of the majority (P_1 in Figure 2); the certainty of the minority (P_2 in Figure 2); and, the proportion of the population in the majority category of opinion (P_4 in Figure 2). Whether the amount of misperception is greater in the majority or in the minority group is an important question. Furthermore, whether it is the majority or the minority which changes in the level of certainty as public opinion develops is also of great interest. The amount of pluralistic ignorance and the rate of change of ignorance is greatly affected by whether it is the majority or the minority that is more certain and whether it is the majority or minority that begins to change first. This point can be shown by calculating what percentage would accurately perceive the majority position if: (a) those in the minority were completely accurate in their perception, i.e., $P_2 = 0$; or (b) those in the majority were completely accurate in their perception, i.e., $P_1 = 1.0$. (If both the minority and majority are completely accurate then $P_1 = 1.0$ and $P_2 = 0$, and 100 percent correctly perceive the majority position.) The results of these two simulations are shown in Table 3.

The effect of uncertainty on the aggregate perception of the majority position is greater if it is the majority which is uncertain. Over time, this principle implies that dramatic changes in the level of certainty of the minority will have comparatively little influence on the match between perceived and actual public opinion. In other words, changes in public opinion due to the spiral of silence will occur

Table 3. Percent Correctly Perceiving Majority Position

	Water Pollution	Air Pollution	Nuclear Regulation
Actual	61%	48%	62%
Minority certain of its position $P_2 = 0$	68	60	68
Majority certain of its position $P_1 = 1.0$	93	88	94

faster when it is the majority that is changing in certainty than when it is the minority becoming more or less sure of its position. This principle might account for some of the patterns described in Noelle-Neumann's article on trends in public opinion (1977).

HYPOTHESIS D: BELIEFS ABOUT FUTURE SUPPORT IN PUBLIC OPINION

Table 1 shows that, for each issue, the predominant view is that public opinion will become more supportive of more vigorous regulation. Again, for either side, the perception of future support is less for air pollution than for the other two issues, but in every case more than 60 percent of those with opinions expect that public opinion will change in the direction of more support for greater regulation.

Hypothesis D states that those in the majority will tend to believe that public opinion will change in the direction of greater support for the majority position and that those opposed to regulation will tend to believe in the opposite trend in public opinion. This hypothesis, like hypothesis C, was based on the theory of pluralistic ignorance, and the looking-glass principle.

Table 4 shows that this hypothesis is not evenly supported in the survey data. Of those who favor more regulation on any issue, about

Table 4. Interest Group Differences in the Expectation of the Future Trend in Public Opinion

	Water Pollution	Air Pollution	Nuclear Regulaton
See more support in future			
Those favoring greater regulation	71%	64%	74%
Those opposed to greater regulation	36	50	57
See more opposition in future			
Those favoring greater regulation	15	21	13
Those opposed to greater regulation	62	44	33
Undecided or don't know about future trend			
Those favoring greater regulation	13	15	13
Those opposed to greater regulation	3	6	10

70 percent believe that public opinion will change in the direction of greater support for regulation. The uneven pattern of support for hypothesis D arises because of the perceptions of the minority—those who favor less regulation. For the water pollution issue, the minority is about as likely as the majority to say that public opinion will eventually change toward greater support for regulation. For the other two issues the minority is more certain of its position—between 50 and 60 percent believe the public will move in their direction.

For each of the three issues—and especially for the water pollution issue—the minority is less certain than the majority of future support in public opinion. This is a different pattern than was found in the analysis of Table 2—the perception of majority support in current public opinion. There, in discussing hypothesis C, we found that the majority and minority were equally certain of their positions.

The differences between issues in the perception of those in the minority may be an important explanatory factor in the analysis of the fourth variable—willingness to express one's opinions. We might summarize the differences between issues in the position of the minority by noting that those opposed to regulation are fairly certain they will eventually lose the water pollution issue; are divided on the future of the air pollution issue (about half believe they will become stronger—this is also the issue where, as shown in Table 2, the anti-regulation forces are more sure of current public support than those who favor regulation); and are fairly certain they will win on the nuclear regulation issue (even though, remarkably, they are a 4:1 minority).

This description of the pattern of certainty does not, of course, answer the more interesting question: Why is there variation in the level of certainty? And particularly, why is the variation in certainty related to minority status, greater for some issues, and primarily limited to perceptions of the trend in public opinion? We will develop some speculative arguments below, but these questions might provide stimulus for further developments in this area of public opinion theory.

PERCEPTION OF SUPPORT AND EXPRESSION OF OPINION:
HYPOTHESES A AND B

Hypothesis A states that those who see a trend toward future support for their position are more likely to be willing to express their opinion. Hypothesis B states that those who see majority support in current public opinion are more likely than those who do not to be willing to express their position.[6] Hypothesis B goes on to state that this pattern is statistically explained by hypothesis A. We lack the sample size to convincingly test this further proposition.

In analyzing the data we find qualified support for each hypothesis. The effects of perceived support depend on whether the respondent is actually in the majority or in the minority position. Not only is there this qualification, but the pattern is not the same for all issues.

Table 5 shows the correlates of willingness to commit oneself for those in the majority on each issue (i.e, those in favor of regulation). For those in the majority, hypotheses A and B—the predictions from the theory of the spiral of silence—are strongly confirmed. For each issue, those in the majority who see support in present public opinion and/or in the future trend of public opinion are more likely to say they would be willing to express their position.

Table 6 shows the level of willingness to express one's opinion for those in the minority on each issue. Hypotheses A and B are not consistently supported for this group. The perception of present and/or future support is strongly related in the hypothesized direction for those in the minority on nuclear regulation, but perceptions are nearly unrelated to support for the issue of water pollution and the variables are related in a negative direction for the issue of air pollution.

What accounts for this pattern of relationships between perception and support among those in the minority position? On each issue, the minority believes it is currently in the majority. This is a thought-

Table 5. Expression of Opinion for Those Who Favor Stronger Regulations

	Water Pollution	Air Pollution	Nuclear Regulaton
Total who would donate money if they could afford it	72%	72%	72%
Perception of public opinion			
Supportive	83	84	87
Opposed	75	69	59
Divided/don't know	33	45	35
Belief about future of public opinion			
Supportive	82	81	83
Opposed	63	70	60
Divided/don't know	27	33	26

[6] A reviewer of an earlier draft of this paper noted that Noelle-Neumann's theory is sometimes specified to apply mainly to those with no opinions or with weak opinions. There is a similar qualification in the literature on pluralistic ignorance: O'Gorman (1975) finds that perception of majority support has a greater impact on the opinions of those who are less certain or less extreme in their views.

Table 6. Expression of Opinion for Those Opposed to Stronger Regulations

	Water Pollution	Air Pollution	Nuclear Regulaton
Total who would donate money if they could afford it	45%	51%	49%
Perception of public opinion			
Supportive	50	47	57
Opposed	46	59	20
Divided/don't know	—[a]	—[a]	—[a]
Belief about future of public opinion			
Supportive	50	46	52
Opposed	46	58	36
Divided/don't know	—[a]	—[a]	—[a]

[a] Too few cases to report reliably.

provoking finding, but since the issues are alike in this respect, it does not offer a clue to the pattern in Table 6.

The issues differ greatly in the minority's assessment of the future trend in public opinion. From the point of view of the anti-regulation minority, public control over water pollution is a lost issue. Very few believe that public opinion will move in the direction of support for less regulation. The 46 percent who would donate money if they could afford it might be intepreted as the minimal amount of support or expression that is owed to a value that is important but sure to lose. The perception of public support or the belief that the majority will eventually favor the anti-regulation position is not strongly enough felt to raise the subjective probability of success enough to inspire much more expression of support.

Air pollution, on the other hand, is perceived by those opposed to regulation to be an issue that is in great conflict. Anti-regulation respondents are more likely than those favoring regulation to believe they are "ahead," and they are about equally divided on the question of whether they will become a stronger majority. The negative relation between perception of support and willingness to express support might come about because those who see a high chance of public opposition see a greater need to support the cause then those who think the issue is sure to win.

The issue of nuclear regulation, in one sense, requires no further explanation because the pattern of relationships is in the direction predicted by the hypotheses and by the theory of the spiral of silence. The issue lacks the special characteristics of the previous two issues and therefore the predictions of the theory hold.

The most interesting question, once again, is: What approach do we take to understanding the incentives and statements of those in the minority? The framework for analysis provided by the theories of pluralistic ignorance and the spiral of silence—at least as the theories have been formalized here—does not provide much further help in explaining the minority position. One immediate suggestion is that with a wider assortment of issues we could determine, at least, whether minority statements become most deviant when the majority position is very widely held—as is the case for the particular issues considered here.

MAJORITY OPINION AND EXPRESSION: HYPOTHESIS E

The fifth hypothesis, derived from the theory of the spiral of silence and the theory of pluralistic ignorance, is that those in the majority are more willing to express their opinions. Those in the majority, we have argued, are more likely to notice changes in public opinion in the direction which favors their position. The perception of favorable change is an additional factor, not included in Figure 1, that leads to willingness to express one's view.

The bottom rows of Table 1 show a strong relationship between belonging to the majority and willingness to express oneself. This pattern supports hypothesis E. We can also ask how much this pattern is explained or reduced by controlling for the other factors in Figure 1—perception of the current mix of public opinion and assessment of the future trend. The partial, or controlled relationship between belonging to the majority and willingness to express oneself can be studied by comparing the percentages in Table 5 with the percentage in each corresponding cell of Table 6. When we hold constant any category of the control variables, we find that there is still a strong difference between those in the majority (Table 5) and those in the minority (Table 6) in willingness to express one's opinions. Hypothesis E is supported for each issue.

Conclusion

For each of the three issues studied we found that both the majority and the minority are certain of current support in public opinion. This confirms hypothesis C: both groups assessed current public opinion in the looking-glass manner. In assessments of the future, however, we found that the self-assurance of the majority is sustained but the self-assurance of the minority is much weaker and depends, to some extent, on the particular issue. This pattern fails to fully support hypothesis D: Those in the majority responded in the looking-glass manner but those in the minority were uneasy—to varying degrees depending on the issue—about future support in public opinion.

Hypotheses A and B were taken directly from the theory of the spiral of silence. According to these hypotheses, perception of support in public opinion (present and/or future) makes people more willing to express their own opinions. These hypotheses were supported for those in the majority but usually not supported for those in the minority. For those in the minority, the relationship between perception of support and willingness to express one's opinion is positive for the nuclear energy issue, negative for the air pollution issue, and close to zero for the water pollution issue.

We developed an issue-by-issue explanation of the pattern of minority expression. Each explanation took note of the incentives for self-expression faced by those in the minority on any particular issue. An issue carries the potential for political conflict when those on both sides believe they can win. Therefore, this is the circumstance when there is the greatest incentive to work for one's position. If the level of confidence in victory becomes too low, the individual begins to worry about the risk of social isolation in expressing his views and begins to question whether or not it is a waste of resources (time, energy, money, etc.) to remain actively committed to his position. On the other hand, if victory seems assured, then the political actor will not take seriously the threat of political opposition and the level of commitment tends to fall off.

The explanatory variable in this argument changes the theoretical underpinning of the spiral of silence a little. Instead of fear of isolation as the motivating factor in self-expression (or self-repression), the arguments and explanations advanced here tend to look at the incentives and expected benefits arising from political expression under particular circumstances. The circumstances of expected benefit are informed by one's view of the level of current and future support in public opinion.

At this point we must reconsider whether or not the particular measure of "expression" used here has biased the results. (The reasons for using willingness to donate money as the indicator of expression are explained in footnote 5.) Certainly the willingness to donate money to a cause will be affected by the kinds of cost-benefit calculations discussed here. The question we must ask is: Will individual calculations about donating money be more sensitive to minority status and the chances of winning than other forms of expression such as attempting to persuade friends, wearing buttons, etc.? It is difficult to say for sure. It would be a welcome contribution to the literature on political participation to learn that different dimensions of participation (e.g., money-oriented vs. symbolic expression) are affected differently by the dynamics of the spiral of silence. On the other hand, it would be a welcome contribution to the literature on public choice and rational action to learn that calculations of expected return influence people's decisions about "spending" for the complete range of personal political resources. In other words, there is a basis for expecting either answer to the question about the appropriateness of the measure used here.

Finally, hypothesis E was confirmed for each issue: controlling for the other factors in the model, we find that those in the majority were more willing to express their opinions.

The theory of the spiral of silence is an important, empirically documented principle that helps answer the more general question of how people's perceptions and expectations can anticipate and possibly influence the outcome in collective situations. The theory of the spiral of silence explains how, in a situation of choice, one side can appear to become dominant in public opinion. As a recent presidential candidate has reminded us, sometimes the appearance of dominance—known as momentum or just "mo" by the cognoscenti—is enough to actually decide an issue. A formal interpretation of this argument is that in elections the appearance of dominance can influence certain elements of the process such as the availability of campaign funding (Committee on House Administration, 1973) or the will to continue the race for those without momentum. The literature on the spiral of silence usually argues, however, that at the end of the race there is not much influence of appearance on the outcome. In the privacy of the voting booth people's votes are rarely affected by their perception of the majority position.

Neighborhood racial tipping is another example of a phenomenon where the buildup of expectations regarding other people's preferences appears to be a decisive factor influencing the outcome. In this case it is the survey respondent himself who is in the position of the candidate needing momentum: The resources to continue, in this case, are the financial investments one might make in keeping up the property or the social investment one might make by deciding to stay in a neighborhood that might tip. In this situation, one's perception of the dominant public opinion—if it is negative—can close out one's willingness to invest in the area (Taylor, 1982a) and/or lead to a situation where people leave "because the neighborhood is tipping" (Taylor, 1982b).

The spiral of silence, particularly when augmented by the observations we have made on pluralistic ignorance and uncertainty, is an important tool for analyzing and explaining people's expectations of the outcomes of collective choice situations. It is only a short step to apply this reasoning to analyze those situations where the anticipated result decisively affects the outcome.

References

Allport, Floyd
1924 Social Psychology. New York: Houghton Mifflin.
Fields, James M., and Howard Schuman
1976 "Public beliefs about the beliefs of the public." Public Opinion Quarterly 40:427–48.
Committee on House Administration, U.S. House of Representatives
1973 Public Opinion Polls, Hearings on the Truth-in-Polling Act (H.R. 5003). Washington, D.C.: U.S. Government Printing Office.
Locke, John
1961 An Essay Concerning Human Understanding, Vol. 1, John W. Yolton (ed.). London: Dent.
Madison, James
1961 "The Federalist No. 49, February 9, 1788." Pp. 338–47 in Jacob E. Cooke, The Federalist. Middletown, Conn.: Wesleyan University Press.
Merton, Robert
1968 Social Theory and Social Structure. New York: The Free Press.
Noelle-Neumann, Elisabeth
1974 "The spiral of silence: a theory of public opinion." Journal of Communication 24:43–51.
1977 "Turbulences in the climate of opinion: methodological applications of the spiral of silence theory." Public Opinion Quarterly 41:143–58.
1979 "Public opinion and the classical tradition: a re-evaluation." Public Opinion Quarterly 43:143–56.
O'Gorman, Hubert
1975 "Pluralistic ignorance and white estimates of white support for racial segregation." Public Opinion Quarterly 39:313–30.
1979 "White and black perceptions of racial values." Public Opinion Quarterly 43:48–59.
1980 "False consciousness of kind: pluralistic ignorance among the aged." Research on Aging 2:105–28.
O'Gorman, Hubert, and Stephen Garry
1976 "Pluralistic ignorance—a replication and extension." Public Opinion Quarterly 40:449–58.
Taylor, D. Garth
1982a "Homeowner capital and the prisoner's dilemma in the market for housing rehabilitation in American cities." unpublished ms., Dept. of Political Science, University of Chicago.
1982b "On micromotives and neighborhood tipping: an analysis of incentives, expectations and actions in racially changing neighborhoods." unpublished ms., Dept. of Political Science, University of Chicago.

PART II

UNDERSTANDING TELEVISION

Concern with what is understood and recalled or, more to the point, what is misunderstood and forgotten, from what is attended to on television has been an important research focus in the past few years, and this topic has cut across a number of different disciplines. Below are reports of studies from advertising and marketing, from the study of news and from developmental psychology, and while the implications these contributors draw from their research go in different directions, in toto their studies elaborate more clearly how much, and what, is not getting through, and in some cases they suggest why.

The first four chapters in this section present and review a study sponsored by the American Association of Advertising Agencies of the extent of miscomprehension of advertising and nonadvertising content and the policy implications of miscomprehension. Jacob Jacoby and Wayne Hoyer, in the first chapter, suggest that a third to a quarter of televised content is, under optimal attention conditions, miscomprehended. In succeeding chapters, Ford and Yalch, and Mizerski raise methodological and conceptual issues from the study, and Jacoby and Hoyer reply.

Gunter and Woodall, Davis, and Sahin concern themselves with the comprehension of televised news. Gunter's brief review focuses on the reasons for poor news recall, and the Woodall, Davis, and Sahin chapter presents two models they suggest should be productive for future research in understanding viewer news comprehension.

Finally, Andrew Collins reviews recent literature from child development on child viewer comprehension to suggest what is required for viewer understanding of television. While what Collins presents applies most clearly to the young, important implications of this work might apply to other populations as well.

This chapter, and the three that follow, are discussions of an American Association of Advertising Agencies study directed at answering the questions of whether television viewers do miscomprehend televised communications and the extent of such miscomprehension, whether commercial advertising is more likely to be miscomprehended than other forms of televised communication, and whether miscomprehension is associated with certain demographic characteristics of viewers. The experiment suggests that a quarter to a third of televised content is miscomprehended, that short segments of entertainment and informational content are more likely to be miscomprehended than advertisements, and that miscomprehension is slightly related to age and educational level. This chapter, and the ones that follow, also discuss the implications of the findings for advertising research and public policy. Jacob Jacoby is Merchants' Council Professor of Marketing at New York University, and Wayne D. Hoyer is assistant professor of marketing at the University of Texas at Austin.

7

VIEWER MISCOMPREHENSION OF TELEVISED COMMUNICATION
Selected Findings

Jacob Jacoby and Wayne D. Hoyer

THE past decade has witnessed an increasing amount of attention paid to the issues of deceptive advertising, misleading advertising, corrective advertising and affirmative disclosure statements. This emphasis, however, has not yet addressed a logically prior set of questions concerning the existence, degree, correlates and causes of message miscompre-

Jacob Jacoby was Professor of Consumer Psychology and Wayne D. Hoyer was a doctoral candidate in the Department of Psychological Sciences at Purdue University at the time this study was conducted. Professor Jacoby is now Merchants' Council Professor of Marketing at New York University and Professor Hoyer is now Assistant Professor of Marketing, University of Texas at Austin. This paper is a highly condensed version of a monograph describing a recently conducted investigation sponsored by the American Association of Advertising Agencies (Jacoby, Hoyer and Sheluga 1980). Readers are directed to this source for answers to any questions this article leaves unanswered. The authors acknowledge with gratitude the many constructive contributions made by the members of the Academic and Industry Review Committees who monitored this project from inception to completion. The members of the Academic Review Committee were Jacob Cohen (New York University), Stephen Greyser (Harvard University) and William McGuire (Yale University). The Industry Review Committee consisted of Rena Bartos (J. Walter Thompson), Seymour Banks (Leo Burnett), Theodore Dunn (Benton and Bowles), and Benjamin Lipstein (originally at SSC&B, now at New York University). It should be noted that the grant was awarded with the written understanding that the results would be made public regardless of the nature of the findings.

hension. The evidence that is available in these regards tends to be fragmentary, anecdotal and impressionistic. At least since Lasswell (1948) comprehension has generally been considered a major result of the process of communication. Further, according to many formulations (Engel, Blackwell and Kollat 1978; Fishbein and Ajzen 1975; Lavidge and Steiner 1961; McGuire 1976), comprehension is assumed to be a logical antecedent to other effects—retention in memory, belief formation and change, attitude formation and change, and behavioral intentions—which are theorized to result from communication.

Miscomprehension—which results when the receiver extracts either an incorrect or a confused meaning from a communication (see Jacoby, Nelson and Hoyer 1982)—is essentially the converse of accurate comprehension. Although comprehension/miscomprehension has been studied extensively in various disciplines such as psychology and education, it is surprising to find little systematic attention to the subject of miscomprehension in regard to the mass media (Pool et al. 1973). Restricting analysis to television, a comprehensive review of 2500 published items in the scientific literature reveals only a handful of studies dealing with comprehension of television content, all of those employing samples of children (Comstock

Jacob Jacoby and Wayne D. Hoyer, "Viewer Miscomprehension of Televised Communication: Selected Findings." Reprinted by permission from *Journal of Marketing*, Vol. 46, No. 4 (Fall 1982), pp. 12-26, published by the American Marketing Association.

et al. 1978, pp. 270–276). Not a single investigation seems to have been conducted that employed adults as respondents.

Implicit in the arguments advanced by some consumer advocates seems to be the assumption that, if they worked at it, advertisers could make sure that their advertisements weren't miscomprehended (Gardner 1975, p. 46). A problem with this view, however, is that it ignores our contemporary understanding of the communication process. An alternative assumption is that virtually *all* forms of communication are subject to being miscomprehended. Stated somewhat differently, there is not necessarily any correspondence between a given communication as conveyed by the source and that same communication as interpreted and remembered by the receiver. This is because the meaning a receiver extracts from a given communication consists of both meaning asserted directly (as expressed in the message) and meaning inferred by the individual receiver. These inferred meanings are a unique function of each receiver's total sum of prior experiences and the set of expectations he/she brings to the situation (cf Harris and Monaco 1978).

If the alternative assumption is correct, then the fundamental question to be resolved is not "Does advertising cause miscomprehension?" but rather, "Is there actually a higher level of miscomprehension associated with advertising than with other comparable forms of mass media communication?" In other words, do advertisements exhibit relatively greater degrees of miscomprehension?

Given the lack of hard benchmark evidence, the Educational Foundation of the American Association of Advertising Agencies decided to fund three investigations on the questions surrounding miscomprehension. This report is a highly condensed summary of the basic findings generated by the first of these investigations. The primary objectives of this investigation were:

- To determine whether viewers do, in fact, miscomprehend televised communications.[1]

- Assuming that some degree of miscomprehension is detected, to determine whether there is a "normative range" of miscomprehension associated with televised communications.

- To determine whether commercial advertising tends to have a rate of miscomprehension that differs from rates for other forms of televised communications.

- To determine whether viewer groups possessing certain demographic characteristics are more

prone to miscomprehending televised communications than are others.

Method

Given these objectives, three core concepts needed to be operationalized. These were communications, viewers and miscomprehension. We concentrate here on describing what was actually done. A detailed discussion of the underlying conceptual rationale is provided in Jacoby, Hoyer and Sheluga (1980, Ch. 2).

Communications

Sixty different communications that had actually been broadcast over TV during the six months spanning the last quarter of 1978 and first quarter of 1979 constituted the set of test communications. These communications were representative of most material being broadcast over commercial television. The set of 60 communications can be grouped into three categories: commercial advertising, noncommercial advertising and program excerpts. Each of these major categories can be further subdivided as shown in Figure 1.

Product/service advertising represents the most common form of advertising appearing on television. These are communications that attempt to persuade the viewer to purchase or use the brand, product or service being advertised. In contrast, image ads are designed simply to enhance the image of the corporate sponsor and do not promote the sale of any specific product or service.

The product/service advertisements were selected on the basis of several criteria. Most important among these was probably the requirement that the ads be highly representative of most commercial television advertising. Accordingly, Bureau of Advertising Re-

FIGURE 1
Types of Communication Studied

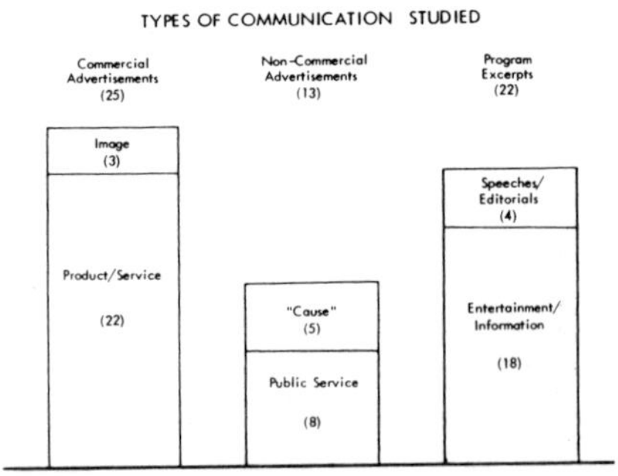

---

[1] Given that the major share of national advertising expenditures is devoted to television and regulatory interest has been most evident in this medium, attention was confined to televised communications.

search data were used to identify the 33 product classes having the highest expenditures for advertising over network TV during 1977. Together these 33 categories accounted for more than 62% of all TV product/service network advertising during 1977. A subset of 11 classes (passenger cars, cereals, beer, headache remedies, cold and cough remedies, department stores, restaurants, heavy duty detergents, cameras, small appliances and medicated skin products) was identified and ads were selected for two different brands from each of these 11 categories. The first three categories alone accounted for 12% of all commercials appearing on network television during calendar year 1977.

Cause advertisements may be distinguished from *public service announcements* on the basis of which party—the source or the recipient of the communication—stands to benefit most if the recipient engages in the advocated action. Cause advertisements (e.g., "Support the United Negro College Fund") are ones from which the source stands to benefit the most, while public service announcements (e.g., "Stay alive, drive 55") are ones from which the viewer stands to benefit most.

Finally, program content was subdivided into a subset of speeches and editorials and a second subset of entertainment and information programs. Examination of *TV Guide* suggested that most regularly scheduled TV content could be grouped into one of the following nine major categories: national news programs, local news programs, comedy programs, adventure/suspense programs, crime/detective programs, interview/talk programs, documentaries, religious programs and educational programs. Two specific programs were selected from each of these nine program categories to comprise the Entertainment and Information subset.

All 60 test communications were 30 seconds in length. This meant that the 38 advertising communications were presented in their entirety. In order to make the 22 program excerpts as equivalent to these communications as possible, the segments tested were all 30 seconds in duration and focused on a "product equivalent" (i.e., a single topic, object or event for which it was possible to assess comprehension; see Table 1 for two examples).[2] It could be argued that this procedure favored better comprehension for advertising compared to program excerpts, since commercial messages are designed to communicate information for a persuasive purpose in exactly 30 seconds. This is rarely the case with programs. However, consider the procedural alternatives.

---

[2]The "product equivalent" refers to a focused, single concrete object or event (such as the discussion of typhoid in the "Quincy" example), whose discrete nature was considered a prerequisite for testing each of the program excerpts studied.

TABLE 1
Two Examples of "Product Equivalent" Segments

"Quincy" Program Excerpt

(Quincy says): Mr. Turner, we're dealing with typhoid fever here. I mean for your protection and for your wife's, I have to know exactly how you made contact with the body.

(Mrs. Turner says): You mean, we might catch typhoid?

(Quincy says): That's possible; typhoid is a contact disease.

(Mrs. Turner says): You mean, ah, if Alan had it and I touched him, that I might get it?

(Quincy says): Well, not necessarily touch, but you could get it by close contact, I mean living together.

(Mrs. Turner says): Well, ah, what should we do? Shouldn't we have shots or something?

(Quincy says): A communicable disease unit will be down here shortly. They'll give you proper medication.

55 MPH Saves Lives (Department of Transportation Advertisement)

(Announcer): At 55 mph you save gasoline, which is real money these days. At 55, you save yourself troubles you really don't need. But 55 mph saves more than that; 55 saves lives.

Since 1974, 55 has been the single biggest factor in reducing highway deaths—by more than 36,000 people. One of them could be you. 55 saves lives.

First, product–service advertisements of 30 minutes' duration simply do not exist. Even if a few did exist, utilizing these would have meant utilizing atypical advertisements, thereby preventing any meaningful generalization to advertising at large.

An alternative, comparing the miscomprehension rates of 30-second commercials to those for 30-minute or one-hour programs, was considered and deemed inappropriate. Clearly, too many serious confounding factors would have been involved in such a procedure. For example, (1) vastly different amounts of information are contained in 30-second vs. 30-minute communications; (2) the vastly different amounts of informational content would have created problems in the sampling of this content for purposes of generating equivalently difficult and exhaustive miscomprehension quizzes; (3) different attention spans would necessarily be involved; (4) even volunteer viewers could not be expected to give equivalent and consistent amounts of attention across such vastly different exposure times; (5) different forgetting curves would be expected, thereby making it especially difficult to test comprehension of material appearing near the beginning of the longer communications. Further, utilizing entire programs rather than segments would have substantially increased the time each respondent had to serve as a subject. Given reliance on volunteer subjects, this alternative would most likely have produced a much more biased sample.

With these problems in mind, it was decided that the best alternative was to locate 30-second segments that could be interpreted easily without viewing the rest of the communication.

Viewers

The sample consisted of 2,700 people, aged 13 years and older. This number of subjects was based on a consideration of the sampling plan for communications and the planned procedural and analytical designs.[3] Sampling quotas ensured that there were equal numbers of males and females tested at each of the following age brackets: 13–17, 18–24, 25–34, 35–44, 45–54, 55–64, and over 65.

When compared to U.S. Census Bureau data, the sample was found to be adequately representative of the U.S. population in terms of years of formal schooling completed, household income claimed for the preceding year, marital status and race. However, as a whole, the sample claimed to be more highly educated and reported a higher level of prior year's income than did the population at large. If anything, these differences could be anticipated to generate higher levels of correct comprehension.

A convenience sample of 225 people was used at each of the 12 central location testing sites. These were situated in shopping malls around the continental U.S. Each viewer was exposed to two of the 60 test communications. Therefore, 30 respondents, each viewing two test communications, were required to obtain one replicate for the full set of 60 test communications. Since it was believed that 90 replicates (or 90 viewers per communication) would be adequate for detecting difference, the total sample required was $(30 \times 90 =) 2,700$ people. It should be noted that all the major analyses were based on *categories* of communication, not on one single communication vs. another. This meant that in virtually no case were there less than several hundred respondents per analysis.

The testing locations were in 12 different shopping malls in New York, Philadelphia, Atlanta, Miami, Detroit, Indianapolis, Kansas City, Oklahoma City, San Antonio, Denver, Los Angeles and San Francisco. The research setting consisted of the testing facilities available at the different malls. All testing rooms were equipped with standard ¾" videotape playback equipment so the communications could be viewed on standard TV monitors.

Miscomprehension

A six-item miscomprehension quiz (patterned after Preston and Scharbach 1971) was administered after exposure to each communication. Each quiz consisted of six brief statements that sampled the universe of

important information content regarding the object of that communication. Viewers were asked to indicate whether each statement was true or false based upon what was stated or implied in the communication.[4] Two of the six statements on each quiz were accurate (i.e., true); four were inaccurate (i.e., false). Half related to objective facts (i.e., they were accurate statements of what had been asserted directly in the communication) and half to inferences that could be drawn from what was stated in the communication regarding the product (or product equivalent). Thus, each quiz consisted of:

- one accurate restatement or paraphrase of an objectively ascertainable fact that was explicitly stated in the communication;

- two inaccurate restatements or paraphrases of objectively ascertainable fact that was explicitly stated in the communication;

- one statement representing an accurate inference that could be drawn from the communication; and

- two statements representing inaccurate inferences that could be drawn from the communication.

How these statements were apportioned is indicated in Table 2, and the quizzes actually used for the two communications cited in Table 1 are provided in Table 3. Subsequent analyses revealed that the tests were of comparable difficulty across the different types of communications. Parenthetically, an early concern was that so much information would be compressed into a single 30-second communication that it would be difficult to determine just which of these items should be represented in the quiz, i.e., there would be a "sampling of information content" problem. In fact, the original intent was to construct quizzes having more than six items. However, the problem of having too much informational content to choose from did not materialize. By restricting attention to the product or product equivalent and focusing on information that would be considered material for evaluation and/or decision making (e.g., the color of the package would *not* be considered an example of material information), we were usually left with just enough useful information out of which to construct a six-item quiz. Our experience in this regard is in keeping with the findings reported by Resnik and Stern (1977). In addition, it should be mentioned that the judgment of "correctness" or "incorrectness" of each statement was judged *independently* by each of three members of the research team. Only items ex-

---

[3]Our thanks to Professor Jacob Cohen of New York University, our statistical consultant on the project, for his invaluable assistance at this and many other points throughout this investigation.

[4]It should be noted that while multiple choice items were considered a potentially attractive mode of questioning, it was felt that the limited content of the segments made multiple choice questions too difficult to formulate.

TABLE 2
Composition of the Miscomprehension Quizzes
(numbers of quiz items)

	Facts	Inferences	Total
Accurate	1	1	2
Inaccurate	2	2	4
Total	3	3	6

hibiting complete agreement across all three judges were included in the quizzes.

It is important to point out that six quiz items does not mean that six different claims or "copy points" were tested. When counting claims or copy points no advertiser includes points that might be inferred—since the number of such inferences that might be made is virtually limitless and often represent the viewer's unique perspective. Thus, the three "factual" items on each quiz were capable of assessing only three different copy points at most. However, since two (and sometimes all three) of these items often addressed the same point, in the majority of instances, each six-item quiz assessed two different copy points at most.

Several points should be made regarding the assessment procedures. First, since interest focused spe-

TABLE 3
Two Examples of Miscomprehension Quizzes*

Quiz for the "Quincy" Excerpt
A/R 1. Typhoid fever can be caught by living with someone who has typhoid fever.
I/R 2. Typhoid fever is *not* a contact disease.
A/I 3. The man in the scene may have caught typhoid fever by touching a dead body.
I/I 4. The husband and wife have been diagnosed as having typhoid fever.
I/R 5. The doctor in this scene will administer the proper medication for typhoid fever.
I/I 6. No cure has yet been found for typhoid fever.

Quiz for the "Drive 55" Advertisement
I/R 1. Driving at 55 miles per hour does *not* save you money.
A/I 2. It is safer to drive at 55 miles per hour than to drive at higher speeds.
I/R 3. The 55 miles per hour speed limit is *not* the single biggest factor in reducing highway deaths.
I/I 4. Motorists should drive at 55 miles per hour at all times.
I/I 5. Since 55 miles per hour is a safe speed limit, seat belts no longer have to be used.
A/R 6. More than 36,000 traffic deaths have been prevented by the 55 miles per hour speed limit.

*Note: A/R = Accurate restatement (fact)
I/R = Inaccurate restatement (fact)
A/I = Accurate inference
I/I = Inaccurate inference

cifically and exclusively on miscomprehension and not on any of the prior (attention, awareness, self-exposure) or subsequent (attitudes, intentions, behavior) effects usually theorized to result from communication, the forced exposure procedure was considered sufficient for ensuring that exposure, awareness and attention had occurred at levels at least as high as those typically achieved under normal viewing conditions.

Second, miscomprehension was assessed immediately after exposure to each communication (rather than after exposure to both communications) because of the rapid decay of memory traces found with such communications. As one example, Bogart (1967, pp. 109–110) cites research to indicate that fewer than 20% of a group of 5,275 respondents could recall the identity of the TV commercial they had viewed just a few minutes earlier. Other problems with delayed recall in advertising research are noted by Percy (1978). Immediate assessment implies that our measurement of miscomprehension was not "pure," i.e., it was confounded with short-term (i.e., one-to-three-minute) recall. However, immediate assessment seemed preferable to measuring comprehension concurrent with viewing, and highly preferable to assessing it 24 hours later when many other extraneous factors could have influenced and diluted the effect.

Third, subjects were told to base their responses on the information contained in the communication, not on what they generally believed. Specifically, the following instructions were read aloud: "Here are a few statements about the (film clip) you just saw. *Based upon* the film clip, please indicate whether the statements are true or false by circling the correct answer. Remember, base your answers only upon the film clip you just saw." The following phrase was repeated at the top of each quiz. "Based on what you've just seen, indicate whether each statement is true or false." It is recognized, however, that in those situations where the audience's prior knowledge was in conflict with the message, the audience may have answered in accord with their prior experience rather than with the message content.

Fourth, the procedures involved two sets of counterbalancing. On the one hand, the order of presentation of test stimuli was counterbalanced for main effects due to order. That is, since each communication was presented a total of 90 times, it was presented first in 45 cases and last in the other 45 cases. On the other hand, to eliminate geographic biases, each of the 60 communications was tested at each site. Since each communication was involved in 90 separate tests, no less than seven nor more than eight of these tests took place at any one of the 12 testing sites.

All interviewing took place from April 17 through May 5, 1979.

Selected Findings

Before discussing the findings as they relate to our objectives, it needs to be pointed out that a series of multiple regression analyses were conducted to determine whether variations in communication complexity, communication familiarity, product awareness-trial-usage,[5] order of testing, or testing site exerted any appreciable effect on the miscomprehension scores obtained. In none of these analyses did these covar-

iates cumulatively explain more than 8.4% of the variation in the scores. This result suggests that, at least for this study, miscomprehension appears to be unaffected by variations in these factors. One possible explanation for this finding may be that complexity varied only slightly across the messages (perhaps because all messages were limited to 30 seconds in duration), such that most were very simple messages.

Objective 1: Does Miscomprehension Occur?

The question "Does miscomprehension occur?" can be rephrased as three separate questions: (a) What proportion of viewers miscomprehended at least some portion of the communications they viewed? (b) What proportion of the meanings in the test communications was miscomprehended? (c) What proportion of the set of 60 test communications was miscomprehended?

Proportion of viewers who miscomprehended. Only 16.8% of the viewers "fully comprehended" (i.e., were able to answer correctly all six quiz items for) either the first or second communication that they viewed. This result means that in 83.2% of the 5,400 viewings (2,700 viewers × 2 test communications

---

[5]Complexity was assessed via a battery of eight separate indices consisting of a copy point index. assessments of both visual and auditory complexity (see Watt and Krull 1974). and an assessment of the difficulty level of the verbal copy (using the Farr, Jenkins and Paterson 1951 version of the Flesch count). Familiarity was assessed with a series of three questions: "(1) To the best of your knowledge. have you ever seen this particular (ad/announcement/segment) before? (2) Approximately how many times have you seen this particular (ad/announcement/segment)? (3) Other than this particular (ad/announcement/segment) have you seen any other (ads/announcements/segments) for this very same (product/service/subject)?" Finally. product awareness, trial and usage were measured with a series of two questions: "(1) Have you, yourself, ever bought the product that was advertised in the commercial you just saw? (2) Whether you've bought the product or not. have you ever used the product?"

FIGURE 2
Extent To Which TV Communications Are
Miscomprehended

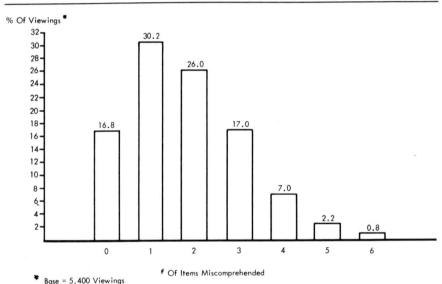

% Of Viewings*

* Base = 5,400 Viewings

Of Items Miscomprehended

FIGURE 3
Extent To Which Viewers Miscomprehended TV
Communications

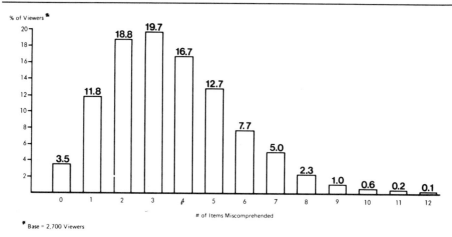

* Base = 2,700 Viewers

each), viewers miscomprehended at least some portion of the communications viewed. However, while perfect comprehension was relatively uncommon, in almost half (16.8 + 30.2 = 47%) of the 5,400 viewings, viewers misunderstood no more than one out of the six quiz items (see Figure 2). Correctly comprehending the content of one communication did not mean that that person was necessarily able to comprehend correctly another communication. In fact, of the 16.8% who fully comprehended one of the test communications (in the sense of answering all six quiz items correctly), most (13.3%) miscomprehended some portion of the second communication that they saw. That is, only 3.5% of the viewers fully comprehended both test communications to which they were exposed (i.e., answered all 12 items correctly; see Figure 3).

Proportions of meanings miscomprehended. One may also ask, "To what extent was the content of the 60 test communications miscomprehended?" In terms of the overall mean, 29.6% of the (2,700 respondents × 2 communications per respondent × 6 quiz items per communication =) 32,400 meanings that were tested were answered incorrectly. Both the median and modal rates of overall miscomprehension were 28%. These averages underestimate the actual amount of miscomprehension since they do not adjust for instances where viewers who did not know the correct

answer managed to guess correctly.[6]

Proportion of communications miscomprehended. The proportion of communications that were miscomprehended was 100%. That is, at least some degree of miscomprehension was associated with every test communication. Across the set of 60 test communications the level of miscomprehension of communication content ranged from a low of 11% to a high of 50% (actually 10.8% and 50.5%, respectively). These are depicted graphically in Figure 4.

In sum, regardless of whether considered in terms of viewers, meanings or communications, the answer to the first research question is a resounding "yes." As assessed here, miscomprehension of televised communications does occur and seems to be far more prevalent than might have been anticipated. Perfect

[6]According to Professor Jacob Cohen, the actual rate of miscomprehension, when corrected for guessing using conventional approaches, is likely to be considerably greater than the rate observed. With an observed miscomprehension rate of .30, the conventional psychometric model for true-false items would estimate the "true" rate of correct comprehension as 2(.70) − 1 = .40, hence the "true" rate of miscomprehension as a substantial .60. Since the conventional model makes rather simplistic assumptions (e.g., comprehension is all-or-none; or, when the correct answer to an item is not known, guessing occurs with .5 expectancy of success), this correction for guessing is not entirely defensible. However, the application of any rational model that corrects for guessing would have yielded miscomprehension rates that were substantially greater than the observed rates.

FIGURE 4
Percent of Miscomprehension Associated With
Each of 60 Test Communications

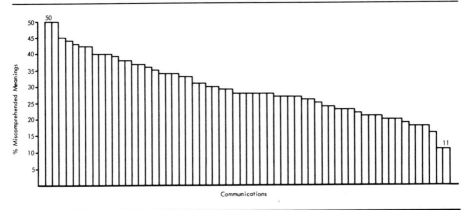

comprehension rarely occurs and may not be generally attainable.

Objective 2: What is the Typical Range of Miscomprehension?

The degree of miscomprehension associated with the most miscomprehended communication was almost five times larger than that associated with the least miscomprehended communication (50% vs. 11%). This raises the question of whether a typical or standard range of miscomprehension can be identified that adequately describes the rate of miscomprehension for most forms of televised communication. The interquartile range (that is, the range encompassed by the middlemost 50% of the test communications) was used to arrive at such an estimate.[7]

Considering the entire set of 60 test communications, the interquartile range was 13%, extending from 23% to 36%. Generalizing from these data suggests that one might expect anywhere from one-fourth to one-third of the material information content contained in communications that are broadcast over commercial television to be miscomprehended.

Objective 3: Is Advertising Less Miscomprehended than Nonadvertising?

Program excerpts vs. commercial advertising vs. noncommercial advertising. Based on the sample of 60 test communications, program excerpts were associated with a significantly[8] higher rate of miscomprehension ($\bar{x}$ = 32.2%) than were either commercial ($\bar{x}$ = 28.3%) or noncommercial ($\bar{x}$ = 27.6%) advertisements. However, this difference is quite small and, though statistically significant, may be considered trivial in practical terms. The interquartile ranges for the three sets of communications are as follows:

Program excerpts	27%–38%
Commercial advertising	22%–34%
Noncommercial advertising	22%–35%

Viewers who miscomprehended program excerpts vs. commercial advertising vs. noncommercial advertising. As might be expected, a similar pattern emerged when the percentage of viewers who miscomprehended the three types of communications was examined. Those communications that tended to be associated with higher levels of miscomprehended content were misunderstood by a larger proportion of viewers. The percent of viewers miscomprehending at least some portion of the communications that they viewed was 84.5% for program excerpts, 81.3% for com-

---

[7]The interquartile range was employed in preference to "plus-or-minus one standard deviation from the mean" for two main reasons: The distribution of miscomprehension scores was decidedly not normal, and the interquartile range lends itself more easily to layman comprehension.

[8]All statements of "significance" refer to statistical significance at the p = .01 level or better.

mercial advertisements and 82.7% for noncommercial ads.

Product-service advertising vs. entertainment information program excerpts. The broad three-category classification system has the potential to obscure what is perhaps the most interesting comparison of all, namely, the contrast between product-service advertising on the one hand and entertainment-information program excerpts on the other. These are the two most frequently broadcast kinds of communication appearing on network television. As noted in Figure 1, this investigation examined 22 exemplars of product-service advertising and 18 exemplars of entertainment and information programs. Are these two kinds of televised communications associated with different levels of miscomprehension?

The answer is "yes." Entertainment-information program excerpts were associated with a small but significantly higher rate of miscomprehension than were product-service advertisements. The mean levels of miscomprehension were 31.0% and 28.8%, and the interquartile ranges extended from 27% to 37% and 22% to 34% respectively. It should be remembered, however, that the program excerpts may be at a disadvantage, since they are incomplete segments.

The miscomprehension of public affairs programming. One interesting finding was the high rate of miscomprehension associated with the restatement of factual information contained in public affairs programs editorials. Since the ramifications of this finding are quite substantial, they caused us to look more closely at these data, particularly the data for the four newscast excerpts. Our concern stems from the following observations:

> When the public focuses on news, television increasingly has received acclaim. In 1960 television was slightly overshadowed by newspapers in being judged by the public as the principal source of news, the provider of the most complete coverage and the most credible source. By 1970 television has become the unambiguous leader on all these counts (Comstock et al. 1978, p. 8).

> Meanwhile, television's popularity as the nation's primary news source has climbed steadily, standing first with 51% in 1959 and with 67% according to the Roper poll for 1978. Audiences for the three TV network newscasts, estimated at slightly more than 35 million in 1968, had grown to more than 47 million by November 1978. Among all media, TV news rated first in credibility, leading newspapers two to one. And this approval was not undeserved (Barrett and Sklar 1980, p. 8).

TABLE 4
Miscomprehension Rates Associated with News-Oriented Televised Communications*

Nature of the Communication**	% Miscomprehension
Local editorial (Indianapolis ABC affiliate)	50%
Local news (Indianapolis ABC affiliate)	43%
President Carter's Press Conference on China (January 1979)	35%
President Carter's State of the Union Address (January 1979)	34%
"Meet the Press"	31%
Local news (Indianapolis NBC affiliate)	30%
Republican response to State of the Union Address (January 1979)	27%
National network news (CBS—Cronkite)	27%
National network news (NBC—Brinkley)	26%
Average % miscomprehension 33.67%	

*Taken from Jacoby, Hoyer and Sheluga 1980, p. 68–69.
**Except as indicated, all test communications had actually been broadcast during November and December of 1978.

Nine of the 60 test communications were segments taken from Presidential addresses, national network news, local news and local editorials (see Table 4). There was greater miscomprehension evidenced among this set of public affairs communications (34.7%) than among the remaining 51 communications (28.7%). The two examples of local news ranked 5th and 25th most miscomprehended (with miscomprehension rates of 43% and 30%), while the two examples of national network news ranked 36th and 40th (with miscomprehension rates of 27% and 26%). If U.S. citizens do indeed rely most heavily on TV to keep informed of the important events occurring in their world, and assuming our data are anywhere close to being a reasonable estimate of miscomprehension, then these data suggest cause for concern.

Objective 4: Are There Demographic Differences Associated with Miscomprehension?

A number of different demographic characteristics were assessed. These included the respondents' sex, age, marital status, employment status, race, years of formal education and household income for the preceding year. Only two of these factors—age ($r = .12$, $p < .001$) and education ($r = -.13$, $p < .001$)—were significantly related to miscomprehension. Both younger and older viewers were more likely to miscomprehend the communications, and miscomprehension appears to decrease (although not appreciably) as amount of formal education increases. Figures 5 and 6 depict these relationships. It can be seen that

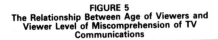

FIGURE 5
The Relationship Between Age of Viewers and
Viewer Level of Miscomprehension of TV
Communications

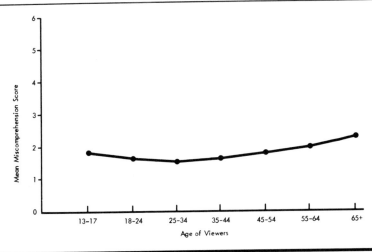

again, while statistically significant, for all intents and purposes these relationships are so weak as to have little practical applicability.

Miscomprehension rates for facts vs. inferences and accurate vs. inaccurate statements. An additional interesting question concerns the differences in miscomprehension rates across different types of questions. Two major findings are worth noting. First, across all 60 test communications the miscomprehension rate was higher for the 240 inaccurate statements (34.7%) than it was for 120 accurate statements (19.4%). Thus, it appears that subjects had greater difficulty answering the incorrect statements. Second, factual statements exhibited a slightly higher rate of miscomprehension (30.78%) than did inferential statements (28.40%). While this difference is statistically significant (due to the large sample size), the magnitude of the difference is quite small.

Discussion

Based upon the assessment procedures used and findings obtained, six specific conclusions appear justified. *First,* a large proportion of the American television viewing audience tends to miscomprehend communications broadcast over commercial televi-

sion. The vast majority (96.5%) of the 2,700 respondents in this investigation miscomprehended at least some portion of the 60 seconds' worth of televised communications that they viewed. *Second,* it would appear that no communication is immune from being miscomprehended. Every test communication was miscomprehended at least some of the time by some of the viewers.

Third, the average amount of miscomprehension associated with each of the 60 test communications was 30% (actually 29.61%). In other words, approximately 30% of the relevant informational content contained within each communication was miscomprehended. *Fourth,* as a preliminary estimate, the typical range of miscomprehension is 29.5% ± 6.5%. That is, typical TV communications seem to have their content miscomprehended at frequencies anywhere from 23% to 36%.

Fifth, nonadvertising communications were associated with significantly higher levels of miscomprehension than were advertising communications. Of particular interest, excerpts of TV programs were miscomprehended at higher levels than were commercial advertisements (for products-brands-services). However, though statistically significant, these differences are practically trivial. *Finally,* for all prac-

FIGURE 6
The Relationship Between Education of Viewers
and Viewer Level of Miscomprehension of TV
Communications

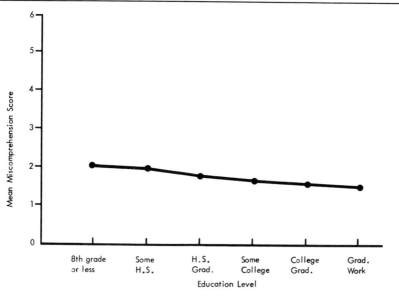

tical purposes no major demographic variables appear to be meaningfully associated with miscomprehension. Miscomprehension seems to be widespread throughout the populace, occurring at all age, income and educational levels in our society and to the same degree.[9]

The Limitations of Our Findings

Inasmuch as this investigation seems to be the first systematic attempt to focus explicitly on the *miscomprehension* of televised communications by adults (see Comstock et al. 1978), *the findings obtained are considered tentative* and in need of corroboration and refinement. They represent preliminary "ballpark estimates" and should be treated as such; that is, they are suggestive, not definitive. In particular, several important limitations must be discussed.

Most importantly, the reliability and construct va-

lidity of the miscomprehension measurements need to be established. This accuracy is especially important because of several factors that may threaten the validity of the present indices. It might be argued that the miscomprehension index is biased because for each quiz, four of the items had false answers and only two had true answers. Since there may be a tendency for individuals to give more true than false answers when there is some uncertainty, this bias would produce a lower miscomprehension score than the 29.6% obtained with quizzes having four true and two false answers. However, the actual amount by which the miscomprehension score would have been lower would have been negligible. Across all 60 communications the average miscomprehension rate for all 120 true items was 19.47% and the average miscomprehension rate for all 240 false items was 34.68%. Thus, a reasonable estimate of what the overall miscomprehension would likely have been for quizzes consisting of three true and three false items would be (19.47 + 19.47 + 19.47 + 34.68 + 34.68 + 34.68 ÷ 6 =) 27.1%. In other words, the expected

---

[9] This finding would suggest that the upward bias in sampling reported earlier did not have a major impact on results of the study.

difference between what was obtained (29.6%) and what might have been obtained (27.1%) is a negligible 2.5%. Also, it is interesting that there was such a large difference in the percent of correct answers (19.5% for true and 34.7% for false). This difference (15.2%) exceeds any other systematic difference in the study and points to the need for additional research.

Another problem with the miscomprehension measure is that the accuracy of the statements was based on the consensus of the three investigators. No independent confirmation was secured, due to the necessity for preserving the anonymity of the 25 commercial communications. Parenthetically, since both the text of the communication and the six-item quiz for that communication are provided in the full report for the 35 noncommercial communications, independent confirmation for these stimuli is always possible. In any event, future research would do well to employ a more objective basis for establishing these judgments.

National advertisements are typically pretested before being broadcast, while other televised communications are not. However, this pretesting generally involves assessing awareness, recall, attitudes and intentions. Although accurate comprehension of the message is generally not assessed, it sometimes becomes apparent that the advertisement is not being properly comprehended. Accordingly, it could be argued that obvious causes of miscomprehension are eliminated from many advertisements, whereas such is not the case with other televised communications.

The possibility exists that viewers may have understood the communications but miscomprehended the test questions. Unfortunately, this cannot be determined from the present data. The only thing that can be said is that if such a possibility did occur, then it was potentially equally distributed across all types of communication. When the above considerations are coupled with the fact that viewers received only one exposure to the communication, it may be argued that the miscomprehension rate has been overestimated. On the other hand, there are compensating factors that may lead to an underestimate of the miscomprehension rate that occurs under naturalistic conditions. The participants were volunteers who underwent a forced, relatively uncluttered exposure procedure. They were, therefore, more motivated, able and likely to attend to the communications than would have been the case had they viewed these communications under normal conditions. This combination of factors should lead to reduced selective attention and reception and improved comprehension. Moreover, we have not adjusted our comprehension rates for guessing. Had we applied any of the conventional models used to correct for guessing on true-false items, the "true" rate of correct comprehension would have been substantially lower, i.e., there would have been more miscomprehension.

It could be argued that comprehension in the real world should be defined in terms of what the audience can recall, not the total message content. In other words, is it important that individuals understand what they cannot remember? Accordingly, the authors are undertaking the examination of responses to open-ended questions that were collected immediately prior to the closed-ended responses reported here.

One final question concerns why the advertisements were not interspersed within actual programs, thereby making the test situation a more faithful analog of the real world. While it would have been advantageous in terms of matching reality, substantial problems are associated with employing such a procedure. Aside from the peculiar and very real problem of being able to employ the same procedure for the program excerpts, the greater the delay between exposure to a test communication and the assessment of its effects, the lower and more distorted the recall of that communication is likely to be. The net result would likely have been higher rates of miscomprehension.

Thus, it is clear that this investigation needs to be replicated by other investigators using other test communications, other samples of respondents, other measures of miscomprehension and other measurement procedures. Only after such systematic exploration is accomplished and the data from these different investigations appear to be in general correspondence will one be able to say that the rate of miscomprehension has been effectively mapped.

Some corroboration has already been accomplished. An earlier investigation by Chaiken and Eagly (1976), using college students and specially designed persuasive communications, obtained a mean miscomprehension rate of 38% for their televised communications (as derived by the present authors from the Chaiken and Eagly data). Another investigation by Lipstein (1980), using in-home testing procedures and content and commercials broadcast over the CBS show "Sixty Minutes," obtained miscomprehension rates of 30% to 42%. Two recently completed investigations by the present authors (one of which used questions and answers from the 1980 televised debate between presidential candidates Carter and Reagan) obtained miscomprehension rates varying from 22% to 29%. Accordingly, the estimate obtained in the present investigation would seem to be an acceptable first approximation.

The Implication of Our Findings

This investigation again reveals a fundamental truth: the mere provision of information does not automatically mean it will have any effect, much less the intended effect (cf Jacoby 1974; Jacoby, Chestnut and Silberman 1977). Rather, the receiver/viewer brings a storehouse of past experience and an ongoing mental set to each communication transaction and tends to interpret and misinterpret communications in terms of these mental phenomena. Given that it is not possible to eradicate either the influence of past experience or the individual's current mental set, it may well be impossible to eradicate miscomprehension. This argument leads directly to a set of implications for public policy makers, educators and researchers alike.

Perhaps the most fundamental implication for policy makers is that just because there is a demonstrable degree of miscomprehension associated with a particular advertisement, it does not necessarily mean that that particular advertisment contains something out of the ordinary to provoke miscomprehension. Such an assumption may be totally unwarranted. Indeed, the findings of the present investigation suggest that a certain frequency of miscomprehension may simply reflect a natural error rate associated with all types of televised communications. The ramifications that this implication has for such regulatory actions as cease and desist orders, corrective advertising and affirmative disclosure orders are substantial.

Of course, a reasonable argument is that the consequences of miscomprehending most TV programs tend to be trivial when compared to the consequences of miscomprehending, and then acting upon, advertising. Hence, the miscomprehension rate for advertising should be lower than that for other forms of televised communication. While the authors might be persuaded that advertising miscomprehension rates are probably unacceptably high, we find completely unreasonable any attempt to use "zero-based miscomprehension" as the criterion for evaluating advertising and as a basis for formulating public policy.

Perhaps the data from the present investigation (assuming corroboration and replication by others) might serve a useful function in this regard. Regulatory interest in correcting misleading and/or deceptive advertising might use the boundary separating the third and fourth quartiles of communications as a triggering mechanism, so that advertising that exceeds this level, while not automatically considered deceptive or misleading, would be targeted for further scrutiny. Of course, any attempt to employ such a cutoff level would have to accommodate the fact that the data adduced here probably underestimate the extent of miscomprehension present under normal viewing conditions. Further, it needs to be recognized that there may be instances (as in the case of over-the-counter and prescription pharmaceutical products) where miscomprehension rates of 10% or even 5% might be deemed totally unacceptable (see Jacoby and Small 1975).

There are parallel implications for advertisers. First, recognizing that some degree of miscomprehension is likely associated with any ad and may, if detected at sufficiently high levels, become the focus of regulatory attention, advertisers might be encouraged to pressure their advertising departments and advertising agencies for lower rates of miscomprehension. Aside from concern over possible regulatory activity, there is a very practical reason for engaging in such research. By lowering the rate of miscomprehension, the advertiser would ensure that more of his/her advertising message has been received as intended. Indeed, it may be that the syndicated advertising evaluation services might be encouraged to devise and provide a "miscomprehension index" along with the other standard communication impact indices that they currently provide.

This concern is not meant to imply that comprehension is the only important measure of advertising effectiveness. Indeed, the other stages of the communication process are equally vital. Rather, it is merely suggested that comprehension is an important step in ensuring the desired message reception and impact. Future research is also needed to determine the causes of miscomprehension. Before miscomprehension can be reduced, advertisers must clearly understand why and under what circumstances miscomprehension occurs. Unfortunately, little insight on this important topic is provided by the present study.

Another implication—one that is consistent with much previous research—is that broadcast advertising may not be a suitable medium for communicating substantial amounts of product information, particularly complex product information. In terms of the classical hierarchy-of-effects conceptualization (Lavidge and Steiner 1961) and more contemporary models of consumer decision making (e.g., Engel, Blackwell and Kollat 1978), perhaps the basic function of advertising is simply to stimulate awareness and generate problem recognition. Labeling and other information sources would seem to be better vehicles for providing the detailed supporting information.

Yet another implication derives from the finding of substantial miscomprehension associated with news programming content. Given that the U.S. populace relies more heavily on TV than it does on any other medium for its daily news (Barrett and Sklar 1980, p. 8; Comstock et al. 1978, p. 8), it should be obvious that considerable effort needs to be expended to make such programming more easily comprehended by the average viewer.

A final word is in order regarding the possibility of reducing miscomprehension rates to zero or near zero levels. The authors believe it will not be possible to reduce miscomprehension to a zero base level. That is, perfect comprehension of televised communication will not be generally attainable. At least four lines of thought lead to this conclusion.

First, language is an imprecise means of communicating meaning. Many words and phrases have multiple meanings, and the particular meaning extracted by one person is often not the same as the meaning extracted by another. Moreover, when words are conveyed only through the audio channel—as is the case with most televised communication—words that are similar or sound alike are even more likely to be confused, thereby exacerbating the problem. In those instances where only one meaning is intended by the source and may be considered the "correct" meaning, extracting some other meaning will necessarily mean that the receiver has miscomprehended the communication.

Second, numerous behavioral science studies have indicated that it is not objective reality but psychological or "perceived" reality that exerts the greater influence over human thought processes and behavior. By virtue of his or her past experiences, every human being brings a unique set of values and expectations to the situation and interprets the objectively presented communication in terms of these subjective factors. Thus, each person's perception and comprehension of a communication has the potential to be different than some other person's perception or comprehension of that same communication. Much the same process is at work when two or more bystanders witness the same auto accident, yet are left with different understandings of what happened. Their perspectives, past experiences and expectations will condition what they "see." One person may have a negative view of business and the capitalistic system, which may cause him/her (perhaps in an unconscious manner) to interpret the accident as having been caused by the driver in "the big black limousine." Another witness may, because of a different set of values and expectations, attribute the cause of the same accident to "the hippie driver in the beat-up old red sports car." In other words, no communication or event is ever interpreted entirely independently of the past experiences, expectations and value structure that the individual who perceives that event brings to the situation.

Third, one must consider the limitations imposed by the type of communication being employed. In contrast to one-on-one, face-to-face interactions in which a two-way flow of communication is established, televised communications are essentially instances of one-way communication. The implications of this are substantial. Perfect comprehension in two-way communication situations is difficult enough. Who among us has not been party to at least one conversation in which one of the parties left the conversation misunderstanding what the other had said? Consider, then, how the problem is made much more complex in one-way communication, where the re-

cipient of the communication has no opportunity to ask clarifying questions, and the source of the communication cannot tailor the message to any perceptions of the receiver's needs and intellectual capabilities.

Fourth, considerable evidence implies that comprehending and storing incoming information is not a rapid process. For example, Simon (1974) reports that the various processes involved in comprehending and storing information usually require a span of time (e.g., five to eight seconds) for each new item of information. Thus the rate at which information is conveyed in televised communication may be such that it is too fast for the individual to comprehend *all* of what is going on, at least for messages of more than a few seconds' duration. Trying to comprehend one particular portion and engaging in the mental effort necessary to file this material in memory (so that it can be recalled even a minute later) may mean that the person will necessarily have to miss something else. In other words, the process of absorbing information may be one where the individual behaves much like a stone skipping across the water, that is, comprehending one item and, while doing so, skipping over several others, then comprehending another, and so on.

For these reasons, it is quite likely that while research may suggest some ways to reduce the level of miscomprehension associated with televised communication (perhaps by making the audio and video components more consistent with each other), the pessimistic but realistic forecast is that perfect comprehension (i.e., zero miscomprehension) will not be generally attainable.

Conclusion

Some may quarrel with the procedural details of this investigation or with the specific findings obtained, arguing, for example, that the 30% miscomprehension rate is too high to be correct, or that commercial advertising is more readily miscomprehended than is TV programming. These arguments may well be correct. No claim is made as to providing definitive answers to the research questions that stimulated this investigation. The authors merely claim that the findings represent preliminary ballpark estimates that are in need of further confirmation and refinement. However, the fact remains that, even with a procedure that should have reduced the rate of miscomprehension, nearly every one of the 2,700 respondents managed to miscomprehend at least some portion of the communications that they viewed, every one of the 60 test communications was miscomprehended, and the average amount of miscomprehension associated with any given communication was an unexpectedly high 30%. Further, these findings were quite robust, holding true for respondents of different ages, income, education levels, sexes and marital status.

The implications of these findings are substantial, particularly since the FTC has ruled in several cases that confusion on the part of as few as 9% of the public is a sufficient basis for taking corrective action (Myers et al. 1981, pp. 4-17 through 4-27). Our evidence implies that to require advertising or any other comparable form of communication to conform to a

"zero base" miscomprehension rate would be totally unreasonable. Further, to contend that advertising is necessarily more prone to miscomprehension than other forms of televised communication is similarly unreasonable. The present findings strongly suggest the need for a programmatic series of research investigations designed to shed considerably greater light on the various questions surrounding viewer miscomprehension of televised communications.

REFERENCES

Barrett, M. and Z. Sklar (1980), *The Eye of the Storm*. New York: Lippincott and Crowell.

Bogart, L. (1967), *Strategy in Advertising*. New York: Harcourt Brace, Chapter 5.

Chaiken, S. and A. H. Eagly (1976), "Communication Modality as a Determinant of Message Persuasiveness and Message Comprehensibility," *Journal of Personality and Social Psychology*, 34 (no. 4), 605–614.

Comstock, G., S. Chaffee, N. Katzman, M. McCombs and D. Roberts (1978), *Television and Human Behavior*. New York: Columbia University Press.

Engel, J. F., R. D. Blackwell and D. T. Kollat (1978), *Consumer Behavior*, 3rd ed., Hinsdale, IL: Dryden Press.

Farr, J. N., J. J. Jenkins and D. G. Paterson (1951), "Simplification of Flesch Reading Ease Formula," *Journal of Applied Psychology*, 35 (May), 333–337.

Fishbein, J. and I. Ajzen (1975), *Belief, Attitude, Intention and Behavior*, Reading, MA: Addison-Wesley.

Gardner, D. M. (1975), "Deception in Advertising: A Conceptual Approach," *Journal of Marketing*, 31 (January), 40–46.

Harris, R. J. and G. E. Monaco (1978), "Psychology of Pragmatic Implication: Information Processing Between the Lines," *Journal of Experimental Psychology: General*, 107 (January), 1–22.

Jacoby, J. (1974), "Consumer Reaction to Information Displays: Packaging and Advertising," in *Advertising and the Public Interest*, S. F. Divita, ed., Chicago: American Marketing Association.

———, R. W. Chestnut and W. Silberman (1977), "Consumer Use and Comprehension of Nutrition Information," *Journal of Consumer Research*, 4 (September), 119–128.

———, W. D. Hoyer and D. A. Sheluga (1980), *The Miscomprehension of Televised Communication*, New York: American Association of Advertising Agencies.

———, M. C. Nelson and W. D. Hoyer (1982), "Corrective Advertising and Affirmative Disclosure Statements: Their Potential for Confusing and Misleading the Consumer," *Journal of Marketing*, 46 (Winter), 61–72.

——— and C. B. Small (1975), "The FDA Approach to Defining Misleading Advertising," *Journal of Marketing*, 39 (April), 65–68.

Lasswell, H. D. (1948), "The Structure and Function of Communication in Society," in *Communication of Ideas*, L. Bryson, ed., New York: Harper.

Lavidge, R. D. and G. A. Steiner (1961), "A Model for Predictive Measurement of Advertising Effectiveness," *Journal of Marketing*, 25 (April), 59–62.

Lipstein, B. (1980), "Theories of Advertising and Measurement Systems," in *Attitude Research Enters the '80s*, R. W. Olshavsky, ed., Chicago: American Marketing Association.

McGuire, W. J. (1976), "Some Internal Psychological Factors Influencing Consumer Choice," *Journal of Consumer Research*, 2 (March), 302–319.

Myers, M. L., C. Iscoe, C. Jennings, W. Lennox, E. Minsky and A. Sacks (1981), "Staff Report on the Cigarette Advertising Investigation," Federal Trade Commission.

Percy, L. (1978), "Some Questions on the Validity of Recall Testing as a Measure of Advertising Effectiveness," in *Current Issues and Research in Advertising*, J. Leigh and C. R. Martin, Jr., eds., Ann Arbor, MI: Graduate School of Business Administration, The University of Michigan.

Pool, I. de S., W. Schramm, F. W. Frey, N. Maccoby and E. B. Parker, eds. (1973), *Handbook of Communication*, Chicago: Rand-McNally.

Preston, I. L. and S. E. Scharbach (1971), "Advertising: More than Meets the Eye?," *Journal of Advertising Research*, 11 (March), 19–24.

Resnik, A. and B. L. Stern (1977), "An Analysis of Information Content in Advertising," *Journal of Marketing*, 41 (January), 50–53.

Simon, H. A. (1974), "How Big is a Chunk?," *Science*, 183 (February), 482–488.

Watt, J. and R. Krull (1974), "An Information Theory Measure for Television Programming," *Communication Research*, 1 (January), 44–68.

This chapter suggests that the Jacoby and Hoyer study is subject to internal and external validity problems that must be taken into account in evaluating its findings. More particularly, Ford and Yalch note that "non-target" respondents were included among experimental subjects, that a naturalistic-condition experiment would be preferable, and that comprehension and recall are insufficiently distinguished. Gary T. Ford is associate professor and chairman of the marketing department at the University of Maryland, and Richard Yalch is associate professor of marketing at the University of Washington.

8

VIEWER MISCOMPREHENSION OF TELEVISED COMMUNICATION
A Comment

Gary T. Ford and Richard Yalch

THE Educational Foundation of the American Association of Advertising Agencies is to be commended for sponsoring research on the important issue of miscomprehension of televised communication. As Jacoby and Hoyer note, to the extent miscomprehension occurs, it has implications for the producers of both advertising and programs, as well as for those who are charged with the responsibility of identifying and regulating deceptive advertising. Since the Jacoby and Hoyer study has such a wide potential audience, it is imperative that its results not be misinterpreted.

Our comment is focused on answering what we believe is the single most important question associated with the miscomprehension study: Is the approximately 30% miscomprehension rate cited likely to be a normative indicator of the miscomprehension one can expect for televised communication under normal viewing conditions, or is it a biased estimate? In addressing our focal question, we examine the miscomprehension study on the criteria of construct, internal

and external validity. Additionally, since to a great extent a study's objectives determine the research design required, we discuss the research objectives listed by Jacoby and Hoyer.

Our remarks are presented in the order in which these issues are usually confronted in the design of a research project. That is, first we discuss the miscomprehension study objectives. Then we evaluate Jacoby and Hoyer's study from the perspectives of construct, internal and external validity, respectively. Our comment concludes with a short summary of what we believe are the appropriate conclusions that can be drawn from their research. Throughout, we offer recommendations for improving research in this area.

Jacoby and Hoyer state their fundamental research question as, "Is there actually a lower level of miscomprehension associated with advertising than is associated with other comparable forms of mass media communications?" They translate this into four specific research questions, which can be paraphrased as:

- Are televised communications miscomprehended?
- Is miscomprehension related to respondent demographics?
- Is commercial advertising comprehended more or less than other televised communications?

- Is there a "normative range" of miscomprehension associated with televised communications?

From an evaluative perspective two critical questions are, "Are these objectives important?" and "What characteristics must the research design possess to realize these four objectives?"

Importance of the Research Questions

To ask whether televised communications are miscomprehended is rhetorical since there is no serious debate about the issue. It is well-recognized that viewers add their own thoughts, biases and other extracommunication factors to the message information and may develop a meaning different from other viewers and different from that intended by the source. Perhaps this selective perception phenomenon caused Jacoby and Hoyer to miscomprehend Gardner's (1975) article, which they claim implies that perfect comprehension is possible. On the page cited by Jacoby and Hoyer, Gardner states, "Gardner and Ross (1973) suggest that any advertisement is going to be deceptive because of the claim-belief interaction specified earlier." We interpret this to mean that there is an interaction between the advertiser's claims and the audience's prior beliefs that may create a meaning not literally provided in the message, i.e., miscomprehension.

The next two objectives, determining the variations in miscomprehension among audience demographic groups and types of communication, seem incompatible with communication practice. For example, the question of whether miscomprehension rates vary with audience demographic characteristics should have included a consideration of who was a member of the target audience and who was not. Clearly, many commercials and programs are intended for specific groups, such as men, women, older persons and children. Furthermore, advertising public policy proceedings have long recognized the importance of defining an advertisement's relevant audience. Thus, we are surprised that Jacoby and Hoyer choose to ignore the most critical audience factor. One consequence of using persons for whom the messages may have had little relevance or interest, we suspect, is to bias upward the miscomprehension rates.

The other incompatible objective concerned whether commercial advertising tends to have a different rate of miscomprehension than other televised communications. We question the importance of this issue because of the vast differences between commercials and other televised communications. Commercials are designed to inform and persuade the audience, whereas programmatic materials rarely have these objectives. Further, commercials are designed to be complete in 30 seconds and are pretested to provide checks on comprehension (e.g., verbatims in the Burke Day After Recall test). Unless one can develop a convincing argument as to why miscomprehension would be to the advertiser's advantage, we would be surprised if the commercials did not have a substantially lower rate of miscomprehension than the other televised communications.

The final research objective was to "determine whether there is a 'normative range' of miscomprehension associated with televised communications." In our opinion, this is the most important objective because of its implications both for those producing and those regulating advertising. However, as discussed in the next section, this objective is difficult to realize.

Issues of Construct Validity

According to Cook and Campbell, construct validity refers to "the possibility that the operational definition of cause and effect can be construed in terms of more than one construct, all of which are stated at the same level of reduction" (1976, p. 238). Jacoby and Hoyer are primarily interested in determining the extent to which televised communications are miscomprehended by viewers. We have reservations about how the construct "miscomprehension" was conceptualized and measured.

First, the authors define miscomprehension as "the evocation of meaning not contained in nor logically derivable from the message—miscommunication as assessed at the juncture of the receiver" (Jacoby, Hoyer and Sheluga 1980, p. 22). In terms of the familiar mass communication model (i.e., source, message, medium and receiver) which Jacoby and Hoyer refer to, the implication of this definition is that all miscomprehension found in the study is attributable to the receiver. There are two major problems with this definition:

- It assumes that all of the televised communications are perfectly clear with no source, message or medium problems such as imperfect transmission.

- It assumes that all communications from the researchers (instructions, quiz items and so on) were also perfectly understood.

In actuality, there is good evidence that the latter factor contributed to the reported miscomprehension rate. The former does not appear to have been a problem but we lack information about commercial messages to make a final judgment of this.

The possibility that the researchers' procedures

resulted in the high level of reported miscomprehension exists partially because of their design. All questions asked of respondents were developed, modified and ultimately accepted for the true-false quizzes by them (Jacoby, Hoyer and Sheluga 1980, pp. 120–21). In our opinion, it would have been appropriate to have the test communications and corresponding quiz items reviewed and tested for convergent validity by linguists, semanticists or others who were expert in meanings of communications and independent of the research study. Jacoby and Hoyer acknowledge that such a strategy would have been desirable but cite as a constraint confidentiality requirements imposed by the suppliers of the commercial advertisements. We find this rationale uncompelling, since consultants routinely are expected to maintain confidentiality. In the absence of impartial judgments, it is hard not to worry that the authors may have constructed (perhaps unknowingly) more difficult test items for the different types of messages. This would account for some of the differences in miscomprehension found between the messages.

Second, based on the described procedures and the results, it is not clear whether the construct being measured is recall or comprehension. The research procedure involved three parts. Initially, the respondents were asked to provide a verbal response to the following question: "What was the main message of the announcement you just saw?," followed by the probe, "What other messages were in the announcement you just saw?" (Jacoby, Hoyer and Sheluga 1980, p. 183). Next, the interviewer asked them three questions about the number of times they had seen this announcement before and if they had ever seen a similar announcement. Then they were given the six-item, paper and pencil true-false quiz, which included both factual and inferential statements and served as the sole measure of miscomprehension. We have several concerns with this approach.

Viewers do not normally store televised communications as verbatim records of the verbal communications, i.e., remember every word and sentence presented. Rather, they store the underlying concepts represented by those words and sentences. Comprehension is then a matter of going from this memory to (generally) a new set of words and phrases that correspond in some degree to the original communication. The verbal "main message" question and subsequent probe probably assess comprehension defined in this manner. Unfortunately, Jacoby, Hoyer and Sheluga (1980, p. 136) report that they did not use them because they could not evaluate these responses with any reliability.

If the inferential statements were well-designed and concentrated on the major points of the message from the perspective of the typical target audience member, they could also evaluate comprehension. However, an examination of the inferential statements reveals that many focused on minor aspects of the message that may not have been easily answered without high recall. Others involved judgments with which many experts might not agree. For example, question six for the "Quincy" excerpt stated that "no cure has yet been found for typhoid fever," which is considered a false implication because the message mentioned that proper medication would be provided. It may be unclear to many whether this medication should be considered a "cure" or merely something to relieve the unpleasant symptoms.

Evidence supports the contention that some quiz items were difficult for respondents because they were either immaterial or poorly worded. Jacoby and Hoyer report that 9% (12 of 132) of the quiz items for the product/service commercials focused on either immaterial or nonproduct related information. Also, 17% of the individual true-false questions were miscomprehended by over 50% of the respondents, and some by more than 80%. Thus, on over 60 of the quiz items more than one-half of the respondents disagreed with the authors' interpretations of the communication. The impact of these questions on the overall miscomprehension rate is substantial. If, for example, 60 items had an average miscomprehension rate of 60%, and these items were deleted from the study, the miscomprehension rate of the remaining items would be 23.55%. This is more than six percentage points less, or a decrease of over 20%, from the overall miscomprehension rate of 29.61% reported in the article.

Of course, items that are missed by large percentages of respondents can be excellent for discriminating between those who comprehended well and those who did not. However, this feature is useful only if one is developing a scale for assessing comprehension difficulty and/or audience rankings of comprehension ability. It is not desirable when one is trying to measure the overall level of miscomprehension. In the process of developing items not easily answered by most viewers, one is necessarily increasing the overall miscomprehension rate.

We also have identified two other sources of upward bias in the miscomprehension measure. In a study of listening comprehension, Newman and Horowitz (1964) found that comprehension was significantly lower when individuals were asked to write, rather than express orally, their understanding of an audio message. Consequently, they recommended using the same mode for assessing comprehension as was used to convey the message. This was the procedure used by Jacoby and Hoyer for the open-ended "main message" points questions, which were not fully analyzed, but not for the true-false quiz.

Jacoby and Hoyer mention that there was a substantial difference in miscomprehension rates between the true and false questions. When "true" statements were presented to the subjects, only 19.4% of the viewers answered incorrectly, whereas when "false" statements were asked, the miscomprehension rate was 34.7%. This is the largest systematic difference reported by the authors and one that might have been avoided. It is most probably the result of a "yea–saying" bias that is associated with respondents who do not know the correct response. Respondents were not informed that they had the option of responding "don't remember" or "don't know," and therefore they were forced to guess, most likely with a tendency to mark true rather than false. Given that the miscomprehension test was constructed with four false and only two true responses, this would result in more than half of the guesses being incorrect.

There are several ways in which the operationalization and measurement problems that we have identified could have been diminished. Comprehension could have been measured conditional upon recall to decrease the effect of guessing. Alternatively, "don't know" or "don't remember" categories could have been included as response options. As the authors acknowledge in their manuscript, unfortunately with little explanation, a multiple choice test may have been a better alternative than their true-false quiz because it can be designed to discourage guessing and would assess alternative interpretations of the message that might be considered "acceptable." Finally, experts in meanings should be asked to assess the relevance and appropriateness of the quiz items. Assessment is especially desirable when one is claiming policy implications for the study's findings and the complete data set is not available for peer review or replication.

Issues of Internal Validity

Internal validity, which refers to the viability of alternative explanations for the experimental results, is the area in which the miscomprehension study is strongest. The authors tested a variety of televised communications to avoid problems with an unusual example of a particular type of communication. The messages were rotated to avoid order effects and an independent research organization blind to the purpose of the study was contracted to collect the data. Additionally, the Flesch test and other measures of message complexity were studied as possible explanatory variables, which is commendable, as were the attempts to control statistically for prior exposure to the communications and for product familiarity. Finally, although a probability sample was not taken, the quota sampling procedure used is employed very commonly in commercial marketing research and resulted in a sample that was essentially representative of the United States adult population that watches television.

Although the study seems free of internal validity problems such as history, instrumentation, statistical regression, maturation and testing, one must be cautious in interpreting some of the results as internally valid. The authors' efforts to determine whether there were significant audience and message differences causing miscomprehension is limited by the laboratory setting, forced exposure and viewing instructions. These constraints would tend to minimize many differences. For example, the presentation of public service announcements in fringe time periods might create special problems for them that would not be captured in this testing procedure.

Also, viable alternative explanations exist for their findings. For example, the authors discuss with great concern the high level of miscomprehension for public affairs programming. However, the most miscomprehended examples of public affairs programming were a local editorial praising the Black History Week celebration in Indianapolis, a local news excerpt about the training of 54 recently elected county prosecutors, and a local news excerpt discussing a federal judge's order to the Indiana State Board of Education that they provide free textbooks to students from poor families. The high miscomprehension of this material may merely reflect the lack of interest and points of reference for viewers from areas outside of Indianapolis.

Issues of External Validity

According to Cook and Campbell (1976), external validity is concerned with "those aspects that focus on generalizing to or across times, settings and persons. . . ." In our opinion, when examined on these criteria the miscomprehension study has serious deficiencies that limit its external validity and in combination render it incapable of realizing the normative range objective.

The normative range objective implies that results from this study can be generalized to the miscomprehension rate expected under normal viewing conditions. Clearly, the laboratory setting and audience instruction differ greatly from a "normal" setting. Additionally, to be useful to advertisers and policymakers, the research should have incorporated multiple exposures, since no conclusions regarding a communication's comprehensibility can be made on the basis of a single exposure. Jacoby and Hoyer argue that the forced exposure, laboratory setting heightened attention and comprehension beyond that reached under normal viewing conditions, and imply that this partially overcomes the single exposure limitation. However, there is no way of knowing whether the heightened attention compensates for the lack of multiple exposures. It would, in our opinion, be inadvisable to make such an assumption without additional research. An appropriate starting point would be to conduct laboratory research and vary the number of exposures. The effect of forced exposure might be assessed by exposing persons to the communications incidental to other tasks so that they would not focus extraordinary attention to it.

Another problem with the research design that limits its generalizability is the lack of consideration of the appropriate target audiences. The effect of not being selective in choosing viewers based on some consideration of their relevance is to bias upward the miscomprehension rates. For example, in addition to the previously mentioned concern about a lack of interest in Indianapolis public affairs on the part of those outside that area, we wonder about female viewers' interest in beer commercials (miscomprehension rates of 37% and 34%) and male viewers' interest in small appliances (miscomprehension rates of 38% and 33%). Perhaps, Jacoby and Hoyer might want to split the sample of viewers for the beer and small appliance commercials into males and females and compute the level of miscomprehension for each sex. If the difference is substantial then it would seem that the failure to specify target audiences has biased the miscomprehension rates.

Public policymakers are well aware of the relevant audience criterion, and routinely account for this factor in advertising regulation proceedings. For example, the impact evaluation of the Listerine corrective advertising campaign was limited to a sample of mouthwash users. Beliefs were compared between Listerine users and users of other brands. Nonusers were specifically not pooled with mouthwash users because of potential selective perception problems.

Thus, when the external validity of the miscomprehension study is evaluated, we conclude that the failure to exclude nontarget viewers coupled with the forced, single exposure procedure, limits the applicability to practical issues of all of the reported findings. The next section presents our conclusions about what can be gleaned from the miscomprehension study.

Conclusions

We have reviewed the project reported by Jacoby and Hoyer and find the intent to investigate how audiences comprehend and miscomprehend televised communications, especially advertising, to be long overdue. Unfortunately, laboratory settings like the one used in this study are primarily of value for determining the causes of miscomprehension and testing theories about why miscomprehension occurs and should not be used to estimate absolute levels of miscomprehension (Calder, Phillips and Tybout 1981). This kind of study should be done under naturalistic viewing conditions, should restrict measurement of miscomprehension to the target audiences, and should include typical levels of exposure to be useful to the producers and regulators of televised communications.

In addition we believe the construct miscomprehension was inappropriately conceptualized, operationalized and measured, and are concerned that similar procedures will be used in the second and third phases of the project. We hope a better understanding of the communications process will be reflected in future research. For example, measures should distinguish recall from comprehension and should not measure comprehension of what is not recalled. Unless more attention is paid to construct validity, the substantial resources invested or budgeted to investigate miscomprehension differences across viewers and communications (e.g., expose many different communications to many different viewers in many different cities) will be wasted.

We hope our detailed evaluation of this project does not discourage other researchers from initiating investigations of the comprehension of televised communications. We agree totally with Jacoby and Hoyer that this is an important area for marketing practitioners and public policymakers. It is important that we develop a better understanding of why individuals miscomprehend communications to reduce miscomprehension and the problems caused by it.

REFERENCES

Calder, Bobby J., Lynn W. Phillips and Alice M. Tybout (1981), "Designing Research for Applications," *Journal of Consumer Research*, 8 (September), 197–207.

Cook, Thomas D. and Donald T. Campbell (1976), "The Design and Conduct of Quasi-Experiments and True Experiments in Field Settings," in *Handbook of Industrial and Organizational Psychology*, Marvin D. Dunnette, ed., Chicago: Rand McNally, 223–326.

Gardner, David M. (1975), "Deception in Advertising: A Conceptual Approach," *Journal of Marketing*, 39 (January), 40–46.

———— and Ivan Ross (1973), "Potential Contributions of Consumer Psychology to Deceptive Advertising Determinations and Corrective Measures," paper presented at the 44th Annual Meeting of the Eastern Psychological Association, Washington, D.C.

Jacoby, Jacob, Wayne D. Hoyer and David A. Sheluga (1980), *Miscomprehension of Televised Communications*. New York: American Association of Advertising Agencies.

Newman, John and M. W. Horowitz (1964), "Organizational Processes Underlying Differences between Listening and Reading as a Function of Complexity of Material," paper read at the annual convention of the Speech Association of the Eastern States; cited in Carl H. Weaver, *Human Listening Processes and Behavior*, Indianapolis: Bobbs-Merrill, 1980

This chapter suggests that the Jacoby and Hoyer findings of a "norm" or "natural error rate" of miscomprehension of televised communication is a measurement artifact. Results from a recent Federal Trade Commission copy test, Mizerski says, imply that the significantly different levels of miscomprehension results of other measurements, such as recall, are included. The chapter also explores the difficulty of providing a valid measure of miscomprehension. Richard W. Mizerski is associate professor of marketing at Florida State University and a former FTC advertising and marketing staff consultant.

9

VIEWER MISCOMPREHENSION FINDINGS ARE MEASUREMENT BOUND

Richard W. Mizerski

IT is important initially to note that the FTC does *not* presently, nor has it *ever*, used a "zero-based" miscomprehension level. Even the most zealous of individuals involved in advertising regulation would agree that some level of miscomprehension occurs. Where opinions diverge is in deciding the level at which either an advertiser or the regulator should limit miscomprehension. In fact, Jacoby and Hoyer recognize that there may be instances tied to health and safety "where miscomprehension rates of 10% or even 5% might be deemed totally unacceptable."

The proposed contribution of their study was that it provides a valid and useful measure of the absolute level of television advertising miscomprehension. Although the findings are admitted as being tentative, Jacoby and Hoyer claim that the levels found were a "norm" or "natural error rate" of miscomprehension. In addition, this rate is suggested to have some significant amount of corroboration that makes it a reasonable approximation to reality. I believe that evidence shows that the levels found in their study were

the result of using a flawed single measurement technique, and that very different levels of miscomprehension would be evident with a more realistic and applicable multiple measurement approach.

Another Test of Miscomprehension

Perhaps the most useful approach to show how the Jacoby and Hoyer level of miscomprehension is idiosyncratic or "measurement bound" would be to report briefly the results of a recent FTC television commercial copy test developed to estimate the level at which potential consumers comprehended a deceptive claim. The product type, brand name and claim cannot be revealed because the full investigation has not yet been published.

Method

The 30-second television commercial tested was chosen because it was felt to be representative of the ads in the allegedly offensive campaign. The product was a popular over-the-counter drug that can be purchased at most grocery and drug stores. The claim investigated would be considered implied or inferred and concerns the brand's efficacy in treating symptoms of a specific type of discomfort. In other words, al-

Richard W. Mizerski is an Associate Professor of Marketing at Florida State University. He was a staff advertising and marketing consultant with the FTC from late 1979 through 1980 and presently works as an FTC consultant on several investigations.

Richard W. Mizerski, "Viewer Miscomprehension Findings Are Measurement Bound." Reprinted by permission from *Journal of Marketing*, Vol. 46, No. 4 (Fall 1982), pp. 32-34, published by the American Marketing Association.

TABLE 1
Answers to Copy Test Questions

Claims	Measures of Net Response			
	Unaided Recall	Aided Recall	Description of Literal Claim	Recognition
Literal claim	60%*	65%	—	98%
Alleged deceptive claim:				
description 1	6	16	7%	95
description 2	1	12	18	74
description 3	—	—	2	not asked
Bogus claim 1	—	3	—	10
Bogus claim 2	—	—	—	4

*Percentage in terms of total number of respondents.

though the claim was not literally mentioned in the ad, it was felt that viewers might believe the claim was made or have their present beliefs reinforced after exposure to the commercial.

What makes this test particularly relevant is the close similarity of its methodology to that used in the Jacoby and Hoyer study. Nonetheless, the FTC test was conducted prior to any reports concerning the miscomprehension study and was in no way affected by Jacoby and Hoyer's project. As with the miscomprehension study, the commercial was tested using a mall intercept technique. Two geographic locations, one in the Northeast and one in the Southeastern United States, were used. The sample consisted of 190 consumers over the age of 18, with 95 interviews conducted at each site. A quota sample technique was used to assure appropriate demographic and usage representation (sex, age, education level and usage of nonprescription products for the relief of the discomforts for which the brand was used). The respondent samples were representative of the population profiles of their respective areas. A market research supplier was used to gather the data.

Shoppers were approached and asked to participate. Each respondent individually was shown the commercial on a television monitor using a single, forced exposure format. After viewing the ad, the respondents were asked a series of questions.[1]

Measures Used

The first question asked was, "Other than getting you to buy the product, what do you think was the main point of the commercial?" This was followed by the

---

[1]These questions and the questionnaire format were developed in cooperation with the research supplier and were found to be free of problems in administration or subject understanding and response in pretests.

probe, "Is there anything else the commercial was trying to get across?" These questions would be considered measures of unaided recall and are very similar to the unaided recall measures used but not analyzed by Jacoby and Hoyer. The next question asked, "What specific discomforts does the commercial say that (brand name) relieves? Is there anything else the ad says (brand name) relieves?" These latter questions were gauges of aided recall.

Those respondents who mentioned the literal claim stated in the ad were next asked, "In your own words, can you tell me what you think the ad means by (literal claim)? Anything else?" This question also may be considered a form of aided recall. Finally, measures of recognition were used and all respondents were asked, "As I read each of the following conditions or discomforts, please tell me, based on what is said or implied in this commercial, which ones do you think (brand name) can relieve?" A total of 10 discomforts were read to the respondents. Unlike the Jacoby and Hoyer study, the respondents were able to provide responses other than true or false, such as "don't know" or "not sure." Responses other than yes/true or no/false never accounted for more than 10% of the total on any item, and only 1% of the total for the alleged deceptive claim. To check for possible order bias in presenting the list of discomforts, two versions of this question were used. No significant differences in responses were detected. In addition, two bogus discomforts, discomforts far removed from the drug's area of effectiveness, were included to assess yea-saying.

Results

The results of this copy test are presented in Table 1. The findings concerning the deceptive claim are broken into the three typical consumer descriptions for the discomfort that the FDA feels are analogous and appropriate to use in advertising. Note the differences between responses to recall and recognition measures. The literally stated claim showed between 60 and 64% of the respondents recalling that discomfort was addressed in the commercial. When a measure of recognition was used, 98% felt that discomfort was mentioned or implied. A 34 to 38% difference in literal claim perception appears to be tied to the measure used. That difference is even more pronounced when viewing the findings for the alleged deceptive claim. For the first description of the deceptive claim, between 6 and 16% of the respondents felt the commercial suggested the brand relieved the discomfort using measures of recall, yet 95% the claim was made using a recognition format. A similar result was exhibited for aided recall of the alleged deceptive claim. Even adjusting for the 10% who felt a bogus claim was stated,[2] the recognition format suggests a significantly different and much higher level of claim comprehension than Jacoby and Hoyer demonstrated.

Implications for Measuring Miscomprehension

Jacoby and Hoyer's "normative level" is easily surpassed using a recognition measure similar to the one they used, yet the level of comprehension/miscomprehension is very different when assessed using unaided or aided recall. Although Jacoby and Hoyer feel they have a reasonable approximation, the FTC example strongly suggests that the level of comprehension is defined by the measure used. Any generalizing from their data to results using other measurement techniques, or perhaps to studies using even slight modification in phraseology from their own, is clearly improper.

Jacoby and Hoyer did have the opportunity to get some gauge of convergent validity by comparing the levels of miscomprehension obtained with the recognition format to the levels measured with recall. It is heartening to note that they have changed their minds about undertaking the examination of these recall responses, as they were quite adamant about not analyzing these data in their original report (Jacoby et al. 1980, pp. 135–136). Their rationale had been that interjudge agreement[3] was unacceptably low for both code classification and judgment of correct allocation, thus it may have been prudent not to report these findings. Yet it does not follow that the remaining measure, the recognition technique developed by the authors, was enough to establish norms that could be generalized across the myriad of techniques usually employed.[4]

Jacoby and Hoyer's problems with the recall measure further suggest a lack of external validity for the miscomprehension study findings for two reasons. First, Hoyer and Sheluga, the junior authors of the original study, may not have had the level of experience and training in coding demanded by commercial research contractors. For example, intercoder reliability for classification of all recall verbatims[5] at Burke Marketing Research averages 98% or better (Tatham 1982). The two junior authors agreed between 61 and 76% of the time.

Secondly, in the typical copy test situation, the levels of comprehension for very specific copy points or claims are crucial, making the establishment of codes and the judgment of correctness for recall responses much more manageable. Obviously, this latter point has an influence on the need for high coder expertise as well. Of course even if Jacoby and Hoyer provided an analysis of the recall scores, it is not clear how to combine the scores from different measurement techniques, and it appears that very different levels of miscomprehension/comprehension will result.

Jacoby and Hoyer have provided some interesting and controversial findings that will certainly spur further investigations in this important area. However, any suggestion that they have established norms or a natural error rate that can be used as a triggering mechanism is not only simplistic but misleading as well.

---

[4]It is interesting to note that the sponsor of the study has said that, "The standard range of miscomprehension (23 to 36%) may not be popular at the FTC, as they have hypothecated a figure of 5 to 10% misunderstanding as being deceptive" (AAAA 1980).
[5]This includes but is not limited to day-after-recall (DAR) use. It should be noted that DAR would probably not be the most suitable measurement of miscomprehension although immediate recall would be useful.

REFERENCES

American Association of Advertising Agencies (1980), "Miscomprehension Study," Washington Newsletter (October).
Jacoby, J., W. D. Hoyer and D. A. Sheluga (1980), The Miscomprehension of Televised Communication, New York: American Association of Advertising Agencies.
Tatham, Ronald (1982), personal communication (Vice President, Burke Marketing Research, Cincinnati OH).

---

[2]Perhaps this could be viewed as the level of miscomprehension.
[3]Agreement was viewed between the junior authors and the subcontractor, and between the junior authors.

Replying to the comments in the previous two chapters, Jacoby and Hoyer note that recall routinely is used as an indicant of recognition, that critics' suggestions of an upward bias in their miscomprehension rate are less compelling than other suggestions of a possible downward bias, and that in some respects, the FTC study cited by Mizerski is less consistent with previous findings than is their own study. Moreover, they remind that when research tradeoffs must be made, it is better to focus on internal than on external validity.

10

ON MISCOMPREHENDING TELEVISED COMMUNICATION
A Rejoinder

Jacob Jacoby and Wayne D. Hoyer

Ford and Yalch

FORD and Yalch structure their commentary around two key questions: Are the four objectives important? Does the research satisfactorily address these objectives?

Objectives

The investigation was "contract research," i.e., research conducted to address objectives specified by a client, in this case the American Association of Advertising Agencies. The members of the Association's Educational Foundation Research Committee had developed the objectives long before the present investigators ever heard of the project. Given that this Committee consisted of prominent academic and industry researchers, there were knowledgeable individuals who considered the objectives important. We would not have undertaken the project if we had not concurred. More importantly, the proposal was reviewed by researchers at the FTC (Drs. Michael Mazis and Debra Scammon) and Food and Drug Administration (Drs. Raymond Stokes and Raymond

---

¹The authors gratefully acknowledge comments on an earlier draft of this rejoinder made by Mark Alpert, Rohit Deshpande and Elizabeth Hirschman.

Schucker, see Bartos 1980). Subsequent meetings with these individuals and their staffs prior to initiating the investigation revealed no problems with the objectives.

Ford and Yalch next consider each objective individually, finding fault with the first three. Regarding the first, they write: "To ask whether televised communications are miscomprehended is rhetorical since there is no serious debate about the issue." If the issue is so obvious, why has it been ignored in virtually all the scholarly literature on TV advertising? They continue, "The next two objectives, determining the variations in miscomprehension among audience demographic groups and types of communication, seem incompatible with communication practice. For example, the question of whether miscomprehension rates vary with audience demographic characteristics should have included a consideration of who was a member of the target audience and who was not." However, simply asserting that an approach is "incompatible with communication practice" does not make this claim true. In fact, this assertion is impossible to substantiate, given the long-standing stream of communication research that considers a wide variety of dependent variables in terms of audience demographics and types of communication (cf Schramm 1973).

The point regarding "target audiences" is well

Jacob Jacoby and Wayne D. Hoyer, "On Miscomprehending Televised Communication: A Rejoinder." Reprinted by permission from *Journal of Marketing*, Vol. 46, No. 4 (Fall 1982), pp. 35-43, published by the American Marketing Association.

taken. Indeed, several problems surfaced when considering how best to incorporate this factor in the design. First, while the term "target audience" may come easily to mind, it defies easy operational definition for many of the communications used (e.g., the NBC Nightly News, the CBS News, President Carter's State of the Union Address, commercials for the United Negro College Fund, the Department of Transportation, etc.). Further, while the notion of target audiences makes considerable sense when dealing with print media, special interest periodicals, or even narrowcast AM and FM radio, this notion is less applicable to TV audiences, where three networks dominate the UHF channels and broadcast to the broadest possible mass audience. Finally, while it might be relatively easy to apply the notion of target audience when studying one or two test communications, given an already complex design involving 60 different communications, attempting to test each with its own relevant target audience presents considerable logistical problems.

Under the circumstances, the approach finally chosen seemed optimal, namely, accepting only qualified TV viewers as respondents and then using regression analyses to examine the effects of previous exposure to that communication and prior usage of the product or service being advertised. Perhaps most telling, if target audiences are so important, why did previous exposure to the communication, previous product experience, and several other related variables account for no more than 8% of the common variance?

Ford and Yalch next question why miscomprehension of commercials was compared with miscomprehension of other types of televised communication, noting: "Commercials are designed to inform and persuade the audience, whereas programmatic materials rarely have these objectives." However, regardless of the differences in objectives, both types of communication are designed to be *understood*—and that is precisely what was tested. Ford and Yalch also write: "Unless one can develop a convincing argument as to why miscomprehension would be to the advertiser's advantage. . . ." The argument they seek is forcefully articulated in an article they themselves cite: "It is perfectly clear, however, that it is logical to assume that those advertisements that are deceptive will produce more sales for the advertiser than he would otherwise expect" (Gardner 1975, p. 46).

Research Design and Findings

Issues of Construct Validity

Ford and Yalch next point out that the definition of miscomprehension that was used "assumes that all of the televised communications are perfectly clear with no source, message or medium problems such as imperfect transmission." Since these assumptions are discussed in the full monograph, and since Ford and Yalch later acknowledge that the clarity of the source-message-medium factors used "does not appear to have been a problem," we fail to understand why they raise this issue at all.

Ford and Yalch surmise that the quiz items and instructions, not the communications themselves, might have contributed to the obtained miscomprehension rate. While this is always a possibility, two points should be noted. First, three of the items in each six-item quiz were restatements of the verbal content contained in that communication. Thus, these items should be as easily comprehended as the communication itself. Second, while the argument might seem to apply to the three remaining "inferential" items, the data suggest otherwise: The inferential items were better comprehended than the "factual" items (miscomprehension rates of 14.2% and 15.4%, respectively).

Ford and Yalch write: "In the absence of impartial judgments, it is hard not to worry that the authors may have constructed (perhaps unknowingly) more difficult test items for the different types of messages." The implication that we might have done so knowingly is rejected. Further, the data reveal that all test items were of equivalent difficulty. As we noted: "Conceivably, more difficult items could have been constructed for one category of communication relative to another. Some perspective on this issue is provided by the data contained in Table 7. From here it can be seen that, though there are some divergences, by and large, the average amount of miscomprehension for each type of quiz item is fairly constant across communication categories. In particular, the two groups which provide the most stable estimates—product/service advertising and entertainment/information program excerpts—reveal a very high degree of consistency across item types" (Jacoby, Hoyer and Sheluga 1980, p. 79).

Ford and Yalch continue: "Based on the described procedures and the results, it is not clear whether the construct being measured is recall or comprehension." This comment is both inconsistent and confusing. When these authors earlier mentioned the "vast differences between commercials and other televised communications," they noted that commercials are "pretested to provide checks on comprehension (e.g., verbatims in Burke Day After Recall test)" whereas other types of programming are not pretested. If they accept recall as a valid means for assessing comprehension 24 hours after exposure, then why do they have difficulty accepting a recall procedure applied 60 seconds after exposure? This comment is also confusing for two reasons. First, as Mizerski indicates, comprehension is the *construct* and recall is an *operational procedure* commonly used to assess this construct. Second, as Mizerski notes, the operational procedure we relied on was recognition, not recall. Hence, the criticism does not apply to our study.

Ford and Yalch continue: "Viewers do not normally store televised communications as verbatim records of the verbal communications, i.e., remember every word and sentence presented." It is important to remember that respondents were required to recognize (not recall) whether a specific point had been made in a communication that they had just viewed. We agree that viewers generally do not store precise verbatim records of verbal content. However, given that fairly exact restatements of these verbal contents were used, it is difficult to understand how using "a new set of words and phrases" would have increased comprehension (particularly since not all viewers would be expected to recode the original content in terms of the same set of "new words and phrases").

Ford and Yalch next question the adequacy of the individual quiz items, pointing out that 9% of the 132 quiz items for the 22 product/service communications focused on nonproduct related information. However, though we would have liked all 132 quiz items to focus directly on product related information, the fact that 9% did not really says nothing about whether viewers correctly or incorrectly comprehended the information offered in these items. Ford and Yalch continue: "Also, 17% of the individual true-false questions were miscomprehended by over 50% of the respondents, and some by more than 80%. Thus, on over 60 of the quiz items more than one-half of the respondents disagreed with the authors' interpretations of the communication." The point of the criticism escapes us. Do Ford and Yalch really mean that the 61 items answered incorrectly by more than 50% of the respondents are necessarily bad items (i.e., have absolutely no validity as indicants of comprehension) and should therefore be discarded? Nothing in the vast literature on tests and measurements would support such a practice. If one found that 80% of a group of second graders responded "false" to the statement, "An equilateral triangle has 3 equal sides," would this mean that the item was bad or would it be faithfully reflecting the level of (mis)comprehension? And what is so magical about 50%; why not 25% or 5%? To carry this argument to its extreme, a quiz could have been constructed in which all the items were answered correctly, thereby revealing no miscomprehension.

More than half the items having miscomprehension rates of over 50% were restatements of verbal content from the communication. Thus, it is easy to reject the contention that "more than one-half of the respondents disagreed with the authors' interpretations of the communication." These respondents disagreed with (miscomprehended) the communication content, not with the researchers.

Ford and Yalch note: "In the process of developing items not easily answered by most viewers, one is necessarily increasing the overall miscomprehension rate." Again, the implication that difficult items were purposely developed is rejected. Had this been our intent, the proportion would have been reversed, i.e., 83% and not 17% of the items would have been answered incorrectly by more than 50% of the respondents. Inspection of the verbatim transcripts and quiz items derived from these transcripts (Jacoby, Hoyer and Sheluga 1980, Appendix E) clearly reveals that the questions were all quite basic and simple.

According to Ford and Yalch, "The impact of these questions on the overall miscomprehension rate is substantial. If, for example, 60 items had an average miscomprehension rate of 60%, and these items were deleted from the study, the miscomprehension rate of the remaining items would be 23.55%." Even if one concurred with the recommendation that these items be deleted (which, it should be remembered, has no justification in the test and measurement literature), the reduction in the obtained miscomprehension rate would be only 6%—from 29.61% to 23.55%.

They continue: "We also have identified two other sources of upward bias in the miscomprehension measure." Their continued emphasis on "sources of upward bias" is understandable but misleading. It completely neglects to mention any of the many and significant counterbalancing sources of "downward bias" that were also operating. Respondents (1) were motivated volunteers, (2) were educationally more upscale than the average citizen, (3) viewed the communication in an uncluttered environment and under forced exposure conditions, (4) were tested for comprehension using true-false recognition questions, and (5) were tested within 60 seconds after they had viewed each communication. Think of how much higher the miscomprehension rates would have been had the sample consisted of non-volunteers who were educationally average or downscale, who viewed the communications under normal cluttered and distracting environmental conditions, and who were tested using either multiple choice recognition or day-after-recall procedures (both of which should lower rates of comprehension).

The first source of upward bias they discuss results from using different media to assess message comprehension and to convey the message. Ford and Yalch write, "In a study of listening comprehension, Newman and Horowitz (1964) found that comprehension was significantly lower when individuals were asked to write, rather than express orally, their understanding of an audio message." We attempted to locate this reference to see exactly what was said and done, especially to determine what controls were employed (e.g., were respondents also required to orally "speak" their understandings of written messages?). Unfortunately, this paper was read at a regional speech association meeting nearly 20 years ago and copies could not be located.

In a follow-up study to the AAAA investigation (which employed six of the same communications to compare comprehension rates across different media), we noted that "there may be a 'methods variance' problem due to the mode of testing" and made the same recommendation Ford and Yalch do (cf Jacoby, Hoyer and Zimmer 1981). However, this recommendation is especially difficult to implement with audiovisual communications. Specifically, how does one assess comprehension of the nonverbal visual component? Regardless, it should be noted that the biases introduced by reliance on written tests should have increased (not decreased) comprehension. Based on a review of the relevant literature, Nieland (1979, p. 29) concludes: "There can be little question of the superiority of the written over the spoken mode of communication" for generating comprehension. Considerable evidence supports this conclusion (e.g., Chaiken and Eagly 1976; Corey 1934; Fisher, Johnson and Porter 1977; Forston 1975; Sales, Elwork and Alfini 1977).

Ford and Yalch next point out: "Respondents were not informed that they had the option of responding 'don't remember' or 'don't know,' and therefore they were forced to guess, most likely with a tendency to mark true rather than false. Given that the miscomprehension test was constructed with four false and only two responses, this would result in more than half of the guesses being incorrect." However, as we have repeatedly noted (Jacoby and Hoyer 1981; Jacoby, Hoyer and Sheluga 1980, p. 64), had any conventional psychometric approach been used to correct for guessing, the miscomprehension rates would have been substantially higher than those reported. According to Professor Jacob Cohen, the statistical consultant on the project: "The actual rate of miscomprehension, when corrected for guessing using conventional approaches, is likely non-trivially greater than the rate observed. With an observed miscomprehension rate of .30, the conventional psychometric model for true-false items would estimate the 'true' rate of correct comprehension as $2(.7) - 1 = .40$, hence the 'true' rate of miscomprehension as a substantial .60. . . . It needs to be recognized that the application of any rational model which corrects for guessing would have yielded miscomprehension rates which were nontrivially greater than the observed

rates" (cf Jacoby, Hoyer and Sheluga 1980, p. 64). Hence, absent an alternative model whose rationale can be justified, accepted psychometric practice suggests our estimates conservatively *underestimate* the actual rate of miscomprehension.

Ford and Yalch continue: "There are several ways in which the operationalization and measurement problems we have identified could have been diminished. Comprehension could have been measured conditional upon recall to decrease the effect of guessing. Alternatively, 'don't know' or 'don't remember' categories could have been included as response options. As the authors acknowledge in their manuscript, unfortunately with little explanation, a multiple choice test may have been a better alternative than their true-false quiz." We would like to make four points in reply.

First, consider the problems involved in making assessment conditional upon recall. How much of each communication would have to be recalled for a respondent to qualify? Would the product, the brand name, one or more copy points, or some other item have to be remembered? Further, would recall have to be "correct"? If so, doesn't relying on "correct" recall then confound the assessment of comprehension? Regardless, given forced exposure and a test environment in which nothing except discussion of the communication intervened between exposure and comprehension assessment, it seems safe to assume that a very large proportion of the respondents would exhibit sufficient levels of recall.

Second, how should "don't know" responses be scored? Would they be deleted from the analysis or would they be scored as incorrect, on the grounds that the respondent failed to grasp what had been communicated?

Third, Ford and Yalch are mistaken: Nowhere in either the complete monograph or the briefer article do we acknowledge that "a multiple choice test may have been a better alternative." True-false items were deliberately chosen in preference to multiple choice procedures because of the massive U.S. Office of Education investigation which revealed that approximately one-third of the American populace was functionally illiterate (Northcutt 1975). Using a multiple choice format (where the probability of guessing correctly is lower than with true-false items) with such individuals would only have increased miscomprehension rates.

Fourth, a recent study (Jacoby, Nelson and Hoyer 1982) provides revealing data regarding the procedures advocated by Ford and Yalch. This investigation used single sentence (print) disclaimers developed by the FTC staff. It seems reasonable to expect that these single sentences would be much less complicated than the full 30-second audiovideo communications into which they were to be inserted. However, using an upscale sample and the advocated multiple choice procedure which permitted respondents to reply "don't know," this investigation found miscomprehension rates ranging from 70 to 90%. Moreover, in both this investigation and the one described by Mizerski, "don't know" and "not sure" options never accounted for more than 10% of the total response to any item. Accordingly, we fail to see how including such options would have appreciably altered the miscomprehension study findings.

Ford and Yalch find fault with the fact that "the complete data set is not available for peer review or replication." We agree and would have preferred making the complete data set available. However, commercial advertisers agreed to participate only after being promised that they would not be identified. Their concern was that any finding, regardless of how small, that revealed their advertising to have been miscomprehended might have provided the FTC with a reason for examining their advertising in greater detail, and possibly bringing them into court at some later time. Be that as it may, we were able to make 35 of our 60 test communications available for peer review. Not only are the verbatim transcripts and quizzes for these 35 stimuli provided in the monograph, but the actual videotapes are available either from the authors or the American Association of Advertising Agencies. Thus, any researcher genuinely concerned with our procedures and findings could easily check these concerns using the same communications. No one has yet asked to see these.

Issues of External Validity

Ford and Yalch write: "Clearly, the laboratory setting and audience instruction differ greatly from a 'normal' setting." Further, Ford and Yalch imply that forced exposure to a communication causes viewers to "focus extraordinary attention to it." Throughout it has been Ford and Yalch's principal contention that the miscomprehension rate we obtained was an upwardly biased estimate. But wouldn't forced exposure, with the "extraordinary attention" which they admit this procedure creates, be expected to *decrease* miscomprehension? Hence, aren't substantial downward biases operating as well?

To achieve greater external validity, Ford and Yalch recommend, "An appropriate starting point would be to conduct laboratory research and vary the number of exposures." We concur and had identified multiple exposure research as the first of several ways in which our work needed to be extended (cf Jacoby, Hoyer and Sheluga 1980, p. 101). However, it is a mistake to assume that laboratory research that varies the number of exposures increases external validity. Recent studies suggest that merely presenting an ad repeatedly in a short amount of time does *not* replicate a real world multiple exposure effect. Rather, subjects become bored and lose interest, thereby not engaging in any processing (Mitchell and Olson 1981).

Ford and Yalch continue: "Public policy makers are well aware of the relevant audience criterion, and routinely account for this factor in advertising regulation proceedings." Not so. They do so only when it suits their purposes. As a case in point consider the study commissioned by the FTC for use in its hearings against the manufacturers of Anacin, Bufferin and Excedrin (Leavitt 1976). At issue was whether advertising had created false beliefs about these products in the minds of consumers regarding their "effectiveness, strength, and speed for relieving pain." In that report, the "relevant audience" criterion was com-

---

TABLE 1
Comparing the Responses of Analgesic Product Users and Nonusers on Ratings of "Speed In Relieving Pain"[a]

	ASPIRIN		ANACIN		BUFFERIN		EXCEDRIN	
	Users %	Nonusers %	Users %	Nonusers %	Users %	Nonusers %	Users %	Nonusers %
Extremely fast	9.3	0.5	17.0	3.4	19.5	4.2	27.5	4.9
Very fast	18.7	8.2	34.0	11.5	30.3	9.1	36.0	9.6
Fairly fast	52.5	32.7	35.4	28.2	40.4	24.6	26.5	19.3
Not fast	13.9	21.4	9.2	7.2	3.7	8.3	3.7	5.6
Don't know	5.6	37.1	4.4	49.7	6.0	53.8	6.3	60.6
Base	375	388	206	557	267	496	189	574

[a]Users of each product are those who, in response to Question 9 ("Thinking about ————'s speed in relieving pain, would you say that ———— relieves pain extremely fast, fairly fast, or not fast?"), stated that they had used that product within the past six months. Nonusers are those who stated that they had not used that product within the past six months. This table was developed from the data collected in Leavitt (1976). An identical pattern of results was obtained for responses to the "effectiveness" and "strength" questions.

pletely disregarded. Not only was there no attempt to measure exposure to this advertising, but the findings for users (the "relevant audience") were lumped together with those for nonusers. However, reanalysis of the data by experts retained by American Home Products, the manufacturers of Anacin, clearly revealed that usage accounted for approximately 50% of the response (see the shifts in "Don't know" responses in Table 1). Perhaps the original analyses were not broken into user vs. nonuser groups because it would have undermined the FTC's contention that it was exposure to advertising (which was not measured) rather than actual usage that determined consumer beliefs.

Ford and Yalch "wonder about female viewers' interest in beer commercials . . . and male viewers' interest in small appliances" and suggest that we "might want to split the sample . . . to compute the level of miscomprehension for each sex." We did so and found no significant differences for either of the two beer commercials or for one of the appliance commercials. The other appliance commercial—for flashlight batteries—did reveal greater miscomprehension for females ($t = 2.92$, $p < .005$). However, given the "appliance" involved (batteries) we would be hard pressed to draw any meaningful conclusions as to why the sexes should differ in their comprehension of this communication. Regardless, Ford and Yalch write, "If the difference is substantial then it would seem that the failure to specify target audiences has biased the miscomprehension rates." Since three of the four differences are not substantial, would Ford and Yalch accept the fact that the failure to specify target audiences has *not* biased the miscomprehension rates?

Conclusions

Ford and Yalch raise a call for research conducted under naturalistic viewing conditions. As was indicated from the outset (Bartos 1980, p. 15), this kind of research has been the intent all along. Moreover, naturalistic measurement would better resolve recall comprehension.

Mizerski

Mizerski's commentary surprises us for three reasons. First, its major thesis—that recognition yields higher estimates of comprehension/learning than does recall—says nothing new. As Maccoby and Maccoby noted nearly 30 years ago (1954, p. 458): "Open questions, in a sense, ask the respondent to *recall* something—to produce it spontaneously. Closed questions, on the other hand, ask the respondent to *recognize* something. The literature on recall versus recognition memory tells us that more will be rec-

ognized than will be recalled, and such proves to be the case with open versus closed questions."

A second surprise is Mizerski's brevity. Given his extensive comments elsewhere (cf Mizerski 1981), it is surprising that none of these issues are raised here. Perhaps our replies to these concerns (Jacoby and Hoyer 1981) have satisfied his objections.

Third, like Ford and Yalch, Mizerski elsewhere criticizes us for failing to provide complete information on 25 of our 60 test communications. Yet Mizerski refuses to identify the brand name, the informational content or even the type of product involved in the study he describes. We feel our research demands stronger refutation than Mizerski offers. His research employed only 190 respondents at two sites, testing only one 30-second communication. In contrast, ours employed 2700 respondents at 12 sites and tested 60 such communications. Other noteworthy differences between the FTC-Mizerski investigation and our own include: (1) Mizerski assessed comprehension of a single copy point; our investigation attempted to assess comprehension of all the relevant elements within the communication. (2) Mizerski used an atypical (allegedly deceptive) ad; none of our communications were considered deceptive. (3) Our investigation examined both what was said and three inferences that could be drawn from what was said; Mizerski examined but a single inference.

Mizerski's principal thesis is that the miscomprehension levels we obtained "were the result of using a flawed single measurement technique, and that very different levels of miscomprehension would be evident with a more realistic and applicable multiple measurement approach." He then goes on briefly to outline his FTC study which employed both recognition and recall measures.

What is it that makes Mizerski's study "more realistic and applicable" compared to our own—especially given his later comment: "What makes this (FTC) test particularly relevant is the close similarity of its methodology to that used in the Jacoby and Hoyer study."[2] Is it simply that he employed both recognition and recall measures, while we have thus far analyzed only our recognition measure? Had his two measures been incorporated in some larger framework (e.g., Campbell and Fiske's (1959) multi-method multitrait matrix), we might be persuaded that his approach was superior. However, such an approach is missing and Mizerski never integrates his two mea-

---

[2]Clearly, then, the litany of issues raised by Ford and Yalch (e.g., the purported confounding of recall and comprehension; the assumption that the communication contained no source, message or media problems; the assumption that the instructions and assessment instrument were understood; the use of laboratory-like settings; the use of forced exposure formats; the use of a single exposure; etc.) apply to the Mizerski-FTC study as well.

TABLE 2
Miscomprehension Findings in Audiovisual Communication Studies

Investigation	Type of Measure*	Number of Test Communications	Rates of Miscomprehension		
			Mean	Median	Range
Chaiken and Eagly (1976)	Recognition (MC)	1	38%[b]	38%	—
Lipstein (1980)	Recognition (TF)	6	32%	30%	30%–42%
Jacoby, Hoyer & Sheluga (1980)	Recognition (TF)	60	30%	28%	11%–50%
Jacoby, Hoyer and Zimmer (1981)	Recognition (TF)	6	25%	24%	19%–32%
Jacoby, Troutman and Whittler (1982)	Recognition (TF)	4	21%	23%	12%–24%
Mizerski	Recognition (MC)	1	2%	2%	—

*TF = true-false; MC = multiple choice
[b]Derived score is based on mean number of MC questions answered correctly.

sures or indicates which of the two is more valid. Later when noting that we have recently begun the major task of examining our recall data, he writes: "Of course, even if Jacoby and Hoyer provided an analysis of the recall scores, it is not clear how to combine the scores from different measurement techniques." Doesn't this comment also apply to his own work?

Just which procedure—recall or recognition—is the more valid? Elsewhere (Allison and Mizerski 1981, pp. 419–420) Mizerski seems to answer when he writes, "There have been many questions raised as to the validity of recall testing as a measure of advertising effectiveness . . . recall may be a necessary and sufficient criteria [sic] for establishing the *persuasive impact* of a communication, rather than a measure of detailed information recall." (italics added) Actually many writers (including Maccoby and Maccoby 1954) have argued that recognition is more valid, and research tends to support this view (cf Belson and Duncan 1962; Dohrenwend 1965; Marquis, Marshall and Oskamp 1972; Schuman and Presser 1981).

Both Mizerski's and our own research used recognition measures, yet obtained different results. We found an average miscomprehension rate of 29.6% and contended that this estimate was an acceptable first approximation. Mizerski, who cites a 2% miscomprehension rate (for the literal claim) doubts that it is an acceptable figure. As Table 2 clearly reveals, a 30% rate is quite consistent with other recognition based findings; 2% is not.

Also directly relevant is the work of Robinson and his colleagues (Robinson and Sahin, forthcoming; Sahin, Davis and Robinson 1981) dealing with the comprehension of complete news stories telecast over the BBC. Separate national probability samples were employed for each of four BBC evening newscasts

aired during June of 1979. Respondents—people who said they had viewed that particular newscast—were interviewed in person within three hours after the telecast. Comprehension of the main point of each story was assessed, using both unaided and aided recall, for each of the 11 to 13 stories contained in the particular newscast. Across all four telecasts and 48 separate news stories, the unaided recall measure revealed an average comprehension rate of *less* than 15%; the aided recall measure yielded a mean comprehension score of *less* than 30%![3]

We fail to see how "problems with [our] recall measure further suggest a lack of external validity for the miscomprehension study findings." None of the findings we report are based on our measure of recall, i.e., the two measures are independent. Accordingly, we fail to understand the argument that problems experienced with our recall measure necessarily imply a lack of external validity for those findings obtained using our recognition measure.

Mizerski writes, "Although Jacoby and Hoyer feel they have a reasonable first approximation, [Mizerski's example] strongly suggests that the confidence interval is defined by the measure used. Any generalizing from their data to results using other measurement techniques, or perhaps to studies using even slight modification in phraseology from their own, is clearly improper." Actually, the differences between our recognition measure and that used by Mizerski involve much more than "slight modification in phraseology." His assessment item reads: "As I read each of the following conditions or discomforts, please tell me, based on what is said or implied in this commercial, which one you think (brand name)

[3]The authors would like to thank Dr. J. Robinson (Director of the Survey Research Center of the University of Maryland) for providing us with an early draft of Robinson and Sahin, forthcoming.

can relieve?'' In effect, this question asks the respondent whether he/she *believes the claim* that the product can relieve certain symptoms. This question is totally different from asking if the person *believes that the ad made the claim* that the product relieved these symptoms. We have already discussed the different questions:

> It should be noted that informational beliefs and, in a parallel sense, inferential beliefs as well, involve two separate questions:
>
> Does the receiver believe the message expresses proposition X?
>
> Does the receiver believe proposition X, i.e., accept it as being true?
>
> These are independent questions. A viewer could respond ''yes'' to the first question and at the same time respond ''no'' to the second (e.g., ''Yes, the commercial did say that this product would remove my freckles'' and ''No, I don't believe the product is capable of doing what it claims''). The exclusive focus of the present investigation is on the first question only. (Jacoby, Hoyer and Sheluga 1980, pp. 38–39).

Clearly, Mizerski's ''slight modification in phraseology'' resulted in his addressing an issue totally different from the one that we addressed. He focused on the second question whereas our study focused on the first.

Mizerski further contends that the external validity of our study suffers because ''in the typical copy test situation, the levels of comprehension for very specific copy points or claims are crucial. . . .'' Let us repeat that we were not concerned with testing commercially meaningful copy points per se, but with assessing comprehension for the entire domain of relevant informational content associated with each of our test communications. Further, nearly half our communications were neither commercials nor public service advertisements and therefore did not have copy points or claims. How should we have assessed comprehension for these communications?

Conclusion

Is our study flawed and biased? Of course it is—which study isn't? Ford and Yalch emphasize Cook and Campbell's (1976) comment on validity. Perhaps they missed those portions of that chapter that read, ''It is unrealistic to expect to control for all the validity threats we mentioned in a single experiment or in a single set of experiments'' (p. 318). ''Some ways of increasing one kind of validity will decrease another kind. . . . These countervailing relationships suggest that a crucial part of planning any experiment has to be an explication of the priority ordering among the four kinds of validity. . . . However, since some trade-offs are inevitable, we think it unrealistic to think that a single piece of research will effectively answer all of the validity questions surrounding even the simplest causal relationship'' (p. 245).

Given that trade-offs must be made, which type of validity is most important? Cook and Campbell are very clear on this point. For both theoretical and applied research, priority must be given to ''the general primacy of internal validity.'' Let us, therefore, conclude with Ford and Yalch's acknowledgment that: ''Internal validity . . . is the area in which the miscomprehension study is strongest.''

REFERENCES

Allison, N. K. and R. W. Mizerski (1981), ''The Effects of Recall on Belief Change: The Corrective Advertising Case,'' in *Advances in Consumer Research*, 8, Kent B. Monroe, ed., 419–422.

Bartos, R. (1980), ''Foreword,'' in *The Miscomprehension of Televised Communication*, J. Jacoby, W. D. Hoyer and D. A. Sheluga, New York: American Association of Advertising Agencies, 13–16.

Belson, W. A. and J. A. Duncan (1962), ''A Comparison of the Checklist and the Open Response Questioning Systems,'' *Applied Statistics*, 2 (no. 2), 120–132.

Campbell, D. T. and D. W. Fiske (1959), ''Convergent and Discriminant Validation by the Multitrait-Multimethod Matrix,'' *Psychological Bulletin*, 56, 81–105.

Chaiken, S. and A. H. Eagly (1976), ''Communication Modality as a Determinant of Message Persuasiveness and Message Comprehensibility,'' *Journal of Personality and Social Psychology*, 34 (no. 4), 605–614.

Cook, T. D. and D. T. Campbell (1976), ''The Design and Conduct of Quasi-Experiments and True Experiments in Field Settings,'' in *Handbook of Industrial and Organizational Psychology*, M. D. Dunnett, ed., Chicago: Rand McNally, 223–326.

Corey, S. M. (1934), ''Learning from Lectures and Learning from Readings,'' *Journal of Educational Psychology*, 25, 459–470.

Dohrenwend, B. S. (1965), ''Some Effects of Open and Closed Questions on Respondents' Answers,'' *Human Organization*, 24 (no. 2), 175–184.

Fisher, L. A., T. S. Johnson and D. Porter (1955), ''Collection of a Clean Voided Urine Specimen: A Comparison Among Spoken, Written and Computer Based Instruction,'' *American Journal of Public Health*, 65 (no. 7), 640–644.

Forston, R. F. (1975), ''Sense and Non-Sense: Jury Trial Communication,'' *Brigham Young Law Review*, 1 (no. 3), 610–611.

Gardner, D. M. (1975), ''Deception in Advertising: A Conceptual Approach,'' *Journal of Marketing*, 39 (January), 40–46.

Jacoby, J. and W. D. Hoyer (1981), "Reply to Mizerski's Criticisms: Some Mislead, Others Misrepresent Facts," *Marketing News*, 15 (July 24), 35–36.

——, —— and D. A. Sheluga (1980), *The Miscomprehension of Televised Communication*, New York: American Association of Advertising Agencies.

——, —— and M. Zimmer (1981), "To Read, View or Listen? A Cross-Media Comparison of Comprehension," working paper no. 81-72, Graduate School of Business, New York University

——, M. C. Nelson and W. D. Hoyer (1982), "Corrective Advertising and Affirmative Disclosure Statements: Their Potential for Confusing and Misleading the Consumer," *Journal of Marketing*, 46 (Winter), 61–72.

——, T. R. Troutman and T. E. Whittler (1982), "Viewer Miscomprehension of the 1980 Presidential Debates," working paper no. 82-31, Graduate School of Business, New York University.

Leavitt, C. (1976), "Public Beliefs about Selected Analgesic Products," report commissioned by the FTC, introduced as exhibit CX-457, FTC hearings on American Home Products Corporation advertising for its brand Anacin.

Lipstein, B. (1980), "Theories of Advertising and Measurement Systems," in *Attitude Research Enters the 80s*, R. W. Olshavsky, ed., Chicago: American Marketing Association, 87–97.

Maccoby, E. E. and N. Maccoby (1954), "The Interview: A Tool of Social Science," in *The Handbook of Social Psychology, Vol. 1*, G. Lindzey, ed., Reading, MA: Addison-Wesley, 449–487.

Marquis, K. H., J. Marshall and S. Oskamp (1972), "Testimony Validity as a Function of Question Form, Atmosphere and Item Difficulty," *Journal of Applied Social Psychology*, 2 (no. 2), 167–186.

Mitchell, A. A. and J. C. Olson (1981), "Are Product Attribute Beliefs the Only Mediator of Advertising Effects on Brand Attitude?," *Journal of Marketing Research*, 18 (August), 318–332.

Mizerski, R. W. (1981), "Major Problems in 4As Pioneering Study of TV Miscomprehension," *Marketing News*, 14 (June 12), 7–8.

Newman, J. and M. W. Horowitz (1964), "Organizational Processes Underlying Differences Between Reading as a Function of Complexity of Material." Paper read at the annual convention of the Speech Association of the Eastern States.

Nieland, R. G. (1979), *Pattern Jury Instructions*, Chicago: American Judicature Society.

Northcutt, N. et al. (1975), "Adult Functional Competency Study: A Four-Year National Investigation," summary report presented to the U.S. Office of Education, Department of HEW. Austin, TX: University of Texas, Division of Extension.

Robinson, J. P. and H. Sahin (forthcoming), *Audience Comprehension of Television News*, London: British Broadcasting Corporation.

Sahin, H., D. K. Davis and J. P. Robinson (1981), "Improving the TV News," *Irish Broadcasting Review*, 11 (Spring), 50–55.

Sales, B. D., A. Elwork and J. J. Alfini (1977), "Improving Comprehension for Jury Instructions," in *Perspectives in Law and Psychology*, B. Sales, ed., New York: Plenum.

Schramm, W. (1973), "Channels and Audiences," in *The Handbook of Communication*, I. de Sola Pool et al., eds., Chicago: Rand McNally, 116–140.

Schuman, H. and S. Presser (1981), *Questions and Answers in Attitude Surveys: Experiments on Question Form, Wording and Content*, New York: Academic Press.

In this brief review, Barrie Gunter suggests that "forgetting the news" is pervasive and that the best recent evidence would suggest that it stems from television journalists' packaging of items to suit their own professional production categories, from ordering effects, and from mismatches between visual and verbal content in news presentation. Gunter is a research fellow at the Independent Broadcasting Authority in Great Britain.

11

FORGETTING THE NEWS

Barrie Gunter

Television news is the most pervasive and influential source of public affairs information in the western hemisphere today and the recent projected broadcasting developments on both sides of the Atlantic mean that its relative importance is destined to grow. In the United States, the network news programmes are continuing to increase their already large audiences, and the 24-hour, seven-days-a-week service called Cable News Network has begun to serve cable systems with an exclusive package of news, current affairs, specialist discussion and news features. In the United Kingdom, meanwhile, the introduction of early morning television with its focus on news and current affairs programming may create a new style of family viewing around the breakfast table which will serve to increase the already considerable general public dependence on television as the most reliable source of news.

The provision of news has long been recognised by broadcasters and public alike as one of the fundamentally important functions of television. The broadcasters maintain elaborate news-gathering facilities and regularly schedule news bulletins among their daily output. Audience research has repeatedly confirmed that the public's need for news is a principle reason for watching television. Yet audience surveys have also shown that people's memory for the content of individual news programmes is often very poor indeed only a few hours or even minutes after viewing. One US survey of several years ago found that some viewers (questioned by telephone in their

From Barrie Gunter, "Forgetting the News," *Intermedia,* Vol. 9, No. 5 (September 1981), pp. 41-43. Reprinted by permission of *Intermedia,* the journal of the International Institute of Communications.

homes about a television news bulletin they had watched earlier that same evening) were able to spontaneously recall only about one of the 20 items (a little over 5%). Indeed, half of the respondents were unable to remember any items at all less than an hour after the programme had been broadcast.

A more recent survey in the USA reported by John P. Robinson of the Communication Research Center, Cleveland State University (in a paper presented to the 1980 Annual Convention of Radio-Television Division of the Association for Education in Journalism in Boston, Massachusetts) indicated a somewhat better overall memory for news. The viewers recalled on average at least some aspects of about half the stories in bulletins containing twelve to twenty items. However, this fairly creditable performance was offset by the viewers' frequent distortions and misunderstandings of important details. Sometimes a viewer merged the content of two stories so that elements of one story became confused with elements from another story.

This forgetfulness is not found only in the USA. Researchers in Sveriges Radio have found that more than half a sample of Stockholm residents who took part in a laboratory study either failed to recall or misconstrued the content of nearly all the items of a simulated seven-minute television bulletin of thirteen stories.

BAD COMMUNICATION

These failures clearly indicate that television bulletins may not be as effective at communicating information about current domestic or world affairs to the public as the pervasiveness of television viewing (for the purposes of news consumption) might lead one intuitively to believe. Why should this be so? The answer may lie partly in the way news is presented and structured by television producers and directors.

Sociological studies of television newsrooms have shown that news editors have quite definite beliefs and opinions about how news programmes can best be organised and presented to facilitate both their impact and the public's ability to recall their content. Yet they tend to be generally ignorant of the audiences' real information 'needs' and learning capabilities. In his book, *Putting Reality Together,* Phillip Schlesinger reported that the people he studied in the BBC newsroom lacked an objective feedback about the public's attitudes and conceptions concerning the news.

The content analysis of UK network news by the Glasgow University Media Group several years ago showed that standardised production routines resulted in clearly identifiable bulletin profiles of limited flexibility. The Glasgow data implied that the organisation of newscasts is neither accidental nor random. It is implicit in these findings that we need to examine the extent to which news recall is related to attributes of presentation and content and to standard presentation practices. In this vein, some recent experimentation has identified a number of specific aspects of news production which may underlie the often extensive and very rapid forgetting of news story content experienced by large sections of the public shortly after watching television bulletins.

Cognitive psychologists have for many years investigated the ways in which presentation formats and the structural attributes of linguistic materials affect our ability to remember things. They have now begun to extend the range of the 'stimulus' materials tested to include broadcast news. The relationships between specific news programming factors and the recall of verbal news information represent an elaborate form of information processing, and are amenable to investigation by proven psychological methods. Recent studies have uncovered two particularly salient aspects of production technique that greatly affect the way we remember news items. The first is the taxonomic packaging of news stories within a single news category (eg, politics, foreign, industry and economics). The second is the use of visual illustrations to support what is read out by the newscaster.

First, let us turn our attention to the organisation of news items in a television bulletin, and to what may be referred to as the 'taxonomic' effect. The routine production of television news is dominated by the need to meet deadlines. Partly as a result, the bulletins are arranged in time slots that are regularly scheduled and strictly defined. The complex functions of the selection, ordering and treatment of news stories for particular newscasts are most economically handled by standardised procedures that embody the requirements of these temporal and spatial limitations. They are aimed more at professional efficiency than audience satisfaction and learning.

Moreover, as noted by Phillip Schlesinger, the newsroom may have little contact with its audience. Whilst there is usually some awareness of the size of the audience for particular programmes, it seems there is generally little knowledge about audience response. Yet, newsrooms apparently abound with commonly held beliefs about the viewers' abilities and motivations to process news information. Any changes in the production format or organisational structure of bulletins are usually the result of an intuitive judgment; and little or no research evidence is sought to find out whether such changes actually improve the quality of information or its comprehensibility.

Clarity and comprehensibility are especially essential qualities for TV news because television reaches a larger and more heterogeneous audience than any other medium. Moreover, much of the information contained in a news bulletin is spoken only once during the programme and, unlike newsprint, cannot be re-studied at the leisure of the consumer. Newsmen are aware of the need for clarity but their ignorance of the basic processes of human verbal learning has resulted in the adoption of production routines which, although designed to make it easier for the public to consume news, are actually self-defeating.

News taxonomy is a very important concept in the production of television newscasts and is especially relevant to the problem of clarity. News stories are classified by journalists and editors, and their producers, into broad semantic or taxonomic domains: politics, industry, foreign, economic, sports, science, human interest, and so on. In *Bad News,* the Glasgow media group showed that the grouping and distribution of news items in bulletins appears to be strongly determined by this categorisation.

One production routine which is supposed to enhance clarity is the grouping together of news items from the same category into homogeneous clusters. A particularly salient version of this production strategy relates to the division of news stories into domestic and foreign categories. It is common practice in the BBC and ITN to have a round-up of news items that share only the characteristic that they are located outside the United Kingdom. Industrial news concerning pay claims or strikes is also frequently treated in this way, and sometimes items on industrial disputes are run in tandem with stories on broader and in actuality unrelatd (although semantically often quite similar) economic issues. The placing implies causal connections that may not exist.

Producers apparently act on the intuitive assumption that this packaging of isolated events into more meaningful combinations makes them more readily learned by the audience. On the evidence of some research done by myself and two experimental psychologists, Colin Berry and Brian Clifford, at the North East London Polytechnic, this reasoning would seem to be fallacious. The attempt to arrive at simplicity and clarity by packaging items into one category of news may in fact represent one of the fundamental reasons why people forget the news that the TV organisations, at tremendous expense and effort, have prepared and distributed.

THE ORDER OF ITEMS

This research began with a relatively simple analysis of the effects on learning of different ways of arranging the order of news items in a bulletin. An analysis of a sequence of fifteen brief news reports showed that the position of an item in a bulletin may have powerful effects upon a viewer's ability to remember it. The practical implications of these findings become clearer when they are considered together with the data from the content analysis of network news output in the UK. The Glasgow media group showed, for instance, that certain types of story were much more likely than others to occupy the first three positions in a bulletin. The favoured topics were political, industrial and foreign news stories. A similar bias occurred in the last three positions which were most often occupied by 'sports' and by human interest and science stories. It is clear that stereotyped production practices encourage strong and consistent biases, specifically in the serial ordering and treatment of news topics, and that these biases may have repercussions in terms of the kinds of news events which are predominantly learned by the audience. Results from the first study on serial ordering showed quite unequivocally that items presented at or near the beginning and at or near the end of a news bulletin were much more likely to be remembered shortly after viewing than were items which occurred in the middle of the sequence (the study took appropriate measures to control for familiarity, emotional impact and the interest value of individual news stories).

The discovery led to further and more detailed investigations of these 'ordering' factors. We discovered powerful effects on learning which have important implications for the production of TV news. A series of experiments was therfore carried out to test the assumption that the arrangement of items in homogeneous sequences enhances the overall clarity and memorability of the bulletin. The specific aim was to examine the effect of 'news packaging' on viewers' ability to recall the news.

A number of people were seated in front of a television monitor, one at a time, and shown a series of four televised news sequences each consisting of three short news reports in a common news category. The bulletin had been recorded several months previously from ITN and BBC-1 news broadcasts. Soon after they had seen each news sequence, the viewers were asked to recall as many of the items as they could, spontaneously and in any order, by writing brief accounts of each news report.

For some viewers, the news category was held constant over all four sequences of items. For instance, in one experiment, the viewer saw twelve items (in four groups of three) about political news events, or twelve items about sports. For others, the category was kept the same for the first three sequences (nine items) and then switched for the fourth sequence (three items). For instance, a switch might be made from three sequences of political news stories (nine in all) to a final sequence of three sports stories.

The viewers' ability to recall what they saw declined over successive sequences of items from the same class, but recoverd whenever a switch was made from one class to another. The decline in memory for the later items in a category was caused by interference from earlier items in the same category. The extent of the decline was quite substantial. It occurred in several different classes of news, including politics, industry, foreign and sports stories. Typically, about 70% of items in the first sequence were correctly recalled but only 40-50% of items in the fourth sequence.

The effect of changing the category of news was remarkable. When the last three items were taken from a fresh category, the viewers' ability to recall the items correctly improved to about 60%. When viewers were shown just one news story at a time, and given the opportunity to concentrate their learning, there were still considerable losses of information within each item as a result of interference from similar types of news material in the same sequence.

This research indicates that, if one wishes the audience to take in information, it may be inadvisable to present news packages consisting of groups of news stories about very similar kinds of events or issues. The result may be extensive forgetfulness. The persistent tendency of television news editors to employ 'packaging' in an attempt to enhance clarity and learning may not so much improve the viewers' memory for new as actually impair it.

It is significant that the largest drop in recall performance usually occurred between the first and second items in a package. Therefore, even groupings of only two very similar types of news story may result in a poor level of recall and learning of the second story. If such pairings occur several times in a newscast they could seriously affect the overall memorability of the programme.

PICTURES AND WORDS

Although the newsreader's verbal presentation is often held to be the essence of a television news bulletin, television remains very much a visual medium. It is always an important consideration whether or not to use this potential and illustrate a news story with newsfilm, photographs or graphics. Some stories, of course, are essentially visual, and need only a rudimentary voice-over commentary. Indeed, most TV newsmen believe in using the visual potential of their medium to the full. Moving pictures are particularly favoured because they create the impression of allowing viewers to witness the news as it actually happens, which is supposed to enhance news impact and learning. But does it?

Some researchers say they have found evidence that film helps viewers gain a better understanding of the news, but the majority of workers in this field have found no such evidence. Our own studies have produced conflicting results. Under certain conditions of presentation and learning, a news item accompanied by film is remembered better than an item accompanied by still photographs, maps or graphics, or an item read by a 'talking-head' in a plain studio setting. Under other conditions, the use of film may actually inhibit the viewers' ability to recall and learn. This converse effect is particularly strong when viewers are required to recall the content of a news story in detail. Thus, there are no unequivocal answers to the question of whether it is better to use film or stills or no visual at all.

The context in which the visual inputs are used is always important. The verbal content of a news item usually plays a dominant 'information' role, and any visualisations should be regarded as relatively subordinate. It is more satisfactory when a fairly precise correspondence exists between the verbal material and picture material, whether film or stills. Film has been regarded by most professionals as the 'natural' means of portraying actuality but research has shown that, where the goal is the effective communication of information, the impact of still photos and graphics can be just as good. In fact, there is no conclusive evidence to support the thesis that film is necessarily more appreciated by the audience than other visual modes of presentation.

From a production standpoint, the use of stills or graphics affords considerably more flexibility and control in the design of individual news items and indeed the bulletin as a whole than does the use of film material. Film is often allowed to dominate production strategy. The availability of appropriate footage may determine which stories are selected and which features should be emphasised whether or not they are relevant to the verbal narrative of the news report. Experiments on the use of newsfilm have shown that film footage that may seem only slightly irrelevant to the narrative can be damaging to learning. Even if the film footage is inconsistent only in part with what is actually being said, the effect upon a viewer's ability to get information from the programme could be considerable.

Of fundamental importance for effective learning is the balanced nature of visual reinforcement. The Swedish researchers Olle Findahl and Birgitta Hoijer have shown that viewers of visually neutral or 'talking-head' presentations are better able to recall 'concrete' facts about the location of news events and the objects or persons involved than the more 'abstract' relationships associated with the causes and consequences of events. The visual reinforcements of concrete information produces imbalanced recall because although it improves the viewers' ability to remember the concrete facts it impairs their understanding of abstract causes and effects.

The reverse is not true. Visual material (pictures, graphics) on causes and effects not only increases the viewer's chances of learning about these abstract matters, but also enhances the viewer's ability to grasp the facts.

A balanced recall and a proper understanding is therefore heavily dependent upon the careful and selective use of visual illustration. They should be made to fit the story narrative rather than predominating over what is said, as is so often the case, especially where film is involved. Indeed, the greater control afforded by using stills and specially designed graphic material, when matching visuals to the story text, favours the more extensive deployment of these kinds of visual inputs.

Research on learning from television news broadcasts is still in its infancy, but the first few psychological studies have already shown that certain of the assumptions about a viewer's capacities to learn about a programme's content are often inaccurate. The profiles and presentation formats determined by these assumptions may often inhibit rather than enhance a viewer's memory. With the impending expansion of information programming the time has come for TV executives and producers to have at least some awareness of the elementary principles of human learning and memory, particularly as they operate in relation to television presentations. It may be time to incorporate into TV production structures some feedback channels from research units to broadcast units. The psychologists working in this field would welcome the opportunity to collaborate with the professionals of television news production in a symbictic, investigative relationship. The aim is to produce workable solutions for improving presentation methods and, hence, the audience's acquisition of knowledge from television news broadcasts. Only in that way can both producers and public be generally satisfied.

Woodall, Davis and Sahin argue that while television is relied upon increasingly as a primary source of information, little is known about the ways in which people learn from news broadcasts. Their chapter reviews research on learning from television news and develops a theoretical framework to guide future research. Two models of memory and understanding are considered: episodic memory and semantic network models, and guidelines for research based on both models are offered. W. Gill Woodall is an assistant professor at the University of New Mexico, Dennis K. Davis is an associate professor of communication at Cleveland State University, and Haluk Sahin is associate professor of journalism at the University of Maryland.

12

FROM THE BOOB TUBE TO THE BLACK BOX
TV News Comprehension from an
Information Processing Perspective

W. Gill Woodall, Dennis K. Davis, and Haluk Sahin

The potential of television news broadcasts to provide an electronic window through which viewers can metaphorically step into other worlds is now familiar to many, and not just to those who study the media. The speed, intensity, detail and power of electronic news events is now a part of our everyday lives. What is interesting about this state of affairs is how little we often gather from this human-electronic interface, and more importantly, how little we understand what happens at the interface itself. What is remarkable is that acquiring information from electronic sources may become one of the primary modes of knowledge transmission in the very near future. The combination of visual images, verbal information, structure and pace of presentation with the cognitive abilities and skills viewers bring to the situation makes television news viewing a quite complex communication phenomenon.

Television news viewing has attracted a number of different research interests. Researchers have been concerned with cognitive determinants of media choice and information seeking,[1] cognitive switching,[2] information

Manuscript accepted for publication, September 1982.

[1]Charles Atkin, "Instrumental Utilities and Information Seeking," in *New Models for Communication Research,* ed. Peter Clarke (Beverly Hills, CA: Sage, 1973).

[2]Richard F. Carter and W. Lee Ruggels, "Application of Signalled Stopping Technique to Communication Research," in *New Models for Communication Research,* ed. Peter Clarke (Beverly Hills, CA: Sage, 1973); Thomas A. McCain and Mark G. Ross, "Cognitive Switching: A Behavioral Trace of Human Information Processing for Television Newscasts," *Human Communication Research* 5:121-129 (1979).

From W. Gill Woodall, Dennis K. Davis, and Haluk Sahin, "From the Boob Tube to the Black Box: TV News Comprehension from an Information Processing Perspective," *Journal of Broadcasting,* Vol. 27, No. 2 (Spring 1983). Reprinted by permission.

gain,[3] as well as comprehension.[4] Research that has focused on comprehension of televised news has shown a remarkable lack of consistency in results, with some studies indicating little or no comprehension of televised news and other studies showing considerable news comprehension that is affected by a number of factors. Little attention has been paid to the underlying theoretical and associated methodological issues in this area. The purpose of this article is to indicate how information processing concepts can provide a theoretical account of television news viewing behavior. Such an account, once fully developed, should clarify previous inconsistent evidence and lay a heuristic basis for further investigation.

Processing the News

The bulk of past research in information processing has been confined to narrow laboratory tasks such as word list learning, word pair recall and sentence recognition. However, recently researchers have begun to step beyond these constrained stimulus situations to apply information processing principles to more complex social processes such as person memory, impression formation, conversational management and the attitude-behavior relationship.[5] Television news research is also a likely candidate for information processing models since the basic questions in this area are ones information processing theorists are concerned with: How do viewers process televised

[3]F. Gerald Kline, Peter V. Miller and Andrew J. Morrison, "Adolescents and Family Planning Information: An Exploration of Audience Needs and Media Effects," in *The Uses of Mass Communications: Current Perspectives on Gratifications Research,* eds. Jay G. Blumler and Elihu Katz (Beverly Hills, CA: Sage, 1974); Jack M. McLeod and Lee B. Becker, "Testing the Validity of Gratifications Measures Through Political Effects Analysis," in *The Uses of Mass Communications: Current Perspectives on Gratifications Research,* eds. Jay G. Blumler and Elihu Katz (Beverly Hills, CA: Sage, 1974); Maxwell E. McCombs, "Mass Communication in Political Campaigns: Information, Gratification, and Persuasion," in *Current Perspectives in Mass Communication Research,* eds. F. Gerald Kline and Phillip J. Tichenor (Beverly Hills, CA: Sage, 1972); Keith R. Stamm, "Environment and Communication," in *Current Perspectives in Mass Communication Research,* eds. F. Gerald Kline and Phillip J. Tichenor (Beverly Hills, CA: Sage, 1972).

[4]Mickie Edwardson, Donald Grooms and Peter Pringle, "Visualization and TV News Information Gain," *Journal of Broadcasting* 20:373–380 (Summer, 1976); Haluk Sahin, Dennis K. Davis and John P. Robinson, "Improving the TV News," *Irish Broadcasting Review* 11:50–55 (1981).

[5]Richard Nisbett and Lee Ross, *Human Inference: Strategies and Shortcomings of Social Judgement* (Englewood Cliffs, NJ: Prentice-Hall, 1980); Reid Hastie, Thomas M. Ostrom, Ebbe B. Ebbeson, Robert S. Wyer, Donald L. Hamilton and Donald E. Carlston, *Person Memory: The Cognitive Basis of Social Perception* (Hillsdale, NJ: Lawrence Erlbaum Associates, 1980); Robert T. Craig, "Information Systems Theory and Research: An Overview of Individual Information Processing," in *Communication Yearbook III,* ed. Dan Nimmo (New Brunswick, NJ: Transaction Books, 1979); Sally Planalp and Karen Tracy, "Not to Change the Topic But . . . : A Cognitive Approach to the Management of Conversation," in *Communication Yearbook III,* ed. Dan Nimmo (New Brunswick, NJ: Transaction Books, 1979); Joseph N. Capella and Joseph P. Folger, "An Information Processing Exploration of Attitude-Behavior Inconsistency," in *Message-Attitude-Behavior Relationship: Theory, Methodology and Application,* eds. Donald P. Cushman and Robert McPhee (New York: Academic Press, 1981).

news, what sense(s) do they make of it and what are the determinants of these processes? To the extent that such questions can be approached, both cognitive theorists and media researchers will benefit by a broadened and more thoroughly grounded explanation.

Paying Attention to the News

As with most information processing models, the initial stage to consider has to do with attention-related processes. While memory and comprehension processes are of primary concern here, it is worthwhile to consider what relationships may exist between each of these stages. First, it is important to acknowledge that survey data[6] indicate that viewers are often engaged in other activities while viewing television news, so that viewers probably do not give complete and focused attention to *all* news stories. However, it is also likely that *some* news stories do receive viewers' focused attention. Given a fluctuating attention level to the news, what accounts of attention processing make sense? Several cognitive theorists[7] have characterized attention-related processing as being one of two kinds. *Bottom-up processing* involves information flowing from perceptual features of input information which serve as the focus of attention and lead to larger information units being built. Such attention-related processing is also referred to as *data-driven processing*. *Top-down processing* involves the use of general world knowledge to guide attention and determine the interpretation of low-level perceptual features. Such processing is also referred to as *conceptually-driven processing*. As Anderson[8] has noted, in most situations attention relies on an interaction of *both* bottom-up and top-down processing. A great deal of perceptual features are available from the environment which can only adequately be handled by guiding knowledge structures and frames of reference. Television news viewing should fit this description quite well. Processing of televised news should involve both bottom-up and top-down processing, where both televised visual and verbal information provide features that catch viewers' attention, and at the same time, viewers' frames of reference guide attention-related efforts. Such a position is consistent with earlier research on selective perception by Broadbent,[9] and current research on attention.[10] Recent work

[6]John P. Robinson, Dennis K. Davis, Haluk Sahin and Thomas O'Toole, "Comprehension of Television News: How Alert is the Audience?" (paper presented to the Association for Education in Journalism, Boston, 1980).

[7]John R. Anderson, *Cognitive Psychology and Its Implications* (San Francisco: W.H. Freeman, 1980); P.H. Lindsay and Donald A. Norman, *Human Information Processing* (New York: Academic Press, 1977).

[8]Anderson, *ibid.*

[9]Donald E. Broadbent, *Perception and Communication* (London: Pergamon Press, 1958).

[10]Stephen K. Reed, *Cognition: Theory and Applications* (Monterey, CA: Brooks/Cole, 1982); Anderson, *op. cit.*; Richard Shiffrin and Walter Schneider, "Controlled and Automatic Human Information Processing: II. Perceptual Learning, Automatic Attending, and a General Theory," *Psychological Review* 84:127–190 (March 1977).

on cognitive switching[11] strongly suggests one way that processing may be conceptually driven. McCain and Ross found that viewers of news broadcasts cognitively switched (that is, unitized news information) based on four functional modes: agreeing, disagreeing, thinking and questioning. They further found that viewers exhibited similar cognitive switching patterns under similar processing conditions. While the processing modes identified in this research are rather broad, it is very likely that such modes are based on the use of activated knowledge of viewers since it is difficult to imagine a viewer agreeing or disagreeing with news information without that viewer having relevant knowledge already stored and available. It is also likely that pre-existing knowledge guides, to some extent, which stories in a newscast get paid most focused attention to. This research has given a glimpse of what attention-related processing of televised news is like, and suggests that most of that processing is conceptually driven. At this stage of processing, as well as the other stages to be discussed, a great deal of emphasis is placed on knowledge that viewers have and use to process incoming information. The pivotal role of previously held knowledge suggests a more integrated and less distinctly sequential view of processing than previous models have suggested. We now turn to a closer consideration of memory processes that provide storage and access to what viewers already know.

Remembering Versus Understanding

One fundamental distinction recently developed in information processing theory[12] claims that *remembering* information and *understanding* information are separate and different cognitive processes. Memory processes involve the storage, retrieval and access to input information, while understanding involves an interaction between incoming information and knowledge stored in memory so that stored information is utilized in going beyond input information to make some set of inferences. This distinction allows the possibility of remembering things we don't understand, and understanding things that we can't later remember. Although the two processes are inter-related in human cognitive systems (for example, better initial understanding of information at input to a cognitive system facilitates its later recall) attempts to characterize and conceptualize the processing of news information should keep memory and understanding processes separate while specifying points of interrelatedness.

The distinction between remembering and understanding carries some interesting implications for news comprehension research. First, given this distinction, it seems unclear what the terms "comprehension" as used by past researchers theoretically stands for. Whether the terms "comprehension" of

---

[11]McCain and Ross, *op. cit.*

[12]Andrew Ortony, "Remembering, Understanding and Representation," *Cognitive Science* 2:53-69 (1978).

news information or "learning" of news information in past research has stood for memory processes or understanding processes, or an amalgam of both is quite unclear. For example, Nordenstreng[13] has argued that the final criterion of successful news activity is the audience's *comprehension* of it, and here he means comprehension in terms of understanding, i.e., whether the audience can form a truthful picture of events described. Katz[14] as well emphasizes the importance of citizens' understanding of news, both on the literal level as well as its broader societal implications. However, the empirical work by both these researchers as well as others seems to focus on what and how much viewers *remember* from newcasts,[15] and not on whether and to what extent viewers understood newscast information. It is difficult, and understandably so, to sort out whether comprehension has implied memory or understanding in past research efforts, and thus all the more important to clearly distinguish the two cognitive processes theoretically in future efforts.

Much the same point can be made on methodological grounds. Whether researchers have in the past measured viewers' memory or understanding of television news events, or both, is ambiguous. Researchers have used free recall, aided or cued recall, and multiple choice questions, and each of these measures could potentially tap into either memory for newcasts *or* understanding of them. For example, on open-ended free recall measures, subjects may give responses that indicate simple recall of information contained in a story (the newscaster said *x* happened) as well as understanding of the story and its implications (if what the newscaster said is true, *y* may happen or should have happened). While the account presented here suggests such responses represent different cognitive processes and should be coded as such, it is unclear how other researchers have handled these cases. Similarly, aided or cued recall can elicit memory of or understanding of televised news. In response to "what do you remember about story *x*?," a viewer could respond with "I remember that the newscaster said *z* in story *x*" or "I think the gist of what the newscaster was saying in story *x* was *w*." While the first response indicates simple retrieval of news information, the second indicates interpretation of information based on inference making. Multiple choice items as well, depending upon how they are written (focusing on the story itself versus viewers' thoughts about an interpretation of the story) may measure memory or understanding. Gunter,[16] as well as Edwardson, Grooms and Pringle[17] have used multiple choice questions to measure 'memory' or

[13]Karle Nordenstreng, "Policy for News Transmission," *Educational Broadcasting Review* (Autumn 1971).

[14]Elihu Katz, *Social Research on Broadcasting: Proposals for Further Development* (London, England: British Broadcasting Corporation, 1977).

[15]Nordenstreng, *op. cit.;* Elihu Katz, Hanna Adoni and Pnina Parness, "Remembering the News: What the Picture Adds to Recall," *Journalism Quarterly* 54:231–239 (1977).

[16]Barrie Gunter, "Remembering the Television News: Effects of Visual Format on Information Gain," *Journal of Educational Television* 6:8–11 (1980).

[17]Edwardson, Grooms and Pringle, *op. cit.*

'information gain' from television news broadcasts. However, whether information gain items measure memory or understanding is unclear. From both theoretical and methodological points then, the distinction between memory and understanding as separate processes is an important one for an information processing view of this area. We now turn to a consideration of how viewers may store and retrieve televised news information, and then how viewers understand televised news.

Remembering News Information: Episodic Memory

One line of research which may be applicable to viewers' memory for televised news has been concerned with the effect of contextual information on the retrieval of target or to-be-remembered information. Tulving and his colleagues[18] have distinguished between two basic types of memory: *semantic memory* and *episodic memory*. Semantic memory can be conceived of as consisting of a network of concepts, words, constructs and their interrelationships, and more will be said about this form of memory later. Episodic memory, on the other hand, is an event memory which stores episodes as unique historical traces that consist of target or to-be-remembered information and the context in which the target information was presented or encountered. Carlston[19] has suggested that event memories include behavioral and situational details and preserves the temporal ordering of activity within an event, and that episodic traces are "raw representations of what an observer thinks transpired in a particular episode."[20]

One important corollary of an episodic form of memory offered by Tulving and Thomson[21] is the encoding specificity principle, which holds that:

> Specific encoding operations performed on what is perceived determines what is stored, and what is stored determines what retrieval cues are effective in providing access to what is stored.

Tulving and his associates[22] have shown that contextual cues that are stored as part of the episodic memory trace can act as very effective retrieval cues in recalling information. In a series of studies utilizing the list-learning paradigm,

---

[18]For a review, see Michael J. Watkins and Endel Tulving, "Episodic Memory: When Recognition Fails," *Journal of Experimental Psychology* 104:5-29 (March 1975).

[19]Donald E. Carlston, "Events, Inferences and Impression Formation," in *Person Memory: The Cognitive Basis of Social Perception,* eds. Reid Hastie, Thomas M. Ostrom, Ebbe B. Ebbeson, Robert S. Wyer, Donald L. Hamilton and Donald E. Carlston (Hillsdale, NJ: Lawrence Erlbaum Associates, 1980).

[20]Carlston, *ibid.*

[21]Endel Tulving and Donald Thomson, "Encoding Specificity and Retrieval Processes in Episodic Memory," *Psychological Review* 80:352-373 (September 1973).

[22]Endel Tulving, "Recall and Recognition of Semantically Encoded Words," *Journal of Experimental Psychology* 102:778-787 (May 1974); Endel Tulving and Michael Watkins, "Structure of Memory Traces," *Psychological Review* 82:261-275 (July 1975); Endel Tulving and Sandor Wiseman, "Relation Between Recognition and Recognition Failure of Recallable Words," *Bulletin of the Psychonomic Society* 6:79-82 (July 1975).

subjects were given lists of word pairs in which one word (for example, "ground") acted as context for a target or to-be-remembered word (a target word such as "day"). As can be seen, contextual words were weakly semantically related to target words in the lists. Evidence from these studies indicated that subjects recalled target words (day) when given the context word (ground) as well as when given strongly related cue words (such as "night" for "day"), and were better at contextual cued recall than at recognizing the target words themselves from a list of words that contained the target words. The research shows that contextual cues can act as highly effective retrieval cues in recall situations, and can be more effective than when subjects are given a "copy" of the target information to recognize.

Other studies have validated these findings in broader research settings. Watkins, Ho and Tulving[23] have shown that verbal information (in this case, words) can serve as contextual cues for subsequent recognition of a visual target (pictures of faces). More recently, Woodall and Folger[24] have shown that nonverbal visual cues (such as hand gestures) that co-occur with linguistic information (in this case, short verbal phrases) can act as contextual cues that provide subsequent access to that linguistic information stored in memory. Episodic memory and the encoding specificity principle have been found to be generalizable beyond narrow laboratory situations and can be applied to assessing the storage and retrieval of televised news information. At the same time, in considering the possibilities of how televised news might be stored in human cognitive systems, characteristics of television news itself make episodic storage a highly likely candidate: the information clearly has event-like structure, and can be cast in context and target terms.

For example, assume that a news viewer watches a news story on the Environmental Protection Agency and its efforts to clean up and monitor Atlantic City, New Jersey's water supply. The story could include a reporter's observations about the situation, how the pollution could have occurred and who the polluters might be, interviews with residents of the area and EPA officials, all accompanied by videotape footage of contaminated wells. A number of entries from this story might be episodically stored by a viewer, including what a viewer understood to be comments from residents in the affected area, comments from EPA officials, and the co-occuring visual information associated with each part of the news story, all in roughly the same order as the newscast presented.

The question for this view then becomes, of the visual, vocal and verbal information present in a television news broadcast, what constitutes contextual information and what constitutes the target or to-be-remembered information. What becomes context and target for viewers in a given news story may depend on several factors, including the structure and characteris-

[23]Michael J. Watkins, Elaine Ho and Endel Tulving, "Context Effects in Recognition Memory for Faces," *Journal of Verbal Learning and Verbal Behavior* 15:505–517 (October 1976).

[24]W. Gill Woodall and Joseph P. Folger, "Encoding Specificity and Nonverbal Cue Context: An Expansion of Episodic Memory Research," *Communication Monographs* 48:39–53 (1981).

tics of the story as well as the cognitive set and skills of the viewer. One plausible procedure is to treat visual information as context for target verbal information. Thus, an episodic memory trace of television news could be made up of two parts: the visual context (pictures, film/videotape images, diagrams and graphs) and verbal information that constitutes the target. Given such a trace, the encoding specificity principle would hold that successful recall of verbal target information requires a respondent to be presented with enough of the visual context to match the memory trace. In the EPA example above, contextual cues such as visual information presented in the news story (videotape footage of contaminated wells, for instance) could be used as retrieval cues by viewers to recall story content. While no investigation has yet to use visual retrieval cues as a way to prompt viewer recall of news information, several studies have shown that the presence of visual information in a news story can enhance subsequent unaided recall. Although there is some mixed and contradictory evidence, investigations by Gunter,[25] Katz, Adoni and Parness,[26] and Findahl and Höijer[27] have shown that various kinds of visual information, such as film and videotape footage, still pictures, and graphs and drawings may enhance later recall of news story information. Although no visual retrieval cues were utilized at time of recall in these investigations, the presence of visual information in the original news items may have provided better access to target information at time of recall for viewers. Contextual cues can be generated by viewers themselves rather than presented to viewers, and such self-generated cues could then provide access to stored target information.

At the same time, it is clear that in some news stories, the visual information presented becomes the target to be remembered while accompanying verbal information plays a contextual role. These stories are usually largely visual and words simply serve to provide context for the pictures. While our guess is that the frequency of news stories where visual information plays a target role is less than those in which visual information is contextual, the assignment of target and context is flexible and at least partially dependent on the story structure.

Cognitive Skills

One mediating factor for an episodic memory account of television news retrieval is the cognitive skills of the viewer. Salomon and his associates[28] have

[25]Gunter, op. cit.; Barrie Gunter, "Remembering Televised News: Effects of Picture Content," Journal of General Psychology 102:216-223 (1980); Barrie Gunter, Brian R. Clifford and Colin Berry, "Release from Proactive Interference with Television News Items: Evidence for Encoding Dimensions Within Televised News," Journal of Experimental Psychology: Human Learning and Memory 6:216-223 (March 1980).

[26]Katz, Adoni and Parness, op. cit.

[27]Olle Findahl and Birgitta Höijer, Fragments of Reality: An Experiment with News and TV Visuals (Stockholm, Sweden: Sueriges Radio, 1976).

[28]Gavriel Salomon, "Can We Affect Cognitive Skills Through Visual Media? A Hypothesis and Initial Findings," Audiovisual Communication Review 20:401-423 (1972); Gavriel Salomon and

shown that television viewing involves particular cognitive skills and modes of representation, some of which are imagistic. Salomon has further suggested that the form of the information mode, in this case television, seems to shape the cognitive representational system used to handle and process that information. Thus, televised information, which is largely visual, may be represented cognitively in part with some sort of imagistic or pictoral system. It stands to reason that there will be individual differences in the population in terms of the adequacy and skill with which viewers can represent and handle visual information presented on television. We may find some viewers to be *visually dependent,* i.e., viewers who have good skill and ability to represent, store and retrieve visual information cognitively, while other viewers may be *visually independent,* that is, less developed in skill and ability to represent, store and retrieve viewed visual information. Keep in mind that such information processing skills have only to do with viewers' representation, storage and retrieval abilities in a certain cognitive code. These rather specific skills should not be confused with other broader cognitive style variables such as field dependence-independence,[29] which has to do with whether an individual views the world in a global or analytical manner.

Although there may be a number of implications here, one very clear one in terms of an episodic memory model involves how much visual context is necessary to facilitate retrieval of target or to-be-remembered information. Salomon, in his own research, identified what he termed aptitude-treatment interactions: viewers of films with poor visual representational skills learned more when visual information was supplied to them than when not, and viewers with good visual representational ability learned more when the visual information was not supplied, but were prompted to use their own mediational abilities. In terms of an episodic model of memory then, we might expect viewers who are *visually dependent* to benefit most in terms of recall from being given few but important visual retrieval cues, while those who are *visually independent* would benefit more from being given a greater amount of visual context with which to retrieve target information. The skills and abilities developed as a result of dealing with certain modes of information are an important feature of any information processing explanation. The different levels of those skills and abilities across viewers ought to be used to increase the power of information processing explanation.

In sum, there are several important general points to be made in applying an episodic model of memory to televised news recall. One point is that if

Richard E. Snow, "The Specification of Film Attributes for Psychological and Educational Research Purposes," *Audiovisual Communication Review* 16:225–244 (1968); Gavriel Salomon and Aikiba A. Cohen, "Television Formats, Mastery of Mental Skills and the Acquisition of Knowledge," *Journal of Educational Psychology* 69:612–619 (1977); Gavriel Salomon, "Internalization of Filmic Schematic Operations In Interaction with Learners' Aptitudes," *Journal of Educational Psychology* 66:499–511 (1974).

[29]Herman A. Witkin and Donald R. Goodenough, "Field Dependence and Interpersonal Behavior," *Psychological Bulletin* 84:661–689 (1976).

televised news is stored episodically, then the low levels of recall found in some studies[30] and the general overall inconsistency of results in the research area can be partially explained by failure of researchers to provide contextual retrieval cues to respondents in recall situations. Without retrieval cues, respondents may simply lack adequate cognitive access to episodically stored news information. Thus, these results can be attributed to poor access to stored information rather than poor memory for televised news. As such, conclusions that viewers recall little or nothing from televised news should be carefully reevaluated; viewers may have lacked access to news information, but not the information itself. Similarly, of those investigations that used cued-recall tests,[31] it is unclear whether the information used as prompts to recall would consistute retrieval cues in an episodic sense. Such cues would need to be part of an episode context, or at least allow the viewer to generate the context of an episode to allow recall. Thus, even research using cued-recall tests may have underestimated viewers' memory.

The episodic component of memory presented here suggests that researchers should determine what features and characteristics of news stories may be contextual for viewers and what features constitute target information. Retrieval cues that are context themselves or allow viewers to generate context can then be used in cued-recall or multiple choice formats to prompt access to episodically stored news events. Although the kinds of retrieval cue characteristics that provide access will be further discussed later, there appears to be many useful insights which can be gained by creatively exploring how different types of retrieval cues can aid different types of news viewers in recalling varying forms of information. Such research can help specify more precisely what people do store and later recall after viewing a news broadcast and thus provide important, elementary information about the news viewing experience and the processing of it. We now turn to consider how viewers understand news information within an information processing model.

Understanding the News

In developing an account of viewers' understanding television news we now make reference to the other form of memory mentioned earlier, semantic memory. A number of information processing theorists[32] have conceptualized semantic memory as a complex network of interrelated

---

[30]Nordenstreng, op. cit.; W. Russell Neuman, "Patterns of Recall Among Television News Viewers," *Public Opinion Quarterly* 40:115-123 (Spring 1976); Katz, Adoni and Parness, op. cit.

[31]John P. Robinson, Dennis K. Davis, Haluk Sahin and Thomas O'Toole, op. cit.; Neuman, op. cit.; E. Katz, op. cit.

[32]M. Ross Quillian, "Semantic Memory," in *Semantic Information Processing*, ed. Marvin L. Minsky (Cambridge, MA: MIT Press, 1968); Allan M. Collins and Elizabeth F. Loftus, "A Spreading-Activation Theory of Semantic Processing," *Psychological Review* 82:407-428 (November 1975); Ortony, op. cit.

"nodes" (words, concepts, properties and their interrelationships) that are linked together by types of relations. For example, the node "DC-10" might be linked to the node "airplane" by a class relationship, and to the node "accident" by time and place relationships. Such networks represent the mental thesaurus of human cognitive systems, and can be taken as the pre-existing knowledge that an individual brings to a situation.

The process of understanding involves an interaction between new incoming information (both verbal and visual) and the pre-existing network of nodes. In any particular case, some set of nodes are activated by the input information, and a set of inferences concerning the input information can be made as a result of the activation. As a simplified example, let us suppose that a viewer sees a televised story on federal budget reductions in the Environmental Protection Agency. The story mentions that recent funding reductions may lessen the ability of the EPA to enforce existing environmental laws and gives examples in three locales. Depending upon a given individual's semantic network, some sets of nodes would be activated within the network, and could possibly include the nodes environment, federal agency, clean air and water, federal beauracracy, regulations, laws, enforcement, local communities, cost/benefit ratio, industry, lobbies and supply-side economics. The extent of an individual's understanding of such a story (depressing as it might be) is a function of the subset of activated nodes and the inferences made based on those nodes.

There are several characteristics of this type of semantic network model (even one as generally and roughly sketched as it is here) that make it particularly applicable to the processing of television news. First, the plausibility of the model is enhanced by its emphasis on the importance of pre-existing knowledge for making sense of new information. Several media researchers have already pointed out that viewers with good general knowledge (which can be taken here as having an extensive semantic network) are better able to recall and understand newscast information than viewers with poor general knowledge. Findahl and Höijer[33] found that individuals with high levels of current issue knowledge were able to recall more news program content than those with low levels of current issue knowledge (we are assuming here that higher levels of recall in this case indicates better understanding). In summing up their evidence on news comprehension, Findahl and Höijer characterize the news viewing situation as being one of "news for the initiated." Even more to the point is a study by Stauffer, Frost and Rybolt[34] which compared literate and illiterate adult's recall and understanding of news. Measures used to compare the two groups included unaided recall of news stories, and a multiple choice test with items concerning recall of numbers, visual information and questions requiring inferences from program content. The inference

[33]Findahl and Höijer, op. cit.
[34]John Stauffer, Richard Frost and William Rybolt, "Literacy, Illiteracy and Learning from Television News," Communication Research 5:221–232 (1978).

making items used would clearly measure news understanding as we have discussed it. Results indicated significantly higher scores for the literate viewers on the unaided recall, as well as higher scores on the recall of number, visual, and inference related questions. As such, this evidence fits well within a semantic network model of understanding that places emphasis on pre-existing knowledge. Further, we would expect that stories that deal with matters familiar to most viewers will be well understood because viewers can rely on a well represented network of nodes acquired through daily experi-ence. Several researchers[35] have found that 'human interest' stories that are related to everyday life and directly concern many viewers are well under-stood and easily recalled, supporting such an expectation. The semantic network version of understanding provides an explanatory framework that integrates this evidence, and allows us a way of understanding how and what different groups of individuals may extract as "meaningful" from a news story.

Another feature of the semantic network model is that understanding is not seen as an all-or-nothing process; rather, input information may be processed on several different levels with greater or lesser depth.[36] This depth of processing feature stems from a level of processing theory initially formulated by Craik and Lockhart.[37] These researchers argued that information is processed on three qualitatively different levels (structural, phonemic and semantic levels), and that semantic processing represents the deepest level and results in superior retention. This explanation was developed in part to account for the different levels of retention obtained in previous studies[38] where stimuli were processed on these different levels. Underlying this explanation is the notion that retrieval of information is best when the meaning of input information is semantically elaborated.

While levels of processing theory has had a major impact on memory research and has received a great deal of empirical support,[39] some criticisms of this approach have emerged. One criticism posed by some researchers[40] is that the levels of processing approach involves circular reasoning (different

[35]See, for example, Olle Findahl and Birgitta Höijer, *On Knowledge, Social Privilege and the News* (Stockholm, Sweden: Sueriges Radio, 1974).

[36]Ortony, *op. cit.*

[37]Fergus I.M. Craik and Robert S. Lockart, "Levels of Processing: A Framework for Memory Research," *Journal of Verbal Learning and Verbal Behavior* 11:671–684 (December 1972).

[38]Thomas S. Hyde and James J. Jenkins, "Differential Effects of Incidental tasks on the Organization of Recall of a List of Highly Associated Words," *Journal of Experimental Psychology* 82:472–481 (December 1969).

[39]Laird S. Cermak and Fergus I.M. Craik, *Levels of Processing in Human Memory* (Hillsdale, NJ: Lawrence Erlbaum Associates, 1979).

[40]Allan D. Baddeley, "The Trouble with Levels: A Reexamination of Craik and Lockhart's Framework for Memory Research," *Psychological Review* 85:139–152 (May 1978); Michael W. Eysenck, "Levels of Processing: A Critique," *British Journal of Psychology* 69:157–169 (1978); Thomas O. Nelson, "Repetition and Depth of Processing," *Journal of Verbal Learning and Verbal Behavior* 16:151–171 (April 1977).

rates of forgetting are due to processing at different levels, and different levels of processing are indicated by different recall rates), and that in order to avoid such circular reasoning, an independent index of depth of processing not related to retention needs to be found. Since an adequate measure of depth of processing has not yet been developed, the levels of processing approach remains suspect, these researchers argue. A second criticism is that Craik and Lockhart's original formulation did not explain *why* the semantic code is deeper and thus more effective in terms of retention than the other codes.

In response to these criticisms, depth of processing researchers have provided some theoretical developments and modifications that take account of these difficulties. Lockhart and Craik[41] have conceded that, lacking an index of processing depth, some circularity or argument is present in their formulations. But, they also argue that the possibility of circularity does not render the levels of processing approach scientifically valueless. They point out that, as a guiding theoretical construct, levels of processing has been shown to have heuristic value and remains a strong explanation of a great deal of empirical work. Further, current and future efforts to provide an index of processing depth[42] may prove to be successful. Thus, levels of processing researchers have argued that, potential circularity notwithstanding, the approach remains a viable one.

Several cognitive theorists[43] have also provided a more developed explanation of why semantic level processing is deeper and provides better retention. These theorists have posed a two-part explanation for semantic processing superiority. First, semantic level processing provides more opportunity for elaboration of information through network node activation than other levels of processing. Thus, input information that is elaborated by way of additional association in an activated network leads to *more accessible* memory traces. Second, semantic level processing may provide more *distinctive* memory traces through elaboration, and thus such traces are more easily recallable because they are discriminably different from other stored information. Processing of information at other levels does not seem to provide the distinctiveness that semantic level processing does. A number of studies[44]

[41]Robert S. Lockart and Fergus I. M. Craik, "Levels of Processing: A Reply to Eysenck," *British Journal of Psychology* 69:171–175 (1978).

[42]Reid Hastie, "Memory for Behavioral Information that Confirms or Contradicts a Personality Impression," in *Person Memory: The Cognitive Basis of Social Perception,* eds. Reid Hastie, et. al. (Hillsdale, NJ: Lawrence Erlbaum Associates, 1980); Alan J. Parkin, "Specifying Levels of Processing," *Quarterly Journal of Experimental Psychology* 31:175–195 (May 1979).

[43]John R. Anderson and Lynn M. Reder, "An Elaborative Processing Explanation of Depth of Processing," in *Levels of Processing in Human Memory,* eds. Laird S. Cermak and Fergus I. M. Craik (Hillsdale, NJ: Lawrence Erlbaum Associates, 1979); Lockart and Craik, *op. cit.*

[44]Anderson and Reder, *ibid;* Kitty Klein and Eli Saltz, "Specifying the Mechanisms in a Levels-of-Processing Approach to Memory," *Journal of Experimental Psychology: Human Learning and Memory* 2:671–679 (November 1976); Morris Moscovitch and Fergus I. M. Craik, "Depth of Processing, Retrieval Cues, and Uniqueness of Encoding as Factors in Recall," *Journal of Verbal Learning and Verbal Behavior* 15:447–458 (August 1976).

have provided empirical support for the elaboration and distinctiveness explanation. As Reed has pointed out, even with modifications, the levels of processing framework "remains a useful conception of memory."[45]

As Craik[46] has noted, the elaboration explanation has the additional advantage of explaining how differences within a particular level of processing can occur. For semantic processing, greater spread of activation among cogitive network nodes results in deeper processing within the semantic domain. Thus, the extent and nature of understanding is dependent on the depth at which input information is processed as well as the spread of activation within that level or domain. A key question for the depth of processing feature concerns factors that promote or inhibit the spread of activation and depth at which information is processed. Ortony[47] has claimed that one factor that affects depth of processing is the context in which input information is encountered. When visual information present in news stories is cast in a contextual role, such visual cues can result in deeper processing and more extensive understanding of news stories. However, it is also quite possible that, at times, visual information can inhibit understanding or be misleading. An important element here is the nature of the link between a news story's visual context and its to-be-remembered information.

Visual information should serve to deepen processing and therefore understanding when the visual cues that act as context are closely linked to verbal content by being either repetitive and redundant, or by complementing verbal content by adding new information in some way. In such cases, the visual context should prompt deeper processing by activating more *nodes* within a viewer's semantic network. For example, a videotape of motorists waiting in line to buy gasoline should clarify and increase understanding of a news story about nationwide gasoline shortages. In addition to other information about a gas shortage (facts and figures presented verbally for example), such a videotape could activate nodes related to personal relevance time and place, line waiting experiences, associated feelings and attitudes, causes of such events and how to avoid them.

Visual context that complements and adds information to verbal content prompts deeper processing in a similar manner. The added informational value of the visual context results in a more extensive activation of nodes than would have otherwise been obtained in a semantic network system. For example, news stories about a DC-10 crash in Chicago featured pictures and diagrams of the wing pylon similar to the one that may have cracked prior to the crash. The pictures of the pylon probably resulted in a more extensive node activation because the position of the part and its relationship to other

[45]Reed, *op. cit.*, p. 134.
[46]Fergus I. M. Craik, "Levels of Processing: Overview and Closing Comments," in *Levels of Processing in Human Memory*, eds. Laird S. Cermak and Fergus I. M. Craik (Hillsdale, NJ: Lawrence Erlbaum Associates, 1979).
[47]Ortony, *op. cit.*

plane parts could be observed. Thus, viewers were given a story with a visual context that allowed them to understand a possible cause of the crash in detail, as well as an expanded ability to make inferences about the crash. Long, detailed verbal descriptions of the pylon probably could not have resulted in as great a depth of processing.

Visual context that is loosely linked or ambiguously connected to verbal content may lead to misconstrued understanding of news information. One consequence of loosely linked visual context is that the visual information may activate a separate and unrelated set of concepts than concepts activated by verbal information, which can in turn lead to erroneous inferences. For example, the videotape of motorists waiting in a gas line could be used to highlight a story that discusses what *might* happen if a middle-east war (such as the Iran-Iraq conflict) cuts off oil shipments. Such a story could result in viewers expecting shortages and lines at the pump in the near future, an expectation based on faulty inferences and loosely linked visual context. Another possibility is that loosely linked visual information may simply distract viewers, particularly when the verbal content is complex.

Previous evidence can now be more clearly interpreted in terms of semantic network activation and its link to visual context. Chu and Schramm[48] for instance, concluded that visual cues will improve learning from audiovisual messages where such cues contribute to information contained in the audio track. Several aforementioned studies have also shown that visual information can enhance recall of news. These findings can be interpreted to indicate that visual information that is well linked to a story's verbal content provides greater activation and deeper processing within a semantic network, while poorly related visual context results in shallow processing and misconstrued inferences. The relationship between understanding and visual information hinges, at least in part, on the link between context and information input. Lack of consideration of the link between visual context and verbal content and subsequent effects on processing depth may also account for the failure of some previous research to find a visual enhancement effect.

Concreteness and Vividness of News Information

The depth at which information is processed does not seem to rest solely on the context-content link, but rather on some attributes of the context and content information as well. Information processing researchers[49] as well as attribution theorists interested in everyday inference making strategies[50] have shown that the concreteness of information as well as the vividness of information are attributes that result in what can be taken as deeper

---

[48]Godwin C. Chu and Wilbur Schramm, *Learning from Television: What the Research Says* (Stanford, CA: Stanford University, ERIC for Educational Media and Technology, 1967).

[49]Allan Paivio, *Imagery and Verbal Processes* (New York: Holt, Rinehart and Winston, 1971).

[50]Nisbett and Ross, *op. cit.*

processing in semantic network terms. Concreteness can be defined as the degree of detail and specificity about actors, actions and situational context.[51] Large amounts of concrete information in news stories may prompt deeper processing because such detailed information can activate extensive and personally relevant sets of nodes within a semantic network. For example, Catholic viewers of religious rites depicted during the Pope's trip to Poland should have been more likely to develop a "deeper" understanding of this news information because they could relate the concrete details to their personal experiences and information held in network memory. Similarly, frequent air travelers or those who have suffered accidental disasters could more deeply understand storeis about the Chicago DC-10 crash because of activation of stored information by concrete details.

Evidence from our own investigations[52] as well as research by Findahl and Höijer[53] has shown that viewers are likely to recall certain concrete details of news programs, mainly the who, what and where details (as we would expect given such information is a large part of what is episodically stored). However, concrete details concerning the causes and consequences of news stories are often not recalled. The recall of isolated concrete bits and pieces of news stories has been termed "fragmentation" of the news by Findahl and Höijer. In examining the structure and links between visual information and context in news stories, Findahl and Höijer found that visuals are most frequently used to illustrate the person and place concrete details of news stories which viewers are most likely to remember anyway. When visuals were used to depict and emphasize causes and consequences of news stories, they found that recall improved for isolated details and the story as a whole as well. In terms of a depth of processing explanation, we suspect that visual concrete information that provides an emphasizing context for cause and consequence content results in deeper processing of the story content. In such cases, the concrete visual context activates more semantic network information concerning causes and consequences and allows for an extensive set of inferences to be made about the story by viewers. The story is thus more deeply understood, particularly on a personal implication level. The elimination of "news fragmentation" under these conditions in Findahl and Höijer's results is probably indicative of deeper processing.

Vivid information as well may result in greater depth of processing. Information that is vivid can be broadly defined as information that compels attention and encourages the creation of powerful mental images which can be used to interpret the information.[54] Although verbal information is often

[51]*Ibid.*

[52]Nadine Dyer and John P. Robinson, "News Comprehension Research in Great Britain," (paper presented to the International Communication Association, Acapulco, Mexico, May 1980); Robinson, Davis, Sahin and O'Toole, *op. cit.*

[53]Findahl and Höijer, *op. cit.*

[54]Nisbett and Ross, *op. cit.*

vivid, much of what we encounter on television as vivid is visual, and it is likely that such information prompts powerful mental images concerning news information to be formed. Mental imagery has been shown to play a vital role in understanding by Paivio[55] as well as Bower.[56] Further, information that prompts imagery results in deeper processing. This has been shown to be the case for verbal information[57] as well as for visual information.[58] Vivid visual information as context in televised news may have a strong potential to provoke deeper and more elaborate processing.

Although the impact of vivid information has yet to be considered by media researchers, anecdotal examples do illustrate this theoretical point. People have often argued that opposition to the Vietnam war grew partly because it was presented to us at home every evening at 6:00 p.m. If ever there was vivid visual information, that was it. Such information clearly prompted a more extensive and radically different understanding of those events, as we would expect given the above rationale. Additionally, disasters and accidents shown on television are examples of visually vivid information. Airplane crash stories have a great deal of vivid visual information (film of the crash site, the engine sitting on the runway). Such information is likely to prompt a great deal of imagery and eventually further our understanding as well as memory of those events.

In sum, we have outlined three factors that prompt deep processing of new information: the closeness and clarity of the link between visual context and verbal content, the level of concreteness of visual context and verbal content, and the level of vividness of visual context and verbal content. If Katz[59] is to be taken at his word when he argues that comprehension involves not only understanding of words and concepts but societal understanding and the problems confronting society as well, then depth of processing and the factors that influence it are important and should be carefully considered.

Memory and Understanding Interrelated

Although the distinction between memory and understanding shows these processes to be separate and different, they should not be seen as unrelated. Rather, memory and understanding, as parts of the human cognitive system, are quite independent. There are several ways in which these two processing modes interplay. First, understanding any kind of input information presup-

[55]Paivio, op. cit.

[56]Gorden H. Bower, "Mental Imagery and Associative Learning," in Cognition in Learning and Memory, ed. Lee W. Gregg (New York: Wiley, 1972).

[57]Michael E. Engle, Ranald D. Hansen and Charles A. Lowe, "Humanizing the Mixed-Motive Paradigm: Methodological Implications from Attribution Theory," Simulation and Games 6:151–165 (1975).

[58]Gordon H. Bower and Martin B. Karlin, "Depth of Processing Pictures of Faces and Recognition Memory," Journal of Experimental Psychology 103:751–757 (October 1974).

[59]Katz, op. cit.

poses a capacity for pre-existing knowledge, and as such, understanding relies on storage and access to knowledge in a very basic way. Since the depth at which understanding may occur is dependent on cognitive node availability, the role of previously stored information takes on further importance. Second, input information may activate not only semantic network information, but episodic information as well. A newscast story may activate both a viewer's relevant semantic knowledge *and* episodic information, and stored event information may then be used by the viewer to make inferences about the newscast. In such cases, viewers may develop a very personalized understanding of a news event because personal event information can be used to make inferences about news story content. Thus, links between understanding and both forms of memory discussed previously can be made.

A third way that memory and understanding interconnect is that event information stored episodically may be transferred to semantic store, and thus information encountered in an episode may later be part of pre-existing semantic knowledge that enables understanding of subsequent events.[60] Information gained from television news broadcasts would seem to be particularly likely to be processed in this way. As Ortony has indicated, information a viewer encounters in an event (in our case, a newscast) is embedded in source and modality contexts. For example, one entry in episodic memory as a result of viewing a news story on the EPA might be: the news story claimed that the investigative and enforcement functions of the EPA are being undermined by its top administrators. Over time, such knowledge may be freed from its context, and if it is relevant and can be accorded sufficient subjective truth by a viewer, Ortony suggests it can become part of the semantic store. Thus, the information encountered in one event (a news story) becomes a knowledge claim held in a viewer's semantic memory. When the viewer next encounters another news story on the EPA claiming: almost none of the "superfund cleanup" money appropriated by Congress has been allocated to pollution site cleanups, the viewer can make inferences with pre-existing knowledge transferred from episodic store (i.e., EPA has not spent the money because top-level administrators have hampered investigation and enforcement efforts). While the nature and conditions of episodic to semantic information transfer are yet to be closely examined, it seems probable that a great deal of information gleaned from televised news would be processed in this way.

Finally, Ortony[61] has claimed that understanding an event at time of input occurs prior to storage of the information about the event. However, it would also seem possible that a viewer could store episodic information about a news story and recall the information later in order to develop understanding at greater depth through further analysis and inference making. Given the fast

[60]Ortony, *op. cit.*
[61]Ortony, *op. cit.*

pace of television news, such delayed attempts at processing information at greater depth may be likely to occur, and deserves empirical attention. As can be seen, understanding and memory are distinct cognitive processes that rely heavily on each other. Such interdependence carries particular importance for television news information processing. We next consider ways that these processes can lead to misunderstanding the news.

Misunderstanding and Confusing the News

One important way that an information processing approach may broaden television news research is by suggesting a more thorough analysis of just what viewers actually glean from newscasts. It has already been pointed out that comprehension is not an all-or-nothing process where the viewer either "gets the message of the story" or doesn't. Rather, understanding is an *active* process on the part of the viewer that can occur at greater or lesser depth. As such, the *accuracy* of a viewer's understanding becomes a relative judgment, not an absolute one, and must be assessed according to what some expert or producer of the news (for example, television journalists or communication researchers) say is the "gist" of the message, or what a viewer ought to comprehend. Such assessment procedures have already been adopted in a recent research.[62] However, an 'accurate' understanding may not be what a viewer gets at all, or may be only *part of* the understanding developed by a viewer. Viewers may make many inferences concerning a news story in understanding it, some of which might be characterized as accurate, some characterized as going beyond immediate story content, and some as inaccurate and cases of misunderstanding. Being concerned only with the accuracy of viewers' understanding would seem shortsighted.

It is worthwhile to sort out these possibilities for several reasons. First, investigations by Findahl and Höijer[63] have shown that what viewers recall is often characterized by misconceptions and distortions, and that these inaccuracies are seldom random. Theoretical principles that help explain how viewers process news stories and come to misunderstandings, as well as any set of inferences regardless of their accuracy, should expand the power and scope of an explanation of television news processing, and have the potential to aid news practitioners as well.

A second reason has both roots and parallels in the knowledge gap literature.[64] As television increasingly becomes the primary source for news information, media researchers must become progressively more concerned about existing and widening knowledge gaps. Television news is likely to

[62]Robinson, Davis, Sahin and O'Toole, *op. cit.*

[63]Findahl and Höijer, *op. cit.*

[64]Thomas Childers and Joyce A. Post, *The Information Poor in America* (Metuchen, NJ: Scarecrow Press, 1975); George A. Donohue, Phillip J. Tichenor and Clarice N. Olien, "Mass Media and the Knowledge Gap: A Hypothesis Reconsidered," *Communication Research* 2:3–23 (1975).

contribute to gaps and inequities of information in segments of the population. As already noted, Findahl and Höijer have described television news as "news for the initiated," suggesting that some segments of viewers are unable to develop such understanding. A sufficiently developed theoretical account of television news processing should be able to explain how news-related information gaps develop.

In a recent review of the knowledge gap literature, Dervin[65] points out that researchers in that area are moving towards reconceptualizations of information usuage that emphasize the active and creative use of information by receivers. Such reconceptualization is quite consistent with information processing principles discussed here, and further suggests that an information processing view can provide several links between news processing and knowledge gaps. First, as Dervin[66] has shown, knowledge gap researchers have only been concerned with whether viewers were affected by the message, or "got" the message of information campaigns, much as television news researchers have only been concerned with whether viewers got the "gist" of the news story. Once again, what overall understanding of a news story viewers developed is ignored for the sake of assessing only accuracy. One result of the overconcern with accuracy is an overestimation of the extent of knowledge gaps. Until researchers begin to assess a receiver's overall understanding in terms of inferences made concerning the information, the extent or nature of information gaps will be difficult to determine.

A second way that information processing principles may aid in explaining television news knowledge gaps is to point out that *lack* of pre-existing knowledge relevant to a story's content may prevent or inhibit a viewer's understanding of that story. If a viewer's knowledge of a content area, or more precisely, semantic node availability relevant to that topic is poor, then the level of understanding developed is likely to be shallow. Further, when such stories are encountered, viewers are unlikely to be motivated to pay attention to them since top-down knowledge structures would be lacking to guide attention. Evidence that shows viewers to be more likely to recall and understand television news stories that are personally relevant to them, and less likely to process news stories less relevant to them (such as foreign and international news) supports this view.

As already noted, the link between story content and visual context may also lead to news misunderstanding and knowledge gaps. Visual context information that is loosely linked or not linked at all to news story content can mislead viewers by activating semantic node information unrelated to story content. As a result, viewers might engage in a series of erroneous inferences. If information that leads to misunderstanding is vivid, the consequences could

[65]Brenda Dervin, "Communication Gaps and Inequities: Moving Toward a Reconceptualization," in *Progress in Communication Sciences, Vol. II,* eds. Brenda Dervin and Melvin J. Voigt (Norwood, NJ: Ablex, 1980).

[66]Dervin, *ibid.*

be more serious and long-term. As Nisbett and Ross[67] have pointed out, vivid information may have a dual effect by affecting not only initial inferences, but future inferences as well. Thus, once a story is misunderstood, those inferences can provide a basis for future misunderstanding.

One other source of confusion in processing the news occurs when viewers misremember news stories. In a series of investigations,[68] Gunter and his associates have shown that news items that are similar may interfere with the recall of each other. Similarly, Robinson, Davis, Sahin and O'Toole[69] have noted that viewers' recall of news stories often show a *meltdown* effect, where elements of one story merge or are confused with elements of other similar stories. One implication of Gunter's findings is that news stories should be arranged in a sequence to reduce interference.[70] Both findings suggest that, while it may be useful to draw similarities among stories, providing distinctive features for stories is also important. Unless distinctive features, which may be used as retrieval cues at recall, are present in stories, misremembering news items may be likely. While we have only sketched here how viewers may misunderstand or misremember news, it is important to consider such issues. Above and beyond implications for theory, media-related information gaps and inequities are unlikely to change until careful analysis is brought to bear.

Understanding What News is Being Measured

A source of frustration in developing the analysis in this paper was that it was mostly unclear as to what researchers have been measuring in previous investigations. The advantages and disadvantages of recall and other measures have been weighed by Katz and his associates as well as Findahl and Höijer.[71] Researchers now need to distinguish what measures may be tapping, assuming the memory-understanding distinction is valid. As we stated earlier, free recall, aided recall and multiple choice formats can all be used to measure either of the two processes. It would seem to depend on whether responses focus on what the story itself was versus what viewers understood the story to mean. For free recall, content categorization systems should be developed that would be sensitive to this difference. For aided recall, cues that are used as episodic retrieval cues would clearly tap memory. Cues that prompt retrieval of story interpretations (what do you think was the main point of story *x*, for instance) can be linked to understanding. Finally, multiple choice questions whose phrasing includes episodic retrieval cues, and whose items focus on news event details could be developed to measure memory. One of the main ways of measuring depth of processing may be multiple choice

[67]Nisbett and Ross, *op. cit.*

[68]Gunter, *op. cit.*

[69]Robinson, Davis, Sahin and O'Toole, *op. cit.*

[70]Reed, *op. cit.*

[71]Findahl and Höijer, *op. cit.*

questions whose items are sensitive to different levels of inference making. These distinctions should further sharpen empirical attempts to explore the analysis developed above. If information processing principles are to be given an adequate test in the television news research area, then more attention should be paid to what aspects of the cognitive system are measured.

Conclusion

The primary aim of this paper has been to construct a theoretical framework for television news research. Information processing principles have been used to outline ways in which viewers might process televised news. These principles have suggested that viewers' attention to news items may be guided by an interaction of bottom-up and top-down processing, that memory and understanding processes are distinct and separate aspects of human cognitive systems, that a great deal of televised news information may be stored and retrieved according to episodic memory principles, while semantic network models may provide an explanation of viewers' understanding of televised news. Further implications of these principles indicated that researchers should be concerned not only with accuracy of memory and understanding, but with viewers' misremembering and misunderstanding of televised news as well. While a formal theoretical model was not presented here, the discussion should suggest some paths for researchers interested in television news to follow.

There are social implications for this approach to televised news research as well. It is quite important to recognize that the process of understanding the news is a cumulative process both for the individual and for society. The ability or inability to understand and remember the news presented to viewers on any given day will leave viewers more prepared or less prepared to understand the news tomorrow. Misconceptions of important stories can persist and influence future understanding and decision making. As a society, we make decisions about collective actions based on our understanding of the world around us which we derive in part from news stories. We elect presidents and select homes and jobs on the basis of understandings. which may be linked to our processing of the news. If there is widespread and increasing misunderstanding of certain news stories, we may all make poorer decisions. Similarly, increasing our ability to understand and remember news might well have benefits that are difficult to anticipate. Increasing the public's ability to understand television news could well be as important to our generation as the campaigns for literacy and public education were for earlier generations.

In this review of the recent literature of children's comprehension of televised content, W. Andrew Collins argues that such comprehension is a complex phenomenon, covarying with attention, cognititive development and knowledge of television's exposition forms, "world knowledge" and knowledge of media conventions and formal features. Collins suggests that the active nature of the viewing process has important implications, which are discussed below, for the processing of content and for behavioral effects of the medium on children. W. Andrew Collins is professor and director of the Institute for Child Development at the University of Minnesota.

13

COGNITIVE PROCESSING IN
TELEVISION VIEWING

W. Andrew Collins

The history of mass media research has been dominated by a dual focus on content and audiences. The major themes have been whether, in what ways, and for what parts of the mass audience mass media effects occur (Comstock et al. 1978; Stein and Friedrich 1975). Little attention has been given to what audiences do with television. In recent years, two levels of audience activity have emerged as research foci. One, the uses and gratifications approach (e.g., Blumler and Katz 1974), emphasizes the orientations that guide viewing preferences and patterns of consumption. The other, the topic of this review, concerns viewers' activities relevant to perceiving, remembering, and evaluating the content of particular programs. A major theme in this research is the possibility that viewers of varying ages, abilities, and social backgrounds may respond differently to the content of television programs because of the different ways in which they process the content of the medium.

This view of both the audience and the viewing process has been inspired by several related trends in behavioral science. Under the influence of experimental psychologists, a concept has emerged in which individuals' roles in mental events are seen as active and constructive, rather than passive and associative (e.g., Bransford and Franks 1972). The theme has emerged strongly in developmental and social-psychological research in the past decade.

The implications of these views for the study of responses to television have recently caused many researchers to shift their attention from a focus on program content and outcomes of viewing to an analysis of the cognitive tasks involved in viewing particular programs and the ways in which viewers of different ages, with different cognitive capabilities, might accomplish those tasks. In part, this cognitive-processing perspective recognizes that individual viewers bring to viewing

varied skills and predispositions that result in different representations of the same television content and, further, that these different perceptions may carry important implications for the social impact of programs.

In this review,[1] I attempt to characterize the questions raised and the evidence amassed as a result of this relatively recent vantage point on the process and effects of television viewing. The focus is on studies of cognitive processes—what viewers do, overtly and covertly, in response to what they are watching and the representations of the content that result from their activity. The amount of research is not large—perhaps fewer than 75 published articles and books since 1970. Furthermore, virtually all of the studies involve variations in children's processing of television content; in only a few instances have other segments of the audience, including adults, been addressed. Although the literature appears to be growing in size and scope, the research reviewed here pertains almost exclusively to processing of television content by children of different ages.

The Television Stimulus

Several comments should be made about the nature of the television stimuli that constitute the processing task for viewers, young and old. Television presentations consist of a series of sequential visual and auditory signals, organized in particular ways in different types of programs. In children's programs like *Sesame Street*, the organization consists of a series of disconnected bits, or

[1] Preparation of this paper was facilitated by Grant No. 24197 from the National Institute of Mental Health to W. Andrew Collins. The paper was completed while the author was a Visiting Fellow at the Boys Town Center for the Study of Youth Development, Omaha, Neb.

From W. Andrew Collins, "Cognitive Processing in Television Viewing," in National Institute of Mental Health, *Television and Behavior: Ten Years of Scientific Progress and Implications for the Eighties,* Vol. 2: Technical Reviews (Rockville, MD: National Institute of Mental Health, 1982), pp. 9-23. This work is in the public domain.

scenes; in dramatic programs, the sequence of scenes is subordinated to a plot or narrative. Other types of content differ from both of these in one or several ways. Whether within short bits or across an hour-long plot, television programs commonly share two general characteristics: (1) They contain information that is both *relevant* and *irrelevant* to the theme of the program; and, in most cases, (2) important program information is *explicitly presented*, and sometimes *implied*. For example, in dramatic programs, two scenes showing contrasting circumstances may occur, with the implication that something has occurred to cause or enable a change from the first to the second; often, these linkages are important to understanding the plot—as in the case of the inference that events portrayed early in a program caused a later event. The linkages must be inferred by the viewer, since they are only implicit in the program itself. Thus, representation of programs is considered in recent research as fundamentally depending on abilities for (1) attending to and retaining relevant content that is portrayed amid attention-getting but extraneous information and (2) inferring implicit program events.

Two questions have dominated the research: (1) What are the nature and the determinants of children's attention to television? (2) How much and what kind of content is retained from viewing typical fare? Recently, interest has turned toward the particular processing requirements posed by unique features of television programing and, thus, differences between media in the nature and outcomes of processing.

Attention to Television

Television is both a pervasive presence in children's environments (cf. Medrich 1979; Parke 1978) and a purveyor of complex information that varies in its attractiveness and comprehensibility. It is also considered to have substantial control over children's attention, eliciting their regard through visual and auditory displays that are highly salient for viewers and, thus, making them passive receivers of the content of programs and commercials. Thus, one fundamental question about young viewers' processing is how their attention to the television screen is regulated.[2] A focal question has been the extent to which young viewers' attention is controlled by what is presented to them, rather than by their own active processing of program content.

---

[2] The question is different from the issue of selective exposure, which refers to putting oneself in proximity to an instance of content or deliberately failing to do so (cf. Sears and Freedman 1967); in research on attention the question has been whether a viewer looks at the television screen, given that the set is operating.

In typical studies of this problem, investigators have sought to identify correlates of children's attention to the screen under naturalistic, distracting circumstances; unseen observers monitor children's visual regard in a playroom containing toys and games and/or other individuals. Under most research conditions, of course, it is difficult to assess reliably where a child is looking and to record gaze duration with sufficient precision to permit meaningful interpretation of changes in visual attention. Recent technological advances in laboratory-recording equipment and methodological and statistical innovations have made it possible to record precisely and to analyze many data points over the course of viewing. For example, in one laboratory (Alwitt et al. 1980), children's looking at the television screen is recorded by observers' pressing a key to activate an auditory signal. The signals, recorded in real time, are subsequently played back through an analog-to-digital converter and transformed by computer into times of onset and offset of each "look" at television. These real-time sequential data can then be examined in connection with momentary characteristics of television content and other events. The result has been highly informative chartings of children's attention to television as a function of attributes of television presentations, age, and individual differences.

Attentional Inertia

The activity of even quite young viewers during television viewing becomes apparent in the context of one general characteristic of children's attention. They tend to continue attending to a circumstance or activity, like the television screen, once looking has begun. Anderson, who with his colleagues discovered this characteristic in studies of young children's viewing, labeled the principle "attentional inertia." The conceptual opposite of habituation, inertia refers to the pattern of attention in which the longer children have been looking at the television screen, the greater the probability that they will continue to look. Inertia also characterizes *not* looking: The longer children have directed their attention elsewhere, the less likely they are to begin looking at television. These parallel patterns of children's attention appear in the data of individual children, as well as in group averages; they are not an artifact of averaging across individual attentional styles. They also hold across an age period of 1–5 years and have been replicated on various samples of children and college-age adults (Anderson et al. 1979). Consonant findings come from Krull and Husson's (1978) report that 4–5-year-old children's attention to *Sesame Street* is best accounted for by the focus of their attention in adjacent scoring periods (in this case, 30-second intervals).

Thus, young children show attentional tendencies that may well be characteristic of television viewing generally.

Factors in Attention

Viewers' inertial tendencies do not, however, override either individual differences in viewing styles or the content and presentational characteristics of programs. Even preschool children's attention varies in response to diverse content. Indeed, in the first 2 years of life, capabilities exist for discriminations among televised events, such as recognizing that the direction of action has changed in a videotaped conversation between two adults (e.g., Golinkoff and Kerr 1975). At the same time, several dimensions of individual and developmental variation are apparent.

Viewer Characteristics. Most research on attention has been conducted with children of age 5 or younger, and—not surprisingly—within this restricted age range, there are notable changes in typical attention patterns. Six-month-old infants attend to an operating television set only sporadically (Hollenbeck and Slaby 1979), but the sheer amount of time spent looking at an operating television set increases dramatically during the years from 1 to 5. Among 1–4-year-olds watching Sesame Street in Anderson's laboratory, proportions of time spent looking at the screen increased from 12 percent to 55 percent, with the largest increase (25 percent to 45 percent) coming between ages 2 and 3. After this major increase, amount of visual attention increases more gradually up to age 5 (Levin 1976). Linear age trends are also reported for attention to commercials over the preschool and early grade school years (Wartella and Ettema 1974).

The increase in attention to programs was largely due to the greater frequency of older children's looking toward the television, even when they were playing with other toys; as they grew older, children gave longer looks and gave them more frequently (Anderson and Levin 1976; Anderson et al. 1979). Anderson concluded that "children begin purposive, systematic TV viewing between 2 and 3 years of age" (Levin and Anderson 1976), an appraisal buttressed by parents' reports of sharp increases in their young children's television viewing around age 2½ (Anderson et al. 1979). Stable and reliable individual differences among children have been reported, even when age is controlled statistically as well, but their significance is not yet known. For example, reported patterns of viewing differences did not correlate with standard measures of intelligence and personality (Levin 1976).

Content Attributes. Attributes of particular programs also attract (or inhibit) children's attention to the screen when they are looking elsewhere and help to maintain or interrupt attention when children are already viewing. Despite the powerful general effects of distractors, age and individual viewing patterns, and attentional inertia, children are responsive to the content and presentational characteristics of shows.

The most detailed evidence on this point comes from Anderson and his colleagues (Alwitt et al. 1980; Levin and Anderson 1976), who correlated children's visual regard to the screen with the presence of 44 visual and auditory attributes in segments of children's programing (ranging from Sesame Street and Mister Rogers' Neighborhood to The Flintstones) and general-audience shows heavily viewed by children (e.g., Gilligan's Island). Their results showed that attention was recruited and maintained by attributes like women characters, women's and children's voices, auditory changes, peculiar voices, activity or movement, camera cuts, sound effects, laughing, and applause. Negative attributes—those that terminate looks at television and inhibit further looks—included male voices, extended zooms and pans, animals, and still pictures.

Anderson notes with some surprise the strong effects of auditory cues on visual attention and, in fact, suggests that the attracting and inhibiting force of many visual attributes occurs largely because of their association with sound attributes (Anderson et al. 1979). Undoubtedly, fluctuations in attention as a function of auditory attributes partly—perhaps largely—reflect children's learning that certain types of auditory and visual cues are usually associated with significant on-screen content. Even young children have probably acquired expectations about such associations through their previous exposure to television. It seems likely that, while engaging in other activities, children monitor an operating television set at some level and shift their attention to the screen in response to certain auditory or peripheral-vision cues.

Comprehensibility and Attention. At what level are program attributes being monitored by children so that their attention varies in consonance with them? While Anderson and his colleagues found that attention fluctuates corresponding to specific standard attributes of characters, settings, and presentations, Krull and his associates (Krull and Husson 1978; Krull et al. 1978; Krull et al. 1977), using an information-theory measure of the characteristics of programs, failed to find a relationship between general program complexity and 4–5-year-olds' attention to Sesame Street. Possibly, even these young children are processing program characteristics semantically, i.e., in terms of the meaning of the content. Specific categories of program attributes may elicit children's expectations about the importance of what is on the screen at any given time; the more general and formal characteristics assessed by the information-theory measure, which simultaneously incorporates multiple features of the presentation, may mask the particular cues of significance to young viewers.

Some further findings of Krull et al. (1978) with respect to older children are consonant with this interpretation. Among 7½-8½-year-old viewers of *The Electric Company,* these researchers report 200–300-second cycles of attention that anticipate cycles in the complexity of the program. They hypothesize that the accumulated viewing experiences of these somewhat older viewers have equipped them to anticipate cycles in typical presentations and to regulate their attention accordingly. Perhaps more general and abstract knowledge about the form of the medium is acquired by this later age and is added to knowledge of specific, immediate content-attribute associations that affect the attention of the younger viewers studied by Anderson.

The Comprehensibility-Attention Hypothesis. The apparent reliance of even quite young children on predictable associations among visual and auditory cues led Anderson to question popular conceptions of television's power to capture children's attention. Anderson argued the converse: Children actually attend selectively on the basis of perceived comprehensibility of content. He hypothesized that children respond to auditory and peripheral-vision cues that ordinarily have been associated in their viewing experience with salient and informative action. Thus, young viewers attend to the television screen when they encounter these cues; and when the cues are absent, they are likely not to attend or to turn their attention away from television.

This hypothesis was tested in two ingenious experiments (Anderson et al. 1981), in which the effects of auditory cues on visual attention were more closely examined. The authors found that concrete dialog (i.e., dialog concerned with immediately present objects and persons) elicited visual attention more effectively than abstract dialog or no dialog at all, indicating that young viewers shifted attention in accord with the content-relevance of the auditory cues. The researchers subsequently manipulated the sound and visual tracks of a *Sesame Street* program. In some segments of the hour-long tape, the content was presented normally; in others, the visual track was scrambled by random editing, but the dialog was not; in another, the audio track was played backward, but the scenes were left in their proper sequential order; and, in a fourth, a Greek-language auditory track was substituted for the English track. In a second version of the tape, the scenes that had been per-verted in the first tape were presented normally, and the normal ones were edited to distort either visual or auditory cues. When the auditory track was perverted, there was much less attention to the screen than when the visual channel was distorted or when the segment was presented normally. The authors conclude that the poor comprehensibility of the auditory-track distortions discouraged attention to segments that, in their normal form, attracted children's attention. Thus, children were not captured, nor held captive, by perceptually salient cues when content was incomprehensible; rather, their patterns of attention "reflect the development, with TV viewing experience, of sophisticated strategies for optimally distributing visual attention to the most informative parts of the TV program" (Anderson et al. 1981).

To date, few extensive content analyses have been reported to chart the relationship between formal attributes and the occurrence of significant and informative program events. Such a hypothesis is intuitively reasonable, however, given the stock ways in which characters and devices are employed in much programing (cf. Leifer et al. 1974; Sternglanz and Serbin 1974). Moreover, in a recent content analysis of *Sesame Street,* Bryant et al. (1978) noted that "apparently the producers . . . reserved . . . electronic embellishments of the basic messages for times when critical material was present" (p. 55). Thus, at this point, Anderson's explanation and evidence are compelling. They are particularly noteworthy because of the indication that even very young viewers, who have generally been thought to be controlled by the stimulation of salient perceptual features of programs, in fact allocate their attention in terms of the sense, not merely the form, of television content.

Activity versus Passivity in Viewing. The responsiveness of even very young children to cues about the comprehensibility and informativeness of television content has led Anderson (1979) and others to argue that, far from being a passive experience, television viewing elicits active processing of content early in life. During typical viewing, children shift from low-level monitoring to more focused attention in a manner that parallels specific and general characteristics of the on-screen content of shows. Their responsiveness to the perceptually salient features of programs results at least partly from the high probability that these noncontent features of shows will be correlated with content that is important to the sense of the show. Both Anderson and Wright (Wright et al. 1979) hypothesize that the significance of these formal features is derived from viewing experiences. Wright also proposes that experience leads to habituation to perceptually salient formal features, resulting in an age-related decline in attention to such features for their own sake; as a result, there is a general shift with age away from attention commanded by highly salient perceptual features of programs to attention marshaled in the service of logical search for meaningful aspects of programs.

The evidence to date on children's attention to television, then, supports the notion that children are active in allocating their attention to various parts of a presentation. We turn now to the corollary question of children's capabilities, once they have turned their attention to television, for comprehending the content of typical fare.

Comprehension of Programs

In the past decade, a number of studies have been addressed to comprehension—the encoding, retention, and retrieval of information from a variety of types of shows, including children's shows, general-audience dramatic and news programing, and commercials. Two questions in particular have guided research: (1) How much and what kind of information is retained from the content of typical programs, and (2) what is the nature of common comprehension difficulties, particularly those experienced by young viewers? Research on this problem has been almost exclusively developmental; thus, our perspective is the age-related course of comprehension. Of course, as we shall see, a number of age-related factors in addition to chronological age or maturation per se contribute to the patterns that have emerged.

The question of what is acquired cognitively from television programs is not a new topic for research, of course. Classic early studies of television (e.g., Himmelweit et al. 1958; Schramm et al. 1961) and film (e.g., Holaday and Stoddard 1933) addressed the issue of media impact on children's knowledge levels; and a few later studies of film presentations (e.g., Maccoby and Wilson 1957) reported acquisition of specific information from programs and variations among children in attention to characters and memory for their actions. The implication that viewers might represent television portrayals in varying ways, with potentially different social outcomes, was not generally appreciated at the time of these studies, however.

Variations in viewers' processing of programs are particularly pertinent in the case of dramatic presentations, where a coherent story is presented through a sequential series of scenes over relatively long time spans. At least three cognitive tasks are involved in comprehending such materials: (1) selective attention to central program events; (2) orderly organization of the program events; and (3) inference of information about implicit relations among explicit scenes (Collins et al. 1978). An example

of the latter is the imputation of a causal relationship between two scenes, although the causal connection is not explicitly depicted. The task of inferring content relations across the span of a typical dramatic program has been referred to as "temporal integration" (Collins 1978).

The findings of the past decade essentially confirm that substantial variations in comprehension occur with age, general experience, and knowledge of the television medium. Although many questions remain, several general conclusions have now been well documented.

Retention

In general, children as old as 8 years have been found to retain a relatively small proportion of depicted actions, events, and settings in typical programs; memory for information particularly important to plots and other primary messages (e.g., commercial appeals) improves dramatically across the grade school- to high school-age range, however (Collins 1970; Collins et al. 1978; Flapan 1968; Leifer and Roberts 1972; Newcomb and Collins 1979; Purdie et al. 1980). These age-related trends appear in studies of a range of types and instances of content—children's programs, general audience dramatic programs, public affairs programs, and commercials.

The age-related course of retention has been seen in both types of explicit content that characterize programs: *central* content, or material essential to the sense of the presentation, and *peripheral*, or incidental, nonessential, content. In studies of memory for explicitly presented events in general audience entertainment drama (Collins 1970; Collins et al. 1978; Newcomb and Collins 1979; Purdie et al. 1980), young grade school children (second and third graders) have consistently been found to remember only about 65 percent of the content identified by panels of adult judges as essential to understanding the narrative. Recognition memory improves linearly with age in these studies, however; by eighth grade, viewers are typically found to recall 90 percent or better of the explicitly presented central information. Preschool and kindergarten children's retention of the central content of *Sesame Street* vignettes has also been reported to be quite low (Friedlander et al. 1974; Calvert and Watkins 1979; Reich 1977), despite the presumably age-appropriate content and facilitative production techniques characteristic of this program. Pronounced age differences have also been found in retention of commercials (Wackman et al. 1979) and news stories (Drew and Reeves 1980). Thus, within the sizable child audience, children vary considerably in the completeness with which they retain the content of typical fare.

Factors in Retention. The reasons for poor retention of central content by preschool and grade school children are undoubtedly complex. Studies of retention have, however, revealed some important aspects of age differences in processing. One line of evidence indicates that younger children's difficulties in retention may stem from poor selection and encoding of relevant content. For example, while both central and peripheral, or nonessential, content are increasingly better recalled with age, plot-relevant information accounts for an increasingly larger proportion of what is remembered (Collins 1970; Collins et al. 1978; Calvert et al. 1979). Indeed, in one study (Collins 1970), peripheral-content memory actually bore a curvilinear relationship to age: Recognition measure scores increased until early adolescence and declined thereafter. Whether peripheral retention declines among more mature individuals obviously depends on the interest value and difficulty of the presentation (Calvert et al. 1979; Collins 1970; Hale et al. 1968; Hawkins 1973), but diverging central and peripheral content curves have been found for different instances of typical content, including situation comedies, action-adventure dramas, and a cartoon produced for school-age children.

Poor memory for central content among younger children cannot be attributed simply to greater likelihood of forgetting relevant content or the interference of other program events. Collins and his colleagues (Collins and Westby 1981; Purdie et al. 1980) recently adopted a procedure that involves the interruption of viewing at different points for different subgroups of children and the testing of them on knowledge of explicit content and inferences up to that point. One group of children sees the entire program without interruption and is then tested on the full battery of recognition items to provide a check on possible contamination of post-interruption answers in the other three conditions. The authors report that children tested on content they had seen only minutes before performed no better than children who were asked the same questions at a much later time; throughout the program, second graders' performance was poorer than fifth and eighth graders'. Similar findings were reported in a study of retention of *Sesame Street* content by Friedlander et al. (1974). Thus, preschool and young grade school viewers probably retain essential content poorly partly because they select and encode it inadequately. In fact, the diverging relationship between central and peripheral content has been interpreted as reflecting children's increasingly greater ability to recognize and encode essential content while filtering out extraneous details.

A somewhat different but consonant perspective (Wright and Vlietstra 1975; Wright et al. 1979) is that age differences in dominance of central content reflect a developmental shift from an early tendency for attention to be commanded by highly salient perceptual features of shows (whether essential or peripheral to the plot) to a more mature pattern in which attention is intuitively marshaled in the service of logical search. Wright attributes the shift both to general cognitive development and to the increasing amount of experience with television accumulated as children grow older. According to his formulation, viewing experience results in habituation to salient perceptual features of presentations and also in an induction of the "grammar" of the medium, including the structure of programs generally; in addition, with age, there is likely to be greater knowledge of how individual programs and their segments are ordinarily constructed.

Experience with television is clearly an important source of knowledge and skills relevant to processing of subsequent content. Nevertheless, currently available evidence indicates that retention of even the most important features of shows is relatively poor for young grade school children, despite the many hours of viewing in which a child engages between toddlerhood and the early grade school years. It seems likely that age differences in cognitive processing may be based on some more general determinants of cognitive performance, perhaps of the sort outlined by Piaget in his theory of the development of cognitive structures and operations (which no doubt reflects the effects of a broader range of experiences than television viewing per se). Both the skills acquired through viewing experiences and the cognitive capabilities that enable viewers to find the logic and meaning in presentations contribute to older viewers' more complete representations of programs.

The Role of Segmentation Skills in Processing. One such skill is children's ability to "chunk" the information included in television content. Television programs may be viewed as streams of events of many kinds; and, while some segmentation is imposed by changes of setting and camera changes, an elemental task of processing is segmentation of the stream of program events into discrete units. The information to date is limited, but suggestive. For example, Wartella (1978), following Dickman (1963) and Newtson (1973), found that older children demarcated larger units, often encompassing all or parts of several scenes, while younger children typically chunked program information into smaller units, often less than the duration of a scene. Correspondingly, as in other research, younger children remembered individual scenes better than the relations among them. Mature perception may, however, involve flexibility in segmentation of event streams; adults appear to use small units when necessary to comprehend fine details of action but ordinarily adapt to the need for grosser perceptions of action (Newtson 1973). It may be that in television viewing younger viewers lack sufficient knowledge of the general flow of events and thus search for meaning by attending to details of portrayals. One priority for future research should be further investigation of the development and function of segmentation processes in television viewing.

Inferences

The second major aspect of television comprehension is the coherence with which programs are encoded. Since much of the socially relevant content of programs is only implied by on-screen events, viewers must infer implications and linkages that "go beyond the information given" (Bruner 1957). Typical programs, in which relevant content is portrayed over relatively long timespans, require temporal integration of discrete scenes in order for the plot to be coherently perceived.

In the most extensive series of studies of inferential processes (Collins et al. 1978; Collins et al. 1981; Newcomb and Collins 1979; Purdie et al. 1980), age differences in inferences about implicit events and their relation to retention of explicitly presented content have been examined. The research is conducted by undertaking detailed content analyses of the structure and interrelationships of scenes in programs; with the help of panels of adult judges, the significance of explicit content and implicit relationships are then assessed. Recognition memory instruments are then constructed to test children's inferences as well as their knowledge of the explicit events from which the inferences must be drawn. Additional procedures, both verbal and nonverbal, have been used as checks on the validity of the recognition instrument.

Children tested on recognition memory items derived from this approach show linear improvement in spontaneous inference making about essential program content across ages; however, at each age, the proportion of correct inference answers is lower than the proportion of correct explicit content answers (Collins et al. 1978). The possibility that younger children's poor inferences are only an artifact of inadequate memory for explicit events is ruled out by conditional probability analyses, in which the likelihood of an inference is calculated, given that a viewer knows either all, some, or none of the explicit events on which the inferences are based. These analyses (Collins et al. 1978; Newcomb and Collins 1979; Purdie et al. 1980) indicate that second-grade viewers are significantly less likely than fifth and eighth graders to infer implicit content, even when they know the explicitly presented information from which the inferences are to be drawn. Indeed, younger grade school children have only performed at, or slightly better than, chance level in these studies.

Apparently, older children spontaneously attempt to make discrete scenes coherent by inferring implicit relationships—a change to more abstract, logical processing that is consonant with the qualitative shifts described by Piaget (1954). This shift is undoubtedly partly a function of more sophistication about television plots (Wright and Vlietstra 1975; Wright et al. 1979); but the more coherent, objective quality of the processing required to accomplish this task also reflects increases in general knowledge and skills for abstract inference that parallel other developmental changes in performance during the same age period (e.g., Brown 1975; Flavell 1977).

Methodological Issues. It is often difficult to determine the validity of the indications researchers extract from children—particularly young children—about their mental states. The difficulty is especially great when the only source of data is the children's own statements, which may be constrained by the child's language ability and other referential and expressive skills for reporting the complexities of what they know. While sensitive analysts can often make worthwhile use of such data (e.g., Flapan 1968), results are often compromised by inappropriate procedures for establishing coding categories and assigning children's responses to them.

In one of the few direct comparisons of verbal reports to other methods, Wackman et al. (1979) recently compared recall and recognition item assessments of children's knowledge of commercials. Their results indicate that recall procedures considerably underestimate the retention levels revealed by recognition memory procedures. Most recent studies of television comprehension have involved procedures that are less dependent on children's productive-language capabilities or have included both open-ended interview studies and elicitation procedures. In most instances, the verbal procedures are carefully pretested to avoid confounding comprehension of programs with verbal difficulties in responding to comprehension questions (e.g., Calvert et al. 1979; Collins 1978; Friedlander et al. 1974); in addition, these pretested procedures are supplemented by both verbal and nonverbal procedures that permit internal checks on the indicators of a subject's understanding. Indeed, if there is a bias in the recognition procedures used in most of these studies, it is probably toward an overestimate of what the child understands about the show. Given the very poor comprehension assessments that have uniformly emerged across studies for younger viewers, children's understanding of much typical television content may actually be poorer than the available evidence suggests.

Interventions to Improve Comprehension. The analysis that has guided studies of comprehension of complex television presentations has also been the basis of several attempts to improve understanding of programs. Two general types of strategies have been attempted: (1) pre-viewing instruction to create a set for certain program information, and (2) provision of additional information during viewing by an adult co-viewer. For example, Huston-Stein and her colleagues (Friedrich and Stein 1975; Watkins et al. 1980) conducted several tests of interventions in which adult co-viewers provide cues for young viewers. In one study, Friedrich and Stein (1975) found that stating verbal labels for nonverbal cues improved kindergarten children's retention of visually presented information. Adult co-viewers' statements about the nature of program events and their relationship to other parts of the plot led to improved comprehension of explicitly presented content for both kindergarteners and third and fourth graders (Watkins et al. 1980). Similarly, Collins et al. (1981) reported that second graders' understanding of implicit relations among important instances of explicit content improved when an adult co-viewer stated three fundamental relations at critical points in the plot, although the improvement did not generalize to plot comprehension overall. A condition in which adults merely restated the action of the program did not affect comprehension, however; apparently, it was the implicit content specified by the co-viewers and not the attention-directing function of the statements per se that affected comprehension scores.

There has been less effort to improve children's understanding by providing pre-viewing instructions or training, and results have been mixed. The primary example is the effort of Wackman et al. (1979) to train children in the categories of information about products commonly included in commercials (e.g., what the product looks like, how it works, what it tastes like, etc.). The training sessions lasted about 3½ hours over a period of about 2 weeks. When subsequently tested for their memory of specific commercials, the training groups of both kindergarteners and third and fourth graders showed significantly better retention of concretely presented product information (e.g., how many items of a product are in a package) than the no-training control group; however, the training program did not affect retention of more abstract kinds of product information (e.g., "requires experience and skill"). In contrast, telling children to "try hard to remember as much as possible" from a dramatic program did not lead to improvement of retention by second graders, even when a material incentive was provided (Collins et al. 1978). The authors speculate that the second graders lacked adequate cognitive strategies for improving their comprehension of the program and, thus, could not retain significantly better, even though they had incentives for better performance. Providing labels or statements of implicit information, on the

other hand, appears to facilitate children's comprehension by instantiating parts of the comprehension task that children do not or cannot accomplish spontaneously. Once these critical aspects of processing are made available, young viewers may be able to achieve on their own the other activities necessary for accurate representation of content.

Children's Representations of Content

Thus far, the emphasis has been on what children fail to understand from typical programs. A different and equally important perspective on the problem is what young viewers do understand from the programs they typically see, granted that—compared to older viewers—they comprehend less of the narrative-essential explicit and implicit content of programs.

Most attempts to characterize children's representation of shows have emphasized characteristics of the information that is especially frequently remembered or is relevant to children's own prior knowledge. For example, Holaday and Stoddard (1933), in an early study of retention from films, found that scenes with particularly salient auditory cues and action features were likely to be retained, a result consonant with recent findings (Calvert et al. 1979) that young children remember plot-essential content associated with salient formal features better than plot-essential content presented in less salient ways. In view of the relation between attention and comprehensibility of content (Anderson et al. 1980), these relations are not surprising. There is, however, little satisfactory direct evidence on the effects of attention on comprehension, largely because most measures of attention rely on visual regard as an index and thus do not take account of the important role of auditory monitoring in children's comprehension of content.

Holaday and Stoddard also reported that portrayals of generally familiar settings or events were especially well remembered by school-age viewers. Recent analyses of children's understanding of programs have focused further on retention in relation to children's general knowledge about persons and events. For example, Collins recently suggested that age differences in comprehension are partly attributable to the way in which children deploy their common knowledge in understanding television programs. Analyzing interview protocols in which children described a television program they had seen, Collins and Wellman (1980) found that both older and younger children mentioned events that were common knowledge for most viewers, but only older children took account of aspects of the portrayal that were idiosyncratic to the program. Furthermore, in recognition memory measures, younger children were more likely than older to choose wrong answers that represent stereotypical outcomes of event sequences, rather than errors involving incorrect linkages among explicitly portrayed elements of the program (Newcomb and Collins 1979). It seems likely that both younger and older viewers readily recognize common knowledge sequences in programs. In addition, however, older viewers also recognize—and, perhaps, note the potential importance of—events that deviate from common expectations, while younger viewers appear less likely to notice such deviations or to appreciate their unique significance within the portrayal.

Prior social knowledge appears to underlie individual, as well as developmental, differences in children's comprehension. Individual differences may be especially pronounced within the younger age groups, for whom comprehension of the explicit content of programs is often poor. Newcomb and Collins (1979) recently reported research in which black and white children of lower and middle socioeconomic status in the second, fifth, and eighth grades saw either a program with white middle-class characters or one with black lower-class characters. Comprehension of explicit and implicit events differed for second-grade youngsters in terms of the match between their own previous experience backgrounds and the characters and settings portrayed in the program. Both white and black lower-class children understood the lower-class family portrayal better than the middle-class second graders, while middle-class children of both races understood the middle-class portrayal better than their lower-class counterparts. Apparently, the general knowledge available to the two groups was somewhat different and, for second-grade viewers, permitted differential understanding of the programs. At the two older ages, however, viewers from all groups understood both programs equally well, perhaps because their more extensive and varied social knowledge made it possible for them to understand a range of types of portrayals. Thus, within the younger age group, in which understanding is generally unreliable, there appeared to be individual differences that are accounted for significantly by variables that summarize viewers' previous social learning experiences.

Although we currently know most about the ways in which young viewers are likely to fail in understanding typical television fare, an important direction for future research is the nature of what they are likely to retain and how common assumptions about television effects might be altered by their typical perceptions.

Three Factors in Processing Television Content

Although the most pronounced effects throughout the research on processing of television content concern age-related skills of viewers, a focus on age may mask issues of what viewers of all ages are required to do in comprehending television portrayals—a question that necessarily involves both the nature of the medium and the viewers' knowledge and skills.

In this section, three requisites for the comprehension of typical media programs that have emerged from recent research are discussed: (1) knowledge of common formats for exposition (e.g., narratives, commercial appeals, etc.); (2) general knowledge and expectations about situations and event sequences (i.e., how events and interactions ordinarily proceed), commonly referred to as "world knowledge"; and (3) knowledge of the form and conventions of the television medium. These three types of knowledge are pertinent to most typical television content, although most of the specific references will be to the popular entertainment programing that has been of interest with regard to the social impact of the medium.

Knowledge of Exposition Forms

To understand most television content, viewers must have an operating concept of certain fundamental formats in which information is presented. Most of these formats are taken for granted, but recent research in cognitive psychology and in studies of television indicates that knowledge of one fundamental format, story forms, is at least partly a function of age and experience. For example, in recent research on prose stories (e.g., Mandler and Johnson 1977; Poulsen et al. 1979; Stein and Glenn 1979), preschool and young grade school children's relatively poor recall of story details has appeared to be related to inadequate general structures according to which story details might be parsed. Stein and Glenn reported marked differences between first and third graders in their recall of simple narratives; third graders elaborated significantly more in retelling story details than first graders did, particularly when there was missing information that fit basic categories of story structure that the older children had more adequately mastered. A somewhat different factor has been emphasized by Sedlak (1979) and others (Bower 1978; Schank and Abelson 1977; Schmidt 1976; Wilensky 1978; Worth and Gross 1974). They assume that inferences about connections among an actor's behaviors require that the observer recognize a plan or a point of view behind the action. Sedlak (1977) suggests that young children fail to comprehend the actions and events in an adult-like way because they begin with different interpretations of the various actors' intentions and points of view.

Collins' research (Collins et al. 1978; Newcomb and Collins 1979; Purdie et al. 1980) generally confirms that children's comprehension of programs is affected increasingly with age by the structure of the narrative, although the particulars of processing are also affected by a confounding of structural features of content with complexity of content and the formal-presentational features characteristic of the medium. Other common exposition formats, like news stories and commercials, have not been studied. Recently, however, the importance of format in commercials was underscored by Wackman et al. (1979), who found that training children on types of information ordinarily included in commercial messages leads to improvement in their retention of those details. Thus, the importance of knowledge of exposition format apparently extends to processing of this pervasive type of content. Recent analytic models and empirical studies (Baggett 1979; Berndt and Berndt 1975; Grueneich 1978; Omanson 1979) illustrate methods for considering the structure of expositions in studying the responses of both children and adults to media presentations.

"World Knowledge"

Much of television comprehension—involving as it does a wide range of common and uncommon portrayals, including many implicit features—draws on knowledge derived from general experience of perceptual, cognitive, linguistic, and social phenomena. It has been noted, for example, that children differ—both across age and individually—in their capability for understanding language constructions, which also characteristically vary across typical television content (Reich 1977). Similarly, viewers vary in their expectations and bases for understanding mental events (e.g., psychological causation, cf. Berndt and Berndt 1975) and social events and actions that are often pertinent to comprehension of the circumstances and events of typical programs. The research by Collins and Wellman (1980) and by Newcomb and Collins (1979) indicates some implications of prior knowledge and expectations for comprehension of programs.

At this time, it is not clear how social knowledge is represented and how it enters into comprehension of television portrayals. The most extensive evidence comes from theory and research on prose narratives (Bower 1978; Bower et al. 1979; Mandler and Johnson 1977; Warren et al. 1979; Schank and Abelson 1977; Stein and Glenn 1979), but few details are known, and several contending perspectives at present guide research efforts (Omanson 1979). The most detailed account of the role of prior knowledge in understanding stories is the scripts approach (Schank and Abelson 1977), in which prior knowledge, in the form of stereotypes of event sequences, enables inferences about gaps in the linkages between the actions or states of the story characters. Like other views of the role of schemata in processing of social information (e.g., Cantor and Mischel 1977; Hastie in press; Judd

and Kulik 1980; Taylor and Crocker in press), the script formulation implies hierarchical information structures in which the highest most abstract levels are supported by a rich store of specific experiences or bits of information at lower levels. Such structures affect both encoding (Bower 1976; Markus 1977; Rogers et al. 1977) and retrieval (Cantor and Mischel 1977; Hastie in press; Zadny and Gerard 1974) of information about newly encountered persons and events. Neisser's (1976) characterization applies generally to current views of the effects of structures in social information processing from television:

A schema is like a format in a computer programming language. Formats specify that information must be of a certain sort if it is to be interpreted coherently. . . . Information can be picked up only if it is developmentally format ready to accept it. Information that does not fit such a format goes unused. Perception is inherently selective (p. 55).

Little attention has been given to the assessment of relevant schemata in studies of comprehension of television programs. In most social psychology research, manipulations have been introduced to activate certain commonly available schemata, which have then been observed to affect memory for a stimulus (e.g., Cantor and Mischel 1977; Taylor and Crocker in press). Recently, however, Bower and his colleagues (Bower et al. 1979) and Nelson (1978), the latter working with children, have attempted to specify knowledge of scripts in task materials for memory and language experiments; and social psychologists (e.g. Markus 1977; Rogers et al. 1977) have also examined the nature of certain social schemata and their role in the processing of new social stimuli. Their strategies are potentially applicable to comprehension of important aspects of social portrayals in television narratives. One focus of future research should be further specification of the nature and representation of social knowledge and its role in the processing of newly encountered social stimuli such as those occurring in television programs.

Knowledge of Media Conventions and Formal Features

A third kind of knowledge that affects processing of audiovisually presented narratives is familiarity with certain presentation conventions. Baggett (1979) recently found that an audiovisually presented narrative had identifiable structure and meaningful breakpoints that corresponded semantically to the breakpoints in a prose version of the same narrative; nevertheless, the way in which information was conveyed in the two media differed markedly. Formal features of programs, such as camera angles and the use of background music, and visual techniques for compressing time and signaling breaks in action carry considerable information for those viewers whose experience permits their meaning to be recognized. Gardner (1980) reports preliminary experimental results that, compared to a picture-book story, a televised version constrained reasoning about the narrative. Book-version children not only remembered more about the story than those who saw a televised version but also drew on their own experiences and knowledge to go beyond the explicit details, while television viewers relied more on details of the presentation itself. Thus, reliance on the conventional media formats may obviate mental activity of certain types in viewing—a hypothesis extensively discussed by Salomon (e.g., 1979). Although little is known about the interaction of social knowledge and knowledge of the presentation conventions that are common to television social portrayals, this dimension of televised information is integral to analyses of children's understanding of programs.

Formal features often confound structural analyses of program content (e.g., story grammars) for explaining the variation in children's understanding of programs. In studies of prose narratives, the explicitness with which story elements are stated can be relatively easily controlled, but control is less feasible in audiovisual narratives because of certain dramatic and cinematic techniques that sometimes result in ambiguous portrayal of important cues. For example, the Japanese psychologist Tada (1969) found that children of all ages had difficulty comprehending a portrayal in which symbolism and filmic devices compressed time and content in the narrative. The clarity with which information is presented audiovisually is also related to formal features, such as pacing, activity level, music, and so forth (Huston-Stein 1977; Krull et al. 1977; Watt and Krull 1974), which often cannot be controlled in audiovisual presentations. This becomes clear in the instance of comparing comprehension of the portrayal of an aggressive resolution of conflict and a negotiated resolution of the same situation (e.g., Collins and Getz 1976). The aggressive portrayal would obviously contrast markedly with the negotiation model in formal features like activity level and pacing and probably cannot realistically be constructed to be more comparable to it in these respects. Prose descriptions of the two events could be more closely matched at a formal level, but comparison between children's comprehension of the two different types of televised content would be confounded by the concomitant variation in presentation characteristics.

Thus, with the naturalistic stimuli of concern to television researchers, it is often difficult to observe the operation of important structural elements and functional categories of content in affecting children's comprehension. Indeed, in analyses of items of content that are

particularly easy or particularly difficult for young subjects in Collins' research, the best correlate of comprehension difficulty was the number and abstractness of steps required to infer the relation between scenes in a portrayal, rather than the functional or structural category of the information (Collins 1978). In short, because of the nature of the medium, the goal of research on processing of television content has been to characterize the typical performance of children of different ages in comprehending certain formal categories of content, which have been sampled from across a range of typical programs. The findings thus speak more directly to the issue of how children are likely to represent typical portrayals of social content in dramatic narratives than to the fundamental nature of understanding narratives generally.

Implications for Effects of Television

The emergence of these three factors underscores again the active nature of the viewing process. Typical programs consist of series of discrete scenes, the interrelationships of which imply coherence that must be inferred. Nevertheless, within a vast audience of children—an audience that has been treated monolithically in much research on the effects of television—representations of programs vary considerably. Children as old as 7 and 8 retain the content of typical programs less completely and less coherently than do older children and adults. Although young viewers attend to information that is obviously salient and potentially informative, they apparently lack the strategic cognitive skills necessary for recognizing and retaining less salient plot-essential information and for integrating central events across time in the course of a program. Thus, while viewing is more active and discriminating among even young children than is generally recognized, the strategic skills necessary for mature viewing of complex programs develop markedly over the grade school and early adolescent years.

Implications for Evaluation of Characters. Research on children's discrimination among, and relative liking for, established characters in programs (e.g., Reeves 1978; Reeves and Greenberg 1977; Reeves and Miller 1978) indicates that viewers rely on few simple dimensions in their responses, with little variation across age. Understanding of characters' actions in the context of the plot, however, requires complex processing, particularly when characters are unfamiliar and elements of the portrayals are abstract or indirect and the relations between them implicit. Variations in young viewers' processing of programs are potentially important for the social impact of the medium. For example, Collins and his colleagues reported that the context for violent physical aggression is often not recognized by younger television viewers, despite the fact that the context for aggression is a major basis on which more mature viewers evaluate the action and the character who performs it (Collins et al. 1974; Jones et al. 1971; Purdie et al. 1980). Indeed, when young grade school viewers comprehend the relation between an aggressive portrayal and the antisocial motives and consequences associated with it, their evaluation of the aggressor is notably more negative than when the contextual cues are not grasped (Purdie et al. 1980). Thus, inferences about a character in connection with his actions affect evaluative judgments that potentially may be pertinent to adoption of observed behaviors.

Besides the apparently age-related difficulties in inferring implied connections, there is also ample evidence that, for younger children, the impact of motives and consequences also depends heavily on the ways in which the cues are portrayed separately. For example, young children's ability to employ motive information in making evaluations have been found to be affected by intensity (Gutkin 1972) and valence of the consequences (Costanzo et al. 1973); perceptual salience and explicitness of motives and consequences (Chandler et al. 1973); and order effects and temporal separation (Austin et al. 1976; Feldman et al. 1976). Similar presentation characteristics have been found to affect the extent to which young children can successfully perform other types of social inference tasks (e.g., Kun et al. 1976; Shultz and Butkowsky 1977). Where television comprehension is concerned, effects of presentation characteristics are relevant to what is required when a viewer, particularly a cognitively or socially immature one, attempts to understand varying portrayals of social cues.

Implications for Behavioral Effects. Implications of variations in comprehension of television portrayals for behavioral effects on children and adolescents have been addressed in relatively few studies, and those in which direct measures of both comprehension and of behavior have been taken (e.g., Leifer and Roberts 1972) have yielded null findings. In this regard, the literature parallels discouraging empirical efforts in the areas of attitude-behavior relationships (e.g., Ajzen and Fishbein 1977) and social cognition-behavior correspondences (e.g., Shantz 1975). Nevertheless, in several studies, behavioral differences have been found that, while they do not provide direct ties to measures of comprehension, are suggestive of links between children's representations of programs and subsequent behavior that should be further examined. For example, Collins et al. (1974) found that kindergarten and second-grade children who had watched an action-adventure program had difficulty remembering the relations of the motive and consequences cues in connection with the aggressive action. Although such cues appear to moderate the behavioral effects of observed aggression (Bandura 1965; Berkowitz and Geen 1967; Berkowitz and Rawlings 1963), kindergartners and second graders remembered the aggressive scene but only infrequently knew its links with the motives and consequences. Collins (1973) further reported behavioral differences that ostensibly reflect cognitive-processing differences. This earlier research involved inserting commercials between scenes of negative motives and negative consequences for aggression and the violent scene itself. Under these conditions, third graders' post-viewing tendencies to choose aggressive responses increased, in comparison to children of the same age who saw the three scenes close together in time. The task of inferring relations between aggression and the pertinent motive and consequences cues may have been more difficult for the first group than for the second, presumably because of the temporal separation imposed by the commercials. There was no evidence of behavioral differences among the sixth and tenth graders who saw both types of programs.

It is impossible to estimate what part of the variance in the social impact of television is due to incomplete or distorted comprehension of what children see. Certainly, comprehension is only one factor in a complex equation for television effects. Marked variability, however, has been found in children's comprehension of socially pertinent content during the middle childhood and adolescent years; and there is also suggestive evidence of concomitant effects on social evaluations and on behavior in the laboratory. These two empirical thrusts suggest that cognitive-processing aspects of television viewing should become a term in the equation that guides future research on television effects.

References

Ajzen, I., & Fishbein, M. Attitude-behavior relations: A theoretical analysis and review of empirical research. *Psychological Bulletin*, 1977, *84*, 888–918.

Alwitt, L. F., Anderson, D. R., Lorch, E. P., & Levin, S. R. Preschool children's visual attention to attributes of television. *Human Communication Research*, 1980, *7*, 52–67.

Anderson, D. R. *Active and passive processes in children's television viewing.* Paper presented at the meeting of the American Psychological Association, New York, 1979.

Anderson, D. R., Alwitt, L. F., Lorch, E. P., & Levin, S. R. Watching children watch television. In G. Hale & M. Lewis (Eds.), *Attention and the development of cognitive skills.* New York: Plenum, 1979.

Anderson, D. R., Lorch, E. P., Field, D. E., & Sanders, J. The effects of TV program comprehensibility on preschool children's visual attention to television. *Child Development*, 1981, *52*, 151–157.

Anderson, D. R., & Levin, S. R. Young children's attention to "Sesame Street" *Child Development*, 1976, *47*, 806–811.

Austin, V., Ruble, D., & Trabasso, T. Recall and order effects as factors in children's moral judgments. *Child Development*, 1976, *48*, 470–474.

Baggett, P. Structurally equivalent stories in movie and text and the effect of the medium on recall. *Journal of Verbal Learning and Verbal Behavior*, 1979, *18*, 333–356.

Bandura, A. Influence of models' reinforcement contingencies on the acquisition of imitative responses. *Journal of Personality and Social Psychology*, 1965, *1*, 589–595.

Berkowitz, L., & Geen, R. G. The stimulus qualities of the target of aggression: A further study. *Journal of Personality and Social Psychology*, 1967, *5*, 364–368.

Berkowitz, L., & Rawlings, E. Effects of film violence on inhibitions against subsequent aggression. *Journal of Abnormal and Social Psychology*, 1963, *66*, 405–412.

Berndt, T.J., & Berndt, E.G. Children's use of motives and intentionality in person perception and moral judgment. *Child Development*, 1975, *46*, 904–912.

Blumler, J., & Katz, E. (Eds.) *The uses of mass communications: Current perspectives on gratifications research.* Beverly Hills: Sage, 1974.

Bower, G. *Comprehending and recalling stories.* Paper presented at the meeting of the American Psychological Association. Washington, D.C., 1976.

Bower, G. H. Experiments on story comprehension and recall. *Discourse Processes*, 1978, *1*, 211–231.

Bower, G. H., Black, J. B., & Turner, T. J. Scripts in memory for text. *Cognitive Psychology*, 1979, *11*, 177–220.

Bransford, J. D., & Franks, J. J. The abstraction of linguistic ideas: A review. *Cognition*, 1972, *1*, 211–249.

Brown, A. The development of memory: Knowing, knowing about knowing, and knowing how to know. In H. W. Reese (Ed.), *Advances in child development and behavior* Vol. 10. New York: Academic Press, 1975.

Bruner, J. S. Going beyond the information given. In *Contemporary approaches to cognition.* Cambridge, Mass.: Harvard University Press, 1957.

Bruner, J. S. *Studies in cognitive growth.* New York: Wiley, 1966.

Bryant, J., Hezel, R., & Zillmann, D. Humor in children's educational television. *Communication Education*, 1978, *28*, 29–38.

Calvert, S. L., & Watkins, B. A. *Recall of television content as a function of content type and level of production feature use.* Paper presented at the meeting of the Society for Research in Child Development, San Francisco, 1979.

Calvert, S. L., Watkins, B. A., & Huston-Stein, A. *Immediate and delayed recall of central and incidental television content as a function of formal features.* Paper presented at the meeting of the Society for Research in Child Development, San Francisco, 1979.

Cantor, N., & Mischel, W. Traits as prototypes: Effects on recognition memory. *Journal of Personality and Social Psychology*, 1977, *35*, 38–48.

Chandler, M., Greenspan, S., & Barenboim, C. Judgments of intentionality in response to videotaped and verbally presented moral dilemmas: The medium is the message. *Child Development*, 1973, *44*, 315–320.

Collins, W. A. Learning of media content: A developmental study. *Child Development*, 1970, *41*, 1133–1142.

Collins, W. A. The effect of temporal separation between motivation, aggression, and consequences: A developmental study. *Developmental Psychology*, 1973, *8*, 215–221.

Collins, W. A. Children's comprehension of television content. In E. Wartella (Ed.), *Development of children's communicative behavior.* Beverly Hills: Sage, 1978.

Collins, W. A., Berndt, T. J., & Hess, V. L. Observational learning of motives and consequences for television aggression: A developmental study. *Child Development*, 1974, *45*, 799–802.

Collins, W. A., & Getz, S. Children's social responses following modeled reactions to provocation: Prosocial effects of a television drama. *Journal of Personality*, 1976, *44*, 488–500.

Collins, W. A., Karasov, R., & Westby, S. *Effects of pre-viewing instructions on children's retention and inferences following a dramatic television program.* Unpublished manuscript, University of Minnesota, 1978.

Collins, W. A., Sobol, B. L., & Westby, S. Effects of adult commentary on children's comprehension and inferences about a televised aggressive portrayal. *Child Development*, 1981, *52*, 158–163.

Collins, W. A., & Wellman, H. *Social scripts and developmental changes in representations of televised narratives.* Unpublished manuscript, University of Minnesota, 1980.

Collins, W. A., Wellman, H., Keniston, A., & Westby, S. Age-related aspects of comprehension of televised social content. *Child Development*, 1978, *49*, 389–399.

Collins, W. A., & Westby, S. *Developmental and individual differences in children's responses to television.* Manuscript in preparation, 1981.

Comstock, G., Chaffee, S., Katzman, N., McCombs, M., & Roberts, D. *Television and human behavior.* New York: Columbia University Press, 1978.

Costanzo, P. R., Coie, J. D., Grumet, J., & Farnill, D. A reexamination of the effects of intent and consequences on children's moral judgments. *Child Development*, 1973, *44*, 154–161.

Dickman, H. R. The perception of behavioral units. In R. G. Barker (Ed.), *The stream of behavior.* New York: Appleton-Century-Crofts, 1963.

Drew, D., & Reeves, B. Learning from a television news story. *Communication Research*, 1980, *7*, 121–135.

Feldman, N. S., Klosson, E. C., Parsons, J. E., Rholes, W. S., & Ruble, D. N. Order of information presentation and children's moral judgments. *Child Development*, 1976, *47*, 556–559.

Flapan, D. *Children's understanding of social interaction.* New York: Teachers College Press, 1968.

Flavell, J. H. *Cognitive development.* Englewood Cliffs, N. J.: Prentice-Hall, 1977.

Friedlander, B. Z., Wetstone, H. S., & Scott, C. Suburban preschool children's comprehension of an age-appropriate information television program. *Child Development*, 1974, *45*, 561–565.

Friedrich, L. K., & Stein, A. H. Prosocial television and young children: The effects of verbal labeling and role playing on learning and behavior. *Child Development*, 1975, *46*, 27–38.

Gardner, H. Are television's effects due to television? *Psychology Today*, January 1980, 63–64.

Golinkoff, R., & Kerr, J. *Infants' perception of semantically defined action role changes in filmed events.* Unpublished manuscript, 1975.

Grueneich, R. *Methodology for the development study of moral judgment.* Unpublished manuscript, University of Minnesota, 1978.

Gutkin, D. The effect of systematic story changes on intentionality in children's moral judgments. *Child Development*, 1972, *43*, 187–196.

Hale, G., Miller, L., & Stevenson, H. Incidental learning of film content: A developmental study. *Child Development*, 1968, *39*, 69–77.

Hastie, R. Schematic principles in human memory. In E. T. Higgins, C. P. Herman, & M. P. Zanna (Eds.), *The Ontario symposium on personality and social psychology: Social cognition.* Hillsdale, N. J.: Erlbaum, in press.

Hawkins, R. P. Learning of peripheral content in films: A developmental study. *Child Development*, 1973, *44*, 214-217.

Himmelweit, H. T., Oppenheim, A. N., & Vince, P. *Television and the child.* London: Oxford University Press, 1958.

Holaday, P. W., & Stoddard, G. D. *Getting ideas from the movies.* New York: Macmillan, 1933.

Hollenbeck, A. R., & Slaby, R. G. Infant visual and vocal responses to television. *Child Development*, 1979, *50*, 41-45.

Huston-Stein, A. *Television and growing up: The medium gets equal time.* Invited address to the Divisions on Developmental Psychology and Educational Psychology at the meeting of the American Psychological Association, San Francisco, 1977.

Jones, E. E., Kanouse, D. E., Kelley, H. H., Nisbett, R. E., Valins, S., & Weiner, B. (Eds.). *Attribution: Perceiving the causes of behavior.* Morristown, N.J.: General Learning Press, 1971.

Judd, C. M., & Kulik, J. Schematic effects of social attitudes upon information processing and recall. *Journal of Personality and Social Psychology*, 1980, *38*, 569-575.

Kelley, H. H. The process of causal attribution. *American Psychologist*, 1973, *28*, 107-128.

Krull, R., & Husson, W. G. *The effects of form and content on children's attention: The case of TV viewing.* Unpublished manuscript, Rensselaer Polytechnic Institute, 1978.

Krull, R., Husson, W. G., & Paulson, A. S. cycles in children's attention to the television screen. In B. D. Rubin (Ed.), *Communication Yearbook II.* Brunswick, N.J.: Transaction Books, 1978.

Krull, R., Watt, J., & Lichty, L. Entropy and structure: Two measures of complexity in television programs. *Communication Research*, 1977, *4*, 61-85.

Krull, R., & Husson, W. G. Children's attention: The case of TV viewing. In E. Wartella (Ed.), *Children communicating: Media and development of thought, speech, understanding.* Beverly Hills: Sage, 1978.

Kun, A., Parsons, J. E., & Ruble, D. Development of integration processes using ability and effort information to predict outcome. *Developmental Psychology*, 1976, *10*, 721-732.

Leifer, A. D., Gordon, N., & Graves, S. Children's television: More than mere entertainment. *Harvard Educational Review*, 1974, *44*, 213-245.

Leifer, A. D., & Roberts, D. F. Children's responses to television violence. In J. P. Murray, E. A. Rubinstein, & G. A. Comstock (Eds.), *Television and social behavior* (Vol. 2). *Television and social learning.* Washington: U.S. Government Printing Office, 1972.

Levin, S. R. *Relationships between preschool individual differences and patterns of television viewing.* Unpublished doctoral dissertation, University of Massachusetts, 1976.

Levin, S. R., & Anderson, D. R. The development of attention. *Journal of Communication*, 1976, *26* (2), 126-135.

Maccoby, E. E., & Wilson, W. C. Identification and observational learning from films. *Journal of Abnormal and Social Psychology*, 1957, *55*, 76-87.

Mandler, J., & Johnson, N. Remembrance of things parsed: Story structure and recall. *Cognitive Psychology*, 1977, *9*, 111-151.

Markus, H. Self-schemata and processing information about the self. *Journal of Personality and Social Psychology*, 1977, *35*, 63-78.

Medrich, J. C. Constant television background to daily life. *Journal of Communication*, 1979, *29*(3), 171-176.

Neisser, U. *Cognition and reality.* San Francisco: Freeman, 1976.

Nelson, K. How children represent knowledge of their world in and out of language: A preliminary report. In R. Siegler (Ed.), *Children's thinking: What develops?* Hillsdale, N.J.: Erlbaum, 1978.

Newcomb, A. F., & Collins, W. A. Children's comprehension of family role portrayals in televised dramas: Effects of socioeconomic status, ethnicity, and age. *Developmental Psychology*, 1979, *15*, 417-423.

Newtson, D. Attribution and the unit of perception of ongoing behavior. *Journal of Personality and Social Psychology*, 1973, *28*, 28-38.

Nisbett, R., & Ross, L. *Human inference: Strategies and shortcomings of social judgment.* Englewood Cliffs, N.J.: Prentice-Hall, 1980.

Omanson, R. *The narrative analysis.* Unpublished doctoral dissertation, University of Minnesota, August 1979.

Parke, R. D. Children's home environments: Social and cognitive effects. In I. Altman and J. F. Wohlwill (Eds.), *Children and the environment.* New York: Plenum, 1978.

Piaget, J. *The construction of reality in the child.* New York: Basic Books, 1954.

Poulsen, D., Kintsch, E., Kintsch, W., & Premack, D. Children's comprehension and memory for stories. *Journal of Experimental Child Psychology*, 1979, *28*, 379-403.

Purdie, S. I., Collins, W. A., & Westby, S. Effect of plot organization on children's comprehension of evaluative cues about a televised aggressive portrayal. Unpublished manuscript, University of Minnesota, 1980.

Reeves, B. Children's understanding of television people. In E. Wartella (Ed.), *Children communicating: Media and development of thought, speech, understanding.* Beverly Hills: Sage, 1978.

Reeves, B., & Greenberg, B. Children's perceptions of television characters. *Human Communication Research*, 1977, *3*, 113-127.

Reeves, B., & Miller, M. A multidimensional measure of children's identification with television characters. *Journal of Broadcasting*, 1978, *22*, 71-86.

Reich, I. R. Cognitive and developmental aspects of viewing television (Doctoral dissertation, City University of New York, 1977). *Dissertation Abstracts International*, 1977, 38 (University Microfilms No. 77-20, 519).

Rogers, T. B., Kuiper, R. G., & Kirker, W. S. Self-reference and the encoding of personal information. *Journal of Personality and Social Psychology*, 1977, *35*, 677-688.

Salomon, G. *Interaction of media, cognition, and learning.* San Francisco: Jossey-Bass, 1979.

Schank, R., & Abelson, R. *Scripts, plans, goals, and understanding.* Hillsdale, N.J.: Erlbaum, 1977.

Schmidt, C. Understanding human action: Recognizing the plans and motives of other persons. In J. Carroll & J. Payne (Eds.), *Cognition and social behavior.* Potomac, Md.: Erlbaum, 1976.

Schramm, W., Lyle, J., & Parker, E. B. *Television in the lives of our children.* Stanford: Stanford University Press, 1961.

Sears, D. O., and Freedman, J. L. Selective exposure to information: A critical review. *Public Opinion Quarterly*, 1967, *31*, 195-213.

Sedlak, A. J. Developmental differences in understanding plans and evaluating actors. *Child Development*, 1979, *50*, 536-560.

Sedlak, A. Understanding an actor's behavior: Developmental differences in plan interpretation. Paper presented as a part of a symposium entitled *Cognitive Processing of Television Content: Perspectives on the Effects of Television on Children* at the biennial meeting of the Society for Research in Child Development, New Orleans, 1977.

Shantz, C. The development of social cognition. In E. M. Hetherington (Ed.), *Review of child development research* (Vol. 5). Chicago: University of Chicago Press, 1975.

Shultz, T. R., & Butkowsky, I. Young children's use of the scheme for multiple sufficient causes in the attribution of real and hypothetical behavior. *Child Development*, 1977, *48*, 464-469.

Stein, A. H. & Friedrich, L. K. The effects of television content on young children's behavior. In A. D. Pick (Ed.), *Minnesota symposia on child psychology* (vol. 9). Minneapolis: University of Minnesota Press, 1975, 78-105.

Stein, N., & Glenn, C. An analysis of story completion in elementary school children. In R. Freedle (Ed.), *Advances in discourse processes* (vol. 2). Hillsdale, N.J.: Erlbaum, 1979.

Sternglanz, S. H. & Serbin, L. A. Sex role stereotyping in children's television programs. *Developmental Psychology*, 1974, *10*, 710–715.

Tada, T. Image-cognition: A developmental approach. In *Studies of broadcasting*. Tokyo, Japan: Nippon Hoso Kyokai, 1969, 105–173.

Taylor, S., & Crocker, J. Schematic bases of social information processing. In E. T. Higgins, C. P. Herman, & M. P. Zanna (Eds.), *The Ontario symposium on personality and social psychology: Social cognition*. Hillsdale, N.J.: Erlbaum, in press.

Wackman, D. B., Wartella, E., & Ward, S. *Children's information processing of television advertising*. (Tech. Rep. to the National Science Foundation on Grant No. APR 76–20770), 1979.

Warren, W., Nicholas, D., & Trabasso, T. Event chains and inferences in understanding narratives. In R. Freedle (Ed.), *Advances in discourse processes* (Vol. 2). Hillsdale, N.J.: Erlbaum, 1979.

Wartella, E. *Children's perceptual unitizing of a televised behavior sequence*. Paper presented to the Association for Education in Journalism Annual Convention, Seattle, 1978.

Wartella, E., & Ettema, J. A cognitive developmental study of children's attention to television commercials. *Communication Research*, 1974, *1*, 69–88.

Watkins, B. A., Calvert, S. L., Huston-Stein, A., & Wright, J. C. Children's recall of television material: Effects of presentation mode and adult labeling. *Developmental Psychology*, 1980, *16*, 672–674.

Watt, J. H., & Krull, R. An information theory measure for television programming. *Communication Research*, 1974, *1*, 44–68.

Werner, H. The concept of development from a comparative and organismic point of view. In D. Harris (Ed.), *The concept of development*. Minneapolis: University of Minnesota Press, 1957.

Wilensky, R. *Understanding goal-based stories*. Yale University Department of Computer Sciences, Research Report #140, September 1978.

Worth, S., & Gross, L. Symbolic strategies. *Journal of Communication*, 1974, *24* (4), 27–39.

Wright, J. C., & Vlietstra, A. G. The development of selective attention: From perceptual exploration to logical search. In H. W. Reese (Ed.), *Advances in child development and behavior* (Vol. 10). New York: Academic Press, 1975.

Wright, J. C., Watkins, B. A., & Huston-Stein, A. *Active vs. passive television viewing: A model of the development of television information processing by children*. Unpublished manuscript, University of Kansas, 1979.

Zadny, J., & Gerard, H. B. Attributed intentions and informational selectivity. *Journal of Experimental Psychology*, 1974, *10*, 34–52.

PART III

FEMINISM AND THE MEDIA

A fruitful area of inquiry in media studies in the past dozen years has been media portrayal of social groups and collectivities, and perhaps in no domain of such studies has there been more commentary than in portrayal of women. This series heretofore has not noted such scholarship, a situation we wish to remedy, not only because the topic is important but also, as the chapters below indicate, considerable theoretical vigor and diversity marks the area.

MaryAnn Yodelis Smith reviews recent American scholarship on women and media and offers a research model for further examination for such studies.

Gertrude Robinson directly examines portrayals of women and work in Canadian and U.S. magazines and shows differences across time and across national boundaries in such portrayals.

Angela McRobbie provides a semiotic analysis of a British teen magazine to support her view that the magazine projects a coherent ideology of adolescent femininity.

Finally, Thelma McCormack discusses the evolution of broadcast women's drama to suggest more reliance on structural analyses.

In this review of recent American research on feminism and the media, Yodelis Smith proposes a research model for examining women and the media, analyzes its theoretical bases for feminist researchers, and then considers studies that have examined the process, content, and effects of mass media from a feminist communications research perspective. MaryAnn Yodelis Smith is professor of journalism and mass communications at the University of Wisconsin, Madison.

14

RESEARCH RETROSPECTIVE
Feminism and the Media

MaryAnn Yodelis Smith

Gaye Tuchman, Arlene Kaplan Daniels, James Benét, *Hearth and Home: Images of Women in the Mass Media.* New York: Oxford University Press, 1978.

Ann Douglas, *The Feminization of American Culture.* New York: Avon Books, 1977.

Ellen Carol DuBois, *Feminism and Suffrage,* Ithaca, NY: Cornell University Press, 1978.

Barbara Sicherman and Carolyn Hurd Green, *Notable American Women/The Modern Period.* Cambridge, MA: Belknap Press, 1980.

Marion Marzolf, *Up from the Footnote: A History of Women Journalists.* New York: Hastings House, 1977.

Matilda Butler and William Paisley, *Women and the Mass Media.* New York: Human Sciences Press, 1980.

Maurine Beasley and Sheila Silver, *Women in Media: A Documentary Sourcebook.* Washington, DC: Women's Institute for Freedom of the Press, 1977.

Laurily Keir Epstein, *Women and the News.* New York: Hastings House, 1978.

Although women communicators can trace their history to Dinah Nuthead, a colonial printer in Maryland in 1696, it was not until the early 1970s that a major movement among communications researchers to document fully and analyze seriously that

From MaryAnn Yodelis Smith, "Research Retrospective: Feminism and the Media," *Communication Research,* Vol. 9, No. 2 (January 1982), pp. 145-160. Copyright © 1982 by Sage Publications, Inc.

history could be discerned. The motion to elevate the saga of women communicators from textbook footnotes to the focus of major research accompanied a growing desire to document feminist history in general. Alleging that women were invisible in history, Ann Firor Scott urged women to remedy the situation. She said the "male historians see what their presumptions lead them to see, and they expect women to blend into the scenery. It is important for women to know something about their history in order to have some self-respect." She charged that American women were operating as if they had no history.[1] Women in communications responded to that charge with such vigor that now—nearly a decade later—appears to be a propitious time for a retrospective review of the major feminist communication research of the 1970s, particularly since an argument could be made that such research currently is on the wane. This could mark the demise of the movement and the beginning of backlash or it could signal ultimate achievement so that the topic of women and media no longer requires separate discussion. The integrationists insist that only when feminist perspectives are included as a matter of course in general communication research will women communicators have achieved equality. The pity would be, of course, to mistake token inclusion for integration or, worse, to ignore the signs of regression. Irrespective of philosophical positioning in the separatist or integrationist camp and irrespective of their predictions for the future, however, communication scholars should find a decade's review of the theoretical model for feminist communication research at least provocative. The studies expanded well beyond the pleas of the early 70s for historical documentation treatises of women and media to sociocultural treatises at the decade's close.

Utilizing Gaye Tuchman et al's (1978) seminal study, *Hearth and Home: Images of Women in the Mass Media,* this review first will suggest a research model and analyze its theoretical bases for feminist communications research and then approach the studies according to media institutions, as well as research methodologies. Finally, studies on media affects, such as television as an instrument of socialization, will be reviewed for their implications for the future of women and the media.

RESEARCH MODEL

As noted, the Tuchman et al. study gives promise of being the most fruitful research model for analyzing women and the media.

Tuchman and her collaborators study women as they are portrayed in the primary media, as well as focus on the women (or lack therof) of those media. Finally, in order to propose remedies for the ills documented by the studies, the media—specifically, television—are viewed in terms of effects (see Figure 1). Although significantly based on Tuchman et al.'s conceptualization of research, the model has been broadened substantially. The potential expanded model, therefore, makes clear that, no matter what the current political climate, scores of research questions regarding the relationship of women and the media remain unexplored. Note particularly the areas of analytical history and message analysis, as well as the interinstitutional context.

Generally, the potential research model sketched in Figure 1 was based on the dual hypotheses proposed by Tuchman et al. and the media assumptions underlying those hypotheses. Nearly all communicators accept the Harold Lasswell proposition that the media transmit social heritage—dominant cultural values—from one generation to the next. This may be particularly true of sex roles. Likewise, most also accept the G. S. Lesser thesis that modeling occurs by observing others without either direct reinforcement for learning or actual overt practice. Television, according to Lesser, greatly increases modeling opportunities, particularly for children. With these assumptions in mind, Tuchman et al. establish their major hypotheses: (1) that the mass media reflect dominant societal values in a symbolic manner and therefore offer programs that will appeal to the largest audience and (2) that women are subject to symbolic annihilation in the media, that is, condemnation, trivialization, or absence (Tuchman et al., 1978: 8). They note the symbolic annihilation is most devastating on television because the audience consists of both sexes and all ages. Not only did Tuchman et al.'s study support both hypotheses, but other research referred to subsequently in this review substantiate the Tuchman et al. work. Although Gertrude Joch Robinson's work supports the Tuchman et al. hypothesis, she does report more optimistic findings about magazines than Tuchman et al. did about television. That is, magazines appear to have been more responsive to major issues facing women in the 1970s in contrast to the more severe symbolic annihilation on television (Grewe-Partsch and Robinson, 1980: 106-111). The potential model traces the symbolic annihilation of women in the media in the intrainstitutional context via the scarcity of female processors

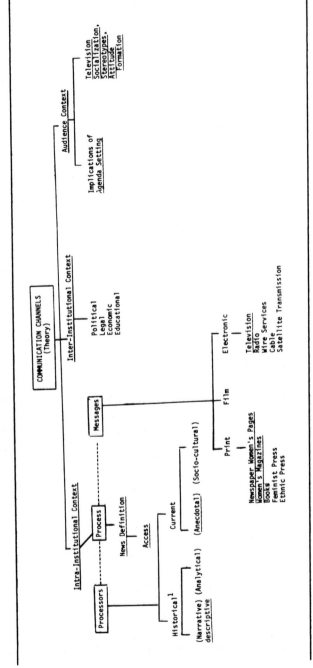

Figure 1: The Research Model—Women and the Media

1. Areas of current research focus are underscored.

to cause change; the process itself, particularly in male-domi-
nated news definitions and female lack of access to the process;
and, finally, via the scarcity of dominant female images in the
media (who are not either trivialized or victimized). The symbolic
annihilation of women in the media gains impetus, too, from
educational, political, legal, and economic factors that interface in
the interinstitutional context, particularly multimedia ownership.
These factors have been largely unexplored in terms of women
and the media although some attention has been paid them in
terms of minority groups and the media.[2] Finally, the devastating
effects of symbolic annihilation are dramatized by the studies of
agenda setting and television socialization. Although both Tuchman et al. hypotheses are supported by all the research—surely to
the despair of thinking men and women—these conclusions do
give rise to recommendations for change in the processors, the
process, and content of the media to at least neutralize, if not
replace, symbolic annihilation of women by the media.

MEDIA PROCESSORS

Women, as processors in the media, have been studied generally via historical descriptive narrative, but more recently in a
more analytical, sociocultural context. Undoubtedly, the sparse
population of women employed by media (and even fewer
women employed or established in positions of power in the
media) has accelerated somewhat the male media managers'
tendency to disregard or denigrate concerns of women. That is,
one might presume (despite the Phyllis Schlaflys of the world) that
women reporters, editors, or producers generally would not be
party to the symbolic annihilation of their sex. Note the history of
the feminist press, for example. Although studies of women as
media processors have increased in number, far too few of them
stray from traditional historical narrative to sociocultural analyses.

In this, feminist communication history is no different from
general communication history, which often has been the target
of barbs from practitioners of history and communication history.
In 1975 James Carey urged a redefinition of communications

history to broaden its scope, and later Garth Jowett (1978: 2) continued to urge: "What we need now is the 'second generation' of studies, those which go beyond the mere narrative details, but start to place these essential details in a meaningful social and cultural context." He added that "very little attempt has been made to integrate into these historical studies the vast amount of important and provocative findings from communications theory."

Though James Baughman's (1981: 9) admonition to deal with less criticizing and analyzing communication history and get on with more writing of it is well taken, there is merit in some comment on the recent historical offerings on women in communications in the context of method. The best response to Jowett's pleas for analytical history probably was made by Ann Douglas (1977) in *The Feminization of American Culture.* The Douglas hypothesis is that the Victorian alliance between women and mostly male clergy, with the resulting popular literature, fostered a sentimental society and the beginning of modern mass culture—the age that gave birth to J. R. and the daytime soaps. Examining carefully the work and times of 30 women writers and journalists and 30 male ministers, Douglas concludes that when women moved from significant roles in family-farm productivity to urban household roles, female labor was devalued and the female identity was correspondingly reconceived. She explains that while the 18th century matron at her spinning wheel had a central role in her own productive unit, the 19th-century urban factory girl was merely a cog in the productive system. The 19th-century female indeed had responsibilities, but Douglas shows that a lady's leisure was treated with more significance. She argues that these women were trained to demand flattery instead of justice and equality. The ministers similarly sought domestic importance to compensate for societal neglect, according to Douglas (1977: 63-88). With documentation from the best-selling magazines and novels of the day, Douglas continues to show how women began to idealize the qualities that kept them powerless (timidity, piety, disdain for competition in the marketplace) and to indulge in the dangerous social preoccupation with glamour and unrestrained consumption. A skillful minibiography of Margaret Fuller as one of the 30 women writers shows Fuller's increasing dedication to writing to give her a more active participation in the changes needed to improve the floundering socioeconomic order (Douglas,

1977: 313-348). Such a framework for history provides the reader with a context for the struggle of the present day toward the goal of human liberation. A mere narrative biography of 60 persons, needless to say, would not have spoken nearly so effectively. Another example is Ellen Carol DuBois's (1978) *Feminism and Suffrage*, which examines the relationships between the feminist press and the suffrage movement. She asserts that the suffrage movement ranks alongside the black and labor movements as one of the major reform efforts in American history.

Nevertheless, biography in its purest form, skillfully written, continues to provide a base for the more analytical discussions. Among the best of brief biographies of women in communication are those in Volume 2 of *Notable American Women/The Modern Period*, edited by Barbara Sicherman and Carolyn Hurd Green (1980). Each well-written and tightly edited biography helps provide thoughtful background for the researcher pursuing more analytical historical questions like Douglas's. The editors purport to present lives that are "important in themselves and suggestive as well of the larger social and cultural issues of their time" (1980: xv). Based on the general four-fold selection criteria (the individual's on her time or field; the significance of her achievement; the pioneering or innovative quality of her work; and the relevance of her career for the history of women (1980: x); the biographical entries are catholic enough to range from Gertrude Edelstein Berg to Frieda Barkin Hennock to Elisabeth May Adams Craig. Some of the biographies present heretofore seldom publicized factual material, that is, that Gertrude Berg of Mollie Goldberg fame was the script writer for the series; and that Judith Cary Waller, the first station manager of WMAQ, Chicago, produced the first play-by-play broadcast of college football in 1924 (1980: 73-74, 716). Other biographies are presented in the context of related sociocultural movements; that is, Charlotta Spears Bass served for more than 40 years as editor of *The California Eagle*, the oldest black newspaper on the West Coast; Irna Phillips, with "Days of Our Lives," "The Guiding Light," and "As the World Turns" to her credit, probably is the single most important influence on the phenomenon of television soaps; and Mildred Edie Brady, early part of the Consumer's Union, "laid the groundwork for the rise of world consumerism" (1980: 61, 543, 102). Other women, more traditionally conceived as journalists, also are included: Frieda Barkin Hennock, the first female Federal Communications Commissioner whose major accomplishment was to insure channels were reserved for educational television; May Craig, the acerbic questioner of government on "Meet the Press"; Aline Milton Bernstein Saarinen, art critic, translator of culture, and NBC news correspondent; Julia de Bergos, poet and Puerto Rican journalist; Alicia Patterson, publisher of *Newsday*; Elizabeth Meriwether Gilmer, the advice columnist (Dorothy Dix); Marguerite Higgins, the first female Pulitzer Prize winner for foreign correspondence; and Clara Savage Littledale, editor of *Parents' Magazine* (1980: 332, 172, 613-614, 123, 529, 275, 340, 422). Because each biography was extensively researched by individual authors, *Notable American Women* makes a more substantive contribution to the literature than similar collections.[3] Each is rich in factual detail, but the detail is integral to a larger sociocultural interpretation.

In a similar historical mode, Marian Marzolf's (1979) *Up from the Footnote: A History of Women Journalists* is a popularized history of women journalists. Although hampered in its usefulness by a lack of footnotes, the Marzolf history at the least provides a compilation of the known history of women journalists from the 14 colonial women printers to the present.

Additionally, a number of works of the decade focus on the current processors in the media, and the stark reality is that although numbers of women employed in the mass media dramatically have increased since the days of Dinah Nuthead, women communicators still are few. They are, of course, more concentrated in the lower ranks of media employes (see, for example, U.S. Commission on Civil Rightrs, 1977: 148-149). However, Gladys Engle Lang suggests that the theatrical quality surrounding promotions of women like Barbara Walters may help break down traditional stereotypes of women and public resistance to women with autonomous status" (Tuchman et al., 1978: 159). Marzolf treats women currently in the media via an anecdotal style. Hers is a survey of women currently working in the communications media and how they feel about being women. A more documented and statistical survey of women currently in the media is provided by Matilda Butler and William Paisley (1980) in *Women and the Mass Media*. The authors devote a chapter to employment that supports the general propositions that men are more likely than women to be in management, to earn higher media salaries, to obtain promotions, and to receive more desirable assignments (1980: 182-230). In addition, *Women in Media: A Documentary Sourcebook* edited by Maurine Beasley and Sheila Silver (1977) provides a useful research tool for exploring conflicts betwwen women employees and the media. For example, there is documentation supporting the challenge to the renewal of WABC-TV (New York) in part because of under-employment of women, as well as documentation supporting the complaint of sex discrimination against women employees of the *Washington Post* filed with the Equal Employment Opportunities Commission (1977: 126, 139). Although the documents in this sourcebook are authentic and often unobtainable elsewhere, the introductions to the documents are not footnoted. While these publications deal extensively with the processors in the media who are female, there remains a good deal to be researched and written. Collective biographies, for example, of women in media would be most useful, as well as further historical analyses of the processors like Douglas's.

THE PROCESS

Primarily, the focus of books on women and process has been on the process of news definition and the related problem of access to the media. Laurily Keir Epstein (1978) edited *Women and the News*, a book notable for its comprehensive discussion of these topics. News generally is defined by male editors and through a male perspective. Therefore, women as a group and individually have difficulty obtaining access to the media to present their views. Related research by Harvey L. Molotch (cited in Tuchman et al., 1978) asserts that there is little treatment of the women's movement in the press because it lacks interest for men who report and edit through a "man's sense of the world" and that more important, the women's pages do not cover events of daily life with which women have to deal. Molotch states that news is defined from a male perspective, "locker-room talk." This process of news definition, he writes, perpetuates old stereotypes, but serves the needs of men who generally own the media. Tuchman et al. (1978: 196) also note that newspapers cover events, not issues, so feminist consciousness raising frequently is ignored. Nevertheless, since a Butler and Paisley (1980: 231-241) proposition is that media portrayals affecting women generally are the result of only an informal process, women and media research could profit by further examination of that process by which media managers define news. The significance of news definition should become more clear as agenda setting by the media is further discussed in terms of its affects on readers and viewers.

Access by women to the press is closely related to the problems of news definition. Gertrude Joch Robinson conceptualizes three kinds of access to facilitate such research: (1) sociological access, which has been already discussed in the section on women as media processors; (2) political access, which is source related and comes to mind more commonly in discussions of access; and (3) symbolic access, which deals with women's ability to find a place on the media agenda. In her view, there was no access to the media while the current feminist movement was organizing, only restricted access (for sensational coverage) in the early 1970s and access routinized to trivialization since then (see Epstein, 1978: 87-98). Nevertheless, Yodelis Smith warns that feminist access cannot be had by frustrating the First Amendment rights of other groups (see Epstein, 1978: 64-81). This delicate legal balance needs to be investigated from other perspectives as well.

THE CONTENT OF THE MESSAGES

Communications research about women and the media also has been fruitfully explored in terms of the content of the media messages or the images projected of women by the media. Although this has been some of the most precise research, it also has been the most depressing to women in that it most thoroughly documents symbolic annihilation. Commenting that the image of women in the mass media is changing for the worse, George Gerbner states that media images are less a reflection of, than a counterattack on, the feminist movement as a social force for structural change. He adds that instead of "mediating even the actual social change that is taking place, the media appear to be cultivating resistance and preparing for a last-ditch defense" (see Tuchman et al., 1978: 46-48).

The message content generally has been analyzed via the specific media institution. In the print media, most attention has been paid by researchers to newspaper women's pages and women's magazines. An early Lazarsfeld and Merton study found that women's pages encouraged women to emulate the upper class and seek high status. Although one might hypothesize that times have changed because newspapers should be responsive to readers in an effort to increase circulation, this generally is not the case. Restrictive news budgets make many women's page editors dependent on national news service, encouraging continued, rigid treatment of sex roles (see Tuchman et al., 1978: 25). In truth, researchers argue about the value of continuing women's pages (or lifestyle, family, or similarly titled sections). Cynthia Fuchs Epstein suggests that "ghettoizing" discussions of human concerns and family and emotional needs suggests that men should bypass these issues, for their needs are met by other presentations of political, occupational, and sports activities. Recognizing this argument for integration of the news, Tuchman et al. (1978: 221, 211; cf. Epstein, 1978: 115), echoed by Leon Sigal, nevertheless suggest that dismantling the women's sections would end the power and autonomy of the women who edit them.

Women's magazines also have been the subject of content analysis, since one would expect that magazines for a female audience would not convey degrading messages. The bulk of the research contradicts this hypothesis. E. Barbara Phillips suggests that even *Ms.* heroines are liberal, but not liberated. She writes that "Ms. heroines, blending the traditionally masculine roles of achievers and traditionally feminine feelings, appear to affirm the hotly debated view that 'anatomy is destiny.'" *Ms.*, she states, implies women are different, but better, and, therefore, given power, would promote a more humane world. At the political level, this view, Phillips complains, merely affirms the existing social order (see Tuchman et al., 1978: 128). Supporting this, Carol Lopate's analysis of women's magazine treatment of Jackie Onassis gives evidence that the magazines, political at the structural level, soften the distinction between the rich and poor and portray work outside the home as negative space between the woman's role of wife and mother (see Tuchman et al., 1978: 139-140). While Robinson expresses much more optimism that women's magazines are beginning to portray women favorably in certain public roles, she does admit that topics like the restructured patriarchal family are omitted. More significantly, however, she notes that these magazine analyses make clear that generation must be added to sex as an additional and crucial predictor of magazine content (see Grewe-Partsch and Robinson, 1980: 110). Also, Butler and Paisley and Marzolf deal with content of women's magazines. Marzolf touches on the content of the feminist press, as well as its personnel, though in no particularly systematic fashion.

Of the electronic media, television content thus far has been most frequently and systematically analyzed by researchers. These include studies of television commercials and children's programming. Like women's magazines, television defines women by the men in their lives—or the lack of them. Judith Lemon's analysis, for example, shows men more dominant (as demonstrated by relevant occupational status) than women, except perhaps in some situation comedies. Stephen Schultz and Joyce N. Sprafkin found that even in Saturday morning spot messages, males dominated in number of appearances and in the level of respect accorded them (see Tuchman et al., 1978: 64-77).

Perhaps the most innovative method of analysis applicable to all media is the Consciousness scale developed by Suzanne Pingree and Robert Hawkins. The scale classifies media images of woman in five ordered consciousness levels, ranging from putting down of women as sex objects, keeping women in traditional home and work roles, appropriating family and work roles for women, acknowledging that men and women can function equally, to recognizing that men and women are nonstereotypic. Needless to say, most media images of women function largely at the first two described levels (see Butler and Paisley, 1980: 148-169). The advantage of the Pingree/Hawkins approach is two-fold: It can be replicated and it is applicable across media. As they suggest, this is a challenging research area for further development.

OTHER INSTITUTIONS

Researchers generally have ignored what the model proposes as the interinstitutional context of media research on women. Such exploration would reflect the political, legal, and economic relationships of other institutions to the media and ultimately its portrayal of women. Here the relationships of the media with other institutions need to be examined. For example, multimedia ownership may have some relationship to the status of women in certain media. Legal questions extend beyond the access issues. The Federal Communications Commission entry into the hiring of women and minorities by broadcasters has not been studied thoroughly. Although the educational philosophy of those who educate the media managers has been dealt with to some extent by Marzolf (1977: 248-265), who recognizes that there is a dearth of female role models for women in communication, one might explore the relationships of the elementary teachers and the sexual stereotypes they promote (as well as those promoted by the textbooks) and the tortured image of women utilized by the media. Political institutions also bear some study in this regard.

EFFECTS ON AUDIENCE

Although determining effects of media on the audience does have pitfalls, this has been an area probed rather successfully by researchers investigating the relationship of such effects and the image of women projected by the media. The studies generally have been focused in two major areas: agenda setting and effects of television viewing on children.

While agenda-setting research is intertwined with news definition as part of the process, some findings are appropriate to include here because they show the devastating effects of the agenda-setting process on women. Bernard Cohen perhaps said it best: While the mass media may not tell us what to think, they undoubtedly tell us what to think about. Based on that assumption, Maxwell McCombs's studies show two findings of great interest to women: (1) newspapers significantly structure our perceptions of which social issues are most important over the long term and (2) television rank orders the issues at the top of the agenda for the short term (see Epstein, 1978: 2-8). Doris Graber's further work substantiates the importance of McCombs's assertions that personal agenda setting by men and women differs only slightly, but newspaper content shows women's interest items with less frequency and in less prominent positions. She suggests that women must develop the ability to monitor their own interests and affect the agenda-setting process (see Epstein, 1978: 28-32). Clearly, agenda setting by media managers has an effect on women.

Additionally, effects of television viewing on children particularly have been extensively studied. Because television is intelligible even to illiterate persons and because it is omnipresent, the important question is whether girls model their behavior and attitudes on the symbolically annihilated and dominated television woman. Joyce N. Sprafkin and Robert M. Liebert make clear that girls do just that. They tend to select programs that feature women behaving in stereotypic ways. Ellen Wartella found that children perceive Ingalls, the most prosocial and unidimensional television mother in her study, as realistic (Grewe-Partsch and Robinson, 1980: 76-83). Other research claims that television may have a greater affect than reality (Tuchman et al., 1978: 238-250). Pingree and Hawkins have devoted a full chapter to the same topic in the Butler and Paisley book. Their piece is particularly excellent for its summary of current research literature.

FUTURE RESEARCH

Having briefly categorized and summarized research on women and the media according to the proposed model, it is clear there are remedies women generally might pursue, as well as further research. Perhaps the most effective remedy was most forcefully proposed by James Benét, who wrote that if women media owners began to exercise their powers as owner, "the effect on the media's image of women could be profound" (Tuchman et al., 1978: 271). The Grewe-Partsch and Robinson collection has excellent beginning anayses of women as managers. Also the

Butler and Paisley text, designed as a textbook/source book, has a substantial chapter on legal and other remedies women should consider both in increasing employment equity in the media and in affecting the stereotypes of women portrayed by the media. At least some of their recommendations are based on successful practical experiences.

Although this essay has alluded briefly to areas of research pursued already under the general framework of the potential model, some studies necessarily had to be omitted. Nevertheless, even those areas need further study. For example, men and women could benefit from further consideration of the process of news definition. While newspapers, women's magazines, and television have had more attention, radio, cable, film, and other media institutions have not. Even strong analytical histories of the feminist press are few. Further, interinstitutional relationships noted on the model hardly have been explored. Again, while the affect of television on children has been a popular topic for researchers, there are other effect studies to be done. It would be a loss, indeed, if women and the media were ignored in the communications studies of the 1980s, because perhaps public attention to such work seems to be receding. Both men *and* women would continue to be frustrated by their continuing to perceive stereotypes in place of reality.

NOTES

1. Ann Firor Scott, Professor of History, Duke University, lecturing at the University of Michigan, Ann Arbor, in 1972.

2. Although women are a sociological minority, numerically they constitute over half the American population and are not included in the term *minority group* when it is used in this essay.

3. Book-length biographies of individual female journalists published in the last decade are not discussed in this review because those are the more common form of historical presentation.

REFERENCES

BAUGHMAN, J. (1981) "Columbia lion becomes Wisconsin mole." CLIO (Winter):
    9.
BEASLEY, M. and S. SILVER (1977) Women in Media: A Documentary Source-
    book. Washington, DC: Women's Institute for Freedom of the Press.
BUTLER, M. and W. PAISLEY (1980) Women and the Mass Media. New York: Hu-
    man Sciences Press.
CAREY, J. (1975) AEJ address (August).
DOUGLAS, A. (1977) The Feminization of American Culture. New York: Avon
    Books.
DuBOIS, E. C. (1978) Feminism and Suffrage. Ithaca, NY: Cornell Univ. Press.
EPSTEIN, L. K. (1978) Women and the News. New York: Hastings House.
GREWE-PARTSCH, M. and G. J. ROBINSON (1980) Women, Communication, and
    Careers. New York: K. G. Saur.
JOWETT, A. (1978) "The state of journalism history." CLIO (Fall): 2.
MARZOLF, M. (1977) Up from the Footnote: A History of Women Journalists. New
    York: Hastings House.
SICHERMAN, B. and C. H. GREEN [eds.] (1980) Notable American Women/The
    Modern Period (Vol. 2). Cambridge, MA: Belknap Press.
U.S. Commission on Civil Rights (1977) Window Dressing on the Set: Women and
    Minorities in Television. Washington, DC: Government Printing Office.

*How media "actively create and recreate" social reality and construct an image of women and work is
explored in this chapter. By examining the life and work characteristics of magazine heroines in
women's magazines and the types of themes related to women in and outside the home, this study
addresses three questions: (1) whether there is a difference between pre- and post-1970s portrayals of
working women; (2) the kinds of differences in various media portrayals of working women; and (3)
whether there is a difference between Canadian and U.S. magazine portrayals of women. Gertrude
Joch Robinson is professor of communication at McGill University, Montreal.*

15

CHANGING CANADIAN AND U.S. MAGAZINE PORTRAYALS OF WOMEN AND WORK
Growing Opportunities for Choice

Gertrude Joch Robinson

In every society, sex-gender associations are the most pervasive aspect of socialization. They associate values and attributes with feminine and masculine behavior which are particularly inflexible in North American and European Judeo-Christian societies. In these societies the private realm is the woman's and the public realm is the man's, which means with respect to employment that work outside the house is negatively evaluated. Women's life planning consequently is fraught with contradictions. It must try to harmonize notions of "proper" with prestigeous career choices, "fulfilling" work with marriage and childbearing. For many women these choices are mutually exclusive and therefore difficult to make. Adequate career training and preparation are consequently often neglected ultimately preventing women from developing autonomous roles outside the home.

Within living memory these public roles have however been socially and legally sanctioned in both North America and Western Europe. World War I gave females the vote and the second war legitimized middle class married women's participation in the labor force for the "national good". As a result of these and other lifestyle changes (*Ridley*, 1968)[1] by 1976 over half of all U.S. and Canadian women between 18 and 64 were working. In addition, most of these women were married and had pre-school children. In the last decade as a matter of fact, working mothers with children under six were the fastest growing segment of the work force in a North American economy increasingly requiring information processing rather than production skills (*Tuchman*, 1978).[2] Such a transformation affects not only women themselves, but their families and their co-workers. In the light of these massive social changes the media portrayal of women's working lives becomes a topic of great social concern. Have the media

From Gertrude Joch Robinson, "Changing Canadian and U.S. Magazine Portrayals of Women and Work: Growing Opportunities for Choice," in Marianne Grewe-Partsch and Gertrude J. Robinson, eds., *Women, Communication and Careers: Communication Research and Broadcasting No. 3*, pp. 93-113 (Munich: Internationales Zentralinstitut für das Jugend- und Bildungsfernsehen, 1980). Copyright by K. G. Saur Verlag KG, Munich. Distributed in the United States and Canada by The Shoe String Press, Inc., Hamden, Connecticut. Reprinted by permission.

kept up with women's new public roles or are their portrayals still dominated by traditional values left over from an earlier age?

Two complementary types of answers have been offered as to why the media are important. The first notes that the media select, structure and evaluate what is considered important and good in the public discussion agenda (*Shaw* and *McCombs*, 1977).[3] All media and especially television which seems to be the only institution creating messages for *all* of us, help in the public definition and legitimation of life and work in a variety of ways. They grant notice of the existence of certain kinds of work activities. They also specify, contrast and describe the work behavior of different groups of people and they bestow approval or censure on this behavior. Public recognition, description, and legitimation are essential for women who wish to challenge and upgrade their public right to work (*Gusfield*, 1966).[4]

In addition, the media serve as "reference groups" for audience members. "Reference groups" are groups with which a person compares him- or herself in making a self-judgment. Mass media portrayals thus are important because they help define the appropriateness of certain kinds of jobs for women, the satisfactions women may expect from work outside the home and how it should fit in with their traditional family responsibilities. All of these in turn influence the choosing, planning and execution of careers for those young women who will be filling available jobs in the 1990s.

Media portrayal of women and work: Alice in her Wonderland

A variety of writers have noted that the media are selective and that they tend to reflect the dominant and socially accepted values. Two major theories explain this media selectivity. They are based on divergent assumptions about the nature of media functioning and social reality. The more prevalent one supported by network personnel and advertisers asserts that social reality is fixed and that the media simply "objectively" and passively "reflect" certain aspects of this reality. The media in this view are like fun house mirrors, providing a somewhat distorted picture of what is "out there". The other position asserts, following *Burke* and *Cassirer*, that social reality is actively created and recreated through the different meanings people attach to it (*Burke*, 1963).[5] Media portrayal in this view is a "construction" process in which what is selected is not random. It is instead the product of bureaucratic practices which stress organizational needs more than personal outlooks (*Robinson*, 1978).[6] Media content, consequently does not reflect a looking-glass likeness, but takes on an "Alice in Wonderland" distortion full of unmapped "black holes" which obliterate issues and attitudes which do not fit in with prevailing values and norms.

This paper adopts the second position and explores both the constructions and the unmapped "black holes" in the portrayal of women's lives in order to explain why they are what they are. In line with the "construction" theory it inquires more specifically into three questions: (1) whether there are differences in different media portrayals of working women; (2) whether there is a difference between pre- and post-1970s portrayals, and (3) whether there is a difference between Canadian and U.S. renditions and outlooks.

A variety of studies have noted that television, the most ubiquitous medium, is also the one most likely to "ignore" women through lack of coverage in its news presentations or trivialization in advertising and situation comedies (*Tuchman, 1978*).[7] The reason given is that this medium programs for a large heterogeneous audience, not particularly concerned with women's lives. In contrast, newspapers with their women's sections, or women's magazines sponsored by advertisers wishing to attract a female audience, should be more responsive to changing attitudes toward work. Furthermore, socio-linguists like *Labov* have noted that there is a time lag in the appearance of changing private values in public discourse (*Labov*).[8] For the portrayal of women's changing work activities, this might mean that there is less evidence of women's changing public roles before 1970 than after. We would expect to find more emphasis on women's home roles during the 1940s through 1960s than after the rise of the women's movement and its support for women's careers, egalitarian pay and freer lifestyles. Finally, it is worth finding out whether the emerging portrayals of women's roles is similar in North American and Western European societies where women's participation in the public realm was differentially supported depending on whether the vote was granted in the 1920s or later (*Black, 1978*).[9]

To test these three hypotheses concerning the portrayal of women in their home and work roles, two types of research were undertaken. The first scrutinized short stories in women's magazines and updates earlier studies investigating the life and work characteristics of magazine heroines in the pre-1970s period. The second is broader and more ambitious. It maps for the first time whether and how women's changing lifestyles are being portrayed in non-fiction articles. This pilot study investigates the prevalence of and preferred themes related to women in and outside the home between 1970 and 1977. In doing so we will be able to determine whether this coverage is broader than that offered by television and to discover possible differences in themes and emphases in Canada and the United States where women (except in Quebec) received the vote early.

Magazine images of women and work before 1970: The "happy housewife heroine"

To get at the pre-1970s data, the existing American research literature was scanned and evaluated. This evaluation revealed that little has been written on the magazine portrayal of women's lives. As few as seventeen articles cover this topic broadly defined. Nearly one-third of these (six articles) concentrate on the characteristics of magazine heroines.[10] Another third (five articles) investigate social norms, sex roles and passivity in working class romance and middle class magazines.[11] Two deal with women's magazines in general and their growth and change.[12] Three investigate children's awareness of occupational differences between the sexes as well as occupational advice and problems of working women.[13]

Out of this collection we decided to focus on the life characteristics of magazine heroines in order to determine implicit attitudes towards work. Betty *Friedan*, the first to analyze short story heroines, discovered that women with careers declined drastically in the twenty year period between 1939 and 1959. In 1959 most of the heroines of *Ladie's Home Journal, McCall's, Good Housekeeping* and *Woman's Home Companion* were career women. Ten years later only one in three of the heroines had a career and by 1959 only one woman in a hundred even had a job. The happy housewife heroine was clearly dominant (*Friedan*, 1963).[14]

Bailey's update of 1957 and 1967 heroines in the same publications adds that the anti-work trend continued and that heroines were getting younger. In the ten years there was a further decrease of characters with careers from 9 % to 4 %. Career women who did appear, were moreover never sympathetically portrayed. They were usually pictured as "unwomanly" and were seen most often in the act of threatening some "true" woman's marriage (*Bailey*, 1969).[15]

Another study by *Franzwa* of the same magazines adds detail on the extent of sex-stereotyping found in the heroines' jobs. Following generally accepted notions of "proper" work for women, most magazine heroines were employed in low status jobs, if they worked at all. 51 % were employed as secretaries, clerks or in service positions. 38 % were in medium rank positions such as nursing, primary school teaching, flight attendant or writer. An infinitesimal 7 % had professions entailing long preparation like college professor, geologist or museum director. A few characters earned a substantial income as interior decorators or owners of businesses (*Franzwa*, 1974).[16] This researcher reiterated that about two-thirds of all female characters were married and that of the married women in the stories only a small 11 % held jobs outside the house.

My own study, designed to further elucidate the relationship between marital status and work in the same U.S. plus two Canadian magazines (*Chatelaine* French and English versions) further corroborates and extends the *Franzwa* findings.[17] In the 1968 to 1970 period the typical magazine heroine was white middle class (91 %), under 35 years of age (78 %), married (58 %) and living in marital bliss (71 %). Only 33 % of all characters were single, divorced or widowed, with the remaining 8 % having an unspecified status. For most heroines (58 %) the level of education was not indicated, whereas the educational achievements of males were generally noted. Most of the married women were housewives (73 %) with only 15 % working outside the home. Generally the heroines had no stated goals in life (52 %) though if a goal was mentioned, it was love-oriented (27 %). Only 2 % of the heroines had career goals.

In all of the stories the possibility of dual roles was implicitly rejected by the mere fact that only 15 % of the heroines were both homemakers and worked. Furthermore, dual-role lives were generally portrayed as "fragmented". Consequently, even in the 1970s these heroines tended still to give up their job in favor of full-time home-making and motherhood. In case this route was not chosen, the heroine is portrayed as the evil career woman, inhuman and unwomanly, defying the "laws of nature" (*Robinson*, 1971).[18] To top it all off, only one out of 125 married characters feels discontented with her housewife role, but this "delusion" lasts only as long as her 24-hour flu. Seventeen years after *Friedan's Feminine Mystique* none of the heroines had as yet recognized "the problem that has no name".

Conclusions: To work is "unwomanly"

In spite of changing social mores, magazine fiction up to 1970 reflects a strong bias in favor of the homemaking role for woman. It extolls the "passive" female as the ideal, irrespective of class and culture. Such passivity reflects itself according to *Flora* in ineffectuality, non-initiative in problem solving, non-participation in the labor force and lack of social mobility (*Flora*, 1971).[19] Magazine fiction furthermore defines women in terms of men and families rather than in terms of work. As such it tends to denigrate married working women which by now constitute a sizable minority of the 1970's work force. In the United States 41 % of the female labor force were married in 1970 and six years later in Canada the figure is even higher, 54 % (*Waite*, 1976).[20]

The fiction furthermore reiterates that work does and should play a secondary role in women's lives. This runs counter to the fact that women with husbands in the lowest and mean brackets must seek employment to supplement inadequate family incomes (*Connelly,* 1976).[21] In addition, working mothers are placed in a double bind. They are portrayed as causing the disintegration of their family's life if they persist in working. Yet, eroding family incomes and increased consumer goods orientations indicate that women's salaries are vital to maintaining a North American middle class life style in the 1960s (*Bell,* 1976).[22]

The negative evaluation of work extends even to single magazine heroines, only about half of which work. The rest of these women study (8 %), engage in leisure activities (15 %), are home-makers (4 %), or have this area of their lives unspecified in the fiction (14 %) (*Robinson,* 1971).[23] The cumulative impact of such a description of women's lives is not only highly selective and out of tune with reality, but negative and discouraging in terms of the example it sets. It fails to provide alternative outlooks for women readers struggling to gain insight into the changing nature of their surroundings.

The portrayal of women's changing lifestyles in the 1970s

To begin to understand whether women's roles in and outside of the home are more broadly covered since the rise of the women's movement, the second and more ambitious pilot project gathered data of a different sort. Interviews with magazine editors such as Doris *Anderson* of *Chatelaine* indicate that magazine fiction is perhaps not the best index of a magazine's attitude and understanding of women's lives, because it is produced by freelancers over whom the editor has little control. *Anderson* herself longs "for the day when the consciousness raising exercises in the analytic and scholarly books are translated into fiction." Yet as editor she cannot do more than encourage her freelancers to incorporate modern trends into their stories (*Anderson,* 1971).[24]

Our study was therefore designed to systematically map post-1970 non-fiction articles in three types of magazines to assess what kind of an interpretation of women's roles they offer. Three different kinds of magazines, women's, elite and general news, were selected because one of our initial hypotheses suggested that women's magazines may be most responsive to women's changing lifestyles.

In order not to have to sample total magazine content, it was decided to focus on a few themes which are judged relevant and indicative of modern outlooks.

Such an analysis however hinges on a distinction between traditional and non-traditional content which is difficult to make. Only one author, *Guenin's* study of changing women's sections in daily newspapers attempts such a definition (*Guenin,* 1975).[25] Based on interviews with modern lifestyles editors, it isolates 24 topics of potential interest to modern women. Our study utilized 8 of these to begin mapping modern trends and "blind spots" in magazine interpretations of women's public lives in the 1970s. *Guenin* categories adopted are: work, women's movement, feminism, equal rights, marriage and divorce, single life, population control and education. In addition three more categories were suggested by our own research: women in politics, history, and art.

Table 1 indicates that the nine magazines in the three types were chosen for their large circulation, their prestige as determined by age and Canadian or U.S. representation. The general magazines are: *Time, Reader's Digest* and *Maclean's* (Canadian). The elite magazines are *Atlantic Monthly* and *Saturday Night* (Canadian), and the women's magazines include: *Good Housekeeping, Ladies' Home Journal, McCall's,* and *Chatelaine* (English version). These magazines constitute not only the leaders in their field, but were also the sources for the magazine heroine studies mentioned above. Some comparability between the findings of the pre- and post-1970s is thus provided.

Table 1: U.S. and Canadian magazines and their circulations

Categories	Magazine names	Circulation 1977	Original publication year	Yearly issues
General News:	Time	4,2 mi.	1923	52
	Reader's Digest	17,7 mi.	1922	52
	Maclean's (Canadian)	6,7 mi.	1895	12
Elite:	Atlantic Monthly	325,000	1857	12
	Saturday Night (Canadian)	100,000	1887	12
Women's:	Good Housekeeping	6,0 mi.	1895	12
	Ladie's Home Journal	7,0 mi.	1882	12
	McCall's	6,5 mi.	1870	12
	Chatelaine (Canadian)	1,0 mi. (Engl.) 275,000 (French)	1919	12

Source: National Research Bureau, Working Press of the Nation, Vol. II Magazine and Editorial Directory, Chicago, 1978 pp. VII, 1-82.

Our nine magazines in the pilot study are of course not a representative sample, since there are upward of 980 consumer magazine titles listed in the 1978 Working Press of the Nation's *Magazine and Editorial Directory*.[26] They do however provide a first approximation for indicating potentially different patterns of coverage in the three magazine groups. They also provide evidence for differences in national approaches. According to the *Magazine and Editorial Directory,* general magazines are the largest category with 120 titles. Women's magazines are second with 63 publications, and news magazines are one of the smaller sub-categories with 30 entries. All together the three contain 213 titles, approximately one quarter of all listings. In our pilot study the year, title, topic, sex of author, length and placement, as well as the evaluative dimension (writer's attitude toward the topic) were scored for each article. These provide data for an assessment of the impact of a writer's sex on coverage as well as for yearly fluctuations. All in all a total of 1316 issues were scanned and 948 articles analyzed.

Work, marriage and feminism capture primary attention

To begin to understand what is "newsworthy" and interesting about women's lives in the 1970s, Table 2 provides data on the most heavily covered topics in the three magazine groups. Leaving out content concerned with such traditional themes as children, health, home, food, and beauty, it appears that there are four high scoring areas of coverage. In order of priority these are: women and their work situation: 261 stories; marriage and divorce: 205 stories; issues of feminism: 126 stories, and women's activities in politics including 81 stories. Though these categories are generally self-explanatory, it is important to note that the topic of "feminism" subsumes articles on consciousness raising, women's changing awareness in relation to the outside world as well as the issue of rape. The "women's movement" topic in contrast includes only articles dealing with *organized* women's groups, their progress, issues, conventions, and relationships.

Table 2 shows additionally that general news magazines also feature women and work in first place, though they place feminism second, and marriage and divorce third. Elite magazines in contrast have as their most covered topic "woman in art"; doubtlessly as a result of the fact that these magazines are published for an urban elite in the art centers of New York and Toronto. The topics of work and feminism however follow in second and third place, as in the other two magazine groups. Women's movement stories are in fourth place.

Table 2: Magazine topics by magazine type 1970–1977 (Nos. of Stories)

Topics	General Magazines				Women's Magazines			Elite Magazines		Totals	
	Time	Digest	Maclean's	McCall's	Good House-keeping	Ladies' Home Journal	Chatelaine	Atlantic Monthly	Saturday Night	Nos.	%
Women and work	45	25	38	30	18	65	26	10	4	261	(28)
Women's movement	21	4	2	0	3	–	3	7	1	41	(4)
Feminism	32	15	29	26	4	4	15	–	1	126	(13)
Marriage and divorce	12	58	4	22	13	70	18	7	1	205	(22)
Equal rights	13	5	4	1	2	4	4	6	4	43	
Population control	11	5	–	3	–	–	7	–	–	26	
Single life	1	25	3	4	6	3	2	4	1	49	
Education	3	7	–	1	–	1	9	2	–	23	(20)
Abortion	14	5	2	4	2	–	5	1	1	34	
Day care	1	3	–	1	1	1	6	–	–	13	
Politics	4	9	16	17	7	14	8	3	3	81	(9)
History	–	2	–	–	2	4	–	4	3	15	(1)
Art	–	–	11	3	1	–	–	10	6	31	(3)
Rape	–	–	–	–	–	–	–	–	–	–	
Sub Total/ Group	157	163	109	112	59	166	103	54	25	948	(100)
		429				440			79		

When total number of articles are converted into percentages, Table 3 indicates that the public discussion agendas of the three magazine types are surprisingly similar, an outcome which had not been expected. They all cover the same topics though in slightly different orders of priority. Such a finding suggests that it is both premature and difficult to argue that women's magazines are more responsive to women's needs *in general* than general news or elite magazines. The only point that can be made is that women's magazines concentrate the most *total* attention on the four topics and that they are most concerned with the problems of working women. An overwhelming 71 % of all women's magazine articles are devoted to work, movement news, feminism, marriage and divorce. General news and elite magazines on the other hand concentrate only 66 % and 51 % of all articles respectively on these topics. In addition, women's magazines do the most work coverage, nearly a third of the total (31 %) of their articles are devoted to such stories. General news magazines have one quarter and elite magazines less than a fifth (18 %) work articles.

Table 3 offers the additional insight that general news and elite magazines provide more *variegated* coverage of women's affairs than the women's magazines which are still heavily pre-occupied with the issues of marriage and divorce (28 %). The topics of equal rights, single life and sexual equality, abortion and population control garner better coverage in the magazines written for a mixed female/male audience.

Table 3: Magazine topics by magazine type 1970–1977 (in %)

Topics	General News Magazines	Women's Magazines	Elite Magazines
1. Women and work	25	31	18
2. Women's movement	6	1	10
3. Feminism	18	11	10
4. Marriage and divorce	17 (66)	28 (71)	13 (51)
5. Equal rights	5	3	1
6. Population control	4	3	0
7. Single life	7	3	6
8. Education	2	3	3
9. Abortion	5	2	3
10. Day care	1 (24)	2 (16)	0 (13)
11. Politics	6	10	7
12. History	1	1	9
13. Art	3 (10)	2 (13)	20 (36)
	100	100	100

The similarity of topics selected in all three magazine groups suggests that audiences are possibly less important in determining content than the professional judgements of staffs. Such an interpretation would fit in with substantial evidence that producers try to protect their "monopolies of knowledge" from outside influence and criticism. This is achieved by the fact that producing staffs form elites which know each other and furthermore share the same work techniques (*Tuchman*, 1966).[27] They also structure audience surveys in such a way that these polls query only preferences among *available* rather than *possible* content categories. All of these factors encourage similar topic selection among different magazine types produced for different audiences.

Global figures however provide only a first approximation for evaluating the question of quality. May it be that women's magazines are more detailed and variegated in their portrayal of women's work problems than the general news and elite publications written for a mixed audience? To unravel this issue the following section will provide a more detailed content analysis of the "women and work" articles.

Women and work: The struggle for job equality

Previous tables show that "women and work" had the highest total number of articles, 261 out of 948 and that this topic was most heavily covered by the women's magazines. Considering the many possible ways of covering such a topic, it is however extremely interesting to note that Table 4 confirms that *all* articles of whichever magazine type have only two major foci: 46 % of all stories cover the struggle for job equality, and 24 % of all articles concentrate on work discrimination. A staggering 70 % of all interest is thus placed on such issues as: equal pay for equal work and improved access to male jobs as well as discrimination at the work place. Three additional topics: dual role problems, first women, and profiles constitute the remaining topics of discussion. Such a finding does not permit us to conclude that women's magazines provide a broader and more sensitive portrayal of women's work problems.

Selected titles of job equality articles indicate that women's entry into sex segregated positions, a broadening of career possibilities, and a concern with career planning are the primary issues discussed in *all* three magazine groups. "She thinks like a man: Women move in business," *(Saturday Night)*; "Women in the boards" *(Time)* about the lack of corporate representation of women; "Police woman on patrol," *(Reader's Digest)*; "Which professions pay off for women," *(Chatelaine)*; "Return of the mid-wife" *(Good Housekeeping)* and "Guerilla

Table 4: Numbers of "women and work" articles by theme in three magazine types

Magazine type	Job discrimination	Job equality	Family and work	First woman	Profile	Row total
Elite:						
Atlantic Monthly	3	2	2	0	1	8
Saturday Night	1	3	1	0	1	6
Sub total	4 (28%)	5 (37%)	3 (21%)	0	2 (14%)	14
General News:						
Time	15	22	0	1	5	43
Reader's Digest	3	15	5	0	4	27
Maclean's	2	14	3	0	19	38
Sub total	20 (19%)	51 (47%)	8 (7%)	1 (1%)	28 (26%)	108
Women's:						
Ladies' Home Journal	28	23	5	4	8	68
Mc Call's	2	23	4	1	0	30
Good Housekeeping	1	3	4	0	7	15
Catelaine	7	14	3	0	2	26
Sub total	38 (28%)	63 (45%)	16 (12%)	5 (3%)	17 (12%)	139
Grand total	62 (24%)	119 (46%)	27 (10%)	6 (2%)	47 (18%)	261

guide for working women" *(McCall's)* give an inkling of the coverage. Job discrimination situations and their remedies are recounted in "All those thinkies, all those thoughts" *(Atlantic)* about women in academia; "The hand that rocks the cradle rules the newsroom" *(Maclean's)*; "Father make her a priest" *(Time)*; "How the trade unions let women down," *(Chatelaine)* and "You can fight sex discrimination on the job" *(Good Housekeeping)*.

Profiles with 18 % of all articles constitute the third focus of "women and work" stories. This is a relatively safe category permitting editors to talk about "first women" in a particular post or recounting an exceptional woman's entry into public, artistic and political life. Cynically viewed, such reporting is a form of tokenism, satisfying the need to show that women are moving out of the home and are "making it" in the world that counts. The relative dearth of "first women" stories, which are very prevalent in daily newspaper reporting, however provides cause for rejoicing. It indicates that magazine editors at least feel that by now women have penetrated into virtually every job category and that this penetration in itself is far less important than the kind of treatment females encounter in the work world.

The most interesting and potentially explosive topic "family and work" however garners only a miniscule 10 % of all article attention. Why do so few articles refer to dual role stress which affects more than half of all working women? Interestingly enough the articles do not even reflect this fact, but talk primarily about the plight of single women or heads of households juggling both jobs and children. One might speculate that the potential implications of work equality for family life are entirely too revolutionary to contemplate. A careful treatment including the equalization of housework and childcare would raise questions about the implications of the paternalistic family system which even socialist countries have not been willing to face *(Scott, 1974)*.[28]

In analyzing "women and work" articles we were additionally interested in determining whether magazine type, sex of author, readership, and article length are systematically related to positive evaluation. Table 5 tracing these interconnections indicates that in women's and elite magazines, where the majority of articles are written by women, positive evaluations are as frequent as in general news magazines, many of which do not indicate authorship. Length furthermore is associated with type of magazine rather than with topic. General news magazines carry overwhelmingly (77 %) short articles of less than 75 square inches. Women's magazines had 52 % medium articles of 76–150 square inches and elite magazines had 79 % of their articles in the large, over 150 square

Table 5: Author's sex, evaluation and location of "women and work" articles in three magazine types

Magazine Category		Author's Sex			Evaluation			Length			Type of Article		
		F	M	Not listed	+	−	0	lg	med	sht	ed.	feat.	gen. art.
General News	No	37	28	43	76	10	22	15	10	83	0	37	71
	% (108)	34%	26%	40%	72%	8%	20%	14%	9%	77%		34%	66%
Women's	No	109	10	20	78	5	56	34	71	34	12	52	75
	% (139)	78%	7%	15%	56%	4%	40%	24%	52%	24%	9%	37%	54%
Elite	No	8	6	0	11	1	2	11	2	1	2	4	8
	% (14)	57%	43%		79%	7%	14%	79%	14%	7%	14%	28%	58%

inch category. Since all of the readers in our nine magazines are middle class and no investigation of editorial attitudes was made, it is impossible to tell whether these factors are positively associated with pro-coverage or not. These findings correspond closely to those of *Farley,* who found that there were no correlations between author's sex, length of article, and positive evaluation. In her analysis of equal rights legislation coverage in women's magazines, positive correlations did however emerge between editorial policy, large circulation, and middle class readership (*Farley,* 1978).[29]

Conclusions: Cautious optimism

How does our evidence fit in with other researchers' findings on the portrayal of women's lives in the 1970s? One study summarizing recent investigations paints a very grim picture. It speaks of the "symbolic annihilation" of women in television, about women's magazines carrying the message "marry and don't work," and about newspapers retaining the notion that women are important only as consorts to famous men (*Tuchman,* 1978).[30] *Corea* rounds out this dismal picture by adding six additional as well as depressing criteria, which explain women's newsworthiness in the press. They are: beauty, victimization, political significance, performance in the arts or athletics, special home-maker abilities, and first woman status (*Corea,* 1973).[31]

As we noted elsewhere, such newsvalues tend to make women-related items rarer, shorter, and lower in the line-up of typical television newscasts.[32] They also encourage the selection of female newsmakers of lower status, e.g. without organizational affiliation, and portray their activities as less important. Women in broadcasting this study confirms are disproportionately associated with human interest events, disasters or women's activities, all of which are not rated "top of the news" (*Robinson, 1978*).[33]

While symbolic annihilation and victimization are certainly the lot of women in television portrayals, our comparative magazine data suggest a more optimistic picture. Magazines in contrast to the broadcast media seem to be more responsive to the major issues facing women in the 1970s. Contrary to expectations, this includes not only women's, but all three magazine types.

Comparing the pre-1970s heroine studies with post-1970s non-fiction coverage, our evidence shows that the dictum "marry and don't work" has in fact been modified. Popular concern is today focused on women and work, changing marriage and divorce, as well as issues of feminism and the womens' movement. Such an ordering of the public discussion agenda suggests more than a "quiet concern" for women's changing roles. What we are witnessing is the widespread acceptance of certain egalitarian tenets of the women's movement reflecting the desires of both men and women to provide equal opportunity for choice of life style. Among these are everyone's right to work if they wish, a concern with making marriages more congruent with both partners' needs, the desirability of encouraging women to re-think their own roles, and the acceptance of those feminist values stressing self-knowledge and development which will ultimately ensure a better life for all.

The substantial coverage accorded women in politics, history, and art suggests furthermore that certain public roles are not only well established, but approved for women as well as for men. Studies of news coverage suggest that this acceptance is a result of their being a part of the traditional beat structure in daily press and television news gathering, which have historically legitimated male politicians, artists, and historical figures (*Robinson, 1978*).[34] Women as latecomers are beginning to reap the social prestige associated with these institutionalized media roles.

The remarkable shift to greater acceptance of women's search for new roles outside the home, including greater work participation, our evidence suggests, is however linked with a concomitant reluctance to investigate how this equalization of work and other opportunities is to be *practically* achieved. Our identification of minor themes in Table 2 indicates that there are six themes which together receive only 20 % of total coverage in all magazine groups. These minor themes give us clues as to the "blind spots" in magazine coverage. They refer to the areas of equal rights legislation, population control, single life, educational equality, abortion, and day care.

In the same vein our more detailed analysis of work articles indicates that our society is not yet ready and willing to publicly explore the practical implications of dual roles on marriage and children. We are not yet clear about the rules according to which nurturing roles will be divided in the future. On what basis and by whom career and work sacrifices are going to be made and how paternity and maternity leaves are going to be arranged.

Our survey of "blind spots" thus suggests that what is being covered in all magazine types are those themes with which we feel more comfortable, and for which there is greater public consensus. Topics which raise real challenges about the restructuring of the patriarchal family set-up are generally left out. As *Huber* notes "Lenin and the early feminists were optimistic about the contributions of technology in liberating women. Yet, 'technological change' resulted in men's monopolizing the exchange of valued goods and services, while women monopolized increasingly trivialized domestic work and second class jobs owing to their childbearing responsibilities." (*Huber*, 1975)[35]

Cautious optimism that the "symbolic annihilation" of women at least in the magazine field is slowly coming to an end is finally found in a series of articles assessing the impact of the women's movement today (*Tuchman*, 1978).[36] Out of eight, only two articles entitled "Requiem for the women's movement" (*Harper's*, 1977) and "Beyond sisterhood" (*Weekend Magazine*, 1977) come to the conclusion that the women's movement "has narrowed to a pallid lobby for equal rights." Using such tactics as discrediting, isolating, and undercutting, which are tactics still successful in television, these articles attempt to ridicule the legitimate claims of an out-group which constitutes 51 % of the total population (*Gerbner*, 1978).[37]

The majority of articles however paint a more serious and careful picture. They draw attention to the legal, work, political, and social changes which have resulted from the movement and comment that it has become an integral part of most people's lives. The headlines note: "The women's movement is alive and kicking" (*Chatelaine*, 1977), "Lib lives" (*Homemaker's Magazine*, 1977), "Ten years of women's liberation" (*Weekend Magazine*, 1978), "Moving on and reaping the rewards of the women's movement" (*New York Times Magazine*, 1978) and "Building the feminist network" (*Saturday Night, 1978*).

Bonnie *Kreps* summarizes their message in "Lib lives" and indicates how coverage has broadened since 1970, when the topic first received public notice (*Robinson, 1978*).[38] In 1977 it is possible to evaluate the women's movement in the following sympathetic way: "For the first time in history, as far as we can tell, we have a movement with no overall structure, with no membership cards, with no leaders, with no one, agreed upon political platform, with no hierarchy. That is the great strength and beauty of this movement. It is a movement intended to bring about a transformation in our most basic human values and as such it cannot be evaluated in the usual way, on the basis of quick success in gaining a power base, or in terms of the tired and stale rhetoric of our competing political parties. It is to the change in the very fabric of women's lives that we must look for success, and any public fight that can be seen as leading toward that goal is worth fighting" (*Kreps, 1977*).[39]

Cautious optimism, finally, is warranted with respect to the narrowing gap between material conditions and changing attitudes toward women's entry into public life and work. More and more evidence is now available that younger generation women have a more liberal value outlook toward sex roles than their mothers. In 1977, a New York Times CBS news poll found that fully three-quarters of those aged 18 to 29 preferred the idea of shared marriage roles and believed that women should work. In the 45 to 64 age bracket only 41 % and 48 % respectively were of these opinions. *Ingelhart* believes that these differences are permanent results of socialization patterns of generations of people growing up in particular environments (*Ingelhart, 1971*).[40]

Black's comparison of US and Canadian attitudes on women's participation in public life found similar generational differences in outlook. Once again generational attitudes towards the statement that "politics should be left to men" show women and men aged 65 and over in partial agreement with the statement while those in their thirties, twenties and teens disagree strongly. The figures for women are 50 %, 65 %, 72 % and 78 % disagreement while the comparative figures for men are: 52 %, 63 %, 68 % and 67 % (*Black, 1977*).[41] *Black* concludes that "it is the young women of this generation who have encouraged the breaking down of the barriers between private and public, making sexuality a political matter with their demand for an end to legal restrictions on contraception and abortion, making childcare a public obligation with their demand that it be provided for all parents. In generational terms, the "acquisitive" women of the post suffrage period staked out women's claim to access to men's public realms. But it is post-bourgeois women who are opening up the private realm to men and thus to all of us. Men should be sympathetic to this endeavor.[42]

Such similarities in North American outlook suggests that U.S.-Canadian differences in the portrayal of women's lives is probably minimal, because both countries adopted women's suffrage about the same time. Support of women's legal right to enter the public arena has existed for over fifty years in both countries. Table 6 which compares *Maclean's, Chatelaine,* and *Saturday Night* themes with U.S. averages in the three types of magazines confirms this hunch. Canadian magazines cover the same themes in the same order as their counterparts south of the border. 5 % to 10 % differences exist however in "women's movement" and "marriage/divorce" coverage and in feminism, politics, and art. Whether these fluctuations from the average are significant is however not determinable from our small sample.

Two types of conclusions for future comparative research emerge from these findings. The first notes that "generation" must be added to "sex" as an additional and crucial predictor of magazine content. All of our magazine groups, irrespective of whether they were edited for female or mixed audiences, defined women's changing roles in the same manner, because they have to attract more

Table 6: Canadian-US comparison of magazine topics (in %)

Topics	Gen. News Mags.		Women's Mags.		Elite Mags.	
	Maclean's	U.S. aver.	Chatelaine	U.S. aver.	Sat. Night	U.S. aver.
Women/work	35	25	26	31	16	18
Women's movement	2	6	3	1	4	10
Feminism	26	18	15	11	4	10
Marriage/divorce	4	17	17	28	4	13
Minor Categories						
Women in politics	15	6	8	10	12	7
Women in history	0	1	0	1	12	9
Women in art	10	3	0	2	24	20

Based on data in Tables 2 and 3.

readers from the younger/middle than the older, after 55 year generations. The second conclusion suggests that nationality differences too are perhaps tempered by inter-generational similarities. The reason for this is that both the North American and the Western European countries gave women the vote about sixty years ago and thus laid the foundation for the public legitimation of changing female roles. Young men and women alike have internalized these more egalitarian value outlooks and are beginning to apply them to the private and the public realms on both sides of the Atlantic.

Footnotes and References

[1] *Ridley, Jeanne Claire:* Demographic change and the role and status of women. In: Annals of the American Academy of Political and Social Science, 375/1968/1, pp. 15–25.

[2] *Tuchman, Gaye:* The symbolic annihilation of women by the mass media. In: Tuchman, Gaye (ed.) et al.: Hearth and home. Images of women in the mass media. New York: Oxford Univ. Press 1978. p. 4.

[3] *Shaw, Donald L.; McCombs, Maxwell E.:* The emergence of American political issues. The agenda-setting function of the press. St. Paul: West Publishing Co. 1977. X, 211 p.

[4] *Gusfield, Joseph:* Symbolic crusade, status politics and the American temperance movement. Urbana, Ill.: Univ. of Illinois Press 1966. pp. 1–15.

[5] *Burke, Kenneth:* The grammar of motives. Los Altos: Hermes Publications 1963.

[6] *Robinson, Gertrude Joch; Sparkes, Vernone:* International news in the Canadian and American press. A comparative news flow study. In: Gazette, 22/1976/4, pp. 203–218.

[7] *Tuchman, Gaye,* op. cit., p. 7.

[8] *Labov, William:* On the mechanism of linguistic change. In: Giglioli, Pier (ed.): Language and social context. Harmondsworth: Penguin Editions, 1970.

[9] *Black, Naomi:* Changing European and North American attitudes towards women in public life. In: Journal of European Integration, 1/1978/2, p. 227.

[10] The six articles are: *Friedan, Betty:* The feminine mystique. New York: Del Publishing Co. 1963. pp. 26–63. *Bayley, Margaret:* The women's magazine short story heroine in 1957 and 1967. In: Journalism Quarterly, 46/1969/2, pp. 364–367. *Robinson, Gertrude Joch* (coll.); *Gardiner, Christine* (coll.); *Kirmayer, Wendy* (coll.) et al.: The image of women in American and Canadian magazines. Montreal, Québec: McGill Univ. 1971. *Johns-Heine, P.; Gerth, H.:* Values in mass periodical fiction, 1921–1941. In: Public Opinion Quarterly, 13/1959/1, pp. 105–113. *Franzwa, He-*

len: Working women in fact and fiction. In: Journal of Communication, 24/1974/2, pp. 104–109. *Phillips, Barbara E.:* Magazine heroines. Is MS just another member of family circle? In: Tuchman, Gaye (ed.) et al.: Hearth and home. Images of women in the mass media. New York: Oxford Univ. Press 1978. pp. 116–130.

11 The five articles are: *Flora, Cornelia Butler:* The passive female. Her comparative image by class and culture in women's magazine fiction. In: Journal of Marriage and the Family, 23/1971/8, pp. 435–444. *Gecas, Victor:* Motives and aggressive acts in popular fiction. Sex and class differences. In: American Journal of Sociology, 77/1972/4, pp. 680–696. *Smith, Dwayne; Matre, Marc:* Social norms and sex roles in romance and adventure magazines. In: Journalism Quarterly, 52/1975/3, pp. 309–315. *McCallum, Pamela:* World without conflict. Magazines for working class women. In: The Canadian Forum, –/1975/55 654, pp. 42–44. *Haymes, Howard:* Post-war writing and the literature of the women's liberation movement. In: Psychiatry, 38/1975/11, pp. 328–332.

12 The two sources are: *White, Cynthia L.:* Women's magazines 1893–1968. London: Joseph 1970. 348 p. *Ferguson, Marjorie:* Women's magazines. The changing mood. In: New Society, 29/1974/3, pp. 475–477.

13 The three articles are: *Clarke, P.; Esposito, V.:* A study of occupational advice for women in magazines. In: Journalism Quarterly, 43/1966/3, pp. 477–485. *Boef, Ann:* Doctor, lawyer, household drudge. In: Journal of Communication, 24/1974/2, pp. 142–145. *Hatch, Marya G.; Hatch, David L.:* Problems of married and working women as presented by three popular working women's magazines. In: Social Forces, 37/1958/1, pp. 148–153.

14 *Friedan, Betty,* op. cit., pp. 30–37.

15 *Bailey, Margaret,* op. cit., p. 366.

16 *Franzwa, Helen,* op. cit., p. 106.

17 All of these studies were based on a sampling of *McCall's, Ladies' Home Journal* and *Good Housekeeping* short and short short stories with a well-defined female character. Novels and novelettes were excluded because they were often not written specifically for women's magazines. Content categories include: marital status, appearance, economic class, education, major occupation, number of children, residence, housing, quality of marriage, goals and problems on which story is based.

18 *Robinson, Gertrude Joch* et al., op. cit., pp. 3–6.

19 *Flora, Cornelia Butler,* op. cit., p. 540.

20 *Waite, Linde:* Working wives 1940–1960. In: American Sociological Review, 41/1976/2, p. 65.

21 *Connelly, Patricia M.:* The economic context of women's labor force participation in Canada. Halifax: St. Mary's Univ. 1976. p. 4.

22 *Bell, Carolyn Shaw:* Working wives and family income. In: Chapman, Jane R. (ed.): Economic independence of women. New York: Sage 1976.

[23] *Robinson, Gertrude Joch,* 1971 op. cit., p. 5.

[24] *Anderson, Doris:* Real women in fiction where are you? In: Chatelaine, 14/1971/9, p. 1.

[25] *Guenin, Zena Beth:* Women's pages in American newspapers. Missing out on contemporary content. In: Journalism Quarterly, 52/1975/1, pp. 66–69, 75.

[26] Working press of the nation. In: Magazine and editorial directory, vol. 2. Chicago: National Research Bureau, Directory Division 1978.

[27] *Tuchman, Gaye:* Objectivity as strategic ritual. In: American Journal of Sociology, 77/1972/1, pp. 660–670.

[28] *Scott, Hilda:* Does socialism liberate women? In: Experiences from Eastern Europe. Boston: Beacon Press 1974. Chapter 3.

[29] *Farley, Jennie:* Women's magazines and the ERA. Friend or foe. In: Journal of Communication, 28/1978/1, pp. 188, 190.

[30] *Tuchman, Gaye,* op. cit., pp. 3–4.

[31] *Corea, Gena:* Writer says papers biased in covering news of women. In: Editor and Publisher, 106/1973/April 21, p. 62.

[32] A woman-related item is one which either has a female newsmaker, a female reporter or falls into women's content as defined by Guenin.

[33] *Robinson, Gertrude Joch:* Women, media access and social control. In: Epstein, Laurily Keir (ed.): Women and the news. New York: Hasting House 1978. pp. 93–97.

[34] Ibid., pp. 89–90.

[35] *Huber, Joan:* Toward a socio-technological theory of the women's movement. Urbana, Ill.: Univ. of Illinois 1975. p. 1.

[36] *Tuchman, Gaye:* The newspaper as a social movement's resource. In: Tuchman, Gaye (ed.) et al.: Hearth and home. Images of women in the mass media. New York: Oxford Univ. Press 1978. pp. 186–217.

[37] *Gerbner, George:* The dynamics of cultural resistance. In: Tuchman, Gaye (ed.) et al.: Hearth and home. Images of women in the mass media. New York: Oxford Univ. Press. 1978. pp. 46–50.

[38] *Robinson, Gertrude Joch:* Women, media access and social control. In: Epstein, Laurily Keir (ed.): Women and the news. New York: Hasting House 1978. pp. 97–103.

[39] *Kreps, Bonnie:* Lib lives. In: Homemakers magazine, –/1977/Sept., p. 112.

[40] *Inglehart, R.:* Changing value priorities and European integration. In: Journal of Common Market Studies, –/1971/Sept.

[41] *Black, Naomi,* op. cit., p. 238

[42] Ibid., pp. 237–238.

In this semiotic analysis of a British teen magazine, Angela McRobbie identifies the central features of its production style and content that provide an ideology of adolescent femininity. McRobbie notes that this teen magazine focuses almost exclusively on the "personal" aspects of being a teenage girl with romantic individualism as the ethos for girlhood. Angela McRobbie prepared this study while she was at the Centre for Contemporary Cultural Studies, Birmingham, England.

16

JACKIE
An Ideology of Adolescent Femininity

Angela McRobbie

Jackie: Cultural Product and Signifying System

Another useful expression though, is the pathetic appealing look, which brings out a boy's protective instinct and has him desperate to get you another drink/help you on with your coat/give you a lift home. It's best done by opening your eyes wide and dropping the mouth open a little looking (hanging your head slightly) directly into the eyes of the boy you're talking to. Practice this (*Jackie*, 15 February 1975).

One of the major reasons for choosing *Jackie* for analysis is its astounding success. Since its first appearance in 1964 its sales have risen from an initial weekly average of 350,000 (with a drop in 1965 to 250,000) to 451,000 in 1968 and 605,947 in 1976. This means that it has been Britain's longest selling 'teen' magazine for over ten years. *Boyfriend*, first published in 1959, started off with sales figures averaging around 418,000 but had fallen to 199,000 in 1965 when publication ceased. *Mirabelle*, launched in 1956, sold over 540,000 copies each week, a reflection of the 'teenage boom' of the mid 50s, but by 1968 its sales had declined to 175,000.[1]

However my aim here is not to grapple with those factors upon which this success appears to be predicated, instead it will be to mount a rigorous and systematic critique of *Jackie* as a system of messages, a signifying system and a bearer of a certain ideology; an ideology which deals with the construction of teenage 'femininity'.

Jackie is one of a large range of magazines, newspapers and comics published by D.C. Thomson of Dundee. [. . .] With a history of vigorous anti-unionism, D.C. Thomson is not unlike other large mass communica-

From Angela McRobbie, "*Jackie*: An Ideology of Adolescent Femininity," in Bernard Waites, Tony Bennett, and Graham Martin, eds., *Popular Culture: Past and Present*, (London: Croom Helm, 1982). pp. 263-283. Reprinted by permission.

tion groups. Like Walt Disney, for example, it produces predominantly for a young market and operates a strict code of censorship on content. But its conservatism is most overtly evident in its newspapers which take a consistently anti-union and 'law and order' line. The *Sunday Post*, with a reputed readership of around 3m. (i.e. 79% of the entire population of Scotland over 15) is comforting, reassuring and parochial in tone. Comprised, in the main, of anecdotal incidents drawn to the attention of the reader in 'couthie' language, it serves as a 'Sunday entertainer' reminding its readers of the pleasure of belonging to a particular national culture.[2]

One visible result of this success has been, at a time of inflation and of crisis, in the publishing world, 'enviably' high profit margins of 20% or more. More than this, D.C. Thomson has expanded into other associated fields, with investments for example in the Clyde Paper Co. (27.15%) and Southern TV (24.8%).

Two points should be made in this context. First, without necessarily adhering to the 'traditional' conspiracy plot thesis, it would be naive to envisage the 'interests' of such a company as being purely the pursuit of increased profits. D.C. Thomson is not, in *Jackie*, merely 'giving the girls what they want'. Each magazine, newspaper or comic has its own conventions and its own style. But within these conventions and through them a concerted effort is nevertheless made to win and shape the consent of the readers to a set of particular values.

The work of this branch of the media involves 'framing' the world for its readers, and through a variety of techniques endowing with importance those topics chosen for inclusion. The reader is invited to share this world with *Jackie*. It is no coincidence that the title is also a girl's name. This is an unambiguous sign that its concern is with 'the category of the subject',[3] in particular the individual girl, and the feminine 'persona'. *Jackie* is both the magazine and the ideal girl. The short, snappy name itself carries a string of connotations: British, fashionable (particularly in the 60s); modern; and cute; with the pet-form 'ie' ending, it sums up all those desired qualities which the reader is supposedly seeking.

Second, we must see this ideological work as being grounded upon certain so-called natural, even 'biological' categories. Thus *Jackie* expresses the 'natural' features of adolescence in much the same way as, say, Disney comics are said to capture the natural essence of childhood. Each has, as Dorfman and Mattelart writing on Disney point out, a 'virtually biologically captive, predetermined audience'.[4] *Jackie* introduces the girl into adolescence outlining its landmarks and characteristics in detail and stressing importantly the problematic features as well as the fun. Of course *Jackie* is not solely responsible for nurturing this ideology of femininity. Nor would such an ideology cease to exist should *Jackie* stop publication.

Unlike other fields of mass culture, the magazines of teenage girls have not as yet been subject to rigorous critical analysis. Yet from the most cursory of readings it is clear that they, too, like those more immediately associated with the sociology of the media — press, TV, film, radio, etc. — are powerful ideological forces.

In fact women's and girls' weeklies occupy a privileged position. Addressing themselves solely to a female market, their concern is with promoting a feminine culture for their readers. They define and shape the woman's world, spanning every stage from childhood to old age. From *Mandy, Bunty* and *Judy*, to *House and Home*, the exact nature of the woman's role is spelt out in detail, according to her age.

She progresses from adolescent romance where there are no explicitly sexual encounters, to the more sexual world of *19, Honey* or *Over 21*, which in turn give way to marriage, childbirth, home-making, child care and the *Woman's Own*. There are no 'male' equivalents to these products. 'Male' magazines tend to be based on particular leisure pursuits or hobbies, motor-cycling, fishing, cars or even pornography. There is no consistent attempt to link 'interests' with age (though readership of many magazines will obviously be higher among younger age groups) nor is there a sense of a natural inevitable progression or evolution attached to their readers' expected 'careers'. There is instead a variety of possibilities with regard to *leisure* [...], many of which involve active participation inside or outside the home.

It will be argued here that the way *Jackie* addresses 'girls' as a monolithic grouping, as do all other women's magazines, serves to obscure differences, of class for example, between women. Instead it asserts a sameness, a kind of *false* sisterhood, which assumes a common definition of womanhood or girlhood. Moreover by isolating out a particular 'phase' or age as the focus of interest, one which coincides roughly with that of its readers, the magazine is in fact creating this 'age-ness' as an ideological construction. 'Adolescence' and here, female adolescence, is itself an ideological 'moment' whose *connotations* are immediately identifiable with those 'topics' included in *Jackie*. And so, by at once defining its readership *vis-à-vis* age, and by describing what is of relevance, to this age group, *Jackie* and women's magazines in general create a 'false totality'. Thus we *all* want to know how to catch a man, lose weight, look our best, or cook well! Having mapped out the feminine 'career' in such all-embracing terms, there is little or no space allowed for alternatives. Should the present stage be unsatisfactory the reader is merely encouraged to look forward to the next. Two things are happening here. 1) The girls are being invited to join a close, intimate sorority where secrets can be exchanged and advice given; and 2) they are also being presented with an ideological bloc of mammoth proportions, one which *imprisons* them in a claustrophobic world of jealousy and competitiveness, the most unsisterly of emotions, to say the least.

Jackie and Popular Culture

There are several ways in which we can think through *Jackie* magazine as part of the media and of mass culture in general.

The first of these is the traditionalist thesis. In this, magazines are seen as belonging to popular or mass culture, something which is inherently inferior to 'high' culture, or 'the arts'. Cheap, superficial, exploitative and debasing, it reduces its audience to a mass of mindless morons,

> the open sagging mouths and glazed eyes, the hands mindlessly drumming in time to the music, the broken stiletto heels, the shoddy, stereotyped 'with it' clothes: here apparently, is a collective portrait of a generation enslaved by a commercial machine.[5]

Alderson, writing explicitly on girls' weeklies, takes a similar position. Claiming, correctly, that what they offer their readers is a narrow and restricted view of life, she proposed as an alternative, 'better' literature, citing *Jane Eyre* as an example.[6]

The problems with such an approach are manifest. 'High' culture becomes a cure for all ills. It is, to quote Willis, 'a repository of quintessential human values',[7] playing a humanising role by elevating the emotions and purifying the spirit. What this argument omits to mention are the material requirements necessary to purchase such 'culture'. And underpinning it is an image of the deprived, working class youngster (what Alderson calls the 'Newsom girl') somehow lacking in those qualities which contact with the arts engenders. Mass culture is seen as a manipulative, vulgar, profit-seeking industry offering cheap and inferior versions of the arts to the more impressionable and vulnerable sectors of the population. This concept of culture is inadequate because it is ahistorical, and is based on unquestioned qualitative judgements. It offers no explanations as to how these forms develop and are distributed. Nor does it explain why one form has a particular resonance for one class in society rather than another.

The second interpretation has much in common with this approach, although it is generally associated with more radical critics. This is the conspiracy thesis and it, too, sees mass culture as 'fodder' for the masses; the result of a ruling class plot whose objective it is to keep the working classes docile and subordinate and to divert them into entertainment. [. . .] By this logic, *Jackie* is merely a mouthpiece for ruling class ideology, focused on young adolescent girls. Again, mass culture is seen as worthless and manipulative. Not only is this argument also ahistorical, but it fails to locate the operations of different apparatuses in the social formation (politics, the media, the law, education, the family, to name but some) each of which is relatively autonomous, has its own *level* and its own specific material practices. While private sectors of the economy do *ultimately* work together with the State, there is a necessary separation between them. Each apparatus has its own *uneven* development and one cannot be collapsed with another.

The third argument reverses both of the first two arguments, to the extent that it points to pop music and pop culture as meaningful activities: 'for most young people today . . . pop music and pop culture is their only expressive outlet'.[8]

Such a position does have some relevance to our study of *Jackie*. It hinges on the assumption that this culture expresses and offers, in albeit consumerist terms, those values and ideas held by both working class youth and by sections of middle class youth. Youth, that is, is defined in terms of values held, which are often in opposition to those held by the establishment, by their parents, the school, work, etc. Such a definition does not consider youth's relation to production, but to consumption, and it is this approach which has characterised that huge body of work, the sociology of culture and of youth, subcultural theory, and which includes, too, delinquency theory.

To summarise a familiar argument which finds expression in most of these fields: working class youth, denied access to other 'higher' forms of culture, and in any case associating these with 'authority' and with the middle class, turns to those forms available on the market. Here they can at least exert some power in their choice of commodities. These commodities often come to be a hallmark of the subcultural group in question but not exactly in their original forms. The group *subverts* the original meaning by bestowing additional implied connotations to the object(s) thereby extending the range of its signifying power. These new meanings undermine and can even negate the previous or established meaning(s) so that the object comes to represent an oppositional ideology linked to the subculture or youth grouping in question. It then summarises for the outside observer the group's disaffection from the wider society. This process of re-appropriation can be seen in, for example, the 'style' of the skinheads, the 'mod' suit, the 'rocker' motor bike, or even the 'punk' safety-pin![9]

But this approach, which hinges on explaining the choice of cultural artefacts — clothes, records or motor bikes etc., — is of limited usefulness when applied to teenage girls and their magazines. They play little, if any, role in shaping their own pop culture and their choice in consumption is materially extremely narrow. And indeed the forms made available to them make re-appropriation difficult. *Jackie* offers its readers no active 'presence' in which girls are invited to participate. The uses are, in short, prescribed by the 'map'. Yet [. . .] this does not mean that *Jackie* cannot be used in subversive ways. Clearly girls *do* use it as a means of signalling their boredom and disaffection, in the school, for example. The point *here* is that despite these possible uses, the magazine itself has a powerful ideological presence as a *form*, and as such demands analysis carried out *apart from* these uses or 'readings'. [. . .]

While the argument made here will include strands from the positions outlined above, its central thrust will represent a substantial shift away from them. What I want to suggest is that *Jackie* occupies the sphere of the personal or private, what Gramsci calls 'Civil Society' ('the ensemble of organisms that are commonly called Private').[10] Hegemony is sought uncoercively on this terrain, which is relatively free of direct State interference. Consequently it is seen as an arena of 'freedom', of 'free choice' and of 'free time'. This sphere includes:

> not only associations and organisations like political parties and the press, but also the family, which combines ideological and economic functions.[11]

[. . .] *Jackie* exists within a large, powerful, privately owned publishing apparatus which produces a vast range of newspapers, magazines and comics. It is on this level of the magazine that teenage girls are subjected to an explicit attempt to win consent to the dominant order − in terms of femininity, leisure and consumption, i.e. at the level of culture. It is worth noting at this point that only three girls in a sample of 56 claimed to read any newspapers regularly. They rarely watched the news on television and their only prolonged contact with the written word was at school and through their own and their mothers' magazines. Occasionally a 'risqué' novel like Richard Allen's *Skingirl* would be passed round at school, but otherwise the girls did not read any literature apart from 'love' comics.

The 'teen' magazine is, therefore, a highly privileged 'site'. Here the girl's consent is sought uncoercively and in her leisure time. [. . .] While there is a strongly coercive element to those other terrains which teenage girls inhabit, the school and the family, in her leisure time the girl is officially 'free' to do as she pleases. And as we have seen, teenage girls show a marked lack of interest in organised leisure activities, showing instead a preference for dancing or merely 'sitting about'. Otherwise the girls in the sample defined their leisure interests in terms of consumer goods − clothes, make-up, magazines, records and cigarettes. It is on the open market then that girls are least constrained by the display of social control. The only qualification here is the ability to buy a ticket, magazine or Bay City Roller T-shirt. Here they remain relatively uninterfered with. [. . .]

Commercial leisure enterprises with their illusion of freedom have, then, an attraction for youth. And this 'freedom' is pursued, metaphorically, inside the covers of *Jackie*. With an average readership age of 10 to 14, *Jackie* pre-figures girls' entry into the labour market as 'free labourers' and its pages are crammed full of the 'goodies' which this later freedom promises. *Jackie* girls are never at school, they are enjoying the fruits of their labour on the open market. They live in large cities, frequently in flats shared with other young wage-earners like themselves.

This image of freedom has a particular resonance for girls when it is located within and intersects with the longer and again ideologically constructed 'phase' they inhabit in the present. Leisure has a special importance in this period of 'brief flowering',[12] that is, in those years prior to marriage and settling down, after which they become dual labourers in the home and in production. Leisure in their 'single' years is especially important because it is here that their future is secured. It is in *this* sphere that they go about finding a husband and thereby sealing their fate. [. . .]

The World of Jackie

What then are the key features which characterise *Jackie*? First there is a 'lightness' of tone, a non-urgency, which holds true right through the magazine, particularly in the use of colour, graphics and advertisements. It asks to be read at a leisurely pace, indicating that its subject matter is not wholly serious, is certainly not 'news'. Since entertainment and leisure goods are designed to arouse feelings of pleasure as well as interest, the appearance of the magazine is inviting, its front cover shows a 'pretty' girl smiling happily. The dominance of the visual level, which is maintained throughout the magazine, reinforces this notion of leisure. It is to be glanced through, looked at and only finally read. Published at weekly intervals, the reader has time to peruse each item at her own speed. She also has time to pass it round her friends or swap it for another magazine.

Rigid adherence to a certain style of lay-out and patterning of features ensures a familiarity with its structure(s). The girl can rely on *Jackie* to *cheer her up, entertain her, or solve her problems each week.* The 'style' of the magazine, once established, facilitates and encourages partial and uneven reading, in much the same way as newspapers also do. The girl can quickly turn to the centre page for the pin-up, glance at the fashion page and leave the problems and picture stories which are the 'meat' of the magazine, till she has more time.

Articles and features are carefully arranged to avoid one 'heavy' feature following another. The black and white picture stories taking up between 2½ and 3 full pages are always broken up by a coloured advert, or beauty feature, and the magazine opens and closes by inviting the reader to participate directly through the letters or the problem pages.

This sense of solidness and resistance to change (*Jackie*'s style has not been substantially altered since it began publication) is reflected and paralleled in its thematic content. Each feature (as will be seen later) comprises workings and re-workings of a relatively small repertoire of specific themes or concerns which sum up the girls' world. These topics saturate the magazine. Entering the world of *Jackie* means suspending interest in the 'real' world of school, family or work, and participating in a sphere which is devoid of history and resistant to change.

Jackie deals primarily with the terrain of the personal and it makes a 'turning inwards' to the sphere of the 'soul', the 'heart', or less metaphorically, the emotions. On the one hand, of course, certain features do change — fashion is itself predicated upon change and upon being 'up to date'. But the degree of change even here is qualified — certain features remain the same, e.g. the models' 'looks', poses, the style of drawing and its positioning within the magazine and so on. All that does change is the length of the hem, shade of make-up, style of shoe, etc.

Above all, *Jackie*, like the girl she symbolises, is intended to be 'looked at'. This overriding concern with visuals affects every feature. But its visual appearance and style also reflect the spending power of its readers. There is little of the extravagant or exotic in *Jackie*. The paper on which it is printed is thin without being wafer-thin. The fashion and beauty pages show clothes priced within the girls' range and the adverts are similarly focused at a low budget market featuring, principally, personal toiletries, tampons, shampoos and lipsticks rather than larger consumer goods. [. . .]

The Code of Romance: the Moment of Bliss

> The hero of romance knows how to treat women. Flowers, little gifts, love letters, maybe poems to her eyes and hair, candlelit meals on moon-lit terraces and muted strings. Nothing hasty, physical. Some heavy breathing . . . Mystery, magic, champagne, ceremony . . . women never have enough of it.[13]

Jackie picture stories are similar *in form* to those comic strips, and tales of adventure, time travel, rivalry and intrigue which regularly fill the pages of children's weeklies. Yet there is something distinctive about these stories which indicates immediately their concern with romance. First the titles clearly announce a concern with 'you', 'me', 'love' and 'happiness'. Romantic connotations are conveyed through the relationship between titles and the names of 'pop' songs and ballads. (*Jackie* does not however use the older *Boyfriend* technique of using a well-known pop song and its singer to both inspire the story and give it moral weight!)

The title, then, anchors the story it introduces. In our sample these include:

'The Happiest Xmas Ever', 'Meet Me On The Corner', 'As Long As I've Got You', 'Come Fly With Me', and 'Where Have All The Flowers Gone?'

This concern with romance pervades every story and is built into them through the continued use of certain formal techniques and styles.

For a start, the way the characters look indicates clearly that this is serious, not 'kids' stuff'. They are all older and physically more mature than the intended reader. Each character conforms to a well-established and recognisable standard of beauty or handsomeness and they are all smart, fairly sophisticated young adults, rather than adolescents or 'teenagers'.

The most characteristic feature of 'romance' in *Jackie* is the concern with the narrow and restricted world of the emotions. No attempt is made to fill out social events or backgrounds. The picture story is the realm, *par excellence*, of the individual. Each story revolves round one figure and the tiny web of social relationships surrounding him or, usually, her. Rarely are there more than two or three characters in each plot and where they do exist it is merely as part of the background or scenery — in the cafe, at the disco or in the street.

Unlike comic strips, where the subject is fun, excitement or adventure, these stories purport to deal with the more serious side of life — hence the semi-naturalistic style of the drawings and the use of black and white. This, along with the boldness of the drawings, the starkness of stroke and angularity of the figures, conspires to create an impression of 'realism' and seriousness. The form of the stories alone tells us that romance is important, serious and relevant. Yet simultaneously in the content, we are told that it is fun; the essence and meaning of life; the key to happiness, etc. It is this blend which gives the *Jackie* romance its characteristic flavour. In general terms this is nothing new, these stories owe a great deal to popular cinema romances, and to novelettes. For a start the characters closely resemble the anonymous but distinctive type of the 'film star' — dewy-eyed women and granite-jawed heroes. Their poses are equally soaked in the language of film — the clinch, the rejected lover alone by herself as the sun sets — the moon comes up — to name but a few. But this cinematic resemblance is based on more than just *association*. The very form of the comic strip has close links with the film. Strung together, in a series of *clips*, set out across and down the page, the stories 'rise' to a climax and resolution, graphically illustrated in larger images erupting across the page.

From these clips we can see clearly that the emotional life is defined and lived in terms of *romance* which in turn is equated with **great moments** rather than long-term processes. Hence the centrality and visual impact of the clinch, the proposal, the wedding day. Together these *moments* constitute a kind of orchestration of *time*; through them the feminine career is constructed. The picture stories comprise a set of visual images composed and set within a series of frames laid out across the page to be 'read' like a text. But these frames communicate *visually*, resemble film-clips and tell the story by 'freezing' the action into sets of 'stills'. Unlike other comics (*Bunty* or *Judy*), *Jackie* stories do not conform to the convention of neatly mounted images set uniformly across the page. Instead a whole range of loose frames indicating different kinds of situations or emotions is used. This produces a greater continuity between 'form' and 'content', so that as the pace of the story accelerates, the visuals erupt *with* the breathless emotional feelings, spilling out over the page.

Each separate image which makes up the story is 'anchored' with sets of verbal messages illuminating the action and eliminating ambiguity. [. . .] Thus the moment of reading and looking are collapsed into one, and the reader is spared the boredom of having to read more lengthy descriptions; she merely 'takes it in' and hurries on to the next image. The techniques through which this relay operates are well known; — dialogue is indicated by the use of balloons issuing from the mouths of the speakers and filled with words; — and thoughts are conveyed through a series of small bubbles which drift upwards away from the character's mouth — thinking being associated with a 'higher' level of discourse, an 'intellectual' pursuit.

The central and most dramatic incident in each story is specified by the spilling out of one visual image over the page. This image sums up graphically the fraught nature of the moment; the moment when the timid shy heroine catches sight of her handsome boyfriend fascinated by her irresistible best friend at a party which she stupidly invited her to; or when the girl, let down by her boy, rushes out of the coffee bar across the street to be hit by a passing car . . . and so on.

Each frame represents a selection from the development of the plot, and is credited with an importance which those intervening moments are not. Thus the train, supermarket, and office have meaning, to the extent that they represent potential meeting-places where the girl *could well* bump into the prospective boyfriend, who lurks round every corner. It is this which determines their inclusion in the plot; the possibility that everyday life could be transformed into *social life*.

Within these frames themselves the way the figures look, act, and pose contributes also to the ideology of romance. For a start there is very little variation in types of physical appearance. This homogeneity hinges on a blend of modernity and conservatism which typifies the *Jackie* 'look'. The girls are 'mod' but neat and conventional, rarely are they 'way-out'. Boys may look acceptably scruffy and dishevelled by displaying a kind of managed untidiness.

This appearance is matched by language. Deriving seemingly from the days of the teenage commercial boom it has a particularly 50s ring about it. Bereft of accent, dialect, slang or vulgarity it remains the invention of the media – the language of pop, and of Radio 1 disc jockeys. Distinctly modern it is also quite unthreatening, peppered with phrases like:

'rave', 'yacked', 'zacked', 'scrummy hunk', 'dishy', 'fave', 'come on, let's blow this place', 'I'm the best mover in town',

all of which convey an image of youth 'on the move', of 'a whole scene going' and of 'wowee dig the slick chick in the corner', 'a nice piece of talent', teenagers 'doing their own thing'. But these teenagers are a strangely anonymous and unrecognisable grouping, similar only, perhaps, to the 'Young Generation' seen on TV variety shows or the young people in Coca Cola or Levi Jeans adverts. It is a language of action, of 'good times', of enjoyment and of consumerism. The characters in *Jackie* stories and in Coca Cola TV adverts at least seem to be getting things done. They are constantly seen 'raving it up' at discos, going for trips in boyfriends' cars, or else going on holiday. And yet as we shall see, the female and male characters in *Jackie* are simultaneously doing nothing but pursuing each other, and far from being a pleasure-seeking *group*, in fact these stories consist of isolated individuals, distrusting even their best friends and in search of fulfilment only through a partner. The anonymity of the language then parallels the strangely amorphous *Jackie* girls. Marked by a rootlessness, lack of ties or sense of region, the reader is unable to 'locate' them in any social context. They are devoid of history. Bound together by an invisible 'generational consciousness' they inhabit a world where no disruptive values exist. At the 'heart' of this world is the individual girl looking for romance. But romance is not itself an unproblematic category and what I will be arguing here is that its central contradiction is glaringly clear and unavoidable even to the girl herself who is so devoted to its cause. This contradiction is based round the fact that the *romantic moment*, its central 'core', cannot be reconciled with its promise for *eternity*. To put it another way, the code of romance realises, but cannot accept, that the man can adore, love, 'cherish' and be sexually attracted to his girlfriend and simultaneously be 'aroused' by other girls (in the present or the 'future'). It is the recognition of this fact that sets all girls against each other, and forms the central theme in the picture stories. Hence the girl's constant worries, as she is passionately embraced; 'can it last?' or 'how can I be sure his love is for ever?'

Earlier we asserted that *Jackie* was concerned with 'the category of the subject', with the constitution of the feminine personality. Indeed 'personality' itself forms an important organising category in the magazine. Each week there is some concern with 'your' personality, how to know it, change it or understand those of your friends, boyfriends, families. In the picture stories 'personality' takes on an important role alongside 'looks'. The characters depend for their meaning on well-known stereotypes. That is, to be 'read' correctly the reader must possess previous cultural knowledge of the 'types' of subjects which inhabit his or her social world.

Jackie boys fall into four categories. First, there is the fun-loving, grinning, flirtatious boy who is irresistible to all girls; second, the 'tousled' scatterbrained 'zany' youth who inspires 'maternal' feelings in girls; third, the emotional, shy, sensitive and even 'arty' type; and fourth, the juvenile delinquent usually portrayed on his motor bike looking wild, aggressive but 'sexy' and whom the girl must 'tame'.

In every case the male figure is idealised and romanticised so that there is a real discrepancy between *Jackie* boys and those boys who are discussed on the Cathy and Claire page. The central point here is that *Jackie* boys are as interested in romance as the girls.

> 'Mm! I wish Santa would bring me that for Christmas . . . so how do we get together?'

and this, as countless sociological studies, novels and studies of sexual behaviour indicate, simply does not ring true. Boys in contemporary capitalist society are socialised to be interested in *sex*, although this does not mean they don't want to find the 'ideal' girl or wife. [. . .]

Female characters, significantly, show even less variation in personality. In fact they can be summarised as three opposite or contrasting types. The 'blonde', quiet, timid, loving and trusting girl who either gets her boy in the end or is tragically abandoned; and the wild, fun-loving 'brunette' (often the blonde's best friend) who will resort to plotting and conniving to get the man she wants. This 'bitch' character is charming and irresistible to men although all women can immediately 'see through' her. Finally, there is the non-character, the friendly, open, fun-loving 'ordinary' girl (who may perhaps be slightly 'scatty' or absent-minded). She is remarkable in being normal and things tend to happen *to* her rather than at her instigation. Frequently she figures in stories focusing round the supernatural.

Most of these characters have changed little since the magazine first appeared in 1964. Their 'style' is still rooted in the 'Swinging London' of the mid-60s. The girls have large, heavily made-up eyes, pale lips and tousled hair, turned up noses and tiny 'party' mouths (à la Jean Shrimpton). They wear clothes at least partly reminiscent of the 60s, hipster skirts with large belts, polo neck sweaters and, occasionally, 'flared' trousers. Despite the fact that several of these girls introduce themselves as 'plain', their claims are contradicted by the accompanying image indicating that they are without exception 'beautiful'. Likewise the men (or boys) are ruggedly handsome, young versions of James Bond (to the extent that some even wear 'shorty' raincoats with 'turned-up' collars). They have thick eyebrows, smiling eyes, and 'granite' jaws.

While some of the stories seem to be set in London, the majority give no indication of 'locale'. The characters speak without an accent and are usually without family or community ties. They have all left school, but 'work' hovers invisibly in the background as a necessary time filler between one evening and the next or can sometimes be a pathway to glamour, fame or romance. Recognisable 'social' backgrounds are rare. The small town, equated with boredom, is signified through the use of strangely anachronistic symbols — the coffee bar, and the motor-bike and the narrow street. The country, on the other hand, is where the girl escapes *to*, following a broken romance or an unhappy love affair. But when her problems are resolved, she invariably returns to *the city* where things 'really happen'. But it is a city strangely lacking a population that these teenagers inhabit. There are no foreigners, black teenagers, old people or children. No married couples and rarely any families or siblings. It is a world occupied almost solely by young adults on the brink of pairing-up as couples.

The messages which these images and stories together produce are limited and unambiguous, and are repeated endlessly over the years. These are (1) the girl has to fight to *get* and *keep* her man, (2) she can *never* trust another woman unless she is old and 'hideous' in which case she doesn't appear in the stories anyway and (3) despite this, romance, and being a girl, are 'fun'.

No story ever ends with *two* girls alone together and enjoying each other's company. Occasionally the flat-mate or best friend appears in a role as 'confidante' but these appearances are rare and by implication unimportant. A happy ending means a happy couple, a sad one — a single girl. Having eliminated the possibility of strong supportive relationships between girls themselves, and between people of different ages, *Jackie* stories must elevate to dizzy heights the supremacy of the heterosexual romantic partnership.

This is, it may be argued, unsurprising and predictable. But these stories do more than this. They cancel out completely the possibility of any relationship other than the romantic one between girl and boy. They make it impossible for any girl to talk to, or think about, a boy in terms other than those of romance. (A favourite story in both picture form and as a short story, is the 'platonic' relationship which the girl enjoys. She likes him as a friend – but when she is made jealous by his showing an interest in another girl, she realises that it is *really* love that she feels for him and their romance blossoms.)

Boys and men are, then, not sex objects but romantic objects. The code of romance neatly displaces that of sexuality which hovers somewhere in the background appearing fleetingly in the guise of passion, or the 'clinch'. Romance is about the public and *social* effects of and implications of 'love' relationships. That is, it is concerned with impressing one's friends with a new handsome boyfriend, with being flattered by the attention and compliments lavished by admirers. It is about playing games which 'skirt about' sexuality, and which include sexual innuendo, but which are somehow 'nicer', 'cleaner' and less 'sordid'. Romance is the girls' reply to male sexuality. It stands in opposition to their 'just being after the one thing'; and consequently it *makes* sex seem *dirty*, *sordid*, and *unattractive*. The girl's sexuality is understood and experienced not in terms of a physical need of her own body, but in terms of the romantic attachment. In depicting romantic partnerships, *Jackie* is also therefore constructing male and female roles ensuring that they are separate and as distinct as possible. They are as different as they 'look' different and any interchange between the sexes invariably exudes *romantic* possibilities. What *Jackie* does is to map out all those *differences* which exist between the sexes but to assert that what they do *share* is a common interest, indeed devotion to, 'romance'.

So far, I have outlined in some detail the organising principles around which this discourse (the picture story) is structured. Now, while I would not hold the separation of form and content as being either possible, or necessary for analysis, there are a number of recurring themes which can be identified through a process of extrapolation from both the image and the accompanying text. Thus, temporarily holding constant the formal features of the picture story – the 'balloon' form of dialogue; the action through 'relay'; and the style of illustration – we can go on to deal with the patterns, combinations and permutations of those stock situations which give *Jackie* its characteristic thematic unity.

The stories themselves can be categorised as follows:

(1) the traditional 'love' story;
(2) the romantic/adventure serial;
(3) the 'pop' special (where the story revolves around a famous pop star);

(4) the 'zany' tale; and

(5) the historical romance.

But those story-types are worked through and expounded by the use of certain conventions or devices and it is through these that the thematic structure can be seen most clearly.

The first of these is the convention of *'time'* or of *'the temporal'*. Under this heading four different modes can be categorised, including the *flashback*. Here the opening clips signify 'aloneness' conveyed through images of isolation; a single figure against, say, a rugged, beautiful threatening landscape. Along this same chain of signifieds and following 'aloneness' comes the explanation — that is — 'alone-and-rejected-by-a-loved-one', or 'separated-from-a-loved-one'. Next comes the elucidation; what has caused such a state of unhappiness or misery, and this is classified and expounded upon through the use of the *flashback*. 'I remember only a year ago and it was all so . . .' 'But Dave was different from the others even then.' The reader is transported into the narrator's past and confronted with scenes of love, tenderness, excitement etc. The difference between the past and present state is emphasised by changes of *season*, and particularly by changes of *expression*. Warm weather, for example, goes with smiling, happy faces gazing in mutual pleasure at one another.

From this point onwards different conventions intervene to carry the story along, and it is neatly concluded with a return to the present, and a 'magical' or intentionally un-magical resolution. (The boy re-appears, or doesn't, or a new one takes his place —.)

Through this device the reader is invited to interpret her life, past and present, in terms of romantic attachments — her life has meaning through *him*.

The second temporal device is the diary. Again this allows the reader access to the innermost secrets of its writer, sometimes mediated through a plotting, and a guilty best friend reading her friend's outpourings. But it is the third convention, *'History'*, which is without doubt the most popular.

By locating the characters in a specific 'period' the scriptwriter and artist are provided immediately with a whole string of easy, and ideologically constructed, concepts with which they can fill out the plot. History *means* particular *styles of clothing, 'quaint' language, strange customs and rituals*. Thus we have the Victorian heroine connoted through her dress and background dissatisfied with her life and bored by her persistent suitor. When she is transported, magically, into the present she is, however, so horrified by 'liberated' women (policewomen and girls in bikinis) that she is glad to return to her safe and secure environment. Thus, culturally defined notions of the Victorian period are used to glamourise the past and criticise the present which is, by implication, bereft of romance. (Bikinis and uniforms don't connote frailty, passivity and fragility.) *At the same time*, this story is incorporating popularised notions of present phenomena which threaten the established order, and in doing so it is thereby diluting and ridiculing them. [...]

Likewise the Edwardian period, again recognisable through costume and this time carrying connotations of more active women, is used to relate a simple story of love, jealousy and reconciliation, with its participants (literally) carrying out their romances on bicycle saddles.

But history is not just novelty, it is also used to demonstrate the intransigence of much-hallowed social values, and 'natural resistance' to change. When a patrician (in the setting of Ancient Rome) falls for a slave girl he can only die for her thereby allowing her to escape with her slave boyfriend; he cannot escape or be paired off with her. Similarly, when a flower girl is attracted by a gentleman her thoughts only become romantic when she discovers that he is not *really* a gentleman but rather a bohemian artist. A nineteenth-century woman and her child arrive at the doorstep one Christmas but are turned away. Two guests help them and it emerges that the woman is the disinherited daughter of a wealthy man ... The messages are clear; love conquers and simultaneously renders unimportant poverty — which at any rate only 'exists' in the past (and is thus contained and manageable). People marry into their own class and their own race. (When a nurse falls for a wounded German prisoner in wartime Britain she knows her love cannot be fulfilled ... and the prisoner returns to Germany.) Similarly, social class, too 'controversial' an issue to appear in stories set in the present, can be acknowledged as *having* existed in the past.

History then provides the *Jackie* team with a whole set of issues which are more safely dealt with in the past; social problems, social class, foreigners and war. But history also means unchanging *eras* characterised primarily by splendid costumes (the code of fashion), exoticism (language and customs) and adventure. And yet despite this the reader can derive reassurance which lingers on a recognition of the *sameness* which links past and present. Underpinning all the adventures and historical tableaux is *romance*, the young girl in pursuit of it, or being pursued by it. Love, it is claimed, transcends time and is all-important, and history is, again, denied.

The fourth and final temporal device is that of the *'seasons'*. The importance of weather in reflecting 'moods' and creating atmosphere is a feature throughout the stories. 'Love' takes different forms at different times of the year, and holiday romances give way to autumnal 'blues'.

The second set of conventions we will be looking at are those which relate to the exigencies of plot. Thus we have (1) the 'zany' tale where romance is blended with comedy. Here the drawings are less dramatic and are characterised by softer lines. The plots revolve around unusual, unlikely events and coincidences resulting in romantic meetings. At their centre is the 'zany' boy whose bizarre hobbies lead him through a number of disasters until eventually he finds a steady girl who 'tames' him. ('Now they're crazy about each other.')

'Zany' girls of this type are rare. Girls are not really interested in anything outside the confines of femininity, besides which, no girl would willingly make a public spectacle of herself in this way. Often, perhaps instead, animals, always the subject of sentiment, figure strongly in these stories. A camel escapes from the zoo, is caught by a young girl in the city centre who has to await the arrival of the handsome, young, zookeeper. Another favourite centres around the ritual of walking the dog and taking an evening stroll in the local park where numerous handsome young men are doing the same thing or are willing to be pestered by *her* dog – and so on. 'Hmm, funny names you call your cats.'

Again the message is clear – a 'zany' absent-minded boyfriend is a good bet! He is unlikely to spend his time chasing other girls and is indeed incapable of doing so, he is the lovable 'twit', who needs mothering as well as loving. (Some Mothers Do 'Ave 'Em!)

Second, there is the plot which depends on a recognisable social locale. The hospital appears frequently here and carries rich connotations of romance and drama. A girl, for example, is recovering from a throat operation and discovers her boy is going out with someone else, but she overcomes her disappointment by meeting someone new in the hospital.

In another story a dashing young man catches sight of a pretty girl and follows her to her place of work, a bloodbank. Terrified to sign up to give blood he thinks of ways of getting to know her . . .

But hospitals are not the only places where romance can happen; at the bus-stop, on the bus, in the park, in the flat downstairs, depending on luck, coincidence or 'stars'. 'He must be on day release . . . he's on the train Mondays and Wednesdays but not the rest of the week.' And there is a moral here, if love strikes, or simply happens 'out of the blue' then all the girl needs to do is look out for it, be alert without actively seeking it. In fact this allows her, once again, to remain passive, she certainly can't approach a young man, only a coincidence may bring them together (though she may work on bringing about such a coincidence). At any rate she certainly can't hang about the bus-stop or street corner waiting to be picked up.

This convention of *place* also, by implication, deems leisure facilities for youth unnecessary. There is no need for them, if *your* boy is on the bus or train each morning. There are no stories set in youth clubs, community centres, even libraries or evening classes, and discos only appear as a backdrop where a girl is taken *to* by her boyfriend. Youth means individuals in search of or waiting for a partner and when this occurs all other leisure needs evaporate.

The third convention takes the idea of luck or coincidence one step further by introducing unambiguously *supernatural* devices. This way the reader is invited to share a fantasy, or 'dream come true'. These include magazines, leprechauns, magic lamps and dreams themselves.

But the dream or fantasy occupies a central place in the girls' life anyway — to an extent *all* the picture stories are fantasies, and escapist. Likewise real-life boys are frequently described as 'dreamy'. Day-dreaming is an expected 'normal' activity on the part of girls, an adolescent phase. But dreaming of this sort is synonymous with passivity — and as we have already seen, romance is the language of passivity, *par excellence*. The romantic girl, in contrast to the sexual man, is *taken* in a kiss, or embrace. Writing on the development of female sexuality in little girls, Mitchell describes their retreat into the 'Oedipus complex' where the desire *to be loved* can be fulfilled in the comforting and secure environment of the home.[14] Likewise in *Jackie* stories the girl is *chosen*,

'Hmm, this mightn't be so bad after all — if I can get chatting to that little lady later'

is taken in an embrace,

'Hmm, I could enjoy teaching you, love ... very, very much.'

And is herself waiting *to be loved*.

'I must be a nut! But I'm really crazy about Jay.
If only I could make him care.'

Finally there is the convention based round personal or domestic life. Here the girl is at odds with her family and siblings (who rarely appear in person) and eventually is *saved* by the appearance of a boyfriend. Thus we have a twin, madly jealous of her pretty sister, who tries to 'steal' the sister's boyfriend when she has to stay in bed with flu.

'Story of my life! Just Patsy's twin. He doesn't even know my name, I bet. Just knows me as the other one. The quiet one.'

Another common theme (echoed in the problem page) is the girl with the 'brainy' family. In one case such a girl is seen reading Shakespeare in the park, by a handsome young man. When he begins to take her out she insists on going to art galleries and museums, but gives herself away when his 'clever' friend shows that she doesn't know what she's talking about. Breaking down she admits to reading cheap romances inside the covers of highbrow drama! Through this humiliation and admission of inferiority (the daughter of another 'clever' family) she wins the true love of the boy. So much for *Jackie*'s anti-intellectualism. All the girl needs is a good personality, 'looks' and confidence. Besides which boys don't like feeling threatened by a 'brainy' girl.

Jackie asserts the absolute and natural separation of sex roles. Girls can take humiliation and be all the more attractive for it, as long as they are pretty and unassertive. Boys can *be* footballers, pop stars, even juvenile delinquents, but girls can only be feminine. The girl's life is defined through emotions — jealousy, possessiveness and devotion. Pervading the stories is an elemental fear, fear of losing your boy, or of never getting one. Romance as a code or a way of life, precipitates individual neurosis and prohibits collective action as a means of dealing with it.

By displacing all vestiges or traces of adolescent sexuality and replacing it with concepts of love, passion and eternity, romance gets trapped within its own contradictions, and hence we have the 'problem page'.

Once declared and reciprocated this love is meant to be lasting, and is based on fidelity and pre-marital monogamy. But the girl knows that where *she*, in most cases, will submit to these axioms, there is always the possibility that her boy's passion will, and can be, roused by almost any attractive girl at the bus-stop, outside the home, etc.

The way this paradox is handled is to introduce terms like resignation, despair, fatalism — it's 'all in the game'. Love has its losers, it must be admitted, but for the girl who has lost, there is always the chance that it will happen again, this time with a more reliable boy. Girls don't, then, fight back. Female 'flirts' always come to a 'bad end'; they are abandoned by their admirers who quickly turn their attention to the quiet, trusting best friend who had always been content to sit in the background.

Conclusion

What, then, are the central features of *Jackie* in so far as it presents its readers with an ideology of adolescent femininity? First it sets up, defines and focuses exclusively on 'the personal', locating it as the sphere of *prime* importance to the teenage girl. It presents this as a totality — and by implication all else is of secondary interest to the 'modern girl'. Romance problems, fashion, beauty and pop mark out the limits of the girl's concern — other possibilities are ignored or dismissed.

Second, *Jackie* presents 'romantic individualism' as the ethos, *par excellence*, for the teenage girl. The *Jackie* girl is alone in her quest for love; she refers back to her female peers for advice, comfort and reassurance *only* when she has problems in fulfilling this aim. Female ·solidarity, or more simply the idea of girls together — in *Jackie* terms — is an unambiguous sign of failure. To achieve self-respect, the girl has to escape the 'bitchy', 'catty' atmosphere of female company and find a boyfriend as fast as possible. But in doing this she has not only to be individualistic in outlook — she has to be prepared to fight ruthlessly — by plotting, intrigue and cunning, to 'trap her man'. Not surprisingly this independent-mindedness is short-lived. As soon as she finds a 'steady', she must renounce it altogether and capitulate to *his* demands, acknowledging his domination and resigning herself to her own subordination.

This whole ideological discourse, as it takes shape through the pages of *Jackie*, is immensely powerful. Judging by sales figures alone, *Jackie* is a force to be reckoned with by feminists. Of course this does not mean that its readers swallow its axioms unquestioningly. And indeed until we have a clearer idea of just how girls 'read' *Jackie* and encounter its ideological force, our analysis remains one-sided.

For feminists a related question must be how to go about countering *Jackie* and undermining its ideological power at the level of *cultural* intervention. One way of beginning this task would be for feminist teachers and youth leaders to involve girls in the task of 'deconstructing' this seemingly 'natural' ideology; and in breaking down the apparently timeless qualities of girls' and women's 'mags'.

Another more adventurous possibility would be the joint production of an alternative; a magazine where girls are depicted in situations other than the romantic, and where sexuality is discussed openly and frankly; not just contraception, masturbation and abortion, but the *social relations* of sexuality, especially the sexism of their male peers. Likewise girls would be encouraged to create their own music, learn instruments and listen to music without having to drool over idols. Their clothes would not simply reflect styles created by men to transform them into junior sex-objects, products of male imaginations and fantasies. But most of all, readers would be presented with an *active* image of female adolescence — one which pervades every page and is not just deceptively 'frozen' into a single 'energetic/glamorous' pose as in the fashion pages and Tampax adverts in *Jackie*.

Notes

1. See G.L. White, *Women's Magazines, 1963-1968* (1970), Appendix IV.

2. See G. Rosei, 'The Private Life of Lord Snooty', *Sunday Times Magazine*, 29 July 1973, pp. 8-16.

3. L. Althusser, 'Ideology and Ideological State Apparatuses: Notes Toward an Investigation' in *Lenin and Philosophy, and Other Essays* (New Left Books, London, 1971), p. 163.

4. A. Dorfman and A. Mattelart, *How to Read Donald Duck* (I.G. Editions Inc., New York, 1975), p. 30.

5. P. Johnson, *New Statesman*, 1964.

6. C. Alderson, *The Magazines Teenagers Read* (Pergamon Press, Oxford, 1968), p. 3.

7. P. Willis, 'Symbolism and Practice: a Theory for the Social Meaning of Pop Music', Centre for Contemporary Cultural Studies, stencilled paper No. 2, p. 2.

8. Ibid., p. 1.

9. J. Clarke, S. Hall, T. Jefferson and B. Roberts (eds.), *Resistance Through Rituals* (Hutchinson, London, 1976), p. 55.

10. S. Hall, B. Lumley and G. McLennan, 'Politics and Ideology: Gramsci', *Working Papers in Cultural Studies*, no. 10 (1977), p. 51.

11. Ibid., p. 51.

12. R. Hoggart, *The Uses of Literacy* (Chatto and Windus, London, 1957), p. 51.

13. G. Greer, *The Female Eunuch* (Paladin, London, 1970), p. 173.

14. See J. Mitchell, *Psychoanalysis and Feminism* (Penguin, Harmondsworth, 1974).

Thelma McCormack suggests that soap operas since the 1930s have evolved, in their treatment of women, from images of woman as mother to images as wife and finally to images of woman as consumer. She recommends that future research on "soaps" place less emphasis on sex-role stereotypes and more on structural analysis and raises the question of whether men should be studying media that have female audiences, whether their views on female audiences are not inevitably their views on women. Thelma McCormack is professor of sociology at York University and a member of the Canadian Research Institute for the Advancement of Women.

17

MALE CONCEPTIONS OF FEMALE AUDIENCES
The Case of Soap Operas

Thelma McCormack

I

A recent large-scale study of U.S. television viewers documented once again the fact that program preferences are strongly influenced by sex differences (Frank and Greenberg, 1980). Now, as in the past (Steiner, 1963), women view more television than men, and the patterns of gender preferences remain largely what they have been: Women are the primary audiences for programming that is domestic and cultural in content, while men are drawn to programs dealing with money, adventure, and power. There is nothing surprising in the findings; they merely serve to remind us of what we already know: As sex roles go, so go program preferences.

Our interest here, however, is neither with the choices made by men or by women, nor with the methodology of the studies. Rather it is with the theories that have been used to interpret the findings. What concepts have been used? Have the concepts themselves inadvertently reflected prevailing sex stereotypes? For example, when women write letters to television personalities, such behavior is regarded as childish, an inability to differentiate fact from fiction, an all-to-willing suspension of disbelief. Consider the following (Kinzer, 1973, p. 46):

> They write letters to fan magazines anxiously inquiring about the personal lives of the stars, threatening mass defection should Mark marry Suzy and leave

Mamie, weeping over the death of a special character, and pouting about an actor who has been replaced.

When men, however, write to a newscaster, an act at least as naive as writing to fan magazines, it is dignified by being called "audience feedback," and, according to Gans (1980) taken seriously by network executives. Gans's (1980, p. 228) picture of women who write is of the few who "write love letters to anchormen," and in case we miss the point about their deviant or infantile character, he adds that some of these women write every day.[1]

In this chapter I want to examine the problem of bias in our knowledge by looking at programs designed for women which have overwhelming female audiences. For this purpose I have chosen studies of the daytime serials.

First, I want to make a few preliminary comments about the soap opera genre and its evolution from a folk form of culture to a commodity designed for women listeners and women viewers. I also want to raise the question of what constitutes a feminist criterion for evaluating their content. For example, is the new direction toward more explicit sex in the programs a measure of liberation?

Second, I want to suggest that implicit in the research are three models of women: mother, wife, and consumer—or, traditional, modern, and postmodern. I prefer the latter set of terms because these modes are broader and more historically grounded than are sex-role stereotypes. Further, I want to suggest that these three images correspond to three class positions and three different modal processes of communication: projection, identification, and cognitive.

In the final section, I want to outline an alternative paradigm for feminist research on popular culture that examines content in terms of a patriarchal social structure using two measures: dependency and privatization.

II

The soap opera, or daytime serial, is one of the oldest forms of popular entertainment. Serialized stories and regular storytelling have always been part of folk cultures, but the form as we know it today—a form specifically made for women with all the help of product testing and market research skills—was, if not first, then most fully developed, on radio. The enormous popularity of the radio "soaps" during the Great Depression of the 1930s and later during the 1940s was carried over into the 1950s or postwar period and into television, where the programs were moved from the morning period to the afternoon.

By all accounts the soap operas are profitable for the networks.[2] Compared to evening or prime-time TV, the costs of daytime serials are minimal. Sets are inexpensive (mostly interior), the action is almost exclusively conversation (Katzman, 1972), and the casts are made up of "pros" who require little rehearsal or retake time.

Although the audiences are women, it is men who write the stories, men who produce the shows (Downing, 1974), and men who make the managerial decisions about them. Far from being cynical, many of the people who work in this genre believe in it and regard it as both important and, on the whole, realistic (Lipton, 1981, p. 59):

> If our heroines sip coffee and worry about their children or their love affairs or the fidelity of their husbands, it is because our viewers sip coffee and worry about their children or their love affairs or the fidelity of their husbands. That soap operas are in large part domestic drama is undeniable, but we are, in large part, a domestic society.

Within this "realistic" domestic drama there are more roles for men than women, and women have more dialogue (Katzman, 1972). Thus, as in other forms of theater, men have more employment opportunities and are not as often required to be young, thin, and beautiful.

It is not clear what the socioeconomic status of the audience is. Most writers suggest that the women at home have a lower standard of living than those on the screen, but what the significance of this is—whether it is a vicarious upward mobility for the viewer or a form of social devaluation—is never spelled out. Given the trend toward middle-aged and middle-class women remaining in or returning to the labor force, future audiences for daytime television may be more bimodal: the very rich and the very poor, the very young and the very old.

For our purposes, a more relevant consideration is whether these popular afternoon dramas have changed over time, whether they have kept up with changes in the society. There is certainly a greater sexual liberation in the plots and more explicit sex in the various segments. If, then, the sexual revolution is taken as the measure of progress, the soap operas have moved in that direction. Similarly, there has also been a more frank and open discussion of divorce, abortion, alcoholism, and illegitimacy and other social problems, subjects that would have been taboo in the more sublimated thirties.

However, this progress may be only superficial. The stories still hinge on issues of morality, and transgressions of conventional morality are still punished as predictably today as they were a quarter of a century ago (Sutherland and Siniawsky, 1982). More significant, with respect to patriarchy the trend may be negative. The independent women of *Ma Perkins* or *Big Sister* were models of women who were in charge and coping. They have been replaced by women who are more dependent socially and emotionally, by women who are more sexually active but who are also more masochistic. In other words, using measures of dependency in male-female relations, the situation may be worse than it was. Similarly, if we take the private/public dichotomy and the privatization of women as the distinguishing feature of patriarchal societies, there has been no change. Women are still seen in the domestic sphere at home or in hospital settings that become debureaucratized and homelike. The problems women have are interpersonal; they can be solved by changes in attitude among the persons involved, not by changes in social structure. If they cannot be solved by changes in attitudes, they cannot be solved at all; they are absolute, part of the universal human condition.

In short, the question raised here concerns the criteria of liberation, whether they are derived from a model of liberal secularization or from a model of feminist liberation. If my observation is correct that on a liberation scale the women in the soaps have lost ground, we can further speculate that as the competition among the networks increases for the disappearing consumer dollar, we will see still more dependency neatly embedded in formula softcore pornography.

III

A. Traditional:
Soap Operas for Motherhood

Shortly after World War II, Warner and Henry (1948) conducted an in-depth study of one popular radio serial: *Big Sister.* They analyzed the scripts as well as two groups, regular listeners and a group of nonlisteners who were recruited to participate in the study as listeners. Both groups of listeners were given various types of projective tests in order to tap some of their deeper anxieties which they might not normally discuss or even be aware of. No surprisingly, they found a high degree of correspondence between the worries and concerns of faithful listeners and those acted out in the stories.

For Warner and Henry, the soap opera was a folk story similar to those found by anthropologists in small preliterate societies. These contemporary folk stories functioned as art and religion did in the small-scale societies: to maintain normative cohesion. More Durkheimian than Marxist, Warner and Henry approve of the domestic content of many of the stories since it helps to strengthen and stabilize "the basic social structure of our society, the family."

The strains within the family are, as they see it, like the strains within a larger traditional social system, basically normative. Thus, Warner and Henry (1948: 64) see the interactive experience of women listeners and the radio serials as symbolic resolutions of moral conflict. "Essentially, the Big Sister drama," they write, "is a contemporary minor morality play which expresses . . . the feelings and beliefs of its audience by use of idealized symbols of good and evil and of things feared and hoped for."

But apart from the universality of the folk story and apart from the continuing need for normative cohesion, there is a specific situation to which the soap opera is an effective response. Traditional women who are the backbone of the society because of their commitment to motherhood are, according to the authors, threatened by the image of women who work outside of the home—not women of their own class whose employment may reflect economic necessity and with whom they share the same value system, but by the professional woman. The latter is not just anyone; she has special talents, skills, and education that are beyond the capacities of ordinary women. While Warner and Henry do not begrudge the elite professional woman her career, they postulate that she has an undesirable effect on the others who envy her but could not hope to match her accomplishments. Biology may not be destiny for all women, according to Warner and Henry, but it is for most. Under these circumstances, then, the majority of women could become chronically dissatisfied with the role of motherhood while being innately incapable of anything else (Warner and Henry, 1948, p. 64):

> Our society, by offering a choice to women between being housewives or career women . . . frequently creates a dilemma for them. The career woman's role is attractive because it is usually of higher status than the occupation of the Common Man level and offers more moral and emotional freedom. On the other hand, such a role is often frightening, demands hard work, ability to buck the system and the capacity for self initiated action.

Confronted by this paralyzing conflict, the soap opera listener finds in *Big Sister* and similar stories a way of resolving the conflict in favor of the traditional role which suits her limitations and satisfies the needs of the society for reproduction. "The Big Sister program," Warner and Henry write, "plays up the importance of the role of the wife and therefore obliquely depreciates the role (career women) the ordinary listener has avoided nor been able to take."

The female listeners Warner and Henry describe are traditional, pre-modern women whose lives center on moral rather than pragmatic issues and sacred rather than secular values. These women are threatened more by the professional ethos of the professional woman than by her wealth or freedom, although neither of the latter is totally rejected. They are also lower-class women whose opportunities for upward mobility are so blocked that they retreat into moralistic and highly bizarre fantasy, a regressive process of projection without any ego strength that might lead to a more critical view of class realities. These women are victimized by the pronatalism which, according to Warner and Henry, is the deeper message of *Big Sister* and its sister shows.

B. Modern:
Soap Operas for
Upwardly Mobile Wives

At about the same time as the Warner and Henry study, two other studies of daytime serials were carried out. Arnheim (1944) examined the content of forty-three stories, while Herzog (1944) interviewed regular listeners; that is, women whose radios were tuned in every morning to one story after another: *Our Gal Sunday, Helen Trent,* and *Ma Perkins.*

Arnheim described the extent to which the soap opera universe was unrepresentative of the real world. Almost all of the characters, but especially the leading ones and those who were particularly attractive, were middle-class. In that sense, the soap opera world was not unlike the rest of popular culture. Just how seriously Arnheim took the discrepancy to be was not stated; it is not clear whether he believed, as many did in the 1940s, that there was a potential political danger when people aspired to higher class positions than they could realistically hope to achieve. Status frustrations on a large scale could lead, it was thought, to fascist or other reactionary social movements.

At the very least this one-class, middle-class world was oversimplified. The same lack of complexity was found in the way people were depicted. Good or bad, selfish or unselfish, faithful or unfaithful, honest or dishonest, their motivations were unambiguous and one-dimensional. The problems soap opera women confronted were almost always interpersonal in origin and were resolved within the narrow world of family, neighborhood, or small town. Luck, moral conversions, death, and good intentions rather than planning, research, and sustained collective effort provided the happy endings. The predictability of the two or three formulas made the stories very comforting, but they did not, according to Arnheim, provide their listeners with the self-knowledge and self-criticism that are the prerequisites for autonomy and control over one's own life.

Although Arnheim concluded that the message of the soap operas was a conservative, uncritical one, the listeners were not the passive, depoliticized women his analysis implied. Herzog's findings disclosed an active woman-listener, a coper, a woman who did not question her social role or the social system, but who was not a spineless victim. If grief was to be her destiny, she would face it with courage; if sorrow was a woman's fate, excessive self-pity would not help matters. Traditional religion gave sympathy but was too flaccid. Listeners as well as the characters in the soap operas were more energetic, more independent, and more determined not to give in to every setback that came along.

What was most impressive in Herzog's findings was the extent to which faithful listeners were doing more than either bracing themselves for the unexpected tragedies of life or vicariously enjoying the lifestyles of the rich and well-to-do. These gratifications were abundantly available in the scripts, but the women who listened faithfully were also seeking information and advice about health, child rearing, marital relationships, and other problems. In some instances they were confused; in others, they just wanted to improve themselves. What Herzog and Arnheim saw from the interviews with listeners was that the soaps were eductional and that listeners were being educated informally and without a didactic environment. The process of social learning or anticipatory socialization was through identification with the strong women characters in the stories. Thus, the stories could not be described entirely as superstructure providing wish-fulfillment fantasies for women whose lives were impoverished; the stories were to an extent adult education, and the women who turned to them for information were not always desperate. Many were the spouses of upwardly mobile men who appreciated their wives' skills in household management and who understood the necessity of acquiring a new etiquette appropriate to a new social status. The initiatives taken by these wives reflected the isolation of the North American, middle-class nuclear family. Mother and married daughter were separated by both social and physical distance, so that mothers and other traditional role models were either unavailable or out of synchronization. If anything, married daughters became role models for their mothers.

C. Postmodern:
Soap Operas for the
"New Middle Class"

A recent study (Compesi, 1980) looked at a television soap opera, *All My Children,* and a sample of its viewers. Data on the program indicated that the educational and income levels of listeners were high; only 9 percent reported having less than high school completion. For these viewers, then, upward mobility was no longer salient; it had been achieved, and whether they were employed or not, they had enough leisure to watch both this and at least two other serials regularly.

When Compesi presented his sample with a list of fifty-two gratifications statements, the responses were of a different nature from those of the previous two studies. Entertainment was the primary factor. The profile Compesi found suggested a woman who was relatively detached, someone more independent and self-sufficient than either of the other two earlier groups, a woman engaging in some kind of game that was mentally absorbing but not necessarily emotionally involving. It could be turned on or off without any great sense of loss or anxiety. Like any other fad activity, television viewing of soap operas could shift from *All My Children* to gourmet cooking and televised classes in yoga.

Compesi found that the educational possibilities of soap operas were unimportant for this group of women—not surprising, since educated women apparently do not require daytime serials to give them advice on health and child rearing when other and better sources of information are available.

The women here resemble the modal figure of contemporary cognitive psychology. They turn inward, not to introspection, but to their own mental processes. They turn away from reality and avoid the effort required to build social meaning. They are people "who are free to engage in internal mental activity—to plan, decide, wish, think, organize, reconcile and transform con-

TABLE 1: Female Audiences

Patriarchal Social Structure	Modal Communication Process	Class Position	Social Role
Traditional	Projection	Lower Class	Mother
Modern	Identification	Upwardly mobile	Wife
Postmodern	Rational information processing	"New middle class	Consumer

flicts and contradictions within their heads—and yet who remain relatively impotent or apparently unconcerned . . . about producing actual changes in their objective social world" (Sampson, 1981, p. 736).[3]

To summarize, then, the three patterns described here are symptomatic in different ways of different stages of patriarchal social structures. Table 1 may help to demonstrate the interconnections. The three patterns sketched here are not intended to be seen as pure types. The purpose of the diagram is to illustrate the way the patriarchal structure in its various stages and transformations (traditional, modern and postmodern) interlocks with class structure, social roles and modal communications processes.

A similar analysis could be done on the basis of male audiences and male programming, but it is our contention that there would be greater emphasis on communication processes that presuppose ego strength. For example, when men watching a sports event become overinvolved, yelling at the umpire or cheering in the living room for a player on the screen, the responsibility for his foolishness is placed in part on the game itself and, in particular, the sportscasters (Bryant, et al., 1977; Comisky, et al., 1977). When women become too involved in a soap opera, the responsibility, as we noted earlier, is placed entirely on them.

The patterns described here are either prefeminist for antifeminist. The first reinforces the traditional family; the second legitimates a contemporary division of labor; the third is the detached woman who belongs nowhere. Barring sudden conversions, these women are far from the ranks of feminists. Some might well be potential recruits to antifeminist movements.

IV

Feminists have often commented informally on the soap operas but have not devoted systematic attention to the genre, even less to the audiences. In theory we would expect a criticism of the functionalist analysis of the family implicit in the Warner and Henry study. In theory, too, we would expect skepticism about the emphasis on social learning found in the Arnheim and Herzog studies. In the first instance, the family would be regarded as an exploitative system; in the second, the "education" is a combination of technical information and ideological indoctrination, rather than intelligent consciousness raising.

Carol Lopate (1976) discusses the idealization of the family in the soap operas where it is treated as "the sole repository of love, understanding, compassion, respect and sexuality." The soap opera universe is bounded by the family. "Inside the soaps," she says, "there is no way to be outside the family." This emphasis on the family she attributes to the loneliness of women at home. Thus, the soap opera family is a total institution but not in the sinister Goffmanesque sense of that term. It is a secure land where each one is equal; there is no repression. "No soap opera father," Lopate says, "is a disciplinarian; no husband a wife-beater . . . women and men in the soap operas are probably more equal than in any other form of art or drama or in any area of real life" (p. 81). Whether her observations are correct or not about the equality, it is the beginning of a feminist analysis of this special genre of popular culture. Lopate's emphasis on the isolation and loneliness of the housewife may have to be revised in terms of more recent demographics about women in the labor force, as indicated earlier in this chapter. Meanwhile, it seems to me unwise to continue to conjure up the 1950s image of a suburban housewife seeking compensatory gratifications through fantasies of family togetherness and kinship compatibility. There will be some who fit the description, although they are becoming fewer and fewer.

V

Feminist studies of communication must start by altering the stereotyped images of female audiences as women who are still searching, like children, for their identity; of women whose socialization—again, like children—is not yet complete; of women who are less intelligent than men whose viewing habits with respect to sport are open to question concerning maturity.

Second, insofar as our understanding of women derives from theories of patriarchal social structures, we must begin to specify more clearly whether the patriarchal social structure is traditional, modern, or postmodern. If we do not, we may fall into the trap noted here of confusing liberal secularization or modernization with feminist liberation.

Third, I have suggested that a preoccupation with sex-role stereotypes may obscure structural relationships based on dependency of women and their privatization. I am not suggesting here that we cease to do studies of sex-role stereotypes, but that we give them a rest while we concern ourselves with measures of class, status, and power. Although it is obvious, it perhaps bears repeating that the soap opera is the quintessential version of the privatization of women's status, of energies dissipated in attempting to manipulate inter-personal relationships, of individualized responses to problems that require collective effort. To ignore this by focusing either on the stereotypes or on the new "pop" aesthetics of popular culture is to miss the deeper meaning of this genre for female audiences.

Finally, the most difficult questions, difficult and embarrassing, must be raised: Should men be doing research in this field at all? As we have noted, much of the professional literature in the research on female audiences has been by men, and their views have often been adopted by women in this field uncritically. While I believe men may do good research, I suggest that there is a deeper kind of flaw when men are studying female audiences, whether it is for soap operas, game shows or Harlequin romances: It is to see the female audience as they see women.

NOTES

1. In fairness, it might be argued that interpretations offered by scholars reflect their judg-ments about the nature and quality of the programs and not about the audiences the programs attract. Programs that appeal to the mind require their audiences, male or female, to think, while those that appeal to the heart elicit emotional responses. Still, one wonders whether there is not an element of preconception, an image of a typical viewer that influences the descriptions of the pro-grams and the interaction of audience and program. Suppose, for example, men were avid viewers of daytime serials and women of public affairs programs. Would studies show how the cognitive, decision-making male uses soap operas to evaluate hospitals and learn about crisis management, while the expressive female was using public affairs programs as a form of escape from the mon-otony and boredom of housework and to enjoy a good cry?

2. According to one report, *Another World* was returning a profit of $3 million per month; at the same time NBC's *Days of Our Lives* was returning $2 million a month (Cole, 1981).

3. The game aspect of the soap opera has been used as a teaching device. Students in a course in the sociology of the family were presented with simulation scripts in Soap Opera Game, where a series of marital crises are presented to the two students chosen to be spouses. This perhaps says more about the way courses in the family are being taught than it does about the soap operas (see Levinson, 1980).

REFERENCES

ARNHEIM, R. (1944) "The world of the daytime serial," pp. 38-45 in P. F. Lazarsfeld and F. N. Stanton (eds.) Radio Research: 1942-1943. New York: Duell, Sloan & Pearce.
BRYANT, J., P. COMISKY, and D. ZILLMANN (1977) "Drama in sports commentary." Journal of Communication 27, 3: 140-149.
COLE, B. [ed.] (1981) Television Today: A Close-Up View. New York: Oxford University Press.
COMISKY, P., J. BRYANT, and D. ZILLMAN (1977) "Commentary as a substitute for action." Journal of Communication 27, 3: 150-153.

COMPESI, R. J. (1980) "Gratifications of daytime TV serial viewers." Journalism Quarterly 57, 1: 155-158.

DOWNING, M. (1974) "Heroine of the daytime serial." Journal of Communication (Spring): 130-137.

FRANK, R. E. and M. G. GREENBERG (1980) The Public's Use of Television. Beverly Hills, CA: Sage.

GANS, H. J. (1980) Deciding What's News. New York: Vintage.

HERZOG, H. (1944) "What do we really know about daytime serial listeners?" in P. F. Lazarsfeld and F. Stanton (eds.) Radio Research: 1942-1943. New York: Duell, Sloan & Pearce: 3-33.

KATZMAN, N. (1972) "Television soap operas: what's been going on anyway?" Public Opinion Quarterly 36, 2: 200-212.

KINZER, N. S. (1973) "Soapy sin in the afternoon," Psychology Today 7, 3,

LEVINSON, R. M. (1980) "The soap opera game." Teaching Sociology 7, 2: 181-190.

LIPTON, James (1981) "Soap operas are for real," pp. 58-60 in B. Cole (ed.) Television Today: A Close-Up View. New York: Oxford University Press.

LOPATE, C. (1976) "Daytime television: you'll never want to leave home." Feminist Studies 3 (Spring/Summer): 69-82.

SAMPSON, E. E. (1981) "Cognitive psychology as ideology." American Psychologist 36, 7: 730-743.

SUTHERLAND, J. C. and S. J. SINIAWSKY (1982) "The treatment and resolution of moral violations on soap operas." Journal of Communication 32, 2: 67-74.

WARNER, W. L. and S. E. HENRY (1948) "The radio day time serial: a symbolic analysis." Genetic Psychology Monographs 37: 3-71.

PART IV

MEDIA AND CULTURE

The four chapters included here embody similarities and differences. All build backwards from cultural products toward generalities about cultural systems, and three of the four pay particular attention to the material and economic determinants of culture—"culture as resource," in the felicitous phrase of one of the authors.

Nord, in the first of these contributions, attempts to demonstrate that much American writing on popular culture is hampered by a tautology concerning audience taste and the popular culture of a period, and much of it is dependent on unsophisticated economic models of culture production. What is needed, he says, is a realization that the understanding of convention and formula in popular culture production says more about the economics of that production than about audience tastes.

In examining culture as resource, Tuchman notes that the interplay between economic and cultural processes can be manifested in examination of such conventions and formulas in concrete settings; her data points are taken from a study of how Victorian novel manuscripts were selected.

In the most abstract of these chapters, Rosengren theoretically and empirically shows that literary "frames of reference" or epochs and their waxing and waning can be fitted to sociometric curves, to the benefit of more conventional literary history.

In the final chapter, Dick Hebdige, through his examination of "Americanization" of British taste between 1935 and 1962, demonstrates that taste subcultures themselves are not necessarily passive consumers of cultural products; they have an active hand in adapting them to their own devices. Culture is for them "resource" in a slightly different way.

David Nord wishes, in this chapter, to demonstrate that much current work in popular culture is marred by tautological thinking and to show that some of it is marred by simplistic economic analysis. His further goal is to show that the use of conventions and formulas in popular culture studies says more about the economics of publishing, moviemaking, and broadcasting than it does about audience values. Nord is an assistant professor of journalism at Indiana University.

18

AN ECONOMIC PERSPECTIVE
ON FORMULA IN POPULAR CULTURE

David Paul Nord

Studies in the history of American popular culture often are based either on a grand tautology or on a dubious economic assumption. The tautology usually takes the following form: The United States was, say, an individualistic society in the nineteenth century. Thus, individualistic heroes were popular in novels and magazines. But how do we know that the United States was an individualistic society? Because individualistic heroes were popular in novels and magazines. In somewhat more subtle fashion—and, of course, dealing with many things besides individualism—this tautology runs through much of the traditional historical work on American popular culture. More sophisticated studies of popular culture avoid tautology, but often only by basing their arguments on a dubious economic assumption. This assumption is that demand automatically creates supply, that the audiences of popular literature and art pretty much "get what they want." In short, much of the edifice of popular culture scholarship rests on the notion that popular art forms—mass magazines, books, films, songs, etc.—reflect the values, interests, or characteristics of the *society,* or that they at least reflect the values, interests, or characteristics of the *audience.*

In some ways, of course, this notion is patently true. Cultural products almost by definition must reflect something about the culture. But exactly how and to what extent popular art forms reflect the culture (or even the audience) is an empirical question that demands empirical study.[1] Too often this question has been answered by assumption. To suggest one way of moving beyond tautology and assumption is the aim of this paper. Specifcally, the paper will have three goals: First, to demonstrate the tautological character of some standard works in popular culture history; second, to show how even sophisticated work in this area is marred by simplistic economic thinking; and third, to propose an alternative way of looking at convention and formula in popular literature and art. This new approach will suggest that the use of conventions and formulas may tell us more about the economics of publishing, movie making, and broadcasting, than about audience values.

II

From the beginning of scholarly interest in popular culture, researchers and critics have been interested more in what might be called the psychology of audiences than in the sociology of popular literature or art.[2]

From David Paul Nord, "An Economic Perspective on Formula in Popular Culture," *Journal of American Culture,* Vol. 3 (Spring 1980), pp. 17-31. Reprinted by permission.

Most of the early work in mass communication research, growing out of propaganda studies in World War I, assumed that media had direct and powerful influence over their audiences. Harold Lasswell concluded in 1927 that the mass media were the "new hammer and anvil of social solidarity."[3] The apparent power of the new media alarmed critics, who attacked the debasing and narcotizing influence on the mass mind of magazines, movies, radio, and popular literature.[4] This view, that mass media can manipulate the audience directly, has now faded and been replaced by the complex transactional perspectives of social psychology. Seldom is it now argued that mass media can directly change (or pervert) basic cultural values.[5]

The other side of this same influence paradigm, however, is still very much alive in the work of historians of popular culture. This approach holds that popular literature and art have been directly influenced by, or have reflected, the values and the characteristics of the society from which they have come. This idea seems plausible and even almost true by definition, when stated in general terms. The link between popular culture and society would seem to be the main subject for empirical investigations in this field. Unfortunately, many studies, far from establishing the extent and the dimensions of this link empirically, have explained the link tautologically. They have "discovered" that popular literature and art reflected past society. But the evidence for their assertions about what past society was really like has come largely from the content of the popular culture itself.

A good example of this sort of tautological approach is James Hart's classic, *The Popular Book*. Hart proposed to study "the connection between popular books read for pleasure by adult Americans and the times in which those books were read." He argues that "in some way or another, the popular author is always the one who expresses the people's minds and paraphrases what they consider their private feelings."[6] Hart's approach is to spend a few paragraphs of each chapter talking about the spirit of the times and then to discuss the books of the times. Evidence for what was the spirit of the times often comes either from vague historical stereotypes or from the popular literature itself. For example, Hart sees the rise of a "new woman" in middle-class America around the 1840s and '50s, and this helps explain the success of woman-and-family-centered romances written by women in those years.[7] But what is his evidence that a "new woman" appeared? It is simply that such women were commonly portrayed in popular fiction. At another point, Hart asserts that the nation "dreamed and sentimentalized" at mid-nineteenth century.[8] How do we know? Well, the novels were dreamy and sentimental. In general, Hart finds that books became popular when they satisfied a need of some kind. But time and again, the popularity of a particular book or style is used to infer the need. And thus in the end Hart has not even the beginning of a predictive answer to the key question, "What makes a best seller?"[9]

Lewis Jacobs' classic history, *The Rise of the American Film*, written in 1939, suffers from this same sort of tautological reasoning. Jacobs asserts, for example, that "most people have become social-minded and have developed a more realistic attitude toward life's problems." He adds that "individualistic retreat" was out of fashion.[10] This attitude was reflected in the cycle of gangster pictures in the early 1930s and in pictures dealing with war, nationalism, and democracy. But the '30s was also the era of the musical and especially the "screwball" comedy. "In these films," Jacobs says, "the rebel, the individualist, is once more respected."[11] When the films themselves provide most of the evidence for what the society was like, it is easy to have it both ways—social-minded or individualistic. Other historians of film have followed Jacobs' lead. Arthur Knight, for instance, in his well-known history, suggests that the popularity of gangster films in the early '30s reflected a feeling that "the only escape from depression-bred despair was to live outside the law." On the other hand, the popularity of Frank Capra's comedies reflected a feeling that "if everyone were kind and generous to his fellow man, the depression would soon be overcome."[12] Once again, the evidence for inferences about the society comes from the movies themselves.

The problem of inferring social attitudes about the Depression from movies has its counterpart for historians of the comic strip. Here, too, the argument is often tautological—sometimes almost humorously so. Pierre Couperie and Maurice C. Horn point out that the Depression was virtually ignored in popular comic strips—a situation very different from the movies. Why? Because the Great Depression "upset the American's world too deeply for him to wish to see it in the comics."[13] How do we know the American's world was so profoundly upset? Because the Depression was not covered in the comics. If Depression material had filled the comics, Couperie and Horn likely would have reached the same conclusion: The Depression upset the American's world so deeply that even light diversions such as the comics (like the movies) were greatly affected.

Even the now standard history of popular culture in America, Russel Nye's *The Unembarrassed Muse,* suffers from tautological reasoning. Though the book is really more of a catalog than an interpretative history, Nye does state the thesis that "popular art has been an unusually sensitive and accurate reflector of the attitudes and concerns of the society for which it is produced."[14] Yet the book offers very few sensitive and accurate reflections of society. The few it does offer are tautological. Nye suggests, for example, that the unsettled, doubtful state of society after World War I had much to do with the theme and tone of the "hardboiled" detective story.[15] Yet other kinds of popular literature, with very different themes and tones, existed at the same time. In this case, and in other cases as well, Nye infers the state of society from the literature (or other art forms) itself.

The problem with all of these works lies in the fact that a tautological theory cannot be "falsified." In other words, no case can be conceived that would invalidate the argument. In the case of Depression movies, for instance, one cannot conceive of a film that would not reflect the society to the satisfaction of movie historians. If a very different sort of film had appeared, it would have brought along its own evidence that it reflected a social need or concern. Had film themes been completely random during the '30s they could still be explained just as easily along these lines. Such explanations are at best trivial, at worst tautological.

III

Most sophisticated students of popular culture avoid tautology by focusing specifically on the *audiences* of a particular art form rather than trying to say something in general about the spirit of the times. These scholars recognize that the great diversity of popular culture makes it something less than Nye's "sensitive and accurate reflector" of society. However, they do hold to the belief that popular magazines, movies, and the like at least reflect the artistic tastes of their particular audiences—though the psychological or sociological nature of the audiences' tastes, needs, and interests may be difficult to specify. This belief is based on the economic assumption that people are free to choose; therefore, their demand creates a supply of the artistic commodity they want.[16]

A good example of a scholar consciously confronting the problem of establishing the link between popular art and society is Andrew Bergman's *We're in the Money: Depression American and Its Films*. Bergman criticizes Siegfried Kracauer's pseudo-psychological study of films in Weimar Germany *(From Caligari to Hitler)*. Kracauer talks loosely of the "collective mentality" of Germany leading up to the Hitler take-over. In Bergman's view the book demonstrates "how difficult and dangerous it is to draw direct lines between moviemakers and 'popular thought.' "[17] Popular thought is too private and too diverse to be easily packaged as "collective mentality." Yet Bergman is willing to assume that the box office popularity of a film or type of film reflects the interests and preferences of the audience and thus in some ways of the culture. He concludes that the various "cycles" of film themes in the 1930s grew out of changing attitudes of the audience toward the Depression.[18]

One of the best recent studies of popular culture in America, John Cawelti's *Adventure, Mystery, and Romance*, also deals seriously with the problems of linking popular art and society. In his first chapter, Cawelti asks the key question: "Can we infer from the popularity of a work that it reflects public attitudes and motives, or is it impossible to go beyond the circular observation that a story is successful with the public because the public finds it a good story?"[19]The answer is not a simple one. As Cawelti explains, at least three different approaches have been applied to this rather impenetrable problem: (1) impact or effect theories; (2) deterministic theories; and (3) symbolic or reflective theories.[20] Cawelti finds serious fault with all three. Effect theories, as I have noted already, have been largely abandoned by communication researchers as too simple-minded. Deterministic theories, usually Marxist or Freudian, are also too simplistic in that they depend on *a priori* assumptions about human behavior. They also tend to equate literary experience with other experience, an equation which may be quite invalid psychologically. The symbolic approach has never been able to demonstrate convincingly that there is a direct connection between literary symbols and other forms of behavior.[21]

Despite these problems, Cawelti does assume that the popular arts reflect the culture in certain ways. And the key to understanding this link is the concept of "formula," which he develops in detail in the book. According to Cawelti, "formulas are ways in which specific cultural themes and stereotypes become embodied in more universal story archetypes."[22] A particular literary formula is successful, not because it creates or captures the collective mentality, but because it maximizes a great number of psychological, social, and artistic dynamics. He begins with the phenomenon of enjoyment:

While the psychology of literary response is certainly not without its mysteries, it seems safe to assume that people choose to read certain stories because they enjoy them. This at least gives us a straightforward if not simple psychological connection between literature and the rest of life.... The basic assumption of this theory is that conventional story patterns work because they bring into an effective conventional order a large variety of existing cultural and artistic interests and concerns.[23]

The bulk of the book is concerned with the definition of specific formulas, especially the detective story and the western. But underlying the descriptive chapters are several hypotheses about the relationship between formulaic literature and the culture that produces it.[24] The evidence that Cawelti marshals in support of these hypotheses is derived from a study of the formulas themselves. He hypothesizes, for example, that readers of formulaic detective stories "share a need for a temporary release from doubt and guilt, generated at least in part by the decline of traditional moral and spiritual authorities."[25] The strength of this inference rests upon the assumption that people have a need or desire for this particular kind of story, or they would not buy it. This is an economic assumption that may not be warranted.

IV

Cawelti's formula approach to the study of popular culture is clearly a useful method for the classification of popular story forms. He nicely defines and organizes concepts that other popular culture scholars have used haphazardly. He also makes a strong case (as does Nye) that enjoyment, escape, and fantasy are the central features of popular literature and art. But the argument that *specific* formulas, such as the detective story and the western, reflect the specific needs and interests of the audience is perhaps going a bit too far. Perhaps the assumption that people "get what they want" is unwarranted. Of course, the assumption is at least partly true, at least in America and Western Europe. But it may not be true enough to make the inferences that Cawelti and others make.

The task of the remainder of this paper will be to develop an alternative theory to explain the role of formula in popular magazines, books, movies, and the like. This theory will be based on the assumption that consumers may not always get what they want, that procducers of popular culture sometimes exert strong control over the market and use this control to their own advantage. I will offer a general hypothesis which, if true, would be more consistent with this theory than with Cawelti's. And I will offer some impressionistic evidence that this hypothesis is true.

A good case study of the limitations of the assumption that people get what they want is Theodore Greene's book, *America's Heroes: The Changing Models of Success in American Magazines*. Greene believes "that a more complex, more precise sense of changing values in our past can be gained from a sustained analysis of general magazines."[26] He assumes that the larger a magazine's circulation in a period, the more closely it reflected the attitudes and values of the nation in that period. The study is a content analysis of the four most popular magazines in four periods, 1787-1820, 1894-1903, 1904-1913, and 1914-1918. By focusing on the kinds of people treated in biographies in these magazines, Greene hopes to infer something about the characteristics of "America's heroes." Briefly, he finds a decline in the importance of individualism in the American hero by 1918.[27] In the period 1787-1820, the typical hero of magazine biographies was something of a patriot, a gentleman, and a scholar. From 1894-1903, the hero was a Napoleonic individualist, the master of his environment. From 1904-1913, the individualistic hero was more socially conscious and was likely to have been a politician or social reformer. In the period 1914-1918, the hero was no longer an individualist at all but was now an organization man.

Greene infers from all this that these were America's heroes and that these heroes reflected popular values and ideals. Even if Greene's assumption that popular magazines reflected popular values is accepted, his conclusions remain unsupported. First, he never offers any reason for believing that the *biographies* were part of what made these magazines popular. Biographies were a small and decreasing part of the content of these magazines over the years. They may have been highly unrepresentative of popular content, and we would never know it. Second, Green's last period of study, 1914-1918, was a time of war. At best all he has found in the end is that individualism decreased and group solidarity increased in wartime. This is a well-known phenomenon, and Greene's re-discovery of it adds little to our understanding of the general trend in individualism in popular thinking over time—which is what he set out to study.

But suppose that Greene's assumption that general magazines reflected popular values is not valid. Suppose we assume instead that magazines did provide their readers light, bright entertainment, but that the specific values conveyed were those of the publishers and not necessarily of the audience. The evidence collected by Greene himself seems much more consistent with this view than with his view. Greene never seems to ponder the significance of the fact that the publishers of the magazines in each period looked remarkably like the heroes of the biographies. In summarizing changes in the business of publishing over time, Greene writes:

The economics of magazine publishing passed from a stage of virtual patronage to one of independent entrepreneurship and finally to that of large corporate organizations catering to mass audiences for the benefit of other large corporate advertisers. The editors of magazines changed from independent professional men to independent businessmen and finally to managers employed to keep the constituent parts of vast publishing empires running profitably.[28]

This might just as well be a summary of the changing characteristics of the heroes. In the period 1787-1820, Greene finds "magazines by gentlemen, for gentlemen, and containing biographies of gentlemen." In the 1890s, he finds "energetic entrepreneurs ambitiously carving out successful careers in the promising new field of popular magazines." In the early 1900s, he finds magazines dominated by independent publishers and socially-conscious writers, such as Steffens, Tarbell, and Sullivan. After 1914, he notes that magazines were becoming large-scale organizations dominated by advertisers, managers, and other organization men.[29] These changes in magazine management correspond almost exactly to changes in magazine biographies. Yet Greene never seems to get the point: The biographies are of the *publishers'* heroes.

Evidence abounds of the increasing market power of large magazines in the early twentieth century. This market power meant that supply need not have responded directly to demand, that magazines need not have closely reflected popular values. Greene himself notes that the rise of the popular mass magazines in the 1890s was first associated closely with price competition, not with competition in content.[30] By World War I, the concentration of national advertising in a handful of general magazines assured their success. They could offer a good product and more of it at a lower cost.[31] They had only to offer what the people would accept, not necessarily what the people wanted. Interestingly, Greene is aware that the content of large magazines came to be more and more in tune with advertisers' values.[32] Yet he resists the implication. The data that he himself collects are much more consistent with an assumption of market control by mass magazine publishers than with the assumption that the values in popular magazines responded in a free market to the values of the American people.

Greene's book, as well as the work of Cawelti, Nye, and others, is marred by a faulty understanding of the economics of popular culture. The producers of popular literature and art will, almost invariably, attempt to maximize their profits. But this does not mean they will necessarily "give the people what they want." In broadcasting, and to a lesser extent in publishing, much of the expense of production goes into the making of the first "unit." Each additional copy of a book, magazine, record, or picture-print sold costs comparatively little to make.[33] In broadcasting, the cost of delivering a program to an additional listener is zero.[34] Furthermore, for media that depend on advertising and that can increase their ad rates with increased circulation, marginal revenues actually increase as marginal costs decrease. In such situations, economies of scale are very large and very important. The incentive is to produce a lot of the same thing—to circulate each book, magazine, or television show as widely as possible. Each new sale at the margin is largely profit. It was the publishers of the new mass-circulation magazines of the 1890s—S.S. McClure, Frank Munsey, Cyrus Curtis—who first learned this simple lesson in the economics of publishing and advertising.[35] It was the builders of the three broadcasting networks in the twentieth century who refined the techniques to a precise and exceedingly lucrative science.

Of course, publishing is not a classic monopoly industry for several reasons. First, people prefer and will, within limits, pay for deviations from a standardized product. Second, most advertisers have an incentive to concentrate their efforts on specialized segments of the general public. Third, and perhaps most important, paper, ink, postage, and diesel fuel are not free and have boosted costs greatly in recent years. Nevertheless, the decreasing-cost character of publishing (especially ad-based publishing) has fostered at least a measure of oligopoly in most sectors of the industry today, and was even more important in the past, when mass magazines carried the national advertising now carried by television. It can safely be said that in most cases the aim of a profit maximizer has always been to standardize the product, to control risk and thus control initial costs, and to expand to the limit sales of each type of product. In the area of popular culture, what would best serve these interests? The answer is clear: formula production.

What I am proposing might be called a "risk theory" of formula in popular literature and art.[36] At one extreme, each consumer in the country would probably like to have his own individual style of popular art. At the other extreme, each producer would like to sell the exact same product to everyone. The compromise is the formula. A formula is something the audience will accept. The producer will avoid risk by staying with the "acceptable," though this may only approximate what the people "really want." In sticking with tested formulas (or imposing them), the producer lowers costs by standardizing production, and he avoids risk. Revenue will also be steady or increasing because the market has already been established (or "softened" as they sometimes, revealingly, say). The writer of formula stories has the same advantages. Writing formula stories is low cost (in time especially) and low risk since a market already exists. All the most prolific writers of fiction have written to formula. For both publisher and writer, formula stories may not be run-away bestsellers, but they usually will not be complete flops either. Minimum risk means steady profits. Consumers have their own risk calculus. They may not get exactly what they want in a particular formula, but at least they know what to expect. They won't be completely disappointed.

This concern with producer control of the content of popular culture is not new, of course, though it has been neglected by some of the historians of popular culture working today.[37] Gilbert Seldes makes the point in a critique of television content. It is misleading to argue, he says, that television gives the people what they want:

> The average man does not know the specific way in which his wants may be satisfied. He shops around among the entertainment offered to him. The desire for "escape" may be satisfied by a western movie or a slapstick farce or a polite comedy.... By offering their wares, the mass media create audiences. When the wares are withdrawn, the audiences cease to exist; they become only potential audiences. When the wares which could satisfy a particular want are not offered and others are offered in profusion, the latent desire for the unoffered kind may dwindle or disappear.[38]

In other words, all we really know is that people want to be entertained. They may choose the specific formulas they do partly because they have little choice and partly because they don't want to risk something new.

The main argument here is that formulas are largely the creation of producers rather than audiences, that producers frequently are not under strong market pressures from audiences, and hence formulas are, if anything, more likely to reflect producers' rather than audiences' values. A key hypothesis can be posed that will allow a test of this theory against the theory that formulas reflect audience needs and desires, as stated by Cawelti, Nye, and others. The hypothesis is this: *The greater the market power a producer has (the greater the opportunity to control risk), the tighter and more standardized will be the formulas.*[39]

Neither Nye's nor Cawelti's theories would predict the relationship posed by this hypothesis. If formula is the product of audience tastes and needs, it should have nothing to do with producer market control. If producers are engaged in giving the people what they want, the organization of production should have little impact. The evidence, however, is otherwise. The business history of book and magazine publishing, film making, song selling, comic stripping, and radio and television broadcasting provides evidence in support of this hypothesis.

As book publishing became more consolidated and "rationalized" in the twentieth century, the market power of the producers increased in some lines of popular book publishing and the formulas became more predictable and rationalized. The popular formulas of the nineteenth century—family romance, historical romance, and the like—seem to have been broader, looser categories than the tight twentieth-century formulas such as the classic western, the detective story, and the "hardboiled" detective story. At the same time, through massive advertising campaigns, book clubs, saturation paperback distribution, phoney bestseller lists, and the like, publishers were able increasingly to control the market and to create demand. Even James Hart admits that demand has sometimes followed supply in twentieth-century publishing.[40] A particularly good example of market power in action is the career of Edward Stratemeyer. As Stratemeyer's syndicate came to dominate the juvenile field in the early twentieth century, the juvenile formulas became tighter than ever. Stratemeyer used assembly-line techniques to turn out hundreds of volumes of the Rover Boys, Tom Swift, the Hardy Boys, and other famous series.[41] It was a publisher's dream come true: low cost, low risk, high volume, steady profit. The key was tight, easily duplicated formulas.

The history of the rise and fall of the mass magazine in the twentieth century also offers evidence to suggest the connection between market power and formula. In the pre-World War II era, when giants like *Life, Look, Colliers,* and the *Saturday Evening Post* dominated the magazine market through their control of national advertising, the formulas were quite standardized: light fiction, news and people features, news and feature photography, and bland editorials. The aim of the mass magazines was to offend as few people as possible, to serve the status quo, to stick with the tried and the true. All the mass magazines were highly imitative in the manner that the television networks are today.[42] The national magazines not only adhered to tested formulas in their stories and features, they also frequently reflected directly the interests and values of the publishers and large advertisers. Theodore White, for example, tells about his days on *Collier's* in the mid-1950s when he did two kinds of stories, political and advertising. The political stories were those he wanted to do; the advertising stories were those he had to do from time to time to keep some big advertiser happy. If travel and airline advertising were falling off a bit, he was assigned to do an aviation story, and the aviation industry was duly notified of *Collier's* continued interest and devotion.[43]

Television destroyed the market power of the large national magazines in the 1950s and '60s. As general national advertising moved out of the magazine field into television, the publication of mass-circulation national magazines became uneconomical.[44] The market power of the large magazine producers declined, and the magazine industry became increasingly fragmented. The industry itself did not die, however; in some ways it was revitalized. There had always been specialized magazines. But with the death of the giants, the market for these smaller magazines with specialized content for specialized audiences boomed in the 1960s and '70s. Some observers of the magazine industry, such as Roland Wolseley, talk about the impact on the magazine market of the changing tastes of the American reader, as if audiences themselves grew less standardized after the 1950s.[45] This may have an element of truth to it. But surely the more important change was in the magazine industry, not in the magazine audience. Readers accepted the standardized formulas of the mass magazines as a compromise between preference and price. A formula from the heyday of *Life, Look,* and *Post* did not necessarily reflect the specific values or interests of what was really a heterogeneous mass audience; it merely did not offend.

The history of film making in America also tends to support the hypothesis that market power breeds standardization and formula. Movie making is expensive, and as the great studios began to monopolize production and distribution in the 1920s, they sought ways to avoid risk. As Russel Nye puts it: "With millions riding on each major picture, studios could afford few mistakes; like other industries they had to standardize the product to minimize risks and maximize profits."[46] The main techniques of standardization were the "star" system and formula stories.[47] The years of the greatest market power of the studios, the 1930s and '40s, were also the years of the tightest formulas. With the rise of independent production in the late 1950s and '60s, and the outlawing of distribution controls such as block-booking, the formulas loosened considerably. Today the old studios have less market power, and films are much more diverse and non-formulaic than in the 1930s and '40s.

It also seems likely that during the height of studio power in the 1930s, the movies more clearly than ever reflected the values of the producers. Andrew Bergman argues persuasively that in the '30s "the movies made a central contribution toward *educating* [my italics] Americans in the fact that wrongs could be set right within their existing institutions."[48] Even the gangster films portrayed something like a traditional American success model. In an era of fairly popular radicalism, the movies continued to reflect the conservative values of the monopolistic, capitalistic studios.[49]

Even the usually forgotten history of popular songs lends some support to the hypothesis that increased market control leads to tighter formulas. Song writing and selling has never been tightly controlled by an oligopoly like the movie studios. And as a result there has been much more diversity and less formula. But when a sector of the music industry has been able to organize and rationalize its production and distribution techniques to gain some market control, the tendency has been for formula to tighten. A good example is the control Tin Pan Alley had over popular song writing and sheet music sales in the 1890s and early 1900s.[50] In recent decades, the large recording companies have wielded greater market power at some times than at other times, and pop music and rock 'n' roll has been more formulaic during the periods of greater control. Like other popular culture producers, the contemporary pop music industry has tried its best to restrict the market and to conventionalize its output, but with only moderate success.[51]

The business history of the comic strip is similar to that of movies. Again, the tightness of the formula corresponds to the market power of the producers. Comic strips are contemporaries of movies, beginning in American newspapers in the late 1890s. For comic strips the great age of diversity was 1900-1910. One history calls it

a great age, filled with astonishing innovations, exciting experiments, and daring attempts. This period of 1900-1910 is considered by some to be the golden age of the comic strip. In any event it was the golden age of the cartoonists, who were not yet laboring under the difficulties nowadays imposed upon them and who were able to give free rein to their originality, talent, and imagination.[52]

Then came the syndicates. As in any decreasing cost industry, the tendency is toward consolidation, standardization, and expansion of sales. Most of the strips had been created by local newspaper artists. Now they were taken up by big business and marketed nationwide. And as a result American comics became increasingly formulaic. The aim, as usual, was not to give the people what they wanted, but to give them what they would accept—and to displease no one. Comics even took up movie formulas.[53] As the power of the great syndicates has declined somewhat in the last twenty years or so, several very different, very innovative strips have emerged and have proven quite popular.

The history of radio and television broadcasting may provide the best evidence that market power is associated with tight formula. Much of the critical writing about television today deals with the lack of diversity in its programming, the unrelenting sameness of its formulas. The very same charges were made against radio forty years ago. In both cases the same villains are pointed out: the networks. As radio and television programming came to be dominated by the three great networks, program content became more stereotyped and predictable and formulas became more rigid. Despite an explicit FCC policy goal favoring diversity in programming, the networks have long persisted in the production of the most standardized and formulaic of all popular arts. Why? To some observers, network behavior smacks of a sinister conspiracy. Bryce Rucker writes:

The networks have stifled competition, used their tools to propagandize for and against causes, formed large holding corporations which supply their own needs, built industrial empires whose tentacles penetrate every sphere of commerce; they wield tremendous political influence, wheedle from the government rights and concessions private citizens could not hope to win, pressure public opinion to do their bidding—the charges are endless.[54]

Though all these charges are probably as true today as they were ten years ago when Rucker made them, conspiracy theories are not needed to explain network behavior in programming. Since television broadcasting is what economists call a "public good" (i.e., it costs nothing, or almost nothing, to add another consumer because consumption does not "use up" the product), there are enormous economies of scale. Audience-maximizing equals profit-maximizing. The struggle for the One Big Audience coupled with the drive to avoid risk has led the networks, logically and inexorably, into program duplication and dependence on formulas.[55] As formulas evolve gradually on one network, they are seized quickly by the other two. More than in any other popular medium, the need is not necessarily to please but to avoid giving offense.

It seems likely that a relaxation of network control would mean a relaxation of formula programming. At least this is the consensus of most advocates of expanding channels through cable television.[56] This would be the other side of the coin. If market power breeds standardization and formula, competition should breed diversity.

V

The argument presented in this paper does not hold that people do not enjoy popular magazines, books, and television shows. Nor does it hold that audience preferences have no influence over what is produced. In most areas of popular culture, there is a spectrum of choice, and the consumer can indeed vote with his dollars. The choices available are greater in some fields (such as books and modern magazines) than in others (such as movies and television). What this argument does hold, however, is that the economic characteristics of popular culture give the producers a great incentive to standardize and formula-ize the product. And the business history of popular culture seems to indicate that this incentive has had its effect. Oligopoly and market power seem to have been associated with more standardization and more rigid story formulas.[57] Systematic empirical research is needed, however, to give this hypothesis a genuine test.

The implication of this argument for the study of literary formulas is obvious. Formulas, of course, are shaped by the culture that produces them, and they nicely serve what is probably the necessary purpose of balancing novelty with familiarity.[58] Cawelti's explication of the psychological role of conventional forms in general is persuasive. But specific formulas are not shaped directly by audience preferences. They emerge in the contention between consumers and producers, whose interests and whose preferences are not the same. The use of standardized formulas will evolve differently in a competitive market compared with a tightly controlled market like television or pre-television national magazine publishing.

What we require is a more sophisticated understanding of the interaction between consumers and producers in the creation of popular literature and art. This creation is a complex process of communication that is only partly economic. But economic factors cannot be ignored. Cawelti, Nye, and others concentrate their efforts on explaining *what* popular culture is, rather than on explaining *how* it is created. They assume it is somehow created in response to audience needs and desires. But producers, like audiences, also have needs and desires, and in the real world of business the customer is not always right.

Notes

[1]Bruce Kuklick, "Myth and Symbol in American Studies," *American Quarterly*, XXIV (Oct., 1972), 445; Donald Dunlop, "Popular Culture and Methodology," *Journal of Popular Culture*, IX (Fall, 1975), 381.

[2]I.C. Jarvie, *Movies and Society* (New York: Basic Books, 1970), pp.xiii, 6-11; Andrew Tudor, *Image and Influence: Studies in the Sociology of Film* (New York: St. Martin's Press, 1975), chapter 4.

[3]Harold D. Lasswell, *Propaganda Techniques in the World War* (New York: Alfred A. Knopf, 1927), p.221. This stage of mass communication research is summarized in Melvin L. DeFleur and Sandra Ball-Rokeach, *Theories of Mass Communication* (3rd ed.; New York: David McKay, 1975), chapter 6.

[4]See, for example, the essays of Dwight Macdonald, Ortega y Gasset, T.W. Adorno, Irving Howe, and others in Bernard Rosenberg and David Manning White, eds., *Mass Culture: The Popular Arts in America* (Glencoe, Ill.: The Free Press, 1957).

[5]See DeFleur and Ball-Rokeach, *Theories*, chapter 7; R.Serge Denisoff, "Content Analysis: The Achilles Heel of Popular Culture," *Journal of Popular Culture*, IX (Fall, 1975), 457-58. For reviews of recent mass communication research projects that suggest the diversity and complexity of communication effects, see Sidney Kraus and Dennis Davis, *The Effects of Mass Communication on Political Behavior* (University Park: Penn State University Press, 1976); George Comstock, *et al.*, *Television and Human Behavior* (New York: Columbia University Press, 1978); Paul M. Hirsch, Peter V. Miller, and F. Gerald Kline, *Strategies for Communication Research* (Beverly Hills, Calif.: Sage Publications, 1978).

[6]James D. Hart, *The Popular Book: A History of America's Literary Taste* (Berkeley and Los Angeles: University of California Press, 1961), pp.283 and 285. The book was originally published in 1950.

[7]*Ibid.*, p.86ff.

[8]*Ibid.*, p.104.

[9]*Ibid.*, pp.283-88.

[10]Lewis Jacobs, *The Rise of the American Film* (New York: Teachers College Press, 1968), p.506 The book was originally published in 1939.

[11]*Ibid.*, p.536.

[12]Arthur Knight, *The Liveliest Art: A Panoramic History of the Movies* (New York: Macmillan, 1957), pp.257 and 260. This same kind of argument can be found in much recent writing on film history published in journals such as the *Journal of Popular Film*.

[13]Pierre Couperie and Maurice C. Horn, *et al.*, *A History of the Comic Strip* (New York: Crown Publishers, 1968), p.173.

[14]Russel Nye, *The Unembarrassed Muse: The Popular Arts in America* (New York: Dial Press, 1970), p.4.

[15]*Ibid.*, p. 257.

[16]It has become customary for writers on popular culture history to include an economic caveat—to remind the reader that popular art forms are produced to make money. But the implications of this caveat are not usually explored. Usually something like a free market is assumed. See, for example, David Manning White and John Pendleton, eds., *Popular Culture: Mirror of American Life* (Del Mar, Calif.: Publisher's, Inc., 1977), pp.viii—8; and Alan R. Havig, "American Historians and the Study of Popular Culture," *Journal of Popular Culture*, XI (Summer, 1977), 180.

[17]Andrew Bergman, *"We're in the Money: Depression America and Its Films* (New York: New York University Press, 1971), p.xiii; Siegfried Kracauer, *From Caligari to Hitler: A Psychological History of the German Film* (Princeton, N.J.: Princeton University Press, 1947).

[18]Bergman, *We're in the Money*, pp. xv-xvi. Other recent historians of film have also wrestled with the relationship between movies and audiences. See, for example, Robert Sklar, "Windows on a Made-Up World," in *Popular Culture: Mirror of American Life*; Sklar, *Movie-Made America: A Social History of American Movies* (New York: Random House, 1975), chapter 12; Tudor, *Image and Influence*, chapters 7-8; and Garth Jowett, *Film: The Democratic Art* (Boston: Little, Brown, 1976).

[19]John G. Cawelti, *Adventure, Mystery, and Romance: Formula Stories as Art and Popular Culture* (Chicago: University of Chicago Press, 1976), p.21. See also Cawelti, "Notes Toward a Typology of Literary Formula," *Indiana Social Studies Quarterly*, XXVI (Winter, 1973-74); and Cawelti, *The Six-Gun Mystique* (Bowling Green, Ohio: Bowling Green University Popular Press, 1971).

[20]Cawelti, *Adventure, Mystery, and Romance*, pp.21-22.

[21]*Ibid.*, pp.22-29.

[22]*Ibid.*, p.6.

[23]*Ibid.*, p.30.

[24]*Ibid.*, pp.35-36.

[25]*Ibid.*, p.104.

[26]Theodore P. Greene, *America's Heroes: The Changing Models of Success in American Magazines* (New York: Oxford University Press, 1970), p.8.

[27]*Ibid.*, p.335.

[28]*Ibid.*, p.7.

[29]*Ibid.*, pp.33, 59, 171, 290-91.

[30]*Ibid.*, p.65.

[31]*Ibid.*, p.289.

[32]*Ibid.*, p.287.

[33]Broadcasting and some kinds of publishing have some, though not all, characteristics of a "public good"—a good where the cost of production is independent of the number of consumers. See, for example, Bruce M. Owen, Jack H. Beebe, and Willard G. Manning, Jr., *Television Economics* (Lexington, Mass.: D.C. Heath, 1974), pp.15-16; Bruce M. Owen, *Economics and Freedom of Expression* (Cambridge: Ballinger, 1975), pp.16-20; and Roger G. Noll, Merton J. Peck, and John J. McGowen, *Economic Aspects of Television Regulation* (Washington: Brookings Institution, 1973), pp.10-11.

The theory of "public goods" has been worked out by economists over the past two decades, led by Paul Samuelson. See Paul Samuelson, "The Pure Theory of Public Expenditure," *Review of Economics and Statistics*, XXXVI (Nov., 1954); Samuelson, "Aspects of Public Expenditure Theories," *Review of Economics and Statistics*, XL (Nov., 1958); James Buchanan, *The Demand and Supply of Public Goods* (New York: Rand McNally, 1968); Jora R. Minasian, "Television Pricing and the Theory of Public Goods," *Journal of Law and Economics*, VII (Oct., 1967); and Harold Demsetz, "The Private Production of Public Goods," *Journal of Law and Economics*, XIII (Oct., 1970).

Very little attention has been paid in popular culture studies to the role of economic markets. One of the few studies is Paul DiMaggio, "Market Structure, the Creative Process, and Popular Culture: Toward an Organizational Reinterpretation of Mass Culture Theory," *Journal of Popular Culture*, XI (Fall, 1977), 436-52.

[34]Actually, even in broadcasting, where the public goods model is most appropriate, it does cost more to *attract* more viewers, but the assumption of no additional cost for an additional viewer is not far from reality. See Noll, Peck, and McGowen, *Economic Aspects*, pp.10-11, 11n.

[35]The best account of the rise of the national magazine in America is still Theodore Peterson, *Magazines in the Twentieth Century* (Urbana: University of Illinois Press, 1964), chapters 1-4.

[36]A similar economic analysis is developed by DiMaggio, "Market Structure," p.438.

[37]Cawelti is quite aware of the economics of formula production. (See *Adventure, Mystery, and Romance*, p.9) He does, however, neglect the implications of this economic factor. Some writers who do give more attention to the economics of audience-building are Tudor, *Image and Influence*, p.70; Dunlop, "Popular Culture and Methodology," p.378; and Herbert J. Gans, "The Creator-Audience Relationship in the Mass Media: An Analysis of Movie Making," in *Mass Culture: The Popular Arts in America*, pp.315-16. See also Gans, *Popular Culture and High Culture* (New York: Basic Books, 1974).

[38]Gilbert Seldes, "Media Managers, Critics, and Audiences," in *Sight, Sound, and Society: Motion Pictures and Television in America*, ed. by David Manning White and Richard Averson (Boston: Beacon Press, 1968), p.33. Former FCC Commissioner Nicholas Johnson states this position even more bluntly: "To say that current programming is what the audience 'wants' in any meaningful sense is either pure doubletalk or unbelievable naivete." *How to Talk Back to Your Television Set* (New York: Bantam Books, 1970), p.19. See also Jeffrey Schrank, *Snap, Crackle, and Popular Taste: The Illusion of Free Choice in America* (New York: Dell, 1977).

[39]DiMaggio, "Market Structure," p.438.

[40]Hart, *The Popular Book*, p.286. On the mass market paperback book industry in recent years see Clarence Petersen, *The Bantam Story: Thirty Years of Paperback Publishing* (revised

ed.; New York: Bantam Books, 1975).

[41]Nye, *The Unembarrassed Muse*, pp.76-87.

[42]Peterson, *Magazines in the Twentieth Century*, pp.445-46; Roland E. Wolseley, *The Changing Magazine: Trends in Readership and Management* (New York: Hastings House, 1973), p.34.

[43]Theodore H. White, *In Search of History: A Personal Adventure* (New York: Harper and Row, 1978), pp.410-15. See also Wolseley, *The Changing Magazine*, pp.68-69.

[44]The decline of the national magazines, described in most texts on American mass media, is nicely summarized by White, *In Search of History* pp.419-36. See also Otto Friedrich, *Decline and Fall* (New York: Harper and Row, 1970). It's the decline and fall of the *Saturday Evening Post*.

[45]Wolseley, *The Changing Magazine*, chapter 1.

[46]Nye, *The Unembarrassed Muse*, p.374.

[47]*Ibid.*, p.366. See also Robert Stanley, *The Celluloid Empire: A History of the American Motion Picture Industry* (New York: Hastings House, 1978).

[48]Bergman, *We're in the Money*, p.167.

[49]*Ibid.*, pp.167-73; Sklar, *Movie-Made America*, pp.196-97.

[50]Nye, *The Unembarrassed Muse*, pp.314-16. See also David Ewen, *All the Years of American Popular Music* (New York: Prentice-Hall, 1977).

[51]Nye, *The Unembarrassed Muse*, pp.358-59; Richard A. Peterson and David Berger, "Cycles in Symbol Production: The Case of Popular Music," *American Sociological Review*, 40 (1975), 158-73. See also Steve Chapple and Reebee Garofalo, *Rock 'n' Roll Is Here to Pay: The History and Politics of the Music Industry* (Chicago: Nelson-Hall, 1977).

[52]Couperie, Horn, *et al.*, *A History of the Comic Strip*, p.29.

[53]*Ibid.*, pp.45 and 61.

[54]Bryce W. Rucker, *The First Freedom* (Carbondale, Ill.: Southern Illinois University Press, 1968), p.140. See also Ben H. Bagdikian, *The Information Machines* (New York: Harper and Row, 1971), chapter 8.

[55]For good discussions of the economics of oligopolistic competition in television network programming see Owen, Beebe, and Manning, *Television Economics*, chapter 3; and Christopher H. Sterling and John M. Kittross, *Stay Tuned: A Concise History of American Broadcasting* (Belmont, Calif.: Wadsworth, 1978), pp.453-63. See also Owen, *Economics and Freedom of Expression*, chapter 3; Peter Steiner, "Program Patterns and Preferences, and the Workability of Competition in Radio Broadcasting," *Quarterly Journal of Economics*, LXVI (May, 1952); Jerome Rothenberg, "Consumer Sovereignty and the Economics of TV Programming," *Studies in Public Communication*, IV (Fall, 1962); John J. McGowen, "Competition, Regulation and Performance in Television Programming," *Washington University Law Quarterly* (Fall, 1967); and Harvey J. Levin, "Program Duplication, Diversity, and Effective Viewer Choices: Some Empirical Findings," *American Economic Review*, LXI (May, 1971). The classic work on oligopolistic competition is Harold Hotelling, "Stability in Competition," *The Economic Journal*, XXXIV (March, 1929).

A differing view that stresses the influence that audiences do have on producers can be found in Martin H. Seiden, *Who Controls the Mass Media: Popular Myths and Economic Realities* (New York: Basic Books, 1974).

[56]See Owen, Beebe, and Manning, *Television Economics*, chapter 5; and Noll, Peck, and McGowen, *Economic Aspects*, chapter 7.

[57]Paul DiMaggio makes a similar argument. See DiMaggio, "Market Structure," p.437.

[58]Cawelti, *Adventure, Mystery, and Romance*, p.1.

In the previous chapter, Nord introduced economic notions to be applied in the study of popular culture. In the present one, Gaye Tuchman uses a particular idea of "culture as resource" drawn from Raymond Williams and her own previous work to examine the selection of novel manuscripts in Victorian literature. This study, she demonstrates, shows how economic and cultural processes are embedded in one another. Gaye Tuchman is professor sociology at Queens College and the City University of New York Graduate Center.

19

CULTURE AS RESOURCE
Actions Defining the Victorian Novel

Gaye Tuchman

In *Marxism and Literature*, Raymond Williams offers a challenging reconceptualization of what orthodox Marxists term base and superstructure—or what
mainstream sociologists call society and culture. Following Gramsci, Williams
(1977: 76, 82) discards the 'proposition of a determining base and a determined
superstructure'. That notion, he argues, obfuscates 'specific and indissoluble real
processes'. It belittles the contribution and potentiality of human agency (cf.
Giddens, 1976). Most important, it ignores that economic and cultural processes
are simultaneously accomplished—or, in the terms Williams prefers, are produced
and reproduced—by the activities of 'practical consciousness'. Williams neither
defines practical consciousness nor tells us how to observe it.

I will provide an expanded illustration of practical consciousness in action by
examining some aspects of the production of mid-nineteenth-century novels. I will
focus upon the activities of John Morley, who recommended rejection or acceptance
of roughly 75 per cent of the novels submitted over the transom to London's
Macmillan and Company between November 1868 and the late 1880s.[1] I will argue
that, in the course of his work, Morley drew on notions of culture and aspects of
culture-producing institutions as resources with which to differentiate what we now
call high culture from what is today identified as popular culture. My use of the
term 'culture' is limited to these sociological categories or high culture and popular
culture and does not include notions of culture developed by anthropologists.[2]

My examination presupposes a theoretical perspective. I propose that the
institutions of the consciousness industry—Enzensberger's (1974) term for the
communications industry—may be seen as a framing or structuring of consciousness, and culture itself may be seen as a material resource. Let me explicate
these terms.

I prefer consciousness industry to communications industry, because it suggests
the phenomenon already nascent in the nineteenth century, that the media
propose ways of seeing or of framing the world that have the potential of becoming
modern myths. Contemporary media unite their markets in collective mourning,

---

[1] Discussion is based upon examination of Readers' Reports for 1867, 1868, 1877, 1878 and 1888 found in the
Macmillan Archives at the British Library. A quantitative analysis of the fate of over-the-transom manuscripts is
found in Tuchman and Fortin (1980). See also the discussion of these reports in Sutherland (1976).
[2] Two anthropological treatments of culture that raise many of the issues considered here are Sahlins (1976) and
Geertz (1973). I do not consider anthropological meanings of the term 'culture', since in the 1860s, 'art' and
'anthropological culture' had not yet been differentiated.

as occurs on the deaths of presidents; collective celebration, as in the United States bicentennial celebration; collective concern, such as that shown over the plight of the Iranian hostages. Like the nineteenth-century novels which explore 'the substance and meaning of community' and in the process helped to constitute the meaning of community (Williams, 1970: 11), these media portray the relationships among individuals and institutions. Most important, some people use them as both entertainment and tools with which to approach the problematics of everyday life. Some college students report, for instance, seeing analogies between a decision they face and the plot of a specific television episode. Psychiatrists report patients who compare their families to the idealized families characteristic of situation comedies in the 1950s. In the 1930s, literary critic Amy Cruse spoke of the eagerness with which in the 1880s she and her young friends consumed novels as philosophic and moral discussions—guides to life (Colby, 1970: 5). Inasmuch as the media are tools for understanding and for acting, they sell consciousness to 'consumers' conceived as 'markets'.

This notion of tool also informs my identification of culture as a material resource. I see culture as social presences differentially accessible to women and men of various social classes which may be used to construct both their identities and their social worlds. Indeed, this notion of culture as tool informs both common conceptions of the 'worth' of the humanities—high culture as an elucidation of life—and the 'worthlessness' of popular culture—television programs as lessons in crime for the uneducated. Just as nineteenth-century publishing includes a notion of readers as markets, so too these ideas about the worth of specific novels crop up in the readers' reports I will consider. Additionally, the idea of culture as tool appears in sociological discussions of class. Following Bourdieu, DiMaggio and Useem (forthcoming) write of high culture along this vein. They speak, for instance, of the cultural capital used by upper classes to maintain their position of power. They might equally well write of the stratification of cultural knowledge within other social classes or within hierarchical institutions.

The term 'structure or structuring of consciousness' is meant to capture this possibility. It suggests that cultural institutions are palimpsests, historically constructed and layered. These institutions are not simply parchments upon which society has writ. As with the palimpsest, at different historical moments, varying and even conflicting inscriptions may emerge and fade, battle for attention, provide or prevent clarity. The institutions themselves are formed by the stratified organization of work, including the stratified ability of social factors to exert human agency; by institutional goals and intents; by the product or commodity manufactured by the institutions; and by the intersection and interaction of the institutions with one another. Each of these factors both creates and is a product of consciousness; each is differentially accessible to other factors in a stratified work-setting; each is differentially accessible to members of the market(s) for which the product is intended.

I take these definitions to be responsive to Williams's treatment of practical consciousness, for in Williams's discussion 'practical consciousness' informs and is formed by productive and cultural processes. It constitutes and is constituted, as seen in the following excerpt on language and literature in which Williams comes closest to defining his concept:

. . . we can add to the necessary biological faculty of language as *constitutive* an equally necessary definition of language development—at once individual and social—as historically and socially *constituting*. What we can then define is . . . the *changing practical consciousness of human beings*, in which the evolutionary and historical processes can be given full weight, but also within which they can be distinguished in the complex variations of language use. It is from this theoretical foundation that we can go on to distinguish 'literature', in a specific socio-historical development of writing, from the abstract retrospective concept . . . which reduces it, like language . . . , to a function and then to a 'superstructural' by-product of collective labor (1977: 43, 44).

I would add two concepts: resource and limitation (Tuchman, 1978). Within the consciousness industry, people use both the culture that they and others produce and facets of the institution itself as resources, even as they must work within or combat institutional and cultural constraints upon their activities. Institutions differentially distribute these resources and limitations.

The increasingly complex structure of nineteenth-century publishing

Nascent aspects of the contemporary consciousness industry may be seen in the rôle of the publisher's reader in the production of the nineteenth-century novel.[3] Hired to advise about the quality and potential sales of manuscripts and sometimes to suggest revisions, these readers increased the internal bureaucracy of publishing firms and so also decreased the potentially direct relationship between authors and audience.[4] Equally important, the publisher's reader became a stand-in for the readers (audience) themselves. In their capacities as both potential judge of a manuscript's viability as a book and stand-in or substitute, the publisher's reader shaped manuscripts, shaped interpretations of the qualities constituting 'good' novels, and so (re)produced culture itself. The very existence of the publisher's reader, whether paid by a retainer or on a piece-work basis, anticipated the awesome separation of the author and the 'user' of culture characteristic of the division of labor in today's consciousness industries.

As is the case of any institutional innovation, the estrangement of author from audience did not arise overnight. For instance, in the mid-eighteenth century, some publishing practices, including new methods of distribution, increased the separation of author and audience. Fewer patrons supported authors.[5] Publishing by subscription—as many as 100 or more patron-readers promising to buy a book upon its issue—began to be replaced by direct payment from publisher-booksellers who singly or jointly purchased copyrights for generally small sums. Authors were at the mercy of publishers. Although some eighteenth-century authors earned significant sums, by and large to be a novelist required independent wealth, the willingness to be a 'Grub Street hack', or the desperation and fortitude to seek one's fortunes with one's pen. This was attempted by some bankrupt industrialists in the 1790s and more frequently by impoverished married ladies and widows who sought to avoid the socially ambiguous position of governess or even more demeaning forms of wage-labor (Tompkins, 1961). Indeed, the very term 'Grub Street hack' with its denotation of pen for hire indicates the dependence of many authors upon the bookseller-publishers of the day. So too, one then common

---

[3] See in particular Sutherland (1976) and Gettman (1960: 187–230), upon whom I heavily rely.
[4] I will use the term 'audience' for those who read books, so as not to confuse the general reader and the publisher's reader. Good material on authors and readers is found in Collins (1928) and Mumby and Norrie (1974).
[5] Material in this paragraph is drawn from Collins (1928), Tompkins (1961) and Mumby and Norrie (1974).

practice reveals both the disdain of publishers for both author and audience and the publishers' rôle as intermediary: if a book failed to sell, a publisher might reissue it with a new title or reassign authorship to yet another pseudonym.

The estrangement of authors from readers (audience) is, of course, implicit in the use of pseudonyms, a practice which also bespeaks the problematic status of writing. Some authors guarded their identity from their publisher. For instance, some women novelists communicated with the Minerva Press through advertisements in newspapers (Blakey, 1939: 49). Fanny Burney arranged for the publisher to whom she had submitted *Evelina* to leave word of its acceptance or rejection at a coffee house and sent her brother in disguise to retrieve the message (Hemlow, 1958: 60).[6]

Additionally, new methods of distribution contributed to the separation of author and audience (reader). Consider the circulating library which 'rented' books for a set yearly fee. Invented in the 1740s, the circulating library facilitated reading by the expanding middle class, since books were too expensive for most of these people to buy. In the 1770s,

[i]f a man in the lower bracket of the white neck-cloth class—an usher at a school for instance, or a merchant's clerk—had a taste for owning books, he would have had to choose between buying a newly published quarto volume and a good pair of breeches (each cost from 10s to 12s), or between a volume of essays and a month's supply of tea and sugar for his family of six (2s6d). If a man bought a shilling pamphlet he sacrificed a month's supply of candles. A woman in one of the London trades . . . could have bought a three-volume novel in paper covers only with the proceeds of a week's work (Altick, 1957: 51, 52).

Although the circulating library increased readership, by the mid-1880s Mudie's Circulating Library, which dominated the Victorian distribution system, also acted as censor and could virtually control the sales and so the form and content of a novel.[7] Mudie's Circulating Library maintained publishers' profits. The standard price of a three-volume novel, 31s 6d, was exhorbitant for all but the very wealthy. Rather than risking 'mass' publication at a 'moderate' price, publishers would be guaranteed a profit if Mudie's purchased a sufficient number of copies at a high price, albeit a negotiated discount. Indeed, Mudie's might buy half a standard run of a novel that Charles Edward Mudie expected to be popular.

Literary historians (especially Gettman, 1960; Griest, 1970; Sutherland, 1976) stress that as a powerful distributor, Mudie's helped to shape the novel. Although some two-, four- and five-volume novels were published in the mid-nineteenth century, Mudie's preferred the three-volume novel and so publishers could minimize economic risk by producing 'three-deckers'. The form constrained authors. Some struggled to push their work into three volumes, while others worked to expand slim material. Mudie's insisted that the volumes he carried could be read by adolescent girls and servants. Authors were forced to comply. Geraldine Jewsbury revised a passage of *Zoë* to provide the heroine with 'a more liberal distribution of spotted muslin' (Tillotson, 1962: 60, 61) and even then Mudie's thought her novel potentially injurious to the young and so condemned it. In 1894, after the death of the three-volume novel, finally killed by Mudie's decision to discontinue stocking that form, Kipling wrote an often-quoted satire on what Mudie's forbade:

[6] It is even more significant that Burney hid from her family the fact that she was writing a novel. Also, it is incorrect to assume that nineteenth-century authors used pseudonyms as a common practice, when dealing with their publishers. The Macmillan Archives reveal that almost all authors corresponded and submitted work in their own names.

[7] These comments are drawn heavily from Griest (1970) and Gettman (1960).

We asked no social questions—we pumped no hidden shame—
We never talked obstetrics when the little stranger came:
We left the Lord in Heaven, we left the fiends in Hell . . .
No moral doubt assailed us, so when the port we neared.
The villain had his flogging at the hangway and we cheered
                                                (Quoted in Gettman, 1960: 245).

Ultimately, as we shall see, the power of Mudie's—his hegemony—was both a resource and a constraint upon the publisher's reader, an added element to be taken into account when judging manuscripts.

The rise of the circulating library was gradual. So too, the activities of the publisher's reader and his or her intercession between author and audience slowly became more important. As early as 1799, Dr John Aiken served as a reader for Cadell and Davies. William Gifford started reading for John Murray's firm in 1808. These and other early publisher's readers brought as qualifications having been 'bred up in the profession or trade of publishing' (Gettman, 1960: 189). Accordingly, one may infer that they were viewed as extensions of their employers, qualified because they were 'familiar with the problems involved in the making and selling of books' (ibid.).

By the 1850s, the publisher's reader was also said to serve as an extension of the general reader (audience). Many were authors. Publisher George Smith fed Charlotte Brontë one volume at a time of Thackeray's *Esmond* 'so as to get the library reader's response' (Sutherland, 1976: 109). In the 1860s, novelist and *Athenaeum* critic Geraldine Jewsbury read for Bentley's; poet and novelist George Meredith for Chapman and Hall; critic and editor John Morley for Macmillan. Needless to say, these recognized authors are hardly the typical library reader. Instead, they must judge quality and give their assessment of what a typical library reader's response to a manuscript might be. On occasion, they based their recommendations on their own experiences as authors. After Mudie's distaste for her novel *Zoë*, Jewsbury demanded revisions in manuscripts whose morality Mudie might condemn. Meredith's recommendations to Thomas Hardy for revising his first novel, *The Poor Man and the Lady* echo criticisms of Meredith's own earlier *The Ordeal of Richard Feverel* (ibid.: 216). Author-readers stand between author and audience.

These publisher's readers are theoretically significant in three ways pertinent to framing consciousness. First, as Habermas (1964) might put it, this increasingly complex structure of publishing transforms a public in the eighteenth-century sense of educated people who know one another and personally discuss ideas and policies into a 'market'—a category of people whose tastes are presupposed by industrial forces and who do not necessarily know one another or get to make a choice as to what will be published. To be sure, many writers are from the same social class as some readers of their work. Also, authors read one another's books and essays and so constituted audiences for one another, even publics. Indeed, some of them had a major editorial influence on their colleagues' manuscripts. Others presented their work to friends or neighbors who might be deemed a 'common reader'. But, the business of publishing, both production and distribution, is increasingly geared toward the formation of a market. And, the concepts 'market' and 'public' connote different formations of consciousness.

Second, whether the publisher's reader earns additional income as a critic, journalist, editor or novelist, the institutionalization of the occupation 'reader' feeds the development of criticism as the activity of literary middlemen. These readers are *de facto* critics. In *The Rise and Fall of the Man of Letters,* John Gross (1970) stresses how literary criticism became a profession in nineteenth-century Britain—much as other cultural activities were wrested from the domain of talented amateurs. Critics, such as Macmillan's reader John Morley, were to carve out a 'Great Tradition' of English literature that eventually reified literature, deprecated excluded writers and speakers, and by identifying the critic rather than the novelist as both author and authority, even deprecated those whose writing was included in the Great Tradition (see Williams, 1977: 43, 44). The critic is to assume that authority of interpreter of the world, as frequently demonstrated by the articles in today's *New York Review of Books.* There the ostensible *raison d'être* of reviewing is transformed into an occasion for a critic to make comments about the topic of an author's book. Here, too, the distinction between critic-authority and author-authority captures a shift in the structure of consciousness.

Third, the publisher's readers themselves reproduce the hierarchies within the publishing industry; that is, they reproduce the existing stratification of culture. Put somewhat differently, publishers choose readers with an eye to their own particular market(s), as well as to pleasing Mudie's. Primarily a specialist in fiction, much of it consumed by women, Bentley employed Jewsbury at a set sum for every manuscript reviewed. By the 1870s, Bentley also paid five other women-novelists to read manuscripts on a piece-work basis. However, Macmillan and Company, which specialized in non-fiction but had a substantive fiction list, resisted the requests of women novelists to serve as readers—even when approached by best-selling women-authors whose work it published.

Finally, when considering this increased industrial configuration, one must note that the novel itself was becoming increasingly differentiated. Literary historians (see, e.g., Tillotson, 1962) agree that from 1840 through 1890, the novel was in the process of becoming the prototypical bourgeois form and that the popular novel was becoming separate from the high-culture novel. It is dangerous to reify that split. Consider Mrs Oliphant's satiric *Miss Majoribanks* (1866). At the time of its publication, it was considered a popular novel, but Q. D. Leavis (1969) has recently termed it a minor classic, i.e. a high-culture novel. Yet, the very existence of such a work as Matthew Arnold's *Culture and Anarchy* (1869), with its advocacy of diffusing 'the best knowledge' and the 'best ideas' to the middle classes in order to edify them socially, politically and culturally (in Arnold's work the three are clearly intertwined) is helping to produce the concept of high-culture as 'culture' by naming it and the phenomena with which it is associated. Of course, Arnold is today held to be *the* Victorian critic and *Culture and Anarchy* was published just after John Morley had joined the firm of Macmillan and Company. Thus, to view practical consciousness in action, it is more than appropriate to turn to how in the 1860s, the publisher's reader helped to constitute a concept of 'culture'—of what 'good' literature is.

I have stressed that the rôle of publisher's reader was part of the increased complexity of publishing and participated in the increased estrangement of the author from his market. In making judgements, these publisher's readers used notions about both those industrial configurations and culture as resources and constraints for determining the fate of manuscripts. However, merely to state that the publisher's readers, like publishing itself, blend art and commerce is to miss the significance of their activities. Rather, in the selection of manuscripts, cultural and economic processes are embedded in one another. They perpetually inform and shape one another, as seen in the Reader's Reports submitted by John Morley to Macmillan and Company. Since a firm and its readers are themselves part of a stratified industry, I will describe Macmillan and Company and John Morley before turning to Morley's reports.

Macmillan and Company

Most of the successful nineteenth-century publishers became established after the British crisis of the 1820s, when many houses had failed, and after the invention of new printing technologies and the formulation of new tax policies for paper. For instance, Chapman and Hall, which specialized in circulating library novels, started in 1830. And, in 1832, after three years as Henry Colburn's junior partner, Richard Bentley founded the house of Bentley, which mainly published fiction. Both Chapman and Hall and Bentley's started in London. Macmillan was founded in Cambridge in 1843 by two Scots brothers Daniel and Alexander.[8] (Since Daniel died young, my future references to Macmillan indicate Alexander.)

Although Macmillan and Company had its idiosyncrasies, by and large its activities followed the general pattern of publishing at the time. Accordingly, it is a good house to study sociologically. Equally important, because it was an elite firm, it displayed concerns pertinent to the separation of popular and high-culture novels. Literary historians describe Macmillan and Company not only as a leading publisher of non-fiction, but also as one of the seven Victorian houses whose novels are read today. (Two of the others are Bentley and Chapman and Hall, to whose readers' reports I will make passing references.)

From its founding, Macmillan's was an academic house. In 1843, the brothers founded a bookstore and drew on its scholarly clientele as authors and as contacts to meet others authors. Alexander held 'at homes' to enlarge the circle of intellectual acquaintances. Like the brothers, some of their authors were advocates of muscular Christianity. For instance, the Macmillans were friends with the Kingsley brothers. In 1853, Alexander was to publish Charles Kingsley's *Westward Ho!* and for many years, Henry Kingsley contributed to *Macmillan's Magazine.* In 1843, these publishing ventures lay ahead. But, from the first, Macmillan associated with intellectuals and academicians and engaged in such academic enterprises as publishing prize essays and poems. From 1843, until a 'friendly parting in 1881' (Morgan, 1943: 68), the firm was the home of Oxford's Clarendon Press. The association was sufficiently meaningful to be mentioned prominently in the firm's advertisements.

Macmillan's growth followed the logic of economic expansion as Alexander sought to produce the recognized components of a top publishing house. Successful publishing houses had magazines. They also reissued serialized stories as novels. In 1859, after several years of consciously working toward that aim, Alexander founded *Macmillan's Magazine* both to reap the profits of monthly circulation and to have its own potentially influential intellectual showcase. How much Macmillan cared about the quality of the magazine is indicated by his selection of its first editor. He was David Masson, one of the first professors of

---

[8] Material on Macmillan is drawn from Morgan (1943), Nowell-Smith (1967), Morley (1917), Packer (1963) and materials in the Henry A. and Alberta A. Berg Collection of the New York Public Library, as well as the Archives in the British Library. Some material here is also found in Tuchman and Fortin (1980).

English literature in Britain, and holder of successive prestigious posts at University College, London, and the University of Edinburgh. The second editor, George Grove, editor of *Grove's Dictionary of Music,* was a recognized intellectual highly praised in Victorian circles.

There was also profit and, increasingly, prestige in novels. From the 1840s, the proportion of published books that were novels increased rapidly. And, as mentioned, novels were in the process of becoming the dominant genre of that period. Macmillan at first issued a few novels that reflected Alexander's taste and contacts, such as *Westward Ho!* (1853) and Thomas Hughes's *Tom Brown's School Days* (accepted in 1857). In 1863, when the firm purchased John W. Parker's list upon his bankruptcy, it gained such financial staples as Charlotte Yonge's *Heir of Redclyffe,* as well as associations with some of Parker's authors. For instance, Yonge was to edit for Macmillan a religious series for children and, as reader, to review some religious works. That same year, Macmillan moved to London, the center of the publishing industry and much intellectual life, a change he had been working toward for some years. There, as in Cambridge, he maintained friendships with intellectuals.

John Morley also travelled in intellectual circles, although unlike that staunch Christian Alexander Macmillan, Morley's closest ties were with positivists, radicals and agnostics. Morley's friends included Leslie Stephen, George Meredith, George Lewes, whom he replaced as editor of *Fortnightly Review*, and John Stuart Mill at whose home he was a frequent guest for Sunday dinner. A solidly 'second-rank' man of letters in the estimation of John Gross (1970), Morley wrote intellectual biographies and books that might now be classified as works within the history of ideas. His life and activities were part and parcel of the growth of literature as a profession. For instance, in the 1870s, Morley edited for Macmillan the multi-volumed series 'English Men of Letters' which an *Athenaeum* critic correctly perceived as heralding an age of 'literary middlemen' (*Athenaeum*, 1878: 11). These volumes on noted writers were penned by then-famous writers, most of whom Morley knew personally. Additionally, Morley was a politician associated with Chamberlain. For years, he flirted with running for Parliament. His political career, like his literary career, was solidly second-rank, culminating in the title Viscount and the post of Secretary of State for India.

Needless to say, this somewhat formidable and often acerbic literary middleman was familiar with the prevailing standards for literature. In keeping with the dictates of his age and his own somewhat 'feminine sensibilities' (Hamer, 1968: 57), Morley deplored immodesty. Some scenes, his reader's reports comment, are 'too strong'. He praised faithfulness to life—'realistic' novels, 'true to nature' and displaying intellectual depth and good writing ('a practised hand'). He was also familiar with literary institutions, including the limitations Mudie's placed upon the novel, as were such other Macmillan employees as business-manager George Lillie Craik, who eventually married novelist Dinah Mulock.

Let me turn, then, to Morley's comments on manuscripts.[9] They reveal his typifications of all the actors in the literary system—Mudie's preferences, Alexander Macmillan's concerns, critics' potential responses, the tastes of readers and his assessment of authors and genres. Especially in his first years with the

[9] Morley's comments are found in a series of copybooks at the British Library. I shall, however, give references to his judgements by using the number assigned a manuscript in the Manuscript Ledgers, also at the British Library.

company, one sees Morley using his understandings of Macmillan's concerns about profit and prestige to impose his own notions of literature. These understandings, his typifications and his own reputation and position with literary and intellectual circles are Morley's resources.

Morley's reports on manuscripts

A learned man, Morley was ubiquitous. He read manuscripts in virtually every area except religion and technical aspects of science and medicine. Although most of the manuscripts submitted to Macmillan were non-fiction, Morley reviewed more fiction than non-fiction works. Apparently, whoever sorted manuscripts into those warranting immediate acceptance, those deserving immediate rejection and those which Morley should see found it easier to determine the quality of non-fiction than fiction (see Tuchman and Fortin, 1980). The pattern of sorting seems to reveal that the standards for judging the quality of non-fiction were more concrete, better developed and more generally known than were those for fiction.

Reviewing non-fiction, Morley concentrated upon both quality and potential profit. Needless to say, both concerns were interrelated. Generally, Macmillan strove to develop a profitable backlist and Alexander was willing to carry a book for decades until it caught on, if he was convinced of its intellectual contribution. One of his business strategies seems to have been investment in good non-fiction that might simply break even, or even show initial losses rather than turn a quick profit. Macmillan seems to have viewed his reputation as an economic asset. By issuing prestigious books, Macmillan announced to potential authors that his was the house to choose when mulling about the submission of a manuscript. He announced to libraries and readers (audience) that his were important books, works to stock or to borrow. Morley's reviews of non-fiction consistently display Macmillan's strategy. The phrase 'not suitable for your list' runs through his assessments of non-fiction. And, he comments with adequate frequency that a book will bring no profit but 'will be a credit to your list'.

Although concerned with potential profit, Morley did not advise Macmillan about the appropriate price for an author's copyright, as Geraldine Jewsbury would on occasion advise Bentley. For instance, in September 1867, Jewsbury told Bentley of Mr Fulham's 'Time Will Tell': 'You know whether Mr. Fulham's former novels have succeeded, if they have this is quite as good as any of them and you may take it,' if he does not want too much . . . '.[10] Similarly, she wrote of Miss Annie Thomas's 'Lance Urquant's Lover': 'It would be perhaps worth your while to take if the lady were not likely to require a large sum for the Ms!' (Bentley Archives, volume 98: 78). Paid on a piece-work basis for every report, frequently adding to her letter-reports the address of a friend she is to visit so that manuscripts may find her, Jewsbury depended for income on appearing to be indispensable. Paid on a retainer and keeping office-hours at Macmillan's, Morley may have delivered monetary estimates in the course of conversation and therefore they may not appear in his formal reports.

Nonetheless, when reviewing novels, Morley is concerned with profit. Simultaneously, he is locating the realistic novel as high culture, while trying to build the

[10] The archives of the house of Bentley, held at the British Library and other major research libraries, have been issued on microfilm by Chadwyck-Healey, Ltd. This quotation (Bentley Archives) is from vol. 98, p. 61, Part 1 of the microfilms. For a study of Jewsbury's reports, see Fahnestock (1973).

literary reputation of his employer's list. Mostly, Morley rejects manuscripts, including over 90 per cent of the novels he sees. Most of his comments, like those Jewsbury mailed to Bentley and Meredith entered in the copybook for Chapman and Hall, are negative and sometimes scathing. Here, too, Morley's reports seem to fit a pattern. According to Gettman (1960: 107), 'The employees at Chapman and Hall used to await the arrival of Meredith's reports with his pungent comments on poor work. Some of Miss Jewsbury's were equally incisive and sarcastic. She concluded her opinion of one novel with the statement, "Reading it is like walking thro' a field of stiff clay on a rainy day."'

Whether sarcastic or merely condemnatory, literary critic John Morley makes literary judgments. Countess von Bothemer's 'Strong Hands, Steadfast Hearts' is 'of a very conventional stamp' (manuscript no. 185). Morley ranks quality, calling Miss Rhodes's 'Ralph Redfern' 'a very fair novel of the second rank' (manuscript no. 43). He praises manuscripts for an ineffable presence of culture, saying of Mr H. Watherston's 'Gossamer': 'fair, but I don't find it remarkable in any respect. Of course, there are signs that the writer is a man of culture and the book is readable' (manuscript no. 6). Similarly, literary values supersede the profits to be gleaned from an author's popularity. Morley condemns Fanny Kemble's novel as an 'old ladies' gossip' in parts, 'an oasis of the possible in a desert of intolerable twaddle' (manuscript no. 2340). However, now and then, Morley combines his concerns with quality and profit, as in his review of Mr R. Thyme's 'Ravendale': 'It is a novel which might take, but which would be of no particular credit if it did' (manuscript no. 49).

At least in his written reports, Morley insisted that manuscripts stand on the quality that they presented, not on the quality to be infused through editing. Although Geraldine Jewsbury recommended specific revisions in some of her reports, Morley did not do so after an unfortunate experience early in his tenure with Macmillan and Company. He had read Mrs Campbell's 'Life of Scarpi' three times, offering what were for him long reviews and suggestions for revisions. The fourth time he saw the manuscript, he commented in despair, 'Miss Campbell has certainly succeeded in bringing the book a little further out of chaos . . . but even now it is only in the raw state. . . . The authoress' mind is made out of wood and further advice is useless' (manuscript no. 44). At best, as in the famous case of Thomas Hardy's first novel, Morley might suggest rejection, while adding that Macmillan should take a hard look at any future work of a promising young author.

To make his points about quality, Morley offered comparisons. Sometimes he invoked past publishing houses or periodicals, whose books might evoke mid-nineteenth-century sneers, as well as contemporary competitors. For instance, Miss Horner's 'Isolina' has 'too much of the ordinary Minerva Press stamp', although 'of course, one has read worse books' (manuscript no. 13). B. R. Green's 'Pride' is 'excellently suited for the London Journal. I don't think it would do for you at all' (manuscript no. 174). At the time, the circulation of the *London Journal* had reached six figures. Or again, '. . . the interest of the rest [of Mrs Russell's "Mabel Stanhope"] is of the kind one has in a London Journal story . . . I presume you don't want to take an ordinary three-volume novel' (manuscript no. 22). Such references to 'ordinary' but popular work necessarily imply distinctions between high culture and popular culture. So does a later comment that a book is suited for Tinsley. Tinsley, like Chapman and Hall, built his profits on the 'ordinary' three-volume circulating library novel, though both firms published some famous novels. Chapman and Hall published Dickens.

Indeed, in his reports, Morley identifies the circulating library novel with mediocrity and profit, not with quality. He dislikes Reverend J. B. Wells's 'The Wilverdeens of Summerdown'. It's 'worth publishing, *not* however by you. I think it is too little above the average Circulating Library' (manuscript no. 71). Similarly, a fragment of Mr M. Penrose's 'Mrs Milbank's Management' has 'very much the air of the ordinary novel of the Circulating Library' (manuscript no. 197). In Williams's terms, Morley is arguing that culture as a phenomenon is, or should be, devoid of economic considerations. He is part of the community working to impose culture on anarchy. Yet, Morley is also defining a market position for Macmillan and Company. In her reports to Bentley, Jewsbury is less likely to condemn a novel for being ordinary or suited only for the circulating library. Much of Bentley's profit came from novels bought by circulating libraries. Similarly, Jewsbury may recommend a manuscript for a specific 'line' that Bentley carries, sometimes approving of genres or authors disliked by Morley.

Consider Morley's comments on Miss E. G. Walker's 'Martin Deane'. He damns it by comparison to Bentley authors and by references to romance. 'The authoress has written a story which is readable enough as the stories of Mrs. Riddell or Mrs. Wood [both sell well] are readable . . . worth printing by anyone who wanted a romance in his list, not otherwise' (manuscript no. 197). Jewsbury had recommended without hesitation Mrs Wood's *East Lynne*, although she had criticized the grammar. Although Bentley had refused Mrs Riddell's early novels, he published much work by both Wood and Riddell.

However, the contrast between Morley's reactions and Bentley's publications does not mean that Morley and Macmillan were concerned with quality, while Jewsbury and Bentley cared only for profit. Rather, Morley is actively engaged in excluding the genre of romance from acceptable culture. Thus, for instance, Morley praises and dismisses Rosamond Harvey's 'romance pure and simple'. He advises Macmillan that it is 'full of ability of the story-telling kind . . . exceptionally coherent and well-written. The plot is excellently kept and its secrets excellently kept back. The characters are well-drawn. The dialogue . . . unusually good and careful. But remember that all these virtues are in a field that is not the highest. . . ' (manuscript no. 236). To use a contemporary example, it is as though a critic were to condemn Doris Lessing's Shikasta series for being science fiction. Lessing is a major writer while Harvey is not, but Lessing is sufficiently defensive about how that series will be seen to justify the claims of the genre in a preface to volume three, *Shikasta*.

Finally, Morley reaffirms his concern for culture and for 'men of culture' in his invocation of the ultimate market: readers. They come in several varieties in his reports: ordinary, ladies, gossipers and people with taste. All but the last group, whom Morley supposedly represents, is slighted. Each is differentiated in terms of implied taste and potential sales. Again some examples. 'Credit' is not enough to warrant publication of Emily Ponsby's 'Lord Latimer'. Morley warns, 'I fear the majority of ordinary readers would find the story too tame for lack of action and variety, yet . . . it is a creditable piece of work' (manuscript no. 4). After his first four months with the firm, Morley advises of E. G. Nisbett's 'My Brides': 'If you want a novel, it strikes me more in your line than I have yet seen. But mind, it is very, very simple, emphatically a novel for ladies' (manuscript no. 37). Reverend Tyrwhitt's novel about Oxford has limited economic and critical appeal, although it has the virtues of gossip for those who like gossip: it 'will languidly interest a good many people belonging to university circles for a short season' (manuscript no. 2309).

But taste—that is, good taste—resides in 'the virtuous part of the public' (from review of manuscript no. 225) with whom Morley identifies. And, for them as for Morley, books should have an impact upon the mind. Thus, Morley criticizes Miss Dillwyn's two-volume novel: 'Like all Miss Dillwyn's writing the book before me is brisk, fresh, smart, and humouristic; yet somehow it doesn't have enough of these qualities to make a mark on one's mind' (manuscript no. 5313).

Morley is very concerned about that mark on one's mind that constitutes the promise of culture. He sees it as a masculine virtue, a supposition in itself significant; for at the time, women authors were slowly being edged out of their opportunity to have high-culture novels accepted. Or more accurately, as the very idea of the high-culture form became institutionalized, women were relegated to the popular novel which had long been their domain (Tuchman and Fortin, 1980). That damnation of feminine sensibility is ironic, since both Morley and Macmillan seem to have been enlightened about women's rights—at least for men of their times. But, disdain of feminine sensibility appears sufficient for Morley to engage in the collective treatment of author, manuscript and potential readers. Take Morley's comment on Miss E. Eyre's 'Gabrielle and Her Guardian': 'There is a real idea at the very centre of this story . . . the treatment of it is very fair . . . but it is not masculine and robust. . . . There is a fluttering of petticoats and a billing and cooing among women . . . it is like five o-clock tea in three volumes' (manuscript no. 196). The comment on Mrs Molesworth's 'Heathercourt Rectory' similarly identifies novel with readers. 'Few men would get through it and the ladies who read it would hardly think the better of their own minds if they liked it strongly' (manuscript no. 2482).

Jewsbury also associates light entertainment with women readers, even though, as typical of her generation of women novelists (Showalter, 1977), she favoured strong professional women while holding to traditional Victorian notions about the separation of spheres. Consider the following juxtaposition in a recommendation to reject she penned in the late 1860s: 'there's ability in the author, *but* the novel is not an entertaining one. I do not think any lady reader would be found to go thro' the first half of the first volume of plot' (Bentley Archives, volume 98: 77). In the sample of Macmiilan Readers' Reports that I have read, I could not find reviews that similarly damned men. Men who wrote slight novels were termed 'young'.

Almost all of the Macmillan reviews I have cited are from the late 1860s. The tone of subsequent reviews was to change somewhat, as were the standards used for comparisons. Later, in 1877, Morley presumes shared standards with his employer, rather than the need to instruct him. He feels free to say of Miss Keary's 'One Spring', after finding some limited merits for the ordinary reader, 'but to you and me [it] is mediocre to the quick' (manuscript no. 2465). The evaluations of institutions change with shifts in the structure of the publishing industry. In the late 1860s, Morley referred to the ordinary circulating library and its ordinary reader. After the demise of Mudie's as a powerful institution, a new reader slights books by saying that they are only suitable for Mudie's Circulating Library. Similarly, although Morley mocked slight and feminine writing, in the 1890s and later, an unidentified reader working for Macmillan (possibly Mowbray Morris) advises the firm that the quality of works by women writers has deteriorated.

Morley had advised rejecting many popular women writers of his day, so that this retrospective praise of women penned in the 1890s may be read as a method for rejecting contemporary women novelists. In the 1890s, when Macmillan published a Colonial Library, the slurs upon Americans and Australians increase—although to be sure, Morley had never mentioned the writers of either country in a complimentary way. Nonetheless, throughout the Readers' Reports I read, one sees at work the same definitional processes: using his understandings of quality, literature, his employer, the competition and the market as resources, the reader 'makes sense' of both manuscripts and the everyday world. He displays 'practical consciousness', as he makes a rôle for himself.

The rôle of the reader expands and is limited. Morley does not see every manuscript. Both the creams and the dregs seem to have been accepted and rejected without his advice. Although Morley is an invaluable employee, he gets overruled. After all, the firm belongs to the Macmillan family who care about both market-position and prestige; both are, ultimately, of monetary value. And, one may suppose, Macmillan pays more attention to the promise of profit than does Morley, for at the beginning, Macmillan overrules Morley on literary questions of potential economic significance, especially the valuation of genres. Although Morley greatly dislikes romances, four of the eight works of fiction accepted over-the-transom in 1867, 1868, 1877 and 1878 are romances. I do not know how Macmillan came to disagree with Morley on these four works: Edith Milner's 'The Rose of Raby', Miss Rowsell's 'Through the Twilight', Mary Allan-Olnery's 'La Comtesse Estelle', or Miss Walker's 'The Connells of Connell Castle' (all published pseudonymously, some also with changed titles.) Sales were certainly a factor in the case of Miss Walker's 'melodramatic romance' which Morley had described as a 'mysterious complex plot—with blood and madness and dead man's bones . . . ought to be published and would sell—but certainly not of your style of publication' (manuscript no. 65). Indeed, such disagreements seem to suggest that Morley is working to tell Macmillan what his 'style of publication' is—or should be. Sales and assessment of the market must have also been a factor in Macmillan's acceptance of Hugh Harrie's novel in 1888. That report states, 'It is a story of the moment and the occasion. It describes the ignoble nature of wire-pulling at elections . . . Of course, the book is not of the highest class. It will not live six months. But considering its actuality I should think it might have some small run and be worth risking' (manuscript no. 5391). Although in fiction, as in non-fiction, Macmillan preferred to publish a book that would last a long time and so to reap the benefits of an active backlist, he apparently was not always adverse to turning a quick profit.

I assume that Macmillan learned to read carefully the remarks of his employees and to fasten on what praise existed, just as George Bentley noticed Geraldine Jewsbury's faint praise for some books. Additionally, Macmillan may also have read the manuscripts after seeing Morley's reports and have used his own sense of the market and potential reception from critics to decide which manuscripts were worth risking. Alexander Macmillan clearly read some books that had not come in over-the-transom and listened to the opinions of his friends (Morgan, 1943). Certainly, Macmillan frequently listened to Morley. In the early 1890s, Alexander sought out Morley after Morley's successor had damned a novel highly praised and recommended by a member of Alexander Macmillan's social circle. Macmillan valued Morley: he hired as a successor to Morley the literary critic Mowbray Morris, reputed to have been even more of a curmudgeon than Morley. Since Macmillan could have hired a novelist, as done by some of his competitors, he must have been satisfied with Morley's work. Indeed, that Macmillan hired another critic, while Bentley hired additional novelists to supplement Jewsbury, affirms that each had faith in the sort of reader he had selected, even as it affirms the increasing internal structure of publishing.

Morley in turn greatly praised his employer. He lauded his tolerance for Morley's agnosticism and termed him a 'statesman' and a 'Minister of Letters' in his auto-biography (Morley, 1917, vol. 2: 34)—high compliments from a 'literary middle-man' turned politician. Ultimately, Morley seems to have understood, his rôle was to advise, not to dictate, to use his understandings of the literary scene and his own reputation as resources to make a case and to work out his estimations of literature and of Macmillan's list on a case by case basis. In other words, Morley saw himself as engaged in practical work. Morley does indeed engage in a practical literary activity. Part of a commercial enterprise, he tried to make rational recommen-dations about markets and distribution. Simultaneously engaged in the rôle of critic, he advocated realistic novels, damned romance and sought to differentiate high culture from popular culture, forceful literature from 'slight feminine work'. Morley is an agent of cultural process.

In Morley's activities as Macmillan's principal reader, one sees economic and cultural processes embedded in one another and united in Morley's practical activity. One sees how culture or understandings of it may serve as a tool or resources and how cultural institutions constitute themselves as frames or structures of consciousness.

Art and commerce, superstructure and base

Of course, there is a more conventional interpretation of Morley's activities and those of other readers. The reader is said either to choose or to compromise between the supposedly contradictory demands of art and commerce. Thus, for instance, writing the official history of Chapman and Hall, Waugh (1930: 144) claims that George Meredith spoke for literature and ignored the mammons of the marketplace. Scholars demur from this interpretation of readers' activities, even as they affirm that art and commerce are supposedly antithetical. For example, Gettman (1960: 200) says, 'Meredith's reports on manuscripts show that he was constantly aware that publishing is half business and half art'. With its even balanced assessment of publishing (half and half) and its approving agreement of Meredith's awareness, Gettman's comment suggests that publishing requires a compromise between opposites. To be sure, this set of opposites is conceptually identical to neither base and superstructure nor the more traditional sociological distinction between structure and attitude. But, in its connotative juxtaposition of money and feeling, lucre and purity, it is reminiscent of them.

This echo is meaningful inasmuch as it captures one element of the history of publishing: the class-based bias of the gentleman and gentlewoman against turning a profit by commerce and the definition of payment for writing as commercial earnings. Consider one tale about an eighteenth-century poet, while recalling that poetry was a more genteel genre than the newly invented novel. Thomas Gray seemed to feel that payment for poetry was improper. Thus, although he accepted 40 guineas for two poems in 1757, he 'held a Quixotic notion that it was beneath a gentleman to take money for his inventions from a bookseller [publisher]' (Edmund Gosse quoted in Mumby and Norrie, 1974: 157). Gray went to some effort to make sure that he would not profit from the publication of *Elegy, Written in a Country Churchyard*. Similarly, women of 'good birth' or 'acceptable' family background might be amateurs in the eighteenth century, but not professional writers—at least not while maintaining 'good' reputations in society. Fanny Burney's elaborate ruse to learn whether *Evelina* had been accepted was intended to protect her own name, as well as the reputation of her family. The general practice of pseudonymous publication had a similar intent.

Rather than pointing to the opposition of economic and cultural processes, as conventionally believed, Morley's activities and those of other readers demonstrate how economic and cultural processes are embedded in one another. The very rôle of publisher's reader increases the structuration of the publishing system, augments the separation of author and audience and helps to shift the voice of authority from author to critic. It enables us to see that system as a structuration of consciousness. Additionally, Morley's reports demonstrate how culture or under-standings of it may serve as a tool or a material resource in the ever-changing estimation of what is to be defined as 'culture'—high culture. One sees publishing and literature as palimpsests, historically constructed and layered, culture and economy united in the practical activity of human factors. One sees, in that sense, practical consciousness.

This mutual embeddedness of culture and economic process clearly continues in the twentieth century. Today, tarred by corporate economics, television is damned with the same harsh cries that Morley once applied to romance. I do not wish to defend television, although I do see it as contemporary society's popular culture and so, in a way, the equivalent of the nineteenth-century novel—albeit a contem-porary form with a much larger audience drawn from more social classes. Today, also, from the small galleries in New York's SoHo to New York's museums and concert halls, what will sell or attract an audience helps to determine what will be presented as high culture. Rather than damning these developments, one might find it worthwhile to track the mutual embeddedness of cultural and economic processes in the galleries and concert halls of the past. I conclude that the mixture of cultural and economic processes—their mutual embeddedness and enactment through practical consciousness—may be found in nineteenth-century publishing. Capitalist culture, even high culture, has never been devoid of economic concerns—has never been 'pure'. Base and superstructure are not discrete and causally ordered phenomena.

Acknowledgments

The research on which this paper is based has been supported by grants from the Ford Foundation, the National Endowment for the Humanities and the PSC–BHE faculty research awards of the City University of New York. An earlier version was delivered to the Seminar on Media Mythologies chaired by Mary Douglas and Karen W. Steinmetz at the New York University for the Humanities. I appreciate the comments of Paul DiMaggio.

Bibliography

ALTICK, R. D. (1957). *The English Common Reader: A Social History of the Mass Reading Public, 1800–1900*, Chicago, University of Chicago Press

Athenaeum (1878). No. 2645, 6 July

Bentley Archives. Published on microfilm, Cambridge, Chadwyck-Healey

BLAKEY, J. (1939). *The Minerva Press, 1790–1920*, London, Bibliographic Society

COLBY, V. (1970). *The Singular Anomaly: Women Novelists of the Nineteenth Century*, New York, New York University Press

COLLINS, A. S. (1928). *The Profession of Letters: A Study of the Relation of Author to Patron, Publisher and Public, 1780–1832*, London, George Routledge

DIMAGGIO, P. and USEEM, M. (forthcoming). Culture and the Reproduction of Social Class, in Apple, M. (ed.), *Culture and Economic Reproduction*. Boston, Routledge, Kegan Paul

ENZENSBERGER, H. M. (1974). *The Consciousness Industry*, New York, Seabury Press

FAHNESTOCK, J. M. (1973). Geraldine Jewsbury: the power of the publisher's reader, *Nineteenth-Century Fiction*, vol. 28, no. 3

GEERTZ, C. (1973). *The Interpretation of Culture*, New York, Harper and Row

GETTMAN, R. A. (1960). *A Victorian Publisher: A Study of the Bentley Papers*, Cambridge, Cambridge University Press

GIDDENS, A. (1976). *New Rules of Sociological Method*, New York, Basic Books

GRIEST, G. (1970). *Mudie's Circulating Library*, Bloomingon, Indiana University Press

GROSS, J. (1970). *The Rise and Fall of the Man of Letters*, New York, Collier

HABERMAS, J. (1964). The public sphere: an encyclopedia article, reprinted (1974) in *New German Critique*, vol. 3, Fall

HAMER, D. A. (1968). *John Morley: Liberal Intellectual in Politics*, Oxford, Clarendon Press

HEMLOW, J. (1958). *The History of Fanny Burney*, London, Oxford University Press

LEAVIS, Q. D. (1969). Introduction, in Oliphant, M. O. W., *Miss Majoribanks*, London, Chatto and Windus

Macmillan Archives. British Library

MORGAN, C. (1943). *The House of Macmillan*, New York, Macmillan

MORLEY, J. (1917). *Recollections* (2 Volumes), Macmillan New York

MUMBY, F. A. and NORRIE, I. (1974). *Publishing and Bookselling*, New York, Jonathan Cape

NOWELL-SMITH, S. (ed.) (1967). *Letters to Macmillan*, New York, St Martin's Press

PACKER, L. M. (ed.) (1963). *The Rosetti-Macmillan Records*, Berkeley, University of California Press

SAHLINS, M. (1976). *Culture and Practical Reasoning*, Chicago, Chicago University Press

SHOWALTER, E. (1977). *A Literature of Their Own: Women Novelists from Brontë to Lessing*, Princeton, Princeton University Press

SUTHERLAND, J. A. (1976). *Victorian Novelists and Publishers*, London, Athlone Press

TILLOTSON, K. (1962). *Novels of the Eighteen-Forties*, Oxford, Clarendon Press

TOMPKINS, J. M. S. (1961). *The Popular Novel in England 1770–1800*, Lincoln, University of Nebraska Press

TUCHMAN, G. (1978). *Making News: A Study in the Construction of Reality*, New York, Free Press

TUCHMAN, G. and FORTIN, N. (1980). Edging women out: some suggestions about the structure of opportunities and the Victorian novel, *Signs: Journal of Women in Culture and Society*, vol. 6, no. 2

WAUGH, A. (1930). *A Hundred Years of Publishing*, London, Chapman and Hall

WILLIAMS, R. (1970). *The English Novel from Dickens to Lawrence*, New York, Oxford University Press

WILLIAMS, R. (1977). *Marxism and Literature*, New York, Oxford University Press

Karl Erik Rosengren offers in this chapter an example of the sort of work he advocated in his chapter in Volume 2 of this series, the use of mass media content as cultural indicators. Here Rosengren uses Swedish literary reviews as indicators of the rise and fall of literary frames of reference, or literary periods. continuations of such studies, he suggests, can amplify and make more precise more traditional studies of literary history. Rosengren is professor of sociology at the University of Lund, Sweden.

20

TIME AND CULTURE
Developments in the Swedish Literary Frame of Reference

Karl Erik Rosengren

I

There is no dearth of theoretical definitions of the concept of culture (Bernardi, 1977). Precise and explicit empirical definitions are less numerous, for the study of culture to a large extent has proceeded by way of ad hoc case studies. The notion of cultural indicators, inaugurated by George Gerbner in 1969 (Gerbner, 1969; cf. Gerbner et al., 1980; Hirsch, 1980; Gerbner et al., 1981) opens up the possibility of a fruitful interplay between theoretical and empirical studies. Obvious parallels to this possible development may be found in the long history of economic indicators, and in the much shorter history of social indicators. The possibility of combining economic, social, and cultural indicators in comparative studies looms on the horizon—indeed a challenging vista (Rosengren, 1981a).

In the humanities, the study of culture has often been narrowed down to the study of "high culture," while the social sciences have had a broader, almost all-encompassing approach. Common and central to both approaches are the notions of cognition and value. Culture tells you what is and what ought to be, what is related to what and what is important. Culture is the cognitive and

From Karl Erik Rosengren, "Time and Culture: Developments in the Swedish Literary Frame of Reference," in G. Melischek, K. E. Rosengren, and J. Stappers, eds., *Cultural Indicators: An International Symposium* (Vienna: Austrian Academy of Sciences, forthcoming). Reprinted by permission of the publisher and the author.

evaluative framework within which human beings act, think, and feel. It is an immaterial social phenomenon, having material correlates, being carried by competing and cooperating groups in society, and at the same time characterizing whole societies. It is the task of cultural indicators studies to provide precise measurements of that framework and its development over time in different societies, so that its nature can be better understood and explained.

Although culture is a wider phenomenon than high culture, the latter is part and parcel of the former. Therefore, the present attempts to construct and apply cultural indicators should encompass also indicators in the field of high culture. In this chapter, a technique for measuring certain aspects of literary high culture will be presented and applied to the Swedish literature of the 1880s and 1960s.

II

An activity central to literary culture is literary criticism: the interpretation and evaluation of literature. In Sweden, as in many other modern societies, the dominating type of literary criticism is found in the daily press: the reviews of newly published literary books. Reviewing, like other forms of literary criticism, is carried out against the background of a shared frame of reference, a set of common ideas: cognitions and values.

The literary frame of reference, then, may be regarded as having two principal components: a set of values and a set of cognitions. Both values and cognitions are connected with various authors and writers (and with groups or categories of authors and writers) who represents and exemplify them. Therefore, an important element of the literary frame of reference is the "lexicon" of authors and writers available to critics and reviewers: the stock of classic and modern, minor and major poets and writers, whose *oeuvres* embody the literary tradition and its present-day continuation. Indeed, that lexicon is so central to the literary frame of reference that its various characteristics can be used to measure important aspects thereof. That is, the lexicon can be used as a proxy for the literary frame of reference. Its various characteristics could be used as indicators of characteristics of the literary frame of reference. In what way could we empirically study that lexicon of authors and writers?

In their reviews, reviewers of literature often mention, refer to, or allude to writers other than the one under review. Such cases will here be called "mentions." A mention may be regarded as an expression of an association made by the reviewer. It is a commonplace observation often made by historians of literature that if during a given period of time a given writer obtains many mentions, it may be inferred that he or she has some topicality during this period.

Now, if a mention may be regarded as an expression of an association made by the reviewer, and if the mentions of one specific writer can be used as an indicator of the topicality of that writer, all the mentions made in all reviews of the daily press in a country during a given time period (or in a representative sample thereof) may be regarded as an expression of the lexicon of authors and writers available to the reviewers and constituting a central element of the literary frame of reference of that period. It could be used to characterize important aspects of the literary frame of reference used by the reviewers of the period, as well as the differential positions of various writers in the frame of reference. By means of the mentions, which offer large quantities of easily identified and characterized units of measurment, the size, age, geographical composition, structure, and rate of change of the reviewers' frame of reference can be reliably measured and related to other phenomena within, and outside of, the literary system.

The mentions technique may be regarded as an application of psychological association theory (Desse, 1965) to literary sociology. Similar techniques have been used in the sociology of science and in the emerging field of "scientometrics" (Price, 1963; Small and Crane, 1979; Garfied et al., 1978). It has been applied to Swedish literature of the 1880s and the postwar period by Rosengren (1968, 1981b), and to literature and film by Rosengren and Arbelius (1971). Rosengren's work has been discussed and criticized by, for instance, Aspelin (1975), Kepplinger (1975), Sammons (1977), and Zima (1977).

In this chapter the mentions technique will be applied to Swedish literature of the 1880s and the postwar period. It will be used to study an important aspect of literary culture: time.

III

The first thing to note about time and the literary frame of reference is that there is a considerable range of variation along the dimension of time in the frame of reference. At the time of the mention of a given writer in a literary review, 30 years may have elapsed since the birth of the writer, or 300, or 3,000. What can we tell about the distribution of the mentions over this huge span of time, about the "temporal ecology" of the literary frame of reference?

The main technique used by traditional history of literature to handle the problem of time is periodization. History is divided into large chunks of time, characterized one way or another, and the individual writer is said to belong to this or that period, to by a typical (or nontypical) romantic, realist, or whatever. The aim of such a periodization, of course, is to structure the history of literature into meaningful and tractable units. But it may also be used in order to give structure to the literary frame of reference as here conceived, and to its development over time. One could ask, for instance, what proportion of the literary frame of reference during a given period of time is dedicated to writers from this or that literary period—say, to writers from classical antiquity, from the romantic era, etc.? The mentions technique offers an opportunity to answer such questions.

Suppose that all mentions in literary reviews in the daily press of a given country and a given period of time were characterized with respect to the literary period in which the writer mentioned lived and worked (operationalized as the year of birth of the writer in question). How would the mentions be distributed over the different literary periods? That is, in a given years—1976, say—what proportion of the frame of reference would be dedicated to writers from the various periods: antiquity, the Middle Ages, the Renaissance, etc.? Figure 1, based on Table 1, provides an answer to that question. It provides an historical atlas of the Swedish literary frame of reference. We can see the various literary traditions waxing and waning in the literary frame of reference, sometimes slowly, but often at a very quick pace. All in all, a complicated, highly dynamic pattern emerges. The task of bringing some order to the complicated pattern is a stimulating one. It will help us to understand better the delicate balance between continuity and change prevailing in the literary frame of reference. Before turning to this task, however, some background information must be provided.

The source material behind the data stems from representative samples of reviews of literary books published in leading Swedish newspapers during the periods 1876-1892 and 1953-1976, two important periods of change in the history of Sweden and her literature. The 1880s were the period of the "Modern Breakthrough" in Swedish literature (Gustafson, 1961), while in the 1960s Sweden underwent much the same social and cultural upheavals as did many other Western countries.

Most of the data concerning the modern period have been collected within the literary subproject of the research program, Cultural Indicators: The Swedish Symbol System, 1945-1975 (CISSS), funded by the Bank of Sweden Tercentenary Foundation. (For presentations of the CISSS, see Rosengren 1981a and 1981b.) The rest of the data were collected within an earlier research project (Rosengren, 1968). The data have thus been collected during two different periods of time, with an interval of about ten years. Because of the relative simplicity of the mentions technique, however, reliability is comparatively high. Consequently, comparability is satisfactory. (This, of course, is crucial to the very concept of cultural indicators.) Further details about the source material, data collection techniques, sampling procedures, sample sizes, and the like may be found in Rosengren (1968, 1981b, forthcoming).

The periods represented in Table 1 and Figure 1 were chosen so as to satisfy two demands. The periods should divide the mentions material into reasonable proportions: not too large, not too small. And the periods should be meaningful from the point of view of literary history. The first demand necessitated rather long periods for the ancient epochs and then gradually shortening

TABLE 1. Proportion of Mentions (%) Given to Writers Born in
          Different Periods

Year of Mention	-1249	1250-1748	1749-1815	1816-1875	1876-1915	1916-
			Year of Birth of Writer Mentioned			
1876	2.3	9.7	60.5	27.4		
1877	1.8	10.2	56.2	31.7		
1878	1.2	13.8	49.0	35.9		
1879	1.7	8.8	49.7	39.8		
1880	2.8	7.4	51.0	38.8		
1881	3.6	10.0	44.6	41.9		
1882	6.7	8.4	42.1	42.7		
1883	1.4	8.3	33.1	57.3		
1884	1.7	6.6	27.4	64.3		
1885	2.3	8.0	27.8	62.0		
1886	3.1	10.0	32.4	54.4		
1887	4.9	8.6	21.5	65.0		
1888	2.7	7.2	33.9	56.3		
1889	.8	5.5	27.4	66.4		
1890	4.8	8.5	33.5	53.2		
1891	2.4	8.6	30.3	58.8		
1892	2.6	7.1	33.2	57.0		
1953	2.1	5.0	11.1	23.2	52.0	6.5
1954	5.8	6.1	8.6	22.7	48.9	7.9
1955	2.9	4.2	11.2	24.3	48.5	8.8
1956	1.6	6.2	11.1	22.8	46.7	11.5
1957	2.1	8.1	8.1	22.0	49.4	10.2
1958	3.5	5.7	8.3	20.6	49.2	12.7
1959	2.6	6.3	11.1	20.1	49.9	10.0
1960	2.9	6.7	6.1	21.9	51.3	11.0
1961	5.5	6.7	12.7	17.0	44.5	13.6
1962	.9	4.2	5.3	17.8	52.5	19.2
1963	1.9	3.7	6.0	15.1	51.3	21.9
1964	1.7	4.5	6.7	14.2	45.8	27.2
1965	1.6	5.8	6.5	15.3	43.5	27.4
1966	2.8	5.5	5.7	13.3	47.0	25.8
1967	.9	6.0	5.8	14.1	42.6	30.6
1968	3.2	5.6	7.2	16.2	40.4	27.4
1969	2.2	3.8	5.1	16.9	44.4	27.5
1970	1.4	5.5	7.8	15.7	43.0	26.6
1971	2.3	4.6	4.6	18.9	47.1	22.6
1972	2.0	5.6	8.3	16.1	38.6	29.3
1973	3.0	6.3	6.1	15.4	42.4	26.8
1974	3.0	4.2	5.8	17.8	42.1	27.1
1975	3.2	4.5	4.1	14.8	45.9	27.5
1976	3.1	3.1	4.6	17.3	43.1	28.9

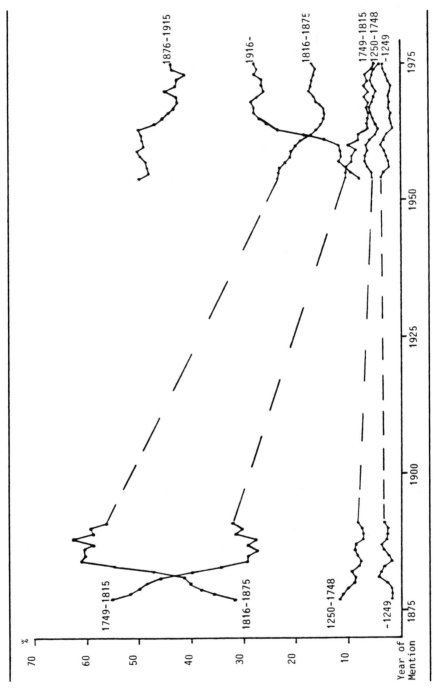

Figure 1: Proportion of Mentions Given to Writers Born in Different Periods of Time (3 years' moving averages)

periods as we approach our own time. The second demand led to minor adjustments at the demarcation lines between the periods. The results were as follows. (Note that the periods are based upon *the birth year of the writer mentioned.*)

Antiquity and the Middle Ages had to be lumped together in order to evade minimal, wildly fluctuating proportions of mentions. The line was drawn, however, as early as 1250, which enables us to treat the Italian literary renaissance of the thirteenth and fourteenth centuries (Dante, b. 1265; Petrarca, b. 1304; Boccaccio, b. 1313) together with its transalpine counterparts of the fifteenth and sixteenth centuries. Besides the Renaissance, our second period, covering writers born in the period 1250-1748, includes also writers in the traditions growing out of the Renaissance: the periods of the baroque and classicism.

The next period, writers born 1749-1815, covers romanticism, neoclassicism, and early realism, the starting year being chosen so as to place Goethe (b. 1749) in the period in which he played such a dominating role. The following period, 1816-1875, covers realism, naturalism, and *fin-de-siècle* symbolism; the next one, 1876-1915, modernism and what might be called the neorealism of the interwar period. The last period is open and covers contemporary writers born in 1916 or later.

It will be noted that the periods grow gradually shorter, diminishing from a couple of thousand years, to roughly 500 years, to 60 and 40 years, respectively. The final period is open, but in reality it also covers about 40 years, since the writers born in the beginning and the middle of the 1950s just got their first mentions in the middle of the 1970s, when the period under study ends.

It is obvious that this categorization is highly schematic. No doubt, examples of writers not easily squeezed into the categorization could be found without too much difficulty. The proponent of such examples, however, would miss the point. The point is not to render as faithfully as possible the myriads of minute details of the development of the literary frame of reference. The point, on the contrary, is precisely the opposite one: to produce an overall picture of the main features of that development. Figure 1 represents a step in that direction.

It shows, for instance, how the proportion of mentions given to writers born 1816-1875 and representing realism, naturalism and *fin-de-siècle* grew rapidly during the 1880s, while the attention bestowed upon writers born 1749-1815 and representing romanticism, neoclassicism, and early realism was rapidly diminishing. In the 1960s, the "contemporary writers" (b. 1916-) were on the advance, while those born 1876-1915 and 1816-1875 were on the wane, the former more rapidly so—but at a higher level—than the latter. During both periods, the writers representing antiquity and the Middle Ages (born -1249) as well as those representing the periods of Renaissance, the baroque, and classicism (b. 1250-1748) were dwindling almost imperceptibly. In the modern period they were joined—roughly at the 5 to 10 percent level—by the romanticists (b. 1749-1815).

Three main features of the development stand out immediately. The first one among these has already been mentioned. The picture of the development offered is highly dynamic. Second, the proportions of the literary frame of reference obtained by representatives of the various literary periods and traditions do not wax and wane linearly and symmetrically. Rather, the data suggest comparatively short periods of relative fast growth, followed by long periods of gradually retarded obsolescence. Third, we find minor, probably more or less randomly distributed oscillations imposed upon these basic patterns of growth and decay. (In Figure 1, these oscillations have been partly dampened by the three years' moving averages used in the figure.)

Figure 1 opens up several possibilities for an increased understanding of the change processes occurring in the literary frame of reference. Two main roads offer themselves: a comparison between the 1880s and the 1960s, and an attempt to grasp the general tendencies supposedly underlying the intricate fluctuations of the raw data. Special interest should be given to the "leading" tradition or traditions, the cohorts of writers dominating the frame of reference during a given period of time (i.e., the group of writers obtaining the greatest proportion of the mentions of each year of that period).

The main difference between the 1880s and the 1960s in this respect is that in the 1880s a shift in the leading traditions occurred, while no such thing happened in the 1960s. From 1882 onward, realists and naturalists, and their contemporaries of other schools, occupied the largest share of the frame of reference. Their advance stagnated rather soon thereafter, however, and in 1890 their decline had already started. In the early 1950s, when our data start again, they had long since been surpassed by the modernists and their contemporaries (who, by the way, were then already on the decline).

The romanticists and their contemporaries (b. 1749-1815)—surpassed in 1882 by the realists and naturalists—were on the decline already when our data start. Their decline continues through the 1950s and the 1960s, when they join forces with the writers belonging to the periods of antiquity, the Middle Ages, the Renaissance, and the Baroque in forming the definitive past of the literary frame of reference.

That no major shift occurred in the 1960s fits in well with other observations made in the project, indicating that the literary change of the 1880s was more thoroughgoing than that of the 1960s (see Rosengren 1981b, forthcoming). The question immediately comes to mind, however, How often do such major shifts really occur? In order to evaluate the difference found between the 1880s and the 1960s in this respect, that question should be given an answer.

Connecting the curves of the 1880s with the corresponding curves of the modern period—the broken lines of Figure 1—we can see that another major shift must have occurred somewhere between 1900 and 1950, when the modernists and their contemporaries (b. 1876-1915), being on the rise, must have passed the realists and naturalists (b. 1816-1875), then in decline. Similarly, another major shift may be coming in the 1980s or 1990s, when the modernists, on the decline, probably will be passed by today's writers (whatever label will be put on them by later historians of literature). Is it possible to say something more precise about these two hypothetical major shifts, the data of which are not yet collected? These possibilities rest with our chances of extracting the regularities supposedly underlying the somewhat erratic patterns of Figure 1.

IV

The phenomena under study are phenomena of growth and decay. One possibility, therefore, is to try to fit the empirical data of Figure 1 and Table 1 to existing theoretical curves of growth and decay, thus giving expression and increased visibility to the central tendencies fo the empirical data, otherwise hidden by the accidental and more or less random fluctuations always found in such cases. Fitting our empirical data to the theoretical curves also gives us increased information about what probably happened, and probably will happen, in periods not covered by our data.

There are several theoretical growth and decay curves available in the literature, commonly used to give a concise expression to the central tendency of the empirical data describing the growth and/or decay phenomena under study in the given cases. Figure 2 presents three such curves. Common to all three curves is the valuable characteristic that they may be turned into straight lines by means of logarithmic transformation. (The equations for the curves, in their linear form, are given in the figure.) When the curves have been transformed to straight lines, we may apply the usual straight-line regression technique (least squares). It is then easy to find the straight line best expressing the central tendency of the transformed data. Having transformed the results back to the original notation, we may draw the curve corresponding to the original, untransformed data.

In a trial-and-error process, the curves of Figure 2 were systematically tested on the data of Table 1 and Figure 1. It soon turned out that no single type of curve sufficed to express the central tendencies of the various growth and decay processes. After a large number of test runs, it was found that the best combination was to express the growth processes in terms of the S curve and the decay processes in terms of the exponential curve. Figure 3 does so for the cohort of writers born 1816-1875 (the realists and naturalists and their contemporaries).

In order to produce Figure 3, some decisions must be taken and some assumptions made. The basic decision is to assume that the growth process tends to follow the S curve, and the decay process, the exponential curve. The next decision is to arrive at the maximum of the S curve. In this case, the

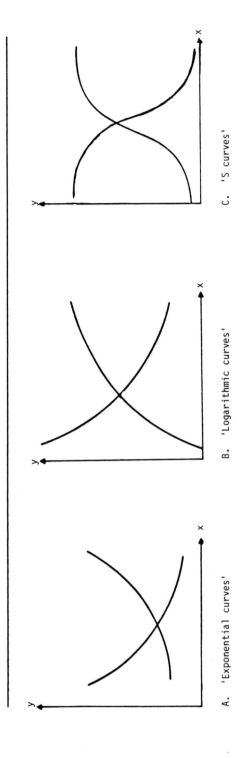

A. 'Exponential curves'

Eq. A: $\ln y = \ln a + bx$

B. 'Logarithmic curves'

Eq. B: $y = a + b \ln x$

C. 'S curves'

Eq. C: $\ln \left(\dfrac{y}{c-y} \right) = a + bx$

Legend: a = the intercept of the transformed curve with the y-axis

b = the slope of the transformed curve

c = the maximum of the S curve

NOTE: See, for instance, Chatterjee and Price (1977).

Figure 2: Three Theoretical Curves of Growth and Decay

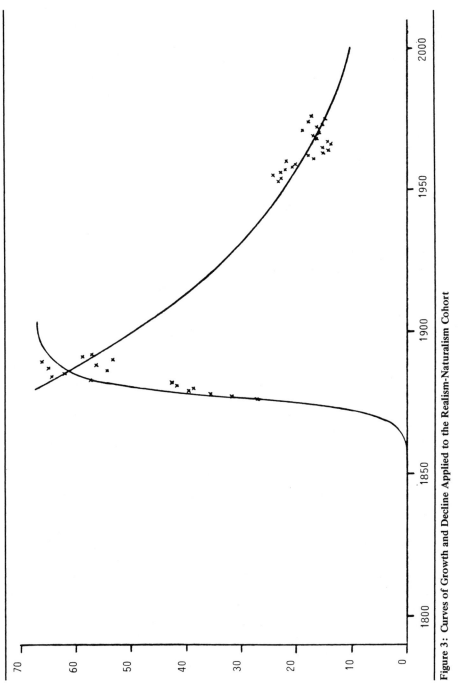

Figure 3: Curves of Growth and Decline Applied to the Realism-Naturalism Cohort

empirical maximum is 66.4 percent, the value for the 1816-1875 cohort in 1889 (see Table 1). The theoretical value was therefore put at 67 percent, and the S curve was based on the empirical values of years 1876-1889. For the exponential decay curve, no maximum has to be inserted. The decay curve was calculated on the empirical values of the years 1884-1892 and 1953-1976. The two curves, then, were calculated on partly overlapping data. In Figure 3 this calculation procedure has its correspondence in the two curves crossing each other and continuing in different directions. It is as if, for a time, the two processes of growth and decay were going on contemporaneously, the incipient decay process preventing the growth process from reaching its theoretical maximum.

The fit of the empirical data to the theoretical curves may be expressed as the Pearsonian r's for the two straight regression lines corresponding to the curves of the figure. The fit is very good for the decay curve ($r = .98$) and good for the S curve ($r = .84$). Between them, then, the two theoretical curves of Figure 3 well express the central tendencies of the empirical data.

The fact of the good fit makes it natural to put some reliance on the curves also for the periods not covered by empirical data: 1860-1875, 1893-1952, 1977-2000. It may be hypothesized that for these years, the development of the proportion of mentions given to the cohort of writers born 1816-1875 would have followed (and will follow) roughly the two curves of Figure 3. No doubt, for most years the actual empirical values would not have fallen exactly on the curves (although some would probably have done so—just as in Figure 3). For some years, the residuals—the distance between a given empirical values and the theoretical values given by the curve—would probably have been rather large, just as in Figure 3. But it is a reasonable hypothesis that the central tendency of the data missing from Figure 3 is fairly well expressed by the two curves. This opens up some interesting possibilities. Suppose we calculated the theoretical curves for all the cohorts of Figure 1 and Table 1. What results would be get? Figure 4 gives the answer. Before commenting upon the results, however, we must clarify the procedures behind the figure.

Basically, Figure 4 is constructed in the same way as Figure 3. That is, growth processes are fitted to the S curve, decay processes to the exponential curve. (Thus, the curves for the cohort 1816-1875 are exactly the same as in Figure 3, except that both curves end at their meeting point.) The curves of the figure are based upon the empirical data of Table 1, in combination with some additional assumptions and deductions. These are partly technical, partly institutional, partly literary. Let us treat each of the three types, one at a time, starting with the technicalities.

The cohort of writers from antiquity and the Middle Ages (born before 1250), together with the cohort of writers from the periods of the Renaissance, the boroque, and classicism (b. 1250-1748) play a rather insignificant role in the literary frame of reference of the 1880s and the 1960s. Together, they get

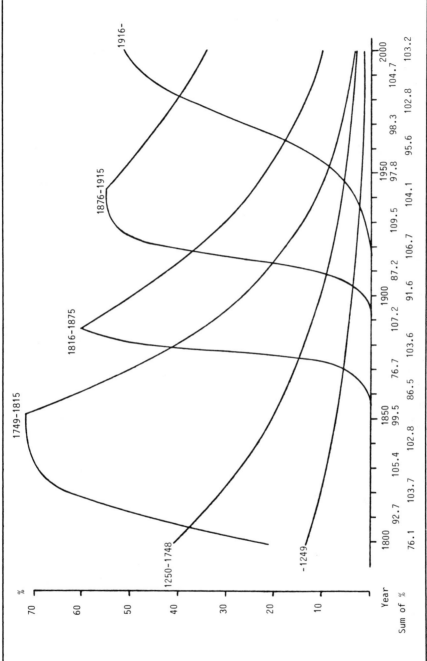

Figure 4: The Literary Frame of reference: Theoretical Curves of Growth and Decay for Six Cohorts of Writers

some 5 or 10 percent of the mentions. But once they must have dominated the literary frame of reference completely. As late as, say, the late 1760s or early 1770s, when the first romanticists were in their early twenties. The writers born before 1749 must have occupied close to 100 percent of the literary frame of reference. We do not know how these 100 percent were divided between them, of course, but a reasonable assumption might be about 25 percent to antiquity and the Middle Ages and about 75 percent to the rest. (That is more than antiquity and the Middle Ages would get, if we were to use the fact that around 1250, they must have had 100 percent of the frame of reference and would calculate the corresponding exponential decay curve.) Assuming that for the period 1755-1775 we had this distribution for the two cohorts (75-25), and combining this assumption with their empirical values, we get the two curves of Figure 4. For the other three decay curves we do not have to make any such assumption; here the empirical data suffice.

For all the S curves, maximum must be inserted (the parameter c in Figure 2). For the cohort of realists and naturalists (1816-1875), this maximum is provided by the data themselves (see above); for the other three it had to be assumed or calculated one way or the other. For the romanticists (b. 1749-1815), the culmination must have occurred at about 1850, for before that their exponential curve reaches absurd heights. This points to a maximum of around 70 percent. After some test runs, the maximum was put at 72 percent, assumed to have occurred in 1855. The "minimum" was assumed to have occurred in 1774, when it was assumed that the cohort of romanticists got their first percentage point of the literary frame of reference. The growth curve of the cohort was then calculated on these two values alone. (This curve, of course, is an entirely theoretical construction, the plausibility of which must be judged from the way it fits in with the curves based on empirical values. We will return to this question later on.)

The growth curve for the 1816-1875 cohort has already been discussed. For the 1876-1915 cohort, the maximum was put at 55 percent, roughly the space available in 1940, when the other curves, based upon empirical data, have got their due. The minimum was put at 1 percent in 1900, analogically with the procedure for the cohort of romanticists. Again, this is an entirely theoretical curve, to be justified later by the way it fits in with the rest of the data. For the cohort of "contemporary writers" (b. 1916 and later), the maximum was put at 55 percent, the same as for the previous cohort. The curve was then calculated on the empirical values for the years 1953-1976. (It was assumed, then, that the tendency to stagnation observable for this cohort from 1965 onward did not continue after 1976.)

These, then, are the technical assumptions behind Figure 4. The main assumptions are that the S curve and the exponential decay curve together describe the processes of growth and decay in the literary frame of reference. The assumptions about the starting points and maxima of the growth curves are fairly reasonable or even self-evident: Most writers do not enter the literary frame of reference until some time between the age of twenty and twenty-five, and a cohort of writers cannot occupy a larger portion of the frame of reference than is left over by the other cohorts. Together, however, the basic assumptions and the additional smaller ones may appear rather audacious. Fortunately, there is a way of testing their plausibility.

It has already been pointed out that the fit between the empirical data and a theoretical curve may be expressed as the Pearsonian correlation coefficient. For the three exponential decay curves based exclusively on empirical data (cohorts 1749-1815, 1816-1875, 1976-1915), these coefficients are high or very high ($-.97$, $-.98$ and $-.70$, respectively). For the two decay curves in which empirical and assumed values are mixed (-1249, 1250-1748), they are also very high ($-.87$ and $-.97$, respectively). The S curve for the cohort (1916-), where only empirical data have been combined with an assumed maximum, also has a very high r (.88). The r for the S curve where the maximum was empirically given (cohort 1816-1875) has been presented above (.86). (For the two theoretically derived S curves, the r's are, of course, perfect: 1.0.)

That all the coefficients of correlations are high or very high suggests that each single curve offers a good expression of the central tendency of the empirical data. The whole set of curves, including the theoretically derived ones, gets support in another way. In this case, the test builds on the simple fact that for each year, the values of all the curves ideally should sum up to 100 percent. The actual results for every tenth year are given at the bottom line of Figure 4. It will be seen that they tend to cluster round the value of 100 percent, ranging from 76.1 to 109.5 (with a mean of 97.9). This is an indication that the "strain" in the model of the development of the literary frame of reference offered by Figure 4 is low to moderate. It tells us that the assumptions made may not have been wildly wrong, but instead, fairly reasonable. From a technical point of view, then, Figure 4 seems to offer an acceptable picture—a descriptive model, if you will—of the development of the literary frame of reference during two centuries, from 1800 to 2000. What about the institutional assumptions of the model?

An institutional assumption made in Figure 4 is that the frame of reference, measured by means of mentions in the literary review of newspapers, has a functional equivalent in periods when the interpretation and evaluation of literature was carried out mainly in other forms than by means of reviews in the daily press (such as academic lectures or essays in scholarly magazines). It is also assumed that in such periods the development of the literary frame of reference is characterized by the same central tendencies as it is in periods with a developed system of literary reviewing in the daily press.

The first of the two institutional assumptions seems to be a very reasonable one. It amounts to saying only that the function of literary criticism may be fulfilled in various institutional settings (see Escarpit, 1968: 419). The second assumption is more audacious. No doubt the institutional setting interacts with the subtantive content of the literary milieu and its frame of reference. For instance, reviewing in the daily press probably tends to stress the more "topical" components of the frame of reference, at the expense of the more "classical" parts. But there is a limit to such interactions, and we my hypothesize the probable direction of their influence. The conclusion of this argument, then, would be that the parts of Figure 4 covering the period before 1830-1840 (when the modern daily press was introduced into Sweden) should be treated especially carefully, since in these parts the older components of the frame of reference may be somewhat underestimated. This conclusion leads to the literary assumptions behind Figure 4.

The main literary assumption behind Figure 4 may be exemplified by the last cohort, the writers born after 1915. Do they really form a meaningful cohort of their own, in the same sense that they make up a common tradition comparable to, say, the realists and naturalists born in the period 1816-1875? Or are they, perhaps, just inheritors, or even epigones, of the modernist tradition (1876-1915)? An experiment with two alternative cohorts (1976-1935, 1936-) resulted in relatively low fit and considerably increased strain—indirect support for the cohort partition used. But the fact remains that, unlike the writers from the other periods, the writers of this period have not yet to any considerable extent been made subject to full-scale, detailed analyses by the historians of literature. This brings us to the basic literary assumption behind Figure 4. The figure assumes that the cohorts in a meaningful way represent literary traditions. Thus, it is dependent on traditional history of literature. Taking that history as a starting point, the technique used in Figures 1 and 4 can then add information concerning the proportion of the literary frame of reference allotted to the various traditions, their rise and decline over time, and regularities to be found in these processes. This information makes it possible to characterize the development of the literary frame of reference in a way not otherwise possible.

The characterization, of course, depends on the partition of the material into cohorts, which can be made in varioius ways. The cohorts can be made large or small, and the demarcation lines between them can be somewhat differently drawn. The partition used in Table 1 and Figures 1 and 4 is assumed to be meaningful. There are other meaningful possibilities, however. In this connection, variation in the size of the cohorts is probably more essential than the place of the demarcation lines, which may be moved about a year or two without altering the picture very much.

Graphs based on cohorts of differential size could be compared to photographs or X-ray pictures with differential levels of resolution. In Rosengren (forthcoming) an alternative to Figures 1 and 4 will be presented, based on ten cohorts instead of six. Space does not permit the inclusion of this alternative here. It turns out, however, that the development of these (smaller) cohorts tends to follow the same pattern as the one in Figure 4: S curves for the phase of growth, exponential curves for the decay phase. Again, the fit of the data to the single theoretical curves—measured by Pearsonian r's—as a rule is high or very high. Also, the "strain" of the overall model, measured as the percentage sums of every tenth year, is low to moderate. So the basic assumptions behind this type of analysis seem to hold also for cohorts of other size and composition than those of Figures 1 and 4. This result allows us to continue our discussion of Figure 4 with some confidence that the pattern it suggests is not entirely incidental.

In order to discuss the pattern of the figure, we need a typology and a corresponding terminology. Two types of phenomena are clearly discernible in the figure: *phases,* delimited by *critical events.*

In the career of a cohort, there are at least four critical events:

— *arrival:* the first year the curve becomes the highest one;
— *breakthrough:* the year the curve becomes the highest one;
— *culmination:* the year the curve teaches its all-time high; and
— *departure:* the year the curve is passed by the following curve.

The arrival marks the beginning of the curve. The culmination divides the curve into two main phases: the growth and decay phases. These two phases refer to the internal development of the curve itself. The other two critical events delimit phases that relate the development of the curve to that of the surrounding curves. There are three such phases:

— *ascendance:* between arrival and breakthrough;
— *dominance:* between breakthrough and departure; and
— *fading:* from departure onward.

The critical events of breakthrough and departure thus delimit the phase of dominance, the phase during which the curve of the cohort receives a larger proportion of the mentions than that of any other cohort. It is fairly obvious that this is the most important phase of the cohort. It is followed by the phase of fading, when the cohort gets gradually less attention in the frame of reference and later cohorts get gradually more. Before the phase of dominance comes the phase os ascendance.

All three phases, of course, could be divided into subphases. Especially for the phase of ascendance, this may be fruitful and necessary in later stages of the analysis. For our present purposes, however, the three phases suggested here will suffice.

Figure 5, based on Figure 4, presents the development of the literary frame of reference in terms of phases and critical events. The fading phases are the longest, while the relative length of the phases of dominance and ascendance varies considerably. Variations between the cohorts in the relative length of the phases may be used to characterize the development of a given cohort. (This variation depends on the degree of peakedness of the curve itself and on the degree of peakedness of its neighbor curves.) Similarly but inversely, the situation in the literary frame of reference during a given period of time may be characterized by means of information about the phases of the various cohorts. This brings us to the substantive interpretation of Figures 4 and 5.

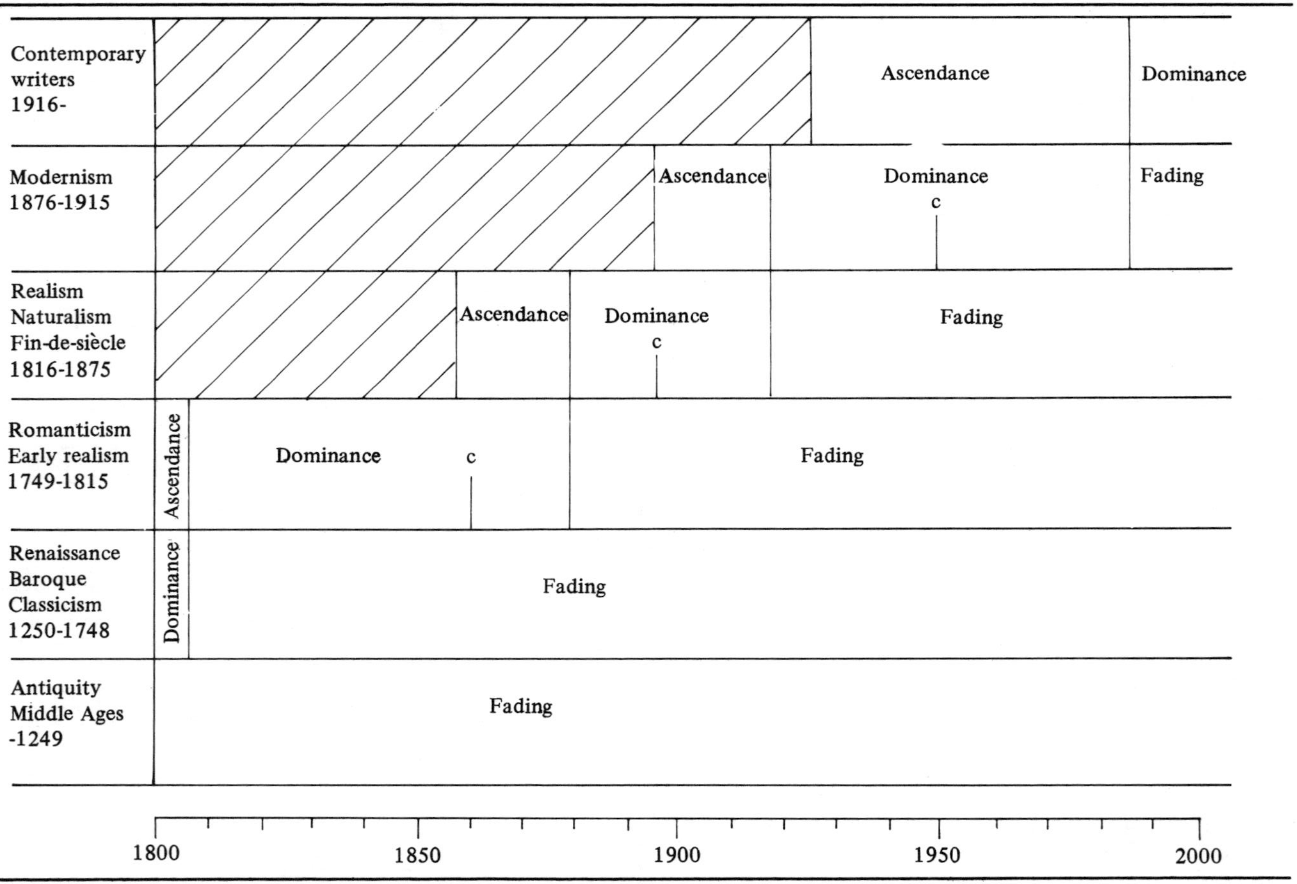

Figure 5 Critical Events and Phases in the Development of Six Cohorts in the Literary Frame of Reference

V

The two figures yield information ranging from broad generalizations to minute particularities concerning the history of Swedish literature and its frame of reference. Let us start with the more general, nomothetic results, moving gradually to the more particular, ideographic ones.

The figures give rather strong support to the hypothesis that developments in the literary frame of reference tend to follow a regular pattern of growth and decline. The central tendencies of that pattern may be described by means of S curves for the growth phenomena and exponential curves for the phenomena of decline. Cohorts of writers entering the literary frame of reference tend to follow the S curve; cohorts leaving the frame of reference, the exponential curve. This pattern seems to hold true for at least the last 150 or 200 years and for cohorts ranging in extension from centuries to decades.

The interpretation of the parameters of the equations for the two types of theoretical curves (see Figure 2) above is straightforward: The height and slope of the curve have their parameters (a, b). In the case of the exponential decay curve, the logarithmitization ensures that the influence of time on the proportion of mentions decreases asymptotically. It has already been pointed out that the S curve required yet another parameter, fixating the maximum of the curve (c). The term $\ln(cy/c-y)$ simply ensures the S shape of the curve: slow-rapid-slow growth. Thus, the equations used do not require nonintuitive concepts alien to common sense.

Using cohorts of differential extension, it is possible to describe the development of the literary frame of reference with differential degrees of resolution. In such descriptions, special interest should be given to major shifts in the frame of reference—cases where one cohort succeeds another in being the phase of dominance, that is, obtaining the largest proportion of the mentions. We have already noted that according to Figure 1 there was one such major shift in the early 1880s and none in the 1960s. Accepting the assumptions made in Figure 3, we find that other major shifts occurred about 1810 and 1920. If the writers born after 1915 are accepted as a cohort representing a specific literary tradition, another major shift will occur in the early 1980s. If this cohort, on the other hand, is divided one way or the other so that part of it is incorporated into the previous cohort, the major shift will be the more delayed the greater part of the cohort that is added to the previous one.

As mentioned above, an alternative structuring of the source material, using ten cohorts instead of six, will be presented in Rosengren (forthcoming). The "degree of resolution," of course, affects the importance of the major shifts. The smaller the cohorts, the less major and the more frequent the major shifts, so that the meaning of the shifts can be more precisely interpreted. Variations in the degree of resolution may thus be used to obtain the level of precision necessary for the argument at hand. The degree of resolution used in Figure 4 probably marks one endpoint of the range of resolution possible. With less resolution, the perspective would probably grow too grandiose. Using more than ten cohorts, on the other hand, probably would mean that the perspective would get lost among details.

Turning to the left-hand part (the earlier periods) of Figures 4 and 5, we note that the major shifts occurring about 1810, 1880, and 1920 fall within three well-known periods of dramatic change in the Swedish history of literature: the take-over of the literary scene by romanticism, naturalism, and modernism, respectively (see Gustafson, 1961; Brandell, 1975). This lends increased credence to the theoretical curves and to the extrapolations made by means of them. It is a validation also of the general notion of the literary frame of reference and of its relevance to the understanding of literary development in general, for literary history is written mainly on the basis of the literary works of art, while we have analyzed the frame of reference by means of mentions in reviews. That the major shifts, including those based on long-term extrapolations, fall where according to history of literature they should fall, shows that there is a close relationship between the development of the literary frame of reference as it has been defined here and the historical development of literature itself. Thus, a close study of the former will contribute to an increased understanding of the latter.

In Figure 5, for instance, one may note the comparatively short period of dominance of the realism/naturalism/*fin-de-siècle* cohort, which is much shorter than are those of romanticism-early realism and modernism. This may be due to very specific, perhaps unique, historical circumstances, but all the same it may tell us something essential about the development of Swedish literature around the turn of the century. It does invite further questions about possible regularities in the relations between literary change and continuity, literary form and content, and societal development at large. Do romantic traditions tend to live for longer periods of time in the literary frame of reference than do realistic traditions? If so, what would that imply about the nature of literary change and about the relations between literature and society?

If nothing else, such questions at least touch really big problems. Our data, however, also call forward questions about the individual writer and his career. The careers of individual writers may be better understood against the background of "literary atlases" such as that of Figure 4. Strindberg, for instance, making his début in the beginning of the 1870s, had to wait for his naturalistic breakthrough until 1879, when the literary frame of reference the cohort of the realists-naturalists were about to pass by the cohort of romanticists and early realists. But did not Strindberg himself create the naturalistic breakthrough in Sweden? Did not the literary frame of reference change because of his creative efforts, rather than the other way around? Up to a point that is true, of course. But only up to a point. Figure 4 tells us that when accomplishing his breakthrough, Strindberg was riding on a wave in the literary frame of reference having started to grow at least fifteen years earlier and approaching dominance of the scene precisely in the years when he wrote his *Red Chamber.*

The further pursuit of such ideographic problems, dealing with the interplay of the individual writers and the periodization of the overindividual system, would offer rich opportunities for applied studies. Such studies would by no means have to be limited to confirming the picture of traditional literary history, working it out in greater precision and detail. A challenging case at hand, for instance, would be the relationship between the cohort of modernism in the frame of reference and various Swedish poets belonging to different generations and showing different tinges of modernism—say, Lagerkvist (b. 1891), Ekelöf (b. 1907), and Lindegren (b. 1910). The three poets had their individual breakthroughs about 1920, 1930, and 1940, respectively, and each time it has been felt that modernism also had something of a breakthrough, about 1930 it was approaching its culmination, and about 1940 it was culminating and starting to decline. The exact profile of the curve, of course, remains to be established. The completion of that task and the close scrutiny of the relationship of the individual modernist writers to the surrounding system would no doubt add significantly to our understanding both of the period and its individual writers. Such studies, however, must of necessity fall outside the frames of the present work.

VI

Continued studies along the lines suggested in this chapter would probably increase our understanding of the nature of cultural change in general and literary change in particular. They might also contribute to our understanding of individual writers and their interaction with the culture surrounding them.

A natural task of such studies, of course, would be to fill out the lacunae of Figures 1 and 4, primarily the period 1893-1952. But continued studies would also have to entail the combination of quantitative data about the literary frame of reference and qualitative data from traditional history of literature. They should be carried out to advantage within a general theory of literary change, such as the one, say, being developed by Martindale (1975, 1981). They should be carried out on a comparative basis, juxtaposing data from several countries. They should also be tied in with studies using cultural indicators of other types, so that the phenomenon of literary change could be seen in a broader context. Ultimately, the results of such studies should be combined with longitudinal research based on social and economic indicators. Only then would we arrive at a really penetrating understanding of literature and literary change, embedded in the immaterial phenomenon on culture and dependent upon society's material development.

No doubt, the road is long. The present discussion is an outcome of a sub-project within the research program, Cultural Indicators: The Swedish Symbol System, 1945-1975, an effort to start walking that road.

REFERENCES

ASPELIN, K. (1975) *Textens dimensioner. Problem och perspektiv i litteraturstudiet.* Stockholm: Norstedts.
BERNARDI, B. [ed.] (1977) *The Concept and Dynamics of Culture.* The Hague: Mouton.

BRANDELL, G. (1975) *Fran forsta varldskriget till 1950.* Stockholm: Aldus.

CHATTERJEE, S. and PRICE, B. (1977) *Regression Analysis by Example.* New York: Wiley.

DEESE, J. (1965) *The Structure of Associations in Language and Thought.* Baltimore: Johns Hopkins University Press.

ESCARPIT, R. (1968) The Sociology of Literature, in *International Encyclopedia of the Social Sciences,* vol. 9, pp. 417-425.

GARFIELD, E., M. V. MALIN, and H. SMALL, (1978) Science Data as Science Indicators, in Y. Elkana et al. (eds.) *Toward a Metric of Science.* New York: Wiley.

GERBNER, G. (1969) Toward "Cultural Indicators": The Analysis of Mass Mediated Public Message Systems. *AV Communication Review* 17: 137-148.

GERBNER, G. et al. (1980) The Mainstreaming of America, Violence Profile No. 11. *Journal of Communication* 30: 10-27.

GERBNER, G. et al. (1981) Final Reply to Hirsch. *Communication Research* 8: 259-280.

GUSTAFSON, A. (1961) *A History of Swedish Literature.* Mineapolis: University of Minnesota Press.

HIRSCH, P. M. (1980) The Scary World of the Nonviewer and Other Anomalies: A Reanalysis of Gerbner et al.'s Findings on Cultivation Analysis. *Communication Research* 7: 403-456.

KEPPLINGER, H. M. (1975) *Realkultur und Medienkultur. Literarische Karrieren in der Bundesrepublik.* Freiburg: Verlag Karl Alber.

MARTINDALE, C. (1975) *Romantic Progression: The Psychology of Literary History.* Washington, DC: Hemisphere.

MARTINDALE, C. (1981) Evolutionary Trends in English Poetry. *Perspectives in Computing* 1: 17-22.

PRICE, D. de S. (1963) *Little Science, Big Science.* New York: Columbia University Press.

ROSENGREN, K. E. (1968) *Sociological Aspects of the Literary System.* Stockholm: Natur och Kultur.

ROSENGREN, K. E. (1981a) Mass Communication as Cultural Indicators: Sweden, 1945-1975, in G. Wilhoit and H. de Bock, eds., *Mass Communication Review Yearbook,* Vol. 2, pp. 717-737.

ROSENGREN, K. E. (1981b) Measurement of Invariance and Change in the Literary Milieu: Sweden in the 1880's and the 1960's. *Zeitschrift für Literaturwissenschaft und Linguistik, Beiheft Literaturwissenschaft und Empirische Methoden:* 52-73.

ROSENGREN, K. E. (forthcoming) *The Swedish Literary Climate, 1953-1976.* Lund: Studentlitteratur.

ROSENGREN, K. E. and ARBELIUS, B. (1971) Frames of Reference as Systems: Size and Other Variables. *General Systems* 16: 205-210.

SAMMONS, J. L. (1977) *Literary Sociology and Practical Criticism.* Bloomington: Indiana University Press.

SMALL, H. G. and CRANE, D. (1979) Specialties and Disciplines in Science and Social Science: An Examination of Their Structure Using Citation Indexes. *Scientometrics* 1: 445-461.

ZIMA, P. V. (1977) Le texte comme objet: une critique de la sociologie empirique de la littérature. *Homme et societé* 43: 151-170.

The following, on English popular culture in the recent past, relies theoretically on Walter Benjamin and mainly examines the "Americanization" of British taste. Changes in English popular culture, Dick Hebdige suggests, tended to be associated with changes in the composition of the "culture market" but should not be interpreted as the wholesale adoption of American popular culture. Rather, the cultural images adopted are refracted indirectly through a "mythical America," and the appropriation of American cultural symbols involves their re-creation and reassembly into distinctive British subcultural "tastes." Hebdige is on the faculty at Middlesex Polytechnic in England.

21

TOWARDS A CARTOGRAPHY OF TASTE
1935-1962

Dick Hebdige

*"To an ever greater degree the work of art repro-
duced becomes the work of art designed for
reproducibility. From a photographic negative,
for example, one can make any number of prints;
to ask for the 'authentic' print makes no sense.
But the instant the criterion of authenticity
ceases to be applicable to artistic production, the
total function of art is reversed. Instead of being
based on ritual, it begins to be based on another
practice — politics."*
Walter Benjamin, *"The Work of Art in the Age of
Mechanical Reproduction".*

In Evelyn Waugh's trilogy, *"The Sword of
Honour"* (1955) there is a minor character called
Trimmer. *"Trimmer".* The name is a synecdoche:
the short, clipped vowels sum up the man exactly
He is meticuloursly neat: he has a clipped
moustache, wears tightly waisted suits and two
tone shoes. He has worked as a hairdresser
(trimmer) on a Transatlantic liner but through a
certain native cunning by skilfully using his
knowledge of the forms (he reads fashion magazines and studies accents), he has managed to
insinuate himself into the officer class. Once
there he takes his place alongside the protagonist,
Guy Crouchback, the sole surviving male in an
old English Catholic family of impeccable lineage
(there are connections with Italy, with the most
antique of antique traditions). Crouchback, with
his fine sense of honour and decorum, represents
a doomed elite. And when the awful Trimmer
sleeps with Crouchback's estranged wife Virginia,
whom he meets one night in a cocktail bar in
Glasgow, the inference is clear: here is a hopeless
future, a post-War future in which we are
destined to witness the inevitable supercession
of the Old Order by the new — the replacement
of the divinely authorised caste-system by the
'democratic sham', of a noble but effete aristocracy by modern man who is quite clearly a
vapid imposter.

Trimmer bears not the remotest relation to a
'true' officer and gentleman. His aspirations are
offensively transparent, he is a little too
echamcleon-like: when on leave in Scotland he
dons a kilt, calls himself Major McTavish and
pins a *"pair of major's crowns on his shoulders
(he . . . changed them for his lieutenant's stars in
the train lavatory)"*[1] Trimmer is far too slick and
amenable to be properly convincing. His hair is
too perfect; his accent a little off-key; his manner
a little too contrived. His tie is too carefully

chosen. His suits fit just too well.

For Waugh what is at stake here in the drama
of Trimmer's impertinence is the sanctity of the
established social order — its inalienable right to
perpetuity. At a time when the structure of
inequality underlying that order had been laid
bare by the Depression years, when the sheer
visibility of the gulf between rich and poor was
beginning to seem unacceptable or at the very
least embarrassing to all but the most intransigent
reactionaries, Waugh sets himself in retrospect in
the teeth of history; defends the indefensible by
resurrecting the most archaic, inegalitarian criteria
— the rule book of the snob. For Waugh, the
Trimmers may inherit the post war world but
because they lack the 'backbone', the 'calibre' of
the people they replace they will squander the
inheritance . . .

In this paper I want to consider some of the
changes in British social and cultural life during
the period 1935–62 to refer these changes back to
the emergences of new patterns of consumption
and new technological developments, particularly
to the qualitative transformations which automation was seen to have effected and to examine
some of the conflicting interpretations of these
changes offered in contemporary accounts.

What we call 'popular culture' — a set of
generally available artefacts: films, records,
clothes, TV programmes, modes of transport etc
— did not emerge in its recognisably contemporary form until the post War period when new
consumer products were designed and manufactured for new consumer markets. Paradoxically,
in many of the debates about the impact and
significance of popular culture, these profound
social and economic transformations have been
mediated through aesthetic concepts like
'quality' and 'taste'. These words are passionately
contested. Different ideologies, different discourses — we could cite at random here the
'sociological', the 'art historical', the 'literary
critical', as well as the discourses of marketing
and industrial design cut across these words at
different angles producing different meanings at
different moments. Underneath the discussion of
an issue like 'discrimination', complex moral,
social even economic options and strategies are
more or less openly examined and the issue of
taste — of where to draw the line between good
and bad, high and low, the ugly and the beautiful, the ephemeral and the substantial — emerges
at certain points as a quite explicitly political

From Dick Hebdige, "Towards a Cartography of Taste 1935-1962," *Block,* Vol. 4 (1981), pp.
39-56. Reprinted by permission.

one.

From the 30's to the 60's, the debates about popular culture and popular taste tended to revolve, often obsessively, around two key terms: 'Americanisation' and the 'levelling down process'. We shall see how a number of cultural critics and commentators working out of cuite different traditions equated the expanded productive potential opened up by the automation of manufacturing processes with the erosion of fundamental 'British' or 'European' values and attitudes and further associated this 'levelling down' of moral and aesthetic standards with the arrival in Britain of consumer goods which were either imported from America or designed and manufactured 'on American lines'. I shall open by mapping out the connections between certain varieties of cultural conservation focussing on the *"spectre of Americanisation"* and indicating some of the ways in which the ideologically weighted separation of the 'serious' from the 'popular' was undertaken. I shall then analyse the formation of those connotational codes which framed the reception given by certain key elites to imported streamlined products and popular American music. Finally, I shall attempt to assess how far the fears concerning the impending 'Americanisation' and 'homogenisation' of British society were borne out by empirical work in the sociological and market research fields. This paper deals, then, with some of the controversies surrounding the emergence from 1935-62 of new cultural forms and patterns of consumption.

The full complexity of the relations between such a heavily loaded series of debates and the larger set of historical transformations to which, however indirectly, they refer can hardly be adequately treated in a paper of this length. But by pursuing a limited number of themes and images across a fairly wide range of discourses it may be possible to reconstruct at least some of that complexity. Such an approach must by definition be eclectic and based on intuitive and what, at times, will seem arbitrary criteria. It may also require the reiteration of histories which are already familiar to the reader. Anothe review of the streamlining debate, for instance, may seem redundant to a design historian and yet I hope that by placing that debate against parallel developments in other disciplines it may be possible to modify the received wisdoms through which a phenomenon like streamlining is conventionally understood. It is perhaps only in this way by outlining the connections and breaks between groups of separate but interlocking statements that we can begin to imagine the particular dimensions of a language which is now largely lost to us and to appreciate not only the historical conditions under which that language was originally constructed but also the social conflicts and shifts in power which were registered inside it and which ultimately led to its dispersal and decline. Moreover, it is only through such a process that we can begin, albeit tentatively, to specify the conditions under which a project as elusive and forbidding as a 'cartography of taste' might be developed.

Waugh and the War of Position

As the example from *"Officers and Gentlemen"* indicates, the work of Evelyn Waugh is relevant to this project in so far as it both symptomatises and parodies the complicity between definitions of 'good taste', class origin and social and political position. For this novelist, the aesthetic boundaries were coterminous with the cultural and moral boundaries and these ran along the same lines which separated the social categories of class. The preservation of the natural order depended for Waugh upon the continual patrolling of these boundaries by a vigilant, incorruptible soldier like himself. In this context, Waugh's depiction of Trimmer as literal detritus – dirt for Mary Douglas is *"matter out of place"*[2] – is peculiarly telling. Although Waugh was distanced from the British upper classes both by his background and his misanthropic disposition, perhaps because both these factors qualified him more clearly for the role of court jester than palace spokesman, his savage revelations can serve as an illuminating counterpoint to the more guarded statements of his peers.

Like all militant reactionaries, Waugh delineates a previously submerged set of values, preferences and assumptions by attempting to exulpate them at the moment when those values and the interests they embody are in crisis, on the point of disintegration. In fact, the growing belligerance of Waugh's prose from 1945, the year in which *"Brideshead Revisited"* was published, onwards dramatically signals the extent to which the cultural consensus had shifted against him during these years, transforming the language of power and control, moving away not only from the kind of caricatured elitism that Waugh himself represented but also – and more gradually – from the 'gentler' patrician and paternalist ideologies which had found favour during the inter War period. David Cardiff has demonstrated how these shifts had already registered at the BBC by the late 30's in the evolution of characteristic styles of presentation in radio talks, in the demarcation of the boundary between the 'serious' and the 'popular' and in the debates about who should speak for the 'common man', in what voice, how often and in support of whose interests[3]. The spectacular trajectory of Waugh's later career in which he posed as the obstinate and unrepentant defender of privilege throws into stark relief the ground on which discussions concerning 'high' and 'low' culture, 'popular' and 'classical' values were initially conducted in the years immediately after 1945. The iconoclasm which motivated Waugh's choice of persona here can only be fully appreciated when it is placed against the emergent orthodoxies of progress, moderation and reform.

Of course, in 1945 the Atlee's Government had been lifted to power on a wave of left wing populism and had succeeded in inaugurating the welfare and nationalisation programmes which made possible the transition to the corporate post War State. With the institutionalisation in the pledge to full employment and the provision of secondary schooling of the rights to work and to free education, the quasi-feudal structures on which Waugh's vision of British society rested were if not entirely swept away then at least seriously disfigured. A social anachronism, Waugh's only possible role was the one to which, finally, he was most temperamentally suited — that of *'Anastasias contra mundum'* — a kind of cultural Canute, and this eventually led him to codify the rituals of exclusion through which the power of an already superceded ancien régime had been perpetuated.

During the mid 50's he helped to specify some of the key signifiers of 'breeding' in an exchange with Nancy Mitford over 'U' and 'Non U' (he corrected her on points of detail[4]). The cartography of taste here took on an aggressively reactionary flavour. The codification of the system of U and non-U was designed to clarify and redefine boundaries rendered opague by post War 'affluence'. It was meant to deter would-be climbers by exposing their charades through the identification of speech mannerisms so habitual and diverse that under normal circumstances they could not be adequately monitored still less adjusted. The sheer density of signifiers, themselves inextricably bound into modes of perception, expectation and belief, to the irrefragable facts of 'social background' militated against the aspirations of even the most versatile pretender. Though ostensibly ambivalent, U and non-U (particularly Waugh's pungent contribution) testified to the persistence of class differences, the survival of the particular configuration of power and value which Waugh chose to defend could not by no means be permanently assured and elsewhere he succumbed to a different set of certainties. In his last book *"The Ordeal of Gilbert Pinfold"* (1957) written some 9 years before his death, we find locked away in the usual labyrinth of irony, his keenest fear: that together affluence and universal education will fulfil the promise or rather the threat of democracy by removing the fact of difference which alone confers value:—

"... *His strongest tastes were negative. He abhorred plastics, Picasso, sun-bathing and jazz — everything in fact that had happened in his own life-time. The tiny kindling of charity which came to him through his religion sufficed only to temper his disgust and change it to boredom . . . He wished no one ill, but he looked at the world 'sub specie aeternitatis' and he found it flat as a map; except when, rather often, personal arrogance intruded. Then he would come tumbling from his exalted point of observation. Shocked by a bad bottle of wine, an impertinent stranger or a fault in syntax . . . "[5]*

Waugh's list is revealing: *plastic* (ie festival of Britain/'inauthentic' mass culture); *Picasso* (Continental modern art/subversive high culture); *sun-bathing* (increased leisure/national inertia/a 'soft' obsession with cosmetics/*"immoralism,*

naturism . . . non-conformism"[6a], and *jazz* (American negro/subversive 'low' culture). Together Waugh suggests, these items and the shifts in taste and value which they embody form part of that process whereby the contours of achievement produced by a tradition based on privilege, and have been progressively planed down until the world for Waugh seems as *".flat as a map".*

This provides a starting point. For Waugh merely stood in the vanguard of a widespread backlash against the confident post War rhetoric of reconstruction and equal opportunity — a backlash which spread across the entire field of cultural criticism during the 1950's.

Hoggart and Orwell: A Negative Consensus
The critical space in which this reaction took pl ace had already been opened up by the literary tradition of dissent and polemic which Raymond Williams describes in *"Culture and Society"* (1961). Though different political perspectives coexist within that tradition, the 'levelling down process' associated with 'mass culture' provided a radical populist like Orwell, a self-confessed elitist such as T.S. Eliot and a social democrat like Hoggart with common cause for concern.

Cultural if not political conservatism drew together writers who were prepared to take opposing sides on issues which at the time were more openly contentious (eg the role of education in the State). Though there was never any agreement as to what exactly should be preserved from the pre-War world, there was never any doubt amongst these writers that clearly *something* should. Whereas Eliot and Leavis were pledged to defend the immutable values of minority culture against the vulgar inroads of the popular arts, to defend in Arnold's terms 'culture' against 'anarchy', Orwell and Hoggart were interested in preserving the 'texture' of working class life against the bland allure of post War affluence — television, high wages and consumerism. The blanket hostility with which the former set of writers greeted the advent of mass culture requires little explanation or critique. It has become part of the 'commonsense' of cultural studies.

However, the more complex and ambivalent resistance to cultural innovation offered by Hoggart and Orwell is frequently bracketted off in the face of the more lasting and positive contributions both writers have made. (Orwell, in this particular context, tends to be remembered for *Road to Wigan Pier* (1937), Hoggart, for his portrayal of the pre-War working class community in the early chapters of *The Uses of Literacy* (1958). In fact both writers castigate the emerging 'consumer culture' on roughly the same grounds. They both equate the classless tone of the glossy advertisements with the erosion paradoxically of personality and choice.

Both Orwell and Hoggart, use the image of the holiday camp as a paradigm for working class life after the War. Orwell imagines a modern design for Coleridge's Kubla Khan consisting of air-conditioned caverns turned into a series of tea-grottoes in the moorish, Caucasian and Hawaiian styles. The sacred river would be dammed up to make an artifically warmed bathing pool and, playing in the background there would be the constant pulse of muzak *"to prevent the onset of that dreaded thing – thought"*. [6b]

In the same way, to achieve the same effects, Hoggart sets one of his parodies of the cheap romantic fiction of the 50's in a place called the Kosy Holiday Kamp complete with *"three dance halls, two sun-bathing parades and lots of milk bars"*[7] in which the Imaginary female narrator *"drools"* over a *"hunk of luscious manhood"* who combines the dubious appeal of *"Marlon Brando and Humph. Bogart"*[8]. Strangely enough, then, despite the ideological gulf(s) which separate these two writers from a man like Evelyn Waugh, there are common themes and images linking what they all wrote on developments in the field of popular culture in the post war years. Where Waugh saw a decline and fall, a flattening out of social and aesthetic criteria, Hoggart and Orwell see the substitution of an *"authentic"*, *"vigorous"* working class community by the idea of a community; the replacement of *"real"* values by what Hoggart at his most evocative calls a *"shiny barbarism"* . . . *"the ceaselss exploitation of a hollow brightness'* . . . *"a spiritual dry-rot"* . . . a *"Candy Floss World"*[9]

Though they spoke from quite different positions, these three writers share a language which is historically determined and determining. They are loosely linked in this particular context through a largely unspoken because largely unconscious (Waugh for reasons I have indicated is the exception here) *consensus* of taste even if that consensus is organised around a list of negatives – ie round those things that they do *not* like.

The Spectre of Americanisation

Increasingly, as the fifties wore on, this negative consensus uniting cultural critics of all persuasions began to settle around a single term; Americanisation. References to the pernicious influence of American popular culture began to appear whenever the 'levelling down' process was discussed and the concept of 'Americanisation' was swiftly and effortlessly absorbed into the existing vocabulary of the 'Culture and Society' debate. Many of the Fritz Lang-like fantasies of an inhuman, fully automated society which lurk behind so much of this writing drew their urgency and power from the ubiquitous spectre of 'Americanisation'. Although during the Cold War, the *prospect* of Soviet territorial ambitions could provoke similar indignation and dread, American *cultural* imperialism demanded a more immediate interpretative response. Whenever anything remotely 'American' was sighted, it tended to be read at least by those working in the context of education or professional cultural criticism as the beginning of the end whether the imagined apocalypse took the form of Huxley's *Brave New World*, Fyvel's *'subtopia'*, Spengler's

'megalopolis' or at a more mundane level, Richard Hoggart's Kosy Holiday Kamp where we will all float together, *"A great composite . . . of the unexceptional ordinary folk: minnows in a heated pool."*[10] America was seen by many of these writers as the prime mover in this terrifying process, as the homogenising agent and from the 1930's onwards the United States (and its productive processes and scale of consumption) began to serve as the image of industrial barbarism; a country with no past and therefore no real culture, a country ruled by competition, profit and the drive to acquire. It was soon used as a paradigm for the future threatening every advanced industrial democracy in the Western world.

Unfavourable depictions of the 'American way of life' and the American way of business such as these were of course hardly novel (for example Matthew Arnold on American anti-intellectualism and 'philistinism' or T.S. Eliot's poem *"Burbank with a Baedeker; Bleistein with a Cigar"*) but during the War and immediately afterwards these depictions broke more decisively into the arena of public, explicitly *populist* discourse and were circulated in a wider number of printed and broadcast contexts. This wider 'official' resistance to American influence can only be understood in the light of particular historical developments – the American military presence in Britain from the early 1940s onwards and Britain's increasing dependence on American economic and military aid. The first *direct* experience of American popular culture for most 'ordinary' Britons occured during the War through informal contact with American servicemen stationed on British bases. It is difficult to estimate the impact of this dramatic encounter though reactions seem to have been ambivalent: curiosity, envy and resentment are blended in those popular representations of American soldiers which stressed their 'affluence' and their relaxed and 'casual manner' (and bv inference their 'easy morals')'

Despite the fact that a good deal of frequently illegal commerce did take place between American troops and the civilian population – perhaps indeed because of it – the American GI began (surreptitiously at first) to be presented in the Press as a 'folk devil', as the enemy at home – a subversive and unsettling influence. It was not only German propaganda dropped behind British lines which played upon the fears and resentments of British soldiers separated from their girlfriends and wives. British journals and newspapers often resorted to similar tactics.

The American serviceman with his dollars and chewing gum, listening to jazz on the A.F.N., buying favours with candy, stockings, cigarettes and beer became a familiar stereotype – one which was easily assimilated into existing mythologies – superimposed on the stock image of the American tourist in Europe. One US chaplain writing home described the typical GI:–

"There he stands in his bulging clothes . . . lonely, a bit wistful, seeing little understanding

WHAT SOME BRITISH RESENT

Different Manners
...

Higher Pay
The lowest-ranking U.S. private is paid 80 dollars (£20) a month, five times the amount it is in Germany.

Different Technique
The American is freer in public with girl friends than the average Englishman.

less — the Conqueror with a chocolate bar in one pocket and a package of cigarettes in the other . . . The chocolate bar and the cigarettes are about all that he, the Conqueror has to give the conquered . . . "[11]

After the War, this covert hostility persisted and was exacerbated by new factors: by Britain's declining status as a world power, the disintegration of the British Empire coupled with the simultaneous rise in America's international prestige and the first indications of American imperial ambitions. In addition the War Debt and the continuing reliance on the American military presence in Europe provided a dual focus for popular resentment.

In magazine articles and newspaper reports, Britain's austerity was frequently contrasted against the booming American economy and the strong dollar. In July 1948 to celebrate the launching of the Queen Elizabeth the *Picture Post* carried a report of a transatlantic crossing entitled prophetically *"The American Invasion"* which displayed a thinly veiled contempt for the new disposable' culture:—

> "Deck-sweepers are filling buckets with five inch cigar butts and quarter-smoked cigarettes, unconsidered debris from the land of not-yet-too-much-plenty".[12]

This was followed by an image which was guaranteed to grate with a *Picture Post* readership still subject in 1948 to the rigours of strict rationing:—

> "In the forward bar two loose-shouldered young men apparently limited to six words an hour, four of which are 'Steward' are spending a morning-long dice-session just for the hell of it".[13]

These themes were elaborated in further articles which appeared throughout the late 40's and early 50's (see for instance *"The Truth about GI Town"* (May 21, 1949) in which *"GI boredom"* is explained through the absence in the North of England of *"juke boxes, television, soda fountains and drive-in cinemas"* see also *"London's American Colony"* (30 June 1951) which includes photographs of *"ostentatious"* Americans playing dice

SHOWING OFF IN PUBLIC is a natural ordeal for the practices of the young spiv. Immaculately dressed, he seeks admiration from girls.

in an illegal London gambling club).

American Music and the British Media
The articulation of these historically localised dissatisfactions in a journal as determinedly 'popular' as the *Picture Post* must have helped to condition the reception given to American cultural imports during the period by the official arbiters of good taste — by the BBC and the literary and artistic establishments. But a chilly reception was already guaranteed by the varieties of cultural conservatism prevalent in official quarters. According to archive research now in progress[14], BBC policy statements throughout the late 40's and early 50's lay down detailed guidelines as to how much American material should be presented and in what context. The content and quality of American comedy shows was apparently subjected to particularly intense scrutiny and ideally the image of America received by the British public was to be filtered through the paternalistic framings of professional commentators like Alastair Cooke. At a time when a tremendous upsurge of popular radicalism,

a popular demand for change coincided with severe material shortages, BBC personnel — programmers and policy makers alike — appear to have been perfectly aware of the 'damaging' indeed potentially subversive impact which American cultural artefacts (particularly popular music: swing, crooning and jazz) could have on public 'morale'. By 1956, when the 'threat' of left-wing populism was hardly a significant political factor, and memories of austerity were beginning to recede, these practices had become firmly sedimented and institutionalised.

Despite the relaxation in the tone and style of BBC broadcasting allegedly affected by the advent of commercial television in 1954, rock 'n roll was deliberately ignored and resisted by the BBC radio networks. British balladeers and cabaret-style singers were systematically favoured and in 1956 the year when Elvis Presely's *Hearbreak Hotel* was released, not one single rock 'n roll record was featured in the annual review of popular songs. A similar pattern of more or less explicit censorship has been observed by Iain Chambers in the music press where throughout the 50's notions of 'quality' and 'taste' were consistently opposed to the 'commercial' blandishments of *"ersatz"* rock 'n roll. (Melody Maker resisted readers' requests to run a weekly 'top ten' until 1956). The following was, apparently, a typical response:—

> *"Come the day of judgement, there are a number of things for which the American music industry, followed (as always) panting and starry-eyed by our own will find itself answerable for to St. Peter. It wouldn't surprise me if near the top of the list is 'Rock-and-Roll'... Viewed as a social phenomenon, the current craze for Rock-and-Roll material is one of the most terrifying things to have had happened to popular music...*
> *The Rock-and-Roll technique, instrumentally and vocally, is the antithesis of all that jazz has been striving for over the years — in other words, good taste and musical integrity."*
> (Melody Maker).

Historical 'authenticity' and/or stylistic sophistication served as the criteria for distinguishing the acceptable forms (ie the 'natural' blues, folk and Trad; sophisticated swing, balladeering etc.) from the unacceptable (ie rock, rhythm and blues). As Chambers remarks, *"What in hindsight appear to be the most arbitrary distinctions were at the time fiercely patrolled aesthetic parameters"*[15] and the passion with which those distinctions were defended and maintained indicates once more the extent to which the values they embodied were felt to be at risk in this case from the *"monotony of incoherence"*[16] which early rock 'n roll was seen to represent. When the broadcasting authorities eventually capitulated to popular demand, the music was subject to the same elaborate monitoring and framing procedures laid down in the early post War years. *6.5 Special, Thank Your Lucky Stars* and *Juke Box Jury* on television, *Saturday Club* and *East Beat* on radio were all hosted by already-established 'professional' presenters (eg Pete Murray, David Jacobs). *Juke Box Jury* was in fact a study in mediation: new musical product was processed through a panel of *"well-known show business personalities"* who submitted it to a brief barrage of witty, frequently barbed but always self-consciously lighthearted commentary. Jack Goode's *Oh Boy!* was the only programme in which the more delinquent connotations of the music were permitted to creep through unremarked (and this, perhaps significantly, appeared on the commercial channel).

Milk Bar Horrors and the Threat of Youth

The gate keeping and policing functions undertaken as a matter of course by the BBC were, as we have seen, assumed with equal seriousness elsewhere in the broader currents of cultural and aesthetic criticism. By the early 50's, the very mention of the word 'America' could summon up a cluster of negative associations. It could be used to contaminate other words and concepts by sheer proximity as in *"Americanised sex"*, *"the false values of the American film"* etc.[17] Once more an example from the *Picture Post* indicates just how far the Americanisation thesis had infiltrated the more 'respectable' reaches of popular journalism. In an article entitled *"The Best and Worst of Britain"* (Dec 19, 1953), Edward Hulton, the editor describes the emergence of a new race of *"machine minders and comic-strip readers"*[18] He quotes a Welfare Officer who compares a group of factory girls who *"put pieces of paper into slots for 8 hours a day"* to *"chickens pecking corn"* and when asked about religion confesses:—

> *"They prefer Victor Mature to God because they can understand Victor — and he relieves the monotony of their lives; as far as they know, God doesn't?"*[19]

Hulton concludes with references to the *"Growth in juvenile crime"*, talks ominously about young *"thugs... who revel in attacking old men and women, and hitting people when they are down"* and the article ends with this solemn warning:—

> *"We are on the brink of that horrible feature of American life where, in many a shady district, thugs go round from shop to shop demanding the payment of 'protection money' or 'else'"*...[20]

Here, the way in which images of crime, disaffected youth, urban crisis and spiritual drift are anchored together around 'popular' American commodities (Victor Mature, comic strips) suggests a more completely structured responses than those we have so far encountered — a fixing of a chain of associations (between youth, the future, America and crime) which has since become thoroughly sedimented in British common sense. As we have seen, such typifications emerge only slowly; meanings coalesce around particular configurations of attitudes, values and events and are gradually naturalised as they circulate in different contexts. By isolating two distinct moments in the formation of this structure, — one from Hoggart, one from Orwell

PIN TABLE SALOONS AND AMUSEMENT ARCADES ARE THE GANG BOYS' IDEA OF LEISURE.   COLIN DONELLAN, ⁴
YOUNG MAN WITH A LIST OF CONVICTIONS, WAITS FOR FRIENDS

– the process of naturalisation can itself be arrested and examined.

In Hoggart's description of the 'juke box boys' (1958), the associations which had begun to congregate around the term 'Americanisation' are organised to the point where they are about to be translated into fully-fledged connotational codes. Hoggart describes a group of young men *"aged between 15 and 20, with drape-suits, picture ties and an American slouch"* who spend their evenings listening to *"nickelodeons"*[21] in the *"harshly lit milk bars"*. The snack bars are associated with an unprecedented spiritual and aesthetic breakdown and the depressing picture is completed by what Hoggart calls the *"hollow cosmos"* effect of early rock 'n roll. Summing up, Hoggart attributes the decline to some received notion of America:–

"Many of the customers – their clothes, their hair-styles, their facial expressions all indicate – are living to a large extent in a myth-world compounded of a few simple elements which they take to be those of American life".[22]

Hoggart closes on a note which establishes once and for all the links between a number of emotive images and ideas: the equation between America and mass culture, between Americanisation and homogenisation, between America's present and Britain's future. At the end of this section on the juke box boys, Hoggart writes:–

"The hedonistic but passive barbarian who rides in a fifty horse power bus for threepence to see a five million dollar film for one and eight is not simply a social oddity; he is a

portent."[23]

The impression created is one of monstrous disproportion (threepence, 5 million dollars, one and eight), dislocation ('hollow cosmos', myth world) and disharmony (rock 'n roll) and together these images form a menacing amalgam which collapses the threat of 'mindless', 'violent' youth into the larger threat of the Future (bland and alien).

To trace the origins of these connotational codes back a little further we need only turn to George Orwell's *"Coming Up for Air"* (1939) in which the same 'artificial', 'alienated' environment is made to serve in exactly the same way as a metaphor for moral and aesthetic entropy. George Bowling, the disillusioned middle-aged narrator, suspecting that something has gone badly wrong with Britain, returns to the village in which he was born (now a sprawling industrial estate) to find his suspicions confirmed – indeed realised and reified – in the emergence of the flashy new milk bars:–

"There's a kind of atmosphere about these places that gets me down. Everything slick and shiny and stream-lined: mirrors, enamel and chromium plate whichever direction you look in. Everything spent on the decorations and nothing on the food. No real food at all. Just lists of stuff with American names, sort of phantom stuff that you can't taste and can hardly believe in the existence of"[24]

In both Hoggart and Orwell, the words 'soft' and 'streamlined' are virtually synonomous and stream-lined products made out of 'shiny' 'modern'

materials are frequently used by these writers as
a kind of shorthand for all manner of imagined
decadence. Once they had been defined as signs of
the perfidious *"American influence"* the very
invocation of such commodities in a piece of
journalism or cultural criticism could be used to
stand in for any combination of the following
ideological themes:— the rebellion of youth, the
'feminisation' of British culture, the collapse of
authority, the loss of Empire, the breakdown
of the family, the growth in crime, the decline
in attendance at places of worship etc. though
none of these are necessarily present in the
example from Orwell. In this way the very
mention of a word like 'streamlined' at a particular historical moment could be used to mobilise
a whole set of ideologically charged connotations
from a number of different sources. To appreciate the complexity of this process we have to
consider the way in which the word 'streamlining'
itself came to be applied to industrial products
by those working within the professional design
milieu and to try to tease out some of the
meanings *encoded* into streamlined artefacts at
the design and production stages. In this way it
becomes possible to turn at last to those
discourses in which the issues of quality and
taste were *overtly* confronted and discussed.

*The Streamlining Controversy (1) The Blasphemy
of "Jazz Forms"*

References to 'streamlining' first began appearing on a regular basis within American design
discourse in the 1930's (though Harold van
Doren cites the submission as early as 1867 of a
patent for a 'streamlined train'). To begin with
the smooth cigar shapes to which the word
'streamlining' referred were associated exclusively
with aviation technology where it was argued
that they served a specific function-facilitating
speed maximalising air flow etc. However these
visual motifs were by the early 30's being carried
over into American car design. (The 1934 Chrysler
Airflow, for instance, was modelled on Douglas
aircraft designs). Streamlining soon constituted
in this new context a popular, *"eye catching
vocabulary"*[25] — one which clashed with the
purist architecturally based idioms of classical
European modernism. The ideals of which in this
particular field were most clearly embodied in
the angular designs by Walter Gropius for the
German Adler Company. (For example, the
1930 Adler Cabriolet is often quoted in books
on design theory as the apotheosis of 'tasteful'
car design.)

By the end of the decade streamlining was
beginning to be applied to commodities totally
outside the transport field in which it had found
its initial rationale. Edgar Kauffman's example
of a scotch-tape dispenser 'naively echoing' tail-
plane 'fairing' is probably, thanks paradoxically
to Reyner Banham[26] the most 'notorious'
instance of the 'improper' usage of aviation
motifs. By 1940 Harold van Doren could write:—

*"Streamlining has taken the modern world by
storm. We live in a maelstrom of streamlined
trains, refrigerators and furnaces; streamlined*

1940's Streamlined Toaster

1937 Electrolux Cylinder Cleaner and 1939
Upright Montgomery Ward by Teague.

*bathing beauties, soda crackers and facial
massages . . . "*[27]

The ensuing controversy surrounding these
allegedly 'improper' applications of streamlining
lasted for more than two decades and constitutes
perhaps the most famous, and certainly one of
the most protracted and comprehensively documented debate to have occured in professional
design circles. It still remains in effect the
decisive, determining 'moment' in the formation
of much current academic discourse on design
(eg formalism/anti-formalism; aesthetic/

commercial; 'good' design/'popular' design). Its interest for us lies in the fact that it acted as the medium through which the hegemony of the modern school (Corbusier, the Bauhaus etc) which had shaped much of the critical theory of industrial design since its inception as a professional discipline in the early 20's was challenged and eventually broken (we are now, for instance, or so the rubric goes, living in the *"Post modernist Age"*). By exploring the controversy within design over the streamlining issue it may be possible to determine how the ideologically charged distinctions between the 'serious' and the 'popular' between 'good' and 'bad' taste came to be articulated in a particular discursive field between the years 1935-55, to examine how far they paralleled similar distinctions produced in other areas at more or less the same time and to relate these developments back to changes in the modes of industrial production, distribution and consumption.

The response of the European design Establishment to the indiscriminate streamlining of imported American products was immediate and uniformly hostile. A streamlined refrigerator was interpreted as an act of provocation in direct defiance of the most fundamental principle of 'good design' – that *"form follows function"*. Such an object was plainly blasphemous: a hymn to excess. It was 'decorative', 'decadent' and its offensiveness as far as the European design authorities were concerned hinged on its arbitrariness. The intrusion of an expressive design vocabulary which bore no *intrinsic* relation to the commodities it shaped was plainly subversive. It introduced the possibility of an *intertextuality* of industrial design – of the unrestricted passage of signifiers across the surfaces of a whole range of unrelated products without any reference whatsoever to 'essential' qualities such as 'function' and this ran absolutely counter to the prevailing 'modern' orthodoxy. (The fact that so much Modern Movement rhetoric was based on an equally arbitrary analogy with architectural idioms was hardly considered. Moreover an alternative 'European' style of streamlining which had its roots in Italian futurism was apparently permissible so long as it remained 'tasteful' and restrained. Once again we encounter the entrenchment and preservation of what in hindsight appear to be peculiarly untenable distinctions.)

The differences between dominant European and American conceptions of the place of 'good taste' in product design stemmed from the different infrastructural links which had been established on the two continents between manufacturing industry, design practice and design theory. American design had been firmly placed on a commercial free-lance footing and was studio and consultancy-based. The most prominent figures in the American design field – van Doren, Bel Geddes, Loewy, Dreyfuss and Teague – ran their own design agencies and while they all subscribed to ideal notions of 'form', 'harmony' and 'proportion', the market continued to exert a major determining influence on both their theory and practice[28]. In Europe on the other hand, national bodies had been set up at least in Britain and Germany to promulgate the principles of 'good design' but, in Britain, there were few integral links with industry, and when design teams were eventually formed they tended to be permanently attached to a single company or corporation. This separation of theory and , practice had direct consequences on the formation of the dominant European design aesthetic. (In America the very notion of privileging 'aesthetic' principles over considerations of market demand and 'popular' taste tended to be regarded as an expensive indulgence).

In Britain the Design for Industries Association (DIA) which had been established in 1915 and was modelled on the Deutscher Werkbund pursued a policy rooted in the ideals of William Morris and the Arts and Crafts Movement. DIA statements had a strongly paternalistic flavour (see for instance early issues of *Design for Today*) which reflected how far it was institutionally and ideologically identified with Government rather than industrial interests. Its influence on British design was minimal and by the late 30's the DIA was under siege from an Evangelical group of Modern Movement proponents led by Nikolaus Pevsner and John Bertram. Both wrote influential books – Pevsner's *"Pioneers of Modern Design"*; Bertram's *"Design"* – which were published eventually as Pelican Specials and which soon found favour and support amongst the dominant taste-making elites. Stephen Bailey has indicated that by the late 30's, institutions like London Transport and the BBC principally through *The Listener* were actively promoting the principles of modern design. The austere, patrician values of the Continental Modern Movement were perfectly compatible with the definitions of 'good taste' which were then becoming prevalent in broadcasting circles. The writings of Pevsner and Bertram were full of references to 'progress' and 'quality', to the 'challenge' of technological change and the need for cultural continuity. Moderation in aesthetics was combined with a commitment to social democracy in a way which fitted in with the more liberal ethos of control which was emerging during this period.[29] (For a similar, roughly contemporaneous development in a different field, see for instance John Grierson's essays on documentary in which the film maker eulogises the 'power' of industry and the 'dignity' of work reconciling a paternal interest in 'ordinary' life with the demand to produce 'good', affirmative and accessible work.[30]) The serious and responsible tone in which questions of popular taste and popular culture were discussed within the Modern Movement closely paralleled the new, more democratic accent – the 'accent on change' – which the BBC sought to adopt in the late 30's, and significantly, Bertram's book was based on a series of radio talks entitled *'Design in Everyday Things'* which he presented in 1937. This is not to say, of course, that in other countries, other contexts, the aesthetic principles of the Modern Movement were necessarily identified with moderate social democratic ideologies. John Heskett, for example, has demonstrated how, in Germany, design forms and concepts normally associated with the Bauhaus and with the Weimar Republic were used just as fully and successfully as German folk and craft forms by the Nazi's[31]. Even Pevsner recognised that there was no *intrinsic* relation between 'well-made' forms and those programmes for social change which he personally supported:—

> "In Germany the post war Labour Government fostered the modern style . . . In Italy modern architecture and modern design enjoy the special furtherance of the Government as being a expression of Fascism.
> In Russia the same style was, after some years of State approval, given up as an outcome of latter-day bourgeoisie, and a decidely conventional and threfore probably more popular style was launched. The reaction of art to changes within our civilisation thus remains indeterminate . . . "[32]

What is however, clear is that the manner in which modernist principles were predominantly interpreted *in Britain* by people like Pevsner, the kind of intervention which the early British popularisers of modernism imagined they were making (Pevsner, for instance, refers in the same sentence to the *"levelling up of class contrasts . . . the raising of standards of design"*[33]) fitted in exactly with the more liberal and progressive ideologies which were then just beginning to find favour amongst certain key elites (eg the BBC).

Both Bertram's and Pevsner's writings contain lengthy polemics against the philistinism of British industry, the vulgarity of popular taste and British reticence in the face of the 'new' and 'well-formed'. Bertram's book is perhaps more purely 'Continental' in tone: attacks on domestic kitsch (*"The sewing machine . . . decorated with gold transfers of ornament borrowed from Gothic altar-pieces"* .... the *'bijou-baronial'* and *'Tudoristic'* bungalow etc[34]) alternate with clusters of adjectival positives: *"practical, honest, cheap, lasting and beautiful"*[35]

The excesses of American streamlining were then hardly likely to be welcomed by this new design oligarchy, and when Pevsner accuses *"modernism in its jazz forms"* . . . of spoiling the market . . . *"for more serious modern work"*[36] one suspects he is referring specifically to American imports or American-influenced designs (the words 'jazz' and 'American' are virtually interchangeable in this kind of writing throughout the 20's and 30's). The disjunction between British and American traditions — the different relationships with industrial practice and the State formed by the respective design elites provides some explanation for the emergence of discursive polarities between what was defined

as 'commercial' and 'responsible' work and for the development of quite different criteria in America and Europe for judging what constitute 'good' design. But in order to obtain a more adequate account of these differences and to appreciate their wider historical importance we have to go beneath and beyond the terms in which the debate was originally conducted and to consider changes both in the production process and in the scale of consumption.

The Streamlining Controversy (2) the Shape of the Future
The emergence of streamlining from 1930 to the late 50's as *the* popular style — 'popular' in the sense of being simultaneously 'commercially successful' and 'democratic', 'anti-purist', 'running counter to the classical' etc can be explained by reference to two major developments: the refinement of pressed steel technology and the creation of new consumer markets. The development of pressing and stamping techniques (whereby sections of a product could be stamped out whole and subsequently welded together) can be seen as an integral part of that process of accelerated automation and rationalisation through which in the years immediately before and after the War, financial and technological resources became concentrated into progressively larger and more efficient units. In other words it was just one of the many technological innovations which enabled monopoly capital to become consolidated in the period.

In this context, the movement away from fabricated, geometric forms to pressed or stamped ones, from what van Doren calls 'rectilinear' to 'curvilinear' forms[37] signalled a more general shift within industrial production towards a greater output of a more limited range of items for a larger domestic market at a lower unit cost. The fact that stamping technology made it easier to produce curved forms, that in Banham's words it *"works most efficiently with broad, smooth envelope shapes"*[39] meant that this innovation and the increased rationalisation of the production process which went with it could literally *declare itself in form*, could advertise through its very newness those quantitative and qualitative breaks that had been made in the production process, in the scale of production and the size of the potential market to which 'streamlined' products were to be directed.

This is not to return to some crude technological determinism. Commercial pressures remained paramount here. The range of design options available continued to be structured by market as well as productive forces. Designers continued to provide appealing and commercially viable designs which at the same time were intended to maximalise the potential for formal and stylistic change opened up by the new technology. And as the American designer Raymond Loewy put it in 1945 ultimately the only streamline aesthetic which was likely to impress the directors and the shareholders continued *"to consist of a beautiful sales curve shooting upwards"*.[39]

But the potential for stylistic experimentation opened up by a new technological 'advance' such as stamping could be cashed in in the market place precisely through the deliberate exaggeration of stylistic *difference*, through the extent to which the new products could be clearly marked off by their very 'newness' and 'uniqueness' — in this case by their *"curvilinear"* qualities — from those already available. It was largely through the vocabulary of style and form then that adaptations in the technical apparatus were mediated to the new mass of consumers.

Advertisements for streamlined products appealed directly to popular conceptions of an irresistable "scientific progress" and frequently drew their inspiration from contemporary science fiction and science faction genres — for instance, from those popular magazines of the 30's which presented utopian futures "based half on fact and half on prophecy"[40]. Streamlining became synonomous with the 'shape of the future', with a romantic exultation in the power of the New and its vocabulary simultaneously influenced and was influenced by what Robin Spencer has called the "popular imaginative concept of tomorrow's world"[41] The significance and appeal of this concept, as Spencer points out "has nothing to do with established art forms"[42a]. The futurist manifestoes and the popular imagery of progress shared only "the bright innocence of technological aesthetics"[42b] but that aesthetic and the meanings constructed round it were transformed as they passed across from high to low, from the lofty assertions of an artistic avant garde to the context of consumption and use — the domain of the popular.

The innocent enthusiasm for technological progress was not confined solely to the reception end of design aesthetics in America. Even a respected designer such as Henry Dreyfuss whose works always followed months of sober market research could succumb just as uncritically as his public to the attraction of crystal-ball gazing. Sometimes, inevitably, these predictions were a little off the mark:—

"In less than half a century it will be AD2000. Who can say what life will be like then? One can only speculate knowing that for all the incredible scientific progress of the last 50 years, limitless vistas lie ahead . . . Mail will probably be dispatched across the country by guided rockets . . .[43]

Increasingly, American product design became the art of imaginative projection as the pressures to overcome the law of the declining rate of profit necessitated the constant stimulation of demand through the production of ever 'newer', more fancifully and 'futuristically' styled commodities. In turn, the competition between manufacturers determined to make an impression on an increasingly heterogeneous market grew more intense as consumers became more status-conscious and more responsive to visual criteria. As John Heskett has indicated, (here in the context of German manufacturing industry "after

Cadillac, 1950's. Advertisement in Ladies Home Journal

the American model") . . . the work of designers became predominantly oriented towards the creation of artificial and superficial differences between products"[44] these intensified market pressures led to a new direction in product design which was subsequently dubbed "consumer engineering"[45].

The Streamlining Controversy (3) From Borax to Pop

The production spiral was most marked in the American car industry. By the 1950's the policy of "planned obsolescence" which was admitted, indeed openly paraded in Detroit as a positive factor both in design and 'consumer-satisfaction' led to what can only be described as the 'creation' of some of the most outlandish and, as it turned out, provocative examples of 'dream' styled

1959 'Chevy'

artefacts to have yet rolled off a production line. (The 1953 Cadillac El Camino was in fact advertised as everybody's *"Dream Car"*).

Harvey J. Earl, head of General Motors styling department was responsible for many of the more outrageously somnambulent designs. His most controversial innovation involved the transposition in 1949 of the Lockheed Lighting tailfin to the rear bumpers of the Cadillac range – a move which he justified by claiming that it conferred *"visible prestige"* on the car owner. In the furore which these 'unwarranted' and 'ostentatious' features caused in European design circles many of the themes of the original streamlining debate of the 30's were recapitulated but with the shift in the post war years from a production to a consumer economy, the issue of impending 'Americanisation' was far more clearly foregrounded:–

"Streamlining is the jazz of the drawing board – the analogy is close, both are U.S. phenomena, both are 'popular' in their appeal, both are far removed from their characteristic sources – negro music and aero-dynamics and finally both are highly commercialised and use the star-system"[46]

British and 'classical' American designers united to protest the arrival of General Motors' *"short-term, low-rent chromium utopia".*[47]

The term 'borax', which had been coined in the American furniture industry to denote *obviously heavy forms and elaborate ornament,*[48] was taken over by the dissenters and used to refer to the kind of terminal styling represented by Detroit. (There was even an adjective – 'borageous'). And as Reyner Banham has pointed out the very presence of such terms in journals as clearly devoted to Modern Movement principles as *The Architectural Review* implies a simple Cold War logic: *"borax is bad . . . elegant is good, stylised is bad, functional is good"*[49]. Indeed the introduction of tailfins which were subsequently described as the 'Vietnam of product design'[50] was even (apparently) blamed for *"the fact that America lagged behind Russia in the space-race. Whilst the Russians had been developing 'Sputnik' . . . the Americans had been debauching themselves with tailfins."*[51]

Nonetheless by this time (as Banham's confidently satirical voice here indicates) the opposition was growing in strength and articulacy: the modernist consensus was being attacked from within (Banham was a former student of Pevsner). The New York Journal *Industrial Design* began to carry arch and generally appreciative reviews of new Detroit product and there were attempts on the part of certain sections of the New York intelligentsia as early as 1951 to have Earl's creations reassessed as art in inverted commas (eg the Hollow Rolling Sculpture exhibition at the Museum of Modern Art). In London the emergence of a similarly ironic sensibility – a sensibility which was eventually to produce both 'Pop Art' and Tom Wolfe's New Journalism – was signalled in the

formation of the Independent Group and the mounting in 1956 at the Whitechapel Art Gallery of the *This is Tomorrow* exhibition which revelled in the despised iconography of the new popular culture.

Once again these discursive shifts and breaks within the art and design world(s) reproduced transformations in the intersecting spheres of cultural criticism and popular journalism and these were in turn written out of and against the prevailing ideologies of 'Americanisation', the 'levelling-down process' 'cultural decline' and 'consumer affluence'. And to trace the connections one stage further (and one stage back), all these shifts occurred out of or in response to changes in the composition of the market and the forces of production. The 'borax' controversy which extended and accentuated the resistance on the part of dominant European elites to American 'streamlined' products helped to crystallise with exceptional lucidity within the confined space of a professional 'discipline' the issues which were felt to be at stake; the significance of form in everyday life, the need for a 'responsible' interpretation of popular demand, the place of public taste in design practice. The Cadillac of the 1950's merely acted as a catalyst for a clash of values and interests which had been building up since the development in America in the first two decades of the 20th Century of mass production technology. It represented the concretisation in form of conflicts between different definitions of legitimacy and taste. It was an object which *invited* strong reactions.

Towards the Streamlined workforce

In America of course, the Cadillac was, as the El Camino advertisements acknowledged, the embodiment in chrome of the American Dream. Throughout the 50's and 60's it represented the aspirations precisely of the *"disadvantaged American"*[52], and it was the blatant expression of these aspirations in their raw state – untouched by the paternalistic mediations of European 'good taste' – which had proved so divisive. This was of course what made the Cadillac so 'vulgar'. It was the levelling down process-in-car-nate. It was the tangible elimination of value and distinction (in the twin senses of 'difference' and 'distinguishing excellence') achieved paradoxically through the 'pretentious' claims made on its behalf to 'social status'. (This was the car for the 'upwardly mobile'). This was the culmination of the whole pernicious process. Here, in the 1950 Cadillac it was quite evident that the 'hallmarks of distinction' had been at last replaced by the fetish of stylistic variation.

Nor was this interpretation confined solely to conservative cultural critics though the imagined erosion of class differences which affluence was supposed to have produced was subject to a different inflection on the Left. Marcuse, who in *"One Dimensional Man"* (1964) describes what amounts to a 'streamlined' workforce cites the example of *"the negro who owns a cadillac"* along with *"the typist who is as attractively made up as the daugher of her employer"* (sic)[53] to demonstrate the extent to which subordinate groups have been assimilated and won over by 'passive consumerism' to dominant modes of thought and action.

The work of Marcuse — the European Marxist in California — is of particular interest here because it represents a conscious attempt to draw together strands and themes elaborated in the context of a number of different discourses — sociological, aesthetic, literary, and psychoanalytical — and to bring these to bear directly on the question of the *"transubstantiation of labour power"*[54] supposedly effected by the automation of the work process. Marcuse takes the suggestion put forward by amongst others Vance Packard and Charles Walker that the tendency to rationalise and standardise the production process together with the rise in wages associated with it leads to *"the strengthening of the position of management, and increasing impotence and resignation on the part of the workers"*[55]. Interestingly enough, he uses the example of the *"Americanised Caltex refineries at Ambes France"* to illustrate Serge Mallet's notion of 'voluntary integration'[56]: the factory as the micrososm of an enclosed consumer society — a society which works like an efficient, unstoppable machine (c/f *Metropolis* and incidentally Foucault's 'panopticon').

The image of a class of 'privatised', affluent workers locked into a closed circuit of production and consumption, *"watching the same TV programmes and visiting the same resort places"*[57] as their employers, struggling only to purchase the products of their own alienated labour informs much of the critical sociological discourse of the 50's and 60's. And as Crichter has pointed out, here referring to Goldthorpe and Lockwood's classic study of Luton car workers, *"The Affluent Worker in the Class Structure"* (1968), the evidence of these changes, in this case:

> *"changes in economic circumstances (increased incomes and access to consumer goods with consequent changes in life styles); changes in the technology and management of work (the decline of manual labour the new 'technician' roles involving greater teamwork and integration into the goals of management); changes in the ecology of cities (increased owner-occupation, suburbanisation and the redevelopment of the inner city"*[58].

tends to be assumed rather than assessed. The authors concern themselves with discovering *"whether, in those situations where most of these 'new' factors are most apparent, they have the effects attributed to them"*[59].

The Evidence of Change

The evidence which *can* be assembled here is, in fact, conflicting, fragmentary and flawed. Many of the available statistics on consumption after the War, for instance, emanate from the new consumer-oriented industries of market-research and advertising, and while these can be extremely useful in delineating general trends, the evidence they provide is sometimes questionable (see below).

Of course there *were* real changes in patterns of consumption from 1935 to 1962. Quite apart from a steady rise in the availability of a wider ranger of consumer goods throughout the period, there was a particularly dramatic transformation in the scale of working class expenditure on leisure in terms both of time and money. For example, Paul Wild has traced the development of new forms of consumption — principally the spread of cinemas and dance halls — in one provincial town, Rochdale, from 1900-1940. During these years leisure provision became increasingly centralised (eg by 1929 British Gaumont owned 300 cinemas up and down the country, by 1945 the Rank group had opened a further 500 and owned the Ealing and Shepherds Bush studios[60]) and American and American-influenced products began to dominate the 'popular' market. Wild characterises the following broad trends: the growth of recreation oligopolies (eg Rank and after the War, EMI), the removal of leisure provision from popular control, a tendency towards greater specialisation in what had previously been communal or class-based rituals, and a swing on the part of a working class audience dominated by a less gruelling work schedule and *"increasingly lured into a world of novelty and the appearance of glamour towards American style entertainments"*[61] But as yet very little work has been done on how working class people themselves perceived these developments how they *used* the new facilities, and to what extent they really were, (as Wild implies in the phrase *"lured into"*), deradicalised by the inter War restructuring of popular leisure.

After the War, changes in patterns of specifically *teenage* consumption attracted a perhaps inordinate amount of attention. One market researcher, Mark Abrams in *"The Teenage Consumer"* (1959) — together with Colin MacInnes in books like *"Absolute Beginners"* — was largely responsible for constructing the influential paradigm of the hedonistic, working class teenager prepared to spend a large proportion of his or her income (which Abrams calculated to have risen to twice its pre War value) on leisure. But subsequent research carried out by sociologists (eg Smith's Bury sample (1966)) threw many of these assertions into question (Smith found that some 40% of the 18 year olds he interviewed spent less than 75p per week on clothes, drink, and going out etc (see Brake 1980[62])

Nonetheless, the 'myth of affluence' and the accompanying ideologies of 'classlessness' and 'incorporation' representing, as they did, attempts to provide coherent explanations for changes in the phenomenal forms of working class life and the formation in particular of the new 'popular culture' ran directly parallel to the 'Americanisation' thesis: the assumed eradication of traditional differences remained largely intact. Abrams

for instance claimed that:—

"Under conditions of general prosperity the social study of society in class terms is less and less illuminating. And its place is taken by differences related to age"[63]

However, there was a good deal of confusion here. Abrams went on to insist that by 1959:—

". . . not far short of 90 per cent of all teenage spending is conditioned by working class taste and value"[64]

Most of the more dramatic developments as far as adolescent consumption was concerned — eg increased provision of leisure facilities (discotheques, boutiques, Wimpey bars, Ten Pin Bowling Alleys etc) and magazines (*Fab, 19* etc) aimed at a specifically teenage market did not fully emerge until the early to mid 60's. But even here amongst the young, consumption rituals, far from being classless continued to take place within a culture sharply divided precisely round the class — related questions of quality and taste. In 1971 the National Board of Prices and Incomes reported that the distribution of earnings remained more or less the same as in 1886: material hardship may have diminished but relative deprivation still persisted. Before 1962, teenage consumption where it wasn't organised through church youth clubs, voluntary associations (and involuntary ones — National Service continued until 1958) tended to be a largely subterranean affair occurring, at least for working class males in the interstices of the parent culture, on the street corners, in Arcades, cafes and dance halls. And the most conspicuous evidence of change — the emergence in the early 50's of flamboyant sub-

cultures like the teddy boys — of groups whose tastes were most clearly conditioned by exposure to American imports, to American popular music and American films, (the style according to Barnes[65] was strongly influenced by Hollywood gangster and Western stereotypes), served to accentuate rather than annul class differences. The teds, after all, were drawn more or less exclusively from the 'submerged tenth' of lower working class youth[66].

According to one survey conducted by the *Picture Post* at the Tottenham Mecca ballroom in 1954, a teddy boy's wages could range from as little as £4.17.6d per week (an apprentice) to as much as £12.00 (a skilled cabinet-maker) whilst the made-to-measure drape suit which was compulsory wear (described by Fyvel as a *"theatrical outfit . . .un-English . . . simply wierd"*[67]) cost £17.00—£20.00, a *"good poplin shirt"* £2.00 and a pair of 'beetlecrusher' shoes £3.00.[68] In other words, becoming a teddy boy was not something which could be undertaken lightly. Far from being a casual response to 'easy money', the extravagant sartorial display of the ted required careful financial planning and was remarkably self-conscious — a going against the grain, as it were, of a life which in all other respects was, in all likelihood, relatively cheerless and poorly rewarded.

But these groups were hardly representative. They served for most contemporary observers of the scene as the *"dark vanguard"*[69] and were perceived as traitors on the shore of the imagined sea of comics, quiffs and bubble gum which threatened to overwhelm the singularity of British culture unless *"something"* (rarely specified) was done. The piece from Hoggart on the *"juke box boys"* gives some indication of how these forms of cultural 'desertion' could be read as *"the most advanced point of social change"*[70] — the shape of things to come.

Beyond the Shock of the New
It is now possible to reassess the broader political and cultural implications of the debates on taste, American cultural influence and the 'quality of life' which took up so much critical space from the 30's to the 60's. Discourses evolved in a wide variety of relatively autonomous professional contexts are linked together paradigmatically through recurrent ideological themes, images and issues. Specifically we have seen how a number of ideologically charged connotational codes could be invoked and set in motion by the mere mention of a word like *"America"* or *"jazz"* or *"streamlining"*. Groups and individuals as apparently unrelated as the British Modern Design establishment, BBC staff members, Picture Post and music paper journalists, critical sociologists 'independent' cultural critics like Orwell and Hoggart, a Frankfurt-trained Marxist like Marcuse, even an obsessive isolationist like Evelyn Waugh all had access to these codes. Together they form a language of value which is historically particular. With the appearance of imported popular phenomena like 'streamlining' and 'jazz' this language — not only the terms themselves: 'excellence', 'quality', 'distinction' and so on — but the structure of expectations and assumptions which lay behind them — the desirability of cultural continuity, and social stability, the existence of moral and aesthetic absolutes — was thrown into crisis.

The challenge represented by shifts in the organisation of market and productive forces was registered at the level of form in the appearance of new recorded musical genres (rock 'n roll, r & b etc) and a new order of commodities differentiated from each other by superficial stylistic features. Just as the Afro-American musical language emerged from a quite different cultural tradition to the classical European one, obeyed a different set of rules, moved to a different time and placed a far greater emphasis on the role of rhythm, participation and improvisation, so the new economy based on the progressive automation and depersonalisation of the production process and the transformed patterns of consumption it engendered disrupted and displaced the old critical language. This new economy — an economy of consumption, of the signifier, of endless replacement, supercession, drift and play, in turn, engendered a new language of dissent. Those terms which had been negatively defined by the established cultural elites were inverted and made to carry oppositional meanings as they were appropriated (in the way that Marcuse had recommended) by the (counter-cultural) advocates of change and converted into positive values — hedonism, pleasure, purposelessness, disposability etc. However, this displacement of one language, of one set of discourses by another set did not occur simply or solely through the mysterious 'dispersal' of epistemological categories and *'regimes of truth'* but by the irruption into a historically particular realm of meaning through the agency of *real* objects, a new range of material commodities — of another message, written, so to speak, in a quite different 'language'. This message spoke another set of transformations, and emanated from a zone which is, *"in the last instance"* more decisive and determining than language — the sphere precisely of production. As the opening quotation from Walter Benjamin suggests, there is a more grounded explanation for the way in which that 'message' was received, and for the conflicting definitions of 'good taste' with which this paper deals . . .

We have seen how streamlining constituted the explicit declaration in form of technological innovations (eg stamping and pressing techniques) which made the production of an increasingly standardised and uniform range of commodities possible. Streamlining came to be used as a metaphor for industrial barbarism, stylistic incontinence and excess. The proliferation of 'jazz forms' was cited by European cultural commentators to simultaneously connote: *"popular taste"*, the *"look of the future"* and *"Americanness"* — all of which were negatively defined. On the other hand, for designers and advertisers of streamlined products and for the 'public at large' the vocabulary of streamlining was used to signal a positive improvement in the 'quality of life' which in turn entailed a massive expansion in the productive base and in the scale of 'conspicuous consumption'. Quality and quantity were indistinguishable here — the clash over issues of taste was inextricably linked to conflicting definitions of material progress, and the rhetoric of modernism with its references to *"beautiful machines"* and *"well-made objects"* served only to obscure the extent to which mass production technology under 'free market' conditions *necessarily* entailed the transformation and displacement of traditional aesthetic criteria and established social distinctions.

It was the simultaneous articulation of the fact of *accessibility* and *reproducibility* (a million streamlined Chevrolets, a million streamlined radio's) which finally proved disturbing to so many cultural critics. A run of different commodities rendered indistinguishable through the identical lines which enfolded them represented in Banham's words, *"a chromium horde bearing down on you"*[71] for a group of European intellectuals educated in a tradition which placed (and still continues to place) — value on the 'authentic', the 'unique' or at the very least the 'honest' and the 'functional'. It was Walter Benjamin who foresaw most clearly the transformation of aesthetic criteria which mass production would eventually necessitate:—

> *". . . the technique of reproduction detaches the reproduced object from the dimension of tradition . . . by overcoming the uniqueness of every reality"*[72]

Writing in the same spirit at more or less the same time, Gramsci produced a remarkably cogent critique of the response of the Italian intellectual bourgeoisie to the first tentative signs of 'Americanism'. He predicted that the introduction into Italy of American-style mass production technology ('Fordism') would lead to the intensification of economic exploitation and eventually to the more effective penetration of the State into every aspect of private and public life — to a subtler, more developed ideological and 'moral coercion' of the masses. But he refused to deplore the changes in the *phenomenal* forms which inevitably accompanied such structural adaptations. He pinpointed the source of the resistance to American cultural influence precisely:—

> *"In Europe it is the passive residues that resist Americanism (they represent 'quality') because they have the instinctive feeling that the new forms of production and work would sweep them away implacably".*[73]

In the image of a streamlined car, in the snatch of 'hot' jazz or 'ersatz' rock 'n roll blaring from a streamlined speaker cabinet, the cultural conservatives of 1935 or 1965, irrespective of their overt politcal affiliations were right to perceive what Benjamin described as *"the destructive, cathartic aspect, that is, the liquidation of the traditional value of the cultural heritage"*[74]. They were right to perceive that what was at stake was a future — their future.

Conclusion

It would, finally, be misleading to end a discussion of some of the conceptions of 'popular taste' which prevailed from 1935-62 without making at least some reference to the alternative definitions of America and American influence which were circulating at the time or attempting to assess the actual extent of American cultural penetration during this period.

As we have already seen, where changes in taste and patterns of consumption did occur, they tended to be associated with changes in the *composition* of the market (ie the 'intrusion' into the sphere of 'conspicuous consumption' of the working class and the young), and these changes in turn were linked to objects and environments either imported from America or styled on American models (eg film, popular music, streamlined artefacts, milk bars, hair styles and clothes). There can be no doubt that America, particularly in the post War period began to exert considerable cultural and economic influence on European culture though those statistics which are readily available tend to fall outside the period covered by this paper (eg in 1973 it was estimated that 50% of the world's screen time was taken up with American films, and that American-made programmes accounted for more than 20% of total TV transmission time in Western Europe; that 20-25% of British manufacturing output was American controlled and that eight of the leading advertising agencies were owned by American companies[75]).

But there is little evidence to suggest that the eradication of social and cultural differences imputed to these developments by a generation of cultural critics has taken place at least in the form they predicted. For instance, the sheer plethora of youth cultural options currently available (eg the rockabillies, heavy metal enthusiasts, ted revivalists etc) most of which are refracted however indirectly through a *"mythical America"* seems to suggest that the early fears about the homogenising influence of American culture were unfounded. Rather American popular culture — Hollywood films, advertising images, packaging, clothes and music — offers a rich iconography, a set of symbols, objects and artefacts which can be assembled and re-assembled by different groups in a literally limitless number of combinations. And the meaning of each selection is transformed as individual objects — jeans, rock records, Tony Curtis hair styles, bobby socks etc — are taken out of their original historical and cultural contexts and juxtaposed against other signs from other sources. From this perspective, the style of the teddy boys can be interpreted less as the dull reflex of a group of what Hoggart called *"tamed and directionless helots"*[76] to a predigested set of norms and values than as an *attribution* of meaning, as an attempt at imposition and control, as a symbolic act of self-removal — a step away from a society which could offer little more than the knowledge that *"the fix is in and all that work does is to keep you afloat at the place you were born into".*[77]

In the same way, positive images of America did persist throughout the period though these were generally constructed and sustained underneath and in spite of the 'official' authorised discourses of school and State. Of course, even in 1935 there existed a positive mythology of the 'New World' — perhaps a remnant of much earlier, romantic myths in which America and Americans were depicted as young, innocent, dynamic and vigorous. In the early 60's the Kennedy brothers were portrayed as personifying these qualities. For instance Christopher Booker in his study of post War Britain, *"The Neophiliacs"* has described how the vocabulary and imagery of the Kennedy era were imported into Britain and used to bolster up the myths of 'Swinging London' and Harold Wilson's 'dynamic' leadership.[78] But until the 1960's the romantic affirmation of American culture tended to be left to such unashamedly 'popular' weeklies as *Titbits* and to the undergrowth of literature — the novelettes, comics and Hollywood ephemera — which were aimed at a predominantly working class market. And by 1960, this market — at least significant sections of it, particularly amongst the young — had swung again — away from the exuberant vocabularies of streamlining and rock. In 1962, Len Deighton's "Ipcress File" appeared. It contained the following passages:—

". . . I walked down Charlotte Street towards Soho. It was that sort of January morning that has enough sunshine to point up the dirt without raising the temperature. I was probably seeking excuses to delay; I bought two packets of Gauloises, sank a quick grappa with Mario and Franco at the Terraza, bought a Statesman, some Normandy butter and garlic sausage . . . In spite of my dawdling I was still in Lederer's Continental coffee house by 12.55 . . . Jay had seen me of course. He'd priced my coat and measured the pink-haired girl in the flick of an eyelid. I knew that he'd paid sixty guineas for each of his suits except the flannel one, which by some quirk of tailor's reasoning cost fifty eight and a half . . . (Later in a strip club) . . . Finally he went to the Gents excusing himself with one of the less imaginative vulgarisms. A cigarette girl clad in a handful of black sequins tried to sell me a souvenir programme. I'd seen better print jobs on a winkle bag, but then it was only costing twelve and six, and it was made in England. . . . 'I'll have a packet of Gauloises' I said ...."[79]

What is so remarkable here — unsurprising perhaps in a genre which as Amis pointed out is so unremittingly brand and status-symbol conscious as the British spy novel of the 60's — is the defection of a man like Harry Palmer not to Russia — still less to America — but to Italy (*'Mario', 'Franco', 'grappa'*), to the Continent (*garlic sausage, 'Normandy butter'*, all those *'Gauloises'*). It is perhaps the final irony that when it did occur rhe most startling and spectacular 'revolution' in British 'popular' taste in the early 60's involved the domestication not of the brash and 'vulgar' hinterland of American design but of the subtle *"cool"* Continental style which had for so many decades impressed the British champions of the Modern Movement. Fyvel writing in 1961 had recorded the switch from the teddy boy style betraying in the process a set of preferences which should require little explanation):—

"Step by step, through various deviations, the clothes and haircuts grew less eccentric and extreme, until at the end of the fifties they had become unified in the rather attractive 'Italian style', which had become normal

walking-out wear for the working-class boy; and by 1960 this had blended with 'conservative cool', or just very ordinary but well-cut clothes".[80]

It was not to be long before the first 'ordinary' (ie working class) disciples of the Modern Style in their Italian suits on their Italian motor scooters, moving to black American modern jazz and black American soul were swarming over Soho. And Harry Palmer with his proletarian origins, his eye for detail (*his* world is hardly as 'flat as a map'), his refined and discriminating tastes (a 60 guinea suit . . . a 58½ guinea suit) and his confident appropriation of Italy (Guy Crouchback's sacred Italy!) is a fictional extension of mod just as Trimmer — the thoroughly contemporary master of appearances bore attenuated traces of the 1950's spiv. What is more, the 'spy masters'. Burgess and MacClean (followed later by Philby) — motivated, or so the story goes, by a profound contempt and loathing for America, for American cultural, economic and military imperialism, for the 'Americanisation' of the globe had flown the roost leaving men like Palmer to take care of things. Needless to say, Gilbert Pinfold would have been appalled.

Notes and References

1. Evelyn Waugh, *Officers and Gentlemen* (Chapman & Hall, 1955).
2. Mary Douglas, *Purity and Danger* (Routledge & Kegan Paul, 1966)
3. David Cardiff, *"The serious and the Popular: Aspects of the evolution of style in the radio talk 1928-39"* in Media, Culture and Society, 1980 2.
4. Nancy Mitford and Evelyn Waugh, *U & Non U* Penguin 1955.
5. Evelyn Waugh, *The Ordeal of Gilbert Pinfold* (Chapman & Hall, 1957).
6.a Bevis Hillier, *The World of Art Deco.* (Dutton, 1971).
6.b George Orwell, *"Pleasure Spots"* in Collected Essays — Journalism and Letters of George Orwell Vol 4, 1945-50; S. Orwell & 1 Angus (eds) (Penguin, 1979)
7. Richard Hoggart, *The Uses of Literacy* (Pelican, 1958).
8. ibid
9. ibid
10. ibid
11. Rev. Renwick C. Kennedy quoted in Eric Goldman, *The Crucial Decade and After: America 1945-60* (Vintage 1956).
12. *"An American Invasion"* in Picture Post (July 31, 1948)
13. ibid
14. D. Cardiff, P. Scannell, N. Garnham (Polytechnic of Central London) research into BBC Written Archives 1928-1950 (to be published)
15. Iain Chambers, *"Pop Music and Popular Culture: From Heartbreak Hotel to Summer Holiday, British Pop Music 1956-63"* (to be published).
16. quoted ibid.
17. This last comes from G. Orwell, *"Th Decline of the English Murder"* in The Decline of the English Murder and Other Essays (Penguin 1970). Orwell couples the decline of the English country house murder

mystery with an apparent drop in the figures for passionate domestic homicides and attributes both to the pernicious influence of American culture. He sees one particular case – the Cleft Chin killings – in which an American army deserter and his 'moll' murdered a number of people and robbed them *"of a few shillings"* during a drunken spree in 1944 – as symptomatic of this decline. The murderers reflected in their sordid crimes, the *"false values of Hollywood films"* and pulp detective fiction. The essay is especially interesting as an early example of explicit anti-Americanisation. Orwell ends on this ominous note:– *"Perhaps it is significant that the most talked-of English murder of recent years should have been committed by an American and an English girl who had become partly Americanised."*

18. Edward Hulton, *"The Best and Worst of Britain"* (3) Picture Post (Dec 19 1953)
19. ibid
20. ibid
21. R. Hoggart (op cit 1958)
22. ibid
23. ibid
24. George Orwell, *Coming up for Air* (Penguin, 1962)
25. Reyner Banham, *"Design in the First Machine Age"* (1960) extracted in S. Bayley (ed) *In Good Shape: Style in Industrial Products, 1900-1960* (Design Council 1979).
26. Reyner Banham, *"Detroit Tin Revisited"* in *Design 1900-1960; Studies in Design and Popular Culture of the Twentieth Century* (ed) T. Faulkner (Newcastle upon Tyne Polytechnic 1976).
27. Harold van Doren in Bayley (1979)
28. see S. Bayley, *"Industrial Design in the Twentieth Century"* in S. Bayley (ed) 1979.
29. see D. Cardiff (op cit 1980)
30. John Grierson, *Grierson on Documentary* (ed) F. Hardy (Faber, 1979)
31. John Heskett, *"Archaism and Modernism in Design in the Third Reich"* Block 3 1980.
32. Nikolaus Pevsner, *"An Enquiry into Industrial Art in England"* (1937) extracted in S. Bayley (op cit 1979)
33. ibid
34. Anthony Bertram, *"Design"* (1938) in S. Bayley (1979)
35. ibid
36. N. Pevsner (op cit 1979)
37. Harold van Doren, *"Industrial Design-A Practical Guide"* (1954) extract in S. Bayley (1979).
38. R. Banham (op cit 1979)
39. Raymond Loewy, *"Industrial Design – the Aesthetics of Salesmanship – An American View"* letter to The Times 19 Nov 1945 reprinted S. Bayley (1979).
40. Robin Spencer *"Designs for Silent Rides over Rough Roads"* in Faulkner (ed) 1976.
41. ibid
42. ibid
42.b Stanley Mitchell: *"Marinetti and Mayakorsky: futurism, fascism, communism"* in Screen Reader (Sept. 1977).
43. Henry Dreyfuss, *"Designing for People"* (1955) extracted in Bayley (1979)
44. J. Heskett (op cit)
45. Donald Bush *The Stream lined Decade* (Braziller, 1975).
46. Edgar Kauffman, *"Borax or the Chromium Plated Calf"* (1950) quoted in Banham (1976)
47. Richard Hamilton, *"Persuading Image"* Design (no 134, Feb 1960) extracted in Bayley (op cit 1979)

48. R. Banham (1976)
49. ibid
50. ibid
51. ibid
52. ibid
53. Herbert Marcuse, *One Dimensional Man* (Routledge & Kegan Paul, 1964).
54. ibid
55. Charles Walker, *Toward the Automatic Factory* (1957) quoted ibid.
56. Serge Mallet, *"Arguments no 12-13"* (1958) quoted ibid.
57. H. Marcuse (op cit 1964)
58. Chas Crichter, *"Sociology, Cultural Studies and the Post War Working Class"* in *Working Class Culture* (eds) J. Clarke, C. Crichter, R. Johnson (Hutchinson, 1979)
59. ibid
60. see Paul Wild, *"Recreation in Rochdale"* in J. Clarke et al (eds) 1979
61. ibid
62. Mike Brake, *The Sociology of Youth and Youth Culture* (Routledge & Kegan Paul, 1980)
63. Mark Abrams, *The Teenage Consumer* (London Press Exchange, 1959)
64. ibid
65. Ken Barnes, *Coronation Cups and Jam Jars* (Hackney Centreprise, 1979)
66. see T. Jefferson, *"The Cultural Meaning of the Teds"* in S. Hall, J. Clarke, T. Jefferson, B. Roberts (eds) *Resistance Through Rituals* (Hutchinson 1976)
67. T.R. Fyvel, *The Insecure Offenders: Rebellious Youth in the Welfare State* (Pelican 1963)
68. *"The Truth abou the Teddy Boys (and Teddy Girls)"* Picture Post May 29, 1954.
69. George Melly, *Revolt into Style* (Penguin, 1972).
70. S. Hall, J. Clarke, T. Jefferson, B. Roberts, *"Subculture, Culture and Class"* in Hall et al. (1976).
71. R. Banham (op cit 1976)
72. Walter Benjamin, *"The Work of Art in the Age of Mechanical Reproduction"* in J. Curran et al (eds) *Mass Communication and Society* (Arnold, 1977).
73. Antonio Cramsci, *"Americanism and Fordism"* in *Selections from the Prison Notebooks* (Lawrence & Wishart, 1971).
74. Benjamin (op cit 1977)
    The wise young narrator of Colin MacInnes's cult novel *"Absolute Beginners* (Allison & Busby, 1959) puts the same point rather more succinctly: *"It's a sure sign of total defeat to be anti-Yank"*
75. see for instance T.A. Gurback, *"Film as International Business"* in *Journal of Communication* (Winter 1974) and COEBigsby, *"Europe, America and the Cultural Debate"* in CWEBigsby, (ed) *Superculture: American Popular Culture and Europe* (Paul Elek, New York 1975).
76. Hoggart (op cit 1958)
77. Tom Wolfe, *"The Noonday Underground"* in *The Pumphouse Gang* (Bantam 1968)
78. Christopher Booker, *The Neophiliacs* (Collins 1969).
79. Len Deighton, *The Ipcress File* (Hodder & Stoughton 1962)
80. T.R. Fyvel (op cit 1963)

I would like to thank Barry Curtis, Tim Putnam and John Walker for the comments and corrections they made to the draft of this article.

PART V

MASS COMMUNICATORS

The past decade has seen a resurgence of research concern with the individuals, organizations and institutions that produce media. While this volume cannot do justice to the breadth and depth of that research, in this part of the volume and the one which follows, we do offer some examples of research operating at different levels of analysis and from differing theoretical perspectives to give some indication of its range.

In the first of these chapters, Dimmick and Coit take the notion of differing levels of analysis as a beginning point and show that clarification of levels (they isolate nine applicable to mass communicator studies) and of the nature of influence within and between them is valuable in organizing the research literature and in the construction, extension, and testing of theories about mass communicators.

In second offering, Kepplinger suggests that what appears to be happening at one level of analysis, as when an institution is obligated to present an "objective" account of election candidates, may be frustrated at another, as when individuals, in his case cameramen, consciously or unconsciously depict those candidates "as they actually saw them."

Whitney and Becker present experimental evidence that a supraorganizational influence on gatekeepers, the wire services' structuration of the days' news, is a more powerful explanation of news selection than a competing one, that of shared news values among the individuals who do the selection.

Powell and Friedkin likewise are interested in supraorganizational influences, as well as intraorganizational ones, in their description of what accounts for what gets programmed on American public television.

Finally, Peter Dreier is concerned with charting what Dimmick and Coit might consider societal-level influences, but here the focus is on the location and potential influence on society of the press. By identifying linkages of newspaper corporations to the U.S. power structure, he argues that the nation's elite press helps to maintain and reinforce an ideology of corporate liberalism.

John Dimmick and Philip Coit propose a taxonomy consisting of nine levels of analysis and two forms of influence that operate within and between these levels. Together with a multilevel research strategy, the taxonomy and the types of influence form a framework for the analysis of complex media decision systems. Data from a national sample of reporters are used to illustrate the multilevel research strategy. Results indicate that experience and the industry in which reporters work explain more variance in autonomy than organization size. John Dimmick is associate professor of communication at Ohio State University. Philip Coit is on the research staff at On-Line Computer Library Center, Inc., and is a doctoral candidate in communication at Ohio State University.

22

LEVELS OF ANALYSIS IN MASS MEDIA DECISION MAKING
A Taxonomy, Research Strategy, and Illustrative Data Analysis

John Dimmick and Philip Coit

In the years since the publication of White's (1950) original gatekeeper study, there has been an increasing awareness of the complexity of decision making in mass communication. The focus has shifted from a molecular emphasis on individual psychology, as in White's study, to an awareness of the importance of employing more molar levels of analysis. For example, in a case study of decision making in television network news, Bailey and Lichty (1972: 229) conclude that, "The organization was the gatekeeper." Even larger levels of analysis are apparent in Gerbner's

---

AUTHORS' NOTE: *We would like to thank Professor John Johnstone for permission to analyze the data from a national sample of United States journalists.*

From John Dimmick and Philip Coit. "Levels of Analysis in Mass Media Decision Making: A Taxonomy, Research Strategy, and Illustrative Data Analysis," *Communication Research,* Vol. 9, No. 1 (January 1982), pp. 3-32. Copyright © 1982 by Sage Publications, Inc.

(1967) use of the term "message system," in DeFleur and BallRokeach's (1975) "production subsystem," and in Donohue et al.'s (1972) "mass media systems." Despite the differences in approach of these researchers, their common use of the word *system* denotes a recognition of the complexity of decision making in the mass media. As Melody (1977: 27) points out, systems analysis replaces the doctrine of reductionism with what he calls the "doctrine of expansionism," in which objects and events are treated as the micro-details of a macro-system.

The usual definition of a system emphasizes the interrelatedness and interdependence among the system components (Laszlo, 1972). Unfortunately, the ability to engage in research on a system and explain its behavior is negatively related to the system's complexity. In order to make the study of complex systems a more tractable task, it is necessary to find some method or organizing the complexity. The crucial question, as formulated by McPhee (1963: 8) is "how to have our complexity and analyze it too?" The taxonomy and the research strategy outlined in the following pages represent one way of answering this question.

In searching for an organizing principle in media decision-making processes, we may make use of Herbert Simon's (1969: 87) observation that complexity is often manifested in the form of hierarchy. A hierarchic system, as defined by Simon, is composed of sybsystems organized in a hierarchical manner. Simon shows that the concept of hierarchic structure is abstract and general: Hierarchic systems in such diverse areas as chemistry, history, biology, and human symbol systems share properties in common. The concept of hierarchial systems provides a potentially powerful tool for analyzing decision making in the mass media of communication.

The purpose of this article is to employ the concept of hierarchic structure in formulating a taxonomy of research areas in media decision making and to propose and demonstrate a research strategy for incorporating different levels of analysis into the design of research. The system of hierarchic levels presented here are a revised version of a taxonomy presented in an earlier article (Dimmick, 1978).

The taxonomy presented in the following pages explicitly utilizes the concept of hierarchy by ordering the system levels from the most molar or supranational level to the molecular or individual level of decision making. At each of the nine levels in the hierarchy, extant research will be reviewed briefly to demonstrate the influence exerted at the level of that particular subsystem. The taxonomy aims at being relatively exhaustive or complete in specifying levels, but it is necessarily incomplete in cataloging variables within each level.

The media decision-making system is hierarchic not only in the sense that the unit of analysis increases in size as one ascends the hierarchy, and vice versa, but is also hierarchic in the sense that decisions made at one level may influence or place constraints on decision makers at the lower levels of the system. The levels higher in the hierarchy constitute the environment—or rather environments—in which media decision makers operate. This conceptualization does not ignore the fact that decision units located at the lower levels may exercise influence at the more molar levels. For example, industries—through their trade associations—may attempt to influence legislation or rule making by regulatory bodies at the societal level on issues affecting their interests. Likewise, organizational subunits may negotiate agreements with firm management and individuals may bargain with their immediate superiors. Answering questions concerning the evolution of such influences is the task of longitudinal studies. Once decisions are made, however, the legislation, the rules, policies, or informal agreements have the effect of influencing or constraining behavior. The taxonomic structure is an explicit acknowledgment that while decisions concerning media content are made by individual gatekeepers acting in sequence and by interacting groups of gatekeepers in an organizational setting, the parameters of the decision process and the very structure of the organization are shaped by influences operating at more molar levels, such as the industry in which the organization operates, and at the level of the society itself.

FORMS OF INFLUENCE

Before presenting the taxonomy, however, it is necessary to clarify the concept of influence and its relationship to the levels of analysis used in the taxonomic structure. Simon (1969) used the term *hierarchy* in two distinct ways—in the formal sense denoted by an organizational chart and in the sense of an informal hierarchy such as the sociometric mapping of interaction patterns. Both uses of the term imply an influence process whether the influence resides in the formal superior-subordinate relationship or in the less formal interinfluence process which occurs among people who interact across time. The term *influence* must include both kinds of hierarchial relationships. Concepts originally formulated by Deutsch and Gerard (1955) and elaborated by King (1975)—normative and informational social influence —will be used to distinguish between the two forms of influence. Normative social influence—what other theorists have called power—is generally a conscious attempt to influence on the part of X the power-holding decision unit (a decision unit may be an individual, a group, an organization, or an industry) and is accepted by another decision unit Y because X controls the allocation of resources. (The term *resources* is used to mean rewards or sanctions in other than a purely social sense.) While stating the relationship in this rather bald way conjures up images of brute force and coercion, such actions are rare. Power relationships are a great deal more subtle and complex as Luhmann's (1979) analysis clearly shows.

Normative influence or power occurs largely *between* levels of analysis. Normative social influence is apparent, for example, when the executives of broadcast stations at the market or community level accept the edicts of the Federal Communications Commission (FCC) at the societal level in order to preserve their licenses and livelihood. Similarly, between-level influence is manifested when the supraorganization—group or chain management—sets the operating budget of the newspapers or broadcast stations it controls. Normative influence is most often manifest is such hierarchical relationships due to the ubiquity of what Luhmann (1979: 132) calls "action chains" in which X has power over Y who in turn exercises normative influence over Z.

In certain cases, however, powers exist when there is no clear hierarchy or action chain involved yet X controls resources which Y needs. For example, advertisers—through their agencies—control the advertising expenditures on which the television networks depend for their survival. Dependence clearly exists, but it is not the dependence of the subordinate on the superior. Likewise, news sources (see Chibnall, 1975) control the vital resource of information upon which the reporter depends. Fortunately, it is possible to specify where such "failures of hierarchy" will occur. As the examples indicate, it is at the boundary of the decision unit where one unit's control or discretion ends and another's begins that these normative influences due to dependency arise (see Pfeffer and Salancik, 1978). In such cases it is the dependency, of course, rather than hierarchy which gives rise to the opportunity to exercise normative influence.

The other major form of influence—informational—occurs when decision units accept information from another in order to reduce uncertainty and arrive at a decision. In this form of influence the source of the information may or may not be attempting to influence behavior. Informational social influence generally operates *within* levels of analysis.

A major vehicle for conveying informational influence is the social network (see Rogers and Agarwala-Rogers, 1976). Within the organization, for example, informal social networks arise which convey informational influence. For example, in Stark's (1962) study of a metropolitan daily, the newsroom was divided into two mutually exclusive social systems which Stark dubbed the "Pros" and the "Local." While social networks are most often studied at the organizational level, networks exist at larger levels of analysis such as the industry. In network television, the agents employed by different organizations form what could be called a liaison network, performing the task of linking the producer and talent subsystems with the network program departments. This liaison network diffuses and collates information which ultimately results in "packages" of talent and story ideas for presentation to the networks (see Shanks 1976: 119). Although these examples are drawn from the industry and the organizational level of analysis, informational influence can occur at lower levels such as the group or dyad as well.

Collectively, the two forms of influence together with the taxonomy and research strategy presented in the following pages form an analytic system for asking and we hope, answering questions concerning decision making in mass communication.

THE TAXONOMY

LEVEL 1: SUPRANATIONAL AND PAN-NATIONAL LEVELS

At this, the most molar levels of analysis, one can ask how media decision making within nation-states is influenced by forces external to the society?

Supranational influences are those exerted formally by international agencies with the intention of influencing the policy levels of national systems. For example, Rahim (1977) and Beltran (1977) have outlined how UNESCO and other international agencies have stimulated research in communication policy and planning as an initial phase in formulating national level policies.

Pan-national influences, on the other hand, are those exerted by one nation or another by virtue of the influencing nation's possession of the skilled personnel as well as the ideational and technological resources necessary to produce and disseminate media content. Currently, nations in the developed world exert influence on media decision making in the third world by exporting what Golding (1979) calls "media ideologies" as well as disseminating actual media content such as television series and news copy (Tunstall, 1977).

LEVEL 2: SOCIETAL-LEVEL INFLUENCES

At this level of analysis, one can ask: How does the society define and constrain the activities of its mass communication institutions and specialists? Here, the most important questions pertain to the legal definitions of the media in society and to the allocation of resources to the media.

In the legal realm, the power vulnerability of media industries—their relative susceptibility to government influence—affects the elaborateness and explicitness of the codes of these industries. The differences in power vulnerability which follow from differences in legal definitions can be demonstrated by contrasting the newspaper industry and broadcasting. As an industry, newspapers are insulated from government control by the First Amendment. Ostensibly, broadcasting is also protected from censorship by the Communications Act of 1934. However, the broadcast industry is susceptible to government influence because stations are licensed by the FCC. This susceptibility has been demonstrated by research on the news departments of the television networks. Warner (1968) found that one major responsibility of the executives in charge of network news is to worry about the FCC. Further, in Lowry's (1971) study of network evening newscasts before and after then— Vice President Agnew's speech attacking the networks, the data show changes in the way events were reported. Lowry concluded that while government officials may have no de jure control of television network news, they may in reality exercise considerable influence. Similarly, Porter (1976) provides extensive evidence on the pressures exerted on the news by the Nixon administration. Porter's analysis shows that the effectiveness of that administration in inhibiting the television networks can be traced to the government's licensing power and the attendant rules and regulations under which American broadcasting operates. Newspapers, on the other hand, are not generally suscep- tible to the same pressures. Bagdikian (1971) reports that the government agencies which collect and report statistics on all industries do not do so for newspapers because they consider the medium "untouchable." The evidence indi- cates that at the societal level of influence (except on the economic dimension), newspapers are not susceptible to normative influence while the broadcast industry is highly susceptible to such influences. Occasional government influences on newspapers such as the Failing Newspaper Act and President Kennedy's successful attempt to in- fluence the *New York Times* in the Bay of Pigs fiasco are well-known exceptions which seems to prove the general rule.

The importance of economics is demonstrated by what McCombs (1972) calls the Principle of Relative Constancy. The Constancy Principle states that the level of spending by consumers and advertisers is highly related to some overall indicator of the economy such as the gross national product. One implication of constancy is that since the amount of money allocated to the media as a whole is fixed, media industries play a zero-sum game: New media industries succeed at the expense of the older media.

LEVEL 3: INDUSTRY LEVEL OF
INTERORGANIZATIONAL RELATIONS

Here, the basic question becomes: How does the industry system in which media organizations exist shape decision processes?

The term *industry system* is used here to mean both the set of competing organizations (e.g., the three television networks) and the relationship of these competing firms to other organizations (e.g., advertisers, program suppliers, and affiliated stations).

The influence of competing firms on each other is demonstrated by Dominick and Pearce's (1976) study of trends in network television. Their study shows that, as in other cases of oligopolistic competition, program diversity has decreased markedly over the history of the medium. In addition, competing firms within the same industry tend to have similar decision structures and similar ways of doing business (Hirsch, 1972; Peterson and Berger, 1975; McPhee, 1963).

The importance of other organizations, aside from competitors, is indicated by Gerbner's (1967) institutional approach to decision making and by Hirsch's (1972) use of the concept organization set: Both focus attention on the importance of interorganizational relationships. For example, Turow (1977) found differences between firms which publish children's books for the mass market and those which publish for the library market. Apparently, these firms have evolved different organizational structures as a result of their relationship with different clients (librarians versus buyers for bookstores) even though the ultimate audience—children—is ostensibly the same.

Finally, the technologies which industries share and the state of that technology at any particular time has a profound affect on decision-making patterns. Currently, technological changes in both the television industry (Broadcast Management, 1977) and daily newspapers (Bagdikian,

1971) are fomenting changes in organizational behavior. In newspapers, computer technology is enabling a greater centralization of decision making, while in television portable video technology are changing decision-making patterns in the entire industry.

LEVEL 4: SUPRAORGANIZATIONAL INFLUENCES

Since it has been estimated that two-thirds of the news personnel in the country work for organizations tied to newspaper chains or broadcast groups or networks (Johnstone et al., 1976), it is important to ask: What are the constraints imposed on an organization's gatekeepers by virtue of their ownership or control by media conglomerates, broadcast chains, or newspaper groups? These constraints may pertain to policies which directly affect media content or may be related to other organizational matters such as personnel policies or pricing decisions (ad rates).

The widespread ownership and control of media organizations (Moeller, 1968; Bishop, 1972; Bagdikian, 1971) points to the importance of the relationship between individual organizations and higher level decision units. The influence of supraorganizational management management may be restricted, as one case study of a broadcast group demonstrated, largely to financial matters with a great deal of latitude in other decisions delegated to local management (Howard, 1976). Other studies (Wackman et al., 1975) indicate that organizations controlled by the same management structure purvey quite similar content or that significant changes in content may be wrought when a chain acquires ownership of a newspaper (Thrift, 1977; Fawcett, 1972). The existence and scope of supraorganizational policies, or other kinds of participation in decision making, are a measure of the autonomy or discretion in decision making: They define the degrees of freedom of decision makers in local markets or communities.

LEVEL 5: COMMUNITY OR MARKET INFLUENCES

The general question here focuses on the influence exerted on gatekeepers by the community or market in which they enact their roles and by the behavior of other media organizations within the market.

Organizational policy, for example, may be influenced by the fact that media executives (Miller, 1963; Donohew, 1965; Edelstein, 1964; Dunn, 1969) are integrated into the community power structure. Likewise, the definitions of news held by lower level gatekeepers may be affected by their integration into the community (Hirsch, 1975). Attributes of the community such as market size affect how conflict is handled by the press (Donohue et al., 1972) and the frequency of publisher interference in newsroom decisions (Bowers, 1967). Other market variables affecting content include such factors as the degree of competition among media organizations (Stempel, 1973).

In addition, the content of the other media organizations in the market may be influential. Studies by Buckalew (1974) and Liebes (1966) indicate that within a community, the content of newspapers may influence the content of radio news and vice versa.

LEVEL 6: INTRAORGANIZATIONAL INFLUENCES

At the level of the organization, the general question asks how gatekeepers' decisions are shaped by organizational variables? The important sets of influences are organizational policy, organizational structure work routines and goals, and the political process within the organization.

Breed (1955) was perhaps the first to point out the importance of policy in shaping gatekeepers' decisions. While he conceived policy as a negative influence on the flow of information, policy is more generally and usefully conceived (in light of such positive aspects of organizational policy as the use of background boxes in daily newspapers) as the organization's attempt to define its "product."

The influence exerted on news content by organizationally mandated work routines has been documented by Tuchman (1973) and by Fishman (1980). Work routines, which March and Simon (1958) would call "programs," are designed to allow beat reporters—for example, who are assigned to cover large and complex bureaucracies such as a municipal court system—to generate a substantial number of stories and still meet the deadlines imposed by the news organization.

Another important set of influences concerns how the organization is structured to accomplish its task—how decision-making roles and functions are defined and how these decision making roles are coordinated by higher level gatekeepers, the organization's executives. Warner (1968) and Epstein (1973), for example, have provided such descriptions of the news departments in the television networks.

A related question asks what are the goals or criterion variables on which organization assesses its performance is economic ways. For example, in television each network aspires to a 30% audience share in each time period. The audience-shared goal is instrumental in attaining a market-share goal of 30% or one-third of advertising billings in network television. In the same industry, noneconomic goals include such aims as airing programs with "prestige" and "looking first-class" (Brown, 1971).

Within the organization, debates over goals and competition for scarce resources—air time or space in the paper, money, or personnel—occur along departmental or subunit lines and figure prominently in decisions concerning media content. Blumler (1969) and Burns (1969) have described such conflicts in the BBC, and Sigal (1973) found strong competition among the desks for page-one placement of stories in two leading American papers. Debates over goals and competition for resources in such a regular and recurring feature of organizations that Cyert and March (1963) have characterized organizations as political coalitions and the executives as political brokers.

LEVEL 7: FORMAL OR INFORMAL GROUP INFLUENCES

What are the influences on media content which derive from the interaction of gatekeepers in formal or informal groups?

Brown (1971), for example, has described the formal negotiation of a network prime-time schedule by executives from several network departments. Similarly, Sigal (1973) analyzed the meetings of editors on two major newspapers which are held to decide the journalistically crucial matter of which stories will receive page-one play. In both cases, media content was not determined simply by executive fiat but was decided in the give and take of group discussion.

Media content is also influenced by less formal interaction among groups of gatekeepers. Studies by Dunn (1969) and Grey (1966) of reporters who cover the same "beat," for example, have shown that an interinfluence process leads to a similarity of news judgment among reporters. Crouse (1973) observing the same phenomenon on the campaign trail uses the epithets *pack* or *herd journalism* to describe what is otherwise a classic depiction of the process of creating social reality in a group context.

LEVEL 8: THE INFLUENCE OF DYADIC COMMUNICATION

What are the influences on gatekeepers' decision making which are attributable to face-to-face contact with other individuals?

Tuchman (1974), for example, found that the substance of the on-camera conversation between the talk show host and his guest stars is negotiated beforehand between the guest star and a member of the television talk-show staff.

One important source of influence on media content at the level of the dyad is the relationship between reporters and their news sources. Studies by Chibnall (1975), Gieber (1960), and Dunn (1969) demonstrate the impact of this form of interaction on newspaper content.

LEVEL 9: INTRAINDIVIDUAL OR COGNITIVE LEVEL

How do individual gatekeepers make decisions concerning media content? What are the criteria or dimensions of chóice which gatekeepers use to evaluate potential media content (e.g., "pilot" programs or news copy). If more than a single dimension is involved, the question of the decision models used to combine or weight the dimensions is relevant. In addition, it is important to ask whether the dimensions of choice and the decision models employed by gatekeepers vary from situation to situation and how they change over time. Studies by White (1950), Snider (1967), and Flegel and Chaffee (1971) have documented the importance of individual criteria in media decision making.

However, it is important to separate—indeed, this is one purpose of the taxonomy—decision criteria which are individual from those which are in some sense mandated by the decision makers' environments. For example, the procedures used by news directors to identify potential employees for positions in television news derive from FCC-required equal opportunity programs (Dimmick and Becker, 1980).

A RESEARCH STRATEGY

The nine levels of analysis which comprise the taxonomy are quite general—they apply to the media decision-system as a whole. The taxonomy should not be construed to mean that influence will operate both within and between levels in all media decision situations. That is an empirical question.

However, since influences on decision making *may* operate at several different levels of analysis, it is important to have the capability of incorporating different levels into the design of research.[1] This seems to be the lesson of Argyris's (1974) attempt to improve the effectiveness of a daily metropolitan newspaper. One possible reason for the failure of the intervention is the analyst's focus on a single level of analysis—the interpersonal level. As Lorsch and

Morse (1974) have empirically demonstrated, accounting for the effectiveness of an organization requires measurement of variables at three levels—the environment in which the organization functions, the members of the organization, and the organization itself. Hence, Argyris's intervention may have failed because it was confined to a single level of analysis.[2]

Clearly, what is required is a research strategy which enables the analyst to engage in an active search for between-level influences. Unfortunately, the social science literature relevant to such methods is quite sparse.[3] However, a beginning has been made by Przeworski and Teune (1970) in the area of comparative politics, and their work provides a basis for suggesting a strategy for multilevel research in media decision making.

The design logic which seems most appropriate for dealing with sources of influence at different levels of analysis lies in the difference between two analytic paradigms which Przeworski and Teune contrast as a "most similar systems" design and a "most different systems" design. The former design is based on the belief that the "best" samples are composed of systems which are similar on as many attributes as possible. The design logic of the "most similar systems" paradigm is that attributes shared by systems are conceived as being controlled, whereas differences between systems are viewed as being potential explanations. If salient differences between systems emerge from research on similar systems, then the number of factors associated with these differences will be small— small enough to justify explanations in terms of these differences. Both research paradigms can deal with variables at different levels of analysis, but the important difference is that the "most similar systems" design requires an assumption, prior to the research, concerning the system level at which the important influences operate. Once the measurement is carried out, alternative levels cannot be considered.

In contrast, the "most different systems" paradigm does not require as assumption as to which level is most influential but, instead, seeks to answer this question empirically. The "most different systems" design begins by measuring behavior at the most molecular level which is feasible. Generally, this is at the individual level but the measurement could be performed at the level of decision-making groups, organizations, or at other levels indicated by the research question. Instead of assuming that influences from particular levels of analysis, the analysis proceeds on the familiar assumption that a population is homogeneous with respect to the relationship between independent and dependent variables *at the level at which behavior is actually measured.* If a relationship does exist, the next question concerns whether the relationship is the same across all subpopulations or levels of analysis. As Przeworski and Teune state:

> To the extent that identifying the social system [level of analysis] does not help predict individual characteristics, systemic factors [levels] are not important. The total population is homogeneous, and further research is not distinct from investigations customarily conducted within a single social system [level of analysis]. The analysis can proceed at the level of individual characteristics without resorting to any system-level variables [1970: 40].

However, if the assumption that the relationship does not vary across levels or subpopulations can be rejected, then the system levels or what Przeworski and Teune (1970) call "systemic factors" are relevant to the explanation of the observed differences.

ILLUSTRATIVE DATA ANALYSIS

In order to illustrate the use of the research strategy outlined in previous sections of the article, secondary analyses were performed using data from Johnstone's national sample of journalists. The goal of the analyses was to provide empirical examples of the use of the taxonomy to answer prototype questions concerning (1) whether a relationship is invariant across taxonomic levels or subpopulations and (2) which levels are most strongly related, in terms of explained variance, to a criterion variable. In both cases, the dependent variables are measures of autonomy since determining which levels influence gatekeepers' autonomy or discretion in decision making is one central purpose of the taxonomy.

As an illustration of the first type of question, the substantive relationship investigated in the secondary analysis concerned whether the relationship of the political beliefs of journalists and the extent of their autonomy in selecting and writing news stories is invariant across levels of analysis. This relationship is important in view of the evidence (Bagdikian, 1974; Bogart, 1974) that media owners and managers tend to be politically conservative while their staffs tend to be more liberal. As Breed (1955) and Bowers (1967) have found, the political, social, and economic beliefs of owners and managers may be translated into the organization's policy and thereby become constraints on the reporting process.

To illustrate the second type of research question, variables representing several levels of analysis were compared in order to assess which levels are the best predictors of journalistic autonomy. Johnstone (1976) presented data which indicated that reportorial autonomy varied inversely with organizational size. In a reexamination of the same data set, Becker (1978) noted that the univariate trends in the data could be interpreted to mean that differences in organizational type (i.e., newspapers, broadcast, or wire service) are a more important predictor of autonomy than organizational size per se. The differences in interpretation of the data by Johnstone and Becker can be viewed as a disagreement over which level of analysis—the organizational or industry level—is more important in its relationship to autonomy. Hence, the present analysis will use variables from several levels in attempting to determine which levels are the best predictors of autonomy.

The national sample of journalists contained respondents who indicated that they did reporting "regularly" or "occasionally" and were employed by daily newspapers, television or radio stations, or by weekly newspapers. Comparisons between these groups represent the industry level of analysis. In hierarchical order the variables available from the Johnstone survey to represent other levels of analysis were:

(1) whether the reporter's firm was owned by a larger enterprise ("chain" or "nonchain," a supraorganization level variable)
(2) the size of the chain or the number of news organizations owned by the parent company ("supraorganizations size," a supraorganization level variable)
(3) the size of the market served by the reporter's firm ("market size," a community/market level variable)
(4) the size of the editorial staff ("organization size," an intra-organization level variable)
(5) the reporter's professional experience measured in years ("years experience," an individual-level variable).

Two measures of reporters' perceived autonomy were used in the data analysis: Story selection autonomy, measured on a four-point scale, was defined as "how much freedom [does the reporter] have in selecting the stories [the reporter] work(s) on . . . (1) almost complete freedom (2) a great deal (3) some or (4) none at all?" Content autonomy, measured on a three-point scale, was defined as "how much freedom [does the reporter] have in deciding which aspects of a story should be emphasized . . . (1) almost complete freedom (2) a great deal or (3) not too much?"

Respondents' political orientation, a variable Johnstone called "political lean," was assessed on a five-point scale on which the extreme left position was scored I and the extreme right position was scored 5 with the midpoint of the scale, middle of the road, scored as 3.

The first question to be answered in the analysis is whether the relationship between the two forms of autonomy and political lean changes differs with the level of analysis one employers. First, the Pearson product-moment correlation between each type of autonomy and reporters' political lean was computed for all respondents. Second, respondents were separated into groups within the industry level of analysis—dailies, television-radio, and weeklies— and the correlations were computed for each of these groups. Third, respondents were further separated into subgroups within each industry according to whether they worked for a chain-owned or nonchain organization. Finally, partial correlations were used to determine if the original Pearson correlations are changed by introducing the remaining level variables as controls. Table 1 and 2 show the results of these analyses.

Table 1 shows the relationship of story selection autonomy and political lean for five levels of analysis. The pattern of negative correlations in the table indicates that lower levels of autonomy are associated with a left political orientation. For reporters on chainowned weekly newspapers[4] and particularly broadcast reporters, autonomy appears to be more markedly affected by their political beliefs than is the selection autonomy of daily newspaper reporters. The inverse relationship between autonomy for reporters with left-leaning political beliefs also appears in Table 2 which shows the correlations between story content autonomy and political lean. In Table 2, however, the relationships are weaker than in Table 1 as indicated by correlations of lower magnitude and fewer statistically significant correlations. In both tables there are substantial differences in the magnitude of the correlations for the sample and some of the entries representing various levels of analysis, especially in the case of broadcast reporters.

In summary, the differences in magnitude of the correlations in the cells of Tables 1 and 2 and the overall correlation for the entire sample of reporters seem to demonstrate that the relationship between autonomy and political lean is not the same for all subgroups of reporters. Consistent with the logic of the research strategy outlined earlier, the data seem to warrant the conclusion that the

TABLE 1

Relationship Between Story Selection Autonomy and Political Lean in a National Sample of Reporters
(sample r = −.158, N = 727, p = .000)

Partial r's	Dailies (N=548) −.10 (p<.02)		TV/Radio (N=116) −.33 (p=.000)		Weeklies (N=63) −.29 (p<.02)	
	Chain (N=448) −.11 (p<.02)	Non-Chain (N=96) −.06	Chain (N=85) −.34 (p<.001)	Non-Chain (N=29) −.31 (p<.10)	Chain (N=11) −.50 (p<.10)	Non-Chain (N=45) −.23
Supra-Organization Size	−.11 (p<.02)	---	−.35 (p<.001)	---	−.60 (p=.05)	---
Market Size	−.10 (p<.05)	.004	−.35 (p<.001)	−.23	−.68 (p=.02)	−.25 (p<.10)
Organization Size	−.10 (p<.05)	−.01	−.36 (p=.001)	−.35 (p<.10)	−.52 (p=.10)	−.22
Years of Experience	−.07	−.03	−.29 (p<.01)	−.30	−.42	−.10
Supra-Organization Size/ Market Size	−.10 (p<.05)	---	−.36 (p=.001)	---	−.70 (p<.05)	---
Supra-Organization Size/ Organization Size	−.10 (p<.05)	---	−.36 (p=.001)	---	−.67 (p<.05)	---
Supra-Organization Size/ Years of Experience	−.07	---	−.30 (p<.01)	---	−.54	---
Market Size/ Organization Size	−.10 (p<.05)	.00	−.36 (p=.001)	−.34 (p<.10)	−.68 (p<.05)	−.25 (p=.10)
Market Size/ Years of Experience	−.05	.05	−.29 (p<.01)	−.17	−.62 (p<.10)	−.14
Organization Size/ Years of Experience	−.05	.03	−.30 (p<.01)	−.36 (p<.10)	−.44 (p<.05)	−.11
Supra-Organization Size/ Market Size/Organization Size	−.10 (p<.05)	---	−.36 (p<.001)	---	−.72 (p<.05)	---
Supra-Organization Size/ Market Size/ Years of Experience	−.04	---	−.30 (p<.01)	---	−.66 (p<.10)	---
Supra-Organization Size/ Organization Size/ Years of Experience	−.04	---	−.31 (p<.01)	---	−.60 (p<.10)	---
Market Size/Organization Size/ Years of Experience	−.04	.05	−.30 (p<.01)	−.32 (p=.10)	−.61 (p<.10)	−.14
Supra-Organization Size/ Market Size/ Organization Size/ Years of Experience	−.04	---	−.31 (p<.01)	---	−.67 (p<.10)	---

TABLE 2
Relationship Between Story Content Autonomy and Political Lean in a National Sample of Reporters
$$(\text{sample } r = -.076, N = 727, p = .04)$$

	Dailies (N=548) −.03		TV/Radio (N=116) $-.27_{(p=.004)}$		Weeklies (N=63) −.10	
	Chain (N=448) −.02	Non-Chain (N=96) −.02	Chain (N=85) −.26 (p=.01)	Non-Chain (N=29) −.32 (p=.08)	Chain (N=11) −.08	Non-Chain (N=45) −.10
Partial r's						
Supra-Organization Size	−.02	---	−.27 (p=.01)	---	−.28	---
Market Size	−.01	−.02	−.27 (p=.01)	−.19	−.15	−.11
Organization Size	−.02	−.02	−.28 (p=.01)	−.36 (p=.05)	−.10	−.10
Years of Experience	−.03	−.02	−.23 (p=.03)	−.31 (p=.10)	−.03	−.04
Supra-Organization Size/ Market Size	−.01	---	−.27 (p=.01)	---	−.29	---
Supra-Organization Size/ Organization Size	−.02	---	−.28 (p=.01)	---	−.35	---
Supra-Organization Size/ Years of Experience	.03	---	−.24 (p=.03)	---	−.21	---
Market Size/ Organization Size	−.02	−.02	−.28 (p=.01)	−.27	−.15	−.11
Market Size/ Years of Experience	.05	.02	−.24 (p=.03)	−.14	−.11	−.06
Organization Size/ Years of Experience	.04	.02	−.25 (p=.02)	−.35 (p=.07)	−.05	−.04
Supra-Organization Size/ Market Size/Organization Size	−.01	---	−.28 (p=.01)	---	−.35	---
Supra-Organization Size/ Market Size/ Years of Experience	.05	---	−.24 (p=.03)	---	−.24	---
Supra-Organization Size/ Organization Size/ Years of Experience	.04	---	−.25 (p=.02)	---	−.29	---
Market Size/ Organization Size/ Years of Experience	.04	.02	−.25 (p=.02)	−.23	−.11	−.05
Supra-Organization Size/ Market Size/ Organization Size/ Years of Experience	.04	---	−.25 (p=.02)	---	−.29	---

relationship is affected by the levels of analysis and, hence, the levels are relevant to explaining these observed differences.[5]

The second question addressed in the analysis concerned the relative efficacy of the level variables—especially industry and organizational size—in explaining reportorial autonomy. In order to answer this question, the variables representing the levels were entered in a forward stepwise regression analysis using dummy variables where measures of the independent variables were at the nominal level of data analysis.[6]

As Table 3 shows, four variables make a statistically significant contribution to explaining the variation in story selection autonomy while only two level variables make significant contributions to the explanation of content autonomy.

Collectively, the level variables shown in Table 3 explain less than one-tenth of the variance in the two forms of autonomy while years of experience alone explains over half the total variance (.053 in selection autonomy and .042 in content autonomy) explained by the entire regression model. For both types of autonomy, the industry in which reporters practice their craft is the second most important influence on autonomy while organization size is not a significant influence on either form of autonomy.

DISCUSSION

In Table 1 the correlations between selection autonomy and political lean are, in general, higher and a larger number are statistically significant than in Table 2 which shows the correlations between content autonomy and political lean. This suggest that where the political beliefs or reporters result in constraints on their autonomy, the control is exercised more strongly on the reporters' freedom to select the stories on which they work and less strongly on

TABLE 3
The Influence of Seven Levels of Analysis on Selection and
Content Autonomy: Summary of Stepwise Regression Models

	Variable	F	df	p
Story Selection Autonomy (N = 719)	Years Experience	41.560	1	<.05
	Industry	10.122	2	<.05
	Political Lean	7.835	1	<.05
	Market Size	4.643	1	<.05
	Organization Size	.476	1	n.s.
	Supra-Organization Size	.347	1	n.s.
	Chain/Non Chain	.349	1	n.s.
	Error		710	
	Model R^2 = .096			
Story Content Autonomy (N = 718)	Years Experience	32.198	1	<.05
	Industry	8.919	2	<.05
	Market Size	2.215	1	n.s.
	Supra-Organization Size	2.076	1	n.s.
	Chain/Non Chain	.689	1	n.s.
	Organization Size	.029	1	n.s.
	Political Lean	.004	1	n.s.
	Error		709	
	Model R^2 = .072			

the reporters' writing and structuring of facts. From the viewpoint of organizational management, this is no doubt an effective control strategy. Given the high value reporters place on autonomy (Johnstone, 1976), such indirect control exercised at this early stage of the news-gathering process is less likely to provoke overt conflict and produce morale-damaging consequences than more direct measures such as killing or editing stories which contravene policy in the later stages of the news production process.

In Tables 1 and 2, the relationship between political lean and selection and content autonomy is consistently statistically significant in both tables only for television and radio reporters. The tendency for broadcast reports with left-leaning political beliefs to be subject to a greater degree of control may be due to relatively stable and enduring features of the industry. It is also possible that the data exhibit, in the language of cohort analysis, a period effect. Johnstone's data were collected in 1971 following two years of attacks on the news industries by the Nixon administration (see Porter, 1976; 37-80, for details of the offensive against the press in 1969 and 1970).

Given the conservative nature of the administration and the power vulnerable status of the broadcast industry discussed earlier in this article, reporters with left-of-center political beliefs would be most likely to be constrained by their managements in response to the administration's criticisms. If future studies find relationships between autonomy and political lean of the magnitude shown in Tables 1 and 2, then perhaps the explanation lies in the structure of the broadcast industry. On the other hand, if future studies find substantially weaker correlations, such findings would support the period-effect interpretation.

Table 3 shows that industry is a more important influence on autonomy than organizational size which supports the hypothesis raised by Becker's (1978) univariate analysis. However, it is an individual-level variable—experience in journalism—which in this analysis plays the most important role in explaining autonomy. Breed's (1955) analysis would suggest that experienced reporters are left alone precisely because they have absorbed news policy and can be trusted to conform to its dictates. However, Garvey's (1971) study shows a much more complicated and less clear-cut relationship between experience and conformity to news policy than Breed's study would indicate. While Breed's analysis may be correct, it is also possible that the higher autonomy accorded reporters with greater experience is a reflection of the strong craft norms in journalism in which on-the-job experience is valued highly and, as a result, the work of the neophyte or "apprentice" is closely monitored while the more experienced journalists are relatively un-supervised. In other words, autonomy may be more a function of an industry-level norm—work experience—than of conformity to organizational news policy. Further research is necessary to decide between these competing interpretations.

SUMMARY

The purpose of this article has been to present a taxonomy of influences on decision making in the mass media and to illustrate the use of the taxonomy and research strategy in a quantitative analysis of between-level influences on decision antonomy in a national sample of reporters. Other studies (Dimmick and Becker, 1980; Becker and Dimmick, forthcoming) have employed the taxonomy in largely qualitative case study of analysis in media personnel decision making. Although a good deal of conceptual and empirical work remains to be done, these studies seem to demonstrate the potential of the taxonomy and research strategy in mapping and testing the significance of influences on decision making in the mass media.

NOTES

1. The idea, however, that social research may be conducted at several levels of analysis is not universally accepted. Galtung's (1967) typology of levels of analysis, if accepted, would severely restrict the ability to conduct multilevel research. To Galtung, the basis of social research is face-to-face interaction and the individual is the basic unit from which larger units of analysis are formed. He defines a typology consisting of three levels: primary, secondary, and tertiary collectivities. The primary collectivity is exemplified by the group in which all individuals or elements are strongly connected. Secondary collectivities or systems are composed of elements which are only weakly connected. The tertiary level is composed of categories (e.g., persons of the same age) in which the elements are unrelated. The strength of the relationship among the elements declines as one moves from the primary through the tertiary levels. Galtung argues that once one reaches the tertiary level, there is no interaction occurring

and, hence, no possibility of forming meaningful units beyond the secondary collectivities.

Galtung provides no rationale or justification, however, for the a priori choice of the "group," "system," and "category" as the elements of the typology. Further, no rationale or empirical evidence is adduced to justify the assertion that the relationships between elements necessarily weaken at the system level and disappear entirely at the level of the category. Beyond pointing out these deficiencies, little else can be said concerning these aspects of Galtung's typology: Unstated arguments are peculiarly invulnerable to criticism. It is possible, however, to show that Galtung's central assumption—the necessity for face-to-face contact—is unnecessarily restrictive. Influence, the core concept in the taxonomic structure presented earlier, can occur despite the lack of face-to-face contact between decision makers. Normative and informational social influence may occur in the absence of actual interaction. Broadcast station managers conform to FCC rules without ever speaking to a single members of the commission, and the *New York Times* exercises its influence on the news judgements of far more gatekeepers than ever that paper's large staff could possibly encounter face to face. In light of these considerations, Galtung's attempt to restrict research to the microlevels does not seem to be a serious impediment to conducting research on media decision making at more molar levels.

2. The fact the question of levels of influence has not been consistently raised is clearly demonstrated by research conducted by one school of organizational theory. Hirsch (1975) criticized this research tradition for taking the small group as the unit of analysis and treating the organization as a more or less unrelated set of decision-making groups unconnected to each other, to the organizational hierarchy, or to the organization's environment. While, as Simon (1969) shows, departmental boundaries "insulate" groups from each other, these groups are not totally independent. In news organizations, for example, normative social influence in the form of the news policy contains decision making on policy-related stories but does not exercise a similar effect on policy-irrelevant news items. On non-policy-related stories, what Cyert and March (1963) have called local rationality prevails—an organizational subunit is left alone to accomplish its task. For example, on daily newspapers each subunit, such as the national or city desk, fills its own "news hole" (page one and policy-related stories excepted) without reference to the organizational hierarchy.

3. One obvious reason for the lack of research designs explicitly formulated to deal with multiple levels of analysis is that the social science disciplines have factored the study of human behavior into its component levels. Particular levels of analysis are associated with specific social science disciplines—the cognitive or individual level with psychology, and the organizational and societal level with sociology and anthropology. Further, as Paisley (1972) has pointed out, particular levels or disciplines are associated with specific methods. Given the fact that interdisciplinary research is still rare, the division of labor in social research has no doubt inhibited the formulation of methods for dealing with multiple levels of analysis.

4. While the n's are moderately high and statistically significant, caution in interpretation is urged not only by the small N but also because the cluster-sampling technique used to select respondents makes it quite probable that these reporters represent an even smaller number of organizations.

5. This analysis is somewhat hampered by the lack of a clear-cut method of testing the significance of the difference between a Pearson r and a partial correlation. However, the magnitude of the differences between the overall sample r's and the correlations in the table for broadcast reporters in Tables 1 and 2 and reporters for chain weeklies in Table 1 seem to be large enough to justify the conclusion that specifying the level of analysis makes a difference.

6. The degree of collinearity was determined by testing the matrices comprised of all possible combinations of the independent variables and no determinant was found to be fatally near zero. As might be expected, organization size and market size were the two variables displaying the highest bivariate r. Examination of Table 3 shows, however, that even if the variance accounted for by "market size" and "organization size" were pooled to represent a single variable, that variable would still have been entered into the forward stepwise regression after "industry." Hence, neither "market size" nor "organization size" would be a stronger predictor of autonomy than "industry."

REFERENCES

ARGYRIS, C. (1974) Behind the Front Page. San Francisco: Jossey-Bass.

BAGDIKIAN, B. (1974) "Professional personnel and organizational structure in the mass media," pp. 122-142 in W. P. Davison and F.T.C. Yu (eds.) Mass Communication Research. New York: Praeger.

——— (1971) The Information Machines. New York: Harper & Row.

BAILEY, G. A. and L. LICHTY (1972) "Rough justice on a Saigon street: A gate-keeper study of NBC's Tet execution film." Journalism Q. 49: 221-229, 238.

BECKER, L. B. (1978) "Organizational variables and the study of newsroom behavior: A review and discussion of U.S. research." Presented at the 11th Annual Conference of the International Association for Mass Communication Research, Warsaw, Poland.

BELTRAN, S. L. (1977) "National communication policy in Latin America: A glance at the first steps," pp. 185-234 in S. Rahim and J. Middleton (eds.) Perspectives in Communication Policy and Planning. Honolulu: East-West Center.

BISHOP, R. L. (1972) "The rush to chain ownership." Columbia Journalism Rev. (November-December): 10-19.

BLUMLER, J. G. (1969) "Producers attitudes toward coverage of an election campaign," in P. Halmos (ed.) The Sociology of Mass Media Communicators. The Sociological Review: Monograph 13. Staffordshire, England: Univ. of Keele Press.

BOGART, L. (1974) "The management of mass media," pp. 143-170 in W. P. Davison and F.T.C. Yu (eds.) Mass Communication Research. New York: Praeger.

BOWERS, D. (1967) "A report on activity by publishers in directing newsroom decisions." Journalism Q. 44: 43-52.

BREED, W. (1955) "Social control in the newsroom: A functional analysis." Social Forces 32: 326-335.

BROWN, L. (1971) Television: The Business Behind the Box. New York: Harcourt Brace Jovanovich.

BUCKALEW, J. (1974) "The radio news gatekeeper and his sources." Journalism Q. 51: 602-606.

BURNS, T. (1969) "Public service and private world," in P. Halmos (ed.) The Socio-logical Review: Monograph 13. Staffordshire, England: Univ. of Keele Press.

CHIBNALL, S. (1975) "The crime reporter: A study in the production of commercial knowledge." Sociology 9(January): 49-66.

CROUSE, T. (1973) The Boys on the Bus. New York: Ballantine.

CYERT, R. M. and J. G. MARCH (1963) A Behavioral Theory of the Firm. Englewood Cliffs, NJ: Prentice-Hall.

DeFLEUR, M. and S. BALL-ROKEACH (1975) Theories of Mass Communication. New York: David McKay.

DEUTSCH, M. and H. GERARD (1955) "A study of normative and informational social influence upon individual judgement." J. of Abnormal and Social Psychology 51: 629-636.

DIMMICK, J. (1978) "Levels of analysis in mass media decision-making: A taxonomy and research strategy." Presented at the meeting of the Association for Education in Journalism, Seattle, Washington.

——— (1977) "Canons and codes as occupational ideologies." J. of Communication 27(Spring): 181-187.

——— L. B. BECKER, and JANE F. BRODERICK (1980) "Personnel decisions in TV organizations: A multi-level analysis." Presented at the meeting of the International Communication Association, Acapulco, Mexico.

DOMINICK, J. and M. C. PEARCE (1976) "Trends in network prime-time programming, 1953-74." J. of Communication 26(Winter): 70-80.

DONOHEW, L. (1965) "Publishers and their influence groups." Journalism Q. 42: 112-113.

DONOHUE, G. A., P. J. TICHENOR, and C. W. OLIEN (1972) "Gatekeeping: Mass media systems and information control," in F. G. Kline and P. J. Tichenor (eds.) Current Perspectives in Mass Communication Research. Beverly Hills, CA: Sage.

DUNN, D. (1969) Public Officials and the Press. Reading, MA: Addison-Wesley.

EDELSTEIN, A. and J. B. SCHULTZ (1964) "The leadership role of the weekly newspaper as seen by community leaders: A sociological perspective," in L. A. Dexter and D. M. White (eds.) People, Society and Mass Communication. New York: Free Press.

EPSTEIN, E. J. (1973) "The values of newsmen." TV Q. 10(Winter): 9-21.

FAWCETT, D. (1972) "What happens when a chain owner arrives," Columbus Journalism Rev. (November-December): 29-30.

FISHMAN, M. (1980) Manufacturing the News. Austin: Univ. of Texas Press.

FLEGEL, R. C. and S. H. CHAFFEE (1971) "Influences of editors, readers and personal opinions on reporters." Journalism Q. 48: 645-651.

GALTUNG, J. (1967) Theory and Methods of Social Research, New York: Columbia Univ. Press.

GARVEY, D. E. (1971) Social Control in the Television Newsroom. Ph.D. Dissertation, Stanford University.

GERBNER, G. (1967) "An institutional approach to mass communication research," in L. Thayer (ed.) Communication Theory and Research. Springfield, IL: Charles C Thomas.

GIEBER, W. (1960) "Two communicators of the news: A study of the roles of sources and reporters." Social Forces 39(October): 76-83.

GOLDING, P. (1979) "Media professionalism in the third world: The transfer of an ideology," pp. 291-308 in J. Curran et al. (eds.) Mass Communication and Society. Beverly Hills, CA: Sage.

GREY, D. L. (1966) "Decision-making by a reporter under deadline pressure." Journalism Q. 43: 419-428.

HIRSCH, P. M. (1975) "Organizational analysis and industrial sociology: An instance of cultural lag." Amer. Sociologist (February): 3-12.

——— (1972) "Processing fads and fashions: An organization-set analysis of cultural industry systems." Amer. J. of Sociology 77: 639-659.

HOWARD, H. (1976) "Cox broadcasting corporation: A group ownership case study." J. of Broadcasting 20(Spring): 209-231.

JOHNSTONE, J.W.C., E. SLAWSKI, and W. BOWMAN (1976) The News People. Urbana: Univ. of Illinois Press.

——— (1972-1973) "The professional values of American newsman." Public Opinion Q. 36: 522-540.

KING, S. W. (1975) Communication and Social Influence. Reading, MA: Addison-Wesley.

LASZLO, E. (1972) The Systems View of the World. New York: George Braziller.

LIEBES, B. H. (1966) "Decision-making by telegraph editors—AP or UPI?" Journalism Q. 43: 434-442.

LORSCH, J. and J. MORSE (1974) Organizations and Their Members: A Contingency Approach. New York: Harper & Row.

LOWRY, D. (1971) "Agnew and the network TV news: A before-after content analysis." Journalism Q. 48.

LUHMANN, N. (1979) Trust and Power. New York: John Wiley.

MARCH, J. D. and H. A. SIMON (1958) Organizations, New York: John Wiley.

McCOMBS, M. (1972) "Mass media in the marketplace." Journalism Monographs 24 (August).

McPHEE, W. (1963) Formal Theories of Mass Behavior. New York: Free Press.

MILLER, D. C. (1963) "Town and gown: The power structure of a university town." Amer. J. of Sociology 68: 432-443.

MOELLER, L. G. (1968) "Journalism education, the media and the 'new industrial state.'" Journalism Q. 45: 496-508.

PAISLEY, W. (1972) Communication Research as a Behavioral Discipline. Stanford, CA: Stanford University, Institute for Communication Research.

PETERSON, R. and D. G. BERGER (1975) "Cycles in symbol production: The case of the popular music industry." Amer. Soc. Rev. 40: 158-170.

PFEFFER, J. and G. R. SALANCIK (1978) The External Control of Organizations. New York: Harper & Row.

PRZEWORSKI, A. and H. TEUNE (1970) The Logic of Comparative Social Inquiry. New York: Wiley-Interscience.

RAHIM, S. (1977) "The scope of communication policy and planning research," pp. 5-24 in S. Rahim and J. Middleton (eds.) Perspectives in Communication Policy and Planning. Honolulu: East-West Center.

SHANKS, B. (1976) The Cool Fire. New York: W. W. Norton.

SIGAL, L. (1973) Reporters and Officials. Lexington, MA: D. C. Heath.

SIMON, H. A. (1969) The Sciences of the Artificial. Cambridge: MIT Press.

SNIDER, P. (1967) "Mr. Gates revisited: A 1966 version of the 1949 case study."

Journalism Q. 44: 419-427.

STARK, R. (1962) "Policy and the pros." Berkeley J. of Sociology 7: 11-31.

STEMPEL, G. H. (1973) "Effects on performance of a cross-media monopoly." Journalism Monographs 29(June).

THRIFT, R. (1977) "How chain ownership affects editorial vigor of newspapers." Journalism Q. 54: 327-331.

TUCHMAN, G. (1974) "Assembling a network talk show," in G. Tuchman (ed.) The TV Establishment. Englewood Cliffs, NJ: Prentice-Hall.

——— (1973) "Making news by doing work: Routinizing the unexpected." Amer. J. of Sociology 79: 110-131.

TUNSTALL, J. (1977) The Media Are American. New York: Columbia Univ. Press.

TUROW, J. (1977) "Client relationships and children's book publishing: A comparative study of mass media policy in two marketplaces," in P. Hirsch et al. (eds.) Strategies for Communication Research. Beverly Hills, CA: Sage.

WACKMAN, D. G., D. M. GILLMOR, C. GAZIANO, and E. DENNIS (1975) "Chain newspaper autonomy as reflected in presidential campaign endorsements." Journalism Q. 52: 411-420.

WARNER, M. (1968) TV Coverage of International Affairs. TV Q. 7(Spring): 60-75.

WHITE, G. M. (1950) "The gatekeeper: A case study in the selection of news." Journalism Q. 27: 383-390.

Based on the results of an interrogation of cameramen who were considered experts on the appli-cation of camera techniques, a content analysis of camera positions in presenting the two candidates for chancellor of the Federal Republic of Germany in the 1976 election was carried out. In addition, all verbal statements by journalists on positive and negative reactions were analyzed. Visual biases could be found evaluating the application of camera techniques by judgments of camermen and confronting verbal and visual contents of television campaign coverage. Hans Mathias Kepplinger is professor of communication research at the University of Mainz, Federal Republic of Germany.

23

VISUAL BIASES IN TELEVISION CAMPAIGN COVERAGE

Hans Mathias Kepplinger

I

Television news programming is based on conventions of verbal and visual storytelling which are rooted in literature and cinema. But, as Tuchman (1978: 110) points out, certain differences are essential: "Like the construction of a newspaper story, the structure of news film claims neutral-ity and credibility by avoiding conventions associated with fiction." As a consequence, time and space are not normally manipulated by using slow motion and extreme camera angles. One can assume, on the other hand, that violations of these general rules indicate a lack of neutrality: Camera techniques may be used to express individual views of a person or an event. Television news films have visual and verbal dimensions and normally the two will present the same or a similar picture of reality. If there are significant

From Hans Mathias Kepplinger, "Visual Biases in Television Campaign Coverage," *Communication Research,* Vol. 9, No. 3 (July 1982), pp. 432-446. Copyright © 1982 by Sage Publications, Inc.

differences between verbal and visual contents, only one of the two presentations can be appropriate. Again, one can assume that the visual content reflects underlying individual views of a person or an event held by those who produce the television news films.

Differences between visual and verbal content may occur, and extreme camera techniques may be used especially when reporting on important events with high emotional involvement such as election campaigns. Investigations of the television election campaign coverage undertaken so far dealt almost exclusively with verbal statements of journalists (Buss and Hofstetter, 1976; McLure and Patterson, 1974; Ruhland, 1979) and candidates (Graber, 1976; Weiss, 1976). On the other hand, all those means of representation which are specific for the television medium, such as camera position, image cutting, lighting, and sound, were mostly not taken into account. The present investigation is an attempt to analyze certain camera techniques and to compare verbal and visual contents of television news films. For this purpose four substudies were carried out:

(1) An interrogation of cameramen. The cameramen were considered experts for the application of camera techniques who might point out the possibilities of a positive or negative display of politicians.
(2) A quantitative content analysis of the camera position in presenting the two candidates for the office of the Chancellor of the Federal Republic of Germany in the 1976 elections, Helmut Schmidt (SPD) and Helmut Kohl (CDU).
(3) A quantitative content analysis of all statements by journalists on positive and negative reactions of the public toward Schmidt and Kohl.
(4) A quantitative content analysis of the visual display of positive and negative reactions of the public toward Schmidt and Kohl.

II

The interrogation of the cameramen was carried out by Willy Loderhose at the suggestion of Percy H. Tannenbaum in the summer of 1979 (Loderhose, 1980). All cameramen of two regional stations of the two nationwide television channels (n = 116) and a random sample of all cameramen of the Federal Republic of Germany (n = 200) were contacted. From this number of contacts, 151 cameramen returned the completed questionnaire and 19 had died, moved to an unknown address, or were on a journey. Thus the returns after adjusting the sample amounted to 51%.

Nearly all the cameramen—and it is justified to speak of "men" because there was only one woman among the 151 persons surveyed—believe that "a cameraman using merely optical means is able to make any person appear in a particularly positive or negative way": 78% answered in the affirmative to the statement "This is definitely possible," while 22% stated "This might be possible." Only one of the persons interviewed suggested "This is hardly possible." To, "which are the means concerned?" the cameramen answered rather definitely: Two-thirds of them would shoot a politician at eye level, another quarter from slightly above or below. No one, however, would choose a full top or bottom view (Table 1).

The opinions of the cameramen as to the effects of different camera angles were determined by asking them which perspective they would select to produce certain effects. A list of six negative and six positive effects was presented to the cameramen. In each case they were to check off which perspective they would choose in order to produce the effect mentioned. It was not intended, with the aid of this question, to determine whether the effects were actually obtained—which is possible only by experiments (Tiemens, 1969-1970; Mandell and Shaw, 1972-73; Schulz et al., 1976; McCain et al., 1977; Davis, 1978)—but whether the replies to the first question were valid. The answers of the camermen confirmed that a camera position at eye level is preferred to achieve positive effects while a full top or bottom view is mainly used to produce a negative effect. The

TABLE 1

Statements of Cameramen as to the Means of Shooting
Technique to Present a Politician as Positively as Possible

Question: "Imagine that you were in a situation to make a shot of a person whom you find rather sympathetic, for instance a person of public life, or a politician you think much of. This person is very nervous on the shooting day, his hands are in constant motion. How would you make appear this person on the screen? Which means of presentation would you use?"

- Possible answers -

Shot Sizes		Perspectives		Camera movements	
Close-up	38	Eye level	66	Static	53
Face shot	27	Slight bottom view	19	Zooming	26
Mid-shot	18	Slight top view	5	Camera movement	11
Full-length shot	9	Clear bottom view	0	Camera pan	1
Extreme close-up	0	Clear top view	0		
No statements	8	No statements	10	No statements	9
Total	100%		100%		100%

N = 151

only exception is the use of the full bottom view to create the impression of "power" (Table 2).

In German television, cameramen have a remarkable but limited influence on the production of news films. Their influence is remarkable because they alone or in cooperation make most of the decisions during shooting. Of all cameramen surveyed, the majority stated that cameramen and journalists in cooperation select shooting sizes (63%), camera movements (57%), and perspectives (52%). The minority stated that they alone make the decisions mentioned (33%, 39%, 46%). Some noticed that the journalists alone select shooting sizes (2%) and camera movements (1%) or gave no concrete answer (Loderhose, 1980: 101). Their influence is limited because the final decisions are made by the journalists who are responsible for the film and who supervise the editing process (Elster, 1979). The films therefore essentially reflect the viewpoints and decisions of

TABLE 2
**Statements by Cameramen on the Intended Effects
in Using Various Perspectives**

Question: "Perspectives can show rest, excitement, weakness, power, etc. What would you like to attain with bottom or top view shots? Please tick off the means of shooting technique corresponding to your opinion."

	Top view		Eye level	Bottom view	
	clear	slight	view	slight	clear
Positive					
Rest	9	16	54	5	1
Sympathy	3	8	60	11	0
Ease	5	12	46	14	1
Power	4	1	11	15	51
Liveliness	3	8	36	25	3
Skill	8	11	36	19	2
Total	32%	56%	243%	89%	58%
Negative					
Excitement	11	9	7	31	22
Antipathy	15	13	3	8	44
Tenseness	22	14	9	15	16
Weakness	52	16	5	6	5
Emptiness	40	12	15	3	11
Clumsiness	19	23	13	10	11
Total	159%	87%	52%	73%	109%

N = 151

the journalists. We can use the answers of the cameramen as criteria for evaluation of the films. They indicate if the final films were more or less favorable for the candidates according to expert criteria.

III

For the content analysis the election campaign coverage of the two nationwide television channels "ARD" and

"ZDF" between April 1 and October 3, 1976 was used. The election took place on October 3. The analysis comprised eight political magazine series of the two channels and all special election telecasts. These magazines were telecast in part every week and in part every other week. As to their character they roughly correspond to "60 Minutes" by CBS.

In the content analysis a difference was made between "reports," "contributions," and "shots." A *report* in the sense of the investigation is the representation of a subject of limited content which can consist of several different contributions such as interviews and speeches. A report is usually presented and/or terminated by a moderator. A *contribution* is a technically homogeneous part of a report. A difference was made between the following types of contribution: speeches, street interviews, studio interviews, rounds of talks and other types. A report can consist of one or several contributions on one or several politicians. Each contribution of every politician was coded on one code sheet each. Several formally equal contributions on one politician in different phases of a report were combined into one contribution. A *shot* is a representation of a person defined by the camera position, size of shot, and direction of shooting. A difference was made between three camera positions, that is, clear bottom view, clear top view, eye level; three directions of shooting: from the front, from the side, and from the rear; and six shot sizes: extreme closeup, close up, face shot, mid-shot, full-length shot, long shot (Millerson, 1978: 57). Slight bottom and top views were coded as eye level since according to the survey results, no different intentions or effects can be expected. If one of the three characteristics is modified by zoom, pan shot, or cut, this results in a new type of shot. In the case of zooming and moving the camera, the beginning and the end of the motion was coded as shot while the intermediate phases were not coded. The reports were coded by four teams consisting of two people each. After two weeks of training, the intercoder reliability was above C.R. = 70 for all categories presented here.

The two television channels have shown the candidates in their election campaign coverage in 795 shots. Surprisingly, one channel (ARD) showed the challenger Kohl more frequently than governing Federal Chancellor Schmidt. However, the Federal Chancellor was, most probably, more frequently on the screen in other telecasts not directly concerned with the election. In the great majority of shots the camera was at eye level or slightly below or above. There were, however, distinct differences in presentation of Schmidt and Kohl. Whereas Schmidt was shown in only 31 shots from the full bottom or top view, Kohl was presented in 55 shots from these perspectives. If the portion of shots is calculated from the total number of shots, it becomes clear that the ZDF—reputed to be conservative—presented the conservative candidate Kohl from the full bottom or top view more often than the progressive Chancellor (Table 3).

IV

Election campaigns are ritualized conflicts with the aim of gaining approval for persons and programs. A candidate meeting with approval of the public during his campaigning tours has good chances, whereas a candidate who is again and again disapproved of by the public has only very slim chances. Therefore, reports of approving or disapproving reactions of the public are, simultaneously, commentaries on the success or failures of the campaigners (Landy, 1972; Duck and Baggaley, 1975; Baggaley et al., 1980: 3-32, 50-52). The television coverage of the reactions of the public toward Schmidt and Kohl were investigated in the following manner: on the one hand the journalists' verbal statements on the reaction of the public were determined, on the other the optical displays of the reactions of the public were analyzed. All *statements* by journalists on the reaction of

TABLE 3

**Number of Shots of Different Perspectives for the Presentation
of Schmidt and Kohl in the ARD and ZDF Channels from
April 1 up to the Election on October 3, 1976**

Shots	ARD[1]		ZDF[2]		TOTAL[3]	
	Schmidt	Kohl	Schmidt	Kohl	Schmidt	Kohl
Clear bottom view	9	16	0	7	9	23
	20	26	11	29	31	55
Clear top view	11	10	11	22	22	32
Eye level	105	152	237	215	342	367
Total	125	178	248	244	373	422

1. χ^2 = 0.1106; df = 1; n.s.
2. χ^2 = 9.1388; df = 1; $p < 0.01$.
3. χ^2 = 4.5764; df = 1; $p < 0.05$.

Calculated for differences between negative (top and bottom view) and positive (eye level) perspectives.

the public—independent of the shots—and all *shots* in which the reactions of the public were optically displayed were coded. The reason for the selection of different recording units was that journalists frequently give their commentaries in only a few shots while reactions of the public are shown visually in a great number of differing shots. In order to record as far as possible all the journalists' statements, these statements, that is, grammatically complete sentences, were selected as recording units.

Reactions showing approval by the audience were ascertained according to six categories:

(1) acoustic (audible), nonverbal approval (clapping and other forms of applause)
(2) acoustic (audible) verbal approval (cheers, approving statements)

(3) visual (optical) approval (gestures, symbols, banners)
(4) successful interaction between candidate and audience (conversations, hand-shaking, gestures to which the audience responds in a friendly manner)
(5) attention, interest among the audience (eager posture, conscious turning toward the candidate)
(6) consent in the audience (gestures and statements expressing consent).

The statements of the journalists on the reactions of the public were determined according to the respective categories. In their election campaign reports the journalists of the two television channels commented surprisingly seldomly on positive reactions of the public. They mentioned somewhat more frequently positive reactions to Kohl than to Schmidt. The differences, however, are not significant. The number of shots in which positive reactions of the public were optically displayed exceeded the number of statements on positive reactions of the public by a factor greater than 10. Thus the shots offered a much greater amount of information than the statements. However, they gave the same impression to the audience as the verbal comments: The positive reaction of the public to Kohl was a little more frequent than to Schmidt (Table 4).

Reactions showing disapproval by the audience were also ascertained according to six categories:

(1) acoustic (audible), nonverbal disapproval (whistling, hissing, booing)
(2) acoustic (audible) verbal disapproval (calls, disapproving statements)
(3) visual (optical) disapproval (gestures, symbols, banners)
(4) missing, failed interactions (attempt to converse with no response or unfriendly response, waving and other gestures with no or unfriendly response)
(5) inattention, lack of interest in the audience (turning away from the candidate, conversations in the audience, disparaging gestures)

TABLE 4

Positive Reactions of the Public to Schmidt and Kohl in the ARD and ZDF Channels from April 1 up to the Election on October 3, 1976: Number of Shots and Number of Statements (in braces)

Presented, (mentioned) reactions of the public	ARD Schmidt	ARD Kohl	ZDF Schmidt	ZDF Kohl	TOTAL Schmidt	TOTAL Kohl
Acoustic nonverbal approval	49 ⎫	82 ⎫	87 ⎫	93 ⎫	136 ⎫	175 ⎫
Acoustic verbal approval	2 ⎬ (4)	3 ⎬ (7)	1 ⎬ (3)	0 ⎬ (3)	3 ⎬ (7)	3 ⎬ (10)
Optical approval	2 ⎭	14 ⎭	3 ⎭	11 ⎭	5 ⎭	25 ⎭
Successful inter-action	19 (2)	34 (5)	16 (1)	8 (1)	35 (3)	42 (6)
Attention, interest	9 (3)	16 (2)	33 (1)	42 (4)	42 (4)	58 (6)
Agreement within the public	0 (0)	1 (0)	0 (1)	0 (1)	0 (1)	1 (1)
Total	81 (9)	150 (14)	140 (6)	154 (9)	221 (15)	304 (23)

(6) conflict in the audience (gestures and statements expressing differences of opinions).

The statements of the journalists about the reaction of the public were determined again with the aid of respective categories. In their election campaign reports the journalists of the two television channels commented even more seldomly on negative than on positive reactions of the public. Negative and positive reactions to Kohl were mentioned somewhat more frequently than toward Schmidt. However, the case numbers are so insignificant that a trend hardly can be made out. The number of shots in which negative reactions of the public were shown again exceeded the number of statements on the negative reaction of the public by a factor of more than 10. In contrast to the journalists' statements, the shots gave a rather biased impression on the reactions of the public. Both television channels showed considerably more frequent shots with

TABLE 5

Negative Reactions of the Public to Schmidt and Kohl in the ARD and
ZDF Channels from April 1 up to the Election on October 3, 1976:
Number of Shots and Number of Statements (in braces)

Presented (mentioned) reactions of the public	ARD		ZDF		TOTAL	
	Schmidt	Kohl	Schmidt	Kohl	Schmidt	Kohl
Acoustic nonverbal disapproval	0	12	1	42	1	54
Acoustic verval disapproval	0 (1)	1 (2)	1 (0)	8 (2)	1 (1)	9 (4)
Optical disapproval	0	8	0	0	0	8
Lacking, unsuccessful interaction	0 (0)	1 (2)	3 (0)	23 (0)	3 (0)	24 (2)
Inattention, desinterestedness	0 (0)	1 (0)	2 (0)	1 (0)	2 (0)	2 (0)
Conflicts within the public	0 (1)	2 (0)	0 (0)	0 (0)	0 (1)	2 (0)
Total	0 (2)	25 (4)	7 (0)	74 (2)	7 (2)	99 (6)

negative reactions of the public to Kohl compared to Schmidt.
Thus the optical coverage possessed a clear bias (Table 5).

If the statements of journalists on negative and positive
reactions of the public are taken as a whole, there are no
significant differences between Schmidt and Kohl: In both
cases the portion of statements on negative reaction of the
public of all statements on the reactions of the public is
similar (Table 6).

However, the situation regarding the optical presentation
of negative and positive reactions of the public is quite
different. The portion of shots with negative reactions of the
public of all shots showing reactions of the public is
significantly higher for Kohl than for Schmidt. Thus Schmidt
was presented as the candidate who nearly exclusively
received the approval of the public whereas Kohl was
displayed as the candidate who met relatively frequent
disapproval by the public (Table 7).

TABLE 6
Statements of Journalists as to Positive and Negative Reactions
of the Public to Schmidt and Kohl

	ARD[1]		ZDF[2]		TOTAL[3]	
	Schmidt	Kohl	Schmidt	Kohl	Schmidt	Kohl
Positive	9	14	6	9	15	23
Negative	2	4	0	2	2	6
Total	11	18	6	11	17	29

1. $\chi^2 = 0.0679$; df = 1; n.s.
2. $\chi^2 = 1.2363$; df = 1; n.s.
3. $\chi^2 = 0.5942$; df = 1; n.s.

SUMMARY AND INTERPRETATION

The content analysis of the visual presentation of the two candidates for the office of the Chancellor of the Federal Republic of Germany in the 1976 election campaign reveals that the CDU/CSU candidate Kohl was more frequently given a negative image on the screen than the SPD candidate Schmidt. Kohl was more frequently shot from perspectives that a majority of cameramen said they would use if they wanted to bring out the excitement, antipathy, tenseness, weakness, emptiness, or clumsiness of the candidate rather than rest, sympathy, ease, power, liveliness or skill. Moreover, negative reactions of the public—acoustic verbal and nonverbal disapproval, visual disapproval, missing or failed interactions, inattention or lack of interest in the audience and conflict in the audience—were displayed more often. The television coverage of the election campaign had a visual bias. On the other hand, no tendency could be found in the verbal statements of journalists concerning the candidates, the reaction of the public, and individual political subjects (Kepplinger, 1979). How can these facts be explained?

TABLE 7
Optical Displays of Positive and Negative Reactions
of the Public to Schmidt and Kohl

	ARD[1]		ZDF[2]		TOTAL[3]	
	Schmidt	Kohl	Schmidt	Kohl	Schmidt	Kohl
Positive	81	150	140	154	221	304
Negative	0	25	7	74	7	99
Total	81	125	147	228	228	403

1. χ^2 = 12.8237; df = 1; p $<$ 0.001.
2. χ^2 = 40.4790; df = 1; p $<$ 0.001.
3. χ^2 = 48.1396; df = 1; p $<$ 0.001.

The television channels of the Federal Republic of Germany are obligated to telecast a balanced program. Therefore, they are not supposed to give a one-sided support either to the parties in power, SPD and FDP, or their candidate, or to support the opposition parties, CDU and CSU, or their candidate Kohl. However, the political opinions of the journalists of the television channels were by no means balanced: some 70% favored the SPD or FDP and only 20% favored the CDU and CSU while the rest were undecided or did not express a preference for any party. In contrast to the population three months before the election, the majority of journalists (76%) were of the opinion that Schmidt would win the election. At this time, however, Kohl still had the same number of followers as Schmidt, as was revealed by opinion polls (see Noelle-Neumann, 1980a: 233, and 1980b: 69, 105, 108).

If the results of the content analyses are considered with this background, the following interpretation presents itself: The television journalists endeavored in their verbal statements to give a balanced presentation of the election campaign. In this connection they accurately complied with the program target of the television channels since the verbal content of the reports were analyzed and checked by the management of the stations and the political parties. However, with the aid of optical means, the television journalists presented—deliberately or unconsciously—the two candidates as they actually saw them: Since they considered Kohl a poorer politician than Schmidt, they frequently accepted more unfavorable shots of the former. Since they viewed Kohl with disfavor and expected him to lose the election, they showed negative reactions of the public more frequently. The opinions of the journalists could, in this connection, be displayed with relative freedom since the video coverage was exactly analyzed and checked neither by the management nor by the parties. This tendency was more pronounced at the ZDF since the management of this channel is more conservative than that of the ARD. The journalists could articulate their political opinions by spoken commentaries even less than the ARD and, therefore, used the means of "optical commentary" more frequently.

REFERENCES

BAGGALEY, J., M. FERGUSON, and P. BROOKS (1980) Psychology of TV Image. Westmead, England: Gower.

BUSS, T. F. and R. HOFSTETTER (1976) "An analyst of the logic of televised campaign advertisements: The 1972 Presidential campaign." Communication Research 3: 367-392.

DAVIS, L. K. (1978) "Camera eye-contact by the candidates in the presidential debates of 1976." Journalism Q. 55: 431-455.

DUCK, S. W. and J. BAGGALEY (1975) "Audience reaction and its effect on perceived expertise." Communication Research 2: 79-85.

ELSTER, I. (1979) "Journalisten zweiter Klasse. Die staendigen freien Mitarbeiter der Rundfunkanstalten" pp. 142-165 in H. M. Kepplinger (ed.) Angepasste Aussenseiter: Was Journalisten denken und wie sie arbeiten. Freiburg, Federal Republic of Germany: Alber-Verlag.

GRABER, D. A. (1976) "Press and TV as opinion resources in presidential campaigns." Public Opinion Q. 40: 285-303.

HENCKELS, D. W. (1978) Fernsehredakteure und Fernsehtechniker. Ph.D. dissertation, University of Hamburg.

KEPPLINGER, H. M. (1980) "Optische Kommentierung in der Berichterstattung ueber den Bundestagswahlkampf 1976," pp. 163-179 in T. Ellwein (ed.) Politikfeld-Analysen 1979. Koeln, Federal Republic of Germany. Westdeutscher Verlag.

—— (1979) "Ausgewogen bis zur Selbstaufgabe? Die Fernsehberichterstattung ueber die Bundestagswahl 1976 als Fallstudie eines kommunikationspolitischen Problems." Media Perspektiven Heft 11: 750-755.

LANDY, D. (1972) "The effect of overheard audience's reaction and attractiveness on opinion change." J. of Experimental Social Psychology 8: 176-288.

LODERHOSE, W. (1980) "Zum Einfluss von Kameraleuten auf Fernseh- und Filmproduktionen." Unpublished master's thesis. Institut fuer Publizistik, Universitaet Mainz.

MANDELL, L. M. and D. L. SHAW (1972-1973) "Judging people in the news—unconsciously: Effect of camera angle and bodily activity." J. of Broadcasting 17: 353-362.

McCAIN, T. A., J. CHILBERG, and J. WAKSHLAG (1977) "The effect of camera angle on source credibility and attraction." J. of Broadcasting 21: 35-46.

McLURE, R. D. and T. E. PATTERSON (1974) "Television news and political advertising: The impact of exposure on voter beliefs." Communication Research 1: 3-31.

MILLERSON, G. (1978) TV Camera Operation. New York: Focal/Hasting House.

NOELLE-NEUMANN, E. (1980a) Die Schweigespirale. Oeffentliche Meinung—unsere soziale Haut. Muenchen: Piper-Verlag.

—— (1980b) Wahlenscheidung in der Fernsehdemokratie. Freiburg, Federal Republic of Germany: Ploetz.

RUHLAND, W. (1979) Fernsehmagazine und Parteien. Die Darstellung der Parteien in den innenpolitischen Magazinen des deutschen Fernsehens im Bundestagswahlkampf 1976. Berlin: Spiess.

SCHULZ, W., R. van LESSEN, C. SCHLEDE, and N. WALDMANN (1976) "Die Bedeutung audiovisueller Gestaltungsmittel fuer die Vermittlung politischer Einstellungen. Medienanalytische und experimentelle Untersuchung am Beispiel sozialkundlicher Filme." AVforschung 15: 49-210.

TIEMENS, R. K. (1969-1970) "Some relationships of camera angle to communicator credibility." J. of Broadcasting 14: 483-490.

TUCHMAN, G. (1978) Making News: A Study in the Construction of Reality. New York: Free Press.

WEISS, H.-J. (1976) Wahlkampf im Fernsehen. Untersuchung zur Rolle der grossen Fernsehdebatten im Bundestagswahlkampf 1972. Berlin: Spiess.

In this chapter, Whitney and Becker present experimental evidence from television and newspaper editors to suggest that by presenting more news in some categories than in others, the wire services cue such editors as to what the important categories of news are. They offer an interpretation that wire service shaping of the news agenda outweighs shared news values among wire service editors and local news editors as an explanation for the structure of their data. D. Charles Whitney is research assistant professor in the Institute of Communications Research and assistant professor of journalism at the University of Illinois at Urbana-Champaign, and Lee B. Becker is professor of journalism at Ohio State University.

24

"KEEPING THE GATES" FOR GATEKEEPERS
The Effects of Wire News

D. Charles Whitney and Lee B. Becker

▶ An enduring concern in the study of journalistic practice is the degree to which news is standardized. A number of commentators have noted that various constraints reduce the variability of news available to audiences. Most of these constraints are tangible, concrete and relatively well documented, such as time, "news hole," or space, money, standardized sources, organizational policy and craft norms.[1] Others are considerably less apparent, and one such "unseen" constraint is the subject of this paper.

Two recent commentaries have reexamined White's classic 1949 "Mr. Gates" study of the news selection behavior of one Midwestern wire news editor.[2] Both have argued that more remarkable than White's finding that the editor engaged in idiosyncratic, subjective selections and rejections of news items was that the editor apparently unconsciously mirrored selections already made for him by the wire services. Classifying the news available from the wire service into seven content categories (labor, accidents and disasters, crime and vice, human interest, national, political, international), McCombs and Shaw[3] note a Spearman's rho of .64 between ranks of seven news item content categories supplied by the wires and ranks of stories selected by "Mr. Gates," and a Spearman r of .80 for a replication study of the same editor 17 years later.[4]

Gold and Simmons, in a study of 24 Iowa daily newspapers relying solely on one AP wire circuit for state, national and international news found overall coefficient of concordance of .915 between ranks of proportions of content supplied by the wire service and ranks of proportion of content used by the newspapers in 13

[1] For time, see Robert L. Jones, Verling C. Troldahl and J.K. Hvistendahl, "News Selection Patterns from a State TTs-Wire," JOURNALISM QUARTERLY, 38:303-12 (1961); and Guido H. Stempel III, "How Newspapers Use the Associated Press Afternoon A-Wire," JOURNALISM QUARTERLY, 41:380-384 (1964); for space, see Gaye Tuchman, *Making News: A Study in the Construction of Reality* (New York: Free Press, 1978) and David Manning White, "The Gate-Keeper: A Case Study in the Selection of News," JOURNALISM QUARTERLY, 27:383-390 (1949); for money, see Edward J. Epstein, *News from Nowhere* (New York: Vintage, 1973); for standardized sources, see Warren Breed, "Newspaper 'Opinion Leaders' and Processes of Standardization," JOURNALISM QUARTERLY, 35:277-284, 328 (1955); but for a contrary view, see Guido H. Stempel III, "Uniformity of Wire Content in Six Michigan Dailies," JOURNALISM QUARTERLY, 37:45-48, 129 (1959); for policy, see Breed, "Social Control in the Newsroom: A Functional Analysis," *Social Forces*, 33:326-35 (1955), and John Dimmick, "The Gate-Keeper: An Uncertainty Theory," *Journalism Monographs* No. 37 (November 1974); for craft norms, see Tuchman, "Objectivity as Strategic Ritual," *American Journal of Sociology*, 77:660-679 (1972).

[2] Paul M. Hirsch, "Occupational, Organizational and Institutional Models in Mass Media Research: Toward an Integrated Framework," in Hirsch, Peter V. Miller and F. Gerald Kline, eds., *Strategies for Communication Research* (Beverly Hills, CA.: Sage, 1977), pp. 13-42, and Maxwell E. McCombs and Donald L. Shaw, "Structuring the 'Unseen Environment'," *Journal of Communication*, 26:18-22 (Spring 1976).

[3] *Op. cit.*, p. 21.

[4] Paul Snider, "'Mr. Gates' Revisited: A 1966 Version of the 1949 Case Study," JOURNALISM QUARTERLY, rr:419-427 (1967).

From D. Charles Whitney and Lee B. Becker, " 'Keeping the Gates' for Gatekeepers: The Effects of Wire News," *Journalism Quarterly*, Vol. 59, No. 1 (Spring 1982), pp. 60-65. Reprinted by permission.

categories.[5]

Stempel, in a 1959 content analysis of wire stories used by six small Michigan dailies, found agreement to be relatively low, with only eight of 764 stories used by all papers and with overall agreement at 31% of stories across papers.[6] His 1964 study of 21 metropolitan papers offers findings more directly relevant to the research reported here.[7] Average use of AP A-wire items by all papers was 22% ranging from a low of 11% by a New York paper to 34% by the *Rochester* (N.Y.) *Times-Union*. In the study period, the afternoon AP A-wire transmitted 97 Washington, D.C.-datelined stories (17% of all stories), 298 U.S.-datelined stories (54%) and 159 foreign-datelined stories (29%). While the numbers and proportions of stories bearing these datelines varied substantially, proportions selected by papers within categories did not: 22% of the D.C.-datelined stories, 20% of the U.S.-datelined stories and 24% of the international stories were selected by the papers.

These findings suggest that wire service editors, in broad terms, "set the news agenda" for newspaper news editors, by suggesting the proper "news mix" and proportions within news categories such as accidents and disasters, crime and vice and human interest news. Two possible explanations present themselves. The first is that the structure of each day's wire file, independent of proportions of content, influences editors' selections. For example, "soft news" such as human interest stories may be transmitted early in a wire cycle, leading to a higher proportionate selection for such early-moving copy, while "hard news" might move closer to deadline.[8] While in an absolute sense editors might value later-moving stories more highly as news, they might not ordinarily alter previously-made news judgments.

Whitney, for example, recorded several such non-substitutions in story play in news scripts in a large metropolitan radio newsroom.[9]

A second and perhaps more plausible explanation of the correspondence between wire copy provided editors and their editorial choices is that wire service editors and news editors in media outlets share highly similar news values, and thus a finding that each select news items in similar proportions in news content categories merely reflects similarity of judgment.

If Gold and Simmons and the "Mr. Gates" studies are correct, the wire services "set agendas" for the news play "mix" of these various sorts of stories by transmitting them in varying proportions: if 5% of what is transmitted is labor news, then 5% of what is selected should be as well. Also implied is that the proportions in categories are consistent across time. The proportion of news within the content type becomes an added piece of information for editors to use in making story selections, information that would be absent if equal proportions of news were transmitted in each category.

An adequate test of an hypothesis that wire service editors' assignment of items in varying proportions to news categories influences other editors' selections of a subset of those items in similar proportions, then, would require variations in the wire file proportions assigned to various news categories. Where the file is "stacked," or proportioned much as news is routinely transmitted, editors' selections should mirror proportions transmitted. Where the file is "balanced," several outcomes, amenable to varying interpretations, are possible: a) if selections mirror the "balanced" nature of the "balanced" wire file, the outcome strongly supports the notion that wire editors "set the agenda" for news editors; b) if selections instead follow the proportions of news normally assigned by ᵉeditors of both wire services and newspaper and television editors, the plausible interpretation is that in normal circumstances, both editors are applying the same

[5] David Gold and Jerry L. Simmons. "News Selection Patterns Among Iowa Dailies." *Public Opinion Quarterly* 29:425-430 (1965).

[6] *Op. cit.*

[7] *Op. cit.*

[8] Cf. Jones, Troldahl and Hvistendahl, *op. cit.*

[9] D. Charles Whitney. "'Information Overload' in the Newsroom: Two Case Studies." Unpublished Ph.D. dissertation. University of Minnesota. 1978.

news values; c) if, however, selections in a "balanced" condition reflect neither the "usual" proportions nor the "balanced" proportions, this invites an "added information" interpretation—that where the proportioning approximates "normal" wire service distributions in the categories, it is followed, but when it does not, idiosyncratic selection will apply.

Methods

Editorial managers of the morning and evening newspapers in Columbus and Dayton, Ohio, and of the three Columbus and two Dayton commercial television stations with regularly-scheduled news broadcasts of 30 minutes per day or more were asked for lists of news employees whose duties included selecting wire service news one or more days per month. Fifty-two such editors were identified, and 46 (88.5%) agreed to participate in the study. Fieldwork dates were May 1-14, 1979, and each editor completed a news selection task and answered a dozen personal interview items. Administration was completed at subjects' offices at the beginning or end of their working days, and about 30 minutes was required of each. Fieldworkers were journalism graduate students.

The selection task was as follows: Two dummy files of what the editors were told were lead paragraphs of wire service news stories were printed on cards. Each file included 98 news items, roughly the number of items that a content analysis of a week of the Ohio AP newspaper wire indicated would be transmitted during a typical day's morning or evening newspaper cycle. About 275 items were selected from current and old newspaper files, from four-year-old wire service items and from fictionalized accounts similar to the newspaper and wire items. Omitted were sports, state and local items, weather and stock market quotations[10] and items of especially important current interest. References to a day of the week were altered to "yesterday" or "today." Stories were coded into the seven categories mentioned in the "Mr. Gates" studies: labor, accidents and disasters, crime and

vice, human interest, national, political and international. Stories which could not be reliably coded into a single category by two judges were excluded. When the story files were completed, items were tentatively assigned to two decks. In the first, or "balanced" deck, 14 items were assigned to each of the seven categories; in the second, or "unbalanced" deck, proportions of items were used approximating those reported by Snider for wire items read by "Mr. Gates": labor 5 items (5.1%); accidents and disasters, 7 items (7.1%); crime and vice, 11 items (11.2%); human interest, 14 items (14.3%); national, 16 items (16.3%); political, 21 items (21.4%); and international, 24 items (24.5%). All items were presented to a panel of five Ohio State University journalism faculty and staff members with news editing experience for ranking on a Likert-type 1-5 "newsworthiness" scale. Their mean item rankings were then used to balance the overall "newsworthiness" within each category across the two decks.

A repeated measures counterbalanced design called for the experimental subjects (the news editors) to select 21 stories, or about the number of wire service items that the largest newspaper in the two cities ran in an average day, from each file. Fieldworkers decided by a coin toss whether the first subject to whom they administered the selection task would select stories from the "unbalanced" or "balanced" deck, or file, first; in subsequent administrations, each fieldworker systematically varied the order of administration. Twenty-four editors selected from the "unbalanced" day first, and 22 from the "balanced."

Results

Of the 46 editors who participated, 38 (82.6%) were male and eight (17.4%) were

[10] Gold and Simmons, op. cit., found such categories to be invariably applied by newspapers, which used a fixed proportion of such copy regardless of what was coming in. Whitney, op. cit., pp. 8-9, has referred to such stories as "policy" stories, since the rules for their selection or rejection are fixed and noncontemporaneous: A weather forecast for a particular region or state has a .0 or a 1.0 chance of being selected for a particular newspaper, regardless of its content on a given day, and the Dow-Jones averages will, or will not, be used by a particular evening newscast, regardless of whether they are up, down or unchanged.

FIGURE I

Percentages of stories in wire files, and percentages selected by editors, in balanced and unbalanced files in seven content categories.

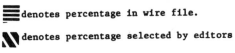

denotes percentage in wire file.

denotes percentage selected by editors

1-A: Balanced Condition

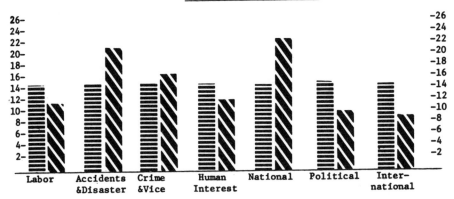

1-B: Unbalanced Condition

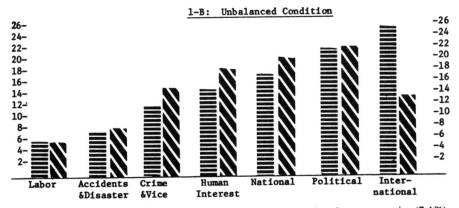

female; 29 (63%) were newspaper editors with the remaining 17 (37%) working for television stations. The editors spend a mean of 4.04 days per week editing wire news. They had been wire editors for a mean of 7.5 years with the most senior editor having been one for 28 years, and they had been professional journalists for a mean of 13 years.

Editors showed considerable variability in their selections of 21 stories from both sets of news leads: in the "balanced" deck, only six stories (6.1%) were selected by no editors, 19 (19.4%) were selected by 25% of

the editors, and only seven stories (7.1%) were selected by as many as half editors. In the "unbalanced" deck, only two stories (2%) were not selected, and 24 (24.5%) were selected by as many as half the editors. The most favored stories in the "balanced" and "unbalanced" set were selected by 38 and 36 editors, respectively. A test for an order-of-administration effect was performed by computing t-tests on the mean number of items selected within each content category by order of administration ("balanced" or "unbalanced" first). In none of the 14

TABLE 1

Proportions in Wire File and Proportions Selected by Editors in
"Balanced" and "Unbalanced" Conditions

	Balanced Condition		Unbalanced Condition	
	% in wire file	% selected by editors	% in wire file	% selected by editors
Labor	14.3	11.0	5.1	5.3
Accidents & Disasters	14.3	20.7	7.1	7.3
Crime & Vice	14.3	16.0	11.2	14.5
Human Interest	14.3	11.7	14.3	17.9
National	14.3	22.2	16.3	19.8
Political	14.3	9.7	21.4	21.7
International	14.3	8.7	24.5	13.4
	100.1%	100.0%	99.9%	99.9%

comparisons was the t-value significant at the .05 level (pooled variance estimate). Thus an order of administration effect was considered unlikely.

Proportions of stories in the content categories in the "unbalanced" conditions by and large serve as excellent predictors of editor selections within the categories; only international news varies substantially from the proportion of incoming news, and international news was the *least* favored category in, the balanced condition. (Figure 1).

A Pearson correlation coefficient between number of items incoming and number selected in the categories in the "unbalanced" set is $r = .71$ (p=.037, n=7); the Spearman rank-order r is .62 (p = .025, n =7). For newspaper editors the Pearson r is .71; for broadcast editors, Pearson r is .66. Since there is no variation in the number of stories presented to the editors in the "balanced" set, correlation coefficients between number of incoming and selected items in the "balanced" deck cannot be computed.

The notion that wire editors and news editors share similar conceptions of how many stories should be selected within each of the seven categories can be tested by comparing the number of incoming stories in the unbalanced set with the number of stories selected by editors from the balanced set. As both examination of Figure 1 and reference to correlations

suggest, this is not the case; the Pearson r is -.41 (n.s.) Spearman r is -.33 (n.s.). Examination of the rankings of selected stories in the "balanced" condition reveals no particular pattern of selection, although, as previously noted, it shows that generally editors are least likely to select international news, the category of news that in both White's 1949 and Snider's 1966 "Mr. Gates" studies accounted for the highest proportion of incoming wire news. A final internal check compared editors' selections in the unbalanced condition with selections in the balanced condition; they were virtually unrelated (Pearson $r = -.046$, n.s.; Spearman $r = .07$, n.s.), indicating that selection influence was not closely related to editors' news values.

Further Analysis. Newspaper editors were more likely in the balanced condition to select accident and disaster, crime, human interest and international stories than were their television counterparts, and the TV editors were more likely to select political, labor and national stories. In the unbalanced condition, newspaper editors and television editors are virtually identical in their selection patterns, except that newspaper editors were much more likely to pick human interest stories (T = 2.34, 44 d.f., p = .02), and TV editors were more likely to select national news items.

Several content variations seem counterintuitive and in some cases contradictory to previous research. Becker has noted that broadcast newsmen are more likely to report they cover controversy and conflict than are print journalists,[11] and Buckalew has noted that for television editors, a visuality news determinant must be added to the list of traditional news elements judged by print journalists.[12] As such, then, the content variations may represent structural variations not controlled in the experiment.

Summary

Forty-six Columbus and Dayton, Ohio, editors cooperated in a counterbalanced-design field experiment to test whether proportions of news items in seven content categories transmitted by wire services served to cue editors as to proportions which should be selected from these categories. Support for such an hypothesis was found, but little support for an alternative explanation that wire editors and newspaper and television editors share an ongoing set of news values was found. In addition, it was suggested that international news was less valued by the newspaper and television editors than was anticipated.

Gold and Simmons, in a reexamination of content analysis data of small Iowa daily newspapers, finding a similar pattern, noted that "This similarity in patterns of news emphasis may represent similarity of news judgments. An alternative interpretation is that the pattern of emphasis of the wire service, represented by the frequency with which various types of stories are set out, is more or less uncritically accepted by these...daily newspapers for their own patterns of emphasis." This study undercuts the notion that the wires and the editors routinely share news values. It supports the idea that news as routinely transmitted in stock categories is indeed "uncritically accepted" in newspaper and television newsrooms.

Sprinkled through the recent research literature on the role of the mass media in setting the political agenda are references to the nagging question of how the media formulate the agenda they present to their audiences.[13] This study suggests quite strongly that the local media, at least, are influenced greatly by the decisions of a relatively few editors operating at the regional, national and international bureaus of the wire services. In other words, the agenda being presented by the media audiences is influenced by the newsgathering procedures of the media and the relationships among the media. The local media are hardly acting alone in shaping the political agenda.

[11] Lee Becker, "Organizational Variables and the Study of Newsroom Behavior." Paper presented to the International Association for Mass Communication Research, Warsaw, Poland, August, 1978, p. 10.

[12] James K. Buckalew, "A Q-Analysis of Television News Editors' Decisions," JOURNALISM QUARTERLY, 46:135-137 (1969).

[13] Maxwell E. McCombs and Donald L. Shaw, "The Agenda-Setting Function of Mass Media," Public Opinion Quarterly, 37:176-187 (1972); Shaw and McCombs, The Emergence of American Political Issues (St. Paul, Minn.: West, 1977).

This study of American public television programming argues that when public television is compared with commercial television, influences over what gets on the air differ markedly. External influences on what gets shown and how it is presented appear greater than in commercial television, and recent changes in funding and technology appear likely to lead to less autonomy for public television programmers than they currently enjoy. Walter W. Powell is assistant professor of sociology at Yale University, where Rebecca Friedkin is a doctoral student.

25

POLITICAL AND ORGANIZATIONAL INFLUENCES ON PUBLIC TELEVISION PROGRAMMING

Walter W. Powell and Rebecca Friedkin

Public broadcasting is one of the few widely accessible alternatives to commercial television. The standard criticisms of commerical television are by now familiar: It is an extremely profitable, oligopolistic industry that promotes capitalist commodities and consumerist values; it is a "wasteland" offering bland, homogeneous fare; and the combination of industry concentration and a limited range of programming results in little that is innovative as well as a failure to present a diversity of views.[1] Public television is sometimes held up as a different entity; its stated mission is to strive for both "excellence and diversity." The extent to which public television meets that challenge is an important questions.

In this chapter we examine how external political forces and internal organizational factors shape the type of programs that are shown on public television. We draw upon interviews and fieldwork at WNET-TV (New York City and Newark, New Jersey) and CPTV (Connecticut), a consortium of five small stations.[2] We discuss a range of factors that determine what programs get on the air. We begin with an analysis of the environment of public television and the processes involved in financing and distributing programs. We

NOTE: Research support was provided by the Program on Non-Profit Organizations at the Institution for Social and Policy Studies, Yale University. We wish to thank Paul DiMaggio and John Simon for helpful comments on a draft.

then turn to an examination of the organizational structure of two major public television stations and show how departmental arrangements, staff politics, and program characteristics shape decision making.

An important characteristic of public television is the lack of clear criteria for decision making and evaluation. In contrast, commercial television operates according to a simple set of rules: Programming decisions are responsive to a market system based on ratings. Lacking objective tests of efficiency or effectiveness, public television is insulated from the benefits and penalties of a market-based price system. Public television must cope with diverse and uncertain funding sources and respond to multiple, and sometimes incompatible, goals. The history of public broadcasting reveals a basic lack of agreement on what it is and on what its mandate should be.[3] The stated mission tries to offer all things to all people: that the needs of minority and specialized taste groups be met and that the Federal Communication Commission's goal of localism, or community control, be met. Recently, basic questions about legitimacy have been raised: Are the costs for public broadcasting justified given the size of the audience reached? Our research was conducted at a time when public television confronted these questions about its mission and purpose, while facing sharp reductions in operating revenues as a result of federal budgetary cutbacks.

The public television system operates on two levels. At the local level there are some 280 public stations. These stations can be roughly divided into two types. A few large stations regularly produce programs for national broadcast. WNET is the largest public television station in the country and is often considered the system's "flagship" station. However, the vast majority of stations are small and produce only a few hours of local programming each week. These "consuming" stations purchase virtually all of their programming. CPTV falls into this category.

At the national level, the Corporation for Public Broadcasting (CPB), the Public Broadcasting Service (PBS), the National Association of Public Television Stations (NAPTS), and National Public Radio (NPR) are the organizational entities that centrally administer and link the public system together. The Corporation for Public Broadcasting is a private nonprofit organization financed by the federal government. CPB is the main conduit through which federal monies flow to public television. It distributes money directly to stations, finances program development and production, and provides funds for PBS and NPR. The Public Broadcasting Service operates the statellite interconnection and distributes programming to member stations. NAPTS is the station membership organization that serves planning needs and provides national representation for the stations. National Public Radio fulfills all of the foregoing functions for public radio stations. Although public radio and television are separate operations, NPR obtains its major source of financing from CPB, thus setting the stage for disputes with public television over funding allocation criteria.

The public broadcasting system is both administratively complex and loosely organized. "Turf battles" are not uncommon. Conflicts over the relationship between CPB and PBS, between radio and television, and between larger producing stations and small consuming stations are frequent and acrimonious. Power struggles are ongoing, as each element in the system jockeys to use the rapid changes taking place in public broadcasting to its own advantage. We will not review these disputes here; however, we do examine the infuence that these various organizations have on the public television decision-making process.

In addition to the many organizations that make up the public television system, there are other constituencies to which public television turns for resources and support. We know that the differences in the structure and output of an organization can be explained by variations in the flow of resources and control over the resource allocation processes (Pfeffer and Salancik, 1978). For example, profit-seeking managers depend on the market for earned income, government agencies or government-funded organizations rely on state support, and nonprofit organizations depend on contributions from key status groups, be they cultural elites, community groups, or civic-minded volunteers. Public broadcasting, however, incorporates elements from each of these ideal types. It represents a peculiar hybrid of economic constraint and political control. Public television operates like a public agency in that as much as 65 percent of the budget of a small station comes from federal, state, and municipal governments. Public stations also receive approximately 25 percent of their financial support from members, and considerable effort is expended on membership and fund-raising drives. In this manner, public television resembles voluntary associations. Other key constituencies are independent producers, artists, private foundations, and corporate sponsors. Recent shifts in the financing of public television and the composition of its key supporters have created considerable uncertainty for public television.[4] Station autonomy has been lessened, and funding sources exert more influence on program development.

SOURCES OF FUNDING

A major source of uncertainty for public television is the precarious and turbulent nature of its funding sources. Not only is money scarce, but external funding relationships are unpredictable. The yearly funding cycle increases the possibility that funding decisions influence program content. A great deal of time and energy must be spent by station executives in developing, maintaining, and smoothing relationships with key funders. There are five major sources of funds for public television: the federal government, state and local governments including state colleges and universities, private foundations, corporations, and membership contributions and other individual donations.

We briefly describe each funding mechanism, its importance, and the unique contingencies and problems it poses.

(1) The *federal government,* although not the largest funder in absolute terms, is the most important continuous source of support for public television. The federal government supplied 27.2 percent of the income for public broadcasting in fiscal year 1979 (Lee, 1981). The federal government is the only funder that directly affects the entire public television system, through its appropriation to the Corporation for Public Broadcasting. Currently, 50 percent of CPB's budget must be "passed through" directly to the stations, proportionate to their ability to raise matching, nonfederal funds. Known as community service grants (CSGs), these are one of the few "no strings attached" grants to PTV stations.[5]

The degree to which funding is uncertain is well illustrated by the history of federal support for public television. There has long been concern that funding for public broadcasting be insulated from political interference and have a self-sustaining and long-term funding mechanism to allow for the planning necessary to produce quality television. The current administrative and funding arrangement was established by the Public Broadcasting Act of 1967, on the recommendation of the Carnegie Commission on Educational Television. The commission explicitly voiced these concerns and recommended funding via a tax on television sets (as in England) to meet them. Intensive lobbying by television set manufacturers killed this proposal, and no alternative was found; CPB was funded from general revenues on a year-to-year basis. Although these appropriations increased substantially from $5 million for fiscal year 1969 to $172 million for fiscal year 1982, neither long-term security nor insulation from political maneuvering has been achieved.

The most vivid case of political interference occurred in 1972, when President Nixon vetoed a two-year, $155 million authorization for CPB. Although the official reason given for the veto was that local stations needed a greater voice in the public television system (see *Public Papers of the President: Richard Nixon,* 1972: 718), it was widely known that the administration was displeased with the content of many programs, especially public affairs series such as *The Great American Dream Machine*—a political cabaret with a strong antiwar bent—*Washington Week in Review,* and *Black Journal.* The Nixon veto led to a reduction in the level of funding (to $110 million) and demonstrated the political vulnerability of public broadcasting.[6]

In response to the Nixon veto, Congress began appropriating funds for CPB up to three years in advance, beginning in 1975 for fiscal years 1976-1978. This mechanism was intended to provide a more stable and insulated system of federal support and to allow public broadcasting to engage in more effective long-term planning. The principle of advanced funding has not operated consistently. Although funds have generally been appropriated at least two years in advance, recent budget cuts by the Reagan administration have proved to be the most serious shock to the system since the 1972 veto. The original Reagan budget proposals recommended the rescission of appropriations already made for fiscal years 1982 and 1983. Congress rejected budget reductions for 1982 but cut the 1983 CPB appropriation by 20 percent. The hoped-for stability of advance funding has been destroyed.

The budget reductions create obvious financial problems, but the protracted political bargaining intensifies an already high level of uncertainty. For example, in a four-month period in 1981, the fiscal year 1984 budget was reduced from $172 million to $137 million to $130 million to $105.6 million, and the adminstration recommended a further cut to $95.5 million. In a curious and unanticipated manner, we believe the advanced funding mechanism has exacerbated public television's budget problems. For the past several years the federal government has been operating under continuing resolutions rather than actual budgets. This means that no budget figures are actually fixed. They can be changed every time Congress extends the continuing funding resolution. Under such a process, the fact that PTV funds are set in advance only means that there is more opportunity to change them.

Additional federal support for public television comes from the national endowments for the arts and humanities, the National Science Foundation, the National Institutes for Health, and other agencies. These grants are typically for the development and production of specific programs rather than for discretionary funds. Program-specific funds are also available through CPB.

Two important points are worth noting about program-specific funding from federal agencies. First, the process of obtaining funding is labor-intensive and extended, sometimes taking several years. Proposals for funding must often be reviewed by a panel of experts, and a consensus must be arrived at before final approval is received. Second, federal funding of this sort is often used as "seed money" and usually *requires* matching funds from nonfederal sources. Partial funding from the government lends legitimacy and prestige to a proposal that is then submitted to foundations or corporations for additional support.[7] Thus, even small reductions in federal spending have a wide-ranging impact on public television programming. Moreover, budget cuts may lead public television to become more risk-averse in order not to jeopardize future funding.

(2) *State and local governments* together comprise the largest source of financial support for public television (40 percent of the budget for the entire system in fiscal year 1979). At the state level, direct political pressures, or fear of such pressures, most clearly affect stations, particularly small consuming stations. Through both overt and implied means, state governments place strong constraints on public affairs programming. According to a former WNET executive, the restrictions are greatest at state-operated stations.[8] "Most of them simply can't do public affairs shows that look critically at their

own state government because of the funding constraint. There is a terrible baggage that comes with state money." Even at community-owned stations, such as WNET and CPTV, there is considerable stroking of state officials. The previously cited WNET executive noted that despite WNET's diverse sources of support, "We have to ask the majority leader of the State Assembly to come on the air and answer questions. We do this stroking simply because we want the money from Albany," CPTV executives were proud of their legislative coverage, noting that it was a service not provided by commercial Connecticut stations, but acknowledged the value of such coverage in obtaining state funds.

(3) *Private foundations* used to be the single largest source of contributions to public television. Most notably, the Ford Foundation provided $292 million in support (Magat, 1979), including construction grants, from the early 1950s to the mid-1970s. During public television's early years, Ford grants literally kept the system alive. However, Ford Foundation support was phased out, ending in fiscal year 1977, and other foundation grants now constitute less than 5 percent of the system's support.

As a rule, foundation grants are available for the support of specific programs or artists. Foundation support has been crucial to bringing innovative, "risky" programming to public television. A notable project is the TV Laboratory at WNET, established in 1972 with grants from the Rockefeller Foundation and the New York State Council on the Arts. Additional support has come from the Ford Foundation and the National Endowment for the Arts. The TV Lab was created to explore the artistic and technological potential of television through research, experimentation, and the creation of innovative projects for broadcast. The Lab has run an artists-in-residence program and has produced or funded such diverse programs as *Making Television Dance,* an attempt by Twyla Tharp to make television and dance work together; *Lathe of Heaven,* a speculative fiction program; abstract programs exploring video graphics; and numerous powerful documentaries such as *Vietnam: Picking Up the Pieces* and *Health Care: Your Money or Your Life.* The TV Lab is the major contact between public television and independent filmmakers. Recently, the TV Lab coordinated a series by independent producers entitled *Non-Fiction Television.* The series included hard-hitting documentaries on the CIA and U.S. foreign policy and the use of deadly force by the police.

(4) In the early 1970s, as foundation support declined and federal support became politically contentious, public broadcasting turned to major corporations for *corporate underwriting.* It was not a role that corporations actively sought for themselves. Corporate support for public broadcasting has grown from 4 percent in 1973 to more than 10 percent at present. However, a much larger percentage of the total budget of producing stations comes from corporations. For the period 1977-1982, corporate underwriting accounted

for 22 to 25 percent of WNET's total revenues. More important, almost half of the national programming on public television is underwritten in part or in full by corporate support. Corporations generally fund the production and presentation of a continuing series such as *Great Performances* or *Masterpiece Theatre* rather than contributing discretionary or development money. The logic behind these policies is clear: A major series has high visibility.

Corporate underwriting grew dramatically during the 1974 oil crisis, at which time American oil companies came under heavy public criticism. Support of public television provided the oil companies, who remain the primary corporation contributors to public television, with a partial remedy to their legitimacy problems.[9] Future increases in corporate support for public television are problematic. More nonprofits now compete for corporate dollars, and pay and cable television offer alternatives for corporations that wish to use the television medium to develop a corporate image or deliver a message to upscale audiences.

Some researchers suggest that corporate giving is motivated more by hopes of favorably influencing public opinion than by a sense of social responsibility. Ermann (1978) argues that the operative goal for corporate philanthropy is "milieu control," or image management. Burt (1980) found that those corporations most involved in philanthropy are in industries dependent on individual consumption. Philanthropy is also positively related to general advertising expenditures, a more straightforward form of image building.

The underwriting of public television shows can be seen as a form of specialized advertising. Audiences for the types of shows supported by corporations are well educated and have high incomes (Ermann, 1978; Office of Communication Research, 1981). Barnouw (1978: 68) argues persuasively, and our research substantiates, that most corporations interested in image enhancement want their names associated with noncontroversial, high-quality shows that he labels "safely splendid." The director of public affairs programming at WNET said that the biggest difference between public affairs shows and cultural programming involves problems with underwriters. He noted ironically that, "Exxon had the right idea doing *Live from Lincoln Center.* Mobile Oil had the best idea when they funded *Upstairs, Downstairs.* These are benign shows. They are not offensive, they are not going to get anyone angry. Public affairs shows get underwriters angry."

There is a direct relationship between program content and corporation underwriting. Nothing quite comparable exists in commercial television. Although advertisers on network television will on occasion drop a series because of program content, thus influencing the program's chances for renewal, such actions are unusual for commercial television.[10] In public television, the return on investment to underwriters is vaguely defined and subjectively evaluated, only occasionally reinforced by "objective" information such as ratings. Furthermore, corporate underwriting is highly concentrated among a handful of firms. These factors combine to give the companies considerable leverage, if they choose to exercise it, over program content. Given these constraints, station personnel correctly assume that most corporations will fund only a certain type of programming—prestigious cultural fare, well-balanced public affairs shows like *The MacNeil-Lehrer Report,* or those shows that appeal directly to corporate executives as viewers, such as *Wall Street Week* or *Firing Line.* Proposals for other types of shows are seldom submitted to large corporations for consideration.

(5) *Member contributions* are another primary source of funding. This support has increased in recent years, due primarily to more strenuous and sophisticated solicitation by the stations. In 1979, subscribers contributed 11.8 percent of total public broadcasting income (Lee, 1981: 17). Nevertheless, fewer than 5 percent of the regular viewers contribute to station support. The nationwide fund-raising drive in spring 1982 generated 7.4 percent more money than the previous year, but the number of contributions dropped 2.5 percent (*New York Times,* June 20, 1982). Generating subscription dollars requires considerable expenditure of time, money, and volunteer effort. There is ongoing tension between the need for on-air promotional events, such as pledge drives and auctions, and the possibility of so irritating viewers with extended interruptions that they become disaffected. Connecticut Public TV recently conducted a pledge week with a "soft sell" campaign, for which they received much praise but little money. The vice-president for development quoted a friend when he commented on that fund-raising drive: "Compliments mean trouble. It means you're not getting money, you're getting compliments."

It is widely recognized that most sources of funding have strings attached. As PBS President Lawrence Grossman has stated, "Every source of money is tainted. With federal funds we worry about becoming a governmental broadcasting arm. Corporate money makes you steer away from controversy. Membership money means you cater to upper middle class viewers. The saving grace is that we have diversified sources" (*Newsweek,* November 20, 1948, p. 139). The mix of funding sources, and the political tensions within the PVT system combine to influence the parameters of program content, as wel shall illustrate in our analysis of the program distribution system.

PROGRAM DISTRIBUTION: ADMINISTRATIVE CONSTRAINTS

How does a program get shown on public television? Although public television is not operated as a network, there is a core of programs that are aired by most of the stations across the country. These core programs are obtained by stations via two mechanisms, the Station Program Cooperative (SPC) and free distribution by PBS to member stations.

SPC, run by PBS, was established in 1974 to decentralize decision making in public television and give more voice to the many small consuming stations. Each year producers, including public stations and independent producers, put forth several hundred program proposals on a wide variety of topics. The stations go through several rounds of bidding to narrow the number of selections to thirty or forty proposed programs. The final cost of a program to a station is based on the number of other stations purchasing the show and the size of the station's community service grant. Producers modify their proposals during the early rounds to try to accommodate stations' needs and garner support. Stations are not committed to the purchase of a program until the final round of bidding, and only those stations that purchase a program may air it. The entire proposal and selection process takes about six months.

The SPC has been widely criticized (see, among many, Katzman and Wirt, 1976; Reeves and Hoffer, 1976). The SPC is slow, administratively cumbersome, and very conservative—in contrast to its intended free market character. Katzman and Wirt (1976: 255) found that purchased programs "reflected at least one or two and often all three of the following characteristics: (1) prior national or multi-station exposure, (2) a low price and/or an exceptionally good value per unit time, and (3) a bandwagon effect." As Katzman and Wirt point out, the SPC does not necessarily reflect the desires of the stations; conservative choices can be artifacts of the selection process. "If 15 new programs are each supported in the voting by 10 stations, none of the new programs would be purchased even though the 150 stations all wanted something new." The SPC is not the only reason few new programs are shown on public television—established programming is easier to obtain underwriting for and helps retain audiences—but it does exacerbate the situation.

The SPC is dominated by large producing stations that have reputations for not being responsive to the needs of the smaller stations. The SPC buyer at CPTV complained about the purchasing power of the large stations that "because of their size, and the pricing formula, they can out-vote anyone because they have so much money." Large stations include administrative overhead costs in their program budgets that are then passed on to underwriters and other stations through the SPC. This makes the cost of station-produced shows higher than programs produced by independent film-makers, a fact resented by most small stations with limited budgets. Small stations also complain they are not fairly credited for their role in supporting the production of large stations. The station manager at CPTV state that "the system is collectively financed by everyone, but WNET and WGBH get all the credit." However, the SPC buyer for CPTV pointed out that there is a strong incentive to buy programs through the SPC, rather than through individual acquisition, because the transmission process is handled by PBS, and thus there are few technical problems involved in airing SPC material.

The SPC was intended to alleviate the powerlessness of small stations and institute a more democratic choice process for nationwide programming. Although generally recognized as an improvement over the previous, more centralized decision process, the SPC has not lived up to expectations. An essentially conservative mechanism the SPC primarily finances "meat and potatoes prime-time" programming.

Free distribution by PBS is a second source of programming and one that delivers a mixed bag of goods. Fully underwritten programs do not go through the SPC but are made available to all stations free of charge. Individual stations must choose to air such a program, but there is clearly a strong financial incentive to broadcast free material. This arrangement gives the underwriter more control over program content. The popular series *Masterpiece Theatre,* funded by Mobil Oil, is an example of a core prime-time program distributed in this manner. Interestingly, WGBH, the producing station, did not want to acquire the highly successful selection "Upstairs, Downstairs" for *Masterpiece Theatre,* but was pressured into doing so by Mobil (Carnegie Commission, 1979: 108).

Free program offerings can lead to other problems between large and small stations. For example, several major corporations sponsored *Free to Choose,* a series by conservative economist Milton Friedman that extolled the virtues of the free market. The series was produced by the Erie, Pennsylvania, public station. By making the program freely available, the Erie station got national exposure much more readily than by going to the SPC for funding. In such situations there is pressure on large stations to carry the free program. The director of broadcasting at WNET noted that the producing station "may not care whether Cleveland picks it up, or Portland. But they most definitely want it to be seen in New York, and if WNET turns down these shows, especially those that are free, we are seen as unresponsive to the system."

The programs purchased through the SPC or provided free by PBS are generally the "tried and true" of public television. They constitute the core of national broadcasting, are generally of high quality, and receive the great majority of corporate underwriting funds and program-specific government grants. Two other major sources of programming provide more varied and less expensive choices for the stations. The Interregional Program Service (IPS), formerly the Eastern Educational Network, operates as a mini-market for programs somewhat like the SPC, but in several important respects it is different. First, IPS makes available programs that have already been produced, while the SPC offers program proposals and occasional pilots. A program buyer at WNET jokingly described the difference between the SPC and the IPS: "At the IPS you can watch what it is you are going to buy. At the SPC you read a proposal and try to guess if the station can really deliver it. They might promise Liza Minnelli in a song series, but then they'll get someone off the streets and say 'well, actually she's the same size as Liza.' So, at IPS it's an easier choice." Second, programs acquired through IPS are generally cheaper because the primary costs of production have already been paid. Third, the IPS is more flexible than the SPC because it meets frequently, has fewer participants and does not involve a bidding process. IPS programs constitute a small proportion of a station's prime-time schedule, so there is less urgency and political bargaining than at the SPC. Finally, IPS and regional networks provide programs that are more suited to a local market than the programs nationally broadcast by PBS, for which PBS requires clearance for broadcast in all PTV markets. Stations in large metropolitan areas, such as WNET, often purchase programs considered too risqué, because of language or nudity, for a PBS national feed.

Stations also acquire programs directly from such sources as foreign television producers and networks, independent producers, and other public stations that sometimes sell programs on a station-by-station basis. An example of this is the provocative documentary *Police Tapes,* taped on location in the South Bronx. The show won numerous awards, had extensive international distribution, and got exceptional ratings in New York. It was eventually purchased by ABC for network broadcast, but it was not purchased through the SPC, because it was considered too controversial. Rather than making it freely available, WNET sold *Police Tapes* to about twenty public stations directly.

Small stations depend almost exclusively on the SPC and free PBS distribution for their programming, partly because they cannot afford the operating costs of long broadcast days and lack the discretionary funds for independent acquisitions. Because of the conservatism and bandwagon effects of the SPC and the financial incentive to air free programs, consuming stations exercise little discretion over prime-time schedules. In contrast, large stations have considerably more program options. Longer broadcast days provide greater scheduling flexibility and more opportunities for special acquisitions. Also, large stations have historically had more discretionary funds with which to make special acquisitions.

Large stations have greater influence on program content due to their direct involvement in program production. The large stations are responsible for most national programs. In contrast, consuming stations produce a few hours a week of local programming, usually public affairs or news shows. However, these types of programs can be strongly shaped by local political realities. Moreover, locally produced programs are generally difficult to underwrite because of their small viewing audience. During the past several years, many stations have had to cancel or drastically reduce their local programming. Nevertheless, these shows are perceived to be an important component of public television's mandate. The station manager of CPTV noted that local programming is necessary to maintain a good staff and thus a strong station. "Cutting local programming kills the station. It kills us in terms of what our mission should be, what our staff wants to be doing, and retards our building for a stronger future."

The role of the independent producer in public television deserves special comment. Although public television has been a major forum for independent producers, the relationship between producers and stations has been strained. Despite frequent criticism, however, independent producers often prefer public to commercial television because public television is willing to broadcast a documentary in its entirety. Network television, on the other hand, uses only short segments of a documentarian's footage, usually weaving them into the evening news.[11] The CPB has attempted to improve relations with independent producers by offering them direct program grants. Although direct funding of independents may provide more financial support, the lack of direct, sustained contact with stations during the production phase may ultimately mean the independents' work is not suitable for broadcast through PBS. This was the case with a segment of Peter Davis's documentary, *Middletown,* which dealt with teenagers and their frank discussions of sex and drugs. PBS required that cuts be made from the final segment if it was to be aired. The producer refused and withdrew the last show. Disturbed by the ensuing public controversy, PBS attempted to provide balance by offering an "objective" commentary on the series as a final replacement show.

In sum, relations between independent producers and public television remain strained, and access to the public airwaves is restricted. Only about 5 percent of the programs shown on public television are made by independent producers. These tensions illustrate the widely divergent demands made on public television by various constituencies who seek to use the system for their own purposes. Programming decisions are influenced by financial conditions at local stations, the amount of underwriting money available for particular shows, the need to placate various supporters, concerns over station morale, and poor relations between stations and creative artists.

Given the extreme financial dependence of public television as well as perennial questions about legitimacy, there appears to be little opportunity for choice or control over programming. This state of affairs obtains for smaller stations; however, the larger stations can and do exercise some power over programming decisions. The major producing stations, such as WNET and WGBH, produce about 25 percent of the programs shown on public television. An analysis of the internal organization of a large public station such as WNET illustrates how decisions are reached as to what types of programs to produce for national broadcast.

STATION ORGANIZATION:
INTERNAL CULTURES AND CONFLICTS

A large public television station is a loose federation of various autonomy-seeking groups. Most public stations have multiple and often conflicting goals. In fact, the notion of goal-oriented behavior may imply a rational, instrumental direction that is inappropriate for public television. A more accurate view would emphasize the multiple uses pursued by various groups on both the inside and the outside. For artists as well as corporate funders, public television is a vehicle for delivering a message. Thus, it is a resource that interest groups seek to capture and use. The managers of public television stations have their own goals and visions and are, naturally, concerned with the continued existence of their stations. Moreover, recent developments—(1) the proliferation of new channels, such as cable, satellite television, video cassettes, and low-power television stations, which offer viewers more alternatives and open new labor markets for artists and producers; and (2) budgetary reductions and their associated staff layoffs and program cutbacks—add to the difficulties that public television executives face in trying to pursue a coherent set of policies.

The most salient internal conflict that has consequences for program choice and content is a basic one: at WNET and CPTV there have been ongoing disputes between programming staff, responsible for the development and production or acquisition of programs, and the underwriting staff, charged with obtaining program-specific grants from corporations, foundations, and federal agencies.[12] While specific administrative arrangements vary from station to station, this internal conflict is common. Indeed, it is a basic organizing problem in most nonprofit organizations in which the product development or service delivery is separated from fund raising. Programming and underwriting or development are, to a considerable degree, separate tasks driven by different motivations. As a general rule, programming staff are primarily concerned with the quality of program content and feel that the underwriting staff should be supportive of all types of programs. Personnel responsible for raising money are more concerned with the ease with which financial support for a program can be secured and the maintenance of long-term funding relationships, and they want programs to be developed with these aims in mind.

Perhaps the clearest example of the programming/development conflict was at CPTV, where, because of the small size of the station, the problem is a person-to-person battle rather than a general interdepartmental issue. The director of programming was quite explicit about this conflict, describing it as "a power thing." She noted, "I get power from choosing programs, in terms of reaching people. The development department gets more power internally, from deciding which programs get funded." She went on to point out the differences in priorities between programming and development. "We evaluate our activities differently. Development is concerned with how much money and membership are generated by a program. I am concerned with audience. If 17,000 people watch *Monty Python,* that's good. I'm not as concerned with how many of them give money."

The conflict between these two organizational functions occurs in three areas that may affect programming: decisions about program content, program scheduling, and program-funding strategies..

(1) *Program Content.* Most decisions about the content of specific programs, as well as ideas for program development, are the purview of the programming department. At WNET, underwriting personnel are frequently displeased with program decisions and desire greater influence in these matters. The most common complaint of the underwriting officers at WNET is that programming does not consult with them enough during the program development stage. One underwriting officer bluntly stated, "Program development is not a two-way street. If it were, funding would be easier to obtain. We know what kinds of programs the corporations and foundations want." During our field observations, changes were introduced to increase the input of underwriting staff in program decision making. An executive in charge of underwriting described these changes as follows:

> It used to be that programming would decide they wanted to do a show on dance. They would develop it and then we would get, through the interoffice mail, a sheet saying, "We're going to do this dance program," and then we would have to go out and sell it. That has changed. Now, from the very outset of serious discussion about a project, someone from my department is involved with programming in the discussion of the likelihood of funding, the content of the show, the direction of the show, what sort of competition there is for the show, and so on.

This executive stressed the collaborative nature of the relationship between programming and underwriting. His staff, however, painted a less rosy picture. One underwriting officer described her limited input into program development:

> We have ideas for programs, we send them to programming, but we don't get anything back until the show has been decided upon. In some cases I'll have some input into marketing. There was a summer musical series that they wanted to do. I told them that if you want to sell this series you need to add four cities to the sites, and that will make the shows much more appealing to underwriters. So, really, my input is catch-as-catch-can.

Another underwriting officer recalled an instance when a major corporation was interested in supporting a national public affairs show, but he could not go to programming and say, "Look, I have a corporate sponsor; let's produce another show." He was distressed that WNET could not respond to opportunities such as this, but he did not consider whether or not WNET *should* produce another public affairs show, given its current mix of productions and program schedule. Another underwriting staff member stated that "a lot of the program ideas circulated around the station don't fit well with corporate interest."

The underwriting officers were pleased by the new arrangements that increased their role in program decisions. One officer noted:

> Someone from underwriting is there from the start so that major decisions are made in conjunction with us. I would know we couldn't raise $500,000 for a one-hour show so I would tell them to cut the money in half. Or I would explain that a particular program should have a host, because you can take a host on a ten-city tour to raise money. Or I might tell them to get the program developed by October since there's a foundation deadline in mid-October.

A member of the publicity department also expressed a need for marketing input into program decisions: "For example, with the *Dick Cavett Show* I'll tell the producer that the ratings sweeps are coming up and Cavett should schedule the best possible guests. The production units simply aren't aware of the importance of ratings. They're only *starting* to accommodate these requests."

The foregoing comments illustrate the widely held view among non-programming employees that program development should take into account potential audience size and the chances for obtaining underwriting support. Some underwriting officers showed little concern for program content. One stated that she found "no moral imperative in public TV." Other staff were more inclined to balance financial and marketing concerns with respect and pride in high-quality programming. One marketing employee commented that "at a commercial station, program content would never be separated from marketing issues, as they are at WNET." In public television, she said, "programming is more important than sales, whereas in commercial TV programming is a slave to sales." One underwriting officer spoke of the need, in theory, for a balance: "I care about the substance—and, of course, the goal for all of us is good programming—but right now, money's really my main concern."

Programming employees, by contrast, feel that program development and content are their specialty and prerogative. A programming director at WNET, commenting on the high quality of public television programming and on his disdain for concern over ratings, lamented, "People in public broadcasting used to think they were doing God's work. They felt they were doing good, worthwhile shows, and that audience size was not something that was relevant to a decision about program content."

(2) *Program Scheduling.* The interests of programming and underwriting or development departments often conflict during quarterly fund-raising drives. Public television has devoted a great deal of market research to the analysis of what types of programs generate the most membership dollars. Based on this information, the director of development at CPTV feels he "should be able to determine what gets on the air—particularly during fund-raising weeks." Local programming is usually dropped during pledge weeks because it has been shown to attact few new members. This practice runs counter to the programming department's priorities. In explaining a pledge-week schedule, the programming director pointed out that "at 7 p.m. we will *not* drop local programs. They are usually bumped during membership weeks, but I am concerned with keeping my staff happy, and I want those programs on the air."

The major determinant of program scheduling is the mix of programs purchased by a station through the SPC. These programs are scheduled by PBS, but some flexibility is retained at the station level. Most nationally distributed programs are "fed" by the PBS satellite several times during the week. A station may air a show at one of those times or tape it and air it another time. However, it is easier and cheaper to air programs when PBS feeds them. Thus, SPC purchases generally set a good portion of a station's schedule. At CPTV, the director of programming entered a recent SPC purchase round with two lists of programs. The A list was her first priority and the B list was to be purchased with whatever funds remained. In drawing up her lists, she was guided by personal preference and viewer appeal. A show's prospects for obtaining local underwriting did not influence her choices. In fact, she deliberately included some programs that were difficult to underwrite in her A list. She noted that the development department was displeased with her plan but said, "That's the way *I* want to do it, and as long as I get support from high enough places, I'll do it this way."

A final example of scheduling considerations involves the decision to counterprogram against commercial stations. A programming executive at WNET noted that Sunday at 10:30 p.m. is an awkward time slot. "If someone is watching commercial TV at 10:00, the chances of them changing the channel to WNET at 10:30 are slim, since no commercial shows end at that time." He complained that he cannot convince other people at the station of the importance of lead-ins and scheduling issues, even though these concerns are commonplace in commercial television. By contrast, another programming executive believed that WNET has a core, loyal audience that is different from the audience that watches commercial television, and that "trying to schedule against the networks is not a winning game for WNET."

(3) *Program-Funding Strategies.* Programming staff tend to resent pressures to concentrate on "fundable" shows. They feel that only a narrow range of programs appeal to corporate underwriters and do not wish to restrict their work to such shows. Programming personnel believe their charge is to create excellent alternative shows that should be supported on the basis of their quality, not marketability. Of particular concern to programming is the "inordinate" amount of time underwriting officers spend on a small handful of national productions.

A marketing person at WNET expressed a different view when he stated that "underwriters want younger male audiences because they're more influential, which is why *The MacNeil/Lehrer Report* is so popular with corporations. Science shows have high marketability for this same reason." Interest in specific target audiences by corporate underwriters means that many programs receive little or no attention from the underwriting department. A WNET proposal for a children's program, partially funded by a CPB matching grant, is a good illustration of the problem. Although half of the money was secured by programming, underwriting was very slow to pursue the additional funds. After several months of inactivity, a programming officer began pressuring underwriting. However, he was all too aware of the realities of the situation, noting that "kids' shows are hard to fund, since kids don't go running to their parents telling them to buy Exxon."

Local programming also receives little attention from underwriting departments. Virtually all corporate support goes for nationally broadcast programs. Underwriting maintains that local programs are not comparable in quality, have smaller audiences, and thus are difficult to underwrite. Programmming people counter that funding does not even try to finance local shows. This problem is particularly acute at CPTV, and on occasion programming secures financing for local productions on its own, much to the displeasure of the development department. In one instance, a programming employee learned from a friend at an insurance firm that the company had considered underwriting a program and would be interested in a musical variety show with appeal to minority audiences. The company's interest was well suited to a weekly music program produced by the station that featured local ethnic musicians. The development department complained that a major company's support was "wasted" on a "small-potatoes show." Development would prefer to approach a company for a larger sum to help underwrite the costs of purchasing an expensive national show.

There is also conflict over what types of business firms are appropriate underwriters and worth the efforts of the development department. At CPTV, *Monty Python's Flying Circus* was underwritten by Nimbus Waterbeds, an atypical business supporter. Although programming supports such an arrangement and wants more support from small business, development prefers to devote its time to courting large corporations that can provide more money.

Decisions about the allocation of underwriting officers' time also determine the prospects of one-shot programs. These programs, not incorporated within a series, are seldom supported. One underwriting officer at WNET stated, "It's simply not worth my time to go to a corporation to ask for money for a small, one-shot show. I only go to corporate underwriters if I have a particularly attractive package and I can give them good service so they can see how public TV works, and potentially they might become a big underwriter." Underwriting officers at WNET were very concerned that good relations be maintained between the station and corporate supporters. One underwriting officer described her job as "servicing" corporations. She noted:

> The station must have a commitment to their corporate underwriters. We should let them know what the programs are about, and who the guests will be. We should send them reviews and clippings of the shows. Servicing involves stroking them, it involves inviting them to special events, it involves lots of other possibilities for entertaining them. In short, you have to fully execute the contract. I see my job as sales. There is a lot of prejudice here about the mission of public TV and many people here don't want to be bothered with the job of raising money.

The same underwriting officer emphatically stated that corporations do not influence program content, "although clearly you can't find underwriting for programs that are biased in viewpoint or very advant-garde." However, she did not appear to be concerned about the limited range of proposals submitted to corporate underwriters and the effects this has on program variety. The extent of her self-censorship was evident in her approach to corporations:

> Some corporations have a negative opinion about public TV. I don't sell programs to these corporations until I know what message they would like to get across.... If we want corporations to get involved, we have to give them more. A proposal should simply list the priorities for the corporation. What are the things that could be gained from underwriting this show? I am constantly pressing this station with the idea that corporations have to have something visible in return for underwriting a show.

Disagreements between programming and funding staff at the two stations illustrate the pluralistic character of public television. Not only are there many coalitions and subcultures within a station, but these groups have divergent views about public television's purposes. Personnel involved in program underwriting view programs in terms of underwriting appeal. The programming staff at CPTV and WNET place underwriting a distant second to their primary focus on program content.

At WNET the programming staff has a strong commitment to the station's flagship role as a major national production center. WNET, the largest station in the public television, is perceived to have an obligation to set systemwide policy by example. This requires a commitment to quality and innovation. The director of programming pointed out that the station is also accountable to its local viewers whom he believes are the "smartest and most stringent in their demands of any public broadcasting audience in the country." He went on to comment that the station's location in New York gives it a dual role: "We have to meet the needs of New York City, a small, self-contained world unto itself, and we must, *because* it is New York, meet the expectations of other stations, the federal government, and the national viewing audience for public TV." Program producers also believe WNET must take risks in order to lead the way for the entire system. A clear example of this role is the station's airing of controversial documentaries. Even if most public stations refuse to air a controversial program, WNET will usually run it. In 1982, *Blood and Sand* was shown in New York, although few other stations aired it. Several years ago the controversial *Death of a Princess* threatened diplomatic relations with Saudi Arabia. According to a WNET executive, "it was absolutely never, never an issue as to whether or not we would show it." Such commitment is necessary in order for WNET to maintain a strong programming staff; nevertheless, these same programming strengths create difficulties in obtaining outside funding.

THE INFLUENCE OF FUNDING SOURCES OF PROGRAMMING

The lack of adequate funding for public television creates a situation of dependency for public TV stations.[13] Those sources that provide the limited available funds naturally have their own reasons for contributing to public television. Each funding source has its own biases about what it wants to support and what it expects to receive in return. No one would suggest that one single source of funding is preferable to the present complicated mix of support. One WNET executive said that multiple funding sources and multiple responsibilities certainly create headaches, but "it is easier to attempt to partially satisfy a number of different people, than to try to totally please one person." Another executive noted, "Sure, we try to be all things to all people—that guarantees that sometimes we win and sometimes we lose. I prefer that to an either/or situation."

The diversity of funding sources permits some leeway to be exercised by the large producing stations. The mix of sources is, however, costly in terms of the amount of effort that must be spent raising funds and placating different funding sources. Funding sources routinely make requests of public television; many are reasonable from the funder's point of view. We discuss how these demands influence program development and content below, but it is important to note that funding sources rarely demand specific changes in program content. It is very difficult to point to situations where a program was altered because of a direct request by a funder. As March (1981) argues, the presumption of intentionality is difficult because it is seldom the case that a consistent set of preferences guides the actions of individuals. Few social actors have preferences that are clearly formed or consistently held. Rather than dictate policy, funding sources set boundaries within which program development has to work if the relationship between funder and the station is to last more than a year.

We use the series *Dance in America* to illustrate the complicated web of relationships necessary to produce a public television program. *Dance in America* (DIA) was part of a larger series, *Great Performances* (GP), a major effort to produce public television programs of comparable quality to programs produced in Britian. British programs had long been the staple of American public television. Not only were British shows of high quality; they were inexpensive to acquire. GP and its DIA segment received wide critical acclaim. The DIA programs were successful in part because WNET producers won the support of an initially dubious dance community. Dance companies found that following their appearances on DIA, ticket sales increased. The DIA programs were funded by a variety of sources: Exxon, the National Endowment for the Arts, the Corporation for Public Broadcasting, the sale of DIA to other public stations through the SPC, and funds generated by WNET. We conducted interviews at WNET during the planning period for the 1981-1982 DIA season, its sixth year of production.

DIA was a reasonably successful government, business, dance community, and public television partnership. Each of the funding sources provided generous support. Exxon had given approximately a half million dollars a year since DIA's inception. This is only a small portion of the corporation's overall support of about $3 million a year for public television. The National Endowment for the Arts contributed a comparable amount; in fact, the Exxon money was a required match to the government funding. CPB provided approximately $250,000 for DIA, and the sale of the series through the SPC brought more than $1 million. However, while funding was stable, production costs rose by more than 100 percent over the five-year period. (This inflation was not restricted to DIA—other public, as well as commercial, productions faced similar cost increases.) The problem, however, was not simply the difficult task of trying to produce high-quality shows on an inadequate budget. The issue was much more thorny: How could WNET cope with the multiple demands of artists, funders, and other public television stations when resources were shrinking?

With the success of DIA came lofty expectations. NEA felt the time was ripe to show all kinds of dance—experimental, ethnic, jazz, tap, and so on—on public television. It wanted to include documentaries in the series to help educate the viewing public about new dance forms. In short, NEA was a champion of stylistic pluralism. Exxon asked how DIA would continue to live up to its standard of excellence. Exxon's deal was to have Balanchine and

Baryshnikov. CPB was concerned that more regional dance companies be involved in DIA and urged that WNET consider coproductions with other public stations around the country. This would add regional diversity and open the door to obtaining money from state arts agencies and local foundations. The New York dance community wanted to present postmodern avant-garde dance works. Other public television stations wanted popular dance segments to increase the size of the viewing audience. In essence, WNET was an access point for a host of groups who wanted to use DIA to achieve their own ends. In the past, conflicting demands had been met by producing a wide range of shows, matching the range of interests of DIA's diverse constituencies. These were WNET's "bargaining chips," to use the words of one DIA producer. With declining resources, it was simply not possible to meet the divergent demands of the various participants. The number of original productions in the series had to be reduced, and inexpensive acquisitions (programs already produced) were used as replacements. However, this made it more difficult to meet the creative interests of funders. It was also much more difficult to present an exciting lineup of shows each season. As a result, audience ratings remained fixed or declined, and other public stations complained about the high cost of a series that was becoming increasingly narrow and less interesting each year.

As the participants became less satisfied with the end product, they attempted to exert more influence over the programming process. For example, Exxon, which had no interest in low-cost regional productions, held off on its support until it could see the complete roster of productions. CPB stated it could no longer contribute to the series unless more diversity were added. CPB also wanted dance productions specifically designed for a television format. The various participants began proposing ideas for DIA, thus weakening WNET's role as producer and placing the station in a reactive position. The proposals were seldom compatible with one another. One producer said, "Exxon proposed three programs that were their cup of tea—but none was NEA's bag." Producers at WNET complained they could not come up with a season of productions without knowing how much money they had to work with; however, funders would not allocate their money unless they knew what the lineup of productions was. The funding situation reached a crisis when it became difficult to satisfy the desires of the various funders with a less expensive series of dance programs.

To complicate matters further, one of the principal directors for DIA left WNET to join CBS Cable in a similar capacity. He left because he was tired of "coping with contingencies in public TV." He noted he "just wanted to work and not have to worry about finances." (It is ironic that CBS Cable has now been discontinued; the service ran up $30 million in losses in its first year of operation.)

Dance in America illustrates the peculiar nature of public television. We have not mentioned the added complexities of how decisions regarding DIA also affect the planning and budgeting for other programs, influence the quality of relations between WNET and funding sources, and determine how much money will be spent by other stations in the annual Station Program Cooperative. Other stations count on WNET's success in order for them to have programs to broadcast. The financial complexity and the personnel turn-over that are endemic in public television result in, to quote the director of the TV Lab, "the sad fact that nothing that is successful on public TV endures." For the 1981-1982 season, the *Dance in America* segment of *Great Perform-ances* was cut back considerably. Only three programs, each featuring the work of Balanchine, were broadcast. This reduced scale was agreed to by NEA and Exxon.

At the outset of the series *Dance in America,* the participants shared a common goal—program success—and the funders adopted the strategy of let-ting WNET and the dance community make program decisions. With success came increased expectations, but this coincided with declining resources. Public television is a system in which it is difficult to measure success in any other manner than whether or not participants report satisfaction with the result. (It is worth noting, however, that DIA was very successful in bringing dance into the cultural mainstream. Several years ago, CBS broadcast *Baryshnikov on Broadway* during prime-time, and it was rated one of the top ten shows of the week. This success was, in part, attributable to the "research and development" work done by WNET with DIA.) The increased demands for influence on the content of DIA can be viewed as a loss of control by WNET. The station was no longer able to balance resources and thus have some autonomy. To continue with DIA, WNET needed NEA money, but the NEA grant is subject to a fifty-fifty matching funds provision. Thus, without the Exxon money, the coffers were empty. In addition, CPB was willing to support independent producers rather than WNET because independents have lower overhead costs. At the same time, the dance community and WNET's pool of talented producers and directors, as well as corporate under-writers, began to see cable television as an alternative forum. WNET lost its position as the exclusive domain for quality dance programming. Both artists and funders had more choices; as a result, they exerted more influence on WNET. The reduced output of WNET in the area of dance is a reaction to its limited control over needed resources.

SUMMARY

Given the financial constraints under which public television operates, it is sometimes surprising that any controversial or innovative programming is produced. However, in addition to the need to sustain smooth, ongoing ties with various funding sources, a station, particularly a producing one, must maintain contact with many artistic communities. If program development is not ongoing, it is unlikely that stations can retain the creative producers and directors currently on their staffs. For a station to remain viable, management must allow program producers and artists some latitude to develop program ideas free of undue financial constraint. In this respect, public television has produced a lengthy list of high-quality programs in a working environment that is heavily politicized and short on resources.

The current financial crisis also threatens public television in other ways. Good ideas may go unexploited for lack of resources. The scramble for funds and the time spent on negotiations leave little lead time for thoughtful planning. Both the opportunity posed by the new technologies and the decline in program development required by budget cutbacks may cause productive staff members to leave public television for better working conditions elsewhere. The staff that remains will have to do more with less, and they may be less capable of making do with fewer resources. More talented and marketable employees will have greater opportunity for exit.

Compared to commercial television, public television has offered more opportunity for voice on the part of both funding sources, such as major corporations and governmental agencies, and creative artists, such as the dance community and independent producers. In contrast to commercial television executives, public television managers lack the resources, and the power associated with them, to map strategies and execute them. A public television station is more an assortment of mini-organizations, each with different purposes, composed of a staff with their own priorities who have varying amounts of allegiance to public television. Caught between shrinking budgets and new communications possibilities, public television must survive on less federal support. Stations will turn to their members, corporate underwriters, and their own initiatives to make up for lost federal dollars. The case of *Dance in America* suggests that with declining resources, public television will become even less autonomous and more subject to outside control.

NOTES

1. Kellner (1981) provides the best recent summary of the impact of network television on American society. He states that the networks "determine the structure and content of news and information, as well as the dominant forms, values, and ideologies in television entertainment." Kellner contends that American network television is "one of the most far-reaching communication apparatuses and information and entertainment transmitters that has ever existed."

2. The interviews and fieldwork at the two stations were conducted by Powell. He was assisted at Connecticut Public TV by Marguerite Schaffer. At WNET-TV, Claire Sokoloff helped with the interviewing and fieldwork. Rebecca Friedkin collaborated on the analysis of the data and kept track of numerous reports and statistics on public television finances.

3. This lack of agreement is even reflected in the language used—prior to 1967, noncommercial television was referred to as educational television; since then the common name has been public broadcasting.

4. The recent controversies over public television documentaries—*Middletown, Matters of Life and Death, Blood and Sand—War in the Sahara,* and *From the Ashes . . . Nicaragua Today*—point to the way in which financial uncertainty has increased tensions within the public television community. There is friction between CPB and PBS and concern that PBS has become too eager to rein itself in. There are fears among program producers that PBS is soft-pedaling controversial material and hoping to survive on safe cultural and scientific shows aired in high-visibility time slots. Moreover, critics charge PBS is using its control over program scheduling to force changes in the content of completed programs. PBS maintains that growing financial constraints require PBS to concentrate its focus and "plan, develop, coordinate, and deliver the best possible Prime Time national program service" with the capacity to attract nationwide audiences (Public Broadcasting Service, 1982, p. 3). Many of the smaller PTV member stations heartily support PBS's effort to centralize control. The smaller stations prefer that the hard choices about their future be made by PBS. In sum, their preference is for a network. However, both independent producers and large stations are opposed to the moves by PBS to increase its control over decision making. The large stations see their influence slipping and fear loss of support and money for the programs they produce. Independent producers, as well as production centers at producing stations, worry that a new era of timidity has set in as a consequence of budgetary cuts.

5. Half of CPB's budget is passed through to stations; an additional 15 percent goes toward specific program grants. The remainder is used to operate CPB, to fund PBS and the Station Program Cooperative, and to fund public radio.

6. For a detailed discussion of the Nixon veto, see Avery and Pepper (1976) and Carnegie Commission (1979).

7. For example, an underwriting officer at WNET spoke of the need to obtain some National Science Foundation support for a proposed series, *The Brain.* "Can you imagine how hard it would be to peddle this show to major firms without the imprimatur of NSF? It's not that the federal money is that large, but NSF funding serves as leadership dollars and better enables us to obtain additional funds. Without NSF support, other funders will be suspicious."

8. There are four types of governance mechanisms among public television stations: state or municipal control, college- or university-operated, community-owned stations, and control by public school systems. The difference is a matter of licensing, that is, to whom the Federal Communications Commission grants a charter to operate a television station, as well as governance. Depending on the nature of the legal charter, the composition of a station's board of directors will vary. Both WNET and CPTV are "community-owned" stations.

9. Although on-air advertising by corporate underwriters is restricted by FCC regulation, there are no prohibitions against off-screen advertising. Corporations back up their programming contributions with large promotional budgets. For example, Mobil gave $3.5 million for programs in 1978 and allocated another $2 million for advertising. Gulf alloted $1.4 million for its sponsorship of *National Geographic Specials* in 1978 and spent $1.8 million.

10. *The Lou Grant Show* shown on CBS is a recent example. See Wall Street Journal (1982) and Dow and Talbot (1982).

11. Bill Moyers, who has his own public affairs shows on both commercial and public television, captures the comparative costs and benefits of the two in the following statement made in the *New York Times,* April 11, 1978: "The commitment to quality is high in both places. On CBS there are first class journalists, but they don't get the time on the air. On public broadcasting, they have the time on the air, but they don't have the resources. The one has the money, but not the time, the other has the time, but not the money."

12. At WNET a recent reorganization, from a functional structure to a multi-divisional structure with three programming divisions—national, local, and educational—and a for-profit enterprises division, was implemented to help reduce conflict and enhance cooperation among programming and fund-raising staff. Each division has its own programming, underwriting, and publicity departments. Furthermore, the separate for-profit division is both an effort to generate profits and an attempt to keep the other divisions "pure." On paper, the reorganized structure should reduce the tension between programming and fund-raising. In practice, conflict has not been eliminated; but disputes are no longer exacerbated by the fact that personnel are located in different departments and report to different bosses. Most of our interviews took place prior to the reorganization or shortly after its initial implementation.

13. Lee (1981, pp. 23-24) notes that in 1978, American public broadcasting revenues (radio and television combined) totaled $552 million, whereas commercial broadcast revenues were over $9.5 billion. The per-person cost differences are also quite large: $10.64 for commercial radio and $.37 for public radio; $24.09 for commercial television and $2.15 for public television. However, public television production costs are much more comparable. Estimates vary, but most producers suggest that public television costs per hours were approximately 40-50 percent that of the costs per hour of commercial television production.

REFERENCES

AVERY, R. K. and R. PEPPER (1976) "Interconnection disconnection: the evolution of the CPB-PBS relationship." Public Telecommunications Review 4, 5: 6-17.

BARNOUW, E. (1978) The Sponsor: Notes on a Modern Potentate. New York: Oxford University Press.

BURT, R. S. (1980) "A note on corporate philanthropy." Survey Research Center Working Paper 36. Berkeley: University of California.

Carnegie Commission on the Future of Public Broadcasting (1979) A Public Trust: The Report of the Carnegie Commission on the Future of Public Broadcasting. New York: Bantam.

DOW, M. and D. TALBOT (1982) "Asner: too hot for medium cool." Mother Jones (August): 6-13.

ERMANN, D. S. (1978) "The operative goals of corporate philanthropy: contributions to PBS, 1972-1976." Social Problems 25: 504-514.

KATZMAN, N. with K. WIRT (1976) "Program funding in public television and the SPC," pp. 251-274 in D. Cater (ed.) The Future of Public Broadcasting. New York: Praeger.

KELLNER, D. (1981) "Network television and American society." Theory and Society 10: 31-62. (Reprinted in D. C. Whitney and E. Wartella, eds., Mass Communication Review Yearbook, Vol. 3. Beverly Hills, CA: Sage, 1982.)

LEE, S. Y. (1981) Status Report of Public Broadcasting 1980. Washington, DC: Corporation for Public Broadcasting, Planning & Analysis.

MAGAT, R. (1979) The Ford Foundation at Work: Philanthropic Choices, Methods, and Styles. New York: Plenum.

MARCH, J. G. (1981) "Bounded rationality, ambiguity, and the engineering of choice." Bell Journal of Economics 9: 587-608.

Office of Communication Research (1981) Review of 1980 CPB Communication Research. Washington, DC: Author.

PFEFFER, J. and G. SALANCIK (1978) The External Control of Organizations. New York: Harper & Row.

Public Broadcasting Service (1982) Key Program Elements of Four-Year Plan. March 24-25.

REEVES, M. G. and T. W. HOFFER (1976) "The safe, cheap and known: a content analysis of the first (1974) PBS program cooperative." Journal of Broadcasting 20, 4: 549-565.

Wall Street Journal [western edition] (1982) "Kimberly-Clark pulls ads from Ed Asner TV show." May 6: 46.

This chapter examines links between the U.S. power elite and the U.S. press by looking at institutional affiliations including corporate directorships, business and trade associations and policy groups, nonprofit civic groups and social clubs, of the directors of the nation's 24 largest newspaper-owning companies. The data reveal a web of affiliations that link all these corporations to the nation's power structure, but they also reveal that some newspaper-owning corporations are more linked than others. Those firms most closely linked to the power elite are those with the greatest journalistic and political influence. These, in turn, display and are distinguished from most other newspapers by a "corporate liberal" ideology that reflects the viewpoint of the "inner group" of the capitalist class, Dreier argues. Peter Dreier is on the sociology faculty at Tufts University.

26

THE POSITION OF THE PRESS
IN THE U.S. POWER STRUCTURE*

Peter Dreier

A great deal has been written about the "power of the press," but little is known about the position of the press within the power structure of the United States. This paper examines the relationship between the U.S. business elite and 'the mass media elite. The mass media play two critical roles in society. First, they are profit-seeking firms; their owners, directors, suppliers, and advertisers are interested in the economic health of these firms. Second, they are ideological institutions. The media set the agenda of political, social, and economic debate. They shape public opinion on crucial issues; socialize individuals to social roles and behavior; and can legitimate or undermine powerful institutions, individuals, and ideas. Who controls these organizations is an important area for research.

Observers of and spokespersons for the mass media both view it as unique among U.S. industries. They view the media as a "fourth estate," standing apart from other institutions and segments of society, putting its public role and its social responsibility above the unfettered pursuit of profits. Publishers, editors, and journalists alike claim that their organizations are not beholden to any special interests except the pursuit of truth. The prime function of the press, according to the canons of the American Society of Newspaper Editors, is "to satisfy the public's need to know" (Udell, 1978:24). Because of their unique function in society, the mass media are, alone among U.S. industries, protected by the Constitution through First Amendment guarantees of "freedom of the press" (Bagdikian, 1971).

The media's special status is codified in an ideology extolling objectivity and impartiality. According to this ideology, the media should not reflect the views of any particular segment of society, but should try to provide a balance of all perspectives and points of view (Schudson, 1978; Tuchman, 1978). These norms are institutionalized in the daily practice of journalism. To guarantee that journalists' judgments are not colored by their own affiliations, newspapers encourage, and often require, that journalists avoid potentially conflicting commitments. The code of ethics of Sigma Delta Chi, the Society of Professional Journalists (whose officers are usually high-level editors of influential newspapers) states: "Journalists and their employers should conduct their personal lives in a manner which protects them from conflicts of interest, real or apparent. Their responsibilities to the public are paramount." Most journalists espouse these professional norms (Johnstone *et al.*, 1976).

* The Fund for Investigative Journalism provided financial assistance for this research. The author thanks Shelly Sandberg, Tom Stern, and Steve Weinberg for help in collecting the data, *Social Problems'* editor and reviewers for improving the manuscript, and Maureen DeVito for typing. Correspondence to: Department of Sociology, Tufts University, Medford, MA. 01255.

From Peter Dreier, "The Position of the Press in the U.S. Power Structure," *Social Problems,* Vol. 29, No. 3 (February 1982), pp. 298-310. Reprinted by permission of the Society for the Study of Social Problems.

While the Sigma Delta Chi statement includes employers (media executives) as well as journalists in its proscription against conflicts of interest, interviews with and letters from newspaper board directors, as well as their statements in various articles, reveal contradictory norms and practices among newspaper firms regarding executives' institutional affiliations (Dreier and Weinberg, 1979; Ingrassia, 1979; Morgenthaler, 1970; Rockmore, 1977). Some believe that all such affiliations compromise the credibility of the press and thus should be prohibited or discouraged. For example, the chairman of one of the nation's largest newspaper firms (who requested anonymity) said: "I have turned down directorships of major banks, saving-fund societies, life insurance companies, fire insurance companies, graduate business schools, hospitals, art museums, orchestra, and Port Authority, to avoid conflict of interest and the mere appearance of conflict of interest, direct or indirect (as in news coverage of strikes against such institutions)" (personal letter to author). Ben Bradlee, editor of the *Washington Post*, believes that newspaper company editors and executives should not join "any civic groups, clubs, or institutions" (personal interview). Otis Chandler, publisher of the *Los Angeles Times*, has resigned from all his corporate directorships, citing the desire to avoid conflict of interest, although fellow board members at the parent Times–Mirror Company have not followed suit. Some firms prohibit affiliations only with profit-seeking corporations. Even among those who prohibit or discourage outside involvements, some apply such standards only to "inside" directors (employees of the firm) and not "outside" directors. Others view such involvements as part of a newspaper's role as an active "citizen" of the community, even suggesting that such involvements improve news coverage by allowing executives to feel the community's pulse. Still others suggest that affiliations related to the media's business operations, such as corporate directorships or business policy groups, are entirely separate from its journalistic activities and thus do not reflect potential conflicts of interest. Allen Neuharth, chairman of Gannett (the largest chain in terms of number of newspapers), explained that "I accepted the Marine Midland (bank) directorship because it has branches in all our communities in New York State . . . It's a good way for our company, through me, to be in touch with the business communities in the cities where we publish. You learn a lot of things about business developments that you might not otherwise know about" (personal interview).

During the past decade, sociologists have developed a growing interest in the upper echelons of business and political power, but they have not focused on the press as a special segment. At the same time, interest in the mass media and its inner workings has also grown. Research, however, has centered on the day-to-day activities of the newsroom itself and the processes of identifying, gathering, writing and editing the news. This has provided a wealth of insight into the social construction of news and the pressures on news media personnel (Dreier, 1978; Epstein, 1973; Fishman, 1980; Gans, 1979; Tuchman, 1972, 1978). But this research has not penetrated the upper echelons of the newspaper hierarchy, the top decision-makers or the boards of directors of newspaper-owning corporations. Much of what we know about these individuals comes from official and unofficial biographies of publishers, histories of particular newspapers and journalistic accounts of the "lords of the press" (Gottlieb and Wolt, 1977; Halberstam, 1979; Lundberg, 1936; Roberts, 1977; Talese, 1969). While these studies suggest that publishers and board members can have an influence on the general tone of a paper as well as upon specific stories, there has been little systematic research on the characteristics of these individuals and how (or if) they are connected to other sectors of the U.S. power structure.

In the most recent and comprehensive survey of media management, Bogart (1974:170) notes that "the people who run such major media organizations are super-elites, notoriously difficult for social scientists to study first-hand." In this paper, I systematically examine the media elites' position in the web of institution affiliations that comprise the U.S. power structure. First, I examine the *extent* of the press' affiliations with other institutions. Despite their occupational code and ideology, the press is deeply involved in the power structure network. Second, I describe the *distribution* of affiliations, particularly between inside and outside directors, a distinction mentioned by several executives as the critical difference in terms of outside involvements. Third, I look at the different *patterns* of affiliation between newspaper firms. Some companies are more closely linked to the power structure than others. There is a small subset of influential papers whose affiliations are significantly greater than the others. This distinctive pattern corresponds to the ideological outlook of the pinnacle of the corporate elite, an outlook termed "corporate liberalism."

THE U.S. POWER STRUCTURE

Following Domhoff (1970, 1979), Dye (1976), Useem (1978, 1979) and others, I defined the U.S. power structure as the top positions in the institutional structure of the society, especially the elite institutions in four major sectors — corporations, business policy groups, non-profit civic organizations, and social clubs. Research has found that, despite divisions among the members of the power structure, overlapping memberships in these elite institutions form a network, or web, of inter-relationships that allows a high degree of cohesiveness within the capitalist class. At the pinnacle of this network is what Useem (1978, 1979), Zeitlin *et al.* (1974), and others call the "inner group" within the capitalist class. This inner group includes those individuals connected to several major corporations who seek to protect the general welfare of large corporations as a class rather than the narrower interests of particular corporations, industries or regions. This inner group is the general voice of big business. Members of the inner group are disproportionately represented in institutions that promote class cohesiveness and integration, such as civic organizations, business policy groups, clubs, and high-level government posts (Useem, 1979, 1980). This paper examines the press' position within the U.S. power structure and its links with this inner group.

METHODS

I defined the newspaper elite as the directors of the 25 largest newspaper companies in the United States (in terms of daily circulation) during 1978 and 1979 (Morton, 1980). The top 25 companies accounted for over one-half (53.5 percent) of the total daily circulation in 1979. In that year there were 1,764 papers in the United States with a combined circulation of 62.2 million (Compaine, 1979:13). The top 25 companies owned 425 daily papers with a total circulation of 33.3 million. These included most of the major metropolitan papers (including 20 of the 25 largest dailies) and many small- and medium-sized papers as well. The top 25 newspaper companies dominate the industry. This reflects the long-term trend, accelerated in the postwar period, toward concentration, conglomeration, and centralization within the newspaper industry (Bagkidian, 1978; *Business Week*, 1977; Compaine, 1979). While many of these companies are diversifying, they are still primarily engaged in newspaper publishing (Compaine, 1979:32). Of the top 25 companies, all except Newhouse (the third-largest chain) provided me with a list of its board of directors for 1978 and 1979. I checked the lists of directors against information from annual reports (for those that publish them) and public references such as Standard and Poor's *Register of Corporations*. Because the list of Newhouse's board could not be obtained directly or indirectly (*Business Week*, 1976a, noted the company's exceptional secrecy), this research focuses on 24 of the top 25 chains.

This method netted a total of 290 individuals. Their names and affiliations (revised and updated here) appear in Dreier and Weinberg (1979). I examined affiliations with elite institutions, as defined by Bonacich and Domhoff (1977), Domhoff (1970), Dye (1976), and Useem (1978,

1979).[1] I obtained information on the affiliations of these 290 individuals from the following sources: Standard biographical data on 60 percent of the directors was obtained from *Who's Who in America*, the regional edition of *Who's Who, Who's Who in Business and Finance*, and several other similar reference books in ethnic and minority group members, educators, government officials, and lawyers. The reference books were consulted for 1975 to 1979. While the individuals listed in these public reference books provided their own, often incomplete, biographical information, what information that is there is generally considered reliable. G. William Domhoff provided recent membership lists of the major business policy groups and of eight nationally prominent social clubs. Many of the directors listed membership in these (and other) business policy groups and social clubs in their *Who's Who* biographies, but some affiliations missing from official biographies were added using the complete membership lists. I checked each individual in the *Business Periodical Index*, which indexes all major business periodicals from 1975 to 1979; articles about or mentioning them were consulted. Finally, I sent each newspaper company a questionnaire requesting biographical information (including institutional affiliations) on their board members. The questionnaire included all information already obtained on each individual and asked that errors be corrected. Mailed questionnaires were followed up by phone calls to public relations directors (or their closest counterparts) in each company. This elicited additional information from some chains and individuals. The data may overlook non-elite affiliations (which are least likely to be caught in this research net), but this is not a significant problem for this research. In addition, I interviewed more than 20 newspaper company directors and many journalists.

TOTAL ELITE AFFILIATIONS

Dreier and Weinberg (1979) found that newspaper firms are actively involved in their local communities. This confirms Molotch's (1976:315) view of the newspaper as one of the key actors

---

1. In terms of *corporations*, the elite institutions are defined as the 1,000 largest industrial corporations and 50 of each of the largest banks, insurance companies, financial companies, utilities, retail companies, and transportation companies in 1979, as listed by *Fortune* magazine. In a society in which economic power is highly concentrated, these 1,300 corporations control the overwhelming share of the nation's economic assets, and thus its economic power. In terms of *business policy groups*, the elite institutions are defined as the 15 major groups that prior research indicates play a critical role in establishing a common position among the major corporations on major issues. These 15 organizations were established to provide a forum for the discussion, articulation and promotion of policies that affect most major companies, regardless of industrial sector or geographic region. They draw their members from the top ranks of a broad range of corporations and include, in some cases, academics, attorneys and other professionals involved with and sympathetic to the business community (Eakins, 1969; Domhoff, 1970, 1979; Hirsch, 1975; Shoup and Minter, 1977). In terms of *non-profit civic organizations*, elite institutions are defined as the 12 private colleges and universities with the largest endowments. There are two reasons for isolating colleges and universities to represent this sector. First, among this sector, college and university board members are the largest sub-category (compared with cultural organizations, research and scientific institutions, philanthropic foundations, health-related organizations, charitable groups) and thus make it easier to see variations by newspaper companies. Second, identifying the "elite" institutions in the other sub-categories of the civic sector is more problematic. For example, it is difficult to determine which cultural institutions in the world of art, music, theater and related activities are the most powerful and prestigious. These 12 colleges and universities control over half (54 percent) of the resources available to private higher education and these institutions (although some of the more prestigious public universities such as Michigan and California and small private colleges such as Amherst and Reed are not included). The trustees of these 12 institutions "exercise a significant influence over higher education and thus over the quality of life in America" (Dye, 1976:133). A disproportionate number of the nation's top leaders attended one of these institutions, which attract a disproportionate number of the inner group members to their boards (Useem, 1979). In terms of *social clubs*, elite institutions are defined in terms of the 47 exclusive clubs identified by Domhoff (1970) and Bonacich and Domhoff (1977) as those that draw their membership from a nation-wide pool of elites, linking together individuals from across the country, disproportionately from the inner group. The author will supply lists of the specific institutions upon request.

TABLE 1

Elite Affiliations by Newspaper Company

	No. of Inside Directors (No. of Affiliations)	No. of Outside Directors (No. of Affiliations)	*Fortune* Interlocks	Business Policy Groups	Elite University Trustee-ships	Elite Clubs	Total Affilia-tions
Dow Jones	11 (3)	9 (54)	24	19	2	12	57
N.Y. Times	6 (12)	5 (35)	23	14	3	7	47
Washington Post	8 (17)	4 (24)	12	17	3	9	41
Times Mirror	9 (18)	6 (22)	24	7	0	9	40
Field Enterprises	4 (16)	8 (20)	15	4	5	12	36
Gannett	14 (5)	7 (25)	17	4	1	8	30
Knight-Ridder	14 (14)	4 (15)	12	2	2	13	29
Minn. Star and Tribune	9 (23)	3 (3)	6	7	1	12	26
Media General	4 (3)	5 (19)	9	7	1	5	22
Hearst	19 (20)	0 (0)	3	2	0	15	20
Tribune	9 (2)	2 (17)	12	1	3	3	19
Thomson	6 (1)	4 (15)	9	4	1	2	16
Harte Hanks	7 (1)	3 (14)	13	2	0	0	15
Capital Cities	10 (10)	2 (3)	8	2	0	3	13
Affiliated	7 (5)	3 (3)	0	1	1	6	8
Scripps	10 (8)	0 (0)	1	1	0	6	8
Cox	8 (5)	0 (0)	2	1	0	2	5
Copley	11 (4)	0 (0)	1	2	0	1	4
Lee	8 (0)	3 (4)	3	0	0	1	4
Independent	11 (3)	0 (0)	1	0	0	2	3
Central	6 (2)	1 (1)	1	0	1	1	3
Evening News	9 (1)	0 (0)	0	0	0	1	1
News America	7 (0)	1 (0)	0	0	0	0	0
Freedom	12 (0)	0 (0)	0	0	0	0	0
Total	220 (173)	70 (274)	196	97	24	130	447

in local affairs, its interests "anchored in the aggregate growth of the locality." Social science and journalistic case studies have also revealed the involvement of local papers and their executives in community affairs (Banfield, 1961; Burd, 1977; Devereux, 1976; Hayes, 1972). But as the newspaper industry has shifted from local to chain ownership, and as parent corporations have become large diversified enterprises, those who control these corporations wield power and influence across local and regional boundaries. One would expect these media elites to become more integrated into the web of affiliations that form the national power structure, if they follow the pattern of other industries.

In fact, the data indicate that the nation's major newspaper firms *are* heavily linked with the nation's power structure. As Table 1 shows, the 24 newspaper companies have 447 ties with elite organizations, including 196 with *Fortune's* 1,300 largest corporations, 97 with the 15 major business policy groups, 24 with the 12 major private universities, and 130 with the 47 elite social clubs. Banks and other financial institutions account for the largest number of corporate interlocks compared with other industries, a pattern found in other interlock studies (Palmer, 1981:7). This is not surprising, given the newspaper industry's rapid growth and expansion in the postwar period and these firms' need for capital (Halberstam, 1979:811).

The power elite influences government policy not only through lobbying, campaign contributions, and policy groups and think tanks, but also by placing representatives (drawn disproportionately from the inner group) in high-level appointed positions in government (Domhoff, 1970, 1979, Dye, 1976; Mintz, 1975; Salzman and Domhoff, 1980; Shoup and Minter, 1977). Table 2 shows that the newspaper industry shares in this pattern of "revolving door" links between the

TABLE 2

Individual Affiliations with High-Level Positions in
the Federal Government (Past and Present)*

Newspaper Company**	Number of Individuals Appointed		
	Inside Directors	Outside Directors	Total
N.Y. Times	2	4	6
Field Enterprises	1	3	4
Minneapolis Star & Tribune	3	1	4
Times–Mirror	2	2	4
Washington Post	0	3	3
Dow Jones	0	3	3
Media General	1	2	3
Gannett	0	2	2
Cox	2	0	2
Knight Ridder	0	1	1
Capital Cities	1	0	1
Tribune	0	1	1
Thomson	0	1	1
Evening News	1	0	1
Total	13	23	36

Notes:
* High-level federal government positions include: first- or second-level cabinet secretary, ambassador, presidential advisory commission, advisory committee to federal agency, and regional Federal Reserve Bank board.
** The other companies have no high-level federal government affiliations.

private sector and government. Thirty-six directors have been appointed to at least one (past or present) high-level federal government position. These posts include cabinet posts, presidential advisory commissions, advisory committees to federal agencies (U.S. Congress: Senate, 1977), and regional boards of the Federal Reserve Bank. Individuals with extensive and high-level experience in the federal government provide useful resources for newspaper companies, because these companies engage in activities (such as broadcasting and mergers) that are closely regulated by government. For example, Allen Neuharth, Gannett's chairman, explained:

> (William) Bill Rogers is in a position to make major contributions to Gannett in its dealings with government, on anti-trust matters, with the FCC (Federal Communications Commission), whatever. He's been on the inside and can help top management understand what can be done and what can't be done (personal interview).

Distribution of Affiliations

Affiliations with power structure institutions are not equally distributed among the 290 directors. As Table 3 indicates, some directors are highly integrated into the network, others are marginally integrated, while others are not integrated at all. Indeed, 157 directors have absolutely no ties to any of the elite institutions of the national power structure; 108 have one to five affiliations; 20 have six to nine affiliations; and five have 10 or more (13 being the highest) affiliations. In other words, 25 of the 290 directors (8.6 percent) account for 204 of the 447 (45.6 percent) elite affiliations.

Moreover, as Table 3 shows, the newspaper companies' outside directors account for a disproportionate share of the linkages with the national power structure. Although outside directors account for only 70 of the 290 (24.1 percent) newspaper company directors, they account for 274 of the 447 (61.2 percent) total elite affiliations. Of the five directors with 10 or more elite affiliations, all are outside directors; of the 20 directors with six to nine affiliations, 15 are outside directors. In addition, as Table 2 shows, 23 of the 70 outside directors (32.8 percent), compared

TABLE 3

Distribution of Elite Affiliations

No. of Elite Affiliations	No. of Inside Directors	No. of Outside Directors	Total No. of Directors
0	146	11	157
	(0)	(0)	(0)
1–5	69	39	108
	(138)	(105)	(243)
6–9	5	15	20
	(35)	(113)	(148)
10–13	0	5	5
	(0)	(56)	(56)
Total	220	70	290
	(173)	(274)	(447)

Note:
Numbers in parentheses give the total number of elite affiliations for each cell.

with only 13 of the 220 inside directors (5.9 percent) have been appointed to high-level positions in the federal government.

This data indicate that the newspaper companies' ties with the U.S. power structure come primarily from outside directors brought onto their boards for a variety of reasons, and that a relatively small group of these outside directors account for a disproportionate share of these elite affiliations. This pattern suggests that a division of labor may exist within the boards of these newspaper firms. The inside directors, with some exceptions, run the day-to-day operations of the newspaper-owning firms (or simply benefit through trusts as beneficiaries). Their affiliations, also with some exceptions, are with industry-related activities — boards of the Associated Press, or newspaper executives' organizations, press clubs, awards committees, and so on — and reflect an industry-oriented outlook. These are mainly professional managers who either climbed the newspaper corporate ladder or were brought in from outside to provide specific kinds of expertise. The exceptions to this rule are those inside directors who are part of the owning families — Katherine Graham of the *Washington Post*, Arthur Sulzberger of the New York Times, John Cowles and John Cowles, Jr., of the *Minneapolis Star and Tribune*, Marshall Field of Field Enterprises, Helen Copley of Copley Press, William Taylor of Affiliated Publications, and William R. Hearst, Jr., of Hearst Corporation, for example. Members of owning families tend to be part of both the social aristocracy of the nation (Baltzell, 1964; Domhoff, 1970; Roberts, 1977; Swanberg, 1961) and the network of the U.S. power structure. Thus, they share more in common with the outside directors than with the professional executives hired to run the newspaper companies on a day-to-day basis. With few exceptions, even the members of the owning families are not as heavily involved as the outside directors; they are less likely, for example, to have directorships on major corporations (Roberts, 1977:460). As members of "old wealth" families, however, many are likely to retain memberships in the exclusive social clubs and civic groups that form an important part of the power structure (Baltzell, 1964; *Business Week*, 1980; Domhoff, 1974; Lundberg, 1968). There are also professional executives — inside directors are part of the owning families — who are heavily involved with the elite institutions, but as a proportion of affiliations they take a back seat to the outside directors.

The outside directors provide a bridge between the newspaper companies and the capitalist class and its institutions. Some, as bank directors, may oversee their banks' investment in newspaper firms. Some, as former government officials, may provide expertise on government matters. But beyond these specific roles, these outside directors — many of them members of the inner group at the pinnacle of the capitalist class — provide a link to the broader interests of the business community with which the newspaper companies' future is tied. They provide important links to the major corporate decision-makers and the larger corporate world. Thus, while they may represent stockholders' interests (*Business Week*, 1979), or banks, or other institutions in the narrow sense, they also provide a link to the central decision-making networks within the capitalist class.

DIFFERENCES AMONG NEWSPAPER COMPANIES

As Table 1 indicates, not all newspaper companies are equally linked with the power structure. Four companies — Dow Jones Company (57 affiliations), the New York Times Company (47), the Washington Post Company (41), and the Times–Mirror Corporation (40) — together account for 185 (41.6 percent) of all elite affiliations. The next four companies account for 27.1 percent, the next four 17.2 percent, the next four 9.8 percent, the next four 3.5 percent, and the final four less than one percent. How can this disproportionate share at the top be explained? What distinguishes the companies with the most elite affiliations, and therefore the strongest institutional integration within the national power structure, from the other companies?

The literature on interlocking directorates suggests that interlocks are relationships between corporations and that directors are agents of these relationships. Organizations seek such ties in pursuit of their interests. Indeed, there is evidence that different interlocks perform different functions, including access to general information about corporations' environments, specific information about corporate plans and procedures, and explicit coordination between interlocked firms (Allen, 1974 and 1978; Burt, 1980; Levine, 1972; Mariolis, 1975; Palmer, 1981; Ratcliff *et al.*, 1979). Interviews with and statements by the newspaper directors under study indicate that all of these factors help to explain specific interlocks for each firm. But these do not explain why the Dow Jones Company, New York Times Company, Washington Post Company, and the Times–Mirror Corporation have a significantly greater share of elite affiliations, of which corporate interlocks are only one type. Alternative hypotheses drawn from the literature do not explain this pattern. These four companies are not the largest in terms of sales or profitability, which are found to be correlated with interlocks (Bunting, 1977; Pennings, 1980), as found in the Dunn and Bradstreat *Million Market Directory* and as found in Morton's (1981) analysis of newspaper firms' average after-tax profit margins over a five-year period. (See also *Business Week*, 1976b and 1978.) Neither are these four companies the largest in terms of total daily circulation, number of newspapers, or number of market areas in which their newspapers circulate, as indicated by the 1980 *Editor and Publisher Yearbook*.

What is clear, however, is that these four companies own the four most prestigious and politically-influential newspapers in the United States, the *Washington Post*, the *Wall Street Journal* (Dow Jones), the *Los Angeles Times* (Times–Mirror Corporation), and the *New York Times* (Bagdikian, 1971; Emery and Emery, 1978; Gans, 1979; Merrill, 1968; Merrill and Fisher, 1980; Tebbel, 1961).

Journalistic influence and prestige probably accounts for the pattern of elite affiliations. There is a perfect correlation between the four newspaper companies with the most elite affiliations and the four most influential newspapers. The data does not explain the causal relationship. Outside directors may be co-opted onto the boards of newspapers seeking access to capital or decision-making elites. Then too, the most powerful corporations and other elite institutions may be co-opting these four powerful papers to ensure their conformity with the power structure's long-term views (Rockmore, 1979). In fact, both of these processes are plausible. Moreover, some individuals may be motivated to join the boards largely for the prestige of affiliating with a highly visible and powerful institution.

Voices of the Inner Group

The four firms/papers with the closest ties to the U.S. power structure—the *New York Times,* the *Washington Post,* the *Wall Street Journal* and the *Los Angeles Times*—are distinguished from most other daily newspapers by their ideological outlook. These four papers reflect a "corporate liberal" perspective. This is the outlook identified with the inner group of the capitalist class (Block, 1977, 1980; Domhoff, 1970; Weinstein, 1968). While leaders of small and medium size businesses have characteristically opposed unions, social welfare, foreign aid, and government regulation in all forms, leaders of the major corporations (the inner group) have sought to forestall challenges from below and stabilize the long-term foundations of capitalism by implementing strategic reforms to co-opt dissent. Concerned with the stability of the entire system rather than the narrow interests of any one industry, corporation, or region, the leaders of the major corporations have conceded the need for some government regulation of business, as well as trade unionism, civil rights and social welfare legislation, foreign aid to promote free trade and stability, and other related policies. Corporate-sponsored think tanks and business policy groups generally adhere to this "corporate liberal" outlook.[2]

Most U.S. newspapers are relatively narrow and parochial in outlook. Few have offices in Washington, D.C., or in foreign capitals. They emphasize local or regional news and economic development and growth (Molotch, (1976). Newspaper publishers traditionally have been politically conservative, reflecting a small-business outlook of government intervention in the marketplace, foreign aid and trade, defense policy, labor relations, and other policies. For the past 40 years, the overwhelming number of daily papers have supported the Republican party. In every presidential election since 1940, with the exception of 1964, most U.S. newspapers (between 57.7 percent in 1960 and 71.4 percent in 1972) endorsed the Republican candidate. This parochialism continues to this day (Emery and Emery, 1978).

There is evidence, however, that as newspapers and newspaper companies grow as corporate entities (and as competition between papers decline, leaving most dailies without any direct competition), they begin to broaden their political outlook. Today there are few independent, locally-owned dailies. Gradually, chains have purchased independent papers and large chains have purchased smaller chains (Bagdikian, 1978; *Business Week,* 1977; Compaine, 1979; Louis, 1978; Rosse *et al.*, 1975). As the chains grow, their high-level employees and executives make links outside the local community. They are no longer under the strong personal control of individuals such as William R. Hearst (Lundberg, 1936; Swanberg, 1961) or Col. Robert McCormick (Waldrop, 1966). Moreover, as newspaper competition declines, monopoly or near-monopoly newspapers must appeal to a broader audience. These reasons are clearly responsible for the increasingly corporate liberal outlook of both the *Chicago Tribune* and the *Los Angeles Times,* once bastions of extreme conservatism (Dreier, 1976; Gottlieb and Wolt, 1977; Halberstam, 1979). Many papers, especially the *Wall Street Journal,* the *New York Times,* and the *Washington Post,* wish to appeal to the "upscale," affluent readers, the target for both advertisers and opinion-leaders. One indication of newspapers' increasingly "statesman-like" role is the steady increase in papers making no presidential endorsements at all—from only 13.4 percent in 1940 to 25.6 percent in 1976 (Emery and Emery, 1978:483).

---

2. Corporate liberal ideology and policy—which is most evident during periods of social unrest, such as the Progressive era, the Depression, and the 1960s—can also be seen as a product of the steady expansion of U.S. corporate and political power in the first three-quarters of this century. Although proponents of corporate liberalism were ascendant within the capitalist class during much of that period, they did meet resistance from other segments of the class. The success of corporate liberalism, moreover, rested on continued corporate and political expansion, a trend that was challenged in the 1970s, both domestically and abroad. The decline of U.S. power in the world economy (Kolko, 1974) and the domestic fiscal crisis of the state (O'Connor, 1973) created difficulties for proponents of corporate liberalism.

Although daily newspapers are moving away from narrow parochialism, the four papers with the closest links to the power structure best reflect the corporate liberal viewpoint. They have taken the lead, among major daily papers, in exposing corporate wrongdoing and government corruption. They regularly investigate corporations and government actions that violate what Gans (1979) calls "responsible capitalism." The *New York Times* published the Pentagon Papers, the *Washington Post* and the *Los Angeles Times* took the lead in the Watergate exposé, and the *Wall Street Journal* was the first major paper to investigate the foreign policy views and business ethics of Reagan advisor Richard Allen, to question the State Department's view of the ties between El Salvador's insurgents and both Cuba and the Soviet Union, and to expose many corporate scandals that corporate officers would have preferred to remain secret. These papers were among the first to reflect the disenchantment with the Vietnam War among the inner group of the business community (Joseph, 1981). Other papers also do such investigations and reporting, but none as consistently and with such national influence as these four papers. What this suggests is that these papers' corporate liberal outlook transcends the narrow interests of any one industry, corporation, or region. The corporate liberal press may criticize or expose *particular* corporate or government practices as harmful to the legitimacy and thus long-term stability of the entire system, or *particular* corporations or elected officials for the same reason. They take the long view. Thus, while at first it may seem paradoxical that the papers and firms with the *most* elite connections are the most likely to expose corporate and government practices, from the standpoint of their role as corporate liberal spokesmen for the inner group, it makes perfect sense.

In examining how the mass media functions, sociologists have usually explained the tendency of newspapers to reflect the outlook of the powerful in terms of the routines of newsgathering and the ability of powerful institutions and individuals to gain regular access to journalists. Or, they point to the attitude of journalists that those in positions of power and influence are more "responsible" news sources (Dreier, 1978; Epstein, 1973; Fishman, 1980; Gans, 1979; Molotch and Lester, 1974; Sigal, 1973; Tuchman, 1972, 1978). Certainly these factors help explain why newspapers in general reflect the world view of the powerful, but they cannot explain *variations* in ideology and world view, between newspapers, since the routines of news gathering are similar on most papers. That is why factors external to the newsroom, including the social, political, and corporate ties of newspaper directors, must be considered in explaining why some newspapers are different than others.

Our data confirm that the nation's leading newspaper companies are all linked to outside institutions. Of the 24 firms, 22 are linked to at least one elite institution of the *national* power structure. Moreover, these links are primarily through outside directors, who serve as the major link to the business community. The patterns of affiliations also suggest that four companies—those that publish the *New York Times*, the *Washington Post,* the *Los Angeles Times*, and the *Wall Street Journal*—represent the newspaper industry's part of the national power structure. These four papers speak not only for the directors and owners, but also for the inner group of the larger capitalist class. This is not to deny that they have a degree of autonomy and independence; they are not mere "tools" of this class (Dreier, 1982). But the structural links help to maintain and reinforce the ideology of corporate liberalism that these papers share with the inner group.

REFERENCES

Allen, Michael
    1974   "The structure of interorganizational elite cooptation: Interlocking corporate directorates." American Sociological Review 39:393-406.
    1978   "Economic interest groups and the corporate elite structure." Social Science Quarterly 58:597-615.
Bagdikian, Ben
    1971   The Information Machines. New York: Harper.
    1978   "Conglomeration, concentration and the flow of information." Proceedings of the Symposium on

Media Concentration. Federal Trade Commission, Bureau of Competition. Washington, D.C.: U.S. Government Printing Office.

Baltzell, E. Digby
1964   The Protestant Establishment: Aristocracy and Caste in America. New York: Random House.
Banfield, Edward
1961   Political Influence. New York: Free Press.
Block, Fred
1977   "Beyond corporate liberalism." Social Problems 24:252-261.
1980   "Beyond relative autonomy." Socialist Register: 227-242.
Bogart, Leo
1974   "The management of mass media." Pp. 143-170 in W. Phillips Davidson and Frederick Yu (eds.), Mass Communication Research. New York: Praeger.
Bonacich, Phillip and G. William Domhoff
1977   "Overlapping memberships among clubs and policy groups of the American ruling class." Paper presented at the meetings of the American Sociological Association, Chicago. August.
Bunting, David
1977   "Corporate interlocking, part III: Interlocks and return on investment." Directors and Boards 1:4-11.
Burd, Gene
1977   "The selling of the sunbelt: Civic boosterism in the media." Pp. 129-150 in David Perry and Alfred Watkins (eds.), The Rise of the Sunbelt Cities. Beverly Hills: Sage Publications.
Burt, Ronald
1980   "Testing a structural theory of corporate cooptation." American Sociological Review 45:821-841.
Business Week
1976a   "America's most profitable publisher." Jan. 26:56-69.
1976b   "Behind the profit squeeze at the New York Times." August 30:42-49.
1977   "The big money hunts for independent newspapers." Feb. 21:56-62.
1978   "Dow Jones joins the media conglomerates." Nov. 13:60-72.
1979   "End of the directors' rubber stamp." Sept. 10:72-83.
1980   "The all-male club: Threatened on all sides." August 11:90-91.
Compaine, Benjamin M. (ed.)
1979   Who Owns the Media? White Plains, N.Y.: Knowledge Industry Publications.
Devereux, Sean
1976   "Boosters in the newsroom: The Jacksonville case." Columbia Journalism Review (January/February):38-47.
Domhoff, G. William
1970   The Higher Circles. New York: Vintage Books.
1974   The Bohemian Grove and Other Retreats. New York: Harper and Row.
1979   The Powers That Be. New York: Random House.
Dreier, Peter
1976   "The Urban Press in Transition: The Political Economy of Newswork." Unpublished Ph.D. dissertation, University of Chicago.
1978   "Newsroom democracy and media monopoly: Dilemmas of workplace reform among professional journalists." Insurgent Sociologist 7:70-86.
1982   "Capitalists vs. the media: An analysis of an ideological mobilization among business leaders." Media, Culture, and Society forthcoming.
Dreier, Peter and Steven Weinberg
1979   "The ties that blind: Interlocking directorates." Columbia Journalism Review 18:(November/December):51-68.
Dye, Thomas
1976   Who's Running America? Institutional Leadership in the United States. Englewood Cliffs, N.J.: Prentice Hall.
Eakins, David
1969   "Business planners and America's postwar expansion." Pp. 143-171 in David Horowitz (ed.), Corporations and the Cold War. New York: Monthly Review Press.
Emery, Edwin and Michael Emery
1978   The Press and America. Englewood Cliffs, N.J.: Prentice-Hall
Epstein, Edward Jay
1973   News From Nowhere. New York: Random House.
Fishman, Mark
1980   Manufacturing the News. Austin: University of Texas Press.
Gans, Herbert
1979   Deciding What's News. New York: Pantheon.
Gottlieb, Robert and Irene Wolt
1977   Thinking Big: The Story of the Los Angeles Times, Its Publishers and Their Influence on Southern California. New York: G. P. Putnam's Sons.

Halberstam, David
1979   The Powers That Be. New York: Knopf.
Hayes, Edward C.
1972   Power Structure and Urban Policy: Who Rules in Oakland? New York: McGraw-Hill.
Hirsch, Glen
1975   "Only you can prevent ideological hegemony: The Advertising Council and its place in the American power structure." Insurgent Sociologist 5:64-82.
Ingrassia, Lawrence
1979   "Owners of newspapers stir debate by taking a role in public affairs." Wall Street Journal, Aug. 24:1, 26.
Johnstone, John W., Edward Slawski and William Bowman
1976   The Newspeople. Urbana: University of Illinois Press.
Joseph, Paul
1981   Cracks in the Empire. Boston: South End Press.
Kolko, Joyce
1974   America and the Crisis of World Capitalism. Boston: Beacon Press.
Levine, Joel
1972   "The sphere of influence." American Sociological Review 37:14-27.
Louis, Arthur M.
1978   "Independent dailies are an endangered species." Fortune, June 19:160-166.
1981   "Growth gets harder at Gannett." Fortune, April 20:118-129.
Lundberg, Ferdinand
1936   Imperial Hearst: A Social Biography. New York: The Modern Library.
1968   The Rich and the Super-Rich. New York: Lyle Stuart.
Mariolis, Peter
1975   "Interlocking directorates and the control of corporations." Social Science Quarterly 56:425-439.
Merrill, John C.
1968   The Elite Press. New York: Pitman.
Merrill, John C., and Harold A. Fisher
1980   The World's Great Dailies. New York: Hastings House.
Mintz, Beth
1975   "The president's cabinet, 1897-1972: A contribution to the power structure debate." Insurgent Sociologist 5:131-148.
Molotch, Harvey
1976   "The city as a growth machine: Toward a political economy of place." American Journal of Sociology 82:309-332.
Molotch, Harvey and Marilyn Lester
1974   "News and purposive behavior." American Sociological Review 39:101-112.
Morgenthaler, Eric
1970   "Some question ethics of putting a newsman on a corporate board." Wall Street Journal, Sept. 4:1, 15.
Morton, John
1980   Financial Profile of the Newspaper Industry. Washington, D.C.: John Muir and Company.
1981   Newsletter. Washington, D.C.: John Muir and Company, Jan. 31.
O'Connor, James
1973   The Fiscal Crisis of the State. New York: St. Martin's Press.
Palmer, Donald
1981   "Broken ties: Interlocking directorates, the interorganizational paradigm and intercorporate coordination." Unpublished research paper No. 595. Stanford University Graduate School of Business. Stanford, California.
Pennings, Johannes M.
1980   Interlocking Directorates. San Francisco: Jossey Bass.
Ratcliff, Richard, Mary Gallagher, and Kathryn Ratcliff.
1979   "The civic involvement of bankers: An analysis of the influence of economic power and social prominence in the command of civic policy positions." Social Problems 26:298-313.
Roberts, Chalmers M.
1977   The Washington Post: The First 100 Years. Boston: Houghton-Mifflin.
Rockmore, Milton
1977   "How activist should a publisher be?" Editor and Publisher, Nov. 12:74-75.
1979   "How does an outside director contribute?" Editor and Publisher, April 21:24-37, 44.
Rosse, James N., Bruce M. Owen and James Dertouzos
1975   Trends in the Daily Newspaper Industry, 1923-73. Studies in Industry Economics, No. 55. Stanford, California: Department of Economics, Stanford University.
Salzman, Harold and G. William Domhoff
1980   "Corporations, non-profit groups and government: Do they interlock?" Insurgent Sociologist 9:121-135.

Schudson, Michael
  1978   Discovering the News: A Social History of American Newspapers. New York: Basic Books.
Shoup, Laurence H. and William Minter
  1977   Imperial Brain Trust: The Council on Foreign Relations and United States Foreign Policy. New
          York: Monthly Review Press.
Sigal, Leon V.
  1973   Reporters and Officials. Lexington, Ma.: D.C. Heath.
Standard and Poor's Corporation.
  1975–   Standard and Poor's Register of Corporations, Directors and Executives. New York: Standard
  79   and Poor's Corporation.
Swanberg, W. A.
  1961   Citizen Hearst. New York: Scribner's.
Talese, Gay
  1969   The Kingdom and the Power. New York: World.
Tebbel, John
  1961   "Rating the American newspaper." Saturday Review, May 13, 44(19):59–62; June 10,
          44(23):54–56.
Tuchman, Gaye
  1972   "Objectivity as strategic ritual." American Journal of Sociology 77:660–679.
  1978   Making News. New York: Free Press.
Udell, Jon G.
  1978   The Economics of the American Newspaper. New York: Hastings House.
U.S. Congress: Senate
  1977   Federal Advisory Committees. Committee on Governmental Affairs, Subcommittee on Reports,
          Accounting and Management. Washington, D.C.: U.S. Government Printing Office.
Useem, Michael
  1978   "The inner group of the American capitalist class." Social Problems 25:225–240.
  1979   "The social organization of the American business elite and participation of corporate directors in
          the governance of American institutions." American Sociological Review 44:553–572.
  1980   "Which business leaders help govern?" Insurgent Sociologist 9:107–120.
Waldrop, Frank C.
  1966   McCormick of Chicago. Englewood Cliffs, N.J.: Prentice-Hall.
Weinstein, James
  1968   The Corporate Ideal in the Liberal State. Boston: Beacon Press.
Zeitlin, Maurice
  1974   "Corporate ownership and control: The large corporation and the capitalist class." American
          Journal of Sociology 79:1073–1119.
Zeitlin, Maurice, Richard Ratcliff and Linda Ewen
  1974   "The 'inner group.' " Paper presented at meetings of the American Sociological Association, Mont-
          real. August.

PART VI

MEDIA PERFORMANCE AND STATE STRUCTURE

This section may be viewed as an extension of the previous one, in that for the authors here, the media are appropriately viewed as institutions, and the contributors here are particularly interested in relationships between media institutions and state power. All four contributions, moreover, have something to say about these institutions in time of crisis, and we feel that a comparative reading of these four chapters is a valuable intellectual exercise.

Olien, Donohue, and Tichenor review their work, and those of others, on the knowledge gap. American (and other) research leads them to believe that structurally, such studies are best contextualized by placement in a systems perspective that emphasizes media performance as reinforcing entrenched institutions, even in times of crisis.

Schlesinger looks at broadcast performance in a particular crisis, the take-over of the Iranian Embassy in London in 1980. The role of media, particularly that of the BBC, was closely allied with that of the government; this, he suggests, has disturbing future implications.

Goban-Klas's crisis is that of the rise of labor discontent in Poland in the summer of 1980, and the media he critically examines are those allied with the Polish state and the alternative media created by the new labor movement to fill the void the former media could not fill.

Moragas, in examining the functions of media in post-Franco Spain, in the move to a parliamentary democracy, demonstrates a lively concern with the proper function of media in meeting the information needs of a democracy and pays attention to the establishment of political legitimacy, particularly in the "establishment" of a political opposition.

The present chapter is a latter-day discussion of Tichenor's knowledge gap hypothesis which suggests that under routine conditions, media dissemination of information on an issue serves to broaden the gap between the information held by high-status individuals and low-status individuals. Here Olien, Donohue, and Tichenor summarize recent research on the knowledge gap and tie it to notions of social control; as they note, media systems are intimately tied, even in times of conflict, to reinforcement of existing power structures.

27

STRUCTURE, COMMUNICATION AND SOCIAL POWER
Evolution of the Knowledge Gap Hypothesis

Clarice N. Olien, George A. Donohue, and Phillip J. Tichenor

Knowledge as a principal basis of social power has historically been the focus of social control measures. Exclusive employment of scribes by kings, restricted use of the Gutenberg press by the church, and control of vast bodies of financial data by banks are manifestations of this emphasis. What is transmitted to whom has always been at the crux of maintenance or enhancement of the status of the more powerful segments of society.[1])

Advances in communication technology as well as geometric increases in the knowledge base create a need for revision of existing modes of knowledge control. Scientists, educators, politicians, and theologians, as well as leaders in other sectors of society, have traditionally justified information campaigns as essential to providing people with public knowledge for their own development or welfare. This apparent altruism reinforces the belief that maximum diffusion of knowledge would tend to equalize knowledge among the different groups in the social system.

The equalizing effect of information dissemination, while a desirable goal in some social philosophies, is not supported by the empirical research findings that groups gain access to and acquire knowledge at differential rates. The relationship between current knowledge level and differential rates of knowledge growth has been a continuing concern of the research program in Ru-

ral Sociology at the University of Minnesota since the mid-1960's. This research on mass communication of information has evolved from an initial emphasis on status-based flow of information to an emphasis on structural factors and knowledge differentials among interest groups. In effect it is a movement from a micro subsystem analysis to a more macro subsystem perspective of the effect of community organization upon patterns of mass media communication

The initial hypothesis

Early analyses of mass communication in our research emanated largely from the social organization aspects of the Westley-MacLean model, which had the advantage of emphasizing linkages between the source, channel and audience components of the communication subsystem and their implications for information flow and acquisition. [2,3]) Early on, analysis of data underscored the importance of characteristics of community structure in determining the success which a purposive source would achieve in placing information in newspapers. Usage of county agricultural agents' purposive messages by newspapers was greater in small, more homogeneous communities where agriculture was a dominant part of the local economy. Community structural characteristics were more related to

From Clarice N. Olien, George A. Donohue, and Phillip J. Tichenor, "Structure, Communication and Social Power: Evolution of the Knowledge Gap Hypothesis," *Massacommunicatie*, Vol. 10, No. 3 (June 1982), pp. 81-87. Reprinted by permission.

newspaper usage of information than were personal interactions between editors and agents.[4])

A structural perspective appeared to provide a fruitful framework for addressing a fundamental question about why mass media information campaigns often fail to achieve their desired objectives.[5,6]) The structural approach, rather than assuming information campaign failure, provided the hypothesis that:

As the infusion of mass media information into a social system increases, segments of the population with higher socio-economic status tend to acquire this information at a faster rate than the lower socio-economic segments, so that the gap in knowledge between these segments tends to increase rather than decrease.

This hypothesis concentrated on formal education as an indicator of group status. The hypothesis does not contend that lower status groups stay "information poor" or "get poorer" in an absolute sense, but that *relative* disparities in knowledge increase as the flow of information increases.[7])

Relevant evidence supporting that initial hypothesis came from a variety of sources. The gaps in knowledge about outer space research, between more and less educated segments, increased as predicted from the early 1950's to the early 1960's, during a period of high publicity on this topic. A secondary analysis of Samuelson's data on a newspaper strike suggested that temporary suspension of a newspaper may lead to a temporary decrease in the public affairs knowledge gap.[8]) A field experiment in Minnesota indicated higher knowledge gaps for topics that had received higher levels of coverage in the press, compared with those receiving lower levels of coverage. These gaps are consistent with a print media system which mirrors the existence of differentials in the social system.

Evidence from other studies

Other investigators in a number of cultural settings provided evidence supportive of the knowledge gap hypothesis.[9,10,11,12]) Several of these researchers studying agricultural diffusion programs in developing countries found that inequities in knowledge often emerge in previously egalitarian societies as a result of programs for diffusion that intentionally distribute information to higher status segments. Beltran's analysis illustrates the extent to which the disparity-increasing consequences of developmental programs have become a major issue in third world nations.[13]) Saxer reported knowledge gaps from studies in several different nations.[14]) These works indicate that if a program of dissemination consciously denies access to information among certain groups, disparities will occur. The knowledge gap hypothesis indicates that it need not be conscious, but that the elements of the social system will operate to deny equal levels of access and accrual of knowledge.

Fry concluded that dependence of high status individuals on newspapers, which are media oriented to high status groups, was one of the operative factors in knowledge gaps about public affairs.[15]) Bultena, Rogers and Conner found that coordinated programs on a conservation project in Iowa led to relatively greater information gain among more educated groups.[16]) Schreiber suggested not only that increasing publicity leads to knowledge gaps, but that the gap has direct relevance for opinion changes on such issues as support for a woman for the U.S. presidency.[17])

Several studies produced evidence that television may have the same effect on knowledge gaps as newspapers. Werner reports a study in Norway, in which televised messages promoting books for children succeeded in reaching five times as high a proportion of middle class families as working class families, even though the working family children were the intended audience.[18]) Katz, Adoni, Parness and Cohen found that economic news reporting on Israeli television increased disparities in knowledge between more and less educated groups.[19]) In the American televised election debates of 1976, the apparent outcome was increased knowledge gaps. Several studies in Europe reported evidence of this effect, including those cited by Nowak in Scandinavian nations.[20,21,22])

Structure and information control

Initially, the knowledge gap hypothesis was derived from a social systems framework. Further elaboration of the structural factors underlying the knowledge gap awaited further analysis. As indicated in a basic theoretical statement published in Journalism Quarterly in 1973, knowledge is controlled primarily in the interest of system maintenance.[23]) The system being maintained might be the media subsystem itself or a source subsystem with which the media have interdependent relations such as a unit of government, business, medicine, academia, or the social system as a whole. System control occurs through two different but overlapping processes within the media subsystem, feedback-control and distribution control. Feedback-control refers to reactive communication, which serves a regulatory function for other subsystems and for the total system. For example, media reporting of (a) one politician challenging another and (b) responses of interest groups to media reports are different aspects of the feedback process. Distribution-control, which can occur independently or jointly with feedback-control, serves a maintenance function through selective dissemination of information and withholding of information. Censorship in this perspective is but one type of distribution-control. Editorial choices constitute another type. A third would be strategic announcing of acts of business or government as accomplished facts, which while distributive in origin may of may not have feedback consequences, depending on the organized capabilities of interested publics to respond.

The structural hypothesis about these processes is supported by data indicating that the distributive aspect of system maintenance will tend to be the overriding concern of media in structures that are less differentiated and more dependent upon primary communication and consensus in decision-making.[24]) A corollary is that the more differentiated a system, the more likely media are to perform a feedback-control as well as a distributive function. Conflict is structurally inherent in highly differen-

tiated structures, such as large urban communities. As differentiation and conflict situations increase, the primary, face-to-face type of interaction of the more homogeneous community becomes inadequate for meeting the information needs of the constituent interest groups. The more differentiated structure, therefore, is more likely to have a press and other mass media that report conflict and to have a variety of formal mechanisms such as labor-management negotiations and other bureaucratic procedures that serve to moderate conflict without disrupting the system itself. Less differentiated structures depend on a relative absence of overt conflict, reinforced by media such as weekly papers that play down or avoid conflict. Data from 88 newspapers provided strong support for this model. The form and function of the media are related to the needs of the structure rather than to the needs of the media subsystem itself.

Other considerations in the knowledge gap hypothesis

Analysis of the fundamental characteristics of social structure, and communication processes within those structures, created the need to specify conditions under which knowledge gaps would be greater or lesser in magnitude. Empirical analyses included conflict, the intensity of the conflict atmosphere, and the pattern of media coverage which is determined by the organized forces that initiated the conflict itself.[25])

Further analysis indicated that within any given structure, conflict is a major factor in knowledge differentials. The higher the proportion viewing the issue as conflictive, the lower the knowledge gap.[26]) As an illustration, one community had been put on a "mercury danger list" by a state health agency report, implying that the town's popular fishing and resort lake was so polluted that fish from its waters should not be eaten. Local leaders claimed publicly that the community had been unfairly singled out by the report and stood to suffer economically as a result. The "whole town talked" about this issue and knowledge was fairly uniform across different levels of education. On the other hand, the gap between high and low educational groups was wider in another community where regionalization of political boundaries was an issue of conflict among the leaders but not the public at large. While there has been relatively little research elsewhere on the effects of conflict as a variable in knowledge gaps, Bonfadelli concludes from European research that structures with greater degrees of conflict have smaller knowledge gaps.[27]

While characteristics of community structure and conflict conditions are important, other characteristics of information programs are equally important in the magnitude of gaps. In applying the structural perspective to an experiment on nutritional information for children, it was found that the degree of organizational support in the school nutrition education program was more important than socio-economic characteristics of the family.[28] But any information program that whishes to reduce disparities must be organized in such a fashion as to counter the existing structural factors that lead to differential accrual of knowledge. Shingi and Mody reported evidence from India, as did Galloway from Australia, that diffusion programs do not lead to increasing knowledge gaps in all cases. The type of knowledge and the way in which the information program is structured can limit or reduce those gaps.[29,30]

Media structure, leader roles and gaps in power

Most of the studies on the knowledge gap concentrated on differentials between higher and lower status groups. The consequences for maintaining the relatively low social power of groups was clear in a variety of programs, including the rural development programs mentioned earlier. In the U.S., the enthusiasm behind the War on Poverty in the 1960's was dampened by findings that projects designed to ameliorate differences actually increased power status for groups that were initially more

advantaged. Project Head Start, Model Cities programs, and the internationally-distributed "Sesame Street" were all found to increase the relative advantage in skills among middle-class groups, over the more deprived and lower status target audiences.[31,32]

Given that social power is the basic issue in the knowledge gap phenomenon, research in recent years has shifted to a more general question about knowledge distribution. The emphasis goes beyond concentration on differences among status groups per se to knowledge differentials among all types of groupings that have vested interests in generation, dissemination, acquisition and utilization of information. This suggests that media organization be analyzed in terms of consequences for (a) power distributions within communities and (b) the power of a particular community vis-a-vis other communities within the larger social system.

At least one other research group, Genova and Greenberg, demonstrated empirically in the mid-1970's that topical interest among individuals was more closely related to knowledge than was education.[33] Interest is a collective concern, the initiating point for social action groups. Power of special interest groups is dependent on relationships with other groups, including mass communication systems that have networks with groups throughout the system.

Pursuit of these structural considerations has led to serious questioning about whether newspapers, or other media, serve as the autonomous channels that a "Fourth Estate" philosophy might imply. Media are as integral to the system as are churches, schools, businesses, or any other social agency. Media reflect the dominant perspectives of the system, and that means the perspectives of the dominant centers of power. In American society, the general outlook of the media channels, especially newspapers, has been described frequently as conservative and pro-business in character.[34,35,36,37,38,39]

This is not to deny that they have also been described by threatened power figures as liberal or even radically leftist. The extent to which established power groups themselves may recognize the support they get from media has been investigated. In two communities, public officials and leaders of citizen groups were interviewed, as members of other established groups or less-established, emerging groups. They were asked whether media were "harmful" of "helpful" to their organizational goals. The results were clear. The established leadership group was far less likely to perceive "harmful" media impact on their organizations than were the less established citizen group leaders. Similarly, members of a newly-organized agricultural protest group were more critical of newspaper coverage of a "tractorcade" demonstration than were leaders of government agricultural agencies or older, established farm organizations.

The clear implication of this research is that media, which are structurally constrained channels reporting on public issues, systematically project definitions of issues which are conducive to the interest of established power groups. By doing so, they reinforce or increase, through their feedback and distributive functions, the gaps in social power between established groups and other groups.

Media support of the status quo may not be apparent in highly charged conflict situations. Intense conflict often produces criticism of media by members of the status quo as "unstabilizing influences" or "sensation mongers" that "blow issues out of proportion". Media as social mirrors reflect perspectives not merely of power alone, but of power *relationships* in society. Where power is vested in a small group, monarchical or oligarchical, media will exclusively project that groups' perspective unless another group develops a countervailing power base for organized media strategies. Serious challenges lead to uncertainties in power relationships, and reporting these uncertainties elicits criticisms from groups whose power is in question. Even in periods of great political instability, media reporting supports the basic institutions and agencies deemed central to survival of the system. In the American system, this means reinforcement of the courts, legislative bodies and executive offices whose authority goes basically unquestioned. The debates are over role performance *within* those bodies, and not whether they should exist or not. In reporting these debates, the weight of media coverage is structured in large part to reinforce the status quo, and therefore the existing power structure.

Media structure and knowledge

The media system, or media mix, is a component of community structure that has implications for the knowledge levels of communities. Just as knowledge control has implications for power differentials among groups *within* communities, the knowledge control outcomes of media structures have implications for communities as they relate to other communities and to centers of political and economic power. Outlying communities of 5,000 or less in the American system are generally served by weekly newspapers, and cities of 10,000 or more generally by daily papers. Suburban communities have varying types of local newspaper systems, some weekly and some daily.

Differences in media structure, as an aspect of total community structure, appear to have considerable impact on levels of knowledge about public affairs. Generally, level of knowledge about *local* issues is highest in urban centers that have daily papers, compared with small, more homogeneous communities served by weeklies, or suburbs where strictly local news is confined primarily to a weekly that has a secondary or tertiary role in the media mix. Included in this research is the question of the structure of media ownership and patterns of journalistic performance under different ownership arrangements. Leadership marginality in media ownership provides a structural basis for active media reporting that may have profound ramifications for community knowledge about matters of civic concern. Hence, it has implications for the power position of the local community vis-a-vis external agencies and other communities with whom there is competition for political and economic resources.

Editor marginality, born of the interdependence between community and larger society, may lead to a pattern of newspaper reporting that is unlikely to occur where the ownership has either an entirely localite orientation *or* an entirely external orientation. Preliminary results from a study of 83 Minnesota newspapers indicates that daily newspapers which are non-locally owned tend to report less controversy than those locally-owned. Given the demonstrated tendency for a conflictive at-

mosphere to lead to a higher public awareness of issues, external ownership may well be a factor suppressing knowledge of public affairs issues. Such ownership might therefore contribute to a knowledge gap between communities, compared with those communities in which the editorial leadership fulfills the type of marginal role that is oriented toward drawing attention to public affairs issues. In an era when local communities and regions find themselves increasingly dependent on external sources of control, the relative disparities in knowledge between communities and other power centers has become a matter for widespread social concern in the world at large. It might be well for research on knowledge differentials to focus on the direct implications for differentials in social power among principal constituent segments of a society.

REFERENCES

1. See, for example, Ben H. Bagdikian, *The Information Machines: Their Impact on Men and the Media,* New York, Harper and Row, 1971; J. McDermott, "Knowledge is power", *Nation,* April 14, 1969; Robert E. Park, "News as a form of knowledge", *American Journal of Sociology,* 45:669-86, 1940; Fritz Machlup, *The Production and Distribution of Knowlegde in the United States,* Princeton, N.J., Princeton University Press, 1962; Sanford A. Lakoff, "Knowledge, power and democratic theory", *Annals,* 394:4-8, 1971, and John K. Galbraith, *The New Industrial State,* Boston: Houghton Mifflin, 1967.
2. G.A. Donohue, P.J. Tichenor and C.N. Olien, "Mass media functions, knowledge and social control", *Journalism Quarterly* 50:652-659, 1973.
3. B.H. Westley and M.S. MacLean, Jr. "A conceptual model for communication research". *Journalism Quarterly* 34:31-8, Winter, 1957.
4. P.J. Tichenor, C.N. Olien and G.A. Donohue, "Predicting a source's success in placing news in the media", *Journalism Quarterly* 44:32-42, Spring, 1967.
5. P.J. Tichenor, G.A. Donohue and C.N. Olien, "Mass communication research: Evolution of a structural model", *Journalism Quarterly* 50:419-425, 1973.
6. See for example, S. Star and H.M. Hughes, "Report of an educational campaign: The Cincinnati plan for the United Nations", *American Journal of Sociology* 55:389-397, 1950; H.H. Hyman and P.B. Sheatsley, "Some reasons why information campaigns fail", *Public Opinion Quarterly* 11:413-423, 1947; J. Klapper, *The Effects of Mass Communication,* New York, Free Press, 1963.
7. P.J. Tichenor, G.A. Donohue and C.N. Olien, "Mass media flow and differential growth in knowledge", *Public Opinion Quarterly* 34:159-170, 1970.
8. M.E. Samuelson, "Some news-seeking behavior in a newspaper strike", Ph.D. Dissertation, Stanford University, 1960.
9. Niels G. Röling, Joseph Ascroft and Fred Wachege, "The diffusion of innovations and the issue of equity in rural development", *Communication Research* 3:155-170, 1976.
10. E.M. Rogers, "Social structure and communication strategies in rural development", paper presented to Cornell-CIAT International Symposium on Communication Strategies for Rural Development, Cali, Columbia, March, 1974.
11. Emile G. McAnany, "Does information really work?" *Journal of Communication,* 28:84-90, 1978.
12. Elina Suominen, "Who needs information and why", *Journal of Communication* 26:115-119, 1976. See also Thomas Childers and Joyce Post, *The Information Poor in America,* Metuchen, N.J., Scarecrow Press, 1975.
13. Luis Ramiro Beltran, "Research ideologies in conflict", *Journal of Communication* 25:187-193, 1975.
14. Ulrich Saxer, Medienverhalten und wissenstand — zur hypothese der wachsenden wissenskluft, pp. 35-70 in *Buch und Lesen,* Gutersloh, W. Germany: Bertelsman, 1978.
15. D.L. Fry, "The knowledge gap hypotheses and media dependence: An initial study". Paper presented to Assn. for Education in Journalism, Houston, Texas, August, 1979.

16. G.L. Bultena, D.L. Rogers and K.A. Conner, "Toward explaining citizen knowledge about a proposed reservoir", *Journal of Environmental Education* 9:24-36, 1978.
17. E.M. Schreiber, "Education and change in American opinions on a woman for president", *Public Opinion Quarterly* 42:171-182, 1978.
18. Anita Werner, "A case of sex and class socialization", *Journal of Communication*, 25, 4:45-50, 1975.
19. See, Elihu Katz, Hanna Adoni and Prina Parness, "Remembering the news: "What the picture adds to recall", *Journalism Quarterly*, 54:231-239, 1977; Hanna Adoni and Akiba A. Cohen, "Television news and the social construction of economic reality", *Journal of Communication* 28:61-70, 1978.
20. George F. Bishop, Robert W. Oldendick, and Alfred J. Tuchfarber, "Debate watching and the acquisition of political knowledge", *Journal of Communication* 28:99-113, 1978.
21. Kjell Nowak, from "Information gaps to information potential", chapter in M. Berg, P. Hemanus, J. Ekecrantz, F. Mortensen and P. Sepstrup, editors, *Current Theories in Scandinavian Mass Communication Research*, Grenaa, Denmark: GMT, 1977.
22. Elihu Katz, "On conceptualizing media effects", pp. 119-142 in Thelma McCormick, ed., *Studies in Communication*, vol. 1, Greenwich, Conn.: JAI Press, inc., 1980.
23. Donohue, Olien and Tichenor, "Mass media functions, knowledge and social control", op. cit., 1973.
24. C.N. Olien, G.A. Donohue and P.J. Tichenor, "The community editor's power and the reporting of conflict", *Journalism Quarterly*, 45:243-52, 1968. See also J.S. Nichols, "Function of the Cuban mass media in social conflict: Prospects for the 1980's. Paper presented at conference, "Cuba in the 1980's". Harvard Univ., Cambridge, Mass., April 1981.
25. G.A. Donohue, C.N. Olien and P.J. Tichenor, "Communities, pollution and fight for survival", *Journal of Environmental Education* 1:29-37, 1974.
26. G.A. Donohue, P.J. Tichenor and C.N. Olien, "Mass media and the knowledge gap: A hypothesis reconsidered". *Communication Research* 2:3-23, 1975. See also W.R. Neuman, "The patterns of recall among television news viewers", *Public Opinion Quarterly*, 40:115-123, 1976.
27. Heinz Bonfadelli, Zur "Increasing knowledge gap" Hypothese, pp. 71-90 in Bertelsman Texte 7, *Buch und Lesen*, Gutersloh, W. Germany: Bertelsman, 1978. See also D.K. Davis, "Assessing the role of mass communication in social processes: A comment on 'Decline and Fall at the White House' ", *Communication Research* 4:23-34, 1977.
28. C.N. Olien, G.A. Donohue and P.J. Tichenor, Can ETV programs change dietary habits of children?" *Sociology of Rural Life* 1:4-5/8, June, 1978.
29. P.M. Shingi and Bella Mody, "The communication effects gap: A field experiment on television and agricultural ignorance in India", *Communication Research* 3:171-190, 1976.
30. See Brenda Dervin, "Communication gaps and inequities: Moving toward a reconceptualization", Chapter 3 in Brenda Dervin and M.J. Voigt, eds., *Progress in Communication Sciences II*, Norwood, N.J.: Ablex, 1980; J.S. Ettema and F.G. Kline, "Deficits, differences and ceilings: Contingent conditions for understanding the knowledge gap". *Communication Research*, 4:179-202, 1977; and J.J. Galloway, "The analysis and significance of communication effects gaps". *Communication Research* 4:363-386, 1977. J.W. Brown, J.S. Ettema and R.V. Luepker, "Knowledge gap effects in a cardiovascular information campaign", Assn. for Ed. in Journalism, East Lansing, Mich., 1981.
31. G. Bogatz and S. Bell, "The second year of Sesame Street: A continuing evaluation". Princeton, N.J.: Educational Testing Center.
32. T.D. Cooke, H. Appleton, R.F. Conner, A. Shaffer, G. Tamkin, and S.J. Weber, *Sesame Street Revisited*. New York: Russell Sage Foundation, 1975. See also Thomas Childers and Joyce A. Post, *The Information-Poor in America*, Metuchen, N.J.: Scarecrow Press, 1975.
33. B.K.L. Genova and Bradley S. Greenberg, "Interests in news and the knowledge gap". *Public Opinion Quarterly* 43:79-91, 1979.
34. K. Davis, H.C. Bredemeier and M.J. Levy, Jr., *Modern American Society-Readings in the Problems of Order and Change*, New York: Rinehart and Co. 1949.
35. L. Sigal, *Officials and Reporters: The Organization of the Politics of Newsmaking*, Lexington, Mass.: D.C. Heath & Co., 1973.
36. B. Hennessy, Public Opinion, 4th edition, Monterey, Calif.: Brooks/Cole, 1981.
37. W. Breed, "Mass communication and social integration", *Social Forces* 37:109-116, 1958.
38. G.A. Donohue, C.N. Olien and P.J. Tichenor, "Feedback to newspaper sources in different communities". Paper presented to Conference of Midwest Assn. for Public Opinion Research, Chicago, Ill. October 1981.
39. P.J. Tichenor, C.N. Olien and G.A. Donohue, "Community control and care of scientific information". *Communication Research* 3:403-424, 1976.

In his discussion of television's role (to say "television coverage" is, as the chapter amply demonstrates, too narrow) in the takeover and subsequent recapture of the Iranian embassy at Princes' Gate, London, in April 1980, Schlesinger raises important questions about the relationship between state and media at the time of political crisis during peacetime in a democracy. While prevention of loss of life is a crucial aim both of the government and the media, he notes that analysis of both media and state performance must proceed meaningfully beyond this concern. Philip Schlesinger is a member of the faculty of social sciences at Thames Polytechnic, England.

28

PRINCES' GATE, 1980
The Media Politics of Siege Management

Philip Schlesinger

'Now that the euphoria following the Iranian Embassy siege has abated, the doubters step in. But where you ask? In the letter columns of the *Guardian,* we answer. Yesterday that newspaper published a fascinating array of letters which pose some very proper questions. One complains his televised snooker was interrupted by the *coup de grâce* of the siege, and we sympathise; another grumbles about the role of television in the affair, and here there must be at least one embryonic thesis.'[1]

The siege at the Iranian Embassy in Princes' Gate, Kensington, between the 30 April and 5 May 1980 was a media event *par excellence,* covered from the outset by a veritable circus of newsmen. It had a bloody conclusion: for the first time the élite Special Air Services regiment (SAS) was used in an overt police action on the British mainland and killed five of the six hostage-taking gunmen. Millions of British television viewers watched the dénouement live. For many media professionals, such as Alan Protheroe, the BBC's Editor of Television News, it was one of television's 'finest hours'[2] and a 'definitive example of just how high standards of broadcast journalism really are in this country'.[3] Others were less enchanted, and had serious doubts about the value of the television reporting. The novelist John Le Carré, eschewing Protheroe's sub-Churchillian rhetoric, pointed out that both television channels actually failed to interpret correctly what was going on during the busting of the siege, and that

> '... the ITN commentator risked a most perilous theory about what was going on: a disaster theory, a theory of total ignominious failure on the part of the authorities. Assuming – as many of us benighted viewers *did* assume – that the explosions had been set off by the captors, he floated the idea that the captors had been panicked by the sight of masked men on the outside of the building.'[4]

The BBC's commentary was even less informative. Indeed, the moment of the siege-busting made the limitations of television actuality programming

---

1 Leader in *The Daily Telegraph* 10 May 1980.
2 An observation made on BBC television's *The Editors,* broadcast on 16 June 1980. Quotations are taken from the BFI Education Department's transcript of this programme.
3 Alan Protheroe 'The Authorities were reluctant to trust the Media: The Iranian Embassy siege' in *The Listener* 22 May 1980 p641.
4 John le Carré 'Introduction' to *Siege: Six Days at the Iranian Embassy,* London, MacMillan 1980 p2. This book was written by *The Observer*'s reporting team and published on 30 May. Extensive use is made of this account below, hence referred to as *Obs.*

From Philip Schlesinger, "Princes' Gate, 1980: The Media Politics of Siege Management," *Screen Education,* Vol. 37 (Winter 1980-1981), pp. 29-54. Reprinted by permission of the Society for Education in Film & Television, Ltd.

plain for all to see. In the excitement of seeing it 'for real', one is apt to forget how important was the absence of interpretation.

John le Carré puts television's communication failure down to the confusion of the reporters, a fact which needs some explanation. The available evidence suggests that the broadcasters were actually in a position to know broadly what was going on *at the time it was happening.* It also seems that they – at least senior editors, particularly in the BBC – had received briefings on government policy and were aware of the likely outcome of the siege. These contentions are documented below. Commenting on the television coverage, *Broadcast* (the television and radio industry's journal) observed how both ITN and BBC news 'went live from the scene only *after* SAS men stormed the building, amidst fire and explosions.' The moment of entry was videotaped, and ITN's report began four and a half minutes after this, and the BBC's only after eight minutes. *Broadcast* speculated,

> 'Given the close links between the broadcasters and the security forces during the siege, and bearing in mind that the hostages' captors may have had access to a television set inside the embassy, it is likely that the broadcasting organisations were actually warned off going live during this period for fear of giving the game away.'[5]

The suggestion that the transmission time was subject to consultation seems well founded. But I am doubtful that the authorities were worried at *this* stage of the siege about television coverage 'giving the game away'. There is no evidence from any of the accounts of the siege that *television* played any significant role in the hostage-takers' monitoring of the responses to their demands. All references to their concern with broadcasting mention radio coverage exclusively. Given the sophisticated monitoring devices being used by the security forces, it would have been known if the captors and their captives had also been watching television. Neither reports so far nor the reconstruction based on hostages' accounts have mentioned this possibility. It therefore seems reasonable to assume that control of television coverage of the siege-busting was as much concerned with the information available to the mass audience as to those inside the embassy. (Had they been watching television, they would have known about activities on the roof and the presence of monitoring equipment from the start, as these were disclosed by ITN on *News at Ten* on the first night of the siege.'[6])

These introductory points raise crucial questions about the extent of state control over the media during the siege. They also raise the question of what role was played by the media, and by broadcasting in particular. I shall try to answer these questions, insofar as published sources permit. My aim is not to chart in detail the media coverage of the siege – that is the purpose of the article by Cary Bazalgette and Richard Paterson – but to bring out the process of control and set this in the context of the British State's strategies for the control of 'news about terrorism'[7] during the past decade.

---

5 'After the siege: How TV covered the Kensington Gore' in *Broadcast* 12 May 1980.
6 *News At Ten* 30 April 1980.
7 The term 'terrorism' is inevitably value-laden. In the official discourse of the West, largely reproduced by the media, it refers to violent anti-state activities, but is never (or hardly ever) used of the repressive activities of states themselves, except those in the Communist bloc. For a more detailed account, see my essay ' "Terrorism", the media, and the liberal-democratic state: a critique of the orthodoxy' in *Social Research,* special issue 'On Violence', forthcoming.

Using the media

In the siege at the Iranian embassy, both the State and the hostage-takers had conscious strategies for making use of the media. The six gunmen who held twenty-six persons as prisoners in the embassy were members of an autonomist guerrilla movement from the predominantly ethnically Arab area of Iran. This region is called 'Khuzistan' by the Iranian central government and 'Arabistan' by the autonomists. The group's central goal was to draw attention to the oppression and exploitation of their area – the principal source of Iran's oil wealth – by the Khomeini regime. As it is frequently argued that acts of terrorism are inherently irrational, it is worth pointing out that the seizure of the embassy had a clear political rationale.[8] This was explained by 'Oan', the leader of the hostage-takers, in an interview conducted by the journalists Moutafa Karkouti and Mohammed Hashir Faruqi, who were also among the hostages:

> Question: What is the immediate goal you think you will achieve by carrying out this operation here and now?
>
> Oan: It will be publicity, propaganda and information outside. I realise that this operation or any similar operation which might happen in the future will not achieve our legitimate rights and might not force the Iranian government to grant Arabistan its autonomy, but what we can achieve from this kind of operation is to make our voice heard by world public opinion, especially in the light of the information blockade which the central government in Teheran is encircling us with, in addition to most of the Arab countries as well as the world media.[9]

a grievance by using extreme means, the guerrilla group also held certain Apart from this conscious and evidently rational intention to communicate assumptions about the British media: apparently not realising that 'information blockades' are not the sole prerogative of the Iranian government. Moustafa Karkouti, interviewed after the siege, recalled one of his conversations with the gunmen thus:

> 'They talked about the freedom of speech and said they thought it was more respected in Britain than in the rest of the world. They made it clear that they thought the media here are stronger than anywhere else in the Western world – they believed the British media and the British population would give their cause a fair hearing.'[10]

But their conception of the media, in particular during the exceptional circumstances of siege coverage, was naive in the extreme – hardly surprising as they appear to have had virtually no real knowledge of British politics and society. As the British media were, in effect, absorbed into the siege-breaking operations of the state, the Arabistan autonomists did not find it easy to get their message across. For the control of communications is one of the key weapons in the struggle between the security forces and those who challenge the authority of the State by actions of this kind. The account

---

8 See Conor Cruise O'Brien 'Liberty and Terror: illusions of violence, delusions of liberation' in *Encounter* vXLIX, n4 October 1977 for a cogent presentation of the orthodox liberal view.

9 An interview quoted in *Siege! Insight on the Great Embassy Rescue,* London, Hamlyn 1980 pp61-62. This is the *Sunday Times* reporting team's account which is also extensively used later hence referred to as *ST.*

10 *Obs* pp76-77.

which follows, therefore, necessarily has psychological warfare as one of its central themes. Aside from these two contradictory communicative strategies, there is another way in which the siege is especially illuminating about points of connection between the media and the State. The capture of two BBC Television newsmen, Chris Cramer, a news organiser, and Sim Harris, a sound technician, meant that the BBC was not just a reporter of the action at Princes' Gate, but also an actor of some significance, as I show below. With its own men on the inside, the Corporation's existing special significance to the State was enhanced. The presence of British journalists inside the embassy probably also had a more general effect on the media, encouraging the already considerable co-operation which had been built up in previous years.

The press and broadcasting were subject to general guidelines issued by the police on the second day of the siege. The request for self-censorship by the press went thus:

'During the course of the current hostage situation at the Iranian Embassy, the Commissioner seeks your co-operation in refraining from publishing or broadcasting details of the deployment of personnel in the immediate vicinity of the Embassy or the use of specialist equipment. The publication or broadcast of such information can provide valuable intelligence to the hostage-takers and by so alerting them could seriously jeopardise the safety of the hostages and the success of the operation. This memo will be cancelled as soon as operational circumstances permit.'[11]

The insistence that newspapers should not publish such details seems odd, given that the police were not going to allow them into the Embassy. It could presumably be justified on the ground that the police wished to control all publicity in case foreign radios picked up information which could assist the gunmen, or alternatively, to prevent press stories from being developed which the British broadcasting media would feel compelled to follow. Broadcasting seems to have been controlled more precisely than the press:

' "We worked more than closely with the authorities throughout the siege," an ITN spokesman said. And the BBC's involvement with the security forces became inevitable as soon as it became clear that two BBC men were actually among the hostages at the beginning.'[12]

After the siege, William Whitelaw, the Home Secretary, expressed his satisfaction at the broadcasting media's self-censorship:

'Inevitably events such as these are a matter of major public concern. They are bound to be covered by TV and radio. Had there been a moment when it was necessary to ask the authorities to exercise restraint then that restraint would have been asked for. But . . . such an occasion did not in the final event arise.'[13]

Such co-operativeness did not emerge out of the blue. There has been a long build-up.

---

11 *ST* p42.
12 *Broadcast* op cit. *Newsnight* (6 May 80) revealed that the police had asked the television organisations not to show the plans of the embassy.
13 ibid.

The State Security Background

The handling of the Iranian Embassy siege cannot be understood in isolation. As the journal *State Research* has pointed out, it reflects the State's current rethinking of 'administrative, policing and military aspects of internal security. Considerations of terrorism and those of demonstrations and strikes have both influenced the outcome'.[14] We should therefore look briefly at some recent observations on the emergence of a 'strong state' in Britain.

The development of what Nicos Poulantzas has termed an 'authoritarian statist' form of rule derives from at least two key intractable problems.[15] First, there is the continuing economic crisis, with its concomitant industrial relations struggles. The current 'monetarist experiment' of the Thatcher government involves the restructuring of capital by following the path of mass unemployment. Given this policy, as Andrew Gamble has observed, 'if the economy is to remain free, the state has to become strong; and nowhere stronger than in its dealings with organised labour'.[16] But although it is under the present administration that the armed forces and the police have been given a more overtly prominent role in countering 'subversion', their strengthening began in the not-too-distant Keynesian days, when other economic policies were being pursued. The second key problem is the persisting failure to achieve a solution to the socio-political problems of Northern Ireland. Against this backdrop, the outlines of Britain's 'secret state' (in E P Thompson's telling phrase) have become clearer during the past decade.

Its significant features include:
– the refurbishing of a 'parallel' emergency state apparatus for use against external attack and internal disorder;
– major shifts in the practice of policing including the emergence of a paramilitary 'third force' and the strengthening of the political police;
– the increased use of high technology surveillance against loosely-defined 'subversives' involving, for instance, uncontrolled data-banks and bugging devices;
– the use of official secrecy legislation against journalists;
– jury-vetting in political trials;
– restrictions upon, and aggressive policing of, demonstrations and picketing; and
– the trial use of repressive technology and special forces in Northern Ireland and the gradual application of the lessons learned in Britain itself.[17]
Although I cannot survey all the relevant material here, it is worth mention-

---

14 *State Research* 'How SAS ended the Princes' Gate Siege' in Bulletin n18 June-July 1980 p117.
15 *State, Power, Socialism* London, New Left Books 1978; see especially part 4.
16 'The Free Economy and the Strong State' in *The Socialist Register* 1979 p15.
17 Restricting oneself to books alone, information on all of these issues may be found in the following: Carol Ackroyd, Karen Margolis, Jonathan Rosenhead and Tim Shallice. *The Technology of Political Control* (2nd edn) London Pluto Press 1980; Tony Bunyan *The History and Practice of the Political Police in Britain* London Quartet Books 1977; Tom Bowden *Beyond the Limits of the Law* Harmondsworth, Penguin 1978; Peter Hain (ed) *Policing the Police* vv1 and 2 London John Calder 1979 and 1980; David Leigh *The Frontiers of Secrecy* London Junction Books 1980; E P Thompson *Writing by Candlelight* London The Merlin Press 1980. The *State Research* Bulletins are an indispensable source.

ing in passing that such evidently accelerating repressive tendencies within the liberal-democratic state-form should not be assumed necessarily to be irreversible.[18] But it is certain that without an effort to defend against such encroachments of existing political space, democratic freedoms eventually will be seriously imperilled.

Most relevant for my argument here are some of the changes in the State's emergency apparatus, the increased role of 'military aid to the civil power', and the unceasing efforts to control the media, especially broadcasting, in the reporting of political violence. Control of the Iranian Embassy siege was vested in the Civil Contingencies Committee (CCC). This body, called the National Security Committee (NSC) until 1975, was created in 1972 after the government's failure to break the miners' strike. The NSC drew together military, intelligence, police, Home Office and Department of Trade and Industry personnel, and was serviced by a full-time staff. Its tasks were two-fold: 'to prepare short-term contingency plans for emergency situations, and to redraw the standing 'War Plan' to meet a possible internal threat to the security of the state'.[19] From 1972 to 1975 a National Security Plan was worked out, involving the military in which preparations for intervention were made for situations ranging from limited strikes to civil war or invasion. As Tony Bunyan points out, this Plan is actually 'directed at an internal rather than an external enemy' and is basically concerned with effective counter-revolution.[20] The NSC/CCC drew up new guidelines about the occasions on which the Ministry of Defence could assist the police and the civil power. During the Iranian Embassy siege the SAS were brought in under the rubric of 'military aid to the civil power' (MACP), an arrangement which had been used on previous occasions against armed terrorists.

Although the SAS action at Princes' Gate may have been unprecedented, the use of an élite military unit in an urban action represents no more than the latest stage in the growing co-operation between police and army. The police have become increasingly prominent and vociferous over recent years as they have become involved in confrontations with political demonstrators, trade unionists and racial minorities, and as various forms of political violence have been encountered and have required suppression. The political imperative to control such 'law-and-order' problems has led to the construction of the 'third force' which has lately emerged to take up the paramilitary ground between the army and the more traditional functions of civil policing. Most controversial, probably, has been the activity of the Special Patrol Groups; despite official denials, these are armed paramilitary units, highly mobile and trained in riot control. But the SPGs are only the most visible part of the new 'third force'. According to *State Research,* there are now over 12,000 riot-trained police organised as Police Support Units and there has also been a growth in specialist units such as the anti-terrorism squad and the diplomatic protection group:

'The police's answer to providing a "third force" in the UK has been

---

18 See the interesting essay by Alan Wolfe 'Political Repression and the liberal democratic state' in *Monthly Review* December 1971, pp18-37, where this is argued more fully. Martin Kettle has argued for a cautious assessment of current trends in Britain in 'The Drift to Law and Order' in *Marxism Today* October 1980 pp20-27.
19 Tony Bunyan op cit p293.
20 ibid p277.

double edged. The anti-terrorist role is carried out by SPGs, newly formed Tactical Firearms Units . . . *and, as a last resort, by the army's Special Air Service (SAS)*. The public order role of a "third force" is undertaken by the Police Support Units and the SPG. Taken together this means that a qualitative change in the role of the police has . . . occurred.'[21]

It is clear from this analysis that the use of the SAS *in extremis* should be seen in the context of a drift toward tougher policing in the era of the 'technological cop'. The higher profile largely forced on the police by social change has created an atmosphere in which the deployment of troops becomes acceptable.

During the past decade, both Labour and Conservative governments have brought the SAS into operations, first in Northern Ireland, and now on the British mainland. The SAS's post-war role was primarily in the field of counter-insurgency actions during the gradual dissolution of the Empire. It became a bogeyman in Northern Ireland, where it was important both in combat against the IRA and in intelligence work.[22] The SAS's specific anti-terrorist role on the home front dates back to 1972, when the British government, like other Western European administrations, became concerned about the growth of political violence in the aftermath of Munich Olympics. A special 'counter-revolutionary warfare' (CRW) team was developed within the SAS. This was first deployed in Britain during the hijack of an aeroplane from Manchester in January 1975.[23] In December 1975, the SAS were present during the Balcombe Street siege; the mere announcement of their presence was apparently sufficient to make the cornered IRA men surrender. In that same month, the 'Europeanisation' of the anti-terrorist campaign gathered steam when, at a European Council meeting in Paris, it was decided that the European interior ministers should discuss how to combat terrorism. Meetings were held in June 1976 and in May 1977, and agreement was reached on the exchange of information about terrorism and techniques for dealing with terrorist incidents. The exchange of information and personnel between national security forces was also agreed. The first occasion on which this arrangement came into operation was in October 1977, when an SAS liaison team assisted the West German anti-terrorist unit GSG-9 to bring an end to the Lufthansa aircraft hijack at Mogadishu. Joint military co-operation of this kind would seem to be well-established now. A further instance was the SAS's involvement in the hunt for Aldo Moro, the kidnapped Italian Christian Democratic leader; the West German police also assisted in this.[24] Although it went unreported by the British media, the head of GSG-9, Ulrich Wegener, came to London during the Iranian

---

21 *State Research* Bulletin n19 August-September 1980 p152; emphasis added. This issue provides a searching analysis of these developments under the title 'Policing the Eighties: the Iron Fist'.
22 For a circumspect account see Tony Geraghty *Who Dares Wins: the story of the Special Air Service* London, Arms and Armour Press 1980 Ch 6.
23 Ibid pp168-169.
24 *State Research* Bulletin n5 April-May 1978 pp83-84; Bulletin n11 April-May 1979 pp84-85. The convergence over policing has a legal dimension too. The UK has extended the grounds for political extradition by its Suppression of Terrorism Act which ratifies the Council of Europe's Convention on the Suppression of Terrorism. *State Research* Bulletins nn4 and 8 February-March 1978 pp63-65 and October-November 1978 pp6-7.

Embassy siege.[25]

The full-scale commitment of the SAS to a domestic policing role resulted from a decision by the Callaghan government, after the successful military action at Mogadishu, to increase the CRW force substantially.

'From now on, each squadron was committed in turn to the CRW role on rotation, between tours in Northern Ireland and training sessions abroad. The implication of the decision was that *Britain was now a potential SAS operational zone in a way not previously contemplated*'.[26]

The commitment of resources has been significant, with the SAS receiving sophisticated weaponry, more training facilities (such as the 'Killing House' where close-quarter battle is practised), and the specialisation of CRW units in 'assault' and 'perimeter containment'.[27] These developments lie behind the dramatic eleven minute SAS action which took place on 5 May 1980.

'Law and Order' News and the State

State security actions such as the breaking of the Iranian Embassy siege are reported within a specific ideological framework, that of 'law-and-order' news. Stuart Hall and his colleagues have pointed out how this form of news has developed during the past decade within the context of a growing 'crisis of hegemony' in the British state. The continuing inability of governments to discipline labour and restore adequate profitability to capital has led towards a more authoritarian structure of rule, aspects of which were outlined earlier. The role of the media in winning consent for this shift from the social democratic consensus to the 'exceptional' law-and-order state has been crucial.[28] In a convergent analysis, Steve Chibnall has demonstrated the especial significance of the focus upon 'violence' in media discourse – in particular, the way in which it is used to police the boundaries of legitimate dissent. Within the media – created artefact of 'the violent society' wildly differing activities, with quite distinct causes, have come to be classified as fundamentally the same, as 'violent'. Thus 'mugging', the Angry Brigade bombings, IRA terror campaigns, criminal shootings of the police, football hooliganism, picketing and political demonstrations are represented within the dominant media discourse as the symptoms of an underlying social malaise – one for which the big stick of coercion becomes an increasingly attractive policy option.[29]

Winning consent for actions like those taken by the SAS at Princes' Gate involves an exceedingly complex process which is by no means just a cognitive one. Hijacks, assassinations, sieges and bombings – especially where they are directed against important people like Lord Mountbatten or Airey Neave – can provoke a sense that the entire society is under threat, and,

---

25 Reported by ABC network news on 2 May 1980.
26 Geraghty op cit p173; emphasis added.
27 Ibid pp174-175.
28 Stuart Hall *et al Policing the Crisis: Mugging, the State and Law and Order* London MacMillan 1978, esp chs 8 and 9. Also Stuart Hall *Drifting into a Law and Order Society* Cobden Trust Human Rights Day Lecture 1978.
29 Steve Chibnall *Law-and-order News: An Analysis of Crime Reporting in the British Press* London, Tavistock 1977. A splendidly succinct account.

as Philip Elliott has pointed out, they evoke ritualised responses from the media. For instance, where IRA activities have taken place on the British mainland, Elliott argues, the press and broadcasting have carried out 'affirmatory rituals' which emphasise the integrity of the social order. In Britain itself, it has been possible to presume adherence to a common symbolic order articulated by those in authority, whereas in Northern Ireland, given the social divisions there, such a mobilisation of common sentiment has proven impossible.[30] Similarly, Yves Lavoinne has argued that in cases of hostage-taking the dominant discourse emanating from the State and reproduced by the media stresses social consensus. Like Elliott, he points to the utilisation of a discourse which is quasi-religious, through which assaults on hostages are taken as affronts to the social collectivity, requiring terrorism to be evaluated as inhuman and irrational, as the very embodiment of chaos.[31]

All these analyses either conceptualise media coverage of violence in terms of its ideological effects, or alternatively as ritual performances which are simultaneously ideological practices. Although knowledge of how audiences perceive such accounts of violence and terrorism remains fragmentary, the evidence is stronger when it comes to the efforts made by State agencies to control media coverage. This suggests the background to the strategems adopted during the course of the Princes' Gate siege: the long-term efforts to control the flow of information and to secure a privileged place in media representations for the agents of the State. Two instances are briefly covered here: Sir Robert Mark's media strategy and the *de facto* partial censorship of broadcast news and current affairs coverage of Northern Ireland.

The Mark strategy

The degree of compliance shown by the British media during the Iranian Embassy siege derives in part from an initiative taken in 1972 by Sir Robert Mark, then Commissioner of the Metropolitan Police. Mark decided that his force should be more accessible to journalists, keeping back information 'subject only to *judicial restrictions, the right to individual privacy,* and the *security of the state*'.[32] The Metropolitan Police and the national media agreed upon the new terms of reference, and the Home Office ratified them. Mark's objective, as he later said in a General Memorandum issued on 24 May 1973 was to improve the police's relationship with the news media and 'consequently a better understanding on their part and that of the public of the force's problems and policies'.[33] But the new 'openness' was coupled with a determined effort to secure a measure of control over journalists. The General Memorandum made reference to a new press identity card. This

---

30 Philip Elliott 'Press Performance as Political Rituals' in H Christian (ed) *The Sociology of the Press and Journalism* The Sociological Review Monograph, Keele University, forthcoming.
31 Yves Lavoinne 'Presse et cohésion sociale: le case des prises d'otages' in *Revue Française de Communication* n2 Winter 1979 pp35-41.
32 Sir Robert Mark 'The Case of Great Britain' *Terrorism and the Media* International Press Institute 1980 unpaged; his emphasis.
33 Sir Robert Mark *Policing a Perplexed Society* London, George Allen and Unwin 1977 pp123-129.

enabled the police to sift the accredited journalists who hold the card from among the non-accrediated, and so to those they deemed unhelpful, in particular members of the radical press. Efforts by the National Union of Journalists to ensure that its card alone should constitute acceptable accreditation have so far been unsuccessful.[34] In September 1975, Mark organised a conference at Scotland Yard for the editors of the national media aiming to work out agreed procedures for 'mutual aid in dealing with kidnapping'. It was stressed that the lives of victims should be the principal concern and that 'any self-denying measures adopted by the press should apply to all'.[35] A distinction was made between 'commercial' and 'political' kidnappings and hijackings, 'political' offences being excluded from the agreement.[36] Hardly had this initiative been taken when Sir Robert's media policy was tested on three occasions with results that evidently satisfied him greatly. Two of the incidents were sieges and the third involved the news blackout of a kidnapping.

The sieges are obviously of greater interest here: what were their continuities with, and differences from, Princes' Gate? Unlike the latter, both the 1975 sieges were under the sole operational control of the Metropolitan Police. At the Spaghetti House in Knightsbridge, a group of three black gunmen held up the managers of a restaurant chain as they were about to bank the day's takings. The gunmen and their hostages were cooped up in the basement for the duration of the siege. The police put into operation a plan devised over the previous two years. The area was sealed off; the Home Office supplied liaison officers and psychiatrists to assist in the bargaining. The liaison officers were present in case troops were required and because some Italian nationals had been taken hostage. The police refused to bargain over the gunmen's demands, but provided them with a radio to help 'make clear to them, not only in shouted conversation, but through the news broadcasts, that they were going nowhere except to a cell, or by implication, to a mortuary, if they preferred that.'[37] The police were able to monitor activities inside the basement, first through sound recordings and later through a television picture supplied by surveillance devices developed by C7, Scotland Yard's technical support branch. The police found the media exceedingly co-operative. The editor of the *Daily Mail,* David English, agreed to kill a scoop about the arrest of one of the gunmen's accomplices. Mark sought the suppression of this information as he did not want it broadcast over the radio. Although Scotland Yard thanked the *Mail* and the rest of the press this was not published, provoking from Mark the disingenuous comment that 'It was almost as if they felt that there was something wrong in suppression of news in the interest of saving human life'.[38]

The Balcombe Street siege in December 1975 was a more clearly political event. The successful conclusion at the Spaghetti House – where no one was killed – gave the police added confidence in dealing with it. This siege was the climax to a bombing and shooting campaign by the IRA in Britain. The

34 *State Research* Bulletin n9 December 1978 – January 1979 pp29-30 and Bulletin n12 June-July 1979 pp106-7.
35 Sir Robert Mark 'The Case of Great Britain' op cit.
36 Peter Harland 'Terror and the Press. Politics and Greed: when lives are at stake where is the difference?' *IPI Report* v26 n10, November 1977 pp5-7.
37 Sir Robert Mark *In the Office of Constable* Fontana/Collins 1979 p199.
38 ibid p201.

police had set an ambush for the Provisional IRA active service unit involved, and after a chase from Mayfair four of its members were cornered in a private flat in Balcombe Street. The siege was handled according to the principles established a mere two months earlier. Once again, the Home Office sent a liaison officer, this time the SAS were moved in, and a team of psychiatrists was organised. The police controlled communications by cutting off the telephone and sending in a field telephone. The police strategy was, again, to play a waiting game, using time to wear down the resistance of the gunmen. Sir Robert Mark noted the important role played by the media:

> 'They asked, at our prompting, loaded questions such as "What about the safety of the hostages?" which enabled me to reply, "The best guarantee of their safety is the swift and ruthless retribution that will follow any harm that befalls them.'[39]

As the siege wore on, and the likelihood of sending in the SAS to shoot things out increased, the ambiguities of the media presence became obvious. On the one hand the police did not want any 'gory end to the siege' shown on the screen, and so they blocked off the view of the cameras. On the other hand, the media were again open to manipulation. As the flat was blocked off from the cameras 'coincidentally, both the *Daily Express* and the BBC disclosed that the SAS were there. This was, of course, broadcast on radio for the encouragement of the terrorists. Thereafter they could hardly surrender fast enough'.[40] In another account Mark says quite bluntly that the presence of the SAS was 'leaked' to the media – so there was little that was 'coincidental' about the disclosure.[41]

The police scored a further success in their relations with the media over the kidnapping for ransom of a Greek Cypriot girl, Aloi Kaloghirou, in November 1975, when Mark described their behaviour as 'opening a new era in police-press relations'.[42] Editors were requested not to publish the story in the public interest. In order to maintain the media's compliance, the police gave daily news conferences at Scotland Yard to inform journalists of progress. This news black-out was sustained for ten days until the girl was released unharmed. Chibnall has noted that many journalists were disenchanted by their end of the bargain. He also makes the point that such 'stops' are common practice in Britain, the only unusual feature being the extent of co-operation on this occasion.[43] After the Met's success with 'voluntary co-operation', The Home Office extended the London model of 'guidelines' to editors of the provincial press. However, these guidelines make no distinctions between 'political' and 'commercial' terrorism, and had in some cases been very widely interpreted by Chief Constables to mean that they can ask for a news blackout whenever publicity might endanger life.[44] Clearly, the establishment of such common procedures helped the authorities in their eventual handling of the Princes' Gate siege.

39 ibid p193.
40 ibid p194.
41 'The Case of Great Britain' op cit.
42 ibid.
43 Chibnall op cit pp186-187.
44 Harland op cit p7. It is worth noting that the Met's pressure on the media has continued. An important instance occurred when the Met tried to obtain censorship rights over programmes about the police after the controversy following the BBC television programme *Law and Order*. For details see *The Leveller* n28 July 1979.

Northern Ireland

The prime focus of 'news about terrorism' in recent years has been Northern Ireland.[45] Coverage in the British media, as Philip Elliott has pointed out, has tended to simplify violent incidents, to avoid historical background, to concentrate upon human interest stories, and to rely upon official sources. Even during periods of intense political activity, the story has been pre-eminently one of violence – and irrational, inexplicable violence at that.[46] Apart from weaknesses in the journalistic practice of the British media, there can be little doubt that the one-dimensional coverage reflects, at least in part, the effective long-term strategy of attrition waged by the State in its psychological warfare campaign. Most critical attention has been focused upon the British State's repeated efforts to control broadcast news and current affairs coverage without stepping over that fatefully delegitimising line into overt censorship. It is a struggle which has been waged patiently and with skill, despite an orchestrated series of apparently intemperate rows. On the other hand, there are indications that the pitch of intimidatory rhetoric has risen of late, and overt intervention looks more likely than ever.

The immediate relevance of this Northern Ireland coverage to the Iranian Embassy siege is that it had led to strained relations between the BBC and the Thatcher government. Two incidents involving the television reporting of political violence were the cause. The first was a *Tonight* interview in July 1979 with a representative of the Irish National Liberation Army, the group which assassinated the Tory Northern Ireland spokesman, Airey Neave. This resulted in representations to the BBC from the Northern Ireland Secretary, Humphrey Atkins, questions in the House of Commons, shocked reaction from Neave's widow, criticism from the Opposition Northern Ireland spokesman Merlyn Rees, and Mrs Thatcher's comment that she was 'appalled'. The BBC defended its action as responsible, in part by arguing that 'We believed that this was an exercise in exposing the enemies of democracy, not condoning them' and by pointing out that this was only the fourth member of a proscribed organisation to be interviewed in ten years.[47] Mrs Thatcher asked the Attorney-General to consider taking legal action. Later, reference was made to Section 11 of the Prevention of Terrorism Act – a new departure in English jurisprudence.[48] Under Section 11 it is a criminal act not to disclose information to the police about sus-

---

45 See Philip Schlesinger *Putting 'reality' together: BBC News* London Constable 1978, esp Ch 8; Anthony Smith 'Television Coverage of Northern Ireland' in *Index on Censorship* n2 1972; John Howkins 'Censorship 1977-78' and Chris Dunkley 'Programmes on Northern Ireland' in *Official Programme of the Edinburgh International Television Festival 1978*; *The British Media and Ireland* Campaign for Free Speech on Ireland 1979, and *Media Misreport N Ireland'*. Belfast Workers' Research Unit 1979.

46 Philip Elliott 'Reporting Northern Ireland' in *Ethnicity and the Media* Paris, Unesco 1977.

47 Ian Trethowan, Director-General of the BBC, in a letter to the Editor of *The Daily Telegraph*, 14 July 1979.

48 See Dorothy Connell, 'Reporting Northern Ireland, 1979-1980' in *Index on Censorship* v9 n3 June 1980.

pected terrorism, with the attendant possibility of five years' imprisonment or an unlimited fine, or both.

The reverberations had hardly died away before the second incident in which the BBC disgraced itself in the government's eyes, this time by filming an IRA roadblock in Carrickmore. Again, this led to frenzied declamations in Parliament against the BBC, which had not even transmitted the film, and which invariably gives painstaking attention to any decision to screen manifestations of IRA strength. On this occasion, after saying that it was time the BBC 'put its house in order', Mrs Thatcher said that the film would not be shown. The police – for the first time – seized an untransmitted copy of the film under the Prevention of Terrorism Act. The threat of a prosecution under the PTA hung over the BBC until July 1980. One immediate response was to tighten up further the guidelines on Northern Ireland reporting: there is little doubt that the exemplary intimidation of the BBC raised widespread anxiety among journalists about the legality of contacts with paramilitary organisations. The government's views became clear in August 1980, when, in a letter to BBC's Chairman, Sir Michael Swann, the Attorney-General, Sir Michael Havers, said that he thought both incidents constituted offences under Section 11 of the Prevention of Terrorism Act (1976). While denying any intent to censor, Havers accused the BBC of aiding terrorist propaganda and decried the fact that BBC personnel had not attempted to 'contact the appropriate authorities to pass on the information required' to apprehend or prosecute terrorists.[49] As the government has not chosen to test its arguments in the courts, the legal standing of its view remains obscure. Nevertheless, this pressure on the BBC to 'behave' forms part of the background to the period of the Iranian Embassy siege, and may have influenced the BBC in its eventual interpretation of its proper role as that of a model corporate citizen.[50]

The role of the media during the siege

'It is perhaps unreasonable to expect the police to think first of the press, though in this case they thought very carefully about the press because . . . they realised . . . that they were part of the game.'[51]

How, in detail, did the state authorities and the gunmen pursue their respective communicative strategies? In what ways was publicity a crucial factor in the management of the siege? My analysis is provisional; I merely seek to clarify the role of news broadcasting and of BBC personnel. It is also restricted by being based largely upon the accounts provided by the *Observer* and *Sunday Times* 'instant' books,[52] which are obviously in-

---

49 *The Guardian* 2 August 1980.
50 Perhaps the BBC's final expiation came when on 6 October 1980 it broadcast a eulogistic drama-documentary entitled *Airey Neave: A Will of Steel*. The title picked up a phrase of Mrs Thatcher's who, suitably enough, had the last word too.
51 Professor John Gunn, psychiatric adviser to the police during the siege, speaking on *The Editors* op cit.
52 In the development of the argument which follows I have tied particular statements to accounts given in the two 'siege' books. I have read them with particular questions in mind concerning the role of the media, whereas the books have been written with that as an important, but subordinate issue. The critical reading offered below points up some crucial moments which were left rather implicit in the books, and as it traverses controversial ground, especially concerning the relationship between broadcasting and the State, it is crucial to provide evidence for each turn in the argument.

complete. A good deal more of the 'story' of the siege has yet to come out. Nonetheless, the books do provide a great deal of material which illuminates, in particular, the importance attached to broadcasting. As I pointed out in the introduction, radio reporting seem to have been of paramount significance, as the gunmen and the hostages had receivers. There is no clear evidence whether any television viewing went on, but it seems reasonable to suppose that it did not. Newspapers were not allowed into the Embassy (*ST* p115).

The growth of the Civil Contingencies Committee (CCC) as part of the emergent 'strong state', which I noted earlier is of especial importance here, since, unlike the Spaghetti House and Balcombe Street sieges, operational control was vested in the Civil Contingencies Committee rather than in the police. It is also worth recalling that since the early 1970s the British government has refused to countenance the escape of hijackers and hostage-takers – a policy in keeping with the emergent European position on anti-terrorism – and has increasingly made the SAS a part of domestic policing under the formula of 'military aid to the civil power'. In the present case, the unit used was the Special Air Services' Special Operations Group, SAS-SOG.[53] The deployment required the formal request of the Metropolitan Police Commissioner, Sir David McNee. The police decision eventually to call on these crack troops, however, can only be understood by recognising the guiding framework of constraints which emanated from the Civil Contingencies Committee, or 'COBRA', as it was labelled by the media. From the start the siege was correctly perceived to be political in character. It was a calculated gesture aimed at the Iranian government, and, given the complex international ramifications, this meant that direct British government involvement was inevitable. The CCC was chaired by William Whitelaw, the Home Secretary, and had fifteen staff members drawn from relevant Departments of State, the Civil Service and the security and intelligence forces. The Foreign and Commonwealth Office was represented by Douglas Hurd, and the Ministry of Defence by Barney Heyhoe (*Obs* p23; *ST* p43).

DAY 1: WEDNESDAY 30 APRIL The Embassy was seized at 11.32 am. At noon, the commercial radio's IRN broadcast a report about the seizure; shortly afterwards, they indicated in an eye-witness report from the scene that the police were on the Embassy roof (*ST* p20). The gunmen's leader, Oan, was evidently upset by a BBC report early in the afternoon which suggested that he and his group were Iraqis (*ST* p30). He wished to correct this view. At this point, *The Guardian* made contact through the Embassy's telex and managed to establish that the group were Arabistan autonomists before Oan terminated the interview (*ST* p31; *Obs* p25). It was the *journalists* among the hostages who suggested that their captors make contact with the media. At 2.45 pm the Syrian journalist Moustafa Karkouti managed to get in touch with the BBC's External Services at Bush House, and explained that

> 'he was a hostage acting under orders to pass on a message. The men holding him wanted ninety-one prisoners in Arabistan to be released. And the BBC should also note that the hostage-takers were from Iran – not Iraq' (*ST* p31; *Obs* p25).

---

53 *State Research* Bulletin n18 op cit p118.

This was the first time this demand was transmitted. The Metropolitan Police received details of the demands at 3.15 pm according to their log. Either they were already tapping the line, or alternatively the BBC made them available (*ST* p32). At 3.45 pm Karkouti spoke to the BBC's External Services again, and Oan relayed his demand that the ninety-one prisoners be released the next day or the Embassy and the hostages would be blown up. Some fifteen minutes earlier, Chris Cramer, the captured BBC news organiser, had telephoned or telexed BBC Television Centre listing the gunmen's demands. Apart from the threat to blow up the Embassy, there was a request for Arab ambassadors to mediate between the gunmen and the British government and a promise that the non-Iranian hostages would not be harmed. The request for mediation was suppressed, at the request of the police, for three days (*ST* p33; *Obs* pp26-27, 137-138). Before the first day ended, the telephone links had been used to make several personal calls, and in addition the gunmen had spoken to the Iranian foreign minister, Sadeq Ghotzbadeh, who had refused any compromise (*ST* p33).

Although the gunmen were able to make use of their access to the media to put across their aims during this first day, these were not relayed in full detail at the request of the police. According to the editor of BBC Television News, the telex from Cramer was immediately made available to the police.[54] The contacts with Bush House probably were as well – given the position of its two men inside the Embassy, the BBC had assumed a crucial role. Even without this chance the Corporation was apparently considered important by the gunmen. In his account of the siege, Chris Cramer notes:

> 'Barely a matter of minutes after the firing and the shouting had stopped, I chose to identify myself to the gunmen as a BBC journalist... On reflection, I was taking a stupid risk by singling myself out as representing what, to many worldwide, is a less than perfect organisation. The crazy thing was that it actually worked. The BBC's credibility rating is obviously high with terrorists.... They seemed to know the time of every bulletin in English, Persian and Arabic. Without that kind of worldwide publicity things might have got very nasty.'[55]

DAY 2: THURSDAY 1 MAY   Only some of the press acceded to the police request not to mention the noon deadline for the release of the prisoners in Iran – namely *The Times, The Guardian* and *The Daily Telegraph* (*Obs* p44). But this was of little note; once again, the BBC was of paramount importance. At 6.20 am, at Oan's request, Karkouti again telephoned Bush House to remind the British public that the noon deadline stood, but that the non-Iranian hostages would not be harmed in the meantime. The duty editor of *Radio Newsreel* managed to engage Oan in a lengthy interview which was subsequently broadcast on early morning domestic bulletins (*ST* pp35-39; *Obs* pp45-47, 138). Alan Protheroe, has surmised, presumably on an informed basis, that this recording was made available to the police before it was broadcast.[56] The gunmen evidently kept listening to the radio,

54 'In the case of the telex that was sent to us from Chris Cramer on the first day, the contents of that were, in fact, made immediately available to the police. The police had copies of the telex. They talked to the people who had received the telex at this end.' Alan Protheroe in *The Editors* op cit.
55 'Inside the embassy' in *Broadcast* 19 May 1980.
56 *The Editors* op cit.

because they heard Karkouti's voice on the BBC, and also mentioned that Tehran radio had broadcast the rejection of their demands (*Obs* p48). Chris Cramer, who had been taken ill overnight, was released by the gunmen at 11.20 am. He was evidently an important source of information for the police; for instance, he told them that PC Lock, the Diplomatic Protection Squad Officer held captive, still had his gun (*Obs* p52; *ST* p41). Cramer says nothing about what he told the police. He had promised the gunmen, obviously under duress, not to reveal anything.[57] However, his unconstrained attitude is revealed in this comment:

> 'After my release, lying in a hospital bed, I mentally pleaded with all the broadcasters to do exactly what the gunmen wanted, to co-operate fully with the Police and the Home Office . . . if necessary to broadcast complete lies. Anything to get the remaining hostages out and to safety. That thought process is completely alien to all my professional beliefs. But, as one of my close BBC friends said last week, professional beliefs don't save lives.'[58]

By the afternoon of the second day, the gunmen had modified their position. They dropped the demand for the release of the prisoners, and asked instead that their demands be broadcast and that three Arab ambassadors arrange for a plane to fly them out. Such a solution was closed off by the security policy of the British State. The government, operating through the CCC, did not want any Arab mediators it could not control. It was worried about the requested use of the Iraqi ambassador, given Iran-Iraq tensions. And it did not want to seem to be endorsing the seizure by taking a soft line (*Obs* pp58-59; *ST* pp43, 45). Karkouti, an astute observer, is quoted as noting retrospectively that

> 'from the second evening, I felt it was being treated by those outside the Embassy as a security problem and it was going to end in a critical situation. It was no longer a political situation and that was very frightening' (*Obs* p57).

In truth, it had been defined as a security situation *from the very beginning*, in line with the developments in anti-terrorist policy since the early 1970s. During the second day the police cut off the telex and telephone links, and the gunmen were entirely dependent upon the police field telephone or conversations through the window for communications (*Obs* p50; *ST* p46). By the end of the day, therefore, the media had no direct access to informants inside the Embassy, and could reveal nothing of the changing intentions of the gunmen.

DAY 3: FRIDAY 2 MAY   It was on this day that the BBC became directly involved as an intermediary between the gunmen and the police, although much is not yet known about the precise role of its personnel. Cutting off communications caused the gunmen intense frustration, and led to the first death threat against a particular hostage. However, despite the plea of PC Lock that there was 'a man about to be killed' unless Oan was allowed to talk to the media by telephone or telex, again this request was refused. Oan modified his demand, and asked to speak to someone at the BBC known

---

57 A point he made during an interview on the BBC television programme *Newsnight*, 5 May 1980.
58 *Broadcast* op cit.

to Sim Harris. Apparently, this idea originated with Sim Harris, the BBC sound recordist, who had suggested the previous night that his captors speak to a senior BBC executive to find out why their demands had not been broadcast.[59] The police had then said no-one was available, which was false.

After the death threat, however, the police did contact the BBC, asking for the Television Home News Editor, John Exelby. As it turned out, the Managing Editor of Television News, Tony Crabb, took his place and departed for the Embassy at 9 am (*Obs* pp73-74; *ST* p47). By 9.30 Crabb was talking to Harris at the Embassy (*Obs* p74; *ST* p51 differs, and presumably wrongly says this conversation did not take place until the afternoon).[60] Harris asked why the gunmen's demands had not been broadcast. Crabb asked 'What demands?'; this seems odd, as Cramer had telexed them through to Television Centre on the first day. Although the *Observer* team comments that 'it was never clear why the police had decided to keep from the Press the fact that gunmen had demanded the presence of Arab ambassadors to act as mediators' (*Obs* p74) their own evidence indicates that the BBC *did* have this information (*Obs* p27 and p131). *So the BBC alone of all the media colluded with the police in keeping this crucial demand secret.*[61]

Crabb had been told by the police that he could offer nothing, and that he should keep the content of the conversation to himself. At the centre of this request was the suppression of the key demand for the intervention of the Arab ambassadors; this apparently 'neither surprised nor particularly upset' Crabb (*Obs* pp74-75). He took notes of the gunmen's demands:

> 'Oan said he wanted:
> 1) a coach to take gunmen, hostages, and one Arab ambassador – unnamed – to Heathrow;
> 2) the non-Iranian hostages to be released at Heathrow;
> 3) an aircraft to take the remaining hostages, gunmen, and Ambassador to a Middle East country – again unspecified – and there released.' (*ST* p52)

It appears that the communication of their aims now obsessed the gunmen, who did not doubt that they would be allowed a safe passage. It was only at 11.30 that night that a BBC bulletin referred to the new demands.

> 'But, to Oan's fury, the BBC not only truncated his statement, but got it wrong. The broadcast said that the gunmen wanted the three Arab ambassadors to negotiate not with the *British* government, which was the fact, but with Iran.' (*ST* p52)

---

59 According to his diary printed in *The Day of the SAS: The inside story of how Britain ended the siege of Princes' Gate*. This war comic is *The Daily Express*'s siege special. On the whole its interest is iconographic rather than factual.
60 Harris' diary supports *The Observer* version.
61 Given the importance of this point the evidence for it should be quoted in full: 'At 5.30 Karkouti and Cramer were allowed to use the telephone again. Karkouti called the BBC World Service at Bush House and Cramer BBC Television at Shepherd's Bush, dictating the statement of the gunmen's demands, the threat to blow up the Embassy if they were not met, *a request for Arab ambassadors to mediate,* and a promise that the non-Iranian hostages would not be harmed . . . the demand for Arab ambassadors to mediate was concealed for three long days.' (*Obs* p27) Astonishingly, even media pundits like Simon Jenkins of *The Economist,* who chaired *The Editors* discussion, seem not to have grasped this point: Jenkins said on the programme: '. . . there was an occasion when the police failed to communicate . . . with the media that the gunmen were demanding that their ambassadors act as liaison officers. Now, why didn't the police communicate that to the broadcasting authorities, even though they didn't want it to be broadcast?' Well, in one case at least they didn't need to.

This error seems quite extraordinary, unless, of course, it was an intentional one. But the two books differ about this incident. The *Observer* account contains no reference to a BBC bulletin late on Day 3, but reports that at the beginning of Day 4 Oan

'. . . was listening, as ever, to what the radio had to say about the siege, preoccupied with the demand for three ambassadors which the police had not yet made public. He heard Radio Tehran say that the ambassadors were needed to negotiate with the Iranian government, not the British.' (*Obs* p81)[62]

This indicates that, rather than getting the demands wrong, the BBC did not report them at all – a point which merits further inquiry.

DAY 4: SATURDAY 3 MAY   By the late morning, the gunmen were evidently getting edgy about the non-broadcasting of their demands, as well as the non-appearance of any ambassadors. They demanded to see Crabb once more. As tension mounted, the police realised that something had to be done about a public statement, and made urgent efforts to find Crabb, who was unavailable until the afternoon (*Obs* pp82-83). The bugging of the Embassy was obviously important in providing intelligence, not least in allowing the police to monitor the gunmen's reactions to the radio reporting. The police apparently knew 'how disastrous the previous night's inaccuracies had been' (*ST* p56), whether these are attributed to the BBC or Tehran radio.

Tony Crabb reappeared at the Embassy just before 2 pm. He was clearly an intermediary for police demands, and, during the hour before he again spoke to the gunmen, seems to have received a briefing.

'The police asked me to stress that anything they did for the gunmen had to be reciprocated by an act of goodwill from them. I was asked to emphasise that my own presence at the Embassy was a concession from the police.'

To Harris's question about why the statement had not been broadcast, Crabb replied that there had been a 'misunderstanding'. Given the evident anger of the gunmen's leader, the police negotiator on the spot said that the statement would be taken down correctly. Either the police officer or Crabb took down the statement (*ST* p56; *Obs* p84): the accounts conflict. The gunmen demanded that the statement be broadcast accurately. Crabb hesitated, but the police agreed the terms provided that two hostages were released (*Obs* p84; *ST* p56). There were delays before the statement was broadcast, caused by the time taken by the CCC in evaluating its consequences. Oan threatened to kill a hostage unless the statement was published, but was prevailed upon to release one instead. 'Almost immediately, the police rang back to say thank you and told Oan that the statement would be released in full on the BBC World Service at 9.00.' (*Obs* p84-85; *ST* 56-57). This formulation suggests very close co-operation.

At 8.35 pm Deputy Assistant Commissioner Peter Neivens, the police spokesmen, read the statement at a press conference. He prefaced it with the comment that: 'It is very important, and I stress very important, that it is given maximum amount of coverage.' (*Obs* p85)

In addition to this, according to Alan Protheroe, even as the statement

---

62 This account accords with Sim Harris's diary, *Daily Express,* op cit p56.

was being read to the assembled newsmen

'... there came one high-level call to me, underlining just how urgent the broadcasting of those demands was ... In the event everybody ran the story – but it was run because it was a good story-development. Little had come out of the siege; here was a top cop spelling out the newest demands, and again asking for the maximum publicity for it. There was, frankly, no need to stress the urgency: a journalistic assessment had already been made concerning the story, and TV News, BBC Radio News, ITN and IRN/LBC were in there, running the story as a news flash.'[63]

Inside the Embassy, the radios were tuned in to IRN and the BBC World Service. IRN broadcast the statement at seven minutes to nine. The captors and their captives also listened to BBC Radio 4 and to the BBC World Service. Both the books and Sim Harris's diary describe the immense relief inside the Embassy as the gunmen's objective was realised. Subsequently a further hostage was released. The statement assured the British government and people that no harm was intended towards the hostages; that three Arab ambassadors were required for the purposes of negotiating the safety of all concerned; and that the reason for the seizure of the Embassy was to draw attention to the plight of Arabistan (ST pp85-87).

DAY 5: SUNDAY 4 MAY The high-water mark of media involvement had been reached on the previous day. The early news bulletins spoke of the Arab ambassadors being willing to assist and of the Red Cross standing by. (Obs p88) The British government stuck to its policy, however and could not reach a working agreement with any of the Arab ambassadors. It refused to permit the gunmen to go free, and was not prepared to allow the ambassadors to negotiate. It wished them merely to convey the terms of surrender. That evening a further hostage was released, and now the gunmen demanded one Ambassador and a safe conduct. (ST p76) During the day, the Iranian foreign minister had suggested that thousands of Iranians were ready to storm the Embassy. Although the BBC's engineers had decided after studying its aerials that the Embassy was capable of receiving Tehran radio, no reference was made to Ghotzbadeh's speech. Alan Protheroe has commented that this was to 'avoid provoking the gunmen'[64] and has added that there had been 'requests not to broadcast things' which he had known were on Tehran radio.[65]

DAY 6: MONDAY 5 MAY This day began with anxiety about the non-appearance of the Arab ambassadors and with the gunmen's intense awareness that security preparations were going on all around the Embassy. Both Harris and PC Lock pleaded with the police negotiators to make some progress over the ambassadors, which they could hardly do as the issue was out of their hands. One of the negotiators assured them that discussions were still going on and that they should listen to the BBC World Service at 12 o'clock for confirmation. (Obs p108; ST p82) This news broadcast reported meetings at the Foreign Office, but nothing about any decisions being reached.[66] The stalemate produced a decisive action from the gunmen: they

63 The Listener op cit.
64 ibid.
65 The Editors op cit.
66 According to Sim Harris, Daily Express op cit p60.

shot a hostage. This ensured the eventual entry of the SAS.

What emerges from this reading of the best existing accounts of the siege is that the BBC was of especial significance. Two aspects of its role need to be considered further: the use of its personnel for mediation, and to the extent to which the Corporation may have received special briefings.

The role of Tony Crabb was obviously important, and it is worth noting the ways in which it was described. According to *Broadcast,* he

'. . . at one stage acted as go-between for security authorities. (He later explained "At no time did I act as a negotiator, but I willingly abstained from taking any journalistic advantage of my involvement in order to be of some help to the negotiators").'[67]

Alan Protheroe echoes this formula in his article on the siege:

'Crabb, for three days, deliberately and honourably stopped working as a journalist and remained at the disposal of the police. He at no time acted as a negotiator, but his presence may have been helpful in defusing a tense situation, and the advice he was able to give the negotiators was crucial in the resolution of the siege.'[68]

Crabb himself is quoted elsewhere as commenting that 'although the gunmen felt that I was a journalist, I didn't feel that I was there in that capacity.' (*Obs* p83)

All these statements reveal an anxiety to play down the BBC's involvement. The way in which Crabb took no journalistic advantage of the situation was presumably by deciding not to broadcast the demands on Day 3. But the BBC was already in possession of the crucial demand for mediation. although not, of course, the specific demands about the arrangements for the safe conduct. In any case, Crabb could not himself have taken journalistic advantage. He would have had to refer the matter upwards, at least to the Director of News and Current Affairs, if not the Director-General. The suppression of the information must have been a policy decision. If Crabb was not there as a journalist, then what was his role? Protheroe suggests that his advice was crucial to the police, but does not say how. The *Guardian* (6.5.80) suggests that the use of Crabb as 'an independent, non-police representative' was important in securing the gunmen's trust, and indeed that would seem to be so. Similar suggestions were made in television broadcasts during the siege. *Nationwide* (2.5.80) described Crabb as a 'recognisable BBC figure', but added that he had 'joined the police team'. *News at Ten* (2.5.80) reported on the arrival at the Embassy of John Exelby, the BBC Television Home News Editor who was there 'to prove that not everyone surrounding the embassy are police'. *Newsnight* (2.5.80) said that Crabb had established rapport with the hostage-takers. These characterisations suggest the importance of the role played by the BBC's quasi-negotiator – delaying tactics on the third and fourth days were clearly assisted by his presence. The cautious descriptions of Crabb's role probably reflect anxiety within the BBC over its entanglement with State agencies, and about the effect on its credibility on the future. Looking back the day after the ending of the siege, *Newsnight* insisted that Crabb was not involved in the negotiations. But although Crabb was not a fully-fledged negotiator in that he was not empowered to offer anything, he did help to secure the release of two

67 *Broadcast* op cit.
68 *The Listener* op cit.

hostages as a trade-off for broadcasting the gunmen's demands on Day 4. His self-ascribed role, if not journalistic, must have been that of a responsible citizen assisting the State in the maintenance of law and order. This setting aside of journalistic professionalism *in extremis* echoes Chris Cramer's sentiment in the quotation cited earlier.

The other noteworthy aspect of the BBC's role concerns the extent of its contacts with the State. Alan Protheroe has deplored 'the reluctance of the Authorities to trust the media, and to recognise that we are, actually, immensely experienced and honourable individuals.' The whole tenor of his argument is that the authorities ought to trust the media more, and that there might be 'some kind of system where much more information can be given to editors'.[69] He denies that there was a 'hot line' by which instructions from Higher Authority caused the suppression of information', stressing instead the ability of journalists to work out the State's strategies for themselves.

> 'It was possible, for example, by deduction from hints and straight information, to establish that the gunmen were infinitely more professional than, say, the 'hoods' of the Spaghetti House, or the IRA men of Balcombe Street. Our assessment, made at the earliest stage, turned out to be absolutely correct: *we were sure that this siege could not be resolved without the intervention of the SAS or a similar group.*'[70]

How could they be so sure? Undoubtedly, there is something to be said for journalistic experience. Many of the reporters at Princes' Gate had been at the previous London sieges, and from the beginning there was speculation about the SAS being brought in. Reporters noticed a Landrover with a Herefordshire number plate (the SAS are based in that county), and were suspicious of the 'gasmen' digging up the road near the embassy. But what Protheroe says seems to go beyond this reportial conventional wisdom, for he has amplified his opaque reference to 'hints' by talking of 'certain briefings which I had received as an individual' which made him conclude that the siege would result in violence.[71] This seems pretty incontrovertible evidence of top-level links between the BBC and the security forcs, and calls into question the argument that journalistic experience alone produced the right decisions. Also puzzling is Protheroe's confident assertion that he knew the television coverage of the final intervention could not damage the operation. Indeed, he seems to have had a good idea that the SAS were going to be used when he said:

> 'I don't think there was any possibility of bodies coming out ... I am utterly convinced from the dispositions of troops and policemen that it was extremely unlikely that anybody would walk out of there unless he was surrendering.'[72]

If detailed briefings were not available, Protheroe's own military intelligence background could have led him to such inferences, along with contributory assessments from other BBC defence experts like Peter Snow and Christopher Wain.

---

69 *The Editors* op cit.
70 *The Listener* op cit; my emphasis.
71 *The Editors* op cit.
72 ibid.

The BBC has frequent informal consultations with members of the military and police establishments. One occurred some six months before the Princes' Gate siege at the closed Abingdon Conference on *Politics Extremism, the Media and the Law,* held on 16-18 November 1979. This brought together top media personnel, Civil Servants, soldiers, policemen and politicians from Israel, West Germany, the USA and Britain. It was sponsored by the BBC together with the International Press Institute and the Ford Foundation. Amongst the participants were the BBC's Director of News and Current Affairs, Richard Francis, and Kate Adie, the reporter who covered the SAS's taking of the Embassy. Another participant was Deputy Assistant Commissioner John Dellow, the officer in charge of operations during the siege. According to the report by *State Research*:

> 'One of the Case Studies in which those present participated concerned the seizure of hostages in a Western capital by a dissident movement from the Middle East. The dénouement of this case study was a shootout, organised by the Government, which, although it had carried on talking had throughout never intended to allow the hostage-takers to escape. Discussion centred on whether a newspaper, which had been told that the hostage-takers were in the end to be ambushed and shot rather than any deal being struck, should release the information.'[73]

Knowledge of such scenarios, coupled with Protheroe's 'certain briefings' and 'hints', suggest that top broadcasters could hardly have been unaware of the government's intentions on the occasion of the Princes' Gate siege, and that some of these expectations must have been transmitted, via briefings, to the reporting teams.

But if this is so, then why was the actual live courage so incoherent? The trade magazine *Broadcast* has noted that it was

> '. . . obvious for at least half an hour before the assault took place that a turning-point had been reached in the siege. Both ITN and BBC News had broadcast news flashes at 19.14 and 19.11 respectively, announcing that the body of a man, probably a hostage, had been pushed out of the embassy. Newspaper reports speak of increased police activity toward 19.18.'[74]

On the face of it, well-briefed reporters familiar with previous anti-hijack and anti-siege actions should have been able to interpret the event more adequately than they did. Admittedly, the 'frame charges' used by the SAS to blow out the windows were a new element, but the 'stun grenades' were familiar from the Mogadishu hijack rescue in 1977. Also unclear is the significance of ITN's camera at the rear of the Embassy, ingeniously smuggled in on the last day of the siege in defiance of the police, who had wanted the preparations round the back to be unobserved. Oddly enough, no reports of police or Home Office displeasure at this have emerged. The ITN director in the field was aware of the immediate build-up to the SAS attack three minutes before it happened. (*ST* p116)

A final point about the television coverage is that the most complete

73 *State Research* Bulletin n18 op cit p119. The two other scenarios discussed at the conference concerned the reporting of extreme Left and Right politics and the question of how to handle torture allegations against the security forces in Northern Ireland.
74 *Broadcast* op cit.

programme available is undoubtedly that in the hands of the security forces. Throughout the siege, events at Princes' Gate were continuously monitored by police cameras. Television viewers who knew what to look for could see them, and in the 'aftermath' coverage there was film of the cameras being dismantled. A police helicopter was flying overhead throughout the ending of the siege. Such helicopters are generally fitted out with television cameras, and six months after the siege viewers of the BBC's *Nine O'Clock News* saw some of the pictures taken from this vantage point. A further source of televised material is the BBC. It is reliably reported that videotapes of the SAS action have been made available to the regiment. On previous occasions, the BBC has been rather sensitive about such co-operation. For instance, there was concern in top editorial circles about the Royal Ulster Constabulary having 'pirated' a videotaped recording of a controversial programme about 'The Republicans' shown in December 1977, as this could give the appearance of collusion with the security forces. The BBC's minutes noted that the

> 'BBC must respond to any formal legal requests for access to transmitted material but in all other cases it always considered most carefully the consequences of making it available, both in relation to the BBC's own position and to that of individual members of staff'.[75]

During the same meeting Alan Protheroe said that the BBC had given film for 'instructional purposes' to the Ministry of Defence and the Metropolitan Police.

It is unclear at present whether ITN also co-operated by releasing film of the siege, but it is known that they would not have raised objections had they been asked. Such requests are largely a matter of form as television coverage can anyway be monitored and taped by the police. Evidently the SAS had their own videotape of the rescue. Mrs Thatcher, who was visiting their tactical headquarters for a celebration party on the night of the action, was invited to watch a recording.[76] Of special interest to the authorities would be the pictures not being transmitted, especially those from ITN, which switched between cameras at the front and the rear of the Embassy. Somewhere there must exist a fascinatingly detailed compilation tape of the way the SAS stormed the Princes' Gate Embassy – one which will never receive a public showing.

Some conclusions

Sieges, hijacks, and hostage-takings raise major problems for the media. There is strong pressure on them from the State, supported by public opinion, to act 'responsibly' in order to save life. Such pressure is perhaps most intense on radio and television, whose transmissions may be directly monitored by the gunmen. In the Iranian Embassy siege, radio news was of unquestionable importance as the gunmen were aiming to obtain airtime for their views: the broadcasting of their demands undoubtedly saved several lives. The BBC became particularly involved in the bargaining process on two days of the siege, and although its representatives have played down

75 *News and Current Affairs minutes* 7 March 1978, n115.
76 Geraghty op cit, p181.

their contradictory position, the Corporation seems to have put the demands of safeguarding law and order before any journalistic imperatives. The presence of two BBC men among the hostages gave them good institutional reasons for this; less clear is whether there will be any future consequences of such close compliance with the security forces' aims. Alan Protheroe's plea for greater 'trust' from the authorities could surely result in an even greater absorption into the crisis-management apparatus of the State. A somewhat different position has been taken by the editor of *The Observer*, Donald Trelford, who suggested in *The Editors* on BBC TV that 'better communication' was needed between the police and journalists, but reserved the right of editors to decide what to use. Such a position is plainly more tenable for newspapers which are not so proximate to the state as broadcasting.

It would be dangerous to accept too readily the public rhetoric of State officials about the need to save life. Without being too cynical – such humanitarian concerns are certainly not totally absent – they do have other priorities. Foremost among them are State security and the maintenance of political credibility by stamping firmly on any manifestation of 'terrorism'. The duality of official attitudes is well-illustrated by some remarks from Sir Robert Mark. When agreeing procedures for covering kidnapping with editors in 1975, he 'emphasised at the outset that *the safety of the victims should be the primary concern* of the police and, hopefully, of the Press'.[77] Compare this with his reflections on the Balcombe Street siege:

> 'Though we were deeply concerned about the safety of the hostages I did not consider for one moment that they were not expendable. I felt heartfelt sympathy for Mr and Mrs Matthews but felt that *human life was of little importance when balanced against the principle that violence must not be allowed to succeed.*'[78]

Raison d'état thus guides the actions of State agencies; it would therefore seem appropriate to evaluate carefully all requests for total co-operation. Otherwise the media are apt to become tools of a given 'psywar operation', and this would foreclose any basis for criticism of the deficiencies in the State's conduct.

Although it is not my purpose in this article to raise detailed questions about the conduct of the Iranian Embassy siege, it is worth noting that it was not an unmitigated success. Most obviously, there was loss of life – five gunmen killed by the SAS and two hostages killed by the gunmen. The eventual shoot-out stemmed from the British government's determination not to allow the gunmen to go free. As the *Sunday Times* team comment: 'in the final analysis, the Government was prepared to sacrifice the lives of the hostages if necessary rather than give in.' (*ST* p71) The deaths were politically acceptable, because, to be blunt, they did not involve any of the British hostages. Indeed, this 'invisibility' of the non-British hostages characterised the handling of the story, coupled with the adulation for the undoubted bravery of PC Lock. (This is dealt with in detail in the article which follows.)

To their credit, several newspapers – the *Observer*, the *Sunday Times*,

---

77 'The case of Great Britain' op cit; emphasis added.
78 *In the Office of Constable*, op cit p193; emphasis added.

and the *Guardian* – did raise questions about the circumstances in which the SAS killed the gunmen, and about the wisdom of the government's policy in not bringing in the ambassadors earlier. On the first question, using hostages' accounts, both *The Observer* and *The Sunday Times* revealed that after killing a second hostage, and attempting to kill two more, three of the gunmen threw away their arms and surrendered. (*Obs* pp119-120; *ST* pp124-128) Two of these gunmen, having been identified by the hostages, were shot by the SAS. Both the *Sunday Times* and *Observer* writers expressed unease about the circumstances in which this took place, but both papers argued that there was little else the SAS could have done, given the un-certainty about whether the men were still armed or whether they could blow up the embassy. Tony Geraghty, the *Sunday Times*'s defence corres-pondent (and historian of the SAS), had no reservations:

> 'The only way of saving the hostages' lives . . . was to kill the terrorists unless it was unequivocally clear that they were identifying themselves for what they were and were very plainly surrendering. This was far from clear at the time. . . .'[79]

Nevertheless, questions do remain. The *Observer* team asked 'Did the SAS team have orders to take no prisoners – and if so who issued them?' (*Obs* p119) This question obviously runs across the purely situational explanation offered for the SAS's action – that in the battleground which was the em-bassy they had no choice but to eliminate the enemy. The *Sunday Times* investigators were at odds with their defence correspondent:

> 'The crucial question is, had the gunmen dropped all of their weapons and genuinely surrendered before they were shot? And if so, can their killings possibly be justified on any legal and moral basis?' (*ST* p127)

Tony Geraghty has, in fact, suggested that there certainly was a strong legal basis for the action:

> '. . . the SAS is stringently subject to the rule of law, for which the police are responsible. The Army's CRW (counter-revolutionary war-fare) teams are reminded of this by a litany of ground rules, more elaborate even than the "Yellow Card" governing the rules of engage-ment for soldiers in Northern Ireland. It travels with the team for dis-play in their tactical operations room near the scene of the siege.'[80]

This observation adds to our knowledge; when *State Research* tried to find out more about these regulations, the Ministry of Defence would not even comment on their existence. To know that they exist, however, is not to know what they detail. Nor does it reveal whether they were observed – it seems that they have not on occasions in Northern Ireland.[81] At the time of writing, some six months after the siege, these questions have not been pursued by the British media; at any rate, nothing has been published.

What of the FCO's refusal (at the behest of the CCC) to let the ambas-sadors mediate? Obviously, this was a matter of high-level political calcu-lation, in which the possibility of a negotiated solution that allowed the gun-men to escape was rejected. The deterrent effect of a hard line seems a plausible enough argument if hostages' lives are not the top priority. It is

79 Geraghty op cit, p180.
80 ibid, p169.
81 Bulletin n18 op cit, p118.

surely a matter of public interest, though, that the BBC, which, alone of the British media was privy to the demand for diplomatic intervention, aligned itself uncritically with government anti-terrorism policy. By keeping quiet about the Arab ambassadors, the Corporation played a crucial role in facilitating the pursuit of the government's strategy for three days. It is extraordinary that this has occasioned no comment – indeed, has evidently gone unnoticed. Did the Corporation have no doubts about the wisdom of the government's aproach? Its unique status in the affair was also reinforced by the way in which the BBC's personnel – Tony Crabb on the outside and Sim Harris on the inside – assisted in the exchange of publicity for hostages, and in contributing to the attrition of the gunmen's will. The BBC was certainly in a difficult position: it *had* to co-operate extensively with the security operation and was rightly concerned for the safety of its personnel. At the same time, the siege undoubtedly represented a further milestone in the peacetime exercise of State control over broadcasting in a moment of crisis. Perhaps the configuration of circumstances was unique: equally, it could have enduring consequences.

No doubt from the siege-managers' point of view a partial censorship is better than none at all. But although successful in practice, the present British model has a paradoxical long-term consequence. The very absence of total censorship makes it possible for interested parties to reconstruct the details of siege operations, including the role of communication media – as I have done here. This means that the security forces have to think out a new 'game plan', at least on the most pessimistic assumption that future hostage-takers will be literate and will understand how things work in Britain. At the extensive debriefing of all those involved in the security side a week after the conclusion of the siege, the question of whether it would be 'necessary to change contingency plans to counter terrorist incidents because of the extensive television coverage of the siege including "blacked up" SAS men storming the building' was considered.[82] Although total censorship remains unlikely, and would anyway be utterly unacceptable to both media and public, a clear code of practice governing media-state relations on such occasions is needed. Fudging the reality of existing *ad hoc* agreements (as with the BBC in this case) is of course the preferred British way out. But it is hardly the most democratic: we have a right to know just how compliant the media propose to be at given moments, and why they choose (or are constrained) to be so.

Finally, the overall coverage of the siege, discussed in the following articles, does give cause for serious concern. The episode was generally treated in patriotic, even chauvinistic, terms. A violent solution was favoured, even glorified. From the point of view of civil liberties, this is worrying indeed. The operation seems to have given the use of the SAS in Britain's cities some legitimacy at a time when social turbulence is likely to increase. Will this mean that strong-arm tactics for dealing with political problems will become an accepted part of our political culture? Not a single politician, and most especially not one of those usually most vociferous in defence of civil liberties, dared to raise a voice in criticism of the SAS action. As we go forward into the Eighties, we may come to consider this silence an index of the drift towards authoritarianism.

---

82 *The Daily Telegraph,* 11 May 1980.

In this propitious chapter, Tomasz Goban-Klas outlines the use of communications during the rise of the Solidarity movement in Poland's momentous summer of 1980. As he notes, the official channels of mass communication and official policy were insufficient to contain a popular movement, and the unfolding events have a great deal to say about the structure and function of mass communication in political crisis. The development of informal channels of communication during that summer's strikes, he notes, was necessitated by workers' feelings that their communication needs were unmet, but could be. Tomasz Goban-Klas is a staff member of the Press Research Center, Cracow, Poland.

29

INFORMATION AT THE TIME OF SOCIOPOLITICAL CRISIS
Poland in the Summer of 1980

Tomasz Goban-Klas

THE STARTING POINT

In early summer 1980, the main channel of information for the majority of people in Poland was the evening television news, transmitted simultaneously by two channels and watched every day by about 60 percent of the adult population. Newspapers were read by about 40 percent of adults, and radio news had a slightly smaller audience—about one third of Polish adults.[1] The total audience—the public—of each of the three mass media was of course considerably greater: television had a reach of 95 percent; radio, 90 percent; and daily newspapers, 80 percent of the population.[2] The readership of the press could have been greater, but the number of copies printed did not satisfy demand.[3]

This does not mean, however, that the information in the press and on radio and television, especially on domestic affairs, was evaluated highly. On the contrary, confidence in the mass media had showed a downward tendency in the recent past, especially since 1976, and was very low.[4] The main reason for low credibility was excessive exposure, especially on television, of economic achievements while the hardships of everyday life and work were con-

Tomasz Goban-Klas, "Information at the Time of Sociopolitical Crisis: Poland in the Summer of 1980," original manuscript. Copyright © 1983 by Sage Publications, Inc.

tinuously growing. The "Propaganda of Success,"[5] as it was called, departed more and more from the people's feeling, thus intensifying the frustration of almost the whole nation.

At the same time, a growing percentage of the population, particularly the younger and better educated, looked for information in alternative, that is, unofficial, channels. These were first of all the foreign broadcasting stations, especially those that broadcast in Polish.[6] In some intellectual circles, photo-copied bulletins, sometimes even books, printed without censors' prior permission, either according to the rules of censorship or despite them, were also gaining growing popularity.

This alternative circuit of information was of great importance in the forma-tion of social views and public opinion as well as for the appearance of opinion leaders without the official stamp. The issues of conversation, especially in intellectual circles, relied on this unofficial information rather than on information from the mass media, widening the gap between the public and underground circuits of information; the generality of the latter helped to overcome individuals' fears and public taboos, thus forming influential unof-ficial opinions that had no chance of public expression in the mass media.

Nevertheless, these opinions found partial expression in some movies, the so-called moral anxiety movies, theater plays, literary productions, socio-logical essays and dissertations, and sometimes articles in magazines of low circulation, which in a veiled but quite readable way, for more perceptive recipients, presented the judgments that were officially negated or silenced.

It should be stressed, however, that the main factor diminishing social optimism, which in turn directly affected the credibility of official optimistic appraisals in the mass media, were the ever-worse conditions of living of almost all social strata, mainly in the large cities, and news about growing ten-sions and crises around the world.

THE LAST STRAW

As the authorities took no decisive measures against the deterioration of the economic situation, social discontent became universal. The following is a list of average percentages of affirmative responses to the question, "Will standards of living improve in the near future? for the years 1973 to 1980:

1973-1974	60%
1978	45%
1979	39%
February 1980	44%
July 1980	22%

Against this background it is no wonder that the popular mood was close to revolt if not to revolution. In the first days of July, the officially concealed decision to increase prices for some brands of meat was the spur for mass protest. Workers in some plants in eastern Poland were furious when they saw the new prices in their canteens. Being together, they felt strong enough to demand appropriate compensation to meet the new prices; when refused it, they went on strike.

The authorities took up trade negotiations in an effort to localize the conflict, but this slowed a solution and helped to disseminate rumors about workers' demands. Thus it formed a basis for further strikes in other parts of Poland. They came soon. In an atmosphere of universal protest, the reasons for some strikes is sometimes purely symbolic. One reporter's article about a strike in a formerly quiet time was under the headline, "A Strike Which Was Wanted by Nobody": "It was provoked by a Comrade O. in the tool-house because she treated the women with greater contempt than usual."[8]

Frequently, a disdainful opinion of a manager about his staff, a demonstration of personal power, were the crystallizers of an outbreak of discontent: "Workers couldn't forgive the director for what he said in an interview for *Tygodnik Plocki* [a local newspaper] last week. . . . He accused them of sloppy work."[9]

Moreover, the unfortunate statements of local authorities, such as strong disapprovals of strikes, accusing strikers of causing tremendous material and moral losses, frequently prolonged and broadened the protest: "In reply, the workers took over control of the plant and the wire broadcasting center."[10]

In many instances, press editorials, especially in local and plant newspapers, instead of appeasing the emotions, acted as catalysts of protest:

> In addition, the articles and information in the local·press about the Roller-Bearing Plant also aroused objections. There were too many good news stories, and this clashed with the actual economic situation and emotional dispostion of the workers. People read there that their factory had made considerable achievements, that rioting Gdańsk workers hindered exports, that the success of their plant was the result of efficient management, flourishing social life, unrestricted freedom of thoughts, opinions and criticism, far-reaching autonomy and competent management. The workers read also that they had no intention of joining any irresponsible protests.[11]

Reaction to such declarations made on behalf of workers in the situation of acute crisis in the whole country was a predictable one; workers went on strike, which cost about 100 million zlotys in production losses.

One result of publishing such editorials was also the lowering of the prestige of journalists. In some cases it reached a real low: "I move that journalists should be excluded from our meeting of the striking committee. . . . Who is against this motion? One one hand goes up."[12]

INFORMATION BLOCKADE

Blocking of all bad news was the fundamental principle of official communication policy in July and the first twentý days of August 1980. It was generated by the assumption that such news might only extend discontent and escalate workers' claims, thus slowing the solution of industrial conflict in the whole country. The blockade of communication channels as well as embargoes on news was therefore applied quite frequently.

In the period before strikes—that is, for almost a decade—the policy was actualized in restriction of criticism in the press, radio, and especially on television. There were even efforts to withhold from the consumers' knowledge the consecutive hidden price rises by stopping the practice of publishing the information about them. But, as the Reverend Chmielewski wrote in the eighteenth century in a Polish encyclopedia under the entry "horse," "What it is like, everybody can see." Such facts could not be kept secret for long. Everyday shopping reminds people of them continuously.

When the strikes started, various measures were taken to limit the flow of information, especially between revolting areas and the "quiet" remainder of the country. At first, the central authorities tried to overcome the troubles by not speaking about them. Central official channels carried no information about the strikes for more than two weeks. But "news about strikes was spread in secret, from mouth to mouth."[13]

Later, when it became impossible to cover up any longer, the official channels timidly confirmed the news about "disturbances in the rhythm of work" or "pauses in work." The word "strike" was taboo at that time, but only when used in relation to the Polish situation. Commentaries indicating disastrous economic effects of strikes outnumbered by the few pieces of information about striking plants and their demands.

Various measures were also taken to limit the interpersonal flow of information. For instances, some railway connections were suspended and long-distance telephone calls broken. The latter measure was taken in Gdańsk in the first two days of strikes: "Since Friday, August 15, we could not get a connection with any place," recalled a journalist.[14] But this had soon to be given up, because it proved inefficient; besides, the workers made restoration of telephone connections a condition for any negotiations.

Later, the embargo on news changed its character; there was information about strikes but no information about strikers' demands. This, however, did not yield the expected results, because the people's expectations were focused on the universal discontent embodied in the strikers, so citizens demanded more detailed information.

In such situations, looking for more information becomes almost an addiction. Here are some examples from journalistic descriptions of these later days:

> The strikes were on the Baltic Coast and we suddenly couldn't take our eyes off the TV screen.[15]

The tension is growing. Never before have the people waited for the TV evening news so impatiently, so nervously. During the past few days this broadcast has become the most awaited event of the day, as if something very important, giving hope, could be found in it overnight.[16]

But neither the TV news coverage nor ardio and press news met the expectations of audiences. "TV news from the Coast," wrote a reporter, was becoming more and more nervous . . . There is also a news report about repairs on the biggest furnace at the Lenin Steelworks [near Cracow] . . . This information is to tell something else. It means that the plant is working. For in Cracow, in Warsaw, in other cities, a nervous rumour has been spreading: 'The Steelworks went on strike.' "[17]

The rumour proved true—the Steelworks had gone on strike. But even after the Fourth Plenary Assembly of the Central Committee of the Polish United Workers [Communist] Party announced important top leadership changes and promised "a fundamental turn in Party policy," neither the Steelworks nor other plants in Poland, especially the Lenin Shipyard in Gdańsk, had any intention to stop strikes. Why? The workers' answer at that time was, "Why are the Coast workers still on strike? We don't know their demands. We don't know on what matters they cannot come to terms with the authorities. Thus we are striking."[18]

The situation was similar in main mining center in Poland, in Silesia. When the negotiations at the Coast were coming to an end, Silesian mines decided to go on strike. The reason? There were many, but one of the most important was the embargo on news. A Silesian correspondent to central newspaper wrote later: "Local propaganda organs—press, radio and TV—absolutely subordinated to the local Party Committee, became the object of ridicule" because the news about strikes that they carried was scarce and the comments implied that strikes were the works of antisocialist plotters. This clashed not only with the Silesian miners' common sense but also with the stand of the state officials as presented by the central mass media, in *Trybuna Ludu*, an organ of the Party Central Committee, and in television news bulletins.

That is why, as the correspondent continued, "In order to learn about the situation in the country, people sought for newspapers published outside the region, as the local ones were instructed not to print any critical or controversial articles."[19]

It shows that a centralization of the mass media in Poland which had been effected in the 1970s had also some unforeseen consequences. Namely, it made any regionalization of conflicts impossible; thus, a critical situation in one part of the country soon generated some strain in the whole country when even scarce news passed by the nationwide television news.

In Silesia the embargo on news was introduced after the first strikes had already started, a few days later than in the Coast. Representatives of the Inter-Plant Strike Committee explained: "We demanded that competent and well-disposed people be sent as negotiators because the former team denied us the right to information about what is going on in the Lenin Shipyard. As we wanted to know exactly what was happening on the Coast, to know their demands and we wanted to make it known to the miners. We also wanted to make known to the whole of Poland that Silesia took the side of the dockyard workers. But at that time, in August, they kept us under a hat so that no real truth reached Silesia and no real truth could leak out from here. . . . That is why they say in Jastrzebie, in Silesia, the strikes lasted longer [until September 3]: For Silesian honour's sake."[20]

Another miner's remark: "What was the saddest? . . . Well, that Poland did not know anything about us. . . . They said in the TV news that we went on Solidarity strike and the strikes stopped immediately."[21]

It wasn't always like that. Lack of detailed information about the acceptance of workers' demands at the Coast prolonged the protests in other regions. A worker in Wroclaw, in western Poland, said: "The TV evening news informed us about the signing the Gdańsk agreement on Sunday . . . but its contents were not quoted. . . . The Inter-Plant Strike Committee waited with the decision to end the strike until late at night, till the information was confirmed by telephone call and telex."[22]

In some cases the distrust of the official media was so great that the strikers did not believe even in television news or press reports about the signing of the agreement in Gdańsk, and it was not before their special envoy brought a confirmation directly and personally from Gdańsk that they gave up doubts.

MISINFORMATION

Where there is a severe conflict, there is always a temptation to present one's own situation in better light by stressing favourable facts or even by making them up. Luckily, at the time of initial phase of social crisis in Poland in summer 1980, there were not so many instances of patent misinformation. The facts were silenced or favorably interpreted rather than fabricated. The media tried to influence public opinion by limiting information rather than by plain misinformation.

Locally, however, there were attempt at misinforming people. For instance, in some plants the "old" trade unions posted announcements or distributed leaflets warning that discontinuation of membership would cause a withdrawal of all social benefits, which was not true. In general, such misinformation did not have the expected effect and frequently even contributed to an escalation of the conflict.

Some local authorities resorted to similar measures. In some plants on strike leaflets were distributed among workers or even scattered from a helicopter. These sheets depicted the dismal consequences for the workers themselves, for their families, and for the whole nation. Sometimes unknown people distributed provocative leaflets.

The strikers' usual response to these actions was to issue their own leaflets, which flatly denied the false charges and invited people to come and learn the workers' real stand on the spot, in the factory: In some cities, for example in Plock, a virtual "leaflet war" broke out:

> On Friday afternoon a plane appeared. . . . A minute later, a shower of white sheets fell down. . . . "People in the town are against your strike." Signed by Municipal Authorities. . . . Striking workers started issuing a photocopied bulletin, ending with the appeal: "Citizens of Plock, do not believe false information." On Saturday, a leaflet signed by the mayor of Plock was posted. The Strike Committee's repartee appeared on the same day.[23]

Some elements of misinformation can be found in the arguments used in commentaries on strikes published by the press, radio, and television. A recurring theme in these articles was the picture of enormous losses in the national economy caused by the strikes. At the same time, no mention was made of the losses caused earlier and for years by irregular material supplies, energy shortages, mismanagement, and so on. A correspondent from Szezecin wrote:

> Despite press information, neither roadstead nor the hinterland was crowded with ships or merchanidise. . . . The port's reloading capacity fell by 600,000 tons, that is, just as much as was overclaimed by the official plan for the past seven months.[24]

The miners similarly denied the official information that after the strikes their yield was much smaller. The change in statistics was due to reporting of honest data.

The general awareness of the inefficiency of economic management was most probably the main cause of an almost unanimous consent of the public opinion to the strikes, as was shown by nationwide public opinion polls conducted by the Public Opinion Research Center at Polish Radio and Television in September 1980 and by the Press Research Center in December 1980 and later. Thus, the propaganda campaign based on the argument that strikes were causing the collapse of the national economy fell on deaf ears.

STRIKE INFORMATIONAL SERVICES

Poland's best experts on organization and management, even governmental experts like Professor K. Dektór, agreed that in general the strikes were very well organized.[25] This, and the fact that there was in no case rioting, disturbances, or accidents, do credit to the proficient informational services. This is demonstrated by the first day of strikes in Gdańsk Shipyard.

A journalist recalled, "Everybody was aware that even a provocation was not necessary, and unconfirmed rumor would suffice to change these several thousand people into a panic-stricken mob."[26] Thus, one of the first actions of the strikers was to take over the plant wire broadcasting service. "They were aware," the journalist wrote, "that the rumor about strike would quickly spread in the city. A crowd of mothers, wives, and friends eager to learn something, to see their relatives, to pass some food, clothes, a mattress, a sleeping bag, was expected at the shipyard gate in the afternoon. This crowd at the gate, although friendly and ready to help, could create disturbances in the city, and this was what the strike leaders wanted to avoid at all costs. The broadcasting center gave a chance of control over the families and onlookers at the gate."[27]

The plant wire radio informed the people gathered outside about the situation in the shipyard. Through this radio, all announcements were read, and through it the individual workers were called to the gate when family members wanted to see them.

The strike organizers who did not include the wire service in their informational network at the very start soon found out how important it was. "The main weak point of the strike at Domel [in western Poland] was lack of control over the plant radio service," wrote one of the members of staff. "Lack of current information led to misinformation. A provocative leaflet distributed in the plant by unknown people also revolted workers and caused unnecessary informational confusion.[28] Thus, the wire broadcasting centers turned out to be of strategic importance and the struggles to get control over them reminded one at times of putsches in Latin America.

The plant radio also rendered it possible for all strikers to participate at least passively in the negotiations. One of the most fortunate decisions of the Gdańsk Inter-Plant Strike Committee was to make the conference and bargaining public. Microphones were put in the conference room, and all statements were broadcast live through the loudspeakers set up in offices and in the yard. A reporter observed:

> In this micro-scale the actual power of the communication media ws revealed. The loudspeakers and giant loudspeakers focused the life of the shipyard. I risk nothing claiming that one of the most important decisions of the Gdańsk Inter-Plant Strike Committee was to make the bargaining public. It helped to keep order in the shipyard and outside. Honest and reliable immediate information was again the basic condition of keeping the workers' confidence in their leaders.[29]

It should be added, however, that when the negotiations were coming to an end, the broadcasts, with the workers' consent, were discontinued because the publicness of discussion affected the liberty of statements and arguments.

The Gdańsk example was imitated in other plants; for example, in the Elblag Metalworks factory the negotiations were also broadcast to the end. Nevertheless, the radio transmissions, being limited in space and unduring, were not sufficient:

> Hunger for information among the workers was enormous all the time. Almost from the very start, a photocopying machine continuously duplicated leaflets

carrying the texts and more important announcements and pronouncements. The written word had a very important function despite the direct broadcasts from the conference of the Strike Committee and later from the negotiations. Spoken words disappear in the air, while written matter can be read once more, considered from all sides. On the tenth day of strike a decision was made to issue a information bulletin called *Solidarity.* Until the time the workers resumed work, fourteen issues of the paper appeared. The role of printed word become manifested once more.[30]

The striking workers made use also of other means of propaganda. The range of visual communication was the most abundant. The workers on orderly duty wore white and red arm bands [the national flag colors]; other functionaries were different colors; the emissary's cars carried lance pennons; the gates were decorated with flags, pictures, portraits (often religious), national emblems, flowers. An eyewitness wrote, "The lance pennons on cars, even on the private ones, and flags and banners on hospital buildings created the feeling that one should not stand aside, that one should joint the movement."[31] There were many banners bearing slogans that in a few words stated the aims of the strike, the attitudes of the workers, and their demands and expectations. The most famous slogan, on the gate of the Lenin Shipyard in Gdańsk, read: "Proletarians of all plants, unite." In Woclawek, a town in central Poland, slogans on the fence of the Municipal Transport Enterprise read: "The MPK workers stand in with the workers on the Coast," "Yes to socialism; no to deformations," and "God help Poland and the nation."[32]

Sometimes slogans were painted on houses and factories, such as "21 times YES," referring to the twenty-one workers' postulates and at the same time to the postwar referendum on nationalization. The most unusual channel of visual propaganda was established between the Coast and the mining center in Silesia. The coal railway cars, shown usually in the television evening news as a symbol of growing national economy in the 1970s, were painted in Gdańsk with slogans that ridiculed the Silesian miners and workers for their timidity and lack of solidarity. It appears that the influence of these slogans was greater than could have been expected from their content and form. Laughter is sometimes an extremely effective propaganda weapon.

In some of the large plants, the workers decided to accredit Polish and foreign journalists:

> Assuming that reliable information helps to keep peace and prevents insinuations, especially in the foreign press, it was decided to let the assembled reporters in [to the shipyard]. This meant that a press service had to be organized. First of all, interpreters had to be found. Soon, besides white and red armbands of the orderly service and the white bands of the members of the Strike Committee, there appeared yellow armbands with names of languages, worn by the interpreters. Toward the end of the strike, although the number of foreign journalists exceeded 100, nobody had any difficulty with finding an interpreter.[33]

Moreover, the accreditation of journalists and the presence of foreign television crews strengthened a feeling of security among the workers.

THE BIRTH OF THE WORKERS' AWARENESS
OF THE RIGHT TO COMMUNICATE

The agreement signed in Gdańsk on August 31, 1980, on behalf of striking workers at the Coast and valid for the whole country, stated, among other things:

> Concerning point three, which reads, "To observe the freedom of speech, printing and publication guaranteed in the Constitution of the Polish People's Republic, and thus not to prosecute independent publications, to give access to the mass media to representatives of all creeds," the following has been agreed: "Radio, television, and press and publications should serve to express the diversity of opinions, ideas and views. They should be submitted to the social control."[34]

Both in the third point of the strikers' demand and in the agreement with the government, there appears the issue of the right to information and to communicate. Such demands were of course put forward in postwar Poland several times before, but mainly by intellectuals, not by the workers. It now remains to determine the causes of such change.

There were suggestions that this demand had been "planted" in the workers' demands by the intellectuals. This is probably true, but it does not explain why even after this suggestion was made, workers continued to stick to the demand. The briefest answer is that it was caused by a spectacular failure of official propaganda. For many years, workers as well as employees were told by official media that everything was going well, the welfare was growing, that prosperity was near. Suddenly, this was shown to be untrue, and the people lost their confidence in the mass media altogether. The summer 1980 crisis was manifested in a rapid change in values ascribed to persons, issues, and problems. Good guys became bad guys; Poland—a prosperous nation, a member of the cosmic club, the tenth leading economic power—proved to be poor and deeply in debt. This is why the demand to make the official activities public, as an assurance against the future lawlessness and willfulness of the authorities, was so strongly supported.

The previously mentioned cases of withholding information about price increases and worsening living conditions in the preceding few years also had their consequences. The scope of the matters subjected to press criticism was limited to what caused a growing gap between the official perspective of the state of the nation and the people's feeling. Against this background, the demand for full and true information, and access to it, appears as a generalization of everyday experiences. A journalist's observation supports this opinion:

> For instance, when I asked them what they thought about censorship, it turned out that they [the workers] connected this world with withholding information

about meat prices, food shortages, and so on. Censorship of culture was rather an unfamiliar idea to them.[35]

Moreover, one-sided information and argumentation about strikes created demands for full access to the mass media, especially to television: "Why do they show on TV various fellows saying that our independent unions are their idea," complained a striking worker, "and why don't they let us say there that these are our, the workers', affairs?"[36]

In this way, through such experiences, was formulated and disseminated the postulate of the right to communicate as an essential element of human rights and as an equally essential element of socialist democracy. It was as the workers repeated in Lenin's words from 1919:

> True freedom and equality would be such a system as constructed by the communists where it would be impossible to grow rich at the cost of others, where there would be no objective possibility of either direct or indirect subordination of the press to the power of the money, where there could be no obstacles for every working man or group of people, no matter what their number, to have an equal right to use common printing houses and common paper and to realize this right.[37]

Nevertheless, the demand for access and freedom of information was understood in a limited manner. Therefore it did not postulate an abolition of the censorship, in view of particular Polish internal and external situations, but rather to put it under social control. Thus the Gdańsk agreement stipulated the special prevention of state, economic, and technological secrets, protection of religious beliefs, and prevention of the distribution of morally harmful materials.

POSTSCRIPT

This article was written in December 1980. Therefore it deals only with the very first phases of Polish events, before the declaration of martial law. At that time there was no coherent communication policy for coping with acute political crises, nor were there concrete demands for changes in this policy. Hence this article, using primarily the opinions of journalists and treating them as social experts on political matters, shows mainly the "boomerang effects" of official communications and the cleverness of the striking workers in using group communication methods and "little media."

NOTES

1. "Komunikowanie masowe w Polsce. Próba bilansu lat siedemdziesiatych," *Zeszyty Prasoznawcze,* 1981, no. 1, p. 60.

2. *Ibid.,* p. 61.

3. Nevertheless, the total circulation of Polish dailies per capita was, and still is, higher than in many European countries, such as France. Cf. UNESCO, *Statistical Yearbook 1980.*

4. "Komunikowanie," *op. cit.,* p. 74.

5. This notion was advanced in the early 1970s to name the policy of publicizing all facts proving and praising the achievements of the political leadership and the whole nation.

6. "Komunikowanie," *op. cit.,* p. 74.

7. From the documentation of public opinion polls conducted by the Public Opinion Poll Center at Polish Radio and Television, Warsaw.

8. E. Wróbel, "Strajk, którege nikt nie chcial," *Zycie Gospedarcze,* 41 (October 12, 1980).

9. M. Beldryk, "Mechanizm sredniege szczebla," *Literaturea* 37 (October 2, 1980).

10. *Ibid.*

11. E. Wróbel, *op cit.*

12. E. Berberyusz, "Drugi krok," *Kultura* 40 (October 5, 1980).

13. A. Jakubowicz, "Nie sposób rzeźbić w zbutwialym drzewie," *Polityka* 40 (October 11, 1980).

14. W. Dabrowski, "18 dni sierpnia 1980," *Student* 20 (October 9, 1980).

15. D. Terakowska, "My z Jastrzebia," *Przekrój* 42 (October 19, 1980).

16. D. Terakowska, "Huta Lenina 19-20 sierpnia," *Przekrój* 42 (October 19, 1980).

17. *Ibid.*

18. M. Blaut, "Slazacy nie sa od Was ani gorsi, ani glupsi," *Polityka* 40 (October 11, 1980).

19. *Ibid.*

20. D. Terakowska, "My z Jastrzebia," *op. cit.*

21. *Ibid.*

22. A. Jakubowicz, "Nie sposób rzeźbić," *op. cit.*

23. M. Beldryk, "Mechanizm," *op. cit.*

24. J. Baczynski, "Szczecin—nie tak jak dawniej," *Przeglad Techniczny-Innowacje* 42 (October 12, 1980).

25. K. Dektor, "Inna propozycja bycia obywatelem," *Kultura* 39 (September 28, 1980).

26. A. Walawski, "Gdańsk—czas tworzenia," *Przeglad Techniczny-Innowacje* 42 (October 12, 1980).

27. *Ibid.*

28. A. Jakubowicz, "Nie sposób rzeźbić," *op. cit.*

29. A. Walawski, "Gdańsk," *op. cit.*

30. *Ibid.*

31. W. Dabrowski, "18 dni," *op. cit.*

32. D. Kedzierska, "Wloclawek—dlaczege?" *Przeglad Techniczny-Innowacje* 42 (October 12, 1980).

33. A. Walawski, "Gdańsk," *op. cit.*

34. Porozumienie Gdańskie, *Zycie Warsawy,* September 2, 1980.

35. A. Jakubowicz, "Nie sposób rzeźbić," *op. cit.*

36. D. Terakowska, "Huta Lenina," *op. cit.*

37. V. Lenin, "Z tez i referatu e demokracji burzuazyjnej i dyktaturze probletariatu," *Pravda,* March 6, 1919; translated into Polish in *Dziela* 28, p. 481.

This study of Spanish mass media from the death of Franco to 1980 offers evidence that the "liberalization" of media in that nation has wrought important changes in the structure and function of that nation's communication system. Of particular importance, Moragas notes, is that television has been allowed to evolve in ways conducive to state legitimation, while the newspaper press has declined in circulation and the periodical press has turned to mass-audience appeal to the "lowest common denominator," combining pornography and political alienation. Miquel de Moragas Spa is on the faculty of Information Sciences at the Autonomous University of Barcelona.

30

MASS COMMUNICATION AND POLITICAL CHANGE IN SPAIN, 1975-1980

Miquel de Moragas Spa

The objective of this study is to describe the communications conditions that have determined the management of public opinion in the political process of dismantling the Franco regime and building parliamentary democracy. Based on the data presented here, I would like to elaborate several hypotheses that would permit the interpretation of the relationship between the communications media and democracy in the 1975-1980 period. A knowledge of the economic, sociological, political, and judicial aspects of communications and the analysis of communications stereotypes that accompanied the development of this political process will permit a more profound interpretation than that of the Spanish press, which took recourse in simplifications of "Francoism" or "disenchantment," or that of the international press, with its admiring comments and references to the political maturity of the Spanish population.

The data in Tables 1, 2, and 3, providing comparisons with the Western European countries, permit the assertion that with the exception of the feeble presence of the press in the communications environment of Spain, the development of audiovisual media, while low, approximates the European average.

From Miquel de Moragas Spa, "Comunicación de masas y transito en España, 1975-1980," *Communicacion y Cultura,* Vol. 7 (Enero 1982), pp. 151-174 ("Mass Communication and Political Change in Spain, 1975-1980, *Communication and Culture,* Vol. 7, January 1982), pp. 151-174. Reprinted by permission. Translated by Roberta J. Astroff, Institute of Communications Research, University of Illinois at Urbana-Champaign.

TABLE 1.   The Communications Infrastructure of Certain Western European
           Countries in 1975

	Number of Radios per 1000 Inhabitants	Number of Television Sets per 1000 Inhabitants	Daily Newspapers, Copies per 1000 Inhabitants
Belgium	397	260	239
Denmark	353	308	341
France	325	268	214
Federal Republic of Germany	316	311	319 (1970)
Italy	230	217	113
Holland	286	267	315 (1970)
Portugal	172	65	70
Spain	261	184	98
United Kingdom	699	316	388
European average	337	244	233
Spanish media in relation to the European average	0.77	0.75	0.42

SOURCE: *Anuario estadistico,* UNESCO 1977.

TABLE 2.   The Use of Radio and Television in Spain, 1978

	Radio	Television
Every day	39.7	76.6
Several days a week	11.5	6.4
One day a week	4.6	1.9
Hardly ever	28.6	4.1
Never listen or watch	15.6	8.0
Number of hours of weekly use for habitual users	13.2	17.0

TABLE 3.   Number of Television Sets and Radio Receivers in Spain

Television Sets	1965	1970	1975	1976
Number of sets (in 1000s)	—	4115	6525	6640
Number of sets per 1000 inhabitants	—	124	184	185

Radio Receivers	1950	1060	1065	1968	1975
Number of sets (in 1000s)	2717	4550	6475	7042	9250
Number of sets per 1000 inhabitants	90	144	144	214	261

SOURCE: *Statistical Yearbook 1970 and 1977,* UNESCO.

Thus, there is a communications apparatus that can adequately serve the requirements for cultural homogeneity and the mass diffusion of such behavior as voting that are indispensable to the very functioning of liberal democracy.

The very experience of political change from dictatorship to democracy in Spain constitutes an example of the necessity of interpreting the crisis of the press from a new perspective, one of the functions of the communications system in each society. The unequivocal necessity of homogenizing the norms of consumer behavior and the standardization of political activity that characterize Western democracies leads to a discussion not so much of a crisis in a particular medium as the adaptation of the system to the new requirements of communications technology.

In terms of the survival and functioning of the democratic system, one cannot talk of the crisis in the press, for example, as a crisis that is capable of being isolated and evaluated at the margin of the general framework of the function of social communication in each historical moment. In this sense, we cannot speak of crisis, in the sense of a loss of influence, of the communications media, but rather must pay attention to the growing influence of these, in order to assure cultural homogenization and standardization in the norms of political and consumer behavior. Spain, understood as a developing society in terms of communications, has the minimum required characteristics that make possible the stability of a political system like that of the capitalist countries of modern Europe.

RADIO IN SPAIN, 1975-1980

In the last years of Francoism and starting with the death of Carrero Blanco (December 1973),[1] the press followed, with logical contradictions, an information policy of support for reform and of the use of local news as an instrument to criticize incompetence and corruption in the system. However, the radio continued to play, in general terms, a clear role in defense of the regime. Nevertheless, a few exceptions did exist, especially among the SER network, such as Radio Barcelona's program *Directo* and *The 25th Hour*, begun before the death of Franco in November 1975. These shows could be considered examples of how private radio attempted to follow the press's model in the use of local news.

The radio functioned in defense of the Franco regime in two ways. On one hand, the state broadcast network of Radio Nacional de España (RNE) had a monopoly on national and international political news. On the other hand, and this involves both the state and the private broadcasters, there was an extremely high percentage of programming dedicated to escapism, entertainment, music, and other amusements.[2]

This situation survived the death of Franco and indeed was intensified during the parliamentary referendum campaign (December 1976) and the earlier period of the first general elections (June 1977).

One of the principal transformations of communications during this stage of political change is to be found, no doubt, in the long battle by private broadcasters and some professionals in state broadcasting to be able to provide political information.

In order to study this process, the following two aspects must be kept in mind: first, the consequences of the elimination of the political news monopoly of the Radio Nacional de España; second, the revision of the kinds and the content of news, especially the use of live broadcasts of leaders of the democratic opposition, who appeared for the first time in flesh and blood before the public. In effect, this can be seen as one of great spectacles of the political transition.

This entire process did not actually start until October 3, 1977, four months after the first general elections were held (June 1977) and the corresponding victory of the UCD [Unión de Centro Democrático—a coalition of centrist parties]. That is the date that the obligatory broadcasting at 2:30 p.m. and at 10 p.m. of the famous "Spoken Newspapers of the RNE" or "Communiqués" was eliminated.

During the months preceding the first elections, the Ministry of Information and Tourism, which was not dissolved until August 1977, when it was transformed into the Ministry of Culture, increased control over all radio broadcasters. These had taken advantage of the first gestures of *apertura*—opening—instigated by [former Prime Minister] Adolfo Suarez (First Amnesty, August 1976) and the passing of reforms in the judicial system (January 1977) to loosen the limits traditionally imposed on Spanish radio by Francosim. But in this preelectoral era, the ministry increased its telephoned "advice" to the directors of the broadcasting stations, established a written record of the Francoist norms on radio news, required the stations to deliver tapes with complete recordings of daily programming, and established a subtle standard on electoral publicity.

From October 1977 on, the radio increased, spectacularly, its informative programs, debates, and interviews and played an important role in political education and democratic participation. In keeping with its logic of competition, even the state radio, RNE, accepted and permitted programs directed by journalists who made room for the leaders of the Left and for union representatives whose presence, on the other hand, was still persistently vetoed on television.

As a consequence, this era, which came to be called the radio boom, signified an important growth in audiences and a progressive increase in advertising revenues in this medium.

If we analyze this process from the perspective of the profitability of this liberalization for the party that won the elections, the UCD, the hypothesis is suggested that this change in communications had as a political function that of attributing democratic credibility to Suarez's party before a public that knew only the Francoist use of the communications media. This advance proved to be irreversible for private radio broadcasters, but it suffered reverses in the case of stations linked to the state, corresponding like each electoral fluctuation to a stop-and-go process.

The dialectic of permissibility and reverse can also be observed in television, as we will see later on. In January of 1978, for example, the directors of the news services of TVE [Televisión Española] were dismissed from their posts. In Catalonia a strict process was initiated of suppressing programs edited and presented by democratic journalists and even some by prominent militants from leftist parties. Once these professionals had lent their services to the task of credibility, they were discharged.

As for audiovisual media, the UCD government found itself at a crossroads that was clearly definitive of the Spanish situation during this transition. On one hand, the government had at its disposal a large communications apparatus inherited from the Franco regime with all the judicial resources, customs, and networks of corruption necessary for propagandistic use in its own favor. The UCD, on the other hand, found itself on the path of transforming the communications system toward the introduction and glorification of the capitalist idea of freedom of and free flow of information. Therefore, the reins were loosened or tightened to the degree to which the UCD could benefit from each situation. The left, opposed to privatization, in fact facilitated the continuance of governmental control over the state communications apparatus. Meanwhile, the communications industry struggled to resolve the problems of planning and infrastructure in order to prepare, in its favor, the debut of privatizaiton that can be read, although with some ambiguity, in the Constitution.

CHARACTERISTICS OF RADIO BROADCASTING IN SPAIN (SUMMARY DATING FROM 1976)

Apart from the already mentioned variations in content and treatment, the principal changes experienced by the radio communications system in the period of transition are the following: the transformation of the networks of the National Movement[3] and of its social organizations (CAR, REM, CES) and their final assimilation into RTVE [Radio Televisión Española]; the appearance of "free" radio and the battle to establish municipal or regional radio; the dismantling of Radio España Independiente; and reduction to a minimum, although always difficult to measure, of the audience of international radio broadcasts.

Although the following organizational chart and the figures given for the Spanish radio infrastructure date from 1976, the same schema is applicable, with minor variations, to the situation in 1980, after the fundamental stages in the political transition.

FREE RADIO

The phenomenon of free radio stations and the vicissitudes of their appearance, the pros and cons, constitute a second reference point for understanding the current scope and the future of the mass media in Spanish democracy.

The free radio stations appears approximately a year after the first appearance of opposition leaders on informational programs on private and state radio. These stations were a response by political groups locating themselves outside parliamentary logic, first from the Left but later also from the extreme Right, to the narrowness of the communications channels that the present social organization offers. The appearance of the free radios also coincided with the moment in the Left-Right debate over privatization, which was more difficult for the Left.

Although the principal argument was that of giving a voice to those on the margins of society, it is interesting to note the very "passion" for alternativity that governed the first proposal. The interest in using a new language, and invasion of colloquial and sectorial language that had been isolated from the linguistic ambit of traditional and institutional radio formats, defines the scope and intention of this alternativity. In fact, the birth of this movement constitutes the first expression of what later on will be called political and social "disenchantment" with the possibilities of parlimentary democracy.

The free radios are not, properly speaking, continuing the long tradition of clandestine communications in Spain; they are demanding above all else their legalization. They do not hide and they broadcast their own arrests. The taste for the risky use of stencils and small presses has been lost.

This movement followed several months after the *freedom of expression* campaign that came out of the arrest and trial of the theater group *els Joglars,* who were accused of insulting the army; but while the free radio movement subscribes to the popular vindication of freedom of expression, content that could provoke legal action is carefully omitted and all activity is centered on the justification of the existence of free radio as a right. The movement thus seeks the protection of the Constitution.

A second determining context for the appearance and functioning of free radio stations was that of the recuperation of the festival as a sign of identity for popular groups, especially neighborhood associations. It is therefore not a coincidence that the first broadcasts and the moments of largest audience of free radio coincide with the celebration of the national festivals.

It cannot be predicted that the future of radio is to be found in free radio. Rather than imagining the future of radio as a consequence of the communicative power of marginal groups, it seems more appropriate to see the future as a result of the efforts of the big Spanish and multinational communications

TABLE 4.   State, Private, and External Broadcasters

STATE BROADCASTERS
Radio Nacional de España—broadcasting centers

Madrid/Barcelona/Seville/La Coruna/Tenerife/Oviendo/San Sebastian/Zaragosa/Bilbao/
Santander/Malaga/Logrono

These are the most powerful of the state broadcasting stations with 50, 100, 200 and up
to 250 Kw.

Radional Nacional de España—Radio Peninsulares

Commercial Stations

Madrid/Barcelona/Seville/Valencia/Cuenca/Gibraltar/Huelva

With capacities of 5, 10, 25, and 50 Kw (the latter, Radio Peninsular of Madrid)

Broadcasting Stations of the National Movement

Cadena Azul de Radiodifusión—Radio Juventud (CAR): Total number of stations, 29.

Red de emisoras del movimiento—Radio "the voice of . . ." (REM): Total number of broadcasting stations, 16.

Caderna de emisoras sindicales—Radio Centro (CES): Total number of broadcasting
stations, 15.

NOTE: These have an average capacity of 2 to 5 Kw.

SOURCE: Logs dating from 1977 and 1978 of Radio Cadena España.

PRIVATE BROADCASTERS
COPE—Cadena de Ondas Populares

Dependent on the episcopal commission of communications media with a total of 45 broadcasters with an average capacity of 2 Kw.

Sociedad Española de Radiodifusión—Cadena SER

This is the most important private radio network in Spain, with a total of 54 broadcasting
stations that cover praactically all of Spanish territory; 25% of its capital is from the state and
the rest is property of important economic sectors close to the UCD. Stations have an average
capacity of 2 Kw, except for the powerful Radio Madrid, Radio Barcelona, and Radio
Zaragoza, which have 20 Kw.

Other private chains:

Cadena RATO: Four local stations.

Compañia de Radiodifusión Intercontinental: Made up of 5 stations, the only important ones
being Radio Internacional de Madrid and Radio Miramar ín Barcelona.

Radio España: Composed of 8 stations. Among the most powerful is Radio España of
Barcelona.

EXTERNAL BROADCASTING
Radio Nacional de España

Spanish-language service to Australia, North America, South America, maritime areas,
Africa, the Middle East, and Asia. Foreign language service to the United States, Canada,
and the Arab countries.

	1950	*1960*	*1070*	*1973*	*1977*
Total number of hours of external service of the Radio National de España, in hours per week	68	202	251	361	403

Radio Liberty

A U.S. station that broadcasts from Pals (Girona) and Munich, dedicated to U.S. propaganda
to Eastern European countries, especially the Soviet Union. At one point, the station had
acquired 330,000 square meters of land. The land and installations were taken from their
owners and made the property of the Spanish state. Radio Liberty in Pals has 4 broadcasting
connecting stations of 250 Kw each.

TABLE 5.
Basic Chronology of the Free Radio Stations

March 26, 1978	First meeting in Barcelona of a founding group of the movement. The Collective takes the name "Ona Iliure."
September 23, 24	First broadcast, sporadic, for the national festival in Barcelona.
January 1979	The station Osina Arratia in San Sebastian broadcasts for a half hour every two weeks.
April 4, 1979	Ona Iliure starts regular broadcasting, 9 p.m. to midnight.
April-May	Different tapes and rebroadcasts by Ona Iliure.
June 1979	Royal decree that regulates the granting of licenses and puts the future of the new stations in the hands of the administration.

NOTE: Together with the above-mentioned stations and with broadcast irregularities, a total of 9 FM stations can be categorized as "free radio" stations: in Barcelona, *Contra Radio, La Compaña de Gracia,* and *Fuerza Nueva,* on the far Right. In the Catalan regions, *El Avispero* in Sta. Coloma, *L'Estel* in Hospitalet, *La maduixa* in Granollers.
SOURCE: Tesina de Emilio Prado, "Las radios libres," tape recording, September 1979, Bellaterra.

industries that, following the logic of the international communications industry, will no longer look for profitability in concentration in just one medium, be it cinema, radio, television, or the press, but rather will organize media "pools."

The central question will be that of private television. The free radios could also be used as the Trojan horse that would ensure their own expansion in the name of the liberal freedom of information.

In this confused and pessimistic panorama, the socialist and communist parties, which have obtained some municipal power, have already realized that the best way would be the establishment of FM on the municipal and regional level. From a communications viewpoint, it appears to me to be impossible to predict the criteria that the administration would use in granting licenses and responding to these municipal applications. But experience in communications development leads me to predict that commercial initiatives will smother these progressive initiatives.

THE DAILY PRESS, 1975-1980

In 1936, before the civil war, there were approximately 2,000 newspapers in Spain. In Madrid, six dailies produced more than 200,000 copies. The situation of the Spanish press in 1975 was very different. It could be said that the drop in the number of titles has occurred generally throughout Europe, and this is true.

Spain's case in particular is characterized by a low general press run and levels of circulation per thousand inhabitants (see Table 1). The journalistic class, both professionals and management, thought the censorship and lack of liberty imposed by the Franco regime were the determining causes of these low circulation rates. According to such logic, a democratic change should have implied a correction, that is, an increase, in the general diffusion of the press. Things happened very differently.

In November 1975 there were a total of 115 newspapers in Spain, 39 of which belonged to the secretary general of the National Movement. The rest were distributed among a few groups controlled by distinct political and financial families of the regime. This is not the place, however, for a detailed analysis of the relations between the financial oligarchy, the banks, and the companies of the 76 privately owned Spanish newspapers.

I would like to emphasize the variations experienced in control over these media with political change, and propose a hypothesis on the causes of the progressive drop in circulation. The recognition of the changes experienced on the map of distribution of communications power is a good step toward understanding the extent of political change in Spain between 1975 and 1980.

The relation between the press and democracy does not actually start with the death of General Franco. Without needing to refer to the press law of 1966—and even before the dramatic executions of September 1975[4] and especially after the death of Carrero Blanco, with the attempt at *apertura* of Arias Navarro (called the spirit of February 12th)[5] and Pio Cabanillas's term in the Ministry of Information and Tourism—in general the private press positioned itself definitively in favor of a process of political reform and signaled a democratic path. This was done without mentioning explicitly the Franco regime and, even less, Franco himself; an elliptical reference to Franco's advanced age had provoked the closing of the daily *Madrid*.

Without doubt this was also aided by the particular circumstances of a few editorial staffs made up, for the most part, of democratic professionals who found a liberal respite in their dialogue with management. This idyllic situation lasted until the eve of the general elections (June 1977).

At that point, the newspaper managements stopped feeling protected by the severity of the administration and started to position themselves in favor of the parties that represented the center and the right. A stiffening of control over hiring and editorial policy in journalism was then initiated.

I am starting from an hypothesis that states that each medium of communication fulfills a precise function in accordance with the needs of adaptation of the system to political changes. This variation in function is determined, above all, by the nature of the audience of each medium. I will now detail the low level of press circulation in Spain. In these conditions the following hypothesis on the function of the press in this initial period of politcal change can be proposed.

The consumers of the press in Spain coincide basically with the political, intellectual, and economic elite. Forcing this a little, one can recall Lenin's old idea that the press is a collective organizer. Indeed. So that the transition to democracy would be possible, before the correct education of public

TABLE 6.
Evolution of the Ten Highest-Circulation Newspapers

	1970	1975	1976	1977	1978	1975—1978
A.B.C. (Madrid)	209.177	181.437	186.323	156.725	135.492	−25
El Correo Español—El Pueblo Vasco (San Sebastián)	80.452	86.329	89.433	80.684	69.132	19
El Noticiero Universal (Barcelona)	83.184	76.537	60.715	50.693	42.141	−44
El País (Madrid)	no exis	no exis	153.893	128.805	128.338	
Informaciones (Madrid)	— — —	61.197	74.797	52.314	39.527	−35
La Gaceta del Norte (Bilbao)	84.475	84.777	77.525	66.317	54.313	−35
La Vanguardia (Barcelona)	222.164	220.127	205.849	195.555	186.173	−15
La Voz de Galicia	— — —	70.675	73.670	67.054	71.301	+0.9
Pueblo (Madrid)	198.387	179.527	170.254	113.736	79.746	−55
Ya (Madrid)	139.251	168.759	168.035	140.572	124.099	−26

opinion which could be resolved through the demagoguery of televised political propaganda, it was necessary to start up the group machinery of the political parties. The contribution of the Spanish press to democracy was, on one hand, to make possible the move from clandestine to open organization of prohibited parties and, on the other hand, to establish the credibility and democratic image of the political assocations that joined to form the UCD as a political party.

The years 1975 through 1977 were ones of journalistic inflation of political news. They were years of information on the constitution of political groups, of news of machinations, of the granting of notoriety to political leaders, of discussing crises, mergers, leaderships, pacts, and group controversies. This performance, or contribution, to democracy created paradoxically a progressive loss of interest for the readers, who did not have immediate stakes in the polemics and group debates. The last days of 1976 were intensely dedicated to the campaign for the referendum by radio, television, and billboards, which extended to the great mass of people information on and persuasion toward democracy. At the conclusion of the 1977 elections, radio, freed from the former news monopoly, drew the publc even further from press consumption.

The data on the evolution of the diffusion of the daily press (Table 6) support rather than contradict this hypothesis. In 1976 an accelerated decline in press circulation begins.

The problem, in any case, consists of explaining the reasons for the increase in press circulation on the eve of and in the months immediately after the death of Franco. Table 7 permits us, since it goes back to 1974, to delve more deeply into these reasons.

The increases in circulation coincide with a particular class of political events. More precisely, they coincide with those events that create a certain type of anxiety among the population. The evolution of the press in Spain

Table 7

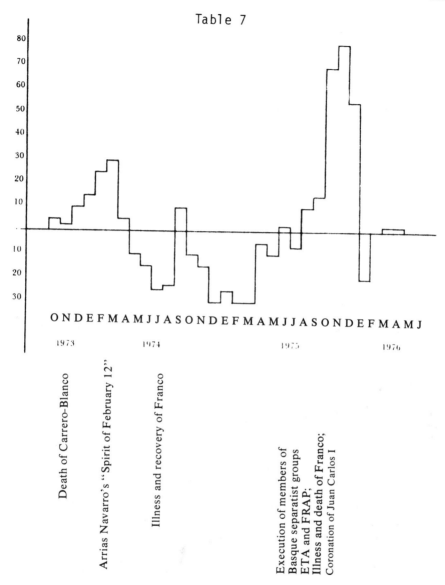

should be studied through the prism of the theory of uses and gratifications. The Spanish population, before the death of Franco, experienced both fear and hope, that is, profound emotions, in relation to its security. Once this unknown was clarified, public opinion contemplated the democratic evolution with increased skepticism, which does not necessarily signify rejection or disregard but simply a feeling of not being personally implicated in these political events. The low levels of participation in the elections and referenda that started in 1977 also support, rather than contradict, the hypothesis proposed here.

THE MOST PROMINENT CHANGES
IN CONTENT IN THE
DAILY PRESS (1975-1980)

Generally speaking, there were few variations in the power structure of the press when compared to earlier times. There were, nevertheless, a series of modifications that gave the press, among all media, a greater mobility. It must be said immediately that if, instead of taking the period 1975-1980, we were to look at the previous five-year period of 1970-1975, we would see comparable if not greater mobility.

At the level of changes in ownership and management of the press in this period, the consequences of the elimination of the secretary general of the Movement must be mentioned. A discussion of this follows. Moreover, changes in the press in this period responded to five major issues:

(1) The need for political groups belonging to historic nationalities to have media of their own available. This is the situation that explains the appearance of three dailies, *Egin* and *Deia* (1978) in the Basque countries and *Avui* (1976) in Catalonia.

(2) Journalistic reorganization of the extreme Right, which is Francoist and a loser in the democratic process. This explains the appearance of the *Imparcial,* an important increase in the circulation of *Alcazar,* and the sale of stock in *Diario de Barcelona,* as the most important events.

(3) Newspapers that resulted from the initial expansion of weeklies. This explains the appearance of *El Periòdico* in 1977 and *Diario 16.*

(4) The need to launch an "independent" newspaper of high quality, with ample documentation, with an interest in making itself a state newspaper that would permit the credible diffusion of the major occurrences of political and administrative life. This is the case of *El Pais,* whose influence in the administration and even in Parliament as a publication devoted to question and answer is undeniable.

(5) We are left, finally, with a question about the leftist press that has little or no answer. If we exclude the case of the marginal *Mundo Obrero,* the leftist press has only one outstanding moment in the increase in circulation of *Mundo Diario* between 1977 and 1978. The profound crisis of the *Mundo* group, which found itself affected by the liberal-democratic policy of the UCD government in financial matters, closes dramatically for the newspaper profession the last episode of the press in the period under study.

THE DISAPPEARANCE OF THE
MOVEMENT PRESS;
THE UTOPIA OF THE PUBLIC PRESS

The study of the evolution of the Movement press is important because it places us at the heart of the principal political dimension of the future of the mass media in Spain: public and semipublic media, freedom of information and objective conditions for its exercise.

As the crisis developed, the hope for a public press, which the socialist and communist parties desired without being able to do anything about it, died. Of the 38 newspapers of the Movement that were in existence in 1975, 25 had

TABLE 8. Newspapers with Circulations under 70,000 (1975-1978)

	1970	1975	1976	1977	1978
AVUI (Barcelona) (entirely in Catalan)			50.591	37.640	32.055
DEIA (Bilbao) (Bilingual Spanish-Basque)					50.283
EGIN (Bilingual Spanish-Basque)					45.731
DIARIO 16 (Madrid)				75.613	58.731
EL IMPARCIAL (Madrid)					51.929
EL PERIODICO (Barcelona)					53.121 (1979)

been started during the civil war as a result of the expropriations of Republican newspapers. Three newspapers appeared in 1939 and the remaining 11 were started before 1945. The Francoist propaganda apparatus, when it had radio and television at its disposal, maintained the Movement press more as an instrument of featherbedding, control, and propagandistic planning than with any true informative intention. In 1975 these newspapers, already old, reached a total daily printing of approximately 451,471 copies, an average of 11,800 copies per newspaper.

With the elimination of the secretary general of the Movement and the simultaneous formation of the autonomous organization called the State Social Communications Media, the continuing survival of these newspapers, which in only the first trimester of 1977 had lost 640 million pesetas, was called into question. The alternative of the workers, unions, and leftist parties was to maintain the newspapers' status as a public press through regionalization. The newspapers would be controlled by representatives of the administration, the regional assembly of members of Parliament, and the communications workers. The proposal was justified above all by the fact that the nationalities (Euzkadi or Basque countries, Catalonia, Andalucia, Galicia, and so on) were demanding the development of autonomous communications media.

In contrast to these hopes, some newspapers had already closed, putting into motion different processes of assimilation into the administration of their former workers. As for the surviving thirty-one newspapers, it seems that the proposed solution by the government will be, finally, the auction. This would resolve the conflict in favor of those who have greater economic power, such as the political bosses of the small capital cities. The dilemma of freedom of information—objective conditions for its exercise—would be resolved in favor of the liberal conception of such freedom.

PICTORIAL MAGAZINES IN THE
PERIOD OF POLITICAL CHANGE

We can start here from a primary and elementary distinction between (1) general information magazines, (2) popular pictoral magazines, (3) erotic publications, and (4) variety, news, sports, comics, and the like.

TABLE 9.   Circulation

General Information Magazines	1974	1975	1976	1977	1978	1974-1978
Blanco y Negro	47.118	67.638	87.848	57.672	44.406	
Cambio 16	42.645	197.276	347.017	— — —	145.487	
Gaceta Ilustrada	83.323	72.083	81.555	59.141	50.594	
Sábado Gráfico	80.602	90.188	71.163	57.019	37.811	
Truinfo	70.302	73.083	87.908	63.108	45.493	

SOURCE: Controles O.J.D.

Between 1975 and the end of 1976, although more slowly than in the daily press, an increase can be seen in the circulation of the weekly political press. From this date on, after the referendum on the political reform and before the first elections were held, this press suffered an obvious decrease in its circulation (see Table 9). It can be confirmed here again that the reading of publications with political content was related to the need to obtain information about the future, the need to deal with anxiety: After Franco, what? This was produced, above all, in the moment of transition from dictatorship to parliamentary monarchy. The most spectacular case of this increase and decrease is without doubt the magazine *Cambio 16,* with a social democratic perspective, which reached the difficult circulation figure of of 350,000 copies, to drop vertically to the level of 100,000 copies in 1979.

The general information magazines that have reached and maintained circulation figures of about 50,000 copies are those published by companies that produce other publications, particularly dailies.

The deep crisis of the leftist press in this period merits special commentary. The exemplary case would be *Cuadernos para el diálogo.* After uniting the democratic sectors during Franco's regime, based on sectors of the Christian Democrats, it became a weekly in 1976, with important participation by leftist professionals. It disappeared in September 1978 after having reached its best professional level, a victim of the dissolution of the unitarist movements.

The Left managed to maintain only two low-circulation magazines in the market, *Triunfo* (45,000 copies in 1975) and *La Calle* (43,000 copies in 1979), and changed the daily *El Socialista* into a weekly as of April 1980. The conclusion can be reached that the liberalization of censorship does not carry with it an increase in the demand for general information publications. This liberalization was noted in the proliferation of small publications, regional in scope, with circulations always below 5,000 copies and enormous difficulties in surviving.

Those that have maintained high circulation figures are the popular pictoral magazines (*Hola, Lecturas, Garbo, Semana,* and their like; see Table 10). A larger increase in those magazines that include erotic copy and commentary can perhaps be observed. Among the popular pictoral magazines, *Pronto* constitutes a case of spectacular increases in circulation, reaching the figure of 830,000 copies in 1979. This magazine, a result like *Interviu* of trial and

TABLE 10. Circulation of the Principal Popular Pictoral Magazines

	1974	1975	1976	1977	1978	1974-1978
Ama	179.891	175.059	151.306	177.493	109.080	−39%
Diez Minutos	332.970	401.448	412.173	383.562	388.003	+16'5
Garbo	124.592	126.019	116.267	103.920	94.497	−24
Hola	428.555	404.118	378.329	364.486	389.861	− 9
Labores del Hogar	126.181	128.883	143.005	162.222	148.111	+17
Lecturas	435.608	483.343	517.482	486.770	490.843	+12
Pronto	149.918	346.439	395.360	368.079	517.683	+245%
Semana	429.192	455.830	407.381	374.203	364.257	−15
Telva	73.723	79.350	76.705	71.122	82.889	−1'7

SOURCE: Controles O.J.D.

error, represents a paradigmatic example of the current structure of mass culture, brief and fragmentary references to the reality constructed by the media themselves (television, cinema, recorded music). The nature of the magazine advertising should be emphasized as a significant detail and indicative of the level of consensus of its readers. Some 47 percent of its advertisements (analysis of the April 13, 1980, issue) are dedicated to ads relating to treatments of the body, to the search for everlasting youth, dieting, methods for breast development, baldness, acne, tanning lotions, and so on.

Among those magazines whose circulation has dropped, sports magazines must be mentioned. They, although to a lesser degree than general information publications, lost ground to the erotic publications (see Table 11), which are the prime beneficiaries of the political change.

In addition to the influence of eroticism in illustrated magazines in general, mention should be made of the appearance of high-circulation magazines such as *LIB* (started in 1977), which reached almost 300,000 copies in 1979, and the appearance of *Penthouse* in April 1978 and *Playboy* in November of the same year, whose circulation is over 200,000 copies monthly.

THE *INTERVIU* PHENOMENON

Interviu is, without doubt, one of the most important communications phenomena of the stage under study. What is truly significant is that this magazine is the result of a journalistic tactic of trial and error, attempted by a business group with little publishing experience. Their first experience in this area had been the bulletin of the Almería firm.

The most noticeable characteristic of this magazine is the semantic mixture of pornography, politics, denunciations of corruption, pornographic investigative journalism, and so on. *Interviu* plays with a continual provocation of the deep resentment that the Spanish reader has after so many years of censorship. The demand responds to the need to overcome the effort and frustration of "reading between the lines." The "new journalism" of *Interviu* consists of inciting the reading of the lines themselves. The passion for the detail, the photographic realism, the daring of pornography are applied photographically (in a manner that is completely foreign to the habitual style of *Paris Match)* to other objects of social life, to blood, to the mangled human

TABLE 11. Circulation of Different Illustrated Magazines
(greater than 70,000 copies)

	1974	1975	1976	1977	1978
Sports and Events					
As-Color	137.145	119.634	103.182	72.578	68.999
El Caso	183.143	154.490	126.588	148.644	161.415
Erotic, Satiric, Humor					
El Papus	74.268	91.528	142.692	82.277	64.820
Lib				219.155	288.559
Varied					
Ser Padres		141.125	144.591	129.903	115.010
Teleprograma	755.528	771.176	792.015	739.015	849.885
Erotic, Political, Blood, Events					
Interviu			296.375	640.524	713.487

SOURCE: Controles O.J.D.

body, to the faithful reproduction of deformation, to the presentation of public figures from unexpected angles (from top to bottom), to the search for the "pornographic" code of political photography, the yawn of the MP, the indiscreet hand scratching a nose, unfocused eyes, and so on.

It would thus be a mistake to attribute the success of *Interviu* to eroticism, which is after all the least pornographic part of the magazine. The levels of permissibility in other semantic fronts overshadow the daring of the erotic treatment.

The first push of *Interviu* can be related to some degree to the need for the democratic credibility of the new regime, as happened later with radio. The hypothesis presented here is that *Interviu*, which first appeared in Spring 1976, experienced its expansion at a time in which Adolfo Suarez made his reputation as an agent of change with the erotic liberalization called the *destape* [literally, "the uncovering"].

The first breasts displayed on magazine covers papering the kiosks of Spain are a result of this era, well symbolized by the summer 1979 issues of *Interviu*, in which nude photos of [performers] Marisol and Nadiuska appeared.

It was a matter, like the first amnesty, of an opening, of a first step, because *Interviu*'s readers had to wait for the period between the general elections (June 1977) and the constitutional referendum (December 1978) to see the pubes of the models of the moment.

This escalation, in 1978, raised the printings of *Interviu* to levels over 700,000 copies. This is the major surprise, in relation to the consumption of magazines, of the political stage we are studying. Only *Teleprograma* and, more recently, *Pronto* have achieved such figures.

The expansion of *Interviu*, in the logic of the contemporary communications industry, could not stop with its own growth. It was time to organize a major communications enterprise, Group "Z," with the launching of a newspaper, *El Periódico;* an important family of magazines, the most significant being the erotic-pornographic magazines *LIB* (1977) and *Penthouse* (1978); and a cinema production company. In February 1978 the management of "Z" made their first declarations in favor of private television and started provisions for the creation of their network.

Finally, *Interviu* began showing a slow decline in 1980, in part brought about by a tough campaign by the extreme Right. That large a communications structure cannot be built without a more strongly rooted economic base, greater financial support, or the support of some multinational communications industry.

THE ROLE OF RTVE DURING
THE CHANGE TOWARD DEMOCRACY

The recent history of the RTVE marks the most negative point in the relations between the communications media and the defense of freedoms and the exercise of democracy.

The greatest resistance to change has been concentrated in television, and that is also where the differences between a project of democratic reform and the democratic breaking with the former regime have been most obvious.

We must not minimize the significant historical fact that the [then] president of the government and the political manager of change, D. Adolfo Suárez, had been general director of TVE and that this position has been occupied by other officeholders in his government, as in the case of two ministers, Sancho Rof of Public Works and Juan José Rosón of the Interior. TVE posts had and still have outstanding political importance. In the case of TVE, the distinction between professionals and politicians cannot be made with any rigor when we are referring to management positions.

The current RTVE inherited a centralized and authoritarian structure that is on a collision course with the new political positions of a democratic and autonomous state. This inheritance, on the other hand, is extraordinarily attractive and useful for the government, which has at its disposal a medium that could guarantee its remaining in power. Everyone now comprehends that television is a fundamental instrument of political power. It is therefore not strange that tension here has been increasing and is still, five years after the beginning of the process of political change, far from being resolved.

Converging in Spanish radio and television are the multiple contradictions derived from a government that has as its objective the consolidation of a communications system in accordance with the ideals of liberal market economics but that has, on the other hand, a powerful communications apparatus, completely controllable, as a consequence of not having altered its system of functioning. I will speak later about the implementation of the statute for RTVE that was approved in January 1980. In any case, the political transition has been accomplished with a television system hierarchically structured, with minor alterations, in accordance with the established order of the previous regime.

Let us go now to the date of the appointment of Adolfo Suárez as president of the government (July 1976).[6]

On the day of his appointment he used television to present the first brushstrokes of a new way of doing politics. Suárez appeared before the audience in an intimate setting, seated on a sofa of his living room. This was the beginning of a political process conducted, step by step, with a semantic strategy transmitted basically by television.

After this first appearance, which would be repeated in accordance with the political necessities of the moment, the most outstanding event in television was, without doubt, the appointment of Rafael Ansón as the new general director of RTVE. With the appointment of Ansón, there was a timid attempt at institutional levels to update the democratic face of television by creating an Advisory Commission—perhaps of British inspiration—but this was in reality in the image of the schema of an organic concept of democracy. Of a total of 51 people, the great majority were members of the administration. The commission never had any influence on programming.

Ansón undertook the task of initiating a major public relations campaign for the new regime, which facilitated the process until the general elections of 1977. This could have been achieved only with the active cooperation of television. The intensity and rigor with which the campaign was planned constitute the most important persuasive phenomenon of the new regime and can only be compared to the Twenty-Five Years of Peace campaign and the 1966 referendum.

The televised campaigns of 1976-1977, which included all of television programming and not just special programs, promoted the reformist leaders indirectly through news about the ministries and general administration activities.

The appearance of the opposition leaders was programmed and rationed with just enough to give the appearance of democratic credibility to the system. Felipe González[7] made his first substantive appearance on television in 1977, the Spanish Communist Party was still illegal, and Jordi Pujol,[8] after hesitations and postponements, appeared in March of the same year.

Before the proclamation of the electoral law, which regulated television political announcement time and was relatively generous with the different opposition parties, there was no democratic control of television, and the appearance of political leaders depended on the criteria of the management, under direct orders from the government. This planning and rationing was not limited to the presence of politicians and the selection of news, but rather was extended to programming in general. Certain programs were withheld for the postelectoral period because of their latent content, while others, for example, anticommunist films, were programmed for strategic moments of the electoral campaigns.

After the June 1977 elections and until the beginning of 1978, a series of actions tending toward the liberalization of the communications system in Spain took place. Amnesty, the dissolution of the secretary general of the National Movement and of the Ministry of Information and Tourism, the move toward consensual democracy, the liberalization of radio and television news, the elimination of the news monopoly formerly held by the RNE, and the screening of the soft-core pornographic film *Emmanuelle* can be noted as the most significant and interrelated points of this period that resulted from the security that its election victory signified for the UCD.

This "spring" was most limited and ended most precipitously in RTVE. In the last months of 1977 and the first of 1978, the doors were closed on the first hopes awakened by the politics of consensus.

The first consequence for television of the constitution of a democratic parliament was the creation, following the appointment of Arias Salgado as the new general director of RTVE, of a Governing Commission for RTVE.

This commission, created in November 1977, was made up of 36 members, 18 of whom were directly named by the government and the rest coming from the different parties with parlimentary representation. This arrangement gave the UCD 25 of the total 36 votes.

The limits of the opening in television were reached in January 1978 with the dismissal of the news directors and the withdrawal of the PSOE from the Governing Commission.

The first sign of democratization of the media, the approval of the new statute for RTVE, had to wait until January 1980. However, the interests and deliberate hesitations that affect this medium were so important that four months after the approval of the statute by Parliament, hindered in various ways, the corresponding parliamentary committees still had not been elected.

The panorama of control must be completed by a secondary analysis, that of the continual denunciations of the corruption of those who run the media. In July 1977 the Anticorruption Committee for television was established, prompted by the medium's workers. Since then the criticisms from diverse sectors have continued. These denunciations culminated with the publication in January 1980 in the newspaper *El País* of an ample report of the Ministry of Finance investigation of RTVE.

Despite the gravity of the accusations, all the top management people of the medium have retained their positions. Although the current situation of RTVE constitutes one of the most important political scandals of this period of political transition, this has not brought about any substantial change.

As was stated, in the discussion of the evolution of radio, the period of greatest liberalization in television, which was always minimal, coincides with the period in which the public relations needs of the UCD and Adolfo Suárez required democratic credibility. This happened between the December 1977 referendum and a few months after the June 1977 elections. After these dates—and including the preparation period of the constitutional referendum, which had half the television effort paid to it that the first referendum had, and very nearly during the new general elections (March 1979), municipal elections (April 1979), and statutory elections (December 1979) as well—television returned to its policy of silencing the opposition and of subtle manipulation of general programming. A good example of the latter is the postponement of the broadcasting of the series *Holocaust* until after the general elections of 1979. The liberalizing period ended definitively after the dismissal in January 1978 of the three directors of the daily news programs who had managed to enliven the news.

It is in the area of political announcements that one would place the greatest contribution of television to the democratic plan; obligated by legislation that, with few precedents for establishing percentages and priorities for regulating the television appearances of political parties, managed to establish a balanced system. The only ones who were harmed, seriously harmed, were the nationalist parties [for example, of the Basque countries or Catalonia] with no state-level representation.

Television has played a decisive role in denying the viability of a *rupturista* course of action and in going along with the distinct phases of reform and continuity.

The appearance of reformist leaders in key moment of political life, the consumate effort to avoid putting the public in contact with critical programs, the establishment of a system of diversion linked to escapism, confused political news based on international anecdotes compounded by a lack of analysis and debate on current events—all this constituted a rigid continuity with the earlier regime and with the style of the principal communications apparatus through which the Spanish obtain their vision of the world.

All these events can be placed once again in the global context of communications policy. The logic of this corruption, the progressive deterioration in programming that reached the extreme point of provoking a loss in audience (on the order of 6.6 to 9.9 percent between June 1978 and June 1979), can be ascribed to the possibility of the creation of private television stations, to the contradictions of a control over television that is compatible with the current democratic system. The result of the current political and economic battle to control this medium is in no way an anecdotal or marginal question; it is a determining factor in the future of democracy and in the establishment of the autonomous regions of Spain.

NOTES

1. Translator's note: Admiral Luis Carrero Blanco was president of Spain's Council of Ministers and was assassinated by the ETA, the Basque separatist organization.

2. Author's note: See my analysis of twenty-four hours of programming of Radio Peninsulares in Barcelona (1976).

3. Translator's note: The National Movement was the Francoist state party.

4. Translator's note: Five people accused of being Basque terrorists were executed by the Spanish government despite international protest.

5. Translator's note: Carlos Arias Navarro was prime minister of Spain and promised reforms even before the death of Franco.

6. Author's note: On the planning of the image of the monarch, see de Moragas Spa, 1980.

7. Translator's note: González is head of the socialist party PSOE, winner of the 1982 elections, and now prime minister.

8. Translator's note: Jordi Pujol is a Catalan nationalist.

REFERENCES

DE MORAGAS SPA, M. (1980) "La propaganda política en España: de la Dictadura al Parlamento," in M. de Moragas Spa (ed.) Sociología de la Comunicación de Masas. Barcelona: Ed. Gustavo Gili.
———(1976) Semiótica y Comunicación de Masas. Barcelona: Peninsular.

PART VII

NEW TECHNOLOGY AND THE INFORMATION AGE

The advent of new technologies, and media technologies may especially be prone to this, are never hard-edged events. As they emerge, their form and meaning, and their structure, organization, and use, are open to experimentation, to change, and to co-optation. If successful, moreover, they are so by altering the very environment in which they emerge.

What we present here is not an overview of the hardware of the new media technologies. Rather, we have four chapters examining from rather different premises how some of these will be organized and used and how the institutional arrangements growing up around them will alter the landscape.

Fombrun and Astley focus on the question of how telecommunications innovations are being managed by major corporate strategy. They note processes of corporate absorption and of intercorporating networking predominate.

Herbert Schiller argues that major players in corporate life are seeking to transform the very nature of the role of information in an emerging corporate economy. His theme is consistent with that of Philip Elliott, who, in the next selection, suggests that subjugation of national and public interests to an international order will, among other things, lead to a disappearance of a "public sphere."

Finally, David Weaver takes a "closer look," in this case a very close one, at how various experiments with cabled television text systems have evolved. One reading of his work would suggest that while such systems are capable of many uses, it takes relatively a short period of time to see systems evolve into rather set uses.

The dynamics of organizational growth in communications and telecommunications, through horizontal integration, vertical integration, and diversification, are discussed in this chapter in the context of technological innovation and institutional evolution. The telecommunications community, Fombrun and Astley note, brings a wide range of traditionally segmented industries into both competitive and collaborative disarray. Driven by technological change, both processes of absorption and networking are taking place, but the future in part depends on the role of outside forces, particularly government. Charles Fombrun and W. Graham Astley are assistant professors of management at the Wharton School, University of Pennsylvania.

31

THE TELECOMMUNICATIONS COMMUNITY
An Institutional Overview

Charles Fombrun and W. Graham Astley

In decades past, the many industrial sectors involved in and around telecommunications in the United States have experienced steady and relatively placid growth, under the careful scrutiny of the Federal Communications Commission. In recent years, however, the telecommunications community has been thrown into a state of turmoil as an accelerating curve of new technologies, the emergence of new markets, and trends toward deregulation have upset established spheres of operation. We are now witnessing a convergence of what were formerly separate industrial sectors, as the activities of organizations as diverse as CBS, Warner, RCA, MCA, Westinghouse, Philips, IBM, and A.T.&T. increasingly interpenetrate and overlap.

Two trends are representative of institutional evolution across the entire industrial landscape (9, 26). First, firms are conglomerating as they vie for the capture of new and profitable market segments; second, they are elaborating their administrative structures through a variety of inter-organizational and inter-industry relationships. This article focuses on these trends as they affect firms in the far-flung telecommunications

Reprinted from "The Telecommunications Community: An Institutional Overview," by Charles Fombrun and W. Graham Astley in the *Journal of Communication,* Vol. 32, No. 4 (Autumn 1982), pp. 56-68. Copyright © 1982 by the Annenberg School of Communications. Reprinted by permission.

community, describing the increasing convergence of diverse industrial sectors and the interdependent actions of government and business firms in that process.

> *The environment of most organizations is itself increasingly made up of organizations.*

Some theorists have drawn attention to the "stakeholders" in the transactional environment with which the organization holds dynamic exchanges and on whom it is dependent for resources (5, 13, 14, 23). These writers stress the behavior of the focal organization. A second group of authors, drawing on the study of industrial organization (24, 25), population ecology (2, 16), and bio-ecology (6), has further examined the "environment" as itself structured and organizational, something which firms both respond to and create. Each of these approaches has strong implications for the adaptive process linking the organization and the environment over time.

Two parallel and complementary approaches to the dynamics of industrial evolution can be identified that deal with (a) the single organization evolving over time, or (b) a group of organizations adjusting to the environment. Led by Alfred Chandler (9, 10), the first line of research focuses on the increasing concentration of economic power in the hands of fewer and larger umbrella organizations. Organizational growth is said to take place through a sequential process involving *horizontal integration,* as the firm spans geographical markets, *vertical integration,* as the firm moves to guarantee its sources of supply and outlets for its outputs, and *diversification* across related and unrelated domains in the process of developing a portfolio of complementary businesses. Following Pennings (22), these stages of growth can be described in terms of a strategic absorption of environmental elements with which the focal organization is, in sequence, horizontally, vertically, and then symbiotically interdependent.[1] Figure 1 diagrams the growth pattern.

The second stream of research has discussed the evolution of a group of organizations from a situation of perfect competition to oligopolistic cooperation and sophisticated network coordination. Rather than stressing the absorption of interdependent functions into the firm, this research suggests the emergence of increasingly complex bilateral and

[1] Horizontal interdependence exists between firms with common markets or products. Vertical interdependence links organizations at different stages of production. Symbiotic interdependence links organizations "that complement each other in the rendering of services to individual clients" (22, p. 434).

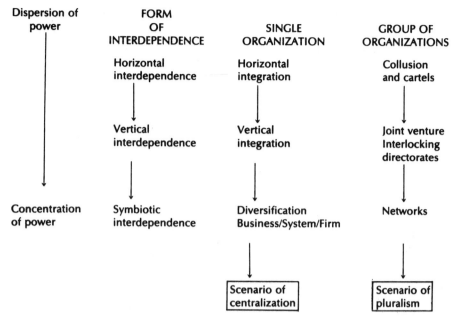

Figure 1: Stages of industrial growth

multi-lateral structures for the coordination of inter-organizational activity that benefits all organizations in the set (15). These structures range from informal discussions and agreements to interlocking directorates, and include cartels, contracts, joint ventures, leadership, and network management (3, 12, 19).

The two processes suggest two different scenarios for industrial evolution in the long run. The first predicts that, as interdependence continues to grow, we will observe the emergence of increasingly complex organizational forms performing broad social functions (26). Following Metcalfe (20), we can label this the "scenario of centralization." Power is concentrated in the hands of a few dominant firms.

The second scenario points to a landscape speckled with organizations, both large and small, performing segmented functional tasks and integrated through a loose network that coordinates the adaptation of single organizations across functional sectors (what Gerlach and Palmer [15] describe as SPINS, or Segmented Polycentric Integrated Networks). This is the "scenario of pluralism" (20), in which power is dispersed across a broad set of organizations whose activities are nonetheless coordinated through a network of interlocks. Figure 1 contrasts these evolutionary scenarios.

The direction taken by any single industry, the telecommunications community in particular, and society as a whole, is largely dependent on social preference and the degree to which government takes on the role of network manager, regulating the growth process and restricting the emergence of one kind of interfirm structure or another. This article will sketch some of the parameters of that interplay between business firm and government in telecommunications.

> *Developments in cable, video, and satellite technologies have produced a scramble for profit through entertainment programming, while also making possible an expanded use of these technologies for the provision of information services to the home.*

The two principal functions performed by the contemporary telecommunications community[2] are entertainment and information manipulation. Home entertainment centered on the TV set is experiencing enormous change. As of 1982, close to 21 million homes (26 percent of all TV homes) have been wired for cable reception (14 million in use), offering more programming choice. Viewers' options are also expanded through the flexibility offered by videocassette recorders (VCRs) and videodiscs. To date, some 2.5 million VCRs and 68,000 videodiscs are in use. Through satellite technology, with reception through sophisticated antennae systems and distribution through a local cable network, such stations as Ted Turner's WTBS can broadcast to national audiences. In the area of home information services, videotex enables TV owners to call forth news and information on diverse subjects, as well as shop, bank, and communicate via the television tube.

These innovative systems are capitalizing on developments in the technological realm that are largely the result of the efforts of a broad range of firms, including IBM, Western Union, A.T.&T., Hughes Aircraft, and RCA. Through significant improvements in transmission technologies and manufacturing efficiency, new products and new markets are creating growth opportunities for small and large firms, both within traditional industry boundaries and with organizations performing complementary functions. Affected firms include motion picture studios, TV networks, newspaper groups, publishing houses, and producers of equipment and technology. Figure 2 diagrams the principal domains that are involved in the delivery of entertainment and information.

As suggested in Figure 2, there is increasing symbiotic interdependence between firms traditionally concerned with the entertainment

---

[2] We purposely distinguish "community" from "industry." An industry brings together firms that are only horizontally interdependent. A community consists of firms related through *all three* forms of interdependence (horizontal, vertical, and symbiotic).

ENTERTAINMENT INDUSTRY	INFORMATION INDUSTRY
SOFTWARE	SOFTWARE

ENTERTAINMENT SOFTWARE	INFORMATION SOFTWARE
Motion picture studios	Wire services
Independent producers (audio, visual print)	Newspaper groups
	Advertising agencies
Magazines	Software producers
Publishing houses	Teletext services
Video game manufacturers	

HARDWARE	HARDWARE
Encoding	Data transmission
TV networks	Common carriers
Pre-recorded cassette manufacturers	Telephone companies
Printing plants	Satellite operators
Rewinding tape manufacturer	Printing plants
Transmission	Data processing
Radio stations	Computer manufacturers (personnel
TV station operators	and main frame)
Cable system operators	Data input/output
Satellite operators	Computer terminals and peripheral
Decoding	equipment manufacturers
Radio sets	
TV set manufacturers	
Video equipment manufacturers	
Theater owners	

Figure 2: Principal firms in the delivery of entertainment and information

sector and firms involved in the delivery and processing of information. This is because of two principal developments: (a) the decreasing cost of microprocessors that make distortion-free digital systems an increasingly attractive and feasible alternative to analog systems; and (b) developments in cable and satellite transmission technology that reduce transmission costs and increase the geographical reach of signals.

These developments have chiseled away at the primary operating domains of many firms. A.T.&T. sees the telephone as only one alternative for transmitting data, with linked computer networks increasingly an option. The Postal Service sees the dominance of hand-delivered correspondence increasingly attacked by telephone contact and "electronic mail" through linked computer systems. Theater owners see video recordings, cable networks, and pre-recorded cassette production as a threat to public screenings. Newspaper groups see cable news and teletext as an alternative to newspapers. Advertising agencies see cable channels and the editing capabilities of cassette recorders as a threat to their advertising effectiveness.

These perceptions (among others) are reinforced by continually evolving technology that speaks to direct broadcasting to the home via satellite, a home entertainment center integrated with the personal

computer, interactive television, and remote shopping. Taken by themselves, each presents a challenge to the basic business strategy of every
firm in the telecommunications community. Taken as a whole, they
constitute a challenge that can only be understood through an awareness
of the collectivity of organizations in the community, their coherence,
and their strategic outlook.

> *To appreciate properly the collective dynamics of the*
> *emerging telecommunications community, it is important*
> *to understand the prior structural configurations*
> *of the constituent groups in the community.*

Figure 2 partitions the telecommunications community in terms of
two dimensions: software versus hardware—the degree to which the
products of the firm involve manufacturing hardware rather than software or content; and entertainment versus information—the primary
social function to which the firm's products are oriented. In Figure 3, the
same functions are represented in terms of a map similar to that
developed by Harvard University's Program on Information Resources
Policy (11) but in which information and entertainment are opposed,
rather than product and service. This was done to remove the manifest
interdependence in their two axes.

As communications and computer technologies join, the broad range
of firms and industrial sectors outlined in Figure 3 is fused into a
community of organizations. Each sector brings with it a prior structure:

PRODUCT

	SOFTWARE		HARDWARE
ENTERTAINMENT	Motion pictures	TV and cable networks	Video equipment
			TV stations
	Entertainment	Pay/subscription	Cable systems
	programs	TV	Radio
	Mass market books	Videotex	Satellite
	Magazines	Video games	
FUNCTION			
			Printing and copying
	College/profes-		Computer
	sional books		hardware
	Advertising	Packaged software	Typewriter
	Directories	Teletext	Personal carrier
INFORMATION	Newspapers	Wire services	Phone/telegraph

Figure 3: Product/function map of the telecommunications community

- Radio is dominated by four broadcast networks and their affiliated stations, controlling 62 percent of all stations (2,803 of 4,497 in 1977).
- Television is dominated by three networks which control 84 percent of all stations (612 of 728 in 1977).
- The top 25 daily newspaper groups controlled 52 percent of all daily circulation in 1976.
- The seven majors controlled 94 percent of all theater film rentals in 1978.
- In computer hardware, IBM controlled 65 percent of worldwide mainframe shipments in 1977, and a leading 12 percent of the software market.
- In telephone equipment, A.T.&T. controlled close to 85 percent of the market, and GTE another 5 percent, in 1979.
- In television sets, 57 percent of the market was controlled by RCA, Zenith, and Philips in 1980.
- Thirty-seven percent of all cable subscribers were serviced by the top eight multiple system operators in 1976.

These basic statistics suggest that relatively few organizations dominate the community formed by the convergence of communications and computer technologies. Different kinds of inter-organizational linkages are forming as the traditionally distinct segments of the community come together through contracts, joint ventures, and outright acquisitions.

A case study of industrial evolution in the video entertainment industry suggests the complexity of the current structural configuration of the "organic" telecommunications community.

Firms involved in the provision of visual entertainment to a wide public include motion picture studios, TV networks, cable system operators, and a host of independent producers, performers, writers, and directors. A high degree of coordinated structuring has characterized the industry ever since the first moving pictures were shown in a New York Kinetoscope parlor in 1894.

Four major functions are performed by firms in the visual entertainment sector: innovation, production, distribution, and exhibition. Initially, innovation and production were the province of a handful of firms that were also the manufacturers of projecting equipment (Edison, Biograph, and Vitagraph). Despite attempts at protecting patents, however, hundreds of producers soon entered the field. Distribution was handled through a system of exchanges that purchased films from producers and rented them to exhibitors. By 1907, some 125 to 150 exchanges operated across the U.S. Consistent with Williamson's (29) arguments, those exchanges minimized the number of transactions producers would have to engage in for the exhibition of their films in the thousands of theaters ("nickelodeons") across the country.

This era of competition among scores of producers, exchanges, and exhibitors ended in 1908 with the formation of the Motion Picture Patents Company (MPCC), a group of ten companies that included all the leading producers and manufacturers of equipment. Through informal collusion, the MPPC coopted Eastman Kodak into exclusive sale of film stock and leased pictures only to those exchanges dealing in licensed films. These exchanges, in turn, could rent only pictures and exhibitors using licensed projectors.

Clearly, the collusive linkages formed early on were designed to absorb uncertainty in the vertical interdependence of the different sectors (see Figure 2). Patent laws guaranteed the legitimacy of the MPPC in its policy activities. The initial networking was replaced in 1910 by direct absorption when, through the General Film Company, 58 exchanges were brought by the MPPC in a direct move toward vertical integration. This move precipitated legal action under the provisions of the Sherman Antitrust Act which, in 1918, resulted in the dissolution of the MPPC.

In 1917, 26 exhibitors organized the First National Exhibitors Circuit to act as purchasing agents, thereby creating countervailing power in the bid for box-office names. By 1925, vertical integration from distribution into exhibition had created an industry dominated by Paramount, First National, Loew's, and Fox. With the advent of sound (the technology for which was developed by A.T.&T.) and the "talkies," Warner and RKO (a subsidiary of RCA) joined the list of dominant companies in the industry by 1930. The capital requirements for the introduction of sound drove out of business all independent producers and exhibitors, leaving a virtual oligopoly of five companies in the industry: Warner Brothers, MGM, Paramount, RKO, and Fox. Each was fully vertically integrated from innovation and production to exhibition.

Roosevelt's New Deal brought the National Industrial Recovery Act, which in turn resulted in the Motion Picture Code of 1933. The Code essentially legitimated the oligopolistic structure of the industry and formalized it through a trade association, the Motion Picture Producers and Distributors of America (MPPDA).

Simultaneously, a struggle over the payment of creative talent, professionals, and executives in the industry resulted in the formation of the Screen Actors Guild in 1937. It was quickly followed by the Screen Writers Guild and the Screen Directors Guild, each a collective body designed to protect the joint interests of its constituent members. They effectively presented countervailing power to the dominant producers.

In 1948, Paramount's defeat in the Supreme Court brought a landmark government decision that directed the five integrated companies to divest their holdings in exhibition. This decision came at a time when the growth of commercial television was transforming the entertainment industry. Between 1948 and 1950, only four million sets were in use. By the late 1950s, 90 percent of all homes in the U.S. had television sets. In the same period, the number of TV stations rose from 7 to 517.

After 1950, an entire industry of independent producers, heretofore discouraged by the dominance of the eight majors, was thriving on the development of television programming. Initially, the majors fought the development of TV through the use of color, 3-D projections, and wide screens. These innovations were insufficient, however, to deal with the drawing power of TV and, by the mid-1950s, the majors themselves were involved in collaborative arrangements with TV that included production and distribution of old film libraries. This early partnership culminated in the made-for-TV film of the 1970s, which involved co-financing of features shown first on television and then in theaters.

Meanwhile, in television, the rise of the networks and their affiliates, coordinated by William Paley (who borrowed the idea from the structure of the radio industry), guaranteed the programming content and advertising revenue of a large number of dispersed TV stations across the U.S. Through control over programming, the networks became a virtual oligopoly in the production and broadcasting of visual entertainment. Simultaneously, the networks diversified into the theater chains that the majors had divested, thereby cementing the entertainment industry into a new configuration with linkages between motion picture operations, broadcasting, and exhibition in the late 1970s.

This description of the development of the video entertainment industry, diagrammed in Figure 4, suggests three general characteristics of structural evolution. First, the nature of collective action varies with the number of organizations vying for competitive positioning. Second, government plays a key role in determining the kinds of linkages that emerge between organizations. And third, organizations pursue strategies that involve *both* internal absorption and external networking as they attempt to control their environmental context.

Institutional management therefore emerges as an important dimension of strategic planning, one that involves a complex set of interactions between business organizations, representative pressure groups within the industry, and government.

> *An additional factor in the growth of the*
> *telecommunications community is the complexity brought*
> *on by technological developments in information handling.*

Changes in three major technological domains are contributing to the turmoil that has created the modern telecommunications community. In video technology, videocassette recording and videodisc playback have created a new outlet for the exhibition of feature films, TV programming,

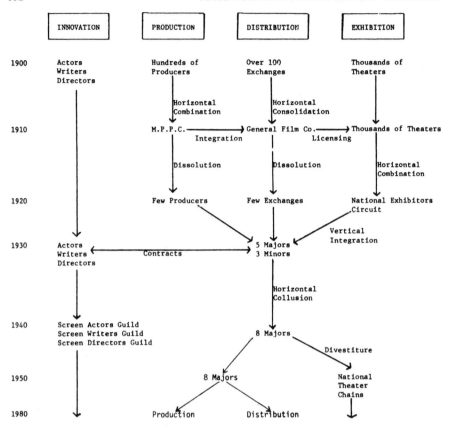

Figure 4: The horizontal and vertical evolution of the motion picture industry

and games. In cable technology, the rapid growth of cable systems has increased the number of channels available to viewers and provides an alternate broadcast medium to TV stations and network programs. At the same time, fiber optical cables are increasing wiring transmission capabilities. Finally, satellite transmission makes it possible to broadcast for national audiences, link up scattered businesses into computer networks, and broadcast directly to homes and businesses. Driven by the decreasing cost of microprocessors and developments in transmission, these three technologies are creating vast threats to the basic businesses of such firms as A.T.&T., the U.S. Postal Service, and Western Union. At the same time, they represent significant opportunities for repositioning vis-à-vis competitors.

For these reasons, numerous relationships have come to mar the long-standing distinction between industrial subgroups and to foster the emergence of an organic community (6). Figure 5 charts a portion of the inter-organizational network linking organizations in the telecommunications community into an organic whole.

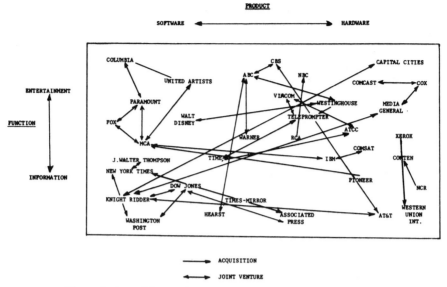

Figure 5: A partial mapping of the telecommunications community

As the figure suggests, both absorption and networking are taking place in the current scramble for positioning. This is largely the result of a governmental stance that favors deregulation and a non-managed process of industrial evolution. This raises two important and related questions for industrial evolution, questions that are now being addressed by the FCC and Congress.

1. As absorption takes place, what will be the degree of concentration after deregulation? This issue could bring on antitrust hostility, although that is not likely, since non-communications firms are diversifying into the community, thereby reducing visible concentration within any single sector. Thus standard industrial classifications belie a true appreciation of concentration across operating domains (26).

2. As networking continues, how will the linkages among organizations affect important outcomes, such as (a) the aggregate rate of innovation (films, inventions, patents); (b) profits of firms; (c) bargaining power of subgroups; (d) quality of product or service output; (e) responsiveness to customer needs in terms of product or service; and (f) social welfare (e.g., reliable phone service, entertainment, access to data processing)?

The telecommunications community brings together a wide range of traditionally segmented industries into both competitive and collaborative disarray. Driven by technological change, both processes of absorption and networking are taking place in this organic collectivity. Where the community will go is largely dependent on the role the Federal Communications Commission and government as a whole choose to play in the·evolutionary process. The implications are vast and difficult to assess but will certainly affect such important outcomes as the free flow of information, the aggregate rate of innovation, and the quality and range of services available to consumers in both national and international markets.

In developing an adequate framework for understanding the structural evolution of the community, this article has not addressed the implications of evolutionary dynamics. One vital concern is the impact of community dynamics on the free flow of information in society. Rather than moving us closer to Marshall McLuhan's vision of the global village, the increasing involvement of multinationals in telecommunications functions may generate an over-abundance of information, the necessity for increased specialization, and a breakdown of effective communication between different sectors of society. In this article we have attempted to sketch a framework for addressing these issues.

REFERENCES

1. Ackoff, R. *Redesigning the Future*. New York: John Wiley & Sons, 1974.
2. Aldrich, Howard. *Organizations and Environments*. Englewood Cliffs, N.J.: Prentice-Hall, 1979.
3. Allen, M. P. "The Structure of Interorganizational Elite Cooperation Interlocking Corporate Directories." *American Sociological Review* 39, 1974, pp. 393–496.
4. Andrews, Kenneth. *The Concept of Corporate Strategy*. Homewood, Ill.: Dow-Jones-Irwin, 1971.
5. Ansoff, H. Igor. *Corporate Strategy: An Analytic Approach to Business Policy for Growth and Expansion*. New York: McGraw-Hill, 1965.
6. Astley, W. G. and C. Fombrun. "Collective Strategy: The Role of Institutional Management." Working Paper No. 125, Wharton Center for the Study of Organizational Innovation, University of Pennsylvania, 1982.
7. Balio, T. *The American Film Industry*. Madison, Wis.: University of Wisconsin Press, 1976.
8. Brock, W. *The Telecommunications Industry*. Cambridge, Mass.: Harvard University Press, 1981.
9. Chandler, A. D. *The Visible Hand: The Managerial Revolution in American Business*. Cambridge, Mass.: Harvard University Press, 1977.
10. Chandler, Alfred. *Strategy and Structure*. Cambridge, Mass.: MIT Press, 1962.
11. Compaine, B. "Shifting Boundaries in the Information Marketplace." *Journal of Communication* 31(1), Winter 1981.
12. Dooley, Peter. "The Interlocking Directorate." *American Economic Review* 59, June 1969.
13. Emshoff, J. R. and R. E. Freeman. "Stakeholder Management." Working Paper 3-78, Wharton Applied Research Center, University of Pennsylvania, 1978.
14. Evan, William. "The Organization-Set: Toward a Theory of Interorganizational Relations." In James Thompson (Ed.) *Approaches to Organizational Design*. Pittsburgh: University of Pittsburgh Press, 1966.
15. Gerlach, L. P. and G. Palmer. "Adaptation through Evolving Interdependence." In P. Nystrom and W. Starbuck (Eds.) *Handbook of Organizational Design*, Vol. 2. New York: Oxford University Press, 1981, pp. 323–381.
16. Hannan, Michael and John Freeman. "The Population Ecology of Organizations." *American Journal of Sociology* 82, March 1977.
17. Huettig, M. *Economic Control of the Motion Picture Industry*. Philadelphia: University of Pennsylvania Press, 1944.

18. Lawrence, Paul R. and J. W. Lorsch. *Organization and Environment: Managing Differentiation and Integration.* Boston: Graduate School of Business Administration, Harvard University, 1967.

19. Mariolis, Peter. "Interlocking Directorates and Control of Corporations: The Theory of Bank Control." *Social Science Quarterly* 56, December 1975.

20. Metcalfe, J. L. "Systems Models, Economic Models and the Causal Texture of Organizational Environments: An Approach to Macro-Organizational Theory." *Human Relations* 27(7), 1974.

21. Michael, D. *On Learning to Plan and Planning to Learn.* San Francisco: Jossey-Bass, 1973.

22. Pennings, J. M. "Strategically Interdependent Organizations." In P. Nystrom and W. Starbuck (Eds.) *Handbook of Organizational Design,* Vol. 2. New York: Oxford University Press, 1981, pp. 433–455.

23. Pfeffer, Jeffrey and G. R. Salancik. *The External Control of Organizations.* New York: Harper and Row, 1978.

24. Porter, Michael E. *Competitive Strategy: Techniques for Analyzing Industries and Competitors.* New York: Free Press, 1980.

25. Porter, Michael E. "The Contributions of Industrial Organization to Strategic Management." *Academy of Management Review* 6(4), October 1981.

26. Schon, Donald. *Beyond the Stable State.* New York: Basic Books, 1971.

27. Steiner, G. *Top Management Planning.* New York: Macmillan, 1969.

28. Trist, E. L. "Referent Organizations and the Development of Inter-Organizational Domains." Distinguished Lecture, Organization and Management Theory Division, 39th Annual Convention of the Academy of Management, Atlanta, 1979.

29. Williamson, O. E. *Markets and Hierarchies.* New York: Free Press, 1975.

30. Wirth, T. (Ed.) *Telecommunications in Transition: The Status of Competition in the Telecommunications Industry.* U.S. House of Representatives Report to the Majority staff of the Subcommittee on Telecommunications, Consumer Protection, and Finance, Washington, D.C., November 3, 1981.

In this chapter from his book, Who Knows: Information in the Age of the Fortune 500, *Herbert Schiller argues that large business enterprises are consorting to change the nature of public information in the United States. Changing the direction and emphasis of the government's information activity from public to private and from social to commercial, he says, is a key to such enterprises' transforming the role of information in the entire economy. However, he adds at the end of this chapter, there are a few, as yet weak, countervailing forces to such a change. Herbert I. Schiller is a professor at the University of California, San Diego.*

32

THE PRIVATIZATION OF INFORMATION

Herbert I. Schiller

Paul Zurkowski of the Information Industry Association alienated the library community by accusing libraries of imposing 'an iron curtain of free information' over the land.

Library Journal
June 1, 1979, p. 1200.

While the current era is often characterized as an "information age," a more appropriate designation would take note of the fact that the privatization and commercialization of information now have become the distinguishing practices of domestic information exchange. This development is changing the way information is being viewed and handled.

Information has been sold in the past, sometimes in great volume. Yet there have always been enclaves of information generation and dissemination which either were excluded from, or ignored, in profit making. In fact, valiant battles have been waged by popular social movements to extend some of these enclaves. The motivation for these struggles, past and present, has been the belief that information is inherently social.

From Herbert I. Schiller, "The Privatization of Information," Chapter 3 of Herbert I. Schiller, *Who Knows: Information in the Age of the Fortune 500* (Norwood, NJ: Ablex Publishing Corporation, 1981), pp. 47-78. Reprinted by permission.

Now new communication technologies have made it possible to generate, process, assemble, store and disseminate enormous quantities of information. Huge private investments in the facilities to perform these tasks make it possible and profitable to handle information as a salable good. These newly offered opportunities for profit making are responsible for the quickening efforts to undermine and discredit the belief that information is a social good, a vital resource that benefits the total community when made freely available for general public use.*

Along with the attack on this belief, practices which reflect and support it also are being overturned and eliminated. In the drive toward privatization of information, the principle that "information is a commodity" plays a prominent role. Major efforts to banish the idea that information is a social good have been focused on the national government.

The national government is the country's major information generator and disseminator. Once the belief that governmental information is a public good can be disavowed, and the national governmental information supply can be corralled for private use and profit making, the *Fortune 500* have an open road toward dominion of future economic and ideological life.

THE NATIONAL GOVERNMENT AND THE PRODUCTION OF INFORMATION

In addition to a sizable and continuing growth of ordinary, day-to-day operational needs for information, for most of this century the United States Government has been confronted with systemic problems which necessitate information acquisition. Preparations for and waging of world (and local) wars, as well as efforts to stabilize the recurring economic gyrations of a privately owned and administered economy, require continuously more comprehensive and systematic information about natural resources, labor power,

*Anita R. Schiller's paper, "The Idea of the Marketplace and the Marketplace of Ideas" (On-Line Conference, San Francisco, November 13, 1980), states: "What seems most important in attempting to understand current trends, is recognizing the increasing proprietary interest in information as a profitable resource on the one hand, and the diminishing social interest in information, as a shared resource, on the other."

economic, financial, technological, geographical, and physical matters.

Mobilizing for and participating in the second world war vastly extended governmental informational involvements in research and, development, largely for weapons development, resource planning and utilization, psychological warfare, and propaganda. These activities did not slacken at the end of the war. Actually, the tremendous American economic-military power in existence supplied the muscle and the wherewithal for the worldwide expansion of the United States business system.

As American economic interests pushed to the furthest reaches of the globe, the necessity for technical strength in all areas of industrial and military administration and governance demanded the continuation of massive research and development (R & D) expenditures. The government supplied them. What has become known as the "grants economy"—huge infusions of governmental funds to business and academic centers for research and development—became institutionalized.

A Brookings Institution study in 1968 paid tribute to this phenomenon:

> The initiatives the government has taken in accelerating the accumulation of new knowledge and promoting new technologies in selected areas, the responsibility for decision-making which it has assumed, the scale on which it has pursued certain objectives, and the close working relationships it has developed with private institutions—all these have been dynamic elements in the postwar development of American society.
>
> The first application of nuclear energy (to the atomic bomb) was merely the most spectacular of many technological advances achieved under government auspices during World War II. Since then there have been many others. The more dramatic include the jet airplane, supersonic flight, the nuclear-powered submarine with its inertial guidance system, high capacity computers, and sophisticated radar.

The author of this encomium justified all these "achievements" with a familiar cold war rationale: "Radar and computers are components of a variety of weapons systems and, like so many other defense items, are reminders that the nation's security continues to be a major spur to innovation. They demonstrate also the fact that, for good or ill, the cold war is in large measure a war of the laboratories."[1]

A more recent appraisal, from European sources concerned with that area's lagging information industry, saw it this way:

The world leadership of the U.S. industry owes much to the innovative Continental market in which it flourishes, to the immense procurement power of the U.S. federal government and massive financial support which defense and space programs have given to research and development in all branches of electronics.[2]

A European study amplifies this assessment:

The [computer] industry in the United States is the principal world supplier; it has a vast home market which it supplies almost entirely on its own. The main factor in this growth has undoubtedly been the massive orders placed by the Federal Government for more than a quarter of a century. The number of computer installations in Federal Agencies alone represents more than one-third of the total in the whole of the United States.[3]

The result of decades-long, massive governmental R & D expenditures (a congressional committee on governmental printing was informed in 1979), is "that the federal government has become the nation's chief generator of knowledge in just about every field. . .[and] as is plainly evident in Congressional hearings, the government's urgent need for information about the nation's social, economic, and technological problems is the over-arching reason why Congress in recent years appropriated between $26 and $30 billion annually for wide-ranging research projects."[4] Actually, the fiscal year budget for 1981 for the federal government requested R & D funds for 31 federal agencies, which totaled $36.1 billion.[5]

Some of the hardware and software that have come out of these huge outlays has already been noted. The focus here will be only on the *informational output* that these R & D expenditures have generated. Indicative of the magnitude of this output, a 1979 governmental study reports:

Expenditures in the United States for the production, dissemination, and use of scientific and technical information (STI) over the last two decades increased phenomenally. . .from 1960 to 1974 STI communication expenditures increased about 323 percent, and growth is expected to continue. The Federal Government, a major supplier and user of information, spent $4.6 billion of the $10.3 billion nationwide-total spent in 1975.[6]

These outlays, it should be emphasized, are made exclusively for the *publication and dissemination of information* derived from the far larger governmental expenditures on research and development. This publication effort, however, cannot be given enough emphasis. It provides a vast stockpile of information—some raw, some semi-processed, and much processed data—which requires varying capacities, economic and technological, for its effective application and utilization.

Given the preeminent role of corporate business in the American economy, it is to be expected that the projects most likely to utilize this informational reservoir would be undertaken by private firms expecting to make a profit. Indeed, this is the case, as for example, the formation of the private corporation COMSAT, using governmentally financed space communcations technical expertise, hardware and experience, demonstrates. (See Chap. 6, regarding remote sensing, as well.)

But the chain of relationships that this rather recent informational abundance occasions does not stop here. What has become increasingly evident is that the *information itself*, the product of public tax money, could be and is privately appropriated at its point of generation—the Government—and sold at a profit. This is an altogether new opportunity for profit making, hardly considered in the pre-World War II period. How information came into the money-making net is part of a larger story.

Corporate power, resurgent after a brief defensive period imposed on it by militant social struggles during the depression decade of the 1930s, resumed its aggressiveness during and after the war, at home and abroad. Domestically, the Government was made subordinate wherever corporate interest chose to advance its profit-making activities. The governmenntal sphere itself soon became such an area for private aggrandizement.

In 1955, a thoroughly complaisant Administration legitimized corporate forays into the governmental sector and formulated an overt policy of governmental reliance on the private sector. This quickly became the standard against which all future governmental activities were to be evaluated. The rationale for this far-reaching penetration of corporatism into the governmental sphere was nicely put in an executive memorandum written many years after the fact:

> In a democratic free enterprise economic system, the Government should not compete with *its citizens*. The private enterprise system, characterized by *individual* freedom and initiative, is the primary source of national economic strength. In recognition of this principle, it has been and continues to be the general policy of the Government to rely on *competitive* private enterprise to supply the products and services it needs.[7]

Among other inaccuracies in this statement, there is the deceptive identification of individuals and citizens as the beneficiaries of a policy which is formulated for corporate objectives and interests.

Implementations of and additions to this policy have occurred regularly since the time it was first announced in a 1955 Bureau of the Budget Bulletin. The most recent revision is found in Circular No. A-76 Revised, issued by the Office of Management and Budget on March 29, 1979. The central policy aim set forth in this document is: "*Rely on the Private Sector.* The Government's business is not to be in business. Where private sources are available, they should be looked to first to provide the commercial or industrial goods and services needed by the Government to act on the public's behalf."[8]

Initially, this policy was not designed specifically for the governmental information sector. It was intended to affect the general procurement of goods and services increasingly used by a greatly expanded State apparatus. Still, it was inevitable that the policy would be applied to information as that field of governmental activity, fueled by the enormous R & D outlays, became increasingly significant. What has occurred, in fact, is that governmentally funded information generation has become a rich and sought-after treasure trove. Developments in recent years in this field are understood best, therefore by examining how this prize is being appropriated and who is doing the appropriating.

The appropriation process extends from the initial securing of federal funds to generate information, to the actual printing of the newly generated information (and more recently, to taping and filming), and to its dissemination and utilization. At each stage commercial elements, fortified with the doctrine of "reliance on the private sector," are seeking to insert and advance their interests.

Data base producers, information packagers and service suppliers, and many large companies with specific informational interests—e.g., mining, agribusiness, oil, etc.—are moving quickly and aggressively, within and outside political and legislative channels, to preempt the national information supply produced with federal money, and the machinery for its dissemination, as well.

An Ad Hoc Committee, advising the Joint Committee on Printing of the U.S. Congress, in its 1979 report set forth the overarching policy question that is being decided almost by default: "Should the information generated by the government," asked the Committee, "be considered as an economic good to be dealt with in purely economic terms, or as a social good to be dealt with in purely social terms, or a combination of both?"[9]

The private sector has no doubt whatsoever how this question should be answered. Paul Zurkowski, president of the Information Industry Association, in a paper prepared for the National Commission on Libraries and Information Science in 1974, wrote:

> The marriage of the profit motive to the distribution of information is the single most important development in the information field since Carnegie began endowing libraries with funds to make information in books and journals more widely available to the public . . . [Consequently] the government of the U.S. has the responsibility to assure that the opportunity for private sector initiatives is expanded and not contracted.[10]

Another voice of the Information Industry, James B. Adler, president of the private Congressional Information Service, before a congressional committee considering a revision of the law regulating government printing, said flatly:

> One of the points that we are trying to make, Mr. Chairman, is that just as it is presently JCP [Joint Committee on Printing] policy to encourage the use of private facilities in the printing of Government documents, it should be the policy of the Committee to encourage the use of private facilities in the distribution of public information wherever that is practical and consistent with the public interest.[11]

Adler emphasized further that a revised law should be explicit on this matter: "We believe that as a matter of policy Congress should write in policy guidance up front that says that private capabilities which can be used for the public good should be considered in constructing Government printing and distribution activities."[12] The chairman of the Congressional subcommittee, Congressman Hawkins, inquired at this point: "So you are really asking us to go beyond the current law?" Adler replied: "Yes Sir."[13]

The efforts of the relatively recently organized private information industry (IIA) firms to seize the existing public informational stockpile and undertake its further production, processing, and distribution—the IIA is generally content to allow the Government to continue to spend substantial tax moneys to finance the generation of information—are being felt in many undertakings that until a very short time ago were considered non-profit-making activities.

Commercial interest is on the offensive. So much is this so, that the generally unexcitable and rarely aggressive American Library Association, through its Executive Director, made a critical assessment of the direction in which decision-making over public information seems to be moving. Events of the last ten years, Robert Wedgworth stated, "have awakened many Americans to recognition that their government is theirs and the information it provides is available for the asking."

Though these are both questionable assertions, Wedgworth went on to say that a threat to this information's accessibility is

Posed by a group of companies whose services are based on new developments in computer technology, micro-graphics, and telecommunications. While we have to live in the same environment and make use of the service of these companies, I am quite interested in their contention that the federal government as the largest producer and disseminator of information in the U.S. should channel most of its publishing and distribution functions through the private sector rather than through agencies such as the GPO, the federal depository library system, and the National Technical Information Service. . . .Yet in some instances this argument fails to recognize that they may be seeking access to information already collected and organized at public expense. It is maintained that these companies can plan and distribute better quality products more effectively than the government. Yet many of the agencies that are the targets of these arguments, such as the National Institute of Health, *have a statutory mission to print and disseminate information produced with public funds for the public benefit, distributing the cost to all taxpayers rather than to those who are in most urgent need of the information.* This may be the single most controversial issue in the national program for library and information services that we have seen proposed over the last several years.[14]

Wedgworth's statement may be overly generous in its assessment of the Government's responsibility and accessibility to the people. Hegemonic control of governmental information by the private sector has never been absent in the United States. What is different now, however, is the shift from indirect to direct control, accomplished through the market mechanism: the private sale and purchase of government information

Wedgworth is on the mark, though, when he emphasizes the implications for and the peril to *general* accessibility of information when commercial initiatives take over and organize distribution on an individual ability-to-pay basis. When this occurs, not only do those with the ability to pay gain advantaged access, but eventually—and, ultimately most importantly—they become the arbiters of what kind of information shall be produced and what is made available. The market unsentimentally yet inexorably confers this authority on those with the fatter bank accounts. Wedgworth is correct, also, in believing that a vital issue is involved. It is no less than: Who will direct what kinds of information the Government will produce in the years and decades ahead? To what purposes that information will be put will be another basic decision made in the same manner.

Actually, the survival of many frail but crucial institutions which have served to protect or advance the public interest is, if not immediately at stake, threatened. Increasing reliance on the private sector and market forces to organize, process, and disseminate information, already is beginning to erode the functions of several public institutions.

These public activities, it need be repeated, have rarely offered adequate service, and often have provided institutional reinforcement for the status quo. Yet they have also nourished a conception of public interest and social service and, at certain historical junctures, have given support and in turn been supported by progressive social currents. Transforming these institutions into market structures—the objective of the IIA and its promoters—is to remove from society those few agencies capable of systemic melioration and humanization.

Access to and commercial disposal of the already large and continuously growing governmental information hoard are the objectives of the for-profit forces in the economy. In working toward this goal, the governmental informational structures and the many intermediary networks that transmit some of this information are the targets for private takeover or serious reductions in capability.

In what follows, some of these developments are briefly reviewed. Justification for any incompleteness in the discussion is that the onslaughts are relatively recent. They are ongoing and quite complex in their detail; uncertainties are numerous; outcomes are not predestined, and in many cases not yet very clear. Still, some patterns, not very promising to the public's need to know, are beginning to take shape.

The private attack is characterized by an insistence that information is a commodity and that those who wish to use it should pay for it. The battle swirls around those structures and institutions, in the Government and outside it, directly engaged in information generation, publishing (in the most comprehensive sense), and dissemination.

INFORMATION GENERATION

The process of information generation is under commercial siege and private interests have encroached substantially on what once were nonprofit activities producing a wide range of information. Federal laboratories, for example, which once undertook directly a good portion of the Government's research work, have been neglected—relatively and absolutely. An ever larger share of the Federal R & D outlays are channeled to corporate laboratories and academic centers which are developing close commercial connections.[15]

Another side of the post-World War II decline in direct, Federal engagement in research and development work is revealed in a study prepared more than a decade ago. It noted that "the business share of federal research and development work. . .has increased from 26.9 percent of federal expenditures in 1954 to 65.1 percent in 1964 . . . [and conversely] since 1940, the use of federal research and development funds by people employed directly by the government has grown less rapidly than has the government's aggregate program."[16] These trends have continued into the 1970s and nothing on the horizon in the '80s promises to reverse them.

A study published in *Science* reported that "of the 610,000 scientists and engineers engaged in R & D in 1979, more than three-fifths were employed by industry. In dollar terms, industry performs about 72 percent of the total.[17] One of the consequences of this privatization of research (the bulk of which is financed by public money) is that a capability of noncommerical, independent evaluation of R & D outputs is weakened, if not eliminated, as the Federal R & D capacity atrophies. An informational consequence of equal significance is that the information derived from these expenditures on research and development may fail to find its way back into the stream of public information. It may be appropriated by the private sector and further promote the aggrandizement of its appropriators.

One facet of the general tendency of private appropriation of public information is the widespread use of private consultants to perform research and evaluative studies for the government. This is a development strongly encouraged by the OMB policy first enunciated in 1955, which stipulated that there should be government reliance on the private sector for the goods and services required for public administration and performance.

This phenomenon reveals a curious aspect of the alleged age of information. All the attention to the informational character of the society notwithstanding, even the number of private consultants on the public payroll remains unknown. The chairman of the Senate subcommittee on Civil Service and General Services observed in 1979 that "we still do not know how many consultants the Government uses, how much they are paid, or what benefit the Government derives from these particular services."[18]

The amounts involved in these practices, however, are far from trivial. A study conducted by the *Washington Post*, and reported in *Documents to the People*, "showed that the Government spent more than $9.3 billion for consultants and [consulting] contracts, and that 68% of the 16,101 research and consulting contracts advertised in 1979 were awarded without competition."[19]

After this information was published, the *Post* reported that at a Cabinet level meeting at the White House, the Director of the Office of Management and Budget (OMB) "directed all agencies to improve control over the hiring of consultants" but its efforts to enforce this policy are hampered because "OMB has not been able to find out how many outside consultants the government is using and what they are being paid!"[20]

What is known, however, is that the pervasive use of private consultants multiplies the obstacles in the way of public information availability and contributes to further informational inequality in the nation at large. The Ad Hoc Advisory Committee to the Joint Congressional Committee on Printing touched, albeit lightly, on this:

> Many government agencies, in contracting for research/ development and consultant studies, specifically permit the private contractor to copyright the results of this federally funded research . . . The result of this contract procedure is that the research findings are not routinely listed in the MONTHLY CATALOG [the Governmental listing of U.S. publications] and are not distributed to depository libraries. In fact, government-funded libraries and information clearing houses often have to purchase such contract reports from private commercial sector publishers.[21]

With this neat arrangement, private informational enterprises are twice blessed, and public knowledgeability is drastically limited.

Another consequence—perhaps more egregious still—of the use of private consultants to handle and assess public functions can only be mentioned here. This involves the quality and character of the findings and recommendations of private firms and individuals on matters concerning the largest issues of social policy.

It is carrying temptation well beyond ordinary limits to institutionalize arrangements whereby profit-making organizations are called upon to assess and advise on public policy making. When, for example, the Treasury Department of the United States Government asks the leading private accounting firm, Price Waterhouse & Co., and "at least three major New York investment banking firms to help the Government scrutinize the financial rescue plan submitted by the Chrysler Corporation,"[22] the mind boggles at the flagrant disregard for the potential of outrageous conflict-of-interest.

WEAKENING THE GOVERNMENT PUBLISHING AND DISSEMINATION FUNCTION

To recapitulate, a massive shift of Federal R & D expenditures from governmental laboratories to corporate facilities and private contractors has occurred since World War II. Simultaneously, there has been an increased use by the Government of private consultants that offer advice and make studies for governmental policy direction. Both of these developments have led to huge amounts of government-financed data and information which escape or are diverted from freely accessible public channels of distribution. Sometimes the findings embodied in this documentation, processed, and 'enriched', are priced prohibitively and become available only to already-knowledgeable and affluent groups and individuals—mostly the business community—directly concerned with or affected by the information. Less influential and prosperous groups may be excluded and may not even know the information is available.

More recently, the arrangements governing the organization, publication, and dissemination of the information that remains under governmental control—a still very considerable body of data—have begun to undergo significant changes. Though these changes are still occurring and are not easily explicable without detailed elaboration, some general tendencies are observable. What seems to be happening, perhaps accelerating, is the continued weakening of the public publishing function, along with a growing effort to commercialize the Government's information product.

In what follows, it will be useful to keep in mind two separate kinds of developments. One involves the outcomes of the growing influence, deliberately applied, of market forces on governmental publishing and information dissemination. This has been mentioned already but will be elaborated in the subseqent discussion. The other changes involve governmental reorganizations in the fields of public printing and document dissemination. These are being proposed and implemented under the general framework of the revision and amendment of Title 44, United States Code, which establishes the rules for the administration of public printing services and the distribution of public documents.

This latter area of change is affecting the actual organization of governmental entities. To be sure, the two developments are related. In these pages, however, most attention will be given to the impact of market forces on the public publishing and dissemination functions. Where these impacts are detectable, also, in proposed legislative reorganization of governmental entities, they will be noted briefly.

Impacts from these separate but related developments are especially evident in the extensive efforts to diminish the domain of the Government Printing Office (GPO); in the promotion and growth of the National Technical Information Service as a rival to the GPO, and in the continued deficiencies and frailty of the national depository library system. A brief consideration of each of these mini-information wars, follows.

THE GROWING TRIALS OF THE GOVERNMENT PRINTING OFFICE

The Government Printing Office came into being in 1861.[23]. For most of its existence, it handled the bulk of the national government's printing, binding, and distribution of documents requirements in in-house, governmentally owned facilities. All this changed with the tremendous increase of government printing, precipitated by the outbreak of the Second World War. From 1940 on, under the stimulus of heavy defense requirements for printing, commercial firms were increasingly utilized under contract. This practice continued after the war and by 1979, two-thirds of the printing contracts from the GPO went to the private sector and their value exceeded $425 million annually.[24]

The growing appetite of the private information industry firms, however, is not directed especially to the printing function of the GPO, although some commercial companies certainly are not indifferent to that source of revenue. The IIA is concerned mainly with generating, processing, and distributing the government's information. It seeks also to undertake such functions as assembling, indexing, document delivery, and disseminating information in new formats, such as microfiche. It also has been intent on restricting the Government Printing Office from entering into the new fields of information handling and packaging.

To the extent that the IIA is successful in limiting the GPO's activities in processing the output of government agencies while expanding the commercial sector's role, the private information firms also gain distributional control of a tremendous storehouse of publicly financed information.

The economic potential here is substantial. Yet still greater long-range benefits accrue to the for-profit, information sector. *Changing the direction and emphasis of the Government's information activity from public to private, and from social to commercial, is a key to transforming the role of information in the entire economy.* The Government is the central information generator in the system and "the largest user of computer technology in the world."* Once it begins to operate with commercial criteria for information production and dissemination, social considerations in the production and use of information begin to disappear throughout the society.

Accordingly, the issue of charging the user for information has become the focal point of the commercial offensive against the public information sector, and against the GPO and libraries, in particular. The commercial information companies insist, first, that all publicly financed information should be sold and retailed at a price no less than its cost of production. Their second demand is that the for-profit sector should become the main distributional channel.

> The information industry [the IIA asserts,] is a major growth industry of the future providing exciting new products and services today which only yesterday were unavailable. *The capabilities of this industry should be relied on today even in cases where government information activities were undertaken when the industry was not recognized to be capable of providing these services.*[25]

In short, many informational activities and functions which hitherto have been public now, according to the IIA, should become commercial and profit producing. In implementing this objective, the Government Printing Office is first in line for sharply reduced responsibilities. The process of contraction has begun, though not abruptly nor entirely visibly.

Among the elements that assist the IIA and its supporters in their efforts to transform public information dissemination into commercial enterprise are the longstanding deficiencies of the GPO, which are now much more in evidence because information has come to play so large a role in the economy. For one thing, "it is not the central source of government documents for the public that it is supposed to be." For another, "there is much that GPO should be doing that it is not doing at all."[26] Both of these assessments are the direct consequences of the limited, narrow view of public information that has characterized the administration of the GPO for a long time.

---

*President Carter, Letter of Transmittal to Congress on the Report of the White House Conference on Library and Information Services, The White House, September 26, 1980.

Administrators within the GPO have had little enthusiasm for carrying out a policy of supplying the public with socially useful information. "It is clear that to its officials," Shawn Kelly writes, "the Government Printing Office is not considered primarily a source of valuable information, but rather a self-sustaining mail-order business."[27] Still, the GPO's troubles and limitations are not by any means all self-induced. Congress has seen to it that the organization has been underfinanced for years, as well as having made it official policy to contract out the bulk of government printing to private printers. Thus, the rigidities and inadequacies of the GPO, imposed and internalized, make it an easy target for the adversaries of a genuinely public information service.

THE NATIONAL TECHNICAL INFORMATION SERVICE (NTIS)

One of the ways in which the control of public information publishing and distribution has gradually been separated from the GPO has been through the establishment, in 1970, of what has become a rival governmental unit, the National Technical Information Service (NTIS). This agency was given a mandate to publish and make available the government's scientific and technical information output. The NTIS resides, not by chance, in the Department of Commerce, the agency which explicitly is assigned the promotion of the business community's interests.

To describe the growth, activities, and influence of the NTIS would require a volume of its own. Here it is sufficient, I believe, to note that the NTIS has been utilized, not necessarily intentionally, as a force promoting the further commercialization of government information. It has done this, first, by introducing and following steadfastly the principle of selling at commercial prices all the documentation it makes available. Its second contribution to commercialization of government information has been indirect but also damaging. It has served to weaken the position of the GPO as the primary government agency engaged in information handling and dissemination.

The insertion of NTIS into the governmental information network has created the divided and weakened information authority that now exists. A 1979 Congressional Research Service report, based on a survey of governmental information activities, noted:

NTIS is somewhat of an enigma. While the major criteria for submission of documents to NTIS are that they be technical and/or scientific in nature, the survey responses demonstrated that there may be some documents which could just as well be under GPO control, *with easier access by the general public.*

At the same time, the report continued, other agencies "are failing to notify GPO of the documents produced through sources other than GPO," and consequently, "there appears to exist no comprehensive source of the most basic information on Federal publications."[28]

Summing up the ambiguities created by the informational activities of NTIS, the report posed these questions:

How does the public gain access to an index of all publications in the NTIS system? Do the Depository libraries receive copies as part of a free distribution system? What procedures do the agencies follow to determine whether a document should go to GPO or NTIS, or both? Are restrictions placed by NTIS on the agencies with regards to the distribution other than through NTIS?

Does NTIS claim copyright on classes of documents within the system [and finally] to what extent is NTIS in competition with GPO, [and] if there is competition, does it diminish GPO's effectiveness?[29]

Not a result of NTIS' activity, but relevant to the issue of leakage in the national public information system, a 1980 congressional study produced astonishment at the disarray and sieve-like quality of the record of the government's informational output. It reported:

Without an accurate inventory of just what is published by an agency, thousands of useful publications never are forwarded to GPO as is now required by law for inclusion in the official listing of government publications in the GPO's Monthly Catalog. This catalog listing is absolutely essential for librarians and the public to know what is available. . . *perhaps as high as 40 percent of the publications generated* by Federal agencies with tax dollars never are included in the Monthly Catalog so that the public may know they exist and have access to them.[30]

Bertram Gross, in his unique study, *Friendly Fascism,* commented on this gap in the governmental information inventory and views it as part of a much wider information hole that affects almost everyone in the country.[31]

The efforts of NTIS, supported by the Office of Management and Budget, to broaden its influence at the expense of the GPO and to extend a 'sales philosophy' to all government information, continue unabated. For example, in a draft bulletin, No. 78, dated June 30, 1978, the OMB *ignored the GPO completely* and proposed to make the NTIS the agency responsible for disseminating scientific and technical information which resulted from federally funded research and development activities.[32] Following objections of university and documents librarians across the country, as well as critical comments from some other agencies in the Government itself,[33] a revised draft circular on *Improved Management and Dissemination of Federal Information* was released for comment in June 1980.

The preeminent role of NTIS in the dissemination of scientific and technical information was reasserted. The draft also included a curious definition of "public information." Its "distinguishing characteristic," according to the OMB circular, "is that the [governmental] agency actively seeks, in some fashion, to disseminate such information or otherwise make it available to the public."[34] In sum, public information is what any governmental agency deems it appropriate to inform the public about.

The policy principles enunciated in the 1980 OMB draft circular are especially illuminating. Commercialization of government-produced information is the central policy objective. Several of the principles set forth make this quite explicit. For example, Principle (a) announces that "public information held by the Federal Government shall be made available to the public in an effective, efficient and *economic* manner." Principle (c) states: "Information is not a free good." It softens this dictum somewhat, by adding, "however, no member of the public should be denied access to public information held by the Federal Government solely because of economic status. In particular, the Federal Government shall rely upon the depository library system to provide free citizen access to public information."

This assurance is less of a guarantee than it purports to be. The next section, on depository libraries, makes the point that the depository system itself is being subjected to commercial pressure. If the Information Industry Association and the Office of Management and Budget have their way—and little seems to stand in their path at this time—depository libraries will be no less market oriented than NTIS.

Principle (d) states that "information available through a mechanism other than the depository library system shall, unless required by other law or program objectives, be made available at a price which recovers all costs to the government associated with the dissemination of such information." And finally, Principle (e) insists that "The Federal Government shall, in accordance with OMB circular A-76, and where not inconsistent with law, *place maximum feasible reliance upon the private sector to disseminate* public information."[35]

The 1980 OMB draft circular on the management and dissemination of federal information may well be revised again. But what is unlikely to be changed, and what actually may be strengthened, are the endorsement and encouragement, implemented in policy, of the privatization and commercialization of government information.

THE GOVERNMENT LIBRARY DEPOSITORY SYSTEM

The growth of the NTIS *inside* the federal structure as a commercial vendor of government information weakens not only the GPO as the primary agency responsible for information coordination. Another institution as well, in the public information network, is affected. This is the government depository system. Though limited arrangements for the deposit of U.S. Government journals and documents were in effect in the early 19th century, "the real basis of the institution of depositories" was created in a series of resolutions and acts of Congress in the immediate pre-Civil War years, 1857–1859. Amended and expanded by congressional action since, the depository system now in operation "provides for a class of libraries in the United States in which certain Government publications are deposited for the use of the public."[36] There are now 1230 institutions designated as government depository libraries, several located in each state.

There is considerable autonomy in each depository library to select the government documents and publications it feels are of most interest and value to the specific constituency it serves. However, the general intent of the system is to have available, in accessible sites, in every state of the union, several depositories which are able to provide the general public with *comprehensive access to the full spectrum* of governmentally produced information. The depository system, regardless of how actively it has been utilized, must be regarded as an important democratic facility at the disposal of the community.

Any development, therefore, that weakens the system—impairs its capabilities by reducing its comprehensiveness—is not a trivial matter. The informational well-being of the general public is affected. When the availability of government documents becomes uncertain because an unknown amount of material is siphoned off by an agency inside the government, operating commercially, such as NTIS, as well as other massive leakages,* the depository system is undermined.

It is undermined because it no longer is assured of receiving a complete inventory of government documentation. Moreover, it sometimes is unable to afford the prices charged by NTIS if it wishes to secure that agency's publications in the marketplace.[37]

Besides the NTIS, there is another, possibly more serious and growing threat to the depository system. These are the efforts of the private information firms to shift the distribution of documentation to the depositories to a market arrangement. Indicative is the proposal the IIA put before the Joint Congressional Committee on Printing in 1979: "Our Association fully supports continued and increased assistance for depositories; however, we believe that support should be in a more direct form, rather than indirect subsidies."

What the Association had in mind here is the replacement of the flow of free government publications to the depositories--labelled "subsidy" by the IIA--with cash payment which would permit the depositories to choose privately-prepared information packages.

Speaking for IIA, James Adler argued:

> At the moment, the depository requires a library to accept its subsidy [sic] from the government in the form of documents. If it wishes

---

*According to a study by Coopers & Lybrand, a private consulting firm, "GPO performs only about 50% of all government printing . . . . GPO distributes about 40% of the documents it prints." *Analysis and Evaluation of Selected Government Printing Office Operations*, prepared by Coopers & Lybrand, an Independent Consulting Firm, Washington, D.C., under the auspices of the Joint Committee on Printing, Washington, D.C., 1979, p. xix.

to make use of any private competing services, it must use its own funds exclusively to buy these additional services. We are suggesting that it would not strain the ingenuity of the staff and members of Congress, to create any one of a number of alternative systems which would provide a wider choice to depositories in terms of choosing the form and source of the documents they receive than the present system provides.[38]

Replying to this view, Donald Koepp, University Librarian at Princeton, declared on behalf of the Association of Research Libraries:

> I would most emphatically not want a subsidy in lieu of the depository for all sorts of reasons. I have a distinct feeling that that would eventually erode into a situation where our control over the material would evaporate; I emphasize one of the most important things for us is control which permits us to identify the existence of a document.[39]

The IIA's proposal would, if enacted, no longer assure a national uniform core of material, available to the public in the many libraries situated all around the country. The Association of Research Libraries' representative noted further that "probably 50 percent of the basic publications of the Government Printing Office are selected by almost any library, any depository of any size in the country. The variations is [sic] at the margin." Clearly, the emphasis on "choice" for depositories that the IIA stresses is a secondary matter at best. The vital need is to protect the 50 percent uniform core.

There is another, not-so-apparent, but likely consequence if the direct cash payment proposal of the IIA were to be accepted. It would introduce the market mechanism into the depository system itself. The demand for government publications at each depository, under a cash subsidy arrangement, would become a site for competing interests to express their preferences. Little imagination is required to see which interests would predominate in an environment where *Fortune 500* criteria and influence prevail. This expressed preference would, in turn, feed back into the total information generation process and push it still further in the direction of the corporate economy's informational interest.

In the matter of cash payments in lieu of documents to the depository libraries, to date the IIA's views have not prevailed. The provision that was introduced originally in the National Publications

Act of 1979 was rejected.[40] The Act itself, retitled the National Publications Act of 1980, died in the 96th Congress. Still, it would be a mistake to believe that the drive against the social use of public information has slackened. Market criteria are being promoted heavily throughout the system of government document distribution. Though the specific mechanisms are still in formative stages, and the full impact of the shift is yet to be felt, there is reason enough to have anxiety over the enfeeblement of the general system.

The national depository library system, along with other institutional structures representing the public's access to and use of tax-supported governmental information, are pressured relentlessly. Inside the Government the NTIS, and outside the private information sector, tirelessly promote and extend private and commercial arrangements for information distribution.

Withal, the Carter Administration, reporting to Congress on the recommendations of the 1979 White House Conference on Library and Information Services, "promised to strengthen the role of the federal depository system in providing access to government information and pointed to gains made already in this area."[41]

COUNTERVAILING CURRENTS

The trends and changes noted above, which affect the availability of documentation resulting from Federal R & D and other expenditures, reveal a profound shift that threatens an already none-too-secure structure of public information accessibility. Institutions long established to assure public information service have been weakened, disoriented, and sometimes reorganized. Privatization of formerly public functions proceeds almost uninterruptedly under the stimulus of an energetic industry sector as well as a general climate favorable to unchecked private enterprise last observable in the 1920s.

The consequences are twofold. Accessibility to the general public of federally produced information becomes increasingly problematic. At the same time, closure to the public of all kinds of governmental information is occurring more and more systematically. In the latter case, for example, *The New York Times* reported that in the Spring 1980 session of Congress, more than 20 legislative proposals were introduced "that would limit access to Government information."[42]

Matching Congress' moves against its own constituents' vital information needs, federal agencies are making their own substantial contributions to the public's informational deprivation. For example, the Federal Communications Commission, assigned the mandate to protect the public interest in the field of broadcasting, proposed to eliminate the requirement that radio stations "keep detailed logs on their broadcasts for public inspection."[43] In the absence of such records, the ability of public interest groups, and individuals as well, to monitor easily the performance of broadcasters is severely impaired. Social accountability of broadcasting, or any other public function, requires a record available to public scrutiny.

Let me include a personal account of the difficulty now experienced in obtaining what should be easily available information. Almost immediately upon reading that the FCC had published a study, "Preliminary Report on Prospects for Additional Networks," in early 1980, I wrote to the Chairman of the Subcommittee on Communications, of the House of Representatives' Committee on Interstate and Foreign Commerce. This subcommittee oversees the Federal Communications Commission. A short time thereafter, I was informed by the Committee's counsel that the FCC "is out of copies of the network study related report." I then inquired of our University's government publications division, which happens also to be a government publications depository, if the document was available. The following reply was received promptly from a University government publications Librarian:

> The FCC report presents real problems. I called the FCC, and they recognized the title immediately, but they also confirmed that they do not have any copies left. They also confirmed that the report was *not* sent as a depository item to libraries.
>
> They did say that copies of their reports could be purchased from the Downtown Copy Center, 1114 21st St. N.W. Washington, D.C., phone 202-452-1422. (This is a private outfit.) I called the copy center and they too recognized the title; they will provide it at 9 cents per page; the whole report, however, is 1611 pages long; thus the total charge (including $12.82 postage) would be over $150.
>
> I also contacted Government Documents department at San Diego State [University], mainly because they belong to the 'Docu-

ments' Expediting program which is one way non-depository items
can be acquired. They do not have it either. They are going to make
inquiries through the Documents Expediting project, but they didn't
seem very hopeful.[44]

This personal chronicle seems to represent the condition of public
information accessibility at this time though eventually, in this instance, the report did come into the depository library on
microfiche. If these are the experiences of someone academically
close to the field of information, who is assisted by a skilled librarian, in one of the country's distinguished research libraries, what
may be said of the information options of less favorably situated citizens?

The evidence of increasing privatization of and barriers to governmentally generated information is not necessarily confirmatory
of Bertram Gross' vision of an imminent *Friendly Fascism*. Yet it
would be equally mistaken to view these developments as inconse-
quential or reflective of the normal ebb and flow of public affairs.

However, counterbalancing forces are at work. Currently, they
lack strength; still, there are reasons to believe that the principle of
freely available public information may muster more support in the
time ahead. For one thing, the national government itself is no
monolith on this matter. There are disagreements among the many
agencies in the federal structure over the desirability of present
trends. While the departments most associated with the private
sector and most heavily involved with the information industry's
products are generally accepting, if not promoting, of the commercialization of government information, other agencies either try to
adhere to the earlier formula of public accessibility, or, less concerned with principle, wish all the same to keep the information
function under their own wing.

Those federal departments striving hardest to withhold information from the public, and accepting eagerly the commercialization of
what they agree to release, are the most powerful and heavily financed agencies of the Government. They are also, not incidentally,
those parts of the bureaucracy most closely associated with or actually integral to the power centers of the system overall. Not unexpectedly, the Department of Commerce, which houses the NTIS,
the Department of Defense, NASA, and OMB are most outspoken
in their opposition to widening public information accessibility.[45]

.Whatever the internal lack of agreement in its various subdivisions, the Government, acting under executive direction, may be expected to reconsider its present acceptance of the splintered authority over federal information and the consequent huge leakages of documentation from the system's retrieval capacity. The necessity for rapid, comprehensive information, in accessible data bases, under unified means of accessing, will intensify as crises erupt in the future. In this very real sense, information fragmentation imperils systemic survival.

Yet there are very strong potential negative consequences of unification, centralization, and deliverability of information. Better organization of information can serve repressive as well as liberatory ends. Given the present structure and use of power in the United States, there is slight prospect that the emancipatory side of information mobilization will be favored at this time. Still, this cannot be taken for granted. The insistence on maintaining intact, freely accessible public information resources cannot be lessened.

Still another factor that eventually may trigger policy reversals in the information field is the rapidly changing structure of the information industry itself and the conflicts this is producing. In Chapter 2 some of these developments were reviewed. Summarizing these briefly, the competitive nature of the industry, apparent in its early years, is disappearing. The period in which relatively small and extremely vigorous companies were innovating and producing new formats, new hardware, and new packages of information which, in many instances, had not been available earlier in usable forms, is coming to a close. Following a familiar, capitalist developmental course, the movement to merger, consolidation, and conglomeration accelerates.

Both familiar and newly arrived information behemoths are on the prowl. The information industry itself is anxiety ridden. Smaller firms are confronting giant structures. Consequently, their need and willingness to participate in anti-monopoly coalitions are not matters of choice but of survival. A coalition of this kind *may* be an outcome of the developments considered here.

The subversion of what Gross calls the "democratic machinery" has proceeded rapidly in recent years. Yet much of this machinery, however disabled, remains in place. More important, it still possesses substantial allegiance and significant numbers of practitioners. Suggestive of the latent democratic forces in American society, especially in the public information field, which may yet be mobilized and activated, are the libraries and their staffs and friends. Assuredly, the library sector is no Exxon of power in the economy. Yet it cannot be disregarded entirely as a social force with deep roots in the community.

Librarianship has been grounded historically in the idea of public service. The commercialization of information runs counter to this deeply embedded principle. Accordingly libraries, and librarians too, are being subjected to the pressures and compulsions of the drive to extend the market into their domain. What is happening to public libraries, as computerization is introduced and market forces are encouraged as the means to finance the newer systems, is a story of its own. It parallels many of the developments that have been described here affecting government information.

An indication of the concern these trends are producing is revealed, in part, in some of the resolutions adopted at the first White House Conference on Library and Information Service (WHCLIS), convened in November 1979. At least four of the conference's resolutions were related directly to the professions's insistence that free public access to information be maintained and extended. For example, in resolutions supporting a national information policy, "the right of access, without charge or fee to the individual, to all public and publicly supported libraries" was advocated. Similarly, Congress was asked "to continue to foster broad public participation in the federal government by subsidizing the sale of documents and maintaining the system of regional depository libraries." And another resolution "asks for the study and implementation of a national information policy that guarantees all citizens equal and full access to publicly funded library and information services, that ensures federal agencies will do everything they can to make these services available.[46]

Each of these resolutions collides with the positions advocated by the IIA, now being implemented by governmental action. Though the opposition at this time remains limited, apparently confined to the library profession (there, too, it is by no means a dominant current), it is at least imaginable that other public sector fields, also threatened by these developments, may join in common cause against the information privatizers and marketeers.

One more development affecting the pace of privatization and concentration of control of public information may be mentioned.

These are the continuing and far-reaching changes occurring in information and communication technology. Again, this is a double-edged situation. In some instances, the new technology encourages mergers and combinations which enable higher capacities of information handling to be utilized more efficiently and to extend the control of already-giant structures. At the same time, the possibility for long-term consolidation and stabilization are reduced, at least temporarily. The uncertainties attendant on a rapidly changing technology arise from the possibile obsolescence of facilities, from the loss or gain of markets, and possibly from the entrance of new competitors. How the balance eventually will be struck in the information field is not completely predictable at this time. The strength and commanding positions of the giants in the communications sector—especially the equipment producers and media owners—suggest an eventual absorption of the new technologies into the hands of a few super-corporations.

Already a few media combines, including Warner Amex, Westinghouse, The Times Mirror Company, and Time, Inc., have a commanding position in the new cable TV industry.[47] Yet surprises are not out of the question. The uncertainty and instability created, to say nothing of the appearance of continuously enlarged monopolies, create opportunities for debate and public resistance.

The efforts to rewrite the Communications Act of 1934 are richly suggestive of these potential conflicts and ambiguities. Most of the debate and opposition over the rewrite have arisen from competing economic groups—broadcasters, hardware producers, data processors—whose interests collide. But in the attempts to smooth out differences, or at least to minimize disagreement of these major, private interests, the opportunity for public interests to be expressed, if not respected, is sometimes possible. Pertinent here, is the concern of the smaller firms in the information processing and computer services industries about being driven out of business by the few communication behemoths, A.T.&T. in particular.

This fear reflects itself in pressure on Congress to protect their existence. This was manifest early in 1980, when "four trade associations representing a substantial percentage of the U.S. computer industry . . . jointly demanded that the House [of Representatives] Communications Subcommittee make further changes to curb A.T.&T.'s monopoly power in its pending rewrite of the Communications Act of 1934 . . . . If the proposed changes aren't adopted, 'we intend to block passage of the bill and will try to unseat the legislators responsible', CCIA [Computer and Communications Industry Association] President Jack Biddle said."[48]

If this threat were indeed carried out, the ensuing battle would inevitably draw in public interest forces who would seek to broaden the conflict into larger frameworks of public access and general availability of information.

Should a popular, anti-information monopoly opposition actually develop in the future, it may still be more than countered by the information complex. This grouping seems intent on forging still stronger ties within its own already-powerful coalition of corporate, military, and academic interests. A former presidential science adviser, now a vice-president for science and technology of Exxon, calls for "a new synthesis of national, corporate and academic resources to sustain innovation"[49]—the expected outcome of expenditures on research.

Largely to expedite this 'general synthesis', the proposed 1981 Federal budget for research and development allocated an increase of 21 percent to the Department of Defense's "basic research" funds, which, it is hoped, will enable the military to mount "a dedicated effort to re-cement the relations" with the academic community.[50]

The integration of the academic research community into the information complex will be promoted further by contracting enrollments and increasingly limited funds for general education. These developments are likely to lead to further channeling of the production of information as well as to its tighter control and limited accessibility. Major universities are beginning to consider seriously engaging in commercial development of the findings coming out of their academic laboratories.[51]

What is occurring therefore, in the information field, is a pincers movement against the public's knowledgeability. On one side, outputs of public information are being transferred to the marketplace and priced accordingly. On the other, information and message-making from private, corporate sources are expanding and reaching new, large, and national audiences. It is to this second phenomenon—the emergence of dense networks of private message making—that the next chapter is devoted.

Notes

1. Clarence H. Danhof, *Government contracting and technological change*. Washington, D.C. The Brooking Institution: 1968, p. 1.

2. Rex Malik, "Europe moving to protect faltering DP industry," *Computerworld*, January 14, 1980, p. 12.

3. "European society faced with the challenge of new information technologies: A community response," Commission of the European Communities, COM (79) 650, Brussels, November 26, 1979, p. 7.

4. *Public Printing Reorganization Act of 1979*, Hearings, Committee on House Administration, House of Representatives, and the Committee on Rules and Administration, United State Senate, 96th Congress, 1st Session, on H.R. 4572 and S. 1436, July 10, 19, 24, & 26, 1979, Washington, D.C., p. 305.

5. Robert Reinhold, "Research by pentagon scheduled to receive fund increase of 21%," *The New York Times*, January 29, 1980, p. A1.

6. *Report to the Congress* by the Comptroller General of the United States, "Better information management policies needed: A study of scientific and bibilographic services," U.S. General Accounting Office, August 6, 1979, p. 1.

7. Circular No. A-76, revised, Office of Management and Budget, Executive Office of the President, Washington, D.C., March 29, 1979, emphasis added.

8. *Ibid.*

9. *Federal Government Printing and Publishing: Policy Issues*, Report of the Ad Hoc Advisory Committee on Revising Title 44 to the Joint Committee on Printing, U.S. Congress, U.S. GPO, Washington, D.C., p. 63.

10. Paul G. Zurkowski, "The information service environment: Relationships and priorities," paper for the National Commission on Libraries and Information Science, November 1974, Washington, D.C., pp. 5, 26.

11. Hearings, Public Printing Reorganization Act of 1979, pp. 257–258.

12. *Ibid.*

13. *Ibid.*

14. *Documents to the People*, Government Documents Roundtable, American Library Association, November 1979, 7 (6), p. 271, emphasis added.

15. David F. Noble & Nancy E. Pfund, "Business goes back to college," *The Nation*, September 20, 1980, p. 1.

16.   C. H. Danhof, *op. cit.*, pp. 7–9.

17.   Edward E. David, Jr., "Industrial research in America: Challenge of a new synthesis," *Science*, July 1980, *29*, (4), pp. 133–139.

18.   Jo Thomas, "Attempt to count U.S. consultants is called failure." *The New York Times*, October 15, 1979.

19.   *Documents to the People*, Government Documents Round Table, American Library Association, September 1980, *8* (5), p. 225.

20.   *Ibid.*

21.   *Federal Government Printing and Publishing: Policy Issues, op. cit.*, p. 44.

22.   Judith Miller, "Experts' advice on chrysler," *The New York Times*, September 17, 1979.

23.   *100 GPO years: 1861-1961, a history of United States public printing*, GPO, Washington, D.C., 1961.

24.   Congress of the United States, Joint Committee on Printing, Memorandum dated October 17, 1980, announcing open meetings in Los Angeles and San Francisco on the Federal Government's printing and distribution programs. From Augustus F. Hawkins, acting chairman of the Committee.

25.   *"Better information management needed: A study of scientific and technical bibliographic services, op. cit.*, Appendix VII, Report to the Congress by the Comptroller General of the U.S. Information Industry Association letter to Mr. J. H. Stolarow, Director, U.S. General Accounting Office, August 6, 1979, p. 56, emphasis added.

26.   Shawn P. Kelly, *The people's printer: A report on the Government Printing Office*, Washington, D.C., July 1979.

27.   *Ibid.*

28.   Sharon S. Gressle, *1978 Survey of selected publication practices of executive branch agencies*, The Library of Congress, Congressional Research Service, Washington, D.C., April 16, 1979, emphasis added.

29.   *Ibid.*

30.   *National Publications Act of 1980*, Report by the Committee on House Administration of the U.S. House of Representatives, 96th Congress, 2nd Session, House Report No. 96-836, Pt. 1, Washington, D.C., March 19, 1980, p. 21.

31.   Bertram Gross, *Friendly Fascism:* New York: E. Evans, 1980, p. 261.

32.   *Federal Register*, July 25, 1978, *43* (143), p. 32204–5.

33.   *Information Hotline*, Special Issue, March 1979, *11* (3).

34.   Office of Management and Budget, "Improved management and dissemination of Federal information: Request for comment," *Federal Register*, June 9, 1980, *45* (112), pp. 38461–38463.

35. *Ibid.*, emphasis added.

36. *Government Depository Libraries*, Revised April 1978, 95th Congress, 2nd Session, Joint Committee on Printing, Washington, D.C., p. 1.

37. Even to obtain an index of the titles available from NTIS represents a sizable outlay, not easily managed by most depositories which have tightly limited budgets. An NTIS *Retrospective Index* for July 1964 through December 1978, for example, lists more than 750,000 publications and costs $600. A *Current Index*, which is a quarterly cumulation of new publications, costs $400 annually. The NTIS offers a "bargain" rate for the combined purchase of these indexes at $900. The fact that this important and expensive NTIS index did not come initially as a depository item created a furor in library circles. As a result, it eventually was made available by NTIS as a depository publication. *Documents to the People*, Government Round Table, American Library Association, September 1979, *7* (5), p. 182.

38. Hearings, Public Printing Reorganization Act of 1979, *op. cit.*, pp. 260–261.

39. *Ibid.*, p. 266.

40. The National Publications Act of 1979, embodied in House Bill No. 5424, introduced into the House of Representatives on September 27, 1979, included section 707(a)2, which:
    provides that when public documents are made available to depository libraries under 707(a)1, the Director of Distribution Services (formerly, the Superintendent of Documents) shall provide the widest degree of choice both as to format—that is, paper, microform, online, etc.—and as to the source of such documents. For example, if the Director determines that it is more advantageous, cost-effective, useful or efficient to procure such documents from private commercial firms, then such sources may be utilized. *H.R. 5424*, National Publications Act of 1979, Print prepared for the Committee on House Administration, 96th Congress, 1st Session, U.S. GPO, Washington, D.C., October 1979, p. 14.

41. President Carter, letter of transmittal for the Report of the White House Conference on Library and Information Services, The White House, September 26, 1980. Also, *LJ SLJ Hotline*, October 6, 1980, *9* (32), page IX–31.

42. Deirde Carmody, "Measures to shield U.S. data criticized," *The New York Times*, May 4, 1980:

43. Les Brown, "F.C.C.'s move to drop some radio rules," *The New York Times*, March 13, 1980, p. C22.

44. Paul Zarins, University of California, San Diego Documents Librarian, in personal communication to the author.

45. *Hearings* before the Subcommittee on Printing of the Committee

on House Administration, House of Representatives, 96th Congress, First Session, on H.R. 5424, The National Publicationss Act, November 14, 1979, U.S. GPO, Washington, D.C. Note the statements of these agencies in the Appendix of the Hearings.

46.   The White House Conference on Library and Information Services—179 Summary, March 1980, U.S., Washington, D.C. GPO See also, *Information World*, January 1980, p. 17.

47.   Tony Schwartz, "Corporations look to cable TV," *The New York Times*, October 18, 1980, p. 01.

48.   Phil Hirsch, "Groups demand stronger rewrite," *Computerworld*, January 21, 1980, pp. 1, 4.

49.   Edward E. David, Jr., "Industrial research in America: Challenge of a new synthesis," *Science*, July 4, 1980, *209*, pp. 133–139.

50.   Dr. Frank Press, Presidential Science Adviser, in *The New York Times*, by Robert Reinhold, "Research by Pentagon scheduled to receive fund increase of 21%," January 29, 1980, p. A1.

51.   "Harvard considers commerical role in DNA research," *The New York Times*, October 27, 1980. Also, David Noble & Nancy E. Pfund, "Business goes back to college," *op. cit.*

Philip Elliott argues that coming shifts in the distributive forms of mass media, accompanied by a shift in power from nation-states to an international economic system, signal changes for intellectuals as well: They are "about to be robbed of those public forums in which they could engage in their 'culture of critical discourse.' Their toe-hold on power is crumbling under their feet," he argues. Philip Elliott is a research fellow at the Centre for Mass Communication Research, University of Leicester.

33

INTELLECTUALS, THE "INFORMATION SOCIETY" AND THE DISAPPEARANCE OF THE PUBLIC SPHERE

Philip Elliott

This paper attempts to raise a series of questions about intellectuals, the mass media, the current course of technical and economic developments in society and their consequences for the culture.[1] It deals not only with the current situation but also with longer-term trends. Society is at the point when there is about to be another shift in the distributive forms of the mass media. This re-opens many of the questions which have already been discussed about centralized broadcasting, both radio and television, as well as other earlier mass media. It also raises questions about the future of the intellectuals in the sphere of cultural production.

The thesis I wish to advance is in marked contrast to that of Alvin Gouldner (1979), outlined by Philip Schlesinger in the opening paper. My argument is that the shift in the location of power from the nation state to the international economic system is graphically illustrated by current developments in the mass media and so too are the implications of this shift for the intellectual fraction of Gouldner's 'New Class'. It is not just that the 'new class' is destined not to come to power. The intellectuals are about to be robbed of those public forums in which they could engage in their 'culture of critical discourse'. Their toe-hold on power is crumbling under their feet.

The new distributive technologies have already re-opened some of the more enthralling controversies of the past. To take a trivial example, space invader games have already been criticized for taking too much of the time and attention on the young, for introducing them to violence and warfare and even leading them into delinquency to get the money to play the games. Such criticisms are very reminiscent of the worries that have greeted each new type of entertainment which was particularly attractive to youth and/or the lower classes.

More seriously, the battle lines are already being drawn between the cultural optimists and pessimists. There are those who see no reason to expect anything from technological developments than an acceleration of trends they already deplore. As an example we may take the following observation from Joe Weizenbaum, Professor of Computer Science at MIT, in an exchange with Daniel Bell:

We may recall the euphoric dreams articulated by then Secretary of Commerce, Herbert Hoover at the dawn of the commercial radio broadcasting and again by others when mass TV broadcasting was about to become a reality. It was foreseen that these media would exert an enormously beneficial influence on the shaping of American culture . . . . The technological dream was more than realised.

From Philip Elliott, "Intellectuals, the 'Information Society' and the Disappearance of the Public Sphere," *Media, Culture and Society*, Vol. 4, No. 3 (July 1982), pp. 243-253. Copyright: Academic Press Inc. (London) Ltd. Reprinted by permission.

. . . But the cultural dream was cruelly mocked in its realisation. This magnificent technology, more than Wagnerian in its proportions. . . . What does it deliver to the masses? An occasional gem buried in immense avalanches of the ordure of everything that is most banal and insipid or pathological in our civilisation (Weizenbaum, 1980: 553–554).

Weizenbaum goes on to illustrate his argument by taking the home computer as another example of a product for which there is no demand until it exists and computer games as a trivialized, sensationalized version of the great ideal showing how intellectual potential can be transformed into a toy to kill, maim and destroy.[2]

On the other side Daniel Bell (1976, 1980), though he has his moments of general pessimism when considering topics like religion, speaks for the optimists who see the new technology as bringing about a quantum shift in the organization of society, a shift which will increase the scope for individual choice and rational decision. Bell is fond of drawing an analogy between the new computer technology with its communication adjuncts and the Alexandrian Library. This treasure house of knowledge in the ancient world contained all human knowledge as it was then available. The library made it freely available for the general benefit of mankind at that time. Computer science, cable technology and data banks are about to realize this dream on a much grander scale.

As always, it is important to set such technological changes in their social context. In this case the aim is supported by the fact that communication changes have vast implications for the organization of work, the economy, the rôles which people are able to play in society, their relationship to that society and to the polity. The corollary of this is that it is important to look not just at the technology but also at the political economy in which it is being developed, to consider what type of organizations and corporations are associated with the present range of media provision and which with the new technologies that are likely to be introduced, what interests they are likely to pursue, consciously and unconsciously, and the type of social and political structures that they are likely to both promote and reflect. These structural changes are bound to have a profound effect on the organization and content of forms of intellectual work.

The thesis I wish to advance is that what we are seeing and what we face is a continuation of the shift away from involving people in society as political citizens of nation states towards involving them as consumption units in a corporate world. The consequence of this for the culture is a continuation of the erosion of what Habermas called the public sphere or C. Wright Mills the community of publics. The hallmark of both these types of polity were contests between politically expressed demands based on knowledge, information and association in democratic, nation states—a type of society which Habermas sees as typical of the bourgeois moment of capitalism. Instead a mass society develops founded on an acceptable level of comfort, pleasure and control in which people participate as members of the market.

The consequence of relying on the market, as Nora and Minc (1978) argue, is to set very real limits on what people can hope to achieve. The market provides not for participation but for consumption. In other words, there is a sleight of hand in the arguments of Daniel Bell and others who look forward to an explosion of information and communication such as will create an information-based society with a more rational form of culture than we now enjoy. The sleight of hand lies in the assumption that new technologies will increase general access to information and open up new possibilities of two-way communication.

The first problem is one of access; the second, what we mean by information and communication. Access is not just a matter of physical means. It also involves having the rights and resources to make use of them. The analogy of a library is appealing because it suggests an open store of knowledge simply waiting for us to bumble around in. Moreover, the public library system is another of those services, like public education, established in the nineteenth and twentieth centuries, in recognition of a general right to knowledge. However poorly the ideal has been realized in practice, the library system has been inspired by the aim of an informed citizenry.

The weakness of the analogy between the old and the new becomes apparent however as soon as we consider the aims of the new controllers of information. What is in prospect, as Herbert Schiller (1981) has pointed out, is the privatization of information. The new information producers are commercial corporations who have a primary interest in keeping information secret to protect their commercial secrets. Their secondary interest is to produce a commodity for sale in the market. In the pursuit of this end, the American information industry is already putting pressure on the sources of public information, of which the main one is the government, to commercialize its operations. Information which was once available to the public as of right will, in future, be available at a price. As Schiller argues, there is likely to be a knock-on effect. Information for which there is not a market will not be produced. In Britain there is a neat illustration of the coincidence between political convenience and market forces in the gradual disappearance of the poverty statistics.[3]

There are other problems with the library analogy. Even libraries have catalogues—catalogues designed to make it easy to answer some questions and so inevitably more difficult to answer others. Who will be writing the catalogues? Who will be setting the questions and the range of possible answers? Indeed, who will have accumulated the stock of knowledge? Not, I submit, the myriad of individual subscribers at their computer terminals and yet, another characteristic of the technological Utopia will be a further domestication of living functions and privatization of social life.

Privatization in this sense is one of the key processes associated with the Frankfurt School's analysis of the media and their effect on social relationships, not through the messages they carry but the type of interaction they encourage. By concentrating activities within the home, the broadcast media of radio and television set up a type of human group which has no other connection with each other than their common use of the same service. The strong version of the Frankfurt school argument is that this opens up the possibility of manipulation, an argument which has been severely questioned by 'effects' research. A weak version of the argument is that this process of privatization deprives people of the possibility of answering back because it deprives them of the opportunities for association in which common needs might be recognized and demands formulated. Instead, to take a flippant but tragic example of someone who is, as they say, at the sharp end of this process, the modern housewife 'goes rushing for the shelter of a mother's little helper', in the words of the old Rolling Stones' lyric and seeks an individual solution to her problems. The example is not so flippant when you consider that the housewife is the supposed epitome of the isolated individual able to exercise free choice in the cornucopia of the consumer society.

The second problem of Bell's vision of a rational, information-rich society is that much of what we now take as information and as an informative process of communication based on a rational model are anything but, having a high level of symbolic, mythical content and passive, entertainment value. The importance attached to the concept of information owes much to the resilience of the ideal of society as a rational, democratic polity and to the success of intellectuals in promoting the equation information plus rational choice equals social progress. It is an equation which has been much disputed by conservative intellectuals. 'Hayek's law' for example claims that attempts at legislative reform always have opposite effects from those intended. It is only recently, however, that such arguments have begun to carry weight against the interventionist intellectuals of Gouldner's 'New Class' who had insinuated themselves into the machinery of national government as the providers and processors of the information on which the government should act. While the Labour Party and the SDP dispute their right to Tawney's name for a new interventionist, intellectual society, the intellectual initiative has passed to various right-wing societies and institutes.[4] These are able to attract private funds whereas the financial and occupational base of interventionist intellectualism in public sector research and educational institutions is being put under increasing pressure.

Nevertheless, the persistence of the Fabianesque concept of information as a necessary social resource can also be seen in discussions of the mass media. The growth of the press was based on two processes, the provision of useful information, mainly commercial and financial intelligence to interested parties, and political controversy. Print was the medium which underpinned the concept of the public sphere by providing an arena for political debate. Over time, both these functions have been transformed. From its original base in elite information, the commercial function has expanded beyond all recognition and with the transformation of news into a commodity, the political function has been eclipsed. Nevertheless, debates about the press are still carried on in terms of the argument for a free press able to supply the information and reflect the opinions necessary to foster decision-making in a democracy. The recent introduction of a new daily newspaper in Britain, the *Daily Star*, shows clearly that the mass market daily papers are a very different sort of animal. The lead features in the three tabloids on the day on which the *Daily Star* started in publication showed a quite explicit concern with irrationality, magic, extra-scientific potential and play on the sacred and profane dimensions. One featured a round-the-world-yachtswoman and a sex-change witch, the second organized an experiment among its readers to show that metal could be bent by mental power and the third discovered a vicar who painted nudes à la Gaugin.

A similar distinction was drawn by William Randolph Hearst, the American newspaper magnate, when he contrasted 'interesting' with 'merely important' news. 'Important news' was concerned with institutions, organizations and decision-making in society. 'Interesting' was that which appealed to individuals *qua* individuals, as individual members of the human race. This human interest aspect of news is part of the basis for a populist form of culture, one which exaggerates the commonalities between people and plays down structural divisions of interest. Those commonalities are exaggerated which revolve around consumption and the pursuit of pleasure. Consider the shift in meaning of 'us' and 'them'. As described by Richard Hoggart in *The Uses of Literacy*, 'them and us' was a common part of the working-class view of the world in the inter-war period he was describing. He defines 'them' as follows:

'Them' is a composite dramatic figure, the chief character in modern urban forms of the rural peasant-big house relationships. The world of 'them' is the world of the bosses whether those bosses are private individuals or as is increasingly the case today, public officials (Hoggart, 1958: 72).

Compare this with the idea of 'them' contained in a *Sun* editorial on the Notting Hill Carnival of 1977:

What Notting Hill has shown yet again is that violence on the streets is not a case of black against white or rich against poor. It is the yobs against the rest of us. That is true not only in Notting Hill but in Lewisham, Ladywood and in the turmoil that engulfed the Grunwick dispute. The same goes for the louts who disrupt soccer matches and smash up railway trains. It is not society which is on trial in any of these cases but the effectiveness of justice to defend the ordinary peaceful man.

Populist culture cannot magic away the evidence of social division and conflict. Instead it turns it into a question of membership or non-membership of society or even the human race. Non-members 'disrupt' entertainment and 'smash up' property. It is, as the *Sun* so elegantly puts it, a matter of 'the yobs against the rest of us'.

Information and communication are also the catch words used to describe the new type of society which will be ushered in by technological change and developments in electronics, data systems and the new distributive media. The new society, it is argued, will involve changes in the power relations within the mode of production. Those who control the information, intellectuals in one form or another, will have control of one of the means of production and so have a base for class power. The fallacy of this argument becomes apparent if we consider how much power the working class have been able to exercise through their control of another means of production, labour. The point is not who is allowed to contribute to the process of production but who extracts the surplus value from it and so has the resources to control the course of its development. Obituaries for the old class of money and capital to be found in the work of Gouldner *inter alia* seem a little premature. This leopard has changed its spots. The supra-national species has become more important, if less immediately visible, than the more familiar national species which is being extinguished.

National capital and national enterprises are increasingly vulnerable as the economic system becomes more and more internationalized. As Raymond Vernon has emphasized, this process of internationalization involves a complex and intricate network of commercial and financial ties and dependencies, a complexity which makes any attempt to identify a single class of institutions like the multi-national corporations or, more popularly, the 'gnomes of Zurich' liable to gross over-simplification. The complexity provides the old class with a new and effective camouflage in its changed form. Nevertheless, Vernon concludes that while greater economic interdependence is 'indispensable for continued economic growth . . . it seems at times to threaten some of the national goals for which the growth was intended, including national stability, egalitarianism, participation and protection' (Vernon, 1977: 193).

These national goals are ones which have been promoted, if not realized, by intellectuals. Indeed, as Schlesinger points out in his paper in this issue, the history of the intellectuals is that of a group which came to prominence through the promotion of nationalism in this century and the last. The nation state and its political system have given some intellectuals a mechanism through which to promote social policies which intervened in the operation of economic forces and attempted to alter some of their effects. The resurgence of monetarism is only a particularly topical reminder that many intellectuals have actively opposed such interventionism. As Eric Gabus of Nestlés put it in a conference defending the rôle of the multi-national corporations, 'the businessman depends on intellectuals to update the trend of public opinion'. But in so far as intellectuals had an independent hold on power to promote different goals, it was through the medium of the nation state and the attempt to use its political power. The process of technological change in the mass media provides us with a useful case to examine the implications of the shift in power away from the nation state and into the international economic system and the effects this is likely to have on culture, the rôle of the intellectuals and the future of the public sphere in which intellectuality was exercised.

To start with developments in the culture, we have already noted the growth of consumer populism, a development which Daniel Bell is quite pessimistic about for fear that shameless hedonism may overtake the Protestant ethic. One of the common interests which can be promoted on behalf of all 'the ordinary, peaceful citizens' of the *Sun* editorial, quoted above, is 'law and order'. This couplet has acquired a special significance in British culture as a way of turning consumer populism into a repressive form of culture which justifies strengthening the agents of the state, their exercise of power over the citizenry and the erosion of democratic, political control over that power.[5] Thus, in a period of general wage restraint, the police and the army have been consistently privileged, police powers are about to be further increased and the Chief Constable of Greater Manchester, James Anderton, has explicitly called for an end to 'political' scrutiny of the police. The use of 'political' in this and similar contexts has important negative overtones compared, for example, to 'democratic'. It illustrates the process of ghettoizing politics and politicians to which I shall return in discussing the effects of broadcasting on politics below. Another example of the increasing rôle of the repressive forces of the state is the use of military forces in a domestic operation, the Iranian Embassy siege.[6]

Three processes are especially noteworthy as contributions to this repressive culture.

(1) An exaggeration of crime, criminality and violence, as for example, the repeated claim that we live in a particularly violent age.

(2) The process of turning political, industrial and social dissent into a form of criminal activity and identifying such action with violence.

(3) The resurgence of that long-established form of ideological management, the Cold War, or its more recent variant, the War against Terrorism, so that dissent becomes identified with an alien threat to the nation, the Western World or our way of life.[7]

This last process is a timely reminder that these cultural developments are to a large extent international. In most parts of the world repression has gone far beyond the culture. The interests of the international economic order are such that the residual rôle assigned to national governments is to be the keeper of national order. To quote Vernon again, 'Foreign investors have demonstrated an unsurprising preference for a stable and friendly economic environment. In a number of developing countries that preference has meant that multinational enterprises have expanded their activities sharply immediately after a Rightist government has taken power or have reduced their activities immediately after a Leftist regime has taken control' (Vernon, 1977: 144).

These twin features of the contemporary culture—consumptive hedonism and anti-political repression—have a special significance given the implications which the new technology has for structural unemployment and the international reorganization of work and production.[8] People deprived of their only means of being involved in the capitalist system by right—that is by selling their labour power—will have to be involved from the other end by a right to consume. In the eyes of some protagonists of the new international system, this right is already established as the new basis for legitimating the distribution of power. Thus Gabus claims 'in a democratically, decentralised society the Multinational Company . . . can retain its economic power only through the goodwill of consumers who by the daily selection of the products they purchase, judge the usefulness of the Multinational Company and put a value on the services it supplies. The survival of this goodwill depends entirely on profitable dealings with a clientele whose needs the Multinational Company appreciates across national boundaries' (Gabus, 1977: 133). But if the right is established, capitalism is a long way from providing everyone with the means to exercise their rights. As we can see from the current international depression the $64,000 question with which the capitalist system seems unable to cope is how to ensure that supply reaches demand.

The preference, demonstrated by the current monetarist and deflationary policies adopted by most governments, is for a strategy which reduces supply to meet effective demand. Thereby large sections of the national and international population are effectively disenfranchised by their exclusion from the market. This brings the repressive aspect of the culture into play to restrict the scope for dissent of those unable to participate in the consumer society and to support repressive action by state forces against them.

The signs are that the market will be the main mechanism for allowing access to the new media services, either directly through the purchase of discs, tapes or subscription services, such as even the BBC is planning for its satellite transmissions, or indirectly through the sale of international advertising space. Direct sale will disadvantage a growing proportion of the population given that unemployment will prevent them from acquiring adequate means. Indirect sale gives another twist to the international spiral by putting yet more emphasis on cross-border consumerism.

The results of relying on these forms of the market are already apparent in the press where the only viable form of journalism is that founded on definable markets as in the leisure interest magazine field. In the case of the British provincial press monopoly control over a sectionalized market is an added bonus. By contrast the political journal and political content is being squeezed out and with it one locus for the operations of critical intellectuals, one forum through which they have contributed to the formulation of policy within the nation state. In so far as politics is not a consumable product, there is no advertising revenue on which political journalism can rely for the support of its services.

These developments in the press are suggestive of the type of content which is likely to survive in new forms of distributive media dependent on sale of item or sale of audience. The BBC's initial catalogue of video cassettes, for example, covers cooking, gardening and other leisure interests, already familiar topics in the magazine field. Plans to include drama and entertainment packages are held up by negotiations on the rights of performers and producers, but such material is expected to predominate once agreements have been reached. The possibility of political or current affairs cassettes has not been mooted.

Broadcasting in its traditional forms has already had a considerable impact on the political culture. The system of control under which it has operated has left little room for political partisanship. Instead the media of radio and television have given considerable support to generalized notions of public and community. Since its inception broadcasting has treated politics with considerable circumspection. Partisan politics was at first excluded completely and then confined to limited ghettoes and subject to stringent rules of balance. Election broadcasts and party politicals are both special cases in the general run of output. Such programmes are heavily signposted and the editorial control of the broadcasters is relinquished or disputed. In the place of partisan politics, general broadcasting has been particularly influential in developing a general notion of public and community as a way of meeting the requirements of balance and objectivity. Formulae were devised for the discussion of public affairs in, for example, BBC Radio's *Any Questions?* which gave pride of place to prominent citizens who were 'non-political'. One of their main qualifications for taking part was independence of party. In a sense broadcasting was only developing a standard practice of British administration to use those who have achieved prominence in one field to superintend developments in another by appointing them to various boards, committees and commissions. Recent work on the history of broadcasting has shown how the BBC was colonized by intellectuals of the professional middle class.[9] They were attracted by the opportunity to discuss public affairs in talks and feature programmes in terms of a general notion of the public interest. It was this same public interest to which intellectuals appealed to support their interventions in policy making and social engineering. The concept of the public good allowed intellectuals to step outside a straightforward technical rationality of judging the efficacy of means to take on questions of ends as well. Public service broadcasting enshrines such an idea in its very title.

Even such generalized notions are likely to be set aside as the new media limit the scope for political discourse even further. The pressure will be felt in two ways. First, the new distributive forms will simply leave out political discussion and criticism. Actuality programming, topical and with limited appeal, is the type of content most at risk. Second, the development of new distributive systems puts public service broadcasting under severe threat.

At least two conditions were necessary to enable public service broadcasting to develop. The first was the framework of government regulation which required a non-partisan approach. Successive governments have had continued misgivings about the progressivism of the community approach when it raised embarassing questions about current policies. The second was the national basis of distribution so that community was co-terminous with the citizenry of the nation state. To make the connections quite explicit, public service broadcasting can be said to have been a political medium of both the intellectuals and the nation state.

The current threat to public service broadcasting provide us with a very clear illustration of how weak is the intellectuals' hold over power and influence. Public service broadcasting has pursued a number of characteristically intellectual goals such as the preservation of the national culture by promoting broadcast versions of national classics and maintaining domestic production, the guardianship of cultural values by sponsoring non-commercial culture and programming for cultural values, and promoting national debate on public issues through a service of news, current affairs and documentaries. This last goal was pursued against consistent political suspicion and opposition, as Grace Wyndham Goldie (1977) makes clear in her account of the development of political television. As a result the debate has taken on the form outlined above.

Much media sociology has been particularly critical of the form as embodied in television news and emphasized the limited contribution that has made to awareness.[10] But on the other hand factual television in its various forms has been influential in putting issues on the public agenda. It has attracted accusations of left-wing bias and more generally that broadcasting has usurped the role of parliament. The documentary has been an effective way of raising questions about the public good and the documentary and current affairs departments of broadcasting have been successful in recruiting the type of educated elite which has traditionally gone into other intellectual and professional positions. News, as well as longer forms of presentation, has shown people suffering through no fault of their own by, for example, war and other disasters, natural and man-made. More important, there is the implicit or explicit suggestion that someone, national governments or international agencies, should do something about it. Disaster reports, for example, are routinely followed by enquiries into cause, prevention and what is and can be done to provide effective relief.

There is a sense in which such information necessarily has interventionist implications. This is what has led to a critique of the media from the Right. Coverage puts pressure on the authorities to act and it may be pressure to act in directions different from those they wish to take. Suffering stories in particular may make it more difficult for the authorities to maintain the support for the policies which produce the suffering such as going to war, pursuing a deflationary economic strategy or not preparing or providing for natural disasters.

So far this system has kept running on an uneasy combination of control and concession. Control by government ownership and economic influence on the broadcasting authorities to contain the liberal perspective in the public sphere of broadcasting and the acceptance by democratic governments of a responsibility to try to mitigate and contain the effects of various disasters for the comfort and well-being of their subjects. It is hard not to draw the conclusion that both the liberal aspect of the media and the ability and willingness of governments to accept such responsibilities are under threat in the developing crisis.

Of these two the public sphere in the media is clearly the most vulnerable. To a large extent the intellectual space there rests on notions of public service and journalistic responsibility. Public service is no longer financially viable. Broadcasting has exhausted non-advertising revenue as the licence fee becomes an increasingly unacceptable poll tax. Even without advertising revenue, public service broadcasting has had to compete with commercial systems and become less able to pursue different goals and to preserve its own distinct identity. The process is illustrated by the co-production movement or, more recently, by the BBC's agreement with the Rockefeller Centre Inc. to become a cable service supplier in the USA. Overseas the BBC is becoming another commercial media producer and distributor. In the United Kingdom, it is fighting a rear-guard action against moves to cable the country for entertainment, moves which appear to be unstoppable as they are led by the prospect of profit rather than public demand. In the press responsible journalism depends on the willingness of owners to pursue non-commercial goals. Conglomeration has made this less likely. Owners and managers are unable to allow the commercial slack in which journalistic space can develop.

Apart from finance, a second problem is the lack of regulatory will to continue to put national communication policy into regulatory form. The coalition of paternalist interests, to use Graham Murdock's phrase, that set up public service broadcasting—intellectual and cultural elites, politicians anxious to lay down rules of debate and new professionals skilled in the techniques of the new media—has been put on the defensive. While it can rally support against the government on an issue like the BBC external services, it is powerless against commercial interests campaigning in terms of variety and independence. Hence, in the United Kingdom cable franchises have been given to companies with no requirements for access or public service programming and in the United States such commitments are being written out of the Federal Communication Act.

Even given the political will however, a third problem is that national power is no longer adequate to regulate supra-national bodies. This problem is raised most dramatically by satellites but already pirate radio and the difficulties the Dutch and Italians have experienced in keeping control of land-based transmissions and cable systems show the dimensions of the problem. An exhibition of the new technology, organized by Philips, the Dutch electrical company, cites as a virtue of the new system of satellite communication that 'there is no need for the countries covered to give their permission'. A special problem for the democracies will be the difficulty of enforcing any rules of political debate. In so far as it survives it will depend on the ability of the wealthy to buy time, a prospect which clearly underlines the way in which the course of history favours an old, familiar class and not some aspiring newcomer, however well-intentioned.

In other fields it is possible to show separately how the nation state is under threat from internationalization and the intellectual hopelessly insecure in the face of the intelligentsia. The inability to control capital flows provides an illustration of the first and the demand for 'relevance' in education one of the second. Dealing with the media and cultural processes has the advantage, however, of demonstrating how these processes are intertwined. In this paper I have tried to do no more than outline a scenario but the argument should be sufficient to suggest that in this field of the media, which Hall (1977) has identified as the current site of the class struggle, the conflict is likely to be resolved by material rather than ideological processes.

Notes

1. I am indebted to my colleagues at the Centre for Mass Communication Research, Leicester University for discussions on the topics raised in this paper and to Philip Schlesinger, whose paper in this issue provided the final impetus to put pessimism to paper.
2. *The Daily Mirror* (10 April 1982) reported that British Telecom had designed a game of sink the Argentine navy for its Prestel service after the British task force had sailed for the Falkland Isles. Following protests this game was withdrawn.
3. Thus, for example, figures on the take-up rate of means-tested benefits are no longer available and the number below the 'poverty line' is now calculated biennially instead of annually.
4. On the dispute over Tawney's inheritance see Raphael Samuel's Socialist Society pamphlet, published by *The Guardian* (29 March and 5 April 1982). Examples of bodies which have begun to make more of the ideological running are the Institute for the Study of Conflict, the Institute for Economic Affairs, which now includes within it a Unit for Social Affairs, the Freedom Association, the Adam Smith Institute and the Centre for Policy Studies.
5. The work of Stuart Hall has been particularly influential in drawing attention to this process. See, for example, his Cobden Lecture, published in *The Guardian* (5 January 1980) and Hall *et al.* (1978). Other studies include Chibnall (1977) and Taylor (1981).

6. On the siege, see Philip Schlesinger (1980/81).
7. Chomsky and Herman (1979) make some pertinent observations on both these phenomena.
8. On unemployment see Jordan (1982) and Showler and Sinfield (1981).
9. In addition to Brigg's official history of the BBC there is the growing body of work by Scannell (1980) and Cardiff (1980).
10. For a general review see Golding and Elliott (1979). The most publicized critique is that of the Glasgow University Media Group (1976, 1980).

Bibliography

BELL, D. (1976). *The Cultural Contradictions of Capitalism*, London, Heinemann
BELL, D. (1980). The social framework of the information society, in Forrester, T. (ed.), *The Micro-electronics Revolution*, Oxford, Blackwell
CARDIFF, D. (1980). The serious and the popular, *Media, Culture and Society*, vol. 2, no. 1
CHIBNALL, S. (1977). *Law-and-Order News*, London, Tavistock
CHOMSKY, N. and HERMAN, E. S. (1979). *The Political Economy of Human Rights*, 2 vol., Nottingham, Spokesman Books
GABUS, E. (1977). The external relations of multinational companies, in Curzon, G. and V., (eds), *The Multinational Enterprise in a Hostile World*, London, Macmillan
GLASGOW UNIVERSITY MEDIA GROUP (1976). *Bad News*, London, Routledge and Kegan Paul
GLASGOW UNIVERSITY MEDIA GROUP (1980). *More Bad News*, London, Routledge and Kegan Paul
GOLDIE, G. W. (1977) *Facing the Nation: Television and Politics, 1936–1976*, London, Bodley Head
GOLDING, P. and ELLIOTT, P. (1979). *Making the News*, London, Longman
GOULDNER, A. (1979). *The Future of the Intellectuals and the Rise of the New Class*, London, Macmillan
HALL, S. (1977). Culture, the media and the 'ideological effect', in Curran, J. *et al.*, (eds), *Mass Communication and Society*, London, Arnold
HALL, S. (1978). *Policing the Crisis*, London, Macmillan
HOGGART, R. (1958). *The Uses of Literacy*, Harmondsworth, Penguin
JORDAN, B. (1982). *Mass Unemployment and the Future of Britain*, Oxford, Blackwell
NORA, S. and MINC, A. (1978). *L'Informatisation de la Société*, Paris, La Documentation Française
SCANNELL, P. (1980). Broadcasting and the politics of unemployment, 1930–1935, *Media, Culture and Society*, vol. 2, no. 1
SCHILLER, H. (1981). *Who Knows: Information in the Age of the Fortune 500*. Norwood, NJ, Ablex
SCHLESINGER, P. (1980/81). Princes' Gate, 1980: the media politics of siege management, *Screen Education*, no. 37
SHOWLER, B. and SINFIELD, A. (eds) (1981). *The Workless State*, London, Martin Robertson
TAYLOR, I. (1981). *Law and Order*, London, Macmillan
VERNON, R. (1977). *Storm over the Multinationals*, London, Macmillan
WEIZENBAUM, J. (1980). Once more, the computer revolution, in Forrester, T. (ed.), *The Micro-electronics Revolution*, Oxford, Blackwell

Teletext and viewdata are both more and less than an "electronic newspaper," are cause both for optimism and pessimism, and are both so new that it is difficult to say definitively how they will evolve but are old enough to be able to see some of the directions they will take, according to David Weaver. In this chapter, Weaver suggests seven lessons that research and experience have to date offered as to what such forms of "electronic publishing" do, at present, mean. David H. Weaver is associate professor and director of the Bureau of Media Research in the School of Journalism at Indiana University.

34

TELETEXT AND VIEWDATA
A Closer Look

David H. Weaver

Although there is little argument that the technology exists now in many countries for the widespread development of both teletext and viewdata systems, there is much speculation about the possible benefits and drawbacks of such systems for journalists, the larger society, and other media. Most of the thinking and writing with regard to the effects of teletext and viewdata is speculation and conjecture—not surprising given the relative newness and limited diffusion of videotex—and most of it can be classified as either "optimistic" or "pessimistic," with a few views in the "mixed reactions" camp. This chapter reviews some of these views of videotex and pulls together the harder evidence from some of the few systematic studies that presently exist.

THE OPTIMISTIC VIEW

Many of those writing about the possibilities of electronic information delivery, via teletext or viewdata systems, are unabashedly optimistic. They stress the ability of the viewer to select only information that is of interest, increased access for more points of view because of the relatively low cost of becoming an information provider, increased diversity of information resulting from low costs and nearly unlimited storage capacities, and greater power for the individual because of increased control over information

From David H. Weaver, "Teletext and Viewdata: A Closer Look," Chapter 2 of David H. Weaver, *Videotex Journalism: Teletext, Viewdata and the News* (Hillsdale, NJ: Lawrence Erlbaum Associates, 1982). Reprinted by permission.

received, and the ability to provide nearly instantaneous feedback to the sources of various messages.[1]

Many of these arguments about the merits of teletext and viewdata are reminiscent of some of the arguments for the quick adoption of other media, such as motion pictures, radio, and television. Advocates of these media predicted such benefits as increased access to information about current events, strengthened democracy and diminished class distinctions because of the uniformity of information available to all citizens, increased national unity and decreased isolation of all persons, establishment of national forums for political discussion, increased worldwide understanding and international unity, better education, and a better-informed electorate.[2]

The arguments in support of teletext and viewdata systems emphasize diversity of information, rather than uniformity, and individual control and convenience, rather than national unity. There is also an emphasis on the greatly increased *volume* of information that may be accessed in the privacy of one's home. As two journalism instructors from Brigham Young University put it, "The newshole of an electronic newspaper is limited only by the storage capacity of the computer system."[3] This claim was echoed recently by a North Carolina newspaper editor who wrote that "because computer memory space is cheaper than newsprint, stories can run as long as anyone wants them to."[4] A promotion brochure for teletext and viewdata systems in the United Kingdom emphasized that "viewdata will offer limitless specialized information and other services as well as general information."[5]

In addition to the "vast quantities" argument, a closely related theme is that of "immediate access." This claim is especially popular among advocates of teletext (broadcast) systems. As one promotional brochure for British teletext put it, "Teletext turns your television set into a storehouse of up-to-the-minute information, and puts it all instantly at your disposal—literally at your fingertips."[6] In his book, *American Newspapers*

---

[1] For a concise summary of these arguments, I am indebted to Linda Zaradich, a master's student in journalism at Indiana University, and particularly to a paper by her entitled "Electronic Home News Delivery: A Systems Analysis," written for a seminar on mass media and society in April 1981.

[2] See Robert Davis, "Response to Innovation: A Study of Popular Argument About New Mass Media," unpublished dissertation, University Microfilms Inc., Ann Arbor, Michigan, 1976.

[3] Cecelia Fielding and William C. Porter, "Time to turn on the newspaper," *The Quill: Magazine for Journalists*, 69 (April 1981), p. 18.

[4] Mark Ethridge III, "Report from Coral Gables: We can relax. Or can we?" *Electronic Publishing: The Newspaper of the Future?* (Report by the Associated Press Managing Editors Media Competition Committee, November 1980), p. 12.

[5] "Teletext and Viewdata for the World" (Basingstoke, England: Bell Carter Elliot Richards Limited, 1979), p. 1.

[6] "A British TV first! Teletext" (London: Department of Industry, undated), p. 1.

in the 1980s, Ernest Hynds writes that electronic home communication systems will "offer immediate access to vast quantities of information and instant news on demand."[7] A brochure describing the Independent Broadcasting Authority's Oracle teletext system makes this same point even more emphatically:

> As a news medium, ORACLE is ideal. Even for headlines, a conventional newspaper has a copy deadline some hours before actual publication: television can accept copy changes a few minutes before transmission. But ORACLE can be on the air with the latest news only seconds after a story breaks. It is difficult to think of a much better news service than that, and its use in this way could make it the most significant development in communications since Caxton.[8]

Colin McIntyre, editor of the BBC's Ceefax system, sees teletext as, "The quickest public information service any broadcaster has ever had at his command."[9] To support this argument, McIntyre points to Ceefax's coverage of the 1980 Moscow Olympics, where sub-editor Audrey Adams typed sports results and news stories directly into the Ceefax computer 1550 miles away, and to the "real-time" subtitling of President Ronald Reagan's inaugural speech on January 20, 1981, with no advance script, that enabled the Palantype (mechanical shorthand machine) operator to take account of ad-libs and corrections.[10]

McIntyre also asserts that "subtitling was the original trigger for the development of teletext,"[11] and this observation leads naturally to another argument for teletext and viewdata: That those who are deaf or hard-of-hearing will finally be able to enjoy television, whereas those who can hear normally will not be distracted by subtitles at the bottom of the screen. As McIntyre puts it, "All teletext is of benefit to the deaf and hard-of-hearing,"[12] and "can truly be described as revolutionary."[13] McIntyre points out that reading Ceefax before viewing the main BBC television evening news means that those who can't hear well, "will know that the tanks they see in the streets are in Beirut and not in Belfast, or vice-versa; and that the actress appearing on the screen has just arrived in London for a

[7]Ernest C. Hynds, *American Newspapers in the 1980s* (New York: Hastings House, 1980), p. 281.

[8]"ORACLE: Broadcasting the Written Word" (Basingstoke, England: Kempsters, undated), p. 5.

[9]Colin McIntyre, "CEEFAX—an editorial update," *European Broadcasting Union Review,* 32 (March 1981), p. 45.

[10]See Colin McIntyre, "BBC Ceefax Girl the Fastest in Moscow," Ceefax Paper, September 1980; Colin McIntyre, "The Palantype Experiment," Ceefax Paper BB/1, February 1981, pp. 1–6; and Colin McIntyre, "CEEFAX—an editorial update," pp. 46–47.

[11]McIntyre, "CEEFAX—an editorial update," p. 46.

[12]Colin McIntyre, "Making news more than just a picture for the deaf," *Viewdata Magazine,* 4 (July 1979), p. 10.

[13]Colin McIntyre, "Ceefax and the Hard of Hearing," Ceefax Briefing, undated.

film premiere, and has not died, or been divorced, or hijacked."[14] With teletext, McIntyre claims, "Deaf viewers are able to see their own written version of the news and read at their own individual speed, so that news subtitles become much less necessary."[15]

Still another argument in favor of teletext and viewdata is that these systems permit audience feedback and immediate action to be taken as a result. As McIntyre puts it, "The teletext audience is one of the most involved, most committed, most participating of audiences that I have met in 30 years."[16] Even with a one-way teletext system such as Ceefax, McIntyre writes that viewers "demand their say, all the time,"[17] and "we can correct the mistake, if mistake it was, before that very viewer's eyes, while he watches, accompanied for the purpose by admiring members of his family witnessing Daddy's correction of the foolish broadcaster."[18]

This capacity for audience feedback is, of course, considerably enhanced with interactive viewdata systems such as the British Post Office's Prestel. According to one *Sunday Times* writer:

> To the newcomer, Prestel is a marvel. Touch the pocket-calculator-like keyboard of your £600 Prestel set, and the Nine O'Clock News can become a bedtime story, an instant booking form for the Royal Shakespeare Theatre, or a six-color graph of the growth in sterling M3. You can buy with it, sell with it, and even use it to complain about it.[19]

Other possible uses of viewdata systems like Prestel include monitoring homes for fire and theft, providing an electronic school, electronic mail, library services from the home, and electronic funds transfer (banking), according to the Manitoba Telephone System which offers a videotex service to about 50 homes in South Headingley, Manitoba.[20] Still other uses of videotex are foreseen by the Viditel Project Manager of the Netherlands Postal and Telecommunications Services, including the conducting of public opinion polls and electronic voting and referendums.[21]

One of the most basic arguments of all, very possibly the most compelling for teletext and especially for viewdata systems, is economic. As Joseph

---

[14]McIntyre, "Making news more than just a picture," p. 10.

[15]McIntyre, "CEEFAX—an editorial update," p. 47.

[16]*Ibid.,* p. 44.

[17]*Ibid.,* p. 44.

[18]*Ibid.,* p. 45.

[19]Peter Stothard, "Why instant information is slow to catch on," *The Sunday Times,* 25 January 1981, p. 61.

[20]Brad Schultz, "Manitoba Town to Test Viewdata-Type Service," *Computerworld,* August 6, 1979, p. 34.

[21]P.J.G.M. Ruiten, "Videotex Developments in the Netherlands," *VIDEOTEX '81: International Conference & Exhibition* (Middlesex, United Kingdom: Online Conferences, 1981), p. 177.

Roizen, president of a consulting firm involved with both technologies, puts it, "We are looking at a multibillion-dollar industry that, over the next five years, will supplant our current means of telecommunications."[22] Roizen's view is echoed by Kenneth Baker, British Minister for Information Technology, who claims that information technology is going to be "the key growth sector in the British economy."[23]

In addition to the opportunities for *making* money, some of those getting involved with videotex, especially newspaper and magazine publishers, are doing so out of a fear of *losing* money. As one videotex project manager puts it, "There are always a number of information providers who participate simply because their competitors are taking part. Others take part because they are afraid of missing the boat once Viditel (the Dutch viewdata system) really gets going."[24] Donald Sparrow, director of a $600,000 study of electronic information systems by the consulting firm Arthur D. Little, Inc., reinforces this point when he asserts that newspapers are interested in electronic information systems for two reasons: "One is the potential threat to the newspapers, and the second is the potential opportunities to information providers."[25]

Another variant of the economic argument for videotex focuses on the *consumer* rather than the producer of information or the system operator. Martin Goldfarb, head of one of Canada's largest research firms, states that, "As costs go up, as they seem to, the availability of a piece of technology that actually lowers costs will attract consumers, not just to get involved, but to pushing the technocrats to getting on with making it better and more cost practical."[26] To Goldfarb, the cost of videotex is, or will be, "infinitesimally small when you place it in the context of the current cost of distribution of information, goods, and services."[27] George Cox, managing director of the London-based Butler, Cox, & Partners consulting firm, claims that the appeal of viewdata is "very nearly irresistible and it offers a real possibility for adding value to a user's TV."[28]

Another version of the economic argument contrasts the costs of printing information with distributing it electronically, and asserts that both the

[22]Harry F. Waters, Cynthia H. Wilson, and Peter Davies, "TV Turns to Print," *Newsweek,* July 30, 1979, p. 74.

[23]Chris Griffin-Beale, "UK pulls together to push teletext in U.S.," *Broadcast,* 2 March 1981, p. 17.

[24]P.J.G.M. Ruiten, "Videotex Developments in the Netherlands," p. 176.

[25]Bill Kelly, "All The News That's Fit to Compute," *Washington Journalism Review,* April 1980, p. 16.

[26]Martin Goldfarb, "Videotex 2000: Prophesy and Prognosis," *Inside Videotex: Proceedings of a Seminar Held March 13-14, 1980* (Toronto, Canada: Infomart, 1980), p. 118.

[27]*Ibid.,* p. 118.

[28]Don Leavitt, "Study Pinpoints Six Issues Raised by Viewdata," *Computerworld,* February 19, 1979, p. 10.

publishers and the consumers will benefit from eliminating the printing process. Bill Kelly, a Washington free-lance writer, predicts that the electronic newspaper will, "not only be affordable to the reader, but will eventually be cheaper to produce for the publisher."[29] Kelly argues, as do others, that the environmental effects and huge energy requirements of producing and printing newsprint are increasing its costs and diminishing its availability, thus making the elimination of the printing process "a logical step in the history of the industry."[30] He asserts that a single Sunday edition of the New York Times consumes 62,860 trees at the same time that electronic component costs and magnetic storage costs are dropping dramatically. This makes the economics of the electronic newspaper look better "almost by the day."[31] Richard Hooper, director of Prestel, agrees and talks of the "cross-over point" at which the costs of print exceed the costs of distributing information electronically because of the rising costs of materials, energy, and the dipping costs of electrons.[32]

These, then, are the main arguments in favor of teletext and viewdata: Vast quantities of very diverse information will be available cheaply and immediately to nearly all persons (even those deaf or hard-of-hearing) who can respond almost instantly in a variety of ways (including buying and selling goods and services, making reservations, sending messages, transferring money, etc.) using electronic systems that will become huge and profitable industries in themselves. Teletext and viewdata will save energy and result in less damaging effects on the environment than the printing process. As one British publisher recently put it, commenting on the excitement surrounding the development of Prestel in 1977:

> In those dewy-eyed days viewdata promised to be all things to all people; it would revolutionise everybody's life at home, at work and at study. It would allow all points of view to be brought to all, open up society, and do virtually everything except find a cure for cancer. "Better information" was the cry; "accessibility by all" was the message; and for an entry fee of some £2,000 anybody could launch the equivalent of a national newspaper.[33]

Even though there may be "every reason for optimism," in the words of one videotex project manager,[34] there are also many arguments for a more restrained, even pessimistic, view of teletext and viewdata.

---

[29]Kelly, "All The News That's Fit to Compute," p. 16.

[30]*Ibid.*, p. 16.

[31]*Ibid.*, p. 16.

[32]Personal interview with Richard Hooper, director of Prestel, in London, March 16, 1981.

[33]Peter Head, "Prestel—from the Point of View of One Information Provider," *VIDEOTEX '81: International Conference & Exhibition* (Middlesex, United Kingdom: Online Conferences, 1981), p. 138.

[34]P.J.G.M. Ruiten, "Videotex Developments in the Netherlands," p. 177.

THE PESSIMISTIC VIEW

Perhaps one of the most fundamental criticisms of teletext and viewdata is that they are examples of "technological push" rather than "market pull"—that is, there is "as yet very little real evidence that the consumer wants or needs this very different medium."[35] In other words, it may be that electrical engineers have invented something for which there is no real need that is not already well satisfied by more conventional forms of communication such as the printed page, the telephone, and the television. As one German spokesman put it:

> It remains to be seen whether and to what extent the public will use the new services. If the public does use them, everybody will take that for a proof that there is a real need for these services. There is room for suspicion, however, that in the field of electronic communication more often than not the service does not answer a need but the need is created by the service. The secret pacemaker of society's heartbeat is the technician.[36]

Even among information providers to the British Prestel system, there is debate about where viewdata systems fit into the existing information order and which needs they should be trying to meet. In reacting to the change in marketing strategy of Prestel from the general domestic to the more specific business, the "inview" newsletter of Mills & Allen Communications notes that "Prestel is a very general system not well suited to the particular. It is not for example, a real-time system but a system requiring update and inherently incapable of minute to minute accuracy."[37] And the newsletter concludes that "the Gateway—using Prestel as a way into private computer systems—is Prestel's only real hope of a long-term role in the specialist business viewdata market."[38]

An even more global argument against the widespread adoption of teletext, viewdata, and other new technologies is made by Philip Elliott of Leicester University:

> The thesis I wish to advance is that what we are seeing and what we face is a continuation of the shift away from involving people in society as political citizens of nation states towards involving them as consumption units in a corporate world.[39]

---

[35]Gerald Haslam, "Videotex: What is it and where does it fit?" *Inside Videotex: Proceedings of a Seminar Held March 13-14, 1980* (Toronto, Canada: Infomart, 1980), p. 10.

[36]Hans Kimmel, "Germany: A Battle Between Broadcasters and the Press," *InterMedia*, 7:39-40 (May 1979), p. 40.

[37]"One year on...," *Inview, 4* (April 1981), p. 1.

[38]*Ibid.*

[39]Philip Elliott, "Will There Be News in 1991?" Paper presented at a seminar on Manipulation in Mass Communication sponsored by the Foundation for Mass Communication Research, Koningshof Veldhoven, The Netherlands, March 25-27, 1981, pp. 2-3.

Elliott sees a "sleight of hand" in the arguments of Daniel Bell and others who look forward to an explosion of information and communication, and who claim that new technologies such as teletext and viewdata will increase general access to information and open up new possibilities of two-way communication. He argues that access to information is dependent upon the way this information is accumulated and catalogued, and that access from the home will encourage the "privatisation of information," resulting in groups of people who have no other connection with each other than their common use of the same information service. In this way people are more susceptible to manipulation, in Elliott's view, and are deprived of the possibility of answering back because they have fewer opportunities for association in which common needs might be recognized and demands formulated. This view, also known as the "enclave theory," envisions "a nation of new isolationists who are removed from all but the most basic human intercourse in their all-electronic caves."[40]

Elliott is also critical of the claim that people will have access to much more information with new technologies than they do now, because in his opinion, much of what is called "information" on these new systems does not supply the knowledge and opinion necessary to foster informed decision-making in a democracy. Rather, much of the content has a "high level of symbolic, mythical content and passive entertainment value."[41] In other words, much of the content of the British mass market daily newspapers (and presumably of teletext and viewdata systems as well) is "interesting" news, rather than "important" news that "exaggerates the commonalities between people and plays down structural divisions of interest," rather than being concerned with "institutions, organizations and decision-making in society."[42]

James Carey and John Quirk echo Elliott's concern in calling for a distinction between information and knowledge. They maintain that knowledge "can be manipulated like any other commodity" by not only controlling factual information or data, but also by controlling a system of thought, or paradigm, that determines what the standards are for assessing the truth and defining knowledge.[43] "Instead of creating a 'new future,' modern technology invites the public to participate in a ritual of control where fascination with technology masks the underlying factors of politics

---

[40]Harry F. Waters, Cynthia H. Wilson, and Peter Davies, "TV Turns to Print," *Newsweek,* July 30, 1979, p. 75.

[41]Elliott, *op. cit.,* p. 4.

[42]Elliott, *op. cit.,* p. 5.

[43]James W. Carey & John J. Quirk, "The History of the Future," in George Gerbner, Larry P. Gross, & William H. Melody, eds., *Communications Technology and Social Policy* (New York and London: John Wiley & Sons, 1973), p. 500.

and power," according to Carey and Quirk.[44] This is so, they assert, because to participate in computer-based information systems intelligently, "The citizen of the future will have to undergo a continuing, lifelong education in real time, the acquisition of new knowledge when it is needed in time to meet problems as they arise." And these "extraordinary demands" will merely "co-opt him into the technical apparatus with only the illusion of control."[45]

Closely related to this criticism is the charge that electronic information delivery systems, like many other forms of technology, will serve to support the existing political-economic power structures in various societies by co-opting people into believing they have a voice in the running of "the system" through the "two-way" capability of viewdata. By creating an "artificial demand" for teletext and viewdata services that will result in huge profits for media and electronics industries, by continuing to rely on relatively few "official" sources of news and information rather than presenting many views on many issues, and by providing more and more very brief news items that consist of what official sources have said or are doing about particular matters, the resulting "information overload" encourages greater specialization of interests and information-seeking patterns, which in turn contributes to the isolation of people from one another, and provides advertisers with more select audiences.[46]

This concern with increasing specialization is also reflected in the questions raised by those who believe in the value of incidental learning and "agenda-setting" from news media. As Charles Everill of Harte Hanks Communications succintly puts it, electronic retrieval systems work most efficiently, "if the consumer knows exactly what (information) he wants, but so often we don't know what we want."[47] Jay Blumler elaborates on Everill's concern when he asks:

> But I wonder what will happen in the new communications era to those services, mainly provided today by the mass media and especially by the broadcast media, which cater for man in his most general role of all—for his role as a citizen of the nation state, who needs to be kept aware, not only of its main problems of the moment but also of issues preoccupying people beyond its borders in this increasingly interdependent world. Presumably we cannot automatically assume that the new communication technologies will serve that general citizen role well, first because its informational requirements are far more diffuse than those, say, of engineers, techni-

[44]*Ibid.*, p. 501.

[45]*Ibid.*, p. 499.

[46]Linda Zaradich, "Electronic Home News Delivery: A Systems Analysis," paper written for a seminar on mass media and society, School of Journalism, Indiana University, April 1981, pp. 3–13.

[47]Daniel Machalaba, "Hot off the Screen: More Publishers Beam Electronic Newspapers to Home Video Sets," *The Wall Street Journal,* January 2, 1981, p. 7.

cians, firemen trainees, shoppers, etc., and secondly, because it demands the existence of competent, responsible and well-resourced agents able to act for us by scanning the social and political environment and drawing our attention to what we need to know. Which button on the keyboard of his domestic computerized video-display screen should the citizen press in order to be kept in touch with the issues of the day?"

Blumler fears that electronic information delivery systems such as teletext and viewdata might lead to less public exposure to serious information on social and political questions, not only because of the ability of each person to select, but also because channel multiplication will probably mean a decreased share of the audience for any given news organization or channel, and this will mean, in turn, decreased revenue to support serious news-gathering efforts. He concludes that there is, therefore, a case for keeping developments in telecommunications technology under public policy review and regulation to guarantee strong, responsible, and free information agents to serve citizens well.[49]

The argument that teletext and viewdata systems are not well-suited for the presentation of serious social and political information is underscored by Prestel journalist Mike Bygrave, who asserts, "Prestel's encyclopedic nature is illusory. With all its hundreds of thousands of 'pages,' the system cannot actually cope with any lengthy or complex set of information."[50] Bygrave argues that Prestel (and presumably other viewdata systems) must be a highly selective information medium because of the limited capacity of each screenful (or page), and the cost of the people and hardware needed to input large volumes of information. Even with such people and hardware, Bygrave points out that the capacity of one page of Prestel (80 or 90 words) makes one ask "if it isn't going to distort (news) to the point of absurdity. Can you really present any serious issue fairly when you're working at that sort of length?"[51]

He is also skeptical about Prestel (or other viewdata systems) as journalistic media because, "It's hard to see how text on Prestel could be organized to pay. Most news or current affairs media pass on only a portion of their cost to the consumer, making the balance up in advertising revenue. Yet, it's not clear how a traditional 'package' of text and advertisements could work on Prestel."[52] Bygrave doubts further that anyone is even going to think seriously about advertising on viewdata systems until such systems have "succeeded" in terms of numbers of users. Thus, unless advertising does absorb a substantial portion of the costs associated with

"Jay G. Blumler, "Information Overload: Is There a Problem?" in Eberhard Witte, ed., *Human Aspects of Telecommunication* (New York: Springer-Verlag, 1980), pp. 233-34.
"*Ibid.*, pp. 234-35.
50Mike Bygrave, "Writing on an Empty Screen," *InterMedia,* 7: 26-28 (May 1979), p. 26.
51*Ibid.*, p. 27.
52*Ibid.*

teletext and viewdata systems (or unless there is significant support from government), Bygrave thinks that "there is so much free or dirt-cheap news and current affairs around already, who will pay to see more?"[53]

The concern with the ability of teletext and viewdata systems to present information of a lengthy or complex nature in a convenient manner is shared by others. It has been estimated that it would take approximately 70 videotex TV screenfuls to contain as many words as one page of a quality newspaper such as *The Wall Street Journal* does. Furthermore, one cannot take a television set as easily onto a subway or train, or carry it from place to place, as one can a newspaper. The limits of videotex systems in terms of number of words and portability are dramatically illustrated by Professor Edwin Diamond who challenges his engineering students at the Massachusetts Institute of Technology to:

> Design a communications system that is lightweight and easily portable, yet has a capacity of 60,000–100,000 words. Display screen should be no more than 9 inches and fit flat on a desk top. System should have easy access so that even an eight-year-old can plug it in. Should be storable and recallable in seconds. System should be usable in airplanes, autos, and canoes. Cost should be no more than $2 a unit.[54]

If the students succeed, Diamond notes, "Their invention would be the magazine."[55] Presumably, the same could be said for many quality newspapers. Their size would exceed the prescribed 9 inches, but their word capacity might be greater than 100,000 per issue.

There is also the question of the ease of reading from a television screen as compared to the ease of reading from the printed page. The letters on the screen are often not as sharply defined as those on the printed page, and there tends to be some movement or flickering of the letters on the TV screen. Although this question is still open, there are those such as deputy editor Tony Fowler of the *Daily Express* in London who argue, "Whatever happens in the realm of technology, people will always want some permanent form of printed matter that gives them the whole story."[56] And Fowler's claim is reinforced by those who point out that videotex receivers allow for only one user at a time and thus can lead to family conflict over what information is to be sought when, whereas the newspaper can be divided into separate sections and read by several persons simultaneously. Of course, if two-, three-, and four-TV set families are the wave of the future, this problem of family stress may not become a major one, at least not with teletext systems.

---

[53] *Ibid.*, p. 28.

[54] "More on Magazines in the '80s," *Magazine Newsletter of Advertising,* 10 (May 1981), p. 1.

[55] *Ibid.*

[56] Quoted in Ray Chapman, "The State of Fleet Street," *The Quill: Magazine for Journalists,* 69 (May 1981), p. 24.

In addition to costs to the user of teletext and viewdata systems, there is also the argument that the costs of manufacturing and the availability of certain components, especially the "ubiquitous electronic chip," will seriously retard the growth of teletext and viewdata systems. As *The* (London) *Economist* put it in March 1980:

> Since 1960 the semiconductor industry has each year doubled the number of transistors or logic functions on a chip, and cut the price of each function by 28%. The average price of a transistor in 1960 was about $10. Now it is less than one cent. This tumbling cost is why electronics fans talk about an approaching era of 'free' intelligence in which computer power can be introduced into almost any product for practically nothing. Would that it were that simple.
>
> The semiconductor industry can no longer keep up with expanding demand. The capital equipment needed to make today's chips is so expensive that, despite increases in capital spending of 50% in 1978 and again in 1979 (so that capital investment now represents 16% of total sales), the top ten American semiconductor manufacturers have been reporting waiting lists of up to ten months.[57]

The Economist contends that the semiconductor industry "is not earning enough profit to finance its own phenomenal growth," that over the past five years, "the industry has suffered a 31% fall in its average return on equity funds and an 18% decline in pretax profits margins," and that capital financiers are now avoiding this industry.[58] The magazine further argues that "the cost of producing software for an application has risen perhaps tenfold," illustrating, "the constraints that software imposes on the spread of supposedly 'free' intelligence."[59]

Summing up its appraisal, *The Economist* states:

> The idea that a marriage of micro-electronics and telecommunications will produce a revolution, exists largely in the imagination—for the moment. It awaits the widespread use of electronic funds transfer, electronic mail and publishing, armchair shopping, remote control of plant and machinery—and, most dramatic of all in its effect on work—the paperless, minimally staffed office of the future.[60]

In short, these are the major arguments against teletext and viewdata: little real evidence of a public need for these new media, a tendency to further isolate people from each other in their "all-electronic caves," superficial treatment of complex issues and serious news, support of the existing political-economic power structures, a dampening of incidental learning about important issues of the day, an increase in family stress, a diluting of the economic resources devoted to serious news-gathering, relatively high

---

[57]Quoted in John Coleman, "Societal implications and the human factor," *Inside Videotex*, p. 117.

[58]*Ibid.*

[59]*Ibid.*

[60]*Ibid.*

cost to the user, lack of portability, difficulty of reading from a television screen, and relatively high cost of manufacturing.

THE EXPERIENCED VIEW

Even though teletext and viewdata systems are in their infancy in most countries except the United Kingdom, some lessons are being learned from operating and experimental systems, and from studies of these systems and their audiences. In this section, I review what we know now from many of the publicly available reports and studies.

1. The editorial aspects of teletext, and especially viewdata, are proving more complex than intially expected. It is not a matter of simply transferring the content of existing printed media to the television screen.[61]

Many of those who have had experience with or studied videotex systems are beginning to conclude that because a videotex screen has only 2-3% of the capacity of a newspaper page at most, and because people seem to be reluctant to read much beyond one screenful for any given story, this implies "a different treatment that excludes most of the comments and analyses that may be legitimately expected from a newspaper."[62] The publisher of the *Yuma Daily Sun,* in describing its cable news service, put it this way:

> News and information is updated hourly until press time, then a full update. All pages on the system are changed an average of three to four times each day. Sun Cable local news does not have the capacity for detail that the paper holds, so we offer only the basic facts of the story in order to create interest for the intimate details found in the afternoon paper. In a story of major importance, we will not "scoop" ourselves on Sun Cable but "break" the story after the press run starts.[63]

In a study of the first two years of the Prestel system in England, Rex Winsbury estimated that "three-quarters of the material on Prestel comes from outside the traditional publishing industry."[64] He also concluded that "editing for Prestel is not like newspaper editing, and not like computer programming, but a novel and challenging mixture of disciplines drawn from both."[65] Winsbury contends that "videotex . . . is not the prerogative

---

[61] Michael Tyler, "Videotex, Prestel and Teletext: The Economics and Politics of Some Electronic Publishing Media," *Telecommunications Policy,* March 1979, p. 44.

[62] Gérard Eymery, "Teletext in France: Antiope-Services," *European Broadcasting Union Review,* 32 (March 1981), p. 54.

[63] Donald N. Soldwedel, "Opportunities for Small Newspapers," *VIDEOTEX '81,* p. 227.

[64] Rex Winsbury, *The Electronic Bookstall: Push-Button Publishing on Videotex* (London: International Institute of Communications, 1979), p. 19.

[65] *Ibid.,* p. 31.

of traditional publishers, or even a subset of them" because a publisher on videotex may be anyone who possesses information that might be of interest or value to others.[66] He argues that the publishers on Prestel tend to be those who offer specialist information, not the general newspapers that cover the widest possible variety of topics to catch the largest and widest possible audience.

In discussing the kinds of information that Prestel is best suited to carry, Winsbury cites financial data, classified advertising, and other "directory" information—anything that is a list, guide, or table, such as addresses, sports results, houses for sale, retail prices, cinema showings, or train times. As he puts it, "It is less clear whether Prestel is suitable for discussion, analysis, extended description, or a long newspaper story."[67] Winsbury thinks it is "a total mistake to regard videotex as some sort of 'electronic clone' of the newspaper," because this attitude produces, "stiff, dull pages that do not exploit the characteristics of videotex and, in a broader sense, narrows the mind about what can be done and said in the new medium."[68] He cautions newspapers, however, not to ignore videotex because of the inroads it may make into classified advertising revenues and into readers of sports and entertainment information.

Another very important point made by Winsbury is that "the idea of a social and political role is central to newspapers, foreign to computers," and it is not clear at this time that either teletext or viewdata systems will be any more than storehouses of, "rather neutral reference information (typically, train and airline timetables, cinema listings, economic statistics) of a relatively static nature and little, if any, controversial content."[69] This point was echoed recently by Philip Meyer of Knight-Ridder Newspapers when he argued before the Videotex '81 conference in Toronto that "information . . . does not fully define what newspapers do."[70] Meyer contends that by making itself, "a credible, heeded, respected voice in the community," the newspaper can deliver "influence along with the information," and thus both information and the context of information.[71] He questions whether videotex systems can deliver such influence and context along with specialized information, arguing, "Prestel's role is more that of a neutral broker of information than maintainer of community beliefs and values."[72]

Meyer disagrees somewhat with those who argue that videotex systems

---

[66] *Ibid.*, p. 57.

[67] *Ibid.*, p. 61.

[68] *Ibid.*, pp. 61–62.

[69] *Ibid.*, p. 67.

[70] Philip Meyer, "Emerging Opportunities in Electronic Technology: What Can We Learn from Newspapers," *VIDEOTEX '81*, p. 233.

[71] *Ibid.*

[72] *Ibid.*, p. 234.

are capable of delivering only very short news and information items when he points out that reporters from Knight-Ridder's experimental Viewtron system in Coral Gables, Florida, found, "they could deliver local news with greater speed and in more detail than *The Miami Herald*'s semi-weekly zoned section for the area of the country which includes Coral Gables."[73] And he notes that contrary to the reported Prestel experience, they (users) had the patience to read long stories, dutifully pushing the button to turn the pages a dozen times or more."[74] Meyer's experience with longer stories on Viewtron is contrary to the experience with all other teletext and viewdata systems included in this study, and even Meyer acknowledges that newspaper companies experimenting with Prestel are "beginning to find that it is easier to clear the market with small packages of information, frequently updated, aimed at highly specialized segments . . . more readily found in the business community."[75]

This view is supported by a recent study in the Federal Republic of Germany that concludes that viewdata systems are especially good for short, timely news items, sports results, and short political announcements that can be easily updated.[76] Likewise, a review of viewdata and teletext in the United States by George Alexander of *The Seybold Report* (an authoritative newsletter dealing with electronics in publishing) concludes such systems, "are not suited to lengthy text presentations, and their graphics are more like diagrams than photos."[77]

2. Some patterns of use of teletext and viewdata systems are beginning to emerge, suggesting that these media are less suited to browsing than are print media and more suited to the seeking of specific, short items of information than longer analyses and extended discussions.

It is becoming increasingly apparent that just as it is not possible simply to transfer the content of printed media to the television screen, it is also not possible to read words on the TV screen in the same manner that one reads words from the printed page. In a recent study of 125 receivers of a teletext service offered through a subscription TV system near Miami, Florida, Oak Communications found that those who had used their teletext system from 1–3 months were critical of the limited content of a page (about 80 words) especially where one article was continued through several pages. Users also indicated that the information was "choppy," and they were "especially

[73]*Ibid.*, p. 235.

[74]*Ibid.*, pp. 235–36.

[75]*Ibid.*, p. 235.

[76]Forschungsgruppe Kammerer: *Struktur, Spektrum und Potentiale der geschäftlichen Bildschirmtext-nutzung* (Köln, 1981).

[77]George Alexander, "Viewdata and Teletext: New Electronic Home Information Delivery Systems," *The Seybold Report,* 10 (November 24, 1980), p. 14.

critical'' of the page access time, which could run as long as 30 seconds.[78] Charles Eissler of Oak Communications concluded from this study that although the informational content of the teletext system "is the main product," much of the perceived value of such a system, "is the appearance and operating convenience of the hardware.''[79]

More to the point regarding information seeking patterns of users, a recent survey of 609 teletext users in the United Kingdom by Philips Electronics shows that in a typical week, the average teletext user makes use of the service 77 times but spends not quite two hours watching teletext pages.[80] Richard Hooper, director of Prestel, notes that the average use of that service per day is 9 minutes.[81] Both of these findings suggest that teletext and viewdata are "in-and-out" media that are more suited to the presentation of short, specific items than to more lengthy articles that require extended periods of concentration by the reader.

A 1980 survey of 227 users of teletext (from an estimated 70,000 receivers in private homes) in the Netherlands indicates that 63% of those whose prime interest was in reading news pages used teletext mainly for the most recent news of the last couple of hours.[82] But 75% of those reading the news section leafed through other pages besides those where they expected interesting news, suggesting some browsing in the news section. This was not true, however, in the broadcasting section (information about television and radio programs) where 74% claimed to read only those pages where interesting news was expected. It must be remembered, however, than even where browsing did occur, most of the news stories were very short—usually not more than one page (80 words or so) in length. Still, this study suggests that people may be willing to browse through some kinds of material on videotex systems if the individual items are not lengthy.

Browsing on teletext and viewdata systems is not as easy as with printed matter, however, primarily because of the limited word capacity of the television screen and the necessity to press a specific number to get another page. One experiment in England at the Loughborough University of Technology has suggested that although the "menu" (index) approach on

[78]Charles O. Eissler, "Market Testing Video-text: Oak's Miami Teletext System," *VIDEOTEX '81,* p. 69.

[79]*Ibid.*

[80]Philips Teletext Users' Survey (London: Philips Video Division, 1981).

[81]Richard Hooper, "The UK Scene—Teletext and Videotex," *VIDEOTEX '81,* p. 133.

[82]Netherlands Broadcasting Foundation Teletext Survey (Hilversum: NOS, 1981). These data were generously supplied by Dr. Harold de Bock, director of the Audience Research Service of NOS.

[83]T. Stewart, "PRESTEL—How Usable Is It?" in Eberhard Witte, ed., *Human Aspects of Telecommunication* (New York: Springer-Verlag, 1980), pp. 116–17.

Prestel is fairly easy to use, it "can be made faster and use fewer pages if it is supplemented with a printed directory."[13] The results of this study also suggest that people could find specific information more quickly and easily if "a limited keyword facility" was provided where users could enter simple words instead of page numbers.

3. The expenditures for teletext and viewdata services by the general public for home use have been very modest so far, and they are likely to remain so in the foreseeable future.

There is evidence that despite the recent development of many communications devices, "the share of information goods and services in household expenditure remains modest."[14] There is also data to suggest that the proportion of household income devoted to communication media has remained rather constant over the past 40 years or so.[15] Tyler writes that in 1976 the average British household spent about £4 a month on printed media, about £3½ on telecommunications and postage, about £6 on television and radio receivers and license fees, and about £2½ on tickets to cinemas, theaters, and sporting events. He argues that if a videotex service could be offered for, say, £12 a month for terminal rental and usage charges, the money for such a service would "imply a considerable diversion of expenditure from other information-related items in the household budget; or, if the diversions hypothesized are to be kept within reasonable limits, we must assume some diversion of other kinds of discretionary expenditures (say, luxury clothing or leisure automobile trips) in favour of Videotex."[16]

In a more recent article based on quantitative models of videotex markets developed by Communication Studies and Planning International (CSP), Tyler writes that although there is evidence emerging for a mass residential market for electronic publishing and transaction services, "the levels of expenditure per household associated with substantial market penetration—say 25% or more of households—are likely to be low—of the order of $5–10 per month, depending on the range of services offered."[17] He claims, however, that there are limited market segments, such as hobbyists or professional and business people working from home, that will pay much more. And Tyler thinks, "While videotex has some limitations as an advertising medium, it is highly cost-effective for classified advertising and many classes of transactions."[18]

[13]Tyler, "Videotex, Prestel and Teletext," p. 46.

[14]Maxwell E. McCombs, "Mass Media in the Marketplace," *Journalism Monographs*, 24 (August 1972).

[15]Tyler, *op. cit.*, p. 47.

[16]Michael Tyler and Paige Amidon, "Prospects for Videotex: An Independent Perspective," *VIDEOTEX '81*, p. 469.

[17]*Ibid.*

A report from a British government-organized private conference on a national commitment to teletext and viewdata in January 1981, reinforces Tyler's view that people are not likely to pay much for the use of teletext and viewdata systems in their homes. The report concludes that teletext systems in Britain are "too expensive" at £3–£5 above the regular monthly rental price of an ordinary television set, and argues that "with a rental premium of £1 per month and a retail premium between £30–£50 Teletext would become a standard feature not only for the replacement market, but also for second sets and first time purchases."[89] The report maintains that cost is a problem for widespread teletext diffusion, "but certainly not an intractable one."[90]

With regard to the Prestel viewdata system, the report admonishes that "the same unfortunately cannot be said for Prestel,"[91] implying that cost may indeed be an unsolvable obstacle to the widespread diffusion of Prestel in the domestic home market. As the report puts it, "There is still no real evidence that there will ever be a mass residential market for Prestel."[92] This conslusion is elaborated on by "information to hand" that suggests that interest in Prestel "only starts when the rental premium falls to £10 per month" (it was £15 at the time of the conference). The report also states that "at a premium of £7 per month (£200 retail) one third of the potential users would be interested; and only when the premium falls to £4 per month (£120 retail) does significant interest ensue, i.e., four out of five people."[93] As for maintenance of a Prestel receiver, "£1 per week running costs seems to be an acceptable figure."[94] Whether or not costs can be brought down to these levels is questionable because, as the report puts it, "We are now faced with a chicken and egg situation where costs cannot come down significantly until set sales and usage increases (sic), which they won't do until costs come down, etc., etc."[95]

In the United States, a study by Oak Communications of its experimental teletext system near Miami, Florida, suggests that about three fourths of approximately 125 users would be willing to pay for a teletext service, but only between $5–$25 per month.[96] Edgar Gladstone, who directed a study of consumer entertainment and information systems for Quantum Science Corporation, states that one of the major conclusions of the study was that

---

[89]"Teletext & Viewdata: The Commitment Conference" (London: Department of Industry and National Economic Development Office, 1981), p. 1-3.

[90]*Ibid.*

[91]*Ibid.*

[92]*Ibid.*, p. 1-4.

[93]*Ibid.*

[94]*Ibid.*

[95]*Ibid.*, p. 1-5.

[96]Eissler, "Market Testing Video-text," *VIDEOTEX '81*, p. 69.

such systems "must provide a package of free and paid-for information" and that "in the end, shopping from home and other transactions will be the real economic justification for home-information services" because profits from those activities will justify offering free services to get people to buy sets with decoders.[97]

Thus, the evidence to date suggests that most people are not likely to pay much beyond a few dollars per month for teletext and viewdata services in their homes. This may be because, as one study concluded, "People are accustomed to paying for entertainment, but not for using the library."[98] Unless videotex services offer features in addition to information, such as shopping from home, electronic banking, etc., most people are not likely to pay much for them.

4. In addition to cost, other factors such as awareness, ease of use, and perceived utility suggest a mass market for teletext systems and a largely business or elite market for viewdata systems, at least in the near future.

According to Brian Champness of Plymouth Polytechnic in England, recent studies of teletext and viewdata use in homes in the United Kingdom suggest that teletext, "has a good chance of taking off, but that there will only be a residential market for Prestel if it becomes as cheap as teletext."[99] There is also some indication from these studies that viewers don't see the need for the nearly 200,000 pages of information provided by Prestel on their televisions. This conclusion is supported by a follow-up report from the recent Teletext and Viewdata Commitment Conference in London, which states:

> The active, aggressive, and immediate promotion of Teletext in the consumer market-place, along with Prestel's carefully targetted marketing programme at the business community, will be the best way to accelerate the arrival of mass market Viewdata, as well as consolidate the growth of Teletext.[100]

A large study of electronic information systems by Arthur D. Little, Inc. in the United States suggests that teletext is something that would be of mass appeal, "reaching an unlimited number of people instantaneously and all at the same time," whereas viewdata "will inevitably interest wealthier and more educated people who will be willing to pay for the convenience offered by the system."[101] Another study of the communication behavior of

[97]Scott R. Schmedel, "TV Systems Enabling Viewers to Call Up Printed Data Catch Eye of Media Firms," *The Wall Street Journal,* July 24, 1979, p. 40.

[98]Joseph N. Pelton, "The Future of Telecommunications: A Delphi Survey," *Journal of Communication,* 31 (Winter 1981), p. 181.

[99]Brian Champness, "Social Uses of Videotex and Teletext in UK," *VIDEOTEX '81,* p. 333.

[100]"Teletext & Viewdata: The Commitment Conference" (From Commitment to Action, p. 1).

[101]Kelly, "All The News," p. 17.

1000 persons in two communities in England by the Centre for Mass Communication Research at the University of Leicester arrives at much the same conclusion: "Examining the specific case of Prestel . . . there can be little doubt that members of the higher socio-economic group are likely to be the early adopters."[102]

The conclusion that a viewdata system such as Prestel should appeal more to the up-scale business market than to the mass domestic should come as no surprise when one considers that the information providers, or publishers, on Prestel "are, foremost, the companies who can offer specialist information."[103] If Prestel and other viewdata systems like it are intended to serve a domestic as well as a business market and are to be used by all manner of people, the Leicester study concludes:

> The data base must be truly comprehensive and the information must be presented in a clear and simple manner. Moreover, the data base must include information on all the many topics about which information is required by different groups of people to enable them to cope with their everyday problems and to help them advance their interests and improve their quality of life. This means that a large number of topics will have to be covered, and our research clearly shows that much of the required information is likely to be highly specific, quite detailed, and often local in emphasis.[104]

The study also argues that "the common carrier policy of British Telecom suggests that if the present policy is maintained, it is unlikely that such a comprehensive service will be provided," and "much more planning, direction, and attention to identified needs will be necessary before effective community and recreation information packages can be carried on the service, and before an acceptable proportion of the general public can be persuaded that the adoption of Prestel would be worthwhile."[105]

In addition to these views from the United Kingdom and the United States, a 1980 study of the structure, scope, and potential of the commercial use of viewdata in the Federal Republic of Germany suggests that the system can be used by commercial enterprises for internal communication, distribution of goods and services, and service to customers, as well as for information and entertainment.[106] The study argues that viewdata is especially well suited to mail order businesses, advertisers, and public institutions.

5. Both teletext and viewdata systems probably will not do much to nar-

---

[102]Peggy Gray, "A Study of Communication Behaviour" (Leicester: Centre for Mass Communication Research, University of Leicester, 1981), pp. 103–04.

[103]Winsbury, *The Electronic Bookstall*, p. 56.

[104]Gray, "A Study of Communication Behaviour," pp. 102–03.

[105]*Ibid.*, p. 103.

[106]Forschungsgruppe Kammerer: *Struktur, Spektrum und Potentiale der geschäftlichen Bildschirmtext-nutzung* (Köln, 1981).

row the knowledge gap between lower and higher socio-economic groups. In fact, they may widen this gap.

Although this conclusion is more speculative than the previous four, it is somewhat consistent with them. Considering the very limited word capacity of a videotex screen, the evidence that both teletext and viewdata systems are more suited to the seeking of specific, short items than to the reading of longer analyses and extended discussions, the relatively high cost of teletext and especially viewdata, and the likelihood that viewdata systems such as Prestel will succeed in the business rather than residential market, it is not unreasonable to suspect that these systems will do little to narrow the knowledge gap between the information rich and the information poor.

Although teletext systems such as Ceefax and Oracle do stand a reasonable chance of becoming truly mass media, they are not likely to provide the kind of information needed by many less well-off people to improve their standard of living. The Leicester study of communication behavior in two English cities found that most people needed knowledge about housing, entertainment, travel, taxation, consumer problems, education, pension matters, and welfare questions.[107] And, as mentioned earlier, the study suggested that the required information should be "highly specific, quite detailed, and often local in emphasis."[108] While the teletext systems in the United Kingdom do provide facts about entertainment and travel, they generally provide none about housing, taxation, consumer problems, education, pension matters, and welfare questions. Even the information concerning entertainment and travel is not usually highly specific and local, and it is not likely to be so in the future unless some way is found to increase greatly the number of pages devoted to regional and local data. As it stands now, Ceefax and Oracle are national teletext systems, not regional or local.

The Prestel viewdata system, on the other hand, does have the page capacity (currently about 200,000) to enable it to carry highly specific, local facts on a wide variety of subjects, but at present Prestel concentrates mainly on information of interest to businesses and commercial organizations, and its chances of becoming a mass domestic medium are highly questionable, especially if it continues to emphasize business and commercial material. As the Leicester study put it, with regard to the specific case of Prestel:

It is unlikely that "communication needs of society" will figure prominently in our deliberations if the economics of the market place are allowed to prevail. So, granted these circumstances, the use of Prestel in the immediate future is not likely to do much to close the gap between the information rich and the information poor.[109]

---

[107]Gray, "A Study of Communication Behaviour," pp. 94–95.
[108]*Ibid.*, pp. 102–03.
[109]*Ibid.*, p. 108.

Whether this conclusion applies to teletext and viewdata systems outside the United Kingdom, or whether it will hold for those systems in England in the future, remains to be seen. It may indeed be overly pessimistic at this early stage to argue that teletext and viewdata will not do much to reduce the information gap between lower and higher socio-economic groups. But the lessons learned from experience with and research on videotex systems so far are not overly encouraging.

6. The impact of teletext and viewdata systems on existing communication media has been almost negligible thus far, and the future impact seems to depend on many factors such as cost, legibility, investment by other organizations, ease of use, promotion, and perceived utility.

Although there was much concern among many print-publishing organizations, especially newspapers, when Ceefax and Oracle were introduced in the United Kingdom in the mid-1970s, this anxiety has lessened in recent years, probably because of the lack of advertising on these teletext systems and probably because of the slow growth of the Prestel viewdata system. However, as Michael Tyler notes, "The interests of the print media as such *may* be threatened by competition from new media."[110] Tyler, like others, argues that the kinds of print media particularly at risk are specialized magazines and local newspapers—both highly dependent upon classified advertising in the United Kingdom.

Even though it may be true that those printed media most dependent upon classified advertising may be most vulnerable to economic undermining by teletext and viewdata systems, it is not at all clear when this might happen. A previously mentioned study of electronic information systems by the consulting firm of Arthur D. Little, Inc., concluded that "the electronic services will not be a major threat to newspapers in the next 15 years, the time frame of our study."[111] Donald Sparrow, director of the study, cautions, however, "Beyond 1992 there could be a more severe impact."[112] Another study of electronic information systems conducted by Quantum Science Corporation suggested that one of the major uses of such systems would be advertising and purchasing products and services. Edgar Gladstone, director of consumer studies at Quantum Science, said, "I see it impacting advertising quite a bit."[113] He believes the big newspapers will try to get into the electronic information delivery market first to protect their advertising revenues, and he concludes, "There's going to be a pretty strong impact on newspapers."[114]

[110]Tyler, "Videotex, Prestel, and Teletext," p. 48.

[111]Quoted in Kelly, "All The News," p. 16.

[112]*Ibid.*

[113]*Ibid.*, p. 17.

[114]*Ibid.*

Rex Winsbury, in his 1979 study of the Prestel system in England, maintains, "It will take a long time for the effect of videotex systems to be felt on newspapers."[115] He argues that when it comes, the effect will be "patchy"—felt in some areas but not in others—and that such effects, "Will not spell the doom of the newspaper but add to the pressures for further modification of its role in the electronic era."[116] This view is echoed by Benjamin Compaine in his study of the U.S. newspaper industry, in which he concludes that economic considerations will preclude any major development of the electronic newspaper in the foreseeable future, even though there may be a market for electronic distribution of supplemental news and information to businesses.[117] Compaine believes that display advertising in newspapers is fairly secure but that classified advertising does lend itself to potential new forms of delivery. Yet, he argues, "The form of the newspaper by the year 2000 should be remarkably similar to the newspaper of 1980," and "the paper may be thinner as certain sections may be replaced by electronic distribution."[118]

Robert Johnson, vice president and general manager of *The Columbus (Ohio) Dispatch,* writes that since *The Dispatch* began to be delivered electronically to home video terminals via the CompuServe system in July 1980, the management has concluded that "electronic publishing of the daily paper is not of significant value in the local market—we are in competition with ourselves at a much higher price for a less complete product."[119] Johnson also asserts that *The Dispatch* "will always include a substantial portion of our daily paper in the (CompuServe) data base because it costs next to nothing to provide, and the preliminary evidence shows it is of substantial interest outside our circulation area."[120]

As for classified advertising, it seems from *The Dispatch* experiment that programming such advertising is more complicated than programming news for the computer. Gary Wilson of *The Dispatch* explains that whereas news is on the system for a 24–hour cycle and then replaced, classified can be on one day, two days, a week, or until forbidden. Wilson also notes that the indexing becomes difficult: "If you are looking for a Chevrolet, and a Ford dealer has a used one, it has to be a complex program to handle all of the possibilities."[121] At any one time, according to Wilson, *The Dispatch* can

[115]Winsbury, *The Electronic Bookstall,* p. 54.

[116]*Ibid.*

[117]Benjamin M. Compaine, *The Newspaper Industry in the 1980s: An Assessment of Economics and Technology* (White Plains, N.Y.: Knowledge Industry Publications, 1980).

[118]*Ibid.,* pp. 222–23.

[119]Robert M. Johnson, "Electronic News Delivery—The Dispatch/CompuServe Experiment," *VIDEOTEX '81,* p. 240.

[120]*Ibid.,* p. 241.

[121]Quoted in Ray Laakaniemi, "The Computer Connection: America's First Computer-Delivered Newspaper," *Newspaper Research Journal,* 2 (July 1981), p. 67.

have up to 10,000 classified ads in its system, making the indexing a very difficult programming assignment.

In spite of the difficulties involved in the programming of classified advertising, there is evidence to suggest that, as Philip Meyer, formerly of Knight-Ridder Newspapers, puts it, "The main threat to newspapers is not competition for information, but competition for advertising."[122] Even though Winsbury, in his study of Prestel, argues that it will take a long time for videotex systems to affect newspapers, he also concludes that viewdata systems such as Prestel will be good at delivering financial information, classified advertisements, and "routine information" such as sports scores and statistics, weather forecasts, entertainment guides, births, and deaths, and "anything that is a list or guide or table."[123]

In order for videotex systems to take classified advertising away from newspapers and specialist magazines, however, there must be widespread penetration of the communities served by these newspapers and magazines. In other words, videotex systems must be accepted by most of the people now being reached by various newspaper and magazines. Considering the other lessons learned from experience and research, widespread acceptance seems to be dependent upon legibility and ease of use, low cost, ready availability, perceived need, and a change in the way people regard the tele-vision—from primarily an entertainment medium to a sometime provider of information. As Winsbury puts it, "The TV screen was not designed for reading but for TV movies."[124] And, as he points out, the cost, availability, ease of use, and content of videotex systems will depend heavily on the scale of investment by the public telephone and telecommunication authorities, TV set manufacturers, information providers, software and system designers, and other parties.[125]

All of these factors suggest one central question—how fast will teletext and viewdata systems be accepted? Or, to put it in Winsbury's words, how fast will these systems become "user-friendly"?[126]

7. Although it is impossible to study the future empirically, the estimates based on present studies suggest that the adoption of viewdata systems in in-dustrialized countries is likely to happen rather slowly as compared to the adoption rate of television.

A recent Delphi study of "some 150 experts around the world" by Joseph Pelton finds that about 84% of those responding to the survey believed that

[122]*Ibid.*

[123]Winsbury, *The Electronic Bookstall,* pp. 59–61.

[124]*Ibid.,* p. 55.

[125]*Ibid.,* p. 54.

[126]*Ibid.,* p. 55.

viewdata would be in use in 5-10% of homes in the O.E.C.D. (Organization for Economic Cooperation and Development) countries by 1985 to 2000.[127] Pelton points out that even though various market studies have predicted that the more sophisticated viewdata systems such as Prestel, Antiope, and Telidon can be expected to grow rapidly in the O.E.C.D. countries in the next few years, there are a number of inhibiting factors such as the level of sophistication required of the user, the costs to the user, the kind of information or services the user will pay for, and the fact that viewdata systems are in competition with other systems already delivering information electronically (computerized data bases, specialized mail services, and cable TV systems). Pelton concludes that if the Delphi experts are correct, "it will be some time before a significant portion of the public (that is, more than 10%) acquires the viewdata habit."[128]

A review of recent studies of teletext and viewdata use in homes by Brian Champness of Plymouth Polytechnic in England "provides some comfort for CEEFAX and ORACLE providers, but little joy for those who believe that the information revolution is around the corner."[129] Champness argues that the impact of both viewdata and teletext in the United Kingdom on the population at large "can better be described as a gentle evolution rather than a technological revolution. Current evidence suggests that it will stay that way."[130] A recent study of the commercial use of viewdata in the Federal Republic of Germany, drawing on a nationwide sample of 220 experts, finds that viewdata is not a basic innovation and that its acceptance will happen rather slowly, more like the acceptance of the telephone than the television.[131]

Efrem Sigel, editor in chief of Knowledge Industry Publications and first author of a recent book on videotex, writes, "It is well to understand that none of the videotext systems discussed in this book will necessarily succeed on a large scale."[132] Siegel identifies four "natural obstacles" to the growth of teletext (use of TV for entertainment, difficulty of reading from a TV screen, lack of portability of a TV set, and low cost of newspapers and magazines), and argues that many of these same problems face viewdata systems. He also sees additional problems for viewdata systems, including the high cost of specially-equipped TV sets, the "bewildering profusion" of information on such systems that contributes to lack of focused marketing

---

[127]Pelton, "The Future of Telecommunications," p. 180.

[128]*Ibid.*, p. 182.

[129]Champness, "Social Uses of Videotex and Teletext," pp. 332–33.

[130]*Ibid.*, p. 339.

[131]Forschungsgruppe Kammerer: *Struktur, Spektrum und Potentiale der geschäftlichen Bildschirmtext-nutzung* (Köln, 1981).

[132]Efrem Sigel, *Videotext: The Coming Revolution in Home/Office Information Retrieval* (White Plains, N.Y.: Knowledge Industry Publications, 1980), p. 129.

efforts, and the resulting lack of a clear identity for such systems in comparison with printed publications. Sigel does see "undeniable promise" in both teletext and viewdata systems, but he believes that the changes they entail in the established ways of doing things "are so profound that they will never take place in a period of months, or even in a year or two."[133]

Even in the United Kingdom, where teletext and viewdata systems were first begun on a regular operating basis, the projections for the future growth of teletext and viewdata imply rather slow acceptance. The 1981 Teletext and Viewdata Commitment Conference report suggests 300,000 teletext TV set sales in 1981, 700,000 in 1982 and 1.2 million in 1983.[134] These projected sales, limited as they are in comparison to the 19 million or so licensed TV sets in the United Kingdom, stand in sharp contrast to the track record so far—113,000 teletext sets and 7000 adaptors sold between 1977 and the end of 1980.[135] This record also compares poorly with about 1.3 milllion color TV sets sold in the first four years after introduction in 1968.[136]

The conference report also suggests a goal of 50,000 business Prestel set/adaptor installations in the next 18 months (by July of 1982), and 1 million Prestel users by the end of 1985.[137] Again, these projections stand in marked contrast to the nearly 11,000 viewdata sets and adaptors sold in 1979 and 1980,[138] and to the nearly 200,000 color TV sets sold in the first two years of availability.[139]

Thus, these figures from the Commitment Conference report suggest that teletext sets, and especially viewdata sets, will not diffuse nearly as rapidly throughout the United Kingdom as did color television after its introduction in 1968. There is no guarantee that either teletext or viewdata sets will achieve the same overall widespread penetration that color television has, either in the United Kingdom or in other countries.

But, as Sigel points out:

Since the U.S. has by far the largest number of computers, computer terminals, telephones and TV sets of any country in the world, it seems safe to make the following prediction: if videotext is viable at all, it will spread wider and faster in the U.S. than elsewhere, even if it comes two or three years later.[140]

---

[133]*Ibid.*, p. 134.
[134]"Teletext & Viewdata: The Commitment Conference," p. 1-8.
[135]*Ibid.*, pp. 1-9 and 10-2.
[136]*Ibid.*, p. 3-3.
[137]*Ibid.*, p. 1-8.
[138]*Ibid.*, p. 1-9.
[139]*Ibid.*, p. 3-3.
[140]Sigel, *Videotext*, p. 8.

SUMMING UP

In this chapter, I have reviewed the major arguments for and against teletext and viewdata systems, and attempted to isolate seven major lessons learned from experience with and research concerning these systems. It should be clear to the reader by now that much of the writing and discussion of videotex as a medium is highly speculative because of its very early stages of development and because of the concerns over its future impact on other media and on the society at large. Only time will tell whether the optimists are more or less correct than the pessimists, and what effects teletext and viewdata will have on the existing media order and on other aspects of our societies.

Another point to be remembered is that the findings summarized in the seven lessons presented in this chapter are based on present uses and technology of teletext and viewdata systems. The technology is certain to change in various ways in the coming years (the resolution of characters on the screen will be made much sharper, the screen size may be expanded, the access time for particular pages will be cut considerably, etc.) and these changes may mean dramatic shifts in the content and uses of these systems. If such shifts in functions do occur, these lessons learned may seem curiously outdated and shortsighted in years to come. Yet, if teletext and viewdata systems continue to develop in the shadow of older media, and are designed to take over many of the functions of these older media without substantially changing these functions, then these lessons may stand the test of time rather well.

PART VIII

AMERICAN TELECOMMUNICATIONS POLICY

The four selections in this part are treatments of current issues surrounding broadcasting and telecommunications in the United States at a time in which the current administration is moving generally in a direction of "deregulation," or the freeing of many sectors of the American economy from governmental oversight. Deregulation is not without controversy, particularly in spheres, such as broadcasting, that clearly are affected by diverse public interests. The four authors here provide varying perspectives on the presuppositions of deregulation.

Dallas W. Smythe, taking radio as a case, argues that the rhetoric of deregulation is based on abstract and fallacious premises.

Willard D. Rowland, Jr., identifies in recent FCC policy reviews the impetus for deregulation as issuing from those forces already in control of American communications, the largest corporations owning the communications infrastructure.

However, Mark Fowler and Daniel Brenner in their chapter, and Richard Wiley in his, argue that marketplace forces and minimal regulation better serve a public interest where competition is possible.

Dallas W. Smythe seeks to demonstrate in this chapter that deregulation of American radio as currently practiced by the Federal Communications Commission rests on two flawed assumptions: First is that a nonmarket will behave as an imaginary perfect, abstract market of perfect competitors with priced transactions; second is that a reified and fictitious "scarcity" is somehow the basis of public regulation of radio broadcasters. Smythe is professor of communication at Simon Fraser University.

35

RADIO
Deregulation and the Relation of the Private and Public Sectors

Dallas W. Smythe

"Deregulation" is the flag currently flown in a powerful campaign to redefine the relation of the private to the public sectors in the United States. In support of it, the "market," "market forces," and the "discipline of the market" are the principal slogans used to rally the troops, and to seem to legitimize the resulting actions taken in the name of government. These slogans are philosophically idealist in nature, and seem to drop from the sky, self-evidently justified and without historical context. My purpose here is to explicate and describe the development of these slogans as they have been applied to a unique public resource— the radio spectrum. They have been promoted in the name of economic theory as apolitical quick fixes for what ails the U.S. by people who use economic jargon, consciously or unconsciously, for partisan political purposes. They are not partisan in the sense of serving one or the other

From Dallas W. Smythe, "Radio: Deregulation and the Relation of the Private and Public Sectors," *Journal of Communication,* Vol. 32, No. 1 (Winter 1982), pp. 192-200. Copyright © 1982 by Dallas W. Smythe. Reprinted by permission.

of the two major parties, for deregulation began under a Democratic administration and is being pursued by the Republicans.

The current debate over deregulation is only the latest phase of a struggle of the private and public sectors present since Jeffersonians and Hamiltonians argued over the terms of the Constitution and how it would be implemented. By the late nineteenth century, farmers and workers were fighting the rising giant corporations for public ownership of basic industries, especially the telegraph, railroads, and telephones. Government regulation did result because big business invited it in order to avoid nationalization. While this government regulation did protect the public in important ways, the regulated industries were also able to make use of the government regulators to facilitate their pursuit of corporate security and profit. And the struggle continues through the current deregulation campaign.

In order to understand the current argument for deregulation, especially as applied to the radio spectrum, the relevant aspects of the history of economic theory and doctrine must first be recalled. Classical economists from Adam Smith to John Stuart Mill called themselves political economists and considered themselves responsible for analyzing evenhandedly both the private and public sectors. The standard history of political economists' work indeed bears the term "economic doctrines" in its title to warn the reader that belief and faith (and therefore politics) rather than science and truth are inevitably salient when one deals with the proper sphere of activity for the public and private sectors (see 2). In the latter part of the nineteenth century the neoclassical economists dropped the term "political economy" and narrowed the scope of their professed expertise to the private sector. For them the public sector was regarded as off-limits, the zone of what came to be called "externalities." Neoclassical economists, from Jevons to Alfred Marshall, Pigou, and F. H. Knight, generally observed these limits. The founder of the Chicago school of economics, Herbert Simon, however, frankly broadened the scope of his professional work to include in substance political economy.

His views, as expressed in 1948, were strikingly consistent with those of John Stuart Mill and with the democratic political values that had prevailed in the United States after 1776:

> *The great enemy of democracy is monopoly, in all its forms: gigantic corporations, trade associations and other agencies for price control, trade-unions—or, in general, organization and concentration of power within functional classes. Effectively organized functional groups possess tremendous power for exploiting the community at large and even for sabotaging the system (5, p. 43).*

It is precisely "monopoly" as Simon described it that powers and profits by the deregulation drive now underway. It is true also that while Simon rejected public regulation of private monopolies as a long-term policy, he favored it as expedient for railroads and public utilities, and when it failed, he favored public ownership for them:

> *Political control of utility charges is imperative, to be sure, for competition simply cannot function effectively as an agency of control. We may endure regulation for a time, on the dubious assumption that governments are more nearly competent to regulate than to operate. In general, however, the state should face the necessity of actually taking over, owning, and managing directly, both the railroads and the utilities, and all other industries in which it is impossible to maintain effectively competitive conditions (5, p. 51).*

After Simon, the new Chicago school political perspective switched about 180 degrees. With Milton Friedman's *Capitalism and Freedom*, published in 1962, the Chicago school made a political commitment to private monopoly in preference to either public ownership or public regulation where the technical conditions exist by which competition destroys itself, producing monopoly (1, p. 28).

> *From the standpoint of economic theory (neoclassical or other), the application of a general theory of market behavior to the real world must begin with the identification of the market.*

What is the principal product or service that is the object of transactions? Who supplies it for a price? Who buys it for a price? In the case of radio, the principal product or service that is the object of transactions in the radio market is audience-power. It is produced and sold for real prices by broadcasters. It is bought at real prices by advertisers for whom it is useful and is used to complete the marketing of the advertisers' end products. As an intermediate producers' good, audience-power is consumed, just as is the gasoline in the truck that delivers the advertisers' products to the retail outlet.

What is the nature of radio programming in relation to the real radio market? It is the lure or bait provided to the population to gather people into audiences that are measured, packaged, and put on the market to sell to advertisers. There is no market for station *time* for advertising, *absent the prospective audience-power to be produced by the broadcaster.* A broadcast station located in unpopulated Antarctica would have lots of time but *nothing* to sell.

Thus audience-power as bought by advertisers is as productive as is the labor-power of the truck driver carrying goods to the market. Audience-power seems to be a peculiar commodity because the fact that it exists and is an economic fact of life has so long been shrouded in mystery. Public regulation of the terms on which broadcast station licensees might use the public property known as the radio spectrum has provided modest protection to the conditions under which broadcasters may produce, and advertisers use, audience-power. By attacking the very existence of such public regulation of broadcasting, the new Chicago school economists illustrate the impact of the rationale for deregulation on audience-power.

> *In its* Inquiry *and* Decision *in favor of radio deregulation
> in 1980, the FCC misunderstood two main concepts—the
> nature of the real market and the nature of the radio spectrum.*

After preliminary attempts in the preceding decade to use the legislative route to deregulation of broadcasting had failed to produce the desired revision of the Communications Act, deregulation was taken up by the FCC. To this end, an *Inquiry and Proposed Rulemaking: Deregulation of Radio* was published by the FCC in the *Federal Register* on October 5, 1979. Despite the lack of publicity given to this proposal, an amazing 22,000 comments were received by the FCC. Of these, 8 percent were from the industry and favored the proposal, while 89 percent were from individuals and other nonbroadcast industry sources and opposed the proposal. After considering these comments the FCC issued a *Decision* on the matter on February 24, 1981.

Both the *Inquiry* and the *Decision* argue that a vague and unanalyzed market somehow reflects a fictitious "consumer sovereignty" in the relations between broadcasters, programs, and listeners (*Inquiry*, paras. 133–134, and *passim*; *Decision, passim*). The argument is essentially (though precision is lacking) that advertisers somehow represent a *derived demand* from that of the radio audience. But derived demand is derived from a *real* market in which there are transactions with prices. Thus one can speak of the demand for steel as derived in part from the automobile market where automobiles are traded for money. But one cannot speak of the market for steel as derived from the market for "status" or "style" unless one leaves hard market phenomena.

The *Inquiry* plunges us into a subjective swamp of metaphors about "consumers," "consumer satisfaction," "consumer preferences," "demand for programs," etc., where no corresponding hard reality exists for lack of a "market" between broadcasters and listeners. The *Inquiry* openly displayed the weakness of the analysis by indulging in fanciful attempts to apply to the station-listener axis the theory of consumer behavior in real competitive markets (paras. 133–150). In flat contradiction of the feasibility of such theorizing, however, it conceded,

> *Some consumers value a particular product more highly than others and as a consequence are willing to pay more for the item. If there is no price tag on the item, there is no way to take into account the intensity of demand felt by the individual consumers* (para. 94).
>
> *Of even greater concern, however, is the fact that, by providing programming at zero price, the [radio] market is unable to measure the intensity of demand for particular programming. . . . Under the present system, there is no way to distinguish between programming that consumers would be willing to pay for, if necessary, and that which consumers would take for free, but not pay for* (para. 137).

And then, by yet another flip-flop, the *Inquiry* tried to resuscitate the fantasies about "demand" for programs from radio "consumers" with the unexplained assertion that "using either assumed values or actual empirical data for the variables outlined above, it is possible to analyze how well radio markets will satisfy consumer wants" (para. 142).

The *Decision* attempted to rebut some of this criticism (p. 13910, para. 7; p. 13912, para. 19), saying: "The key point is not whether a price mechanism exists, but whether the market has an incentive structure that is responsive to consumer demands" (para. 19). This is to evade the issue and to deny the elementary precepts of neoclassical economic theory about markets. If market forces and market discipline mean anything, they mean price-motivated behavior: no prices, no incentive structures.

In addition to the alleged market between stations and listeners, the *Inquiry* made much of the argument that radio programs are "quasi-public goods" (paras. 100–105, 130–132). Radio programs were analogized to public parks, public buildings, national defense, etc. However, public goods or quasi-public goods are end products, sufficient unto themselves. Radio programs are not end products. They are the lure or bait used to produce audience-power which is sold by the stations to advertisers for the latter's use in completing the production and marketing of their products. The FCC *Decision* did not discuss this criticism, but it did drop the quasi-public goods argument.

The conclusion to be drawn from this analysis of the theory of markets as it concerns the relation of radio broadcast stations to audiences is that it is impossible to show that these relations are a market or amenable to the discipline of the market, as that term is known in neoclassical economic theory. The elements that make up a market simply do not exist on the broadcaster-program-audience axis. We are left therefore with metaphors—figures of speech, repeated by rote—that conceal the reality.

> *The other essential foundation of the FCC's*
> Decision *concerns whether scarcity or public*
> *ownership of the radio frequency assignments*
> *is the basis of regulation of radio broadcasting.*

The new Chicago school economists are biased in favor of market solutions to all problems. When they approached the question of whether scarcity or public ownership of radio frequencies is the basis of regulation of their use, it might seem that they would have examined the state of affairs when market forces actually were *completely* in control of radio broadcasting. Such a period existed for a little less than a year in 1926–1927 after a Federal court held that under the Radio Act of 1912 the Secretary of Commerce had no power to regulate radio licensees who met the citizenship requirement (*U.S.* v. *Zenith Radio Corp.*, 12 F[2d] 614 at 618 [1926]; 35 *Ops. Atty Gen.* 126 at 132 [July 8, 1926]). Here was a natural laboratory situation in the real world in which to test their theory of the competence of the market to regulate radio broadcasting. Had they studied it, they would have found that the market spoiled the possibility of a radio broadcasting system. It was a perfect example of Hardin's "tragedy of the commons" (3).

The characteristic of common property (such as the radio spectrum, fisheries, forests, etc.) is that when used as if it were private property there is an inevitable tendency to destroy the capacity of the resource to serve either the individual user, the market, or society as a whole. When the Zenith case was decided there were about 500 radio stations. A "gold rush" ensued and in the less than a year before the Radio Act of 1927 was enacted, some 200 new broadcast stations crowded onto the air—an increase of about 40 percent. "By this time it was impossible in most places to receive any kind of consistent broadcast signal," says Head (4, p. 158). President Coolidge called for new radio legislation to eliminate the "chaos ... most urgently" (4, pp. 158–159). The most pressing problem facing the new Federal Radio Commission in 1927, according to Head, was "to reduce sharply the number of stations in operation," and it cut back most sharply among stations authorized to operate at night (when skywave interference was present). The sequence was: free market forces spoiled the market for everyone because they generated interference; the subsequent reduction in station numbers (relative scarcity) was caused by the interference.

But the 1980 FCC *Decision* buries the primary significance of interference as the basis of all radio regulation by a twofold shift in frames of reference. Whereas scarcity had been the effect of interference when attention was given to AM service to *communities*, and still is, the FCC argument based on the alleged disappearance of scarcity rests on (a) the later degradation of AM service areas in order to create more primary *markets*, and (b) the advent of FM stations, educational stations, and TV stations. In the view of the FCC the disappearance of "scarcity" has nothing to do with *serving communities*, but everything to do with selling audiences to advertisers in *markets* (*Decision*, p. 13911, paras 14–16). In short, the intended result of the proceeding, deregulation, is the basis for the alleged abundance of service, an inversion of the ostensible procedure. The FCC's use of "scarcity" therefore collides with the technical, legal, and political grounds for maintaining previous FCC policy because it is designed to protect the public interest in the use of public property. Secretary of Commerce Herbert Hoover, in opening the fourth radio conference, said:

> *Some of our major decisions of policy have been of far-reaching importance and have justified themselves a thousand-fold. The decision that the public, through the Government, must retain the ownership of the channels through the air with just as zealous a care for open competition as we retain public ownership of our navigation channels has given freedom and development in service that would have otherwise been lost in private monopolies* (6, p. 1).

That the 1980 FCC *Decision* is able to quote some comments by congressmen and judges that identify "scarcity" as the basis of regulation is not surprising.

> **The law and the practice of using the radio spectrum as common and state property prevails all over the world and has done so since its use began.**

In pushing their ideological line, the new Chicago school economists ignore why this is so. My *Statement* in support of comments of the Office of Communication, United Church of Christ, in FCC *Inquiry*, June 30, 1980, said:

> *The radio spectrum differs from other natural resources in possessing certain characteristics either uniquely or to a greater degree. These characteristics combine to produce the public policy objectives which have emerged to distinguish the radio spectrum from the private property which is the basis of economic life in the private sector. The unique characteristics are:*
>
> *1. The radio spectrum's original and still its principal use is the act of sharing information between transmitter and receiver, i.e.,*

communication. Minor exceptions prove the rule, e.g., radar and geodectic exploration. For no other resource is the principal function the transmission AND retention of information or anything else.

2. For one nation or class of users to use it, all nations and classes of users must also be able to use it with equipment built to compatible standards. Worldwide cooperation is therefore necessary for the radio spectrum to be used by anyone and everyone.

3. It is nondepletable and self-renewing. To be sure there is interference between users (which international regulation minimizes) but this "pollution" disappears immediately the interfering transmitters cease interfering.

4. Measurement of rights to use the radio spectrum are probabilistic rather than discretely specifiable. This alone is a major bar to establishment of a free market in transferable rights to use the spectrum.

5. Because the radio spectrum is used to communicate information and because the control of the flow of information is the basis of political power, the control of the use of the radio spectrum lies close to the seat of sovereignty in the nation state. No other resource has this order of political significance. At the same time, the necessary joint decision-making by all nations at the world level has for almost a century substantiated the fact that by international and national law, title to the radio spectrum rests not with individuals or nations but in all humanity (Statement, pp. 2–3).

The FCC commented as follows on the part of my statement above which they did quote:

The first four properties appear to involve economic issues and can be examined using economic analysis. The last property is concerned with political power; if true, it could represent, in our constitutional system, a rationale for removing allocation from government control altogether rather than requiring the government to allocate the resource (*Decision*, p. 13911, para. 13, emphasis added).

In this second sentence is the clear intent to deny to the national government the function of planning the use of the radio spectrum that is absolutely essential to sovereignty. It is an assertion that the "market" could perform *all* government functions. And in considering it we must take note of other similar statements in the *Decision*. In introducing the discussion of the rationale for the deregulation proceeding, the FCC said,

we have not rejected a pure marketplace solution because of any inherent weakness in the marketplace theory as applied to broadcasting. Rather, we have determined from a reading of the full record that the implementation of a pure market approach would not be in the public interest at this time [sic] *due to administrative complexities and possible legal difficulties involving individual vs. market-wide responsibilities (Decision, p. 13909, para. 1).*

And in a footnote, the FCC offered this proceeding as "a good initial basis for decisionmaking" by Congress that "might consider" the elimination of "legal difficulties" impeding a full marketplace approach to broadcasting in revising the Communications Act. The program that is perceivable is: today—partial deregulation of radio broadcasting; tomorrow—total deregulation of radio and TV broadcasting and direct broadcast satellites; day after tomorrow—market forces to administer allocation of the spectrum as a whole.

In this article I have limited myself to the basic theory of regulation as the FCC seeks to apply it to radio broadcasting. It rests on two transparently shoddy and fraudulent foundations: (a) that a nonmarket will behave as an imaginary perfect, abstract market of perfect competitors with priced transactions is assumed by idealist philosophers to work; and (b) that a reified and fictitious "scarcity" is somehow the basis of public regulation of radio broadcasters. If this FCC *Decision* survives further challenges (from the courts and the public), it appears that the public which owns the radio frequencies will be deprived of protection of its rights to receive radio service necessary for its educational, social, cultural, and political welfare—rights won in struggles in the Congress, the regulatory agency, and the courts over more than half a century. Such an outcome of this struggle over radio deregulation would have multiplied political effects in all aspects of the private/public sector struggles going on outside the communication field. For although the new Chicago school economists try to denigrate it as "political," the hard facts of life about control of the benefits flowing from the use of the radio spectrum rest at bottom on the proposition that the power to control the flow of information is the basis of all political power.

It follows that the strategic pivot on which rests the outcome of the struggle to redefine the border between the public and private sectors in the U.S. in general lies precisely in this debate over radio broadcasting.

REFERENCES

1. Friedman, Milton. *Capitalism and Freedom.* Chicago: University of Chicago Press, 1962.
2. Gide, Charles and Charles Rist. *A History of Economic Doctrines.* London: D. C. Heath, 1947.
3. Hardin, Garett. "The Tragedy of the Commons." *Science,* December 13, 1968, pp. 1243–1248.
4. Head, Sydney W. *Broadcasting in America* (2nd ed.). Boston: Houghton Mifflin, 1972.
5. Simon, Herbert. *Economic Policy for a Free Society.* Chicago: University of Chicago Press, 1948.
6. U.S. Government. *Proceedings of the Fourth National Radio Conference and Recommendations for Regulation of Radio.* Conference called by Herbert Hoover, November 9–11, 1925. Washington, D.C.: U.S. Government Printing Office, 1926.

Rowland suggests that deregulation trends in American broadcasting argue less for the "failures" of efforts to rewrite principal communications legislation than for an incremental process of change shaping a new policy environment. The result of this approach, he says, has been principally to benefit the major corporate interests and further to reify conditions favoring them. Willard D. Rowland is research assistant professor in the Institute of Communications Research at the University of Illinois at Urbana-Champaign.

36

THE FURTHER PROCESS OF REIFICATION
Continuing Trends in Communication Legislation and Policymaking

Willard D. Rowland, Jr.

For nearly fifty years after passage of the Radio Act of 1927, there were virtually no serious, widely supported efforts to change the principal statutory provisions of federal policy for telecommunications. To be sure, the Radio Act (PL 69-632), dealing only with broadcasting and providing for an ambiguously conceived Federal Radio Commission, was supplanted by the Communications Act of 1934 (PL 73-416). However, that law did little more than consolidate and formalize federal regulatory authority in telecommunications, readopting almost in their entirety the broadcasting provisions of the Radio Act and folding into the new Federal Communications Commission (FCC) authority for aspects of otherwise unchanging common carrier regulation and policy. Characteristic of much New Deal legislation, the new law did not so much change general public policy as reinforce and expand prior bipartisan federal measures in antitrust and administrative law, carrying forward the rhetoric of a poorly understood fiduciary doctrine (the "public interest") that had embedded in it a fundamental government commitment to existing terms of economic order and industrial structure.

During the period between 1934 and 1978, hundreds of bills were introduced, and in nearly every session of Congress there were one or more hearings on proposed legislation and on related aspects of broadcaster, common carrier, and regulatory performance.[1] For example, bills would regularly appear dealing with political broadcasting, network-affiliate relationships, televi-

Willard D. Rowland, Jr., "The Further Process of Reification: Continuing Trends in Communication Legislation and Policymaking," original manuscript. This chapter is a revised and updated version of an article in the *Journal of Communication,* Vol. 34, No. 2 (Autumn 1982), pp. 114-136.

sion content, telephone rates and service, and the terms of FCC authority. Typically, however, such bills were not the product of any comprehensive review of all the complicated facets of policy options for telecommunications. Unlike the situation in most other industrialized democracies, the United States was not, at least until the mid-1960s, much interested in any sort of authoritative a priori process for reviewing the terms of national policy for broadcasting. Traditional laissez-faire ideology produced slight American disposition to develop the equivalent of high-level, royal commissions to examine policy options, especially in communications matters, with all their First Amendment implications. Furthermore, with the expansion of the federal regulatory apparatus and its presumed attention to all facets of the public interest, there already appeared to exist an adequate means for such policy review. Any legislation introduced in Congress was therefore the product of quite a differnt process. It usually emerged from lobbying by one or more specially interested parties, most often within the regulated industries, and it tended not to reflect any widespread public debate or expression of need.

On the whole, of course, there was little serious political interest in significantly changing federal policy for broadcasting and telecommunications. Excepting various particular issues of concern, the overall level of public discontent always seemed rather low. Moreover, the general terms of purpose and patterns of organization, ownership, and control in electronic communications were of substantial benefit to most political and industrial forces. Any proposal to change the legislation raised the possibility of upsetting the generally acceptable status quo; therefore, few presidents or congressional leaders felt compelled to pursue new initiatives. As a result, most bills, even those promoted by industry, tended not to earn nuch White House support, and in Congress they regularly failed to find their way out of committee or at most secured passage in only one house.

There also existed other opportunities for congressional policy review. With the power to accept or reject appointments of new members to the FCC, the Senate periodically had occasion to debate communications issues. Through the annual budgetary process and oversight hearings for regulatory and other federal agencies involved in communications matters, both houses had even more frequent opportunities. Rather than actually passing amendments or new laws, Congress generally tended to prefer to guide communications policy through the "raised eyebrow" process associated with these various forms of hearings and related committee reports, brandishing the threat of formal legislation, all the while expecting that such warnings would be sufficient to lead to "voluntary" regulatory and industry action. Executive branch policy concerns were typically reflected through Commission appointments and Budget Bureau reviews of agency funding requests. Meanwhile, reflecting the system of U.S. public policymaking at large, the administrative agenda was constantly guided by an endless, often intense negotiation process among the several governmental offices and the interested industries.

From time to time, amendments to the Communications Act were in fact passed by Congress and signed by presidents, and there were provisions of other legislation that had variously direct or indirect impact on details of the communications law. For the most part, however, such adjustments were technical—for example, the 1959 Fairness Doctrine clarifications or the administrative procedures changes of 1946—constituting relatively minor accommodations to practical problems associated with interpretation of the 1934 statute or other aspects of administrative law. With the possible exception of the 1967 Public Broadcasting Act (PL 90-129), none of these amendments represented any significant change in federal communications policy. The central doctrines remained largely inviolate: predominantly private ownership and commercial purpose, fiduciary licensing under the spectrum scarcity principle, common carrier monopoly and universal service, and preemptive federal regulatory authority for some aspects of some services (common carrier) and for all aspects of others (broadcasting).

By the late 1970s, that period of legislative and executive branch avoidance of legislative review had come to an end, and the possibility of the adoption of substantially revised communications legislation appeared to be greater than at any time since the passage of the basic radio law a half century before. The reasons for this shift were several. They related to a series of developments beginning in the mid-1960s that included the increasingly rapid emergence of newer technologies of electronic communications, attendant new forms of industrial competition and realignment, a variety of attacks on the regulatory process, continuing general anxieties about the societal impact of electronic media, and struggles between Congress and the White House over a wide variety of policy issues.

The technological changes involved a general process of continuing hardware miniaturization, increasing computation speed, and larger transmission capacity—the pattern of ever smaller and cheaper tools performing ever larger and faster tasks. In specific terms, these changes were reflected in new opportunities for telecommunications transmission and associated competitive pressures on the telephone monopoly; the spread of broadband cable television; the adoption of satellites in various forms of commercial enterprise; introduction of home video recording and playback equipment; experiments with videotex systems in broadcasting and cable; and, through it all, a process of convergence and reconfiguration—the steady evaporation of the distinctions among broadcasting, telecommunications, and the print and film media. Nearly all the major industrial interests in the broadcasting, cable, electronic common carrier, program production, data transmission, and computing and publishing fields were beginning to jockey with one another, seeking to reposition themselves as advantageously as possible for exploitation of the emerging communications forms. To the extent that the existing communications legislation and regulatory process tended to favor one party or another, such interests did not seek policy changes. But to the degree that the policy conditions were either too slowly or too quickly changing according to the different needs of the contending parties, pressures began to build for major adjustments within the established regulatory structure or, failing that, for more sweeping legislative measures.

Adding to these often conflicing pressures for policy redefinition were the broader societal uncertainties associated with the civil rights, antiwar, consumer, and other reform movements, which, taken together, seemed to imply a certain need to reassess the adequacy of electronic communications, particularly the performance of broadcast television. During the late 1960s and early 1970s, the communications-oriented branches of the citizens' action or public interest group movement appeared to be achieving significant success in challenging broadcast station license renewals and in forcing the FCC to adopt in all its regulatory activities somewhat broader definitions of the "public interest" standard and the notion of "parties at interest" than had been its wont theretofore. These groups were making inroads by working within the terms of the Communications Act and the existing regulatory process, using the Commission's own internal procedures (generally mandated by statute) and the courts to reverse many aspects of the industry-regulatory accommodations that had been at work since 1927. Reflecting various societal concerns about television and electronic communication—about portrayals and employment of minorities and women, adequacy of content for children, effects of advertising, levels of violence and pornography, and the extent of media concentraton and cross-ownership—the reform groups were threatening to force the regulatory process into ever-more activist, adversary relationships with the broadcast industry. There were even indications that such efforts might be expanded to encompass the entire field of telecommunications, including cable and common carrier services.

In fact, since at least the early 1960s, various technological changes (computers, microwave transmission) and related new business needs (new terminal equipment, more long-distance data transmission and other specialized services) had already led the FCC to begin reconsidering the "natural monopoly" conditions of telecommunications and to issue a series of court-sustained rulings that in turn had begun to introduce certain forms of competition into the common carrier field (Wiley, 1981). Coupled with a renewed spirit of consumer activism, such regulatory trends had the makings of a relatively significant set of policy adjustments. Whatever the extent of possible changes, it was increasingly clear that in telecommunications and broadcasting, respectively, various entrepreneurial and reform interests had begun to use the Communications Act and the regulatory process, the very means used in the past for policy favoring existing industries, precisely against those interests. By the early 1970s, the established industries not only had taken notice; they were also searching for ways to stem the tide.

The policy review process was never officially commenced. No single party directed that it be undertaken, set its agenda, or established its timetable, but the review did begin to proceed simultaneously and haltingly in a number of different official and unofficial channels, with events in various forums directly or indirectly affecting one another. There was neither a mutually agreed-upon order to the process nor any prior arrangements about which forums would predominate at which stages. Events were tending to be responsive to forces and conditions that often were extraneous to any specifically clear considerations about communications policy.

In retrospect, however, it is possible to see three distince (though closely related), relatively self-conscious, and rather widely encompassing phases of the policy review process beginning in the mid-1960s and extending to the present. The first phase emerged during the decade extending roughly from 1967 to 1977, as a series of presidential and other high-level commissions or task forces. Each typically issued a report on a broad range of communications policy matters, and each was usually based on a growing body of foundation, private, and federally sponsored technical, social, and policy research.

The second phase, still developing in the early 1980s, involved the direct, official entry of Congress. It began in 1976 and 1977, principally in the Subcommittee on Communications of the House of Representatives, and has continued with an increasing involvement by the Senate communications subcommittee. These congressional efforts have consisted of various reports and hearings reviewing federal policy toward cable, broadcasting, and telecommunications, and a growing flood of drafts of new communications legislation— some involving wholesale "rewrites" of the 1934 act, others constituting more specialized revisions of only portions of it.

Overlapping both of these periods has been a simultaneous third phase, principally involving the FCC. Since the early 1970s, the Commission has been trying to adjust to aspects of the developments in the other phases, undertaking inquiries and even major regulatory changes in reaction to or anticipation of the policy signals emanating from the other areas.

The task force review phase beginning in the mid-1960s appeared to represent something of a departure in American communications policymaking. Marked heretofore by an ad hoc, piecemeal approach by Congress and an even more laissez-faire posture by most administrations, the process now seemed to be opening up somewhat, using the official and semiofficial presidential or other special commission mechanism to pursue a relatively more comprehensive review of policy options. The apparent shift began in 1966, with the creation of the Carnegie Commission on Educational Television (1967) and shortly thereafter the President's Task Force on Communications Policy (1969). The Carnegie Commission was neither selected nor funded by the government, but the president, Lyndon Johnson, gave its formation a great deal of encouragement, his staff saw to it that certain of the Commission's members were appointed with an eye to their influence in the White House and Congress, and he quickly helped guide several of its recommendations into enactment as the 1967 public broadcasting amendments to the basic communications legislation.

The President's Task Force was more official. It was appointed by Johnson; it was government-sponsored; its chairman, Eugene Rostow, and other appointees carried the authority of a group with a mandate to help sort out White House and congressional options; and several of its recommendations were actually implemented by Johnson's successor, Richard Nixon. Of course, the special commission review had become an increasingly frequent device during the Kennedy and Johnson administrations, and it turned out that its use often had to do with objectives unrelated to the specific recommendations of any single report (Popper, 1970).

During the Nixon and Ford administrations, the task force mechanism continued to be used, particularly in regard to cable issues. The seventies saw reports issued by such groups as the Sloan Commission (1971), the Conference Board (1972), the Committee for Economic Development (1975), the U.S. Cabinet Committee on Cable Communications (1974), the Aspen Institute for Humanistic Studies, and the Rand Corporation. These reports dealt with the importance of the changes taking place in electronic communications technology, stressing particularly the implications of broadband cable, the challenges to conventional broadcasting, the changes in telecommunications service options, and the inadequacies of the federal regulatory response.

The President's Task Force seemed oriented primarily toward trying to encourage a greater degree of government awareness of the changing technological environment, promoting better, more widespread use of those technologies, and rationalizing the executive branch communications policy review capacity. Indeed, the Task Force recommendations along these lines led to the creation in 1970 of the Office of Telecommunications Policy (OTP) and in 1977 of its successor agency, the National Telecommunications and Information Administration (NTIA) in the Department of Commerce. But as related to the principal policy trends during the 1970s, the more significant aspects of the report came in its discussions of regulation, competition, and the relative roles of government and industry.

> Government cannot and should not take over the function of private business. Indeed, in certain areas, we recommend that policy rely more on market force, and less on regulation, than in the past [U.S. President's Task Force on Communications Policy, 1969, p. 8].

In the wake of the Great Society legislation of the 1960s and as part of a trend stretching back to the 1880s, the size and role of the federal government were continuing to grow. But against this still rising tide there was beginning to run a strong undertow of neolibertarian, deregulatory thinking that would be increasingly felt throughout the 1970s. Not yet a call for sweeping deregulation, the Task Force report encouraged a significant policy role for government. In fact, increased government capacity was a major recommendation. But there was also no mistaking the ultimate goal.

> Among the most pervasive of our findings, therefore, is the need to strengthen governmental capabilities, both in the FCC and the Executive Branch, to develop and implement policies which will enable the private sector to reach its full potential [U.S. President's Task Force on Communications Policy, 1969, p. 9].

As early as the time of the Task Force report, there was growing unease in policy circles about the FCC's mid-1960s decision to restrict the development of cable on the grounds of its competitive threat to broadcasting. Reflecting growing awareness of the tendency of regulatory agencies to protect their client industries, the several reports contained successively stronger indictments of the FCC for its protective behavior toward existing broadcasting interests. Less clearly acknowledged in these analyses was the extent to which the Commission was always constrained by the failure of Congress, itself all too sensitive to the needs of broadcasters, to provide any other mandate for the Commission.

The subsequent flood of high-level official and quasi-official task force reports increasingly emphasized the presumed benefits of broadband cable, invoking high expectations for content diversity, including a wider range of informational, educational, economic, and in-home services. Such celebrations were not always without caution. The Sloan Commission (1971, pp. 2-3) was quick to note that the "notion that technological advance is synonymous with progress has lost its old attraction, and there are many who will assert that it is quite the opposite that is true." The U.S. Cabinet Committee report (1974, p. 16) was also not dewy-eyed: "We have not treated [cable] as a modern-day Rosetta stone capable of unravelling the complex problems facing this society."

Nonetheless, the Sloan vision (1971, p. 47) and that of most of the reports was essentially optimistic:

> The cable system that this Report has postulated promises a television of abundance, very nearly as copious as the press, providing all that has come to be expected of conventional television and an endless range of new services to the home, to the institutions society has erected to serve its needs, and directly to the public itself.

Following the historical pattern of academic and popular response to all previous electronic communications developments, most of the high-prestige reports on cable, and the press accounts of them, did in fact characterize the medium as a potential remedy for many contemporary social and political ills. The cautions notwithstanding, cable became invested with the ability to end alienation from the political process by providing better means for public access, personal interaction, and expression of "the community voice." It would even stem urban congestion and information chaos by providing wider dissemination of information and reductions in the need to travel.

Again, not all the reports were quite so panaceatic, and there were some other differences among them. There was, for instance, virtually no consensus on the exact mix of cross-ownership restrictions, if any, to impose among broadcasting, cable, and telephone interests, on the relative separations necessary between programming services and distribution facilities, or on the extent of the relative regulatory authority among local, state, and federal governments. More significant, however, is that all the major studies tended to accept as appropriate, or at least as inevitable and beyond need for discussion, the traditional patterns of predominantly private ownership and profit-making purposes for cable and the other new communications technologies.

In this light it is perhaps not surprising that, as signaled in the 1967 Task Force study, the principal theme running throughout these reports was an expression of faith in the operations of the marketplace and the need to enhance that mechanism. Again and again, previous federal policy came under attack. But the emphasis tended to be primarily upon the FCC's patterns of protectionism for broadcasting and the need to permit cable to compete. Representative of the various reports, the Cabinet Committee (1974, p. 16) "simply conclude[s] that cable has much to offer, and it should be given an opportunity to prove its worth to the American people in the marketplace of goods and services and in the marketplace of ideas."

The commission reports would occasionally take note of such needs as those of ethnic and taste minorities, women, and other interests associated with diverse public service interpretations of the fiduciary principle, and they would variously invoke the images of "open access," "freedom of expression," and "fair competition" and make recommendations for such things as better, more permanent funding for public broadcasting or cable ownership by community-based, nonprofit organizations. But by and large, such recommendations were not central to the reports, and it was seldom clear how those provisions were realistically expected to be implemented and fully developed against the imposing counterweight of mass media and telecommunications systems already so heavily entrenched in commercial, private enterprise foundations.

By the late 1960s, the executive branch initiatives in these matters had slowed somewhat. The Watergate period and the evidence of attempts to use White House agencies to influence the print and electronic media and the regulatory process for baldly partisan purposes focused attention on problems of communications policymaking created by the rise of a more powerful executive. It also raised questions about the need for reassertion of legislative interests. Meanwhile, the membership and leadership in Congress had begun to change significantly in all areas, including communications. Throughout the 1970s, each new Congress brought a proportionately larger share of newer members with new committee assignments. By 1976 such a principal figure as Senate Communications Subcommittee Chairman John Pastore (D-R.I.) had retired, and his House counterpart, Torbert Macdonald (D-Mass.), had died. With such changes there were no longer the same understandings among key legislators, old regulatory processes, and the various conflicting industrial and other interests about the specific terms of the previous accommodations. New communications subcommittee members and chairpersons meant new staffs, new patterns of influence, and, at least for some, opportunities to undertake new policymaking initiatives. As a result of all these factors, there was a certain degree of renewed communications policy leadership in Congress, first in the House and then in the Senate.

During the first, task force phase of the policy review period, broadcasters had become both alarmed at the license challenge successes of public groups up through the early 1970s and tantalized anew by an old dream of greater license security. An apparently new judicial environment was forcing the FCC to take relatively drastic measures in denying television license renewals. To seek some relief, the broadcasters became involved with Congress, the White House, the Commission, and citizens' groups in a complex pattern of pressures and counterpressures.

One of the expedients the industry had used to help stem the tide of license challenges had been the "settlement agreement," in which, in exchange for withdrawal of a challenge by a citizens' group, the broadcaster would meet certain programming, service, and employment demands (Cole and Oettinger, 1978). Such agreements had become so prevalent and so costly that the industry was becoming anxious to secure some regulatory limitations on them. Beyond that, and in order to protect itself from what it saw as the threatening influence of reform-minded tendencies in the courts and the Commission, the industry sought a more permanent form of statutory assistance. The objective here was legislation that would extend license renewal periods, make the renewal process more perfunctory, and make challenges even more difficult than they had been before the mid-1960s.

There was considerable congressional support for many of these measures. Despite continuing demonstrations of political concern about media concentration, television violence, effects of children's advertising, and generally limited interpretations of public interest obligations by the industry, the broadcasters still wielded substantial influence in both houses of Congress, and traditional regulatory tendencies toward protectionism were not entirely discouraged. However, the power of the critique of FCC restrictions on cable was growing with every new high-level task force report, and it was becoming increasingly evident to the broadcasters that if they were to retain any maneuvering room in the effort to stave off the license renewal challenges, they were going to have to reach some accommodation with the policymakers on the issues of cable and network programming standards.

The initial bargain was struck in 1971. It consisted of an OTP-guided Consensus Agreement—a compromise with the cable industry on the terms of a long-delayed new copyright law and of revised cable rules. The subsequent new FCC cable regulations in 1972 (36 FCC 2d 141) revitalized the economic attractiveness of cable in the nation's largest cities and encouraged a new phase of large scale investment and expansion. Once over that barrier and now increasingly influenced by a growing executive and congressional deregulatory mood, the FCC relatively quickly dropped most of its 1972 rules and by the late 1970s had virtually totally deregulated the cable industry. The next bargain, struck in 1975, was an agreement with the chairman of the FCC, Richard Wiley, to initiate the so-called family reviewing hour. That arrangement provided for the networks to avoid scheduling in the earliest prime-time viewing period program material unsuitable for the entire family. Written into the NAB Code, the family viewing policy eventually became tied up in legal action, and as a partial consequence of that activity it was effectively ignored. For the moment, however, it was an important concession by the industry.

But the most significant negotiating step the broadcasters took was to agree to begin discussing with members of Congress and others the possible terms of new, more broadly ranging communications legislation. Always publicly opposed to the "rewrite," the broadcasters nonetheless began to explore the grounds for legislative accommodation, for compromises wherein the growing policymaker need to deal with the rapidly changing technological environment could be traded for some measure of traditional protection for broadcast industry interests.

Meanwhile, the telecommunications industry had not remained idle. AT&T's hegemonic situation had long made it more vulnerable than broadcasters to calls for certain forms of more rigorous regulatory control. Indeed, since the early twentieth century, "Ma Bell" had been cast in much political and popular rhetoric as the archetypal monopoly, and the natural monopoly and public utility features of wired communication had fostered regulations in such areas as rates and services. While public ownership and the most serious regulatory constraints were never realistic options, the Commission had finally become willing to permit introduction of some competition into telecommunications, particularly in equipment and transmission services. In this policy it had had tacit, if not always explicit, congressional support. Meanwhile, in 1974 the Department of Justice had instituted a new antitrust suit seeking, among other things, to force AT&T divestiture of Western Electric and other subsidiaries.

Accordingly, during the mid-1970s, as AT&T felt the initial consequences of the FCC decisions and as it observed the increasing tilt of the general political mood toward deregulation, it too began to seek a legislative accommodation. The result was a concerted effort in 1976 to effect passage of a law that would preserve as much as possible AT&T's traditional dominance in most facets of telecommunications. Ostensibly introduced on behalf of small independent telephone companies, the bill was entitled the Consumer Communications Reform Act. It was, in fact, so pro-AT&T that it came to be called the Bell Bill. The bill was widely opposed by consumer groups and did not survive. Unsuccessful at getting its entire way, AT&T had nonetheless indicated a willingness to entertain the possibility of negotiating the terms of new legislation. More important, by stealing a march on the policy development process, it had greatly influenced the agenda of possible options (see Sirico, 1979; Krasnow et al., 1982, pp. 241-244).

During the early 1970s, neither the House nor the Senate communications subcommittees had paid much attention to the breadth and far-reaching implications of the technological developments in communications. They had seemed content to stick to their traditional commitments to the broadcasting and telecommunications industries, holding hearings on such matters as the Fairness Doctrine and violence on television, but otherwise generally steering to a status quo public policy course. By the mid-1970s, however, in the wake of the task force reports, other critiques of the FCC and federal communications policies, and the Bell Bill episode, Congress began to pay more attention to the changing technological environment.

The initial signs of movement came in the House, where Chairman Macdonald announced a reorganization of his communications subcommittee, in which its oversight responsibilities in power and energy would be divested and its staff would be enlarged for increased attention to FCC and communications matters. The changed emphasis was reflected first when, in July 1975, the subcommittee held hearings on the extent of telecommunications research and policy development activities in the federal government. Those hearings were soon followed by a detailed subcommittee staff report on cable and related regulatory and policy problems (U.S. Congress, House of Representatives, 1976a), which set the stage for an exhaustive series of hearings on cable beginning the following spring (U.S. Congress, House of Representatives, 1976b). The cable hearings had been planned by Chairman Macdonald and his staff but, due to serious illness, Macdonald resigned as chairman in favor of Lionel Van Deerlin (D-Cal.). The subcommittee continued the cable review, but it also soon began to expand the inquiry, by the advent of the 95th Congress substantially increasing its budget and staff for that effort. The expanded activity led to publication in May 1977 of the *Options Papers,* a large collection of staff studies encompassing a wide-ranging series of communications policy issues facing Congress (U.S. Congress, House of Representatives, 1977). In June 1977, the Senate Communications Subcommittee, though somewhat more reluctantly, joined the review by holding its own hearings on cable. For several years thereafter, from 1978 to at least 1982, every session of Congress was marked by serious attempts in both houses to rewrite nearly all or at least major portions of the 1934 law.

It is impossible here to account for all the important issues and problems raised in the rewrite effort. So far it has involved hundreds of witnesses and submissions in scores of hearings on dozens of proposed new bills. However, it is perhaps possible to trace several of the key themes and issues in this extended legislative debate.

The House subcommittee's staff report on cable and the subsequent *Options Papers* were written with the clear intention of guiding Congress toward new legislation. Building on the previous task force studies, especially the Cabinet Committee work, the staff reports criticized the FCC's prior policies toward cable, calling for regulation of cable "in its own right" and more reliance on marketplace forces. The *Options Papers* discussed a vast array of procedural, structural, and institutional issues in spectrum management, broadcasting, common carrier telecommunications, cable, and many other areas. The common carrier section represented something of a critique of the Bell Bill, raising many of the complex questions about rate structures, efficiency, interstate and local cost separations, the continuing need for primacy of universal service goals, the developing terms of equipment and intercity service competition, and the possibilities for structural change within the industry that the AT&T legislation had tried to finesse.

The broadcasting sections of the *Papers* in fact contained relatively few extensive statements of policy options, but they did discuss structural restrictions to encourage diversity and such options as extending license renewal periods, leasing spectrum space, treating broadcasters as public utilities, and instituting mandated access time or limited common carrier status. Underlying these alternatives, however, was the more general policy issue already moving to center stage. Arguing that in 1927 and 1934 Congress did not opt for minimal, largely technical regulation "because it viewed the marketplace as imperfect," the *Papers* contended that "Congress still has a basic choice as to how to implement its public policy objectives. Simply stated, Congress can choose to impose restrictions on the broadcaster (direct regulation) or to stimulate the marketplace generally (indirect regulation)" (p. 44).

Deregulation views had thus come to prominence in much congressional communications thinking and, while there remained considerable wariness about how to apply such an approach in telecommunications, there was a growing interest in trying to implement it in broadcasting and cable. But the various interested parties among the industries, government, and public groups would all likely have many different views about acceptable terms of deregulation. Therefore, the broadcasting portions of the first sweeping version of the rewrite (HR 13015), introduced in 1978, were built on a fundamental compromise.[2] Drawing on the license lease notion in the *Option Papers* and other federal policies involving natural resources, the bill proposed that, for a substantial amount of deregulation—including elimination of the public interest standard and the Fairness Doctrine, virtually permanent license renewals, and the effective gutting of the FCC—the broadcasters and other spectrum users would agree to pay a fee. This "spectrum use fee" would generate a "public dividend" that would cover the costs not only of regulation but also of such special services as public and minority group broadcasting. In common carrier matters, the bill called for the "maximum feasible reliance on marketplace forces" and urged that regulation encourage establishment of "full and fair competition." To this end it made a distinction between "competitive" and "noncompetitive" services, with the intention of maintaining regulation only for the latter.

As part of the policy tradeoffs involving AT&T, the bill would force Bell to divest itself of its manufacturing subsidiary, Western Electric, thus breaking up an important portion of the vertical integration in the telecommunications industry. But the bill would also have permitted AT&T to acquire interests in other telecommunications services, thereby permitting it to engage in a broad range of unregulated electronic media enterprises, presumably including cable and videotex, and to escape a 1956 consent decree agreement with the Department of Justice that had barred Bell from providing data processing and other services not defined as regulated common carrier communications.

In retrospect, it is clear that, as early as the release of the *Options Papers,* the major broadcasting interests were unwilling to strike the sort of bargains required by the rewrite (Lucoff, 1980). Moreover, it turned out that (for quite different reasons) there was little consensus about the bill among many other interested parties—the FCC, public broadcasting, citizens' groups, cable, AT&T, and other common carriers (see, for example, Rowland, 1980).

As a result of all the opposition to it, the bill was scrapped, and in March 1979 another version (HR 3333) was introduced. Its terms still involved important tradeoffs, although the costs to the industry were beginning to diminish. For instance, the bill reinstated some references to the public interest standard, but the emphasis was slight, and the dominant focus remained on marketplace forces. In broadcasting the bill retained a spectrum fee, but the fee was to be substantially reduced and the bill would still grant permanent licenses, the end of comparative license application and renewal hearings, and other aspects of the virtually total, nontechnical deregulation of radio and television. The first bill had worried about commercialization of public broadcasting; this version would now permit it to carry advertising. In telecommunications the second bill retained the notion of separating services into regulated and unregulated categories. The former, dubbed "dominant carrier" (meaning essentially AT&T), would remain subject to federal oversight, but now, while Bell would still be permitted to move into unregulated services, again overriding the 1956 consent decree, it would not be required to divest Western Electric.

Such changes reflected a process of frantic jockeying in which it was beginning to appear that the subcommittee leadership, especially Chairman Van Deerlin and his majority staff, were willing to make any bargain to effect passage of a bill. But this desperate search for compromise revealed a continuingly serious lack of consensus both within the subcommittee and among the major interested parties, and it just hardened the opposition of many. While anxious to secure many of the promised concessions, the major industrial parties came to realize that, the exhortations of the chairman and his staff notwithstanding, the prospects for forcing through a bill were increasingly dim and that by delay they could probably improve the odds for much better terms. Under these circumstances the idea of a comprehensive rewrite had become severely discredited and by July 1979 the second effort had been abandoned.

Meanwhile, the Senate subcommittee had also entered the legislative review process. After its own cable hearings in 1977, its members introduced two "renovation" drafts in March 1979, just ahead of the House's second effort. One, S. 611, represented the position of the subcommittee's Democratic majority under Chairman Ernest Hollings (D-S.C.) and had a policy rationale based on "full and fair competition." The other, S. 622, represented the Republican majority and was based on an even more explicit "marketplace competition" policy. The broadcasting amendments of these bills were brief, including the S. 611 provisions for indefinite radio and five-year television license renewals in exchange for a "public resource fee" to be based on the market value of the spectrum space used and to generate funds in excess of the costs of regulation. In S. 622 there were similar license renewal extensions, plus other provisions making license challenges more difficult and additional terms of deregulation for radio, television, and cable. There also was a spectrum fee provision, but this "Commission fee" was much more modest, to be sufficient only to underwrite the costs of regulation. Neither bill replaced the public interest language in the broadcasting portions of the 1934 act, but in the new general introductory sections the marketplace and deregulatory emphasis was unmistakeable. In telecommunications the bill carried forward the original House draft concept of separate competitive (unregulated) and noncompetitive (regulated) services. Both also provided means for getting around the consent decree, and, in keeping with the second House draft, they softened the AT&T divestiture requirements.

While still somewhat split on broadcasting and other provisions, the House and Senate subcommittees seemed reasonably close on telecommunications matters. Therefore, in December 1979, in an effort to reach an accommodation with the increasingly crucial Senate subcommittee and to salvage at least some legislation, Chairman Van Deerlin secured agreement among a number of his colleagues to permit introduction of a new draft (HR 6121), this time without any broadcast provisions. After being reintroduced in January 1980 and subsequently revised, the bill was reported out of the full commerce committee. However, the House leadership put off final consideration of the bill by referring it to the judiciary committee, where it was rejected, in large part because of concern about the bill's impact on the still pending Department of Justice antitrust suit against AT&T. In June, the Senate subcommittee took up a new bill of its own (S. 2827), which in telecommunications matters represented something of a compromise between S. 611 and S. 622 and reiterated many of the evolving HR 6121 features. Unlike the House draft, the Senate bill contained broadcasting provisions, including extended license renewal periods (five years), random selection procedures for new license assignments (lottery), relaxed comparative hearings procedures for contested renewals, revisions of Section 315, and requirements that the FCC move toward deregulating radio by reducing or eliminating rules on program content, commercial lengths and frequencies, program logs, and format and ascertainment requirements. The bill retained some restrictions on AT&T involvement in cable and permitted the FCC to impose other limitations on cable concentration and cross-ownership. However, there was no spectrum fee provision, and the bill left that possibility only marginally open by calling for an FCC study of the subject.

With the approach of the 1980 elections, the goal of achieving consensus on the major provisions of any of the rewrite drafts was becoming increasingly unlikely. The uncertainties associated with the possibilities for change in the White House and Congress contributed to the caution that had characterized the attitude of many subcommittee members in both houses since 1978. Sensing that the new conditions might continue to enhance their positions, most of the key industry lobby groups also called for delay, even though, as in broadcasting, the concessions were becoming greater and greater. As a result, the rewrite was to be deferred until the new Congress arrived in January 1981. As it happened, two broadcasting measures, which strictly speaking were not part of the rewrite effort, were passed by the full House just a month before the elections.[3] However, due to the upheavals in the Senate immediately following them, there was no real opportunity for the lame duck Democratic leadership to secure passage of a comparable statute. Hence, after four years of extensive efforts to secure new communications legislation, the 96th Congress ended with no revisions.

Despite the absence of legislation, however, aspects of the new policy trends were well on their way to implementation all during the middle and late 1970s, as manifested by the activities of the FCC. The deregulatory undertow had begun to affect federal policy in many areas, and all during the Nixon, Ford, and Carter administrations the FCC had begun to adjust to the new current. As reflected as early as its *Carterfone* decision (13 FCC 2d 420 [1968]) and its *First Computer Inquiry* (28 FCC 2d 267 [1971]), the Commission had begun to introduce a certain pro-competitive tendency into its common carrier efforts. In conjunction with the later Justice Department antitrust suit against AT&T, these decisions suggested something of the extent of the shift apparently beginning to take place within the actual operations of the government.

Meanwhile, in 1972 under Chairman Dean Burch, the Commission created a Reregulation Task Force, initiating a process of regulatory review that, while initially focused largely on technical rules involving broadcasting, came eventually to play an important role in much of the FCC's deregulatory activity during subsequent years. Under a new Republican chairman, Richard Wiley, the Commission had created a Cable Television Deregulation Task Force in 1974, and all during the mid-1970s, without much explicit guidance from Congress, the FCC had moved ahead to substantial deregulation in cable, pay television, and satellite communications.

These efforts were continued during the tenure of Democratic Chairman Charles Ferris, and the developing competition and marketplace imagery came to underlie much of the Commission's approach to its second computer inquiry decision (77 FCC 2d 384 [1980]) and the staff work in its third Network Inquiry (1980). In the former, the Commission actually tried to read and anticipate the central telecommunications provisions of the various rewrites by, among other things, reinterpreting the 1956 consent decree and deregulating "enhanced" (data processing) services and customer equipment sales. The latter critically reviewed past FCC network regulation policies, finding them actually to have contributed to the restrictive network practices they were meant to contain, and arguing for deregulation in this area to create conditions for more networks and hence more programming competition. Altogether, then, by the early 1980s the FCC was not merely well in tune with the dominant tendencies in federal policy thinking; it was in some cases running ahead of them.

Deregulation positions seemed to be strengthened by Ronald Reagan's capture of the presidency, the emergence of a Republican majority in the Senate, and the changed makeup of the House. In the Senate the communications subcommittee chairmanship fell to Barry Goldwater (R-Ariz.), a coauthor of one of the 1979 renovation drafts and a principal architect of the 1980 compromise bill, and leadership of the parent commerce committee went to

Robert Packwood (R-Ore.). However, since the former Republican minority had managed to control much of the subcommittee's approach during the 1978-1980 period, its emergence as the new majority did not actually much change the Senate's posture. In the House the Democratic majority remained, but it had slipped considerably, and Subcommittee Chairman Van Deerlin, the single most insistent congressional proponent of the rewrite, failed to win reelection. Former Commerce Committee Chairman Harley Staggers (D-W.Va.) had retired, and his successor was John Dingell (D-Mich.). Van Deerlin's replacement in the subcommittee chair was Timothy Wirth (D-Colo.), but because the political balance in the House was even more tenuous than it had been during the previous Congress, the lack of consensus that had been apparent in the subcommittee since the introduction of the first rewrite in 1978 showed little sign of abating. Furthermore, as part of the congressional reorganization and budget realignments associated with the new Congress, Wirth's subcommittee was reassigned additional responsibilities, from some of which it had divested itself in 1975. Renamed the Subcommittee on Tele-communications, Consumer Protection, and Finance, it would no longer have the luxury of focusing exclusively on communications issues.

Meanwhile at the FCC, Chairman Ferris was soon to be replaced by a Reagan appointee Mark Fowler. Several other appointments also became available to the new president, and within a few months the Commission had been redefined even more in the administration's image. Quickly announcing a desire to hasten the process of deregulation, Chairman Fowler invoked a policy of "unregulation" and began to articulate the terms of an explicit "marketplace approach to broadcast regulation" (Fowler and Brenner, 1982).

Though somewhat delayed by the election and the need to assess the possibilities in the light of the new political conditions, the legislative review process never really stopped, and early in the 97th Congress, several new communications bills were introduced. In January 1981, however—even before formal congressional action recommenced—the FCC issued a major radio deregulation order that had figured in the earlier legislative proposals. Completing action on a rulemaking that had been proposed by Chairman Ferris in 1978 and adopting part of the broadcasting deregulation provisions from S. 2827 in 1980, the Commission eliminated rules for radio stations dealing with ascertainment, program logs, and nonentertainment program and commercial time guildelines. Almost immediately thereafter, in the Republican-controlled Senate a bill was introduced to codify the FCC's radio deregulation package as well as to provide for indefinite radio license periods, a random license selection process in place of comparative renewals, and a prohibition on regulation of program formats. Simultaneously, a similar House bill was introduced (HR 1297), along with another (HR 1298) that would further restrict FCC authority to review license applications and would extend license periods to ten years for radio and five for television.

Within a month Senator Goldwater introduced a television measure (S. 601), in effect reiterating the general provisions of S. 270 and extending television license renewals to five years. In March, Senator Packwood proposed a bill (S. 821) that would require imposition of license fees, which, however, were set at such a level as to cover only one-half the costs of FCC regulation. In the House, Subcommittee Chairman Wirth permitted inclusion of a similar provision in the annual FCC funding bill (HR 3239). Also circulated was a bill (HR 4726) that, in addition to the various radio and television deregulatory and license renewal changes common in the Senate and House Republican drafts, would have the FCC establish a point system through which broadcasters might earn renewals by carrying certain amounts of "public interest" programming.

As the battles over President Reagan's first budget (fiscal year 1982) became more intense, telecommunications matters were put aside, save for their discussion in a set of hearings on the status of competition and deregulation held by the House subcommittee in May 1981. That effort would lead to an important report in November, which, for the first time in a number of years, would raise a series of systematic doubts from within a congressional subcommittee about the actual operational merits of much of the deregulatory thinking (U.S. Congress, House of Representatives, 1981a). The primary agenda in both houses, however, continued to center on the S. 270, 601, and 821 sorts of broadcasting changes, plus new measures to extend "long-range" funding for public broadcasting.

The confusions attendant on the complex, bitter struggle over the Reagan budget turned out to provide the Senate Republicans, especially Chairman Packwood, an opportunity to secure passage of certain communications measures. Arguing that their provisions would save $4 million in government regulatory spending, Senator Packwood and his colleagues, over objections by House Telecommunications Subcommittee Chairman Wirth, managed to get leadership approval for including several of the communications measures in the massive budget legislation, the Omnibus Budget Reconciliation Act of 1981 (PL 97-35). This maneuver permitted a number of the more controversial measures, particularly S. 270 and 601, to be worked into the budget legislation in such a way that not only did they not have to be formally debated and reported out of committee, they could also avoid the normal House-Senate conference process on individual bills. In the end chairmen Dingell and Wirth were successful in placing some brakes on the Senate effort, and the budget conference committee members deleted many of the major provisions that remained in the House and Senate bills, taking out, for instance, the radio deregulation package, the comparative license renewal elimination, and the tradeoff between indefinite license renewals and license fees. In the final budget legislation, however, broadcasters did emerge with one important concession—license term extensions (seven years for radio, five for television). The bill also authorized the FCC to begin using a lottery system for initial license assignments. Furthermore, it extended public broadcasting authorizations for fiscal years 1984-1985, although it substantially cut funding levels and facilities support.

The legislation hardly represented the sort of complete coup commercial broadcasters had been seeking. Their agenda had long included, at minimum, such items as confirmation of the FCC's radio deregulation package and its extension to television, plus longer license periods and the end of comparative license renewals; at maximum, deletion of the Fairness Doctrine, permanent license renewals, and, ultimately, elimination of the public interest standard, the hook on which most of the objectionable regulations hung. Nevertheless, the 1981 budget bill was a significant victory for the broadcasters. In exchange for the extended license renewals, they gave up nothing. Although the public interest standard remained in the old legislation, the spectrum fee failed once again, confirming the emerging pattern that "small" regulatory and legislative changes in the industry's favor could be accomplished without any new policy concessions on its part. This was an endorsement of the industry's perception since the early phases of the rewrite that it had little need to engage in any wide-ranging set of policy compromises, that it could oppose a comprehensive effort confident that better terms could be obtained on a piecemeal basis.

In September 1981, the FCC issued a package of proposals for further broadcast legislative revisions. The proposals were organized along two "tracks," the first of which contained relatively, though not entirely, noncontroversial technical, "housekeeping" changes in regulations governing certain Commission practices and conditions. By far more significant were the Track II proposals, which included endorsement of the marketplace-over-regulation policy, elimination of the equal time and fairness doctrines (Section 315), reasonable access (312 [c] [7]) and equitable distribution (307 [b]) provisions of the 1934 act, deletion of the comparative license renewal process, and codification of the earlier set of FCC radio deregulations. The public interest criterion was retained, but only barely. It had been eliminated in preliminary drafts and was reinstated only by special motion during the Commission's formal adoption of the package.

The remaining months of 1981 saw another flurry of broadcast legislation proposals, including some to enact various of the FCC's Track I provisions. But as had been clearly indicated during the fight over the budget bill amendments and as was becoming clear in the competition study, there remained among some in the House subcommittee majority a considerable lack of enthusiasm about the drive for further broadcast deregulation. In light of the budget bill experience, there was concern by Chairman Wirth and others that seemingly innocuous bills on Track I matters not be used to provide the Senate subcommittee and the House minority with platforms to introduce further, more significant changes.

The strategy of building at least a partial dam against the full force of the deregulatory current was reiterated when Chairman Wirth released the staff report on competition in November. The report concluded that, with a few exceptions, the telecommunications and broadcasting industries were still largely uncompetitive and that powerful, dominant market forces still rested with a relatively small group of interests (U.S. Congress, House of Representatives, 1981a, p. 5). The report argued that Congress should reconsider some of the assumptions in deregulation and entertain the possibility of pursuing stronger structural regulations, such as ownership restrictions and mandated access, as opposed to content regulation. This reconsideration theme was underscored in a December hearing, when Energy and Commerce Committee Chairman Dingell restated the traditional principle that "the airways are a public trust . . . , that they do belong to all the people," and that the primary obligation of broadcasters is to serve the public interest and only secondarily to earn a profit (U.S. Congress, House of Representatives, 1981b, p. 63).

Such long-unvoiced views were highly unlikely to stem the entire deregulatory tide. But since the broadcasters' agenda depended on continued efforts to build the case against the spectrum scarcity and fiduciary principles, they had to keep up the pressure and meet even this rearguard action. Accordingly, their representative at the hearing, Erwin Krasnow, felt the situation demanded that he argue that the doctrine of public ownership of the spectrum was "a shibboleth of fiction" (U.S. Congress, House of Representatives, 1981b, p. 121). While this view was not yet central to the congressional perspective, and although it ran against Sections 301 and 309 (h)(1) of the 1934 act and a half century of judicial opinion, it was far more plausible than it had been a decade before, and that it could now be voiced in a congressional hearing suggested that the central policy agenda had shifted much closer to the industry's side. It certainly was being echoed at the FCC, where Chairman Fowler and his legal assistant had been preparing a formal law review paper on broadcast deregulation (Fowler and Brenner, 1982).[4] A brief for a purer marketplace approach, the paper constituted a frontal assault on the spectrum scarcity rationale for regulation and on the fundamental fiduciary principle. It avoided the "unregulation" rubric used in the Chairman's earlier policy statements, but for all intents and purposes the terms of the approach outlined here were the same. The paper discussed the possibility of a spectrum fee, especially as a means for funding public broadcasting. But although the chairman was to tout the concept widely in industry circles, promoting it as a political expedient, the paper was explicit that the spectrum fee should represent no quid pro quo for broadcast deregulation (Fowler and Brenner, 1982, p. 256). It made the argument for the wholesale shift to a marketplace mechanism on the standard libertarian grounds of constitutional protections for speakers (broadcasters) and of minimal government interference in private enterprise.

Accordingly, the pressure for broadcasting deregulation remained strong. Early in 1982, during the second session of the 97th Congress and with strong industry support, broadcasting deregulatory measures were introduced that would encompass and in some cases actually go beyond the Track I and Track II provisions of the 1981 FCC legislative recommendations. In March 1982, the full Senate passed S. 1629, to codify the radio deregulation package, abolish comparative renewals, and direct the FCC to encourage more competition and services in broadcasting. A floor amendment establishing limited license fees was also passed with the bill. By the end of the session the House proved unwilling to adopt a companion bill, though in August both houses and the President did approve a thoroughly revised version of HR 3239, which now contained a number of Track I, license lottery clarification, and other relatively minor, noncontroversial matters. Simultaneously Congress passed and the president signed another large budget reconciliation measure (PL 97-253), which included a provision reducing the size of the FCC from seven to five members, beginning in 1983. Meanwhile, in July the Senate Commerce Committee had readily passed and sent to the floor a bill (S. 2172) that would severely restrict local and state regulatory authority over cable systems.

The activity involving telecommunications legislation was no less complex during the 97th Congress. In 1981, the Senate actually passed a bill (S. 898) that, picking up on provisions of the earlier S. 2827 and HR 6121, provided for a limited restructuring of AT&T and deregulation of certain services. In the House, Chairman Wirth and others in the subcommittee majority remained reluctant to pass a comparable bill, though in December 1981 they finally agreed to introduce a somewhat more restrictive measure (HR 5158) which, while withdrawn in July 1982, could yet serve as the basis for accommodation with the Senate during the next Congress. Meanwhile, the Reagan administration had been attempting to change the government's position in its antitrust suit against AT&T. During prior administrations the Department of Justice had opposed efforts to override the 1956 consent decree, insisting that AT&T remain out of unregulated services absent substantial divestitures within the Bell system. Under the new administration the Department stance shifted, and in January 1982, Justice announced a settlement that, as finally approved in August by Federal Judge Harold Greene and as provided in the FCC's earlier Computer II decision, permits AT&T to enter unregulated data processing services in exchange for spinning off its local (Bell) operating companies.

CONCLUSION

This review of legislative and regulatory activities in recent years suggests something of the obvious but little-discussed way American communications policy has been developing. Masked by all the commotion over the various rewrite efforts and their "failures," the reality of the situation is that there has been under way for some time an incremental process of change shaping a new policy environment.[5] Congress and the White House have so far passed three pieces of legislation. Though each is rather limited, altogether they point toward the terms of the new conditions. In part, the process has involved the public debates over the provisions of the various rewrites. But it has also consisted of a continuing set of private negotiations, primarily between the government and the principally interested industrial parties, during which the policy agenda has been severely constrained. Since the time of the *Options Papers,* the "options" have in fact been relatively narrow and have drifted steadily toward the industry positions.

Simultaneously, the terms of these negotiations have been imposed through the normal process of FCC oversight. The Commission has been regularly and ritualistically denounced by all sides; yet it has served a crucial function for the political process through its efforts to anticipate the legislative intent and to maintain the momentum of policy development. Important conflicts between aspects of the still-existing 1934 legislation and the newer policy trends do remain, and it is possible that, as was the case in the late 1960s and early 1970s, various dissenting parties will turn from the Commission to the courts for resolution. At that point the incentive for some more or less comprehensive legislative package might again arise. But many of the compromises among the more powerful parties that would be necessary for such a package might have already been negotiated, while the weaker interests would have continued to be pushed aside. Therefore, whether the process is comprehensive or piecemeal, the general tendencies of the principal policy provisions are clear, and their adoptions are likely to follow the traditional pattern.

The more thoroughgoing marketplace (unregulation) policy since the 1980 election has been seen by some to constitute a significant shift away from the trends of the previous decade. It is suggested that, more than being just an acceleration in the deregulatory efforts, the new approach is rather a wholesale attack on all facets of regulation (Wiley and Neustadt, 1982). An implication of this concern is that, as it is being applied, unregulation may have consequences that are at odds with the avowed purposes of earlier forms of deregulation. The issue here is whether the stronger marketplace position is merely an intensification of deregulation, wherein the basic goal remains the enhancement of competition, or represents an effort to use the imagery of deregulation to disguise what is in effect nothing more than an effort to secure the dominant position of the preexisting industrial interests. Analysis of FCC decisions such as those in *Computer II* or in the 9Khz AM radio bandwidth case suggests that, not unlike the situation before the advent of deregulation, much current FCC and federal policy does not contribute to as much increased competition as it might.

American public policy in communications and in most other areas continues to emerge through the continuous pressure-cooker process of governmental-industrial interaction. Many parties to the communications rewrite effort may have genuinely contemplated achieving important public service benefits from the full range of tradeoffs. However, the results of the incremental policy adjustment process have been increasingly to the benefit of the major corporate players. For instance, the AT&T settlement resolves certain technological and business anomalies, rationalizing the aspects of communications as commerce, but the divestiture burden on Bell is, next to doing nothing, the least expensive and onerous option the government might have chosen. It is not the same as forcing AT&T to give up Western Electric or Bell Labs. Additionally, just as the settlement terms are minimal, they have the effect of forestalling more serious congressional measures. Once AT&T begins to divest itself of its local companies in 1983, it will be difficult for Congress to make any other major structural—and significant policy—changes. Furthermore, while aspects of competition may indeed be introduced and redound to the benefit of large enterprises involved in massive volumes of data transmission and processing, there remain serious questions about the costs for small, individual telephone users.

A major rationale for broadcasting and cable deregulation had been to foster more voice and access and to remove the danger of government interference implied in FCC authority to review licensee performances. The public interest was to have been preserved by eliminating the public interest standard. In exchange for deregulation, a public dividend of both services and fees was to have been delivered. Under deregulation, however, the emerging terms of industry structure and of program and service content would appear to be leading to results closely resembling the long-term trends in American broadcasting and other media—the steady enhancement of national, commercial entertainment markets. In the meantime, with every incremental step toward deregulation, the spectrum fee is always in danger of elimination. Even though it remains in various current drafts, the fee is established at the most modest levels and designed to accomplish the most limited public service ends.

It may well be, then, that there are contradictions not only in unregulation, but also in the basic terms of deregulation itself. As suggested by the 1982 House majority staff report, there are in fact broader, independent marketplace forces that tend to lead precisely to the anticompetitive conditions deregulation is supposed to avoid. Furthermore there is a long and telling history in these matters that much of the current debate tends to ignore (Smythe, 1972).

In light of these unspoken social and economic assumptions behind the policymaking process, it is possible to reinterpret the meaning of much of the policy adjustments in the last ten to fifteen years. Beginning with the task force phase, the communications policy review process has been doing little more than seeking a means for negotiating the conflicting needs of the major industrial interests already in control of most aspects of American communications. With bows here and there to potential problems of concentration, the needs of various minorities, and the goals of improving access and public participation, the principal policy attitudes expressed in the various reports, rewrite drafts, and regulatory inquiries have echoed the traditional American libertarian view that the principal barrier to free expression and diversity of viewpoint rests in government regulation. Far from actually encouraging any truly new or pluralistic approaches to owning, controlling, and developing the next generation of U.S. telecommunications, the policy review effort has actually tended to reify the major characteristics of the prior conditions.

Contrary to the standard accounts about the newness of the deregulation trends, one can now observe that they are not all that radical. For all the concerns about government interference and anitcompetitiveness often correctly perceived in much public regulation, the long-term consequences of the U.S. administrative apparatus have actually been to preserve a fundamentally private enterprise economy. Deregulation may call for more competition and therefore for more diversity of voice and choice, but it contemplates that competition only within a standard commercial context, without a vision of how to promote true diversity in the broad sense of the term. To the extent that deregulation fosters more competition only among large, national, profit-driven, corporate interests, it represents a relatively small group of actors with a notably narrow range of purposes, a communications process that is still highly contralized and unidirectional, and a rather shallow level of cultural and political experience.

Therefore, after the current phase of intense communications policymaking review reaches some plateau of closure, after all the complex negotiations over all the endless details of the legislative and regulatory options, it may well be true that certain changes will have occurred among the specific technologies available to users and the precise allocation of telecommunications ownership and services. Nonetheless, seen at some distance, those changes will be relatively small and few, and they will represent merely technical adjustments within the framework of a general American communications policy commitment that was well established long before the Radio Act of 1927 and that has since been reinforced through the policymaking process.

NOTES

1. While obviously now dated, a 1958 House subcommittee report (U.S. Congress, House of Representatives, 1958) remains one of the best reviews of congressional legislative activity and its relationship to FCC regulation. Many of the conditions that report described have persisted during the quarter-century since its release.

2. Primary sources for analysis of the rewrite efforts include the bills themselves and the various staff analyses and hearings on them. For discussion of aspects of the events and principal policy issues during the initial effort (1978-1979), see Haight (1979), Krasnow et al. (1982), Lucoff (1980), and Rowland (1980). For the period since, the major secondary sources are the almost weekly trade press accounts in *Broadcasting, Telecommunications Reports,* and *Television Digest.*

3. One (HR 6228), introduced by Al Swift (D-Wash.), would have codified existing FCC cross-ownership rules while also exempting multimedia licensees from renewal challenges on such grounds. The other would have repealed the archaic Lea Act forbidding strikes or collective bargaining by studio musicians. A third measure, involving the perennial attempts to secure a commercial VHF frequency assignment for New Jersey, did not pass in the full House. In 1982 such a measure did pass the Senate as an amendment to the Cannon bill (S. 1629).

4. Editors' note: This article, as well as Smythe, 1982, and Wiley and Neustadt, 1982, is reprinted elsewhere in this volume.

5. There are several other closely related and highly important streams of communications policy review activity currently under way. These include legislative efforts, court suits, and FCC inquiries variously involving such matters as copyright, privacy, electronic mail, home video recorders, low-power television, videotex, and direct broadcast satellite communications. Space does not permit treating them all. However, it would be fair to presume that the conclusions reached here about the significance of the communications policy developments that have been discussed would apply equally well in these other realms.

REFERENCES

Carnegie Commission on Educational Television (1967) Public Television: A Program for Action. New York: Harper & Row.

COLE, B. and M. OETTINGER (1978) Reluctant Regulators. Reading, MA: Addison-Wesley.

Committee for Economic Development (1975) Broadcasting and Cable Television: Policies for Diversity and Change. New York: Author.

Conference Board (1972) Information Technology: Some Critical Implications for Decision Makers. Report 537. New York: Author.

Federal Communications Commission, Network Inquiry Special Staff (1980) New Television Networks: Entry, Jurisdiction, Ownership and Regulation: Final Report. Washington, DC: Author.

FOWLER, M. S. and D. L. BRENNER (1982) "A marketplace approach to broadcast regulation." Texas Law Review 60, 2: 207-257.

HAIGHT, T. R. [ed.] (1979) Telecommunications Policy and the Citizen. New York: Praeger.

KRASNOW, E. G., L. D. LONGLEY, and H. A. TERRY (1982) The Politics of Broadcast Regulation. New York: St. Martin's Press.

LUCOFF, M. (1980) "The rise and fall of the third rewrite." Journal of Communication 30, 3: 47-53.

POPPER, F. (1970) The President's Commissions. New York: Twentieth Century Fund.

ROWLAND, W.D., Jr. (1980) "Public broadcasting: the federal regulatory and policymaking process." Journal of Communication, 30, 3: 139-149.

SIRICO, L.J., Jr. (1979) "Horse trading with Ma Bell: who benefits?" in T. R. Haight (ed.) Telecommunications Policy and the Citizen. New York: Praeger.

Sloan Commission (1971) On the Cable: The Television of Abundance. New York: McGraw-Hill.

SMYTHE, D. W. (1982) "Radio: deregulation and the relation of the private and public sectors." Journal of Communication 32, 1: 192-200.

U.S. Cabinet Committee on Cable Communications (1974) Cable: Report to the President. Washington, DC: Government Printing Office.

U.S. Congress, House of Representatives, 97th Cong., 1st sess., Committee on Energy and Commerce, Subcommittee on Telecommunications, Consumer Protection, and Finance (1981a) Telecommunications in Transition: The Status of Competition in the Telecommunications Industry. Majority Staff Report, November 3. Washington, DC: Government Printing Office.

U.S. Congress, House of Representatives, 97th Cong., 1st sess., Committee on Energy and Commerce, Subcommittee on Telecommunications, Consumer Protection, and Finance (1981b) Hearing: Broadcast Reform Proposals, December 9. Washington, DC: Government Printing Office.

U.S. Congress, House of Representatives, 85th Cong., 2d sess., Committee on Interstate and Foreign Commerce, Special Subcommittee on Legislative Oversight (1958) Regulation of Broadcasting. Study, November. Washington, DC: Government Printing Office.

U.S. Congress, House of Representatives, 94th Cong., 1st sess., Committee on Interstate and Foreign Commerce, Subcommittee on Communications (1976a) Cable Television: Promise versus Regulatory Performance. Staff Report, January. Washington, DC: Government Printing Office.

U.S. Congress, House of Representatives, 94th Cong., 2d sess., Committee on Interstate and Foreign Commerce, Subcommittee on Communications (1976b) Hearings: Cable Television Regulation Oversight, Parts 1 and 2. May, July, August, September. Washington, DC: Government Printing Office.

U.S. Congress, House of Representatives, 95th Cong., 2d sess., Committee on Interstate and Foreign Commerce, Subcommittee on Communications (1977) Options Papers. Staff Report, May. Washington, DC: Government Printing Office.

U.S. President's Task Force on Communications Policy (1969) Final Report. Washington, DC: Government Printing Office.

WILEY, R. E. (1981) "Competition and deregulation in television: the American experience," in L. Lewin (ed.) Telecommunications in the U.S.: Trends and Policies. Dedham, MA: Artech House.

WILEY, R. E. and R. M. NEUSTADT (1982) "U.S. communications policy in the new decade." Journal of Communication 32, 2: 22-32.

Fowler and Brenner argue that the time is overdue for a national communications policy that will account for market forces in radio and television and accommodate the First Amendment rights of those who operate commercial stations. They propose that a trusteeship model of broadcast regulation by which the Federal Communications Commission has regulated program content yield to a deregulated marketplace approach; new program responsibilities could then be assigned to noncommercial broadcasting in a deregulated environment for commercial radio and television. Mark S. Fowler is chairman of the Federal Communications Commission, and Daniel L. Brenner is legal assistant to the FCC chairman.

37

A MARKETPLACE APPROACH TO BROADCAST REGULATION

Mark S. Fowler and Daniel L. Brenner

I. Introduction

Regulation of radio and television by the Federal Communications Commission remains a frequent target for administrative law reformers. The vague licensing criterion provided by Congress—the standard of "public convenience, interest, or necessity"[1]—has provided a starting point for critics dissatisfied with the last fifty-five years of regulatory performance in this area. In applying this criterion, the Commission has built a series of legal fictions into a regulatory environment altogether different from that faced by the media ventures that preceded radio and television, or those that are now being introduced.

The Commission's world of regulation is not without intricacy. To be sanctioned as a licensee, an applicant has to prove it has investigated its community through "ascertainment."[2] Having adduced the needs

---

The views expressed are those of the authors and do not necessarily reflect Commission views. It is not the intent of the authors to express any conclusions about the merits of specific actions currently before the Commission or decided during their tenure.

1. 47 U.S.C. §§ 303, 307(a) (1976).

2. *See* Ascertainment of Community Problems by Broadcast Applicants, 57 F.C.C.2d 418 (1975), *modified*, 61 F.C.C.2d 1 (1976); Primer on Ascertainment of Community Problems by Broadcast Applicants, 27 F.C.C.2d 650 (1971). The ascertainment process includes interviews with community leaders, general public opinion surveys, and demographic studies. Compliance with the Commission's engineering, ownership, and financial requirements must also be shown.

---

and interests of the community, the applicant is expected to propose programming that meets those needs and interests. If the applicant seeks a television license, the Commission's guidelines also require the programming to include a dose of news and public affairs.[3] A further maze of rules details the procedures to be followed[4] if the applicant owns more than one broadcast outlet or is involved in the cable television business,[5] employs more than four people,[6] happens to be an alien,[7] or believes that partisanship, not objectivity, should characterize station programming.[8]

Broadcasting in the United States conforms little to the model contemplated in the Commission's licensing philosophy. Most television stations affiliate with one of the three major commercial networks and delegate many programming decisions to the networks.[9] Acceptable ascertainment by applicants for license renewal or new licenses can amount to five-minute interviews with community leaders and a generic summary of community demographics prepared by a commercial

3. See 47 C.F.R. § 0.281(a)(8)(i) (1981).

4. See, e.g., id. § 73.642(a)(3), (f)(3) (1981); id. § 73.643(a). Deregulation of over-the-air pay television has been underway since 1977, see, e.g., Second Report and Order in Docket No. 21,502, 85 F.C.C.2d 631 (1981) (establishing comparative criteria for subscription television proposals in mutually exclusive application proceedings). The Commission's lease-only policy regarding decoders for subscription television and other restrictions, see Further Notice of Proposed Rule Making in Docket No. 21,502, Subscription Television Service, 88 F.C.C.2d 213 (1981), have recently been eliminated. See FCC News, Mimeo No. 4684 (June 18, 1982).

5. See OFFICE OF PLANS AND POLICY, FCC, POLICY ON CABLE OWNERSHIP (1981).

6. The Commission has required a broadcast station having more than four full-time employees to file an equal employment opportunities (EEO) program consistent with the policy set forth at 47 C.F.R. § 73.2080 (1981) (adopted in 1976, Nondiscrimination in the Employment Policies and Practices of Broadcast Licensees, 60 F.C.C.2d 226 (1976)), and annual EEO reports, FCC Form 395, 98 RAD. REG. (P & F) 395-1. The Commission first adopted formal regulations requiring nondiscrimination and affirmative action in 1969, see Petition for Rulemaking to Require Broadcast Licensees to Show Nondiscrimination in Their Employment Practices, 18 F.C.C.2d 240 (1969), and extended these protections to women in 1971, Equal Employment Program, 32 F.C.C.2d 831 (1971). This Article does not specifically address the Commission's EEO efforts. However, we do note that racial discrimination distorts ownership and employment opportunities in the marketplace and that EEO efforts attempt to remedy this distortion. Commission programs to promote equal treatment of all potential participants in broadcasting, both in employment and ownership, are consistent with a marketplace approach because they ensure that all have an opportunity to compete.

7. 47 U.S.C. § 310(b) (1976). See generally Watkins, Alien Ownership and the Communications Act, 33 FED. COM. L.J. 1 (1981).

8. See 47 U.S.C. § 315(a) (1976); 47 C.F.R. § 73.1910 (1981); Brandywine-Main Line Radio, Inc. v. FCC, 473 F.2d 16 (D.C. Cir. 1972), cert. denied, 412 U.S. 922 (1973).

9. See En Banc Programming Inquiry, 44 F.C.C. 2303, 2314 (1960); 2 OFFICE OF NETWORK STUDY, FCC, SECOND INTERIM REPORT, TELEVISION NETWORK PROGRAM PROCUREMENT 199 (1965) ("[T]he composition of the network schedule, as a real matter, becomes a highly limiting factor in the licensee's ability to serve his community."); see also 1 NETWORK INQUIRY SPECIAL STAFF, FCC, NEW TELEVISION NETWORKS: ENTRY, JURISDICTION, OWNERSHIP AND REGULATION 298 (1980) ("[E]ach of the network forms considered in this chapter that use interstate facilities to distribute programs appears to have, or likely may have, a substantial impact on the broadcast service delivered to viewers.").

research firm. The ascertainment process typically produces a perfunctory listing of community needs and of standard programs to fulfill those needs, often compiled in Washington by the broadcaster's attorney or the attorney's paralegal. The process also borders on the unseemly from a constitutional standpoint, since the Commission's zeal in reviewing program proposals treads on the editorial independence guaranteed by the first amendment to broadcasters. But year in, year out, the Commission has urged broadcasters to conduct these exercises and to carry public affairs programs that broadcasters may not want to carry and, apparently, few viewers elect to watch. Both the license renewal rate and the profits for most of the broadcasting business have been so high that neither the regulated nor the regulators have been anxious to challenge the system.[10]

The Commission's fiduciary approach to broadcast regulation may be ending at last. Competition to over-the-air broadcasting from new media has led to an awareness that traditional broadcasting is just one of many information delivery systems.[11] Technological plenty is forcing a widespread reconsideration of the role competition can play in broadcast regulation. And regulators and others have become increasingly aware that regulatory processes have infringed the first amendment rights of broadcasters without a sufficiently compelling constitutional justification.

This Article proposes a new direction for governmental regulation of broadcasting in the United States. The ideas raised are not entirely new, but they have been ignored by those who have been busy raising and lowering the drawbridge of licensing. Our thesis is that the perception of broadcasters as community trustees should be replaced by a view of broadcasters as marketplace participants. Communications policy should be directed toward maximizing the services the public desires. Instead of defining public demand and specifying categories of

10. *See generally* B. COLE & M. OETTINGER, RELUCTANT REGULATORS 36-49 (1978). The industry's renewal record is nearly perfect, standing at about 99%. In the last 40 years, only two licensees have lost licenses as a result of petitions to deny, *see* Office of Communication of United Church of Christ v. FCC, 425 F.2d 543 (D.C. Cir. 1969); Alabama Educ. Television Comm'n, 50 F.C.C.2d 461 (1975). These cases provide slim precedent for predicting renewal activity because the offending practices in both cases involved overt racial discrimination. Since the advent of television, only two licensees have been denied renewal in favor of a competing applicant on a purely comparative basis. *See* Greater Boston Television Corp. v. FCC (WHDH-TV), 444 F.2d 841 (D.C. Cir. 1970), *cert. denied*, 403 U.S. 923, *reopening denied*, 463 F.2d 268 (D.C. Cir. 1971); Simon Geller (WVCA-FM, Gloucester, Mass.), FCC Report No. 17,007, Mimeo No. 4193 (May 21, 1982).

11. *See* Report and Order on Direct Broadcast Satellite Service, FCC News, Mimeo No. 4775 (June 23, 1982). *See generally* NATIONAL ASS'N OF BROADCASTERS, NEW TECHNOLOGIES AFFECTING RADIO AND TELEVISION (1981).

programming to serve this demand, the Commission should rely on the broadcasters' ability to determine the wants of their audiences through the normal mechanisms of the marketplace. The public's interest, then, defines the public interest. And in light of the first amendment's heavy presumption against content control, the Commission should refrain from insinuating itself into program decisions made by licensees.

A. Economics and Broadcasting

The proposition that consumers are best off when society's economic resources are allocated in a manner that enables people to satisfy their wants as fully as possible permeates all sectors of our economy.[12] Depending on what goods or services are involved, consumer satisfaction is enhanced by freedom of choice in the price, quality, or variety of products. We increase social utility by promoting competition, removing artificial barriers to entry, preventing any one firm from controlling price or eliminating its competitors, and in general establishing conditions that allow the price of goods to be as close as possible to their cost of production.[13]

Although we have relied on free markets to provide most of the goods and services in our society for over 200 years, this has not been the case in the broadcast industry. For a variety of reasons, the Commission has traditionally refused to recognize the undeniable fact that commercial broadcasting is a business. But it is a business, one that faces increasing competition in the years ahead for the eyes and ears of its audience.[14] The first step in a marketplace approach to broadcast regulation, then, is to focus on broadcasters not as fiduciaries of the public, as their regulators have historically perceived them, but as marketplace competitors.

B. Spectrum Markets

A threshold difficulty in applying a marketplace approach to commercial broadcasting lies in the definition of the market. Broadcasters differ from some other information providers because they receive exclusive use of an assigned frequency; the frequencies reserved for broadcasters are not available for nonbroadcasting uses regardless of

12. *See* A. SMITH, AN INQUIRY INTO THE NATURE AND CAUSES OF THE WEALTH OF NATIONS, (1st ed. Edinburgh 1776), *reprinted in* ADAM SMITH (R. Hutchins ed. 1952); *see also* R. BORK, ANTITRUST THEORY AND PRACTICE 92-106 (1981); B. OWEN, ECONOMICS AND FREEDOM OF EXPRESSION 26-31 (1975).

13. *See* R. BORK, *supra* note 12, at 93-94.

14. "Glamour and social influence not withstanding [sic], television is a business." B. OWEN, J. BEEBE & W. MANNING, JR., TELEVISION ECONOMICS 3 (1974).

demand. In a true marketplace, broadcasters would compete with all potential users of the airwaves for the exclusive right to use a particular frequency, just as they must compete with other businesses for land, labor, buildings, equipment, and other factors of production. The spectrum market would consist of those buying and selling rights to use frequencies on an exclusive, protected basis.

It is difficult to define frequency rights in familiar terms. Those who hold rights to occupy a plot of land or to mine the minerals beneath its surface can establish precisely the dimensions of their claims, but broadcast frequencies are intangibles that exist only in conjunction with the technical apparatus for transmission and reception. The difficulty in defining the right to a frequency has led, on the one hand, to nearly mystical assertions about particulate flowing in the "ether"[15] and, on the other hand, to an unproductive debate over who "owns" the airwaves, the public or the broadcaster.[16]

Yet the Commission has allocated radio frequencies for a long time and spectrum users have accepted the system. The user's right is based in the government's provision of exclusivity to a patch of spectrum with sanctions, both civil and criminal, meted out to those who "trespass" with the user's exclusive enjoyment. Having said this, the broadcasting marketplace comes into focus: it consists of those seeking government-granted *exclusivities*.

A marketplace approach to exclusive use of radio frequencies would open all positions in the electromagnetic spectrum to bidding by those who want them. As with the allocation of other goods in society,[17] the highest bidder would acquire exclusive rights to a particular frequency. In the fully deregulated marketplace, the highest bidder would make the best and highest use of the resource.[18] R.H. Coase set forth the contours of this approach to the electromagnetic spectrum,

15. This point of view appears in discussions of the legal status of airspace, *see, e.g.,* C. ALEX-ANDROWICZ, THE LAW OF GLOBAL COMMUNICATIONS 27-28 (1971) (citing author's translation of SIBERT, 1 TRAITE DE DROIT INTERNATIONAL PUBLIC 848 (1951) ("Can a State which is between the two above States (i.e., between the State of origin of waves and the State of their destination) stop the passage of radio waves which are in transit above its territory?").

16. *Broadcast Reform Proposals: Hearings on H.R. 4726, H.R. 4780, and H.R. 4781 Before the Subcomm. on Telecommunications of the House Comm. on Energy and Communications*, 97th Cong., 1st Sess. 63 (1981) (remarks of Rep. Dingell). *Contra* Jaffe, *The Editorial Responsibility of the Broadcaster: Reflections on Fairness and Access*, 85 HARV. L. REV. 768, 783 (1972).

17. Such arrangements should not seem peculiar. Putting aside zoning considerations, a plot of land theoretically will be purchased by whichever user can make the highest and best use of it. If the land is twice as valuable when used for a six-story apartment building than for a gasoline station, the apartment builder will pay more for it in a competitive economy. Similarly, if a particular radio frequency is more valuable to a company offering car phone service than to an independent UHF television outlet, the former would outbid the latter in a deregulated market.

18. R. BORK, *supra* note 12, at 98.

and broadcasting in particular, in 1959.[19] Professor Coase observed that producers generally obtain more of a desired resource when buying it on the open market. If forced to bid for unused frequencies or to buy them from existing users, broadcasters would draw the frequencies away from other industries only if they paid more for them, and vice versa.[20] The pricing mechanism would bring the costs of spectrum use in line with those of other factors of production used in broadcasting or any other business.[21]

Commenting on Coase's argument, Professor Harry Kalven concluded that "the perspective is so radical by today's views that although I am persuaded of its correctness, I am not clear how it can be used in public discussion."[22] More than fifty years of regulatory precedent, now compounded by the settled expectations of the public and the broadcasting industry, would make it difficult to conduct an auction of the entire electromagnetic spectrum. And to its credit, the system of centralized grants probably contributes to the development of more efficient uses of frequency bands, forcing users to develop better tuners and transmitters to enhance their signal rather than consume more spectrum on the perimeter.[23]

In any event, Congress early on decided to abandon market forces in determining grants of exclusivity to the spectrum. Probably because commercial radio had already established squatter's rights to some frequencies, Congress reserved a portion of the spectrum (and, in fact, not a very large portion in terms of the frequencies that could be used for broadcasting) for radio and later television. This was the original electromagnetic sin. Regardless of what the marketplace would have man-

19. Coase, *The Federal Communications Commission*, 2 J.L. & ECON. 1 (1959). Some of the ideas presented in Coase's article first appeared in Note, *Old Standards in a New Context: A Comparative Analysis of FCC Regulation*, 18 U. CHI. L. REV. 78 (1950); *see also* Herzel, *Public Interest and the Market in Color Television Regulation*, 18 U. CHI. L. REV. 802 (1951).

20. Adoption of a pricing mechanism for exclusive use might require the government, a heavy user of the radio spectrum for military and civilian purposes, to pay its way, although such uses could remain exempt from such market forces. *See* M. MUELLER, PROPERTY RIGHTS IN RADIO COMMUNICATION: THE KEY TO THE REFORM OF TELECOMMUNICATIONS REGULATION 38 (Cato Institute Policy Analysis Series, 1982).

21. Coase, *supra* note 19, at 20-22.

22. Kalven, *Broadcasting, Public Policy, and The First Amendment*, 10 J.L. & ECON. 15, 30 (1967).

23. Spectrum-saving techniques have been particularly adapted to land mobile radio. One system, amplitude compandered single sideband transmission (ACSB), enables two-way radio to transmit over channels five kilohertz wide. Voice channels have traditionally been five or six times as wide. The number of channels could increase in that part of the spectrum—from low band through 800 megahertz—from 1,600 to 8,313. *See* Wilmotte, *ACSB: Spectrum Efficiency for the Future?*, TELOCATOR, June 1980, at 20. Cellular radio, which provides a service similar to land mobile radio, primarily through car telephones, also employs spectrum-saving technology.

dated, broadcasting was to be entitled, as of right, to a number of exclusive channels.

II. The Trusteeship Model

Instead of being exchanged as a property right, exclusivity to a radio frequency has been assigned by the Commission on the amorphous "public interest" standard. Broadcaster responsibility officially runs to the viewing public as defined by the Commission, not to shareholders, sponsors,[24] or even the users of the sponsors' products or services who indirectly finance the stations. Two considerable evils have come from this arrangement: "broadcasters take advantage of the public-interest myth to promote a variety of protectionist policies, motivated in fact by economic self-interest . . . [and] . . . the public at large is misled in its perception of the role and function of broadcasting in America."[25] In short, by abandoning a marketplace approach in the determination of spectrum utilization, the government created a tension, in both first amendment and economic terms, that haunts communications policy to this day.

A. *The Origins of the Model*

The trusteeship model of broadcast regulation can be traced to the beginning of radio regulation in the United States in the early part of the twentieth century. Federal regulation of radio broadcasting emerged in the early part of the century out of the congestion in ship-to-shore and ship-to-ship communications, which the Department of the Navy described as an "etheric bedlam produced by numerous stations all trying to communicate at once."[26] Congress perceived spectrum scarcity to be a significant enough problem to justify federal oversight and abandonment of market techniques in spectrum management, and enacted the Radio Act of 1912,[27] which forbade operation of a radio apparatus without a license from the Secretary of Commerce and Labor. The limited regulatory power of the Commerce Department, however, did not extend beyond the role of nondiscriminating

24. The role of the sponsor's influence on program decisionmaking is detailed in E. BARNOUW, THE SPONSOR (1978).

25. B. OWEN, J. BEEBE & W. MANNING, JR., *supra* note 14, at 12.

26. "Mischievous and irresponsible operators seem to take great delight in impersonating other stations and sending out false calls. It is not putting the case too strongly to state that the situation is intolerable, and is continually growing worse." S. REP. No. 659, 61st Cong., 2d Sess. 4 (1910).

27. Ch. 287, 37 Stat. 302 (1912), *repealed by* Communications Act of 1934, ch. 652, § 602(a), 48 Stat. 1064, 1102.

registrar,[28] and the result was a frequency free-for-all in the mid-1920's, that doomed the 1912 scheme.[29]

The Radio Act of 1927[30] represented Congress' response to fifteen years of inadequate regulation. The Act was largely replicated in the Communications Act of 1934,[31] which transferred the powers of broadcasting regulation to a new federal agency, the Federal Communications Commission. The Act empowered the Commission to license radio stations in the "public convenience, interest, or necessity," providing for a "fair, efficient, and equitable distribution of radio service" to all communities.[32] The licensing scheme, with its inquiries into program service, received broad approval from the Supreme Court in the 1943 decision, *NBC v. United States*.[33] As Justice Frankfurter viewed it, the "confusion and chaos" existing prior to 1927

> was attributable to certain basic facts about radio as a means of communication—its facilities are limited; they are not available to all who may wish to use them; the radio spectrum simply is not large enough to accommodate everybody. There is a fixed natural limitation upon the number of stations that can operate without interfering with one another.[34]

The Supreme Court has described the "public convenience, interest, or necessity" standard as a "supple instrument for the exercise of discretion by the expert body which Congress has charged to carry out its legislative policy."[35] In reality, the meaning of this standard may be closer to the views of a commentator who concluded in 1930 that it meant "about as little as any phrase that the drafters of the Act could have used and still comply with the constitutional requirement that there be some standard to guide the administrative wisdom of the li-

---

28. Secretary of Commerce Herbert Hoover attempted to limit the number of radio licenses by using his authority under the Act of 1912. The courts, however, held that the Secretary lacked the power to refuse license applications or to choose the wavelength that a licensee could use. *See* Hoover v. Intercity Radio Co., 286 F. 1003 (D.C. Cir. 1923), *appeal dismissed*, 266 U.S. 636 (1924); United States v. Zenith Radio Corp., 12 F.2d 614 (N.D. Ill. 1926).

29. Judicial limitations imposed on the Commerce Department led to a rush for radio licenses. In the nine months following United States v. Zenith Radio Corp., 12 F.2d 614 (N.D. Ill. 1926), *discussed in* note 28 *supra*, more than 200 stations went on the air. The result was widespread signal interference. *See* Coase, *supra* note 19, at 51. *See generally* 1 E. BARNOUW, A HISTORY OF BROADCASTING IN THE UNITED STATES: A TOWER IN BABEL 94-122 (1966). At least one state court delineated private property rights in radio frequencies during this period. *See* Tribune Co. v. Oak Leaves Broadcasting Station (Cir. Ct., Cook County, Ill. 1926), *reprinted in* 68 CONG. REC. 216 (1926).

30. Ch. 169, 44 Stat. 1162, *repealed by* Communications Act of 1934, ch. 652, § 602(a), 48 Stat. 1064, 1102.

31. Ch. 652, 48 Stat. 1064 (codified in scattered sections of 47 U.S.C.).

32. 47 U.S.C. §§ 303, 307(a), 307(b) (1976).

33. 319 U.S. 190 (1943).

34. *Id.* at 213 (footnote omitted).

35. FCC v. Pottsville Broadcasting Co., 309 U.S. 134, 138 (1940).

censing authority."[36]

Over the years the Commission has gradually developed the trusteeship approach, fleshing out the programming obligations of broadcasters under the "public convenience, interest, or necessity" standard. In 1946 the Commission published the so-called "Blue Book," named after the hue of its cover, entitled *Public Service Responsibility of Broadcast Licensees*.[37] Although never actively enforced, the Blue Book stated that the Commission "proposes to give particular consideration" to four types of programming: (1) local and network programs that were carried on a sustaining (i.e., noncommercial) basis; (2) local live programs; (3) programs devoted to discussion of public issues; and (4) station efforts to limit the amount of time it devoted to hourly advertising.[38]

The Commission's next major effort to influence broadcaster service appeared in the *Report and Statement of Policy* in its *En Banc Programming Inquiry*,[39] which it issued in 1960 in the wake of the quiz show scandals on network television.[40] The 1960 *Statement* emphasized the importance of broadcaster service to the community: "The principal ingredient of such obligation consists of a diligent, positive and continuing effort by the licensee to discover and fulfill the tastes, needs and desires of his service area. If he has accomplished this he has met his public responsibility."[41] The *Statement* recognized that the

---

36. Caldwell, *The Standard of Public Interest, Convenience or Necessity as Used in the Radio Act of 1927*, 1 AIR L. REV. 295, 296 (1930).

37. FCC, PUBLIC SERVICE RESPONSIBILITY OF BROADCAST LICENSEES (1946). The Commission invoked this policy statement in several renewal decisions, *see, e.g.,* Eugene J. Roth (Mission Broadcasting Co.), 12 F.C.C. 102 (1947); Howard W. Davis, 12 F.C.C. 91 (1947); Community Broadcasting Co., 12 F.C.C. 85 (1947). The Blue Book is discussed in Deregulation of Radio, 84 . F.C.C.2d 960, 994-95 (1981).

38. In 1949, the Commission issued an additional content pronouncement, which encouraged stations to express their editorial viewpoints on the air. Editorializing by Broadcast Licensees, 13 F.C.C. 1246 (1949). At that time, the Commission created the two-pronged "fairness doctrine," which obligated licensees to cover controversial issues of public importance and afford coverage for contrasting viewpoints. Congress subsequently codified the doctrine in 47 U.S.C. § 315(a) (1976). *See generally* Note, *The Future of Content Regulation in Broadcasting,* 69 CALIF. L. REV. 555, 561-66 (1981). Until 1981 the right to editorialize applied only to commercial broadcasters. Under 1981 amendments to the Communications Act, a noncommercial educational broadcast station may engage in editorializing if it does not receive a grant from the Corporation for Public Broadcasting. Omnibus Budget Reconciliation Act, Pub. L. No. 97-35, § 1229, 95 Stat. 357, 730 (1981) (amending 47 U.S.C. § 399 (1976)).

39. 44 F.C.C. 2303 (1960).

40. The scandals resulted from the proliferation of prime-time quiz programs offering large financial prizes. Some of these were rigged in order to prolong the appearances of the most intriguing contestants. Curiously, the only alleged "crimes" involved charges of perjury before the House of Representatives and New York City investigators. *See Hearings on Television Quiz Shows Before A Special Subcomm. on Legislative Oversight of the House Comm. on Interstate and Foreign Commerce* (pt. 1), 86th Cong., 1st Sess. (1959).

41. 44 F.C.C. at 2312.

Commission "may not condition the grant, denial or revocation of a broadcast license upon its own subjective determination of what is or is not a good program."[42] Yet, because the broadcaster is required to act in the public interest, the Commission did not view itself as "barred by the Constitution or by statute from exercising any responsibility with respect to programming."[43]

The *Statement* articulates fourteen "major elements [of programming] usually necessary to meet the public interest, needs and desires of the community . . . ."[44] The major change established by the *Statement* was the insertion of the ascertainment exercise into the application process.[45] Ascertainment was supposed to be the way for a station to factor the fourteen major elements into its program service. In order to enable broadcasters and their lawyers to prepare initial and renewal applications with adequate specificity, the Commission has issued a series of primers that articulate an acceptable scheme for determining community needs.[46] Since 1960, the Commission has adopted percentage guidelines for news and public affairs programs, which were eliminated for radio but remain in effect for television.[47]

---

42. *Id.* at 2308.

43. *Id.* at 2309. The schizophrenic tone of these introductory remarks characterizes the response of the 1960 *Statement* to the problem of regulating programming content without doing so directly. This on-again, off-again approach also appeared in the discussion of licensee responsibility for broadcasts. Thus, the Commission initially stated, "This duty is personal to the licensee and may not be delegated." *Id.* at 2313. But in the next paragraph it observed that licensees place " 'practical reliance' on networks for the selection and supervision of network programs which, of course, are the principal broadcast fare of the vast majority of television stations throughout the country." *Id.* at 2314.

44. *Id.* These major elements are: (1) opportunity for local self-expression, (2) development and use of local talent, (3) programs for children, (4) religious programs, (5) educational programs, (6) public affairs programs, (7) editorials by licensees, (8) political broadcasts, (9) agricultural programs, (10) news programs, (11) weather and market reports, (12) sports programs, (13) service to minority groups, and (14) entertainment programs. *Id.*

45. *Id.* at 2316. The 1960 *Statement* provided generalized requirements for stations for the determination of tastes, needs, and desires, and the manner in which the licensees could propose to meet them. Subsequent efforts to articulate with specificity the steps necessary to perfect this generalized ascertainment requirement have led to overregulation. *See supra* notes 2-8 and accompanying text.

46. The 1981 radio deregulation order eliminated this scheme for AM and FM licensees, but it remains in force for television licensees. 84 F.C.C.2d 960 (1981).

47. Television deregulation has been proposed along the lines of radio deregulation. *See infra* note 155.

The other major content-related pronouncements, both issued in 1974, avoid specific content obligations for broadcasters. *See* Children's Television Report and Policy Statement, 50 F.C.C.2d 1 (1974), *aff'd sub nom.* Action for Children's Television v. FCC, 564 F.2d 458 (D.C. Cir. 1977); Handling of Public Issues Under the Fairness Doctrine and the Public Interest Standards of the Communications Act, 48 F.C.C.2d 1 (1974), *reconsideration denied*, 58 F.C.C.2d 691 (1976), *aff'd sub nom.* National Citizens Comm. for Broadcasting v. FCC, 567 F.2d 1095 (D.C. Cir. 1977). A 1979 report criticized commercial broadcasters for failing to make a meaningful effort to air programs for children, and explored a myriad of regulatory alternatives. OFFICE OF PLANS AND

The Commission thus has not hesitated to consider program content and prescribe categories of desirable programming when defining the duties of licensees. Governmental guidance in broadcast decision-making, the fundamental characteristic of the trusteeship model, sets it apart from a marketplace approach.

B. The First Amendment and the Model

The first amendment to the Constitution and section 326 of the Communications Act[48] both forbid censorship of broadcasters. There is a tension between these prohibitions and the Commission's examination of past or proposed programming to determine which of several competing applicants should receive a license.[49] The Commission does employ noncontent criteria to distinguish among applicants, e.g., in considering whether an applicant already has media properties in the community,[50] whether station owners will be involved in the daily management of the station,[51] and whether the applicant's record in providing equal employment opportunity is adequate.[52] But if all other

POLICY, FCC, TELEVISION PROGRAMMING FOR CHILDREN: A REPORT OF THE CHILDREN'S TELEVISION TASK FORCE (1979).

48. 47 U.S.C. § 326 (1976).

49. 47 C.F.R. § 0.281(a)(10) (1981). The Commission's policies concerning the weight to be given past or proposed programming in renewal proceedings have been vexing. The Policy Statement on Comparative Broadcast Hearings, 1 F.C.C.2d 393 (1965), established criteria for initial licensing. The Commission subsequently held that this statement governed the introduction of evidence in comparative renewal hearings, Seven (7) League Productions, Inc. (WIII), 1 F.C.C.2d 1597, 1598 (1965), but the criteria to be used and the weight to be accorded each criterion has remained in a state of flux. The Commission unsuccessfully attempted to establish a policy to assure renewal to incumbent licensees whose past program performance was deemed "superior." Policy Statement Concerning Comparative Hearings Involving Regular Renewal Applicants, 22 F.C.C.2d 424 (1970). Under this scheme, renewal would be guaranteed:

  if the applicant for renewal of license shows in a hearing with a competing applicant that
  its program service during the preceding license term has been substantially attuned to
  meeting the needs and interests of its area, and that the operation of the station has not
  otherwise been characterized by serious deficiencies . . . .

Id. at 425 (footnotes omitted). This statement was nullified in Citizens Communications Center v. FCC, 447 F.2d 1201 (D.C. Cir. 1971), on the ground that it violated § 309(e) of the Communications Act of 1934, 47 U.S.C. § 309(e) (1976), which requires a hearing by anyone seeking to compete for an application. *See* Brenner, *Toward A New Balance in License Renewals*, 17 J. BROADCASTING 63, 71 (1972-1973). The Commission has clarified with ardor the weight to be given past program service in a comparative proceeding for renewal. *See* Cowles Broadcasting, Inc., 60 F.C.C.2d 372 (1976), *clarified*, 62 F.C.C.2d 953 (1977), *vacated and remanded sub nom.* Central Fla. Enters., Inc. v. FCC, 598 F.2d 37 (D.C. Cir. 1978), *decided on remand*, Cowles Broadcasting, Inc., 86 F.C.C.2d 993 (1981), *aff'd sub nom.* Central Fla. Enters., Inc. v. FCC, No. 81-1795 (D.C. Cir. July 13, 1982). The Commission recently began a review of its renewal policies. *See* Formulation of Policies Relating to the Broadcast Renewal Applicant Stemming from the Comparative Hearing Process, 88 F.C.C.2d 21 (1981).

50. 47 C.F.R. § 0.281(a)(1) (1981); Policy Statement on Comparative Broadcast Hearings, 1 F.C.C.2d 393, 394 (1965).

51. Policy Statement on Comparative Broadcast Hearings, 1 F.C.C.2d 393, 395-98 (1965).

52. 47 C.F.R. § 0.281(a)(5) (1981); *see supra* note 6.

criteria are equal, the Commission looks at the content of proposed programs. Historically, the Commission has attempted to avoid content criteria. Nevertheless, because these criteria most directly predict what service to expect from an applicant, the Commission cannot avoid considering such criteria under the judgmental directive of the "public interest."

The mandate for intrusion into program service of a licensee under the public interest standard was best formulated, and legitimated, by Justice Frankfurter in *NBC v. United States*.[53] Justice Frankfurter stated that the Commission is more than a "traffic officer, policing the wave lengths to prevent stations from interfering with each other. . . . [T]he Act does not restrict the Commission merely to supervision of the traffic. It puts upon the Commission the burden of determining the composition of that traffic."[54] As Justice Frankfurter explained, the Commission's licensing function goes beyond finding an absence of technical objection to the granting of a license: "If the criterion of 'public interest' were limited to such matters, how could the Commission choose between two applicants for the same facilities, each of whom is financially and technically qualified to operate a station?"[55]

The times were perhaps different when Justice Frankfurter considered these matters. A Supreme Court Justice in the 1940's could not ignore the importance of a news service during wartime, nor could he easily dispute the public policy of mandating broadcaster "responsibility" in such times. Then, too, Justice Frankfurter was asked in *NBC v. United States* to consider the first amendment rights of broadcasters in a case having nothing to do with broadcasters as journalists. At issue instead were the Commission's "chain broadcasting" rules, which restricted what were perceived to be anticompetitive practices of the radio networks.[56]

The first amendment implications of governmental inquiry into broadcast service are evident today, even if they were obscure in 1943. For example, the Commission compares a television station's programming with "guidelines" about the percentage of news, public affairs, and other nonentertainment programs a station should carry, although the Commission does not consider the content and scheduling of these

    53. 319 U.S. 190 (1943). Known as the "Network Case," the decision caused NBC to divest itself of one of its two radio networks, which in turn paved the way for creation of ABC.
    54. *Id*. at 215-16.
    55. *Id*. at 216-17.
    56. For a discussion of these rules in the early days of network broadcasting, see 2 NETWORK INQUIRY SPECIAL STAFF, *supra* note 9, at 60-63.

programs.[57] A similar review would be forbidden if made of column inches in a newspaper or magazine to determine whether to grant newsrack or newsstand space, or permission to publish. So long as program review is part of the licensing process—and, under the Frankfurter formulation of public interest, it will remain so—first amendment problems will persist.

C. Economic Implications of the Trusteeship Model

Besides undermining the first amendment rights of broadcasters, the trusteeship role of the Commission has also distorted competition in the broadcasting marketplace. On the ground that advertiser support of over-the-air broadcasting is essential, courts have ordered the Commission to consider the competitive consequences of market entry. Despite the Supreme Court's admonition in 1940 in *FCC v. Sanders Brothers Radio Station*[58] that competition, not regulation, should characterize broadcasting, the D.C. Court of Appeals in *Carroll Broadcasting Co. v. FCC* held that the Commission should engage in limited vigilantism against newcomers to a local market.[59]

Under the *Carroll* doctrine, when an existing licensee offers proof of the detrimental economic impact of a new station, the Commission must consider such evidence and, if substantial, deny the competitor's license. The application of this formula to another industry would seem ludicrous. Imagine a city council attempting to bar the addition of a second motion picture theater on the basis of an existing theater's claim that the town was not big enough for both. But in effect this is how the court of appeals insisted that the Commission oversee entry into broadcasting. Although the Commission has never used the *Carroll* doctrine to foreclose issuance of a new license, it remains part of the arsenal used by existing licensees to forestall competition.

Other efforts to protect existing broadcasters from competition turned up in the Commission's policies to stunt the development of cable and subscription television. These policies raised barriers to entry and discouraged rather than encouraged more service offerings.[60]

---

57. 47 C.F.R. § 0.281(a)(8) (1981). The Commission declined to adopt percentage standards as a condition for renewal, but proceeded instead on a case-by-case basis. Formulation of Policies Relating to the Broadcast Renewal Applicant Stemming from the Comparative Hearing Process, 66 F.C.C.2d 419 (1977), *aff'd sub nom.* National Black Media Coalition v. FCC, 589 F.2d 578 (D.C. Cir. 1978).

58. 309 U.S. 470, 474 (1940); *see infra* text accompanying note 115.

59. 258 F.2d 440 (D.C. Cir. 1958). The Department of Justice rejected the Commission's request to appeal this decision to the Supreme Court.

60. *See* HOUSE SUBCOMM. ON COMMUNICATIONS OF THE COMM. ON INTERSTATE AND FOR-

Their misguided premise was that trustees could carry out their stewardship only in an environment protected from "ruinous" competition. Abandoned by the Commission in the late 1970's,[61] these policies evidence yet another downside to the trusteeship model.

The responsibilities imposed under the trusteeship model turn an operator into a super-citizen, with obligations that go beyond providing goods and services that the public wants. The system promotes "taxation by regulation," as one commentator called it.[62] The incidental costs of licensure would vanish if there were no program-tied licensing criteria. Furthermore, because the licenses have become imbued with a "community service" character, they have lost some of their marketplace attributes. Consequently, broadcast licensees have been subjected to restrictions that bear no relation to the marketplace. For instance, even though the Communications Act authorizes the President to shut down a radio frequency during a national emergency or the threat of one,[63] aliens have always been denied the right to become licensees.[64] No similar condition attaches to other important forms of mass communication.[65] Most significantly, broadcasting stations cannot be bought and sold freely. Licensees who acquire broadcast properties solely for quick resale can be accused of "trafficking" in the properties and the Commission can set aside their transfer of ownership.[66] The Commission must also approve a transfer before a new owner can assume control, again thwarting efficient management. This insistence on voluntary transfers, comparable to equerries exchanging stud horses for the betterment of the sport, has deflated prices for some broadcast properties. Unlike other business entities, broadcast stations cannot be the objects of unfriendly takeovers.

EIGN COMMERCE, 94TH CONG., 2D SESS., CABLE TELEVISION: PROMISE VERSUS REGULATORY PERFORMANCE (Subcomm. Print 1976).

61. Cable Television Syndicated Program Exclusivity Rules, 71 F.C.C.2d 951 (1979); Inquiry Into the Economic Relationship Between Television Broadcasting and Cable Television, 71 F.C.C.2d 632 (1979). These reports led the Commission to eliminate its distant signal and syndicated exclusivity rules, which had restricted the types of programs cable systems could carry. Cable Television Syndicated Program Exclusivity Rules, 79 F.C.C.2d 652 (1980), affirmed sub nom. Malrite T.V. v. FCC, 652 F.2d 1140 (2d Cir. 1981).

62. Posner, Taxation by Regulation, 2 BELL J. ECON. & MGMT. SCI. 22, 23 (1971).

63. 47 U.S.C. § 606(c) (1976).

64. Id. § 310(b) (1976).

65. See K. CROWE, AMERICA FOR SALE (1978). Efforts by foreigners to control the American press range from the short-lived attempt to buy the New York Trib., which was the object of an aborted takeover by the South African government as part of a plan to gain influence abroad, Wash. Post, Apr. 3, 1979, at A1; id. Apr. 8, 1979, at A19, to the much-publicized endeavors of Australian Rupert Murdoch, currently owner of the New York Post.

66. The Commission has authorized its staff to deny licenses to those accused of having a history of short-term buying and selling of broadcast properties. 47 C.F.R. § 0.281(a)(2) (1981). But see infra note 164.

The grandest myth of the trusteeship concept is the belief that the value of licenses has remained unchanged since their granting. The Commission has ignored the fact that tremendous wealth attaches to the most desirable licenses, whose value far exceeds the tangible assets of the stations holding them.[67] Instead of adopting regulations that would reflect the actual value of these licenses, the Commission has buried its head deeper into the regulation books and considered additional behavioral rules. Such efforts have merely produced more obligations for these special public stewards who, in turn, are usually willing to comply with whatever the Commission asks, as long as the cost of compliance is slight.

D.   The Flawed Rationales Supporting the Model

1. Defects of the Scarcity Rationale. —Spectrum scarcity always has been the cornerstone of the justification for abandoning the marketplace approach and reducing first amendment protection for broadcasters. The Supreme Court pointed to spectrum scarcity in its ratification of the trusteeship model in *NBC*, and the Court has cited scarcity in some of its other, although not in all, pronouncements supporting Commission content regulation.[68] But the use of spectrum scarcity to justify "public interest" determinations over licensees is fraught with serious logical and empirical infirmities.

First, virtually all goods in society are scarce. In most sectors of the economy, the interplay of supply and demand regulates the distribution of goods. If a good becomes especially scarce, its price is bid up. Ideally the highest bidder will make the best use of the resource. The application of the trusteeship model to broadcasting is a substantial deviation from the ordinary allocation of scarce goods and services in society.[69]

One might argue, however, that deviations from the market should occur with regard to communications media. For instance, in wartime the government might be justified in regulating the amount of newsprint any one paper received. The supply of newsprint could be re-

67. *See* 47 C.F.R. § 0.281(a)(2) (1981). This provision curiously calls attention to sellers who will "realize" a profit on the sale of their broadcast station. *See generally* H. LEVIN, THE INVISIBLE RESOURCE: USE AND REGULATION OF THE RADIO SPECTRUM (1971); Greenberg, *Television Station Profitability and FCC Regulatory Policy*, 17 J. INDUS. ECON. 210 (1969).

68. *See, e.g.,* Red Lion Broadcasting Co. v. FCC, 395 U.S. 367, 399 (1969). *Contra* FCC v. Pacifica Found., 438 U.S. 726 (1978); *cf. id.* at 770 n.4 (Brennan, J., dissenting) ("The opinions of my Brothers POWELL and STEVENS rightly refrain from relying on the notion of 'spectrum scarcity' to support their result.").

69. *See supra* text accompanying notes 17-23.

duced for newspapers intending to print only comics or other purely entertainment features. But no factors remotely comparable exist in broadcasting today. Yet the trusteeship model results in broadcast regulation that resembles this hypothetical.

Apart from this basic misunderstanding of scarcity, other factors should lead to a rejection of the belief that a condition of true scarcity prevails in broadcasting. Scarcity is a relative concept even when applied to the limited spectrum earmarked for broadcast use. Additional channels can be added, without increasing the portion reserved for broadcast, by decreasing the bandwidth of each channel.[70] Technology is an independent variable that makes scarcity a relative concept. At some point, quality becomes so reduced or costs so great that new channels should not be added. But until that point is reached, saturation of the spectrum has not occurred. The continued evolution of spectrum efficiency techniques makes it difficult to say with certainty that saturation of channels will ever be permanent in any market.

Channels can also be added by revising the interference rules. The Commission has traditionally shied away from this solution because of concerns about the risk of degrading signal quality.[71] Under the pres-

---

70. For instance, FM bandwidth could be narrowed, although a narrower channel could affect the quality of the FM signal. Bandwidth reduction techniques might be available that would not reduce quality significantly. Single sideband and amplitude companding have been suggested for use in land mobile communications. *See supra* note 23. Application of these techniques to broadcasting could increase the number of FM channels five- or seven-fold. These techniques, however, would require more expensive tuners and massive investments by existing broadcasters.

In television, bandwidth could be reduced from six to four megahertz without impairing quality significantly, thereby allowing more signals in markets with channel saturation under existing allocations. OFFICE OF PLANS AND POLICY, FCC, UHF TASK FORCE REPORT, TELEVISION BANDWIDTH REDUCTION 2 (1978). Bandwidth compression has been achieved through digital techniques and has been commercially used in video conferencing. One system permits up to 30 simultaneous color video links to be established on a single satellite transponder. Com. Daily, Dec. 29, 1981, at 2, 2-3. Bandwidth reduction would require consumers to acquire new receivers, an investment whose aggregate cost may exceed the benefits from new service. Still, cost considerations do not alone make the broadcast band ineluctably "saturated."

Additional channels could also, if desired, have been created in AM service. It has been proposed (but rejected by the Commission) to reduce channels on the AM band from 10 to 9 kHz, creating an additional 12 channels on the band. 9 kHz Channel Spacing for AM Broadcasting, 88 F.C.C.2d 290 (1981). One of the reasons for rejecting the shift was the expense that the changeover would have entailed to broadcasters and listeners.

The Commission could also consider reassigning portions of the spectrum neighboring the broadcast frequencies now used for other civilian or military uses. For example, the AM band could be expanded in this way, and the 1979 World Administrative Radio Conference has urged this change. *See* F.C.C. Public Notice, Mimeo No. 25,215, at 5-6 (Jan. 15, 1980).

71. The Commission could turn the question of interference over to the marketplace. A party suffering interference from another would be able to pay to terminate objectionable interference. This, of course, could lead to nuisance interference for purposes of extortion, but it is reasonable to assume that the marketplace would allow a spectrum user to pay to clear a frequency. Resolution of interference problems resembles the settlement process among competing

ent allocation scheme, the Commission assigns frequencies for television and FM radio to localities throughout the United States. The Commission created a master "table of allocations" to accomplish this purpose.[72] New assignments are added to the tables quite frequently in FM and occasionally in television. In addition, less than full strength service, such as low-power television, which radiates in an area as small as one-tenth of the typical television service area, can be added to the existing allocation scheme without creating destructive interference.[73]

The Commission's approach to AM radio has been to allow new stations to "shoe-horn" in, based on predicted levels of interference with existing stations.[74] By allowing this expansion of AM service, the Commission has acknowledged that new outlets can be brought to the market without the need for finite limits. The stream of new AM stations is proof of the dubiety of scarcity in that band. Indeed, the Commission is considering a similar demand-based approach to the FM band.[75] In short, the theoretically scarce airwaves continue to absorb more and more new channels and could accommodate additional channels. The only major factor limiting expansion—other than unacceptable levels of interference—is the cost of accommodating those new channels.

The scarcity rationale focuses on the wrong scarce resource, megahertz, instead of advertising dollars. Even in the indirect marketplace of over-the-air commercial broadcasting, the number of stations depends on the amount of advertising dollars or on other funding sources in the community. Except in the largest cities, where the Commission's allocation policies have limited the number of outlets, advertising support or subscriber dollars restrict broadcast opportunities more than does the number of channels.

---

applicants for a broadcast frequency, in which applications are mutually exclusive to each other. *See* 47 U.S.C. § 311(c) (1976); 47 C.F.R. § 73.3525 (1981); NBC, Inc., 26 RAD. REG. 2d (P & F) 951 (1964). Often during the application process all parties except one will drop out, content to receive reimbursement for costs incurred in seeking the license. Similarly, unauthorized interference could be "solved" by paying the offending broadcaster an amount equal to the expense of shielding the signal.

72. The Commission created the table in order to comply with the mandate of the Communications Act, 47 U.S.C. §§ 151, 307(b) (1976). The objectives of Congress were to provide television service as far as possible to all people in the United States and to establish a fair, efficient, and equitable distribution of stations throughout the country. *See* Television Assignments Amendment of § 3.606 of the Commission Rules and Regulations (Sixth Report and Order), 41 F.C.C. 148 (1952).

73. *See* Inquiry into the Future Role of Low-Power Television Broadcasting and Television Translators in the National Telecommunications System, 47 Fed. Reg. 21,468 (1982).

74. 4 C.F.R. § 73.37 (1981).

75. Modification of FM Broadcast Station Rules to Increase the Availability of Commercial FM Broadcast Assignments, 78 F.C.C.2d 1232 (1980).

In addition, scarcity is not the only reason behind the present limited number of VHF television stations (channels 2-13), which are the most profitable outlets. The Commission's allocation of only three VHF commercial outlets in most communities is hardly an unavoidable product of the limited ether; rather, it derives from the Commission's landmark allocation scheme for television, the *Sixth Report and Order*.[76] The goal of the *Sixth Report* was to ensure as far as possible that most communities in the United States would have at least one local television channel, preferably VHF.[77] The arrangement, however, has resulted in a national distribution system in which at most only three VHF commercial outlets prevail in most markets.[78] As Commission studies have found, this "three to a market" approach of the *Sixth Report* assures the dominant position of the commercial television networks.[79] At the very least, one can hardly explain the availability of only the three VHF television outlets carrying the three commercial networks as a force of nature caused by a limited spectrum.[80] It should serve instead as a basis for authorizing more outlets, not for regulating those that already exist.

The scarcity upon which the trusteeship model relies exists only in some, not all, markets. Even under the current allocation scheme,

---

76. 41 F.C.C. 148 (1952). *See generally* Schuessler, *Structural Barriers to the Entry of Additional Television Networks: The Federal Communications Commission's Spectrum Management Policies*, 54 S. CAL. L. REV. 875 (1981).

77. *See* 41 F.C.C. at 151 (citing 47 U.S.C. 307(b) (1976)).

78. The 1952 allocation scheme issued four or more VHF assignments in only 7 of the top 50 markets; 20 markets received three VHF assignments, 16 received two VHF assignments, and 2 received only one VHF assignment. Five of the top 50 markets had only UHF assignments. One network could reach 45 of these markets with VHF stations, and the second network could reach 43 markets. A third network could reach only 27 and a fourth network had access to VHF stations in only 7 of the top 50 markets. MAJORITY STAFF OF THE SUBCOMM. ON TELECOMMUNICATIONS, CONSUMER PROTECTION, AND FINANCE OF THE HOUSE COMM. ON ENERGY AND COMMERCE, 97TH CONG., 1ST SESS., TELECOMMUNICATIONS IN TRANSITION: THE STATUS OF COMPETITION IN THE TELECOMMUNICATIONS INDUSTRY 247 (Comm. Print 1981) [hereinafter cited as TELECOMMUNICATIONS REPORT].

79. *See* 2 NETWORK INQUIRY SPECIAL STAFF, *supra* note 9, at 27-30; HOUSE COMM. ON INTERSTATE AND FOREIGN COMMERCE, NETWORK BROADCASTING, H.R. REP. No. 1297, 85th Cong., 2d Sess. 195 (1958) [hereinafter cited as the Barrow Report].

80. The Commission could have chosen a scheme that did not emphasize the concept of a local VHF outlet quite so much. Indeed, the Commission had before it the Dumont plan, which would have used regional stations to allow more than three outlets to service larger areas. AD HOC ADVISORY COMM. ON ALLOCATIONS TO THE SENATE COMM. ON INTERSTATE AND FOREIGN COMMERCE, 85TH CONG., 2D SESS., ALLOCATION OF TELEVISION CHANNELS 98-101 (Comm. Print 1958). *See generally* Schuessler, *supra* note 76, at 921-26. The Commission could have allocated television frequencies exclusively in the more plentiful UHF band (channels 14-83) or prohibited the mixing of UHF and VHF channels in the same market. *See id.* at 886-930. Perhaps the most interesting wrinkle to the Commission's choice is that both CBS and ABC had stressed the undesirability of any extended operation in the VHF band. ABC urged the Commission to move all commercial television to UHF, with VHF frequencies to be used for technical development directed at improving television on the UHF frequencies. *See* Barrow Report, *supra* note 79, at 20.

which assigns fewer channels than could be accommodated on the available spectrum, channels outside larger cities go wanting for lack of a taker.[81] This situation is especially true for allocations in the UHF band, where some channels have remained unclaimed for decades. It is capricious to justify regulation of broadcasters in nonsaturated markets by claiming that their operation employs a scarce resource unavailable to potential entrants in other markets.

Scarcity does exist in the sense that there is no more room for additional full-power VHF stations in the largest markets under current levels of permitted interference. Yet one can always buy an existing station, just as one may be likelier to consider buying an existing newspaper operation than trying to launch a new one. Furthermore, the current complement of VHF stations exceeds the number of daily newspapers in large cities, and the total number of broadcast outlets far exceeds the number of daily circulated newspapers.[82] So a relatively low number of outlets in one medium should not lead to content-based rules in another.[83]

Finally, the scarcity notion also fails to recognize the substitutes for over-the-air distribution. In audio service, cassette and phono disc recordings vie with AM and FM channels and their subcarrier services like Muzak. Cable television, low-power television, multipoint distribution service, cassette and disc, and, in the future, direct broadcast satellites provide substitutes for over-the-air video service in many

81. The Commission periodically issues a report listing channels allocated in the UHF and VHF bands that have not been applied for or assigned. FCC Public Notice, Mimeo No. 3331 (Apr. 16, 1982).

82. Only 35 cities are served by two or more competing daily newspapers. In contrast, very few American communities have only one radio or television station. TELECOMMUNICATIONS REPORT, *supra* note 78, at 263; *see also* OFFICE OF PLANS AND POLICY, *supra* note 5, at 62 (citing data from ARBITRON, TELEVISION MARKETS AND RANKINGS GUIDE 1979-1980 (1979)). Yet no one has seriously suggested that the relative scarcity of newspapers justifies the regulations that have been imposed on broadcasters. Contrary to daily newspaper trends, the number of broadcast outlets is steadily rising; since the Court decided *Red Lion* in 1969, the number of radio outlets has increased by 38% and the number of television outlets by 21%. By 1981, there were 9060 radio and 1035 television stations. FCC News, Mimeo No. 3510 (Sept. 22, 1981). In contrast, the number of daily newspapers, which currently totals about 1750, has remained fairly constant over the past 35 years. TELECOMMUNICATIONS REPORT, *supra* note 78, at 263-64.

83. Professor Emerson argues that the significant comparison among media is the number of printing presses versus the number of persons who wish to use broadcast facilities, not the number of newspapers versus the number of stations. T. EMERSON, THE SYSTEM OF FREEDOM OF EXPRESSION 662 (1970). Because the number of printing presses or copying machines is not limited by spectrum slots, television is the "scarcer" medium. But this distinction fails to distinguish between a medium of individual communication and a medium of mass communication. The distribution available by mimeograph and paper pales next to the circulation of a major daily paper; it is not an adequate substitute for the reach of a daily. Just because anyone has access to a copier does not mean that he can start a successful daily paper. The limiting factor in broadcasting is the same as in print: economic support.

markets. A five-meter backyard satellite dish can, for those who can afford them, bring in more channels "off the air" than a television antenna picks up in a city with the greatest number of stations on the air.

Nonspectrum-utilizing distribution modes like cable and video cassette provide virtually limitless diversity of scheduling and content. Where new high-capacity cable systems are in place, no scarcity exists with respect to the television spectrum. What may inhibit the number of cable channels, is again, a scarcity of dollars to support advertiser-based or subscription channels. Similarly, choice in video cassette programming is completely determined by what the consumer is willing to spend for software.[84] Thus, the scarcity rationale, as used to justify the regulation of broadcasting in a different manner than other media, misperceives what scarcity is in a free economy. Moreover, it ignores the practical realities that go a long way toward explaining the limited number of channels in some markets.

Even if one assumes that the absence of more television channel space in the largest markets justifies a licensing policy in those markets, this assumption establishes nothing about the form the regulations should take.[85] The trusteeship model endorsed the giant leap from scarcity to the current panoply of federal regulation over all broadcasters, not just those in saturated markets. Logic, however, does not support the assumption that the trusteeship scheme is more likely to maximize consumer welfare, even in markets without available outlets, than would a system relying on the judgment of marketplace players.[86]

2. Other Justifications

(a) The "prior grant" theory.

—A more rational justification for continued government regulation is the bootstrap argument that rests on broadcasters' enjoyment of "the fruits of a prior government

84. In evaluating the "scarcity" of outlets for information, it is important to consider all information providers, from broadcast outlets and newspapers to magazines, paperback books, direct mail fliers, billboards, posters, handbills, sound trucks, and tee shirts. All of these provide some form of expression and each undercuts the significance of broadcast stations as necessary outlets for expression.

85. Judge Bazelon has suggested that when regulations are required, they should be structural regulations, such as cross-ownership limitations and content-neutral access requirements. *See* Bazelon, *The First Amendment and "The New Media"—New Directions in Regulating Telecommunications*, 31 F. Com. L.J. 201, 209-13 (1979).

86. *See* C. Schultze, The Public Use of Private Interest 6 (1977):

Finally, and perhaps most important, we usually tend to see only one way of intervening [in the marketplace]—namely, removing a set of decisions from the decentralized and incentive-oriented private market and transferring them to the command-and-control techniques of government bureaucracy. . . . Instead of creating incentives so that public goals become private interests, private interests are left unchanged and obedience to the public goals is commanded.

grant." The Supreme Court advanced this rationale in *Red Lion Broadcasting Co. v. FCC*[87] after acknowledging "gaps in spectrum utilization." The Court stated that "the fact remains that existing broadcasters have often attained their present positions because of their initial government selection in competition with others before new technological advances opened new opportunities for further uses."[88] Since the government has aided the market strength of incumbent licensees, it may under the "prior grant" rationale regulate some aspects of the conduct of those licensees in order to guarantee the best service to the public.[89]

This reasoning leads equally well to a market approach as to the trusteeship model, because it does not follow from licensing that the government also must affirmatively regulate licensee conduct. Once the Commission concludes that the best service for the public lies with a market system, where licensees can air programs designed to attract the largest audiences for advertisers or the largest subscriber base, it can refrain from reviewing programming and other licensee decisions. Moreover, now that broadcasting outlets face more competition from new media delivery outlets, activistic "grandfathering" of early licensed stations with trusteeship duties makes even less sense.

(b) FCC v. Pacifica Foundation: *"impact" theories.*—The Supreme Court has identified other reasons for regulating broadcast content under the public interest standard, and they appear most strikingly in *FCC v. Pacifica Foundation*.[90] The Court was confronted with a Commission policy statement prohibiting indecent broadcasting that allegedly applied to the airing of a comedy monologue by George Carlin on an FM nonprofit station in New York City. *Pacifica* upheld the Commission's determination that "indecent" broadcasts, as identified in congressional statutes and defined by the agency, could be punished.[91] The Court minimized the relative first amendment claims of broadcasters as compared to the right of the audience, particularly chil-

---

87. 395 U.S. 367, 400 (1969).

88. *Id.*; *see also* Office of Communication of United Church of Christ v. FCC, 359 F.2d 994, 1003 (D.C. Cir. 1966).

89. The "prior grants" especially benefit the networks with ownership of radio and television stations in the largest markets. ABC, NBC, and CBS each own AM, FM, and VHF-TV outlets in the three largest markets, New York, Los Angeles, and Chicago. These three markets alone comprise 16.6% of all television households. *See* 1982 BROADCASTING CABLECASTING YEAR BOOK, at B-76.

90. 438 U.S. 726 (1978); *see also* CBS v. Democratic Nat'l Comm., 412 U.S. 94, 116 (1973); Brandywine-Main Line Radio, Inc. v. FCC, 473 F.2d 16, 49 (D.C. Cir. 1972), *cert. denied*, 412 U.S. 922 (1973).

91. 438 U.S. at 731-32, 735-41.

dren, to avoid exposure to offensive materials. The Court noted that "the broadcast media have established a uniquely pervasive presence in the lives of all Americans."[92] Likening reception of offensive broadcast signals to an indecent phone call, the Court surmised that listeners and viewers cannot insulate themselves from offensive program content. Second, the Court concluded that regulation of broadcasting content was justified because broadcasting is "uniquely accessible to children, even those too young to read."[93]

Neither argument, however, adequately distinguishes broadcasting from other mass media. Broadcasting may have a pervasive presence in the "lives of all Americans," but that says very little about the operation of a particular station, which is, after all, the unit of regulation under the licensing scheme. Under the Court's rationale, program producers have a "presence"—measured, for example, by having two or more network series on the air at the same time—far more "pervasive" than the operator of an individual station. Furthermore, it is unlikely that any viewer watches a single station's entire daily broadcast. The assertion of the pervasive influence of individual licensees is a gross exaggeration of the licensees' real impact.

Moreover, other media are also "pervasive." One can hardly argue that a one-newspaper town is not "pervaded," "uniquely," by the orientation of its paper. A blockbuster motion picture, unlike a typical television or radio broadcast, is repeated for weeks on end in a community. Its exhibition is also more likely to pervade the community's consciousness than a single television (or, as in *Pacifica*, a nonprofit FM afternoon) broadcast.

The fact that broadcasting is usually received in the home adds no support to the continued application of the trusteeship model to broadcasting. A large number of television programs probably offend some portion of the home audience. For example, evangelical programs may offend those whose faith is grounded in a different theological perspective,[94] but the annoyance caused to some viewers by these programs

92. *Id.* at 748.
93. *Id.* at 749.
94. The Commission's inclusion of religious broadcasters among groups eligible for noncommercial, reserved licenses was questioned in a petition requesting rulemaking to explore the entire matter of religious broadcasting in America. This petition, which the Commission declined to adopt for rulemaking, led to an avalanche of mail from listeners of religious broadcasting. Revision of Rules Permitting Multiple Ownership of Non-Commercial Educational Radio and Television Stations in Single Markets, 54 F.C.C.2d 941 (1975). Controversy has long surrounded religious broadcasting, starting with the Federal Radio Commission's refusal to renew the license of Reverend Shuler because of defamatory and otherwise objectionable utterances made over his Los Angeles radio station. *See* Trinity Methodist Church, S. v. Federal Radio Comm'n, 62 F.2d 850 (D.C. Cir. 1932), *cert. denied*, 288 U.S. 599 (1933).

hardly justifies government intervention to ascertain where the public interest lies in such matters. The viewer always retains ultimate control over what enters his home; he may choose to turn the channel.

In fact, religious programming is market-oriented, since only religious broadcasters who can afford to purchase time for their messages appear regularly on the air. There is every reason to believe that the marketplace, speaking through advertisers, critics, and self-selection by viewers, provides an adequate substitute for Commission involvement in protecting children and adults from television's "captive" quality.[95]

Indeed, those who would justify regulation by pointing to a program's potential to offend viewers stand the first amendment on its head. Those who deliver popular, acceptable speech have little reason to fear the rebuke of the majority. Only words and ideas that trouble or confound need the special aid of constitutional protection.[96] A licensing scheme justified by the avoidance of offensive programs is inconsistent with a society dedicated to free inquiry and expression.

Undoubtedly many children below the age of literacy watch television. This situation may justify regulation of indecent materials carried over the air. Indecent material can be withheld from distribution to children if it is in the form of print or film,[97] and scheduling of adult programs for late-night viewing can and does give parents more control over what their children watch. But these narrow restrictions do not justify a broad-scale trusteeship approach with its power to grant and revoke licenses based on content, any more than a trusteeship approach should be sustained over bookstores because they might at some point carry indecent materials on their shelves.[98]

In a separate opinion in *Pacifica*, Justice Powell argued that the different treatment of broadcast media for first amendment purposes is justified because children and adults have equal access to whatever is

95. Under *Pacifica*, the Commission can establish time of day standards for programs that might be inappropriate for children. Furthermore, the Commission can mandate warnings to advise parents of the potential offensiveness of a broadcast. *See* Pacifica Found., 56 F.C.C.2d 94, 98 (1975), *reconsideration granted*, 59 F.C.C.2d 892 (1976), *rev'd*, 556 F.2d 9 (D.C. Cir. 1977), *rev'd*, 438 U.S. 726 (1978). Curiously, the broadcast in *Pacifica* was carried early in the afternoon on a school day on a noncommercial station unlikely to attract a large audience of children.
96. *See* Kingsley Int'l Pictures Corp. v. Regents of the Univ. of New York, 360 U.S. 684 (1959); Pacifica Found., 36 F.C.C. 147 (1964).
97. *See* Ginsberg v. New York, 390 U.S. 629 (1968).
98. No one has ever seriously argued that broadcasters should air only what is fit for the youngest viewer. The child audience argument must give way to the realities of a pluralistic society. *See Pacifica*, 438 U.S. at 768-69 (Brennan, J., dissenting); Butler v. Michigan, 352 U.S. 380, 383 (1957). Justice Brennan observed in *Pacifica*: "As surprising as it may be to individual Members of this Court, some parents may actually find Mr. Carlin's unabashed attitude towards the seven 'dirty words' healthy and deem it desirable to expose their children to the manner in which Mr. Carlin defuses the taboo surrounding the words." 438 U.S. at 770 (Brennan, J., dissenting).

broadcast.[99] This differs from a bookstore where access to store shelves can be monitored by a clerk. Yet Justice Powell's lament applies equally well to other materials in the home, such as the pictorials carried in Sunday newspapers, advertising circulars received through the mail,[100] and weekly or monthly subscription magazines, which do not depend upon literacy or access to a television set for their influence. Cause for alarm about either these materials or television is unjustified. In a free marketplace, whether broadcast or print, advertisers and subscribers will not eagerly support materials, whether delivered on the air or on the doorstep, that are as likely to offend as to attract potential customers. Similarly, there is no reason to assume that the Commission is a better clearinghouse for passing judgment on programs than advertisers or the subscribers who support them or the viewers who ultimately decide whether to watch their programs.

III.   The Marketplace Approach in Broadcasting

The reasons articulated by the Commission and the courts for the trusteeship model are hardly convincing, let alone compelling, when poised in a constitutional balance against the rights of broadcasters.[101] Scarcity analysis is theoretically misguided and, in many cases, factually erroneous. Other facets of broadcasting, such as intrusiveness, failure to segregate child and adult audiences, and "captiveness," do not call for government involvement. There is reason to believe that marketplace forces can, and indeed do, affect the success or failure of television programming, just as they affect the content of nonbroadcast media.

A scheme that empowers the Commission to judge content on these speculative rationales should be rejected, for the consequence has been and continues to be a level of first amendment protection for broadcasters that is not simply "different"[102] but substantially weaker than the protection given other media. In the meantime it has led to

---

99. 438 U.S. at 757-59.

100. "When I was a boy the sight of a girl's knee occasioned lewd thoughts, and *La Vie Parisienne*, a long-dead precursor of *Penthouse* and similar magazines, drove young males mad with pictures a good deal less explicit than today's department store advertisements of brassieres and bikinis." Gellhorn, *Dirty Books, Disgusting Pictures, and Dreadful Laws*, 8 GA. L. REV. 291, 298 (1974).

101. "[O]nly a compelling state interest in the regulation of a subject within the State's constitutional power to regulate can justify limiting First Amendment freedoms." NAACP v. Button, 371 U.S. 415, 438 (1963). The inadequacy of the trusteeship approach is especially glaring in light of Professor Kalven's admonition that the starting place in this analysis should be the constitutional rights of broadcasters. *See* Kalven, *supra* note 22, at 37.

102. *See* Joseph Burstyn, Inc. v. Wilson, 343 U.S. 495, 503 (1952).

the exclusion of new entrants who might have met unserved communications needs. A marketplace approach to broadcast regulation, on the other hand, emphasizes the role of new competitors, and new competition among existing firms, to ensure service in the public interest.

A. The Current Marketplace in Broadcasting

Market forces have not been totally absent under the trusteeship approach. Nor has the trusteeship philosophy had a devastating effect on broadcasting in America. First, despite the deviation from the marketplace approach that has occurred in broadcast regulation, the American system of broadcast service generally compares well with those of other nations.[103] Entertainment programming produced for domestic television, while not always aimed at the highest of brows, enjoys enormous audiences at home, and overseas demand for these shows is substantial. Network and local news departments have pioneered techniques of electronic news gathering and news coverage. Anyone proposing changes in our licensing system must concede the comparatively high quality of our domestic productions.[104]

Second, despite its content-oriented rules and the not-infrequent protest against its rulings, the Commission's actual impact on programming has probably been slight. There have been some close calls, but the Commission's bark has been worse than its bite.[105] The Commission has shown little desire to censor programming. This is not to give a ringing endorsement to the broadcast industry's less than strident defense of its first amendment rights, or to the Commission's ability to shut its regulatory jaw. Nevertheless, broadcasting has generally enjoyed widespread, sustained consumer acceptance and the Commission's regulation has rarely been overbearing.

Third, we must emphasize the twin idiosyncrasies of a market analysis applied to a business like broadcasting. The first has already

103. The average American household watches 6 hours and 45 minutes of television per day, according to Nielsen statistics. Recent public opinion surveys indicate that 51% of the public think that television is the most believable news source. *See* 1982 BROADCASTING CABLECASTING YEAR BOOK, *supra* note 89, at A-2.

104. An informal comparison with the television service provided by other nations indicates that, with the exception of teletext services, the United States provides the greatest number of distribution channels of television programming. *See* R. NEUSTADT, THE BIRTH OF ELECTRONIC PUBLISHING 19 (1982).

105. "One embarrassment in attacking seriously the topic of free speech in broadcasting is that the admitted benignity of the FCC has made it difficult to mount appropriate indignation." Kalven, *supra* note 22, at 19. Yet broadcasters are subject to news and other nonentertainment program guidelines, the fairness doctrine, access rights for federal candidates, and other regulations that would be impermissible if imposed on newspapers. *See infra* notes 129-30 and accompanying text.

been noted: a key resource in broadcasting, exclusivity of radio spectrum, is allocated by governmental decision, not by price. Prices, therefore, are not allowed to allocate frequencies in the same way they allocate other resources in the marketplace.[106] The second crucial idiosyncrasy of commercial broadcasting is that with the exception of subscription television, consumers cannot vote with dollars to get the programs they want.[107] With over-the-air, advertiser-supported broadcasting, it is impossible to measure directly the intensity of demand individual consumers feel for the programs they watch. Competitive markets easily determine what people want and how much they are willing to pay for it: consumers with the most intense demand for a scarce good outbid those with less desire for that good. But in the broadcasting market, where viewer or listener intensity cannot be measured accurately, this process cannot occur. Broadcasting, therefore, is an atypical market from the point of view of both the broadcaster as supplier and the viewer as consumer.[108]

Over-the-air broadcasting relies on an indirect market mechanism. Advertisers sponsor programs that they expect to appeal to the viewers they want to reach with their messages. In a sense, the advertiser acts as the representative for consumers, sometimes for all consumers, sometimes for demographic subgroups. This representative form of program selection is well served—but further distanced from traditional pricing mechanisms—by the fact that a program, once broadcast, is available to additional consumers without cost.[109] The broadcaster cannot collect fees from additional consumers who watch the program.[110]

Thus, the broadcasting marketplace is indirect and imperfect, but

106. B. Owen, The Economics of Diversity in Broadcasting (Studies in Industry Economics No. 60, 1976); Owen, *Regulating Diversity: The Case of Radio Formats*, 21 J. Broadcasting 315 (1977); *cf.* M. Friedman & R. Friedman, Free to Choose 13-24 (1980) (describing the role of price in the marketplace).

107. Owen, *supra* note 106, at 316-17; *see* Brenner, *Government Regulation of Radio Program Format Changes*, 127 U. Pa. L. Rev. 56, 69-72 (1978); Parkman, *The FCC's Allocation of Television Licenses: Regulation with Inadequate Information*, 46 Alb. L. Rev. 22, 39 (1981).

108. In this instance, the "market" refers to programming that listeners desire. Because broadcasting is advertiser-supported, the product in the market consists of listeners. The buyer in this instance is the advertiser, the seller the broadcaster, with programming serving as the largest factor of production needed to generate an audience.

109. Products with this characteristic are called "public goods." *See* B. Owen, J. Beebe & W. Manning, Jr., *supra* note 14, at 15-16.

110. As a practical matter, advertisers pay either a fixed rate to broadcasters for each spot they run or receive guaranteed minimum numbers of audience exposures, with additional viewers coming as a bonus. A program that generates a larger audience than anticipated creates a windfall for the advertiser. On the bright side, from an efficiency viewpoint the broadcaster's marginal cost for serving that extra customer is zero. Owen, *supra* note 106, at 316-17.

we know that it generally works. The stations and networks that carry programs with the highest viewing ratings can charge the highest rates for advertising. Producers with programs that are in demand by the public can charge networks and stations the most for their productions.[111] Actors engaged in hit television series can, or at least can try to, obtain higher salaries. Although the advertiser, rather than the consumer, pays for the program, market forces still move the key resource—time on an exclusive broadcasting frequency—toward its highest and best use. The real issue is not whether the marketplace is fully efficient; rather it is whether the Commission, by ignoring until recently the realities of the broadcasting business, has substituted a system of regulation by trusteeship that has caused more harm than good.

B. Legal Basis For a Marketplace Approach

The Commission, as much as possible, should rely on market forces rather than its judgments on program service or other licensee decisions to determine where the public interest lies in broadcasting. The Supreme Court has interpreted the Commission's broad statutory mandate as granting wide discretion to the Commission for determining the public interest.[112]

Approval of the market approach first appeared in the Supreme Court's 1940 review of the Commission's decision in *FCC v. Sanders Brothers Radio Station*.[113] A station operator had protested that licensing an additional radio station in its community would cause it economic harm. The Court upheld the Commission's denial of the protest on the ground that such injury to a rival station was not "in and of itself" an element that had to be considered when passing on a broad-

---

111. All of this is necessarily imprecise. Even though a program generates the largest number of viewers for a particular period of time, its success says nothing about the intensity with which viewers prefer it over a competing program or whether they would prefer a type of programming not offered at all. Furthermore, the amounts advertisers pay do not represent income that might be collected directly from viewers if they could pay. Still, popular programs do receive advertiser support regardless of the intensity of their popularity. Less popular programs tend to fail to achieve adequate advertiser support and other programs are substituted to make better use of the time period. *See* Note, *supra* note 38, at 558; *see also* Deregulation of Radio, 84 F.C.C.2d 968, 983 (1981).

Another important factor in a program's success is its placement on the network schedule. Networks juggle series into different time slots in order to place a program within the overall flow that suits it best. This process helps a program "find" its audience or, conversely, prevents it from getting a regular following. Sometimes critical acclaim or viewer writing campaigns can influence a network to give a program a longer time to develop an audience. CBS may have retained "The Waltons" despite weak ratings in part because of a sustained write-in campaign. The show subsequently became a ratings leader.

112. *See, e.g.,* FCC v. National Citizens Comm'n for Broadcasting, 436 U.S. 775, 795 (1978); NBC v. United States, 319 U.S. 190, 218 (1943).

113. 309 U.S. 470 (1940).

cast license application.[114] The Court found that the 1934 Act recognized:

> that the field of broadcasting is one of free competition. . . . *The Commission is given no supervisory control of the programs, of business management or of policy.* In short, the broadcasting field is open to anyone, provided there be an available frequency over which he can broadcast without interference to others, if he shows his competency, the adequacy of his equipment, and financial ability to make good use of the assigned channel.[115]

This is surely strong language in support of the free market approach, especially considering that Justice Frankfurter's *NBC* decision, which validated the broad regulatory powers of the Commission, would emerge three years later. *Sanders Brothers* does backpedal following this portion of the opinion and suggest that the Commission could consider whether the addition of a new station would cause both an existing and the proposed outlet to go under, or whether dividing the field among two stations would result in inadequate service by each.[116] But the Court rejected the licensee's claim of too much competition.

The Court's concern with the effect of a new station on existing stations and service now appears myopic.[117] The market that a new station enters comprises not simply existing broadcast facilities, but all competitors for the advertising dollar, from newspapers to billboards. Consistently applied, the Court's rationale would lead the Commission to be equally concerned that an additional newspaper in a community might lead to ruinous competition between existing broadcast properties and the newspaper. More generally, a policy of preserving existing service arbitrarily favors established editorial voices over new ones, an approach never sanctioned by the Supreme Court.

If competition, not entry control, is to determine the provision of mass communications service in the United States, as it already does in all media save broadcasting, the FCC should not worry about either of the possibilities identified in *Sanders Brothers*. The case reveals the heavy emphasis the Court and the Commission placed on the role of open competition in broadcasting and the scant authority they found for Commission supervision of programming or station business policies.

---

114. *Id*. at 473.
115. *Id*. at 474-75 (emphasis added).
116. *Id*.
117. The D.C. Circuit resurrected this view in 1958. *See* Carroll Broadcasting Co. v. FCC, 258 F.2d 440 (D.C. Cir. 1958); *see supra* text accompanying note 59.

In *FCC v. WNCN Listeners Guild*,[118] decided in 1981, the Supreme Court expressly sanctioned the Commission's discretion to invoke market forces in its regulatory mission. In *WNCN* the Court found no inconsistency between the first amendment and the Commission's decision that the public interest in radio is best served by promoting diversity in entertainment formats through market forces and competition among broadcasters. The Court noted that the Commission had admitted that the marketplace would not necessarily achieve a perfect correlation between listener preferences and available entertainment programs.[119] But given the choice of regulating format changes or leaving those decisions to the marketplace, the Court concluded that the Commission acted reasonably in adopting the latter. The Court recognized that the Commission was within its range of discretion in preferring a market approach to achieve the Communication Act's goal of providing "the maximum benefits of radio to all the people of the United States."[120]

The Supreme Court admittedly did not express any enthusiasm for open competition in broadcasting in the forty-one years between *Sanders Brothers* and *WNCN*. Instead, in 1969 in *Red Lion Broadcasting Co. v. FCC*[121] and, most recently, in 1981 in *CBS v. FCC*,[122] the Court reaffirmed the viewpoint of Justice Frankfurter in *NBC v. United States* that the Commission bears the "burden of determining the composition of . . . traffic" over broadcast frequencies.[123] None of these three cases, *NBC*, *Red Lion*, or *CBS*, directly involved the conflict between the marketplace and trusteeship approaches to broadcasting. Only in *WNCN* did these policies collide.[124] Presented with the question, the Supreme Court held that the Commission could rely on marketplace forces to ensure that licensees satisfy the public interest.

Under the Supreme Court's view of the Communications Act, then, the Commission can apply a free market model to broadcasting, particularly where it finds that the costs of content-oriented regulations outweigh their benefits. This approach differs from a trusteeship model, under which the Commission would require broadcasters to air programs—from public affairs shows to responses to station editorials—that might not be aired voluntarily, and that consumers, insofar as

---

118. 450 U.S. 582 (1981).
119. *Id.* at 596.
120. *Id.* at 593-94 (quoting NBC v. United States, 319 U.S. 190, 217 (1943)).
121. 395 U.S. 367 (1969).
122. 453 U.S. 267 (1981).
123. 319 U.S. 190, 216 (1943).
124. *See* 450 U.S. at 604.

they can be heard in the advertiser-supported marketplace, do not demand.

The market perspective diminishes the importance of the Commission's past efforts to define affirmatively the elements of operation "in the public interest." It recognizes as valid communications policy, well within Commission discretion, reliance on voluntary broadcaster efforts to attract audiences—whether by specialized formats, as in the case of major market radio, or with a mix of programs, as in the case of television—and to provide the best practicable programming service to the public. It concludes that governmental efforts to improve the broadcast market have led to distortions of programming that have merely yielded a different programming mix, not a better one, and that the costs of government intrusion into the marketplace outweigh the benefits. Important first amendment interests support this conclusion as well.

C. The First Amendment and the Marketplace Approach

1. The First Amendment Rights of Listeners and Viewers Under the Speech Clause. —The Supreme Court's recently repeated formulation of the hierarchy of values in broadcasting—that "the right of the viewers and listeners, not the right of the broadcasters . . . is *paramount*"[125]—is central to a first amendment analysis of broadcast regulation. Under this hierarchy, initially set forth in *Red Lion*, the rights of listeners "to receive suitable access to social, political, esthetic, moral and other ideas and experiences"[126] outweigh the first amendment claims of broadcasters when the two conflict. This ranking does not, however, create an individual right of access to broadcast time in any single listener or viewer.[127]

Even before *Red Lion*, the Court had subordinated broadcaster claims of first amendment rights to the public's interest in access to 'ideas and information and to rules designed to enhance that interest. In *NBC*, where the issue was the independence of station owners from network control, the Court rejected the broadcasters' claim that the licensing criteria established in the chain broadcasting rules offended their freedom of speech.[128]

The *Red Lion* decision addressed the first amendment question

---

125. *Red Lion*, 395 U.S. at 390 (emphasis added).
126. *Id.*
127. *See* CBS v. Democratic Nat'l Comm., 412 U.S. 94 (1973).
128. The Court described the broadcasters' first amendment claim as a "sort of last resort" argument. 319 U.S. at 226.

more directly. The Court endorsed a right of access to ideas and up-held the Commission's requirement that a radio or television station give an individual time to reply to personal attacks and political editorials. Five years later, in *Miami Herald Publishing Co. v. Tornillo*,[129] the Supreme Court unanimously rejected a similar regulation when applied to a daily newspaper. But the Court in *Tornillo* did not attempt to harmonize the disparate holdings of the two cases.[130]

In *CBS v. FCC*,[131] the Court, relying on *Red Lion*, again concluded that the public interest in access to particular communications outweighed the impact on the editorial functions of the broadcaster. The Court faced a conflict between the broadcaster's first amendment claim and a Commission interpretation concerning presentation of the viewpoints of candidates for federal office under a congressionally created right of "reasonable" paid access. The Court noted that a statutory right of access did not preclude broadcasters from presenting any particular viewpoint or program and sustained the Commission's mandate of air time for the Carter-Mondale reelection committee under the reasonable access provisions.

A divided Supreme Court subordinated the broadcaster's constitutional rights in a different manner in *FCC v. Pacifica Foundation*.[132] *Pacifica* has little to commend its constitutional analysis. The majority lacked support both for its claim that broadcasting "has received the most limited first amendment protection,"[133] and also for maintaining that a sound basis for more regulation is the pervasive "power" of the electronic media. Yet like the other broadcasting cases, *Pacifica* indicated that the Commission can, indeed should, subordinate a broadcaster's claim to editorial freedom to the perceived needs of the general public for access to expression over the airwaves or (as in *Pacifica*) for protection against harm from such expression.

What do the Supreme Court's repeated holdings on the hierarchy of first amendment interests tell us about a marketplace approach to broadcasting? First, it should be noted that the language of the first amendment protects the right of speech, not the right of access to ideas or even the right to listen. The direct concern of the first amendment is

---

129. 418 U.S. 241 (1974).

130. *See* Note, *Reconciling* Red Lion *and* Tornillo: *A Consistent Theory of Media Regulation*, 28 STAN. L. REV. 563 (1976).

131. 453 U.S. 367 (1981).

132. 438 U.S. 726 (1978); *see supra* text accompanying notes 90-100.

133. *Id.* at 748. For a critical assessment of the Court's approach in this case, see Brenner, *Censoring the Airwaves: The Supreme Court's* Pacifica *Decision*, ABA BARRISTER, Fall 1978, at 10.

with the active speaker, not the passive receiver. The listener's interest is certainly enhanced by the exercise of the right of free speech, especially where the first amendment is viewed as a tool for self-governance.[134] But listener rights are not the same as the individual's right to speak, and no such rights exist in broadcasting.[135] Thus, it remains unclear exactly what listener interests are protected under the first amendment, aside from the "values" spilling over from the exercise of free speech.

Even assuming the existence of a protected right of access to ideas under the first amendment, it is illogical to assume that broadcasting, and broadcasting alone, is the exclusive arena for the exercise of this right, as the language in *Red Lion* might suggest. "Crucial" access to ideas pertinent to self-governance or self-fulfillment can be provided by many sources other than the airwaves. Furthermore, broadcasters should not shoulder a broader responsibility for providing important information than other media. The argument that listener access to broadcasting is crucial may prove too much. For if listener rights are deemed "paramount" to broadcaster rights, so the rights of newspaper readers should be paramount to the rights of the publishers and editors and the rights of movie patrons superior to those of exhibitors, distributors, and producers. This is the logical result once one stops analyzing the issue in terms of the rights of individuals under the first amendment.

Finally, even assuming that the interest in access to ideas is more pronounced in radio and television than in other media, it does not follow that only governmental regulations can ensure this access. Again, *WNCN* provides the most instructive precedent, since in *WNCN* the Court confronted the free market approach and the *Red Lion* hierarchy for the first time.[136] The Court rejected the claim that the Commission's laissez-faire policy toward radio format changes[137] conflicted with the first amendment rights of listeners under *Red Lion*. It recognized that *Red Lion* provided individual listeners with no right to control the abandonment of a format and concluded that the Commission's reliance on market forces did not violate listeners' first amendment rights. Rather, the Court found that a station's format generally would reflect listener interests and therefore be consistent

134. A. Meiklejohn, Free Speech and its Relation to Self-Government 88-89 (1948).

135. The rights of listeners, in the form of paid editorial access, were trumped by broadcaster claims based on the first amendment protection of journalistic discretion in CBS v. Democratic Nat'l Comm., 412 U.S. 94, 114-21 (1973).

136. *See supra* text accompanying notes 118-24.

137. Changes in the Entertainment Formats of Broadcast Stations, 60 F.C.C.2d 858 (1976).

with the first amendment hierarchy in broadcasting.[138]

The Court did more than avoid a potential conflict between the rights of listeners and broadcasters in dismissing the *Red Lion* claim. It affirmed the importance of listener rights, regardless of broadcaster rights. But the Court agreed with the Commission that this "paramount" interest is best served when a broadcaster in the marketplace is free to respond to perceived listener demand. In this marketplace approach, the interests of listeners and broadcasters, in the past sometimes in conflict (such as over a right of individual access to the media), converge. The commercial broadcaster maximizes profits by providing the service it believes consumers most desire. In choosing a service that maximizes profit, the licensee serves listener interests because the choice of service is geared to attracting the most listeners. The market approach is superior to the alternatives because it does not put the government between the licensee and the listener it is wooing.[139]

Thus, a Commission policy that equates the functions of the marketplace in commercial broadcasting with satisfaction of listener interests finds support in the Court's analysis of the first amendment rights of listeners. Once the Commission concludes that market forces, rather than its own judgments, are most likely to produce programming that best serves the people, the paramount claims set forth in *Red Lion* are satisfied.

Admittedly, this conclusion reads much from the *WNCN* result, for the *Red Lion* claim is not analyzed at length in the decision. And one can characterize the recent *CBS* case, announced shortly after *WNCN*, as reducing the scope of licensee editorial discretion. But the 1981 *CBS* case dealt with a narrow access statute, itself an exception to the result in the Supreme Court's 1973 decision in *CBS v. Democratic National Committee*.[140] In denying a general right of individual access in the 1981 case, the Commission did not allow licensee discretion to override its own interpretation of the statute's purpose. Absent an express Commission finding that it cannot rely on licensee discretion to carry out its congressional mandate, however, *WNCN* suggests the

---

138. 450 U.S. at 604.

139. Some argue that if the government withdraws from an active licensing role, stations will become the province of the rich, who will use them to mold public opinion. These critics assume incorrectly that national media concentration will go unnoticed by the Commission or the Department of Justice. Moreover, daily newspapers can also affect public opinion and yet have not become the mouthpieces of rich individuals. Finally, media owners with strong views on some subjects can operate news organizations with little bias on the front page, as is shown by the *Christian Science Monitor*, and more recently the *Washington Times*.

140. 412 U.S. 94 (1973).

compatibility of a marketplace approach and *Red Lion*'s emphasis on listeners' rights.

2. The First Amendment Rights of Broadcasters Under the Press Clause.—The marketplace approach emphasizes broadcaster discretion as a way to maximize listener welfare. An independent first amendment interest also protects broadcaster discretion from the dictates of the government. As Professor Kalven has sentiently observed:

> We have been beginning, so to speak, in the wrong corner. The question is not what does the need for licensing permit the Commission to do in the public interest; rather it is what does the mandate of the First Amendment inhibit the Commission from doing even though it is to license.[141]

Application of the first amendment to broadcasting largely dates from dictum in *United States v. Paramount Pictures, Inc.*[142] Justice Frankfurter's analysis in the 1943 *NBC* case, however, suggests that the Court already had recognized that broadcasters have a constitutional basis for objecting to overly intrusive regulation.[143] Despite later dictum in *Pacifica* devaluing the first amendment interests of broadcasters,[144] the Court in *CBS v. Democratic National Committee* championed the editorial freedom of broadcasters. It rejected a claim that the first amendment and the "public interest" standard required licensees to sell time for editorial advertisements. "For better or worse," the Court stated, "editing is what editors are for; and editing is selection and choice of material."[145]

The belated recognition of the first amendment rights of broadcasters may be due to the relatively late development of broadcast journalism as a serious professional calling. News and interpretation have

141. Kalven, *supra* note 22, at 37.

142. 334 U.S. 131, 166 (1948). Justice Douglas argued that broadcasting enjoyed the same first amendment protection as newspapers and magazines, CBS v. Democratic Nat'l Comm., 412 U.S. at 148 (Douglas, J., concurring), as did Senator Proxmire in his efforts to repeal the fairness doctrine, *see, e.g.,* 120 CONG. REC. 36,514 (1974) (remarks of Sen. Proxmire). *See also* Robinson, *The FCC and the First Amendment: Observations on 40 Years of Radio and Television Regulation*, 52 MINN. L. REV. 67, 160-63 (1967). This Article assumes that broadcasters' free speech rights are included in those protected by the press clause.

143. "But Congress did not authorize the Commission to choose among applicants upon the basis of their political, economic or social views, or upon any other capricious basis. If it did, or if the Commission by these Regulations proposed a choice among applicants upon some such basis, the issue before us would be wholly different." NBC v. United States, 319 U.S. at 226.

144. *See supra* notes 132-33 and accompanying text.

145. 412 U.S. at 124. The Court equated the broadcaster's right to reject controversial paid advertising with the corresponding right of the printed media. It concluded that "[c]alculated risks of abuse of editorial power had to be taken in order to preserve higher values"—the right of editors to be free from governmental control. *Id.* at 125.

always been part of radio programming,[146] but both radio and television have remained primarily entertainment media. Until recently, investigative broadcast journalism was scheduled sporadically, and it remains the exception to the rule despite its sometimes significant impact.[147] Questions of entertainment program selection and scheduling, not newsroom judgments, dominate the broadcaster's first amendment activity.[148]

Yet these different activities do bring broadcasting within the rubric of the "press" for first amendment purposes. The constitutional privileges accorded the press in the areas of privacy[149] and defamation[150] apply equally to broadcasters and print journalists. So, too, do rules limiting protection of the secrecy of news sources[151] and reporter access to public facilities.[152] Even the courtroom, once thought to be off-limits to the tools of broadcast journalists, can now be entered.[153] Print and broadcast journalists share as co-venturers in the rights accorded the press by the first amendment.[154]

3. Summary.—The marketplace approach to broadcast regulation has two distinct advantages from a first amendment perspective. First, it does not conflict with *Red Lion*. In basing editorial and program judgments on their perceptions of popular demand, broadcasters enforce the paramount interests of listeners and viewers. Even if licen-

---

146. *See* 2 E. BARNOUW, A HISTORY OF BROADCASTING IN THE UNITED STATES: THE GOLDEN WEB 17-22 (1968). *See generally* A. KENDRICK, PRIME TIME (1969).

147. Among the most celebrated confrontations was a 1971 CBS documentary, "The Selling of the Pentagon," which covered the public relations efforts of the Defense Department. The program's airing led to a showdown between broadcasters and the congressional subpoena power when Congress unsuccessfully tried to obtain nonbroadcast outtakes from the network. *See* E. KRASNOW & L. LONGLEY, THE POLITICS OF BROADCAST REGULATION 82-83 (2d ed. 1978).

148. *See, e.g.,* Bazelon, *FCC Regulation of the Telecommunications Press*, 1975 DUKE L.J. 213, 219-20.

149. Cox Broadcasting Corp. v. Cohn, 420 U.S. 469 (1975) (challenge to television broadcast ofthe name of a rape victim from official court records) (described in Nixon v. Warner Communications, Inc., 435 U.S. 589, 608-09 (1978), as a case involving the "right of access of the press").

150. *See, e.g.,* Gertz v. Robert Welch, Inc., 418 U.S. 323 (1974), in which the Court used the conjunctive "publishers and broadcasters" to describe the class of potential defendants in defamation cases.

151. *See, e.g.,* Branzburg v. Hayes, 408 U.S. 665 (1972), in which the Court considered three appeals from reporters concerning demands upon them for information from grand juries. Two of the appeals involved newspaper reporters; the third appeal involved a Massachusetts television reporter. The Court did not distinguish among the three cases in determining the limits on the obligations of reporters to respond to grand jury subpoenas.

152. *See, e.g.,* Houchins v. KQED, Inc., 438 U.S. 1 (1978) (right of San Francisco television station to photograph prison facility). The Court referred to "the media" as having no special right of access without distinguishing between print and broadcast journalism.

153. *See, e.g.,* Chandler v. Florida, 449 U.S. 560 (1981).

154. *See The Supreme Court, 1980 Term*, 95 HARV. L. REV. 91, 227-28 (1981); Fowler, *Freedom of (Electronic) Speech*, Wash. Post, Sept. 20, 1981, at C7, col. 2.

sees occasionally misperceive the wants of their audiences, the present regulatory system, which is based upon the Commission's judgment of the community's needs, does not ensure a better result. Second, the marketplace approach accords protection to the distinct constitutional status of broadcasters under the press clause. This first amendment interest is, or should be, coextensive with the first amendment rights of the print media, regardless of whether the public is best served by its uninhibited exercise. A broadcaster's first amendment rights may differ from its listeners' rights to receive and hear suitable expression, but once the call is close, deference to broadcaster judgment is preferable to having a government agency mediate conflicts between broadcasters and their listeners.

IV.   Toward a Transition From a Trusteeship Approach to a Marketplace Approach

This Article has discussed the trusteeship model, the consequences of that model during its half-century of existence, and the marketplace approach to broadcast regulation. We now examine new directions that the Commission and Congress can pursue in forging a communications policy that utilizes marketplace theory.[155]

A.   Level I: A Return to the Marketplace

1.   General Approach: Resale.—In light of the fifty-five years of spectrum regulation under the trusteeship model, the problems of applying market techniques to spectrum use are more practical than theoretical. One approach would be to require all spectrum users to retire their licenses. The Commission would hold an auction to select new users and frequency rights would go to the highest bidders, who under a market theory should put the frequencies to their best use.[156] If a higher use for a frequency later emerged, the holder could resell the frequency rights.

---

155. It is beyond the scope of this Article to propose model legislation to accomplish the deregulatory goals advocated here. Some reforms, however, could be accomplished without legislation, since certain offending policies were originally adopted within the discretion of the Commission under the Communications Act. The Commission proposed a package of legislative reforms in 1981, known as Track I and Track II, which addressed many of the problems raised in this Article. Much of Track I, including lottery provisions and lessened financial incentives for licensure, was introduced in H.R. 5008, 97th Cong., 1st Sess. (1982). Track II provisions eliminating the fairness doctrine and political speech rules were introduced in H.R. 5584 and H.R. 5585, 97th Cong., 2d Sess. (1982).

156. *See* De Vany, Eckert, Meyers, O'Hara & Scott, *A Property System for Market Allocation of the Electromagnetic Spectrum: A Legal-Economic-Engineering Study*, 21 STAN. L. REV. 1499, 1512-22 (1969).

Although a good way to have started in the 1920's, an auction would substantially disrupt current service and frustrate the expectations of those who have long held spectrum rights and of their customers.[157] Another way to encourage optimum frequency use would be to allow licenses to be bought and sold freely after the initial grant, regardless of whether the initial grant is determined by auction, lottery, or under the old trusteeship approach. On resale, the seller, rather than the government, would capture the higher value of the frequency,[158] but the allocation of resale profit would not prevent the frequency from reaching its highest use, thereby achieving the market objective.

To some, the major objection to free resale would be the windfall to incumbent licensees. The windfall, to the extent that it actually occurred, would consist of the increased value of a deregulated license created by its release from content and ownership restrictions and its new, freely transferable character. The problem presented by the windfall of free transferability is not entirely novel. Except for distressed properties or those that have never been transferred, the price paid to a transferor under existing assignment rules already reflects the steadily increasing value of the exclusivity. It is almost always greater than the value of the nonlicense assets being transferred. Restricted resales under section 310(d) of the 1934 Act have already occurred several times with respect to many licenses, so that the windfall has been captured.[159]

---

157. Some portions of the reserved broadcast spectrum have been reassigned for land mobile uses. In Land Mobile Use of TV Channels 14 through 20, 23 F.C.C.2d 325 (1970), the Commission authorized a "sharing" that amounted to a shift of two of the lower seven (14 to 20) UHF frequencies from broadcasting to land mobile use in the top ten markets. The Commission later added three other congested markets. In An Inquiry Relating to the Future Use of the Frequency Band 806-960 MHz, 51 F.C.C.2d 945 (1975), aff'd sub nom. National Ass'n of Regulatory Utility Comm'rs v. FCC, 525 F.2d 630 (D.C. Cir. 1976), the Commission reallocated all of the upper 14 UHF channels (70 to 83) for a variety of new land mobile technologies, including trunked and cellular systems. The Sheriff's Office of Los Angeles County has petitioned for additional allocation of UHF frequencies in the lower seven for public safety and other land mobile operations. See FCC Public Notice, Petitions for Rule Making, Mimeo No. 3479 (Sept. 21, 1981).

158. The capital gains tax recaptures some of this value. The elimination of programs and paperwork associated with the trusteeship approach also undoubtedly would reduce costs and lead to increased revenues, but its dollar value, especially in a more competitive environment, is hard to determine.

159. Free transferability eliminates the extra costs associated with the Commission's transfer process. These costs primarily stem from litigation arising out of the petitions of competitors and public interest groups to deny new licenses and the delays associated with the resolution of the petitions. Adoption of a marketplace approach would eliminate the grounds for such petitions because the marketplace model assumes that resale is in the public interest, as it represents transfer of an asset to a higher use as contemplated by the new owner. See generally J. GRUNDFEST, CITIZEN PARTICIPATION IN BROADCAST LICENSING BEFORE THE FCC (Rand Corp. R-1896-MF 1976); Schneyer, An Overview of Public Interest Law Activity in the Communications Field, 1977 WIS. L. REV. 619; Volner, Broadcast Regulation: Is There Too Much "Public" in the "Public Interest?," 43 CIN. L. REV. 267, 280-82 (1974). Under the Communications Act, a competing applica-

More generally, the marketplace approach could be most expeditiously introduced to broadcasting by granting existing licensees "squatter's rights" to their frequencies. These rights embody the reasonable expectation of renewal that licensees presently enjoy for satisfactory past performance.[160] The critical next step, from a market viewpoint, would be to deregulate fully the sale of licenses.

This approach to resale need not preclude the use of lotteries or auctions for new assignments to broadcasters or other spectrum users. Consider the Commission's handling of low-power television service. Announcement of this new service led to the submission of thousands of applications, many mutually exclusive, so that the Commission is faced with choosing among competing applicants. Although the Commission has approved a comparative process to license this new service,[161] initial grants using either a lottery and resale[162] or an auction could inject market incentives into the distribution of this service. Either technique would be likely to raise the frequency exclusivity to its highest use as a broadcast frequency.

2. Eliminating Content and Business Restrictions.—In addition to promoting resale, the marketplace approach requires an end to program regulation. Government oversight of broadcast content arrogates editorial responsibilities protected by the first amendment and interferes with the functioning of market forces as well. The agenda for restoring competition to the television market should include scrapping

tion will not be considered at the time of a proposed license transfer. 47 U.S.C. § 310(d) (Supp. III 1979). The Commission, however, accepts petitions to deny at the time of transfer, since the Commission must make an affirmative public interest finding to authorize the reassignment. This ban on competing applications has been part of the Communications Act since 1952, and was designed to operate so that "in applying the test of public interest, convenience, and necessity, the Commission must do so as though the proposed transferee or assignee were applying for the construction permit or station license and as though no other person were interested in securing such permit or license." H.R. REP. No. 1750, 82d Cong., 2d Sess. 12 (1952). The ban foreclosed future efforts by the Commission under its "AVCO ruling," which it had announced prospectively in Powel Crosley, Jr., 11 F.C.C. 3, 26 (1945), to permit competing applications.

160. *See generally* Note, *The Recognition of Legitimate Renewal Expectancies in Broadcast Licensing*, 58 WASH. U.L.Q. 409 (1980).

161. *See* Inquiry into the Future Role of Low Power Television Broadcasting and Television Translators in the National Telecommunications System, 47 Fed. Reg. 21,468 (1982).

162. The 1981 Omnibus Budget Reconciliation Act, Pub. L. No. 97-35, 95 Stat. 736 (1981) (to be codified at 47 U.S.C. § 309(i)), authorized the Commission to use lottery procedures to choose among mutually exclusive applications for initial telecommunications licenses, subject to criteria specified by Congress. The Commission declined to implement its lottery authority because the statute did not eliminate the administrative burden of examining each lottery applicant under 47 U.S.C. § 308(b) (1976), and because of obstacles to implementing the statutory preference for "groups or organizations, or members of groups or organizations, which are underrepresented in the ownership of telecommunications facilities or properties." Amendment of Part I of the Commission's Rules, 50 RAD. REG. 2d (P & F) 1503 (1982).

the content-oriented regulations that prescribe minimum amounts of nonentertainment programs and limit advertising. Their elimination would allow broadcasters to satisfy consumer desires based on their reading of what viewers want, from all-news to all-entertainment programming. The Commission also should seek repeal of other content regulations, such as the fairness doctrine and the political speech rules, although it might assign access obligations for political candidates and referenda to public broadcasters.[163]

Restrictions that impede resale should be the first barriers abandoned in the move to a market environment. The rule on "trafficking" licenses, which require applications for license assignment or transfer of stock control to be designated for hearing unless the license has been held for at least three years, are particularly perverse.[164] The rule condemns licensees who acquire a station and dispose of it in less than three years. Yet such behavior is not restricted in other segments of the economy. To the contrary, we generally reward those who buy an ailing company and, having turned its fortunes around, sell it. Under a trusteeship approach it is conduct unbecoming a public steward; under a market approach it is conduct rewarded by profit on resale.

The Commission should also consider abolishing rules that restrict growth by existing players or limit entry of new players in any of the competitive video fields. It should place particular attention on its restrictions on ownership of media facilities.[165] For example, the Com-

---

163. In 1981 the Commission recommended that Congress repeal the fairness doctrine, 47 U.S.C. § 315 (1976), and the equal opportunity and equal access requirements for political candidates, *id.* § 312(a)(7) (1976). *See* BROADCASTING, Sept. 21, 1981, at 23. Public broadcasters might be required to provide candidates with opportunities for political speech as part of their mission in a marketplace approach to regulation. *See infra* notes 190-92 and accompanying text.

164. 47 C.F.R. § 73.3597(a)-(d) (1981). "Trafficking" in broadcast licenses and permits was defined as the licensee's acquisition of a station "for the purpose of reselling it at a profit rather than for the purpose of rendering a public service." Powel Crosley, Jr., 11 F.C.C. 3, 23 (1945). In the late 1950's and early 1960's, Congress focused on this issue, *see generally* SPECIAL SUBCOMM. ON LEGISLATIVE OVERSIGHT OF THE HOUSE COMM. ON INTERSTATE AND FOREIGN COMMERCE, 85TH CONG., 2D SESS., REGULATION OF BROADCASTING: HALF A CENTURY OF GOVERNMENT REGULATION OF BROADCASTING AND THE NEED FOR FURTHER LEGISLATIVE ACTION (Subcomm. Print 1958). In 1960 House Subcommittee Chairman Oren Harris proposed in H.R. 11,340 that broadcast license transfers be prohibited within the first three years after a grant unless a public hearing held in the station's service area determined that the transfer was due to "inadequacy of operating capital, death, or disability of key management personnel, or other changed circumstances." H.R. 11,340, 86th Cong., 2d Sess. (1960). The bill died in the 86th Congress, but was reintroduced the next term, H.R. 1165, 87th Cong., 1st Sess. (1961), and remained pending at the time the FCC adopted the trafficking rule. Procedures on Transfer and Assignment Applications, 32 F.C.C. 689 (1962). The Commission recently proposed deleting the trafficking rule. Amendment of § 73.3597 of the Commission's Rules, Applications for Voluntary Assignments or Transfers of Control, 47 Fed. Reg. 985 (1982).

165. *See generally* OFFICE OF PLANS AND POLICY, *supra* note 5; Howard, *Multiple Broadcast Ownership: Regulatory History*, 27 FED. COM. L.J. 1 (1974).

mission has long enforced a "7-7-7" rule, which restricts one licensee to seven AM, seven FM, and seven television outlets, no more than five of which can be VHF stations.[166] The rule stems from the Commission's desire to establish some limit on the number of stations a single licensee can operate. This arbitrary rule has almost certainly promoted inefficiency, for it does not measure a licensee's share of the homes using television nationwide. An operator with twenty-one stations in the bottom twenty-one markets possesses far less market control than the owner of three stations in the top three markets. If national concentration is a concern, the Commission could limit station ownership by the percentage of homes reached rather than by an arbitrary number of stations. But even a percentage approach should have to demonstrate that a limit on ownership bears a close relationship to preventing an identifiable harm.

In revising the 7-7-7 rule, the Commission should consider whether express limitations on concentration are warranted or whether they create undesirable barriers to entry in programming or distribution. Concentration of media outlets, particularly in a local market, can pose special problems. But this fact alone should not subject the media industries to limitations on the ownership rights freely permitted in other concentrated industries.

A less restrictive policy toward group ownership would also aid program diversity. The 1952 allocation scheme led to the development of only three full-time television networks.[167] Significant group ownership in broadcasting exists outside of stations licensed to the networks, but the Commission's regulations have prevented these groups from gaining access to important markets and establishing alternatives to the traditional three-network structure.[168] In its review of the 7-7-7 rule and other ownership limits, the Commission should be aware that the right of group owners to acquire additional stations might make alternative networks viable. It should also consider anew the scrutiny it gives to financial[169] and character qualifications[170] in transfers and at

---

166. *See* 47 C.F.R. §§ 73.240(a)(2), .35(b)(1), .636(a)(2) (1981). The Commission arrived at the 7-7-7 figure by taking as a ceiling the largest number of stations held by any one licensee at the time of the rule's adoption.

167. *See supra* note 78 and accompanying text.

168. "Under the Commission's present Table of Assignments, a potential fourth network could expect to reach only 35.8% of the nation's television households by means of technically comparable affiliates, assuming that all assignments were operational." Schuessler, *supra* note 76, at 998 (footnote omitted).

169. New Financial Qualifications for Broadcast Assignment and Transfer Applicants, 87 F.C.C.2d 200 (1981), lessened the showing required by the Commission in the transfer situation. Under the new standards, an applicant must only demonstrate sufficient capital to consummate the transaction on the closing of the sale and to meet expenses for three months. *Id.* Previously,

renewals. The governing principle in this hard look is whether any Commission rule fosters or undermines market forces, forces designed to discover and meet the public's interest.

B.   Level II: A Cost of Asset Approach: The Spectrum License Fee

1.   Charging for Spectrum Use.—The concept of property is essential to the functioning of a marketplace economy. In a deregulated communications marketplace, the right to a frequency exclusivity for an unlimited period of time would be an intangible property interest. Indeed, the reasonable expectation of license renewal enjoyed by broadcasters today comes close to a property right, in reality if not in name.

The broadcast license, however, had never been deemed a property right, in part because the Commission can take it away for gross misbehavior without compensation. Under a marketplace approach, the grounds for revoking a license would narrow drastically, if not disappear. Lying or other malfeasance toward the Commission or persistent technical violations would be among the few bases on which the Commission would be likely to strip a licensee of its exclusivity.[171] Under these circumstances, whether or not Congress explicitly recognized the proprietary aspects of a broadcast license, the question of its value as property would be inescapable. Who should receive the value? And through what mechanism should it be distributed?

To the extent that the government should receive part of the value of the exclusivity, it is worth considering whether the Commission should charge a spectrum usage fee. The Commission could base a fee

the Commission required applicants to demonstrate an ability to meet expenses for the first year, Ultravision Broadcasting Co., 1 F.C.C.2d 544, 547 (1965); Public Notice, 1 F.C.C.2d 550 (1965), rather than 90 days. The next deregulatory step would be to eliminate all financial qualifications, just as there is no required showing when a buyer seeks to acquire a newspaper by transfer of ownership.

170.   The Commission has wrestled with the question of what constitutes sufficiently good character for a broadcast licensee. The Commission found RKO General, Inc. unqualified to be licensee of its television stations, in part because its nonbroadcast misconduct called into question its character qualifications, in part because of misrepresentations before the agency. RKO Gen., Inc., 78 F.C.C.2d 1, 4, 47-80 (1980), *rev'd in part*, 670 F.2d 215 (D.C. Cir. 1981). The Commission has launched an inquiry directed toward reducing the scope of its character test in broadcasting. *See* Policy Regarding Character Qualifications in Broadcast Licensing, 87 F.C.C.2d 836 (1981).

171.   The Commission has denied license renewal for a station's abdication of control over programs, Trustees of the Univ. of Pa., 71 F.C.C.2d 416 (1979), persistent violation of operating rules, United Television Co., Inc., 55 F.C.C.2d 416 (1975), and clipping network programs to insert local advertising and thereafter misrepresenting this conduct to the agency, Western Communications, Inc., 59 F.C.C.2d 1441 (1976). Revocation has occurred for misrepresentations in connection with fraudulent billing practices. Sea Island Broadcasting Corp., 60 F.C.C.2d 146 (1976).

on a small percentage of a station's profits,[172] or it could levy a flat charge based on bandwidth use.

Merely charging a usage fee for the spectrum admittedly does not instill significant incentives in the broadcasting market. A charge would not lead to the most efficient frequency use because it would not be levied according to each licensee's relative use. A flat charge imposed on an increasingly competitive industry, if set too high, could force marginal broadcasters out of business. Even a fee based on a percentage of royalties would not measure the comparative worth of broadcasting against other spectrum uses.

A spectrum fee is, however, economically attractive because it puts a price on a major input of doing business in broadcasting—the method of distribution. Such a fee would recognize that broadcasters receive something of value in the exclusivity that the government provides them, similar to government franchises for offshore oil rights or food concessions in public parks. Additionally, the fee would end the competitive advantage that broadcasting enjoys over such delivery systems as cable television, which pays a franchise fee to the licensing municipality,[173] a regulatory advantage distinct from the natural

---

172. Congressman Van Deerlin proposed the inclusion of a fee provision in the Communications Act of 1978. The fee would have been based on the costs of processing the license and the value of the spectrum and would have gone to a "telecommunications fund" to support federal regulation, public broadcasting, minority ownership of stations, and rural telecommunications. H.R. 13,015, 95th Cong., 2d Sess. § 413 (1978). The bill also proposed broadcast deregulation, extending television license terms from three to five years for a period of ten years (and becoming indefinite thereafter), and creating indefinite radio license terms. Congressman Van Deerlin viewed the license fee and broadcast deregulation as "trade-offs." *See* BROADCASTING, June 12, 1978, at 29.

An inquiry by the Library of Congress into whether there is a legally certain method to collect more than the costs of administration where radio frequency spectrum is concerned concluded that "if there is, we are not aware of it." Congressional Research Service, The Library of Congress, Memorandum, Legal Analysis of Radio Spectrum Use Charges (Apr. 20, 1979). In 1981 Henry Geller, former General Counsel of the Commission, renewed support for a spectrum fee. *Public Broadcasting Oversight of 1981, Hearings on H.R. 4726, H.R. 4780, and H.R. 4781 Before the Subcomm. on Telecommunications, Consumer Protection, and Finance of the House Comm. on Energy and Commerce*, 97th Cong., 1st Sess. 98-99 (1981). The president of the Public Broadcasting Service, Lawrence K. Grossman, has recommended that spectrum fees be used to support public television. BROADCASTING, Jan. 4, 1982, at 14. In an accompanying editorial, *Broadcasting* urged consideration of Grossman's proposal, although it criticized the size of the fee proposed in H.R. 13,015. *Id.* at 114. The political viability of a fee to support public television thus seems to depend on the amount of the fee. The National Radio Broadcasters Association has proposed fifty-year licenses for radio tied to a spectrum fee of one percent of station revenues. The fee would be earmarked for public radio and minority ownership. The larger rival trade group, the National Association of Broadcasters, opposes a spectrum fee but would support smaller "license" fees, *see, e.g.,* S. 1629, 97th Cong., 2d Sess. (1982). *See generally* BROADCASTING, July 5, 1982, at 60.

173. On the other hand, broadcasting seems to suffer a disadvantage where copyright is concerned. The 1976 Copyright Act required cable operators for the first time to reimburse proprietors of copyrighted works. 17 U.S.C. § 111(d)(2) (1976). Cable systems pay the compulsory fees

advantage it enjoys in avoiding cable's high fixed costs in wiring a community. To be equitable, the Commission would have to impose the fee on all spectrum uses, whether for cable television microwave hops, direct broadcasting satellites, or multipoint distribution operations.

The spectrum fee approach is not free of negative aspects. The right to collect a fee ultimately depends on the supposition that the airwaves belong to the public at large, a premise that has no logical place in determining the degree of regulation permitted over broadcasters. The value of the exclusivity depends on a licensee's investment and ingenuity. The exclusivity granted by the government to a broadcaster is similar to a patent or copyright, for which the holder pays only nominal registration fees. The key to the success of a broadcaster, unlike a concessionaire in a public park, is ingenuity.

Administering a spectrum fee raises other problems. The fee would account for the exclusive frequency received by the licensees to distribute programs and the right to transfer freely the exclusivity. The fee could also cover the services rendered by the Commission in enforcement and licensing.[174] This approach accords with the trend to have the users of government services pay their way. The Commission, however, could not determine the market-clearing price of the spectrum because the spectrum would not be subject to bidding by the full range of potential users. Any fee beyond the value of services rendered by the Commission is thus bound to be somewhat arbitrary and lead to new distortions in the market. Therefore, a spectrum fee would be an inexact method of capturing the perceived windfall. In addition, when stations have been transferred in the past, the sellers already have captured much of the windfall. Consequently, fees imposed on subsequent

---

for carriage of radio and television programs to the Copyright Royalty Tribunal, which disburses them to copyright owners. In 1981, three trade groups, the National Cable Television Association, the National Association of Broadcasters, and the Motion Picture Association of America, agreed on a "great compromise" to amend the 1976 Act. The compromise would have maintained the compulsory license as well as the current copyright fee schedule. The syndicated exclusivity rule, rescinded by the Commission in 1980, would have been reimposed and made applicable to all television markets. See BROADCASTING, Nov. 30, 1981, at 32-33; CABLEVISION, Nov. 9, 1981, at 14. The proposal failed to generate support among members of the associations and eventually broke down. Its failure may be explained by the madcap internal subsidization between broadcasters and cablecasters. Cable television incurs low copyright liability for the off-the-air programming it retransmits, but it has high distribution costs. Broadcasters pay little to distribute programs, but pay both for their own programming (reimbursed by advertisers, of course) and, some argue, for a share of cable's programming costs as well.

174. The Commission has the authority to charge fees, but it must base fees on the "value to the recipient." The Commission may not include fees based on the cost of services that inure to the benefit of the public generally. National Cable Television Ass'n v. United States, 415 U.S. 336 (1974).

owners of these stations to recapture prior windfalls create new unfairness.

Justification for a spectrum fee, thus, depends less on its economic merit and more on how one weighs the relative equities of a deregulated broadcast environment against a spectrum fee that is likely to be somewhat arbitrary. Deregulation does not necessitate a spectrum fee, nor does it exclude it. Ultimately, Congress must decide whether to impose a fee based on its valuation of the interests affected by the grant of exclusivity.

2. Disposition of the Spectrum Fee in the Public Interest.—A congressional decision to apply a spectrum fee would raise the separate question of the proper disposition of the funds collected. On the one hand, the government could collect fees and remit them to the general treasury in obedience to the oft-repeated, though unproductive, contention that the airwaves "belong to the people." On the other hand, the government could pursue the public interest directly and use the fees collected from commercial broadcasters to support a public broadcast service. This concept is not novel,[175] but it has applicability to the marketplace approach to regulation advanced here. This suggestion requires a short digression, one that moves away from the general approach advocated thus far.

After the Commission decided to reserve the broadcasting spectrum for radio and television, it created two classes of broadcasting: commercial and noncommercial.[176] The need for noncommercial broadcasting has been hotly debated.[177] Today's noncommercial service combines instructional radio and television, which originated in the 1950's with the establishment of the Public Broadcasting Service (PBS) by the Public Broadcasting Act of 1967.[178] Over the years public television has never escaped its identity crisis. Should it attempt to reach the broadest audience, on the theory that the tax dollar supporting the system requires an expansive approach? How "commercial" should this system be? Who should be involved in decisionmaking? How repre-

---

175. *See supra* note 172.
176. *See generally* Lindsey, *Public Broadcasting: Editorial Restraints and the First Amendment,* 28 FED. COM. L.J. 63, 64-75 (1975).
177. *See generally* R. COASE & E. BARRETT, EDUCATIONAL TV: WHO SHOULD PAY? (1968). Commercial broadcasting, with the rare exception of special programs, was devoted exclusively to light entertainment. . . . But the citizen, rich or poor, who wanted something more, who happened to be eager to use Sunday night to stretch his mind, to face up to some of the issues of the day or even to enjoy some fine music, had no opportunity to do so.
Id. at 39.
178. Pub. L. No. 90-129, 81 Stat. 365 (codified at 47 U.S.C. §§ 390-399 (1976)).

sentative are the boards of local public broadcasting stations? What is the appropriate mix of funding for public television? And, most basically, should public broadcasting exist at all?

These issues stem from two congressional actions in 1967. First, acting on studies by the Carnegie Commission and the Ford Foundation, Congress almost unanimously passed the Public Broadcasting Act. Second, Congress deferred the determination of how to fund the system. It declined to adopt the Ford Foundation's plan to create a communications satellite system that would provide free interconnection to public stations and establish a profit center for revenues earned by carrying other satellite traffic.[179] It also rejected the Carnegie Commission's recommendation that an excise tax on the sale of television sets be imposed to support the system.[180] Over the years, the question of financing has remained unsettled. Public broadcasting has even faced the danger of being "punished" in the budget process for programs that offended an incumbent administration.[181]

The issue of what type of programming public television should carry has been joined in the marketplace. New cultural channels have been launched on cable on a subscriber or advertiser-supported basis (or a combination of both).[182] PBS, hoping to use its expertise in this segment of the programming market, has proposed its own pay cable service devoted to the cultural and arts field.[183] Revenues from a PBS pay cable channel would support the chronically underfunded system.

What does a marketplace scheme of broadcast regulation portend for this format in public broadcasting? The fundamental question is whether the Commission should continue to maintain two sets of licen-

---

179. *See* Letter from McGeorge Bundy, Ford Foundation, to Rosel Hyde, Chairman, Federal Communications Commission (Aug. 1, 1966), *reprinted in* DOCUMENTS OF AMERICAN BROADCASTING 570 (F. Kahn ed. 1972).

180. CARNEGIE COMM'N ON EDUCATIONAL TELEVISION, PUBLIC TELEVISION: A PROGRAM FOR ACTION (1967), *portions reprinted in* DOCUMENTS OF AMERICAN BROADCASTING, *supra* note 179, at 576.

181. For a discussion of the role of public television before and during the Watergate hearings, see E. BARNOUW, TUBE OF PLENTY 454-55 (1975); *see also* C. STERLING & J. KITTROSS, STAY TUNED 457 (1978).

182. CBS Cable, offered generally as a basic (non-pay) cable service, serves three million homes on over 250 cable systems. Other cultural services, such as Bravo Pay Cable Service, which currently serves 120,000 homes, are offered on a pay basis. *See* CABLEVISION, Nov. 23, 1981, at 191.

183. S. MAHONY, N. DeMARTINO & R. STENGEL, KEEPING PACE WITH THE NEW TELEVISION (1980), reported on the status of pay cable ventures in the cultural sector and advocated a new, nonprofit corporation to provide a pay cable network independent of public television to program for "an elite with specialized tastes." *Id.* at 45. PBS rejected the recommendation to stay out of pay cable and has proposed a public subscriber network to provide additional revenues for over-the-air public television. *See* TELEVISION/RADIO AGE, Feb. 9, 1981, at 49. *See generally* Ginsburg, Book Review, 33 FED. COM. L.J. 309 (1981).

sees. Reserving frequencies, including valuable VHF frequencies, for noncommercial activity distorts the marketplace and deprives non-commercial operators of even the indirect reverberations of consumer demand that advertisers provide.[184] Despite efforts by public television to broaden its circle of decisionmakers, programming choices remain an insulated judgment call by those in power.

Yet as public broadcasters begin to look more like commercial op-erators, aiming programming at wider audiences and adding limited advertising,[185] new problems emerge. Why should a commercial enter-prise be denied a chance to compete for their frequencies? One solu-tion would be to end protection for noncommercial licensing and expose existing licenses, or at least unclaimed channels reserved for noncommercial broadcasting, to commercial licensure by lottery, auc-tion, or traditional comparative hearing.

A differing viewpoint, however, assumes that noncommercial tele-vision will remain viable. The reservation of certain broadcast fre-quencies reflects a social value beyond market efficiency. Economists have long recognized the existence of "merit goods," which society val-ues although the marketplace cannot explain or justify their reten-tion.[186] Reservation of valuable real estate for public parks, public support for museums and libraries, the special tax treatment accorded religious and eleemosynary institutions, and the system of public edu-cation are all services shielded, to a greater or lesser extent, from mar-ketplace forces. So, too, public television, in spite of the deficiencies in its method of program selection, has been a merit good.

Having distorted the market at the outset by reserving a number of spectrum exclusivities for broadcasting, the Commission can make some provision for programs that might not find their way on the air through market mechanisms. The Commission's long-standing policy of encouraging locally originated programming illustrates this point.[187]

---

184. *See supra* notes 107-11 and accompanying text.

185. Under the Omnibus Budget Reconciliation Act, Pub. L. No. 97-35, § 1232(b), 95 Stat. 357, 732 (1981), Congress created the Temporary Commission on Alternative Financing for Public Telecommunications (TCAF) with a mandate to study the options for new revenue sources for public radio and television. The TCAF has since reported to Congress on new financing schemes, although it did not evaluate spectrum fees. TCAF, ALTERNATIVE FINANCING OPTIONS FOR PUB-LIC BROADCASTING (1982). The TCAF has already authorized an advertising experiment on ten public television stations. FCC Public Notice, Mimeo No. 2746 (Mar. 11, 1982); *see* BROADCAST-ING, July 19, 1982, at 68.

186. *See* B. OWEN, J. BEEBE & W. MANNING, JR., *supra* note 14, at 158-59; Brenner, *supra* note 107, at 88-92.

187. *See, e.g.,* En Banc Programming Inquiry, 44 F.C.C. 2303 (1960):
    Under [§ 307(b) of the Communications Act] the Commission has consistently licensed stations with the end objective of either providing new or additional programming ser-

The desire to weave the nation's broadcasting system into a community's infrastructure may not reflect the desires of a majority of the broadcast audience, but Congress may nonetheless find it desirable to preserve local service. This judgment, after all, undergirded the 1952 television allocation plan.[188] Unlike satellite-distributed cable or network broadcast service, only a local station can distribute a local program over the air. Locally oriented news, public affairs, and cultural programs will not be provided by the national arts or news channels, but they could be part of a public television or radio service.

Similarly, experimental programming may take longer to develop an audience than the marketplace usually permits, but it can be an enduring objective of public television. One can seriously question whether pay cable cultural and arts channels will support offbeat productions. Pay cable networks, whether public television's or one of the commercial enterprise's, are likely to skim the most popular cultural programs, leaving little support for emerging but less marketable talent.

Public television can also carry a pilot or ongoing basis age-specific programming that does not find sufficient support in the marketplace. Programming for children is a prime candidate. An advertiser-supported system may be unable to meet the demand for children's programs because of the limited range of advertisers wishing to sponsor these programs.[189] Although cable television provides a way for parents to subscribe to programs for children, this service will not be of-

vice *to* a community, area or state, or of providing a new or additional "outlet" for broadcasting *from* a community, area, or state. Implicit in the former alternative is increased radio reception; implicit in the latter alternative is increased radio transmission and, in this connection, appropriate attention to local live programming is required.

Id. at 2311. The ascertainment exercise also directed the broadcaster to determine local problems and describe programs designed to meet those problems. *See supra* notes 44-47 and accompanying text. One Commissioner has defined localism "as the maintenance of a studio for the production of local news and public affairs." Amaturo Group, Inc., 74 F.C.C.2d 299, 315 (1979) (Ferris, Chmn., concurring). Another approach to the "localism" concept starts from the § 307(b) mandate of a "fair, efficient, and equitable distribution" of stations. Localism under this approach relates not to program origination but to local service. *See* Comment, *The Promising Future of Direct Broadcast Satellites in America: Truth or Consequences?*, 33 FED. COM. L.J. 221, 222-32 (1981).

188. *See supra* notes 76-80 and accompanying text. Curiously, though the Commission touts localism in its decisions, it has never required any fixed percentage of local programming despite the suitability of over-the-air television to distribute local programs. *See* Community Television of S. Cal., 72 F.C.C.2d 349 (1979) (noncommercial licensee has wide discretion in fulfilling obligations to serve community needs; complaint that station spent disproportionate amount of funds on nonlocal programming provided no basis for renewal hearing); WPIX, Inc., 68 F.C.C.2d 381, 402-03 (1978) (renewal challenge denied; premise that "local needs can be met only through programming produced by a local station has not only been rejected by the Commission . . . but it also lacks presumptive validity").

189. OFFICE OF PLANS AND POLICY, *supra* note 47, at 41-44.

fered in many communities. For some time to come, some child audiences will remain without access to specialized cable services. Public television's mission could be to provide programming for these viewers. A need also may exist for specialized programs for the elderly, who may be neither economically attractive to advertisers nor wealthy enough to generate a significant quantity of subscription programs for their special needs and interests.

Public television can also become a forum for individual access denied by commercial outlets.[190] Because public broadcasters are government funded, it is more likely that their denial of access to individuals would constitute state action for first amendment purposes.[191] The decision of a government-funded broadcaster to deny access would trigger strict scrutiny under the speech clause.[192]

190. In CBS v. Democratic Nat'l Comm., 412 U.S. 94 (1973), the Supreme Court upheld the Commission's rejection of a claim that individual groups have a right to purchase advertising time to comment on public issues. The concept of an affirmative right of access in broadcasting was set forth in Barron, *Access to the Press—A New First Amendment Right*, 80 HARV. L. REV. 1641 (1967); *see also* Rosenbloom v. Metromedia, Inc., 403 U.S. 29, 47 n.15 (1971).

191. In CBS v. Democratic Nat'l Comm., 412 U.S. 94 (1973), Justice Douglas suggested in a concurring opinion that editorial activities by public broadcast stations did constitute state action. Justice Douglas also stated that a denial of access in such an instance would constitute an abridgment under the first amendment:

> If these cases involved [the Corporation for Public Broadcasting], we would have a situation comparable to that in which the United States owns and manages a prestigious newspaper like the New York Times, Washington Post, or Sacramento Bee. . . . [T]he programs tendered by the respondents in the present cases could not then be turned down.

Id. at 149-50 (Douglas, J., concurring). Justice Douglas' views at least suggest that there would be a smaller burden on proponents of an access scheme to public television than required under *CBS v. Democratic National Comm.* Public broadcasters, insofar as they originate programming, would not necessarily lose first amendment protection. But to the extent that programming decisions by a public broadcaster are state action, the licensee would be bound to disseminate all views within the limits of its time schedule, as Justice Douglas stated. *Id.* at 150. However, *CBS* held only that the 1934 Act and the first amendment do not require broadcasters to accept paid editorial advertisements. It did not hold that carrying the advertisements, in particular on public stations, violated the first amendment. *But see* FCC v. Midwest Video Corp., 440 U.S. 689 (1979) (Communications Act, which prohibits treating broadcasters as "common carriers," 47 U.S.C. § 153(h) (1976), foreclosed imposition of access requirements amounting to common carrier obligations upon licensees).

192. It is beyond the scope of this Article to determine whether there is an individual right of access over public channels, but the exercise of this right doubtless would increase the number of speakers on the air. Yet it does not offend the first amendment rights of broadcasters as much as in the commercial sector, since the government funds the broadcasters in question. Creation of a limited right of access during certain hours on television for individual speakers as well as documentary and entertainment program producers would bring the public forum, long a tradition in American society, to the medium of broadcasting, which has functioned in many ways as the modern equivalent of the soap box in the town square.

In 1979, the Commission rejected a proposal for an access alternative to fairness that, if undertaken by licensees, would be deemed presumptive compliance with the fairness doctrine. The Handling of Public Issues Under the Fairness Doctrine and the Public Interest Standards of the Communications Act, 74 F.C.C.2d 163 (1979). The Commission based its decision on its experience with access programs, particularly the fact that the issues raised in access experiments fre-

This Article cannot discuss all the arguments for and against maintenance of public television. This is properly a question for Congress, which passed the Public Broadcasting Act of 1967 without ensuring the system's financial security, because it involves broader questions about public financing.[193] Maintenance of public television and radio through revenues from a spectrum fee might be part of an overall approach to the spectrum used for broadcasting. Like the national park concessionaire whose fee supports nonprofit park activities, the broadcaster would find his transmission fee used to fund worthwhile activities on adjacent channels.

It may seem somewhat incongruous to require broadcasters to finance a government-sanctioned competitor. Yet, in creating public television stations in the first instance, the government has always used tax revenues, including those from commercial broadcasters, to support public broadcasting. A bolstered public broadcast system operating within a marketplace approach would inject a "best use" strategy for most frequencies while still accommodating the nonmarket considerations that gave rise to the reservation of spectrum initially. Commercial broadcasters would be absolutely free to pursue commercial objectives without lingering trusteeship obligations. At the same time, noncommercial broadcasters would have a clear mandate to provide services as alternatives to, not duplicates of, the programming available over commercial channels.

C. Level III: Deregulation of Broadcasting: No Spectrum Fee

The failure of the spectrum fee concept to generate substantial support over the years may in large measure be due to the inertia of both the regulators and the regulated. From the inception of federal regulation, broadcasters have received their grants without direct fee. The suggestion of imposing a fee for something that has always been a free and renewable resource—an exclusivity granted by the government—generates considerable opposition. And the aggregate cost of the trusteeship form of regulation may be less than the fee charged. Given the choice, many broadcasters might prefer the security of current regulation to true competition and a charge for their frequency exclusivity.

quently fail to concern important public matters. *Id.* at 172-78. Although access in terms of free speech opportunities may be sometimes more valuable in theory than in practice, it offers a safety valve for our proposed broadcasting scheme. Furthermore, it provides a logical alternative to the representative form of broadcasting embodied in the trusteeship approach.

193. *See generally* J. BUCHANAN, THE PUBLIC FINANCES 465 (1970); A. SHARP & B. SLIGER, PUBLIC FINANCE 55 (1970).

Moreover, not all broadcast facilities are profitable.[194] Those who have recently turned the corner would probably find it unfair for the government to charge them for an exclusivity that became valuable only through their persistent efforts. These broadcasters undoubtedly would argue that substantial deregulation of commercial broadcasting should occur without a fee.

The most significant point about fees and public television, in economic terms, is that there should be no quid pro quo for adoption of a marketplace approach. Free resale and the elimination of content and business restrictions do not depend for their validity or effectiveness on the existence of a fee or of a protected public broadcasting system. Congress should separate the fate of the marketplace approach to broadcast regulation from questions of the collection of spectrum fees or the maintenance of public broadcasting. Congressional consideration of the latter notions should not forestall a transition to a marketplace approach.

V. Conclusion

The Communications Act provides the Commission with discretion to translate consumer wants into the programming decisions of broadcasters by invoking marketplace principles. The need for a fresh approach to broadcasting, now spurred by competitive challenges from cable and other video providers, is long overdue. This new approach concludes that broadcasters best serve the public by responding to market forces rather than governmental directives. It restores the broadcasting business to the unregulated status of American enterprise generally. In doing so, it also recognizes that content regulation of commercial radio and television is fundamentally at odds with the first amendment status of broadcasting.

The time has come for Congress and the Commission to recognize the role of broadcasting within overall spectrum usage and adopt a more rational approach to broadcast regulation. One possible, though inessential, approach would be to charge for the exclusivity provided by a government license. Congress must also clarify the purpose of the noncommercial licensing function. Congress should either ratify the mission of public broadcasting in the overall scheme for the reserved broadcast spectrum or instruct the Commission to return its frequencies for reassignment to face the rigors of the marketplace. The end result

---

194. *See, e.g.,* 1 NETWORK INQUIRY SPECIAL STAFF, *supra* note 9, at 77. In 1978, 93% of VHF affiliates and 83% of UHF affiliates were profitable; among independents, 80% of VHFs and 60% of UHFs were profitable. *Id.*

should be a commercial broadcasting system in which market forces rather than trustee duties govern as far as possible the provision of broadcast service to the American people.

Despite a number of problems, the introduction of free enterprise competition into the telecommunications field in the United States has produced great benefits to the public, argues Richard E. Wiley, a former chairman of the Federal Communications Commission. Wiley also suggests that deregulation, where "true" competition can be achieved in telecommunications, fosters enhanced public service, though regulation will remain in force where "natural monopoly" remains a market characteristic. Wiley is a partner in the Washington, D.C., law firm of Kirkland and Ellis.

38

COMPETITION AND DEREGULATION IN TELECOMMUNICATIONS
The American Experience

Richard E. Wiley

The United States is one of the few nations in the world which permits private ownership of public utilities. Of course, this does not mean that policies regarding these critical industries are beyond the reach of governmental authority. Regulatory agencies like the Federal Communications Commission set public policy and oversee the utilities in their implementation of that policy. In general, the primary concerns of telecommunications regulators lie in the areas of rate levels and rate structure, and market entry and exit.

The underlying principle in the regulation of telecommunications in the United States is the realization of certain recognized social goals. These objectives were established by Congress in the Communications Act of 1934, which remains in force today. That Act created the FCC with the mandate to further the development of universal telephone service at affordable rates and to encourage construction of the most modern, rapid, and efficient nationwide telecommunications system possible. These goals were to be pursued, however, in the context of private ownership of telecommunications companies.

At the time the Communications Act was passed, the idea that a "natural monopoly" was an inherent element in universal public telephone service was a widely held belief. While the telephone system did not need to be under a common, national ownership, it was thought that no geographic location could or should be served by more than one telephone company. The overall network consisted of a group of interconnected local or regional monopolies.

From Richard E. Wiley, "Competition and Deregulation in Telecommunications: The American Experience," in Leonard Lewin, ed., *Telecommunications in the United States: Trends and Policies* (Dedham, MA: Artech House, Inc., 1981), pp. 37-59. Reprinted by permission.

In 1934, this "natural monopoly" concept was probably an accurate reflection of the technology of the times. In addition, the perspective of that day had been shaped by decades of chaotic conditions within the telecommunications industry. A brief review of those years provides a better understanding of the thinking which prevailed during the period.

1. THE HISTORICAL BACKGROUND

1.1 Events Before the Creation of the FCC

1.1.1 The Monopoly Era

Practical electronic communications really began in the United States when Samuel Morse invented the telegraph in the late 1830's. A $30,000 Congressional grant nurtured the development of telegraphy and, by 1844, a government-owned telegraph line was in operation between Washington, D.C., and Baltimore, Maryland, a distance of about forty miles. Although the government owned this telegraph line, the Morse telegraph patents were privately held. The majority of the Morse patent holders, however, believed that the government should be totally responsible for telegraph service. They offered to sell the patents to the government for $100,000. Congress, however, rejected the offer and, in 1846, authorized the sale or lease of the Baltimore-Washington circuit to private interests. Thereafter, except for a brief period during World War I, telecommunications in the United States has been largely a private commercial endeavor. While most nations chose to operate their telecommunications system as a public monopoly, usually through the postal authority, the U.S. followed a policy of government regulation of private interests.

In the years following 1846, numerous telegraph companies appeared and disappeared, with frequent mergers and consolidations. By 1866, a company consisting of several merged telegraph carriers — Western Union — had become the dominant carrier. In many places, it was a monopolist — and, all too often, it acted like one as well.

The telephone appeared in the 1870's. Alexander Graham Bell filed for the first telephone patent in 1876. Only three hours later, Elisha Gray, another inventor, made a similar request. A series of patent disputes followed. This patent difficulty was symbolic of the telephone's infant years. In fact, Bell's backers became so discouraged that, in the fall of 1876, they offered to sell the telephone patent to Western Union for $100,000. However, Western Union, believing that the telephone would never be more than a novelty or a toy, declined the offer. This was a decision which it quickly came to regret.

Shortly thereafter, the Bell System's fortunes began to improve. Within two years, Western Union realized that some of its customers were using the telephone in place of its telegraph service. In response to these inroads, Western Union purchased Elisha Gray's patent rights in 1878 and entered the telephone business in competition with Bell. The fledgling Bell company responded by instituting a patent infringement suit against Western Union.

One year later, Western Union and AT&T reached an out-of-court settlement. Under this 1879 agreement, Bell purchased Western Union's telephone equipment, paid Western Union a small royalty, and agreed not to enter the telegraph business during the life of the disputed patents. In return, Western Union agreed to stay out of telephony for the same period, and to drop its patent suits. Thus, Western Union protected its monopoly status in the telegraph sector, and AT&T no longer had to worry about competition in the telephone field from a financially superior rival. This private agreement laid the groundwork for an industry structure which in basic form persists to this day — Western Union is the United States' predominant record carrier and AT&T is the predominant voice carrier.

As a result of this agreement, Bell was able to establish itself in the most lucrative urban markets, to develop a sound corporate and financial structure, and generally to secure a competitively advantageous position. A further by-product of the settlement with Western Union was Bell's purchase of a controlling interest in the Western Electric Manufacturing Company, which Western Union had created. Bell made Western Electric the sole supplier of telephone equipment for the Bell System telephone operating companies. Later, in 1907, AT&T decided to centralize its research and development efforts, and merged its engineering staff with Western Electric's research staff. Thus, Bell Telephone Laboratories was formally incorporated in 1925. AT&T and Western Electric still each hold half interest in Bell Labs, which remains the research and development wing of the Bell System.

1.1.2 The Competitive Era

During its years of patent monopoly, the Bell System developed service in the lucrative urban regions, leaving the less populated regions for others to serve. It also developed a network of intercity lines linking these urban centers. The expiration of Bell's patents in 1893 sparked a more rapid deployment of telephone service than had occurred during the monopoly years, due to the entry of new, and sometimes competing, independent telephone companies. These new companies helped bring telephone service into many small communities and rural areas for the first time.

To meet the competition, the Bell System grew explosively, from about 260,000 telephones in 1893 to over 3,000,000 telephones in 1907. Bell also refused to interconnect its plant with its competitors' lines. Because it controlled the telephone service in many large cities, and generally the long distance circuits connecting the cities, communities not served by the Bell System were isolated from other communities. Many states of the U.S. eventually concluded that Bell's refusal to interconnect was contrary to the public interest and, between 1904 and 1919, 34 of them passed laws which required physical connection of telephone companies.

However, the Bell System continued its attempts to maintain its predominant position by refusing to sell Western Electric equipment to non-Bell companies, by refusing to purchase non-Western Electric equipment, and by filing numerous suits to protect its patents. Bell tried to enhance its preeminence further by attempting to acquire two of the three largest non-Bell telephone equipment manufacturers.

1.1.3 Early Regulation: The Return to Monopoly

In 1910, the Interstate Commerce Commission, an arm of the U.S. government, was given authority to regulate wire and radio communications. Previously, many of the states had tried individually to regulate public communications services. It became apparent, however, that some central federal authority was needed to bring a uniform national policy to the regulatory effort. This regulation grew from a recognition of the importance of telecommunications and a need to protect the public from abuses. The ICC, however, was primarily concerned with transportation regulation and largely ignored communications. Interestingly enough, AT&T supported the move toward government regulation of the telephone industry. AT&T apparently was motivated by a concern over growing support for government ownership of communications facilities, and by the belief that regulation was preferable to competition or government ownership.

With the ascendancy of Theodore Vail to its chairmanship in 1907, AT&T policies changed from aggressive competitiveness to acquisition of competing telephone companies. Vail, for a short period, also changed AT&T's previous policy against selling equipment to independent (that is, non-Bell) telephone companies. The decision to sell Western Electric equipment to the independents came when AT&T

had no significant patent advantages, and was consistent with AT&T's decision to begin acquiring its competitors. The task of integrating new acquisitions into the Bell System would be helped if the independent telephone company was already using Western Electric equipment. Furthermore, in areas too sparsely populated to attract Bell operating companies, AT&T provided technical and financial assistance as well as the right to interconnect with AT&T Long Lines and other Bell System operating companies. By so doing, AT&T expanded the size and value of its interconnected network without having to assume the burden of serving low density or non-remunerative areas.

AT&T's acquisitions, however, were not limited to competing telephone companies. In 1909, it purchased a controlling interest in Western Union, and Vail assumed the presidency of the nation's largest telegraph company. This action, along with AT&T's aggressive purchasing of independent telephone companies, led the surviving independents, along with Postal Telegraph — Western Union's only remaining major competitor — to petition the Justice Department for relief. In 1913, the Attorney General of the United States responded by advising the ICC of the Justice Department's concern over AT&T policies. This Justice Department involvement ultimately led to AT&T's agreement to divest itself of Western Union and to stop acquiring other telephone companies.

In only a few years (in 1921, to be exact), these restrictions were lifted and Bell again began acquiring other telephone companies. In response to industry concern, however, AT&T soon agreed to restrain its acquisition policy. Nevertheless, the Bell System continues to serve most major population centers and provides the preponderance of long distance communications. For example, a 1973 study showed that the Bell System served only about 41% of the land area of the continental United States (excluding Alaska and Hawaii, which also are served by non-Bell carriers), but had over 83% of the nation's telephones. The basic relationship between the Bell System and the independents today may be characterized as complementary, with independents and Bell companies serving as local telephone monopolists interconnecting with AT&T domestic and international Long Lines and Western Electric selling equipment to others only if necessary.

1.2 FCC Regulation

It was with this background fresh in the mind of Congress that the Communications Act of 1934 was enacted, vesting in the FCC the authority to regulate the nation's communications system. Regulation of the private monopoly was viewed as necessary, but the ICC had failed to fulfill that need. It was felt that creation of a separate regulatory body would be more likely to protect the public interest. The FCC regulated the Bell System and Western Union as essentially private monopolies for nearly the next four decades. (Western Union had competition from Postal Telegraph until 1943, when the two companies merged.)

The only service in which carriers directly competed for business was private leased line service, where AT&T and Western Union offered competing interstate lines for high volume communications users. Other than in this market, which comprises only a very small part of the revenues realized by the Bell System and Western Union, the United States' domestic communications industry was properly characterized until the mid-1960's as one where monopolists provided a limited number of homogeneous communications services.

This industry structure was probably appropriate for its time. Little need existed for service other than traditional voice telephone service. The rights-of-way, land costs, and other problems of building competing wireline networks, either between cities or within a city, made competition impractical. Thus, the markets for both transmission services and terminal equipment were well served. The dual national policy objectives of affordable, universal service and the construction of the most rapid and efficient system possible were best fulfilled through this regulated monopoly market structure.

2. THE PRESENT ERA: COMPETITION RETURNS

In the 1960's, technological progress removed many of the elements of telecommunications service which made it a "natural monopoly." In particular, two events occurred which drastically altered the type of market development best suited to meet the national goals. Business user needs for high-speed digital data communications became widespread, and new microwave technology overcame the alleged "natural monopoly" traits of intercity telecommunications transmission.

2.1 Data Communications: A New Public Need

The needs of business for high-speed digital data communications were a result of the invention of the computer. The emergence of this new commercial product began in 1951 when UNIVAC, the world's first electronic digital computer, was delivered to the U.S.

Census Bureau. By 1962, over 10,000 computers were installed in the United States and, by the mid-1960's, about 30,000 were in place. Today, hundreds of thousands of digital computers are operating throughout the world. In just twenty-five years, the computer has become a vital and integral part of the economy of industrialized nations and has virtually revolutionized the manner and efficiency of performing business transactions, analyzing and storing information, performing scientific calculations, controlling complex manufacturing processes, and automating office functions.

In the 1950's and 1960's, changes in computer technology greatly altered the economics of computer usage and vastly increased the reliance of data processing systems on communications. At first, commercial computers were capable of performing only one task at a time. A user got an exclusive block of time during which he actually operated the machine. This mode of operation, however, proved to be very inefficient. This was because the computer, with its massive investment, remained idle while the human was entering information, reading output, or just thinking. The development of remote access data processing, in combination with "time-sharing," eliminated the need for physical transportation of computer inputs and permitted cost-effective interactive computer processing. These developments, of course, were dependent upon communications lines.

Additionally, as more and more computers came into use, the need for computers at different geographic locations to be able to "talk" to each other also developed. The characteristics and requirements of the data communications that takes place between terminals and a central computer, or between computers, are entirely different from the characteristics and requirements of voice communications. Accordingly, the terminal devices and networks optimized for voice communications had some serious limitations for data transmission.

An important companion of the computer revolution was the accompanying progress in electronics in general. Such breakthroughs as the transistor, integrated circuits, and the minicomputer radically increased computer power while rapidly reducing both the cost and size of the equipment. By the mid-1960's, computers and the related technology had many potential applications throughout telecommunications networks, such as message-switching, store-and-forward service, automatic forwarding, address list storage, and so on. Thus, the technological revolution that produced the demand for specialized communications also produced many of the solutions as well. In the process of developing these telecommunications applications for computers, large numbers of firms outside the traditional tele-phone and telegraph industry acquired technical expertise that was directly transferable to communications.

The proliferation of applications for remote access data processing and other emerging specialized communications needs demanded a wide variety of terminal devices. The homogeneity of the terminal market was destroyed by this technological revolution; the simple telephone no longer suitably adapted the public telephone network for all uses. In the face of so obvious a proliferation of special re-quirements and potential suppliers, serious questions arose as to whether it was in the public interest to rely on a single terminal equipment supplier or whether reliance on a competitive marketplace might be more appropriate.

The revolution in computer and electronics technology which began in the early 1960's produced tremendous economic, technical, and operational incentives to combine computers and communications. These incentives, in turn, raised significant issues of public policy re-garding the appropriate boundary between regulated monopoly com-munications activities and unregulated competitive data processing services, and the adequacy of existing communications services and facilities to meet existing or future data communications needs. On the one hand, the FCC was concerned that the Bell System would use its market leverage as the dominant entity in the telephone field to monopolize the data processing industry as well. On the other hand, it appeared that the telephone system was not capable of ful-filling data transmission requirements. The FCC recognized the importance of these issues and, in 1965, it instituted a proceeding known as the *First Computer Inquiry.*

This Inquiry reached four important conclusions: (1) communica-tions facilities and services related to computer/communication ser-vices were in their infancy; (2) timely development of communica-tions services adapted to these special needs was critical to U.S. economic growth and needs; (3) a number of users were dissatisfied with many aspects of the telephone communications capabilities; and (4) special private line capabilities were needed for many data communications applications, particularly high speed data transmis-sions.

Primarily as a result of the findings of the *First Computer Inquiry* [1], the FCC began reassessing the monopolistic market structure which had arisen. The radically new public needs engendered by the development of data communications changed the way in which the social objectives set by Congress in 1934 could best be achieved. While dramatic changes were soon to be wrought in both the terminal equipment and transmission fields, the introduction of competition in each developed separately.

2.2 Terminal Equipment Competition

While communications needs were emerging which the Bell System did not meet, its telephone customers were prohibited from connecting any device to Bell lines — no matter how innocuous — which was not furnished by the telephone company. In one instance, AT&T attempted to enforce this restriction against customers who utilized the Hush-A-Phone, a cup-like device which was placed on the telephone handset to funnel the speaker's voice into the telephone instrument. The device was intended to facilitate private telephone conversations in crowded offices. In 1956, when the FCC refused to order the Bell System to rescind this limitation, the manufacturer of the Hush-A-Phone asked the courts to rule that the FCC had erred in reaching its decision. A United States Court of Appeals agreed and held that AT&T had acted unlawfully in disallowing the attachment of the Hush-A-Phone [2]. In so doing, the court enunciated the principle that telecommunications subscribers have a right to use the telecommunications system in ways which are privately beneficial without being publicly detrimental, and that telephone company regulations which interfere with that right are unreasonable.

After the *Hush-A-Phone* decision, AT&T made some changes in its regulations, but essentially took the position that the *Hush-a-Phone* ruling was limited to its facts. Thus, the general prohibition against connecting customer-provided terminal devices to telephone company lines persisted. The next time this issue arose was when an entrepreneur, Thomas Carter, began marketing to private individuals a device called the "Carterfone." This device acoustically and inductively interconnected mobile radio systems with the national telephone system. In response to the telephone company's refusal to allow its use, the manufacturer of the Carterfone asked the FCC for relief. Thus, the issue of terminal equipment interconnection was presented to the FCC concurrently with its consideration of the *First Computer Inquiry*.

In March 1968, the Commission found: *(a)* that the Carterfone satisfied an unmet communications need, *(b)* that it did not adversely affect the telephone system, and *(c)* that the AT&T tariff prohibiting its use was unreasonable and unlawful [3]. As part of its *Carterfone* decision, the Commission ordered the carriers to submit regulations which were to protect the telephone system against technically *harm-ful* devices, but which otherwise allowed the customer to provide his own terminal equipment. Subsequently, AT&T filed regulations which generally allowed free acoustic and inductive interconnection of customer-provided terminal equipment and communications systems, but which permitted the direct electrical connection of such equipment only through "connecting arrangements" allegedly necessary to protect the network from technical harm.

These connecting arrangements, of course, could only be acquired from the telephone company, and only for an extra monthly charge. Significantly, AT&T contended that their so-called protective devices were not to serve as sources of revenue in order to save the telephone network from economic harm; instead, they were said to be technically necessary to preserve the integrity and usefulness of the network.

In response to such Bell regulations, many users and manufacturers complained that the restrictions on the use of customer-owned terminal devices rendered the telephone company service offerings inadequate to meet the needs of the public for more flexible, efficient and economic access to the nationwide switched telephone network. In the early 1970's, the FCC initiated informal proceedings to explore the technical feasibility of liberalizing these restrictions [4].

A research contractor hired by the Commission as part of this inquiry concluded that, although uncontrolled interconnection of customer-provided facilities to the nationwide telephone system could harm the network, it was technically feasible to liberalize the interconnection provisions of the tariffs without causing any harm by establishing a properly authorized program of certification of customer-equipment.

As a consequence, in 1975 the Commission found that the regulations requiring the use of telephone company supplied connecting arrangements imposed an unnecessary limitation on the customers' right to make reasonable use of the services and facilities furnished by the carriers; that those restrictive provisions constituted an unjust and unreasonable discrimination both among users (or classes of users) and among suppliers of terminal equipment; and that a program adopting standards and procedures to govern the registration with the Commission of protective circuitry and/or terminal equipment would provide the necessary minimal protection against technical harm to the network and will serve the public interest [5]. Accordingly, the Commission adopted a federal registration program for terminal devices. This program allows full competition in the manufacture and sale of all types of terminal equipment, from the simple telephone to highly sophisticated office systems. FCC-registered devices may be connected directly to the telephone network simply by plugging them into a standard interface, just as electric appliances are plugged into a socket.

This new FCC policy has benefited the American consumer by permitting the terminal equipment market to evolve naturally into a multiple supplier market where competitors must utilize state-of-the-art technology and innovative features to capture a portion of the market. In this environment, competitors cannot build or market terminal devices which are overpriced or which are more expensive than consumers wish to purchase.

Prior to the initiation of the FCC's terminal equipment registration program, to mention only one early example of its success, telephone company provided answering machines were quite expensive, costing about $500 in the late 1960's. By 1976, the average wholesale cost of answering devices purchased by industrial users from competing sources was approximately $220. Smaller answering devices designed for individual consumers now cost only about $70. By 1974, there was a total installed base of 150,000 answering devices provided by the telephone companies, while 650,000 customer-provided answering devices were utilized by commercial/industrial users and individual customers. These figures show that the new competitive suppliers, while fulfilling consumer needs, dramatically lowered the price of answering machines. Many similar economic benefits have resulted from the FCC's terminal equipment interconnection policies, including increased innovation and responsiveness on the part of the telephone companies.

2.3 Early Competition in Intercity Transmission

Similar benefits have been realized in the separate area of competitive transmission services. Prior to the 1960's, only the telephone companies and Western Union publicly offered private line service, and those services generally were either telegraph or voice grade circuits. Transmission services were viewed as "natural monopolies." The emergence and proliferation of computers in the 1960's, however, spawned a demand for specialized private line services which were not provided by AT&T and Western Union. The development of a post-World War II telecommunications transmission technology — microwave radio — provided a technological means of overcoming the "natural monopoly" characteristics of intercity leased line transmission.

In the 1950's, when the three newly-established American television networks needed private line service to transmit television signals to their affiliated stations all across the country, AT&T predominately used coaxial cable. However, when these networks began to seriously consider the establishment of their own private microwave network, AT&T switched to microwave for its television signal relay services despite its initial investment in coaxial cable. It did so because privately-owned microwave transmission networks, using towers, dish-shaped antennas, and radio waves, proved to be a competitive threat since they could be more efficient and economical than AT&T's leased coaxial cable service.

In 1956, to obtain the information necessary to the allocation of spectrum for private point-to-point microwave systems, the FCC began an investigatory proceeding. Several issues concerning the use of microwave systems by private businesses were examined, including what effect such systems might have on the ability of common carriers to serve the general public. Based on that proceeding, the Commission issued an Order in 1959 known as the *Above 890* decision [6].

In this decision, the Commission found that an adequate number of microwave frequencies were available to fulfill the reasonably foreseeable needs of both the common carrier and private point-to-point microwave systems. Over AT&T's objections, the Commission further held that there was no reasonable likelihood that the public common carriers would suffer any adverse economic effects from the licensing of private point-to-point communications systems. As a result, the Commission determined that any private microwave system which met proper technical criteria would be authorized to operate even though common carrier facilities existed which could provide service to the private system applicant.

Thus, microwave technology made it economically feasible for large businesses to construct private transmission networks to serve their own communications needs. These private microwave networks were installed by railroads, mining operations, pipelines, and other businesses, generally in areas where wireline facilities were not available from common carriers. Each of these systems was licensed by the FCC, utilizing temporary frequency assignments pending the accumulation of sufficient information on common carrier microwave needs to make permanent allocations of radio frequencies. Thus, AT&T was impelled by competition with private microwave networks to hasten its development of microwave technology for its own network. Despite the fact that, since 1959, some 190,000 miles of private microwave networks have been constructed in the United States, there is no evidence of any adverse impact on telephone industry revenues or on its ability to provide low cost communications service.

2.4 "Specialized Common Carriers"

Although the 1959 decision allocating microwave frequencies for private use brought a kind of competition to telecommunications transmission services, only a handful of very large organizations possessed both the need and the financial resources to install a private system. It was the FCC's authorization of competing microwave service *for hire* that really gave momentum to the move toward competition.

As previously indicated, a dramatic change in the nature of private line communications came in the 1960's with the advent of the computer age and the consequent demand for data communications channels specifically engineered to meet this need. Information flow within and between computers is based upon digital technology. However, the public telephone network, and the private line facilities of both AT&T and Western Union, were designed according to analog technology, which is best suited to meet the particular needs of voice communications — not computer communications. Thus, an intrinsic incompatibility existed between computer communications needs and the facilities available to support them. Out of concern that the new data needs would not be met and that other new and innovative services might not develop, the FCC initiated a rulemaking which culminated in its *Specialized Common Carrier* decision [7].

Prior to the initiation of this proceeding, the Commission already had granted an application by Microwave Communications, Inc. (MCI) to provide specialized common carrier services between Chicago and St. Louis. This decision was based on a finding by the FCC that competition was reasonably feasible and that the system could be expected to provide public benefits. Also pending before the Commission were hundreds of applications for the construction of other microwave facilities to provide special common carrier services in various parts of the country. The agency decided that these myriad applications could be efficiently handled through the development of overall rules in this area.

The *Specialized Common Carrier* decision was significant in that it established a policy in favor of new entry in the specialized communications field. In adopting this policy, the Commission noted that the specialized communications market, particularly for data communications, was growing very rapidly and was expected to continue to expand at very high rates. The specialized common carrier applicants, rather than entering a fixed market with the same services, were seeking to develop new services and markets, and thus could be expected to satisfy demands which were not being met by the existing carriers and to expand the size of the total communications market. Permitting the entry of specialized common carriers would provide data users with the flexibility and wider range of choices they required. Moreover, competition in the private line market was expected to stimulate technical innovation, the introduction of new techniques, and the provision of those types of communications services which would attract and hold customers.

In the *Specialized Common Carrier* inquiry, several questions were raised concerning the effect which multiple entry by specialized carriers might have on existing carriers and their ability to provide communications services to the public. AT&T claimed that the diversion of revenues caused by multiple entry would not be insubstantial. Such a diversion might delay installation of large capacity facilities on high density routes and jeopardize the realization of declining unit costs. The Commission found, however, that given the very small percentage of AT&T's existing total market that was vulnerable to the limited type of competition proposed by the specialized common carriers, in combination with the high growth rate of Bell's basic services and the likelihood that AT&T would obtain a substantial share of the potential market for new specialized services, there was no reason to anticipate that competition would cause a diversion of revenues of the magnitude claimed by AT&T. Likewise, the FCC was not persuaded that Western Union would necessarily suffer any substantial diversion of revenues or other detriment, or that the independent telephone companies would be prejudiced by a policy in favor of new entry.

Arguments of "creamskimming" and "economies of scale" also were raised by opponents of new entry, examined by the Commission, and rejected. "Creamskimming" involves competing in only the most profitable markets and not serving the less profitable. The ultimate result of such competitive entry, the argument went, would be the deaveraging of telephone charges in a way which would thwart continued realization of universal service. Rural telephone users would have to be charged more and urban users less if the telephone company was to respond to creamskimming competition; uniform rates for both would no longer be possible. However, the Commission concluded that creamskimming assumes that the established carriers are already serving the total potential market and responding to all changes in demand and technology at an optimum rate. Accordingly, potential entrants can enter only by taking part of the existing market, and will want to enter only to take the "cream" on the low cost routes.

Charges of creamskimming were thus found to be inapplicable to new entry by specialized common carriers because these carriers were primarily, interested in markets yet to be developed, rather than the "cream" of existing markets. That individual service proposals were of limited geographical scope posed no serious concern. New markets naturally develop gradually, beginning in those submarket areas where maximum demand can be stimulated at minimum cost, and specialized common carriers could not be expected to construct facilities on a total nationwide basis all at one time. Concerning "economies of scale," the Commission pointed out that such economies usually occur, if at all, in markets where technology is stable and consumer demands are homogeneous. By contrast, the market for specialized communications facilities is characterized by rapidly changing applications of improved technology and diverse consumer demands.

The right of other carriers to utilize Bell System local facilities was an early subject of dispute, but it has since been settled [8]. In the *Specialized Common Carrier* decision, the Commission authorized new specialized private line carriers and issued a broad directive to the telephone carriers to make facilities available to such new carriers, on a reasonable and non-discriminatory basis, for the local distribution of the carriers' intercity traffic. Although Bell provided dedicated local private lines to specialized common carriers, it would not interconnect them with the public telephone network for the purpose of providing private line services originating or terminating in the local telephone exchange. Bell argued that the *Specialized Common Carrier* decision did not require such interconnection. The FCC disagreed, however, and ordered the Bell System companies to stop denying specialized carriers reasonable interconnection services similar to those provided to AT&T's Long Lines Department [9].

The Commission reasoned that competition between Long Lines and the specialized carriers in the interstate private line services market would not be full and fair if the specialized carriers were prevented from providing private services which utilize the local telephone exchange by reason of monopoly control by Bell and other telephone companies over local plant. Thus, the Bell System was ordered to permit interconnection of its local public telephone services with the facilities of specialized common carriers. The method of charging for this interconnection is the subject of continuing dispute and negotiations.

2.5 Domestic Satellite Services

In 1972, one year after the *Specialized Common Carrier* decision, the FCC adopted a competitive entry policy toward domestic satellite communications networks as well [10]. The Commission determined that competitive entry was the policy most likely to demonstrate the extent to which satellite technology could provide specialized services more economically and efficiently than could terrestrial facilities. It was the FCC's view that competitive sources of supply for specialized services, both among satellite licensees and between satellite and terrestrial systems, would encourage service and technical innovation, and provide an impetus for efforts to minimize costs and charges to the public.

The Commission recognized that, to realize the objectives of a multiple entry policy, the incentive for competitive entry by financially responsible satellite system entrepreneurs must be meaningful, and not merely token. To ensure that real opportunity for entry would not be frustrated by any particular applicant, the Commission imposed certain conditions on AT&T's entry into the domestic satellite market.

The FCC determined that the public interest required AT&T to have access to satellite technology and to determine its feasibility as an efficient means of providing its basic public telephone services. However, the Commission also recognized that other carriers might be deterred from attempting to enter the specialized satellite service markets by AT&T's existing economic strength and dominance, its unique ability to load a high capacity satellite system with monopoly telephone traffic — thereby controlling the cost of specialized services furnished via that system — and its potential for subsidization of specialized services with revenues from monopoly services. Thus, the FCC prohibited AT&T from utilizing its satellite facilities for private line services for three years.

Since that time, three carriers, RCA, Western Union, and Satellite Business Systems have established domestic satellite transmission systems, and Hughes Communications, Southern Pacific Communications, and General Telephone and Electronics (GTE) have been granted authority to establish systems. AT&T also has a domestic satellite system in operation, which it leases from Comsat General.

The domestic satellite market, along with the terminal equipment field, has become one of the most dynamic and competitive industries in American business.

2.6 "Value-Added Networks" or Resale Carriers

Still another FCC policy of the 1970's has increased competition in telecommunications services. "Value-added networks" (VAN's) first appeared in 1973 with FCC approval of a packet-switched communications network offered by Packet Communications, Inc. [11]. The VAN's were developed to serve data communications users needing more or different services than are available from a leased channel. These carriers provide some additional service — the "added value" — superimposed upon the basic transmission service. The service offered by Packet Communications was characterized as "value added" because it proposed to take channels leased from other carriers and combine them with computers and software to transmit data more efficiently and with less error than would be possible with just the leased channel.

In authorizing Packet Communications, Inc., the FCC recognized that the entry of "value-added" carriers into the communications services market would affect the structure of the communications industry. Nevertheless, it determined that entry should be permitted because it would introduce new and improved means for meeting consumers' data transmission requirements in a manner not available from any other type of carrier. The Commission noted that the findings and philosophy of the *Specialized Common Carrier* decision, dealing generally with the specialized services market, were relevant and supported a competitive environment for the development and sales of the type of services proposed.

The authorization of Packet Communications and other VAN's was folldwed by the FCC's general policy decision favoring resale and shared use of telecommunications facilities. In July 1976, the Commission adopted a policy requiring the abolition of all carrier regulations which ban or inhibit the unlimited resale and sharing of common carrier private line facilities and services [12]. Common carriers traditionally had restricted or prohibited the resale or sharing of their private line facilities and services, with exemptions from such restrictions for certain customers designated by the common carrier. For example, AT&T, while prohibiting resale and sharing in general, voluntarily permitted resale of certain facilities by Western Union and the sharing of AT&T services among the members of certain groups.

The FCC determined that restrictions on the resale and sharing of communications services by subscribers were unjust and unreasonable, and found that unlimited resale and sharing of private line facilities would serve the public interest. However, entities which resell communications services were considered as common carriers and were subjected to regulation under the Communications Act as such.

Among the benefits expected to accrue from expanded resale and sharing of private line services are rates for communications services which are more closely related to costs; better management of the communications network; management expertise in users and communications intermediaries; avoidance of waste of communications capacity; and the creation of additional incentives for research and development of ancillary devices to be used with transmission lines.

3. THE CONSEQUENCES OF THE NEW COMPETITIVE MARKET STRUCTURE

No discussion of the American experience would be complete without addressing the effects of the new policies. In general, the changes have been very beneficial. Competition originally was introduced because the monopoly carriers were not sufficiently innovative and efficient to meet all the public needs. Competition was viewed as a spur to creativity in the design and marketing of terminal equipment and special transmission services, as well as an incentive for the introduction of cost-cutting techniques. It appears that this policy, although in its early phases, is a success. However, due to its relative newness, a few adjustments still may be necessary.

Specifically, the establishment of an open and competitive market in the provision of terminal devices has worked very well. Consumers are free to purchase their own telephones, or to lease them from the telephone company as they always have. While most residential users have continued to get their telephones from the telephone company, many businesses have chosen to purchase office systems, private branch exchanges, or other sophisticated equipment from other sources. No adverse economic impact has been identified by the telephone companies, consumers are free to choose the equipment which best suits their needs, and the terminal equipment market has been infused with new vigor and innovativeness. In particular, more and more office equipment — word processors, telecopiers, even typewriters — is being produced with built-in communications capabilities.

On the other hand, the experience in competitive intercity transmission has been somewhat less successful. While the domestic satellite and value-added carriers are doing well in the competitive environ- ment of their particular submarkets, the more traditional offerings of the specialized carriers have fared less well. Only recently have these carriers become profitable. In a nutshell, the crucial difference be- tween the satellite and value-added submarkets and the traditional leased line service market appears to be that the specialized carriers must compete directly against the Bell System, while the VAN's and satellite carriers have attempted to carve out particularized submar- kets where AT&T does not compete. In the traditional leased line and telephone markets, where AT&T retains about 95% of the business, substantial competition has not developed.

The root of today's problem in establishing competition in intercity services can be stated in one word: cross-subsidy. The heart of the cross-subsidy issue is found in the co-existence of monopoly and competitive markets, with AT&T dominating both. The FCC has been, and continues, struggling to identify a way to permit Bell to offer competitive services but, at the same time, keep those operations separate from its local telephone services. The task is proving extremely elusive.

Full and fair competition means that the FCC has not, and will not, erect protective umbrellas over new suppliers of terminal devices and private line services; but, on the other hand, it also means that the Bell System rate levels for interstate competitive services should be compensatory, i.e., not below cost (including a fair return), and that its practices with respect to competitors must be lawful. If AT&T sets non-compensatory rates for competitive communications ser- vices, it might subsidize those services with revenues collected from users of its monopoly services — the residential and commercial users of local and long distance telephone service — because AT&T ob- viously will attempt to earn its system-wide rate of return. Detecting and preventing this kind of unlawful cross-subsidy between services is critical to protecting users from discrimination, as well as to the assurance of full and fair competition in the specialized markets. The manner in which communications services should be priced to avoid unlawful cross-subsidies is the key to several FCC proceedings.

Although expanding technological developments, unmet communi- cations needs, and the consumer's right to satisfy those needs through means which do not harm the telephone network, prompted the FCC to permit competition in the telecommunications market, initially the Commission was careful to limit the competition to two discrete facets of telecommunications: terminal devices and private line services. In those two areas, the FCC found that full and fair competition would assist in fulfilling the Congressional objectives of universal service and a modern, efficient system.

Recently, however, the Commission made a further finding that the telephone companies should no longer retain their monopoly over long-distance public telephone service [13]. A limited amount of competition has existed in that field since 1976. The telephone companies still will retain their monopoly control over local telephone exchange service and will charge their long-distance competitors for local interconnection. Thus, while this decision will lessen the cross-subsidy problems somewhat, it will not alleviate them entirely.

Because all competing intercity carriers, including AT&T, will utilize the local facilities of the monopoly telephone company to originate and terminate their intercity traffic, some means still must be devised to ensure that AT&T's competing intercity services are not subsidized by its monopoly service. This involves two separate problems. First, all existing plant, over $100 billion worth, must be allocated to either intercity or local exchange. Nearly 40% of these items are not directly attributable to either category of service. Thus, allocation of these common costs — telephone poles, parking lots, etc. — is an important process. This allocation is necessary if the FCC is to be able to examine AT&T's rates for each service and determine whether they are compensatory. After years of effort, the Commission recently resigned itself to adopting a simple cost allocation manual based on the jurisdictional separations process. This decision is subject to review by the court of appeals [14].

The second difficult but necessary task is to devise an accounting and reporting system for AT&T which, in combination with the allocation of existing common plant, will enable the FCC to maintain an up-to-the-minute record of the Bell System's rate base by service category. Again, this process is extremely slow; the goal often seems unattainable.

The final step in the transformation of the American telecommunications industry from a monopolistic structure to a competitive one is "deregulation." This word, meaning the lessening or ending of FCC intervention in the competitive marketplace, seems to have magical powers in Washington these days. In fact, Congress is now considering legislation to deregulate telecommunications substantially.

However, the FCC recently beat Congress to the punch by issuing its *Second Computer Inquiry* decision [15]. In this decision, the FCC

determined that it will not regulate "enhanced" communication services, which it defined to include offerings which incorporate some
element of computer processing. The agency thus has deregulated all
services formerly classified as "hybrid communications" or "hybrid
data processing," as well as other services incorporating store-and-forward or other computer processing applications. In addition, the
FCC determined that all offerings of "customer premises equipment"
should be on an unregulated basis. The *Second Computer Inquiry*
also permits AT&T to offer unregulated enhanced services, as long as
it does so through a separate subsidiary corporation meeting several
requirements for "full" separation. Whether the FCC can take these
deregulatory steps within the parameters of the Communications Act
of 1934 is now up to the courts.

Three principal issues require judicial resolution [16]. First, it must
be determined whether the FCC is correct in concluding that its
"ancillary" jurisdiction extends to all services containing an element
of communications, but that its "Title II" (common carrier) jurisdiction does not apply to any service containing an element of
computer processing. Second, the court will be asked to decide
whether the FCC can forbear from regulation of activities where its
jurisdiction — either ancillary or Title II — applies. Third, the Commission's novel interpretation of the 1956 *Western Electric* consent
decree [17] (which limits AT&T's services to those whose rates are
subject to regulation), must be reviewed. Under the *Second Computer Inquiry*, the FCC's new ancillary jurisdiction and forbearance
from regulation doctrines, in combination, are said to make "enhanced" services "subject to" FCC regulation even though no such
power is exercised. Accordingly, the Commission (contrary to the
views of the Department of Justice) concludes that the consent
decree does not preclude AT&T from offering unregulated "enhanced" services. AT&T has petitioned the federal district court in
New Jersey, which entered the decree in 1956, for a ruling that the
FCC's interpretation is the correct one. This position is opposed by
the Department of Justice and numerous private parties [18].

Regardless of the ultimate outcome of the *Second Computer Inquiry*
litigation, deregulation is an inevitable next step in the evolution of
telecommunications policy. Common sense dictates that regulations
established to protect the public from the abuses of a monopolist
need not be maintained when full competition has supplanted monopoly. Thus, the fields of terminal equipment, domestic satellite
communications, and specialized data transmission services, may no
longer need direct economic regulation by the FCC. Instead, the

Commission's role should shift to that of acting only when necessary to preserve or foster competition. The giant Bell System, however, should continue to be subject to FCC oversight (or stringent separation requirements) in its participation in these competitive markets as well as in its continued provision of monopoly public telephone services.

Precisely how much, and what kind of regulation of the Bell System is necessary to ensure full and fair competition will continue to be the subject of much Congressional and FCC debate. Too little regulation could retard the growth of competition, and too much could unfairly hamper the Bell System's ability to compete. The resolution of these important questions will determine whether the progress made since 1959 can continue to grow and flourish.

4. CONCLUSION

In all, despite the problem identified, the American experience in introducing free enterprise competition into the telecommunications field has produced great benefits for the American public. Moreover, it has made a significant contribution to maintaining and enhancing the world's most advanced telecommunications system.

This chapter is adapted from a lecture given by Mr. Wiley before the Max Planck Institute, Cologne, West Germany, on February 12, 1980. Mr. Wiley was assisted in the preparation of these materials by Danny E. Adams, Kirkland and Ellis, Washington, D.C.

REFERENCES

[1] *Tentative Decision,* 28 F.C.C.2d 291 (1971), *Final Decision,* 28 F.C.C.2d 267 (1971), *aff'd in part sub nom. GTE Service Corp. v. FCC,* 474 F.2d 724 (2d Cir. 1973).

[2] *Hush-a-Phone v. United States,* 238 F.2d 266 (D.C. Cir., 1956).

[3] *Carterfone,* 13 F.C.C.2d 420 (1968), *recon. denied,* 14 F.C.C.2d 571 (1968).

[4] *AT&T (Foreign Attachments),* 15 F.C.C.2d 605, *recon. denied,* 18 F.C.C.2d 871 (1969).

[5] *First Report and Order,* Docket No. 19528, 56 C.C.C.2d 593 (1975), *aff'd sub nom. North Carolina Util. Comm'n v. FCC,* 537 F.2d 787 (4th Cir.), *cert. denied,* 429 U.S. 1027 (1976); *Second Report and Order,* 58 F.C.C.2d 739 (1976), *aff'd sub nom. North Carolina Util. Comm'n v. FCC,* 552 F.2d 1036 (4th Cir. 1977).

[6]   27 F.C.C. 359 (1959).

[7]   29 F.C.C.2d 870 (1971), *aff'd sub nom. Washington Util. and Trans. Comm'n v. FCC*, 513 F.2d 1142 (9th Cir.), *cert. denied*, 423 U.S. 836 (1975).

[8]   While the right of other carriers to interconnect with the Bell System facilities has been established, the terms and conditions of such interconnection are still the source of controversy.

[9]   *Bell System Tariff Offerings*, 46 F.C.C.2d 413 (1974), *aff'd sub nom. Bell Tel. Co. of Pennsylvania v. FCC*, 503 F.2d 1250 (3d Cir. 1974), *cert. denied*, 422 U.S. 1026 (1975).

[10]   *Domestic Communications-Satellite Facilities ("DOMSAT"), First Report and Order*, 22 F.C.C.2d 86 (1970); *Second Report and Order*, 35 F.C.C.2d 844 (1972), *aff'd sub nom. Network Project v. FCC*, 511 F.2d 786 (D.C. Cir. 1975).

[11]   *Packet Communications, Inc.*, 43 F.C.C.2d 922 (1973).

[12]   *Resale and Shared Use*, 60 F.C.C.2d 261, *modified* 61 F.C.C.2d 70 (1976), *recon.*, 62 F.C.C.2d 588 (1977), *aff'd sub nom. American Tel. and Tel. Co. v. FCC*, 572 F.2d 17 (2d Cir.), *cert. denied*, 439 U.S. 875 (1978).

[13]   *MTS and WATS Market Structure*, CC Docket No. 78-72, 81 F.C.C.2d 177 (1980).

[14]   *Manual and Procedures for the Allocation of Costs*, CC Docket No. 79-245, 84 F.C.C.2d (1981), *review pending sub nom. MCI Telecommunications Corp. v. FCC*, Case No. 81-1052 (D.C. Cir.) (filed January 16, 1981).

[15]   *Amendment of Section 64.702*, Docket No. 20828, 77 2d 384 (1980). *recon.*, 84 F.C.C. 2d 50 (1980).

[16]   *Computer and Communications Industry Ass'n v. FCC*, Case No. 80-1471 (D.C.Cir.) (filed May 5, 1980).

[17]   [1956], Trade Cas. (CCH) Par. 68, 246 (D.N.J. 1956). This consent decree was agreed to by AT&T and the United States Department of Justice in settlement of an antitrust suit then being brought against AT&T by the Justice Department. Although the consent decree remains in force, another such suit is now being prosecuted. *United States v. AT&T*, Civil Action No. 74-1698 (D.D.C.).

[18]   Motion for Construction of Final Judgment, Civil Action No. 17-49, (D.N.J.) (filed April 13, 1981).